ARTICLES ON
TWENTIETH CENTURY LITERATURE:
AN ANNOTATED BIBLIOGRAPHY
1954 to 1970

by

David E. Pownall
Hofstra University Library

An Expanded Cumulation of "Current Bibliography" in the Journal Twentieth
Century Literature. Volume One to Volume Sixteen. 1955 to 1970.

KRAUS-THOMSON ORGANIZATION LIMITED
New York, 1976

Pownall, David E   1925-
    Articles on twentieth century literature:
an annotated bibliography, 1954-1970.

    "An expanded cumulation of 'Current biblio-
graphy' in the journal Twentieth century
literature, volume one to volume sixteen, 1955
to 1970."
    1. Literature, Modern--20th century--
history and criticism--Periodicals--Bibliography
I. Twentieth century literature. II. Title.
Z6519.P66   016.809'04   73-6588
ISBN 0-527-72150-6

Printed in U.S.A.

ARTICLES ON
TWENTIETH CENTURY LITERATURE:
AN ANNOTATED BIBLIOGRAPHY
1954 to 1970

by

David E. Pownall
Hofstra University Library

Volume 5

Authors

McAlmon to Pynchon

McALMON, ROBERT

M1   Card, James, "The Misleading Mr. McAlmon and Joyce's Typescript," James Joyce Quarterly, 7:143-7, Winter, 1970.

Robert McAlmon has stated that as the typist of a section of
Ulysses, he haphazardly inserted additional phrases by Joyce into
the typescript rather than in the order Joyce intended. In fact,
McAlmon made none of the changes he describes, and Joyce corrected passages typed out of place. McAlmon's one "contribution"
was to omit ninety-three words from the manuscript. (D.P.)

M2   Dunavon, Robert, "The Man at the Edge of the Photograph,"
Catholic World, 207:116-8, June, 1968.

Robert McAlmon "was a writer of genuine talent; he wrote with
clarity and vigor, and he had an unerring eye for the small details
that reveal character." However, "he was never able to bring his
talent into focus and make a positive statement of life." "McAlmon
carefully identified himself with the revolutionary avant-garde, and
yet . . . he never really understood the deeper, underlying significance of the works of men like Picasso, Joyce or Hemingway."
(D.P.)

MACAULAY, ROSE

M3   Chase, Mary Ellen, "Five Literary Portraits," Massachusetts
Review, 3:511-6, Spring, 1962.

[These are first-hand recollections of Sarah Orne Jewett, Willa
Cather, Gertrude Stein, Dorothy Sayers, and Rose Macaulay.]
(G.C.)

M4   Nicolson, Harold, et al, "The Pleasures of Knowing Rose Macaulay,"
       Encounter, 12:23-31, March, 1959.

       [These are recollections and impressions of Rose Macaulay by
       Harold Nicolson, Rosamund Lehmann, Alan Pryce-Jones, Dwight
       MacDonald, Patrick Kinross, C. V. Wedgwood, Mark Bonham
       Carter, Anthony Powell, William Plomer and Diana Cooper.] (D.P.)

M5   Swinnerton, Frank, "Rose Macaulay," Kenyon Review, 29:591-608,
       November, 1967.

       Rose Macaulay's mind was shaped by her class, the scholarliness
       and religious orthodoxy of her home, the war; she was "a brave,
       kind, honest woman who wrote much that was amusing, much that
       was beautiful, and one classic book, The Towers of Trebizond, in
       which all these influences and all her virtues" were demonstrated.
       (G.S.)

           GOING ABROAD

M6   Bensen, Alice R., "The Skeptical Balance: A Study of Rose
       Macaulay's Going Abroad," Papers of the Michigan Academy of
       Science, Arts and Letters, 48:675-83, 1963.

       "The author's very real concern for human well-being and her
       skepticism regarding the efficaciousness of human efforts have
       expressed themselves here with a largely detached amusement.
       But sometimes one will assert itself more strongly, and sometimes
       the other; these constantly varying degrees of engagement . . .
       prevent any monotony. . . ." (K.M.W.)

           TOLD BY AN IDIOT

M7   Irwin, W. R., "Permanence and Change in The Edwardians and
       Told by an Idiot," Modern Fiction Studies, 2:63-7, May, 1956.

       Both novels treat the interaction of permanence and change in the
       lives of people and society. Theme and form are more nearly
       integrated in The Edwardians than in Told by an Idiot because in
       the former tradition and change are represented as forces in con-
       flict, whereas in the latter their interaction is confusing. (R.A.K.)

VIEWS AND VAGABONDS

M8   Bensen, Alice R., "Ironic Aesthete and the Sponsoring of Causes:
A Rhetorical Quandary in Novelistic Technique," English Literature
in Transition, 9:39-43, No. 1, 1966.

["The ironic cast of [Macaulay's] mind . . . kept her constantly
aware of the antimony inherent in humanistic thinking and, consequently, in 'uplift.' This paper will study certain technical
implications of this ironic consciousness in . . . Views and
Vagabonds (1912), and will indicate that these aspects of the
technique were imposed by the quandary in which she found herself." (D.A.B.)

McCARTHY, MARY

M9   Brower, Brock, "Mary McCarthyism," Esquire, 58:62-7, 113,
July, 1962.

". . . despite all the criticism of her conduct--the many slurs on
her femininity and the attacks on her work--there is a secret admiration for her candor, her audacity, and her stupendous try for
the woman's moon." (K.M.W.)

M10   Cluny, Claude Michel," A propos de Mary McCarthy,"
La Nouvelle Revue Française, 14ᵉ année, No. 159, pp. 527-8,
March, 1966.

Mary McCarthy is a writer who begins again (almost) always the
same work. After The Groves of Academe, the university continues to preoccupy her and her characters and one can say that
all the threads of The Group once again lead back to Vassar.
(T.T.B.)

M11   Fitch, Robert E., "The Cold Eye of Mary McCarthy," New
Republic, 138:17-9, May 5, 1958.

The "cold eye" of Mary McCarthy does not envisage Voltaire's
truths of Reason, Nature, and Humanity. "Its only authority
derives from the self--her own self--and this authority must be
asserted in shrill or in eloquent iteration." For "the quality of
her satire is defined by the cerebro-genital emphasis, which ex-
cludes the affections and the moral emotions." (D.P.)

M12   Niebuhr, Elisabeth, "The Art of Fiction 27: Mary McCarthy,"
Paris Review, No. 27, pp. 58-94, Winter-Spring, 1962.

[This interview probes Miss McCarthy's writing habits, her view of
herself as a novelist, her work in progress and plans for the future,
her political background and activities, as well as her experiences
at Vassar and with Partisan Review.] (D.P.)

M13   Ohmann, Carol B. and Richard M. Ohmann, "Class Notes from
Vassar," Commonweal, 79:12-5, September 27, 1963.

Miss McCarthy writes "as if to record a stretch of the real world's
happenings," but the "visible surface of reality enters [her novels]
through the filter of her characters's minds." (M.G.)

M14   Ross, T. J., "Passion--Moral and Otherwise," New Republic,
139:23-6, August 18, 1958.

Although Dean Fitch insists that Mary McCarthy "has no point of
view at all," and claims that "she gains a false sense of superiority
through snickering at all possible ideals," a powerful, anti-
totalitarian spirit runs through all her work. She has "the born
novelist's eye . . . for catching social types peculiar to her own
time. . . . she is powerfully aware of how often the most educated
tend to be the most brainwashed." (D.P.)

M15   Schlueter, Paul, "The Amoralist: Mary McCarthy," Motive,
25:46-50, December, 1964.

Autobiographical nature of a recurring character, ("whatever
fictional name she is given,") appears in The Company She Keeps,
The Oasis, The Groves of Academe, and A Charmed Life; relationships between these earlier works and The Group are evident.
"Despite the intellectualism, the . . . clarity of insight into character, her novels lack the foundation . . . on which the greatest,
most enduring art must be based." (E.F.S.)

       A CHARMED LIFE

M16   Podhoretz, Norman, "Gibbsville and New Leeds: The America of
John O'Hara and Mary McCarthy," Commentary, 21:269-73,
March, 1956.

"Mary McCarthy and John O'Hara are two of the most consistently
interesting and provocative novelists in America. . . . Each

A CHARMED LIFE (cont'd)

navigates his own course, but both discover the same America.
. . . Sharing O'Hara's angle of vision, one begins to believe that
to learn where a man was born, educated and buys his clothes is
to know virtually all there is to know about him," although in Ten
North Frederick O'Hara acknowledges "that a man's life is more
than his observable behavior." A Charmed Life "is a satiric portrait of a community of intellectuals" in which every man's "movement of his spirit is taken account of and used in evidence against
him." (D.P.)

THE GROUP

M17   Cook, Bruce, "Mary McCarthy: One of Ours?" Catholic World,
      199:34-42, April, 1964.

      The action of The Group "seems to take place in a void. And in
      spite of the catalogs of accoutrements, techniques, and artifacts
      of the 'thirties, of which many critics complained so bitterly, the
      reader . . . receives no special feeling of time or place from the
      book." (D.P.)

M18   McCarthy, Mary, "Letter to a Translator: About The Group,"
      Encounter, 23:69-71, 74-6, November, 1964.

      [This is a detailed response to questions from the Danish translator
      of The Group about style, technique, grammar, and general literary
      method. Miss McCarthy comments on the care, thought and per-
      ceptiveness evidenced by the translator's letter.] (D.P.)

M19   Mathewson, Ruth, "The Vassar Joke," Columbia University Forum,
      6:10-6, Fall, 1963.

      Mary McCarthy's The Group "is a kind of vaudeville, a series of
      comic turns. She has warned us that she is a ventriloquist; some-
      times she seems to be sawing one girl into nine parts." (D.P.)

      THE OASIS

M20   Gottfried, Alex, and Sue Davidson, "Utopia's Children: An Inter-
      pretation of Three Political Novels," Western Political Quarterly,
      15:17-32, March, 1962.

      Hawthorne's The Blithedale Romance, Mary McCarthy's The Oasis,
      and Harvey Swados's False Coin "each has as its subject certain

THE OASIS (cont'd)

utopian experiments carried out in an American setting contemporary with the author's time. The novels offer us a historic view of the American dissent-idealist through the eyes of three highly gifted observers, as they examine the dynamism between a political idea and the individuals and culture in which it takes root." (D.P.)

McCOURT, EDWARD

M21   Baldwin, R. G., "Pattern in the Novels of Edward McCourt," Queen's Quarterly, 68:574-87, Winter, 1962.

McCourt, usually considered as just another Canadian regional realist, is notable for his "applied romanticism" as manifested in his recurrent use of the theme of the salvation of a romantic personality. (G.B.M.)

McCRAE, HUGH

M22   Chisholm, A. R., "Hugh McCrae, O. B. E., 1876-1958," Australian Quarterly, 30:39-41, June, 1958.

Poetry is "the adequate record of a vision that glimpses Reality behind all the shifting realities that surround us. "Hugh McCrae . . . had that part of vision and the ability to record it." (G.C.)

M23   Cowper, Norman, "McCrae the Man," Southerly, 19:67-75, 1958.

[These are biographical details and reminiscences concerning McCrae.] (G.C.)

M24   Fitzgerald, Robert D., et al, "Tributes to Hugh McCrae," Meanjin Quarterly, 17:73-82, April, 1958.

[Four appreciative reminiscences of McCrae are presented here.] (G.C.)

McCULLERS, CARSON

M25   Baldanza, Frank, "Plato in Dixie," Georgia Review, 12:151-67, Summer, 1958.

The "common denominator" that most adequately accounts for the similarities of Carson McCullers's and Truman Capote's parables about physically and spiritually lonely people is the appearance in their works of distinctly Platonic conceptions of love, but they lack Plato's naive assumptions about the rewards of persevering to achieve spiritual love. (W.G.F.)

M26   Dodd, Wayne D., "The Development of Theme through Symbols in the Novels of Carson McCullers," <u>Georgia Review</u>, 17:206-13, Summer, 1963.

The characters in McCullers's novels are lonely hunters in quest for a music of life. For the most part they are unsuccessful and the reasons "for the failure of these lonely souls are found in a suggestive and developmental symbolism which always emphasizes the discreteness of individuals from each other and from God himself." (W.A.F.)

M27   Drake, Robert, "The Lonely Heart of Carson McCullers," <u>Christian Century</u>, 85:50-1, January 10, 1968.

Certainly Carson McCullers possessed "a great talent. However, it was often vitiated not only by technical insufficiencies but also by her failure to live up to [her] precepts. . . ." In her two greatest achievements <u>The Heart Is a Lonely Hunter</u> and <u>The Member of the Wedding</u> "she came near to finding an inevitable and technically unexceptionable embodiment" of her central theme of spiritual isolation, although each of these works suffers "from a considerable degree of incoherence" and a "tendentious exploitation of contemporary southern social problems," defects which become fully evident in her lesser works. (D.P.)

M28   Evans, Oliver, "The Achievement of Carson McCullers," <u>English Journal</u>, 51:301-8, May, 1962.

". . . Carson McCullers is probably the best allegorical writer on this side of the Atlantic since Hawthorne and Melville. Her writing is almost never peripheral, as Faulkner's often is; it goes straight to the heart of its subject, and it rarely fumbles." (D.P.)

M29   Evans, Oliver, "The Case of Carson McCullers," <u>Georgia Review</u>, 18:40-5, Spring, 1964.

"There are . . . three reasons why Mrs. McCullers's work is not more widely appreciated. The first is psychological, and has to do with her [pessimistic] 'message.' . . . The second . . . is her choice of characters and situations." The third reason has to do with her special blend of realism and allegory. (G.C.)

M30   Folk, Barbara Nauer, "The Sad Sweet Music of Carson McCullers,"
       Georgia Review, 16:202-9, Summer, 1962.

       "Musical allusions of one kind or another are to be found in almost
       all McCullers stories, music serving now as architectural frame-
       work, again as extended correlative, often and regularly as minor
       symbol. And in the literary context the use of music and musical
       references is always intelligent, functional and openly reverent."
       (W.A.F.)

M31   Hamilton, Alice, "Loneliness and Alienation: The Life and Work
       of Carson McCullers," Dalhousie Review, 50:215-29, Summer,
       1970.

       Carson McCullers "is writing about the inner isolation that man
       feels when he is frustrated from expressing himself as fully as
       possible." Mrs. McCullers "lives in a world of freaks and ab-
       normalities . . . [in which] something is wrong on the human level."
       (D.P.)

M32   Hart, Jane, "Carson McCullers, Pilgrim of Loneliness,"
       Georgia Review, 11:53-8, Spring, 1957.

       Carson McCullers does not write about the grotesque and abnormal
       simply to capitalize upon a primitive interest in strange things;
       rather she is concerned with a larger vision in which the abnormal
       figures serve a functional purpose in projecting the idea of human
       loneliness with which the author is always preoccupied. (W.G.F.)

M33   Hassan, Ihab H., "Carson McCullers: The Alchemy of Love and
       Aesthetics of Pain," Modern Fiction Studies, 5:311-26, Winter,
       1959-1960.

       "It is upon the unconverted and inconvertible wish, as it seeks
       expression in love and suffering, that the imagination of Carson
       McCullers has fastened. In doing so she has given unique and
       perhaps lasting forms to an impulse that has reigned supreme in
       modern literature, that very impulse which Trilling . . . charac-
       terized as having 'an intense and adverse imagination of the culture
       in which it has being.' And if in its modern adversity the imagina-
       tion of Mrs. McCullers has focused on man's aloneness and sought
       the ambience of his decay, it has done so less in the spirit of Poe
       than in that of . . . Baudelaire. . . ." (D.P.)

M34   Hendrick, George, "'Almost Everyone Wants to Be the Lover':
The Fiction of Carson McCullers," Books Abroad, 42:389-91,
Summer, 1968.

". . . The Heart Is a Lonely Hunter, Reflections in a Golden Eye,
The Member of the Wedding, The Ballad of the Sad Café, Clock
Without Hands, and such stories as 'The Jockey' and 'A Tree, A
Rock, A Cloud' appear to be among the important achievements of
our time." (D.P.)

M35   Hughes, Catherine, "A World of Outcasts," Commonweal,
75:73-5, October 13, 1961.

"The world of Carson McCullers is a world of outcasts; her
universe the realm of extraordinary, rather than 'normal' happenings. Yet for all this, she succeeds in establishing a rapport of
feeling, an aura of shared experience." The labyrinth established
for the McCullers characters "is a world of either/or, in which
there are few half-way measures, where everything is viewed in
nightmarish bold relief. Simultaneously unrealistic and yet supra-
realistic, it is the unique and unforgettable world of Carson
McCullers." (D.P.)

M36   Jaworski, Philippe, "La double quête de l'identité et de la réalité
chez Carson McCullers," La Nouvelle Revue Française, No. 199,
pp. 93-101, July, 1969.

McCullers's work does not evolve from one book to another. Her
world is already in place in The Heart Is a Lonely Hunter. Each
ensuing work will pick up, moderating the form but not changing
the sense, one or several of the motifs of her initial work, for
example, the search for identity and the questioning of reality.
(T.T.B.)

M37   Johnson, J. W., "The Adolescent Hero," Twentieth Century
Literature, 5:3-11, April, 1959.

"Whether the adolescent hero proves to be only a passing fancy
with a few major authors and a host of minor ones, or whether he
will remain as an archetypal figure of our age is yet to be seen.
. . . It is clear that a few writers--notably Wolfe, McCullers,
and Salinger--believe him to be such an embodiment of a cultural
animus." (D.P.)

M38   Lubbers, Klaus, "The Necessary Order: A Study of Theme and
       Structure in Carson McCullers's Fiction," Jahrbuch für
       Amerikastudien, 8:187-204, 1963.

       "The overall theme of Carson McCullers's books is that of man's
       problematic and painful existence with various veerings from its
       proper course. Man's drab life is presented at critical points
       such as adolescence, loss of friendship, oncoming death, and
       leads to types of escape, imaginary and real." (K.M.W.)

M39   McCullers, Carson, "The Flowering Dream: Notes on Writing,"
       Esquire, 52:162-4, December, 1959.

       Mrs. McCullers writes primarily of the spiritual isolation derived
       from the inability to love, choosing anything human for a subject.
       O'Neill, the great Russians, Faulkner and Flaubert are her chief
       influences. The Southerner is rarely cosmopolitan since he is
       "bound to this peculiar regionalism of language and voices and
       foliage and memory. . . ." (D.P.)

M40   McGill, Ralph, "Carson McCullers: 1917-1967," Saturday Review,
       50:31, 88, October 21, 1967.

       "Carson was one of the two or three best Southern writers. She
       belongs with Faulkner." In quality her writings rank with his "and
       in sensitivity to and interpretation of the juxtaposition of loneliness
       and love she excels." (W.K.)

M41   McPherson, Hugo, "Carson McCullers: Lonely Huntress,"
       Tamarack Review, No. 11, pp. 28-40, Spring, 1959.

       The failure of Mrs. McCullers's second play, "The Square Root of
       Wonderful," does not diminish the importance of her earlier works,
       the best of which is Reflections in a Golden Eye. Critics, un-
       fortunately, have not examined her works for meaning. The fact
       of love--an all-encompassing Platonic love--is man's only hope.
       (D.E.W.)

M42   Rechnitz, Robert M., "The Failure of Love: The Grotesque in
       Two Novels by Carson McCullers," Georgia Review, 22:454-63,
       Winter, 1968.

       The "fictional worlds" depicted in Reflections in a Golden Eye and
       The Ballad of the Sad Café are grotesque. "Unwilling to confront
       life in its complexity . . . [the characters] construct a limited

world which they deem to be safe, but which . . . becomes a [grotesquely furnished] prison. . . ." (G.C.)

M43   Robinson, W. R., "The Life of Carson McCullers's Imagination," Southern Humanities Review, 2:291-302, Summer, 1968.

Carson McCullers's is "a moral art, severe originally, humane finally . . . [which] defines the walls within which man as man must exist and affirms that he can love and live within them." (G.C.)

M44   Thorp, Willard, "Suggs and Sut in Modern Dress: The Latest Chapter in Southern Humor," Mississippi Quarterly, 13:169-75, Fall, 1960.

Although the influence of the tradition of early Southern humor on contemporary Southern fiction is difficult to document, much recent Southern writing is humorous. The fantastic, sometimes horrifying, humor of Faulkner, Capote, O'Connor, and McCullers parallels similar fantasies in George Washington Harris and Henry Junius Nott, although much of that tradition of Southern humor was extremely realistic. (D.P.)

M45   Vickery, John B., "Carson McCullers: A Map of Love," Wisconsin Studies in Contemporary Literature, 1:13-24, Winter, 1960.

Only "gradually is the central inviolability of the individual recognized" by the lovers in McCullers's stories, "and when it is, it is seen to be synonymous with that isolation which in the final analysis envelops everyone." (B.K.)

M46   Williams, Tennessee, "The Author: Carson McCullers," Saturday Review, 44:14-5, September 23, 1961.

In Clock Without Hands, her final work, Carson McCullers has placed the capstone on a career which demonstrates "all the stature, nobility of spirit, and profound understanding of the lonely searching heart that make her, in my opinion, the greatest living writer of our country, if not of the world." (D.P.)

THE BALLAD OF THE SAD CAFÉ

M47   Bigsby, C. W. E., "Edward Albee's Georgia Ballad," Twentieth Century Literature, 13:229-36, January, 1968.

THE BALLAD OF THE SAD CAFÉ (cont'd)

Albee's The Ballad of the Sad Café "seems to prove that in sacrific-
ing his own 'voice,' his freedom to define character and situation
through his command of language, he has sacrificed the essence of
his greatness. He has produced a play of disturbing power. . . .
It is a play which finally fails either to live up to the promise of his
earlier work or to reflect the subtle insight which is the essence of
Carson McCullers's particular achievement." (D. P.)

M48   Griffith, Albert J., "Carson McCullers's Myth of the Sad Café,"
Georgia Review, 21:46-56, Spring, 1967.

"To treat of love 'wild, extravagant, and beautiful as the poison
lilies of the swamp, ' Mrs. McCullers has elevated [the] primitive
characters and . . . grotesque action [in The Ballad of the Sad Café]
to the wild, extravagant, and beautiful level of myth." (G. C.)

M49   Moore, Janice Townley, "McCullers's The Ballad of the Sad Café, "
Explicator, 29: Item 27, November, 1970.

In Carson McCullers's The Ballad of the Sad Café, it is notable that
Cousin Lymon, the hunchback, is from beginning to end described
in terms of fowl imagery . . . a progression that reveals Lymon's
propensity toward evil as the story unfolds." (D. P.)

M50   Phillips, Robert S., "Dinesen's 'Monkey' and McCullers's Ballad:
A Study in Literary Affinity, " Studies in Short Fiction, 1:184-90,
Spring, 1964.

Isak Dinesen's "The Monkey" may be seen as "a very probable
inspiration" for McCullers's The Ballad of the Sad Café, and "affords a partial understanding of the sources and invention of a work
which . . . has become a minor though cryptic classic." (P. J. R.)

M51   Phillips, Robert S., "Painful Love: Carson McCullers's 'Parable',"
Southwest Review, 51:80-6, Winter, 1966.

The Ballad of the Sad Café must be read as parable rather than
novel. The characters are deliberately overdrawn, made ludicrous,
and "divorced from life as we know it." McCullers dehumanizes
her characters to isolate the moral dilemmas examined. (P. J. R.)

CLOCK WITHOUT HANDS

M52 Emerson, Donald, "The Ambiguities of <u>Clock Without Hands</u>,"
<u>Wisconsin Studies in Contemporary Literature</u>, 3:15-28, Fall, 1962.

As is true of her other fiction, in <u>Clock Without Hands</u> Mrs.
McCullers portrays characters all of whose outward experience "is
conditioned by a sense of moral isolation, a feeling of despair, and
baffled search for an identifiable Self." She fails, however, in her
attempt to make the characters stand for the whole South. (B.K.)

THE HEART IS A LONELY HUNTER

M53 Carpenter, Frederic I., "The Adolescent in American Fiction,"
<u>English Journal</u>, 46:313-9, September, 1957.

<u>The Catcher in the Rye</u> "concentrates on three days in the life of an
upper-class New York City boy, who has just been expelled from a
private school." <u>The Heart is a Lonely Hunter</u> "describes the
various racial and social tensions of a Southern town, as seen
through the eyes of the young daughter of a poor family over the
period of a year." <u>Cress Delahanty</u> "etches scenes in the life of
a middle-class California girl, over a period of four years. Yet
all three [authors] observe their adolescent protagonist without
sentimentality, and without condescension, but with a deeply sympathetic understanding." (D.P.)

M54 Durham, Frank, "God and No God in <u>The Heart is a Lonely Hunter</u>,"
<u>South Atlantic Quarterly</u>, 56:494-9, Autumn, 1957.

Reinforcing the theme of loneliness in <u>The Heart is a Lonely Hunter</u>
is an ironic religious allegory, which, although not intricately perfected, helps to emphasize the discreteness of human beings, not
just from one another but also from God. (W.B.B.)

M55 Evans, Oliver, "The Case of the Silent Singer: A Revaluation of
<u>The Heart Is a Lonely Hunter</u>," <u>Georgia Review</u>, 19:188-203,
Summer, 1965.

". . . the allegory of <u>The Heart Is a Lonely Hunter</u> is neither
religious nor political but concerns the struggle of individuals to
free themselves from the cells of their beings [and] . . . to identify
themselves . . . with something bigger than themselves and outside
themselves." (G.C.)

THE HEART IS A LONELY HUNTER (cont'd)

M56   Madden, David, "The Paradox of the Need for Privacy and the Need for Understanding in Carson McCullers's The Heart Is a Lonely Hunter," Literature and Psychology, 17:128-40, Nos. 2-3, 1967.

"The validity of McCullers's vision of the psychic realm of her characters, or of man, depends a great deal upon the accuracy and consistency with which she achieves a very acute psychological understanding of her characters and of the nature of loneliness which moves them grotesquely." (J.M.D.)

M57   Moore, Jack B., "Carson McCullers: The Heart is a Timeless Hunter," Twentieth Century Literature, 11:76-81, July, 1965.

The Heart Is a Lonely Hunter employs the myth of initiation retold "in convincingly contemporary terms." (D.P.)

M58   Sherrill, Rowland A., "McCullers's The Heart Is a Lonely Hunter: The Missing Ego and the Problem of the Norm," Kentucky Review, 2:5-17, No. 1, 1968.

"McCullers probes to the sources of human loneliness as the characters attempt to relate themselves to the world of the novel, find no reciprocity from that world, and, without gratification, re-address themselves inwardly . . . to a dream world within which they become hopelessly absurd." (G.C.)

THE MEMBER OF THE WEDDING

M59   Phillips, Robert S., "The Gothic Architecture of The Member of the Wedding," Renascence, 16:59-72, Winter, 1964.

This essay will "define those themes and functional devices which constitute Gothicism in the contemporary American novel" and examine their use in McCullers's novels, which are perhaps the most typical examples of Southern Gothicism in this century. (S.A.)

M60   Tinkham, Charles B., "The Members of the Side Show," Phylon, 18:383-90, Fourth Quarter, 1958.

Mrs. McCullers's Member of the Wedding, like the film "The Quiet One," dramatizes the problem of untold numbers of unhappy people today who seek out artificial happiness in some single system

THE MEMBER OF THE WEDDING (cont'd)

that seems a sweeping solution to all the problems of life and who
hysterically oppose any group that threatens their claim to exclusive
happiness. (W.G.F.)

Mac DIARMID, HUGH

M61   Cookson, William, "Some Notes on Hugh MacDiarmid," Agenda,
5, No. 4-6, No. 1, pp. 35-41, 1967-68.

MacDiarmid's Scots poems are unique because of " 'their special
combination of imaginative power, tenderness, wit, intelligence.'
. . ." The "uneveness of MacDiarmid's later work is to be looked
for in his use of the English language." (G.C.)

M62   Cox, Kenneth, "Hugh MacDiarmid's Neoplatonism," Agenda,
5, No. 4-6, No. 1, pp. 65-71, 1967-68.

". . . neoplatonism most readily indicates the sort of experiences
and ideas central to MacDiarmid's work. . . . Established at the
centre and ignoring the middle MacDiarmid's poetry reaches out to
the remote extremities of the real." (G.C.)

M63   Glen, Duncan, "Hugh MacDiarmid: Supporting Roles," Agenda,
5, No. 4-6, No. 1, pp. 53-8, 1967-68.

". . . the most fruitful of MacDiarmid's personal theory building
has been that which . . . has been important outside his own poetry
in that it has produced the Scottish Literary Revival." (G.C.)

M64   Keir, W. A. S., "Hugh MacDiarmid and the Scottish Renaissance,"
English (London), 16:230-3, Autumn, 1967.

Hugh MacDiarmid, associated for over forty years with the so-called
Scottish Renaissance, "has always been supremely individualistic,
controversial, and provocative, and--for many of his readers--ca-
pricious, inconsistent, and self-contradictory." (D.P.)

M65   Kocmanová, Jessie, "Art and Revolution in the Poetry of Hugh
MacDiarmid," Philologica Pragensia, 5:218-25, 1963.

". . . while MacDiarmid has much in common with the formal
revolt of the English and American poets and writers of the twenties
. . . his purpose and his achievement in his poetry are profoundly

different and considerably more challenging." He has devoted his life "to finding the true synthesis of Art and Revolution." (G.C.)

M66   MacDiarmid, Hugh, "Growing Up in Langholm," Listener, 78:204-6, August 17, 1967.

"After journeying over most of Scotland, England and central, southern and Eastern Europe, as well as America, Siberia and China, I am of the opinion that my native place--the Muckle Toon of Langholm, in Dumfriesshire--is the bonniest place I know: by virtue . . . of the wonderful variety and quality of the scenery in which it is set." (D.P.)

M67   MacDiarmid, Matthew P., "Hugh MacDiarmid and the Colloquial Category," Agenda, 5, No. 4-6, No. 1, pp. 72-8, 1967-68.

". . . in his most ambitious poem ['A Drunk Man Looks At the Thistle,' MacDiarmid] may . . . free himself from the folk-image of the poet . . . even when exploiting folk connotations . . . but his technique and style . . . [conform] to the eighteenth century opinion that modern Scots poetry must be . . . a colloquial poetry." (G.C.)

M68   Milner, Ian, "The Poetic Vision of Hugh MacDiarmid," Landfall, 16:362-71, 1962.

"No other modern poet has looked more deeply or more honestly upon the discords of his own nature, as of his society, and voiced the possible harmonies, than Hugh MacDiarmid . . . . he stands among the great innovating imaginations of our time." (K.M.W.)

M69   Moore, Hugo, "Nationalism and Social Revolution: Hugh MacDiarmid in Politics," Agenda, 5, No. 4-6, No. 1, pp. 59-64, 1967-68.

"Monetary reform, Nationalism, Social Revolution" are "political ideas" valuable "as fertilising influences on the poetry of Hugh MacDiarmid." His is poetry which is "one of the few political forces . . . [the people] have anything to hope from." (G.C.)

M70   Morgan, Edwin, "MacDiarmid at 75," Listener, 78:176-7, August 10, 1967.

The greatest flaw in MacDiarmid's poetry is his lack of human feeling, a deficiency which in another writer would be crippling. However he has created "a poetry that has managed to bring to-gether science, religion, politics, aesthetics, and certainly polemics, and to devise its own Pisa-like tower of simile and allusion, cemented with the loosest syntax known to Christendom, and yet to stand, as impressively in the end as any 20th-century verse." (D.P.)

M71   Scott, Alexander, "Hugh MacDiarmid and the Scots Tradition," Agenda, 5, No. 4-6, No. 1, pp. 42-52, 1967-68.

MacDiarmid "endeavour[ed] to create verse in Scots which expressed higher reaches of spiritual and intellectual concern . . . than the eighteenth-century Scottish bards had aimed at." (G.C.)

M72   Scott, Tom, "Some Poets of the Scottish Renaissance," Poetry, 88:43-7, April, 1956.

Hugh MacDiarmid, greatest poet of the present Scottish Renaissance, among several poets of significance, has developed the song tradition from "folk song and imitation of folk song to art song and the true lyric poem." He has also reintroduced an intellectual and moral content "not present since the Middle Ages." (F.L.)

M73   Singer, Burns, "Scarlet Eminence: A Study of the Poetry of Hugh MacDiarmid," Encounter, 8:49-62, March, 1957.

A grotesque synthesis of perfect Beauty with the merciless arrogance of MacDiarmid's communism was his life-long attempt. He revived the ancient idea of the poet as universal sage and attempted omniscience, and he was therefore left with a "plethora of truths." (D.B.D.)

M74   Smith, Ian Crichton, "Hugh MacDiarmid: Sangschaw and A Drunk Man Looks at the Thistle," Studies in Scottish Literature, 7:169-79, 1970.

Sangschaw "shows quite unmistakably the emergence of a poet of genius. . . ." A Drunk Man "seems to be a turning point in MacDiarmid's work. . . . Before it he wrote hallucinatory lyrics. After it we find him accepting an unorthodox communism. A Drunk Man shows him in an uneasy poise [between the two]." (D.A.B.)

IN MEMORIAM JAMES JOYCE

M75   Morgan, Edwin, "Jujitsu for the Educated: Reflections on Hugh MacDiarmid's Poem 'In Memoriam James Joyce'," Twentieth Century, 160:223-31, September, 1956.

IN MEMORIAM JAMES JOYCE (cont'd)

This poem "is great, and it is also petty; it swings across continents and seas . . . and yet it is also eccentric, home-made, and often self-contradictory." (G.C.)

M76   Morgan, Edwin, "MacDiarmid and Sherrington," Notes and Queries, 10:382-4, October, 1963.

A passage in "In Memoriam James Joyce" is adapted from the fourth chapter of Sir Charles Sherrington's Man on His Nature. (W.G.F.)

LAMENT FOR THE GREAT MUSIC

M77   Scott, Tom, "Lament for the Great Music," Agenda, 5, No. 4-6, No. 1, pp. 19-34, 1967-68.

MacDiarmid, in his lament for the neglected "pibroch music of the MacCrimmons," is "discovering the deepest historic roots of his own psyche, and is inspired . . . to a classical muse which has never been equalled . . . since Milton, in these islands." (G.C.)

McDOUGALL, COLIN

M78   Sutherland, Ronald, "The Vital Pretense: McDougall's Execution," Canadian Literature, No. 27, pp. 20-31, Winter, 1966.

"The artistic qualities of Execution are concordant with the significance of its theme. The style is laconic, touched with poetry on occasion, and ideally suited to the dramatic quality of the material." The novel projects "a total and powerful impression of war--its thrills, its horrors, its glory, its boredom, its madness, and, ironically, its momentary periods of profound peace." (D.P.)

McEVOY, JOSEPH PATRICK

M79   Turner, Darwin T., "Jazz-Vaudeville Drama in the Twenties," Educational Theatre Journal, 11:110-6, May, 1959.

Among American Jazz-Vaudeville plays written in the decade of experimentation between 1920 to 1930, John Howard Lawson's Processional, John Dos Passos's The Garbage Man, J. P. McEvoy's God Loves Us, and Channing Pollock's Mr. Moneypenny are outstanding, although none was completely successful. Probably "the major reason for the death of Jazz-Vaudeville social criticism in drama was the inability of the playwrights to enrich their dramas with thought and significance which would transcend the superficial appeal of the novelty of the technique." (D.P.)

MacEWEN, GWENDOLYN

M80   Atwood, Margaret, "MacEwen's Muse," Canadian Literature, No. 45, pp. 24-32, Summer, 1970.

In Gwendolyn MacEwen's poetry the Muse is "often invoked and described but never named. . . ." He is "the inspirer of language and the formative power in Nature; [he] is male." His function is to achieve "the creation of order out of chaos." (D.P.)

M81   Gose, E. B., "They Shall Have Arcana," Canadian Literature, No. 21, pp. 36-45, Summer, 1964.

[This is an analysis of Gwendolyn MacEwen's novel, Julian the Magician, by means of folkloric and alchemical motifs.] (H.M.)

McFEE, WILLIAM

M82   McFee, William, "The Literary Life at Seventy-Five: A Whine from the Chimney Corner," Saturday Review, 39:7-8, 38-40, July 14, 1956.

"A man who has reached my age reacts against anniversaries out of modesty. He has seen so many reputations rise like balloons and sink out of sight. . . . He becomes increasingly aware of the meretriciousness of all literary fame. He certainly becomes skeptical of his own pretensions." (D.P.)

McGAHERN, JOHN

M83   Cook, Bruce, "Irish Censorship: The Case of John McGahern," Catholic World, 206:176-9, January, 1968.

John McGahern's second novel, The Dark, was banned in Ireland, immediately after it was published in England, as "indecent or obscene." Subsequently, McGahern lost his teaching job and has not, since then, been able to teach in Ireland. It is clear that this censorship is the response to McGahern's intensity of feelings "against priests, father, government, all figures of authority." (D.P.)

M84   Cronin, John, "The Dark Is Not Light Enough: The Fiction of John
       McGahern," Studies, 58:427-32, Winter, 1969.

       "It seems to me that McGahern's first novel, The Barracks . . .
       perfectly achieved his purpose but that The Dark, which attempts
       to present a similar[ly] somber universe in confessional form is
       . . . much less successful. . . . The success and the failure depend
       . . . on form." (D.A.B.)

       McGAHEY, JEANNE

M85   Moore, Rosalie, "The Beat and the Unbeat," Poetry, 93:104-7,
       November, 1958.

       "Beat poetry gives you a false sense of urgency; not that the urgency
       does not actually exist, but that the beatman is substituting pitch for
       the actual work which a poet should do. . . . The main difference in
       the work of Jeanne McGahey seems . . . to lie in her technical
       skill." In her poetry "she tries to excite or move the reader. She
       uses . . . an indirect approach . . . [which] is actually a short-cut
       into the emotional core of the poem, and to the perception of the
       reader." (D.P.)

       McGINLEY, PHYLLIS

M86   Halsey, Louis, "The Poetry of Phyllis McGinley," Catholic World,
       211:211-5, August, 1970.

       The knowledgeable reader will perceive in Phyllis McGinley's poetry
       "the consummate craft, the sharp clarity of her ideas, the artful
       pacing of the rhythms, the quick but kindly wit. the engaging irony,
       the telltale foible neatly forked, the shaped and satisfying conclusion.
       Love and compassion temper her satire and irony." In American
       light verse only Oliver Wendell Holmes "is her equal; in this century
       she is sui generis." (D.P.)

M87   Richart, Bette, "The Light Touch," Commonweal, 73:277-9,
       December 9, 1960.

       Phyllis McGinley follows in a tradition of light verse perfected by
       Robert Herrick, and, earlier in this century, practiced by Dorothy
       Parker and Edna St. Vincent Millay. Miss McGinley adds suburbia
       to love and art as the proper subjects of light verse; she doesn't
       always "realize that light verse has a moral obligation not to make
       a point at the expense of truth. . . . Her variety, her usual . . .

explicitness of observation, her humanity are a tradition in themselves. . . . she is, within her tradition, an important poet. . . ." (D.P.)

M88 Sullivan, Kay, "From Suburbs to Saints: Phyllis McGinley," Catholic World, 185:420-5, September, 1957.

"First and foremost a wife and mother, a superlative cook, sunny and chic, Phyllis McGinley has been acclaimed the best writer of light verse in the United States. She has sent admiring parents to the suburbs and capitulated children with her lovable saints." (D.P.)

MACHADO DE ASSIS, JOAQUIM MARIA--See
ASSIS, JOAQUIM MARIA MACHADO DE

MACHADO Y RUIZ, ANTONIO

M89 Albornoz, Aurora de, "La presencia de Segovia en Antonio Machado," Ínsula, 19:9-10, July-August, 1964.

An unknown poem and a short article remind us that Machado's Segovia period was characterized more by personal friendships and public acts, less by solitary meditations on landscape. (C.O.)

M90 Angeles, José, "El mar en la poesía de Antonio Machado," Hispanic Review, 34:27-48, January, 1966.

Metaphors and other allusions to the sea in Machado's poetry, far from being facile, typify the "extralogical" aspect of most modern poetry, appealing predominantly to the subconscious part of man. (C.O.)

M91 Beceiro, Carlos, "Notas para la poética machadiana," Ínsula, 19:23-4, July-August, 1964.

From the earliest poems, the importance of remembering, of knowing, and of the symbolic value of the afternoon, is clear. (C.O.)

M92 Carbonell, Reyes, "Más notas estilísticas sobre la poesía de Antonio Machado," Duquesne Hispanic Review, 1:11-23, No. 1, 1962.

[This is a look at five stylistic resources of Antonio Machado.] (C.O.)

M93   Carrilla, Emilio, "La poesía de Antonio Machado," Revista Hispánica Moderna, 30:245-56, July-October, 1964.

Time is not only one theme of Machado's poetry, as has been stated repeatedly; it is the theme, standing in fundamental relationship to all other themes, giving a unity and coherence to his total work. (C.O.)

M94   Chapman, J. A., "Antonio Machado's Espejo sin azogue and a Seguiriya gitana," Romance Notes, 6:16-20, 1964.

An unusual image taken from the folksong collections of Machado's father suggests an area of further study in the sources of Machado's poetic material. (C.O.)

M95   Cobos, Pablo de A., "La muerte personal en Antonio Machado," La Torre, 17:53-69, July-September, 1969.

Machado seemed peculiarly unmoved by the fact of personal death. His stoicism was consistent with his characteristic carelessness concerning detail and his absent-mindedness with friends. The great exception centers on the death of his wife, Leonor. (C.O.)

M96   Durán, Manuel, "Antonio Machado, el desconfiado prodigioso," Ínsula, 19:1, 18, July-August, 1964.

Silent, suspicious, and alone, Machado is the one poet of his time who has best achieved communication, and known dialog, trust and love. (C.O.)

M97   Ferreres, Rafael, "Etapas de la poesía de Antonio Machado," Cuadernos Hispanoamericanos, 59:303-19, September, 1964.

[This is a survey of the four periods of Machado's poetry, with emphasis on theme and influences.] (C.O.)

M98   García Blanco, Manuel, "Cartas inéditas de Antonio Machado a Unamuno," Revista Hispánica Moderna, 22:97-114, April, 1956.

Machado's letters to Unamuno concerning the Spanish problem, religion, the First World War, and philosophy reveal the influence of Unamuno's thought on him. (A.C.H.)

M99 Gifford, Henry, "Seven Paragraphs on Antonio Machado," Hudson Review, 15:212-6, Summer, 1962.

Machado "was able to fuse personal tragedy with a landscape." (C.E.N.)

M100 Glendinning, Nigel, "The Philosophy of Henri Bergson in the Poetry of Antonio Machado," Revue de Littérature Comparée, 36:50-70, January-March, 1962.

The relatively few poems of Machado which deal with the idea of things in time make it clear that "Machado used Bergsonian ideas in his poetry for a relatively short period. And it seems probable that the extent of his debt to the French philosopher has been exaggerated." (D.P.)

M101 Gullón, Ricardo, "Distancia en Antonio Machado," Revista Hispánica Moderna, 34:313-29, 1968.

[Gullón studies especially "psychological distances" in its many forms, including irony, in Machado.] (C.O.)

M102 Gullón, Ricardo, "Sombras de Antonio Machado," Ínsula, 19:7, July-August, 1964.

Two "shadows" inhabit the poetry of Machado: that of the complementary self, partner in internal dialog, and that of the various others that Machado "might have become." (C.O.)

M103 Herrero, Javier, "Antonio Machado's Image of the Centaur," Bulletin of Hispanic Studies, 45:38-41, January, 1968.

Machado's centaur is astrology's Sagitarius. Spain, according to Ptolemy, falls under the sign of the Archer, the zodiac-monster, whose violent influence is imprinted in Spanish soil and expressed in Spanish character. (C.O.)

M104 Ilie, Paul, "Antonio Machado and the Grotesque," Journal of Aesthetics and Art Criticism, 22:209-16, Winter, 1963.

"Machado's contribution to the grotesque is best understood in terms of the shift from a moral-aesthetic to an existentialist preoccupation. . . . The grotesque expresses the poet's transcendence of his ego and the equivocal nature of his feelings. Whereas its more objective, Goyesque form is linked to the distortion of external reality, its subjective form foreshadows the psychological practices of surrealism." (D.P.)

M105   Luis, Leopoldo de, "Billetes de ferrocarril para Juan Ramón y Machado," La Estafeta Literaria, No. 434, pp. 10-1, December 15, 1969.

[This is a comparison of the modernismo and dynamism of Jiménez and Machado making use of their written impressions concerning railroad trains.] (T.T.B.)

M106   Mallo, Jerónimo, "La ideología religiosa y política del poeta Antonio Machado," Symposium, 9:339-47, Fall, 1955.

Machado was a traditional Spanish liberal, though less anti-clerical, more apolitical, more solitary than most. (C.O.)

M107   Marra-López, José R., "Antonio Machado: Una presencia ejemplar," Ínsula, 19:11, July-August, 1964.

[This is a personal tribute to an exemplary life and an exemplary work, from a member of the post-war generation.] (C.O.)

M108   Newberry, Wilma, "The Influence of Pirandello in Two Plays of Manuel and Antonio Machado," Hispania, 48:255-60, May, 1965.

In Las adelfas the Machados give their version of the theme of the many-sided nature of truth, but without carrying Pirandello's ideas to the extreme. In El hombre que marió en la guerra they pose the problem of personality, translating it to the Spain of the Generation of '98. (C.O.)

M109   Palley, Julian, "Los tres tiempos de Antonio Machado," Revista Hispánica Moderna, 30:257-60, July-October, 1964.

Machado's three times are (1) historical time or time recalled, (2) present time or time experienced, and (3) subconscious time or time dreamed. For Machado this third time represents a search for God. (C.O.)

M110   Parker, J. M., "The Poetry of Antonio Machado," English Studies in Africa, 7:217-26, 1964.

Machado, one of Spain's greatest modern poets, writes of "the conflict between past splendour and present decay." (R.K.)

M111 Piñera, Humberto, "Tempo de Proust en el tiempo de Machado," La Torre, 13:137-54, January-April, 1965.

The ideas of Bergson and Heidegger are clearly reflected in the ideas of Antonio Machado. But as a poet, Machado is closer to Proust. He feels time in the same way. He makes similar extensive use of memory and dream and creates a similar mood of tedio or tempo lento. (C.O.)

M112 Predmore, Michael P., "J. R. Jiménez's Second Portrait of Antonio Machado," Modern Language Notes, 80:265-70, March, 1965.

Jiménez's second portrait of Antonio Machado, published in Sur in 1941 "displays a rare combination of exact description with rich symbolic elaboration. . . . The style . . . and tone . . . are both sober and dignified--and deadly earnest." ". . . there is a remarkably sustained intensity throughout which results . . . from the singular unity of theme and from the homogeneity of expressive elements." This is "a magnificent symbolic portrait." (D.P.)

M113 Rojas, Carlos, "Machado the Moralist," Emory University Quarterly, 21:32-44, Spring, 1965.

Machado saw that the poet's principal moral responsibility is to recognize every stranger as his brother. (R.K.)

M114 Sánchez Barbudo, Antonio, "El pensamiento de Abel Martín y de Juan Mairena y su relación con la poesía de Antonio Machado," Hispanic Review, 22:109-65, April, 1954.

[This is the conclusion of a major study, here stressing Bergson, Heidegger, and the relation of philosophy and poetry.] (C.O.)

M115 Schwartz, Kessel, "The Sea and Machado," Hispania, 48:247-54, May, 1965.

"Machado views the sea as great poets have viewed it from time immemorial, as a primitive place of potential power, as an alluring call which is difficult to deny, as unfathomable, desolate, mysterious, terrible, as life and death, God and eternity. Machado's sea serves for every mood and occasion and it may be smiling, sonorous, somber, salty, fierce, tranquil, bitter, or loving." (C.O.)

M116   Suárez Rivero, Eliana, "Machado y Rosalía: Dos almas gemelas,"
        Hispania, 49:748-54, December, 1966.

        In spite of regional and chronological differences Rosalía is more
        than a precursor of one of Spain's greatest modern poets; she be-
        comes rather a "twin soul." (C.O.)

M117   Tilliette, Xavier, "Antonio Machado, poète philosophe," Revue de
        Littérature Comparée, 36:32-49, January-March, 1962.

        Bergson, Unamuno, and Ortega y Gasset influenced Machado's
        "poet philosophy" as represented in the characters of Abel Martín
        and Juan de Maireno. Martín, Leibnizian "philosopher of the
        future," praises poetry as a "deliverance from nothingness."
        Mairena, his pupil, is the more sceptical "poet of the present."
        (A.W.)

M118   Torre, Guillermo de, "Antonio Machado a los veinticinco años de
        su muerte," Cuadernos del Congreso por la Libertad de la Cultura,
        No. 86, pp. 51-5, July, 1964.

        The secret of Machado's lyric is that in spite of the technical in-
        novations of his contemporaries and the exegesis of commentators,
        it is formally old-fashioned and conceptually straightforward.
        (C.O.)

M119   Tudela, Jose, "Unamuno y Antonio Machado," Ínsula, 19:8, 26,
        November-December, 1964.

        [Two early letters from Unamuno, and an article by Machado attest
        to their continued friendship and ideological affinity.] (C.O.)

M120   Weiner, Jack, "Machado's Concept of Russia," Hispania, 49:31-5,
        March, 1966.

        "Out of a reverence for Russia as the mother of a universal literature
        seems to have emerged Machado's concept of the Soviet Union as the
        city of universal brotherhood. And one might even say that towards
        the end of his life he turned his eyes to atheist Russia in his search
        for 'the God we all seek but never find'." (C.O.)

        ANOCHE, CUANDO DORMÍA

M121   Foster, D. W., "Estructura poética en tres poemas de Unamuno,
        Machado y García Lorca," Duquesne Hispanic Review, 6:1-13,
        No. 1, 1967.

ANOCHE, CUANDO DORMÍA (cont'd)

[This is an examination of "poetic" language: repetition and accumulation especially, in Lorca's "Canción de jinete," Machado's "Anoche, cuando dormía," and Unamuno's "¿Qué es tu viva. . .?"]
(C.O.)

THE CRIME WAS IN GRANADA--See
EL CRIMEN FUE EN GRANADA

EL CRIMEN FUE EN GRANADA

M122   Wardropper, Bruce W., "The Modern Spanish Elegy: Antonio Machado's Lament for Federico García Lorca," Symposium, 19:162-70, Summer, 1965.

Machado's elegy on Lorca's death, his "El crimen fue en Granada" "is calculated down to every last effect. This means that the poet's angry grief is under the strictest control; it has been dominated by the very act of poetic creation. . . . By recalling, by recreating, Lorca's own poetry after his death, Machado has infused his poem with Lorca's poetic personality." (D.P.)

DE UN CANCIONERO APÓCRIFO

M123   Ciruti, Joan E., "Humor in the Cancionero apócrifo of Antonio Machado," Modern Language Forum, 42:133-40, December, 1957.

Though not characteristic of most of Machado's work, his late "intellectual wit" shows his maturity. The use of incongruous images, fantastic humor and "intellectual shock" is a result of his skepticism. Because of Machado's broad view, he is not "bothered with immortality" and religious seriousness, nor with tragic engagement, and therefore becomes a "humorist." (K.W.)

M124   Gicovate, Bernardo, "El testamento poético de Antonio Machado," PMLA, 71:42-50, March, 1956.

[This is a commentary on Machado's then much neglected De un cancionero apócrifo.] (C.O.)

ES UNA TARDE CENICIENTA Y MUSTIA

M125   Allen, John J., "Suspension of Formal Unities as a Poetic Device in a Poem by A. Machado," Romance Notes, 7:144-8, 1966.

ES UNA TARDE CENICIENTA Y MUSTIA (cont'd)

"Machado has developed an ideal situation for the temporary suspension of the unifying elements of his poem, for the very essence
of his similes is 'lostness,' aimlessness as opposed to order, and
motion as opposed to static symmetry." (C.O.)

FUE UNA CLARA TARDE

M126 Dobrian, Walter A., "Formal and Rhetorical Consciousness in
Antonio Machado," Hispania, 48:452-5, September, 1965.

Poem VI of Soledades, in contrast to the looseness of form and the
theme of joyful recollection in poem VII, "is one of Machado's most
consciously formal and rhetorical lyrical pieces . . . [although]
simplicity remains its dominant aspect. . . . What it is, in essence,
is a series of simple images and signfiicant phrases so skilfully
arranged and repeated that they render a moving impression of the
sentiment of the poet." (D.P.)

M127 Ilie, Paul, "Verlaine and Machado: The Aesthetic Role of Time,"
Comparative Literature, 14:261-5, Summer, 1962.

In comparing Verlaine's "Apres trois ans" with Machado's analogous.
"Fue una clara tarde," we find that "both men were idealists, but
Verlaine attempted to idealize what he felt to be an objective beauty,
while Machado idealized a past which he tried, paradoxically enough,
to objectify by memory." (C.E.N.

M128 Villegas, Juan, "El tema del tiempo en un poema de Antonio
Machado," Hispania, 48:442-51, September, 1965.

An analysis of poem VI of Soledades shows dialog to be the thematic
and formal center, as the poet and the fountain develop the theme of
anguish and monotony. (C.O.)

GALERÍAS

M129 Allen, Rupert C., "Un poema existencialista de Antonio Machado,"
Duquesne Hispanic Review, 2:57-71, Autumn, 1963.

The opposing philosophies of Pythagoras and Heraclitus are the
unifying element in the poem "Galerías," an existentialist vision--
confronting two ways of understanding human existence. Images
fall under two groupings, those of "being" and those of "becoming."
(C.O.)

GALLERIES--See
GALERÍAS

HACIA UN OCASO RADIANTE

M130 Siebenmann, Gustav. "Un poema típicamente machadiano: Analyse
eines Gedichtes von Antonio Machado," Germanisch-Romanische
Monatsschrift, 18:81-90, January, 1968.

In order to determine the significance of the frequent critical comment that a poem is "typical Machado," one may profitably consider
a detailed analysis of Machado's poem "Hacia un ocaso radiante."
(J.R.R.)

M131 Siebenmann, Gustav, "¿Qué es un poema 'típicamente machadiano'?
(Análisis de una poesía de Antonio Machado)," Papeles de Son
Armadans, 53:31-49, April, 1969.

A structural analysis of "Hacia un ocaso radiante . . ." suggests
the great importance of the temporal dimension. Machado's most
typical, i.e. longest, poems depend on careful development and
gradual evolution to a simple close. Neither in structure nor in
technical resources does he resemble the poets of previous generations. (C.O.)

HASTÍO

M132 Moody, Michael W., "A Stylistic Analysis of 'Hastío' by Antonio
Machado," Romance Notes, 8:161-4, 1967.

["A running analysis shows how successfully the poet has achieved a
sensitive equation of form and content . . . to advance the concept
of life on the decline."] (C.O.)

JUAN DE MAÑARA

M133 Ackerman, Stephen H., "The Machados and Don Juan," Revista de
Estudios Hispánicos, 1:157-82, 1967.

In the Machado brothers's drama, Juan de Mañara, Don Juan achieves
a kind of salvation, not through the intercession of a good woman, but
thanks to his own awareness of the consequences of his licentious life.
(C.O.)

JUAN DE MAÑARA (cont'd)

M134   Dominicis, María Canteli, "Antonio y Manuel Machado y su Don Juan de Mañara," Hispania, 46:730-4, December, 1963.

[This is a running commentary on the Machado version of the Don Juan play.] (C.O.)

MUERTE DE ABEL MARTÍN

M135   Turner, Dorothy, "Machado explicado por Machado," Ínsula, 19:8-9, July-August, 1964.

Machado's "Muerte de Abel Martín," may be understood by citing key lines from other Machado poems. It is neither lament nor resignation, but rather, the recognition of an act of will at life's end. (C.O.)

OUT OF AN APOCRYPHA SONGBOOK--See DE UN CANCIONERO APÓCRIFO

POEMA DE UN DÍA

M136   Morrow, Carolyn, "An Analysis of 'Poema de un día': The Philosophy of Bergson in Machado's Concept of Time," Romance Notes, 2:149-53, 1961.

"The influence of Bergson has developed the intuition of time seen in Soledades into the profound philosophy of 'Poema de un día.'. . . The rather laconic manner of the 'Poema' . . . [suggests] the terse refinement to come. . . . Perhaps it is [Bergson's] new ideas . . . which evoke in Machado the need for a new style." (D.P.)

POR UN VENTANAL, ENTRÓ LA LECHUZA

M137   Very, Francis, "A. Machado and the Oil-Drinking Owl," Modern Language Notes, 78:200-2, March, 1963.

The belief in the oil-drinking habit of the oliba and the lechuza "appears largely in Southern France, Catalonia, and Spain. . . . it appears . . . limited to Catholic countries. "In 'Por un ventanal, entró la lechuza' from Nuevas canciones Machado has "in cameo fashion, employed it as the means of exposition of the virtue of love toward the humblest creature in its need, even at the expense of the external adornments of the Christian faith." (D.P.)

SIESTA

M138 Enjuto, Jorge, "Comentarios en torno al poema 'Siesta' de Antonio
Machado," Ínsula, 19:13, July-August, 1964.

"[Machado] shows us, with his offering and with his life, the face of
true Being and the path to its discovery." (C.O.)

SOLEDADES

M139 Ribbans, Geoffrey, "Antonio Machado's Soledades (1903): A
Critical Study," Hispanic Review, 30:194-215, August, 1962.

[This is the first extended critical discussion of this "first volume,"
showing also the beginning of themes and modifications to be found
in later works.] (C.O.)

LA TIERRA DE ALVARGONZÁLEZ

M140 Foster, David William, "'La tierra de Alvargonzález': una con-
tribución machadeana al romance español," Duquesne Hispanic
Review, 4:65-77, Fall, 1965.

Although the ballad form was little cultivated by Machado, this 712
line composition uses the fragmentary and impressionistic nature of
the Spanish ballad to develop one central theme--the triumph of a
land over its poor inhabitants. The bitter tragedy here portrayed
reveals again Machado's relationship to the Generation of '98. (C.O.)

MACHADO Y RUIZ, MANUEL

M141 Carbonell, Reyes, "Textura de un verso de Manuel Machado,"
Romance Notes, 3:9-12, Autumn, 1961.

[This is an intensive metrical and phonological examination of one
line from Machado's Adelfas.] (G.B.M.

M142 Newberry, Wilma, "The Influence of Pirandello in Two Plays of
Manuel and Antonio Machado," Hispania, 48:255-60, May, 1965.

In Las adelfas the Machados give their version of the theme of the
many-sided nature of truth, but without carrying Pirandello's ideas
to the extreme. In El hombre que marió en la guerra they pose the
problem of personality, translating it to the Spain of the Generation
of '98. (C.O.)

JUAN DE MAÑARA

M143 Ackerman, Stephen H., "The Machados and Don Juan," Revista de Estudios Hispánicos, 1:157-82, 1967.

In the Machado brothers's drama, Juan de Mañara, Don Juan achieves a kind of salvation, not through the intercession of a good woman, but thanks to his own awareness of the consequences of his licentious life. (C.O.)

M144 Dominicis, María Canteli, "Antonio y Manuel Machado y su Don Juan de Mañara," Hispania, 46:730-4, December, 1963.

[This is a running commentary on the Machado version of the Don Juan play.] (C.O.)

MACHEN, ARTHUR

M145 Matteson, Robert S., "Arthur Machen: A Vision of an Enchanted Land," Personalist, 46:253-68, Spring, 1965.

Machen's theme was "the mystic vision, and his musical prose is outstanding. . . . his books are almost entirely Idea and Style. Few of them have flesh and blood characters and even his better books have little that could be called plot." (D.P.)

M146 Sweetser, Wesley D., "Arthur Machen: A Bibliography of Writings About Him," English Literature in Transition, 11:1-33, No. 1, 1968.

[This is an annotated bibliography of over 200 books, articles, and unpublished theses on Machen.] (K.M.W.)

M147 Sweetser, Wesley D., "Arthur Machen," English Literature in Transition, 13:65-7, No. 1, 1970.

[These are additions to Professor Sweetser's annotated bibliography of writings about Machen which appeared in ELT, vol. 11, 1968. (D.P.)

M148 Tyler, Robert L., "Arthur Machen: The Minor Writer and His Function," Approach, No. 35, pp. 21-6, Spring, 1960.

The minor writer sometimes shows how literary changes come about, points to a new style, a new mode of sensibility. Machen's significance lies in his near misses. (A.F.)

M149   Vodrey, Joseph Kelly, "Arthur Machen," <u>Princeton University Library Chronicle</u>, 26:114-8, Winter, 1965.

Arthur Machen's "distinctive style" and his " 'gift of vision' " continue to attract the attention of scholars. (D.P.)

THE ANGELS OF MONS

M150   John, Alun, "Arthur Machen and 'The Angels of Mons'," <u>Anglo-Welsh Review</u>, 14:10-4, 1964-65.

"The Angels of Mons" is a short story dealing with "spiritual powers coming to the aid of earthly arms" become a "war legend." (G.C.)

McKAY, CLAUDE

M151   Cooper, Wayne, "Claude McKay and the New Negro of the 1920's," <u>Phylon</u>, 25:297-306, Fall, 1964.

"In his prose, McKay stressed the value of the common Negro and joined other Negro Renaissance writers in a rediscovery of Negro folk culture. But . . . in his poetry, he best expressed the New Negro's determination to protect his human dignity, his cultural worth, and his right to a decent life." (D.P.)

THE HARLEM DANCER

M152   Collier, Eugenia W., "I Do Not Marvell, Countee Cullen," <u>CLA Journal</u>, 11:73-87, 1967.

"From the Dark Tower" by Countee Cullen "is a restrained, dignified, poignant work. . . ." Sterling A. Brown's "The Odyssey of Big Boy" is "an art ballad, uniting several aspects of folk experience." "The Harlem Dancer," by Claude McKay encases "the wild and lascivious world of the Harlem nightclub." These poems "represent some of the principal themes of the Negro poetry of the 1920's. . . ." (D.P.)

HOME TO HARLEM

M153   Arden, Eugene, "The Early Harlem Novel," <u>Phylon</u>, 20:25-31, Spring, 1959.

Dunbar's <u>The Sport of Gods</u> is the first novel to treat Negro life in New York seriously and at length. Van Vechten's <u>Nigger Heaven</u>, in

HOME TO HARLEM (cont'd)

spite of being sensational, "had much of serious interest to say
about the urban Negro." McKay's Home to Harlem and Thurman's
The Blacker the Berry established a stereotype Negro whose existence "seemed confined to drink, sex, gambling, and brooding about
racial matters. . . ." Fisher's The Walls of Jericho and Cullen's
One Way to Heaven launched a counter movement in realism. (D.P.)

M154   Larson, Charles R., "Three Harlem Novels of the Jazz Age,"
Critique: Studies in Modern Fiction, 11:66-78, No. 3, 1969.

Claude McKay's Home to Harlem, Carl Van Vechten's Nigger
Heaven, and Countee Cullen's One Way to Heaven document the
cultural birth of the urban Negro and give a panoramic picture of
the complexity of Negro life in Harlem during the 1920's. (B.K.N.)

TRUANT

M155   Turpin, Waters E., "Four Short Fiction Writers of the Harlem
Renaissance--Their Legacy of Achievement," CLA Journal,
11:59-72, September, 1967.

Jean Toomer, Rudolph Fisher, Langston Hughes and Claude McKay,
all associated with the Harlem Renaissance, have each produced
works of short fiction which represent "a kind of legacy which the
young contemporary Negro writer may draw on with profit." (D.P.)

MacKAYE, PERCY

M156   Ritter, Charles C., "Percy MacKaye's Civic Theatre Philosophy as
Revealed in His Speeches," Quarterly Journal of Speech, 53:349-53,
December, 1967.

In the early years of this century "by means of the civic theatre
ideal MacKaye prophesied the integration of the unartistic energy
of many diverse movements current at the time. . . . MacKaye's
concept of communal drama was based on the principle of neighbor-
liness. Through the exercise of this principle, he hoped that the
civic theatre could act as a great instrument of national unity."
(D.P.)

MACKENZIE, COMPTON

M157   Fytton, Francis, "Compton Mackenzie: Romance versus Realism,"
Catholic World, 182:358-63, 1956.

". . . Mackenzie is a great romantic writer, a sort of Sir Walter
Scott in the manner of Jane Austen. . . . [He] has been true to the
great romantic tradition of Smollet and Scott," a tradition the
contemporary English novel could benefit from. (G.C.)

M158   Mackenzie, Sir Compton, "The Art of Memory," Listener,
69:199-200, January 31, 1963.

"What happened nearly eighty years ago is still happening. Therefore I have no nostalgia for the past, no regrets for friends who
have passed away; I never make the mistake of revisiting places
that influenced my youth because I know that their magic would
have faded and that I should be disillusioned by material changes."
(D.P.)

MACKENZIE, KENNETH IVO

M159   Clarke, Donovan, "Seaforth Mackenzie: Novelist of Alienation,"
Southerly, 25:75-90, No. 2, 1965.

The "socially alienated" Mackenzie used in his four novels the
broad theme of alienation. Failure to publish his Dead Men Rising
(1951) in his native Australia depresses his reputation there. (S.T.)

M160   Cowan, Peter, "Seaforth Mackenzie's Novels," Meanjin Quarterly,
24:298-307, September, 1965.

Kenneth Ivo (Seaforth) Mackenzie's "four novels show him to be one
of the most clearly individual and mature writers Australia has
produced." These novels reveal a "facility with words, [and] a
refusal to be satisfied with the simpler levels of experience."
(G.C.)

M161   Davis, Diana, "A Checklist of Kenneth Mackenzie's Works, Including Manuscript Material," Australian Literary Studies, 43:398-404,
1970.

[This is a listing of Mackenzie's published works, studies of
Mackenzie and manuscript material held in Australian libraries.]
(G.C.)

MACKENZIE

M162   Davis, Diana, "The Genesis of a Writer: The Early Years of Kenneth
Mackenzie," Australian Literary Studies, 3:254-70, 1968.

This paper considers "the forces which, in the backwater Perth of
the late twenties and early thirties, impelled Mackenzie to take up
writing as a profession at a time when Australian society, utilitarian
in the choice of purposes to which wealth might be devoted, gave only
rare opportunities for a professional life in literature." (D.A.B.)

M163   Geering, R. G., "Seaforth Mackenzie's Fiction: Another View,"
Southerly, 26:25-39, No. 1, 1966.

Mackenzie's "unpublished papers confirm the impression given by
the complete novels--that of a genuine artist struggling to come to
terms with himself and trying to discover which areas of his experience were truly meaningful. All his prose writings reveal, too, his
search for that elusive adjustment between the teller and the tale
which holds both in the perfect balance." (D.A.B.)

M164   Jones, Evans, "A Dead Man Rising: The Poetry of Kenneth
Mackenzie," Australian Quarterly, 36:70-9, June, 1964.

Mackenzie's early poetry was influenced by his Sydney friends; it is
fluent, lacks discipline, most particularly a moral discipline.
". . . in his later poems, one finds a man straining to find his way.
His themes become silence, isolation, the contemplation of death:
and his discipline becomes much more stringent." There is a
"serenity that is strained towards, and . . . is achieved. We have
very little poetry of the calm certainty of Mackenzie at his best.
. . ." (D.P.)

MACKENZIE, SEAFORTH--See
MACKENZIE, KENNETH IVO

MACKINTOSH, ELIZABETH

M165   Conklin, Matthew T., "The Tragic Effect in Autumn Fire and Desire
Under the Elms," Modern Drama, 1:228-35, February, 1959.

"Although each author treated the same themes and used a similar
set of characters in a rural setting, the tragic effects of the two
plays are so vastly dissimilar as to warrant a comparative study."
(C.K.L.)

M165   2444

McLAVERTY, MICHAEL

M166   Cronin, John, "Ulster's Alarming Novels," <u>Eire: Ireland</u>,
        4:24-34, No. 4, 1969.

        "Ulster, with its segregated schools, its residential ghettoes and
        its neanderthal politics produces novelists [like Michael McLaverty
        Brian Moore, Forrest Reid or Maurice Leitch] who reflect its
        sectarian schizophrenia." (G.C.)

MacLEISH, ARCHIBALD

M167   Edwards, Clifford W., "From <u>Everyman</u> to <u>Superman</u> in Archibald
        MacLeish," <u>Catholic World</u>, 210:165-9, January, 1970.

        "In <u>J. B.</u> MacLeish pictured life as meaningless, but the miracle of
        love in a man's heart as a way out. In <u>Herakles</u>, man faced by the
        absence of God must look to himself for the meaning of life, but
        . . . MacLeish has perhaps begun to discern a new humanity beyond
        the Hebrew <u>Everyman</u> and the Greek <u>Superman</u>." (D.P.)

M168   MacLeish, Archibald, "The Poet and America: A Discussion of His
        Development as a Poet," <u>Carolina Quarterly</u>, 9:5-13, Winter, 1957.

        In his poems MacLeish searches for "the definition of the American
        idea." Ultimately, this "idea of America" is identified as "an idea
        of human integrity set in a rich land, with the greatest of all man's
        dreams to live by--the dream of a whole and generous freedom."
        (G.C.)

M169   Sickels, Eleanor M., "MacLeish and the Fortunate Fall," <u>American
        Literature</u>, 35:205-17, May, 1963.

        Through his first treatment of "the myth of the lost Paradise in the
        verse play <u>Nobodaddy</u>" through "the proud humanism of <u>Songs for
        Eve</u> and the tragic reconciliation of <u>J. B.</u>," MacLeish's Fall "is
        fortunate because without it man is a mere animal. . . . MacLeish's
        redemption is in all human good achievement, and in the very yearn-
        ing for the infinite which caused the Fall." (D.P.)

M170   Worth, Katharine J., "The Poets in the American Theatre,"
        <u>Stratford-upon-Avon-Studies</u>, 10:86-107, 1967.

        Archibald MacLeish, Robert Lowell, William Carlos Williams and
        e. e. cummings "have made their names as poets outside the theatre,

and . . . in coming into the theatre, have usually been regarded as attempting or making a second reputation." "Their very sense of isolation, by providing them with a theme, has drawn them into the main stream of modern drama. They may exist . . . on the extreme fringe of the American theatre, but their subject matter is central, the isolation of the individual in the world of his imagination, the desperation of his attempts at communication." (D.P.)

ARS POETICA

M171 Blanke, Gustav H., "Archibald MacLeish: 'Ars Poetica',"
Jahrbuch für Amerikastudien, 13:236-45, 1968.

"The following interpretation is intended to show that the devaluation of 'meaning' in favor of 'being' cannot be interpreted as a condoning of an absence of 'significant meaning' or even simply of 'meaning'; rather, MacLeish is concerned with coming to grips with a literary work 'which has a palpable design upon us' (Keats.") (J.R.R.)

M172 Sullivan, Harry R., "MacLeish's 'Ars Poetica'," English Journal, 56:1280-3, December, 1967.

MacLeish's "Ars Poetica," which is a "poem about the meaning of poetry does not simply tell us what it is; it succeeds in actually becoming what it purports to demonstrate. Importantly, the poem . . . images life in its ambiguities, paradoxes, and ironies." (D.P.)

DOVER BEACH--A NOTE TO THAT POEM

M173 Zigerell, James, "MacLeish's '"Dover Beach"--A Note to that Poem'," Explicator, 17: Item 38, March, 1959.

The mature mind does not want unchanging fullness. (B.K.)

THE END OF THE WORLD

M174 Kocher, Annis Cox, " 'The End of the World' for a New Beginning," English Journal, 55:700-2, September, 1966.

"In the sonnet 'The End of the World,' Archibald MacLeish in his octave piles up concrete details of the circus in a breathless series, only to destroy the whole with matter of fact: 'Quite unexpectedly the top blew off.' . . . Even more disturbing . . . the sestet [which follows] shocks with the prolonged horror of great, dark, unbelieving emptiness." (D.P.)

THE HAMLET OF A. MacLEISH

M175 Gottesman, Lillian, " 'The Hamlet of A. MacLeish'," CLA Journal, 11:157-62, December, 1967.

"MacLeish's 'Hamlet' is a commentary on [Shakespeare's] play, an adaptation, and a series of associations. The poem is made up largely of fleeting meditations. Lines quoted from Shakespeare are adapted and used in a new context." Other sources "especially the Grail Legend and T. S. Eliot's poetry" provide "allusions and symbols." (D.A.B.)

HERAKLES: A PLAY IN VERSE

M176 Eberhart, Richard, "Archibald MacLeish's Herakles," Virginia Quarterly Review, 43:499-503, Summer, 1967.

MacLeish's Herakles is a "play of poetic ideas. . . . The litheness, leanness, and efficiency of the language is everywhere apparent and in this play MacLeish has given us great quickenings of poetic imagery, flashes of profound insight set forth with staccato force, a vehicle of language so pliable and sharp as to catch the Greek spirit of lightness and truth." (D.P.)

M177 Sandeen, Ernest, "This Mortal Story," Poetry, 112:199-201, June, 1968.

Archibald MacLeish's Herakles: A Play in Verse shows man "striding toward God-like Power" through his knowledge of science, but "trailing the Jungian shadow." Herakles is a better play than J. B. it entrusts more to the audience. In its use of language and verse it reveals its author's experienced craftsmanship. (F.L.)

HYPOCRITE AUTEUR

M178 Joost, Nicholas, "MacLeish's 'Hypocrite Auteur'," Explicator, 11: Item 47, May, 1955.

In "Hypocrite Auteur" we see "the debt of MacLeish to the French symbolists. First . . . he tells us that the poet creates metaphors which themselves are images quarried from the inexhaustible wealth of meanings in men. Second, MacLeish proceeds to demonstrate this esthetic doctrine by making 'Hypocrite Auteur' itself such a metaphor. The poem is a large metaphor constructed of a series of smaller metaphors, all with subtly interlocking relationships. . . ." (D.P.)

J. B.

M179   Bond, Charles M., "J. B. is not Job," Bucknell Review, 9:272-80, March, 1961.

"Not only does MacLeish fail to see the real problem of Job, he fails also to understand God as the author of the Book of Job understands him." (G.C.)

M180   Caspar, Leonard, "The Godmask of MacLeish," Drama Critique, 1:11-2, November, 1958.

"For the undiscerning and undemanding, J. B. will be consoling. It makes God man's scapegoat by claiming that man has always been God's; it argues that man is the more admirable for being not only less guilty than God, but more loving as well. For others J. B. will raise ponderable questions. Does J. B. actually love, or first trust and then fear his God? If he loves, is it the love of oversight . . . or of gratitude. . . . Above all, would such questions exist . . . if J. B. had been intimately characterized through the course of the play?" (D.P.)

M181   Christensen, Parley A., "J. B., the Critics, and Me," Western Humanities Review, 15:111-26, Spring, 1961.

Despite a paradoxical critical response--"nearly all [critics] found in it unresolved problems, distressing ambiguities"--J. B. can be said to be "true in spirit to the great tragedies of literature. . . . [it] shows us how through terrible affliction a theist becomes a humanist. . . ." (G.C.)

M182   Ciardi, John, "J. B. Revisited," Saturday Review, 43:39, 55, January 30, 1960.

"MacLeish . . . has taken the Job legend out of a God-centered universe and reset it in a naturalistic universe. Stricken, J. B. cries out to the blank spaces for Justice, but . . . all God has to say is that He is bigger than a man. But J. B. . . . had asked for justice, not for size. And there . . . J. B. bows his head and forgives God, for he realizes that size is the only answer the universe can give back." (D.P.)

J. B. (cont'd)

M183 D'Arcy, Martin C., S. J., "J. B.: Wrong Answer to the Problem of Evil," Catholic World, 190:81-5, November, 1959.

In J. B. "Mr. MacLeish appears to mean that it is useless to call upon divine justice or love, but there remains human love, and that is enough. . . . Not only the theologians have missed this point which MacLeish makes, but also Job and the Writer of Job as well. MacLeish has read into the story what is not there." (D.P.)

M184 Dunkel, Wilbur Dwight, "Theology in the Theater," Theology Today, 16:65-73, April, 1959.

". . . while one praises J. B. as an artistic masterpiece, even in its denial of the Christian faith, the Christian must regret that the early premises of this work of art were not fulfilled." James Forsyth's "Heloise deals with the theology of Abelard . . . rather than the letters of this articulate pair of lovers." The dramatization of Greene's The Power and the Glory by Dennis Cannan and Pierre Bost "develops forceful theological concepts." Compassion is "the pervasive quality of O'Neill's latest play, A Touch of the Poet." Budd Schulberg and Harvey Breit's The Disenchanted "poses the theological question . . . : 'What has happened to Me?'" "In The Shadow of a Gunman Sean O'Casey . . . still tilts his lance at the Roman Catholic Church and its ritual. . . ." These recent productions share great attention to theological principles. (D.P.)

M185 Gledhill, Preston R., "J. B.: Successful Theatre versus 'Godless' Theology," Brigham Young University Studies, 3:9-14, Winter, 1961.

J. B. is magnificent theatre, and although there is occasional unevenness in the verse, the play does include "hauntingly beautiful poetry." Yet for all that, J. B. is characterized by a "negativistic and unchristian philosophy." J. B. is not a religious play. (D.P.)

M186 Grebstein, Sheldon Norman, "J. B. and the Problem of Evil," University of Kansas City Review, 29:253-61, June, 1963.

". . . Job must be tested so that he can see God, who is best seen from an ash-heap. Instead, it is from his ash-heap that J. B. performs the heroic act of forgiving God, of starting again, with the realization that the same terrors could again befall him." (K.M.W.)

J. B. (cont'd)

M187   Hall, Donald, "Archibald MacLeish: On Being a Poet in the Theatre,"
Horizon, 2:48-56, January, 1960.

Verse plays can be successful on the modern stage if the dramatic
form is suited to the verse form. J. B. was made successful by
the happy consolidation of many theatre people, notably Elia Kazan.
(J.P.H.)

M188   Hamilton, Kenneth, "The Patience of J. B.," Dalhousie Review,
41:32-9, Spring, 1961.

In accepting the romantic humanism of Matthew Arnold, MacLeish
"fails to come to grips with the religious realism of the Book of
Job." (R.K.)

M189   Kazan, Elia and Archibald MacLeish, "The Staging of a Play: The
Notebooks and Letters of Elia Kazan's Staging of Archibald
MacLeish's J. B.," Esquire, 51:144-58, May, 1959.

[This is an extensive exchange of letters between Kazan and
MacLeish concerning the reshaping of the play for its New York
appearance.] (D.P.)

M190   Krutch, Joseph Wood, "The Universe at Stage Center," Theatre
Arts, 42:9-11, August, 1958.

"J. B. and his wife are . . . recognizably modern Americans,
though they are sufficiently generalized to represent an Everyman
and an Everywoman." In "the action Job's calamities fall upon him
one after another in short, swift scenes sufficiently particularized
to be humanly compelling, sufficiently typical to symbolize adequately
Misfortune itself. . . . The verse is strong enough, compact enough,
and rich enough to be rewarding when read. . . . J. B. makes its
mark because it never fumbles. . . . the execution matches the
intention." (D.P.)

M191   Lynch, William F., "Ritual and Drama," Commonweal, 71:586-8,
February 26, 1960.

Among recent cinematic explorations of the ritual imagination are
the Mexican One-Eye and He Who Must Die, the film version of
Kazantzakis's The Greek Passion. In MacLeish's J. B. "the cart
of sensibility and thought is way out in front of the action. . . . It

M191   2450

J. B. (cont'd)

is a new Job we are given, a thoroughly romantic one." In the end
we cannot believe in the new dichotomy of "a Christian theology that
is transcendental and on the other hand a new poetic and non-theo-
logical experience that is in touch with reality." (D.P.)

M192   MacDonald, Dwight, "Masscult and Midcult," Partisan Review,
        27:203-33, 589-631, Spring, Fall, 1960.

". . . Masscult is at best a vulgarized reflection of High Culture
and at worst a cultural nightmare, a Kulturkatzenjammer."
Hemingway's The Old Man and the Sea, Wilder's Our Town,
MacLeish's J. B., and Benet's John Brown's Body are typical Midcult products. ". . . each has won the Pulitzer prize, has been
praised by critics who should know better, and has been popular
. . . with the educated classes. Technically, they are advanced
enough to impress the midbrows without worrying them. In content,
they are 'central' and 'universal' in the line of hollowly portentous
art. . . ." (D.P.)

M193   McLaughlin, John, S. J., "J. B.: Under What Sign?" National
        Review, 6:563-4, January 18, 1959.

"Mr. MacLeish's J. B., I am saying, considered in its totality, is
subversive of Christian principle and worthy of bold-face type in our
era's sterile lexicon of secularism. . . . In J. B. the message is,
regrettably but unmistakably, anti-supernatural." (D.P.)

M194   MacLeish, Andrew, "The Poet's Three Comforters: J. B. and the
        Critics," Modern Drama, 2:224-30, December, 1959.

The pejorative criticism of latter-day critics sees J. B. as a mis-
representation of the Book of Job and fails to recognize that the
Book of Job provides a "suggestive framework for a modern and
broadly universal statement." Rather, the play is "an illustration
of man's existence within the Christian tradition. . . ." (C.K.L.)

M195   MacLeish, Archibald, "The Men Behind J. B.," Theatre Arts,
        43:60-3, April, 1959.

"The Book of Job is a human triumph. Its answer is not a dogma
but an act--Job's act, Job's doing, Job's picking up his life again.
And the myth of Job is a myth for our time because this is our
answer also: the answer that moves so many of us . . . [to] pick

J. B. (cont'd)

up our lives again after these vast disasters and go on--go on as men." [This is followed by brief statements by Alfred de Liagre, Jr., producer of J. B., Elia Kazan, director and Boris Aronson, designer.] (D.P.)

M196 Montgomery, Marion, "On First Looking into Archibald MacLeish's Play in Verse, J. B.," Modern Drama, 2:231-42, December, 1959.

While "MacLeish has demonstrated that he is aware of the technical complexities of play verse . . . J. B. has the feeling, despite some interesting stage manipulations, of a humanistic sermon and a pep-talk." (C.K.L.)

M197 Siegel, Ben, "Miracle on Broadway: And the Box-office Magic of the Bible," Modern Drama, 2:45-6, May, 1959.

J. B.'s warm success on Broadway, against the publicity limitations of a New York newspaper strike, appears due, in part,to planned and fortuitous coverage by national television and the fact that by and large the nation's conforming intellectuals had queued up "with pant-ing eagerness to witness a graphic reaffirmation of the durability of the ancient verities." (D.P.)

M198 Stock, Ely, "A Masque of Reason and J. B.: Two Treatments of the Book of Job," Modern Drama, 3:378-86, February, 1961.

MacLeish's J. B. "is resolved in an affirmation that love can grow in a world where there is apparently no love. . . . Frost's point [in A Masque of Reason] . . . is that if you consider the problem of evil in a purely rational way . . . all you can do is laugh." (D.P.)

M199 Stroupe, John H., "The Masks of MacLeish's J. B., " Tennessee Studies in Literature, 15:75-83, 1970.

"The Satanmask and Godmask underline the fiction of creator and devil and at the same time heighten the reality of J. B. . . . . The metaphorical blindness of God and Satan are ironic counter-points to the physically blinded J. B., who gains the only true vision in the play. And . . . he gains his vision through his own efforts and his own suffering." (K.M.W.)

J. B. (cont'd)

M200 Terrien, Samuel, "J. B. and Job," Christian Century, 76:9-11, January 7, 1959.

"While Mr. MacLeish's verse drama is a brilliant re-creation of the story of Job, the character of J. B. is completely foreign to that of the hero who speaks in the biblical poem." (D.P.)

M201 Thelen, Mary Frances, "J. B., Job, and the Biblical Doctrine of Man," Journal of Bible and Religion, 27:201-5, July, 1959.

MacLeish did not intend his play "as a vehicle for ideas, as one more attempt to solve the problem of theodicy; but he would have us respond to it as a study of human experience, an exploration of how a man of our time might react to the extremes of misfortune and pain. . . . [Thus] our proper subject . . . is, first, the character of Job and of J. B. and the different ways in which authors have conceived them, and second, an analysis of the doctrine of man in the Book of Job in the light of biblical anthropology in general." (D.P.)

M202 Vann, J. Don, "MacLeish's J. B.," American Notes and Queries, 2:150, June, 1964.

"In the prologue of Archibald MacLeish's verse play J. B., Nickles, who is to play Satan, attempts to convince Mr. Zuss that he should wear the dramatic mask in playing the part of God," relating his view of the character Mr. Zuss is to play through a song, which at first glance seems almost a nonsense verse. . . ." (D.P.)

M203 Weiner, Herbert, "Job on Broadway: MacLeish's Man and the Bible's," Commentary, 27:153-8, February, 1959.

"The questions which Job asks, and which J. B. also claims to ask, call for an accounting between man and God. They cannot be resolved by advice 'to blow on the coal' of the human heart. If there is no divine heart, then there would seem to be more 'glory' in the man who, if not cursing, at least refuses to bless." (D.P.)

M204 White, Jean, "Will to Live is Key to MacLeish's 'J. B.'," Library Journal, 84:36-7, January 1, 1959.

MacLeish explains to a Washington (D.C.) reporter that he turned to the Book of Job because it is "the great ancient myth that contains the problem of today, the voice of man crying out for reason and justice in the universe." (W.G.F.)

J. B. (cont'd)

M205   White, W.D., "MacLeish's J. B.--Is It a Modern Job?" Mosaic, 4:13-20, Fall, 1970.

". . . in its fundamental thrust, in the formulation of its basic problem, and in the suggested answer to its major questions, J. B. is far removed from its biblical model." (G.C.)

M206   White, William S., "MacLeish and the Broken Major," Harper's, 218:77-80, April, 1959.

Archibald MacLeish's J. B. was an indifferent success in the theatre because the audience expected answers when the author only meant to ask a great question. The play's fate is less a measure of its greatness than a measure of audiences who rebel at depth in the theatre. (F.L.)

MacLENNAN, HUGH

M207   Chambers, Robert D., "The Novels of Hugh MacLennan," Journal of Canadian Studies, 2:3-11, August, 1967.

"The willingness to start from scratch, to assume nothing and provide all, is the initial fact to grasp about MacLennan's fiction. It explains why students of Canadian history and society turn to his books for a 'sense of period'." (D.A.B.)

M208   Goetsch, Paul, "Too Long to the Courtly Muses; Hugh MacLennan as a Contemporary Writer," Canadian Literature, No. 10, pp. 19-31, Autumn, 1961.

A truly balanced historical estimate of MacLennan needs concentration on his characteristic blend of traditional and contemporary elements. His theme is incomplete man's striving towards a full affirmation of life. With acceptance of both tradition and the modern experience MacLennan wrestles for a positive solution to this problem. (J.S.)

M209   Woodcock, George, "A Nation's Odyssey: The Novels of Hugh MacLennan," Canadian Literature, No. 10, pp. 7-18, Autumn, 1961.

MacLennan's novels interpret Canada's maturing society in terms of universal myth of the Odyssey, and his deliberate adaptations illuminate the growth of national consciousness. He does not always maintain the proper balance between theme and mythical structure, but he is still developing and improving his unique contribution. (J.S.)

M210 Woodcock, George, "A Nation's Odyssey: The Novels of Hugh MacLennan," Review of English Literature, 2:77-90, October, 1961.

MacLennan "has steadily widened and varied his portrayal of the character of Canadian life. Ultimately, perhaps, he is best as a social novelist, using his central myth to demonstrate the underlying universality of the personal and national experiences he recreates. . . . no writer has yet come nearer to writing a Canadian Comedie Humaine." (R.J.G.)

BAROMETER RISING

M211 New, William H., "The Storm and After: Imagery and Symbolism in Hugh MacLennan's 'Barometer Rising'," Queen's Quarterly, 74:302-13, Summer, 1967.

MacLennan's novel is essentially allegorical in structure, depicting the emergence of Canada as an independent nation. (S.T.C.)

M212 O'Donnell, Kathleen, "The Wanderer in Barometer Rising," University of Windsor Review, 3:12-8, Spring, 1968.

"Hugh MacLennan's novel opens with the statement that 'there is yet no tradition of Canadian literature' and proceeds to offer a creative vision of the Canadian environment and character. Dealing with the subject of a returned Canadian soldier in 1917, the author conveys his idea of the special attraction of this nation and of the traits peculiar to its people." (D.A.B.)

EACH MAN'S SON

M213 Tallman, Warren, "Wolf in the Snow, Part One: Four Windows on to Landscapes," Canadian Literature, No. 5, pp. 7-20, Summer, 1960.

The characters Philip Bentley in Ross's As For Me and My House, Brian O'Connal in Mitchell's Who Has Seen the Wind, David Canaan in Buckler's The Mountain and the Valley, Alan MacNeil in MacLennan's Each Man's Son and Duddy Kravitz in Richler's The Apprenticeship of Duddy Kravitz share a profound sense of isolation

EACH MAN'S SON (cont'd)

which may be traced "to the ways in which each is alienated from the natural childhood country of ordinary family life." (D.P.)

RETURN OF THE SPHINX

M214   New, William H., "Winter and the Night-People," Canadian Literature, No. 36, pp. 26-33, Spring, 1968.

Return of the Sphinx "is a frustrating novel, because it promises so much and wavers so much too. For MacLennan scholars it will be a key work, one which shows not only his descriptive abilities but also his consciousness of the tragic possibilities in modern life. . . . But for very few [readers], unfortunately . . . will it be the impetus for seeing the world with eyes that have been made fresh." (D.P.)

THE WATCH THAT ENDS THE NIGHT

M215   Farmiloe, Dorothy, "Hugh MacLennan and the Canadian Myth," Mosaic, 2:1-9, Spring, 1969.

In The Watch That Ends the Night MacLennan "has gone back to examine what he feels are the character-shaping protoforms of the Canadian identity as exemplified by the fur trader. In one magnificent chapter . . . in which the boy Jerome escapes down the wilderness river in his canoe . . . MacLennan is giving us his version not only of the Canadian character, but of the Canadian myth." (D.A.B.)

M216   MacLennan, Hugh, "The Story of a Novel," Canadian Literature, No. 3, pp. 35-9, Winter, 1960.

Our basic attitudes to society have changed and the external action of the traditional novel is both inaccurate and inadequate. The basic human conflict is within the individual. MacLennan set out to write The Watch that Ends the Night with the determination to write a book which depended on this spirit-in-action, rather than character-in-action, concept. (I.F.B.)

M217   New, William H., "The Apprenticeship of Discovery," Canadian Literature, No. 29, pp. 18-33, Summer, 1966.

Richler's comic treatment of the theme of "the apprenticeship of discovery" in "The Apprenticeship of Duddy Kravitz differs in many

THE WATCH THAT ENDS THE NIGHT (cont'd)

respects from MacLennan's use of it in The Watch that Ends the
Night. . . . MacLennan's work lacks the vivacity of the other, but
it aims for and achieves an entirely different tonal effect. . . . For
both MacLennan and Richler, the mastery to which the apprenticeship leads necessitates a recognition of the self both by the individual
and by others." (D.P.)

M218   Thorne, W. B., "The Relation of Structure to Theme in The Watch
that Ends the Night," Humanities Association Bulletin, 20:42-5,
Spring, 1969.

"The three major figures of the novel discover themselves against
the vast panorama of [. . . historical and social forces and] their
individual past experience. Correspondences in structure, characterization, and theme are continuously focused in the first person
narrative of George. They begin and end in him, and the other two
main characters, though they experience their own rebirth, are
again reborn in the multiple personality of Everyman George, who
has at last learned how to retire meaningfully into himself and 'die
into life'." (D.A.B.)

MacLOW, JACKSON

M219   McCord, Howard, "Jackson MacLow," Research Studies
(Washington State University), 34:242-6, December, 1966.

MacLow's techniques "largely derived from modern music,
especially the work of John Cage . . . [thrust] upon the reader or
hearer a responsibility for creation which before had been jealously
and exclusively possessed by the artist." (D.A.B.)

MacMANUS, FRANCIS

M220   McMahon, Seán, "Francis MacManus's Novels of Modern Ireland,"
Eire: Ireland, 5:116-30, Spring, 1970.

MacManus "was one of the few literary figures who stayed in Ireland
. . . when others ('finding the mores of the new state too confining')
left the country. . . . The theme of all his work [was] 'Praise God
for Ireland' [;] yet he did so [with] a healthy, unblinking acceptance
that urged him to stand and give challenge." (D.A.B.)

M221 Sheridan, John D., "Francis MacManus, 1909-1966," Studies, 55:269-76, Autumn, 1966.

In all his books MacManus "showed himself not only a gifted writer but a disciplined one. He had learned to subordinate the incidental to the essential. . . . He was conscious all the time of a plan and a purpose to which everything must conform. His decorative work was functional. . . ." (D.P.)

MacMECHAN, ARCHIBALD

M222 Chittick, V. L. O., "A Footnote to Tales of the Sea," Dalhousie Review, 36:275-8, 1956.

[This is an account of a parallel between a passage in Whitman's "Song of Myself" and MacMechan's report of "deep-sea heroism" in "The Sarah Stands By."] (G.C.)

M223 McBrine, R. W., "Archibald MacMechan, Canadian Essayist," Dalhousie Review, 50:23-33, Spring, 1970.

MacMechan "was the first writer in this country to make the familiar essay his forte. . . . he was also the most prolific . . . and . . . his essays in general are unquestionably among the best of his time." His essays are characterized by "convictions about the dignity and worth of the human spirit and his delight, unspoiled by sentimentality with the conditions of his own life." (D.P.)

McMURTRY, LARRY

M224 Davis, Kenneth W., "The Themes of Initiation in the Works of Larry McMurtry and Tom Mayer," Arlington Quarterly, 2:29-43, Winter, 1969-70.

The aim of the southwestern writers McMurtry and Mayer is knowledge--recognition and confirmation in the world to which the actions of the work must tend. (T.T.B.)

M225 Peavy, Charles D., "Coming of Age in Texas: The Novels of Larry McMurtry," Western American Literature, 4:171-88, Fall, 1969.

"The themes of loneliness and lost love are recurrent themes in McMurtry's novels, but the most important theme is the achievement of manhood (with its accompanying loss of innocence)," through the protagonist's relations with women who are older or more emotionally mature. (W.G.F.)

M226   Peavy, Charles D., "A Larry McMurtry Bibliography," Western
American Literature, 3:235-48, Fall, 1968.

[This is a list of McMurtry's works, including letters, book reviews,
and unpublished material.] (W.G.F.)

THE LAST PICTURE SHOW

M227   Peavy, Charles D., "Larry McMurtry and Black Humor: A Note
on The Last Picture Show," Western American Literature,
2:223-7, Fall, 1967.

"McMurtry's satire of small town sexuality should not be viewed as
sensationalism . . . but as a development of the humor that was
evident in his writing as early as his witty spoofing of Houston's
Astrodome." (W.G.F.)

MacNEICE, LOUIS

M228   Allen, Walter, "Louis MacNeice," Essays by Divers Hands,
35:1-17, 1969.

MacNeice combined within himself traits of the aristocrat and the
peasant, a dichotomy which "comes out strongly in his poetry and
formed indeed the basis of his view of things." ". . . he seems to
me essentially a Thirties poet and to have remained one." By
Poems, his second volume of poetry, "he was the master of his
medium, and, I believe, a totally original poet." (D.P.)

M229   Auden, W. H., "Louis MacNeice," Encounter, 21:48-9, November,
1963.

"In my opinion, Louis MacNeice's later poems, while continuing to
exhibit the technical excellence and delicacy of ear which had always
been his from the beginning, are both more moving and more original
than his earlier." "He was a pleasure to be with. It is a pleasure to
remember him. He was, and always will be, a pleasure to read."
(D.P.)

M230   Brown, Terence, "Louis MacNeice, 1907-1963: His Poetry,"
Studies, 59:253-66, Autumn, 1970.

"MacNeice the sceptic, reared to exile and loneliness, perhaps
maimed into fundamental scepticism by childhood experience, trans-

cends his limitations, to write poems of unique vision, of stoical, tense, secular joy, a poetry of paradox and opposites, of creative dialectics." (D.P.)

M231   Curnow, Allen, "Louis MacNeice," Landfall, 18:58-62, 1964.

"The long discursive poems--not only Autumn Journal, but also . . . the later, longer, more personal, and more philosophical poem called Autumn Sequel . . . [are] MacNeice's most durable and original contributions to the poetry of our times." (G.C.)

M232   Elman, Richard M., "The Legacy of Louis MacNeice," New Republic, 149:19-21, October 26, 1963.

"MacNeice believed poems should be articulate about a wide range of human experience. He was a 'modernist' who alternated between poems of private sensibility and public subject matter nearly all of his career, but he did not limit himself as to methods." (W.F.)

M233   Fauchereau, Serge, "Louis MacNeice, Un poète pendant les années 30; un poète de la radio," Critique, No. 225, pp. 131-49, February, 1966.

MacNeice, as well as W. H. Auden, Stephen Spender and Cecil Day Lewis, placed himself in the service of the revolution. Contrary to common opinion, MacNeice shows an evolution in his works. From Blind Fireworks (1929) to The Burning Perch (1963) there is an obvious evolution in his honesty and clairvoyance, a refusal of temptations to trick about his feelings. (T.T.B.)

M234   Gitzen, Julian, "Louis MacNeice: The Last Decade," Twentieth Century Literature, 14:133-41, October, 1968.

"Summarizing the movement from structural images to parable, from autobiographical to impersonal viewpoint, from conversational to rigid meters, and from complex to simplified diction, it becomes apparent that the efforts of MacNeice's last years were marked by a more severe discipline, a tortured simplicity, resembling that of the aging Yeats." (D.P.)

M235   Hamilton, Ian, "Louis MacNeice," London Magazine, 3:62-6, November, 1963.

"What is charming in [MacNeice's] early poems is a fractional immediacy of perception, a developed gift for projecting the momen-

tary visual complex . . . and a passive liveliness to the sheer
plenitude and variety of experience." Subsequently he "got suddenly arrested by the public calamities of his time and forced into
new, hardly congenial, directions--into abstract discourse, rhetorical self-examination." MacNeice "could never finally accept that
he 'loved the surface but lacked the core'." (D.P.)

M236 Heppenstall, Rayner, "A Demise of Poets, " London Magazine,
6:57-65, January, 1967.

[These are recollections of an acquaintanceship and friendship with
MacNeice, dating from 1935 to 1963.] (D.P.)

M237 Irwin, John T., "MacNeice, Auden, and the Art Ballad, "
Contemporary Literature, 11:58-79, Winter, 1970.

Both MacNeice and Auden have written sophisticated "art" poems
on top of preexisting folk ballads "with part of the meaning of the
art poem depending on the reader's knowledge of the meaning and
tone of the folk-ballad model. " (K.H.B.)

M238 Longley, Michael, "A Misrepresented Poet, " Dublin Magazine,
6:68-74, No. 1, 1967.

"Louis MacNeice found his voice very early. This doesn't mean, of
course, that he didn't develop. . . . But a poetic personality which
was so soon assured and recognisable meant that critics and anthol-
ogists found their voices very early when they came to deal with
him. . . . MacNeice seems to me to be a severely misrepresented
poet." (D.A.B.)

M239 McKinnon, William T., "The Cad with the Golden Tongue, " Essays
in Criticism, 20:109-15, January, 1970.

Although MacNeice is badly undervalued today he is able "to recreate
and communicate, perhaps better than any other poet I know, the
human situation both in the 60's and in the 30's. The cad with the
golden tongue was . . . a stern moralist of rare intellectual distinction. . . ." (D.P.)

M240 McMahon, Seán, "A Heart that Leaps to a Fife Band: The Irish
Poems of Louis MacNeice, " Eire-Ireland, 2:126-39, Winter, 1967.

Although MacNeice was born in Ireland and used Irish subjects in
some twenty five poems, he has been neglected in Ireland. In these
poems "MacNeice had marvelous things to say about Ireland and

. . . for all his years in England . . . the Irishness in him is as clear, as continuous, and as irremovable as a mica fault in a granite cliff." (D.P.)

M241   MacNeice, Louis, "Childhood Memories," Listener, 70:990, December 12, 1963.

[These are recollections of MacNeice's early years in Carrickfergus, where his father was Church of Ireland rector, remembrances of his sister, the ancient gardener. It was a rather lonely childhood, one that encouraged MacNeice to read a lot.] (D.P.)

M242   Smith, William Jay, "The Black Clock: The Poetic Achievement of Louis MacNeice," Hollins Critic, 4:1-11, April, 1967.

"It is not until the poems in The Burning Perch that MacNeice listens with full attention to 'the black clock that strikes when it has stopped,' and confronts his Loneliness and Otherness head-on. . . . And in the direct confrontation of loneliness and death, he became not only a real, but also a great, artist. . . ." (D.A.B.)

M243   Spender, Stephen, "The Brilliant Mr. MacNeice," New Republic, 156:32-4, January 28, 1967.

In his autobiographical The Strings are False, MacNeice analyzes people with a cool detachment, a detachment MacNeice accorded me at a social gathering we both attended. In Autumn Journal and Autumn Sequel this detachment manifests itself in a concern for metrics quite isolated from content. Only rarely in his poetry, for example when he writes of death, does MacNeice's subject order his form. (D.P.)

M244   Wain, John, "MacNeice as Critic," Encounter, 27:49-55, No. 5, 1966.

"Tolerance, decency, acuteness, the honest facing of difficulties: these are the marks of MacNeice's criticism, and when they are added to his initial advantages--a good education . . . and the imagination of a practitioner--the result is criticism which has few equals in our time. One other quality should be added: the courage to tackle a large general subject." (D.P.)

BLIND FIREWORKS

M245 Brennan, Moya, "A Poet's Revisions: A Consideration of
MacNeice's Blind Fireworks, " Western Humanities Review,
23:159-71, Spring, 1969.

"A survey of the rejected poems [in Blind Fireworks] may be
instructive in two ways: firstly because it demonstrates MacNeice's
own self-criticism and secondly because it demonstrates his deeper
and perhaps only half-conscious motives for making such a drastic
revision; i.e., to edit his earlier writing so as to correspond more
clearly with his later conception of his poetic role. " (D.A.B.)

PERSEUS

M246 Cope, John I., "MacNeice's 'Perseus', " Explicator, 26: Item 48,
February, 1968.

"We see only by the light of our own eyes and in the limits of that
vision we turn experience to stone. " (D.P.)

THE RIDDLE

M247 Dorrill, James F., "MacNeice's 'The Riddle', " Explicator,
29: Item 7, September, 1970.

"With admirable economy Louis MacNeice conveys, in 'The Riddle, '
a compelling sense of life's abiding mystery in the face of inevitable
mutability." "For expert fusion within brief compass, of . . . wry
comment on the superficiality of modern life and haunting evocation
of the wonder at the heart of things--this brilliant little poem could
hardly be bettered. " (D.P.)

ROUND THE CORNER

M248 Brown, Terence, "MacNeice's 'Round the Corner', " Notes and
Queries, 17:467-8, December, 1970.

A review by MacNeice of a volume of Rex Warner's translations of
poems by George Séféris provides thoughts which were developed
into MacNeice's "Round the Corner, " "where the sea is suggested
as a constant by which the fluctuating despairs of life can be
measured and appeased. " (D.P.)

SNOW

M249   Barry, Sister M. Martin, O. P., "MacNeice's 'Snow'," Explicator, 16: Item 10, November, 1957.

In MacNeice's "Snow" the emphasis is chiefly "upon the vitality, the oddity, the ambiguity, the many facets of sense experience and of material things, which combine to make up 'world'." (D.P.)

M250   Borroff, Marie, "What a Poem Is: For Instance, 'Snow'," Essays in Criticism, 8:393-404, October, 1958.

By being a representation of the train of thought of a fictional speaker, "Snow" produces in the reader a gradual awareness of the speaker's experience, and thus the poem can act as a "moral exhortation," enlarging our perception of the world around us. (D.B.D.)

M251   Borroff, Marie, "'Snow' and Poetic Theory," Essays in Criticism, 9:450-1, October, 1959.

Messrs. Collins and Draper have implied in their objections to my essay on "Snow" that "detailed criticism should be directed toward the elucidation of complex and problematic texts." However, "in writing about 'Snow,' I was concerned with . . . the process by which a reader responds to the successive lines of an effective poem, the importance of multiple implication in this process, and the differences between genuine philosophic propositions and statements in poetry which superficially resemble them. The choice of a relatively simple poem as an example made it possible to proceed at once to the real subject of the essay. . . ." (D.P.)

M252   Collins, P. A. W. and R. P. Draper, "Miss Borroff on 'Snow'," Essays in Criticism, 9:209-11, April, 1959.

". . . Miss Borroff's lengthy account of 'what, primarily and in the literal sense, "Snow" is' . . . is indeed an impressive performance, but the reader may ask where such an elaborate critical apparatus is intended to lead him." "Snow" is "one of those poems where the criticism is best kept brief and pithy." (D.P.)

McNULTY, MATTHEW EDWARD

M253   Rosset, B. C., "McNulty's 'How I Robbed the Bank of Ireland'," Shaw Review, 7:47-53, May, 1964.

Bernard Shaw's principal companion in his youth was Matthew Edward McNulty, who persuaded Shaw to become a writer, rather than devoting his energies to creating a new religion. McNulty remained a petty bank official, who wrote several plays, some worthy of production at the Abbey Theatre. [Reprinted here is his gothic story "How I Robbed the Bank of Ireland."] (D.P.)

MacORLAN, PIERRE

M254   Besson, Ferny, "Portrait de Pierre MacOrlan," La Revue des Deux Mondes, 140, No. 13, pp. 31-42, July 1, 1968.

A visionary with a genius for epithet and a profound pessimism, MacOrlan was a master of poems in prose, souvenirs and novels. (T.T.B.)

M255   Bloch, Adèle, "Pierre MacOrlan's Fantastic Vision of Modern Times," Modern Language Quarterly, 24:191-6, June, 1963.

MacOrlan's "originality lies primarily in the creation of a universe supernatural in essence, but adorned with the attributes of real life." (G.S.)

M256   Gascó Contell, Emilio, "Pierre MacOrlan, poeta de la aventura," La Estafeta Literaria, No. 376, pp. 12-3, August 12, 1967.

MacOrlan is the last of the great witnesses of the artistic Bohemia of Montmartre in the early years of the century, as well as that of the life of the underworld. (T.T.B.)

M257   Lanoux, Armand, "Un romantique en chandail écossais: Pierre MacOrlan," A la Page, No. 17, pp. 1633-9, November, 1965.

The hero of MacOrlan is never the war but the soldier. The ethics of adventure color his inspirations, which, plus the decor, constitute what is constant in his very diverse work, which he calls the social fantastic. (T.T.B.)

MacPHERSON, JAY

M258 Reaney, James, "The Third Eye: Jay MacPherson's The Boatman,"
Canadian Literature, No. 3, pp. 23-34, Winter, 1960.

Miss MacPherson deals, in The Boatman, "with a great variety of
topics in a carefully modulated variety of ways," arranging her
lyrics in suites and building them up "around a consistent and observable variety in poetic effects." The myth of things within
things--Man within Leviathan within God--is the essential design.
(I.F.B.)

MACRÍ, ORESTE

M259 Ricciardelli, M., "Oreste Macrí: The Critic as a Writer,"
Books Abroad, 42:535-7, Autumn, 1968.

Macrí's critical writings are "profound and conscious, complex and
refined, original and comprehensive. . . ." ". . . besides being
an engaging work of criticism, Realta del simbolo becomes a necessary tool for all those interested in deepening their knowledge of
hermeticism." (D.P.)

MADARIAGA, SALVADOR DE

M260 Predmore, Michael P., "Madariaga's Debt to Unamuno's Vida de
Don Quijote y Sancho," Hispania, 47:288-94, May, 1964.

Although "Unamuno is passionate, impressionistic, and unorganized"
while "Madariaga is objective, analytical, and coherent," there is
ample evidence to indicate that "much of the material in at least one
half of the eleven chapters of Guía del lector was inspired by the
perceptions and intuitions of Unamuno, expressed in Vida de Don
Quijote y Sancho twenty years earlier." (D.P.)

M261 Sedwick, Frank, "Madariaga, El enemigo de Dios, and the Nature
of Charity," Hispania, 43:169-73, May, 1960.

Madariaga's novel "shows how, under certain conditions, conventional
morality can hinder pure charity." (A.C.H.)

MAETERLINCK, MAURICE

M262   Brachear, Robert, "Maurice Maeterlinck and his 'Musée Grévin'," French Review, 40:347-51, December, 1966.

As playwright and theoretician, Maeterlinck was in the vanguard of the revolt of the idealist theatre against the dramatic conventions wherein the actor himself might be replaced by symbolic forms, even to the idea of a theatre freed from human presence. (T.T.B.)

M263   Décaudin, Michel, "Une année Maeterlinck," Revue de Littérature Comparée, 38:426-31, July-September, 1964.

"The award of sainthood to Maeterlinck and its inevitable counterpart, denigration have been manifested in studies of recent years as his centenary approached." Recent Maeterlinck studies are numerous, many are important, and many break new ground. (D.P.)

M264   Evans, Calvin, "Maeterlinck and the Quest for a Mystic Tragedy of the Twentieth Century," Modern Drama, 4:54-9, May, 1961.

Maeterlinck's theatre "represents the first moderately successful effort in the last three decades of the nineteenth century to employ the stage for something other than a platform from which to damn social wrongs." (C.K.L.)

M265   Mahony, Patrick, "The Maeterlinck Centenary: 1862-1962," Personalist, 43:487-92, Autumn, 1962.

Maurice Maeterlinck was a titanic figure "who created a new style of drama which brought a new thrill to the theater. All his work was based on a search for truth and beauty. . . . the charm and lucidity of his fancy were always controlled by the scruples of a fastidious artist. . . . What is best in him is wholly inimitable." (D.P.)

M266   Mallinson, V., "A Vindication of Maeterlinck: A Centenary Appraisal," Modern Languages, 43:46-52, 109-14, June, September, 1962.

[This is a two-part appraisal of Maeterlinck's work: part one, poetry and essays, part two, plays.] A harsh critic might deny that his works can seriously be considered as philosophy, but he must admit that they have a genius and a very great beauty. (G.C.)

M267   Osborn, Catherine B., "Maeterlinck, Predecessor to Ionesco,"
        French Review, 41:660-8, April, 1968.

        Most of the characteristics of Ionesco's dramatic art are already in
        Maeterlinck: the relationship between the spectator and the play,
        simultaneous involvement and distance, and a sense of mystery.
        (S. L. K.)

M268   Perruchot, Henri, "La roman de Maurice Maeterlinck et de
        Georgette Leblanc," A la Page, No. 45, pp. 422-9, March, 1968.

        [These are biographical details of Maeterlinck's life between 1895
        and 1911, and the influence of his actress-interpreter, Georgette
        Leblanc.]   (T.T.B.)

M269   Pouilliart, Raymond, "Maurice Maeterlinck et Carlyle," Revue de
        Littérature Comparée, 38:337-58, July-September, 1964.

        The early influence of Carlyle on Maeterlinck is demonstrated in an
        article by Maeterlinck published in La Revue générale in October
        and November of 1889. Carlyle was to remain a major influence on
        Maeterlinck for the rest of his life. (D.P.)

M270   Renard, Raymond, "Maurice Maeterlinck et l'Italie," Revue des
        Langues Vivantes, 24:3-19, 99-112, 195-212, 283-315, 1958.

        Maeterlinck was foremost among the French symbolists who directly
        influenced the formation of the school known as "crepuscularism" of
        Italian symbolist poets. (D.P.)

M271   Stimson, Frederick S., "Lo invisible: Azorín's Debt to Maeterlinck,"
        Hispanic Review, 26:64-70, January, 1958.

        "The drama reveals a direct influence in the borrowing of symbols.
        . . . This new treatment, this purification, of French symbolism,
        helps to make Lo invisible what Azorin calls superrealista."
        (A.C.H.)

                        PELLÉAS ET MÉLISANDE

M272   Kosove, Joan Pataky, "Maeterlinck's Pelléas et Mélisande,"
        French Review, 40:781-4, May, 1967.

        Maeterlinck's Pelléas et Mélisande "is neither about youth nor
        beauty, neither about love nor death. Pélleas et Mélisande deals

PELLÉAS ET MÉLISANDE (cont'd)

with an intriguing and complex irony, the presentiment of disaster at the moment of happiness and calm. To the extent that the work succeeds, we experience . . . a modal effect appropriate to a realization about life that is part sad and part comic, part startling and part puzzling, but totally inevitable." (D.P.)

MAEZTU, RAMIRO DE

M273 Sisto, David T., "A Note on the Philosophy of Ramiro de Maeztu and Carlos Reyles," Hispania, 41:475-9, December, 1958.

Maeztu and Reyles began as Nietzschean radicals and became increasingly conservative in their later works. "Hispanidad in Maeztu is like uruguayismo in Reyles." (A.C.H.)

MAGGIORE, GUISEPPE

M274 Ringger, Kurt, "Der Gatopardo und seine angebliche Vorlage-- zu Giuseppe Maggiore 'Sette e mezzo'," Germanisch-Romanische Monatsschrift, 14:101-11, January, 1964.

Detailed comparison of Lampedusa's Leopard (1960) with Maggiore's "Seven and a Half" (1952) provides no basis for the recent talk of plagiarism. The two works "have in common that which two works naturally can have in common when their authors have similar inclinations, know one another and speak with one another about their work. The two novels are divided however by the abyss which gapes between a work of art and an attempt from which even the true poet perhaps may have drawn material here and there." (J.R.R.)

MAIAKOVSKIĬ, VLADIMIR VLADIMIROVICH

M275 Annenkov, George, "The Poets and the Revolution: Blok, Mayakovsky, Esenin," Russian Review, 26:129-43, April, 1967.

[These are excerpts on Blok, Mayakovsky, and Esenin from Annenkov's reminiscenses Dnevnik moikh vstrech. Tsykl tragedii.] (D.P.)

M276   Ehrenburg, Ilya, "People, Years and Life," <u>Partisan Review</u>,
        28:494-514, May-June, 1961.

        [These are Ehrenburg's recollections of artistic figures of the
        1920's in Russia; especially of the poet Mayakovsky.] (R.K.)

M277   Erlich, Victor, "The Dead Hand of the Future: The Predicament
        of Vladimir Mayakovsky," <u>Slavic Review</u>, 21:433-40, September,
        1962.

        ". . . it is primarily as an embattled artist that he [Mayakovsky]
        refused the entrance ticket to the world he never made. Yet in his
        headlong rush toward a future worthy of a poet, he had propelled
        himself into a situation that rendered all genuine poetry impossible."
        (G.C.)

M278   Goncharov, B., "Maiakovskiĭ v krivom zerkale sovetologii,"
        <u>Voprosy literatury</u>, 14:100-12, March, 1970.

        Contemporary Western literary criticism of Maiakovskiĭ is no
        longer objective; critics such as Humetsky and Moser are subjective,
        tendentious, false and outright anti-Soviet in their latest appraisals.
        (V.D.)

M279   Gusev, V. I., "Na Stykax Poètičeskix Pokolenij (Xudožestvennyj
        opyt Maiakovskogo i molodaja poèzija 20-x godov)," <u>Voprosy
        literatury</u>, 13:56-74, June, 1969.

        Young poetry of the twenties, searching for its identity, found a
        great resource in Maiakovskiĭ. Such poets as S. Kirsanov, Ja.
        Smeljakov, A. Surkov, and L. Martynov repeatedly found in
        Maiakovskiĭ's poetry inspiration, guidance, and abundantly rich
        material. (V.D.)

M280   Holquist, Michael, "The Mayakovsky Problem," <u>Yale French
        Studies</u>, No. 39, pp. 128-38, 1968.

        Quotations from Lenin, Bunin, Andrey Sinyavsky, Pasternak, Max
        Eastman, Trotsky and Stalin provide "some minimal data for com-
        ing to grips with the problem of a great poet in time of revolution."
        (G.C.)

M281   Jakobson, Roman, "The Generation That Squandered Its Poets
(Excerpts)," Yale French Studies, 39:119-25, 1968.

[These are excerpts from "The Generation That Squandered Its
Poets," translated by Dale E. Peterson.] (K.M.W.)

M282   Moser, Charles A., "Mayakovsky and America," Russian Review,
25:242-56, July, 1966.

"Unlike his predecessors Korolenko and Gorky, Vladimir
Mayakovsky came to America as an unabashed publicity agent for
his fatherland, transformed as it was by the October Revolution."
(G.C.)

M283   Muchnic, Helen, "Vladimir Mayakovsky," Russian Review,
17:115-27, April, 1958.

"An immoderate and violent man, he had no capacity for analysis
or detachment: he did not criticize, he damned; he did not love,
but worshipped; he could hate and despise, but not dislike. He was
intransigent in his opinions, and as uncompromising in his relations
with himself as with others." (R.G.L.)

M284   Pertsov, Victor, "The Pioneers: Notes on the Creative Method of
Gorky and Mayakovsky," Soviet Literature, No. 10, pp. 136-41,
1968.

Although they took different roads, Gorky and Mayakovsky "upheld
life against decadence, truth against falsehood, realism against
modernism. The essence of their work in twentieth-century art is
the same, its social roots are identical and it represents two
pinnacles of one and the same artistic school, the art of social
realism." (D.P.)

M285   Peterson, Dale E., "Mayakovsky and Whitman: The Icon and the
Mosaic," Slavic Review, 28:416-25, September, 1969.

"The two poets share in common the fact that each purveyed in verse
an exaggerated image of man." However, "Whitman's 'self' is a
'caresser of life wherever moving'; Mayakovsky's 'Man' is a home-
less angel, trumpeting apocalypse to a deaf universe." (G.C.)

M286   Pickel', Faina N., "Muzestvo poezii," Voprosy literatury,
       12:24-45, July, 1968.

       Maiakovskiĭ's poetry is based on reason; the basis of his creation is
       "the esthetics of struggle and victory." His poetry is thus filled
       with internal heroic themes. (V.D.)

M287   Soskice, P. D., "Some Trends in Russian Futurist Poetry,"
       New Zealand Slavonic Journal, pp. 2-17, 1970.

       Russian Futurist poetry was a reflection of diverse trends, such
       as the rejection of tradition, the coinage of new words for poetry,
       and (exemplified by Maiakovsky) the synthesis of the auditory and
       the visual. (A.S.W.)

M288   Terras, Victor, "Majakovskij and Time," Slavic and East
       European Journal, 13:151-63, Summer, 1969.

       Majakovskij created many original time images. He, like many
       other Russian revolutionaries, "flees into an abstract and fantastic
       'cosmos' in order to escape real life, real history, and real time."
       (V.D.)

M289   Thomson, R. D. B., "Mayakovsky and His Time Imagery,"
       Slavonic and East European Review, 48:181-200, April, 1970.

       "The basic conflict of Mayakovsky's works is a sort of cosmic
       struggle between past and future with the soul of the present as the
       main issue at stake." (G.C.)

M290   Usakov, Aleksandr M., "Maiakovskiĭ i Grosz," Voprosy literatury,
       12:46-56, July, 1968.

       "The similarities between the graphic art of a prominent German
       artist (Grosz) and the creativity of a great poet of the revolution
       (Maiakovskiĭ) are obvious." Maĭakovskiĭ knew G. Grosz and used
       many of his ideas and techniques, i.e., hyperbole. Both artists
       used satire to unmask the enemies of the people. (V.D.)

       THE BEDBUG--See
       KOP

KOP

M291   Derzhavyn, Volodymyr, "A Dubious Soviet 'Cultural Achievement'--
        V. Mayakovsky's Farce on the Moscow Stage again," Ukranian
        Review, 4:55-7, 1957.

        ". . . The [Bed] Bug is a fairly crude farce, in which a poor attempt
        is made to cover up the lack of scenic effects and the superficiality
        of the plot by means of feeble jokes, long-winded moralising . . .
        and various circus-like effects." (G.C.)

MAILER, NORMAN

M292   Baldwin, James, "The Black Boy Looks at the White Boy: Norman
        Mailer," Esquire, 55:102-6, May, 1961.

        [This is Baldwin's intimately critical account of himself and of his
        "very good friend," Norman Mailer.] (G.C.)

M293   Clecak, Peter, "Social Criticism and Illusions of the Open Society,"
        Massachusetts Review, 10:247-79, Spring, 1969.

        ". . . American [social] criticism is essentially a mode of adjustive
        therapy and only incidentally a catalyst of qualitative social change.
        As symbolic action, criticism relieves intellectual, moral, and
        emotional guilt and frustration. As a prelude to political action,
        it frequently creates false hopes. . . ." Mailer's work "is both
        a symbolic act which organizes and partially releases tensions, and
        a critical act designed to diagnose social and psychological diseases.
        Yet Mailer . . . abandons the hope of reforming or revolutionizing
        economic, social, and political institutions through a combination of
        criticism and politics." (D.P.)

M294   Cook, Bruce A., "Norman Mailer: The Temptation to Power,"
        Renascence, 14:206-15, 222, Summer, 1962.

        "What Norman Mailer is most interested in is power--power both
        as a subject and object. In each of his three novels his protagonists
        struggle for it and against it, and in each struggle they lose." (S.A.)

M295   DeMott, Benjamin, "An Unprofessional Eye . . .: Docket No. 15883,"
        American Scholar, 30:232-7, Spring, 1961.

        The matter of Norman Mailer's assault on his wife with a pocket
        knife in November, 1960 created considerable journalistic interest

at the time, but no implications were drawn in the context of his fiction. Mailer's work has not been discussed in any connection with the world of ideas, although he has been credited with possessing an "extraordinary novelistic equipment." His preoccupation in his novels with violence did not seem to have an intellectual base, although his essay "The White Negro," posits an elite character in which "the desire to murder and the desire to create" have "come to bed." (D.P.)

M296 Foster, Richard, "Mailer and the Fitzgerald Tradition," Novel, 1:219-30, Spring, 1968.

"This pattern of affirmative and idealistic impulses reflexively renewed or reborn in the face of disillusioning experience, plus the contemporaneous American subject matter which is the characteristic substance of their imaginative visions not only connects Fitzgerald and Mailer importantly, but puts both of them in the main stream of American writers. . . ." (D.P.)

M297 Galligan, Edward L., "Hemingway's Staying Power," Massachusetts Review, 8:431-9, Summer, 1967.

"We have become accustomed to imitators of Hemingway . . . and they have made us forget how radical and unconventional a writer he really was. Mailer, Bourjaily, and Algren know better; so each produced in response to him a book which is so deeply personal and metaphorical, that it fits into none of the conventional categories. Mailer speaks for all three of them when he explains that Hemingway was a visionary whose writings 'were parts of a continuing and . . . comprehensive vision of existence into which everything must fit'." (D.P.)

M298 Glicksberg, Charles I., "Norman Mailer: The Angry Young Novelist in America," Wisconsin Studies in Contemporary Literature, 1:25-34, Winter, 1960.

If Mailer exalts the nihilistic gospel of Hip instead of mastering the form of the novel, he will hasten his death as a novelist. (B.K.)

M299 Glicksberg, Charles I., "Sex in Contemporary Literature," Colorado Quarterly, 9:277-87, Winter, 1961.

Norman Mailer, the "prophet" of "Hip," is a writer of important literary potential whose "energy that should go into the making of his books is dissipated in evangelical exhortation." (J.N.P.)

M300   Goldstone, Herbert, "The Novels of Norman Mailer," English
        Journal, 45:113-21, March, 1956.

        "In the final analysis Mailer has not described a big enough or rich
        enough world. His is too narrow and onesided, for he does not have
        a view of human experience that does any real justice to man's
        potentialities for feeling and action. More than that, he has not
        been able to create, as good novelists do, his own world which en-
        compasses all he sees in a personal vision." (D.P.)

M301   Hoffman, Frederick J., "Norman Mailer and the Revolt of the Ego:
        Some Observations on Recent American Literature," Wisconsin
        Studies in Contemporary Literature, 1:5-12, Fall, 1960.

        "Mailer's writings explicitly state the terms of the modern revolt
        against conventional society": the major impulse is to express
        passion through instinctive acts free both of established conventions
        and all ideological complication. (B.K.)

M302   Krim, Seymour, "An Open Letter to Norman Mailer," Evergreen
        Review, No. 45, pp. 89-96, February, 1967.

        Although he has demonstrated that he is a dramatic artist Mailer
        now risks becoming a monologist. His Cannibals and Christians is
        wide ranging, varied, and holds to an uncompromising point of view.
        Nevertheless it duplicates the repetitious and mechanical form of
        Advertisements for Myself. Mailer's procedure of publishing first
        in magazines and newspapers, and then collecting these efforts for
        book publication results in making the works appear piecemeal and
        the voice behind them shrill. (D.P.)

M303   Langbaum, Robert, "Mailer's New Style," Novel, 2:69-78, Fall,
        1968.

        In 1965 with American Dream and in 1967 with Why Are We in
        Vietnam? Norman Mailer has broken through to a new, metaphor-
        ical style which may be described as "hallucinated realism." How-
        ever, "Mailer still adheres to the large realistic tradition of the
        novelist as a chronicler of his time. He remains political and uses
        his new style to project those unconscious pathological forces that
        are . . . the main determinants of political behavior, especially in
        American now." (D.P.)

M304 Lakin, R. D., "D. W.'s: The Displaced Writer in America,"
<u>Midwest Quarterly</u>, 4:295-303, 1963.

The young writer soon discovers that "the business of producing
literature in our country is far more tangled and dangerous than
envisioned in those early dreams of hard won but ultimate acclaim.
The career of Norman Mailer currently illustrates this truth."
(K.M.W.)

M305 Leverett, Ernest, "The Virtues of Vulgarity--Russian and American
Views: (Dostoevsky, Scott Fitzgerald, Marlon Brando, Norman
Mailer, Beats and Buffoons)," <u>Carleton Miscellany</u>, 1:29-40,
Spring, 1960.

"In America the word 'vulgar' . . . is used largely as an epithet to
describe the opposition, whoever it may be." A recent Marlon
Brando movie about Japan, Norman Mailer's <u>Advertisements for
Myself</u>, in which he apparently proposes to be the penultimate beat,
demonstrates against the great concern with vulgarity of characters
in Dostoevsky, "how little the beats have done . . . to deal with the
terrors of the underground, to cope with the tragedy of human insuf-
ficiency . . . [although] beats are basically good, virtuous-vulgar
American heros. . . ." (D.P.)

M306 Mailer, Norman, "Advertisement," <u>Forum</u> (Houston), 3:21-2,
Fall, 1959.

[This is an analysis of the effect upon himself of the success of <u>The
Naked and the Dead</u>; excerpted from <u>Advertisements for Myself</u>.]
(J.P.H.)

M307 Mailer, Norman, "Norman Mailer versus Nine Writers," <u>Esquire</u>,
60:63-9, 105, July, 1963.

[These are Norman Mailer's opinions on the recent works of William
Styron, James Jones, James Baldwin, Saul Bellow, Joseph Heller,
John Updike, William Burroughs, J. D. Salinger, and Philip Roth.]
(K.M.W.)

M308 Marcus, Steven, "Norman Mailer--An Interview," <u>Paris Review</u>,
No. 31, pp. 28-35, Winter-Spring, 1964.

[This interview concentrates on the beginnings of Mailer's writing
career, literary and non-literary influences on his writings, his
methods and procedures of writing, the extent to which his charac-

ters are modeled on real people, the way craft can keep good writers from becoming great writers.] (D.P.)

M309 Mudrick, Marvin, "Mailer and Styron: Guests of the Establishment," Hudson Review, 17:346-66, Autumn, 1964.

After promising first novels, Styron--quietly--and Mailer--noisily --have sold out to the "drawing-rooms of the establishment." (C.E.N.)

M310 Newman, Paul B., "Mailer: The Jew as Existentialist," North American Review, 2:48-55, July, 1965.

"The best standard of comparison [for An American Dream] is still The Naked and the Dead, which illustrates the right combination of the ironic and the tragic that Mailer needed in order to make his existentialism convincing." (D.A.B.)

M311 Podhoretz, Norman, "Norman Mailer: The Embattled Vision," Partisan Review, 26:371-91, Summer, 1959.

Mailer has shown both moral courage and technical variety in grappling with what he himself calls "the sickness of our times . . . this damn thing that everything has been getting smaller and smaller and less and less important, that the romantic spirit has dried up. . . ." (R.K.)

M312 Rambures, Jean-Louis de, "Norman Mailer, l'enfant terrible des lettres américaines," Réalités, No. 269, pp. 95-105, June, 1968.

From The Naked and the Dead to Why Are We in Vietnam? Mailer has been caught in the trap of American mythology. The need to remain a rebel writer and to play a successful writer is his permanent contradiction. In An American Dream, Americans have recognized their own dreams and their own nightmares. (T.T.B.)

M313 Richler, Mordecai, "Norman Mailer," Encounter, 25:61-4, July, 1965.

Norman Mailer's "one outstanding virtue," apparent in An American Dream along with its embarrassing faults, is his "astonishing narrative skill." Mailer seems to have committed himself to becoming a personality rather than a writer, but there is still hope that he may in time write a good novel. (D.P.)

M314   Schrader, George Alfred, "Norman Mailer and the Despair of
        Defiance," Yale Review, 52:267-80, Winter, 1962.

        What Mailer calls "the philosophy of Hip" and "good orgasm,"
        Kierkegaard named the "despair of defiance." Mailer's concept
        of redemption evades or postpones the problem of ethical and
        religious choice. His personal as well as his literary life exem-
        plifies this evasion. (F.L.)

M315   Schroth, Raymond A., "Mailer and His Gods: Norman Mailer Goes
        to War," Commonweal, 90:226-9, May 9, 1969.

        ". . . Mailer has interpreted his generation's wars and warriors as
        manifestations of deeper tensions in civilian life. Since, for Mailer,
        man is most himself in crisis . . . conflict is the condition in which
        his nature can best be explored. In his Manichean vision of the
        universe, Mailer's paradoxically gentle, religious hero's freely
        plunging into violence is most likely to bring him into contact with
        God." (D.P.)

M316   Schulz, Max F., "Mailer's Divine Comedy," Contemporary
        Literature, 9:36-57, Winter, 1968.

        Despite his unorthodox methods, Mailer is essentially in the tradi-
        tion of eighteenth and early nineteenth century English and American
        primitivism in moral view. (P.J.R.)

M317   Stern, Richard G., "Hip, Hell, and the Navigator: An Interview
        with Norman Mailer," Western Review, 23:101-9, Winter, 1959.

        [This interview with Mailer took place on May 6, 1959.] (G.C.)

M318   Tanner, Tony, "On the Parapet: A Study of the Novels of Norman
        Mailer," Critical Quarterly, 12:153-76, Summer, 1970.

        "Since the Second World War Norman Mailer has demonstrated an
        unflagging ability to convert environmental pressures into lexical
        gestures which makes him one of the most resilient of recent
        American novelists." The question of who runs things "is certainly
        Mailer's main concern, and his first three novels can be seen as
        studies of three different kinds of power and their distinctive mani-
        festations or modes of operation." (D.P.)

M319   Toback, James, "At Play in the Fields of the Bored," Esquire,
70:150-5, 22-36, December, 1968.

[These are recollections of a series of encounters with Mailer,
including meetings in bars, a television interview of Mailer conducted by Toback, and an account accompanied by photographs of
the filming in East Hampton of Mailer's Five Day Party, a venture
in which Toback had a part.]   (D.P.)

M320   Toback, James, "Norman Mailer Today," Commentary, 44:68-76,
October, 1967.

"Mailer holds himself together . . . by virtue of his work. Through
creation he is able to come closer to the unattainable goal of total
victory in the struggle which is the metaphor for his vision of life.
Even if we do not believe in it ourselves, even if we are impatient
with [his] intellectual naivete . . . and even if we are annoyed by
the heavily flawed style of his prose, we can still learn from, and
be moved by, this belligerent prophet."   (D.P.)

M321   Trilling, Diana, "Norman Mailer," Encounter, 19:45-56,
November, 1962.

Mailer, the "anti-artist," conceives of his role as writer as "more
messianic than creative." His "driving need to turn . . . experience
to social use" has caused him to follow a curious "religious route":
from "Moses to Marion Faye, with a stop-over at Marx." (G.B.M.)

M322   Weatherby, W. J., "Talking of Violence: An Interview with Norman
Mailer," Twentieth Century, 173:109-14, Winter, 1964-65.

[This interview, carefully edited by Mailer, centers on Mailer's
views of violence--personal, social violence, violence as it relates
to our time: ". . . the interest in violence brings literature closer
to athletics--we want to break records."]   (D.P.)

M323   Winn, Janet, "Capote, Mailer and Miss Parker," New Republic,
140:27-8, February 9, 1959.

The recent Truman Capote, Norman Mailer and Dorothy Parker
television program moderated by David Susskind turned into a
debate between Capote and Mailer on virtually every topic discussed. Miss Parker contributed little to the occasion beyond her
presence. Capote made excellent sense, demolishing Mailer's
remarks at every point, albeit politely.   (D.P.)

M324 Witt, Grace, "The Bad Man as Hipster: Norman Mailer's Use of Frontier Metaphor," Western American Literature, 4:203-17, Fall, 1969.

"An examination of Mailer's use of frontier metaphor reveals a departure from the traditional use of frontier-as-possibility and the frontiersman as a symbol of resistance, individualism, courage, and self-reliance. Mailer's work . . . gradually transforms the resolute and courageous pioneer into the bad man, who, in the guise of Hipster, becomes the hero of An American Dream." (W.G.F.)

ADVERTISEMENTS FOR MYSELF

M325 Bone, Robert A., "Private Mailer Re-enlists," Dissent, 7:389-94, Autumn, 1961.

Mailer's Advertisements for Myself demonstrates that "if suicide is the ultimate tendency of Hip, and combat its beginning, what could be more damaging to its claims on the literary imagination? A myth so confining can perhaps give structure to certain kinds of human experience. It can produce, for example, a great war novel. But it cannot provide the foundation of a mature art." (D.P.)

M326 Dupee, F. W., "The American Norman Mailer," Commentary, 29:128-32, February, 1960.

"Advertisements for Myself is chaotic; its tone is uncertainly pitched between defiance and apology." It "is a confessional document of considerable interest and an engrossing document of the postwar literary life. It is also an extremely funny book, for Mailer's gifts as a humorist are among his most reliable gifts. (D.P.)

M327 Howe, Irving, "A Quest for Peril," Partisan Review, 27:143-8, Winter, 1960.

Mailer's Advertisements for Myself "is a rowdy intense and exciting book [which] . . . systematically sets out to assault the decorums of liberal moderation. . . . In both the best and weakest sections of the book, one is struck by Mailer's absolute unwillingness to settle into his achievement, his impatience with a style as soon as he comes close to mastering it, his devotion to restlessness as a principle of both life and work." (D.P.)

ADVERTISEMENTS FOR MYSELF (cont'd)

M328   Mailer, Norman, "Advertisements for Myself on the Way Out: Prologue to a Long Novel," Partisan Review, 25:519-40, Fall, 1958.

"My passion is to destroy innocence, and any of you who wish to hold to some part of that warm, almost fleshly tissue of lies, sentimentality, affectation and ignorance which the innocent consider love must be prepared instead for a dissection of the extreme, the obscene and the unsayable." (D.P.)

AN AMERICAN DREAM

M329   Bersani, Leo, "The Interpretation of Dreams," Partisan Review, 32:603-8, Fall, 1965.

Mailer's An American Dream is "a dazzling performance, a recklessly generous yet disciplined exercise in self-exposure and self-invention. . . . It is an intensely private novel. . . . Mailer in An American Dream is somewhat like Balzac in his attitudes towards social maneuvering and power. . . ." (D.P.)

M330   Boyers, Robert, "Attitudes toward Sex in American 'High Culture'," Annals of the American Academy of Political and Social Sciences, No. 376, pp. 36-52, March, 1968.

"Probably the most talented, serious, and proclaimed champion of apocalyptic sexuality in this country is Norman Mailer, whose . . . An American Dream is a pop-art caricature of . . . banal and ludicrous" ideas, although "his imagination is teeming with invention and his metaphors have the reach of genius." Jeremy Larner's Drive devotes considerable attention "to the possibilities of apocalyptic orgasm." In his One Flew over the Cuckoo's Nest Kesey's solution . . . is . . . the releasing of . . . the twin resources of laughter and uninhibited sexuality. . . ." Barth's The End of the Road treats "sex as a means of relief from painful reality, though not as a means of transforming that reality. . . ." James Purdy's Cabot Wright Begins "is a novel about a rapist, and incidentally about everything in the modern world. . . ." Philip Roth's "Whacking Off" "recounts an adolescence and a young adulthood tainted by the spectral presence of masturbation and the fear of exposure." In our most gifted writers "human sexuality cannot be considered apart from other essential elements of the human personality." (D.P.)

AN AMERICAN DREAM (cont'd)

M331   Corrington, John William, "An American Dreamer," Chicago
Review, 18:58-66, Spring, 1965.

"An American Dream is a flawed masterpiece. . . . But it is revivifying to read a novel which aims at fiction's ultimate virtue:
the rendering of the uncommunicable. . . ." (W.G.F.)

M332   Normand, J., "L'Homme mystifié: Les héros de Bellow, Albee,
Styron et Mailer," Études Anglaises, 22:370-85, October-
December, 1969.

"Man in America holds roughly the same position he has in earlier
generations. Events are actually controlled by "a social sclerosis
which impedes a spirit of acceptance and resignation among writers."
As a consequence Bellow's Herzog "is a synthesis of discordances, a
human mosaic"; Albee's Who's Afraid of Virginia Woolf? shows us "two
neurotics whose existence together is only supportable through an elaborate falsehood"; Cass Kinsolving in Styron's Set this House on Fire "is
a simple, honest American, filled with good intentions, naturally generous, but possessed by a destructive demon which brings most of his
efforts to nothing"; Rojack in Mailer's An American Dream "is a be-
witched, fascinating character, driven by a puritan passion for venge-
ance, a frenetic need for debauchery, and a need to risk all in combat."
(D.P.)

M333   Solotaroff, Robert, "Down Mailer's Way," Chicago Review,
19:11-25, June, 1967.

"What interests me is how inevitable An American Dream . . . was
once Mailer committed himself four years ago to publish an eight-
installment novel in Esquire, and so I shall try to track those paths
through his novels and relevant non-fiction which seem [to reveal] how
the man who wrote The Naked and the Dead at the age of twenty-four
came to write An American Dream sixteen years later." (D.A.B.)

M334   Wagenheim, Allan J., "Square's Progress: An American Dream,"
Critique: Studies in Modern Fiction, 10:45-68, No. 1, 1967-68.

An American Dream "is a brilliantly lighted journey into the secret
recesses of the unconscious, slipping along the edge of psychosis
and revealing . . . the etiology of homosexuality, of sexual violence,
of rebelliousness--the connection, in short, between sexual disturb-
ance and social disorder. Operating on another level, it is a fierce
and terrible myth for our own society. . . . Finally, An American

AN AMERICAN DREAM (cont'd)

Dream is a dream of possible salvation, holding out a small hope
. . . that someday the nightmare will end, and that there will be the
moment of sanity. . . ." (D.P.)

M335   Weber, Brom, "A Fear of Dying: Norman Mailer's An American
Dream," Hollins Critic, 2:1-6, 8-11, June, 1965.

Norman Mailer's An American Dream "is qualitatively the most
substantial of his four novels, a salutary contribution to contemporary American literature, and a repudiation of the sociological
truism that early success inevitably rots artistic talent." (D.P.)

M336   Wood, Margery, "Norman Mailer and Nathalie Sarraute: A Comparison of Existential Novels," Minnesota Review, 6:67-72, 1966.

". . . Norman Mailer's An American Dream is the first American
work of fiction which resembles the existential experimental
European novels of the last ten years. . . . Though it lacks the artistry of the European novels, Mailer's latest novel deserves to be called
'existential' by virtue of its subject matter and tone." (D.A.B.)

ARMIES OF THE NIGHT

M337   Middlebrook, Jonathan, "Can a Middle-Aged Man with Four Wives
and Six Children Be a Revolutionary?" Journal of Popular Culture,
3:565-74, Winter, 1969.

Mailer's "potential American epic," Armies of the Night has at its
heart these values: "patriotism, individualism and private wealth,
a sense of sin, familial responsibility, sexual mysticism, the sense
of America as organic and feminine, jungle intuitions and an existential, autobiographical assertion, I am." In this novel, suitably
and appropriately rewarded by a National Book Award, Mailer becomes a "most reluctant sort of revolutionary, the model for those
Americans caught with their families and forty years. . . ." (D.P.)

THE NAKED AND THE DEAD

M338   Enkvist, Nils Erik, "Re-readings: Norman Mailer, The Naked and
the Dead," Moderna Språk, 56:60-4, 1962.

The Naked and the Dead "captures the same dramatic intensification
of human relationships, the same agony and hatred, the same boredom and fear, and the same tension and obscene horror that has long

THE NAKED AND THE DEAD (cont'd)

been the stock-in-trade of realistic and naturalistic war novelists.
. . . its literary strength lies in structure and characterization and
in the philosophic pattern that Mailer has imposed. . . ." (D.P.)

M339   Gordon, Andrew, "The Naked and the Dead: The Triumph of
Impotence," Literature and Psychology, 19:3-13, Nos. 3-4, 1969.

"Every character in The Naked and the Dead is a projection of and
an advertisement for that grand egomaniac, Mailer himself." (D.P.)

M340   Ross, Frank, "The Assailant-Victim in Three War-Protest Novels,"
Paunch, No. 32, pp. 46-57, August, 1968.

Although Dos Passo's Three Soldiers, Hemingway's A Farewell to
Arms, and Mailer's The Naked and the Dead are dissimilar, they
each attack America's "irrational commitment" to war as a solution
to problems between nations. Each novel reports atrocities committed as a result of military ethics. Men at war are victims of the
same ethics which require them to kill. "War-protest" novels are
written by authors strongly committed to reality. (D.P.)

THE PRESIDENTIAL PAPERS

M341   Gilman, Richard, "Why Mailer Wants to Be President," New
Republic, 150:17-24, February 8, 1964.

By his systematic confusion of art and life, Mailer "has made first
literature and now politics a choice between himself and everything
else." And "he has given us, by the ironic action of his voracious
ego, a new sense of where our own selves are and what we might do
to resurrect them." (W.F.)

M342   Miller, Jonathan, "Black-Mailer," Partisan Review, 31:103-7,
Winter, 1964.

In The Presidential Papers Mailer "has settled for nothing less than
the unconditional surrender of the entrenched values of modern
American culture." In it, "the very tastelessness of his total style
with all its self-advertisement, clotted jargon and so on add up to a
certain barbarous bulk to be set against the general fastidiousness of
all-around. Mailer has been running . . . not just for President of
the United States; he has also been running for President of everything else, President of the World, President of Beefcake and
President of Contemporary Sensibility. . . . He is in a hurry to

THE PRESIDENTIAL PAPERS (cont'd)

establish his claims to greatness without having to wait upon the
natural season of his own supposed genius." (D.P.)

WHY ARE WE IN VIETNAM?

M343   Aldridge, John W., "From Vietnam to Obscenity," Harper's,
236:91-7, February, 1968.

Norman Mailer's Why Are We in Vietnam? is "relentlessy, brilliantly, hilariously obscene, very probably the most obscene novel
ever published in this country. . . ." In this book "Mailer had indeed
managed to bring Vietnam and obscenity together in a marvelous synthesis . . . [designed to tell] us something important not only about
the obscenity of our situation in Vietnam but . . . about the possible
power of obscenity to help alleviate that situation." (D.P.)

M344   Hux, Samuel, "Mailer's Dream of Violence," Minnesota Review,
8:152-7, No. 2, 1968.

"The substance of Why Are We in Vietnam? is in one sense an
allegorical answer to the title. We are there because the Medium
and High-grade Ass-holes are in the ascendancy in America, and
even their sons learn to obey that hard American god who says:
'Go out and kill--fulfill my will, go and kill'." (D.P.)

MAINWARING, DANIEL

M345   Astro, Richard, "Steinbeck and Mainwaring: Two Californians for
the Earth," Steinbeck Quarterly, 3:3-11, Winter, 1970.

Acquaintance with Daniel Mainwaring's novel One Against the Earth
(1933) makes the similar reverence for the earth expressed in
Steinbeck's California novels more comprehensible and less unique.
(W.G.F.)

MAKAL, MAHMUT

M346   Devereaux, Robert, "Anatolian Trilogy," Books Abroad, 31:126-30,
Spring, 1957.

In his three books, and notably in the cause celebre, Bizim Koy,
the young Turkish writer Mahmut Makal has revealed the traditional
peasant life and society in Anatolia. His despair and discouragement
are not "completely unwarranted." (F.E.E.)

MALAMUD, BERNARD

M347   Baumbach, Jonathan, "The Economy of Love: The Novels of
        Bernard Malamud," Kenyon Review, 25:438-57, Summer, 1963.

        Malamud, as a romantic, "writes of heroes": as a realist, he
        "writes of their defeats. . . . Defeat of love is the tragedy." (G.S.)

M348   Bellman, Samuel Irving, "Women, Children, and Idiots First: The
        Transformation Psychology of Bernard Malamud," Critique:
        Studies in Modern Fiction, 7:123-38, Winter, 1964-65.

        "Is there a special point to Malamud's reconstructionist view of
        society, whereby non-Jews turn into Jews and some Jews begin
        turning into Negroes . . . much to their discomfort? Yes . . .
        the world is losing its oxygen and becoming unfit to live in; people
        grow desperate in their plight . . . turn black perhaps, sicken unto
        death, and make a pitiful spectacle as they fight a losing battle."
        (W.G.F.)

M349   Bluefarb, Sam, "Bernard Malamud: The Scope of Caricature,"
        English Journal, 53:319-26, 335, May, 1964.

        ". . . Malamud's caricatures, though perhaps inspired by his sense
        of the moral dilemma, in their final effect . . . imply a morality
        which transcends the immediate intentions of their creator.
        Malamud . . . has given them a life of their own, and though they
        are drawn from life itself, the sustenance that sustains these figures
        has imbued them with . . . the dimensions of allegory. . . ." (D.P.)

M350   Charles, Gerda, "Bernard Malamud: The 'Natural' Writer,"
        Jewish Quarterly, 9:5-6, Spring, 1962.

        Malamud's The Natural and a number of the stories in The Magic
        Barrel possess "an uncanny quality . . ." and A New Life, although
        sometimes vulgar, "has more depth than Kingsley Amis's Lucky
        Jim. . . ." (D.P.)

M351   Eigner, Edwin M., "Malamud's Use of the Quest Romance,"
        Genre, 1:55-75, January, 1968.

        In each of Malamud's first four novels "the cast of characters from
        the Percival myth are identifiable throughout." In The Natural,
        The Assistant, A New Life, and The Fixer, "Malamud has come a
        long way in the sophistication of his escapes--from baseball star-

dom to Spinoza. . . . But so has Malamud's conception of man's
possibilities grown. . . ." (D.P.)

M352 Featherstone, Joseph, "Bernard Malamud," Atlantic Monthly,
219:95-8, March, 1967.

His writings celebrate "not a people but the individual . . . who
endures." His best short stories and novels, usually in a minor
key, reveal him as a gifted and expressive writer with a compassionate view of life as it is daily lived. (W.K.)

M353 Geismar, Maxwell, "The American Short Story Today," Studies on
the Left, 4:21-7, Spring, 1964.

American short story writers such as Updike, Salinger and Malamud
are "too successfully adjusted to their present fame and fortune to
break through their own literary mode." (D.P.)

M354 Goldman, Mark, "Bernard Malamud's Comic Vision and the Theme
of Identity," Critique: Studies in Modern Fiction, 7:92-109,
Winter, 1964-65.

"The search for the real is a function of the quest for identity in
Malamud's fiction. This notion of identity is especially crucial for
the Jewish-American writer, caught between an American ethos,
his manifest subject, and a deeper consciousness of his Jewish self
and world." (W.G.F.)

M355 Goodman, Oscar B., "There Are Jews Everywhere," Judaism,
12:283-94, 1970.

". . . Malamud has . . . utilized Jewishness as an encompassing
image in which concrete human experience transcends abstract
ideals." (D.A.B.)

M356 Gross, John, "Marjorie Morningstar, Ph. D.," New Statesman,
64:921, November 30, 1962.

Malamud and Bellow bring "the intensity of the past . . . into an
ambiguous relationship to present Jewish society. . . . Roth
belongs with slick professionals" such as Irwin Shaw, Weidman,
and Wouk. (D.P.)

M357   Hicks, Granville, "His Hopes on the Human Heart," Saturday
       Review, 46:31-2, October 12, 1963.

       Throughout his works, Malamud "has been greatly troubled by the
       depreciation of the human in modern times as terribly exemplified
       by . . . the Nazi destruction of the Jews. He believes that the
       human must be protected, and the note that he sounds again and
       again is compassion." (D.P.)

M358   Lamdin, Lois S., "Malamud's Schlemiels," Carnegie Series in
       English, 11:31-42, 1970.

       Malamud's "main characters are prototypal anti-heroes--eternal
       victims, born losers, well-meaning bunglers--the sort of men to
       whom bad luck happens. They are fit protagonists in a fiction
       whose central motif is the omnipresence of suffering, for they are
       born to suffering, conditioned by it, and ultimately find the mean-
       ing of their lives in learning to deal with it. As sufferers they
       serve as root symbols for the condition of man." (D.P.)

M359   Mandel, Ruth B., "Bernard Malamud's The Assistant and A New
       Life: Ironic Affirmation," Critique: Studies in Modern Fiction,
       7:110-21, Winter, 1964-65.

       "Both novels offer a similar affirmation for the possibility of human
       salvation and identity through a consciously constructed personal
       ethos. The central character in each book . . . is redeemed . . .
       only after purgatorial fires have refined him during his search for
       self-discipline and a new, meaningful life directed by humanistic
       values." (W.G.F.)

M360   Marcus, Steven, "The Novel Again," Partisan Review, 29:171-95,
       Spring, 1962.

       The work of Malamud and Golding illustrates the shift during the
       past fifteen years from novelistic to poetic forms and assumptions.
       The novel has declined through dedication to fantasy and poetic
       form, a trend partly the result of reaction to the Cold War, which
       has required a maintaining of the status quo. (D.P.)

M361   Mellard, James M., "Malamud's Novels: Four Versions of Pastoral,"
       Critique: Studies in Modern Fiction, 9:5-19, No. 2, 1967.

       "For Malamud, the pastoral mode is his greatest strength as a
       writer of fiction, because it has given him an archetypal narrative

structure of great flexibility, a durable convention of characterization, a consistent pattern of imagery and symbols, and a style and
rhetorical strategy of lucidity and power." (D.P.)

M362   Mudrick, Marvin, "Who Killed Herzog? or, Three American
Novelists," Denver Quarterly, 1:61-97, Spring, 1966.

"Malamud, Bellow, and Roth have taken upon themselves the job of
inventing the contemporary fictional Jew," and "it is difficult not to
be hopeful about all of them, in the impasse to which their energies
have rashly carried them." (A.S.W.)

M363   Pinsker, Sanford, "The Achievement of Bernard Malamud,"
Midwest Quarterly, 10:379-89, Summer, 1969.

"With the publication of The Fixer in 1966 . . . Malamud moved
beyond the built-in ironies that had characterized his earlier fiction
and charted a course more appropriate to the sensibility of the
Sixties," creating an atmosphere of tragic vision rather than "ironic
affirmation." (S.T.C.)

M364   Pritchett, V. S., "That Time and that Wilderness," New Statesman,
64:405-6, September 28, 1962.

For Malamud and Bellow life in America is skin-deep, an abstraction which represents the point of entry to personal nightmares or
private rituals. They are interested in the city; they expect little
from America. Faulkner, however, has created a South in depth,
peopled with black-and-white characters capable, nevertheless, of
a marked humanism. His real mode is comedy. (D.P.)

M365   Raffel, Burton, "Bernard Malamud," Literary Review, 13:149-55,
Winter, 1969-70.

"My own feeling is that as a novelist [Malamud] has on the whole
declined from novel to novel; that as a writer of short stories he
possesses a limited talent; and that he is infinitely more American
than he is Jewish, distinctly to his own disadvantage. Yet he remains
in spite of these literary and cultural judgments, a profoundly disturbing writer." (D.P.)

M366   Ratner, Marc L., "Style and Humanity in Malamud's Fiction,"
Massachusetts Review, 5:663-83, Summer, 1964.

Malamud's work affirms "his belief that through self-scrutiny,
suffering, and sympathy men can recreate their humanity." Through

juxtaposing the surreal and the real, the poetic and the ordinary, Malamud achieves compression and emphasizes his ironic view of life. (D.P.)

M367   Rovit, Earl H., "Bernard Malamud and the Jewish Literary Tradition," Critique: Studies in Modern Fiction, 3:3-10, Winter-Spring, 1960.

Although Malamud uses some of the manner of the traditional Yiddish tale, his technique is poetic and symbolic. He is unwilling to allow Yiddish atmosphere to substitute for, or embody, his vision. The "meaning" of his story is always left to the reader--a clear departure from the tradition of the Yiddish tale in order to meet the demands of the modern short story. (G.O.)

M368   Shrubb, P., "About Love and Pity--The Stories of Bernard Malamud," Quadrant, 9:66-71, November-December, 1965.

Malamud's writing is an achievement of the highest order. Although its mode is comic, the comedy is made to contain revelations of profoundly adult truths, truths about love as "a painful duty." (S.T.)

M369   Siegel, Ben, "Victims in Motion: Bernard Malamud's Sad and Bitter Clowns," Northwest Review, 5:69-80, Spring, 1962.

Malamud's work "is a moral critique, an attempt to explore and reveal the melancholy state of the human condition. . . ." Each of his writings provide "an ironic yet compassionate insight into the dark dilemma that is modern life." (D.P.)

M370   Solotaroff, Theodore, "Bernard Malamud's Fiction: The Old and the New," Commentary, 33:197-204, March, 1962.

"Malamud's Jewishness is a type of metaphor for anyone's life. . . . The surfaces of life still look stable enough, but underneath, massive and fearful changes are obviously at work. . . ." (P.A.R.)

M371   Tanner, Tony, "Bernard Malamud and the New Life," Critical Quarterly, 10:151-68, Spring-Summer, 1968.

In Malamud's novels from The Natural to The Fixer "we can find a recurring pattern which links them very closely together and re- veals a profound consistency in Malamud's vision. . . . his wisdom I take to be a searching insistence on the necessity of growing up.

All his novels are fables or parables of the painful process from immaturity to maturity--maturity of attitudes not of years." (D.P.)

M372 Weiss, Samuel A., "Notes on Bernard Malamud," Chicago Jewish Forum, 21:155-8, Winter, 1962-63.

"The lure of self-surrender, of yielding to others affects Malamud powerfully and constitutes a striking feature of his moral heroes, who are driven to atone some guilty past through expiation and spiritual rebirth." (G.C.)

M373 Weiss, Samuel A., "Passion and Purgation in Bernard Malamud," University of Windsor Review, 2:93-9, Fall, 1966.

"For Malamud the Jew transcends racial identity and becomes a metaphor for all suffering humanity who have gathered from suffering what has been called 'moral intelligence,' a scrupulous regard for fair and humane dealing." (A.S.W.)

THE ASSISTANT

M374 Alley, Alvin D., and Hugh Agee, "Existential Heroes: Frank Alpine and Rabbit Angstrom," Ball State University Forum, 9:3-5, Winter, 1968.

"In both Bernard Malamud's The Assistant and John Updike's Rabbit, Run, there is an emphasis on the alienation of man from an absurd world and his estrangement from his normal society." Both Frank Alpine and Rabbit Angstrom "are haunted by the dryness of their souls and their journeys of despair include fierce encounters with a world whose values are twisted, uprooted, dislocated, and, for them, unintelligible." (D.P.)

M375 Francis, H. E., "Bernard Malamud's Everyman," Midstream, 7:93-7, Winter, 1961.

Malamud's The Assistant "more than a stereotyped vision of the suffering Jew . . . is a work beautifully wrought in lyric language, with fantasy woven into its realism with all the rich suggestiveness of poetry. . . ." "Thus far in his career . . . Malamud has emerged as an artist who has achieved a successful over-all fusion of his view of man and the fantastic-naturalistic elements which portray that view. . . . Though doctrine immediately defines his characters, compassion ultimately does so." (D.P.)

THE ASSISTANT (cont'd)

M376 Hays, Peter L., "The Complex Patterns of Redemption in The Assistant," Centennial Review, 13:200-14, Spring, 1969.

In The Assistant Bernard Malamud, with religious allusion, Mediterranean mythology, sacrificial rites and fertility imagery infusing a philosophy very much like Martin Buber's, has created a modern parable in the form of a naturalistic novel, a story of redemption which expresses perennial realities of psychological and philosophical truth." (D.P.)

M377 Hruska, Richard J., "My Grandfather and Morris Bober," CCC: The Journal of the Conference on College Composition and Communication, 13:32-4, May, 1962.

Morris Bober in The Assistant "died believing he was a failure, while those same men who had once deceived him, now admired him for his personal integrity. He never understood that success lay, not in his objective, but in the method he used to obtain it." (W.G.F.)

M378 Leer, Norman, "Three American Novels and Contemporary Society: A Search for Commitment," Wisconsin Studies in Contemporary Literature, 3:67-86, Fall, 1962.

The "post-modern" novel (exemplified by Malamud's The Assistant, Wright Morris's The Field of Vision, and Kerouac's The Dharma Bums), starting in opposition to the fluid world of mass society, records the search for relationship; implied is that the discovery of individual identity is perhaps the beginning of a larger social commitment. (B.K.)

M379 Mellard, James M., "Malamud's The Assistant: The City Novel as Pastoral," Studies in Short Fiction, 5:1-11, Fall, 1967.

In The Assistant, for his characters, in place of the conventional shepherds [Malamud] uses simple lower-class and proletarian types, often Jewish, whose thoughts and language give [him] an uncluttered, but highly lyrical style, and whose frustrations and privations mirror the basic human condition. A second and more important way in which Malamud implements the pastoral mode is in the pervasive use of nature imagery. . . . nature imagery in The Assistant suggests that the narrative center of the novel lies in the pastoral vegetation myths, rituals, and ceremonies that celebrate the cycles of death and renewal in nature." (D.P.)

THE ASSISTANT (cont'd)

M380   Shear, Walter, "Culture Conflict in The Assistant," Midwest
Quarterly, 7:367-80, Summer, 1966.

In The Assistant, man is caught between the conflicting claims of
the Jewish tradition and the American heritage, and he suffers
"because a fragmented abundance of world-views produces uncertainty about intentions, actions, and roles." (A.S.W.)

M381   Stanton, Robert, "Outrageous Fiction: Crime and Punishment,
The Assistant, and Native Son," Pacific Coast Philology, 4:52-8,
April, 1969.

"Dostoyevsky's Crime and Punishment, Malamud's The Assistant,
and Wright's Native Son all center upon crime and the moral regeneration of the criminal in a world where God's will is no
longer evident. . . . by implication [Malamud and Wright] comment
on and extend some of [Dostoyevsky's] most important and outrageous
ideas." (D.P.)

THE FIXER

M382   Alter, Robert, "Malamud as Jewish Writer," Commentary,
42:71-6, September, 1966.

"Malamud is . . . the first important American writer to shape out
of his early experiences in the immigrant milieu a whole distinctive
style of imagination and . . . a distinctive technique of fiction as
well. . . . in The Fixer the central action is a process of suffering
through violence, torture by inches, complete with the obscene in-
ventions of a jailer's sadism, an attempted poisoning, a suicide,
even Dostoevskian hallucinations. . . . never before has he written
such taut, muscular prose. . . ." (D.P.)

M383   Baumbach, Jonathan, "Malamud's Heroes: The Fate of Fixers,"
Commonweal, 85:97-9, October 28, 1966.

In The Fixer Malamud demonstrates again that he is a "didactic
writer, a moralist." It takes "either courage or madness to write
about the dignity of the individual in the United States in the year of
our Lord 1966." (E.S.)

THE FIXER (cont'd)

M384 Elkin, Stanley, "The Fixer," Massachusetts Review, 8:388-92,
Spring, 1967.

Malamud's "The Fixer is immensely moving. . . . This quality is
at once its supreme achievement and part of its downfall. . . .
There are fewer enigmas in The Fixer than metaphors, less ambiguities than italics. To say that it is moving, then, is to perceive
in it its picturesque qualities." (D.P.)

M385 Frankel, Haskel, "Bernard Malamud," Saturday Review, 49:39-40,
September 10, 1966.

[This interview with Bernard Malamud largely concentrates on The
Fixer:] "If this book isn't about freedom, I don't know what it is
about." Finally, "my work, all of it, is an idea of dedication to the
human. . . . If you don't respect man, you cannot respect my work."
(D.P.)

M386 Freedman, Alan Warren, "Bernard Malamud: The Hero as Schnook,"
Southern Review, 4:927-44, October, 1968.

"In The Fixer Malamud has . . . written a searingly brilliant novel.
His mastery of dialect achieves new heights of artistry in order to
express new depths of misery. . . . Yakov Bok . . . is an archetypal victim with nothing going for him. . . . he is a poor schnook
distinguished only by misery and his sense of victimization. But
because he embraces these, and . . . finds something in himself
and in his life to affirm, he becomes a paradigm of a new kind of
hero--one who given the context of his meaningless, arbitrary world
and his own feebleness, even irrelevance, when confronting it,
triumphs because he endures." (D.P.)

M387 Hoag, Gerald, "Malamud's Trial: The Fixer and the Critics,"
Western Humanities Review, 24:1-12, 1970.

"I believe Bok's psychic troubles could hardly be more familiar to
the twentieth-century reader, and therein lies the daring of the
author's plan. The occupational hazard of the mythologist of contemporary experience is that the reader, like Huck Finn, may just
say 'I been there before'." (D.A.B.)

THE FIXER (cont'd)

M388   Horne, Lewis B., "Yakov Agonistes," Research Studies
(Washington State University), 37:320-6, December, 1969.

"Yakov Bok of The Fixer, like the central figures of Bernard
Malamud's other novels, is a shlemiel . . . an anti-hero lacking
generally those qualities that characterize the man with heavy
shield and glistening armor, the man striding the battlefield of
formal challenge and clanging swords. . . . Yet by the end of the
novel, Yakov Bok, in an assertive and iron-hard and without doubt
bungling way, has conquered the whole Philistine world of Russia.
. . . Like Milton's Samson, Yakov Bok leaves the prison at the
end of the novel . . . and downs great temples. . . . For the
strength of Yakov Bok . . . is basically the same as the strength
of Milton's champion : like Samson, he shows the dual strength of
patience and vision." (D.P.)

M389   Ratner, Marc, "The Humanism of Malamud's The Fixer,"
Critique: Studies in Modern Fiction, 9:81-4, No. 2, 1967.

Although The Fixer "is somewhat marred by a documentary tone
. . . all the events and experiences are finally tuned to Malamud's
central character, Bok. . . ." The nature of human suffering, as
Malamud expresses it in The Fixer,"is that nothing is so individual
and universal in a man's experience as pain. Malamud's hero
moves from being 'fixed' by circumstances and events to being the
'fixer.' He begins with the 'rock of atheism' pain, and ends by affirming his faith in an act of moral engagement." (D.P.)

IDIOTS FIRST

M390   Dupee, F. W., "The Power of Positive Sex," Partisan Review,
No. 31, pp. 425-30, Summer, 1964.

"Like J. F. Powers, Malamud is a wildly conservative force in
writing at present, a fact which he . . . perhaps owes in part to
his interest in the short story, with its necessary economy. . . .
Malamud's ability to persuade us of the reality of his characters--
their emotions, deeds, words, surroundings--remains astonishing.
In most of the twelve stories that make up Idiots First, that ability
is quite . . . evident. . . . The Fidelman stories are beautifully
done, and very funny. Something about them, however, suggests
the rigors of a punitive expedition on the part of the author and
possibly at his own expense." (D.P.)

THE LADY OF THE LAKE

M391   Hill, John S., "Malamud's 'The Lady of the Lake': A Lesson in Rejection," University Review, 36:149-50, Winter, 1969.

Malamud's "The Lady of the Lake" is "a lesson in rejection. Freeman loses his past and his beloved because he shuns his heritage. This lesson is doubly striking for him because not only is Isabella better off for keeping her heritage but, because of it, she is lost to him. . . . Freeman's total loss . . . is the price of his rejection of Self." (D.P.)

THE LOAN

M392   May, Charles E., "The Bread of Tears: Malamud's 'The Loan'," Studies in Short Fiction, 7:652-4, Fall, 1970.

Malamud's "The Loan" reflects in Lieb the baker's crying into the bread to make it sell, the Jewish tradition of misery, which brings strength rather than defeat. Lieb's past misery makes him prosper, as Kobotsky's misery gives him the strength to ask for a loan. However, Bessie's will is stronger than both men; she denies the loan. (D.P.)

THE NATURAL

M393   Freese, Peter, "Parzival als Baseballstar: Bernard Malamuds The Natural," Jahrbuch für Amerikastudien, 13:143-57, 1968.

By making use of the Wasteland motif and by presenting a contemporary version of the grail quest, Malamud, in The Natural, imparts a deeper, mythological dimension and a timeless significance to the realistically described contests of sport. (G.C.)

M394   Greiff, Louis K., "Quest and Defeat in The Natural," Thoth, 8:23-34, Winter, 1967.

"In his novel, The Natural, Bernard Malamud seizes the clichéd image of ballplayer as hero and, in a spirit both playful and serious, recreates it in epic dimensions. The results of this . . . are often bizarre; a mixing together of archetypal patterns, current bits of Americana, stereotypes, and myths. Yet . . . the results are often compelling. . . . For in these strange combinations Malamud seems to have created an appropriate idiom for dealing with heroes and their quests in a modern work of fiction. . . ." (D.P.)

THE NATURAL (cont'd)

M395 Shulman, Robert, "Myth, Mr. Eliot, and the Comic Novel,"
Modern Fiction Studies, 12:395-403, Winter, 1966-67.

"In opposition to Eliot's denigration, however, Malamud [in The
Natural] draws on the techniques and outlook of The Waste Land to
affirm the heroic possibilities of the common life and its representative men, even as he records their failures." "Throughout The
Great Gatsby there is a strong connection between Fitzgerald's
surrealistic techniques, his nightmare visions of breakdown and
fragmentation . . . and similar techniques and broken parties in
The Waste Land." (D.P.)

M396 Turner, Frederick W., III, "Myth Inside and Out: Malamud's
The Natural," Novel, 1:133-9, Winter, 1968.

In Malamud's The Natural "Roy Hobbs is the hero of a mythology,
but ultimately he fails that mythology by his inability to see and act
beyond it without destroying it for himself." (D.P.)

M397 Wasserman, Earl R., "The Natural: Malamud's World Ceres,"
Centennial Review, 9:438-60, No. 4, 1965.

In The Natural "what Malamud has written is a novel that coherently
organizes the rites of baseball and many of its memorable historic
episodes into the epic inherent in baseball as a measure of man.
. . ." (D.P.)

A NEW LIFE

M398 Barsness, John A., "A New Life: The Frontier Myth in Perspective," Western American Literature, 3:297-302, Winter, 1969.

"The ultimate human perversity, even in the West, is to cling
firmly to belief in spite of incontrovertible evidence to the contrary.
If any moral must be drawn about the universe of A New Life, it is
that believing what one wants inevitably forces the ironic tragedy of
getting what one deserves." (W.G.F.)

M399 Elman, Richard M., "Malamud on Campus," Commonweal,
75:114-5, October 27, 1961.

Malamud's A New Life is not convincing, although descriptive
passages are "accurate and exotic." The novel is "as dreary as
the institution it sets out to satirize." (D.P.)

A NEW LIFE (cont'd)

M400   Schulz, Max F., "Malamud's A New Life: The New Wasteland of the
        Fifties," Western Review, 6:37-44, Summer, 1969.

        In A New Life, seemingly another lampoon of academia, Levin is
        "modern man, a hero in spite of himself, willing to allow that
        involvement in life may ennoble, but ready to avow that it inevitably
        damns one." (A.S.W.)

M401   White, Robert L., "The English Instructor as Hero: Two Novels
        by Roth and Malamud," Forum (Houston), 4:16-22, Winter, 1963.

        Both Malamud in A New Life and Roth in Letting Go "examine
        American culture in general": they are not restricted to Jewish
        subject matter and point of view; they deal extensively with the
        academic world. Malamud's novel is limited by the homogeneous
        society it explores, while Roth's characters "represent a wide
        range of American social strata." (D.P.)

        PICTURES OF FIDELMAN

M402   Lefcowitz, Barbara F., "The Hybris of Neurosis: Malamud's
        Pictures of Fidelman," Literature and Psychology, 20:115-20,
        No. 3, 1970.

        "Bernard Malamud's use of a neurotic character in Pictures of
        Fidelman expands the literary potential of mental pathology in a
        highly sophisticated manner. Throughout the six episodes . . .
        that make up the picaresque novella, Malamud both depicts and
        parodies neurosis by juxtaposing two sets of values, the first com-
        posed of the private world of Fidelman as victim and obsessional
        neurotic, and the second of the socio-historical world of Fidelman
        as victimizer. . . . Fidelman's inability to perceive . . . the split
        between private self and public self serves as a major linking motif
        for the six episodes." (D.P.)

        TAKE PITY

M403   Perrine, Laurence, "Malamud's 'Take Pity'," Studies in Short
        Fiction, 2:84-6, Fall, 1964.

        The theme of Malamud's "Take Pity" "is concerned with the tangled
        human emotions of pride and pity. . . . The story underscores the
        ambiguity of human relationships. Eva's refusal to accept charity

TAKE PITY (cont'd)

is at once an evidence of strength and of weakness--of admirable
self-reliance and of self-centered failure to respond to Rosen's
human need. Rosen's desire to help, in one light admirably altruistic is in another not altruistic at all, but a compulsive need of
his own nature which shows its impurity by turning finally to hate."
(D.P.)

M404   Pinsker, Sanford, "A Note on Bernard Malamud's 'Take Pity', "
Studies in Short Fiction, 6:212-3, Winter, 1969.

". . . the schematic structure of Malamud's story bears an uncanny
resemblance to Sartre's No Exit. Indeed, both contain a highly fan-
tasized 'hell,' but, more importantly, both suggest that 'hell is
other people'." (D.P.)

MALAPARTE, CURZIO

M405   Van Eerde, John, "Names in the Works of Malaparte, " Names,
6:88-96, June, 1958.

Malaparte relies often enough in descriptive passages on names
that evoke literary associations to "allow one to recognize in him
a considerable unwillingness to create autonomous imagery"; the
effect of this practice is to make his characterization superficial.
(W.G.F.)

MALEWSKA, HANNA

M406   Bereza, Henryk, "Of Sages and Kings, " Polish Perspectives,
6:35-8, February, 1963.

In her earlier period (The Grecian Spring, The Iron Crown, Stones
Will Cry Out, The Passing Shape of the World), Malewska was
obsessed with the idea of order and harmony. During the past
twenty years, although faithful to her Catholic outlook, her approach
to the problems of man and the world have undergone a radical
change in The Seven Sages, The Refusal of Sir Thomas Moore, and
The Lords of Leszno. (T.T.B.)

MALLEA, EDUARDO

M407   Belloni, Manuel, "The Inner Silence of Eduardo Mallea, "
Américas, 19:20-7, October, 1967.

"Two problems seem fundamental in all Mallea's novels: the autobiography of a question, and the mental imagery of the world. That
is what makes Mallea so Argentine: because he always asks in
silence and because he thinks reality in order to create it." (G.C.)

M408   Flint, J. M., "The Expression of Isolation: Notes on Mallea's
Stylistic Technique, " Bulletin of Hispanic Studies, 44:203-9,
July, 1967.

Mallea assumes a formidable task in giving his characters so
tenuous a motivating force as isolation. It demands a suggestive
style. Metaphor is the principal device used to hint at the psychological state of the characters. (C.O.)

       ALL GREEN SHALL PERISH--See
       TODO VERDOR PERECERÁ

       LA BAHÍA DEL SILENCIO

M409   Lewald, H. Ernest, "Mallea's Theme in La bahía del silencio, "
Hispania, 40:176-8, May, 1957.

"Mallea is doubtlessly concerned with man as an individual and
spiritual being in a century of ever-increasing mass behavior and
superficial values." (A.C.H.)

M410   Shaw, Donald L., "Narrative Technique in Mallea's La bahía de
silencio, " Symposium, 20:50-5, Spring, 1966.

Mallea's novel is "discussion fiction" made popular by Spain's
Generation of 1898. Mallea's autobiographical protagonist, in a
series of test situations, is concerned with the regeneration of
Argentina, human communication, and the need for a life-directing
ideal. (C.O.)

       THE BAY OF SILENCE--See
       LA BAHÍA DEL SILENCIO

HISTORIA DE UNA PASIÓN ARGENTINA

M411 Carrero del Mármol, Elena, "Gálvez y Mallea: Imágenes de la Argentina," Duquesne Hispanic Review, 2:167-78, Winter, 1963.

Gálvez is a writer preoccupied with the national, a preoccupation manifested in the form by which he is able to reconstruct the surroundings in which his characters move. Similarly, Mallea, a man of vast culture, was able to implant in his Historia de una pasión argentina a sharp yet simple division of his country: the existence of a visible and an invisible Argentina. (D.P.)

M412 Petersen, Fred, "James Baldwin and Eduardo Mallea: Two Essayists's Search for Identity," Discourse, 10:97-107, Winter, 1967.

Eduardo Mallea's "'spiritual definition'" of Argentina, his Historia de una pasión argentina (1937), may be compared to Baldwin's Nobody Knows My Name, in his "search for himself . . . as a social being within the web of American life." (G.C.)

M413 Petersen, Fred, "Notes on Mallea's Definition of Argentina," Hispania, 45:621-4, December, 1962.

"As an essayist working within the broad framework of a problem on the national level [in his Historia de una pasión argentina], Mallea joins Sarmiento and Rodó in emphasizing those factors which prevent a nation from optimally developing itself to its highest degree of fulfillment. . . . Mallea . . . places his observations on a spiritual--even mystical--plane which seems to have been reached by way of a personal scrutiny which is . . . 'universal' within the context of Western civilization." (D.P.)

POSESIÓN

M414 Petersen, Fred, "The Relationship of Narrative Technique to Theme in Eduardo Mallea's Posesión," Books Abroad, 38:361-6, Autumn, 1964.

"All three of the stories included in the Argentinian Eduardo Mallea's . . . Posesión, have as their unifying element the idea of possession, in one or another of its aspects." (C.E.N.)

LA SALA DE ESPERA

M415   Gibbs, Beverly Jean, "Spatial Treatment in the Contemporary Psychological Novel of Argentina," Hispania, 45:410-4, September, 1962.

In the contemporary psychological novel of Argentina, as represented by José Bianco's Las ratas, Ernesto Sábato's El túnel, Eduardo Mallea's La sala de espera, Estela Canto's El hombre del crepúsculo, and Carlos Mazzanti's El sustituto, spatiality "forms a special kind of background against which the personalities of the protagonists are delineated, or . . . it is transformed into a psychic phenomenon and serves in the portrayal of the mental and physical patterns of behavior of these individuals." (D.P.)

TODO VERDOR PERECERÁ

M416   Lichtblau, Myron, "El arte de la imagen en Todo verdor perecerá," Revista Hispánica Moderna, 29:120-32, April, 1963.

The rich imagery of this novel is not only decorative. It is used to portray more strikingly the psychological foundation of the work, the progressive emotional decay of the protagonist." (C.O.)

MALLET-JORIS, FRANÇOISE

M417   Delattre, Geneviève, " Mirrors and Masks in the World of Françoise Mallet-Joris," Yale French Studies, No. 27, pp. 121-6, Spring-Summer, 1961.

Mme. Mallet-Joris is possessed of a predominantly visual temperament. When we look at her characters "our eyes are met by their appearance only, that is, by what they are willing to let us see. Their truth lies behind the fortress of lies which they have erected, in a secret realm where they are overcome by fear when faced with their nudity and vulnerability, with what the novelist sometimes calls their soul." (D.P.)

M418   Marshall, Joyce, "Françoise Mallet-Joris: A Young Writer on Her Way," Tamarack Review, 8:63-72, Summer, 1958.

Miss Mallet-Joris has, in House of Lies taken a step forward that indicates her future potentialities. With boldness, idiosyncracy, passion, compression, and sense of theme, she writes of a world of human beings and human values, of individuals seeking individual salvations and satisfactions. (D.E.W.)

M419 Reck, Rima Dell, "Françoise Mallet-Joris and the Anatomy of the Will," Yale French Studies, No. 24, pp. 74-8, Summer, 1959.

Mme. Mallet-Joris is concerned with analysing the will and various forms of self-deception. The only characters who escape the perils of willfulness are those too simple to understand the complexity of life. (K. L.)

MALRAUX, ANDRÉ

M420 Albérès, R. M., "Andre Malraux and the 'Abridged Abyss'," Yale French Studies, No. 18, pp. 45-54, Winter, 1957.

Malraux faces the crucial question, the meaning of existence, and forces the reader to face it with him by forcing identification with the hero and by his stylistic technique of "abridgment." (K. L.)

M421 Baumgartner, Paul, "Solitude and Involvement: Two Aspects of Tragedy in Malraux's Novels," French Review, 38:766-76, May, 1965.

In Malraux's early novels the tragedy of solitude predominates, whereas in the later novels the tragedy of involvement is characteristic. "Since both prototypes are drawn from the principle that the whole is greater than the sum of its parts, and since solitude and involvement hold forth the same ontological absurdity, the same contradiction between action and being, it seems Malraux has not so much moved on to another problem as he has contemplated the same one from a different angle." (D. P.)

M422 Blend, Charles D., "Early Expressions of Malraux's Art Theory," Romanic Review, 53:199-213, October, 1962.

Although André Malraux's books on art only began to appear in 1947, he had been developing his art theory during the years of his literary production, and scattered through his articles, speeches, prefaces and novels were the ideas that later became central in his art books. In those publications, "art as a struggle with destiny is the constant source from which flow all the streams of his art theory." (D. P.)

M423 Blend, Charles D., "The Humanism of André Malraux," Kentucky Foreign Language Quarterly, 1:1-5, No. 1, 1954.

"For Malraux, man finds himself alone in a universe in which he plays a temporary and fleeting role, a part which is without purpose and absurd. Death puts an end to individual human life, and the possible extinction of the species may terminate even the concept of man. . . . The core of his humanism therefore becomes: What to do about man in order to give him some stature, and dignity?" (K.M.W.)

M424   Blend, Charles D., "The Rewards of Tragedy," Yale French Studies, No. 18, pp. 97-106, Winter, 1957.

Malraux conceives of tragedy as an awareness of destiny, or all that defeats man. To face the unknown world with discipline rather than hope for justification is man's task. (K.L.)

M425   Boak, Denis, "Malraux: A Note on Editions," AUMLA, No. 21, pp. 79-83, May, 1964.

Both Les Conquérants and La Condition humaine are, in their final form, considerably revised. These changes are "in the direction of [Malraux's] own evolving political ideas." They indicate also Malraux's "conscious craftsmanship" and demonstrate that his "so-called 'journalistic eye-witness' style is in fact highly conscious and deliberate." (S.T.)

M426   Boak, Denis, "Malraux and T. E. Lawrence," Modern Language Review, 61:218-24, April, 1966.

"Thus we see Malraux's preoccupation with the figure of Lawrence . . . throughout most of his career, his attitude to the older man gradually growing more complex with time. At first Lawrence is seen as the prototype of the adventurer . . . then he is seen . . . as the adventurer/writer, who succeeds in turning his actions into one of the great books of the age; finally, when in many ways Malraux's own development . . . has surpassed Lawrence's own, we find . . . Lawrence shown as a forerunner of Malraux's own vision of the Tragic, man's fight against his destiny and attempt at self-transcendence." (D.P.)

M427   Bromberg, Victor, "Malraux: Passion and Intellect," Yale French Studies, No. 18, pp. 63-76, Winter, 1957.

The conflict between passion and intellect is present in all Malraux's novels, combined with a yearning for a new synthesis to resolve the dilemma. (K.L.)

M428   Bromberg, Victor, "Malraux: Poet of Violence and Destiny,"
Proceedings of the American Philosophical Society, 114:187-90,
June, 1970.

These are the "themes and problems that, almost in obsessive ways,
galvanize Malraux's imagination: man in and against history; man
in extreme situations; destruction and survival; the decline of the
West; the dialectical tension between revolt and morality--and above
all a communion through suffering proposed as the answer to man's
questioning of his undecipherable destiny." ". . . the notion of art
in Malraux's mind is necessarily bound up both with cruelty and
survival." (D.P.)

M429   Collins, Larry, and Dominique Lapierre, "The Remarkable Life of
André Malraux," Saturday Review, 51:20-3, 59-61, April 27, 1968.

"To a whole generation of French intellectuals he has been a symbol
of adventure, of active commitment to the causes they supported.
. . . Malraux seems to have deliberately chosen a life of action
. . . 'To be more than a man in the world of men . . . to escape
from the human condition'." (D.P.)

M430   Cordle, Thomas H., "Malraux and Nietzsche's Birth of Tragedy,"
Bucknell Review, 8:89-104, February, 1959.

"The triumph of tragedy, in Nietzsche's view, was that it seized
and held firm the dissonances of human existence and still cast
over them an illusion of harmony and beauty. The accomplishment
of Malraux's novels could be stated in much the same way. They
join together indissolubly humiliation and failure with proficiency
and the will to conquer and endow their union with an air of indisputable rightness." (K.M.W.)

M431   Davezac, Bertrand, "Malraux's Ideas on Art and Method in Art
Criticism," Journal of Aesthetics and Art Criticism, 22:177-88,
Winter, 1963.

"The defects of Malraux's works on art . . . spring from his intentions. Malraux's body of criticism aims at being a work of art in
itself. . . . He has assembled a frieze, at times fantastic, at times
solemn, of artworks, artists, and styles, and relates them or dis-
solves them at will on the basis of ethical values. . . . in the last
analysis he reduces art to a consumer's goods appealing primarily
on the basis of pleasure. Because his ideas do not suppose the
recognition of scientifically valid principles . . . his analysis of art
is far too dependent on his individual bias. . . ." (D.P.)

M432   Ellis, Lowell B., "Some Existentialist Concepts in Gide, Malraux, and Saint-Exupéry," Bucknell Review, 10:164-73, 1961.

"The use of existentialist concepts by Gide, Malraux, Saint-Exupéry, and others, does not of course prove the influence of these authors on the 'Paris School' of existentialists, but it may suggest that the philosophy deserves further consideration before being declared dead." (K.M.W.)

M433   Feldman, K. F., "André Malraux, Gaullist," Contemporary Review, No. 1112, pp. 66-8, August, 1958.

Malraux enacts in his life the role of his fictional hero, "the engaged man," taking on the vital issues of his day. His intellectual anguish is caused by his century's inability to "reconcile the primacy of the individual with the levelled-up needs of the masses." The dawn he detects in de Gaulle's return is a false one. (F. L.)

M434   Frank, Joseph, "André Malraux: The Image of Man," Hudson Review, 14:50-67, Spring, 1961.

Of writers famous before World War II, Malraux is one of the few the younger generation admires. "Better than any other figure of his epoch, Malraux anticipated and crystallized the post-war Existentialist atmosphere that has become associated with the names of Sartre and Camus." (C. E. N.)

M435   Gershman, Herbert S., "The Structure of Revolt in Malraux, Camus, and Sartre," Symposium, 24:27-35, Spring, 1970.

"The characters of Malraux, Camus, and Sartre were victims of thumb-heavy scales, for the margin of power lay elsewhere. Revolt for all three novelists was a personal decision, not a rule which obliged mankind in general. . . . The insoluble dilemma of Malraux and Camus--how to fight a hopeless revolution which, even if successful, would be a failure--was abandoned by Sartre who, sensitive to new evidence and trapped by theory, preferred to work a parallel mine." (D.P.)

M436   Girard, Rene, "Man, Myth and Malraux," Yale French Studies, No. 18, pp. 55-62, Winter, 1957.

To Malraux each culture is a myth, an effort by man to hide from the truth of his mortal condition. Malraux, however, cannot completely deny concrete experience and open the door to nothingness.

M436   2506

This is the conflict in his novels. The problem he presents in
Voices of Silence--the meaning of art divorced from the myth of
culture--is an extension of the same conflict between the "self and
otherness." (K. L.)

M437 Grover, Margaret, "The Concept of Literary Creation in the
Critical Writings of André Malraux: 1927 to 1935," Romanic
Review, 61:198-208, October, 1970.

Articles, book reviews, and prefaces to books by other writers,
all written between 1927 and 1935, serve "to lay bare some elements
of Malraux's aesthetic in the field of literature at the time when he
is writing his five pre-war novels." In his literary criticism
Malraux is most "conscious of belonging to a new world . . . which
must challenge, yet again, the concept of man handed down to it.
. . . Malraux considers that experience of the East brings Western
man face to face with himself and makes him recognize all that
needs to be changed in his attitudes." (D. P.)

M438 Harrington, Michael, "André Malraux: Metamorphosis of the Hero,"
Partisan Review, 21:655-63, November-December, 1954.

Malraux's "single theme is, of course, man's fate. . . . In this
persistent problem, the constant personality has been that of the
hero. The successive cloaks--the stages of metamorphosis--have
been politics and art. The environment has always been that of
death." (D. P.)

M439 Hertz, Micheline, "Woman's Fate," Yale French Studies,
No. 18, pp. 7-19, Winter, 1957.

The female characters in Malraux's novels develop from objects of
eroticism to the "woman of the future," liberated and the equal of
man--although still subordinated to his needs. (K. L.)

M440 Hoog, Armand, "Malraux, Möllberg and Frobenius," Yale French
Studies, No. 18, pp. 87-96, Winter, 1957.

Malraux has not changed from a man of action to an aesthete; he
has never left the museum. Thus he does not deny the unity of
man, but sees in art a reflection of immortal Man who exists
despite cultural relativism. (K. L.)

M441   Jenkins, Cecil, "Malraux the Romantic," London Magazine,
       8:50-7, March, 1961.

       Throughout his career Malraux largely used "contemporary history
       or pliable fictional material, the 'Revolution' as formal symbolism
       and realism as an idiom of persuasion in the service of a fundamen-
       tally anti-historical vision of the world." (D.P.)

M442   Komatsu, Kyo, "A Japanese Franc-Tireur Talks with Gide and
       Malraux," Centennial Review, 4:115-43, 1960.

       [These are recollections of Komatsu--a Japanese journalist forced
       to leave Japan in 1937 because of his anti-fascist views--of conver-
       sations in France with Gide and Malraux. Komatsu had previously
       translated works of both authors into Japanese.] (D.P.)

M443   Langlois, Walter G., "The Debut of André Malraux, Editor
       (Kra, 1920-22)," PMLA, 80:111-22, March, 1965.

       Malraux's early experience with the publisher Kra was important
       because not only did it constitute "his introduction into the field of
       art-book publishing, but it also revealed his deep sympathy with the
       poetic movements of Symbolism and Cubism. The first two
       Sagittaire series remain a truly remarkable tribute to the energy,
       intelligence, and taste of an editor who was barely twenty years
       old." (D.P.)

M444   Langlois, Walter G., "Young Malraux and the Values of the
       Communist Metaphysic," Southern Review, 3:884-93, October, 1968.

       Through his Indochina experiences "Malraux was drawn to
       Communism because it was the best means of fighting the in-
       justices of the oppressive Colonial government and other govern-
       ments like it. But on a broader intellectual level, Marxism ap-
       pealed to him because he saw it as . . . not so much a political
       and historical theory as . . . the answer to the deep spiritual sick-
       ness afflicting the West. His commitment to the cause . . . was
       really not ideological, but metaphysical; not political, but human."
       (D.P.)

M445   Leavitt, Richard P., "Music in the Aesthetics of André Malraux,"
       French Review, 30:25-30, October, 1956.

       Although Malraux concentrates on painting and sculpture to the
       exclusion of other arts, references to music are scattered through

his writings, most notably Le Temps du Mépris and L'Espoir. In his aesthetic "the great enemy is "le destin." Music, by its close connection with the emotions is an agent of "le destin" and must . . . be outgrown. . . . Music is completely the prisoner of time, and it is in the visual arts that Man's conquest stands forth most clearly, most ideally." (D.P.)

M446   Malraux, André, "Three Speeches," Yale French Studies, No. 18, pp. 27-38, Winter, 1957.

[These three speeches, translated by Kenneth Douglas, were given respectively at the Congress of Soviet Writers, August, 1934; at the International Association of Writers for the Defense of Culture, Paris, November, 1935; and before the same body in London, June, 1936.] (D.P.)

M447   Matthews, J. H., "André Malraux," Contemporary Review, No. 1099, pp. 24-8, July, 1957.

Malraux presents the idea of death's inevitability as the source of all man's fears and inadequacies. Accepting the human condition, Malraux tries to elevate man above it. Action is his answer; revolution, his particular kind of action. The heroic act is important only as it lifts man above the human dilemma. (F.L.)

M448   Maurois, André, "André Malraux," A La Page, No. 38, pp. 1142-56, August, 1967.

Malraux is the precursor of the absurd, in that life is only a stone thrown in the ocean. Malraux is interested more in acts than in doctrines. He has naturally a cosmic mind. His heroes have always been in search of the Grail, the Absolute. (T.T.B.)

M449   Oxenhandler, Neal, "Malraux and the Inference to Despair," Chicago Review, 15:72-4, Winter-Spring, 1962.

[This is a review of Geoffrey Hartman's book André Malraux in which he finds a version of the tragic theme in each of Malraux's novels.] (K.M.W.)

M450   Rao, Raja, "André Malraux among the Gods of India," Texas Quarterly, 4:102-11, Winter, 1961.

[This is an impressionistic account of Malraux's visit to some principal Hindu temples.] (W.G.F.)

M451   Reck, Rima Drell, "Andre Malraux's Theory of the Relation between
       Cinema and Novel," South-Central Bulletin, 22:30, March, 1962.

       Malraux's insights on cinema are contained in his Esquisse d'une
       psychologie du cinèma and various reviews, prefaces, and lectures.
       In his view the cinema rivals and is the inspiration of the modern
       novel. Cinema, having developed entirely within this century,"tele-
       scopes the aesthetic problems of development of the other arts." (D.P.)

M452   Reck, Rima Drell, "The Heroes in the Novels of Malraux: The
       Aesthetes and the Myth of Art," University of Kansas City
       Review, 28:151-7, December, 1961.

       "The hero who engages in aesthetic and cultural speculation, whose
       form of action is primarily reflective, is a recurrent figure in the
       novels of Malraux." (R.G.L.)

M453   Reck, Rima Drell, "Malraux on Cinema and the Novel,"
       Criticism, 5:112-8, Spring, 1963.

       In both theory (Esquisse d'une psychologie du cinèma) and practice
       (Les Conquérants, La Condition humaine, L'Espoir) the writings of
       Malraux reveal fundamental similarity of technique between the
       modern novel and the cinema--the principle of selection and juxta-
       position of facts and scenes, "cutting and editing" to create order
       from chaos. (J.L.A.)

M454   Reck, Rima Drell, "Malraux's Cerebral Eroticism," Forum
       (Houston), 3:44-6, Winter, 1962.

       "In the novels of Lawrence, eroticism is the primary form of man's
       desire to affirm himself. In André Malraux's heroes we find the
       logical successors of the heroes of Lawrence. . . . The cerebral
       eroticism of Perken and Ferral is but one form of their desperate
       metaphysical search to prove that man is superior to his human
       condition." (K.M.W.)

M455   Reck, Rima Drell, "Malraux's Heroes: Activists and Aesthetes,"
       University of Kansas City Review, 28:39-46, Autumn, 1961.

       "Only those characters who are able to separate themselves from
       the world of action by immersing themselves in art escape the
       deceptions of action, and manage . . . to liberate themselves from
       the absurdity which haunts their world." (R.G.L.)

M456   Rees, G. O., "Animal Imagery in the Novels of André Malraux,"
        French Studies, 9:129-42, April, 1955.

        There are 350 tropes drawn from the animal world in six of
        Malraux's works. Only one-third are conventional. He uses strik-
        ing figures in human portraiture (generally pejoratively), the
        animation of objects, and (principally insect images) the rendering
        of ideas or emotions that sustain the main themes of his novels.
        (W.F.)

M457   Rees, G. O., "Sound and Silence in Malraux's Novels," French
        Review, 32:223-30, January, 1959.

        ". . . sounds and silence are, in Malraux's novels, considerably
        more than mere evidence of care in the choice of realistic detail.
        Important as their contribution is to narration and description,"
        they additionally in many instances, constitute "a part of the very
        structure of the work . . . so helping to bring about what Gaëton
        Picon . . . has characterized as 'this intimate and musical fusion
        of all the inspirations of a work, provoked by one of its sharp
        vicissitudes'." (D.P.)

M458   Roedig, Charles F., "André Malraux in Asia," American Society
        of Legion of Honor Magazine, 32:145-63, No. 3, 1961.

        Malraux's "experiences in Asia diverted him for a time from his
        study of art to literature, and they introduced him to . . . the
        anguish of human beings stripped of their human dignity. These
        experiences inaugurated a succession of works . . . imbued with a
        greater humanity." (D.P.)

M459   R[oedig], C. F., "A Bibliographical Note on Malraux's Art
        Criticism," Yale French Studies, No. 18, pp. 129-30, Winter, 1957.

        Malraux decided in 1935 to devote himself to an interpretation of
        man through art, but the "final monumental synthesis" was delayed
        until after World War II. [Included are comments on Malraux's
        publications on art, in French as well as in English translation.]
        (D.P.)

M460   Roedig, Charles F., "The Early Fascinations of Malraux,"
        American Society of Legion of Honor Magazine, 24:21-31, No. 1,
        1958.

        "In the early works Malraux was concerned with the domination of
        his fascinations in order to put them in their correct and harmless

perspective. This done, he was freed to continue his great works which have since dazzled the world." (K.M.W.)

M461 Roedig, Charles F., "Malraux on the Novel (1930-1945)," Yale French Studies, No. 18, pp. 39-44, Winter, 1957.

Malraux thinks the novelist should function no longer as a psychological prober, but as a moralist who points an accusing finger at the world. (K.L.)

M462 Roudiez, Leon S., "Schème et vocabulaire chez Malraux," French Review, 41:304-18, December, 1967.

The structural constants with their deviations have signification in the novels of André Malraux. Malraux's key vocabulary words are surrounded with an air of mystery and seldom retain a specific meaning. (S.L.K.)

M463 Saisselin, Rémy G., "Malraux: From the Hero to the Artist," Journal of Aesthetics and Art Criticism, 16:256-60, December, 1957.

Malraux could change from social reformer to art critic because he sees the revolutionary hero and the artist as both strangers in society, both fighters against destiny as anguish, both heroes. (M.J.O.)

M464 Sonnenfeld, Albert, "Malraux and the Tyranny of Time: The Circle and the Gesture," Romanic Review, 54:198-212, October, 1963.

"Time and immutability, death and immortality, man's inherent limitations and man's need to transcend his human lot . . . pervades all of Malraux's novels. . . . Malraux chooses two recurring visual motifs to embody the essence of this struggle. . . . frequently, Malraux's circle images . . . represent the endless cyclical movement of the universe, the inexorable orbit of time which enslaves, degrades, and eventually annihilates man. . . . all of Malraux's novels also contain essentially linear, symbolic gestures in which a hero ensures his transcendence of death and solitude by bestowing his mission either upon a successor or upon a collective fraternity dedicated to changing the course of history." (D.P.)

M465   Sperber, Manès, "André Malraux und die Politik," Merkur, 23:326-41, April, 1969.

Having learned the price which the intellectual must pay in order to play the politician, Malraux may soon return to poetic and philosophical writings. (J.R.R.)

M466   [Stéphane, Roger], "André Malraux Talks to Roger Stéphane," Listener, 80:571-2, October 31, 1968.

[This interview, based on Malraux's Anti-Memoirs, elicits Malraux's views on man and his actions, his impressions of Nehru, Mao Tse-tung and General de Gaulle, and the irony of Malraux, a left-wing revolutionary functioning as a member of an authoritarian right-wing government.] (D.P.)

M467   Stokes, Samuel E., Jr., "Malraux and Pascal," Wisconsin Studies in Contemporary Literature, 6:286-92, Autumn, 1965.

"It is the mode of expressing metaphysical concerns that creates the 'accent pascalien' which one also detects in Malraux." (P.J.R.)

M468   Turnell, Martin, "Malraux's Fate," Commonweal, 82:410-3, June 18, 1965.

". . . Malraux is a great figure rather than a great writer. His continual urge to find causes mean that he has of necessity identified himself with causes that are phenomenal and that this has had its effect on his fiction. . . . With Man's Fate . . . too much that is ephemeral, too much that is perishable, has gone into the novel, which becomes more dated every year. . . . Man's Hope . . . which is riddled with the political clichés of the nineteen-thirties and the incomprehensible initials of forgotten left-wing organizations, is rapidly becoming unreadable." (D.P.)

M469   Vandegans, André, "Malraux a-t-il fréquente les grandes écoles?" Revue des Langues Vivantes, 26:336-40, 1960.

André Malraux was never registered at l'École nationale des Langues orientales vivantes; he never registered at la Faculté des Lettres de Paris. It remains possible that he followed certain free or public courses to which he had been admitted without registering. He did attend l'École du Louvre, but only in the capacity of an auditor. (D.P.)

M470   Vigée, Claude, "La Mort comme épreuve du réel dans les romans
        d'André Malraux," Modern Language Notes, 83:513-23, 1968.

        "For Malraux, death is not necessarily . . . an empty and vain
        event. Man, this perpetual moribund, must stand erect and act to
        exorcise the emptiness of his mortal nature. . . . The great charac-
        ters in the leading novels of Malraux cannot pass the test of their
        inner reality and that of the world when they are brought to bay by
        death." (D.P.)

M471   West, Paul, "Malraux's Genteel Humanism," Kenyon Review,
        21:623-38, Autumn, 1959.

        Divided and ineffective, Malraux's view turns about a consoling
        humanism, in the tradition of Arnold, Pater and Santayana. His
        later aesthetic makes "art ape ethics" and action become a des-
        perate immersion in the human, at the price of losing not only our
        illusions of control . . . but even self-control. . . ." (K.W.)

M472   Wilkinson, David, "Malraux, Revolutionist and Minister,"
        Journal of Contemporary History, 1:43-64, No. 2, 1966.

        "For seven years now André Malraux has . . . administer[ed]
        culture to the French people; he is also a high priest of their
        history." Malraux has been called on to justify de Gaulle's victory;
        he has also evolved a politics of art in three phases: "the new human
        type, the systematic resurrection of the past, and cultural democ-
        racy." (D.P.)

        ANTIMÉMOIRES

M473   Black, Cyril E., "Malraux: The Unity of Thought and Action,"
        Virginia Quarterly Review, 45:148-51, Winter, 1969.

        Malraux "is one of a handful of men in his generation to have com-
        bined so fruitfully the life of the intellect and the life of action, and
        he understands as few men do this world of societies and individuals
        in conflict." His Antimémoires "are neither narrative biography
        nor confession, but rather a selection of experiences designed to
        evolve through reconstruction of conversation and retrospective
        comments certain salient formative experiences." (D.P.)

ANTIMÉMOIRES (cont'd)

M474   Brée, Germaine, "The Anti-Memoirs of André Malraux,"
Contemporary Literature, 11:269-82, Spring, 1970.

Though the first volume of Malraux's Anti-Memoirs is a solid
literary achievement built around the theme of the voyage, it is
hard to imagine three more such volumes, for "no renewal of the
themes seems possible, so well-rounded is the itinerary." (K.H.B.)

M475   Galantiere, Lewis, "The Last Enemy Overcome," Saturday
Review, 51:45-6, 70, November 16, 1968.

In part Anti-Memoirs "treats two kinds of confrontation, direct and
reflective, with death. . . . Another part of the book is devoted to a
succession of tests of the validity of Malraux's past acts and convictions. . . . Altogether, Anti-Memoirs is a virtuoso performance
of astonishing range and skill. But . . . the whole does not, in the
end, seem . . . to be greater than the sum of the parts." (D.P.)

M476   Gilman, Richard, "Malraux Side-stepping Himself," New Republic,
159:27-30, November, 23, 1968.

"Anti-Memoirs may be a lesson for our time in its grand strategy of
placing the general questions ahead of the ego, of trying to be more
serious than anecdote and personal recapitulation will allow. But
. . . the book's 'philosophy' has no clear ground, and its purpose
has no sustaining energy. It gives off, along with flashes of brilliant
originality and rightness, the sense of a mind too long in the abstractions and predictabilities of the state. . . ." (D.P.)

M477   Grosjean, Jean, "Les Antimémoires d'André Malraux,"
La Nouvelle Revue Française, No. 178, pp. 658-66, October, 1967.

Haunted by the great events of his time and the invisible roots of
every event, Malraux has sought a solution through an unsuspected
hope, thereby trying to stop the imminent catastrophes. In La Voie
royale he plumbed Asia and in Les Conquérants the revolution,
whereas La Condition humaine and L'Espoir continue a combat for
China and Spain. Le Temps du mépris prepares for the war on
Nazism. (T.T.B.)

ANTIMÉMOIRES (cont'd)

M478   Hartley, Anthony, "Malraux and the Myth-maker," Encounter, 30:64-70, June, 1968.

"Thus Antimémoires is at the point of intersection of two aspects of Malraux himself. Not only is he present as the artist imparting meaning to events, but he himself plays the role of leader directing history. . . . Yet Antimémoires is still the work of a great writer and a man of intellectual quality who has not been deluded by his imaginative gifts into concealment of his own innate contradictions." (D.P.)

M479   Langlois, Walter G., "The Anti-Memoirs, Saba, and the Immortality of Man," Southern Review, 5:1019-29, Autumn, 1969.

The confrontation with death "has given meaning to Malraux's own life and helped define for him the limits of the human condition. Not surprisingly, it is this confrontation which emerges as the fundamental element of [the Anti-Memoirs], as it has been in one way or another in all of his previous writings." (J.M.D.)

M480   Lucet, Charles, "Malraux et ses Antimémoires," French Review, 42:1-15, October, 1968.

In his Antimémoires the message of Malraux is that man is unconquerable although he is at the bottom of an abyss which he wishes to regard without vertigo, an abyss explored before by Pascal and Baudelaire as the abode of an uncertain hope. (D.P.)

M481   Riffaterre, Michael, "André Malraux's Antimémoires," Columbia Forum, 11:31-5, Winter, 1968.

Malraux's Antimémoires is "crammed with passages plucked out of [his] older works." Antimémoires is "as different from memoirs as a poem is different from the most brilliant narrative. Where memoirs would explain and describe the author through the settings in which he appears . . . antimemoirs refashion memories to the shape of his mental contours, and deflect the meaning of words in accordance with his inner rules." (D.P.)

LA CONDITION HUMAINE

M482   Groves, Margaret, "Malraux's Lyricism and the Death of Kyo," Modern Language Review, 64:53-61, January, 1969.

LA CONDITION HUMAINE (cont'd)

"Scenes like the death of Kyo [in La Condition humaine] add to the stature of Malraux as a novelist not for what they add to his philosophy of life but for the richness and beauty which they bring to his work. They add to it a complexity and an illogicality borrowed from life itself." (J.R.R.)

M483   Langlois, Walter G., "The Dream of the Red Chamber, The Good Earth, and Man's Fate: Chronicles of Social Change in China," Literature East and West, 11:1-10, March, 1967.

"The Dream of the Red Chamber . . . presents a picture of the old Chinese ruling class. . . . Pearl Buck's book The Good Earth describes the vast agricultural masses of the Middle Kingdom in the early years of the twentieth century, when new, outside forces were beginning to have an effect. The period of turbulence that surrounded the fall of the old China, and the main elements involved in the social revolution that has continued to modify contemporary China are graphically presented in André Malraux's great novel, Man's Fate." (D.P.)

M484   Nelson, Roy Jay, "Malraux and Camus: The Myth of the Beleaguered City," Kentucky Foreign Language Quarterly, 13:86-94, No. 2, 1966.

"The presentation of multiplicity within unity, the adaptation of the traditional novel to an absurd world, is a task which Malraux and Camus attacked and accomplished in a remarkably similar way-- the former in La Condition humaine (1933), and the latter in La Peste (1947)." (D.P.)

M485   St. Aubyn, F. C., "André Malraux: The Syntax of Greatness," French Review, 34:140-5, December, 1960.

The rather long paragraph which occurs early in Part One of La Condition humaine, in a scene between the hero Kyo Gisors and his wife May illustrates through a rich concatenation of stylistic and imagistic structure and detail "the inevitable solitude of the human condition at the heart of love, and what is more significant, of conjugal love." (D.P.)

LA CONDITION HUMAINE (cont'd)

M486   Silverstein, Norman, "Institutional and Individual Reformers: The Existentialist Element in Man's Fate," Ball State Teachers College Forum, 6:37-44, No. 1, 1965.

"Malraux's novel is a paradigm of the responses men make to anguish. As such, it offers no easy solution to the problem of individual reform, except as Kyo and revolutionaries find release from anguish in communicating." (K.M.W.)

DAYS OF CONTEMPT--See
LE TEMPS DU MÉPRIS

L'ESPOIR

M487   Picon, Gaëtan, "Man's Hope," Yale French Studies, No. 18, pp. 3-6, Winter, 1957.

Malraux's Man's Hope is not mere reportage, it is a series of real happenings transformed into poetry. The evocation of the Spanish Civil War is also Malraux's farewell to the myth of revolution. (K.L.)

MAN'S FATE--See
LA CONDITION HUMAINE

MAN'S HOPE--See
L'ESPOIR

LA METAMORPHOSE DES DIEUX

M488   Grunwald, Henry Anatole, "André Malraux: The Gods in Art," Horizon, 1:5-17, 112-7, November, 1958.

"In The Metamorphosis of the Gods, Malraux has pulled together a number of these insights [on art]--chiefly those concerning art as an expression of the otherworldly--and arranged them in what, for him is almost order. The resulting work is breathtaking, irritating, beautifully but densely written, repetitious, humorless, fascinating, and unquestionably brilliant. Every page glows with a passion for art--and . . . it displays a longing sensitivity and an almost professional knowledgeability about religion." (D.P.)

THE METAMORPHOSIS OF THE GODS--See
LA METAMORPHOSE DES DIEUX

LA TEMPS DU MÉPRIS

M489   Hartmann, Geoffrey H., "Camus and Malraux: The Common
Ground," Yale French Studies, No. 25, pp. 104-10, Spring, 1960.

Malraux's novel Days of Contempt was the first "to recognize and
broadcast the danger of Nazism. Yet he sacrificed nothing to
propaganda. His book is neither an indictment nor a cry of hate.
It was concerned with the sources of man's resistance. . . . Camus
defined the metaphysical rebel by the cogito 'I rebel, therefore we
are--alone,' and this 'alone' is the precise tragic dénouement
observed also by Malraux." (D.P.)

LES NOYERS DE L'ALTENBURG

M490   Chua, C. L., "André Malraux's Unfinished Novel, Les Noyers
de l'Altenburg: A Caveat for Critics," Neophilologus, 53:10-3,
January, 1969.

Uncertainties and the inconclusiveness of Malraux's Les Noyers de
l'Altenburg warn us "that critical statements about the form, plot,
or theme of Noyers should be made under the author's own reserva-
tion that the book is offered as an unfinished piece of imaginative
literature." (D.P.)

M491   Frank, Joseph, "Malraux and the Image of Man," New Republic,
131:18-9, August 30, 1954.

"If, for the youthful Malraux, the image of man was becoming extinct,
the mature Malraux [in Les Noyers de l'Altenburg] has now dedicated
himself to keeping this image alive with all the resources of his magnificent gifts. . . . And the genius of Malraux . . . can still light up
the tarnished image of Man with some of the radiance it once had for
Shakespeare and Montaigne." (D.P.)

M492   Reck, Rima Drell, "Malraux's Transitional Novel: Les Noyers de
l'Altenburg," French Review, 34:537-44, May, 1961.

Les Noyers "concluding that action is not the most effective form of
defiance . . . states without compromise man's victory over his
human condition in art." (R.B.W.)

THE ROYAL WAY--See
LA VOIE ROYAL

THE TEMPTATION OF THE WEST--See
LA TENTATION DE L'OCCIDENT

LA TENTATION DE L'OCCIDENT

M493   Douthat, Blossom, "Nietzschean Motifs in Temptation of the
        Occident," Yale French Studies, No. 18, pp. 77-86, Winter, 1957.

        Both Nietzsche and Malraux are aware that the West is crumbling and
        in need of a new myth. Nietzsche finds in tragedy the resolution of
        "insupportable vitality and senseless formalism" and Malraux perhaps
        glimpses a similar solution: the reconciliation of Orient and
        Occident. (K.L.)

M494   Reck, Rima Drell, "Malraux and the Duality of Western Man,"
        Personalist, 48:345-60, Summer, 1967.

        The Temptation of the West (1926) is seminal in Malraux's career
        as novelist, art critic, social philosopher, and humanist. (J.C.)

            LA VOIE ROYALE

M495   Ball, Bertrand Logan, Jr., "Nature, Symbol of Death in La Voie
        royale," French Review, 35:390-5, February, 1962.

        "The jungle is an exteriorization or palpable image of the intangible
        enemy, death, against which the heroes struggle inwardly." (R.B.W.)

M496   Boak, Denis, "Malraux's La Voie royale," French Studies,
        19:42-50, January, 1965.

        La Voie royale, published in 1930 but probably written before 1928,
        is only a partial success. As a pure adventure story it has unusual
        intellectual overtones, but the structure is confused. As a philo-
        sophical novel, it is more effective, but the ethical values are more
        loosely attached to the human condition than in Malraux's later
        work. (D.P.)

M497   Casey, Bill, "André Malraux's Heart of Darkness," Twentieth
        Century Literature, 5:21-6, April, 1959.

        Both Malraux's The Royal Way and Conrad's Heart of Darkness
        portray a single idea: "that of an indifferent universe in which man

LA VOIE ROYALE (cont'd)

is alone, shored up by guides and standards of his own making . . .
which once seen for what they are, fall away and leave only the
conviction of man's moral isolation in a grotesque and meaningless
world." (D.P.)

M498 Cordle, Thomas, "The Royal Way," Yale French Studies, No. 18,
pp. 20-6, Winter, 1957.

The Royal Way, although thought to be the most inferior of Malraux's
novels, is actually an important part of the "Malraux myth." (K.L.)

M499 Dale, Jonathan, "Sartre and Malraux: La Nausée and La Voie
royale," Forum for Modern Language Studies, 4:335-46,
October, 1968.

"La Nausée . . . appears as Sartre's attempt to take Malraux's
themes of La Voie royale to their logical conclusion." (J.R.R.)

THE VOICES OF SILENCE--See
LES VOIX DU SILENCE

LES VOIX DU SILENCE

M500 Darzins, John, "Malraux and the Destruction of Aesthetics,"
Yale French Studies, No. 18, pp. 107-13, Winter, 1957.

"Time and time again [in Voices of Silence] Malraux reverts to his
original humanist thesis and asserts the Promethean autonomy of
the artist, the priority of the individual over the collective style,
the reduction of the cosmos to man." (K.L.)

M501 Frank, Joseph, "Malraux's Metaphysics of Art," Sewanee Review,
70:620-50, October-December, 1962.

In The Voices of Silence "Malraux ultimately fails, then, to dissolve
the disparate qualities of historical cultures and their styles into
the universal apprehension of the liberty of the creative act. But
. . . Malraux has unquestionably written one of the great reaffirma-
tions of humanism in our time. . . ." (D.P.)

LES VOIX DU SILENCE (cont'd)

M502 Hartmann, Geoffrey H., "The Taming of History," <u>Yale French Studies</u>, No. 18, pp. 114-28, Winter, 1957.

[Malraux's ideas about art in <u>Voices of Silence</u> are applied to poetry.] (K.L.)

M503 Lawler, J. R., "André Malraux and <u>The Voices of Silence</u>," <u>Meanjin Quarterly</u>, 19:282-90, September, 1960.

". . . at the centre of <u>Les Voix du silence</u> Malraux has placed his own anguished questioning of fate. . . . It is essentially a grandiose poem of a new kind . . . an unending dialogue between his hope and his despair that can never be wholly resolved, but in the courage and amplitude of which we recognize the note of greatness." (K.M.W.)

M504 Roedig, Charles F., "A Bibliographical Footnote on Malraux's Art Criticism," <u>Yale French Studies</u>, No. 18, pp. 129-30, Winter, 1957.

[This describes the publishing history of <u>Les Voix du silence</u>.] (K.M.W.)

M505 Tint, H., "<u>Les Voix du silence</u> and the Novels of Malraux," <u>French Studies</u>, 11:323-32, October, 1957.

Developed gradually in Malraux's earlier works, the moral implications of <u>Les Voix du silence</u> transcend aesthetics and present, in poignantly nonrational arguments, a search for a moral absolute and a rejection of Spenglerian philosophy. (R.A.B.)

M506 West, Paul, "A Narrowed Humanism: Pater and Malraux," <u>Dalhousie Review</u>, 37:278-84, Autumn, 1957.

André Malraux's <u>Les Voix du silence</u> is "an up-to-date version of the views on art of Walter Pater [although] the Malraux version is of course, wider in range. . . ." (D.P.)

THE WALNUT TREES OF ALTENBURG--See
LES NOYERS DE L'ALTENBURG

MANDEL, ELI

M507   Dudek, Louis, "Two Canadian Poets: Ralph Gustafson and Eli Mandel," Culture, No. 22, pp. 145-51, June, 1961.

There is a dual trend in current Canadian poetry, the abstruse and the realistic. But the lines of division are not entirely clearcut. Gustafson, a metaphysical poet, also manifests the real and actual. Mandel begins with a harsh vision, but in the end achieves imagination and myth. (J.S.)

M508   Ower, John, "Black and Secret Poet: Notes on Eli Mandel," Canadian Literature, No. 42, pp. 14-25, Autumn, 1969.

Eli Mandel's poems "are as strange and knotty as anything in Canadian poetry." His "ethnic background appears significant not only with regard to those poems containing specifically Jewish allusions, but may also serve as a major formative influence upon both the poet's vision and his style. Secondly, Mandel is a poet of spiritual upset and rebellion, and can be appreciated only in the atmosphere of crisis that gave birth to romanticism, existentialism, and contemporary anarchism. Thirdly, he is a myth-maker . . . his poetry shows both the radical imaginative re-arrangement of reality and the plumbing of the unconscious mind which are characteristically interrelated facts of myth-making poetry." (D.P.)

MANDEL'SHTAM, OSIP EMIL'EVICH

M509   Brown, Clarence, "Fourth Prose: Introductory Note," Hudson Review, 23:49-52, Spring, 1970.

Mandelstam's Fourth Prose, never published while he was alive, was a desperate act of self-therapy, as the result of a vicious official attack against the poet. Fourth Prose "preceded and largely made possible the poems dated '1930' and onwards in his collected works." (D.P.)

M510   Brown, Clarence, "Into the Heart of Darkness: Mandelstam's Ode to Stalin," Slavic Review, 26:584-604, December, 1967.

In 1937 "Mandelstam, after a series of misfortunes and tragic sufferings . . . decided that the time had come to sell out. . . . And so he attempted . . . [to write] an adulatory ode to Iosif Stalin . . . . The chief purpose of this paper is to unravel and lay bare some of the metamorphoses of the ode that can be discerned in some twenty-four poems." (D.P.)

M511   Kovac, Anton, "Mandelstam--An Architect of Acmeism,"
New Zealand Slavonic Journal, pp. 67-76, 1969.

In Mandelstam's poetry "the three essentials of acmeist poetry--
clarity, the stress on the real existence of the external world, and
solidity--matured into a unique fruit." (A.S.W.)

M512   Mandelstam, Osip, "From the Noise of Time," Commentary,
40:37-41, October, 1965.

[This is a selection from the memoirs of Osip Mandelstam, a
Jewish-Russian poet and essayist (1891-1938). (G.A.S.)

M513   Mihailovich, Vasa D., "Osip Mandel'shtam and His Critics,"
Papers on Language and Literature, 6:323-5, Summer, 1970.

"In summation, one concludes that the criticism of Mandel'shtam's
works has been sketchy and unsystematic. Only lately have the
critics begun to evaluate him in perspective. . . . Works on
Mandel'shtam can be divided into three groups; those written in
Russian before and after the revolution, and those written abroad.
. . . the definitive view of him and his literary achievement is yet
to come." (D.P.)

M514   Nilsson, Nils Åke, "Osip Mandel'štam and His Poetry," Scando-
Slavica, 9:37-52, 1963.

Mandel'štam has not "achieved the place he deserves in modern
Russian poetry. Perhaps one . . . reason is the label of 'neo-
classicist' attached to him in all surveys of Russian literature.
. . . behind this designation we have a poetry of more complex,
controversial kind than we may have expected." (K.M.W.)

M515   Stuckow, George, "The Fate of Osip Mandelstam," Survey, No. 46,
pp. 151-5, January, 1963.

According to official and unofficial sources, Mandelstam must have
died in the Spring of 1938 in a Vladivostok transit camp, while
awaiting transport to a permanent camp. He had become quite mad,
fearing poisoning by the authorities, and finally ended feeding on
garbage from the refuse heap. (D.P.)

M516 Terras, Victor, "Classical Motives in the Poetry of Osip Mandel'štam," Slavic and East European Journal, 10:251-67, No. 3, 1966.

Mandel'štam "deserves to be called a hellenist . . . for having stepped into the stream of time and retrieved from it . . . genuine fragments of the ancient world, visions of Hellas and Rome which are marvels of historical intuition in the Bergsonian sense." (G.C.)

M517 Terras, Victor, "The Time Philosophy of Osip Mandel'shtam," Slavonic and East European Review, 47:344-54, July, 1969.

". . . Mandel'shtam's time concept is of pivotal importance to his entire philosophy, just as his time percept is characteristic of his poetic vision." The poet "wisely stays with an irrational, metaphoric solution of the antimony, never trying to generalize, or to abstract." (D.P.)

M518 Watstein, Joseph, "Osip Mandelstam: The First of the Soviet Literary Rebels," Western Humanities Review, 20:277-89, 1966.

[This is an examination of the life, times and art of a poet of "rare power and originality."] (G.C.)

M519 Woodward, James B., "Rhythm and Structure in the Alexandrines of Mandel'shtam," Canadian Slavic Studies, 2:1-13, Spring, 1968.

". . . although Alexandrines without the caesura are almost totally absent from Mandel'shtam's verse . . . he was still able to invest it with effective rhythmic variety . . . and adapt it subtly to his purpose." (G.C.)

ACMEIST MANIFESTO--See
UTRO AKMEIZMA

BESSONNICA

M520 Nilsson, Nils Åke, "Osip Mandel'štam's 'Insomnia' Poem," International Journal of Slavic Linguistics and Poetics, 10:148-54, 1966.

"Bessonnica" ("Insomnia"), published in the second edition of Kamen' (The Stone), one of Mandel'štam's best known poems, is linked with the genre of "insomnia" poems. ". . . the poem tells us that Mandel'štam sees in contemporary historical events a parallel to classical history . . . but it also indicates that the poet has come to the conclusion that he cannot stay any longer in the beautiful but fragile world of balance and order he had created for himself in The Stone." (D.P.)

INSOMNIA--See
BESSONNICA

NOTES TOWARDS A SUPREME FICTION--See
VOS' MISTIŠIJA

TRISTIA

M521   Carlisle, Olga, "Four Poems by Osip Mandelstam: An Introduction,"
Southern Review, 4:692-703, July, 1968.

Mandelstam's "poetry made use of neoclassical imagery--yet it was
intensely original. . . ." His "early verse is neoclassic, hermetic,
and yet of crystalline clarity. . . . Mandelstam's poetic magic may
be felt at the level of the line, sometimes even of the word." "The
following four poems are at the core of Tristia. . . ."   (D.P.)

UTRO AKMEIZMA

M522   Brown, Clarence, "Mandelshtam's Acmeist Manifesto, Translated
and with a Note," Russian Review, 24:46-51, January, 1965.

[This article presents a translation of Mandelstam's Acmeist
Manifesto with a brief note indicating the edition used and placing
it in the context of Acmeism and Mandelstam's other criticism.]
(A.S.W.)

VOS' MISTIŠIJA

M523   Brown, Clarence, "Mandelstam's 'Notes Towards a Supreme
Fiction': Text, Translation, Comment," Delos: A Journal on
and of Translation, 1:32-48, 1968.

The Vos'mistišija "leads us into Mandelstam's special poetic."
"At once statement and exemplification, these poems provide us
with concepts that illuminate virtually everything that Mandelstam
wrote." (G.C.)

MANDIARGUES, ANDRÉ PIEYRE DE--See
PIEYRE DE MANDIARGUES, ANDRÉ

MANFRED, FREDERICK FEIKEMA

M524   Kellogg, George, "Frederick Manfred: A Bibliography," Twentieth
Century Literature, 11:30-5, April, 1965.

[This checklist attempts exhaustiveness in reporting "(1) Manfred books (2) Manfred periodical writings (3) Writings about Manfred. It also contains a select list of book reviews." A brief foreward evaluates Manfred's works.]   (D.P.)

M525   Milton, John R., "Frederick Feikema Manfred," Western Review, 22:181-96, Spring, 1958.

"At present he [Manfred] seems to be more at home in the Western historical novel, where it is easier for him to be more creative and objective at the same time than he can be in his longer and more personal works." Furthermore, "his experimenting seems now to be leading to a uniquely American language."   (C.K.L.)

M526   Milton, John, "Interview with Frederick Manfred," South Dakota Review, 7:110-30, Winter, 1969-70.

[This interview elicits ruminations on himself by Manfred, comments on his characters and his search for his own voice in his fiction.] (D.P.)

M527   Milton, John R., "Voice from Siouxland: Frederick Feikema Manfred," College English, 19:104-11, December, 1957.

"Manfred is a regionalist in the broadest sense of the term. He is well on the way to becoming a major American author. His voice speaks from Siouxland, but it speaks to all people."   (D.P.)

M528   Swallow, Alan, "The Mavericks," Critique: Studies in Modern Fiction, 2:74-92, Winter, 1959.

Janet Lewis "is a maverick today, for her style is exact, impeccable, and just, but it does shout for attention." Vardis Fisher is producing "a vast, imperfect, but truly imaginative work. . . ." Walter Van Tilburg Clark has raised the "western story" to serious levels. Frank Waters's writing is "incisive and fundamentally enlightening." Frederick Manfred "is a man of prodigious labor and prodigious ability." Edward Loomis has a "mastery of significant detail, sound emotion, and emerging theme. . . ." These six mavericks "demonstrate the cultivation which is going on in the West today."   (D.P.)

M529   "West of the Mississippi: An Interview with Frederick Manfred," Critique: Studies in Modern Fiction, 2:35-56, Winter, 1959.

[This is the transcript of a taped interview with Frederick Manfred in which the editors of Critique discuss with Manfred "the writer as a product of the area west of the Mississippi, his use of that area in his fiction, and his relation with his contemporaries."] (G.O.)

THE BUCKSKIN MAN'S TALES

M530 Roth, Russel, "The Inception of a Saga: Frederick Manfred's Buckskin Man," South Dakota Review, 7:87-99, Winter, 1969-70.

Manfred's The Buckskin Man's Tales seems influenced by or related to Lawrence's Studies in Classic American Literature, William Carlos Williams's In the American Grain and Faulkner's Yoknapatawpha novels, in that the characters are ridding themselves of their European consciousness in their "search for the true self in a context of an enduring and generic American self." (D.P.)

CONQUERING HORSE

M531 Wylder, D. E., "Manfred's Indian Novel," South Dakota Review, 7:100-9, Winter, 1969-70.

Manfred's Conquering Horse is an exceptional Indian story in that it is not a retelling of the battle of cultures, nor is it naturalistic. In it Manfred "has combined the elements of the tragic and the epic into a unified and honest novel about the Plains Indian at the peak of his culture." (D.P.)

THE GOLDEN BOWL

M532 Bebeau, Don, "A Search for Voice, a Sense of Place in The Golden Bowl," South Dakota Review, 7:79-86, Winter, 1969-70.

Manfred is true to himself and the land he knows in his novel The Golden Bowl. The message of the novel is universal: man will find his identity through establishing roots in the land. (D.P.)

LORD GRIZZLY

M533 Austin, James C., "Legend, Myth, and Symbol in Frederick Manfred's Lord Grizzly," Critique: Studies in Modern Fiction, 6:122-30, Winter, 1963-64.

Through his use of the legend of the mountain-man Hugh Glass and the mythology of the Arickaree and Sioux Indians, Manfred "has given the theme of the opening of the West an epic magnitude that many writers have aimed for without success." (W.G.F.)

LORD GRIZZLY (cont'd)

M534   Milton, John R., "Lord Grizzly: Rhythm, Form and Meaning in the Western Novel." Western American Literature, 1:6-14, Spring, 1966.

"In Lord Grizzly, as in other mature Western novels, form, meaning, and rhythm are synonymous. Neither social problem nor psychological conflict nor philosophical argumentation explains this fiction. It is characterized, rather, by an elemental and almost mystic (at least mythic) fusion of man and land, animal and spirit, the rational and irrational." (W.G.F.)

RIDERS OF JUDGMENT

M535   Milton, John R., "Re-Creation of the Old West: A Post-Script on Riders of Judgment," Western Review, 22:196-9, Spring, 1958.

Manfred's eighth novel, Riders of Judgment, is a visual novel which exudes the life of the Old West. In it, "the religious implications are kept in the background; the symbols are tantalizing but relatively unimportant." (D.P.)

MANFREDI CANO, DOMINGO

M536   Ríos Ruiz, Manuel, "Domingo Manfredi Cano, novelista enamorado de su tiempo," La Estafeta Literaria, No. 430, pp. 21-2, October 15, 1969.

Prolific and astute novelist Manfredi Cano presents themes of contemporary man opposed to tradition, religious vocation, etc., as well as psychological portraits of the middle class and personal struggle between reason and racial instincts. (T.T.B.)

MANKOWITZ, WOLF

M537   Metcalf, John, "Wolf Mankowitz," Atlantic Monthly, 198:86-8, October, 1956.

Wolf Mankowitz is a story-teller "writing about people he knows, building his own idiosyncratic beauty around them . . . drawing his moral from what happens to those people rather than jiggling them about like puppets to make them fit his argument." His gleaming irreverence is in "lively contrast to the gray, general-worthiness of so much English post-war writing." (D.P.)

MANN, HEINRICH

M538   Exner, Richard, "Die Essayistik Heinrich Manns: Autor und
Thematik," Symposium, 13:216-37, Fall, 1959.

Heinrich Mann's essays were actually variations on a theme central
to all his works: Mankind has been created; the dream of Mankind
should not be abandoned in favor of reality. In the end good fortune
will prevail. (D.P.)

M539   Exner, Richard, "Die Essayistik Heinrich Manns: Triebkräfte
und Sprache," Symposium, 14:26-41, Spring, 1960.

[This analysis of the motivating power and style of Heinrich Mann's
essays constitutes the completion of major study begun in the Fall,
1959 issue of Symposium.] (D.P.)

M540   Linn, Rolf N., "Heinrich Mann and the German Inflation,"
Modern Language Quarterly, 23:75-83, March, 1962.

Mann "appraised the turbulent postwar years" of the Weimar
Republic "in one comedy and three novellas that deserve far more
attention than they have received . . . : Das gastliche Haus, Der
Gläubiger, Sterny, and Kobes." (G.S.)

M541   Linn, Rolf N., "Heinrich Mann--heinrich mann," Neue Deutsche
Hefte, 14:17-29, No. 1, 1967.

[This subjective survey of H. Mann's works attempts to show what
is good about this author who does not enjoy great favor but who also
refuses to be forgotten.] (J.R.R.)

M542   Linn, Rolf N., "Portrait of Two Despots by Heinrich Mann,"
Germanic Review, 30:125-34, April, 1955.

In the two novellas, Auferstehung and Der Tyrann, Mann, more
clearly than in his novels, "delineates his concept of the tyrant and
reveals the close relationship of tyranny to decadence." (J.R.R.)

M543   Nicholls, Roger A., "Heinrich Mann and Nietzsche," Modern
Language Quarterly, 21:165-78, June, 1960.

In early works such as Die Göttinnen Mann shows the influence of
Nietzsche's statements concerning decadence, nobility, and amorality;
but he later reacted against Nietzsche, who was linked with the
Hitlerian glorification of power. (G.S.)

M544　Sorensen, Bengt Algot, "Der 'Dilettantismus' des Fin de Siècle und der junge Heinrich Mann, " <u>Orbis Litterarum</u>. 24:251-70, No. 4, 1969.

"No other German writer has concerned himself so intensively with the phenomenon of dilettantism as did the young Heinrich Mann. . . . The phenomenon itself remains an essential component of his work and his existence up to the decisive change around 1905." (J.R.R.)

M545　Weisstein, Ulrich, "Heinrich Mann in America: A Critical Survey, " <u>Books Abroad</u>, 33:281-4, Summer, 1959.

"The following bibliography grew out of an attempt to list all the writings by and about Henrich Mann which have been published in the United States." (M.J.O.)

M546　Weisstein, Ulrich, "Heinrich Mann und Gustave Flaubert: Ein Kapitel in der Geschichte der literarischen Wechselbeziehungen zwischen Frankreich und Deutschland, " <u>Euphorion</u>, 57:132-55, 1963.

"But up to now no one has found it worth the trouble to examine closely what kind of influences these were [of Flaubert on Heinrich Mann], from which works and views of the Frenchman they came and how they manifested themselves in his German admirer." (J.R.R.)

DIE ARME TONIETTA

M547　Weisstein, Ulrich, "<u>Die arme Tonietta</u>: Heinrich Mann's Triple Version of an Operatic Plot, " <u>Modern Language Quarterly</u>, 20:371-7, December, 1959.

The opera <u>Die arme Tonietta</u>, characterized by "sentimentalism à la Puccini . . . blended with certain <u>verismo</u> elements, " is a central and structural "play within a play" in the novel <u>Die kleine Stadt</u>; a second version exists in manuscript outline and the third is a Verga-like novella. (G.S.)

DIE BRANZILLA

M548　Linn, Rolf N., "Heinrich Mann's <u>Die Branzilla</u>, " <u>Monatshefte</u>, 50:75-85, January, 1958.

DIE BRANZILLA   (cont'd)

The novella <u>Die Branzilla</u> "deserves to be rescued from the semi-oblivion into which it has fallen. To demonstrate its merits through analysis of content and form is the purpose of this paper." (J.R.R.)

THE EMPIRE TRILOGY--See
DIE KAISERREICHTRILOGIE

HENRY, KING OF FRANCE--See
DIE JUGEND UND DIE VOLLENDUNG DES KÖNIGS
HENRI QUATRE

IM SCHLARAFFENLAND

M549   Hahn, Manfred, "Zum frühen Schaffen Heinrich Manns,"
<u>Weimarer Beiträge</u>, 12:363-406, May-June, 1966.

H. Mann's novel <u>Im Schlaraffenland</u> marks "the beginning of the German satirical social novel in the epoch of imperialism" and was Mann's first significant step toward becoming a writer of significance. (J.R.R.)

M550   Weisstein, Ulrich, "Maupassant's <u>Bel Ami</u> and Heinrich Mann's <u>Im Schlaraffenland</u>," <u>Romance Notes</u>, 2:124-8, 1961.

"Whatever Heinrich Mann's indebtedness to Maupassant, there is no question that <u>Im Schlaraffenland</u> is considerably more than an imitation of <u>Bel-Ami</u>. . . ." (J.R.R.)

IN THE LAND OF COCKAIGNE--See
IM SCHLARAFFENLAND

DIE JUGEND UND DIE VOLLENDUNG DES KÖNIGS
HENRI QUATRE

M551   Weisstein, Ulrich, "Heinrich Mann, Montaigne and <u>Henri Quatre</u>,"
<u>Revue de Littérature Comparée</u>, 36:71-93, January-March, 1962.

". . . certain formal and structural similarities between [Montaigne's] <u>Essais</u> and Heinrich Mann's epically proportioned narrative . . . reveal the influence which . . . the Frenchman exerted upon his German follower." Aesthetically and psychologically <u>Henri Quatre's</u> "theme is the incompatibility of thought and action, and the conflict in the protagonist between feeling and

DIE JUGEND UND DIE VOLLENDUNG DES KÖNIGS
HENRI QUATRE (cont'd)

intellect. . . . Henri is seen as an individual whose idiosyncracies
make him vulnerable to the blows of fate. . . . The historical
Montaigne matures through constant self-analysis, the hero of the
novel through suffering in action. Montaigne is sophisticated, Henri
naive. Montaigne's triumph shows in his hardwon equanimity,
Henri's defeat in his surrender to passion." (D.P.)

M552 Weisstein, Ulrich, "Humanism and the Novel: An Introduction to
Heinrich Mann's Henri Quatre," Monatshefte, 51:13-24,
January, 1959.

"It is the aim of the present essay to assess the literary value of
Heinrich Mann's Henri Quatre, a novel which, in this writer's
opinion, occupies a position in contemporary German literature
comparable only to that of Thomas Mann's Der Zauberberg and
Hermann Hesse's Das Glasperlenspiel." (J.R.R.)

DIE KAISERREICHTRILOGIE

M553 Hardaway, R. Travis, "Heinrich Mann's Kaiserreich Trilogy and
the Democratic Spirit," Journal of English and Germanic Philology,
53:319-33, No. 3, 1954.

"In Das Kaiserreich, Heinrich Mann definitely concerns himself
with democracy by constantly holding up democratic ideals as
preferable alternatives to the absolutistic spirit; his chief success
. . . is to arouse abhorrence for this spirit; to this extent, by
helping to clear the way for democracy, he has made a highly
valuable contribution to it; he does not, however, whatever the
reasons, present a constructive, inspiring message." (J.R.R.)

KING WREN: THE YOUTH OF HENRI IV--See
DIE JUGEND UND DIE VOLLENDUNG DES KÖNIGS
HENRI QUATRE

DIE KLEINE STADT

M554 Linn, Rolf N., "Democracy in Heinrich Mann's Die kleine Stadt,"
German Quarterly, 37:131-45, March, 1964.

In this novel, set significantly in an Italian locale, Mann subtly
reveals the worth of the self-correcting democratic process. Cor-

DIE KLEINE STADT (cont'd)

ruption and self-serving, hopefully kept within reasonable limits, are the inevitable concomitants of democratic politics. (R.H.L.)

M555   Weisstein, Ulrich, "Die kleine Stadt: Art, Life and Politics in Heinrich Mann's Novel," German Life and Letters, 13:255-61, No. 4, 1960.

"Although full of contradictions and inconsistencies, The Little Town is a milestone on Heinrich Mann's way to artistic maturity and deserves comparison with The Subject and The Blue Angel as a minor classic of modern German literature." (J.R.R.)

THE LITTLE TOWN--See
DIE KLEINE STADT

MADAME LEGROS

M556   Weisstein, Ulrich, "Heinrich Mann's Madame Legros--Not a Revolutionary Drama," Germanic Review, 35:39-49, February, 1960.

Heinrich Mann's Madame Legros is not concerned with subverting the existing order. Her orientation is individual and naive. Mann's indifference toward psychological realism, moreover, obtrudes uncomfortably in this one drama that he took as seriously as his fiction. (R.H.L.)

YOUNG HENRY OF NAVARRE--See
DIE JUGEND UND DIE VOLLENDUNG DES KÖNIGS
HENRI QUATRE

ZOLA

M557   Roberts, David, "'Wirklichkeit oder Gedicht': The Zola Essay of Heinrich Mann," Forum for Modern Language Studies, 6:243-54, July, 1970.

"This essay which grew out of Untertan is its ideal counterpart, and the ideal counterpart to the Kaiserreich trilogy." (J.R.R.)

MANN, KLAUS

M558   Rieck, Werner, "Hentrik Höfgen: Zur Genesis einer Romanfigur
Klaus Manns, " Weimarer Beiträge, 15:855-70, No. 4, 1969.

[The article traces the genesis and evolution of the character
Höfgen from Mann's novel Treffpunkt im Unendlichen.] (J.R.R.)

M559   Walter, Hans-Albert, "Klaus Mann und Die Sammlung, "
Frankfurter Hefte, 21:850-60, December, 1966; 22:49-58,
January, 1967.

Mann's bourgeois attitudes helped distinguish Die Sammlung from
other periodicals published by exile Germans. "When it ceased to
exist, the [writers of the] exile had lost their first and best literary
periodical. " (J.R.R.)

MANN, LEONARD

M560   Vintner, Maurice, "Rediscovery--1: Leonard Mann's A Murder
in Sydney, " Overland, 44:39-40, 1970.

This "good novel lost in the sands, " although often "too rough and
careless in style and construction to realize fully its potential
power . . . has many elements of a great novel, " especially depth
of characterization. (G.C.)

MANN, THOMAS

M561   Adorno-Wiesengrund, Theodor, "Zu einem Porträt Thomas Manns:
Bei Eröffnung der Darmstädter Ausstellung: 24. März 1962, "
Die Neue Rundschau, 73:320-7, Nos. 2 and 3, 1962.

One of the purposes of Mann's irony was dissimulation. A versatile
genius, he had many masks for his dissimulation, for example, that
of the Hanseatic senator's son. Mann's essential nature was in fact
not bürgerlich and his over-emphasized concern with death was
simply his suspicion of man's guilt in existing. (R.H.L.)

M562   Andersch, Alfred, "Mit den Augen des Westens (Thomas Mann als
Politiker), " Texte und Zeichen, 1:85-100, Winter, 1955.

Mann is humanistic and masculine. He realistically acknowledges
but abstains from writing for or against enlightenment, pacifism,
democracy, internationalism. Not allowing dictation by any

current fads, he is the representative of the German people. Mann
is able, usually, to give artistic realism to political happenings.
(M.J.)

M563   Angoff, Charles, "Recollections of Elinor Wylie, Thomas Mann,
Joseph Hergesheimer, James Stevens, Logan Clendening,"
Literary Review, 10:169-79, Winter, 1966-1967.

[An editor of the American Mercury recalls anecdotes concerning
the indicated literary greats; "what I have to say, in some cases,
is not very important in itself, but I believe that such remarks as
I have to make may be revealing in some way or other."] (J.R.R.)

M564   Arnold, Armin, "D. H. Lawrence and Thomas Mann,"
Comparative Literature, 8:33-8, Winter, 1961.

"Lawrence was among the first--if not the first--Englishman to
point out the qualities of Thomas Mann," which Lawrence saw as
an aversion to real life and a "craving for form." (R.J.G.)

M565   Asher, J. A., "Thomas Mann and Goethe: A Rejoinder,"
Publications of the English Goethe Society, 26:92-8, 1957.

Professor Eichner doesn't seem to realize that "an understanding
of Mann's uniqueness cannot be gained by identifying him in any
way with his predecessors, least of all Goethe." (J.R.R.)

M566   Asher, John Alexander, "Thomas Mann's 'Unio Mystica' with
Goethe," Publications of the English Goethe Society, 25:1-20, 1956.

"It is on account of the brilliance of his ironical style--rather than
any supposed 'identification' with Goethe--that later generations
will be attracted to the works of Thomas Mann." (J.R.R.)

M567   Beharriell, Frederick J., "Psychology in the Early Works of
Thomas Mann," PMLA, 77:149-55, March, 1962.

Mann's work before 1900 shows many important anticipations of
psychoanalytic theory, but his view of personality is pseudo-
biological: it "speaks in terms of heredity, degeneration, and
decadence of the genetic strain. . . ." (B.K.)

M568   Berland, Alwyn, "In Search of Thomas Mann," Symposium,
        18:215-28, Fall, 1964.

        The American student has many problems in reaching a rapproch-
        ement with Thomas Mann since, among many other concerns,
        American romanticism is fundamentally optimistic, affirmative,
        and adjusted, whereas Mann's writings are deeply rooted in the
        more pessimistic nineteenth century European romanticism, to
        which Mann adds a particular fascination with disease. (D.P.)

M569   Binger, Norman H., "Thomas Mann's Analysis of Democracy,"
        Germanic Notes, 1:10-2, No. 2, 1970.

        "Perhaps Mann's statement is too 'pointiert,' but the meaning is
        clear: Our goal should be a compromise between the agonale Lust
        of Ancient Greece and the socialism of modern Russia." (J.R.R.)

M570   Blissett, William, "Thomas Mann: The Last Wagnerite,"
        Germanic Review, 35:50-76, February, 1960.

        Mann's earliest Wagnerite characters consciously play, hence
        diminish and parody, Wagnerian roles. In The Magic Mountain
        Mann's Wagnerism attains organizational complexity. Joseph and
        his Brothers, with its web of leitmotifs, is perhaps the most
        Wagnerian work in literature. The distrustful musical generaliza-
        tions in Doctor Faustus are meant for Wagner's music. (R.H.L.)

M571   Blomster, W. V., "The Demonic in History: Thomas Mann and
        Günter Grass," Contemporary Literature, 10:75-84, Winter,
        1969.

        Influenced by Nietzsche, both Mann and Grass accept the existence
        of demonic forces in history. Mann regards them as a highly pro-
        ductive though potentially dangerous force in life and treats them
        symbolically, while Grass argues for the "dedemonization of
        history," treating them as objectively and concretely as possible.
        (B.K.N.)

M572   Blomster, Wesley V., "Thomas Mann and the Munich Manifesto,"
        German Life and Letters, 22:134-46, January, 1969.

        A pivotal period in Mann's life followed the public reaction to
        Mann's lecture on Wagner held at the beginning of the Hitler
        regime. (J.R.R.)

M573   Blume, Bernhard, "Perspektiven des Widerspruchs: Zur Kritik
        an Thomas Mann," Germanic Review, 31:176-90, October, 1956.

        A selective examination of criticism of Thomas Mann follows from
        the assumption that "to the influence of a great author belongs also
        the resistance which he evokes against himself." (J.R.R.)

M574   Brion, Marcel, "Littératures Étrangeres: Thomas Mann,"
        La Revue des Deux Mondes, No. 18, pp. 348-58, September 15,
        1955.

        Not only is Mann a militant humanist, but he employs death as his
        central subject, hidden or obvious. Always a link exists between
        love and death, disease (institutional and individual) and death, and
        artistic creation and death. (L.L.)

M575   Carossa, Hans, "Übersiedlung nach München: eine Erinnerung
        an die Ziet, wo Thomas Mann in München nahe der Isar wohnte,"
        Die Neue Rundschau, 3:294-7, June, 1955.

        Recollections of the time Thomas Mann lived in Munich near the
        Isar shed some light on his work of that period, after World War I.
        (L.L.)

M576   Conversi, Leonard, "Mann, Yeats, and the Truth of Art,"
        Yale Review, 56:506-23, June, 1967.

        Mann and Yeats both face an impasse. Their work can be summed
        up in the statement: "The problem that man (and the artist) faces
        is his knowledge of the problem he faces." The truths or false-
        hoods of a man's being may be real, but they are accidental. "Only
        the dialectic is of the essence." (F.L.)

M577   Crick, Joyce, "Thomas Mann and Psychoanalysis: The Turning-
        Point," Literature and Psychology, 10:45-55, Spring, 1960.

        [This is part one of a two part study on the impact of psychoanalytic
        theory on Thomas Mann and his use of Freudian theory in a late
        work.] Although the relationship between Thomas Mann's "devious
        psychology and psycho-analysis," and between his "so-called 'new
        humanism' and the dry moralism of Sigmund Freud has been taken
        for granted," careful scrutiny reveals a significant gap between
        Mann's acquaintance and approval. (J.M.D.)

M578   Daemmrich, Horst S., "Friedrich Schiller and Thomas Mann:
       Parallels in Aesthetics," Journal of Aesthetics and Art Criticism,
       24:227-49, Winter, 1965.

       "In the present paper I shall show, first, that Thomas Mann turns
       to Schiller for aesthetic concepts . . . second, that Mann's artist
       typology is actually based on Schiller's categories; third, that
       Mann consciously adopts Schiller's reasoning with respect to the
       function and evaluation of works of art." (J.R.R.)

M579   Daemmrich, Horst S., "Mann's Portrait of the Artist: Archetypal
       Patterns," Bucknell Review, 14:27-43, December, 1966.

       "A number of important studies . . . try to account for Mann's
       concept of the artist. . . . they overlook, first, that Mann con-
       ceived of a number of artist types and, second, that he finally
       crystallized his thinking concerning the problem of the artist's
       existence." (J.R.R.)

M580   Deguy, Michel, "Art et consolation selon Thomas Mann,"
       Cahiers des Saisons, No. 30, pp. 569-75, Summer, 1962.

       The virtue of consolation that Mann lends to Art is equivalent to
       that of comprehension that Jung attributes to analysis, that of an
       adaptation. Mann, the bourgeois artist, considers art a consolation,
       but for his heroes it is failure. His theme of election-damnation
       applies to his work and his life. (T.T.B.)

M581   Deguy, Michel, "Vie et roman," La Nouvelle Revue Française,
       10e année, No. 113, pp. 886-94, May 1, 1962.

       To the contrary of Marcel Brion's judgment, the work of Mann is
       the opposite of real esoterism. "The keys are within the work,
       and precisely because they are within the reach of an attentive
       reader and not hidden outside of the work," as Brion claimed, it
       is not esoteric "but the transposition, the cultivated and humor-
       istic mimicry of esoterism." (T.T.B.)

M582   Diller, Edward, "The Grotesque Animal-Heroes of Thomas Mann's
       Early Works," German Life and Letters, 20:225-33, April, 1967.

       "As a response to the world in which one cannot feel at home, then,
       the animal-heroes of these first stories do resemble lost figures
       desiring acceptance and sympathy. They are awkward and misshapen
       creatures who indeed live their lives in 'thoughts and flights of
       fancy'." (K.M.W.

M583   Dyck, J. W., "Thomas Mann and Josef Ponten," <u>German Quarterly</u>, 35:24-33, January, 1962.

"This article attempts to point to this gap of literary criticism [i.e., the failure to examine Mann's strong attraction to Ponten] and to expound the Mann-Ponten relationship in the light of sources other than the well-known <u>Rundschau</u> letter." (J.R.R.)

M584   Ehrentreich, Alfred, "Motivische Wechselbeziehungen zwischen Roman und Novelle bei Thomas Mann," <u>Germanisch-Romanische Monatsschrift</u>, 20:353-6, 1970.

"With Mann novel and novella face one another as much as partners who reciprocally continue the conversation (motif), although . . . individual works--such as <u>Royal Wedding</u> . . . assume more a peripheral position yet remain related to the whole through psychology and style, through the artistic principles of form. . . ." (J.R.R.)

M585   Eichner, Hans, "Thomas Mann and Goethe: A Protest," <u>Publications of the English Goethe Society</u>, 26:81-92, 1957.

"Is it fanciful, in view of these and the many similar passages that will occur to the reader, to point out a parallel between Mann and Goethe from the former's deliberately subjective point of view?" (J.R.R.)

M586   Ellis-Jones, R. B., "The Place of the <u>Bürger</u> in Thomas Mann's Essays," <u>German Life and Letters</u>, 23:347-55, July, 1970.

[Mann's changing view of the bourgeois is used as the touchstone in this survey of the evolution of his socio-politico-cultural outlook.] (J.R.R.)

M587   Erpel, Fritz, "Thomas Mann's Knowledge of Goethe," <u>Germanic Review</u>, 32:311-3, December, 1957.

Mann was not familiar with Goethe's first version of <u>Werther</u>.(C.S.P.)

M588   Exner, Richard, "Some Reflections on a Thomas Mann Exhibit," <u>German Quarterly</u>, 36:197-200, March, 1963.

Thomas Mann would have approved this exhibit of books, letters, portraits and other memorabilia of his life and works which opened at Darmstadt under the patronage of Katia Mann and had been organized by the Federal Republic of Germany, although "he was not quite as solemn a person as this exhibit might suggest." (D.P.)

M589   Exner, Richard, "Zur Essayistik Thomas Manns," Germanisch-
Romanische Monatsschrift, 12:51-78, January, 1962.

The essays "were created masterfully and stand within a tradition
of thinking and writing which never had to fear being wrong, taking
a partisan position, and preserving the light of reason in dark
times." (J.R.R.)

M590   Exner, Richard, "Probleme der Methodik und der Komposition in
der Essays von Thomas Mann und Hugo von Hofmannsthal,"
German Quarterly, 30:145-57, May, 1957.

Essays are essential parts in the works of Mann and Hofmannsthal
and should be treated as such as may be demonstrated by their
essays on Lessing. (C.S.P.)

M591   Faesi, Robert, "Grenzen und Gipfel von Thomas Manns Welt,"
Die Neue Rundschau, 3:373-91, June, 1956.

Mann's world is bound by and reaches the summit of interest in (1)
the degenerate artist type, (2) the once solid but now decaying upper-
class, (3) the son-father, or familial relationship, (4) the analysis
of the psyche. Rarely does he deal with vast social problems, more
rarely with the state as such. (L.L.)

M592   Feuchtwanger, Lion, "Thomas Mann Rode Forth: The Cost of
Greatness," Nation, 181:192-4, September 3, 1955.

Although Thomas Mann could have withdrawn from the confusion
following World War I, he chose to participate vigorously, even
recklessly against the trends of his time. "He fought actively for
his heretical opinions, with lectures, with challenging pronouncements, with the electrifying effect of his personal participation."
"Thomas Mann rode forth and he had to pay the price" through the
"turbulence of exile." (D.P.)

M593   Feuerlicht, Ignace, "Der Erzähler bei Thomas Mann," German
Quarterly, 43:418-34, May, 1970.

The authorial narrative style, in which the author comments on
the plot and characters by direct address to the reader, is one of
the most important characteristics of Thomas Mann's works.
(R.H.L.)

M594   Feuerlicht, Ignace, "On Recent Editions of Thomas Mann,"
        German Quarterly, 33:227-32, May, 1960.

        "But, on the whole, the recent editions constitute a considerable
        improvement" in spite of "the errors that still mar many pages of
        his books." (J.R.R.)

M595   Feuerlicht, Ignace, "Rolle, Dienst und Opfer bei Thomas Mann,"
        PMLA, 77:318-27, June, 1962.

        "The concept of the role has great significance in modern psycho-
        logy, sociology and literature. Three essentially different roles
        can be distinguished. . . . In the life role the limits of the ego are
        fulfilled and expanded. In the social role they are emptied and
        erased. In the art or game role they are transformed and reful-
        filled again and again." [Most of Mann's novels are examined here
        in this light.] (J.R.R.)

M596   Feuerlicht, Ignace, "Thomas Manns mystiche Identifikation,"
        German Quarterly, 36:141-51, March, 1963.

        "Myth and irony, two seemingly opposed concepts . . . in the case
        of Thomas Mann in his 'mythic identification' could produce an
        ironic identification. . . ." (J.R.R.)

M597   Field, George W., "Music and Morality in Thomas Mann and
        Hermann Hesse," University of Toronto Quarterly, 24:175-90,
        January, 1955.

        "So far as possible this comparative study seeks to avoid purely
        technical features . . . and it is our intention to concentrate on
        the meaning of music in its widest sense, the role of music in life,
        its significance in human culture, in other words its relation to
        moral actions and concepts." (J.R.R.)

M598   Frank, John G., "Letters by Thomas Mann to Julius Bab,"
        Germanic Review, 36:195-204, October, 1961.

        These eight letters, now in the Library of Congress, were written
        by Mann between 1909 and 1930 to Julius Bab, the critic who had
        defended the young Mann against the condemnation of Alfred Kerr.
        (R.H.L.)

M599   Fuller, James A., "The Humanism of Thomas Mann," CEA Critic,
       20:1, 6-7, October, 1958.

       "In depicting . . . a continuous struggle of mankind in this world
       . . . Mann is being essentially humanistic. He realizes that . . .
       by enduring hardships and trials and by learning to sympathize with
       one's fellow man, a person becomes a complete individual."
       (G.C.)

M600   Furst, Lilian R., "Thomas Mann's Interest in James Joyce,"
       Modern Language Review, 64:605-13, July, 1969.

       "Mann's interest in Joyce was, then, directed less at his actual
       writings than at what he believed Joyce to represent, namely an
       artist who had successfully grappled with the inherent difficulties
       of twentieth-century art." (J.R.R.)

M601   García Ponce, Juan, "El artista como héroe (Mann, Hesse, Broch),"
       Revista Mexicana de Literatura, pp. 12-34, January-February, 1965.

       Mann, Hesse, and Broch, using the artist as protagonist, do so as
       poets of decadence, of the end of an age. The artist as exile or mis-
       fit searches to regain his place in a world where traditional values
       have collapsed. (C.O.)

M602   Gilman, Richard, "The Journey of Thomas Mann," Commonweal,
       69:93-6, October 24, 1958.

       "Parody, critique and irony are what determines the approaches to
       Mann's art, its defenses, like the moat around a castle. . . . In
       the light of this, Mann's work is, after all, about the relationship
       of art and life, but . . . his writing aims to recover those hidden
       depths where art and life, having recognized their reciprocity, can
       no longer choose to be alone." (D.P.)

M603   Gilman, Richard, "Revelations of the Mind of Mann," Commonweal,
       69:603, March 6, 1959.

       These last essays of Thomas Mann on Schiller, Goethe, Nietzsche,
       and Chekhov tell us at least as much about the author as they do
       about his subjects, since they are the kind of essay which subordi-
       nates "explication and argument to the recording of an encounter
       . . . naturally marked by idiosyncracy and a weighting toward the
       privately valuable, by an anchoring in the mirror." (D.P.)

M604   Glebe, William V., "The Artist's 'Disease' in Some of Thomas
Mann's Earliest Tales, " Books Abroad, 39:261-8, Summer, 1965.

In his early work (e.g., "Little Herr Friedemann") the diseased
artist reflects Mann's later rejected idea that the artist is useless
to men and a misfit. (C.E.N.)

M605   Goes, Albrecht, "Lebensfreundlichkeit: Thomas Mann zum 80.
geburtstag, " Die Neue Rundschau, 3:369-72, June, 1955.

Mann's work will endure because it speaks to Germany in particular
and to Europe and the world in general, and because of its creative
power. (L.L.)

M606   Gronicka, André von, "In Memoriam Thomas Mann, " Modern
Language Forum, 41:108-11, December, 1956.

"Thomas Mann, like Goethe and Schiller before him, speaks out of
a deep faith in mankind, a faith that is alive in Mann's 'loving
irony,' the presence of which cannot be denied even in the parodistic style of Mann's old age." (J.R.R.)

M607   Guthke, Karl S., "Thomas Mann on Heinrich von Kleist: An
Unpublished Letter to Hans M. Wolff, " Neophilologus, 44:121-2,
April, 1960.

[Dated January 19, 1949, this previously unpublished letter summarizes Mann's attitude toward Heinrich von Kleist. Text in
German.] (F.J.P.)

M608   Haile, Harry G., "Thomas Mann und der 'Anglizismus', "
Monatshefte, 51:263-9, October, 1959.

The so-called Anglicisms--really Americanisms--found increasingly
in Thomas Mann's works from the last of the Joseph novels onward
do not necessarily represent wanton violation of German idiom.
Rather they permit Mann one more facet of Distanzierung. (R.H.L.)

M609   Hamburger, Käte, "Der Epiker Thomas Mann, " Orbis Litterarum,
13:7-14, No. 1, 1958.

Mann's "epic works reveal in a higher degree, in a more pregnant
manner than any other of our time the form creating function of
narration." (J.R.R.)

M610　Hartung, Günter, "Bertolt Brecht und Thomas Mann: Über Alternativen in Kunst und Politik," Weimarer Beiträge, 12:407-35, May-June, 1966.

"Posing a simile for the future of Germany, Thomas Mann narrated in the destiny of Pope Gregory the miracle which comes through faith and the grace which awaits the penitent; Brecht wrote 'The Days of the Commune,' likewise an historical piece yet at the same time a primer on how one fights for, secures and builds up a real democracy." (J.R.R.)

M611　Hatfield, Henry, "The Achievement of Thomas Mann," Germanic Review, 31:206-14, October, 1956.

In reviewing Man's career, "he was, and is, more significant as a realist than as a thinker," and his fame will rest "less on the elaborate devices of Doktor Faustus than on simple things." (K.L.)

M612　Hatfield, Henry, "Death in the Late Works of Thomas Mann," Germanic Review, 34:284-8, December, 1959.

With Doktor Faustus, Mann's mood shifts sharply to nihilism and death. This vein continues in The Holy Sinners and The Deceived Woman. A definitive return to affirmation, however, is signaled by Mann's "Essay on Schiller." (R.H.L.)

M613　Hatfield, Henry, "Recent Studies of Thomas Mann," Modern Language Review, 51:390-403, July, 1956.

Recent criticism of Mann reveals (1) the publication of Felix Krull enhanced his prestige in America and England, where it had been in decline since the late 1940's; (2) the criticism "conformed to widely accepted beliefs about 'national characteristics' "; (3) Mann's 80th birthday was the occasion of many positive revaluations; (4) criticism is "turning belatedly to a close study of his style and a more sophisticated analysis of his ideas within their aesthetic context." (W.T.S.)

M614　Hatfield, Henry, "Thomas Mann and America," Salmagundi, 10-11:174-85, Fall, 1969-Winter, 1970.

"The American chapter in Mann's career remains an episode, though an important one. In some ways the story is disappointing and unhappy. Yet Mann put his American experiences to creative use. . . ." (J.R.R.)

M615   Heller, Erich, "The Conservative Imagination: On Thomas Mann's 'Non-Political' Meditations," Encounter, 10:16-56, February, 1958.

The true artist is non-political (Mann claimed in his untranslated Meditations) because he believes morality is the contemplation of reality, and all his creations are Truth. The artist must "withdraw" in spite of the fact that the man who withdraws remains morally unrealized. (D.B.D.)

M616   Heller, Erich, "Parody, Tragic and Comic: Mann's Doctor Faustus and Felix Krull," Sewanee Review, 66:519-46, Autumn, 1958.

Out of his conception of the sterility of modern Germany, and (by extension) of the modern West, Mann constructed Doctor Faustus as a tragic parody, Felix Krull as a comic parody, fashioning each work into at once a résumé and a nullification of these two great literary species of the West. (A.S.)

M617   Heller, Erich, "Thomas Mann and the 'Domestic Perversity'," Encounter, 12:54-6, March, 1959.

Mr. Goronwy Rees's review of my book seems to imply that the Nazi catastrophe meant little to Thomas Mann. One cannot blame Mann "for not having been a Swift," but Mann did, in pamphlets and speeches which fill two volumes, attempt "to rouse resistance to Hitler inside Germany, then to awaken the world to the immensity of the German danger." Finally, his great moral concern about this "little domestic perversity" is imbedded in the pages of Doctor Faustus. (D.P.)

M618   Heller, Erich, "Thomas Mann's Place in German Literature," Listener, 53:1014-6, June 9, 1955.

"Knowledge as the enemy of life, as the tempter to death, as the ally of disease--this is an ever-recurring theme in Thomas Mann's works, and certainly the central inspiration of his beginning. . . . the deep seriousness of this preoccupation is reflected in everything he has ever written. . . ." (D.P.)

M619 Heller, Peter, "Creative Process and Creative Product: Two
Examples of an Analogy," Journal of Aesthetics and Art
Criticism, 12:328-42, March, 1954.

"What was said of Mann applies also to Freud: The author himself
feels that his own activity and being during the creative process
have the same 'meaning' as the result of this process. To both
Mann and Freud the very act of creative thinking has a subjective
meaning which parallels the objective meaning (message, content,
insight) of the creative product." (J.R.R.)

M620 Heller, Peter, "Thomas Mann's Conception of the Creative
Writer: The Pattern of Balanced Ambivalence," PMLA, 69:673-96,
September, 1954.

". . . Mann's metaphysical notions are eclectic, deceptive, and
inconsistent, now too elusive to be defined, now too crude and
simplistic to be taken at face value. They have done damage to
Mann's reputation as an artist. Moreover, the later Mann appears,
at times, in the guise of a somewhat complacent Humanist. The
heaping of antitheses, the ironical dialectics, the oscillations, and
ornate rhetoric of the author are nonetheless inspired by an ideal
of unity and integration which is deeply felt precisely because Mann
is continually aware of the conflicting trends within him. . . .
Mann desires a balance which would not omit or oppress any part
of the human but would include all its elements, and bring them
into lively, vibrant, and fruitful communication with one another."
(D.P.)

M621 Hellersberg-Wendriner, Anna, "The Essence of Thomas Mann,"
Commonweal, 62:583-6, September 16, 1955.

Thomas Mann "had only one theme: the separation of man from
the fertile grounds which condition his existence. His whole vision
is of the majestic darkness, the immutable monotony of a mind
estranged from truth by a long genealogy of error." (R.W.S.)

M622 Henze, Eberhard, "Die Rolle des fiktiven Erzählers bei Thomas
Mann," Die Neue Rundschau, 76:189-201, Summer, 1965.

The acceptance of the fiction of narrator and listener is, in the case
of Thomas Mann, parody. In Der Zauberberg and the Joseph novels,
time and place unities are observed with respect to narrator and
listener; the absence of such unities in Doktor Faustus results in
subtle and difficult complexities. (R.H.L.)

M623 Herz, Ida, "Erinnerungen an Thomas Mann, 1925-1955,"
German Life and Letters, 9:281-90, July, 1956.

[These personal memories of Thomas Mann make a reference to a
number of his works, e.g. The Magic Mountain, Dr. Faustus and
the Joseph novels.] (J.R.R.)

M624 Hirschbach, Frank D., "Götterlieblinge und Hochstapler,"
German Quarterly, 32:22-33, January, 1959.

"Joseph, Goethe, Felix Krull--what opposites to Thomas
Buddenbrook, Johannes Friedemann and Gustav Aschenbach. The
former torn and yearning men who pull themselves together occasionally in order to pay later all the more dearly; the latter
active, commanding, self-assured men whose active and successful lives leave them little spare time for self-analysis." (J.R.R.)

M625 Hughes, William N., "Thomas Mann and the Platonic Adulterer,"
Monatshefte, 51:75-80, February, 1959.

In the Platonic adulterer Mann has created a variation on the central
theme: the relationship between artist and society. This intruder,
as Lieutenant von Throta in Buddenbrooks, Spinell in Tristan, and
Goethe in Lotte in Weimar, effects an unstable artistic unity with
the wife or fiancée of a relatively insensitive bourgeois. (R.H.L.)

M626 Hunt, Joel A., "Mann and Whitman: Humaniores Litterae,"
Comparative Literature, 14:266-71, Summer, 1962.

"Whitman as champion of an incredible theory of political eroticism,
provided weapons of a sort for Mann's humanistic defense of the
Weimar Republic." (C.E.N.)

M627 Hunt, Joel A., "The Stylistics of a Foreign Language: Thomas
Mann's Use of French," Germanic Review, 32:19-34,
February, 1957.

Thomas Mann uses French in his novels and stories as a stylistic
device to suggest, usually in a minor key but with fair consistency,
two major themes. These may be designated roughly, when they
reach a kind of ultimate crystallization, as charlatanry and eroticism." (K.L.)

M628 Jonas, Klaus W., "Eine Begegnung, die nicht stattfand: Rilke und Thomas Mann," Modern Austrian Literature, 2:16-22, Summer, 1969.

Rilke was favorably disposed in print toward Thomas Mann's works and he wanted to meet Mann in person. Such a meeting never occurred. Mann for his part wrote now unfavorably, now a trifle more charitably about Rilke and his works, but the general negative tone is unmistakable. (R.H.L.)

M629 Jonas, Klaus W., "In Memoriam: Helen T. Porter Lowe, 1876-1963," Monatshefte, 55:322-4, November, 1963.

"More than anyone else, she had worked with tireless devotion to win for Thomas Mann's work that international audience and understanding which it now enjoys in the English-speaking world." (J.R.R.)

M630 Jonas, Klaus W., "The Thomas Mann Archive in Zürich," German Quarterly, 35:10-6, January, 1962.

"This is not the place to present a detailed inventory of the treasures assembled in Zürich. Suffice it to mention but a few of them. . . ." (J.R.R.)

M631 Jonas, Klaus W., "Thomas Mann Collections," Monatshefte, 50:145-56, April-May, 1958.

With reference to Thomas Mann's literary remains "little or no information has been available, and the present survey is intended to provide some concrete answers about these repositories of Thomas Mann documents." (J.R.R.)

M632 Kahler, Erich, "Die Erwählten," Die Neue Rundschau, 66:298-311, 1955.

The Holy Sinner and Felix Krull are new forms and further elaborations of the problem developed in Doctor Faustus. Gregory and Krull--like Joseph and Adrian--are an inverse pair. These novels are based upon the paradox of earthly existence, the reciprocal infection of good and evil. Through the convulsing experiences of these two "mongrel men," Mann achieves the impression that everything is not so simple and morally divisible as an earlier age dreamed. (L.L.)

M633   Kahler, Erich, "Gedenkrede auf Thomas Mann," Die Neue
        Rundschau, 67:535-48, 1956.

        Mann best represents the cataclysmic changes that have shaped the
        world since Bismarck. His works are the strong testimony of a
        man who, either directly or indirectly, experienced all the tremen-
        dous discords and dilemmas, all the struggles and irreconcilables,
        all the bedeviled problems of his age. (H.H.V.)

M634   Kakabadse, Nodar, "Paul Thomas macht Verse oder Kommentare
        zur Lyrik des jungen Thomas Mann," Weimarer Beiträge,
        12:461-70, May-June, 1966.

        This examination of Mann's early pseudonymous poems confirms the
        "fact that lyric poetry was not organic to Thomas Mann." (J.R.R.)

M635   Kamenetsky, Christa, "Thomas Mann's Concept of the 'Bürger',"
        CLA Journal, 5:184-94, March, 1962.

        Mann uses the term Bürger (in the sense of Weltbürger) "as an
        ideal term representing highly educated, strong, active, and
        emotionally healthy and stable people"; in the sense of Spiessbürger,
        "the same term may be used in connection with weakness, compla-
        cency, and decay." (B.K.)

M636   Kaufmann, Fritz, "Imitatio Goethe: Thomas Mann and his French
        Confreres," Monatshefte, 48:245-59, October, 1956.

        "In a world of extremes, a world torn and blinded by passions--a
        tearing that went through their own hearts--the way to Goethe proved
        the good way to Thomas Mann and the French writers [Gide and
        Barrès] of his generation." (J.R.R.)

M637   Kellen, Konrad, "Reminiscences of Thomas Mann," Yale Review,
        54:383-91, Spring, 1965.

        Thomas Mann never made outlines for his books and rarely made
        changes in the original drafts. He wrote slowly, and 99 percent of
        his published work appears as first written. He was severely self-
        disciplined and somewhat formal in behavior, even with intimates.
        His work is not "right" in any language but German. (F.L.)

M638 Keller, E., "Thomas Mann and Democracy," <u>AULLA Proceedings</u>, 2:39, 1963.

". . . democracy for him was only a means to an end: the end being that type of freedom in which humanity in its very essence could be realized." (K.M.W.)

M639 Kerényi, Karl, "Thomas Mann und der Teufel in Palestrina," <u>Die Neue Rundschau</u>, 73:328-46, Nos. 2-3, 1962.

Mann was working on <u>Buddenbrooks</u> while on a visit to Palestrina, near Rome, in 1897. This visit also contributed to many ideas in Mann's original Faust plan of 1901, the precursor of the much later <u>Doktor Faustus</u>. Chapter twenty-five is especially of Palestrina. (R.H.L.)

M640 Kurz, Paul Konrad, S.J., "Thomas Mann und die Ironie," <u>Stimmen der Zeit</u>, 179:446-60, June, 1967.

Special attention to Mann's <u>Joseph</u> and <u>Holy Sinner</u> novels as well as to the nature of irony, indicates that "in spite of its Christian content and phrases and in spite of its moral dignity, Thomas Mann's bourgeois-humane irony is on the whole more rejecting than receptive to that which is truly Christian." (J.R.R.)

M641 Lange, Victor, "Thomas Mann: 1875-1955," <u>Saturday Review</u>, 38:26, September 17, 1955.

From Schopenhauer, Wagner, Nietzsche, he learned to respect yet question the elemental claims of life and mind upon each other. The chances of the individual in an increasingly inhuman and crumbling society and the efficacy of the artist therein were his constant theme. He never radically dissolved "the living shape, the recognizable presence of his created figures." (C.P.)

M642 Lehnert, Herbert, "Anmerkungen zur Entstehungsgeschichte von Thomas Manns <u>Bekenntnisse des Hochstaplers Felix Krull</u>, <u>Der Zauberberg</u> und <u>Betrachtungen eines Unpolitischen</u>," <u>Deutsche Vierteljahrsschrift für Literaturwissenschaft und Geistesgeschichte</u>, 38:267-72, No. 2, 1964.

From a number of statements contained in Mann's published writings "one had to conclude that the Krull-novel lay fallow from Spring 1911 and that the writing down of <u>The Magic Mountain</u> had followed immediately upon that of <u>Death in Venice</u>. From letters of that time, however, it can be shown that these dates must be modified." (J.R.R.)

M643   Lehnert, Herbert, "Heine, Schiller, Nietzsche und der junge Thomas Mann," <u>Neophilologus</u>, 48:51-6, February, 1964.

The fact that "like [his fictional creation] Gustav Aschenbach, Thomas Mann 'administered his fame' . . . forces us to great methodical caution" in assigning importance to Mann's self-evaluations. (J.R.R.)

M644   Lehnert, Herbert, "Quellenforschung und fiktive Strukturen," <u>Rice University Studies</u>, 53:13-21, No. 4, 1967.

Literary criticism should follow the lead of the natural sciences and admit that the method of questioning influences results. Such rigor is used in evaluating some of Mann's sources. (J.R.R.)

M645   Lehnert, Herbert, "Thomas Mann-Forschung," <u>Deutsche Vierteljahrsschrift für Literaturwissenschaft und Geistesgeschichte</u>, 40:257-97, 1966; 41:599-653, 1967; 42:126-57, 1968.

["In the first part of this research report the reader is to be instructed concerning present possibilities of achieving a broadened field of view and a clear picture of Thomas Mann via the following sequence: a) research sites (archives), b) editions of the works, c) editions of the letters, d) memoires, e) aids." The second and later following part of this report will give a survey of tendencies in the secondary literature, likewise from the aspect of a newly arising picture of Thomas Mann against the background of old conceptions."] (J.R.R.)

M646   Lehnert, Herbert, "Thomas Mann in Exile 1933-1938," <u>Germanic Review</u>, 38:277-94, November, 1963.

Mann's political activities after his departure from Germany changed some aspects of his thought. While he did not give up his basic position, irony, defended earlier in <u>Betrachtungen eines Unpolitischen</u>, he does envisage and support a non-Marxist socialism rooted in humanity. (R.H.L.)

M647 Lehnert, Herbert, "Thomas Mann in Princeton," Germanic Review, 39:15-32, January, 1964.

Mann located in Princeton in 1938. Here he gave "conferences" and lectures and finished writing Lotte in Weimar. On receiving the degree of Doctor of Letters he replied with a speech (given here) of heartfelt gratitude. He began to write Joseph der Ernährer, which he completed after moving to California in 1941. (R.H.L.)

M648 Lehnert, Herbert, "Thomas Mann und Schiller," Rice Institute Pamphlet, 47:99-118, April, 1960.

"If we look back, we will see that the intensive preoccupation with Schiller and his works [when Mann prepared his Versuch über Schiller] overcame the alienation which Thomas Mann had never completely lost as long as he regarded him as the moralist and the fool of freedom." (J.R.R.)

M649 Lehnert, Herbert, "Tristan, Tonio Kröger und Der Tod in Venedig: Ein Strukturvergleich," Orbis Litterarum, 24:271-304, No. 4, 1969.

"We should seek to determine the artistic value of [Mann's] ambivalence of perspective independent of any progressive stylistic categories." (J.R.R.)

M650 Leopold, Keith, "Point of View in the Novels of Thomas Mann," AUMLA, No. 8, pp. 29-36, May, 1958.

From Buddenbrooks (1901) to Felix Krull (1954), point of view in Mann's works has, with two exceptions, developed from neutral omniscience to an increasingly prominent personal narrator. (F.J.P.)

M651 Leppmann, Wolfgang, "Der Amerikaner im Werke Thomas Mann," German Quarterly, 38:619-29, November, 1965.

Mann makes Samuel Spoelmann in Königliche Hoheit a stereotyped second-generation capitalist. Ken Keaton in Die Betrogene has more dimension, but his characterization reveals Mann's unfamiliarity with the American man-in-the-street. Moreover, although the novel is set around 1923, Keaton is clearly a post-World War II man. (R.H.L.)

M652 Lesser, Jonas, "Einige Bemerkungen über Thomas Manns Verhältniss zu Philosophie und Religion," Die Neue Rundschau, 66:518-23, June, 1955.

Although rejecting him at first in favor of Schopenhauer, Mann later paid homage to Kant. Mann's religious belief, neither Catholic nor Protestant, was influenced by Luther. What is God for Mann? "Is he not the universality, the plastic principle, the omniscient righteousness, the comprehensive love? The belief in God is the belief in love, life, and art." (L.L.)

M653 Lesser, J., "Thomas Mann," Contemporary Review, 189:169-72, March, 1956.

Mann kept within the German literary tradition by writing in the lyrical-metaphysical manner, but he was an innovator in novel structure. His great novels are "musical," not only because of the language, but because their structure resembles complex musical forms, using particularly the Wagnerian leitmotif, and in Doctor Faustus the strenger Satz. (F.L.)

M654 Linn, Rolf N., "Conversation with Thomas Mann," German Quarterly, 33:224-6, May, 1960.

"Because of my interests at the time, a good part of our conversation dealt with Theodor Fontane, one of Mann's favorite authors." (J.R.R.)

M655 Lowe-Porter, Helen T., "Translating Thomas Mann," Symposium, 9:260-72, Fall, 1955.

This was a task accepted reluctantly with many qualms, dropped, then resumed, and completed in triumph. The technical aspects, and some of the personal ones, of this author-translator relationship extending over nearly fifty years Mrs. Lowe-Porter discussed with frankness, modesty, and charm. (J.L.B.)

M656 Lukacs, George, "The Stature of Thomas Mann," Masses and Mainstream, 8:20-6, September, 1955.

Thomas Mann was the last representative writer of critical realism. From within the ken of a middle class, middle world outlook, he developed the view of the doom of the middle class and the inevitable advent of socialism. Not only political, his works are artistic organic wholes; they reflect his judgment on both social and political matters. (A.W.)

M657   Manierre, Virginia, "How Long is a Minute?" New Mexico
Quarterly, 26:238-48, Autumn, 1956.

The individual atmosphere of Mann's books comes from the subjective, back-and forward-extending duration of events. The interrelatedness of time and people gives his universe "an extra dimension," and "his virtue is . . . that he can convey [the relative nature
of time] in his books." (J.L.B.)

M658   Mann, Golo, "Recollections of My Father, Thomas Mann,"
Claremont Quarterly, 5:5-15, Spring, 1958.

"For, when all is said about my father's irony, his skepticism,
his incapacity to choose and to make up his mind, when all this is
said, he was yet, in the last analysis, a moralist. . . . systematic
pessimism is not a moral attitude. It could not be his last word."
(J.R.R.)

M659   Mann, Monica, "Eighty Years of Thomas Mann," Saturday Review,
38:39-40, June 4, 1955.

Mann's writing links life, which he experiences, with what "he does
not experience so that it becomes art." "The genuine is relieved of
its burden by the imitated, depreciated in its worth, but also raised."
Both a fictional "doctor of alchemy" and a real man of life, he has
consummated the marriage of his work and his life. (C.P.)

M660   Marck, Siegfried, "Thomas Mann as a Thinker," Ethics, 67:53-7
October, 1956.

". . . for Thomas Mann as a thinker, the philosophy of Schopenhauer
represented the point of departure for all [his] following reflections."
Mann "was always tormented by the tension between the traditional
elements of his heritage and the deviations connected with his essentially artistic life. . . . the fundamental tension dominating all his
epic and all his reflective writing was that between demonism and
humanism." (D.P.)

M661   Martin, John S., "Circean Seduction in Three Works by Thomas
Mann," Modern Language Notes, 78:346-52, No. 3, 1963.

"To see Mario and the Magician, The Magic Mountain, and Death in
Venice in relation to the myth of Circe and Odysseus . . . enriches
our sense of Mann's well-marked mythical consciousness. Second,
it underlines his long-lasting concern with a single theme, that of

salvation through seduction. Third, with respect to <u>Death in Venice</u> and <u>The Magic Mountain</u>, it adds substance to his statement that he originally conceived the latter as 'a humorous companion-piece' to the former. . . . And finally it enriches our reading of Mann's three works" through an awareness that the extent "to which his characters unconsciously re-enact myth and sometimes fail to live up to their mythical counterparts is an aspect of his irony." (D.P.)

M662 Mason, Eudo C., "Thomas Mann und Rilke," <u>Orbis Litterarum</u>, 13:15-26, No. 1, 1958.

"With both Rilke and Thomas Mann this concept of decadence, elevated into the mythic and the metaphysical, becomes not only a means of private self-interpretation, but even beyond that a basic motif of their own writing and a constituent component of their world view." (J.R.R.)

M663 Mercanton, Jacques, "Thomas Mann," <u>La Nouvelle Revue Française</u>, 4:308-14, February 1, 1956.

Thomas Mann gave to the novel a new significance without breaking down the traditional form and without exhausting novelistic devices. With the passage of time, however, his novel became more of an epic. (M.M.)

M664 Michael, Wolfgang F., "Thomas Mann und Rilke," <u>Archiv für das Studium der neueren Sprachen und Literaturen</u>, 202:112-4, August, 1965.

Rilke's name is strangely absent from Mann's critical writings but the recent publication of Mann's letters makes his views of Rilke quite clear. (J.R.R.)

M665 Mileck, Joseph, "A Comparative Study of <u>Die Betrogene</u> and <u>Der Tod in Venedig</u>," <u>Modern Language Forum</u>, 42:124-9, December, 1957.

There are basic similarities of structure and theme in Mann's most famous and in his last <u>Novellen</u>. The "duality of life and death," the irony, and some of the technical elements are similar. Though the later story is not as "severe" on the "moral aberration" corrupt sexual longing, it too shows "indulgence" punished. (K.W.)

M666 Morse, J. Mitchell, "Joyce and the Early Thomas Mann," Revue
de Littérature Comparée," 36:377-86, July-September, 1962.

Joyce and the early Mann gave similar expression to the artist's
"redemption" through painful withdrawal from the "dance of life."
(A.W.)

M667 Morton, Frederic, "Thomas Mann at 80: Still the Adventurer,"
Nation, 180:504-5, June 11, 1955.

[This interview with Mann shortly after his eightieth birthday
elicits his impressions of America, his assessment of the influence
of American writers on European literature, his present writing
projects, his reading, the uneasy place of the writer today, Mann's
future plans.] (D.P.)

M668 Müller, Joachim, "Thomas Manns Sinfonia Domestica,"
Zeitschrift für deutsche Philologie, 83:142-70, April, 1964.

In terms of subject, narrative technique, intention and style, three
of Mann's shorter works, Herr und Hund, Gesang vom Kindchen,
and Unordnung und frühes Leid, represent an artistic unity. (J.R.R.)

M669 Munk Nielsen, C. A., "Eyvind Johnson and Thomas Mann," Orbis
Litterarum, 13:27-43, No. 1-2, 1958.

In a public letter to Mann in 1945 Johnson expressed his "gratitude
to a man from whose literary production the Swedish poet drew
inspiration and valuable stimuli specifically during the work on his
['Krilon'] novel trilogy." (J.R.R.)

M670 Myers, David, "Sexual Love and Caritas in Thomas Mann,"
Journal of English and Germanic Philology, 68:593-604, No. 4, 1968.

". . . Thomas Mann was artistically uninterested in normal sexual
love. . . . he confirmed his self-confessed fascination with the
pathological by painting predominantly pessimistic pictures of
bizarre and often perverse forms of sexual behavior. . . . Mann's
subordination of sexual love to an almost utopian representation of
pan-eros and caritas [was] his way of indicating a therapeutic
emergence from the pathological sphere. . . . the ethical development of Mann's quester-heroes . . . [was] a movement away from
sexual license towards renunciation and sublimation in a universal,
humane love for mankind." (D.P.)

M671   Nemerov, Howard, "Themes and Methods: The Early Stories of
       Thomas Mann," Carleton Miscellany, 2:3-20, Winter, 1961.

       The protagonists of Mann's early stories are "disappointed lovers
       of life and the world, those whose love has turned to hatred or
       cynicism, those whose love is an abject and constantly tormenting
       surrender in the face of scorn, and those whose love masquerades
       as indifference and superiority which a chance encounter will destroy."
       (W.G.F.)

M672   Neumeyer, Peter F., "Thomas Mann, Jews and Nazis,"
       Midstream, 13:68-71, June-July, 1967.

       ". . . the text of the letter [by Mann from 1921], and the circum-
       stances surrounding its writing and its non-publication go far to
       confirm us in our doubts, and to underline the difficulty of speaking
       without a great deal of qualification about individual motivation in
       the first years of National Socialist stirring." (J.R.R.)

M673   Newton, Caroline, "Thomas Mann and Sigmund Freud,"
       Princeton University Library Chronicle, 24:135-9, Winter, 1963.

       Mann did not read any of Freud's work until after the publication of
       The Magic Mountain (1924), but Mann felt that Freud's influence as
       "the foremost thinker of our time" upon the Zeitgeist had enor-
       mously influenced the novelist's work indirectly. (W.G.F.)

M674   Nicolson, Harold, "Thomas Mann," Die Neue Rundschau, 66:508-10,
       June, 1955.

       Thomas Mann's writings create so deep an impression because "he
       deals acutely and sympathetically with what for us is always the
       most fascinating riddle of the German Character, namely the con-
       trast between the sedative and the dynamic, the Apollonian and the
       Dionysian, the rational and the daemonic." (L.L.)

M675   Nielsen, Birger Hassing, "Thomas Manns Vorarbeiten zu einem
       Drama über Luthers Hochzeit (1955)," Orbis Litterarum,
       20:98-127, No. 1, 1965.

       "It is known that under the impressions of National Socialism and
       the Second World War Thomas Mann had developed into a strong
       critic of Protestant culture and tradition" and had started work on
       a play on the subject of Luther. It is important to "impart an im-
       pression of what we could have expected if Thomas Mann had been
       granted the time necessary to be able to complete the work." (J.R.R.)

M676   N[oth], E[rnst] E[rich], "Farewell to Thomas Mann," Books
Abroad, 29:296, Summer, 1955.

Thomas Mann's "amazingly rich and multi-shaded work was, and
will remain, known and cherished all over the world. Its impact
will continue to be felt. . . . [He was] a great European who became
an American citizen and doubtless was a world figure in German
letters." (D.P.)

M677   Nündel, Ernest, "Der Bogen und die Leyer: Thomas Manns
Äusserungen zur künstlerischen Tätigkeit," Deutschunterricht,
21:42-53, May, 1969.

Mann's comments on the role of the artist show that he believed
that the artist should choose both the bow and the lyre, i.e., he
should use both reason and feeling, objective observation and intuition, nihilism and love. (J.R.R.)

M678   Oliver, Kenneth, "Two Unpublished Letters of Thomas Mann,"
Monatshefte, 51:325-7, December, 1959.

The first of these letters, both from 1951, discusses Mrs. Lowe-
Porter's translations; the second seeks to clarify "various scattered
references to what I called the new or third, humanism in my essays."
(J.R.R.)

M679   Parry, Idris, "Thomas Mann's Latest Phase," German Life and
Letters, 8:241-51, July, 1955.

Mann's latest works, Die Betrogene and Bekenntnisse des
Hochstaplers Felix Krull, both emphasize the triumph of discipline
in life by a negative picture of the fearful consequences of failure.
Rosalie von Tuemmler pays for her social indiscipline with her
life, whereas the brilliant, irresponsible Krull in the picaresque
parody ends up in jail. (W.G.F.)

M680   Peacock, Ronald, "Much is Comic in Thomas Mann," Euphorion,
59:345-60, June, 1966.

Mann "does what, after all, comic writers have always done; he
works from the golden mean of reason. He uses his humanist faith
as the point of reference for his view of the comic fall from grace."
(J.R.R.)

M681 Pearson, Gabriel, "The Heroism of Thomas Mann," International Literary Annual, 1:122-30, 1958.

"Why I want to see [Mann] read is that he is one of the great encouraging facts in contemporary literature. His work stands for the values of the realistic tradition--the values of community and individuality. And he has demonstrated that in the face of catastrophe these values can still hold." (J.R.R.)

M682 Pfund, Harry W., "Zurich's Literary Shrine, the Thomas Mann Archives," American-German Review, 29:14-7, February-March, 1963.

"It seems fitting that such a literary shrine [i.e., the Bodmer House] should house on one of its upper floors the Thomas Mann Archives, including many of the personal belongings, furniture, and papers of the writer to whom Switzerland and particularly the environs of Zurich became a second and deeply beloved homeland." (J.R.R.)

M683 Pike, Burton, "Thomas Mann and the Problematic Self," Publications of the English Goethe Society, 37:120-41, 1967.

"Everywhere [Mann's] art shows evidence of a scrupulous concern for the exact rendering of the world around him. Yet however elaborate this detail, Mann remains, paradoxically, an artist whose primary concern is with the self." (J.R.R.)

M684 Politzer, Heinz, "Thomas Mann und die Forderung des Tages," Monatshefte, 46:65-79, February, 1954.

Mann's career gives answers to the questions: "How did the artist Thomas Mann relate to power? How did he exercise the paternal authority cleared for him by generations of European youth? And how does the creator of Doktor Faustus conduct himself towards politics, towards the demands of our day?" (J.R.R.)

M685 Pollak, Hans, "Kleine Beiträge zur Beurteilung von Thomas Mann," Germanish-Romanische Monatsschrift, 7:394-6, 1957.

[These are brief comments on Thomas Mann and his attitudes on Goethe, Gottfried Keller, and Kleist.] (K.M.W.)

M686   Prausnitz, Walther G., "Thomas Mann: Artist in Exile, "
        Discourse, 8:105-18, 1965.

        "The question whether Mann's political voice will survive at the
        expense of his creative work is an idle and unprofitable one: what
        is more important is the tracing of the development within the artist
        himself of his awareness of the relationship he must have toward the
        society in which he lives. " (J.R.R.)

M687   Pringsheim, Klaus H., "Thomas Mann in America, " Neue
        Deutsche Hefte, 109:20-46, No. 1, 1966.

        [This is a study of Mann's discontent with the America of the
        McCarthy era.] (J.R.R.)

M688   Pringsheim, Klaus H., "Thomas Mann in America, " American-
        German Review, 30:24-34, February-March, 1964.

        "My only justification, then, for writing this article . . . is that I
        knew the great man and have certain personal recollections and
        impressions which have been among the more significant events in
        my life. Also, from time to time, I do feel a desire . . . to set
        things straight. . . ." (J.R.R.)

M689   Pryce-Jones, Alan, "The 'Two Faces' of Thomas Mann, " Listener,
        60:828-30, November 20, 1958.

        "In the essentially private aspects of life--in religion, in human
        relationships--[Mann] seems always to present two faces to truth.
        He maintains his thought and its opposite without the least embar-
        rassment: indeed, the tension between opposites is the stuff of
        which his best work is invariably made. " (J.R.R.)

M690   Reed, T. J., "Mann and Turgenev--a First Love, " German Life
        and Letters, 17:313-8, July, 1964.

        Though Turgenev exerted thematic and stylistic influence discernible
        in Mann's first story, Gefallen, the influence was short-lived.
        (R.B.W.)

M691   Reed, T. J., "Thomas Mann, Heine, Schiller: The Mechanics of
        Self-Interpretation, " Neophilologus, 47:41-50, 1963.

        In assessing self-evaluations such as those by Mann, one must
        remember "however valid for the writer the affinities which his

imaginative sympathy delights to establish, for the critic there must
be a distinction between the asserted and the actual, between a
claimed and a real affinity." (J.R.R.)

M692   Requadt, Paul, "Jugendstil im Frühwerk Thomas Manns,"
Deutsche Vierteljahrsschrift für Literaturwissenschaft und
Geistesgeschichte, 40:206-16, June, 1966.

Mann's early works such as the drama "Fiorenza" (1905) reflect
the influence of art nouveau. (J.R.R.)

M693   Rey, W. H., "Tragic Aspects of the Artist in Thomas Mann's
Work," Modern Language Quarterly, 19:195-203, September, 1958.

Mann's employment of the techniques of decadence (such as "irony
toward both sides") is resolved short of nihilism. The tragic artist-
heroes of Death in Venice and other works are victims "of the unreconciled extremes." They achieve art and knowledge by fusing
the "sensual and spiritual." Their "way to the divine leads through
self-destruction . . . ." (K.W.)

M694   Riley, Anthony, "Notes on Thomas Mann and English and American
Literature," Comparative Literature, 17:57-72, Winter, 1965.

Dickens and Poe influenced particularly Mann's grotesque humor.
(C.E.N.)

M695   Root, John G., "Stylistic Irony in Thomas Mann," Germanic
Review, 35:93-103, April, 1960.

Stylistic irony in the Schlegelian spirit is common in Mann's works.
A species therof, syntactical irony, recurrent, digressive, oscil-
latory, and appositive, occurs in isolation only in Death in Venice
and swings the victory to Müdigkeit. In Tonio Kröger the hero, not
undermined by syntactical irony, may still escape ultimate corruption. (R.H.L.

M696   Rühle, Jürgen, "Die Republik der Unpolitischen: Zur 90.
Wiederkehr des Geburtstags von Thomas Mann," Forum, 12:315-7,
380-3, June-July; August-September, 1965.

"Filled with a tragic yearning for democracy, for what he calls
humanity, Thomas Mann, incontestably the most representative
and most significant figure of German literature between the wars,

has brought to many thousands of pages of paper the unfortunate
relationship of the intellectuals to the democracy of the twentieth
century." (J.R.R.)

M697   Rychner, Max, "Gestalten und Beziehungen in den Romanen,"
Die Neue Rundschau, 66:261-77, June, 1955.

The Gestalt of one novel is based upon and like that of another; in
turn it evokes still another Gestalt. The role of the Gestalt in the
artist structure of the novels is elucidated by a detailed examination
of the various relationships. (L.L.)

M698   Schiffer, Eva, "Illusion und Wirklichkeit in Thomas Manns
Felix Krull und Joseph," Monatshefte, 55:69-81, February, 1963.

Felix Krull, the poseur par excellence, has such an ambivalent
attitude toward his duality that in the end he does not rightly know
who he is. Joseph, on the other hand, knows full well the definitions, even the subtleties of the multi-faceted double roles he plays.
(R.H.L.)

M699   Schneider, Marcel, "La Morte de Thomas Mann," La Revue de
Paris, 62:137-42, October, 1955.

The greatness of Thomas Mann and his work lies in his acceptance
of a complex world. He has never succeeded in formulating a simple
doctrine. Although the antagonism between reality and the world of
philosophy and art may be labeled the principal theme of his work,
it is in the diversity of the humanist tradition that one must seek the
thought of this author. (M.R.)

M700   Schneider, Reinhold, "Kurzer Nachruf auf Thomas Mann," Die Neue
Rundschau, 67:521-7, 1956.

Mann had a single theme: "die Geschichte der Entbürgerlichung."
He pursued the goal of "Hanseatic humanity" as exampled by his
native Lübeck of old. This saved him from decadence and esthetic
isolation; it gave him an artistic conscience, a sense of duty, a set
of ethical principles founded upon bourgeois morality. (H.H.V.)

M701   Schulz, Siegfried A., "Hindu Mythology in Mann's Indian Legend,"
Comparative Literature, 14:129-42, Spring, 1962.

[This is a discussion of Mann's use of the Vetàla stories, a collection of witty and urbane Indian entertainments.] (C.E.N.)

M702   Schumann, Willy, "Theodor Storm und Thomas Mann: Gemeinsames und Unterschiedliches," Monatshefte, 55:49-68, February, 1963.

Theodor Storm was not a major influence in Mann's intellectual and artistic development. But there are several significant common factors which find their reflections in the oeuvres: north German maritime family roots and childhood, prosperous bourgeois background, devotion to work and duty, and discomfort in the great world. (R.H.L.)

M703   Seidlin, Oskar, "Pikareske Züge im Werke Thomas Manns," Germanisch-Romanische Monatsschrift, 36:22-40, 1955.

Mann presents a "new" version of the picaresque in two of his works, Bekenntnisse des Hochstaplers Felix Krull and Joseph und seine Brüder. In Joseph the greatest possibilities of the picaro are realized. (G.C.)

M704   Seyppel, Joachim, "Adel des Geistes: Thomas Mann und August von Platen," Deutsche Vierteljahrsschrift für Literaturwissenschaft und Geistesgeschichte, 33:565-73, 1959.

"However, let it be stressed here from the beginning: we are not concerned with causal influences of the elder [Platen] upon the younger [T. Mann]; the question is one in the purely esthetic sense of the spiritual relationship of two great figures of German culture." (J.R.R.)

M705   Singer, Felix, "Thomas Mann," Trace, No. 36, pp. 25-7, March-April, 1960.

"Mann was neither a philosopher nor novelist, and knew that--but was an ambiguous combination of both, and glorified in this ambiguity." (W.G.F.)

M706   Sonnenfeld, Albert, "Tristan for Pianoforte: Thomas Mann and Marcel Proust," Southern Review, 5:1004-18, Autumn, 1969.

"In the works of Thomas Mann and Marcel Proust, the Wagnerite of the piano bench is an important ironic representation of the authors's own youthful fervor as acolytes at the pagan altars of Bayreuth. And if in later years they were to mock the excessively pious faithful, they never forswore the faith." (J.M.D.)

M707   Sørensen, Bengt Algot, "Die symbolische Gestaltung in den
        Jugenderzählungen Thomas Manns," Orbis Litterarum, 20:85-97,
        1965.

        The transcendence of the symbolic over the realistic was already
        eivdent in Mann's early short stories. At first uncertainly and ex-
        perimentally, he progressed until he had developed his own sym-
        bolic story form; a form he further developed and refined in his
        later works. (K.M.W.)

M708   Stern, Guy, "A Case for Oral Literary History: Conversations with
        or about Morgenstern, Lehmann, Reinacher and Thomas Mann,"
        German Quarterly, 37:487-97, November, 1964.

        Literary facts established through oral history interviews with
        Christian Morgenstern, Wilhelm Lehmann, Eduard Reinacher,
        Thomas Mann and/or their associates demonstrate the great value
        of this new technique for literary historians. (D.P.)

M709   Stern, J. P., "Thomas Mann's Last Period," Critical Quarterly,
        8:244-54, Autumn, 1966.

        During his self-exile from Hitler's Germany, Thomas Mann main-
        tained "a profound and anxious concern for the state of Germany and
        Europe," a concern which "delayed the completion of the Joseph
        tetralogy [and] is imprinted on Doctor Faustus, his last great work."
        The Joseph tetralogy "ranges . . . freely and . . . playfully over
        aeons of time," connected by the encompassing existential and
        literary themes. Doctor Faustus is Mann's "strangest and most
        powerful novel," the tale of a "single solitary man, infinitely mov-
        ing in his proud, chilly isolation, the bearer of a gift that destroys
        him." However, the novel does re-establish "the balance . . .
        between the solitary man and his time and country of desolation."
        (D.P.)

M710   Strich, Fritz, "Schiller und Thomas Mann," Die Neue Rundschau,
        68:60-83, May, 1957.

        There is a basic similarity between Schiller and Mann. Schiller,
        long before Goethe, became a constructive and educative force for
        Mann, whose Novelle, Schwere Stunde (1905), written in defense
        of Schiller's heroic poetry, is a self-portrait. Its theme is "Moral
        des Künstlers," "der Wille zum Werk." (H.H.V.)

M711   Szondi, Peter, "Versuch über Thomas Mann," Die Neue Rundschau,
       67:557-63, 1956.

       Mann's works are based on the antithesis: Geist-Natur. The heroes
       of his early fiction (Tonio Kröger, for example) represent the former,
       while more recently created characters exemplify the latter in a
       spiritualized form. Goethe und Tolstoi marks the turning point.
       [Rather detailed analyses of Der Erwählte and Die vertauschten Köpfe
       are given.] (H.H.V.)

M712   Tuska, Jon, "Thomas Mann and Nietzsche: A Study in Ideas,"
       Germanic Review, 39:281-99, November, 1964.

       Mann, judging Nietzsche by his total effect, could not embrace the
       latter's denunciation of justice. Mann pleaded for a retention of
       reverence for man, and he regarded Nietzsche's support of the
       claims of barbarism as a "grotesque error." (R.H.L.)

M713   Uecker, Heiko, "Ein unbekannter Artikel Thomas Manns in
       norwegischer Sprache," Arcadia, 5:77-83, March, 1970.

       [This is a discussion of an unfamiliar article written by Mann in
       1936 about contemporary theater and never since translated from
       the Norwegian in which it appeared.] (J.R.R.)

M714   Weigand, Hermann J., "Thomas Mann and Goethe: A Supplement
       and a Correction," Germanic Review, 32:75-6, February, 1957.

       "Although I stated in my contribution to the October 1956 Thomas
       Mann memorial issue of Germanic Review that no one of his circle
       'would have interpreted Goethe's literary physiognomy in [unflatter-
       ing] terms such as those quoted in Werther,' Mr. Erich Neumann
       has referred me to a letter from H. G. von Bretschneider, dated
       October 16, 1775, which refutes this. Also, my earlier criticism
       that Mann's residence in America had weakened his use of German,
       as evidenced by his substitution of überall for überhaupt, neglects
       to consider that Mann probably used the term as a conscious archa-
       ism representative of practice in Goethe's time." (D.P.)

M715   Weigand, Hermann, "Thomas Mann zum Gedächtnis,"
       Neophilologus, 40:162-79, July 1, 1956.

       [This memorial to Thomas Mann devotes particular attention to
       Felix Krull and to The Black Swan.] (J.R.R.)

M716   Weigand, Hermann, "Thoughts on the Passing of Thomas Mann,"
       Germanic Review, 31:163-75, October, 1956.

       Mann "transmuted the raw material of his earthly existence into
       works that live." He develops from the young man desiring worldly
       fame, to an archetypal likeness of Goethe in Lotte in Weimar, and
       finally a stylistic identification with Felix Krull. (K.L.)

M717   Werner, Alfred, "Thomas Mann, Priest of Culture," Chicago
       Jewish Forum, 14:214-20, Summer, 1956.

       "There was chaos in Goethe, along with the inherited bourgeois
       tradition of system and orderliness. When these two clashed in
       the poet's soul, they produced dramas and novels, the hero of
       which was always Goethe, in different disguises. The same can be
       said of Mann--one idea formed the central theme of his life work:
       the sensitive artist's groping for a settlement with the cruel pattern
       of human existence." (K.M.W.)

M718   West, Paul, "Thomas Mann and English Taste," Southern Review,
       5:1126-40, Autumn, 1969.

       "The English spirit or mind . . . is too empirical and self-conscious
       to enjoy Thomas Mann, especially the Mann of the longest novels.
       (J.M.D.)

M719   Wilkinson, Elizabeth M., "Aesthetic Excursus on Thomas Mann's
       Akribie," Germanic Review, 31:225-35, October, 1956.

       [This is a discussion of Goethe's and Schiller's theories of form
       and content in relation to Mann's work, with emphasis on the justifi-
       cation of the highly specialized intellectual material included in his
       novels.] (K.L.)

M720   Willecke, Frederick H., "Thomas Mann and Luther," Kentucky
       Foreign Language Quarterly, 5:154-60, Third Quarter, 1958.

       Since Mann expressed two extremely different viewpoints toward
       Luther and the Reformation, the publication of a fragmentary
       dramatic work called Luthers Hochzeit will be of great interest in
       clarifying the novelist's attitude. (W.G.F.)

M721   Wird, Günter, "Bekenntnisse eines Politischen:Thomas Manns Radioreden," Weimarer Beiträge, 16:70-106, No. 1, 1970.

[This is a study of Mann's radio addresses transmitted by BBC to Germany from October 1940 to May 1945.]   (J.R.R.)

M722   Wirtz, Erika A., "Thomas Mann, Humorist and Educator," Modern Languages, 47:145-51, December, 1966.

Making frequent use of irony and parody, Mann "pleaded for a new humanism and for the renunciation of irrationalism and a re-appraisal of Romanticism."   (J.L.A.)

M723   Witte, W., "Thomas Mann and Schiller," German Life and Letters, 10:289-97, July, 1957.

". . . by demonstrating the significance of Schiller's work and thought in the world of today . . . [Mann] repaid the debt he owed to one whose influence on his own development, though less conspicuous than Goethe's or Wagner's, was yet far greater and deeper than appears at first sight."   (J.R.R.)

M724   Woodward, Anthony, "The Figure of the Artist in Thomas Mann's Tonio Kröger and Death in Venice," English Studies in Africa, 9:158-67, September, 1966.

"There were shadows in Mann's work, and his irony served both to hide and to reveal them. It is that other, shadowy side of Thomas Mann's writings that I shall attempt to evoke by means of some brief allusions to two early works, Tonio Kröger and Death in Venice." (J.R.R.)

M725   Wooley, E. O., "Four Letters from Thomas Mann to E. O. Wooley," Monatshefte, 56:15-7, January, 1964.

In letters written during the period 1943 to 1954 Thomas Mann notes his interest in Theodor Storm and the symbolical role of Storm's early works in his, Mann's, life and writings. (R.H.L.)

M726   Yourcenar, Marguerite, "Humanism in Thomas Mann," Partisan Review, 23:153-70, Spring, 1956.

Mann's broad humanism rests on "a philosophy and way of life founded upon human values. A traditionalist in using the past's riches, he is revolutionary in "constantly reinterpreting human thought and conduct." All knowledge is his province. He sees us with respect to life and death, the temporary and the eternal. (J.L.B.)

DER BAJAZZO

M727   Zerner, Marianne, "Thomas Mann's Der Bajazzo, a Parody of Dostoevski's Notes from Underground," Monatshefte, 56:286-90, November, 1964.

"Here, however, the question is limited to whether the Notes from Underground may have stimulated the young author [Mann]--consciously or not matters little--to give through Der Bajazzo (1897) a parody of the theme and intent of Dostoevski's short novel." (J.R.R.)

BASHAN AND I--See
HERR UND HUND

DIE BEKENNTNISSE DES HOCHSTAPLERS FELIX KRULL

M728   Bennett, Joseph, "A Bourgeois Eros," Hudson Review, 8:617-20, Spring, 1955.

"As a novel of high adventure, [Felix Krull] is fascinating. . . [although] the ponderousness with which Mann sets about to philosophize, the windiness of his disquisitions, seem more obvious in this ultimate work than in any other, and utterly irrelevant to the very serious fictional business of keeping this lively story in progress." (D.P.)

M729   Dieckmann, Friedrich, "Felix Krulls Verklärung: Zum zweiten Teil der Bekenntnisse," Sinn und Form, 19:894-934, August, 1967.

Many changes were made in Krull between the original fragment and the completed novel. (J.R.R.)

M730   Fowler, Alastair, "The Confidence Man," Listener, 65:781, 784, May 4, 1961.

The literary idea of the confidence man first appeared in the picaresque literature of the later Middle Ages; "Lazarillo de Tormes was the primary form of the picaresque romance. . . . the genre reaches a new stature in Gil Blas . . . [which] succeeds in formalizing the ingredients of picaresque into a set of accepted conventions."

DIE BEKENNTNISSE DES HOCHSTAPLERS FELIX KRULL
(cont'd)

A notable American example is Melville's The Confidence Man, but
"in The Confessions of Felix Krull, Confidence Man, the symbolic
elements of picaresque are deployed with full consciousness for the
first time." (D.P.)

M731   Guérard, Albert J., "Pleasures in Life Itself," Virginia Quarterly,
Review, 32:291-6, Spring, 1956.

". . . watching the later Mann one could incorrigibly long for . . .
life as life, not life as idea, for less archness and subtlety. The
Confessions of Felix Krull provides these simpler pleasures to a
quite astonishing degree. It is almost continuously entertaining and
lively, though intermittently threatened with seriousness. And this
is the creative drama of the novel: its apparent struggle between the
'novelistic' Mann, vastly amused by the situations he summons up,
and Mann the theorist on art and personal identity, fond of parodying
and echoing Goethe." (D.P.)

M732   Heilman, Robert B., "Variations on Picaresque (Felix Krull),"
Sewanee Review, 66:547-77, Autumn, 1958.

Mann used the picaresque form to portray by implication the artist
as the non-moral picaro, who, living by his wits, wins the confidence
of the respectable and dutiful, and, in tricking them, provides them
with physical or psychical fulfillment. (A.S.)

M733   Kleine, Don W., "Felix Krull as Fairy Tale Hero," Accent,
19:131-41, Summer, 1959.

". . . fairy tale equips the work with a link to its deeper issues.
. . . Mann's novel asks questions about man's role in the universe
which picaresque or social satire simply does not ask. . . .
traversing the light miles that lie between the heart and its wishes,
[Krull] retrieves the unity of human experience." (J.R.R.)

M734   Koch, Thilo, "Vollkommenheit," Texte und Zeichen, 1:133-5,
Winter, 1955.

Mann, a humanist and humorist, positive-biologistic, progressive
picture-maker is unsurpassed. In Bekenntnisse des Hochstaplers
Felix Krull, Mann portrays a swindler, writing as his own life
progresses, and reflecting, throughout, the events of the world

DIE BEKENNTNISSE DES HOCHSTAPLERS FELIX KRULL
(cont'd)

(particularly Germany). Ambivalent, talented Krull shows that man
can be godlike--only through deception. (M.J.)

M735   Lange, Victor, "Betrachtungen zur Thematik von Felix Krull, "
Germanic Review, 31:215-24, October, 1956.

"In the ultimately (1954) resulting totality of the Confessions it is
not difficult . . . to point out most brilliantly interwoven almost all
themes and motifs of Mann's art." (J.R.R.)

M736   Nelson, Donald F., "Felix Krull or: 'All the World's a Stage', "
Germanic Review, 45:41-51, January, 1970.

"In representing the world as a stage Thomas Mann brought into
play a parodistic allusion to the Baroque drama in the tradition of
Calderón and thus enlarged the perspective in which Felix Krull
may be identified with seventeenth-century literary traditions."
(R.H.L.)

M737   Riley, Anthony W., "Three Cryptic Quotations in Thomas Mann's
Felix Krull, " Journal of English and Germanic Philology,
65:99-106, January, 1966.

Late in life Mann showed an increased preference for "cryptic"
quotations, subtly transforming the words of the original to give
the quotation a humorous twist or symbolic significance in the new
work and to perceive "the rich legacy of the literature of the past.
Often the quotations are so . . . cunningly woven into the fabric of
the novel . . . that the quotation can be discovered only by painstaking . . . examination." In the scene in Felix Krull where Krull is
preparing to assume his role as Marquis de Venosta, Mann quotes
verbatim from the memoirs of the Rumanian confidence man
Manolescu. In the hilarious love-scene with Madame Diane Houpflé,
words, somewhat changed, are taken from Victor Hugo's Hernani.
In the earlier scene in which Krull is interviewed by the Swiss
Generaldirektor Stürzli for a job as elevator boy at a hotel in Paris,
Krull paraphrases the last two lines from Béranger's Chansons to
achieve a particular humorous effect. (D.P.)

DIE BEKENNTNISSE DES HOCHSTAPLERS FELIX KRULL
(cont'd)

M738   Sands, Donald B., "The Light and Shadow of Thomas Mann's
Felix Krull," Renascence, 13:119-24, Spring, 1961.

Felix Krull mirrors Mann's "final reflections on the Goethean
spirit." (R.K.)

M739   Schiffer, Eva, "Changes in an Episode: A Note on Felix Krull,"
Modern Language Quarterly, 24:257-62, September, 1963.

Mann revised a chapter in the 1937 fragment to link the 1937 and
1954 versions and to clarify the themes of the book. (G.S.)

M740   Schiffer, Eva, "Manolescu's Memoirs: The Beginning of Felix
Krull," Monatshefte, 52:283-92, November, 1960.

The Memoirs of Manolescu "supplied Mann with certain specific,
superficial elements of plot and character; beyond that, some
acquaintance with it helps to set off delightfully the mastery and
complexity of Mann's narrative technique." (J.R.R.)

M741   Smeed, J. W., "The Role of Professor Kuckuck in Felix Krull,"
Modern Language Review, 59:411-2, July, 1964.

The "palaeozoological and palaeoanthropological" conversation
between Krull and Professor Kuckuck in Book III, chapter 5 of
Felix Krull is not only "an affirmation of life and a recognition
that the very transience and limitations of life are what engage our
sympathy," but the conversation serves also "to broaden the
satirical scope of the novel." (D.P.)

M742   Stilwell, Robert L., "Mann's Confessions of Felix Krull, Confidence
Man," Explicator, 20: Item 24, November, 1961.

"Hermes-Troth, and not the Olympian Hermes alone, is a patron god
of identity-switching Felix Krull." (B.K.)

THE BELOVED RETURNS--See
LOTTE IN WEIMAR

BETRACHTUNGEN EINES UNPOLITISHCHEN

M743   Brock, Erich, "Ein gern vergessenes Buch Thomas Manns
Orbis Litterarum, 13:3-6, Nos. 1-2, 1958.

This work, frequently substantial and enlightening, unfortunately
possesses false, one-sided, and intolerant characteristics. It
contains sections dealing with martial heroism and the metaphysics
of the "Folk" which can serve, and indeed have served, the most
evil causes. (G.C.)

DIE BETROGENE

M744   McWilliams, James R., "Thomas Mann's Die Betrogene: A Study
in Ambivalence," CLA Journal, 10:56-63, 1966.

"As in Der Tod in Venedig where the jungle vision of life in all its
fertility is contrasted with the Stygian world of Venice, ambivalence
is the distinguishing feature of the later novella." (J.R.R.)

M745   Mertens, Gerard M., "Hemingway's Old Man and the Sea and Mann's
The Black Swan," Literature and Psychology, 6:96-9, August, 1956.

Hemingway's The Old Man and the Sea and Mann's The Black Swan
share heroes whose life is at the climacteric, both of whom wage
courageous although unsuccessful battle, both feel betrayed by fate,
both are widowed, both have one true friend. Each story incorporates a mystic dream element. (D.P.)

M746   Rahv, Philip, "The Triumph of Decay," Commentary, 18:82-4,
July, 1954.

The Black Swan "reads like a feeble parody of" Death in Venice.
"Missing are the ardors and rigors of the Venetian tale: the closed
form and classical discipline of style and craft. . . . Moreover, in
The Black Swan the dazzling dialectic of life and art . . . is replaced
by the more restricted polarization of psyche and soma." (D.P.)

M747   Rey, W. H., "Rechtfertigung der Liebe in Thomas Manns
Erzählung Die Betrogene," Deutsche Vierteljahrsschrift für
Literaturwissenschaft und Geistesgeschichte, 34:428-48,
November, 1960.

". . . here the title finally assumes ironic significance. The betrayed woman [Die Betrogene] is in reality the blessed woman.

DIE BETROGENE (cont'd)

Thomas Mann's last narrative presents a defense of love and therewith at the same time a defense of the divine." (J.R.R.)

M748 Schoolfield, George C., "Thomas Mann's Die Betrogene,"
Germanic Review, 38:91-120, January, 1963.

Mann's tale of the passion of a fifty-year-old Rhineland widow for
an uncomplicated young American has generally received harsh, but
quite superficial criticism. Die Betrogene subtly reflects Mann's
residency in America, and his acquaintance with the mythology of
Karl Kerényi as well as with classical antiquity and early Christianity. (R.H.L.)

M749 Szennessy, Mario, "Über Thomas Manns Die Betrogene," Deutsche
Vierteljahrsschrift für Literaturwissenschaft und Geistesgeschichte,
40:217-47, June, 1966.

Mann's farewell work "is a credo to his old homeland and it lay in
the nature of things that the latter didn't want to hear it. . . ."
(J.R.R.)

THE BLACK SWAN--See
DIE BETROGENE

BUDDENBROOKS

M750 Jolles, Charlotte, "Sesemi Weichbrodt: Observations on a Minor
Character of Thomas Mann's Fictional World," German Life and
Letters, 22:32-8, October, 1968.

"Not only does she [Sesemi Weichbrodt] remain firmly imprinted on
our memory in spite of being a very minor character of the world
of Buddenbrooks, but she also is a character who is fully integrated
in the story." (J.R.R.)

M751 Koester, Rudolf, "Is Infallibility Necessary? A Note on the
Chronology of Buddenbrooks," CLA Journal, 11:163-6, 1967.

"While the chronological discrepancies in this work reveal that
Mann is not infallible (perturbing as this thought may be to some
critics), they offer no serious challenge to his reputation for precise workmanship." (J.R.R.)

BUDDENBROOKS (cont'd)

M752   Lucas, Guy, "Die Darstellung der Gesellschaft in Thomas Manns
Buddenbrooks," Revue des Langues Vivantes, 30:195-220,
July-August, 1964.

"From the not a little tempting investigation of the art and manner
with which Thomas Mann presents society in Buddenbrooks, it
becomes clear that the author does not let it appear as a totality, a
mass; rather, it is much more to be found among the traits of some
more or less individual 'representatives,' from whom the reader
has to draw conclusions concerning the manner of living and thinking
of whole groups of people." (J.R.R.)

M753   Nachman, Larry David and Albert S. Braverman, "Thomas Mann's
Buddenbrooks: Bourgeois Society and the Inner Life, Germanic
Review, 45:201-25, May, 1970.

"By implication, Johann Buddenbrook represents the claim of
bourgeois society that it alone provides a completely fulfilled and
materially self-sufficient life. Buddenbrooks, from this point on,
can be considered an examination and criticism of the ultimate
reality of this claim." (R.H.L.)

M754   Scherrer, Paul, "Bruchstücke der Buddenbrooks--Urhandschrift
und Zeugnisse zu ihrer Entstehung 1897-1901," Die Neue Rundschau,
69:258-91, August, 1958.

The author discovered these fragmentary original manuscripts of
Buddenbrooks last summer in the Thomas Mann Archives in the
Confederative Technische Hochschule in Zurich. His discovery
necessitates a revaluation of the chronology and process of composition of Buddenbrooks, free of the conjecture, uncertain references, and tenuous connections which have heretofore been included
in such studies. (R.H.L.)

M755   Stresau, Hermann, "Die Buddenbrooks," Die Neue Rundschau,
66:392-410, June, 1955.

. A detailed discussion of Mann's typical methods of composition
especially concerning Buddenbrooks elucidates much of what he
attempted in that novel. When character, leitmotiv, symbol, and
influences (Schopenhauer, Wagner, Nietzsche) are examined, the
power of life and the power of death are seen to be the interacting
themes which establish the tension. (L.L.)

BUDDENBROOKS (cont'd)

M756 Tollinchi, Esteban, "Schopenhauer y los Buddenbrooks," La Torre, 17:11-33, April-June, 1969.

Mann read The World as Will and Idea as he was about to have Thomas Buddenbrook die. Mann's profound reaction becomes a part of the novel. It can be seen also in later works, such as the Joseph tetralogy and Doctor Faustus. (C.O.)

M757 Weintraub, Stanley, "Castle Corner: Joyce Cary's Buddenbrooks," Wisconsin Studies in Contemporary Literature, 5:54-63, Winter-Spring, 1964.

"As novels of decline of a class, the pattern of development" in both Cary's and Mann's novels is "toward physical decline, moral decline, and the deaths of representative figures in each generation. Although the grim, ironic comedy of Mann . . . becomes ironic farce in Cary, the tone of both works evidences an affectionate respect for partisan tradition. . . ." (W.G.F.)

THE CONFESSIONS OF FELIX KRULL, CONFIDENCE MAN--See
DIE BEKENNTNISSE DES HOCHSTAPLERS FELIX KRULL

DEATH IN VENICE--See
DER TOD IN VENEDIG

THE DILETTANTE--See
DER BAJAZZO

DOKTOR FAUSTUS

M758 Assmann, Dietrich, "Thomas Manns Faustus-Roman und das Volksbuch von 1587," Neuphilologische Mitteilungen, 68:130-9, June, 1967.

"Not the history of Faust is told [in Mann's novel], but that of an artist and human who sees himself as Faust and whose fate receives weight and its representative quality within the Faust legend." (J.R.R.)

DOKTOR FAUSTUS (cont'd)

M759 Berger, Erich, "Eine Dantestelle in Thomas Manns Doktor Faustus,"
Monatshefte, 49:212-4, April-May, 1957.

"The Poet's Address to His Song" used by Thomas Mann in Faustus
is correctly identified as being from Dante but it is not from the
Divine Comedy. (J.R.R.)

M760 Bergsten, Gunilla, "Musical Symbolism in Thomas Mann's Doktor
Faustus," Orbis Litterarum, 14:206-14, Spring, 1959.

The Durchbruch for which Adrian Leverkühn longs, a breakthrough
of subjectivity in a world of imposed artistic and spiritual objective
forms, is reinforced in the novel by allusions to the creative life of
Beethoven. This is only one example of musical history and theory
in the novel. (E.L.)

M761 Blomster, W. V., "Textual Variations in Doktor Faustus,"
Germanic Review, 39:183-91, May, 1964.

The 1948 Vienna edition of Doktor Faustus, the basis of all subsequent editions, shows deletions from the 1947 Stockholm edition
totaling some ten pages. The deletions are mostly musicological
considerations contrary to the ideas of Arnold Schönberg. Whether
the deletions were made to conciliate the Schönberg school cannot
be ascertained. (R.H.L.)

M762 Boeninger, H. R., "Zeitblom, Spiritual Descendant of Goethe's
Wagner and Wagner's Beckmesser," German Life and Letters,
13:38-43, October, 1959.

"It is the purpose of this paper to analyze the character of Zeitblom
as the antipode of Leverkühn-Faustus, and to show his spiritual
descent from two famous earlier antipodes of the German spirit:
Goethe's Wagner and R. Wagner's Beckmesser." (J.R.R.)

M763 Briner, Andres, "Conrad Beissel and Thomas Mann," American-
German Review, 26:24-5, 38, December 1959-January 1960.

[This is an elucidation of Mann's citing the eighteenth century
Pennsylvania-German composer as a predecessor of Leverkühn-
Schönberg.] (J.R.R.)

DOKTOR FAUSTUS (cont'd)

M764   Briner, Andres, "Thomas Mann and The American-German Review,"
       American-German Review, 30:33, February-March, 1964.

       "It now turns out that Mann saved a copy of The American-German
       Review for June 1943 and marked with a pencil an article by Hans
       Theodore David entitled, 'Hymns and Music of the Pennsylvania
       Seventh-day Baptists.' Some of the information which David men-
       tions appears word for word in Mann's novel." (J.R.R.)

M765   Brown, Calvin S., "The Entomological Source of Mann's Poisonous
       Butterfly," Germanic Review, 37:116-20, March, 1962.

       The ultimate source of Thomas Mann's knowledge of the butterfly
       Hetaera esmeralda, that is, of Adrian Leverkühn's "giftiger
       Schmetterling" in Doktor Faustus, is the English naturalist,
       Henry Walter Bates. Mann's symbolism of the butterfly is inherent
       in the generic name, from Greek hetaira "courtesan, prostitute."
       (R.H.L.)

M766   Buisonjé, J. C. de, "Bemerkungen über Thomas Manns Werk
       Doktor Faustus (1947)," Neophilologus, 41:185-99, July, 1957.

       "For Thomas Mann music is often a symbol for something verbal-
       individual. Thus when he turns against music, it is impossible that
       he means such 'music' in his works. It is to be regretted that--as
       far as we can see--Thomas Mann never clearly defined his music
       concepts." (J.R.R.)

M767   Charney, Hanna and Maurice Charney, "Doctor Faustus and Mon
       Faust: An Excursus in Dualism," Symposium, 16:45-53,
       Spring, 1962.

       "Mann and Valéry, incompatible as their interests might otherwise
       be, converge on their way of framing the problem of identity: for
       them both, it presents itself initially in terms of dualism." (R.J.G.)

M768   Devoto, Daniel, "Deux musiciens russes dans le Doktor Faustus de
       Thomas Mann," Revue de Littérature Comparée, 33:104-6,
       January-March, 1959.

       The two Russian musicians who influence Leverkühn are Tchaikovsky
       and Stravinsky. (J.R.R.)

DOKTOR FAUSTUS (cont'd)

M769   Elema, J., "Thomas Mann, Dürer und Doktor Faustus,
Euphorion, 59:97-117, 1965.

[This illustrated article examines Dürer's role in Mann's study of
the failure of German bourgeois intellectuality. Elema concludes,
"Albrecht Dürer belongs in the evolutional series not simply as a
chronological beginning, but also as the bright world of the early
period which already bears the poison within itself."] (J.R.R.)

M770   Engelberg, Edward, "Thomas Mann's Faust and Beethoven,"
Monatshefte, 47:112-6, March, 1955.

". . . I wish to suggest in the following pages that by considering
Beethoven's spiritual and physical struggles we can recover some
of the meaning of Leverkühn's particular plight; Beethoven's image
will help us perhaps to focus once again on the special problems of
Leverkühn's artistic conflict." (J.R.R.)

M771   Frank, Joseph, "Reaction as Progress, Thomas Mann's Doctor
Faustus," Chicago Review, 15:19-39, Autumn, 1961.

"The images of our greatness are far more intimately connected
with those of our misery than we are willing to admit; and it is the
genius of Thomas Mann, sharpened by the tragedy of his culture,
which has discerned and portrayed their inner connection." (J.R.R.)

M772   Friedenberg, Daniel M., "Mann's Obsesssion with the Circle of
Duality," Commonweal, 74:476-7, August 25, 1961.

The keen interest in the background material Mann used for Doctor
Faustus prompted him to write The Story of a Novel: The Genesis
of Doctor Faustus. According to Mann the central motif in Doctor
Faustus is the "obsession with the dual nature of good and evil, of
grace and hell." (D.P.)

M773   Hatfield, Henry, "The Magic Square: Thomas Mann's Doktor
Faustus," Euphorion, 62:413-30, January, 1969.

"Using the hints given by the magic square and the twelve-tone
system, one should envision [Doktor Faustus's] structure both ver-
tically and horizontally. I suggest that there are seven major
themes, or clusters of themes, each of which is operative on seven
levels." (J.R.R.)

DOKTOR FAUSTUS (cont'd)

M774 Heimann, Bodo, "Thomas Manns Doktor Faustus und die Musik-
philosophie Adornos," Deutsche Vierteljahrsschrift für Literaturwissenschaft und Geistesgeschichte, 38:248-66, July, 1964.

"Thomas Mann takes from [Adorno] the articulated perception and
uses it as a symbol. . . . The philosophical-musical constellation
gains both power and freedom by means of multiple references."
(J.R.R.)

M775 Heller, Erich, "Faust's Damnation: The Morality of Knowledge,"
Listener, 67:59-61, 121-3, 168-70, January 11, 18, 25, 1962.

[This is a three part article on the original Faustian doctrine, the
Fausts of Lessing and Goethe, and the Fausts of Paul Valéry and
Thomas Mann.] (K.M.W.)

M776 Höhler, Gertrud, "Der Verdammte, üppig im Fleisch: Ein
Bildzitat in Thomas Manns Doktor Faustus," Euphorion, 62:405-14,
January, 1969.

Leverkühn's tönendes Gemälde in Doktor Faustus is related to
Michelangelo's Last Judgment in the Sistine Chapel." (J.R.R.)

M777 Jørgensen, Aage, "Thomas Mann's Doktor Faustus," Orbis
Litterarum, 20:165-75, No. 2, 1965.

". . . Doktor Faustus is on principle an ambiguous work. . . . any
attempt to characterize the novel which does not emphasize this is
fundamentally one-sided." (J.R.R.)

M778 Kaye, Julian B., "Conrad's Under Western Eyes and Mann's
Doctor Faustus," Comparative Literature, 9:60-5, Winter, 1957.

Mann's novel is consciously and significantly indebted to Conrad's
and has similar techniques and "humanistic values." Both show an
"ironic" and "paradoxical" approval of the liberalism of the West.
The self destructive nakedly "human" and "demonic" hero is seen
from the angle of a good but "unimaginative and passionless" avoidance of "both the diabolical and the divine." (K.W.)

DOKTOR FAUSTUS (cont'd)

M779   Kunne-Ibsch, E., "Die Nietzsche-Gestalt in Thomas Manns Doktor
        Faustus," Neophilologus, 53:176-89, April, 1969.

        "In the person of Adrian only one--even if a very important--aspect
        of the Nietzschean figure is illuminated while 'somehow' much more
        Nietzsche is present in the whole novel." (J.R.R.)

M780   Lehnert, Herbert, "Zur Theologie in Thomas Manns Doktor
        Faustus," Deutsche Vierteljahrsschrift für Literaturwissenschaft
        und Geistesgeschichte, 40:248-56, June, 1966.

        It is doubtful that Mann's fictional treatment of German history could
        objectively clarify his views of Germany and simultaneously permit
        the creation of a fictional world free of its author. (J.R.R.)

M781   Lyon, James K., "Words and Music: Thomas Mann's Tone-Poem
        Doctor Faustus," Western Humanities Review, 13:99-102,
        Winter, 1959.

        Though the leading character of Doctor Faustus was not based on
        Schönberg, "it seems clear that Mann did base most of his theory
        on Schönberg's twelve-tone system via a manuscript" by Dr.
        Theodor Wiesengrund-Adorno; but even here Mann made a large
        number of changes and misrepresentations. (M.H.)

M782   Mann, Michael, "Adrian Leverkühn--Repräsentant oder Antipode?"
        Die Neue Rundschau, 76:202-6, Summer, 1965.

        The prototypes of the political allegory which critics somewhat
        superficially infer in the case of the artist Leverkühn are to be
        found throughout the Mann oeuvre; in Doktor Faustus the formula-
        tion is less unconscious. (R.H.L.)

M783   Mann, Michael, "The Musical Symbolism in Thomas Mann's
        Doctor Faustus," Music Review, 17:314-22, November, 1956.

        "Thomas Mann chose Schönberg's musical world to mirror in it the
        conception of his book and beyond this, to find in it the reflection of
        our present-day cultural crisis in general. . . . The Faustus novel
        is a product of that crisis, not only by virtue of its subject matter
        but even more so by its inner structure, its new approach to literary
        form--in regard to which the principle of montage and the resulting
        overthrow of the novel as an art form have been found symptomatic.

MANN, T.

DOKTOR FAUSTUS (cont'd)

One of the most characteristic forces which are brought into play
in our time . . . is the irrational; and again it is music . . . which
becomes the central symbol for these darker sides of the human
mind. . . ." (D.P.)

M784   Mendelssohn, Peter de, "Tagebuch des Zauberers," Die neue
Rundschau, 66:511-7, June, 1955.

The diary Mann kept while composing Doctor Faustus contains
precise notes of the origin of the idea, compilation of theme and
symbol, techniques and manipulations of the work, private and
public information used, descriptions of acquaintances, distinct
and powerful polemic substantiations, personal difficulties with
composition, notes on the illness which lasted throughout composition, basic motif: nature of sterility, loss of paradise, despair,
the artist and culture. (L.L.)

M785   Müller, Joachim, "Thomas Manns Doktor Faustus: Grundthematik
und Motivgefüge," Euphorion, 54:262-80, No. 3, 1960.

"The epic symbolism, with which the poet can distance himself from
this work which moves him most deeply, and yet remain most deeply
bound to it, surely leaves open the question whether the basic theme
is ultimately religious-theological or human-secular." (J.R.R.)

M786   Nielsen, Birgit S., "Adrian Leverkühns Leben als bewusste
mythische imitatio des Doktor Faustus," Orbis Litterarum,
20:128-58, No. 1, 1965.

"Adrian Leverkühn's psychology and the mythic imitatio of his
predecessor cannot be understood without being acquainted with
Thomas Mann's understanding of the concept of the 'mythic'."
(J.R.R.)

M787   Oates, Joyce C., " 'Art at the Edge of Impossibility': Mann's
Doktor Faustus," Southern Review, 5:375-97, April, 1969.

"The paradox in Mann lies in his commitment to and his strenuous
approval of the dialectical process as a technical means, and his
ultimate mystical belief in the unity of the ego and the world."
(J.R.R.)

DOKTOR FAUSTUS (cont'd)

M788   Peterson, John, "The Role of the Theological Themes in Thomas
        Mann's Doctor Faustus," Discourse, 9:492-515, 1966.

        "These four themes (devil, Apocalypse, Old Testament, and myth-
        ology) play an important role in the understanding of the unity which
        is achieved throughout the novel. To maintain, however, that Mann
        was an expert in these four themes along with all the other motifs
        used would be an ungrounded fallacy." (J.R.R.)

M789   Politzer, Heinz, "Of Time and Doctor Faustus," Monatshefte,
        51:145-55, April-May, 1959.

        "The Faust theme is also deeply committed to the element of time
        . . . external time, the Zeitgeist which shaped and reshaped the
        figure, and internal time, time as a motive and agent of Faust's
        career itself." (J.R.R.)

M790   Puknat, Siegfried B. and E. M. Puknat, "Mann's Doctor Faustus
        and Shakespeare," Research Studies (Washington State University),
        35:148-54, June, 1967.

        "Whether or not the Elizabethan play Love's Labour's Lost and
        sonnets become fully viable in the development of his latter-day
        Faust, Mann left a commentary both on the tantalizing nature of
        the Shakespearean works he chose to manipulate in his fiction and
        on his own narrative techniques in relation to another literature."
        (J.R.R.)

M791   Putz, H. P., "Die teuflische Kunst des Doktor Faustus bei Thomas
        Mann," Zeitschrift für Deutsche Philologie, 82:14-7, No. 3, 1963.

        "Not only the beautiful, but also the real is already possessed by the
        devil and in no other work by Thomas Mann is the boundary between
        artists and so-called solid citizens [Lebensbürger] so blurred."
        (J.R.R.)

M792   Rey, W. H., "Return to Health? 'Disease' in Mann's Doctor
        Faustus," PMLA, 65:21-6, March, 1960.

        "In Doctor Faustus Thomas Mann has laid bare the catastrophe of
        the artist creating out of disease. Should he not for this reason elect
        himself to take the lead toward a new art creating out of health?"
        (D.P.)

DOKTOR FAUSTUS (cont'd)

M793   Rey, William H., "Selbstopfer des Geistes, Fluch und Verheissung
        in Hofmannsthals Der Turm and Thomas Manns Doktor Faustus,"
        Monatshefte, 52:145-57, April-May, 1960.

        Inspired by heroic fearlessness, both authors accept the challenge
        of modern history and make the cultural catastrophe (the disruption
        of spiritual order by chaotic forces) the main theme of their works.
        The question they raise is: Is art still possible in the coming "night
        of mankind" that threatens to swallow up the very image of mankind;
        and what mission befits the artist in this time of extreme danger?
        (K.M.W.)

M794   Schaper, Eva, "A Modern Faust: The Novel in the Ironical Key,"
        Orbis Litterarum, 20:176-204, 1965.

        ". . . Thomas Mann's novels . . . never abandon the outward appear-
        ance of the traditional novel. . . . yet the ironical orientation
        achieves in the end a transformation of this traditional edifice from
        within. . . . For the irony discernible in Thomas Mann's novels
        . . . is not just another aspect of the novel: it is the mode in which
        the whole work in all its complexity is played out." (K.M.W.)

M795   Scher, Steven Paul, "Thomas Mann's 'Verbal Score': Adrian
        Leverkühn's Symbolic Confession," Modern Language Notes,
        82:403-20, October, 1967.

        On pages 207-208 of Mann's Doktor Faustus the "massive yet evanes-
        cent paragraph . . . offers an ingenious 'word picture' of Wagner's
        Prelude [to ACT III of Die Meistersinger von Nürnberg], but simul-
        taneously the emerging musical outline and its various details sym-
        bolically correspond to specific major events and decisions in
        Leverkühn's life." (D.P.)

M796   Sørensen, Bengt Algot, "Thomas Manns Doktor Faustus: Mythos
        und Lebensbeichte," Orbis Litterarum, 13:81-97, 1958.

        A poetically fascinating but entirely one-sided and subjective view
        of German history and the German soul is generated in Doktor
        Faustus by Mann's preference for mythical generalizations in con-
        junction with his fatalism, his inner experiences which he combines
        with external events, and the ideas of Nietzsche, Bertram, Kerényi,
        and others. (K.M.W.)

DOKTOR FAUSTUS (cont'd)

M797   Stout, Harry L., "Lessing's Riccaut and Thomas Mann's Fitelberg,"
German Quarterly, 36:24-30, January, 1963.

Thomas Mann borrowed many elements from the episode which involved Riccaut de la Marlinière in Lessing's Minna von Barnhelm
for his character Saul Fitelberg in Doktor Faustus. The "multiple,
often contradictory aspects of Fitelberg's character give us a portrait
of a person of enormous complexity and significance, beside whom
Riccaut appears extremely uncomplicated." (D.P.)

M798   Tuska, Jon, "The Vision of Doktor Faustus," Germanic Review,
40:277-309, November, 1965.

The American critic Glenway Wescott, taking a narrow view, errs
in wishing to expurgate the "philosophy" in Doktor Faustus. For the
Apocalyptic--not without Nietzschean intermediation--is what informs the total work. (R.H.L.)

M799   Wasserstrom, William, "In Gertrude's Closet," Yale Review,
48:245-65, December, 1958.

In such disparate works as Ulysses and Doctor Faustus, The Castle
and The Stranger, Room at the Top and The Counterfeiters "the essential rhythms inherent in all stories of education reappear." It is
striking to observe "the way Oedipus's restless spirit moves from
cellarage to battlements throughout the drama of our lives and literature, and finally joins Dedalus and Meursault, Leverkühn, Ghost and
Hamlet--in Gertrude's closet." (D.P.)

M800   Wiemann, H., "Thomas Mann and Doktor Faustus," AUMLA,
No. 4, pp. 39-45, 1956.

"It is not true that Thomas Mann with his Doktor Faustus condemned
Germany to all eternity. . . . It is an epoch, a diseased phase in
German history that he condemns, and with it he condemns the er-
roneous beliefs which he himself once held." (K.M.W.)

M801   Williams, William David, "Thomas Mann's Doktor Faustus,"
German Life and Letters, 12:273-81, July, 1959.

"Whether [Mann's] hero, and his country and his race, are damned
or not, is not for him to decide. He has exposed the complex and
insoluble enigma he has taken as his subject, and his task is now
done." (J.R.R.)

DAS EISENBAHNUNGLÜCK

M802 Lainoff, Seymour, "A Note on Mann's 'Railway Accident',"
College English, 18:104-5, November, 1956.

The enlightenment of the narrator of this story has been taken to be
bona fide, but this view can be contradicted if the narrator is understood to be interpreting the events of the accident in a way that ap-
peases his vanity. (E.L.)

ENTTÄUSCHUNG

M803 Geissler, Rolf, "Die verfehlte Wirklichkeit. Thomas Manns
Erzählung 'Enttäuschung'," Wirkendes Wort, 16:323-9,
September-October, 1966.

In this early work Mann is recreating the effect of a confusing
meeting; thus the reader will have to reflect on the references of
isolated remarks in order to grasp the whole. (J.R.R.)

DER ERWÄHLTE

M804 Bercovitch, Sacvan, "Thomas Mann's 'Heavenly Alchemy': The
Politics of The Holy Sinner," Symposium, 20:293-305, Fall, 1966.

"This paper attempts to show that a significant element in The Holy
Sinner--carefully sustained alongside its other, larger themes--is a
political allegory of German guilt and regeneration." (J.R.R.)

M805 Brandt, Thomas O., "Narcissism in Thomas Manns Der Erwählte,"
German Life and Letters, 7:233-41, July, 1954.

"Der Erwählte is Mann himself. His novel is a work of artistry not
of art. It shows a great nobility of form and indifference of substance.
Mann gladly sacrifices truthfulness to beauty, probability to effect,
and objectivity to eclat." (J.R.R.)

M806 Fraiberg, Selma, "Two Modern Incest Heroes," Partisan Review,
28:646-61, Fall-Winter, 1961.

Both Ellison's Invisible Man and Thomas Mann's The Holy Sinner
"are burlesques of the incest myth." In both these tales "the incest
hero rises above the myth by accepting the wish as motive; the heroic
act is the casting off of pretense." (D.P.)

DER ERWÄHLTE (cont'd)

M807   Fürstenheim, E. G., "The Place of Der Erwählte in the Work of Thomas Mann," Modern Language Review, 51:55-70, January, 1956.

Der Erwählte, when studied in the context of Mann's total fiction, is seen as a serious work whose irony is inadequately foiled by humor. (W.T.S.)

M808   Loose, Gerhard, "Glocken über Rom," Modern Language Notes, 74:633-6, November, 1959.

The Kirchenglockenerzgetöse that hails the newly chosen Pope in Thomas Mann's Der Erwählte finds its antecedent more than thirty years earlier in a strong reaction to a musical effect in Hans Pfitzner's Palestrina, Musikalische Legende. (M.J.O.)

M809   McClain, William H., "Ein unveröffentlichter Thomas Mann Brief über den Erwählten," Monatshefte, 54:9-10, January, 1962.

Thomas Mann left little comment on Der Erwählte. In this letter, however, he observes that incest was really a class privilege, as in Egypt, that in ancient Eastern religions the lover was often the son, and that in general this toying with the grotesque ought to be bearable to humanity. (R.H.L.)

M810   Schoolfield, George C., "Thomas Mann and the Honest Pagans," Philological Quarterly, 36:280-5, April, 1957.

For the turning point of his novel Der Erwählte, Mann "looks back to the turning point between the classical and the medieval worlds. It is a twilight world that bears an uncomfortable resemblance to our own." (B.B.)

M811   Stackman, Karl, "Der Erwählte: Thomas Manns Mittelalter-Parodie," Euphorion, 53:61-74, 1959.

The adverse criticism which Mann's Holy Sinner initially encountered was based largely on formal grounds. "If we go beyond the merely formal in this work of Thomas Mann's, we encounter not nihilism, but a totally unreserved opting for the cause of the spirit." (J.R.R.)

DER ERWÄHLTE (cont'd)

M812 Stock, Irwin, "Mann's Christian Parable: A View of The Holy
Sinner," Accent, 14:98-115, Spring, 1954.

"The theme . . . of the close and fruitful relationship of good and
evil is not . . . the novel's only meaning. . . . Before we can have
good and evil at all we must impose a spiritual scheme on the chaos
of Nature. . . ." (J.R.R.)

M813 Wunderlich, Eva C., "Zweimal Gregorius: Thomas Mann und
Hanna Stephan," German Quarterly, 38:640-51, November, 1965.

It appears that among the many other sources of the novel Der
Erwählte, including chiefly the Gregorius of Hartmann von Aue,
one should also include Hanna Stephan's 1940 story Die glückhafte
Schuld. Though there is no hint of ideological identity, there are
several persuasive identities of detail. (R.H.L.)

M814 Wysling, Hans, "Die Technik der Montage zu Thomas Manns
Erwähltem," Euphorion, 57:156-99, 1963.

"Since the sources used by Mann, his notes and pictorial material
are almost completely present and in addition his work on language
and playing with it formed a major charm of this small late work,
it is like no other suited to grant us an insight into Thomas Mann's
manner of creating." (J.R.R.)

M815 Ziolkowski, Theodore, "Hermann J. Weigand and a Letter from
Thomas Mann: The Critical Dialogue," Yale Review, 56:537-49,
June, 1967.

Weigand's comments on The Holy Sinner in Surveys and Soundings
in European Literature drew a letter from Mann which reflects his
admiration for Weigand and plays the game with the critic. With
good humor he points out errors in Weigand's comments on The
Holy Sinner and reveals much of his own source material and
method. (F.L.)

FRIEDRICH UND DIE GROSSE KOALITION

M816   Williams, A., "Thomas Mann's Nationalist Phase: A Study of 'Friedrich und die grosse Koalition'," German Life and Letters, 22:147-55, January, 1969.

"Thomas Mann's way to humanity led through phases of nationalistic rejoicing, patriotic disappointment and personal distress interspersed with moments of acute awareness from which he gained new insight of outstanding value." (J.R.R.)

GEIST UND KUNST

M817   Reed, T. J., "'Geist and Kunst': Thomas Mann's Abandoned Essay on Literature," Oxford German Studies, 1:53-101, 1966.

"Even in this early period, [Mann] was occupied not only with the human or social problem of the artist, but also with the more specific one of the nature of literary art and its function (as distinct from the writer's position in society). And this problem did not resolve itself into the same basic antithesis, but--after a surprising reshuffle--into the new opposition of Geist and Kunst." (J.R.R.)

DIE GESCHICHTEN JAAKOBS

M818   Ewton, Ralph W., Jr., "The Chronological Structure of Thomas Mann's Die Geschichten Jaakobs," Rice University Studies, 50:27-40, Fall, 1964.

"When Mann introduced a vagueness about time into his works it was for an important but rather simple reason: to characterize such a world of myth." (J.R.R.)

M819   Herz, Ida, "Ein Roman wandert aus: Zum Erscheinen von Die Geschichten Jaakobs," German Quarterly, 38:630-9, November, 1965.

There were great difficulties in bringing out the first volume of the Joseph tetralogy in Hitlerian Germany in 1933. The second volume was the last that could be published in Germany. (R.H.L.)

DIE GESCHICHTEN JAAKOBS (cont'd)

M820   Hughes, Kenneth, "Theme and Structure in Thomas Mann's Die
Geschichten Jaakobs, " Monatshefte, 62:24-36, Spring, 1970.

". . . the circularity of the mythical collective is not merely the
theme of the novel; it also contributes the only suitable structure
for its literary representation, and theme and structure are splendidly united as complementary aspects of Die Geschichten Jaakobs. "
(R.H.L.)

GLADIUS DEI

M821   Hoffmann, Ernst Feodor, "Thomas Mann's 'Gladius Dei', "
PMLA, 83:1353-61, October, 1968.

Topical references in this story show that the Munich intellectual
community around 1900 was enacting a "quasi neo-Renaissance, "
and that the central figure is wrong in assuming that the underlying
moral structure of the community agreed with that of the Italian
Renaissance. (R.H.L.)

M822   Stamm, Edith Perry, "Mann's 'Gladius Dei', " Explicator,
23: Item 60, April, 1965.

" 'Gladius Dei' presents a fascinating study in reversals of motifs.
. . . These reversals seem to point to a final interdependence of
the moral and the aesthetic. . . ." (D.P.)

M823   Wolf, Ernest, "Savonarola in München: Eine Analyse von Thomas
Manns 'Gladius Dei'," Euphorion, 64:85-96, No. 1, 1970.

"Hieronymus is a strange reincorporation of Savonarola, who surprisingly appears at the beginning of our century in Munich in the
shape of an Aryan youth. The connections between the hero of
'Gladius Dei' and Savonarola therefore must be gained from allusions
and indirect references. " (J.R.R.)

HERR UND HUND

M824   Braun, Frank Y., "Thomas Mann's Canine Idyl, " Monatshefte,
49:207-11, April-May, 1957.

Scheffauer's statement that the short piece "Herr und Hund" is the
"finest study of the mind of a dog ever written" should be qualified

HERR UND HUND (cont'd)

to read "does contain some of the most literate observations . . .
and . . . intriguing speculations about canis familiaris in German
animal literature." (C.P.)

M825 Mann, Michael, "Allegorie und Parodie in Thomas Manns Idyll
'Herr und Hund'," Monatshefte, 57:336-42, December, 1965-
March, 1966.

This novella is the first artistic reflection of Mann's increased
concern with the bourgeois as a cultural rather than, as in
Betrachtungen eines Unpolitischen, a political creature. We have a
reconciliation between culture and civilization, and a predictive
aversion to idyllic, romanticized nature. (R.H.L.)

    THE HOLY SINNER--See
    DER ERWÄHLTE

    IRONY AND RADICALISM--See
    BETRACHTUNGEN EINES UNPOLITISCHEN

    JOSEPH AND HIS BROTHERS--See
    JOSEPH UND SEINE BRÜDER

    JOSEPH DER ERNÄHRER

M826 Hughes, Kenneth, "The Sources and Function of Serach's Song in
Thomas Mann's Joseph der Ernährer," Germanic Review,
45:126-33, March, 1970.

"Both the West-Ostlicher Divan and the Novelle have contributed
important elements to Serach's song. Nevertheless, the precise
Goethean context into which we must place the song to determine
its structural function is that of the Novelle." (R.H.L.)

M827 Hunt, Thomas, "The Use of Irony in Thomas Mann's Joseph the
Provider," Discourse, 9:367-77, 1966.

"This volume . . . affords the clearest and most complete presentation of Mann's Joseph hero as 'the apotheosis of the ironical life,'
as well as a subtle, tongue-in-cheek presentation by a narrator whose
pompous omniscience is the setting for a half-mocking smile and a
knowing wink." (J.R.R.)

JOSEPH DER ERNÄHRER (cont'd)

M828   Seidlin, Oskar, "Ironische Brüderschaft: Thomas Manns Joseph der Ernährer und Laurence Sternes Tristram Shandy," Orbis Litterarum, 13:44-63, 1958.

Tristram Shandy cannot be regarded as the source of Joseph der Ernährer. However, there is a hidden union between the two writers, a similarity of tone. The gift of humor enables each of them to deal, in the wisest manner possible, with the insoluble problems of human existence. (G.C.)

JOSEPH THE PROVIDER--See
JOSEPH DER ERNÄHRER

JOSEPH UND SEINE BRÜDER

M829   Ackermann, Paul Kurt, "Comments on Joseph und seine Brüder in Some Unpublished Letters from Thomas Mann to René Schickele," Monatshefte, 54:197-200, April-May, 1962.

In the mid-thirties Mann and Schickele exchanged views on Mann's Joseph-novels. Mann esteemed Schickele's critical comments. (R.H.L.)

M830   Apt, S., "Dvoinoe blagoslovenie," Voprosy literatury, 14:133-50, January, 1970.

It is a very difficult task to translate Thomas Mann's tetralogy Joseph And His Brothers, since it contains vocabulary full of Biblical references and an abundant "archeological" lexicon. Also the rhythms within the tetralogy are different and the task of detecting them depends on the erudition of the translator. (V.D.)

M831   Bloch, Adèle, "The Archetypal Influences in Joseph and His Brothers," Germanic Review, 38:151-6, March, 1963.

Mann's interest in mythology was developed only late in life. It was then that he adhered to and gave credit to Jung's theory of archetypes, which is best reflected in the culture-hero Joseph. (R.H.L.)

JOSEPH UND SEINE BRÜDER (cont'd)

M832   Richter, Bernt, "Der Mythos-Begriff Thomas Manns und das
Menschenbild der Josephsromane," Euphorion, 54:411-33, 1960.

The portrayal of the protagonist and the general image of all
mankind in the Joseph tetralogy reflects Mann's socio-pedagogical
intentions and his enlightened humanist strivings. (K.M.W.)

M833   Seidlin, Oskar,"In the Beginning was . . . ? The Origin of Thomas
Mann's Joseph und seine Brüder," Modern Language Notes,
77:493-8, December, 1962.

Although Mann clearly describes the beginnings of his Joseph-saga
as being in 1928 through his re-reading of the biblical passage, and
his recollecting Goethe's statements in Dichtung und Wahrheit on the
Joseph story, other evidence moves the beginning back to 1925.
However, it seems even more likely that the formula of myth and
psychology which guides the tale grew from Mann's reading of "Der
alte Fontane" as early as 1910. (D.P.)

M834   Spininger, Dennis J., "The 'Thamar' Section of Mann's Joseph und
seine Brüder: A Formal Analysis," Monatshefte, 61:157-72,
Summer, 1969.

External evidence, as well as evidence in the Joseph novel, suggests
that the Thamar story may stand as an independent novella. Formal
analysis supports this indication. For example, the closing image
of Thamar complements the initial image of will and decisive character. (R.H.L.)

M835   Sutschkow, Boris, "Roman und Mythos in Thomas Manns Josephs-
legende," Sinn und Form, 21:382-403, March, 1969.

Doubts concerning the nature of man, a burning issue of the 1930's,
are reflected in Mann's Joseph cycle written at the time. (J.R.R.)

M836   Van Doren, Mark, "Joseph and His Brothers, A Comedy in Four
Parts," American Scholar, 26:289-302, Summer, 1957.

Mann's problem in his great comic novel is to make Joseph's vanity
palatable: the triumph of Mann is that we love on every page the
hero that the author himself loves this side of an idolatry that would
destroy the comedy, since comedy admits no gods made on earth.
(W.G.F.)

DER JUNGE JOSEPH

M837   Stockhammer, Morris, "Thomas Mann's Job-Jacob," <u>Judaism</u>,
        8:242-6, 1959.

Mann "so movingly describes the sorrows of Jacob and Joseph,
but, at the same time, humbly bows to the recognition that in spite
of its reprehensibleness, injustice is a divine matter, because it is
a condition of the divine existence of right." (J.R.R.)

KÖNIGLICHE HOHEIT

M838   Frey, Erich A., "An American Prototype in Thomas Mann's
        <u>Königliche Hoheit</u>," <u>Kentucky Foreign Language Quarterly</u>,
        13:125-9, 1966.

"Our investigation points to sufficient parallels to admit the conclusion that the story of the Rockefellers served our author as a
major pattern for his description of the Spoelmanns." (J.R.R.)

M839   Vordtriede, Werner, "A Case of Transposed Heads in Thomas Mann's
        <u>Königliche Hoheit</u>," <u>Modern Language Notes</u>, 74:49-51, January,
        1959.

A misprint of "Greisenkopf" for "Griefenkopf" in most editions of
Mann's story has substituted nonsense for an important ironic symbol. (M.J.O.)

LOTTE IN WEIMAR

M840   Crick, Joyce, "Psycho-Analytic Elements in Thomas Mann's Novel
        <u>Lotte in Weimar</u>," <u>Literature and Psychology</u>, 10:69-75, Summer,
        1960.

The themes of <u>Joseph und seine Brüder</u> lead to the central figures
in Mann's late Goethe novel. Similarly, "in Mann's intellectual
scheme, Freud too holds the balance between the conscious and the
unconscious, and it is Freud who gives Mann the conceptual framework of 'identification' in which to understand his relationship with
his chosen 'father' Goethe." (J.M.D.)

LOTTE IN WEIMAR (cont'd)

M841   Dickson, Keith, "The Technique of a musikalisch-ideeller
Beziehungskomplex in Lotte in Weimar," Modern Language Review,
59:413-24, July, 1964.

The complex of musical-conceptual relationships in Lotte in Weimar,
where "form and content are a perfect unity," justifies Mann's
statement that all his works of art "were always good scores."
(J.R.R.)

M842   Glebe, William V., "The 'Diseased' Artist Achieves a New 'Health':
Thomas Mann's Lotte in Weimar," Modern Language Quarterly,
22:55-62, March, 1961.

In Lotte in Weimar Mann solves the "conflict between art and life";
in the novel Goethe "achieves the great synthesis by transforming
the artist's disease into a creative power. . . ." (G.S.)

M843   Havenith, E., "Bemerkungen zur Struktur des Goetheromans
Lotte in Weimar," Revue des Langues Vivantes, 27:329-41, 1961.

Lotte in Weimar is a study of Goethe's personality in the form of a
novel. Mann attempts to reconcile two opposing aspects of Goethe's
artistic achievement: the Sturm-und-Drang period of Goethe's youth
and the classicism characteristic of the mature artist. (G.C.)

THE MAGIC MOUNTAIN--See
DER ZAUBERBERG

A MAN AND HIS DOG--See
HERR UND HUND

MARIO AND THE MAGICIAN--See
MARIO UND DER ZAUBERER

MARIO UND DER ZAUBERER

M844   Duffy, Charles and Don A. Keister, "Mario and the Magician:
Two Letters by Thomas Mann," Monatshefte, 51:190-2, April-
May, 1959.

In letters to one of the authors in 1945, Mann disavows any symbolical intention in naming Mario's adversary Cipolla. Mann further

MARIO UND DER ZAUBERER (cont'd)

states that Mario carried the pistol--a fact apparently taken for granted in the story--in readiness for someone else, probably a love rival. (R.H.L.)

M845   Hunt, Joel A., "Thomas Mann and Faulkner: Portrait of a Magician," Wisconsin Studies in Contemporary Literature, 8:431-6, Summer, 1967.

Possibly Faulkner's An Error in Chemistry, later reprinted in Knight's Gambit, may show the influence of Mann's Mario und der Zauberer. (P.J.R.)

M846   Matenko, Percy, "The Prototype of Cipolla in Mario und der Zauberer," Italica, 31:133-5, September, 1954.

The prototype of Mann's character Cipolla in Mario und der Zauberer seems to have been the deceitful friar Fra Cipolla in Boccaccio's Decameron (Sixth Day, Story Ten). (D.P.)

M847   Wagener, Hans, "Mann's Cipolla and Earlier Prototypes of the Magician," Modern Language Notes, 84:800-2, 1969.

In Thomas Mann's Mario und der Zauberer "it seems obvious that in his character Cipolla he has taken up literary traditions from Boccaccio's Decameron as well as the universal literary tradition of incorporating politicians as magicians." (D.P.)

MEERFAHRT MIT DON QUIJOTE

M848   Bernd, Clifford A., "Thomas Mann's 'Meerfahrt mit Don Quijote'," German Quarterly, 38:652-9, November, 1965.

This Thomas Mann essay is replete with variants of the typical Mann dichotomy: artist-Philistine. Permeating the whole is the dichotomy in which art, intellect, and meditation are represented by the reading of Cervantes's novel, while vegetative Philistinism is represented by the enjoyment of shipboard life in first class. (R.H.L.)

A RAILWAY ACCIDENT--See
DAS EISENBAHNUNGLÜCK

REFLECTIONS OF A NON-POLITICAL MAN--See
BETRACHTUNGEN EINES UNPOLITISCHEN

ROYAL HIGHNESS--See
KÖNIGLICHE HOHEIT

SCHNEE--See
DER ZAUBERBERG

SCHWERE STUNDE

M849   Daemmrich, Horst S., "Thomas Mann's 'Schwere Stunde' Reconsidered," Papers on Language and Literature, 3:34-41, Winter,
1967.

"A reexamination of the text shows first that the novella is carefully
structured, second, that it skillfully incorporates Schiller's own
accounts of his poor health and the problems he encountered while
working on Wallenstein, and third, that it conveys an accurate portrait of Schiller." (J.R.R.)

SNOW--See
DER ZAUBERBERG

THE TALES OF JACOB--See
DIE GESCHICHTEN JAAKOBS

THEODOR STORM

M850   Bernd, Clifford A., "Keller's Comment on the Schimmelreiter in
Thomas Mann's Essay Theodor Storm: Fact or Fiction?"
Modern Language Notes, 80:635, December, 1965.

In his essay Theodor Storm, Thomas Mann refers to a letter which
"Keller sent to Storm commenting on Storm's Novelle Der Schimmelreiter. But no such letter was ever written." Mann's statement is a
plausible fiction. "What a delightful confusion this is, and what a
splendid example of the dichotomy between art and reality!" (D.P.)

DER TOD IN VENEDIG

M851   Addison, Bill Kaler, "Marlow, Aschenbach, and We," Conradiana,
2:79-81, Winter, 1969-70.

"Marlow in Heart of Darkness and Aschenbach in Death in Venice
both faced death while pursuing life. Wracked with ague, Marlow
looked into impenetrable darkness and did not flinch. . . .
Aschenbach hungered for life so incautiously in cholera-infested
Venice that he fell prey to the disease. . . ." (D.P.)

DER TOD IN VENEDIG (cont'd)

M852 Amory, Frederic, "The Classical Style of Der Tod in Venedig,"
Modern Language Review, 59:399-409, July, 1964.

Mann's knowledge and use of Classical writings and technique increase the discrepancy between form and content in this novella
which can thus be compared with the semi-real autobiographies of
the Alexandrian historians. (J.R.R.)

M853 Baron, Frank, "Sensuality and Morality in Thomas Mann's Tod in
Venedig," Germanic Review, 45:115-25, March, 1970.

Chapter II is essential to the understanding of Aschenbach's development in making form--beauty, sensuality--an end in itself. Thomas
Mann's ideal of equilibrating sensuality and morality may be seen in
his interpretation of Goethe's Wahlverwandtschaften. (R.H.L.)

M854 Braverman, Albert, and Larry Nachman, "The Dialectic of Decadence: An Analysis of Thomas Mann's Death in Venice," Germanic
Review, 45:289-98, November, 1970.

"The profound tragedy of the story lay in the fact that it was, like
Venice, a cul-de-sac; the complete articulation of the problem led
to the inevitable conclusion that there was, after all, no solution."
(J.R.R.)

M855 Church, Margaret, "Death in Venice: A Study in Creativity,"
College English, 23:648-51, May, 1962.

"In Death in Venice Thomas Mann makes some observations about
the artist and his relation to reality which it is the purpose of this
essay to discuss from at least two points of view, the aesthetic and
the psychological." (R.J.G.)

M856 Conley, John, "Thomas Mann on the Sources of Two Passages in
Death in Venice," German Quarterly, 40:152-5, January, 1967.

"The first [passage] is the Latin quotation, which appears in the
opening paragraph. . . . The second passage concerns the image of
the fist and the open hand, which appears in the flash-back and which
might be said to exemplify the whole action of the novelette." (J.R.R.)

DER TOD IN VENEDIG (cont'd)

M857   Cox, Catherine, "Pater's 'Apollo in Picardy' and Mann's Death in
        Venice," Anglia, 86:143-54, Nos. 1-2, 1968-69.

        "Pater's intention in 'Apollo in Picardy' is no less than Mann's in
        Death in Venice; and if Pater's art may suffer by this comparison
        with Mann's, our respect for the theme that he attempted must grow."
        (J.R.R.)

M858   Egri, Peter, "The Function of Dreams and Visions in A Portrait
        and Death in Venice," James Joyce Quarterly, 5:86-102,
        Winter, 1968.

        "The first Joycean and Mannian works in which dreams and visions
        play a decisive role are A Portrait of the Artist as a Young Man and
        Death in Venice. It is not only the autobiographical character of the
        two works, the problem of the relation of the lonely artist to his
        surroundings, the expression of the social, moral and artistic crisis
        in the years before World War I that make a comparison . . . pos-
        sible, but also the fact that the inner exploration of the psychology
        of the artist brought with itself the necessity of laying the basis of a
        new manner of literary representation. The role of dreams and
        visions in building up this new method is the subject of this article."
        (D.P.)

M859   Frey, John R., " 'Die stumme Begegnung': Beobachtungen zur
        Funktion des Blicks im Tod in Venedig," German Quarterly,
        41:177-95, March, 1968.

        The function of glances in Thomas Mann's Tod in Venedig--princi-
        pally those between Aschenbach and Tadzio--is to reflect, anticipate,
        and describe the internal and external events in the story. The
        glance thus serves as a unifying structural force. (R.H.L.)

M860   Gronicka, André von, "Myth plus Psychology: A Style Analysis of
        Death in Venice," Germanic Review, 31:191-205, October, 1956.

        "In the supreme achievement of his Meisternovelle Thomas Mann
        draws equally from . . . the immediate, sensible present and the
        endless vistas of the past, from the fleeting reality of life and the
        timeless reality of art. Throughout he maintains, with an unerring
        touch, a unique equilibrium between the realism of coldly controlled
        observation, of self-critical analysis and that Rausch, that inspired
        creative élan, that 'splendid sensation of uplift' capable of infusing

DER TOD IN VENEDIG (cont'd)

the specters of a mythical past with a new vibrant vitality and thus creates what must be adjudged a masterpiece of 'psychology plus myth'." (D.P.)

M861   Gross, Harvey, "Aschenbach and Kurtz: The Cost of Civilization," Centennial Review, 6:131-43, Spring, 1962.

Conrad's Heart of Darkness and Thomas Mann's Death in Venice "tell of the terrible price man pays for civilization," yet become, through "their stylistic richness and formal perfection," "parables of instruction from which we learn to transform and transfigure the powers which seem, at this anguished moment in history, destined to destroy us." (W.D.)

M862   Hepworth, James B., "Tadzio-Sabazios: Notes on Death in Venice," Western Humanities Review, 17:172-5, Spring, 1963.

Understanding the pervasive use of the myth of Dionysus enables one "to correctly interpret a great amount of the symbolism which hither-to has escaped the eyes of the critics." (R.J.G.)

M863   Kirchberger, Lida, "Death in Venice and the Eighteenth Century," Monatshefte, 58:321-34, Winter, 1966.

There is considerable evidence, both in Thomas Mann's letters and in the work itself, suggesting a link between his Death in Venice and Schiller's uncompleted narrative work, The Ghost-Seer. (R.H.L.)

M864   Kohut, Heinz, "Death in Venice by Thomas Mann: A Story About the Disintegration of the Artistic Sublimation," Psychoanalytic Quarterly, 26:206-28, 1957.

"Death in Venice was written in such a period of stress, and it is the aim of this essay to try to trace in part how the emerging pro-found conflicts of the author were sublimated in the creation of an artistic masterpiece." (J.R.R.)

M865   Krotkoff, Hertha, "Zur Symbolik in Thomas Mann s Tod in Venedig," Modern Language Notes, 82:445-53, October, 1967.

Through Mann's use of poetic license, the multiple meanings of phenomena are made comprehensible. Appearances are clarified in a very literal sense and also associations are suggested to the

DER TOD IN VENEDIG (cont'd)

reader that he might otherwise only suspect to exist but not fully consider. (K.M.W.)

M866   Lehnert, Herbert, "Another Note on 'Motus Animi Continuus' and the Clenched-Fist Image in Der Tod in Venedig, " German Quarterly, 40:452-3, May, 1967.

"It appears likely to me that both sources, Mann's own remembrance of Beer-Hofmann talking about Hofmannsthal and the Goethe passage, were fused." (J.R.R.)

M867   Lehnert, Herbert, "Note on Mann's Der Tod in Venedig and the Odyssey, " PMLA, 80:306-7, June, 1965.

The quotation "oft veränderten Schmuck und warme Bäder und Ruhe" in Mann's Der Tod in Venedig is taken from a German translation of Homer's Odyssey (VIII.249). (D.P.)

M868   Lehnert, Herbert, "Thomas Mann's Early Interest in Myth and Erwin Rohde's Psyche, " PMLA, 79:297-304, June, 1964.

"In Der Tod in Venedig, myth is used with extraordinary effectiveness to complement naturalism." "Thomas Mann's pencil-marked copy of Erwin Rohde's Psyche and . . . excerpts from the book . . . found in notes Mann took" reveal Rohde's book as a major source of mythological material for Der Tod in Venedig. (D.P.)

M869   Lehnert, Herbert, "Thomas Mann's Own Interpretations of Der Tod in Venedig and Their Reliability, " Rice University Studies, 50:41-60, Fall, 1964.

"But most of Mann's self-interpretations view the work on one level while its value lies in its play on several. The simplified aspect always offers some critical insight but it leaves the work tarnished; the reader cannot be blamed for taking the author's interpretations more seriously than those written by others. Therefore, criticising the self-criticism is worthwhile because it helps to set the work free so that it may be viewed in its freshness." (J.R.R.)

DER TOD IN VENEDIG (cont'd)

M870 McClain, William H., "Wagnerian Overtones in Der Tod in Venedig," Modern Language Notes, 79:481-95, December, 1964.

In reading Mann's Der Tod in Venedig "one cannot but be struck by numerous parallels in form and content between his touching account of Aschenbach's passion and death in Venice and the many works of Wagner which tell of individuals who suffered and died for love particularly, of course, his moving version of the Tristan-story and his portrayal of Brünhilde's Liebestod and the end of Götterdämmerung. The exploration of these parallels leads to fascinating new insights into the larger meaning of Mann's strange tale and also enables one to see its final scene in a new light." (D.P.)

M871 McNamara, Eugene, "Death in Venice: The Disguised Self," College English, 24:233-4, December, 1962.

Mann's story "can be read as a parable of the unexamined life and its dangers." (R.J.G.)

M872 McWilliams, J. R., "The Failure of a Repression: Thomas Mann's Tod in Venedig," German Life and Letters, 20:233-41, April, 1967.

"In Der Tod in Venedig, more than any other major work, the author dispenses with the external story-situation and concentrates on the hero's psychic conflict. The tale represents the author's deepest penetration into the psyche of the artist figure and reveals Mann to be strikingly perceptive in the use of the psychology of his time." (K.M.W.)

M873 Mautner, Franz H., "Thomas Mann über Tod in Venedig," Monatshefte, 50:256-7, October, 1958.

"One shudders when one thinks of the rising flood of interpretations now becoming common which have no basis other than the great intellectual agility of the literary interpreter. . . ." (J.R.R.)

M874 Michael, Wolfgang F., "Stoff und Idee im Tod in Venedig," Deutsche Vierteljahrsschrift für Literaturwissenschaft und Geistesgeschichte, 33:13-9, April, 1959.

Having outlined the many sources for material included in Death in Venice "we would much rather turn to only the conceptual content which this material had to serve." (J.R.R.)

DER TOD IN VENEDIG (cont'd)

M875　Moeller, Hans-Bernhard, "Thomas Manns venezianische Götterkunde, Plastik und Zeitlosigkeit," Deutsche Vierteljahrsschrift für Literaturwissenschaft und Geistesgeschichte, 40:184-205, June, 1966.

"Elements from the life of Goethe, of Platen and of Mahler are subordinated to the idea of a novella. . . . On many levels relationships are reflected and refracted so that truths artistically become apparent which can be formulated in direct statements." (J.R.R.)

M876　Seyppel, Joachim H., "Two Variations on a Theme: Dying in Venice," Literature and Psychology, 7:8-12, February, 1957.

Thomas Mann's Death in Venice and Ernest Hemingway's Across the River and Into the Trees reflect the "tragic experience of the 'mystical union' of beauty and death, of sex and death, with which psychologists have long been familiar." (R.A.B.)

M877　Slochower, Harry, "Thomas Mann's Death in Venice," American Imago, 26:99-122, Summer, 1969.

Aschenbach's homoerotic impulses are transformed into his "dream" of falling in love with Tadzio, but this scenario does not reflect the sublimation of Mann's own pathological pressures. More properly, Mann's artistry takes him beyond "substitute gratification" to a point of "secondary autonomy." (J.M.D.)

M878　Stavenhagen, Lee, "The Name Tadzio in Der Tod in Venedig," German Quarterly, 35:20-3, January, 1962.

"Speculation on the vast complex of meanings represented by the boy will be beyond the scope of this paper, but it is clear that any interpretation of Mann's message must take into account the symbolic and allegorical associations of the name Tadzio." (J.R.R.)

M879　Stelzmann, Rainulf A., "Eine Ironisierung Nietzsches in Thomas Manns Der Tod in Venedig," South Atlantic Bulletin, 35:16-21, No. 3, 1970.

"Thomas Mann--so we believe we are able to show--weaves the principal theme of Nietzsche's first period, the already mentioned opposition of the Dionysian and the Apollonian, into the structure of his novella and at the same time ironically keeps his distance from it." (J.R.R.)

DER TOD IN VENEDIG (cont'd)

M880   Stelzmann, Rainulf A., "Thomas Mann's Death in Venice: Res et Imago," Xavier University Studies, 3:160-7, 1964.

"The following essay . . . will represent Death in Venice as an exercise in, and a masterpiece of, Hegelian logic and irony." (J.R.R.)

M881   Tarbox, Raymond, "Death in Venice: The Aesthetic Object as Dream Guide," American Imago," 26:123-44, Summer, 1969.

Mann's work is a notable example of the "depressive response" in literature. Aschenbach finally ejects the "threatening and diseased elements" of mind and enters the "sleep phase" of the "ecstatic suicidal process" where he can "fully relax and enjoy the fantasy of rejoining the mother and sleeping at her breast." (J.M.D.)

M882   Thomas, R. Hinton, "Die Wahlverwandtschaften and Mann's Der Tod in Venedig," Publications of the English Goethe Society, 24:101-30, 1955.

"The fact is that such thematic and stylistic features of Die Wahlverwandtschaften as reappear in Der Tod in Venedig are so transformed as to be unrecognizable without forewarning. . . . We are here touching on a problem central to all Mann's work and thought, the problem of parody." (J.R.R.)

M883   Traschen, Isadore, "The Uses of Myth in Death in Venice," Modern Fiction Studies, 11:165-79, Summer, 1965.

Mann's Death in Venice "embodies two primary myths, the Apollonian-Dionysian and the monomyth. . . . Death in Venice is the first [tale] to use the mythic method as a way of giving shape and significance to contemporary history by manipulating a continuous parallel between contemporaneity and antiquity" an end which Mann achieves by integrating "the monomyth into the Apollonian-Dionysian mythology." (D.P.)

M884   Urdang, Constance, "Faust in Venice: The Artist and the Legend in Death in Venice," Accent, 18:253-67, Autumn, 1958.

Mann embraces the Romantic view of the artist, "cursed as Faust was cursed, by his artist nature," who must "actively seek out and

DER TOD IN VENEDIG (cont'd)

embrace evil" and then be punished for the guilt of his questing nature. Gustav Aschenbach thought he had escaped this fate, "only to find at the end that it cannot be avoided." (F.J.C.)

M885 Vordtriede, Werner, "Richard Wagners Tod in Venedig," Euphorion, 52:378-96, 1959.

"From a work as great as that of Wagner many possible roads lead into the future. One, and the one closest to Thomas Mann, is the road into artistic nihilism as the ultimate consequence of Tristanizing surrender (Auflösung). The experience of Goethe in his education protected Thomas Mann from this." (J.R.R.)

M886 Wysling, Hans, "Aschenbachs Werke: Archivalische Untersuchungen an einem Thomas Mann-Satz," Euphorion, 59:272-314, March, 1966.

The list of works ascribed to Aschenbach at the start of the second chapter of Death in Venice all refer to works planned by Mann during the years 1900-1911. (J.R.R.)

TONIO KRÖGER

M887 Furst, Lilian R., "Thomas Mann's Tonio Kröger: A Critical Reconsideration," Revue des Langues Vivantes, 27:232-40, 1961.

"Yet even long after its weaknesses and one-sidedness have been recognised and rationally acknowledged, Tonio Kröger for better or worse continues to hold a special place in our hearts. . . . who would dare to judge a work of art by the rational standards of the intellect alone?" (J.R.R.)

M888 McWilliams, James R., "Conflict and Compromise: Tonio Kröger's Paradox," Revue des Langues Vivantes, 32:376-83, 1966.

"Tonio comes forth as a fallible human being, who, like all of us, utters words which do not always correspond with his innermost feelings. His ambiguous pronouncements and the extent to which he fails to back them up by deeds reveal a breach in his nature which demands careful investigation." (J.R.R.)

MANN, T.

TONIO KRÖGER (cont'd)

M889 Rosenhaupt, Hans, "Thomas Mann's Interest in Translation,"
History of Ideas News Letter, 3:60-3, July, 1957.

[A report on information given by Mann in 1941 to aid in translating
a passage from Tonio Kröger.] (E.L.)

M890 Swales, M. W., "Punctuation and the Narrative Mode: Some Remarks
on Tonio Kröger," Forum for Modern Language Studies, 6:235-42,
July, 1970.

Tonio Kröger's whole development . . . on the psychological and
human level . . . is articulated in terms of Tonio's relationship to
his whole being . . . ; on the artistic level it is articulated in terms
of a relationship to language. . . . Hence, the narrative mode is a
crucial embodiment of the theme. And perhaps even such a seemingly trivial factor as punctuation, as the use of three dots, helps
to establish that mode and, above all, its supremely important
temporal function." (D.P.)

M891 Weigand, Paul, "Thomas Mann's Tonio Kröger and Kleist's Über
Das Marionettentheater," Symposium, 12:133-48, Spring-Fall, 1959.

"In conclusion, while Thomas Mann's indebtedness to Kleist could
not be demonstrated through external means, Mann's deep and enduring interest in Tonio Kröger clearly speak for the presence of
influence." (B.B.)

M892 Wetzel, Heinz, "The Seer in the Spring: On Tonio Kröger and The
Waste Land," Revue de Littérature Comparée, 44:322-32, July-
September, 1970.

In both Mann's Tonio Kröger and Eliot's The Waste Land, published
respectively in 1903 and 1921 "the presentation of the 'waste land'
and of the reasons for its existence are largely identical. . . ." A
comparison of the works "illustrates the growing universality of
historical consciousness, and of the resignation and lethargy resulting from it between the beginning of the century and the end of World
War I." (D.P.)

TONIO KRÖGER (cont'd)

M893   Wilson, Kenneth G., "The Dance as Symbol and Leitmotiv in Thomas Mann's Tonio Kröger," Germanic Review, 29:282-7, December, 1954.

In Tonio Kröger Mann employs the dance [quadrille] "as symbolic act" and as leitmotiv. In both cases the dance represents the "ordinary human relationships" from which the artist, Kröger, is excluded." (J.R.B.)

M894   Witthoft, Brucia, "Tonio Kröger and Muybridge's Animals in Motion," Modern Language Review, 62:459-61, July, 1967.

Mann seems to have taken as his model for Hans Hansen's horse books in Tonio Kröger Eadweard Muybridge's Animals in Motion (1899). (J.R.R.

THE TRANSPOSED HEADS--See
DIE VERTAUSCHTEN KÖPFE

TRISTAN

M895   Hermand, Jost, "Peter Spinell," Modern Language Notes, 79:439-47, October, 1964.

Peter Altenberg, an almost forgotten turn-of-the-century writer, is the probable model for Detlev Spinell in Thomas Mann's Tristan. (J.R.R.)

M896   Kirchberger, Lida, "Thomas Mann's Tristan," Germanic Review, 36:282-97, December, 1961.

Among such influences on Thomas Mann at the turn of the century as Schopenhauer, Nietzsche, and Wagner, must be included that of E. T. A. Hoffmann. Details in Tristan concerning the nature of the artist are in many cases parallel to those in Rat Krespel and other Hoffmann narratives. (R.H.L.)

M897   Witte, Karsten, " 'Das ist echt! Eine Burleske!' Zur Tristan-Novelle von Thomas Mann," German Quarterly, 41:660-72, November, 1968.

Tristan, in its essence and in Thomas Mann's own words, is a burlesque, the characteristic of which is incongruence of form--opposition between object and treatment. Classic myth and Christian

TRISTAN (cont'd)

symbolism are the principal agents of the pervasive discrepancy. The target of the burlesque is Richard Wagner's Tristan und Isolde. (R.H.L.)

DIE VERTAUSCHTEN KÖPFE

M898   Baum, Georgina, "Ironie und Thomas Manns Erzählung Die vertauschten Köpfe," Weimarer Beiträge, 12:446-59, May-June, 1966.

As in the Joseph tetralogy, Mann here too employs "an ironically superior view which, coming from a sunken past, is turned toward a cheerful future." (J.R.R.)

M899   Schulz, Siegfried A., "Die vertauschten Köpfe: Thomas Manns indische Travestie," Euphorion, 57:245-71, 1963.

Mann's version of the Indian tale introduces substantive changes, which reflect the influence of Schopenhauer, Nietzsche, and Wagner on Mann. (K.M.W.)

M900   Wilhelm, Friedrich, "Thomas Mann über seine indische Legende," Euphorion, 64:399-403, 1970.

Further evidence confirms that Mann did indeed think of Goethe's Paria trilogy when he composed his novella The Transposed Heads. (J.R.R.)

M901   Willson, A. Leslie, "Thomas Mann's Die vertauschten Köpfe: The Catalyst of Creation," Monatshefte, 49:313-21, November, 1957.

The Transposed Heads treats the themes of wickedly innocent seduction, the interrelated influence of mind and body as well as intellect and beauty, and beguilement and guilt. "The catalyst of his imagination has combined beauty and spirit to form truth." (C.S.P.)

A VOYAGE WITH DON QUIXOTE--See
MEERFAHRT MIT DON QUIJOTE

A WEARY HOUR--See
SCHWERE STUNDE

YOUNG JOSEPH--See
DER JUNGE JOSEPH

DER ZAUBERBERG

M902   Basilius, Harold A., "Mann's Naphta-Settembrini and the Battle of the Books," Modern Fiction Studies, 14:415-21, Winter, 1968-69.

"Thus does Thomas Mann weave and crisscross and transmute diverse and disparate materials relating to two early sixteenth century personages (Pfefferkorn and Reuchlin) into projections of two characters (Settembrini and Naphta) in his twentieth century novel." (J.R.R.)

M903   Braun, Frank X., "A Lesson in Articulation in Thomas Mann's Zauberberg," Monatshefte, 58:124-30, Summer, 1966.

An ironic educational detail of this Bildungsroman consists in the omnipresent author's discreet but telling supplementation of his hero's static and indiscriminate description of Peeperkorn. (R.H.L.)

M904   Brennan, Joseph Gerard, "Three Novels of Dépaysement," Comparative Literature, 22:223-36, Summer, 1970.

". . . much literature has been made round the notion that a man's being taken out of his element, finding himself suddenly transported to exotic soil, can lead to an important shift in his moral center of gravity. This special sense of dépaysement is common to André Gide's L'Immoraliste, Henry James's The Ambassadors, and Thomas Mann's Der Zauberberg. . . ." (D.P.)

M905   Eis, Ruth, and Karl S. Guthke, "Naphtas Pietà: Eine Bemerkung zum Zauberberg," German Quarterly, 33:220-3, May, 1960.

A pietà in the regional museum at Bonn must have been the model for the one described in the sixth chapter of Thomas Mann's Magic Mountain. (J.R.R.)

M906   Furst, Lilian R., "Italo Svevo's La Coscienza di Zeno and Thomas Mann's Der Zauberberg," Contemporary Literature, 9:492-506, Autumn, 1968.

"The two novels represent, each in its own way, fundamental investigations into the condition of modern man: both take as the central figure an ordinary man, both envisage the problem in terms of disease and health, and both are major . . . twentieth-century novel[s]." (J.R.R.)

DER ZAUBERBERG (cont'd)

M907   Gaertner, Johannes A., "Dialectic Thought in Thomas Mann's
The Magic Mountain," German Quarterly, 38:605-18, November,
1965.

The dialectical process in The Magic Mountain inevitably produces
cancellations and paradoxes--it leads nowhere, even as overinvolve-
ment does. Mann instead prefers an attitude of balance, of intelligent non-commitment. (R.H.L.)

M908   Guthke, Karl S., "Thomas Mann on his Zauberberg: An Unpublished
Letter to Hans M. Wolff," Neophilologus, 44:120-1, April, 1960.

[This is the German text of a previously unpublished letter dated
November 25, 1950, which supplements Mann's Princeton lecture
on the Zauberberg.] (F.J.P.)

M909   Hallamore, Joyce, "Zur Siebenzahl in Thomas Manns Zauberberg, "
German Quarterly, 35:17-9, January, 1962.

"All these examples are taken from the magic world of The Magic
Mountain and point to the snaring, the magic, the timelessness of
this fairy-tale world." (J.R.R.)

M910   Hatfield, Henry, "Castorp's Dream and Novalis, " History of Ideas
News Letter, 1:9-11, 1954.

". . . the climax of Mann's novel, [The Magic Mountain], Hans
Castorp's vision in the snow, has a prototype in one of the high
points in Novalis's work, the fifth of his 'Hymns to Night' (1800)."
(G.C.)

M911   Hatfield, Henry, "Drei Randglossen zu Thomas Manns Zauberberg, "
Euphorion, 56:365-72, No. 4, 1962.

(1) The translation of a Whitman poem into French created the necessary distance for Castorp to enter an erotic conversation. (2) "In
many a respect Naphta is different from [his model, the Hungarian
critic] Lukács. . . . But one understands The Magic Mountain better
if one is aware of the 'Lukács-components' in Naphta." (3) Qualities
derived from a real person were used as the model for the wounded
officer in Mann's Herr und Hund and subsequently divided between
Castorp and Ziemssen in The Magic Mountain. (J.R.R.)

DER ZAUBERBERG   (cont'd)

M912   Hindus, Milton, "The Duels in Mann and Turgenev," Comparative
Literature, 11:308-12, Fall, 1959.

"Faced with a problem in the resolution of the plot of The Magic
Mountain similar to one found in Fathers and Sons, Mann solved it
in a manner containing so many detailed resemblances to Turgenev's
solution as to suggest clearly that he used the Russian author as his
model." (J.R.R.)

M913   Hirschbach, Frank D., "The Education of Hans Castorp,"
Monatshefte, 46:25-34, January, 1954.

"But one might well . . . ask the question in what respects Hans is
really a changed person when he descends from the Magic Mountain
in the fall of 1914." (J.R.R.)

M914   Hunt, Joel A., "The Walpurgisnacht Chapter: Thomas Mann's First
Conclusion," Modern Language Notes, 76:826-9, December, 1961.

The first conclusion of the Walpurgisnacht chapter of Der Zauberberg
"throws into sharper focus the original [comical and satirical] intentions of Thomas Mann in writing this novel; its deletion testifies . . .
to the alteration of this conception" to make the novel to a greater
extent "a chronicle of the European spiritual crisis of the years preceding the first World War." (D.P.)

M915   Koopmann, Helmut, "Die Kategorie des Hermetischen in Thomas
Manns Roman Der Zauberberg," Zeitschrift für deutsche Philologie,
80:404-22, 1961.

"Important for us is a statement by Thomas Mann that specifically
his 'sanatorium novel' forms a connecting link between Buddenbrooks,
the realistic work of his youth, and the manifestly mythological work
of his advanced age, namely, the Joseph-novels. . . . In the late
work the mytholygising is obvious--where and how could the mythical
already be hiding [in The Magic Mountain], and where does it become
evident?" (J.R.R.)

M916   Kratz, Henry, "A Methodological Critique of W. R. Maurer's 'Names
from The Magic Mountain'," Names, 11:20-5, March, 1963.

"There are two basic considerations in analyzing fictional proper
names. . . . First, one must distinguish between names which the

DER ZAUBERBERG   (cont'd)

author borrows from already existing proper names and those which
the author freely invents. Second, one must exercise every care in
making statements regarding the connotations conveyed by the names
in question." (K.M.W.)

M917   Lehnert, Herbert, "Hans Castorps Vision: Eine Studie zum Aufbau
        von Thomas Manns Roman Der Zauberberg," Rice Institute
        Pamphlet, 47:1-37, April, 1960.

        "Hans Castorp's development experiences a moment where the tradi-
        tion of Goethe becomes vital for him. . . . But . . . he glides down
        with very little resistance into Romantic 'one-sidedness' and seals
        his fall with his surrender to his nation's enthusiasm on the battle-
        field. The realization of Humanität is a question put to the future."
        (J.R.R.)

M918   Loose, Gerhard, "Ludovico Settembrini and Soziologie der Leiden:
        Notes on Thomas Mann's Zauberberg," Modern Language Notes,
        83:420-9, April, 1968.

        In Der Zauberberg not only Ludovico Settembrini but also his father
        and his grandfather have been endowed with traits of the nineteenth
        century historical figure Luigi Settembrini. In Der Zauberberg
        Settembrini echoes ideas on suffering advanced by Franz Carl Müller-
        Lyer in his Soziologie der Leiden, first published in 1914. (D.P.)

M919   Mann, Michael, "Eine unbekannte 'Quelle' zu Thomas Manns
        Zauberberg," Germanisch-Romanische Monatsschrift, 15:409-13,
        October, 1965.

        [Mann's son suggests that his father drew from the text of Mahler's
        "Song of the Earth" in describing Hans Castorp's dream world.]
        (J.R.R.)

M920   Maurer, Warren R., "Another View of Literary Onomastics,"
        Names, 11:106-14, June, 1963.

        Henry Kratz in his "A Methological Critique of W. R. Maurer's
        'Names from The Magic Mountain'," Names, 11:20-5, has provided
        "a rigid set of rules intended to apply with equal precision to every
        author. . . . I consider well-chosen character names to be an integral
        part of a literary work of art . . . best . . . studied by a combination
        of literary criticism and onomastics. . . . their validity can . . . be

DER ZAUBERBERG (cont'd)

enhanced by a conscientious effort to avoid conjecture which isn't
supported either by the author, his circumstances or the work itself."
(D.P.)

M921　Maurer, Warren R., "Names from The Magic Mountain," Names,
9:248-59, December, 1961.

Thomas Mann chose or invented his fascinating character names in
The Magic Mountain with meticulous care. "Whether based on Greek
mythology, history, the Bible, Latin grammar, word play, folklore,
or the animal, vegetable, and mineral realms, they comprise an
important strand of the Romanteppich Zauberberg. . . ." (D.P.)

M922　Norman, Arthur M. Z., " 'Seven' Symbolism in The Magic Mountain,"
Monatshefte, 47:360, November, 1955.

"The insistent use of the seven symbol reiterates the allegorical
nature of the book, pointing up the flow of time as it matures the hero
Castorp. . . ." (J.R.R.)

M923　Passage, Charles E., "Hans Castorp's Musical Incantation,"
Germanic Review, 38:238-56, May, 1963.

The five recorded musical selections which Castorp plays in Chapter
VII of the Magic Mountain have special significance. The first four
recapitulate the novel through the death of Hans's inseparable friend,
Joachim. The fifth presages Hans's battlefield death. (R.H.L.)

M924　Rebelsky, Freda Gould, "Coming of Age in Davos: An Analysis of
the Maturation of Hans Castorp in Thomas Mann's The Magic
Mountain," American Imago, 18:413-21, Winter, 1961.

". . . Hans Castorp, the hero of The Magic Mountain, appears at the
beginning of the book as a person withdrawn from active life, passive,
depressive." In the novel he grows to become a " 'delicate child of
life,' a genius in the world of experience, a more active human being.
. . . he moves from withdrawal to activity and developing competence,
from dependence to independence. . . . he moves through numerous
career choices, intellectual growth, and types of interests to his final
choice of career." However, Hans "never completely outgrew being
'life's delicate child'." (D.P.)

MANN, T.

DER ZAUBERBERG (cont'd)

M925   Roth, Maria C., "Mynheer Peeperkorn in the Light of Schopenhauer's Philosophy," Monatshefte, 58:335-44, Winter, 1966.

Mynheer Peeperkorn in The Magic Mountain reflects at several crucial points, including his suicide, an oblique statement of Schopenhauer's philosophy. This creates a paradoxical tension with respect to the general--and Hans Castorp's--affirmation of life. (R.H.L.)

M926   Schultz, H. Stefan, "On the Interpretation of Thomas Mann's Der Zauberberg," Modern Philology, 52:110-22, November, 1954.

The Magic Mountain has sometimes been interpreted as Mann's declaration of his conversion to democracy, and sometimes as his warning of the bourgeois decadence of the West. However, the protagonist of the novel, Hans Castorp, is a Nietzschean character; indeed, certain Nietzschean ideas seem almost to provide "an outline" for the novel. Mann's imagination was impelled and guided by the Nietzschean vision of the Romantic epoch in Europe, and this provides the true "time" and true subject of the novel. (A.A.S.)

M927   Seidler, Ingo, "Zauberberg und Strafkolonie: Zum Selbstmord zweier reaktionärer Absolutisten," Germanisch-Romanische Monatsschrift, 19:94-103, 1969.

["The following work takes related situations in the prose of Mann and Kafka as the occasion for demonstrating by means of intensive parallel interpretations philosophically significant similarities and methodologically no less significant oppositions between the models, the works and their authors."] (J.R.R.)

M928   Struc, Roman S., "Sanatorium Arktur: Fedin's Polemic Against Thomas Mann's Magic Mountain," Research Studies (Washington State University), 35:301-7, December, 1967.

"Fedin's polemic . . . is misguided and strikes at best at issues on which both authors agree: life as man's trench war against the forces of death. But with a difference: for Fedin sees the forces of life and death as irreconcilable and hostile entities, Thomas Mann sees death as part of a never-ending spiral of decline and regeneration." (J.R.R.)

DER ZAUBERBERG (cont'd)

M929 Struc, Roman S., "The Threat of Chaos: Stifter's Bergkristall and Thomas Mann's 'Schnee'," Modern Language Quarterly, 24:323-32, December, 1963.

"The affinity between these two seemingly so diverse authors is not limited exclusively to similarities between Bergkristall and 'Schnee,' but it also extends to the backgrounds and the philosophical tenets of these two writers." (G.S.)

M930 Stuckenschmidt, Dierk, " 'Schlüsselbilder' in Thomas Manns Zauberberg," Monatshefte, 58:310-20, Winter, 1966.

Certain recurrent images in Der Zauberberg serve to explicate the basic ideas of the novel. Thus the sanatorium is implicitly and inferentially equated with the classical underworld, with a monastery, with a prison, with a net for catching birds--forces which threaten to deprive Hans Castorp of his power of decision. (R.H.L.)

M931 Tate, Lucile C., "Death, the Cradle of Life," Brigham Young University Studies, 8:303-6, 1968.

"Magic Mountain is not only a novel, but a tremendous 'musical' experience, and its message is vital to our day. We desperately need its dream of man rising anew from his state of disease, war and death to a wholeness and harmony." (J.R.R.)

M932 Wilson, John R., M.B., F.R.C.S., "Tuberculosis and the Creative Writer," JAMA, 196:161-4, April 4, 1966.

Three novels, Ships that Pass in the Night, by Beatrice Harraden, published in 1894; The Magic Mountain, by Thomas Mann, published in 1924; and The Rack, by A. E. Ellis, published in 1958, describe the rise and fall of the sanatarium system for the treatment of tuberculosis. Ships that Pass in the Night is the first fictional treatment of the theme, published just ten years after Koch's isolation of the tubercle bacillus. It lacks literary distinction. The Magic Mountain, the most famous sanatarium novel, describes the system at its height just before World War I, with an air of mysterious unreality; and The Rack, which describes sanatarium life with harrowing realism, is the last great novel on the subject. (D.P.)

DER ZAUBERBERG (cont'd)

M933   Zinberg, Dorothy S. and Norman E. Zinberg, "Hans Castorp:
Identity Crisis Without Resolution," American Imago, 20:393-402,
Winter, 1963.

The "amorphous quality of Hans Castorp's self-concept" is implicit
in the formative events of his early life and never resolved in his
later life. Castorp "will do only what is expected of him. He never
faces up to being a person in the real world, his resolution is only
partial." (D.P.)

MANNING, FREDERIC

M934   Hergenhan, L. T., "Novelist at War: Frederic Manning's Her
Privates We," Quadrant, 66:19-29, August, 1970.

An understanding of "the personal experience and attitudes which
determined the particular direction and pervading qualities of
Manning's novel" reveals that "war, to Manning, was not simply
destructive but also a revelation of part of his own identity and of
the nature of his fellows. . . ." (G.C.)

M935   Hergenhan, L. T., "Some Unpublished Letters from T. E. Lawrence
to Frederic Manning," Southerly, 23:242-52, No. 4, 1963.

[Printed here are nine letters, all written from 1930-1934.] (D.P.)

MANSFIELD, KATHERINE

M936   Baldeshwiler, Eileen, "Katherine Mansfield's Theory of Fiction,"
Studies in Short Fiction, 7:421-32, Summer, 1970.

". . . a coolly 'objective' view of one's subject is not enough. . . .
What is essential is to penetrate one's subject, not to take a flat
view of it; thus feelings, and objects as well, must be contemplated
--or rather 'submitted to'--until one is truly lost in them." (K.M.W.)

M937   Bowen, Elizabeth, "A Living Writer," Cornhill Magazine,
1010:120-34, Winter, 1956-1957.

Katherine Mansfield "had no desire whatever to be 'spared' life"
although "her writing already had touched perfection. . . . She would
have been bound to go on experimenting . . . her art was tentative,
responsive, exploratory. . . ." (M.H.)

M938   Brophy, Brigid, "Katherine Mansfield's Self-Deception," <u>Michigan</u>
<u>Quarterly Review</u>, 5:38-93, Spring, 1966.

Miss Mansfield projected a variety of personalities for herself. Her
journal and letters to Murry and Mr. Alper's biography of her reveal
her true personality as "at once more attractive, more cogent, and
more bitingly tragic" than we have believed before. (D.P.)

M939   Garlington, Jack, "Katherine Mansfield: The Critical Trend,"
<u>Twentieth Century Literature</u>, 2:51-61, July, 1956.

[This article surveys the trends in critical reception of Katherine
Mansfield's work from the early 1920's to the present.] In the last
two years of her life, and for some time thereafter, her reputation
was very high; in the late forties onwards the tendency has been to
deplore her "sentimentality," her lack of compression, her "dated-
ness." Her historical importance in the development of the short
story is recognized; she is now less frequently included in antholo-
gies. (D.P.)

M940   Haferkamp, Berta, "Zur Bildsprache Katherine Mansfields,"
<u>Die Neueren Sprachen</u>, 18:221-39, May, 1969.

The manifold function of Katherine Mansfield's imagery appeals both
to the emotions and to the reason of the reader. (J.R.R.)

M941   Hudson, Stephen, "First Meetings with Katherine Mansfield,"
<u>Cornhill Magazine</u>, 170:202-12, Autumn, 1958.

[This is a fictitious meeting between Katherine Mansfield and a "Mr.
Schiff."] (G.C.)

M942   Kleine, Don W., "An Eden for Insiders: Katherine Mansfield's New
Zealand," <u>College English</u>, 27:201-9, October, 1965.

"Expert in the weathers, mental and circumstantial, which authen-
ticate a child's milieu . . . [Mansfield] exerts at times a unique,
puzzling power over the memory, refreshing it to remind us we
forgot, fusing two worlds . . . in a perception of loss at once por-
tended and lamented." (G.C.)

M943   Lea, F. A., "Murry and Marriage," D. H. Lawrence Review,
        2:1-23, Spring, 1969.

        Like Katherine Mansfield, Murry was a social déraciné, devoid
        when they met, not merely of the ease of living which goes with a
        familiar society, but of all those accepted standards of good and
        bad, right and wrong, which most of us assimilate unconsciously
        and few of us ever question." [Includes a letter by Murry on
        marriage.] (D.P.)

M944   Murry, Mary Middleton, "Katherine Mansfield and John Middleton
        Murry," London Magazine, 6:69-71, April, 1959.

        [These are recollections of Katherine Mansfield and her second
        husband, John Middleton Murry.] (D.P.)

M945   Sutherland, Ronald, "Katherine Mansfield: Plagiarist, Disciple, or
        Ardent Admirer?" Critique: Studies in Modern Fiction, 5:58-75,
        Fall, 1962.

        From a close examination of Miss Mansfield's letters, journal and
        scrapbook, along with the complete works of both her and Anton
        Chekhov, it can be determined with some measure of certainty that her
        short stories "were in no significant way influenced by Chekhov." (W.D.)

M946   Wright, Celeste Turner, "Darkness as a Symbol in Katherine
        Mansfield," Modern Philology, 51:204-7, February, 1954.

        In her short stories Katherine Mansfield often used images of tun-
        nels to represent death and "dark water" to convey loneliness and "a
        longing for love." (G.C.)

M947   Wright, Celeste Turner, "Katherine Mansfield's Boat Image,"
        Twentieth Century Literature, 1:128-32, October, 1955.

        Katherine Mansfield had an innate fondness for symbols in her life
        as well as her work. One symbol which persists throughout her
        personal records is a boat image "which for her had various mean-
        ings: escape, the voyage through life, and a triumph over the fear
        of death." (D.P.)

M948   Wright, Celeste Turner, "Katherine Mansfield's Dog Image,"
        Literature and Psychology, 10:80-1, Summer, 1960.

        Many references to dogs in Mansfield's works can be traced to an
        incident that occurred when she was a child. (J.M.D.)

M949   Wright, Celeste Turner, "Katherine Mansfield's Father Image,"
University of California English Studies, 11:137-55, 1955.

"A consistent father portrait shapes itself for the reader of
Katherine Mansfield. . . . In more than twenty narratives her skill,
vitalized by love, hate, pity, and fear turns a business man into a
character that is memorable and . . . poignant. Here is an opportunity to observe the transformation of biography into literature."
(L. L.)

AT THE BAY

M950   Corin, Fernand, "Creation of Atmosphere in Katherine Mansfield's
Stories," Revue des Langues Vivantes, 22:65-78, No. 1, 1956.

"At the Bay" indicates that Mansfield's attitude towards life, her
"tone," is "darkened by . . . [a] tinge of melancholy, pessimism
and irony, giving to the atmosphere . . . created . . . [in the story]
a slight touch of sadness and frustration." (G.C.)

THE FLY

M951   Assad, Thomas J., "Mansfield's 'The Fly'," Explicator,
14: Item 10, November, 1955.

Being the boss had become the boss's "last pleasure." (B.K.)

M952   Bateson, F. W., and B. Shahevitch, "Katherine Mansfield's 'The
Fly': A Critical Exercise," Essays in Criticism, 12:39-53,
January, 1962.

"The Fly," if accepted as a piece of realistic fiction, demonstrates
that "granted the difference of genres, exactly the same critical
procedure is in order for realistic fiction as for a poem." (G.C.)

M953   Bateson, F. W., "More on 'The Fly'," Essays in Criticism,
12:451-2, October, 1962.

"I admire Mr. Greenwood's ingenuity in proposing a functional
justification of [detail] . . . but . . . the reading he proposes is not
for me the natural way to respond to Katherine Mansfield's ironic
specificity. . . . detail is there because it is 'wanted' by the short
story as a genre. . . . " (D.P.)

THE FLY (cont'd)

M954   Bateson, F. W., "A Sort of Answer," Essays in Criticism,
        12:347-51, July, 1962.

        Messrs. Jolly, Copland, and Greenwood "have raised . . . many
        points--several of them . . . eminently sensible ones" in their
        criticism of Mr. Shahevitch's and my effort in EC (12:39-53,
        January, 1962). ". . . I shall not attempt to answer them all. . . .
        What we set out to provide . . . was a 'critical exercise'--not a
        model critical essay." (D.P.)

M955   Bell, Pauline P., "Mansfield's 'The Fly'," Explicator,
        19: Item 20, December, 1960.

        "The Fly" dramatizes a retreat from the fear of death and a return
        to the hope of life. (B.K.)

M956   Boyle, Ted E., "The Death of the Boss: Another Look at Katherine
        Mansfield's 'The Fly'," Modern Fiction Studies, 11:183-5,
        Summer, 1965.

        ". . . only when 'The Fly' is read as the spiritual death of the boss
        can the story be fully liberated from the charge that its symbolism
        is vague and confused." (G.C.)

M957   Copland, R. A., "Katherine Mansfield's 'The Fly'," Essays in
        Criticism, 12:338-41, July, 1962.

        The high value of "The Fly" "lies in its power not merely to surprise
        but to terrify, not merely to expose but to involve; and in its dynamic,
        tragic movement." (D.P.)

M958   Greenfield, Stanley B., "Mansfield's 'The Fly'," Explicator,
        17: Item 2, October, 1958.

        "The fly is not to be equated with any person, but with the boss's
        grief. The theme of the story is that 'Time and Life Conquer Grief'."
        (G.C.)

M959   Greenwood, E. B., "Katherine Mansfield's 'The Fly'," Essays in
        Criticism, 12:341-7, July, 1962.

        In their account of "The Fly" Bateson and Shahevitch (Essays in
        Criticism, 12:39-53, January, 1962) "lay bare their prejudice

THE FLY (cont'd)

against the realistic convention . . . [which is] one means of presenting that element of the concrete, the particular, the perceptual, necessary for [the concrete universal.] But it is just as 'poetic' as any other convention." (D.P.)

M960 Greenwood, E. B., "More on 'The Fly'," Essays in Criticism, 12:448-50, October, 1962.

". . . Mr. Bateson's answer to my criticisms of this 'critical exercise'" is disingenuous. "Katherine Mansfield may have fallen into 'naturalism' in this story but . . . most of it illustrates a striving towards a 'poetic realism' with a concomitant functional use of detail." (D.P.)

M961 Hagopian, John T., "Capturing Mansfield's 'Fly'," Modern Fiction Studies, 9:385-90, Winter, 1963-64.

"Despite the obvious autobiographical sources, to link the meaning of the story to Katherine Mansfield's private life or to other stories is to deny that she has created a self-sufficient work of art. . . . 'The Fly' is an embodiment in language of an emotionally charged, powerfully poignant human experience. . . ." (D.P.)

M962 Jolly, R. A., "Katherine Mansfield's 'The Fly'," Essays in Criticism, 12:335-8, July, 1962.

". . . in this story, as in a good lyrical poem, there are several layers of meaning, some explicit, some implicit, and some meanings in logical contradiction of other meanings. The meaning of the story is a compound of these separate and sometimes contradictory meanings. . . . But the power of the story derives from the fact that it draws upon . . . levels of meaning which speak to us not of the boss but of our predicament." (D.P.)

M963 Oleson, Clinton W., "'The Fly' Rescued," College English, 22:585-6, May, 1961.

In his "Symbol and Parallelism in 'The Fly'," CE, January, 1961, J. D. Thomas "suggests that the fly in Katherine Mansfield's story represents 'a life force . . . fighting with instinctive courage for survival, until finally done to death by human perversity.'. . ." However, the story "should be read as the depiction of the boss's escape from facing the reality of death and the sterility of his own existence." (D.P.)

THE FLY (cont'd)

M964   Peltzie, Bernard E., "Teaching Meaning Through Structure in the
        Short Story," English Journal, 55:703-9, 19, September, 1966.

        "The Fly"and Saki's "The Open Window" "demonstrate how a formal
        characteristic, structure . . . may be used to open up a story."
        (G.C.)

M965   Rea, J., "Mansfield's 'The Fly'," Explicator, 23: Item 68,
        May, 1965.

        "The chief characteristic of the boss in Katherine Mansfield's
        'The Fly' is . . . his inability to recognize that others have a break-
        ing point." (D.P.)

M966   Thomas, J. D., "The Anatomy of a Fly," College English,
        22:586, May, 1961.

        In reading "The Fly" "I [have] made three working assumptions:
        (1) that every part is consistent with every other in all possible
        connections; (2) that Mr. Woodifield bears a significant relation
        to the boss; (3) that the episode of the fly at the end of the story
        has a direct bearing upon the decline of the boss's morbid grief for
        his son." (D.P.)

M967   Thomas, J. D., "Symbol and Parallelism in 'The Fly'," College
        English, 22:256-62, January, 1961.

        The fly is not the symbol of the Boss's dying grief but of his escape
        from the Death-in-Life of Mr. Woodifield to which the Boss thought
        to resign himself. (M.J.O.)

M968   Wright, Celeste T., "Genesis of a Short Story," Philological
        Quarterly, 34:91-6, January, 1955.

        Mansfield's journal, letters and scrapbook clearly indicate that in
        "The Fly" the boss represents her selfish father and a cruel Jehovah.
        The fly represents Katherine. (L.L.)

M969   Wright, Celeste Turner, "Mansfield's 'The Fly'," Explicator,
        12: Item 27, February, 1954.

        " 'The Fly' is explicated by other Mansfield stories, all depicting the
        same strenuous businessman. . . . the fly is Katherine," the "Boss,"
        her father. (G.C.)

THE GARDEN PARTY

M970 Davis, Robert Murray, "The Unity of 'The Garden Party'," Studies in Short Fiction, 2:61-5, Fall, 1964.

By carefully examining the symbols and images of "The Garden Party," and their place in the basic pattern, one can perceive both the diversity and the unity of the story. (P.J.R.)

M971 Iversen, Anders, "A Reading of Katherine Mansfield's 'The Garden Party'," Orbis Litterarum, 23:5-34, 1968.

"'The Garden Party' can be read on several levels: as a social comedy . . . developing into a serious discussion of the relations between two social classes . . . as a penetrating psychological study; as a pattern of archetypal images (the Garden of Eden; the journey to the nether world); and . . . for its autobiographical interest." (D.A.B.)

M972 Kleine, Don W., "'The Garden Party': A Portrait of the Artist," Criticism, 5:360-71, Fall, 1963.

Laura is "'the artistic one'," a "sensitive young romantic," "a prototypical figure in many of Katherine Mansfield's stories." To subordinate the heroine [as a person] . . . to her discovery is to miss the story's central meaning." (J.L.A.)

M973 Robinson, Fred C., "Mansfield's 'The Garden Party'," Explicator, 24: Item 66, April, 1966.

Laura is "presented symbolically as turning into the mythical laurel tree--symbol of drastically protected innocence--just at the height of the Sheridans's preparations . . . for the party which is to establish Laura in the narrow life of the socially protected upper class." (D.P.)

M974 Taylor, Donald S. and Daniel A. Weiss, "Crashing the Garden Party," Modern Fiction Studies, 4:361-4, Winter, 1958-59.

In "The Garden Party" the conflict between a dream world and the real world is satisfactorily resolved on both the realistic and the mythic levels. (W.T.S.)

THE GARDEN PARTY (cont'd)

M975 Walker, Warren S., "The Unresolved Conflict in 'The Garden Party'," <u>Modern Fiction Studies</u>, 3:354-8, Winter, 1957-58.

In spite of its beauty and strength the story often leaves the reader with a feeling of dissatisfaction. It has a structural weakness: the conflict has a dual nature, only partly resolved. (R.A.K.)

HER FIRST BALL

M976 Busch, Frieder, "Katherine Mansfield and Literary Impressionism in France and Germany," <u>Arcadia</u>, 5:58-76, March, 1970.

"Her First Ball" demonstrates that "in Katherine Mansfield's work we find the greatest number of impressionistic devices in the concisest form of fiction, the short story." (J.R.R.)

THE MAN WITHOUT A TEMPERAMENT

M977 Kleine, Don W., "Katherine Mansfield and the Prisoner of Love," <u>Critique: Studies in Modern Fiction</u>, 2:20-33, Winter-Spring, 1960.

[This is an extended analysis of "The Man Without a Temperament."] (G.O.)

MARRIAGE A LA MODE

M978 Kleine, Don W., "The Chekhovian Source of 'Marriage a la Mode'," <u>Philological Quarterly</u>, 42:284-8, April, 1963.

The many similarities between Mansfield's story and Chekhov's "The Grasshopper" "suggest that the latter was for Miss Mansfield a source. . . ." Her story, however, is a "piercing satire" while Chekhov's is a complex character study." (G.C.)

THE MATING OF GWENDOLEN

M979 Garlington, Jack O'Brien, "An Unattributed Story by Katherine Mansfield?" <u>Modern Language Notes</u>, 71:91-3, February, 1956.

"Internal evidence"--theme and style--indicates that "a story entitled 'The Mating of Gwendolen,' which appeared in <u>The New Age</u>, November 2, 1911 (Vol. 10, p. 14), was written by Katherine Mansfield." (G.C.)

MISS BRILL

M980 Gargano, James W., "Mansfield's 'Miss Brill'," <u>Explicator,</u>
19: Item 10, November, 1960.

Miss Brill was named after a European flatfish, a fish with a "blind
side." (B.K.)

M981 Hull, Robert L., "Alienation in 'Miss Brill'," <u>Studies in Short
Fiction</u>, 5:74-6, Fall, 1967.

"The principal theme of Katherine Mansfield's 'Miss Brill' is estrangement. . . . Indeed, Miss Brill's world is more than lonely;
it is also an existential world in which she finds herself in complete
solitude, estranged from God, man, and, more importantly, from
herself." (D.P.)

M982 Madden, David, "Katherine Mansfield's 'Miss Brill'," <u>University</u>
<u>Review</u>, 31:89-92, December, 1964.

"The basic strategy of the story is counterpoint. . . . Nearly every
line has a double intention: to render Miss Brill's observations and
simultaneously to reveal her situation and personality. On the first
level, an atmosphere of delight is created, but it is made increasingly
fragile by an ironic undertone on the second level." (K.M.W.)

M983 Thorpe, Peter, "Teaching 'Miss Brill'," <u>College English</u>, 23:661-3,
May, 1962.

"What happens in the story is that with each main event Miss Brill's
mind moves higher and higher up the hierarchy of unrealities, until
she has reached a point from which she can only fall with a thump
back to the hard ground of the real world of her humdrum life."
(R.J.G.)

PRELUDE

M984 Hale, Nancy, "Through the Looking Glass to Reality," <u>Saturday</u>
<u>Review</u>, 41:10-2, 39-40, November 8, 1958.

Nancy Hale's "The Empress's Ring," E. M. Forster's "The Machine
Stops" and Katherine Mansfield's "Prelude" demonstrate that "the
territory of fiction is . . . the other half of the world of reality; the
dark side of the moon, the mantelpiece mirror that reflects the room,
the dream between the wakings, the shadow within the sunlight." (D.P.)

MANSOUR, JOYCE

M985   Hubert, Renée Riese, "Three Women Poets: Renée Rivet, Joyce Mansour, Yvonne Caroutch," Yale French Studies, No. 21, pp. 40-8, Spring-Summer, 1958.

Among modern French poets, women are very rare. The three young poets, Renée Rivet, Joyce Mansour and Yvonne Carouth cannot be reduced to a common denominator. Found in these poets are "aesthetic discoveries achieved through structure and not blindly groped for amidst lyrical storms." (D.P.)

M986   Matthews, J. H., "The Poetry of Joyce Mansour," Books Abroad, 40:284-5, Summer, 1966.

". . . in her most recent work, Miss Mansour shows signs of an effort toward composition which did not appear . . . when she wrote Cris. With increased control comes greater subtlety, and the promise of even more impressive achievements to come." (K.M.W.)

MANTERO, MANUEL

M987   Hernández, Antonio, "Manuel Mantero," La Estafeta Literaria, No. 429, pp. 38-9, October 1, 1969.

Mantero's poetry, and the philosophy thereof, is Heideggerian, enclosed in the solitude of Mantero's destiny, inserted in the convergent and divergent law of signs, gods and the voice of the people. (T.T.B.)

MAO TSE-TUNG

M988   Grimm, Tilemann, "Zu Mao Tse-Tungs Lyrik, Engagierte Dichtung und klassische Liedkunst," Poetica, 1:85-97, January, 1967.

"Are Mao's poems beautiful? I believe we can answer the question affirmatively--with limitations: where the party leader comes through and contacts the poet, we start to feel alienation but when the poet from the fullness of his life and experience paints pictures and memories with a fleeting ink brush, then he takes us into a realm of beauty which is truly breathtaking." (J.R.R.)

M989   Lanoux, Armand, "Mao avant le livre rouge," À La Page, No. 35, pp. 743-7, May, 1967.

Correspondence and poems of Mao in 1957, written before the Cultural Revolution, cast some light on what is happening today in agitated China. (T.T.B.)

M990 Payne, Robert, "The Poetry of Mao Tse-Tung," Literary Review, 2:77-81, Autumn, 1958.

[This is a character sketch based on a 1946 interview, followed by sixteen of Mao's poems translated by Mr. Payne.] (E.T.)

M991 Ping-ti Ho, "Two Major Poems by Mao Tse-Tung," Queen's Quarterly, 65:251-8, Summer, 1958.

Mao Tse-Tung's combined life of poetry and politics is traditional among Chinese statesmen. His most significant poetry provides "an informal footnote on [his] unusual personality." (G.M.)

MARAGALL, JUAN

M992 Foster, Virginia Ramos, "Examples of La bella dormida in Catalan Literature," Romance Notes, 8:22-8, 1966.

[This is a study of the "Sleeping Beauty" theme in Juan Maragall and Carlos Riga, two modern Catalan poets.] (C.O.)

M993 Mendeloff, Henry, "Maragall's La vaca cega: A Study in Bovine Stoicism," Romance Notes, 8:18-21, 1966.

"Despite the fact that the cow is surely one of the more prosaic members of the animal kingdom, Juan Maragall succeeds in making a blind cow the subject of a lyrical poem of rare poignancy, whose stoical overtones enhance it with the serene dignity which is traditionally associated with the philosophical acceptance of, and resignation to, personal tragedy." (D.A.B.)

M994 Valentí Fiol, E., "Juan Maragall, modernista y nietzscheano," Revista de Occidente, 20:195-221, February, 1968.

Together with Clarín and Yxart, Maragall first displayed the anti-naturalistic reaction known as symbolism. His writings were adapted to modern conditions in order to save middle-class society from the threat of socialism. Paradoxically he echoed the Nietzschean doctrine of the aristocracy of the strongest. (T.T.B.)

MARAÑÓN, GREGORIO

M995   Lain Entralgo, Pedro, "El patriotismo de Marañón," La Estafeta
       Literaria, No. 391, pp. 4-7, March 9, 1968.

       Like almost all his generation, Marañón inherited the critical
       attitude and reforming anxiety so traditional in Spain. His criticism
       lies in the deficiency of Spain's preoccupation for science, which
       resulted in a lack of impersonal and severe criticism, in excessive
       religiosity, social inequity and the distorted configuration of sexual
       life. His criticism is not that of a covered masochism or a sadistic
       examination of improper conduct, but a love of perfection. (T.T.B.)

M996   Sánchez, José, "El doctor Gregorio Marañón: Médico, literato,
       humanista," Hispania, 45:451-7, September, 1962.

       [This is a eulogy and biography of Dr. Marañón.] (C.O.)

MARCEAU, FÉLICIEN

M997   May, Georges, "Félicien Marceau: A Modern Romantic Novelist,"
       Yale French Studies, No. 24, pp. 80-6, Summer, 1959.

       Marceau uses traditional technique and is fundamentally optimistic,
       two things which set him apart from his contemporaries. (K.L.)

MARCEL, GABRIEL

M998   Abraham, Claude K., "L'Amour paternel dans le théâtre de Gabriel
       Marcel," French Review, 34:251-60, January, 1961.

       "I wish to speak here . . . of [Marcel's] idea of the family, and
       especially of fatherly love, which are two important ideas in the
       religious world of the author." In his dramas "Marcel attempts
       to describe an ideal family, but this ideal does not represent more
       than a sort of divine grace, which seems implausible, and still
       less dramatic. For the most part Marcel's characters prefer faith
       to sincerity. . . . A lack of authenticity often occurs when Marcel
       attempts to unite in a family characters who have nothing in common."
       (D.P.)

M999   Cain, Seymour, "Gabriel Marcel's Way," Commonweal,
       73:271-4, December 9, 1960.

       "In his own way, speaking in his own time [Marcel] communicates
       to us in the perennial philosophic quest for contact with reality."

"His way has been . . . like that of the poet or novelist who says and makes what demands to be said and made by him, striving to fulfill in creation an inner demand and urgency which . . . cannot be bodied forth by conscious will alone . . . and which cannot be imaged in advance." (D.P.)

M1000 Collins, James, "Marcel: Christian Socratic," Commonweal, 68:539-42, August 29, 1958.

"Marcel's genius is as deeply artistic as it is philosophical. . . . In his own thought and literary activity, he maintains a zone of free interchange between the concrete presentations of the playwright and the researches of the philosopher. His plays display a meditative dimension, while his philosophical treatises remain close to the drama of the person and his choices." Marcel philosophizes "as a Christian thinker." He "accepts the basic harmony between human experience and the Christian revelation, as well as the illumination which the latter casts upon the personal and social life of man." (D.P.)

M1001 Gallagher, Kenneth T., "Gabriel Marcel: Philosopher of Communion," Catholic World, 195:96-101, May, 1962.

The theme of communion "fills not only Marcel's philosophy, but also his drama. . . . the impetus behind the action of his . . . plays derives from the obstacles that impede man's effort to achieve real communion with others." (G.C.)

M1002 Gerber, Rudolph J., "Gabriel Marcel and Authenticity," Personalist, 48:548-59, Autumn, 1967.

"According to an analysis which runs sporadically through twelve volumes, Marcel presents man's authenticity . . . as the fidelity of man to his ontological appeal." In Marcel's philosophy "man's authenticity consists in his worldly quest for the Being of beings. This quest is frustrated in exclusively pragmatic and-or objectivist modes of thought but satisfied in the ethical experience of the other's person. . . . Being is a felt certitude rather than a noetic acquisition." (D.P.)

M1003 Hazelton, Roger, "Marcel on Mystery," Journal of Religion, 38:155-67, July, 1958.

Marcel "believes that the mysterious can be acknowledged without thereby becoming a mere content of thought, that it is life itself which asks the truly metaphysical questions, and that being asserts itself in the experiences and reflections of the metaphysical thinker." (G.C.)

M1004 Hocking, William E., "Marcel and the Ground Issues of Metaphysics," Philosophy and Phenomenological Research, 14:439-69, June, 1954.

[This is a detailed discussion of Marcel's philosophy, including a review of his preface to the English translation of his Journal metaphysique.] (G.C.)

M1005 Hughes, H. Stuart, "Marcel, Maritain and the Secular World," American Scholar, 35:728-49, Autumn, 1966.

As "philosophers . . . yearning to unite metaphysical certainty with a down-to-earth awareness of actual human relationships, Maritain and Marcel . . . gave twentieth-century anti-Cartesianism a new concreteness, and they did not hesitate to apply it to specific historical situations." (G.C.)

M1006 McGowan, F. A., "Marcel's Early Drama: A Meditation," Renascence, 15:183-94, Summer, 1963.

The incidents in Marcel's dramas up to 1933 "serve as 'positions' for the three factors which Marcel at different times has called 'the approaches to ontological mystery,' 'the experience giving access to being and communion,' 'the situations for response to invocation' --fidelity, hope, love." (S.A.)

M1007 Mason, H. T., "Gabriel Marcel: Philosophical Fragments 1909-1914 and The Philosopher and Peace," Notes and Queries, 13:399, September, 1966.

These two early works will chiefly be of interest to the specialist. Marcel himself regards them as "immature . . . and sees in them only a genetic and anticipatory value when compared with later works." (D.P.)

M1008 Mendoza, Esther C., " 'Being-for-Others' in J. P. Sartre and G. Marcel," Saint Louis Quarterly, 4:5-36, 1966.

"We have, then, in Sartre's and in Marcel's analysis of the existential fact of being-for-others, two mutually exclusive theories, the results of two divergent paths pursued in the attempt to shed light on what is truly human existence. . . . Sartre fails to find any possibility for inter-human communication. . . . [For Marcel] communication . . . constitutes the very grandeur of man as man." (D.A.B.)

M1009 Miceli, Vincent P., "Marcel: The Ascent to Being," Thought, 38:395-420, Autumn, 1963.

"The role of the Christian philosopher for Gabriel Marcel is to extend the horizons of being by witnessing to the need of a world in communion." (G.C.)

M1010 Miceli, Vincent P., "Marcel: The Drama of Transcendence," Thought, 40:195-224, Summer, 1965.

"For Marcel, drama and philosophy, tragedy and dialectics are mutually created in . . . [the] struggle to achieve authentic existence by conquering their temptation to flee into objectivity." (G.C.)

M1011 Mihalich, Joseph C., "Marcel's Ontology of Love: A Background for Literature," Renascence, 13:21-5, 32, Autumn, 1960.

"By the objective standards of traditional philosophy, Marcel has fashioned a mystique rather than a metaphysics. Perhaps the most conclusive evidence of this is the impotency of orthodox criteria of philosophical criticism to measure and evaluate his efforts." (K.M.W.)

M1012 Murchland, Bernard G., C.S.C., "Gabriel Marcel: A Spiritual Realist," Catholic World, 185:340-5, August, 1957.

Although Gabriel Marcel has come to be known as an Existentialist thinker, he prefers the expression "spiritual realist." "This type of realism permits him to see the perplexity and despair that flow from the instability of twentieth century life; it makes him acutely conscious of the concrete human being--the person who suffers, struggles, hopes and loves; but it also enables him to rise above the limitations of man." (D.P.)

M1013 Murchland, Bernard G., C.S.C., "The Philosophy of Gabriel Marcel," Review of Politics, 21:339-56, April, 1959.

"Marcel does not offer a complete philosophy. But he has been an outstanding pathfinder through the obscurities of our existential limitations and his work points significantly to that creative presence and fulfillment that reside beyond the limits. Within a concrete ontology he affirms the validity of human values and the transcendent world of faith." (D.P.)

M1014 Novak, Michael, "Marcel at Harvard," Commonweal, 77:31-3, October 5, 1962.

"In the light of [philosopher, playwright] Marcel's own history, the scientific atmosphere of Harvard seemed suddenly inadequate, and the concrete intellectual histories of the individual men in the departments seemed as significant as their 'objective conclusions.' The timidity and inhibitions of American religious men seemed especially irksome." (P.A.R.)

M1015 Stallknecht, Newton P., "Gabriel Marcel and the Human Situation," Review of Metaphysics, 7:661-7, June, 1954.

"Marcel has presented us with an individualism that is wholly free of the insolence--the hybris--that so often blinds humanists and individualists to the wisdom of gratitude and humility. Thus . . . we may be sure that Marcel has offered us a philosophy genuinely Christian in spirit. Indeed, the ultimate importance of his work may lie in his ability to unite . . . the Socratic with the Christian way of life and of thought." (D.P.)

M1016 Watts, Harold H., "Gabriel Marcel's Theatre of Grace," Drama and Theatre, 7:101-9, Winter, 1968-69.

Instead of being "an embroidery of truths already set down in his philosophical 'journals'," Marcel's theatre "is a form of meditation on human action that the metaphysical journals cannot encompass." Marcel's "'journals' move onward from individual men to dangerously inclusive observations about man [in which] . . . individual men and their gestures suffer . . . depletion. The plays of Marcel are, among other things, an effort to offset this depletion; they are attempts to remain at the level of real event and real choice that philosophical thought . . . drifts away from." (D.P.)

M1017 Wilhelmsen, Frederick D., "The Preoccupations of a Christian Philosopher," Commonweal, 62:623-4, September 23, 1955.

"Marcel's judgments on the social order issue from his sense of being: unless man returns to being he cannot recapture that fidelity to his own existence and to the world which is the source of honor and the sister of hope. . . . But a world increasingly given over to

technological thought . . . is a world increasingly removed from
the order of God's creation. . . . Marcel . . . is primarily concerned with the danger of turning man and the world into a system
of means and a field of objects. . . ." (D.P.)

ARIADNE--See
LE CHEMIN DE CRÊTE

LE CHEMIN DE CRÊTE

M1018 Condon, Mary, "Ariadne and Gabriel Marcel," Renascence,
20:99-103, Winter, 1968.

"In Ariadne Marcel's characters strive for Being but are not able
to transcend their autonomous existence. They are on the first
level of being, incarnation, and are trying to fulfill themselves
through the second level, communion." (S.A.)

MARCH, WILLIAM

M1019 Going, William T., "William March's Alabama," Alabama Review,
16:243-59, October, 1963.

"Without doing violence to his various aesthetic purposes and
methods of storytelling, William March, better than any other
writer of American fiction, has spread before his readers the
state of Alabama. . . ." (D.P.)

M1020 Tallant, Robert, "Poor Pilgrim, Poor Stranger," Saturday Review,
37:9, 33-4, July 17, 1954.

[This is a brief account of March's life and death and reminiscences
of an interview with him.] (G.C.)

THE BAD SEED

M1021 Going, William T., "A Footnote to 'The Bad Seed: A Modern Elsie
Venner'," Western Humanities Review, 18:175, Spring, 1964.

Abigail Ann Hamblen traces the parallels between Holmes's Elsie
Venner and March's The Bad Seed well but she fails to underscore
the "terrifying bit of irony" with which March concludes his novel.
(G.C.)

THE BAD SEED   (cont'd)

M1022 Hamblen, Abigail Ann, "The Bad Seed: A Modern Elsie Venner,"
Western Humanities Review, 17:361-3, Autumn, 1963.

Both The Bad Seed and Elsie Venner embody the conviction that
"evil can possess a human being through no fault of his own; that
his forebears can transmit to him various weaknesses and tendencies of which he becomes the helpless victim." (G.C.)

THE LITTLE WIFE

M1023 Going, William T., "March's 'The Little Wife'," Explicator,
20: Item 66, April, 1962.

"The obvious theme that death is a reality and cannot be pushed
aside," is complemented by the suggestion "that all life is a lonely
journey, wherein communication is impossible." (B.K.)

MARIA DE JESUS, CAROLINA

M1024 Cartey, Wilfred, "The Realities of Four Negro Writers," Columbia
University Forum, 9:34-42, Summer, 1966.

"The absurdity of the question, whether the Negro writer shall write
as a Negro, is particularly patent here; for these are, in effect,
autobiographical novels. The writers have in common the accident
that each is dealing with the same theme--the debut of himself; and
he is a Negro. Whether in South Africa, Barbados, or Harlem, he
speaks from within the castle of his skin." (D.P.)

MARÍAS, JULIÁN

M1025 Vilar, Sergio, "Julián Marías and the Intelligentsia in Spain,"
Books Abroad, 37:252-60, 1963.

[This is a survey of the philosophical ideas of Julián Marías, with
special reference to the trauma of civil war and exile.] (C.O.)

MARISSEL, ANDRÉ

M1026 François, Carlo, "Poésie d'André Marissel," French Review,
39:265-74, November, 1965.

Marissel's poetry is an affair both intimate and personal, incessantly balancing accounts between death and nothingness. Speaking
of death, he attempts to deny it, exorcise it, transcend it. A sense
of error, fear of punishment and total acceptance of martyrdom
permeate the sensitivity of Marissel. (T.T.B.)

MARKANDAYA, KAMALA

M1027 Kumar, Shiv K., "Tradition and Change in the Novels of Kamala
Markandaya," Books Abroad, 43:508-13, Autumn, 1969.

Markandaya's novels, like India itself, are "poised delicately
between a nostalgic idealization of traditional values and a new
compulsive urge for modernity." Her novels derive their "aesthetic
validity" from the "interlocked polarities of religion and science,
possession and renunciation, empiricism and transcendentalism."
(K.H.B.)

M1028 Parameswaran, Uma, "India for the Western Reader: A Study of
Kamala Markandaya's Novels," Texas Quarterly, 11:231-47,
Summer, 1968.

This writer of novels about Indian life in English "limits herself to
a small canvas in each novel and effectively brings out certain social
foibles and certain emotional conflicts faced by average human beings
. . . she does not go deeply into any problem or situation despite her
keen insight and her eye for details." (W.G.F.)

MARKHAM, EDWIN

M1029 Filler, Louis, "Edwin Markham, Poetry and What Have You,"
Antioch Review, 23:447-59, Winter, 1963-1964.

"Markham had been one of the great men of the 1900's. . . . He
had been America's conscience, voicing its concern for humanistic
and humane causes. . . . But as Progressivism slipped away . . .
Markham's fame, and, indeed, the quality of his verse, declined."
(G.C.)

MARQUAND, JOHN PHILLIPS

M1030 Benedict, Stewart H., "The Pattern of Determinism in J. P.
Marquand's Novels," Ball State Teachers College Forum,
2:60-4, Winter, 1961-62.

". . . with the exception of Dreiser, Marquand is perhaps the most rigidly deterministic author who has thus far written in America in this century." (G.C.)

M1031 Brown, John Mason, "John P. Marquand: The Man," Saturday Review, 43:14-5, August 13, 1960.

John P. Marquand "looked the way his books sounded, and sounded like the most colorful of his own Bostonians. He made conversation an experience. . . . His standards were high, his disgust was gorgeous. . . . He had a young writer's enthusiasm. . . . as a man, no less than as a writer, he never went backward except to go forward." (D.P.)

M1032 Driver, Josephine P., "The Young Marquand," Atlantic Monthly, 216:69-72, August, 1965.

[These recollections of Marquand by a lifelong friend center on his shyness, his loneliness in high school in Newburyport, Massachusetts.] (D.P.)

M1033 Geismar, Maxwell, "John P. Marquand: The Writer," Saturday Review, 43:15, 39, August 13, 1960.

This acute and brilliant observer of middle-class suburbia had the sharp eyes of the born reporter, "the sensitive ear for speech, the right gift of creating atmosphere and of projecting social types. He had everything the novelist needs except the intellectual boldness, the moral hardness, the deep insights of the major writer." (W.E.K.)

M1034 Greene, George, "A Tunnel from Persepolis: The Legacy of John Marquand," Queen's Quarterly, 73:345-56, Autumn, 1966.

"John Marquand's success in making credible that new world, which is still our world, is the reason why he continues to deserve attention, not just as a painstaking reporter, but as a poet of the human condition itself." (G.G.)

M1035 Gross, John J., "The Late John P. Marquand: An Essay in Biography," English Record, 19:2-12, No. 2, 1968.

"It is probable that [Marquand's] inability to resolve the question of the meaning of the present through which he was living in terms of a past remembered represented both the tension of his novels and the basis for his failure . . . as a novelist." (A.S.W.)

M1036 Johnson, Robert O., "Mr. Marquand and Lord Tennyson,"
Research Studies (Washington State University), 32:28-38, 1964.

". . . Marquand used Tennyson's poetry to help develop a carefully-
balanced ironic attitude in three of his serious novels. . . . [His]
irony was not an 'outside' attitude, but one that he took pains to
fashion. In his successful works, Marquand did much more than
function as a social reporter." (K.M.W.)

M1037 Marquand, John P., "Apley, Wickford Point, and Pulham: My
Early Struggles," Atlantic Monthly, 198:71-4, September, 1956.

[Marquand discusses his novels The Late George Apley, Wickford
Point and H. M. Pulham, Esquire.] (G.C.)

M1038 Oppenheimer, Franz M., "Lament for Unbought Grace: The Novels
of John P. Marquand," Antioch Review, 18:41-61, Spring, 1958.

"The work of John P. Marquand . . . is concerned with the core of
American civilization and it has diagnosed the degenerative symptoms radiating from that core with clinical insight and constructive
pessimism . . .: loss of organic roots, isolation, anxiety and
nihilistic worship of success." (F.C.T.)

M1039 Roberts, Kenneth, "The Memories of John P. Marquand: Marsh
Mud, Harvard Sawdust and Stuffed Shirts," Saturday Review,
39:14-5, September 15, 1956.

[This is a remembrance of pleasurable excursions in Marquand's
fictional realms.] (G.C.)

M1040 Smith, William James, "J. P. Marquand, Esq.," Commonweal,
49:148-50, November 7, 1958.

Although Marquand is currently underestimated, "he remains one
of our most competent novelists." He offers something rare and
wonderful, the charm of craftsmanship . . . an eye for proportion
and unpretentious decoration . . . sensible comforts and sedate
humor." (J.M.D.)

M1041 Stedmond, J. M., "The Business Executive in Fiction," Dalhousie
Review, 42:18-27, Spring, 1962.

Modern business novels are concerned with "the problem of loyalty"
and the price of material success. Compared to novelists like

Howard Swiggett and Cameron Hawley, Marquand at least deals with these problems provocatively; he does not adopt an easy, uncritical " 'positive' attitude." (G.C.)

M1042 Weeks, Edward, "John P. Marquand," Atlantic Monthly, 206:74-6, October, 1960.

John Marquand "was so observant and had such an accurate inner ear for American idiom that it all came to seem deceptively easy. The critics . . . marked him down for this [but] . . . the downgrading . . . overlooks the credibility which Marquand brought to every line he wrote; it overlooks that fine blend of humor and skepticism which makes one laugh aloud as one reads; it overlooks John's almost infallible prescience." (D.P.)

M1043 White, William, "More Marquandiana, 1956-1968," Serif, 6:33-6, June, 1969.

[This is a bibliography of articles and books about Marquand, 1956-1968, omitting reviews of the novels.] (A.S.W.)

H. M. PULHAM, ESQ.

M1044 MacLean, Hugh, "Conservatism in Modern American Fiction," College English, 15:315-25, March, 1954.

"The Great Gatsby is a conservative book because it denies the possibility of infinite progress. . . . Marquand's H. M. Pulham, Esq. . . . deals with the dangers into which extremist conservatism may fall. . . . The Catcher in the Rye . . . reveals the 'progressivist myth' clearly enough as ludicrous and obscene. . . . 'The Bear', more than Faulkner's other work, depends on ritual myth, and a sense of the past." (D.P.)

THE LATE GEORGE APLEY

M1045 Goodwin, George, Jr., "The Last Hurrahs: George Apley and Frank Skeffington," Massachusetts Review, 1:461-71, May, 1960.

"Much of what is unique in Massachusetts politics stems from the fact that the state received an overwhelming proportion of Irish immigrants. . . ." Both George Apley (The Late George Apley) and Frank Skeffington (The Last Hurrah) "help to explain much" of this uniqueness. (G.C.)

THE LATE GEORGE APLEY (cont'd)

M1046 Gordon, Edward J., "What's Happened to Humor?" English
Journal, 47:127-33, March, 1958.

"If humor has this triple purpose: the reforming of society, the
bringing of self-knowledge, and the presenting of an optimistic view
of life, we . . . have criteria by which we may evaluate changes in
the [comic] tradition." [A comparison of The Late George Apley
with Twain's The Adventures of Huckleberry Finn illustrates these
changes.] (G.C.)

M1047 Hamblen, Abigail Ann, "Judge Grant and the Forgotten Chippendales,"
University Review, 33:175-9, Spring, 1967.

Judge Robert Grant's The Chippendales presages by twenty-five
years Marquand's portrait of prim, proper Boston in The Late
George Apley. Both novels share a slightness in plot, although
they are dissimilar in outcome. Judge Grant's long periods, and
labored humor give way to Marquand's lightly suggestive irony.
But certainly Grant's understanding of integrity and sturdiness of
character is as great as Marquand's. (D.P.)

M1048 Johnson, R. O., "Mary Monahan: Marquand's Sentimental Slip?"
Research Studies (Washington State University), 33:208-13,
December, 1965.

The reappearance of Mary Monahan late in The Late George Apley
is not a sentimental slip on Marquand's part, but a way of reaffirm-
ing Apley's basic sentimentality as well as his thwarted masculinity
and blindness. The episode also shows us that Willing, Apley's
biographer, is not able to understand his subject. (D.P.)

POINT OF NO RETURN

M1049 Van Nostrand, Albert D., "After Marquand, the Deluge," English
Journal, 48:55-65, February, 1959.

As a result of the popular success of Marquand's Point of No Return,
clusters of business novels began to appear, most notably Hawley's
Executive Suite and Cash McCall, Swiggett's The Power and the
Prize, Sloan Wilson's The Man in the Gray Flannel Suit, and George
DeMare's The Empire--and Martin Brill. These novels show startling similarities to Point of No Return; they have sharpened the conflict between the individual and the business system in which he

POINT OF NO RETURN (cont'd)

lives, but the "presiding sense of dilemma" characteristic of
Marquand is missing. Only DeMare's novel "amplifies qualities
found in John Marquand's novel. . . ." (D.P.)

M1050 Van Nostrand, Albert D., "Fiction's Flagging Man of Commerce,"
English Journal, 48:1-11, January, 1959.

Marquand's Point of No Return and Howells's The Rise of Silas
Lapham "both exploit the timely subject and the urgent tone endemic
to American business fiction. In both books a man's livelihood sig-
nalizes the course of his entire life. Together, they demonstrate a
change in their shared subject, a new emphasis in the individual's
response to business, in light of which the presumed popularity of
the businessman . . . is monumentally irrelevant." (D.P.)

TIMOTHY DEXTER REVISITED

M1051 Larrabee, Eric, "Two Gentlemen from Newburyport," American
Heritage, 12:46-9, April, 1961.

Marquand wrote Timothy Dexter Revisited, his last volume, "out of
dissatisfaction with his first effort" on Dexter written in 1925, "and
out of a concern for achieving balanced historical judgment."
(D.P.)

WOMEN AND THOMAS HARROW

M1052 Kazin, Alfred, "John P. Marquand and the American Failure,"
Atlantic Monthly, 202:152-6, November, 1958.

There is a "manifest lack of vital dramatic energy in Marquand's
new novel, in which an increasing impatience and despair have gone
hand in hand with the now ungovernable nostalgia." (G.C.)

MARQUÉS, RENÉ

M1053 Dauster, Frank, "The Theater of René Marqués," Symposium,
18:35-45, Spring, 1964.

"His theater is a complex and peculiarly suggestive metaphor for a
people he regards as guilt-ridden and obsessed with a desire for
self-destruction. The measure of his ability . . . is the fact that
out of this material, he has created plays which are . . . among the
most distinguished in Latin America today." (K.M.W.)

MÁRQUEZ, GABRIEL GARCÍA--See
GARCÍA MÁRQUEZ, GABRIEL

MARQUINA, EDUARDO

M1054 Snyder, Isabel, "A Twentieth-Century Adaptation of Lope's
La Dorotea," Hispania, 42:325-9, September, 1959.

A comparison of Lope de Vega's dialogue novel with Eduardo
Marquina's play reveals that "Marquina's whole work is more
restrained in tone than Lope's. It also ends on a more idealistic
note." (A.C.).

MARQUIS, DON

M1055 Hamblen, Abigail Ann, "Protestantism in Three American Novels,"
Forum (Houston), 3:40-3, Fall-Winter, 1960.

Don Marquis's Sons of the Puritans and Ruth Suckow's The John
Wood Case (as well as Hawthorne's The Scarlet Letter) emphasize
a theory which is a "dark weight on the American consciousness":
that "a man's moral lapse is of concern not only to himself, but to
the group." (J.P.H.)

M1056 Hill, Hamlin L., "Archy and Uncle Remus: Don Marquis's Debt to
Joel Chandler Harris," Georgia Review, 15:78-87, Spring, 1961.

"Marquis used the techniques and methods of native American humor,
especially as he learned them from Joel Chandler Harris; and an
examination of this indebtedness not only adds an important link in
the continuity of this type of humor, but it also explains in part the
neglect Marquis has suffered and the decline into which his reputation has fallen." (R.J.G.)

MARSCHALL, JOSEF

M1057 Moore, J. Michael, "Josef Marschall and His Lyrics," Books
Abroad, 28:299-300, Summer, 1954.

"There are three main characteristics that make up Marschall's
poetry . . . his love for nature, his love for the Greek and Roman
classics, and his love for music." (G.C.)

MARSHALL, ALAN

M1058 Lindsay, Jack, "A Triumph over Adversity: Comments on Alan
Marshall's Writing," Meanjin Quarterly, 29:436-45, December, 1969.

". . . Marshall above all expresses the goodness of men. . . . he
discovers the goodness that lies at the core of their humanity . . .
because he himself is good: because . . . in the moment of recognition and discovery he both loses and finds himself in a pure consciousness of union with his fellows." (G.C.)

MARTIN, DAVID

M1059 Phillips, Arthur A., "The Writings of David Martin," Meanjin
Quarterly, 20:15-24, April, 1961.

A "conflict of two elements within his temperament . . . moves
within [Martin's] work. . . . On the one hand there is a realistic
humanist . . . who writes as a perceptive and sympathetic observer."
On the other, he is "an old-fashioned romantic, responsive to the
influences of Shelley and Blake." (G.C.)

MARTIN DU GARD, MAURICE

M1060 Billy, André, "Historiographes de la Vie Littéraire," La Revue
des Deux Mondes, pp. 431-7, August 1, 1957.

André Salmon's Souvenirs sans fin and Maurice Martin du Gard's
Les Mémorables are of especial interest to the student of the
twentieth century because they reveal so much of the authors themselves. (L.L.)

M1061 Martin du Gard, Maurice, "Les Mémorables," La Revue des Deux
Mondes, 7:39-51, November 1, 1967.

[These are memoirs of Maurice together with souvenirs of Roger
Martin du Gard, André Gide, Jean Schlumberger and Georges
Duhamel.] (T.T.B.)

MARTIN DU GARD, ROGER

M1062 Andrews, Oliver, Jr., "A Chat with Roger Martin du Gard,"
French Review, 32:463-5, April, 1959.

[This is a reminiscence about a talk with du Gard concerning Eugéne
Dabit.] (G.C.)

M1062   2642

M1063 Barberet, Gene J., "A Remembered Talk with Roger Martin du Gard," Books Abroad, 32:379-81, Autumn, 1958.

[This is the report of a conversation in the spring of 1957 with one of the last remaining members of the original Nouvelle Revue Française group.] (W.G.F.)

M1064 Barberet, Gene J., "Roger Martin du Gard: Recent Criticism," French Review, 41:60-9, October, 1967.

"As a precursor of the Existentialists or spokesman for humanity in a world torn by conflicting ideologies, Roger Martin du Gard continues to have relevance to the contemporary scene." (G.C.)

M1065 Bonfantini, Mario, "Martin du Gard, o della perplessità," Il Mondo, 10:9, September 16, 1958.

The predominant sentiment aroused by the works of Martin du Gard is a feeling of inconclusiveness, of confusion in the author's intent which is especially evident in his attitude towards Jacques and Antoine Thibault. (V.R.)

M1066 Camus, Albert, "Roger Martin du Gard," La Nouvelle Nouvelle Revue Française, 34:641-71, October, 1955.

Because of the depth of his creations, Martin du Gard has continued the tradition of Tolstoy. As early as Jean Barois, he announced one of the main themes of twentieth century literature: the portrayal of man, who, having abandoned hope, pits himself against death. Les Thibault introduced the theme of the individual caught between history and God. This man will eventually find consolation in knowing that "All men die at the same time and with the same violence." (M.R.)

M1067 Clouard, Henri, "André Gide et Roger Martin du Gard: correspondance," La Revue des Deux Mondes, 140:435-45, June 1-15, 1968.

Born adversaries and inseparable friends Gide and Martin du Gard disclosed the reciprocal influence that each had on the other's works. The sharpest discussions were on the Tolstoy-Dostoevsky theme; the opposition of the novel of objectivity and average humanity (Martin du Gard's) and the subjective novel of the exceptional human (Gide's). (T.T.B.)

M1068 Grosser, Alfred, "Une Morale sans metaphysique: l'oeuvre de Roger Martin du Gard," Esprit, 10:523-34, October, 1958.

Martin du Gard accepts the universe without systematic pessimism, but with a calm atheism that posits moral law as the only way to self-knowledge and fulfillment. (K. L.)

M1069 Ibert, Jean-Claude, "Un Écrivain solitaire: Roger Martin du Gard," Conjonction, No. 72, pp. 28-9, 1958.

Despite the pessimism resulting from his acute observation of human behavior, Martin du Gard never seems to have lost faith in man's future. (W.G. F.)

M1070 McMurray, George R., "The Role of History in the Works of Roger Martin du Gard," Xavier University Studies, 5:27-36, 1966.

Martin du Gard "depicts the historical process as a series of great events or tides, each of which leaves its imprint on the present generation and erects a barrier between it and the succeeding one." (A.S.W.)

M1071 Martin du Gard, Maurice, "Les Mémorables," La Revue des Deux Mondes, 6:39-51, November 1, 1967.

[These are memoirs of Maurice together with souvenirs of Roger Martin du Gard, André Gide, Jean Schlumberger and Georges Duhamel.] (T.T.B.)

M1072 Martin du Gard, Roger, "Lettres d'André Gide et de Roger Martin du Gard," La Nouvelle Revue Française, No. 180, pp. 1037-54, December, 1967.

[This is correspondence between Gide and Martin du Gard from July 1920 and February 1931.] (T.T.B.)

M1073 O'Nan, Martha, "Form in the Novel: André Gide and Roger Martin du Gard," Symposium, 12:81-93, Spring-Fall, 1959.

"Thus, it can be said that as young novelists Gide and Martin du Gard in turn dreamed separately of a new framework for the novel, and that later as friends they exchanged ideas on novelistic technique which helped them construct a complex form which each man erected in his own image." (B.B.)

M1074 O'Nan, Martha, "The Influence of Tolstoy upon Roger Martin du Gard," Kentucky Foreign Language Quarterly, 4:7-14, First Quarter, 1957.

Martin du Gard's Jean Barois, Les Thibault and other works resemble War and Peace and Anna Karenina in their metaphysical search for an understanding of life. Though they differ in that Tolstoy sought for answers in the realm of the spiritual, while Martin du Gard placed confidence in the social evolution of man, both authors share the belief that "a complete understanding of life is beyond the grasp of the human being." (F.J.P.)

M1075 Picon, Gaëton, "Roger Martin du Gard," Contemporary Review, No. 1116, pp. 329-31, 1958.

[This is a brief review of the literary career of this "most illustrious novelist."] (G.C.)

M1076 Roudiez, Leon S., "The Function of Irony in Roger Martin du Gard," Romanic Review, 48:275-86, December, 1957.

In Roger Martin du Gard's works irony "is first a means of exorcising fate, and second an expression of the transference of the author's masochism to his characters--in itself a reaction to his inherent ambition and pride." (D.P.)

M1077 Roudiez, Leon S., "Situation de Roger Martin du Gard," French Review, 34:13-25, October, 1960.

Roger Martin du Gard has been relatively little studied since his death in 1958. His future probably lies in the evolution of major intellectual currents, and, although generally assigned to a second rank as a writer, his true worth can only be established after a vigorous and detailed examination of all his works. (D.P.)

M1078 Roza, Robert, "Roger Martin du Gard, Master-Builder of the Novel," American Society of Legion of Honor Magazine, 38:73-88, No. 2, 1967.

Roger Martin du Gard, following Tolstoy's example, has kept alive a traditional, unbroken, rational image of man, combining effectively the drama of history and the reality of fiction. (A.S.W.)

M1079 Spurdle, Sonia M., "Roger Martin du Gard's Debt to Ibsen in L'Une de nous . . . and Les Thibault," Modern Language Review, 65:54-64, January, 1970.

"Of all of Ibsen's plays it is Ghosts which seems to have been uppermost in his [Martin du Gard's] mind when he was planning Les Thibault. It appears, moreover, that features from Ghosts have filtered through into his nouvelle, L'Une de nous. . . ." (J.R.R.)

M1080 Vial, Fernand, "Roger Martin du Gard (1881-1958)," American Society of Legion of Honor Magazine, 30:35-51, No. 1, 1959.

Jean Barois and Les Thibault reveal that Martin du Gard "is an author of the past, dealing with problems which are no longer actual. . . . Yet the basis for many of these problems remains unimpaired. . . ." (G.C.)

M1081 Williams, Ena, "Roger Martin du Gard," Contemporary Review, 194:329-31, December, 1958.

Martin du Gard's first novel was published through the intercession of André Gide, and his second, Jean Barois, brought Martin du Gard success. The monumental Les Thibault is "a thoughtful, solid and carefully constructed classic . . . a vast contribution to the history of his time. . . . his immortality [is] assured through the characters he had created." (D.P.)

M1082 Wood, John S., "Roger Martin du Gard," French Studies, 14:129-40, April, 1960.

Martin du Gard "is perhaps the last of the great artisans of the (traditional) novel, who presuppose the reality of the world and who treat man in function of that reality." His characters "measure the present and the future against the heritage of the past. . . ." (G.C.)

LA BELLE SAISON

M1083 Saint-Girons, C., "Une Source inédite de Roger Martin du Gard," Revue d'Histoire Littéraire de la France, 68:91-3, January-February, 1968.

Roger Martin du Gard used newspaper and magazine clippings as a trampoline for his creative imagination. [One such clipping from the Martin du Gard file is compared here to a section of La Belle Saison.] (D.-J.J.)

JEAN BAROIS

M1084 Kaiser, Grant E., "Roger Martin du Gard's Jean Barois: An Experiment in Novelistic Form," Symposium, 14:135-41, Summer, 1960.

The novel should be examined "in order to discover what artistic effects . . . [Martin du Gard] gained or hoped to gain from using the dialogue form." (G.C.)

M1085 Wilhelm, Kurt, "Roger Martin du Gards Dialogroman Jean Barois," Zeitschrift für Französische Sprache und Literatur, 79:97-120, June, 1969.

"The crticial considerations with which Martin du Gard conceived his Jean Barois were the expression of a basic new orientation of his creative productivity." (J.R.R.)

LES THIBAULT

M1086 DeJongh, William F. J., "Unnatural Death in Les Thibault," Romance Notes, 9:190-4, Spring, 1968.

"No study has been devoted to unnatural death in Martin du Gard's works, for the reason, probably, that the subject is indelicate and too bold. A note, however, may well be turned with concentrated attention upon the two kinds of death that extinguish the life of most leading characters in Les Thibault [suicide and euthanasia]." (D.A.B.)

M1087 Jonas, Maurice, "L'Antihéroïsme précurseur de Roger Martin du Gard," French Review, 42:834-45, May, 1969.

The heroism of Jacques in Les Thibault is demythified and made absurd so as to invite the substitution of an authentic heroism. This antiheroism was imitated and developed by Sartre, de Beauvoir, Camus, and Malraux. (A.K.)

L'UNE DE NOUS

M1088 Boak, C. D., "An Early Work by Roger Martin du Gard," AUMLA, No. 20, pp. 318-30, November, 1963.

In L'Une de nous, Martin du Gard "was attempting to find a satisfactory vehicle for his basic themes: death, old age and solitude,

L'UNE DE NOUS   (cont'd)

the moral and intellectual conflict between religious belief and positivistic science, and the problem of evil and suffering." (G.C.)

MARTÍN SANTOS, LUIS

M1089 Díaz, Janet Winecoff, "Luis Martín Santos and the Contemporary Spanish Novel," Hispania, 51:232-8, May, 1968.

The only published novel of Martín Santos marks him as the most important and successful of the new novelists reacting against the two vogues of nouveau roman and "social realism." Unpublished manuscripts should consolidate the position he won with Tiempo de silencio, the only novel published before his death in 1964. (C.O.)

TIEMPO DE SILENCIO

M1090 Eoff, Sherman H. and José Schraibman, "Dos novelas de absurdo: L'Étranger y Tiempo de silencio," Papeles de Son Armadans, 56:213-41, March, 1970.

Tiempo de silencio by Luis Martín-Santos and L'Étranger by Camus both exemplify the absurd novel. A major difference is that Martín-Santos accepts not even the theoretical solution that Camus proposes, an arbitrary "creating one's own independent dignity." (C.O.)

M1091 Ortega, José, "La sociedad española contemporánea en Tiempo de silencio de Martín-Santos," Symposium, 22:256-60, Fall, 1968.

Martín-Santos belongs to the "wounded" generation. His novel is a scathing denunciation of post-war Spanish society in the style of historical realism, somewhat reminiscent of Marxism's socialist realism. (C.O.)

MARTÍNEZ ESTRADA, EZEQUIEL

M1092 Stabb, Martin S., "Ezequiel Martínez Estrada: The Formative Writings," Hispania, 49:54-60, March, 1966.

Martínez Estrada's brilliant essays apprehend reality dialectically and irrationally. Further, they show a remarkable consistency from the earliest to the most recent. Finally, an understanding of his work is essential to an understanding of the Argentine intellectual milieu of the 30's, 40's, and 50's. (C.O.)

MARTÍNEZ FERRANDO, JESUS ERNESTO

M1093 Ballester Segura, Luis, "Martínez Ferrando, historiador y
novelista," La Estafeta Literaria, No. 387, p. 37,
January 13, 1968.

Historian, archivist, translator and novelist, Martínez Ferrando
was a fertile and bilingual writer--in Catalan and Spanish--of more
than a hundred works. An internationally known short story writer,
he was especially noted for his poetic sensitivity and acute observation of characters. (T.T.B.)

MARTÍNEZ OLMEDILLA, AUGUSTO

M1094 Sainz de Robles, Federico C., "Raros y olvidados: Augusto
Martínez Olmedilla (1880-1966)," La Estafeta Literaria, No. 432,
p. 10, November 15, 1969.

Novelist, short-story writer and chronicler, Martínez Olmedilla is
perhaps best remembered for his Apuntes, written under the pseudonym of Teófilo. (T.T.B.)

MARTÍNEZ RUIZ, JOSÉ

M1095 Abbott, James H., "Azorín and Taine's Determinism," Hispania,
46:476-9, September, 1963.

Due to Azorín's early reading of Taine, deterministic and scientific
concepts have played an important part in his literary development,
although he occasionally gives some importance to individual will
power. (C.O.)

M1096 Abbott, James H., "Ya es tarde, se tenía que morir: Azorín and
Death," Books Abroad, 41:409-12, Autumn, 1967.

[These are meditations on the theme of death, on the occasion of the
death of Azorín, March 2, 1967.] (C.O.)

M1097 Alfonso, José, et al., "Azorín: 5 posdatas," La Estafeta
Literaria, No. 366, pp. 34-7, March, 1967.

[These are criticism and souvenirs of Azorín by Alfonso, José de
las Casas Acevedo, Pascual Antonio Beño, Eduardo Robles and
José Álvarez Esteban.] (T.T.B.)

M1098 Ayllón, Cándido, "Experiments in the Theater of Unamuno, Valle-Inclán, and Azorín," Hispania, 46:49-56, March, 1963.

In the twenties these three writers reflect in Spain the experimentation of Pirandello, the expressionists, and the surrealists more than do the Madrid art theaters. They lead directly to the theater of Casona and Lorca. But they fail to take adequate account of the special demands of the stage as an artistic medium. (C.O.)

M1099 Campos, Jorge, "José Martinez Ruiz, 1897," Ínsula, 22:3, May, 1967.

The political opinions of the early Azorín are frankly revolutionary. But they are limited to the printed page. Azorín is a literary "anarchist" who wants only to be left alone with his books. (C.O.)

M1100 Cano, José Luis, "Dos libros de Azorín: España clara, Ultramarinos," Ínsula, 22:8-9, May, 1967.

[This is a book review of two volumes of previously uncollected journalistic pieces.] (C.O.)

M1101 Caro Baroja, Julio, "Azorín," Revista de Occidente, 20:138-53, February, 1968.

Azorín, a great critic and renovator of prose, was not influenced directly by Greek and Roman moralists but was deeply affected by the writings of Montaigne, Vauvenargues and other less well known moralists. (T.T.B.)

M1102 Caro Baroja, Julio, "Azorín," La Estafeta Literaria, No. 392, p. 10, March 23, 1968.

The generation of '98 is a myth. There is no connection between the Azorín of the turn of the century and Machado or the other authors with whom he is now associated so complacently. Similarly, his early years and the bad companions for which he is criticized today had little or no influence on his work over the years. (T.T.B.)

M1103 Castresana, Luis de, et al., "5 visitan a 1," La Estafeta Literaria, No. 365, pp. 4-18, March, 1967.

[These are homage and souvenirs by Castresana, Luis Ponce de León, Manuel Ríos Ruiz, Maria Embeita, José Alfonso, Antonio Fernández Villaverde, Gaspar Gómez de la Serna, Rafael de Penagas, Manuel Alcántara, etc.] (T.T.B.)

M1104 Descouzis, Paul, "Azorín, alférez de Cervantes," Hispania, 52:21-5, March, 1969.

Azorín's most lasting work has been the revivification of the national idol, making of Don Quixote the incarnation of Castilian individualism. (C.O.)

M1105 Domingo, José, "La Valencia de Azorín," Ínsula, 22:7, May, 1967.

Azorín's early years of law study in Valencia are also his introduction to journalism and journalistic criticism. (C.O.)

M1106 Fernández Pombo, Alejandro, "Las mujeres de Azorín," La Estafeta Literaria, No. 376, pp. 8-9, August 12, 1967.

Azorín's city heroines are merry, vital, noisy and laughing. If they turn out to be as fine as princesses it is through some unfathomable mystery. On the other hand, his provincial heroines are sad, delicate and smiling, and die early. (T.T.B.)

M1107 Fox, E. Inman, "Azorín, maestro," Ínsula, 22:1, 11, May, 1967.

The great lesson of Azorín, beyond themes, styles, images, is that of how to read. Azorín reads creatively, making of each piece of literature a new and unique creation. (C.O.)

M1108 Fox, E. Inman, "Lectura y literatura," Cuadernos Hispano-americanos, No. 205, pp. 5-26, January, 1967.

Azorín's literature is inspired, not by observed reality, but by other literature. Thus, in a highly personal way, he ponders the Spanish classics according to a modern esthetics. And much of his creation becomes a re-writing, a re-creating of the great works of Spanish literature. (C.O.)

M1109 García Mercadal, J., "Resurrección de una crítica: El carácter de Azorín," Insula, 22:6, May, 1967.

Early critical response to Azorín was hardly favorable, even from a kindred spirit such as Manuel Bueno. (C.O.)

M1110 González Echevarría, Roberto, "El primitivismo de Azorín," Revista de Occidente, No. 76, pp. 95-103, July, 1969.

The Spanish intellectual and social atmosphere when Azorín began to write was propitious for his cult of the primitive and of the medieval Castilian spirit, which forms part of the general movement in contemporary European art, music and literature. (T.T.B.)

M1111 LaJohn, Lawrence, "Surrealism in Azorín's Theater," Kentucky Foreign Language Quarterly, 10:20-5, First Quarter, 1963.

"The third period of Azorín's literary evolution has been termed 'Sección de Superrealismo.' This period is characterized by a rejuvenation in both his novelistic and dramatic techniques. . . . His theater in the decade 1927-1936 is mainly an attempt to bring into Spain surrealism prevalent in the theater of continental Europe." (S.A.)

M1112 Livingstone, Leon, "The Pursuit of Form in the Novels of Azorín," PMLA, 77:116-33, March, 1962.

Azorín's novelistic career is a pursuit of form, from the earliest autobiographical realism to the self-conscious anti-novel of his later works. (C.O.)

M1113 Livingstone, Leon, "The Theme of Intelligence and Will in the Novels of Azorín," Romanic Review, 58:83-94, April, 1967.

Intelligence destroys will and is superior to it. Azorín's novel moves from the panicked apathy of La voluntad (1902) to the calm submission to a macrocosmic wisdom only superficially tied to chance. (C.O.)

M1114 Lott, Robert E., "Azorín's Experimental Period and Surrealism," PMLA, 79:305-20, June, 1964.

"Considerable disagreement exists about the application of terms like surrealism and expressionism to Azorín's experimental period. This is largely because of a faulty understanding of the true nature of these and other vanguard movements. In view of the present state of critical confusion and a lamentable lack of thorough studies . . . these terms should be used with extreme caution." (C.O.)

M1115 Mainer, José Carlos, "Para un análisis formal de Capricho y La isla sin aurora," Ínsula, 22:5, 11, May, 1967.

These two late novels show that Azorín is unjustly forgotten as a novelist. His philosophy of, and attempts at, fragmentation place him among the technical innovators of the 40's and 50's. (C.O.)

M1116 Marías, Julian, "Marías habla de Azorín," La Estafeta Literaria," No. 393, p. 10, April 6, 1968.

Azorín's style is superficial; it relies on the surface appearance of things in order to study the reality hidden underneath. In Azorín we see the uncertain density of which human life consists. (T.T.B.)

M1117 Miró, Emilio, "Antonio Azorín y algunos de sus hermanos novecentistas," Ínsula, 22:7, 10, May, 1967.

Will-less resignation and existential solitude are typical of the anti-heroes of Azorín and his contemporaries. Thus ideals, melancholy as they are, and ultimately empty, are necessary to the game of life. (C.O.)

M1118 Newberry, Wilma, "Pirandello and Azorín," Italica, 44:41-60, 1967.

"In summary, 'Pirandellism' is an essential component of the work of this important member of the Generation of '98, and Azorín's admiration of and affinity for Pirandello are undeniable. . . . The artistic combination of Pirandellism plus Golden Age Spanish techniques and ideas, plus Azorín's own original art in his experimental plays, certainly symbolizes the tradition plus innovation formula which is so often suggested as the solution to Spain's problems." (D.P.)

M1119 Pageaux, Daniel-Henri, "La Confrontation du passé et de l'actuel chez Azorín," Modern Language Notes, 82:210-21, March, 1969.

Azorín's vision of time is an unresolvable dialectic between past and present. The interplay between a disappearing past and a precarious present forces him to teeter between hope and despair. (C.O.)

M1120 Rand, Marguerite C., "Azorín in 1960 and After," Hispania, 45:32-9, March, 1962.

[These are recollections of an interview with Azorín, followed by a pilgrimage to his birthplace, etc.] (C.O.)

M1121 Rand, Marguerite C., "Más notas sobre Azorín y el tiempo,"
Hispania, 49:23-9, March, 1966.

Recent letters of Azorín show that he continues his well known
preoccupation with the theme of time, but without the anguish of
earlier years. (C.O.)

M1122 Rand, Marguerite C., "Tributo a Azorín," Hispania, 50:923-30,
December, 1967.

"His work represents one of the great literary values of the Spanish
world in the twentieth century. . . . He has created a new lyricism,
notable especially in the case of the poets." (C.O.)

M1123 Saénz, Pilar G., "El interés azoriniano en la literatura francesca,"
Duquesne Hispanic Review, 3:35-47, Spring, 1964.

From his first productive years at the turn of the century to the
present, Azorín has read, quoted, and commented on French
literature. Especially in Montaigne he finds a kindred spirit. (C.O.)

M1124 Torre, Guillermo de, "Azorín, esencial," Ínsula, 22:1, 12,
May, 1967.

Totally a writer, unattached to movements, schools, or commercial
necessity, Azorín delighted always in raising the insignificant, the
instantaneous, the trivial, to the level of art. (C.O.)

DIARIO DE UN ENFERMO

M1125 Livingstone, Leon, "The 'Esthetic of Repose' in Azorín's Diario de un
enfermo," Symposium, 20:241-53, 1966.

This early novel represents a first attempt by Azorín to transcend
finite reality while yet respecting it. The esthetic of repose involves the suspension of the entire movement of existence, a triumph
over the fugacity of the momentary. (C.O.)

DOÑA INÉS

M1126 Durán, Manuel, "Azorín's 'Broken Record Device' in Doña Inés,"
Romance Notes, 4:112-6, Spring, 1963.

The device of the constantly interrupted story reveals Azorín's contention that the flow of time produces violence and tragedy, but sensitivity enables man to transcend history. (S.T.B.)

DOÑA INÉS (cont'd)

M1127 Montes Huidobro, Matías, "Un retrato de Azorín: Doña Inés,"
Revista de Occidente, No. 81, pp. 362-72, December, 1969.

Azorín had the precision of a costumbrista. Like Juan Valera, he
uses the hands of his central character to express motion, emotion
and progress of sentiments and events. (T.T.B.)

LO INVISIBLE

M1128 Stimson, Frederick S., "Lo invisible: Azorín's Debt to Maeterlinck,"
Hispanic Review, 26:64-70, January, 1958.

"The drama reveals a direct influence in the borrowing of symbols.
. . . This new treatment, this purification, of French symbolism,
helps to make Lo invisible what Azorín calls superrealista."
(A.C.H.)

EL LIBRO DE LEVANTE

M1129 Barreda-Tomás, Pedro M., "El libro de Levante: Prenovela
gaseiforme," Hispania, 52:39-44, March, 1969.

In this "pre-novel" (1929), Azorín has suppressed all plot, all
narrative device, to arrive at a pure and formless novel-to-be.
(C.O.)

EL LICENCIADO VIDRIERA

M1130 Rand, Marguerite C., "El licenciado Vidriera, Created by Cervantes,
Re-Created by Azorín," Hispania, 37:141-51, May, 1954.

[This is a running comparison of Cervantes's exemplary novel and
Azorín's gloss (1915).] (C.O.)

PASIÓN

M1131 Pérez de la Dehesa, Rafael, "Un desconocido libro de Azorín:
Pasión (cuentos y crónicas) 1897," Revista Hispánica Moderna,
33:280-4, July-October, 1967.

González Derrano's published prologue to this book, plus other
circumstantial evidence, suggest that around 1897 Azorín under-
went an intellectual crisis which caused him to abandon his earlier

PASIÓN (cont'd)

revolutionary anarchism. Then it is highly probable that he decided against publishing an already promised and completed manuscript. (C.O.)

MARTÍNEZ SIERRA, GREGORIO

M1132 O'Connor, Patricia W., "La madre española en el teatro de Gregorio Martínez Sierra," Duquesne Hispanic Review, 4:17-24, 1965.

The typical mother-figure, once in power, is authoritarian and in-flexible, an unthinking exponent of religious and social traditions. She is an unflattering representative of the conservative classes in contrast, for Martínez Sierra, with the modern, independent, in-tellectually curious woman. (C.O.)

M1133 Young, Raymond A., "A Comparison of Benavente's Rosas de otoño and Martínez Sierra's Primavera en otoño," CLA Journal, 11:206-20, 1968.

"In general Primavera en otoño is more light and gay. Its problems are more easily settled; not so grave as those in Rosas de otoño." (C.O.)

MARTINSON, HARRY

M1134 Johannesson, Eric O., "Aniara: Poetry and the Poet in the Modern World," Scandinavian Studies, 32:185-202, November, 1960.

"Martinson's epic poem is a powerful and unbearably concrete illustration of one of the most acute problems of modern human beings, their estrangement from the natural world, an estrange-ment caused by man's passion to gain power over nature." (E.L.)

MARTYN, EDWARD

M1135 Ryan, Stephen P., "James Joyce and Edward Martyn," Xavier University Studies, 1:200-5, 1962.

James Joyce and Edward Martyn were "poles apart on most issues (ideological, doctrinal, and literary), [and yet] were in complete agreement on the necessity for an Irish theatre which would be European and international in scope, rather than provincial and

national. . . . Joyce was aware of his fellow-countryman's debt to
Continental playwrights, and . . . [held] a continued interest in
Martyn's work. . . ." (D.P.)

M1136 Ryan, Stephen P., "An Unpublished Letter of Edward Martyn, "
Notes and Queries, 7:268-9, July, 1960.

A letter written one month before the publication of Martyn's novel
Morgante "serves as substantial evidence" of Martyn's dislike of
the liberal statesman John Morley, and "indicates that the novelist's
anti-liberal position owes much to the publication, in 1889, of
William Samuel Lilly's A Century of Revolution. . . ." (G.C.)

M1137 Setterquist, Jan, "Ibsen and Edward Martyn, " Edda, 61:97-104,
1961.

"A rather malicious, yet magnificent full-length portrait of Martyn
appears in George Moore's autobiography Hail and Farewell.
Martyn had a "special interest in social and intellectual drama" and
he, "Moore and Yeats were all united in a mutual effort of doing for
Ireland what Ibsen had done for Norway." (G.C.)

THE HEATHER FIELD

M1138 Setterquist, Jan, "The Heather Field, " Edda, 61:82-96, 1961.

"And so Martyn in writing The Heather Field paid homage to the
great Norwegian pioneer, adopting, in his first play, some of
Ibsen's creative principles of the drama." (G.C.)

REGINA EYRE

M1139 Ryan, Stephen P., "Edward Martyn's Last Play, " Studies,
47:192-9, Summer, 1958.

Martyn's "final desperate effort to secure recognition for himself
and his playhouse is a Hamlet in reverse" with parallels to Ibsen's
When We Dead Awaken. "The ignominious failure of Regina Eyre
did much to hasten the Irish Theatre's death. . . . few theatres
could have survived a Regina Eyre--certainly not a theatre already
in the final stages of decline." (K.M.W.)

MARY, ANDRÉ

M1140 Chabaneix, Philippe, "Les Poètes et la poésie," La Revue des
Deux Mondes, 140:371-5, June 1-15, 1968.

[These are critique and souvenirs of Pierre Camo, François
Mauriac and André Mary.] (T.T.B.)

MASEFIELD, JOHN

M1141 Chubb, Thomas Caldecot, "Some Recollections of John Masefield,"
Mark Twain Journal, 14:7-10, Summer, 1969.

[These recollections of a friendship that began in 1920 when Chubb
won the Masefield Prize for poetry include Chubb's recollections of
a visit to Masefield in England and his remembrance of a talk by
Masefield on the hard lot of men before the mast in sailing ship
days.] (D.P.)

M1142 Delany, Paul, "W. B. Yeats to John Masefield: Two Letters,"
Massachusetts Review, 11:159-62, Winter, 1970.

[These two letters dated 1930 and 1932, from Yeats to Masefield,
the first of their correspondence to be published, "reveal something of the warmth and intimacy of their friendship," which began
at the turn of the century.] (D.P.)

M1143 Drew, Fraser, "The Irish Allegiances of an English Laureate:
John Masefield and Ireland," Éire-Ireland, 3:24-34, Winter, 1968.

"The important Irish allegiances of John Masefield are . . . the
personal ties with his wife and with Synge and the Yeats brothers,
and his interest in the Irish theatre and the Irish country scene."
(A.S.W.)

M1144 Drew, Fraser Bragg, "John Masefield and the Manchester Guardian,"
Philological Quarterly, 37:126-8, January, 1958.

". . . the Manchester Guardian has now vouched for the authenticity
of 390 Masefield articles . . . published in its pages between
August 26, 1903 and October 16, 1924. . . ." (G.C.)

M1145 Drew, Fraser, "Poetry and Pugilism: John Masefield's Fights, "
Canadian Forum, 38:155-6, October, 1958.

John Masefield, sailor and poet, was also a sports-lover, as
evidenced by his descriptions and praise of the boxing art. (R.K.)

M1146 Stanford, Derek, "Masefield at Eighty, " Contemporary Review,
194:19-22, July, 1958.

Mr. Masefield's three long works--The Everlasting Mercy, Dauber
and Reynard the Fox are not "easily matched . . . for vigour,
authenticity, and lyrical grace. . . . The stamina of the poet is in
them." (G.C.)

C. L. M.

M1147 Gierasch, Walter, "Masefield's 'C.L.M.', " Explicator,
13: Item 25, February, 1955.

Mother is author of harm to own sex. (B.K.)

CARGOES

M1148 Nault, Clifford A., Jr., "Masefield's 'Cargoes', " Explicator,
16: Item 31, February, 1958.

The poem, which contains anachronistic allusions, exalts the
coaster. (B.K.)

DAUBER

M1149 Couchman, Gordon W., "Masefield's Dauber and Falconer's
'Shipwreck', " Notes and Queries, N.S. 1:124, March, 1954.

"Masefield has drawn on Falconer's poem in the lines in Dauber in
which the Mate celebrates the successful passage around Cape Horn.
. . ." (G.C.)

M1150 Drew, Fraser Bragg, "Masefield's Dauber: Autobiography or
Sailor's Tale Retold?" Modern Language Notes, 72:99-101,
February, 1957.

"Dauber is not . . . basically autobiographical, although its theme
and its descriptive detail are clearly Masefield's own." (G.C.)

MASSON, ANDRÉ

M1151 Hubert, Renée R., "André Masson and His Critics," Comparative Literature Studies, 7:480-8, December, 1970.

". . . Breton sees Masson as a revolutionary. . . . Michel discovers Masson's desire . . . to espouse primitive myths. . . . Sartre . . . examines the dynamic and explosive nature of the lines that . . . reveal man's unbounded desire for liberation." (G.C.)

MASTERS, EDGAR LEE

M1152 Derleth, August, "Masters and the Revolt from the Village," Colorado Quarterly, 8:164-7, Autumn, 1959.

[This is an interview with Edgar Lee Masters at seventy-one.] (G.C.)

M1153 Derleth, August, "Three Literary Men: A Memoir of Sinclair Lewis, Sherwood Anderson, and Edgar Lee Masters," Arts in Society, 1:11-46, Winter, 1959.

[These are Derleth's recollections of his personal relations with Sinclair Lewis, Sherwood Anderson and Edgar Lee Masters, each of whom Derleth knew well and corresponded with, and each of whom played a role in Derleth's own development.] (D.P.)

M1154 Hartley, Lois, "The Early Plays of Edgar Lee Masters," Ball State University Forum, 7:26-38, Spring, 1966.

Masters's seven printed plays show "an ambitious man striving toward literary success. The play proves not to be his medium. Yet through the play he learns something about dialogue, structure --and drama." (G.C.)

M1155 Hertz, Robert N., "Two Voices of the American Village: Robinson and Masters," Minnesota Review, 2:345-58, Spring, 1962.

Edwin Arlington Robinson "is interested in the souls . . . which dramatize the writer's notion of the human condition. Edgar Lee Masters re-vivifies . . . an entire midwestern town, each of whose inhabitants speaks pretty much about his condition alone." (K.L.)

M1156 Masters, Edgar Lee, "Posthumous Poems of Edgar Lee Masters," Texas Quarterly, 12:71-115, Spring-Summer, 1969.

[These poems are selected and edited, with an introduction by Frank Kee Robinson.] (G.C.)

M1157 Narveson, Robert D., "The Two Lincolns of Edgar Lee Masters," Discourse, 4:20-39, Winter, 1961.

Writing with a nostalgic affection for the scenes of his boyhood, Masters paid in The Spoon River Anthology some of the warmest tributes in American literature to Lincoln as a small town man; but by the time Masters came to write the bitterly critical Lincoln: The Man, he had been forced to admit to himself that "Lincoln was no mere pawn to the forces of puritanism and plutocracy" but was "aligned with Masters's bitter political enemies." (W.G.F.)

M1158 Robinson, Frank Kee, ed., "Edgar Lee Masters Centenary Exhibition: Catalogue and Checklist of Books," Texas Quarterly, 12:4-68, Spring-Summer, 1969.

[This is an annotated catalog, indexed and illustrated, of the exhibit at the University of Texas.] (K.M.W.

ACROSS SPOON RIVER

M1159 Putzel, Max, "Masters's 'Maltravers': Ernest McGaffey," American Literature, 31:491-3, January, 1960.

Masters's friend "Maltravers" of Across Spoon River was really Ernest McGaffey, whose "real contribution was to recognize Masters's poetic talent at a stage when it would have been imperceptible to anyone who did not love him as a friend." (K.M.W.)

LICHEE NUTS

M1160 Hartley, Lois, "Edgar Lee Masters and the Chinese," Literature East and West, 10:302-5, September, 1966.

"Masters's understanding of the Chinese minority in two American cities [Chicago and New York] and his reading in Chinese literature led toward the writing of the witty, ironic poems of Lichee Nuts." In the collection Masters wrote satirically "on some of his favorite topics, including national and world politics, aspects of American culture, and Christianity. . . . Lichee Nuts remains one of Masters's more original and absorbing books." (D.P.)

THE NEW SPOON RIVER

M1161 Robinson, Frank Kee, "The New Spoon River: Fifteen Facsimile Pages," Texas Quarterly, 12:116-43, Spring-Summer, 1969.

[Fifteen facsimile pages are presented, along with comments on the history of The New Spoon River and its critical reception.] (K.M.W.)

A ONE-EYED VIEW

M1162 Crawford, John W., "A Defense of 'A One-Eyed View'," CEA Critic, 31:14-5, February, 1969.

Masters's anthology followed the naturalistic tendency to show man in society caught in circumstances which conspire to defeat his potential development. It contains plain statement, disillusionment and exaltation, as well as antithesis, but the basic interpretation of a writer should be determined not by the exceptions to his style, but by the abundance of a given mood. (T.T.B.)

THE PASTURE ROSE

M1163 Burgess, Charles E., "An Unpublished Poem by Edgar Lee Masters," Papers on Language and Literature, 5:183-9, Spring, 1969.

"The Pasture Rose," dated October 23, 1941 and probably unrevised, was written for Edith L. Masters, a first cousin of the poet. ". . . it is another of those poems in which he utilized the characteristics suggested by lives of members of his family for a philosophical poetic sketch." (W.E.K.)

SPOON RIVER ANTHOLOGY

M1164 Crawford, John W., "Naturalistic Tendencies in Spoon River Anthology," CEA Critic, 11:6, 8, June, 1968.

Throughout all the epigraphs in Spoon River Anthology "which illustrate the deterministic interpretation of life, there is an ancient and haunting sense of the poignancy of human disappointment and defeat." (D.P.)

SPOON RIVER ANTHOLOGY   (cont'd)

M1165 Duffey, Bernard I., "Progressivism and Personal Revolt,"
Centennial Review, 2:125-38, Spring, 1958.

The riddle of Western agrarian reform in America covering the
period from about 1870 to the nomination of Woodrow Wilson may
be illuminated through an examination of the imaginative literature
associated with the movement. Hamlin Garland's Main Travelled
Roads "grew very closely out of its author's involvement in the
Granger-Farmers's Alliance-Populist nexus. . . . Masters's
Spoon River Anthology reflects a direct and active commitment to
Bryan Democracy." Finally, Sandburg's Chicago Poems "was
closely associated with Sandburg's attachment to Midwestern
socialism. . . ." (D.P.)

M1166 Earnest, Ernest, "A One-Eyed View of Spoon River," CEA Critic,
31:8-9, November, 1968.

It is dangerous to pigeonhole Masters as a naturalist who believes
that all phenomena may be explained on the basis of determinable
causes. The greatness of the work lies in the variety of its responses to life. The very structure of the work is often that of
antithesis. (T.T.B.)

M1167 Earnest, Ernest, "Spoon River Revisited," Western Humanities
Review, 21:59-65, Winter, 1967.

The appearance of The Waste Land, and the subsequent change in
direction of modern poetry may have caused the decline of Spoon
River's reputation, but "it has a robust, earthy quality that has
been rare in the poetry since its time." (A.S.W.)

M1168 Hahn, Henry, "Evolution in the Graveyard," Midwest Quarterly,
10:275-90, April, 1969.

". . . the apparent 'split personality' of the Anthology arises with
Masters's attempts to capture a living, changing 'scientific' concept
of man and then to entomb that concept in 'graveyard poetry' of an
earlier age." (G.C.)

MATA, GONZALO HUMBERTO

M1169 Urbanski, Edmund Stephen, "Ecuadorian Literary War Over Juan Montalvo," Hispania, 52:102-9, March, 1969.

In the 1960's Gonzalo Humberto Mata spearheaded a critical attack on Ecuador's nineteenth century essayist, Montalvo. His impassioned attacks have been joined by others and have brought Mata a noisy fame. (C.O.)

MATA DOMÍNGUEZ, PEDRO

M1170 Sainz de Robles, Federico C., "Raros y olvidados: Pedro Mata (1875-1946)," La Estafeta Literaria, No. 435, p. 20, January 1, 1970.

Poet, playwright and journalist, Mata launched his great success in prose with Corazones sin rumbo and continued with popular novels of gallantry, writing with a tactful erotic naturalism that avoids extremes. (T.T.B.)

MATTHIESSEN, FRANCIS OTTO

M1171 Gunn, Giles B., "Criticism as Repossession and Responsibility: F. O. Matthiessen and the Ideal Critic," American Quarterly, 22:629-48, Fall, 1970.

"In urging the critic to attend at once to the arts of his own time . . . Matthiessen was largely attempting to rescue criticism from the peripheries of life and return it again to the center. His chief aim was simply to recall critics to their primary obligation--to make of criticism nothing less than an act of the fully responsive and engaged self." (K.M.W.)

MATUTE, ANA MARÍA

M1172 Díaz, Janet Winecoff, "The Autobiographical Element in the Works of Ana María Matute," Kentucky Romance Quarterly, 15:139-48, 1968.

"Despite the importance of autobiographical settings, of rural and agrarian themes, of the themes of solitude and alienation, and of the world of marionettes, the greatest input of autobiographical elements in Matute's work" comes from the Spanish Civil War. (G.C.)

M1173 Jones, Margaret W., "Religious Motifs and Biblical Allusions in
the Works of Ana María Matute," Hispania, 51:416-23,
September, 1968.

Ana María Matute often introduces religious or Biblical material to
express her personal philosophy or to offer additional insight into
character development. Without attacking organized religion, she
castigates the "money changers" who pervert Christian ideology.
She also expresses her sympathy with the lower classes. (C.O.)

M1174 Winecoff, Janet, "Style and Solitude in the Works of Ana María
Matute," Hispania, 49:61-9, March, 1966.

"The recurrent themes of solitude, lack of communication, and
alienation of the individual, the numerous instances of life's meaninglessness and futility, and the apparent impossibility of escape
are, of course, major topics of existentialism. Their prominence
in Matute's writing might be explained in terms of . . . existentialist influence, or as a commentary on life in present-day Spain.
. . ." (C.O.)

M1175 Wythe, George, "The World of Ana María Matute," Books Abroad,
40:17-28, Winter, 1966.

Mansilla de la Sierra, where Ana María Matute spent her summer
holidays as a child, plays an important role in her writings, which
are "enhanced by the extent to which she sees the world through the
eyes of childhood. It is this quality of mystery, of magic, of fairy
tale, combined in a unique mixture with the harsh and bitter realities of life, that gives the distinctive stamp to all of her work."
(D.P.)

PEQUEÑO TEATRO

M1176 Díaz, Janet W., "La 'Comedia dell'arte' en una novela de Ana
María Matute," Hispanófila, 40:15-28, September, 1970.

Her first novel, Pequeño teatro, coincides substantially with the
form of the commedia dell'arte. Even the novel's satire of contemporary Spanish life is disguised under the trappings of traditional
farce. (C.O.)

MAUGHAM, WILLIAM SOMERSET

M1177 Amis, Kingsley, "Mr. Maugham's Notions," Spectator, No. 6941, pp. 23-4, July, 1961.

"Like all writers with energy and a degree of professional pride, Mr. Maugham has managed on occasion to transcend his limitations. His notions of the writer's function and nature . . . [are] patently inadequate as a commentary on his own best work." (R.J.G.)

M1178 Belloc, Elizabeth, "The Stories of Somerset Maugham," Month, 32:67-72, 1964.

Maugham's stories illustrate that he "is one of the real writers of our time, a brilliant craftsman who knows what he has to say and how to say it." (G.C.)

M1179 Burgess, Anthony, "W. Somerset Maugham: 1874-1965," Listener, 74:1033, December 23, 1965.

Maugham possesses a "very considerable art" which learned much from the Victorians and became increasingly supple and economical. His most successful efforts, in keeping with his talent, are in the short story. His most characteristic contribution is the dispassionate man of the world who serves as a first-person author-narrator. His power and elegance has not declined in later years. (D.P.)

M1180 Cordell, Richard A., "Somerset Maugham at Eighty," College English, 15:201-7, January, 1954.

"Somerset Maugham has been ashamed of dullness and obscurity but never of competence. It is this competence . . . which may insure for him a position not far below the major writers of the past half-century. . . ." (G.C.)

M1181 Cordell, Richard A., "Somerset Maugham: Lucidity Versus Cunning," English Fiction in Transition, 1:30-2, No. 3, 1958.

Maugham has been badly underrated by critics since they regard "clarity and intelligibility as lack of subtlety and cunning. . . . his writings afford no puzzles, uncertainties, ambiguities; one looks in vain for allegory, myth, time-themes, labyrinthine motifs, dialectics, myriad perspectives, world of images, metaphor in the plot, and so on." ". . . the cunning scholar-critic might begin by praising lucidity as a virtue rather than condemning it as a vice." (G.C.)

M1182 Cordell, Richard A., "The Theatre of Somerset Maugham,"
Modern Drama, 1:211-7, February, 1959.

Maugham completed his "theatre" twenty-five years ago, and is
now content to be merely a playgoer. (C.K.L.)

M1183 Cosman, Max, "Mr. Maugham as Footnote," Pacific Spectator,
10:64-9, Winter, 1956.

Accurately gauging and gratifying public taste, Maugham has always
been a sure seller. He has treated the topical with the perennial:
love, marriage, religion. Despite nihilism, hedonism, optimism,
and pessimism, his center is common sense. Not first rank, he
will be, one hopes, a large footnote on literary history. (J.L.B.)

M1184 Dobrinsky, J., "Aspects biographiques de l'oeuvre de W. Somerset
Maugham," Études Anglaises, 8:299-312, No. 4, 1955.

". . . the purpose of this article is to evoke the youth of Somerset
Maugham . . . because such an examination will not fail to shed
light on the origin of his vocation and the birth of his temperament as
a writer. In a concern to be objective, we must consider critically
the autobiographical works of Maugham himself." (D.P.)

M1185 Dobrinsky, J., "Les Débuts de Somerset Maugham au théâtre:
Naissance d'une vocation et affirmation d'une personnalité
littéraire," Études Anglaises, 10:310-21, 1958.

"As the themes outlined in the first part of a symphony are picked
up in the finale, the thematic rough drafts of Maugham's first plays
are picked up and integrated in the major works of the mature
period." (D.-J.J.)

M1186 Fielden, John Seward, "The Ibsenite Maugham," Modern Drama,
4:138-51, September, 1961.

". . . Maugham is to a surprising extent an Ibsenite . . . over half
his plays are in varying degrees problem plays . . . [and] as a
social satirist he is by no means greatly inferior to Shaw. . . ."
(G.C.)

M1187 Gerber, Helmut E., "W. Somerset Maugham," English Fiction in
Transition, 1:30-2, 1957.

[This is a listing of the major recent Maugham bibliographies and
items not listed in those bibliographies.] (G.C.)

M1188 Heywood, C., "Somerset Maugham's Debt to <u>Madame Bovary</u> and
Miss Braddon's <u>The Doctor's Wife</u>," <u>Études Anglaises</u>, 19:64-9,
January-March, 1966.

Maugham's use of <u>Bovary</u> was shaped by Braddon's imitative novels.
(C.E.N.)

M1189 Jonas, Klaus W., "W. Somerset Maugham: An Appreciation,"
<u>Books Abroad</u>, 33:20-3, Winter, 1959.

"Somerset Maugham is the last great professional writer of
England. For sixty years he has earned his living exclusively by
his books . . . expressing his opinions heedless of whether his
fellow men agree with him or not." (K.M.W.)

M1190 Jonas, Klaus W., "W. Somerset Maugham Collections in America,"
<u>Jahrbuch für Amerikastudien</u>, 3:205-13, 1958.

Major library collections of Maugham manuscripts, correspondence
and books are held by the Library of Congress, Yale University, and
the New York Public Library. Important collections are also held
by the Princeton University Library, The Pierpont Morgan Library
and Stanford University. Preeminent among private collections are
those of Bertram E. Alanson, Richard A. Cordell and Karl G.
Pfeiffer. (D.P.)

M1191 Krim, Seymour, "Maugham the Artist," <u>Commonweal</u>, 61:284-7,
December 10, 1954.

"Maugham is perhaps only a first-rate 'minor' writer. But . . .
[he] has held his audience through the years, and expanded it by
consistently giving extreme adult pleasure in the realm in which he
became expert; he is the last of the great flower of nineteenth
century professionals in a world in which the writing of fiction no
longer has the stability of a 'profession,' and is slowly but inevitably
changing its character and its ultimate purpose." (D.P.)

M1192 Krim, Seymour, "Somerset Maugham," <u>Commonweal</u>, 61:245-50,
December 3, 1954.

". . . the time seems especially ripe to consider this wise old
literary cat. . . . Not only has Maugham had an unusually long and
productive career . . . his work has persisted among readers of all
tastes with a perversity almost equal to Maugham himself, refusing
to lie down and die despite innumerable burial services. . . .

Maugham is close to being a master of the art of story-telling, and it is hard to conceive of a modern fiction writer of any school who does not appreciate this mastery. . . ." (D.P.)

M1193 Maugham, Somerset, "Looking Back on Eighty Years," Listener, 31:173-4, January 28, 1954.

[This comparison of the habits and customs of the England of half a century ago with present day practices includes a number of auto-biographical digressions.] (D.P.)

M1194 Menard, Wilmon, "Maugham's Pacific," Saturday Review, 50:77-80, March 11, 1967.

Maugham's "most fascinating short stories and novels are those about the lush green islands of the South Seas or about the exotic Orient." His early reading of Moby Dick, Typee, and Omoo had stimulated his interest, and his own extensive travels in the Pacific, where he was able to observe personalities on shipboard and in port, coupled with gossip brought him by his sociable, charming secretary-companion, Gerald Haxton, provided the basis for much of his know-ledge of the Pacific. (D.P.)

M1195 Menard, Wilmon, "Somerset Maugham and Paul Gauguin," Michigan Quarterly Review, 7:227-32, 1968.

[In this interview Maugham discusses his "visit-of-research" to Tahiti.] (G.C.)

M1196 Menard, Wilmon, "Somerset Maugham in Hollywood," Michigan Quarterly Review, 7:207-10, Summer, 1968.

[These are reminiscences of Maugham's Hollywood career.] (G.C.)

M1197 Pollock, John, "Somerset Maugham and His Work," Quarterly Review, 104:365-78, 1966.

"Somerset Maugham used two lines of approach to his subjects. In one, he took . . . the outer psychological values of a real person and wrought them into an imaginary portrait by embodying them in a series of [fictitious] incidents. . . . In the other he took the fundamental values and put them into fictitious persons. . . ." (G.C.)

M1198 Rees, Leslie, "A Meeting with Somerset Maugham," <u>Meanjin Quarterly</u>, 26:452-6, December, 1967.

[This is an account of a meeting of Rees with Maugham during the London theatre sesson of 1933-34.] (G.C.)

M1199 Smith, Harrison, "In the Great Tradition: Maugham the Master Craftsman," <u>Saturday Review</u>, 49:25, January 15, 1966.

Maugham revealed a great intelligence, that was cold and cynical, in a world of mediocre or moronic minds. He had an abysmal knowledge of the middle and upper classes and was a master craftsman of his time in recording society as he, a citizen of the world, saw it. (W.K.)

M1200 Swinnerton, Frank, "Maugham at Eighty," <u>Saturday Review</u>, 37:13-4, 70-2, January 23, 1954.

Now, as Somerset Maugham reaches his eightieth year, he is beginning to receive critical attention for those virtues of lucidity and detachment which were not sufficient to bring him a critical reputation in the unfavourable context of his great popular success. (D.P.)

M1201 Visanath, G. V., "The Novels of Somerset Maugham," <u>Quest</u>, No. 23, pp. 50-2, October-December, 1959.

Maugham's "'realism'" is "in the nature of a magician's trick, where a curtain is whisked aside to reveal the unpleasant reality that lies behind the appearance." (G.C.)

CAKES AND ALE

M1202 Brown, Allen B., "Substance and Shadow: The Originals of the Characters in <u>Cakes and Ale</u>," <u>Publications of the Michigan Academy of Science, Arts, and Letters</u>, 45:439-46, 1961.

[This article identifies probable "real life" prototypes of characters in <u>Cakes and Ale</u>.] (G.C.)

THE CIRCLE

M1203 Fielden, John S., "'Mrs. Beamish' and The Circle," Boston
University Studies in English, 2:113-23, Summer, 1956.

"The Circle is a satirical comedy concerned with showing the
superiority of 'romance' of the free life lived by the emotions, to
the life of dull, over-intellectual conventionality. . . ." (G.C.)

LIZA OF LAMBETH

M1204 Colburn, William E., "Dr. Maugham's Prescription for Success,"
Emory University Quarterly, 19:14-21, Spring, 1963.

Maugham, in his first novel, Liza of Lambeth, doesn't follow his
own recommendation that "a young writer is to write only about the
things he knows." (R.K.)

MRS. CRADDOCK

M1205 Heywood, C., "Two Printed Texts of Somerset Maugham's Mrs.
Craddock," English Language Notes, 5:39-46, September, 1967.

A comparison of the first edition of Mrs. Craddock (1902) to the
Collected Edition of 1937 "sheds light both on the objects of censorship at the turn of the century and on the persistence of Maugham's
interest in his early novel." (G.C.)

OF HUMAN BONDAGE

M1206 Doner, Dean, "Spinoza's Ethics and Maugham," University of
Kansas City Review, 21:261-9, Summer, 1955.

The title of Maugham's Of Human Bondage is taken from Part IV of
Spinoza's Ethics. Further, the underlying structure of the novel is
derived from Spinozian concepts. Philip moves, through the novel,
from unwilling acceptance of his part (bondage) to an understanding
of the true nature of the whole and positive acceptance of his part in
the whole. Understood in Spinozian terms, Philip becomes more
than merely a believer in a meaningless life, but rather a free man.
(A.W.)

ON A CHINESE SCREEN

M1207 Redlin, Rosemarie, "Somerset Maugham: On a Chinese Screen,"
Die Neueren Sprachen, 13:573-81, 1964.

The value and charm of this work stems not only from its conciseness, its classical simplicity and psychological unity, but from its
objectively clear depiction of a person tragically fated to live part
of his life in a completely alien land. (G.C.)

MAULNIER, THIERRY

M1208 Belvin, Robert W., "The Problem of the Literary Artist's Detachment as Seen by Julian Benda, Jean-Paul Sartre and Thierry
Maulnier," Romanic Review, 47:270-84, December, 1956.

Benda believed the intellectual must deprecate "realist" passions
and glorify spiritual values; only on rare occasions should he enter
the world of action. Sartre, on the contrary, believes the whole
life of the intellectual must be in the world of action. Maulnier
represents a mediating force: the intellectual "is not to isolate
himself from his period . . . nor to embrace it, but to see beyond
it." (B.B.)

M1209 Giraud, Raymond, "Maulnier: In and Above the Conflict, "
Yale French Studies, No. 14, pp. 79-84, April, 1955.

Maulnier's La Maison de la nuit lacks unity of tone. Scenes operate
at various levels without creating a pattern of contrast that is
esthetically satisfying. Nevertheless it is an attempt to rise above
polemics ". . . and to produce a work of art and a study of the complexities of motivation and human character." (L.L.)

MAURIAC, CLAUDE

M1210 Galey, Matthieu, "Nathalie et Claude," Cahiers des Saisons,
No. 35, pp. 564-6, Fall, 1963.

Although resembling somewhat Nathalie Sarraute, Mauriac is more
dogmatic, translating into a rigid technique what is, with her, only
the supple instrument of an artist. His more immediate ancestors
are Joyce, Balzac, Rivarol and Dujardin, even to the point of candor,
details, unhealthy minutiae, sincerity and love of new forms.
(T.T.B.)

M1211   Johnston, Stuart L., "Structure in the Novels of Claude Mauriac,"
        French Review, 38:451-8, February, 1965.

        "Claude Mauriac's four novels, which are in reality one novel in
        four parts, are at once a meditation on subjective and objective
        reality in space and time and an exercise in novelistic technique."
        (R.B.W.)

M1212   Mercier, Vivian, "The Immobilization of Time," Nation,
        201:119-21, February 1, 1965.

        Claude Mauriac's tetralogy, Le Dialogue intérieur "can be described
        as unique. By sheer dint of writing, he has worked his way out of
        the derivative and the slick into a personal style and an individuality
        whose existence he himself might paradoxically deny [since] a per-
        sistent theme in the tetralogy is Bertrand's conviction of his own
        lack of individuality, his denial of the uniqueness of each human
        personality, his view of men . . . as replaceable parts."
        (D.P.)

        MAURIAC, FRANÇOIS

M1213   Allen, Trevor, "The Mauriac Novels," Contemporary Review,
        208: 211-5, April, 1966.

        Mauriac's novels, filled with the spiritual conflicts of errant souls,
        not-at-all-certain expiation, and hard-won divine pardon leave a
        feeling that even out of the human "wrack" there comes "the clarity
        of a serene sunset after a storm." His Catholic scruples become an
        implicit part of the story: he is not a "theological romancer."
        (F.L.)

M1214   Audinet, Pierre, "À la lumière de Malagar," À La Page, No. 16,
        pp. 1512-6, October, 1965.

        [These are souvenirs of Mauriac and critique of L'Agneau.]
        (T.T.B.)

M1215   Blot, Jean, "François Mauriac et la forêt magique," La Nouvelle
        Revue Française, No. 199, pp. 80-4, July, 1969.

        Fortune resides in the pine forests that fill Mauriac's universe--
        forests which control the conformity of the characters. In a closed
        society any variation represents a threat. The woman, guardian of

values, plays a privileged role. Any love which risks losing these values is forbidden. (T.T.B.)

M1216 Bost, Jacques-Laurent, ". . . Je suis désabusé," Les Temps Modernes, 17ᵉ année, No. 189, pp. 1197-1201, February, 1962.

Mauriac's diatribes against Vilar and Malraux, which appeared in his notes, are "useless, venomous and vulgar." His antagonism to Dumur's criticism discloses arguments which are contradictory, inasmuch as he is blinded by his fanaticism for de Gaulle. "In other words, he is a schizophrenic." (T.T.B.)

M1217 Chabaneix, Philippe, "Les Poètes et la poésie," La Revue des Deux Mondes, 140, Nos. 11-12:371-5, June 1 & 15, 1968.

[These are critiques and souvenirs of Pierre Camo, François Mauriac and André Mary.] (T.T.B.)

M1218 Davis, R. T., "Reservations about Mauriac," Essays in Criticism, 9:22-36, January, 1959.

Although Mauriac's fiction possesses concentration, point and lucid intensity, his work is marred by a narrowness of range and too often communicates "a sense that living is a distasteful and hellish affair." The failure in Mauriac's imaginative sympathy results in "scrappiness and discontinuity" in his novels, while many aspects of every-day life are entirely absent. (C. O.)

M1219 Eustis, Alvin, "Youth in Mauriac: An Assessment," French Review, 39:536-41, February, 1966.

"Youth leads us . . . to the very heart of the author's universe, to the message that he is trying to spell out for himself in his successive creations, for by its mere existence youth serves his older characters as a catalyst, bringing about profound changes in them." (G.C.)

M1220 Flower, J. E., "The Role of the Natural World in the Novels of François Mauriac," Modern Languages, 49:55-61, June, 1968.

"[Mauriac] uses certain devices . . . to create inner cohesion between subject matter and style . . . in such a way that the metaphysical problems . . . are perfectly contained within the cyclic patterns of a natural and animal world. . . . Noticeable . . . are his use of the weather . . . and a repeated motif regularly associated with an individual. . . ." (J.L.A.

M1221 Fumet, Stanislas, "Les Quatre-vingts Ans de François Mauriac," La Table Ronde, No. 214, pp. 132-5, November, 1965.

Mauriac was a novelist whereas he is still a poet and never so much one as when he became a "journalist." He is no longer forced to conform to the conventional requirements of the novel. (T.T.B.)

M1222 Gallant, Clifford J., "La Mère dans l'oeuvre de François Mauriac," Kentucky Foreign Language Quarterly, 11:79-85, No. 2, 1964.

Mauriac lost his father when he was eighteen months old. He was raised by his mother and was profoundly influenced by her. His work bears the imprint of that experience, as indicated by the maternal characters of his novels, from the most abusive Félicité Cazenave in Génitrix to the loving Blanche Frontenac in Le Mystère Frontenac. (D.-J.J.)

M1223 Graef, Hilda, "Marriage and our Catholic Novelists," Catholic World, 189:185-90, 1959.

Mauriac, Greene and "other outstanding contemporary Catholic authors" depict marriage as "either something horrible or boring, or, if physically satisfactory, necessarily sinful." (G.C.)

M1224 Holdheim, William W., "Mauriac and Sartre's Mauriac Criticism," Symposium, 16:245-58, Winter, 1962.

A detailed analysis of Sartre's "M. François Mauriac et la liberté" (February 1939) "will not only reveal Sartre's virtues and faults as a literary critic, but will lead to a fruitful completion and modification of his Mauriac picture--fruitful because it involves nothing less than the aesthetics of the modern novel in general." (M.G.)

M1225 Jerome, Sister M., I. H. M., "Human and Divine Love in Dante and Mauriac," Renascence, 18:176-84, Summer, 1966.

Among recent writers it is Mauriac who "most consistently demon-strates a preoccupation with [the] relationship between human and divine love. Moreover, his novels when examined sequentially display a development of this theme very similar in its basic prem-ises to that of the great Italian poet." (S.A.)

M1226 Kyria, Pierre, "Une Poète à réinventer: François Mauriac," Cahiers des Saisons, 44:446-8, Winter, 1966.

Novelist, polemicist and moralist, Mauriac is especially a poet. He has no public, absolute truths to give us except that of his art. (T.T.B.)

M1227 Liebling, A. J., "M. Mauriac's Automobile," New Yorker, 34:39-61, June 21, 1958.

Since World War II, Mauriac has consecrated himself to journalism and controversy, "the arts of the age" and has become "more than any other man in our time, the articulate conscience of France." (W.G.F.)

M1228 Mein, Margaret, "François Mauriac and Jansenism," Modern Language Review, 58:516-23, October, 1963.

The prospect of reconciliation between God and man saves Mauriac from the extremes of the Jansenist doctrine which strongly influenced him. (S.T.B.)

M1229 Moloney, Michael F., "François Mauriac: The Way of Pascal," Thought, 32:389-408, 1957.

"In the wake of Pascal the fundamental fact of human life is, for Mauriac, the collision of the Christian ethic with the inclinations of nature." (G.C.)

M1230 Pivot, Bernard, "Un Adolescent d'autrefois," Réalités, No. 278, pp. 103-11, March, 1969.

Mauriac continues writing traditional regional literature--that of sentiments, money, evil and dissatisfied youth. (T.T.B.)

M1231 Reck, Rima Drell, "Mauriac's Inferno," Yale French Studies, No. 32, pp. 118-23, 1964.

"For Mauriac, the modern city becomes the landscape of a spiritual odyssey." "His originality lies . . . in an anterior vision, carefully elaborated through many novels, of an authentic place, the region around Bordeaux, from which his characters often flee, but which remains for them the pendant to the living death they see in Paris. . . . Only the lost seek Paris where they are further lost." (D.P.)

M1232 Robichon, Jacques, "François Mauriac a quatre-vingts ans," À La Page, No. 16, pp. 1504-11, October, 1965.

Mauriac explores the solitude of man in the midst of his likenesses and his facility to delude himself concerning his vices. In these themes he is a moralist. His interpretation of the seamy side of life and the immanence of hell attach Mauriac to the tradition of Pascal, Joubery, Chamford and Montaigne. (T.T.B.)

M1233 Rubin, Louis D., Jr., "François Mauriac and the Freedom of the Religious Novelist," Southern Review, 2:17-39, Winter, 1966.

"Intellectually, Mauriac's Jansenist position would be much closer to that of orthodox Puritans. But emotionally, humanly, Mauriac is drawn toward sinners, and in his very denunciation of sin, in the lurid colors he uses to paint it, he reveals the attraction it holds for him." (J.M.D.)

M1234 Sénart, Philippe, "M. Mauriac et le 'dégagement'," La Table Ronde, 166:95-9, November, 1961.

To write was to bear witness for Mauriac in the beginning. Today it is to pray. Formerly he warned his readers that the "novelist rarely yields to the temptation of silence." Now that he feels nearer God than men, he finds no way to agree with anyone about anything. By realizing that writing and silence are not incompatible, he has solved the problem that old age presented to him. (T.T.B.)

M1235 Smith, Maxwell A., "Mauriac and the Theatre," American Society of Legion of Honor Magazine, 37:101-10, No. 2, 1966.

Although Mauriac's dramatic productions do not loom large in his total oeuvre, his plays do represent a distinctive achievement. "What differentiates his plays from his novels is chiefly their almost complete absence of any religious element. . . . What Mauriac's plays have in common with his novels is their fundamental pessimism. . . ." (D.P.)

M1236 Smith, Maxwell A., "A Visit with François Mauriac," American Society of Legion of Honor Magazine, 34:155-62, No. 3, 1963.

[The conversation is limited almost entirely to Mauriac's literary work. Dr. Courrèges in Le Désert de l'amour is a projection of Mauriac himself. Le Mystère Frontenac expresses the depth of his devotion to his family. Mauriac is a Jansenist with his heart but not with his head.] (D.P.)

M1237 Stoker, J. T., "The Question of Grace in Mauriac's Novels,"
Culture, 26:288-302, September, 1965.

Some of Mauriac's characters, like Yves Frontenac and Marie and
Luc in Le Noeud de vipères, are "born with grace." Others, like
Naémi Pélouegre, have grace thrust upon them, "whilst those who
achieve grace are Jean Pélouegre, Thérèse Desqueyroux and Louis,
the main character of Le Noeud de vipères." (G.C.)

M1238 Stratford, Philip, "One Meeting with Mauriac," Kenyon Review,
21:611-22, Autumn, 1959.

[This is a description of an interview with Mauriac on June 18, 1957.]
(G. C.)

M1239 Turnell, Martin, "The Style of François Mauriac: Sin and the
Novelist," Twentieth Century, 164:242-53, September, 1958.

Mauriac's "is a country of extremes . . . remorseless sun and
torrential rains. These extremes are reflected . . . in his prose
style [and other aspects of his life and work.] . . . You cannot
have a world of extremes without monotony. . . . The contrast
between the monotony of tone and syntax and the violence of imagery
and vocabulary [is significant.] Monotony is the moral element in
Mauriac's work, violence of language his rebellion against it."
(D.A.B.)

M1240 Vial, Fernand, "Paris Letter," Renascence, 7:187-95, 1955.

[Among "some important events of a Catholic character" this
"letter" mentions the Semaine des Intellectuals Catholiques which
dealt with Mauriac's theme "What is man?" and the production of
Port-Royal, Montherlant's play.] (D.A.B.)

M1241 Weightman, J. G., "Mauriac, the Witness," Encounter, 12:71-3,
No. 1, 1959.

"Whatever reservations one may wish to make about [Mauriac's]
quality as a creative artist or about his depth as a thinker, it must
be agreed that he has been a very effective thorn in the side of the
French bourgeoisie." (G.C.)

LES ANGES NOIRS

M1242 Flower, J. E., "Form and Unity in Mauriac's The Black Angels, " Renascence, 19:79-87, Winter, 1967.

In The Black Angels, "Mauriac manages to contain his material in what is for him a new handling of the physical form of his novel, and more importantly by translating the metaphysical problem involved into the terms of a natural cycle." (G.C.)

LE BAISER AU LÉPREUX

M1243 Stratford, Philip, "Chalk and Cheese: A Comparative Study of A Kiss for the Leper and A Burnt-Out Case, " University of Toronto Quarterly, 33:200-18, January, 1964.

The difference between Mauriac's A Kiss for the Leper and Greene's A Burnt-Out Case "is tuberculosis in Les Landes and leprosy in the Congo. Yet . . . they are both poetic in . . . 'the power to suggest human values.' . . . But finally . . . the important thing is that grace is present." (D.P.)

THE BLACK ANGELS--See
LES ANGES NOIRS

LE DÉSERT DE L'AMOUR

M1244 Humiliata, Sister Mary, I. H. M., "The Theme of Isolation in Mauriac's The Desert of Love," Twentieth Century Literature, 7:107-13, October, 1961.

Human isolation, the "impenetrability of souls" is a pervasive theme in many of Mauriac's novels, a theme perhaps best exemplified in The Desert of Love. The theme of isolation is identified by a wide range of imagery, and isolation is here overshadowed by the novel's major theme--"that Divine Love is man's only fulfillment." (D.P.)

THE DESERT OF LOVE--See
LE DÉSERT DE L'AMOUR

L'ENFANT CHARGÉ DE CHAÎNES

M1245 Flower, J. E., "François Mauriac and Social Catholicism: An Episode in L'Enfant chargé de chaînes, " French Studies, 21:125-38, April, 1967.

L'ENFANT CHARGÉ DE CHAÎNES (cont'd)

"Jean Paul's adventures in L'Enfant chargé de chaînes reflect
Mauriac's own reactions to social, literary, emotional or religious
experiences at this time in his life. . . . Yet there is no mature,
serious criticism of Social Catholicism in this novel." (G.C.)

LA FIN DE LA NUIT

M1246 Thornton-Smith, C. B., "Sincerity and Self-justification: The
Repudiated Preface of La Fin de la nuit," Australian Journal of
French Studies, 5:222-30, May-August, 1968.

In his Oeuvres Complètes (Fayard, 1950), Mauriac repudiates the
preface to the first edition of La Fin de la nuit, ostensibly on the
grounds that the character Thérèse had not been converted before
her death, which would scandalize Mauriac's Catholic readers.
Inevitably, the repudiation enhances the value of the original preface
as a means of putting in perspective Mauriac's stated reasons for
not converting Thérèse. (D.P.)

GÉNITRIX

M1247 McNab, James P., "The Mother in François Mauriac's Génitrix,"
Hartford Studies in Literature, 2:207-13, 1970.

"Mauriac's artistic success in Génitrix derives largely from his
creation of perfect consistency between the mother-son relationship
and the World in which it is situated, so that the World stands as a
symbol of the relationship and is inseparable from it." (G.C.)

M1248 Murphy, Eugene F., "Mauriac's Génitrix," Explicator,
13: Item 37, April, 1955.

"An eloquent textual detail that serves to lift this roman-tragédie
above provincial proportions is the abundance of romanisms,
latinisms, and 'classicismes' which Mauriac irresistibly inserts
into the dramatic narrative." (G.C.)

A KISS FOR THE LEPER--See
LE BAISER AU LÉPREUX

LE NOEUD DE VIPÈRES

M1249 Denommé, Robert T., "The Viper's Tangle: Relative and Absolute
Values," Renascence, 18:32-9, Autumn, 1965.

Mauriac dramatically underscores "the absurdity of an existence in
which no absolute value is sought. Despite its exterior form, The
Viper's Tangle is not a novel concerned with relative values; it is a
work concerned with ideals and absolutes." (S.A.)

M1250 Tartella, Vincent P., "Thematic Imagery in Mauriac's Viper's
Tangle," Renascence, 17:195-200, Summer, 1965.

The "systems of imagery that energize the novel," as well as some
of its situations, have "scriptural resonances" which provide "a
rich ground against which Louis's story is the modern, particular
figuring of a timeless, Universal pattern." (S.A.)

M1251 Wentersdorf, Karl P., "The Chronology of Mauriac's Le Noeud de
vipères," Kentucky Foreign Language Quarterly, 13:89-100,
Supplement, 1967.

Throughout Le Noeud de vipères the "many references to people's
ages and to periods of time . . . permit the reconstruction of a chronology for the life of the protagonist that is both detailed and . . .
coherent. The large number of these references suggests . . . a
carefully worked-out time plan." (D.P.)

LA PHARISIENNE

M1252 Heck, Francis S., "Dos mujeres sin alma: La Pharisienne y Doña
Perfecta," Duquesne Hispanic Review, 4:79-89, 1965.

"Is it possible that Doña Perfecta had an influence on La Pharisienne?
Did François Mauriac know the work of Galdós?" (C.O.)

THÉRÈSE--See
THÉRÈSE DESQUEYROUX

THÉRÈSE DESQUEYROUX

M1253 Farrell, C. Frederick, Jr. and Edith R. Farrell, "The Multiple
Murders of Thérèse Desqueyroux," Hartford Studies in Literature,
2:195-206, 1970.

THÉRÈSE DESQUEYROUX   (cont'd)

" . . . Mauriac has created an integral character whose psychological tendencies remain constant throughout her life. . . .
[Thérèse] poisoned Bernard when her frustration reached the point
where fantasy would not relieve it. . . ."   (G.C.)

M1254 Murray, Jack, "Three Murders in the Contemporary French
Novel," Texas Studies in Literature and Language," 6:361-75,
Autumn, 1964.

François Mauriac's Thérèse Desqueyroux, Albert Camus's
L'Étranger and Alain Robbe-Grillet's Le Voyeur disclose "a possible
trend in contemporary French literature toward an increasing dehumanization in the representation of human life." The person is
more and more dissociated from the world around him and his own
personal history. This trend may be the result of "the anachronistic survival of Cartesian psychology."   (W.G.F.)

M1255 Sutton, Geneviève, "Phèdre et Thérèse Desqueyroux: Une
communauté de destin," French Review, 43:559-70, March, 1970.

Thérèse and Phèdre are both captives of place, time, noncom-
munication, and their crimes. They are marked by death from the
beginning.   (A.K.)

M1256 Swift, Bernard C., "Structure and Meaning in Thérèse Desqueyroux,"
Wascana Review, 5:33-44, 1970.

The "suggestiveness" of the novel "arises--not only from details of
circumstance, tone, imagery, atmosphere--but from its persuasive
evocation, through the structure itself, of some ultimate unintelligi-
bility in human acts."   (G.C.)

M1257 Villas, James M., "The Pine Trees in Mauriac's Thérèse
Desqueyroux," Romance Notes, 3:3-9, Spring, 1962.

"An attentive study of the novel's structure reveals the frequently
recurrent image of the pine trees, used by Mauriac to symbolize
the gradual decline and degradation of Thérèse's existence."
(S.T.B.)

VIPER'S TANGLE-See
LE NOEUD DE VIPÈRES

THE WOMAN OF THE PHARISEES--See
LA PHARISIENNE

YOUNG MAN IN CHAINS--See
L'ENFANT CHARGÉ DE CHAÎNES

MAUROIS, ANDRÉ

M1258 Huvos, Kornel, "André Maurois et les États-Unis: Relativisme,
conformisme, sympathie," French Review, 42:825-33, May, 1969.

"Since it is impossible to know absolute truth (relativism), we must
accept the world as it seems to us . . . (conformism)." Relativism
and conformism determine Maurois's attitude toward the United
States. (A.K.)

M1259 Kolbert, Jack, "André Maurois à la recherche d'un genre: La
biographie," French Review, 39:671-83, April, 1966.

As a novelist Maurois's career has not been distinguished. But
through his biographies he has created a powerful human comedy.
(D.P.)

M1260 Kolbert, Jack, "André Maurois 1885-1967," American Society of
Legion of Honor Magazine, 39:9-11, No. 1, 1968.

"André Maurois passed away on October 9, 1967 at the age of
eighty-two. . . . It is not too soon to make initial assessments of
his contributions to contemporary French literature." (D.A.B.)

M1261 Kolbert, Jack, "André Maurois's Esthetics of Biography,"
Bulletin of the Rocky Mountain Modern Language Association,
21:45-51, June, 1967.

"In the opinion of Maurois, biography as a genre is a delicate blend
of history, literary criticism, psychology, social science, and
literary art. . . . [However,] in the final analysis, the biographies
of André Maurois are the products of an incurable moraliste."
(D.A.B.)

M1262 Kolbert, Jack, "A Few Notes on the Short Fiction of André Maurois,"
Studies in Short Fiction, 3:104-16, Winter, 1966.

"Taken as a whole, Maurois's stories form a miniature Comédie
humaine, with their interwoven multiplicity of characters, themes,
and situations." (P.J.R.)

M1263 Kolbert, Jack, "The Worlds of André Maurois," Susquehanna
University Studies, 7:215-30, June, 1965.

"Mauriac merits the attention of a large audience because he is
. . . an exemplary figure who has forged an exemplary existence
from which less exemplary people can learn much. The life of this
author is an eighty-year triumph of the mind and art over the formidable obstacles of everyday life." (D.A.B.)

M1264 LeSage, Laurent, "The U. S. Through French Eyes: André Maurois
and Marcel Aymé," American Society of Legion of Honor Magazine,
39:13-26, No. 1, 1968.

André Maurois and Marcel Aymé died within a week of each other in
October, 1967. Maurois, who knew America intimately, was "a
polite observer of American manners." No one in his country "has
spoken better on our behalf." Marcel Aymé has shown "a derisive
and censorious picture of American life" in a short-story and two
plays. Between them, these two authors illustrate the range between
an unsympathetic and uninformed view of America, typical, unfortunately, of that of many Europeans, and an intelligent and sympathetic point of view. (D.P.)

M1265 Maurois, André, "Il y a cent ans naissait Romain Rolland,"
À La Page, No. 24, pp. 836-51, June, 1966.

Although the distance between their temperaments appears great,
it is only when one knows better Maurois, (pupil of Alain) and
Romain Rolland that one perceives that they have in common the
taste and love for a universal humanism. (T.T.B.)

M1266 Perruchot, Henri, "Les Trois Moments de la vocation littéraire
d'André Maurois," À La Page, No. 43, pp. 20-4, January, 1968.

Influenced most strongly by the works of Hugo and Balzac, as well
as by the instruction and direction of Alain, Maurois entered upon
a writing career instead of embracing the teaching profession. His
services as liaison officer with the English army in World War I
enabled him to understand a foreign point of view and colored his
novels, e. g., Bernard Quesnay and Les Silences du colonel
Bramble. (T.T.B.)

PROMÉTHÉE

M1267 O'Brien, Justin, "Observer of the Human Comedy," Saturday
Review, 49:26-7, July 9, 1966.

Maurois, at the age of eighty, "has published his biography of that
towering genius Honoré de Balzac. No one less than a Rodin could
portray Balzac as he looked to his contemporaries and as he looks
to us; only a Maurois could write his life with the required empathy
and gusto." (D.P.)

M1268 Pommier, Jean, "Balzac 1965: Le Prométhée d'André Maurois,"
Revue d'Histoire Littéraire de la France, 65:657-82, October-
December, 1965.

"Clearly the genre of biography has evolved to new psychoanalytic,
character development, sociological preoccupations, etc., let alone
Marxism. However, we should take this work for what it . . . does
excellently: it is a chronicle of Balzac . . . and not regret the absence of elements characteristic of newer works in the mode." (D.P.)

MAURRAS, CHARLES

M1269 Kedward, H. R., "The Nationalism of Charles Maurras,"
Listener, 79:565-7, May 2, 1968.

"When placed back among the crises and tensions of the Third
Republic Maurras is seen to be the most coherent antithesis to
Republican rule. . . . one can find his ideas diffused throughout
most right-wing movements in . . . France, not least in the numerous fascist groups and in the insular nationalism of . . . de Gaulle." (D.P.)

M1270 Léger, François, "Une visite de M. Taine à Maurras," La Revue
des Deux Mondes, 140:191-200, May 15, 1968.

On December 29, 1890, L'Observateur français published an admiring article on Taine by Maurras. As a result, the philosopher
visited Maurras. This story is the basis for the chapter in Barrès's
Déracinés describing Taine's visit to Roemerspacher. Although the
details of the visit by Maurras may be fallacious, the portrait of
Taine's views is essentially correct. (D.-J.J.)

M1271 Maurras, Charles, "Correspondance de Maurice Barrès et Charles Maurras (1888-1923)," La Revue des Deux Mondes, 142:30-47, January, 1970; 276-91, February, 1970.

[This is commentary on their respective works.] (T.T.B.)

MAVOR, OSBORNE HENRY

M1272 Luyben, Helen L., "James Bridie and the Prodigal Son Story," Modern Drama, 7:35-45, May, 1964.

The Black Eye uses the prodigal son in that the higher transcendence of irrational goodness makes a destiny for the hero in spite of himself. (G.A.S.)

MAY, JAMES BOYER

M1273 Beaudoin, Kenneth Lawrence, "James Boyer May: A Force in Contemporary Literature," Carolina Quarterly, 10:63-71, Spring, 1958.

Already important as a short story writer and a critic concerned with weaning the American public from effete, academic poetry, May merits recognition also as an "abstract" and satiric poet, who, in a tumultuous decade, "has redigested the traditional themes, and at least tentatively restated them in the very teeth of change." (W.G.F.)

MAYAKOVSKY, VLADIMIR--See
MAĬAKOVSKIĬ, VLADIMIR VLADIMIROVICH

MAYER, TOM

M1274 Davis, Kenneth W., "The Themes of Initiation in the Works of Larry McMurtry and Tom Mayer," Arlington Quarterly, 2:29-43, Winter, 1969-70.

The aim of the southwestern writers McMurtry and Mayer is knowledge--recognition and confirmation in the world to which the actions of the work must tend. (T.T.B.)

MAZZANTI, CARLOS

M1275 Gibbs, Beverly Jean, "Spatial Treatment in the Contemporary
Psychological Novel of Argentina," Hispania, 45:410-4,
September, 1962.

In the contemporary psychological novel of Argentina, as represented by José Bianco's Las ratas, Ernesto Sábato's El túnel,
Eduardo Mallea's La sala de espera, Estela Canto's El hombre del
crepúsculo, and Carlos Mazzanti's El sustituto, spatiality "forms a
special kind of background against which the personalities of the
protagonists are delineated, or . . . it is transformed into a psychic
phenomenon and serves in the portrayal of the mental and physical
patterns of behavior of these individuals." (D.P.)

MEDIO, DOLORES

M1276 Díaz, Janet Winecoff, "Three New Works of Dolores Medio,"
Romance Notes, 11:244-50, Winter, 1969.

In Isabel II, El señor García, and Andrés, the author's abiding
concern with the effect of environment on her characters, especially
that of money, is a dominant feature. (A.K.)

M1277 Murciano, Carlos, "Dolores Medio o la experiencia novelada,"
La Estafeta Literaria, No. 408, pp. 8-10, November 15, 1968.

From delightful children's stories and mediocre work lacking in
creative force and imaginative penetration, Dolores Medio has
developed a clipped direct style and has become an exceptional
narrator, alternating the external narration technique with the
interior monologue, after Funcionario público and including such
works as Mañana, Compás de espera, El pez sigue flotando.
(T.T.B.)

M1278 Winecoff, Janet, "Fictionalized Autobiography in the Novels of
Dolores Medio," Kentucky Foreign Language Quarterly,
13:170-8, 1966.

Dolores Medio's works form two groups: "the first, in which
autobiographical elements prevail in setting, plot and characters;
the second, in which plot and characters are no longer drawn from
the novelist's own life. . . ." (G.C.)

MEIRELES, CECÍLIA

M1279 Nist, John, "The Poetry of Cecília Meireles," Hispania, 46:252-8, May, 1963.

One of the outstanding figures of modern Brazilian poetry, adopted by the Modernist Movement, unique in her preference for traditional forms and religious themes (joy, awe), Meireles also serves to link Brazilian poetry with the less radical movements of Portugal. (C.O.)

MEJÍA VALLEJO, MANUEL

M1280 Deuel, Pauline B., "Sound and Rhythm in El día señalado," Hispania, 52:198-202, May, 1969.

"The auditory imagery . . . and its reinforcement through group-ings of rhythmic patterns . . . [bring] a heightened awareness of sound and rhythm in the novel. The rhythm refers specifically to the marked beat of the repetitions, but it could apply to the whole mystique of Mejía Vallejo's style." (C.O.)

MELEZH, IVAN

M1281 Ovčarenko, Aleksandr, "Otzilo li nacional'noe svoj vek?" Voprosy literatury, 11:53-66, December, 1967.

In positive characterizations of their own national heroes, White Russian authors (Dovzenko, Bozenko, and Melezh) contribute to the enrichment of heroes of other nations. The literature of a single nation assumes universal humanitarian traits. (V.D.)

MELL, MAX

M1282 Guder, G., "Der Nibelunge Not: A New Drama by Max Mell," German Life and Letters, 8:285-92, July, 1955.

Founding his two-part drama on the greatest epic inheritance of the Germans, Das Nibelungenlied, Mell strove to answer the urgent question of a corrupt time objectively by revealing that man can overcome his existential insecurity only by renouncing all striving for temporal security and seeking security in the Eternal Law of the infinite. (W.G.F.)

MENCKEN, HENRY LOUIS

M1283 Angoff, Charles, "H. L. Mencken: A Postscript," South Atlantic Quarterly, 63:227-39, Spring, 1964.

[These are recollections of Mencken's relationships with Philip Goodman and George Jean Nathan.] (D.P.)

M1284 Angoff, Charles, "The Inside View of Mencken's Mercury," New Republic, 131:18-22, September 13, 1954.

"Mencken himself--and so powerfully did he impress his personality upon The [American] Mercury that he and it were virtually one as long as he edited it--was a man of few basic ideas, and perhaps half of them were absurd, cheap, and simply not true. . . . But as a journalist his influence was immense. Indeed, he was one of the greatest editors in all our history." (D.P.)

M1285 Angoff, Charles, "A Kansan in Westchester," University Review, 31:283-8, June, 1965.

[These are recollections of Dorothy Thompson--a Kansan in Westchester--and her relations with her husband Sinclair Lewis and with H. L. Mencken.] (D.P.)

M1286 Angoff, Charles, "Mencken as a 'German' American," Chicago Jewish Forum, 25:143-6, Winter, 1966-67.

Mencken held reactionary politico-economic views, and his love of things German led to apparent pro-Nazi sympathies. (A.S.W.)

M1287 Angoff, Charles, "Mencken: Prejudices and Prophecies," Saturday Review, 46:44-5, August 10, 1963.

Mencken's editorial greatness lasted from 1924-1928. With the beginning of the Great Depression in 1929, "he lost his grip, and thereafter till his retirement at the end of 1934, he did little more than fumble." His best years of achievement were golden ones in the history of journalism in the United States. (W.K.)

M1288 Babcock, C. Merton, "Mark Twain, Mencken and 'The Higher Goofyism'," American Quarterly, 16:587-94, Winter, 1964.

Twain and Mencken had much in common, but "the most remarkable difference between them" was that "whereas the former felt at home

with the verbal patterns of unsophisticated people, the latter consistently deprecated the unintellectuality of homely idioms."
(W.G.F.)

M1289 Babcock, C. Merton, "Mencken's Shortest Way with Academic
Nondissenters," University College Quarterly, 12:28-32,
January, 1967.

"H. L. Mencken . . . worked out a sure-fire, double-barreled
method for solving the problems of higher education in America.
He proposed: (a) hanging the professors, and (b) burning the
Universities." (A.S.W.)

M1290 Babcock, C. Merton, "Profiles of Noted Linguists: Henry Louis
Mencken," Word Study, 36:1-4, No. 2, 1960.

[This is a short biographical sketch of the author of The American
Language.] (K.M.W.)

M1291 Babcock, C. Merton, "The Wizards of Baltimore: Poe and
Mencken," Texas Quarterly, 13:110-5, Autumn, 1970.

Although Mencken was reluctant to admit any critical affinity with
Poe, both "were prowling practitioners of the black arts, blas-
phemous profaners of the sacred groves, and bedeviled headhunters
running amuck in the American literary jungle. Both critics would
gladly have throttled the clergy, gagged the pedagogues, barbecued
the transcendentalists, and strangled all fake pretenders to literary
fame." (D.P.)

M1292 Barrick, Nancy D. and Ernest O. Brown, M. D., "Mencken, the
Negro, and Civil Rights," Menckeniana, No. 35, pp. 4-7,
Fall, 1970.

"Mencken grappled with the movement for Negro civil rights, such
as it was before World War II, in as sophisticated a fashion as anyone of his day. In principle he upheld civil rights as guaranteed by
the Constitution. Yet . . . the image of the Negro as a completely
free and equal citizen made him uneasy." (D.P.)

M1293 Bauer, Harry C., "Grand Master of the Word Art," Menckeniana,
No. 27, pp. 4-12, Fall, 1968.

Mencken "fancied himself to be a critic of ideas; but he will chiefly
be remembered as a consummate performing artist in the verbal

category of communications, rather than as an earnest dispenser of brilliant ideas. What made him the Grand Master of the Word Art was his uncanny ability to package old truths, half-truths, and untruths so daintily that they bore and still bear the semblance of astonishing new truths." (D.P.)

M1294 Black, Earl, "Mencken and Individualism," New Mexico Quarterly, 35:215-22, Autumn, 1965.

Menckenian individualism is "a rather bald example of cultural nihilism. Individualism, demonstrated by assailing that which society holds sacred, reduces to iconoclasm, and no occasion is missed to point out that the emperor is, in fact, nude." "The Menckenian individualist observes and ridicules, but he does not participate, and this is his ultimate failure. . . . in the history of American individualism, it is difficult to believe that Menckenian individualism was itself more than a third-rate variety." (D.P.)

M1295 Blodgett, Harold W., "Mencken and Conrad," Menckeniana, No. 29, pp. 2-3, Spring, 1969.

From 1908, when he reviewed Conrad's "The Point of Honor" until after Conrad's death, "Mencken appreciated Conrad's modernity, his technical experimentation, his probing into motives, his ironic detachment that both scorned and underlined involvement, his profound pessimism . . . above all his finding in the alien English language a mastery of style. All these qualities aroused Mencken's own abundant resources of expression. . . ." (D.P.)

M1296 Bloom, Robert, "Past Indefinite: The Sherman-Mencken Debate on an American Tradition," Western Humanities Review, 15:73-81, Winter, 1961.

In the extended debate between Stuart P. Sherman and H. L. Mencken on Dreiser and American literature, Sherman displayed a basic inability to understand the nature of literature and America, while Mencken, if often overshooting his mark, aimed in the right direction. (M.H.)

M1297 Boewe, Charles, "Fable Agreed Upon," Colorado Quarterly, 10:277-83, Winter, 1962.

[This tongue-in-cheek discussion of the need for "truth which transcends mere historical accuracy" analyzes Mencken's "highly publicized bathtub story."] (G.C.)

M1298 Boller, Paul F., Jr., "Purlings and Platitudes: Mencken's
Americana," Southwest Review, 50:357-71, Autumn, 1965.

In his monthly feature "Americana" in the American Mercury
H. L. Mencken used the "fatuous quote," which refuted itself
without the need of comment, to satirize prejudice, religious
bigotry, American chauvinism and anti-intellectualism. (D.P.)

M1299 Buitenhuis, Peter, "The Value of Mencken," Western Humanities
Review, 14:19-28, Winter, 1960.

"As a literary arsonist . . . [Mencken] burned many rubbishly
intellectual constructions and outmoded temples. Thus he prepared
the ground for a good deal of the subsequent honesty and integrity of
American literature." (G.C.)

M1300 Castagna, Edwin, "Loud and Clear: H. L. Mencken the
Communicator," Menckeniana, No. 30, pp. 1-8, Summer, 1969.

Mencken "delighted, shocked and diverted his contemporaries.
Beyond that he gave us splendid lessons in how to use our language
to communicate with each other. . . . He knew how to tell it, maybe
not just the way it was, but exactly as he saw it, and with zest."
(D.P.)

M1301 Cooke, Alistair, "The Baltimore Fox," Saturday Review, 38:13,
63-4, September 10, 1955.

If Mencken "was overrated in his day as a thinker . . . he was vastly
underrated as a humorist with one deadly sensible eye on the behavior of the human animal. . . . He was . . . a humorist by
instinct and a superb craftsman by temperament. So that . . . there
emerged . . . purified and mellowed in later years, a style flexible,
fancy-free, ribald, and always beautifully lucid. . . . " (D.P.)

M1302 Cooke, Alistair, "The Last Happy Days of H. L. Mencken,"
Atlantic Monthly, 197:33-8, May, 1956.

"This is a memoir of those few days at the end of July, 1948, when
[Mencken] frolicked in his favorite sport, politician-baiting. . . ."
(G.C.)

M1303 Cowing, Cedric B., "H. L. Mencken: The Case of the 'Curdled' Progressive," Ethics, 69:255-67, July, 1959.

Mencken was "the epitome of waning progressivism. . . . In reactionary, postwar American the evangelism of the progressives was supplanted by frustration, and in adversity they came to rely more on invective than on popular fervor. Mencken represented the cause in this final stage." (G.C.)

M1304 Dolmetsch, Carl Richard, "H. L. Mencken as a Critic of Poetry," Jahrbuch für Amerikastudien, 11:83-95, 1966.

The general opinion of Mencken as a critic of poetry admits that he was "an ingratiating stylist [but] . . . an irresponsible critic whose criticism was totally without theoretical foundation and based solely upon whim, caprice and ad hominem considerations." Actually, "as one who helped to sweep away much of the claptrap of poetasting that went on in pre-World War I America, who called attention to the works of many excellent new poets . . . and who provoked . . . a movement that has eventually been as dynamic and productive as the New Criticism, Mencken deserves better than he has received in the history of American literary criticism." (D.P.)

M1305 Dolmetsch, Carl R., "Mencken as a Magazine Editor," Menckeniana, No. 21, pp. 1-8, Spring, 1967.

Mencken's accomplishments as magazine editor and a champion of new American writers in the face of financial troubles and a declining magazine public were enormous. (A.S.W.)

M1306 Durham, Frank, "Mencken as Midwife," Menckeniana, No. 32, pp. 2-6, Winter, 1969.

Although DuBose Heyward, John Bennett, and Hervey Allen formed the Poetry Society of South Carolina in part, at least, because of "their outrage at the apparently anti-Southern disquisitions of Henry Louis Mencken," he was really, in his Machiavellian way, attempting to encourage the formation of a Southern literature. He was also responsible for the first appearances in print of Julia Peterkin. (D.P.)

M1307 Durham, Frank, "Mencken As Missionary," American Literature, 29:478-83, January, 1958.

Mencken wrote two letters vainly trying to persuade Henry Sydnor Harrison to sign the Dreiser protest. (W.G.F.)

M1308 Durr, Robert Allen, "The Last Days of H. L. Mencken," Yale
Review, 48:58-78, September, 1958.

Mencken, in his last years, hampered in speech, sight, and memory,
and suffering frequent pain, lived in his Victorian Baltimore home
with his brother August, where he followed a simple daily routine
determined by the weather and his current physical state. Kindly
and considerate toward visitors and neighbors, he belied the general
concept of the whiplash of the twenties. (F.L.)

M1309 Farrell, James T., "Dr. Mencken: Criticus Americanus," New
World Writing, No. 6, pp. 64-76, 1954.

"There is a simple explanation for the fact that Mencken can still
be interesting on subjects dead to us. He loved to write, and unlike
many editors and critics, he liked and respected writers. To
Mencken, the America of the twenties was the biggest circus on
earth." (K.M.W.)

M1310 Fitzgerald, F. Scott, "Six Letters to the Menckens from F. Scott
Fitzgerald," Fitzgerald-Hemingway Annual, pp. 102-4, 1970.

[These letters and notes sent from 1930 to 1935 are concerned
primarily with personal rather than literary matters.] (D.P.)

M1311 Fitzgerald, Stephen E., "The Mencken Myth," Saturday Review,
43:13-5, 71, December 17, 1960.

H. L. Mencken "is not to be easily catalogued. There is Mencken,
the iconoclast, the editor, the writer, the author, the sponsor of
young writers. There is Mencken the musician and connoisseur of
good food. There is Mencken the practical joker, Mencken the
scholar. There is the traveling journalist, complete with portable
typewriter. There is the skeptic [who stated:] . . . 'One horse-
laugh is worth ten thousand syllogisms. It is not only more effective;
it is also vastly more intelligent'." (D.P.)

M1312 Forgue, G., "La Carrière de H. L. Mencken et les critiques,"
Études Anglaises, 12:112-23, April, 1959.

In forty years of criticism Mencken has yet to find his critic: "on
many essential points, the man and the work remain a mystery
which favors the birth of tenacious and specious legends."
(D.-J.J.)

M1313 Forgue, Guy Jean, "Myths about Mencken," Nation, 193:163-5, September 16, 1961.

Mencken has been variously described "as a liberal, an anarchist, and a reactionary. Some see him as an atheist; others a Christian. He has been denounced as a foe of America and as a rabid national- ist; taken for a pacifist, or a warmonger; an optimist, or a pes- simist; a first-rate intellect, or a low buffoon." Most unpleasant of all, he has been charged with being pro-Nazi and anti-Semitic. "That such gross misrepresentations could have been made and be- lieved shows that it is hard to talk sense about Mencken. . . . by their diversity and their persistence [these legends] testify to Mencken's influence and universality." (D.P.)

M1314 Forgue, Guy J., "Quelques 'prejugés' politiques de H. L. Mencken," Études Anglaises et Americaines, 3:101-13, No. 3, 1966.

Baltimore provided the source for Mencken's criticism of the U. S. Mencken considered himself a social rather than a political critic; his work is central to the liberal revolt against the agrarian, religious and conservative thought patterns prevalent at the begin- ning of the century. His political theory that the aristocrat would need to sacrifice himself to the needs of democracy had no effect on events; he attempted unsuccessfully to form a freedom party to protect the U. S. Constitution from change. (D.P.)

M1315 Johnston, Gerald W., "Henry L. Mencken [1880-1956]," Saturday Review, 39:12-3, February 11, 1956.

When Mencken died the world lost "the incomparable reporter, the critic, the philologist, the social historian. . . ." But his friends in Baltimore lamented their loss of "Henry Mencken the unique who, deriding them exalted them, in threatening them encouraged them, in prophesying death and doom gave them a new, strong grip on life." (D.P.)

M1316 Knopf, Alfred A., "For Henry, with Love," Atlantic Monthly, 203:50-4, May, 1959.

[This is a "remembrance" of the Knopf-Mencken friendship, "warmly lit, full of laughter, forthright . . . and endearing. . . ."] (G.C.)

M1317 Krutch, Joseph Wood, "This Was Mencken: An Appreciation," Nation, 182: 109-10, February 11, 1956.

"No doubt it will be some time yet before he will . . . have lived down his popularity and a lack of gentility more absolute than . . . even Mark Twain . . . dared exhibit. He founded no worthy school . . . his style was inimitable. . . . But . . . the time will come when it will be generally recognized . . . that Mencken's was the best prose written in America during the twentieth century." (D. P.)

M1318 McCall, Raymond G., "H. L. Mencken and the Glass of Satire," College English, 23:633-6, May, 1962.

"The main intent of Mencken's satire is not to shock the booboisie but to direct the [intellectual] elite, in the manner of a barker at a carnival, to the choice features of the spectacle." (R. J. G.)

M1319 McHugh, Robert, "Dirge for a Vanished Art," South Atlantic Quarterly, 60:340-4, Summer, 1961.

"Letters to the editors of newspapers, one of the few truly indigenous American art forms, have declined . . . into a disgraceful state of decay." Letters to the editor of the Baltimore Evening Sun by "American Mother" were actually by Holger A. Koppel, royal Danish consul in Baltimore, and a friend of Mencken, and Mencken had a hand in many of his letters which expressed "a somewhat broad caricature of the expressions, alarms, prejudices, and whims of a contemporary mother." (D. P.)

M1320 Manchester, William, "H. L. Mencken at Seventy-Five: America's Sam Johnson," Saturday Review, 38:11-2, 64-5, September 10, 1955.

The most provocative critic of the twenties, he served, as did Johnson, as a parlor conservative when the left was advancing. Both were gargantuan wits and neurotics, and "hard on incompetence, stern with cant, brutal with dishonesty." They were "literary deans who had built solid reputations within the craft and could improve upon the accepted because they had mastered it." (C. P.)

M1321 Martin, Edward A., "H. L. Mencken's Poetry," Texas Studies in Literature and Language, 6:346-53, Autumn, 1964.

Mencken's first book, Ventures into Verse (1903), was a poetic miscellany. His verse, however, "shows a progression and reflection in itself of Mencken's growing awareness of his failure as a poet," but that he "turned away from versemaking and fiction does not mean that his poetic impulses . . . atrophied . . . only that he sought in journalism what for him were more suitable forms of rhetoric." (W.G.F.)

M1322 Martin, E. A., "The Ordeal of H. L. Mencken," South Atlantic Quarterly, 61:326-38, Summer, 1962.

Influenced by the anti-Philistinism of Nietzsche and Shaw, Mencken placed high value on individualism; yet, like Mark Twain, "he was never [really] able to . . . move away from . . . the bourgeois life that had nurtured him." Consequently, he adopted the duplicitous mask of comic satire "to convey . . . deepest feelings about his culture." (J.L.A.)

M1323 Morrison, Joseph L., "Colonel H. L. Mencken, C. S. A.," Southern Literary Journal, 1:42-59, Autumn, 1968.

In spite of Mencken's scolding tone toward the south in many of his essays, his Toryism and Social Darwinism made the ideals and life style of the "old" south of 1750 appealing to him. (A.S.W.)

M1324 Morrison, Joseph L., "Mencken and Odum: The Dutch Uncle and the South," Virginia Quarterly Review, 42:601-15, Autumn, 1966.

Fifty-odd letters of Mencken to Howard W. Odum, the Southerner and pioneer regional sociologist, testify not only to a warm friendship, but to Mencken's influence on and support of a remarkably progressive southern scholar. (D.P.)

M1325 Mott, Frank L., "The American Mercury," Menckeniana, No. 22, pp. 9-10, Summer, 1967.

[This article describes the style and content of The American Mercury.] (A.S.W.)

M1326 Nolte, William, "Criticism with Vine Leaves," Texas Studies in Literature and Language, 3:16-39, Spring, 1961.

Mencken's success as a humorist has made people remember him primarily as a wit rather than an intellectual because "it is a natural human tendency to accord the humorless clod who spouts his nonsense with funereal seriousness a higher position than we give to the hearty rascal who leavens his common sense with laughter." (W.G.F.)

M1327 Nolte, William H., "GBS and HLM," Southwest Review, 49:163-73, Spring, 1964.

Mencken and Shaw "shared much": both "were concerned with ideas"; both loved music, "were concerned with philology," religion, and both were craftsmen in prose. However, "they differed in the fundamental fact that Shaw was essentially a revolutionary." (G.C.)

M1328 Nolte, William H., "Mencken on Prose Fiction," Texas Quarterly, 7:139-53, Autumn, 1964.

Although Mencken "never laid down a set of iron-clad rules concerning the novel or drama or poetry," he "did have a theory of literature and theory of criticism, both of which were rather severely revised between the early years on the Smart Set and the period of the [American] Mercury." (W.G.F.)

M1329 Nolte, William H., "Mencken's Criticism of Criticism," Midwest Quarterly, 6:417-38, July, 1965.

Mencken's essay "Criticism of Criticism of Criticism" places "the critic in the role of . . . catalyst" and "'empiricist'." His "Footnote on Criticism" depicts the critic as "primarily concerned with expressing himself in his individual reaction to the work of art." (G.C.)

M1330 Nolte, William H., "The Smart Set: Mencken for the Defense," South Dakota Review, 6:3-11, Autumn, 1968.

Mencken, through his editorship of The Smart Set, encouraged many young writers and "cleared the way for an aesthetic approach to art free from moralistic dogma." (A.S.W.)

M1331 Porter, Bernard H., "H. L. Mencken: A Bibliography," Twentieth Century Literature, 4:100-7, October, 1958.

[Listed here chronologically in several categories are works by H. L. Mencken, with a final section which reports books and pamphlets on Mencken.] (D.P.)

M1332 Pouder, G. H., "Mencken and Cabell," <u>Menckeniana</u>, No. 15, pp. 1-5, Fall, 1965.

"More than any other force, Mencken was responsible for Cabell's literary emergence forty-five or more years ago. . . . Cabell was very conscious of the powerful assist and frequently acknowledged it in graceful fashion." (D.P.)

M1333 Pouder, G. H., "Mencken and the Dramatic Urge," <u>Menckeniana</u>, No. 21, pp. 9-10, Spring, 1967.

Although no plays of Mencken's were ever actually produced, he did write two or three amusing burlesques which make entertaining reading. (A.S.W.)

M1334 Puknat, Siegfried B., "Mencken and the Sudermann Case," <u>Monatshefte</u>, 51:183-9, April-May, 1959.

Sudermann's works were given a varied reception in America. H. L. Mencken thought the plays and novels lacked direction because Sudermann tried to mix watered-down romanticism into doctrinaire Schlaf-Holz naturalism. But Mencken esteemed Sudermann's <u>Novellen</u>, which offered less range for diffuseness. (R.H.L.)

M1335 Remley, David A., "I Am a One-Hundred Percent American," <u>Carleton Miscellany</u>, 10:96-103, Fall, 1969.

[These are reminiscences of Mencken as a member of the "Saturday Night Club."] (G.C.)

M1336 Rubin, Louis D., Jr., "H. L. Mencken and the National Letters," <u>Sewanee Review</u>, 74:723-38, July-September, 1966.

". . . the phase of Mencken's career that will be adjudged of most significance and usefulness will be the 1910's, when he was composing his monthly literary essays for the old <u>Smart Set</u>. In the 1920's Mencken was a symbol and a symptom; in the 1910's he was a maker and a finder. He will figure in our national letters as the leading dismantler of the Genteel Tradition, the chief crusader against certain venerated nineteenth-century literary attitudes which . . . had to be destroyed if future American writers were to do their best work." (D.P.)

M1337 Stenerson, Douglas C., "The 'Forgotten Man' of H. L. Mencken,"
American Quarterly, 18:686-96, Winter, 1966.

Mencken was both arch-reactionary and libertarian. "Since he took
over concepts from . . . different sources without attempting to
reconcile the assumptions on which they were based, the opinions he
expressed in his social criticism are often strikingly inconsistent."
(W.G.F.)

M1338 Stenerson, Douglas C., "Mencken's Early Newspaper Experience:
The Genesis of a Style," American Literature, 37:153-66,
May, 1965.

Largely through self-education while a young newspaperman,
Mencken "began to perfect a style capable of expressing vividly the
whole range of the ideas and attitudes which later gained fame as
his 'prejudices'." (W.G.F.)

M1339 Stenerson, Douglas C., "Short-Story Writing: A Neglected Phase
of Mencken's Literary Apprenticeship," Menckeniana, No. 30,
pp. 8-13, Summer, 1969.

O. Henry, Kipling and Thomas Huxley strongly influenced Mencken's
early short story writing, which is marked by sentimentality, artistic
unevenness, and an attempt to appeal to a mass audience. These
efforts are chiefly important for the light they shed on his early
critical attitudes. (D.P.)

M1340 Stone, Edward, "Baltimore's Friendly Dragon," Georgia Review,
8:347-53, Fall, 1954.

[This is an account of a visit to Mencken in 1937 following correspondence relating to a Master's thesis on Nietzsche's influence on
Mencken.] (G.C.)

M1341 Swanberg, W. A., "Mencken and Dreiser," Menckeniana, No. 15,
pp. 6-8, Fall, 1965.

The Mencken-Dreiser association ranged from "deep attachment to
total estrangement." Mencken performed countless services in
establishing Dreiser's position in American letters. Major rifts
occurred after Mencken's sulphurous review of An American Tragedy
and after Dreiser joined the Communist Party. (D.P.)

M1342 Turaj, Frank, "The Native Tradition: A Note," Menckeniana, No. 31, pp. 10-2, Fall, 1969.

Although Mencken praised and worked for such authors as E. W. Howe, Joseph Kirkland, Sherwood Anderson, the early Garland, Sinclair Lewis, Ambrose Bierce, Ring Lardner and other American authors who wrote in the modes of pessimistic realism and naturalism, he "never clearly understood the place they occupied within a native development." (D.P.)

M1343 Wagner, Philip M., "Mencken Remembered," American Scholar, 32:256-74, Spring, 1963.

"A worm's eye view of Mencken. . . . He knocked down a whole shooting gallery full of sacred literary sheep and cows. . . . He was equally fascinated by reason and unreason, and happiest taking the latter apart. . . . His philosophy was the bleak and lonely one of an agnostic." (P.A.R.)

M1344 Walt, James, "Mencken and Conrad," Conradiana, 2:9-21, Winter, 1969-70.

Mencken happened on Conrad about the turn of the century and thereafter trumpeted his praise in reviews and longer studies more notable for idolatry, forthrightness, dashing and lucid style than for critical objectivity. (D.P.)

M1345 Walt, James, "Conrad and Mencken--Part II," Conradiana, 2:100-10, Spring, 1969-70.

Mencken was book reviewer for Smart Set from 1908 to 1922, during which time he reviewed many of Conrad's books with enthusiasm, dazzling rhetoric, candor, flashes of insight, and, finally, regret and embarrassment at the decline in Conrad's powers. (D.P.)

M1346 Weintraub, Stanley, "Apostate Apostle: H. L. Mencken as Shavophile and Shavophobe," Educational Theater Journal, 12:184-90, October, 1960.

". . . it is to Mencken more than any other American critic that we owe the popular notion of Shaw as a self-advertising clown and coiner of cheap paradoxes. Mencken consistently treated GBS as primarily a satirist with a slapstick. . . ." (G.C.)

M1347 Weintraub, Stanley, "Mencken to Shaw: 'A Young Man in the Writing Trade' Writes to His Hero," Menckeniana, No. 26, pp. 9-10, Summer, 1968.

Printed here is Mencken's letter to Shaw, intended to announce the publication of Mencken's George Bernard Shaw: His Plays, the first book-length study of Shaw. Later Mencken was to disown his "youthful enthusiasm via irreverent, anti-Shavian polemics. . . ." (D.P.)

M1348 Wilson, Edmund, "The Aftermath of Mencken," New Yorker, 45:107-15, May 31, 1969.

Mencken, as an editor of Smart Set, honestly attempted "to sift out what was valuable from the rubbish of our very own second-rate period--from the eighties to the early nineteen-hundreds--and as he became more self-confident in his heresies he steadily became more impressive." No satisfactory biography exists in English, no sound comprehensive book, although Guy Jean Forgue's H. L. Mencken, l'homme, l'oeuvre, l'influence is a large-scale, satisfactory study, and Sara Mayfield's memoir is a useful antidote to Angoff. Mencken's posthumous Minority Report confirms his lack of coherence. (D.P.)

M1349 Wycherley, H. Alan, "Mencken and Knopf: The Editor and His Publisher," American Quarterly, 16:460-72, Fall, 1964.

"Available records of the relationship suggest that Henry L. Mencken and Alfred A. Knopf enjoyed an unusual and even remarkable friendship in a world wherein malice and pettiness are so often operative." (W.G.F.)

M1350 Wycherley, H. Alan, "Mencken on Teachers," CEA Critic, 26:3, November, 1964.

Among his many targets Mencken heaped a good measure of his scorn upon "teachers in general and professors in particular. . . . he thwacked and bullyragged English teachers whenever the mood was upon him. . . . Mencken's synonyms for professors included pedagogue, obergogue, gogue, imbecile, and idiot." (D.P.)

THE AMERICAN LANGUAGE

M1351 Babcock, C. Merton, "Dancing to the Tune of the Pied Typer,"
Menckeniana, No. 22, pp. 14-5, Summer, 1967.

Mencken put his stamp of approval on the kind of research he often
ridiculed by accepting an erroneous article for use in Supplement
One of The American Language. (A.S.W.)

M1352 McDavid, Raven, "American English," College English, 25:331-7,
February, 1964.

In early editions of The American Language Mencken commented
that the National Council of Teachers of English "seems to be
centered upon an effort to protect the grammar books against the
living speech of the American people." In later editions he noted
with approval "that in the NCTE there was already a strong party
receptive to linguistic realism willing to recognize American standards on their own merits." (D.P.)

M1353 McDavid, Raven I., Jr., "The Impact of Mencken on American
Linguistics," Menckeniana, No. 17, pp. 1-7, 1966.

The influence of Mencken's The American Language may be explained
by its accuracy of observation, its treatment of Americanisms, and
Mencken's "familiarity with source materials and scholarship."
Also, Mencken's "intellectual flexibility," the fact that his book is
well written, his generosity in acknowledging linguistic contributions,
and, finally, his clear understanding "that a language is a living and
developing organism" all contributed to the seminal value of The
American Language. (D.P.)

M1354 McDavid, Raven I., "A New Look at Mencken's Vulgate," Ball
State Teachers College Forum, 1:39-42, Spring, 1960.

[Difficulties involved in editing Mencken's American Language and
bringing it up to date are discussed.] (G.C.)

M1355 Woolf, Henry Bosley, "Mencken Revisited," English Studies,
47:102-18, April, 1966.

[This is a summary and discussion of the 1963 edition of The
American Language.] (G.C.)

NOTES ON DEMOCRACY

M1356 Iversen, Anders, "Democratic Man, the Superior Man, and the Forgotten Man in H. L. Mencken's Notes on Democracy," English Studies, 50:351-62, August, 1969.

In Mencken's Notes on Democracy, it is possible "to show that what ailed him as a thinker was not so much his inconsistency and ir- reverence as the irrelevance of some of his chief ideas and concepts, which made it impossible for him to come to grips with the real problems." (G.C.)

THE PHILOSOPHY OF FRIEDRICH NIETZSCHE

M1357 La Belle, Maurice M., "H. L. Mencken's Comprehension of Friedrich Nietzsche," Comparative Literature Studies, 7:43-9, March, 1970.

In The Philosophy of Friedrich Nietzsche, Mencken reveals his misunderstanding of Apollonianism, Dionysianism, the superman, the will to power, and eternal recurrence. He later used Nietzsche's terms for his own iconoclastic purposes. (R.O.R.)

MEREZHKOVSKY, DMITRIY SERGEYEVICH

M1358 Bedford, C. H., "D. S. Merezhkovsky: The Forgotten Poet," Slavonic and East European Review, 36:159-80, 1957.

Merezhkovsky's "verse is an integral part of [his] whole [work]. Without a knowledge of it, it is impossible to understand his later work fully, for it was on the basis of his poetic creation that the entire structure of his more mature period was raised." (D.A.B.)

MERI, VEIJO

M1359 Laitinen, Kai, "Väinö Linna and Veijo Meri: Two Aspects of War," Books Abroad, 36:365-7, Autumn, 1962.

"The works of [Väinö] are important because they revaluate and correct the conception of Finnish social history. The works of Meri are of man in a world where nothing is certain and nothing can be taken for granted." (C.E.N.)

MERRILL, JAMES

M1360 Brown, Ashley, "An Interview with James Merrill," <u>Shenandoah</u>, 19:3-15, Summer, 1968.

". . . I'm lucky to be a poet rather than a painter or sculptor--they have to think of something new every year. . . . I've yet to see a poem that I can't relate to something at least fifty years old if not two hundred." (D.P.)

M1361 Sheehan, Donald, "An Interview with James Merrill," <u>Contemporary Literature</u>, 9:1-14, Winter, 1968.

[This is the text of an interview with Merrill conducted in Madison, Wisconsin by Sheehan on May 23, 1967.] (G.C.)

NIGHTS AND DAYS

M1362 Ettin, Andrew V., "On James Merrill's 'Nights and Days'," <u>Perspective</u>, 15:33-51, Spring-Summer, 1967.

<u>Nights and Days</u> shows Merrill "as technically more assured, more allusive, more daring, more clearly philosophical, far more complex than in his preceding volumes. . . ." "This splendid combination of emotion; intellect; verbal power; technical virtuosity, daring and sensitivity; and a seemingly infallible ear makes James Merrill clearly one of the most outstanding poets currently writing in English. . . ." (D.P.)

MERTON, THOMAS

M1363 Bacon, Stefan, "Latin America and Spain in the Poetic World of Thomas Merton," <u>Revue de Littérature Comparée</u>, 41:288-300, April-June, 1967.

Merton is nearly unique among English language poets for his know-ledge of and confessed influence by poetry in Spanish. Beginning with Lorca and Vallejo, Merton has imagined a kind of personal anthology of favorite poems. (C.O.)

M1364 Baird, Sister Mary Julian, R. S. M., "Blake, Hopkins and Thomas Merton," <u>Catholic World</u>, 183:46-9, April, 1956.

For Merton "the key to Blake's rebellion" was Blake's attempt "to glorify the transfiguration of man's natural love, his natural powers, in the refining fires of mystical experience." Merton was never enthusiastic about Hopkins, but Father Leahy's biography of Hopkins influenced Merton to become a Catholic. (D.P.)

M1365 Dell'Isolla, Frank, "A Bibliography of Thomas Merton," Thought, 29:574-96, Winter, 1954-55.

[This descriptive bibliography of Merton's works includes listings of his translations and his contributions to books.] (G.C.)

M1366 Fowler, Albert, "Possessed by the Holy Spirit: The Poetry of Thomas Merton and Vassar Miller," Approach, No. 51, pp. 33-42, Spring, 1964.

Monk and layman, Trappist and Episcopalian, each with a leaning toward the Quaker, both bring a special light and grace to a tried and tempted America. (A.F.)

M1367 Fowler, Albert, "A Visit with Thomas Merton," Friends Journal, 7:490-2, December 1, 1961.

Merton's interest in the poem The Fish God led to an invitation to the Trappist monastery in Kentucky where Albert and Helen Fowler discussed with him problems facing the Christian writer today. (A.F.)

M1368 Julie, Sister Rosemarie, "Influences Shaping the Poetic Imagery of Merton," Renascence, 9:188-97, 222, Summer, 1957.

Literary influences on the imagery of Thomas Merton include symbolism, imagism, surrealism, the metaphysical poets, and Gerard Manley Hopkins. Theological influences reflect an early concern with sin, while later works demonstrate an influence from St. John of the Cross and a greater emphasis on positive spirituality. (G.C.)

M1369 Kelly, Richard, "Thomas Merton and Poetic Vitality," Renascence, 12:139-42, 148, Spring, 1960.

Thomas Merton has a vitality lacking in many Catholic poets because he unsentimentally uses his religion to attack the city, the machine, war, and other phenomena of his age. (K.L.)

M1370 Marie, Sister Consuela, S. B. S., "Merton or Toynbee?" <u>Xavier</u> <u>University Studies</u>, 1:34-8, 1961.

"Both Toynbee and Merton . . . strain to point out the desideratum, the oneness of humanity in the world." Toynbee sees danger ahead and "urges a remedy--the unification of the world. Merton . . . comes up with . . . a divinely revealed and a divinely bestowed means of world unification--the Eucharist." (G.C.)

M1371 Materer, Timothy, "Merton and Auden: Setting the Borders of Religious Poetry," <u>Commonweal</u>, 91:577-80, February 27, 1970.

"The lyrics of Thomas Merton and W. H. Auden set the borders of contemporary religious poetry. The struggle to express religious feeling in esthetic form marks the work of each writer. . . . For Auden religious verse is a controlled, impersonal, at times ir-reverently light-hearted statement about man's relationship to his Creator. For Merton, it is a personally felt, unselfconsciously emotional, at times ecstatic witness to the effects of God's grace." (D.P.)

M1372 Mayhew, Alice, "Merton against Himself," <u>Commonweal</u>, 91:70-4, October 17, 1969.

Merton's life has encompassed a series of personal conflicts. His early journals reveal an opposition between his desire to pursue a secular writing career and his wish to live a life of contemplation. Ironically, the success of <u>Seven Story Mountain</u> denied him the solitude he sought. In time he resolved this conflict and his <u>The Geography of Logaire</u> attacks the world's institutions without reject-ing the secular world. (D.P.)

M1373 Stevens, Clifford, "Thomas Merton: An Appraisal," <u>American</u> <u>Benedictine Review</u>, 18:223-6, 1967.

Thomas Merton's writings are the works of a "thoroughly . . . contemporary" man whose works "will stand beside the great spiritual literature of all times." (G.C.)

M1374 Van Doren, Mark, "Thomas Merton, Monk," <u>Columbia Forum</u>, 12:44, Spring, 1969.

Thomas Merton "had a singular power to reach out and touch people with the words he wrote. . . . although he was a complete monk, dedicated to solitude and prayer, there was no limit to the charity

that went forth from him in waves. . . . The vitality in him, the
humor, the common sense . . . these overflowed from him like
masterpieces from a genius. . . ." (D.P.)

M1375 Von Wellsheim, Mother Anita, R. S. C. J., "Imagery in Modern
Marian Poetry," Renascence, 10:176-86, Summer, 1958.

"The spirit of modern traditional Marian poetry may be summed up
as one of loving intimacy, dependence, and reverent familiarity. A
new unity and simplicity are attained through a more direct use of
metaphor and the expansion of images. Modern poets [such as
Francis Thompson, G. K. Chesterton, Robert Lowell, and Thomas
Merton] reveal the inner meaning and beauty of Mary by the power of
identification, the spiritualization of material objects, and a highly
suggestive use of symbolism." Non-traditional Marian poetry
"aims at bringing out truth by contrast or conflict, and differs from
traditional imagery not in degree but in kind." (D.P.)

NO MAN IS AN ISLAND

M1376 Graham, Aelred, "The Mysticism of Thomas Merton,"
Commonweal, 62:155-9, May 13, 1955.

In Thomas Merton's No Man Is an Island "a rare and attractive
combination of gifts display themselves: the readability of an accomplished writer, imaginative and intelligent, with a poet's ear
for the music of words; an instinctive sense of the orthodox blended
with the originality . . . of one who thinks for himself. Added to
these are perceptiveness, compassion, humility and an abounding
common sense. . . ." (D.P.)

M1377 Shaddy, Virginia M., "Thomas Merton and No Man Is an Island,"
Catholic World, 184:51-6, October, 1956.

Merton's No Man Is an Island gives, for the most part, "a one-sided
view, and the strong impression of a strained inhibition, a rigidity,
a stoic sternness. . . . The love of God and of humanity, the deep
and genuine joy that should be the fruit of the contemplative life
. . . are lacking in the over-all effect of the book. . . ." (D.P.)

MERWIN, WILLIAM STANLEY

M1378 Andersen, Kenneth, "The Poetry of W. S. Merwin," Twentieth Century Literature, 16:278-86, October, 1970.

"With his later poetry . . . W. S. Merwin has come of age as an artist. His development, significantly, has been distinguished by . . . those ultimate tragic questions which concern us all. . . . Merwin has created not only diverse works of art but also, within this art, a synthetic philosophy. . . ." (D.P.)

M1379 Benston, Alice N., "Myth in the Poetry of W. S. Merwin," Tri-Quarterly, 4:36-43, Fall, 1961.

Merwin views reality as an "inchoate mass of possibilities." From this chaos he creates his personal myths. He insists that mystery is basic in all life. (E.T.)

M1380 McShane, Frank, "A Portrait of W. S. Merwin," Shenandoah, 21:3-14, Winter, 1970.

"But for the most part Merwin's verse lacks a geographical center: as he has evolved and moved from place to place, so too has his work. It has been a poetry of continuing transformation and development, a passage from one realm of experience to another, often hallucinatory and dreamlike." (D.P.)

M1381 Roche, Thomas P., Jr., "Green with Poems," Princeton University Library Chronicle, 25:89-104, No. 1, Autumn, 1963.

[This is a short overview of Merwin's work, highlighting indications of his growth as a poet. A lengthy bibliography of the poet's publications is included.] (K.M.W.)

LEVIATHAN

M1382 Wild, Paul H., "Hearing Poetry: W. S. Merwin's 'Leviathan'," English Journal, 56:954-7, October, 1967.

"W. S. Merwin's 'Leviathan' is an exciting and useful modern poem for demonstrating the beauty of poetic sound. The theme . . . [that] the transcendent power of primitive nature waits somewhere to be born--seems nearly insignificant beside the achievement of the language." (D.P.)

MEYERSTEIN, EDWARD HARRY WILLIAM

M1383 Watson, Vera, " 'AE' to E. H. W. Meyerstein," English,
12:220-5, 1959.

[Portions of letters from George William Russell (AE) to E. H. W.
Meyerstein are reproduced and discussed.] (G.C.)

MEYNELL, VIOLA

M1384 Maguire, C. E., "Another Meynell," Renascence, 11:175-84,
Summer, 1959.

Alice Meynell's daughter, Viola, is as accomplished a writer as
her mother, but she has been ignored. In her short stories, however, she handles "human hope and suffering with invariable tact
and reverence. . . ." (K.L.)

MICHAUX, HENRI

M1385 Broome, Peter, "The Introversion of Henri Michaux: His Aims,
Techniques and Shortcomings," Nottingham French Studies,
1:34-44, October, 1962.

Michaux "turns his gaze inwards, in the hope of finding some
superior reality. . . . He looks upon this introspection as a means
of preserving his own freedom and individuality . . . and as a way
of approaching a realm of vital, superhuman experience and knowledge. Thus he is not a mere escapist, recoiling farther and farther
simply because life hurts and embarrasses him. . . ." (K.M.W.)

M1386 Broome, Peter, "Michaux and the Exorcism on God," Australian
Journal of French Studies, 2:191-220, May-August, 1965.

". . . there is evidence to suggest that Michaux has recently
accomplished the greatest therapeutic measure of his life and, by
lucidity and science, worked an exorcism on his most nagging
enemy. Whereas in his past failures he has never quelled Perfection, probably because he has never been close enough to penetrate
it, now for the first time he has 'seen through' God and the myth of
the Absolute." (D.A.B.)

M1387 Ellmann, Richard, "A Note on Michaux," Tri-Quarterly, No. 12,
p. 114, Spring, 1968.

In "the new vision of the world which Michaux initiated" he "dis-
avowed the role of writer or of artist; if he fell into it, he did so for
none of the standard reasons. Art was not artifact, at most it might
be self-liberation. . . . To approach literature with suspicion, doubt,
repugnance even, to regard the act of writing as involuntary; to compare it not with la haute magie of the Sar Péladan but with a lower
form born out of desperation and savage wile; these are if not precisely Michaux's attributes, at least the signs of his presence."
(D.P.)

M1388 Hackett, C. A., "Michaux and Plume," French Studies, 17:40-9,
January, 1963.

". . . it was clear that Plume represented many aspects of his
creator's character, in particular the inability to be, or seem to
be, like other people, to conform, to live 'normally'; and also the
whole gamut of conflicting feelings, attitudes, and states of mind
which accompany that inability and protestation." (K.M.W.)

M1389 Kushner, Eva, "L'Humour de Michaux," French Review,
40:495-504, February, 1967.

Unable to find any humor in the universe, the poet creates his
poetic universe in which humor is a liberating element. [This study
examines the sources and manifestations of this humor.] (S.M.K.)

M1390 Mills, Ralph J., Jr., "Char and Michaux: Magicians of Insecurity,"
Chicago Review, 15:40-56, No. 2, 1961.

Char and Michaux "represent in their separate accomplishments the
latest phase in a romantic tradition of poetry which reaches through
Lautréamont and Rimbaud . . . down to the Surrealist movement.
. . ." (D.P.)

M1391 Thomas, Henri, "Henri Michaux contre le rêve," La Nouvelle
Revue Française, No. 207, pp. 446-9, March, 1970.

Contrary to Freud, Michaux's works show that dreams must be
construed in relation to the desires, fears and dominant preoccupations of the current situation. The genius of his poetry and prose is
in an unfettered dream. (T.T.B.)

CHANT DE MORT

M1392 Harvey, Lawrence E., "Michaux's 'Chant de Mort', " Explicator, 20: Item 1, September, 1961.

The poem "suggests to those who may view happiness less in terms of pursuit than of possession and right the forgotten values of suffering and the deeper virtues of a hard realism." (B.K.)

CLOWN

M1393 Bishop, Lloyd, "Michaux's 'Clown', " French Review, 36:152-7, December, 1962.

"Michaux's selection of the clown to embody and translate his pessimism is an attempt at mythopoesis, in particular the universality of myth." (R.B.W.)

MICHENER, JAMES

M1394 Leib, Amos P., "History and Setting in Michener's Story of Norfolk Island: 'Mutiny', " Australian Literary Studies, 4:349-59, 1970.

Michener exaggerates and adds to historical fact in creating a dramatic structure for "Mutiny, " particularly as he alters the history of Pine Avenue on Norfolk Island. (A.S.W.)

MICKEL, KARL

M1395 Wickert, Max A., "Karl Mickel: A Voice from East Germany, " Books Abroad, 43:211-2, Spring, 1969.

Karl Mickel illustrates well the "formidably unpromising" situation facing the writer who has not received official sanction in Eastern Europe. Yet, he "is not only a controversial figure but . . . the best poet now writing in the DDR. . . . Mickel's theme is that the tension between a utopian vision . . . and an untransformed present . . . must lead to a declaration of the reality of vision so that the present can be seen with a transformed consciousness." (D.P.)

MIHURA, MIGUEL

M1396 Arjona, Doris K., "Beyond Humor: The Theater of Miguel Mihura,"
Kentucky Foreign Language Quarterly, 6:63-8, 1959.

"Mihura's humor . . . grows out of his themes, his situations, and
his characters. It is full of the absurdities and tricks of dehumanization, yet it is used in the service of a deep humanity." (C.O.)

M1397 Wofsy, Samuel A., "La calidad literaria del teatro de Miguel
Mihura," Hispania, 43:214-8, May, 1960.

"Within the limits of [Mihura's comic] art he often attains a height
of which the contemporary Spanish theater can well be proud."
(A.C.H.)

M1398 Young, Raymond A., "Sobre el humorismo de Miguel Mihura,"
Hispanófila, No. 36, pp. 21-9, May, 1969.

All of Mihura's comedies contain a mix of irony and tenderness.
Beneath the most grotesque or "absurd" circumstances he treats
profound human problems. All this, plus his tact and consideration,
qualify him as the principal comic dramatist of the day. (C.O.)

MILES, JOSEPHINE

M1399 Beloof, Robert, "Distance and Surfaces: The Poetry of Josephine
Miles," Prairie Schooner, 32:276-84, Winter, 1958-59.

Josephine Miles "sees her world from one of the most difficult of
artistic points of view. . . . she is never aware of it as a great
metaphysical scheme on the one hand, nor, on the other, as a
stream of detail which is itself the ultimate reality. . . . The
primary aesthetic effect of what I have called Miss Miles's 'middle-
distance' perspective is to convert her physical world to one in
which the principal impression is of surfaces and of relationships
of surfaces." (D.P.)

MILLAY, EDNA ST. VINCENT

M1400 Brittin, Norman A., "Edna St. Vincent Millay's 'Nancy Boyd'
Stories," Ball State University Forum, 10:31-6, Spring, 1969.

"The 'Nancy Boyd' stories are all stories of courtship which involve
physical and temperamental attraction and often love. Three

themes are paramount in them: the question of love versus career, the approval of Greenwich Village attitudes, and the overwhelming of men by love." (G.C.)

M1401 Brittin, Norman A., "Millay Bibliography: Additions and Corrections," American Notes and Queries, 8:52, December, 1959.

[Additions to the bibliography of Edna St. Vincent Millay include appearances of poems by Millay, and reviews not previously noted. Corrections include a mistaken attribution of a poem to Millay.] (D.P.)

M1402 Cottrell, Beekman W., "Edna St. Vincent Millay," Carnegie Series in English, 2:25-41, 1955.

"She expresses a side of America as truly as Whitman or Emerson or Benet. American literature owes to Edna Millay a whole new field of free expression for its women writers. . . . No other writer of our time has so completely mastered the sonnet form." "Her harvest--so joyously gleaned, so perfectly understood, so meticulously preserved--offers . . . the splendid sustenance of lyric poetry at its finest and most intense." (D.P.)

M1403 Dell, Floyd, "My Friend Edna St. Vincent Millay," Mark Twain Journal, 12:1-3, Spring, 1964.

[This is Dell's account of his "romance" with Edna St. Vincent Millay.] (G.C.)

M1404 Orel, Harold, "Tarnished Arrows: The Last Phase of Edna St. Vincent Millay," Kansas Magazine, No. 4, pp. 73-8, 1960.

Millay's "ruin as a creative poet began as a conscious act, and in that fact lies her tragedy." With Make Bright the Arrows, "a book of poetry, 'written in furious haste,' 'hot-headed,' 'faulty and unpolished,'" she damaged "her reputation as a perfectionist." (G.C.)

M1405 Patton, John J., "A Comprehensive Bibliography of Criticism of Edna St. Vincent Millay," Serif, 5:10-32, September, 1968.

[This comprehensive unannotated bibliography of Millay criticism in English is arranged alphabetically by main entry. A separate check list of incomplete or doubtful entries is included at the end.] (A.S.W.)

M1406 Patton, John, "An Unpublished Hardy Letter to Millay," <u>Colby Library Quarterly</u>, Series 5, pp. 284-5, June, 1961.

[A presentation of a copy of <u>The King's Henchman</u> to Thomas Hardy elicited a letter from Hardy (published here) in which he refused judgment of a play written for acting and indicated preference for Edna St. Vincent Millay's lyrics.] (D.P.)

M1407 Richart, Bette, "Edna St. Vincent Millay: Poet of Our Youth," <u>Commonweal</u>, 66:150-1, May 10, 1957.

In Edna St. Vincent Millay "there is no richness, no secret tension to relate the mystery of the poem to the mystery of human experience. . . . It was not peace, momentary or eternal that she recorded, but merely the outcry." Yet in some of her sonnets "both love and death, traditionally and formally disciplined, achieve the wan glory of the human condition. . . ." (D.P.)

M1408 Tanselle, G. Thomas, "Millay, Dell, and 'Recuerdo'," <u>Colby Library Quarterly</u>, Series 6, pp. 202-5, March, 1963.

Edna St. Vincent Millay's "Recuerdo" must be excluded from the poems arising from her relationship with Floyd Dell. In the political campaign of 1940, Dell used the stanza form of "Recuerdo," and echoed some of its lines in a response to her "The President with a Candidate's Face." (D.P.)

M1409 Weber, Carl J., "A Poet's Memory," <u>Colby Library Quarterly</u>, Series 4, pp. 265-74, August, 1958.

[These are reminiscences of the June 21, 1937 Colby College commencement during which Edna St. Vincent Millay received the honorary degree of Doctor of Letters.] (G.C.)

M1410 Whittemore, Reed, "Three Reasons," Poetry, 90:52-8, April, 1957.

Three reasons for liking Millay's poetry are: (1) their sentiment, sometimes admittedly excessive, (2) the poet's reducing her sentiment under New Criticism and still surviving, (3) the fact that the evident "control" in the latter poetry did not drive the poet herself out of it. (F.L.)

ARIA DA CAPO

M1411 McKee, Mary J., "Millay's Aria da Capo: Form and Meaning,"
Modern Drama, 9:165-9, September, 1966.

"The medium of commedia dell'arte provides characters through
which we behold the tragic fate common to all men, but with a detachment which transforms frustration into laughter. We see the
protagonists not with sympathy but as caricatures with a purely
stage life. Yet in Aria da Capo these caricatures . . . possess a
strange and terrible significance. The use of commedia dell'arte
in this twentieth-century play has true and vital aesthetic power."
(D.P.)

RENASCENCE

M1412 Minot, Walter S., "Millay's 'Renascence'," American Notes and
Queries, 8:25, October, 1969.

Miss Millay preferred the earliest reading of the line "I turned and
looked another way" rather than the version which appeared in the
second edition of Renascence (line 3). (D.P.)

M1413 Munson, Gorham, "Parnassus on Penobscot," New England
Quarterly, 41:264-73, June, 1968.

Renascence "is a joyous expression of a state of consciousness
induced in the beholder by the 'multi-colored, multi-form beloved
beauty' of the Penobscot scene spread out below Mount Battie. . . ."
(D.P.)

MILLEN, GILMORE

M1414 Robinson, Clayton, "Gilmore Millen's Sweet Man: Neglected
Classic of the Van Vechten Vogue," Forum (Houston), 8:32-5,
Fall, 1970.

"Millen's Sweet Man deserves to be read not only as a sympathetic
treatment of Negro life in the south in the early part of this century,
but as a harbinger of the fiction of the thirties . . . and an historic
point in the development of realistic fiction about the black man's
life in America." (A.S.W.)

MILLER, ARTHUR

M1415 Allsop, Kenneth, "A Conversation with Arthur Miller," Encounter, 13:58-60, August, 1959.

[This is a conversation between Miller and Allsop about the theater and American civilization in general.] (G.C.)

M1416 Barksdale, Richard K., "Social Background in the Plays of Miller and Williams," CLA Journal, 6:161-9, March, 1963.

The American Southland furnishes Williams with those subtle nuances of social decadence needed as background for his titanic character conflict. "Similarly, America, with its fevered dreams of material success and the good life, furnishes a background for Miller's carefully wrought tragedies." (B.K.)

M1417 Blumberg, Paul, "Sociology and Social Literature: Work Alienation in the Plays of Arthur Miller," American Quarterly, 21:291-310, Summer, 1969.

"A persistent thread running through Miller's writing is his concern with the world of work and his effort to illustrate the alienating character of labor in the modern world." His characters "spend much of their time at work, in work-related activities, talking about work or in reaping the (usually negative) consequences of their labor." (W.G.F.)

M1418 Brandon, Henry, "A Conversation with Arthur Miller," World Theatre, 11:229-40, Autumn, 1962.

[In this conversation Miller compares American theatre to theatre around the world, discusses his playwriting practice, his assessment of the McCarthy influence on America, the lack of religious content in American theatre, his views of the development of American drama; finally, his perceptions of future directions of drama.] (D.P.)

M1419 Brandon, Henry, "The State of the Theatre: A Conversation with Arthur Miller," Harper's Magazine, 221:63-9, November, 1960.

[This interview elicits Miller's views on the American "hunger for purpose," Chekhov's art, the evolution of American drama from the end of the First World War to the present, with notable contributions on social and economic problems, moving to a current "dangerous extreme of triviality, " the differences between Sartre and Miller, and the need for American theatre to reach out beyond "the center of the web. "] (D.P.)

M1420 Carlisle, Olga, and Rose Styron, "The Art of the Theatre II: Arthur Miller: An Interview, " Paris Review, No. 38, pp. 60-98, Summer, 1966.

[This interview covers Miller's views of writing short stories and plays, his concept "that tragedy was the basic pillar" of drama, his early playwrighting experiences, his concern that Method acting can distort the meanings of plays, the impact of motion pictures on modern plays, his assessments of his own works, and the importance of his experiences with the Un-American Activities Committee.] (D.P.)

M1421 Cassell, Richard A., "Arthur Miller's 'Rage of Conscience'," Ball State Teachers College Forum, 1:31-6, Winter, 1960-61.

Miller "dramatizes the shattering fragmentation of values in contemporary life, where faith has been lost and both life and death are 'heavily weighted with meaningless futility'." "The central question he asks is, 'How may a man make of the outside world a home?' " (G.C.)

M1422 Corrigan, Robert W., "The Achievement of Arthur Miller, " Comparative Drama, 2:141-60, Fall, 1968.

"Miller's own sense of involvement with modern man's struggle to be himself is revealed in his own growth as an artist and has made him one of the modern theatre's most compelling and important spokesmen. " (D.P.)

M1423 Dillingham, William B., "Arthur Miller and the Loss of Conscience," Emory University Quarterly, 16:40-50, Spring, 1960.

"Man's obligation to assume his rightful place in a world unified by love and a sense of responsibility is . . . the major theme of . . . [Miller's] plays." Those who have lost their "integrity of 'conscience'," who have forfeited their "rightful place[s]" in the world may be observed in his four tragedies. (G.C.)

M1424 Driver, Tom F., "Strength and Weakness in Arthur Miller,"
Tulane Drama Review, 4:45-52, Summer, 1960.

Miller's keen social or "public" approach to the theatre overshadows
or weakens his psychological or "personal" approach to the characters. And without attempting to find some relevant, moral truth,
Miller's characters don't rise to "the level demanded of one who
would break out of the confusion that enveloped Willy Loman."
(S.G.L.)

M1425 Eissenstat, Martha Turnquist, "Arthur Miller: A Bibliography,"
Modern Drama, 5:93-106, May, 1962.

[This bibliography, which includes foreign as well as English
language material, lists books, unpublished plays and articles by
and about Miller and his writings.] (D.P.)

M1426 Flaxman, S. L., "The Debt of Williams and Miller to Ibsen and
Strindberg," Comparative Literature Studies, Special Advance
Issue, pp. 51-60, 1963.

Tennessee Williams and Arthur Miller use themes, characters and
dramatic forms clearly drawn from Ibsen and Strindberg, although
their plays are set in American surroundings. They attempt a
fusion of naturalism and symbolism, and they employ a variety of
expressionistic techniques. Rarely have they reached the heights
achieved by the great Scandinavians. (D.P.)

M1427 Gelb, Phillip, "Morality and Modern Drama," Educational Theatre
Journal, 10:190-202, October, 1958.

[In this interview Miller discusses moral values in drama, the
importance of observing the details of real human behavior in plays,
the dramatic practice of Eliot, Shaw and Tennessee Williams, the
difficulty of not making evil in characters appear overstated, and
comments on the irresponsibility of the Germans, and the need, in
the South, to strongly affirm "the rights of all men to be equal."]
(D.P.)

M1428 Groff, Edward, "Point of View in Modern Drama," Modern Drama,
2:268-82, December, 1959.

The dramatic techniques or methods of such modern dramatists as
Pirandello, O'Neill, Arthur Miller, Strindberg, Brecht, and Wilder
"have a common aim: to make the playform more subjective by

associating the dramatic events with the consciousness of individual
characters who may participate in the action or merely narrate the
story presented on the stage." (D.P.)

M1429 Hayashi, Tetsumaro, "Arthur Miller: The Dimension of His Art
and a Checklist of His Published Works," Serif, 4:26-32, June,
1967.

". . . I have attempted to include all of the known published works
of Arthur Miller. The checklist is divided by genre: Plays, Adaptations, Novels and Short Stories, Articles and Essays, and Reports."
(D.A.B.)

M1430 Hynes, Joseph A., "Arthur Miller and the Impasse of Naturalism,"
South Atlantic Quarterly, 62:327-34, Summer, 1963.

Because they are naturalistic, Miller's plays are not tragedy, as
Miller claims that Death of a Salesman is. Miller is a "man of the
theatre, but . . . not yet a sufficiently mature dramatist." (J.L.A.)

M1431 Kalven, Harry, Jr., "A View from the Law," New Republic,
136:8-13, May 27, 1957.

[This is a view of the legal position of Miller in refusing to provide
the Committee on Un-American Activities with the names of others
who had attended meetings of a small group of Communist writers
in 1947. ". . . Arthur Miller had the worst of the legal issues involved. . . . I doubt if Mr. Miller will win. But I hope very much
I am mistaken."] (D.P.)

M1432 McAnany, Emile G., S. J., "The Tragic Commitment: Some Notes
on Arthur Miller," Modern Drama, 5:11-20, May, 1962.

Arthur Miller is distinguished not only for his association with
"Marxism, Marilyn or misfits," nor for his play about a salesman,
but for "a significant body of dramatic theory and critical comment
on contemporary serious drama." In his most important statement,
the preface to his Collected Plays the hero "is a man intensely committed to a set of values which he will not give up. . . ." Viewed
from the light of Miller's dramatic theory Willy Loman in Death of
a Salesman is eventually destroyed by "the combination of success
and fatherhood. . . ." (D.P.)

M1433 McCarthy, Mary, "Americans, Realists, Playwrights,"
Encounter, 17:24-31, July, 1961.

The realists of the American theater are Arthur Miller, Tennessee
Williams, William Inge, Paddy Chayevsky, the Elmer Rice of Street
Scene and Eugene O'Neill. "Unlike the other playwrights, who make
a journalistic claim to neutral recording, Arthur Miller admittedly
has a message." (G.C.)

M1434 Martin, Robert A., "Arthur Miller and the Meaning of Tragedy,"
Modern Drama, 13:34-9, May, 1970.

[This interview explores Miller's current views on the nature of
dramatic tragedy.] (D.P.)

M1435 Martin, Robert A., "Arthur Miller--Tragedy and Commitment,"
Michigan Quarterly Review, 8:176-8, Summer, 1969.

"This interview . . . is part of a continuing series of conversations,
interviews, and correspondence, which will form the basis of a book
by Mr. Martin on Arthur Miller's plays and his theory of tragedy."
[Here Miller notes "in a tragedy, some way or another, there has to
be the question of the survival of that society."] (D.A.B.)

M1436 Martin, Robert A., "The Creative Experience of Arthur Miller:
An Interview," Educational Theatre Journal, 21:310-7, October,
1969.

[This interview concentrates on Miller's sense that he writes plays
on topics which are "immediate" to him, his comment that he selects
characters for his plays for their relevance to the theme of the play;
that Jewishness, as such, has not influenced him remarkably beyond
the way the Jew tends to stand "at the crack of civilization"; and
finally his sense that nihilism is dangerous.] (D.P.)

M1437 Miller, Arthur, "Arthur Miller Talks: The Contemporary Theatre,"
Michigan Quarterly Review, 6:153-63, July, 1967.

The present commercial nature of contemporary American theatre,
which extends from Broadway to repertory centers in smaller cities,
must be overcome if drama in America is to survive as an art form.
Theatre must educate audiences so they know what to expect of
theatre; new perspectives must be introduced. (D.P.)

M1438 Miller, Arthur, "On Recognition," Michigan Quarterly Review, 2:213-20, October, 1963.

Unfortunately, the American writer achieves recognition as a success instead of as a writer. The few readers in America do not allow a real dialogue to develop between author and reader. American writers should develop a tragic sense. (D.P.)

M1439 Miller, Arthur, "The Playwright and the Atomic World," Tulane Drama Review, 5:3-20, June, 1961.

"But the irony remains that despite our enormous scientific establishment . . . there is evidently an impression abroad . . . that we have little intellectual interest in science. . . . In the field of drama the same sort of irony prevails. . . . one feels the European writer, the critic, and . . . the audience too, are more interested in the philosophical, moral and principled values of the play than we are. . . . The truth is . . . that if there is a leadership in the contemporary play since the Second World War . . . America has it." (D.P.)

M1440 Moss, Leonard, "Arthur Miller and the Common Man's Language," Modern Drama, 7:52-9, May, 1964.

Arthur Miller's greatest effects in his best works come from a purified colloquial language which achieves emotional tension in a dramatic situation. (G.A.S.)

M1441 Mottram, Eric, "Arthur Miller: The Development of a Political Dramatist in America," Stratford-upon-Avon Studies, 10:126-61, 1967.

Arthur Miller's "plays are written for and largely from the point of view of a man whose attitudes are not radical and innovatory but puzzled, confused and absolutely resolved not to break with his fellow countrymen. He has maintained his theatre as nearly popular as an intellectual playwright may. . . ." Typically he has "dealt with his local themes of faith and meaning within the confused national and personal life of America. . . ." (D.P.)

M1442 Newman, W. J., "The Plays of Arthur Miller," Twentieth Century, 164:491-6, November, 1958.

Although no fundamental philosophical attitude can be derived from Miller's plays he is nevertheless concerned with the problem of narrowing the situation of universal man to the concrete example of an individual American man. American family relationships provide Miller with the raw material of conflict between human beings, rather than with his themes. (D.P.)

M1443 Popkin, Henry, "Arthur Miller: The Strange Encounter," Sewanee Review, 68:34-60, Winter, 1960.

Miller's plays are so constructed as to be "a liberal parable of hidden evil and social responsibility. . . . Responding to the political climate, Miller's plays have moved steadily inward. Although each play has probed the impact of large, bewildering issues upon a simple man, the large issues have become increasingly dim." (A.S.)

M1444 Prudhoe, John, "Arthur Miller and the Tradition of Tragedy," English Studies, 43:430-9, October, 1962.

". . . the power of the human will to overcome the forces of evil, or imagined evil, exerted upon it, lies at the centre of Miller's concept of tragedy." (G.C.)

M1445 Reno, Raymond H., "Arthur Miller and the Death of God," Texas Studies in Literature and Language, 11:1069-87, Summer, 1969.

Miller's plays, for all their variations, amount to something of a corporate work, a single sprawling drama revolving around a single theme: the death of God. (M.R.)

M1446 Rovere, Richard H., "Arthur Miller's Conscience," New Republic, 136:13-5, June 17, 1957.

Miller's refusal to bear witness against others before the House Committee on Un-American Activities, although a courageous act, does exhibit "a certain amount of moral and political confusion." "In a free society, any one of us may arrive at and freely express a judgment about the competence of duly constituted authority. But in an orderly society, no one of us can expect the protection of the law whenever we decide that a particular authority is unworthy of our cooperation." (D.P.)

M1447 Schraepen, Edmond, "Arthur Miller's Constancy: A Note on Miller as a Short Story Writer," Revue des Langues Vivantes, 36:62-71, 1970.

"Both stories ['I Don't Need You Any More' and 'The Prophecy'] share a common theme: the knowledge of destructiveness and separateness in oneself with which one has to learn to cope, and the dramatic crises in both stories are, to a degree, worked out in family contexts." (K.M.W.)

M1448 Seager, Allan, "The Creative Agony of Arthur Miller," Esquire, 52:123-4, 126, October, 1959.

Miller undergoes an exhausting effort to write his social dramas, beginning with notes of events, past and present, which relate some-how to a theme. Later, "dialogue and structural notes" are the next stage to be replaced, finally, by the completed play. Miller views his writing "as a constant effort to penetrate to a core of meaning in his material." His plays appear to be developed primarily from feeling rather than intellect. (D.P.)

M1449 Steinberg, M. W., "Arthur Miller and the Idea of Modern Tragedy," Dalhousie Review, 40:329-40, Autumn, 1960.

Miller's tragedies, while moving toward a greater emphasis on character, attempt to fuse a concern with the individual and a con-cern with social forces. (R.K.)

M1450 Trowbridge, Clinton W., "Arthur Miller: Between Pathos and Tragedy," Modern Drama, 10:221-32, December, 1967.

The idea that tragedy deals with paradox is central to Miller's theory of drama. In the course of his career Miller has grown toward trag-edy and away from pathos. (D.P.)

M1451 Tynan, Kenneth, "American Blues: The Plays of Arthur Miller and Tennessee Williams," Encounter, 2:13-9, May, 1954.

Miller's "artistic life is dedicated, like Shaw's, to a belief in prog-ress towards an attainable summit. Williams's aspirations are imag-inative and hence unattainable; therein lies the difference between them. Complementary, yet irreconcilable, Miller and Williams have produced the most powerful body of dramatic prose in modern English. They write with equal virtuosity, Williams about the violets, Miller about the rocks." (D.P.)

M1452 Weales, Gerald, "Arthur Miller: Man and His Image," Tulane Drama Review, 7:165-80, Fall, 1962.

All of Miller's plays treat the theme of "the relationship between a man's identity and the image that society demands of him." Although in places sentimental, the treatment of this theme manages, through effective emotional appeal, to achieve a favorable and sustaining audience reaction. (W.A.F.)

M1453 West, Paul, "Arthur Miller and the Human Mice," Hibbert Journal, 61:84-6, January, 1963.

"Miller's is the drama of human worry. It is intended to restore us to a sense of human and humane responsibility." (R.J.G.)

M1454 Wiegand, William, "Arthur Miller and the Man Who Knows," Western Review, 21:85-103, Winter, 1957.

Miller's college plays "contain the seeds of an important non-political premise" which he developed in his post-war plays. The character who senses that his society is sick is "destined to be trampled upon, yet to arrive at this 'knowing' is a man's only chance of saving his soul." (M.J.B.)

M1455 Williams, Raymond, "The Realism of Arthur Miller," Critical Quarterly, 1:140-9, Summer, 1959.

"The key to social realism . . . lies in a particular conception of the relationship of the individual to society, in which neither is the individual seen as a unit nor the society as an aggregate, but both seen as belonging to a continuous and in real terms inseparable process. . . . The work of Arthur Miller . . . seems to have come nearer than [that of] any other post-war writer . . . to this substantial conception." (J.N.P.)

AFTER THE FALL

M1456 Bigsby, C. W. E., "The Fall and After: Arthur Miller's Confession," Modern Drama, 10:124-36, September, 1967.

"In After the Fall Miller is attempting to come to terms with the fact of violence." (D.P.)

MILLER, A.

AFTER THE FALL (cont'd)

M1457 Brashear, William R., "The Empty Bench: Morality, Tragedy, and Arthur Miller," Michigan Quarterly Review, 5:270-8, October, 1966.

"Miller in After the Fall bursts many bubbles, about social relations, moral nature, and our innermost motives; but they are bubbles that for the tragedian were never there. . . . this kind of scrutiny can be absorbing, meaningful, and important, but carried beyond limits it begins to encroach on the provinces ruled by minds of a deeper and vaster nature, and becomes embarrassing--even ludicrous--to the tragedies. . . ." (W.G.F.)

M1458 Casty, Alan, "Post-Loverly Love: A Comparative Report," Antioch Review, 26:399-411, Fall, 1966.

". . . the quest for love and [the] shift to a deeper penetration of its realities can be illustrated by . . . works from the three different narrative arts: Saul Bellow's Herzog, Arthur Miller's After the Fall, and Federico Fellini's 8 1/2." These also show "the relative state of technique in the three arts today." (J.L.A.)

M1459 Ganz, Arthur, "Arthur Miller: After the Silence," Drama Survey, 3:520-30, Fall, 1964.

"If, in the final analysis, After the Fall is a failure, nevertheless it is still a good deal more than a scandalous pièce à clef. Where before Miller had tended to look at guilt and innocence in rather elementary terms, he has here at least attempted to apprehend the complexities that lie behind moral choices." (D.P.)

M1460 Koppenhaver, Allen J., "The Fall and After: Albert Camus and Arthur Miller," Modern Drama, 9:206-9, September, 1966.

In Miller's After the Fall and Camus's The Fall "the visions of Camus and Miller are essentially the same. The difference lies in the extent to which each man pursues the problem of the fall of man. Camus's vision is of the fall itself, and . . . he describes better the external and internal forces which destroy the human being in our world. Miller shows what can come after the fall, suggesting that there can be an after if we choose to forgive even in the face of idiocy and absurdity." (D.P.)

AFTER THE FALL   (cont'd)

M1461 Moss, Leonard, "Biographical and Literary Allusion in After the Fall," Educational Theatre Journal, 18:34-40, March, 1966.

In After the Fall Miller "extends the relevance of his fictional account by implying that his protagonist's ordeal imitates the crisis 'existing' as an 'objective fact' in his own history, in his earlier plays, and in two major works by other authors." (G.C.)

M1462 Murray, Edward, "Point of View in After the Fall," CLA Journal, 10:135-42, December, 1966.

". . . After the Fall suffers from . . . a faulty and ill-chosen point of view that renders the structure of the play static and repetitious, destroys any effective tension and irony . . . underlines the in-adequacy of Miller's verbal gifts, makes his leading character, Quentin, suspect . . . and, finally, reduces theme nearly to thesis, thus destroying what is in itself a serious and important statement. . . ." (D.A.B.)

M1463 Nolan, Paul T., "Two Memory Plays: The Glass Menagerie and After the Fall," McNeese Review, 17:27-38, 1966.

"It is now commonplace to describe such plays as The Glass Menagerie and After the Fall by the term 'memory plays'; but no critic . . . has yet suggested that this is a separate form built upon a different set of assumptions from the traditional drama-of-action and different too from such mind-searching plays as Strindberg's Dream Play. . . . The new 'memory play,' unlike the dream play and expressionist drama, is a projection of the conscious mind; and unlike the traditional drama-of-action, it is concerned only with that action that is understood and retained in the mind of the protagonist." (D.A.B.)

M1464 Steene, Birgitta, "Arthur Miller's After the Fall: A Strindbergian Failure," Moderna Språk, 58:446-52, December, 1964.

After the Fall is badly realized Strindberg; Miller has not con-vincingly been able to translate his private experience into a public language. The prolonged self-analysis of his characters does not make any universal point. (D.P.)

MILLER, A.

AFTER THE FALL   (cont'd)

M1465 Stinson, John J., "Structure in After the Fall: The Relevance of the
Maggie Episodes to the Main Themes and the Christian Symbolism,"
Modern Drama, 10:233-40, December, 1967.

The symbolic referents of Maggie to Christ are dubious. Although
the second act is not as coherent as it might have been, After the
Fall is Miller's most ambitious drama. (D.P.)

ALL MY SONS

M1466 Boggs, W. Arthur, "Oedipus and All My Sons," Personalist,
42:555-60, October, 1961.

Although Oedipus and All My Sons share many superficial resemblances, only Oedipus is a "true tragedy of recognition." "For
several reasons Miller's tragic muse fails him in this play. Although
the social message of the play, one's responsibility to one's fellow
man, can be a tragic theme, it seldom is. . . . In developing several
strains of action, Miller never clearly focuses his audience's attention upon his tragic protagonist. . . . Worst of all, Miller apparently
never really decides upon his protagonist." (D.P.)

M1467 Loughlin, Richard L., "Tradition and Tragedy in All My Sons,"
English Record, 14:23-7, February, 1964.

The title of All My Sons is intended to emphasize the theme of man's
responsibility for man. Classical and biblical parallels in the play
also support this theme. (D.P.)

M1468 Wells, Arvin R., "The Living and the Dead in All My Sons,"
Modern Drama, 7:46-51, May, 1964.

All My Sons is not a simple thesis play with clear-cut alternatives,
but a complex human drama of misunderstood personal motivations.
(G.A.S.)

M1469 Yorks, Samuel A., "Joe Keller and His Sons," Western Humanities
Review, 13:401-7, Autumn, 1959.

"All My Sons is "a realized internal conflict within the artist . . .
[which] relates to the immemorial strife between clams and their
accretions, national states; between the solitary human being and

ALL MY SONS (cont'd)

the crystallization and concretion of his dreams." Miller's "final
and most firm belief is that private loyalties are supreme. . . ."
(G.C.)

THE CRUCIBLE

M1470 Curtis, Penelope, "The Crucible," Critical Review, No. 8,
pp. 45-58, 1965.

The Crucible is Miller's only play "in which a whole community is
directly, and tragically, implicated. . . . At the same time, the
language is much more flexible, more compelling, than in the other
plays; there is an altogether more adventurous play of metaphor."
(G.C.)

M1471 Douglass, James W., "Miller's The Crucible: Which Witch is
Which?" Renascence, 15:145-51, Spring, 1963.

"Our purpose here will be to determine the nature of Mr. Miller's
treatment [of the witch trials] and its differences from the Salem
viewpoint that it seeks to explain, and finally to compare the two
viewpoints in an effort to arrive at their relative value." (S.A.)

M1472 Fender, Stephen, "Precision and Pseudo Precision in The Crucible,"
Journal of American Studies, 1:87-98, April, 1967.

". . . if one examines the language . . . of the characters in The
Crucible, it becomes clear that it is the speech of a society totally
without moral referents. . . . Proctor must indeed cast off the
terminology of Salem." (D.P.)

M1473 Ferris, Oliver H. P., "An Echo of Milton in The Crucible," Notes
and Queries, 16:268, July, 1969.

Mr. Fred L. Standley's suggestion that Arthur Miller might be indebted to Milton for details of the death by pressing of Giles Corey
in The Crucible is ridiculous, unwarranted, and unjustified. The
episode, as dramatized by Miller, closely follows contemporary
accounts. (D.P.)

THE CRUCIBLE (cont'd)

M1474 Hill, Philip G., "The Crucible: A Structural View," Modern Drama,
10:312-7, December, 1967.

The Crucible has been maligned unduly by critics who do not understand that the climax of the play occurs at the moment Proctor disavows his confession, rather than in the courtroom scene. (D.P.)

M1475 Popkin, Henry, "Arthur Miller's The Crucible," College English,
26:139-46, November, 1964.

Arthur Miller's drama The Crucible "falls short as a play of ideas"
but succeeds in keeping "our attention by furnishing exciting crises
. . . in the lives of people in whom we have been made to take an
interest." (M.G.)

M1476 Standley, Fred L., "An Echo of Milton in The Crucible," Notes and
Queries, 15:303, August, 1968.

A passage in Miller's The Crucible echoes lines from Milton's poem
"Another on the Same," with the principle difference being "the
change of tone and intent from humorous banter to tragic seriousness." (D.P.)

M1477 Walker, Phillip, "Arthur Miller's The Crucible: Tragedy or
Allegory?" Western Speech, 20:222-4, Fall, 1956.

"The play . . . does not achieve full identity as either a personal
tragedy or a political allegory but, rather, contains within itself
the unfulfilled characteristics of both. . . . As a result, one is left
hovering in the no-man's-land between allegory and tragedy . . .
never sure whether a particular line is to be accepted on its own
emotional terms or as a cryptic comment on the activities of
[McCarthy]." (K.M.W.)

DEATH OF A SALESMAN

M1478 Bates, Barclay W., "The Lost Past in Death of a Salesman,"
Modern Drama, 11:164-72, September, 1968.

A major strand of the play is the triumph of the present over the
past. Willy Loman is, in many ways, an anachronism. (R.C.B.)

M1478   2730

DEATH OF A SALESMAN   (cont'd)

M1479 Bettina, Sister M., S.S.N.D., "Willy Loman's Brother Ben: Tragic Insight in Death of a Salesman," Modern Drama, 4:409-12, February, 1962.

In Death of a Salesman "Ben is a most important 'minor' character, a projection of his brother's personality rather than an individual human force. Through him Miller provides for the audience a considerable amount of the tragic insight which, though never quite reaching Willy, manifests itself to them in the dramatic presentation of the workings of his mind." (D.P.)

M1480 Bliquez, Guerin, "Linda's Role in Death of a Salesman," Modern Drama, 10:383-6, February, 1968.

Linda (Mrs. Willy Loman) unwittingly prods Willy to his doom by acquiescing to his faults and encouraging his dreams. This adds dimension to the theme of the disintegration of a family through avoidance of reality. (R.C.B.)

M1481 Couchman, Gordon W., "Arthur Miller's Tragedy of Babbitt," Educational Theatre Journal, 7:206-11, October, 1955.

"Lewis's satire is simply the story of what Babbittry . . . the Worship of Success . . . does to George F. Babbitt. Arthur Miller's tragedy is the story of what it does to Willy Loman." (G.C.)

M1482 De Schweinitz, George, "Death of a Salesman: A Note on Epic and Tragedy," Western Humanities Review, 14:91-6, Winter, 1960.

Death of a Salesman, "while representing vast re-arrangements and shifts of value . . . shows a basically traditional epic and tragic structure," employing as its sources of value American history (New England), the frontier (Alaska and Africa), and the city (New York). (M.H.)

M1483 Goetsch, Paul, "Arthur Millers Zeitkritik in Death of a Salesman," Die Neueren Sprachen, 16:105-17, March, 1967.

Miller "shares the discontent of the leftist dramatists of the 30's, but he can no longer accept the alternatives offered by them for he knows only too well that a transformation of society depends on a transformation of each individual." (J.R.R.)

DEATH OF A SALESMAN   (cont'd)

M1484   Gross, Barry Edward, "Peddler and Pioneer in Death of a Salesman,"
Modern Drama, 7:405-10, February, 1965.

"Death of a Salesman, then, is, from one viewpoint, a search for
identity, one man's attempt to be a man according to the frontier
tradition in which he was raised, and a failure to achieve that identity
because in this time and place that identity cannot be achieved."
(G.A.S.)

M1485   Hagopian, John V., "Arthur Miller: The Salesman's Two Cases,"
Modern Drama, 6:117-25, September, 1963.

Miller's "Death of a Salesman is broadly an indictment of all modern
industrial society. . . ." This "exists mainly in the outer frame of
the play." The "inner drama--Biff's drama . . . has not been sufficiently appreciated as a uniquely American manifestation of the
eternal, humanizing struggle of a man to achieve his own identity,
even if it means the sacrifice of those he loves."   (D.P.)

M1486   Heilman, Robert B., "Salesmen's Deaths: Documentary and Myth,"
Shenandoah, 20:20-8, Spring, 1969.

In spite of chance resemblances of Arthur Miller's Death of a
Salesman to Eudora Welty's "The Death of a Traveling Salesman,"
the two works have different themes. "One hero grieves for an unachieved divinity, the other suffers from an unachieved community.
Loman would triumph, Bowman yearns to belong." In spirit,
"Miller's drama of death drifts toward documentary, Miss Welty's
toward myth."   (D.P.)

M1487   Hynes, Joseph A., " 'Attention Must Be Paid. . .'," College
English, 23:574-8, April, 1962.

Death of a Salesman contains "annoying violations of dramatic
economy," "looseness in conception of character," a lack of self-
awareness in the supposedly tragic hero, etc. "Willy is confused;
but despite the force of this play, Mr. Miller's possible theme lies
buried in his own confusion." (R.J.G.)

DEATH OF A SALESMAN   (cont'd)

M1488 Inserillo, Charles R., "Wish and Desire: Two Poles of the Imagination in the Drama of Arthur Miller and T. S. Eliot," Xavier
University Studies, 1:247-58, Summer-Fall, 1962.

"The tendency of the romantic mind to play endlessly with unrooted
possibility, and so to allow subjectivity to become solipsistic, is
embodied in Miller's [The Death of a Salesman]. Eliot, on the other
hand, exemplifies in [The Family Reunion, The Cocktail Party, and
The Confidential Clerk] the strength of what we may call a 'classic'
orientation toward existence in its fastening upon the fertility of
human possibility that issues from the depth of human limitation
itself." (D.P.)

M1489 Jackson, Esther Merle, "Death of a Salesman: Tragic Myth in the
Modern Theatre," CLA Journal, 7:63-76, September, 1963.

". . . Miller seems to demonstrate a superiority to other American
dramatists in the symbolic interpretation of unusual dimensions of
collective experience." Death of a Salesman is "perhaps the most
nearly mature myth about human suffering in an industrial age."
(G.C.)

M1490 James, Stuart B., "Pastoral Dreamer in an Urban World,"
University of Denver Quarterly, 1:45-57, Autumn, 1966.

"Throughout his play [Death of a Salesman] Miller implies that he
believes in the myth of the American pastoral past. . . . [However,]
in leading us out of the 'evil' city . . . Miller succeeds only in
returning us to that dubious paradise of his own nostalgic dreams."
(D.A.B.)

M1491 Lawrence, Stephen A., "The Right Dream in Miller's Death of a
Salesman," College English, 25:547-9, April, 1964.

"In the Requiem, Happy, Biff, and Charlie all try to grasp at the
essence of Willy, but each of them falls short. Attention must be
paid to [him] because he believes in love. . . ." (M.G.)

M1492 Miles, O. Thomas, "Three Authors in Search of a Character,"
Personalist, 46:65-72, Winter, 1965.

Man as portrayed in Brave New World "enables us to see that unless
the man described" in Death of a Salesman and Exile and the Kingdom

DEATH OF A SALESMAN   (cont'd)

"finds a redemptive factor in his life he will arrive at the point so terrifyingly described by Huxley." (G.B.M.)

M1493 Miller, Arthur, Gore Vidal, et al, "Death of a Salesman: A Symposium," Tulane Drama Review, 2:63-9, May, 1958.

[This is a conversation between Arthur Miller, Gore Vidal, Richard Watts, John Beaufort, Martin Dworkin, David W. Thompson and Philip Gelb on Death of a Salesman.] (D.P.)

M1494 Oberg, Arthur K., "Death of a Salesman and Arthur Miller's Search for Style," Criticism, 9:303-11, Fall, 1967.

Despite Miller's own "obverse comments on poetic poetry or the mood play, his entire dramatic career has been an effort to get beyond a limited realism and a confining prose." Like Tennessee Williams "he is in search of a style that will allow for an unusually expressive speech." (S.A.)

M1495 Siegel, Paul N., "Willy Loman and King Lear," College English, 17:341-5, March, 1956.

Although Death of a Salesman and King Lear are of course of widely different orders of merit, the contemporary play achieves tragedy of the same kind as the Shakespeare play. Both plays have as their theme "Know thyself," and Lear's abasement and self-recognition are paralleled in Willy's degradation and final insistence on his dignity as a human being. (D.B.D.)

M1496 Parker, Brian, "Point of View in Arthur Miller's Death of a Salesman," University of Toronto Quarterly, 35:144-57, January, 1966.

In a way the blurring of realistic and evoked scenes in Death of a Salesman creates a more pointed tragic effect than Miller achieves in his later plays. The greater empathy with Willy that these stage techniques produce heighten the tragic effect of Willy's fall from grace. (D.P.)

AN ENEMY OF THE PEOPLE

M1497 Bronson, David, "An Enemy of the People: A Key to Arthur
Miller's Art and Ethics," Comparative Drama, 2:229-47,
Winter, 1968-69.

Arthur Miller's adaptation of Ibsen's An Enemy of the People
indicates a basic identity of concerns. Miller attempts economy
and concentration, although the original is a richer play. In
Miller's "prosy adaptation . . . he measured out mutually exclusive portions of good and evil and dispensed with the substance of
life, the individuality and extravagance, the irony and grotesque-
ness. . . ." (D.P.)

INCIDENT AT VICHY

M1498 Clurman, Harold, "Director's Notes: Incident at Vichy,"
Tulane Drama Review, 9:77-90, No. 4, 1965.

[These are Clurman's notes on "the action, the adjustment, the
physical movement or business (if any) of each scene" in Miller's
Incident at Vichy.] (D.P.)

M1499 Roth, Martin, "Sept-d'un-coup," Chicago Review, 19:108-11,
Spring, 1966.

Incident at Vichy demonstrates that Miller searches for a substitute
for dramatic form because his literary sensibility is undramatic.
The central tactic of his plays is tantrum; other devices are to gain
attention. (D.P.)

THE MISFITS

M1500 Alpert, Hollis, "Arthur Miller: Screenwriter," Saturday Review,
44:27, 47, February 4, 1961.

The Misfits is "a serious attempt by a major playwright to conceive
a work directly for the screen." The prose version has been followed on the screen "with unusual faithfulness. There is no essential difference between the events as we read about them and as we
see them on the screen," but "the spare, clear prose of the book
is no match for the vividness of the camera." (D.P.)

THE MISFITS (cont'd)

M1501 Ganz, Arthur, "The Silence of Arthur Miller," Drama Survey, 3:224-37, Fall, 1963.

In the eight years since A View From the Bridge, Miller has produced only one work, the screenplay The Misfits. Despite "its
erratic structure and passages of blatantly bad writing" it is an
interesting work. "Miller seems to have recognized the inadequacy
of a rejection or a simplistic criticism of modern society. . . ."
(D.P.)

M1502 Popkin, Henry, "Arthur Miller Out West," Commentary, 31:433-6,
May, 1961.

The Misfits is "a violently forced dramatization of a theme that
Miller has hitherto expressed only in passing and almost inadvertently. The theme is communication, and Miller now attacks it
with a tireless, but also tiresome, patience." (G.C.)

THE PRICE

M1503 Bigsby, C. W. E., "What Price Arthur Miller?: An Analysis of
The Price," Twentieth Century Literature, 16:16-25, January,
1970.

"The Price marks a sharp improvement over Arthur Miller's last
two plays. It avoids the pretentious dialogue of After the Fall and
the simple-minded manipulation of Incident at Vichy. It acknowledges, too, a sense of ambiguity lacking even from his earlier successes. . . . Miller has at last emerged from the personal and
artistic difficulties which he has experienced since the mid-fifties."
(D.P.)

A VIEW FROM THE BRIDGE

M1504 Epstein, Arthur D., "A Look at A View from the Bridge," Texas
Studies in Literature and Language, 7:109-22, Spring, 1965.

"Although Miller considers Eddie [Carbone] a tragic figure, he nonetheless apparently has never had any clearly defined outline of the
emotions toward Eddie which he wanted to elicit from his audience."
He recognizes Eddie's moral flaw, but--typical of his vision of life
--he "cannot ignore the essential humanity of his characters."
(W.G.F.)

MILLER, HENRY

M1505 Armitage, Merle, "The Man Behind the Smile: Doing Business with Henry Miller," Texas Quarterly, 4:154-61, Winter, 1961.

"No man can write with more facility, style, and descriptive richness than Miller. . . . But he never knows how to stop and he never knows how to edit. . . . Few men are so unable to see the truth, or face it." (W.G.F.)

M1506 Barrett, William, "Henry Miller: Man in Quest of Life: His Exuberant Reflections," Saturday Review, 40:9-10, August 3, 1957.

To Miller sex is the "symbol of the violent quest for experience that flung [him] out of an ordinary office job and a bourgeois career into the stews of Paris. As a writer Miller has never dealt with experience as such but with himself having the miraculous adventure of having experience. He is an innocent abroad. . . ." (D.P.)

M1507 Bode, Elroy, "The World on Its Own Terms: A Brief for Steinbeck, Miller, and Simenon," Southwest Review, 53:406-16, Autumn, 1968.

These three writers have not received just recognition from critics because they accept much of life as it is without indulging in the more fashionable escapist exercises. (J.C.O.)

M1508 Capouya, Emile, "Henry Miller," Salmagundi, 1:81-7, No. 1, 1965.

"From childhood innocence to immersion in the modern nightmare, and then an awakening to a second innocence as an artist--that is the legend" Miller stresses in his works. "It is a story of religious conversion. . . . What hope there is for man is the hope of individual rebirth." (G.C.)

M1509 Carse, James P., "Henry Miller and the Morality of Art," Intercollegian, 79:3-5, June, 1962.

Miller's works are distinguished from contemporaries because his Man is projected in "historical" rather than "heroic" terms. He must be considered as a "maker of the myth in which this understanding of man becomes ours.'. . . To find him filthy is to be filthy ourselves. . . ." (E.F.S.)

M1510 Childs, J. Rives, "Collecting Henry Miller," Private Library, 3:34-7, October, 1960.

It is a "gross injustice" to attribute a pornographic purpose to Miller. He is "a bold spirit, venturing to speak his mind in defiance of the cant of our century," and he chooses to use the language he does to express "profound dissatisfaction" with his world. (W.G.F.)

M1511 Hassan, Ihab, "The Literature of Silence: From Henry Miller to Beckett and Burroughs," Encounter, 28:74-82, January, 1967.

Beckett "leaves us with a world so depleted of life that . . . we are close to the absence of outrage. And Miller presents us with a chaotic world . . . [which reflects] the rage of apocalypse. . . . Burroughs is finally led to deny not only the Word but also the Flesh." For all three, "silence is a metaphor of their complex rage." (G.C.)

M1512 Haverstick, John, "Henry Miller: Man in Quest of Life: His Turbulent Career," Saturday Review, 40:8, August 3, 1957.

Since Tropic of Cancer appeared almost a quarter of a century ago Henry Miller, "Brooklyn native, ex-Greenwich Villager, ex-Western Union boy, ex-Paris expatriate, ex-Alaska bound, once seemingly perenially mistress-bound," has published "a score or more other books and pamphlets whose subject matter was generally well-couched in sex, most of which caused large ripples in the avant-garde pond. . . . Since the Thirties, however, Miller's works have tended to take on a milder tone. . . ." (D.P.)

M1513 Highet, Gilbert, "Henry Miller's Stream of Self-Consciousness," Horizon, 4:104-5, November, 1961.

Tropic of Cancer and Tropic of Capricorn are "sections of a non-stop monologue." They are "among the foulest books ever written. . . . Miller's obscenity . . . is closer to the astounding obscenity of Rabelais and Aristophanes, but it is far less wholesome." (D.P.)

M1514 Hoffman, Michael J., "Yesterday's Rebel," Western Humanities Review, 24:271-4, Summer, 1970.

"Do the young consider Miller to be 'where it's at?' Do the professors with their eyes trained down the corridors of history find Miller to be part of a great tradition that they must perpetuate? I am afraid the answer to both questions must be no." (D.A.B.)

M1515 Jackson, Paul R., "Henry Miller's Literary Pregnancies,"
Literature and Psychology, 19:34-49, No. 1, 1969.

The conflicting elements of comic uncertainty and affirmation in
Miller's fiction resolve themselves when we see that his "basic
mode of literary creation involves the transformation of personal
doubt and middle-class uncertainty into a grand myth of personal
regeneration." (J.M.D.)

M1516 Kleine, Don, "Innocence Forbidden: Henry Miller in the Tropics,"
Prairie Schooner, 33:125-30, Summer, 1959.

"This oracular, quixotic, sentimental man is less than a great
writer, he is not an important thinker. But . . . Henry Miller has
never compromised with the Great American Rot. . . . His honor
has never flagged in thirty years of war with a civilization in which
the body . . . can only be a dirty joke." (D.P.)

M1517 Levitt, Morton P., "Art and Correspondence: Durrell, Miller, and
The Alexandria Quartet," Modern Fiction Studies, 13:299-318,
Autumn, 1967.

During their long correspondence and friendship Durrell moved away
from an early dependence on Henry Miller--as exemplified by the
derivative Black Book--to a conception of art and the artist in his
relationship to life, which is the central theme of The Alexandria
Quartet. Quartet repudiated the work of Miller as well as his own
early imitations. Miller the master had remained "constant as man
and artist" while Durrell, through his growing concern for form,
became the conscious literary artist. (D.P.)

M1518 Littlejohn, David, "The Tropics of Miller," New Republic,
146:31-5, March 5, 1962.

Henry Miller "is an individualist so extreme as to seem at times
prehistoric. He is above or below, or beyond, or apart from all
our most intimate social concerns. . . . Miller has been epically
unsuccessful, both denounced and unread for most of his adult life.
But . . . his lifelong 'commitment' has yielded a unique and devastating quality of honesty in almost all his works." (D.P.)

M1519 Miller, Henry, "Obscenity in Literature," New Directions in Prose and Poetry, No. 16, pp. 232-46, 1957.

"Examining my own life, describing it in detail, exposing it ruthlessly, I believe that I am rendering back life, enhanced and exalted, to those who read me. . . . our moral guardians [insist] that access to forbidden literature may cause us to behave like animals. But to think thus . . . makes of passion, man's greatest attribute, a caricature." (D.P.)

M1520 Mitchell, Edward B., "Artists and Artists: The 'Aesthetics' of Henry Miller," Texas Studies in Literature and Language, 8:103-15, Spring, 1966.

"For Miller, the only adequate definition of artist is 'the poet and the seer who are one.'. . . He repeatedly insists that art, as that term is generally understood, must be transcended: . . . 'Art is only a means to life, the life more abundant. It . . . merely points the way. . . . In becoming an end it defeats itself'." (D.P.)

M1521 Moravia, Alberto, "Two American Writers (1949)," Sewanee Review, 68:473-81, Summer, 1960.

Henry Miller is the American Céline--a nihilist and anarchist, whose works are but "the material of all the novels and all the essays that he might have written." Truman Capote's baroque fantasy presents an America "half unripe and half rotting: the skyscrapers of New York and the crumbling colonial houses of the south." (A.A.S.)

M1522 Peignot, Jérôme, "Henry Miller ou le juif manqué," La Nouvelle Revue Française, 12e année, No. 141, pp. 516-25, September, 1964.

The product that Miller offers us is not literary but a drug--all the exoticism of the Occident. With him, for the first time since Walt Whitman, American letters can be both white, normal and happy without being imbecilic. There are tremendous analogies between Miller and Balzac. (T.T.B.)

M1523 Polley, George Warren, "The Art of Religious Writing: Henry Miller as Religious Writer," South Dakota Review, 7:61-73, Autumn, 1969.

Henry Miller writes religious novels or rather, prototypes of what religious novels in the future will be. In Miller's values the "moral" man struggles with evil rather than hiding from it. The truly religious man "is a man of peace who is concerned only, like God, with the individual." (D.P.)

M1524 Renken, Maxine, "Bibliography of Henry Miller: 1945-1961,"
Twentieth Century Literature, 7:180-90, January, 1962.

[The list is arranged chronologically in three sections: books and
brochures; contributions to books and periodicals; books about
Henry Miller and articles and reviews on Henry Miller.] (D.P.)

M1525 Rexroth, Kenneth, "The Neglected Henry Miller," Nation,
181:385-7, November 5, 1955.

Henry Miller--neglected in America but widely read in Europe--
"writes as if he had just invented the alphabet." Untouched by
religion, he betrays no sense of guilt. "Although he often raves,
he never preaches." He is a realist, like Petronius, Casanova, and
Restif de la Bretonne; his pornography is part of his general truth,
and he "rubs your nose in it." "Better the Flesh than the World and
the Devil." (T.C.L.)

M1526 Robischon, Thomas, "A Day in Court with the Literary Critic,"
Massachusetts Review, 6:101-10, Autumn-Winter, 1964-5.

After studying the experts's testimony in the trial of Tropic of
Cancer in Suffolk County (Massachusetts) Superior Court, it appears
that "obscene literature can be defended with an honest and unflinch-
ingly frank claim that the arousal of lustful thoughts and desires is a
legitimate literary purpose, and that this purpose does indeed have a
socially redeeming importance." (K.M.W.)

M1527 Rode, Alex, "Henry Miller: The Novelist as Liberator," Américas,
18:41-3, January, 1966.

Henry Miller has "tried to teach us . . . [to] come to terms with
. . . the ridiculous, the fumbling and ineffectual clown within all of
us, too myopic to be a saint and too ineffectual to be truly evil."
(G.C.)

M1528 Smithline, Arnold, "Henry Miller and the Transcendental Spirit,"
Emerson Society Quarterly, No. 43, pp. 50-6, Second Quarter, 1966.

Henry Miller "represents a continuation of the Transcendental spirit
in contemporary American literature and like the Transcendentalists
he reasserts the basic concepts of the divinity of man, the holiness of
life, and the unlimited possibilities of spiritual freedom." (D.P.)

M1529 Solotaroff, Theodore, " 'All that Cellar-Deep Jazz': Henry Miller and Seymour Krim," Commentary, 32:317-24, October, 1961.

Henry Miller "now appears on the scene as a prophet with a certain grisly honor." He "has not only been serving as one of the father figures of the Beat writers but also as a Vergil to more sophisticated writers like [Karl] Shapiro . . . or Seymour Krim, who . . . are following Miller's lead to liberate their creative selves by a journey into their own tropics of cancer." (D.P.)

M1530 Southern, Terry, "Miller: Only the Beginning," Nation, 193:399-400, November 18, 1961.

Miller's work, in the tradition of the romantic agony, falls dead center in the American cultural grain. As a result, "the work of the American which may finally stand . . . is that of the dreaded dark horse." (W.F.)

M1531 Traschen, Isadore, "Henry Miller: The Ego and I," South Atlantic Quarterly, 65:345-54, Summer, 1966.

"Miller was . . . a prisoner of the crudest necessities--food and sex. . . . But if he was too often preoccupied with such matters, his preoccupation was a source of energy. . . . [Yet] he is a man without consequences. . . . He is the same at the end as he was at the beginning." (J.L.A.)

M1532 Wickes, George, "The Art of Fiction XXVIII: Henry Miller," Paris Review, No. 28, pp. 128-59, Summer-Fall, 1962.

[This interview explores Miller's writing habits, his revision practices, his recollection of his ten years of writing before Tropic of Cancer appeared, the influence of dada and surrealism on his works and the impact of living abroad on his writing. Finally, Miller comments on Durrell, Orwell, D. H. Lawrence, and his interests in painting and the cinema.] (D.P.)

M1533 Wickes, George, "An Exchange of Letters between Henry Miller and Lawrence Durrell," Paris Review, No. 29, pp. 133-59, Winter-Spring, 1963.

[This is an exchange of letters between Durrell and Miller beginning shortly after Durrell had read The Tropic of Cancer and continuing until 1949. The letters concentrate on literary matters.] (D.P.)

M1534 Wickes, George, "Henry Miller at Seventy," Claremont Quarterly, 9:5-20, No. 2, 1962.

[These are excerpts from an interview with Henry Miller published in the Paris Review.] (K.M.W.)

M1535 Williams, John, "Henry Miller: The Success of Failure," Virginia Quarterly Review, 44:225-45, Spring, 1968.

"In what we may think of as a typically American way, with what we may even call Yankee ingenuity, Henry Miller has made a success of his failure." (S.A.)

JUST WILD ABOUT HARRY

M1536 Bedford, Richard, "Full of the Old Harry," East-West Review, 2:115-23, Winter, 1966.

In his first play Just Wild About Harry "Miller has put his theme-- the sole, religious theme central in all his writing--into a different form. He has given us a dramatization of that 'autobiographical document' which is always the account of the metamorphosis which led to his confrontation of that unity of reality, truth, and love, when he finally achieved his own peculiar identity." (D.A.B.)

SEXUS

M1537 Lund, Mary Graham, "Henry Miller: A Fierce Oracle," North American Review, 4:18-21, January, 1967.

Miller's message to young people is that "if sex is not an awakening to happiness, to new vistas of meaning, it is wrong. Each person must work out his own code, must find meaning in his own experience, in this as in every other area of life. If sex is not life and love, it may be whispering death and affirming hate." (D.A.B.)

TROPIC OF CANCER

M1538 Bess, Donovan, "Miller's Tropic on Trial," Evergreen Review, No. 23, pp. 12-37, March-April, 1962.

[This is a report of the obscenity trial of a bookdealer for selling a copy of Tropic of Cancer in Marin County, California.] (D.P.)

TROPIC OF CANCER

M1539 Brown, Ruth, "Cancer and the Cops," Saturday Review, 44:13, June 24, 1961.

Americans will now be able to purchase a copy of Tropic of Cancer in their nearest bookstore with the publication on June 24 of Henry Miller's classic, and Grove press is already planning to publish the remainder of Miller's banned works. (D.P.)

M1540 Foster, Steven, "A Critical Appraisal of Henry Miller's Tropic of Cancer," Twentieth Century Literature, 9:196-208, January, 1964.

"Henry Miller's cause has not been made clear enough to merit spontaneous applause. He must give sharper definition to his vision, clarity to his motives, consistency to his characters. . . . Formless and crude as the novel may be, however, it is the work of a healthy artist. And what it lacks above all is a basic responsibility, not to other artists or to society, but to art itself." (D.P.)

M1541 Jackson, Paul R., "The Balconies of Henry Miller," University Review, 36:155-60, December, 1969; 221-5, Spring, 1970.

"Although throughout [Tropic of Cancer] Miller dramatizes himself as fastidious and manipulated, at best a most incomplete revolutionary; in the balcony scenes he can maintain a comically vindictive scorn; he projects an aggressive alternative to his own conventional hesitations." (D.P.)

M1542 Katz, Al, "The Tropic of Cancer Trials: The Problem of Relevant Moral and Artistic Controversy," Midway, 9:99-125, Spring, 1969.

"Given their frame of reference, the censors were quite correct in regarding Tropic of Cancer as a dangerous book. . . . 'Hard-core' pornographic photographs and stories tend to be boring and uninfluential. . . . Tropic of Cancer . . . allows for substantial intellectual discussion . . . and in some sense provides an alternative vision of existence for those whose minds are either open or groping for such an alternative." (D.A.B.)

M1543 Kaufmann, Stanley, "An Old Shocker Comes Home," New Republic, 145:17-9, July 10, 1961.

Essentially Tropic of Cancer is "a mirror-image of the testimony which is given at revival meetings. There you can hear about men

TROPIC OF CANCER   (cont'd)

who got right with God; this man got right with art and sex and the
use of his brain and time. Like all converts, he is on fire. Like all
converts . . . he is a bit tedious." (D.P.)

M1544 Lowenfels, Walter, "Unpublished Preface to Tropic of Cancer,"
Massachusetts Review, 5:481-91, Spring, 1964.

[The first part is memoirs of Lowenfels's relationship with Miller
and of Miller in Paris. The second is the first publication of
Lowenfels's rejected introduction to the Tropic of Cancer.] (G.A.S.)

M1545 Norris, Hoke, "Cancer in Chicago," Evergreen Review, 6:40-66,
July-August, 1962.

[This is an account of circumstances preceding the trial of suburban
policemen in the Chicago area for illegally suppressing the sale of
Tropic of Cancer; and an account of the trial, which resulted in an
order enjoining the police from interfering with the sale of the
novel.] (D.P.)

M1546 Redman, B. R., "An Artist's Education: Henry Miller's Tropic of
Cancer," Saturday Review, 44:12, June 24, 1961.

In Tropic of Cancer Henry Miller strips bare the follies and foibles
of his companions during the down-and-out days in Paris--and spares
himself no more than his fellows. . . . His sketches of women are
various and vital. . . . He contradicts himself without apology. He
has put into words the education of an artist who believes that 'art is
only a means to life, to a life more abundant.'. . ." (D.P.)

M1547 Yerbury, Grace D., "Of a City Beside a River: Whitman, Eliot,
Thomas, Miller," Walt Whitman Review, 10:67-73, September, 1964.

Passages in Eliot's Waste Land, Dylan Thomas's "Prologue to an
Adventure" and Henry Miller's Tropic of Cancer appear to share as
a source the ideas expressed in Walt Whitman's "Crossing Brooklyn
Ferry." (D.P.)

MILLER, PETER

M1548 Mullins, S. G., "The Poetry of Peter Miller: A Critical Review,"
Culture, 21:398-408, December, 1960.

Characterized in one word Miller's poetry is _stimulating_. His
themes are fresh, his images exciting, his technique sound. Wit
is the hallmark of his style. His talent is at its best in making the
commonplace visually and aurally compelling. This is achieved by
beauty of vision, freshness of form and rhythm. (J.S.)

MILLER, VASSAR

M1549 Fowler, Albert, "Possessed by the Holy Spirit: The Poetry of
Thomas Merton and Vassar Miller," _Approach_, No. 51, pp. 33-42,
Spring, 1964.

Monk and layman, Trappist and Episcopalian, each with a leaning
toward the Quaker, both bring a special light and grace to a tried
and tempted America. (A.F.)

M1550 Fowler, Helen, "Energy versus Excitement," _Approach_, No. 44,
pp. 40-2, Summer, 1962.

The poems of Vassar Miller are acts of faith. Her use of song or
ballad with refrain is particularly noteworthy. She is actively engaged in the action of each poem. (A.F.)

M1551 Owen, Guy, "Vassar Miller: A Southern Metaphysical," _Southern_
Literary Journal, 3:83-8, Fall, 1970.

"Although Vassar Miller has been writing poetry . . . for almost twenty
years . . . she is not in the mainstream of contemporary American poetry. In an age of scepticism and non-commitment, she is passionately
committed to God and Church. Further . . . she preferred . . . to
stick with traditional modes, stressing discipline and control." (D.P.)

MILLER, WALTER M., JR.

M1552 Rank, Hugh, "Song Out of Season: _A Canticle for Leibowitz_,"
Renascence, 21:213-21, Summer, 1969.

Students of contemporary satire should pay more attention to the
many recent religious satires, but especially to Miller's _A Canticle_
for Leibowitz. This book "deserves further evaluation on the basis
of its own intrinsic merits and of its historical position." (S.A.)

MILOSZ, CZESLAW

M1553 Folejewski, Zbigniew, "Czeslaw Milosz: A Poet's Road to Ithaca,"
Books Abroad, 43:17-24, Winter, 1969.

Milosz's later poems are "characterized by a deep, mature tone of
conviction and by a clear, hard texture, free of exaltation in diction
and imagery. . . . The poet's intimate contact with Western literature, his deep concern with the moral and political conflicts--all
this gives his poetry intellectual depth." Although pessimistic "it is
matter-of-fact poetry, filtered through philosophical reflection,
exotic in personal retrospective detail, and universally solid in its
awareness of modern man's problems." (D.P.)

M1554 Gömöri, George, "On the Collected Poems of Czeslaw Milosz,"
Books Abroad, 43:201-2, Spring, 1969.

"The prewar Milosz was neither a genuine classicist nor a modernist.
. . . his lines were sonorous and attractive, but the poetic substance
of his verse was rather thin." Recently, "his net to catch associations is spread more widely, his poems draw heavily on the imagery
of the unconscious, and philosophical paradox is beginning to play an
important part in his outlook." (D.P.)

MILOSZ, OSCAR

M1555 Bellemin-Noël, Jean, "Douze lettres inédites de Milosz à Rolland
Boris," Revue d'Histoire Littéraire de la France, 67:617-21,
July-September, 1967.

"The twelve letters in our possession retrace in an abridged form the
whole evolution of the poet [Oscar Milosz]: young disciple of
Mallarmé, man of letters fascinated with the work of his maturity,
philosopher entirely devoted to esoteric research, such was in fact
the writer; but we especially recognize his refinement, the simplicity
of his friendships, the humor he maintained in spite of his illness,
the authenticity of his intellectual preoccupations." (D.-J.J.)

MIRBEAU, OCTAVE

M1556 Dubeux, Albert, "Le Féroce Mirbeau," La Revue des Deux Mondes,
140, No. 6, pp. 211-25, March 15, 1968.

Mirbeau is in perpetual rebellion against the iniquity of fate. Beyond
his dramatic baggage, which has made his reputation, he has left
short stories and novels which portray his true thoughts, which ana-

lyze the weakness of modern civilization and castigate our democratic regime. (T.T.B.)

M1557 Schwartz, Martin, "Octave Mirbeau et l'affaire Dreyfus," French
Review, 39:361-72, December, 1965.

"Great friend and admirer of Emile Zola, Mirbeau came to the aid
of the master on the occasion of the Dreyfus Affair, and this episode
in Mirbeau's tumultuous and little known life demands to be clarified.
[The] many unpublished letters [presented here] fill a regrettable
lacuna in the study of French writers and of the role they played in
the Affair. At the same time, these documents are a precious statement on an important period during the life of the author, a period
during which he conceived and wrote one of the most ferocious and
bitter novels that French literature of the nineteenth century produced: Le Jardin des supplices." (D.-J.J.)

LE JARDIN DES SUPPLICES

M1558 Burns, Wayne, " 'In the Penal Colony': Variations on a Theme by
Octave Mirbeau," Accent, 17:45-51, Winter, 1957.

In the Penal Colony is based on Mirbeau's Le Jardin des supplices
(1899). Kafka's achievement contrasts with Mirbeau's sadistic
banalities. Kafka gives this story "a depth of symbolic reference
that illuminates the barbarism of our machine civilization." (B.K.)

MIRÓ, GABRIEL

M1559 King, Edmund L., "Gabriel Miró Introduced to the French,"
Hispanic Review, 29:324-32, October, 1961.

[This is an extended review of Jacqueline van Praag-Chentraime's
Gabriel Miró ou le visage du Levant, Terre d'Espagne (Paris,
1959).] (C.O.)

M1560 O'Sullivan, Susan, "Watches, Lemons and Spectacles: Recurrent
Images in the Works of Gabriel Miró," Bulletin of Hispanic Studies,
44:107-21, 1967.

"It is my intention in this article to attempt a brief analysis of three
. . . images--the watch, the lemon, and the pair of spectacles--
from the early work of Miró onwards and to show how the novelist
arrived at the particular value which he attaches to them in his later
major novels." (D.A.B.)

M1561 Parr, Marcus, "El concepto modernista de la palabra de Gabriel Miró," Hispania, 39:68-71, March, 1956.

Miró carries the message of modernism to its culmination in prose by recreating the Spanish language and bringing to it a new lexicon. He uses metaphors and juxtaposes images capable of creating more than themselves in a way which brings to light the pristine qualities of the world. (M.M.)

MISHIMA, YUKIO

M1562 Boardman, Gwenn R., "Greek Hero and Japanese Sumurai: Mishima's New Aesthetic," Critique: Studies in Modern Fiction, 12:103-13, No. 1, 1970.

"This hybrid nature of Mishima's attitudes and symbols--a Zen Buddhist with 'Augustinian' theories, a modern Japanese extolling the ancient Greek Way, a dramatist who offers us a 'Japanese Electra' . . . offers a challenge to the reader. . . ." "There are clues to the meaning in the symbolic colors and gestures and figures of Mishima's fictional universe. . . . But ultimately, the world is the post-war scene so many contemporary Japanese writers . . . describe as one of 'nihilism'." (D.P.)

M1563 Dana, Robert, "The Stutter of Eternity: A Study of the Themes of Isolation and Meaninglessness in Three Novels by Yukio Mishima," Critique: Studies in Modern Fiction, 12:87-102, No. 1, 1970.

Confessions of a Mask, The Temple of the Golden Pavilion, and The Sailor Who Fell from Grace with the Sea "show the work of Yukio Mishima to be a detailed and extensive probing into the problem of human life in a universe which is basically meaningless and disordered. . . . Mishima's novels possess consistency of concern and structure, and an unimpeachable, if grotesque, integrity." (D.P.)

M1564 Falk, Ray, "Yukio Mishima," Saturday Review, 42:29, May 16, 1959.

"Yukio Mishima at thirty-four is Japan's most prolific, gifted, and successful young author--a man quick with an idea, writing of the present for his contemporaries but well read in the classics of his own and Western culture." He "has a knack for giving significance and depth to current events." (D.P.)

M1565 Micha, René, "Les Allégories de Yukio Mishima," La Nouvelle Revue Française, No. 180, pp. 1066-80, December, 1967.

Mishima, author of more than thirty plays, eighty short stories and sixteen novels, is incessantly occupied with new experiments and new researches in language. He is a direct literary heir of the tradition of Turgenev and Dostoevski. (T.T.B.)

CONFESSIONS OF A MASK--See
KAMEN NO KOKUHAKU

GOGO NO EIKŌ

M1566 Goldstein, Bernice and Sanford Goldstein, "Observations on The Sailor Who Fell from Grace with the Sea," Critique: Studies in Modern Fiction, 12:116-26, No. 1, 1970.

"Mishima Yukio's The Sailor Who Fell from Grace with the Sea can be viewed as a novel of dislocation and disconnectedness." In addition it is "an unsettling allegory on the postwar world of modern man." (D.P.)

KAMEN NO KOKUHAKU

M1567 Korges, James, "Gide and Mishima: Homosexuality as Metaphor," Critique: Studies in Modern Fiction, 12:127-37, No. 1, 1970.

"Homosexuality in The Immoralist is a metaphoric index of Michael's ironically increasing self-knowledge, and his increasing self-interest and cruelty. . . . Mishima's Mask [in Confessions of a Mask], on the other hand, is aware of the significance of his fantasies, and of his failures." (D.P.)

KINKAKUJI

M1568 Duus, Louise, "The Novel as Koan: Mishima Yukio's The Temple of the Golden Pavilion," Critique: Studies in Modern Fiction, 10:120-9, No. 2, 1968.

Mishima's The Temple of the Golden Pavilion is based on the act of a young Zen Buddhist acolyte who burned down the revered Golden Pavilion of the Rokuon Temple in Kyoto. Mishima fleshes out the incident "with a detailed account, delivered in the voice of the fictional acolyte, Mizoguchi, of the growth of his obsession with the Golden Temple. . . . one is struck by the curious detachment of the narrator. . . ." (D.P.)

THE SAILOR WHO FELL FROM GRACE WITH THE SEA--See
GOGO NO EIKŌ

THE TEMPLE OF THE GOLDEN PAVILION--See
KINKAKUJI

MISTRAL, GABRIELA

M1569 Dinamarca, Salvador, "Gabriela Mistral y su obra poética,"
Hispania, 41:48-50, March 1958.

Among the poetic works of Gabriela Mistral "Desolación is best:
because of its sincerity, the nobility of its sentiments, the vigor of
its expression and the purity of its language." (A.C.H.)

M1570 Furness, Edna Lue, "The Divine Gabriela," Western Humanities
Review, 10:75-7, Winter, 1955-56.

[This article includes English translations of three poems.] (C.O.)

M1571 Furness, Edna Lue, "Gabriela Mistral: Professor, Poet, Philosopher, and Philanthropist," Arizona Quarterly, 13:118-23,
Summer, 1957.

"While engaged in the punctilious performance of her duties as a
dedicated teacher, Gabriela Mistral found time to read widely, to
think and meditate, and to lay the foundation of her work which
makes a claim to immortality--as a professor, poet, philosopher,
and philanthropist." (A.A.S.)

M1572 Furness, Edna Lue, "A Woman's Work and Words," Western
Humanities Review, 12:188-91, Spring, 1958.

[This is a brief biography and a translated exhortation to all
workers.] (C.O.)

M1573 González, Manuel Pedro, "Profile of a Great Woman," Hispania,
41:427-30, December, 1958.

Vigor and tenderness are Mistral's outstanding qualities. "Nature
and the Bible are the two principal sources of her poetic imagery."
(A.C.H.)

M1574 Sánchez-Castañer, Francisco, "Evocación de Gabriela Mistral. ¿Quién y cómo era?" Die Neueren Sprachen, 15:470-7, October, 1966.

Due to the complexity of her character, Mistral's poems may seem enigmatic, at times disconcerting, "but it can't be doubted that she was an admirable woman, very 'mujer.'. . ." (J.R.R.)

M1575 Silva Castro, Raúl, "Notas sobre los 'Sonetos de la muerte' de Gabriela Mistral," Hispanic Review, 33:57-62, January, 1965.

Of the eleven Death Sonnets, seven have been found and dated with some precision. Of the remaining four, there is no trace. (C.O.)

M1576 Wheelock, Ruth A., "Gabriela Mistral, Voice of the Americas," Catholic World, 186:252-8, January, 1958.

"Set against the background of the tragedy which shaped her life, Gabriela Mistral's works in poetry and prose show her soul's transformation from the depths of bitter despair to the heights of service to mankind and a close personal relationship with her God." (G.C.)

MECIENDO

M1577 Feuerlicht, Ignace, "Gabriela Mistral's Cradlesong 'Meciendo'," Modern Language Journal, 40:150-1, March, 1956.

In this cradlesong thoughts, feelings, images, words, structure, and sounds form an indissoluble unity, which in itself symbolizes contented unity of or with the universe, as well as perfect love and motherhood. (W.G.F.)

¿PARA QUÉ VINISTE?

M1578 Knowlton, Edgar C., Jr., "Mistral's '¿Para Qué Viniste?'," Explicator, 26: Item 66, April, 1968.

The pregnant woman is "psychologically, poetically, and spiritually . . . alone." (D.P.)

MITCHELL, MARGARET

M1579 Byron, Dora, "A Higher Critic Looks at Gone With the Wind,"
Emory University Quarterly, 13:231-2, December, 1957.

"Gone With the Wind is an economic interpretation of the South.
Scarlett represents 'the South,' torn between a love for the planta-
tion economy, symbolized by Ashley, and a love for the economy of
industry and finance capitalism, symbolized by Rhett. Melanie
represents the gracious living of the Old South. . . ." (D.P.)

M1580 Drake, Robert Y., Jr., "Tara Twenty Years After," Georgia
Review, 12:142-50, Summer, 1958.

Gone With the Wind lacks the subtlety of presentation of Young's,
Faulkner's or Warren's Civil War novels, but "its very lack of
subtlety and self-consciousness is in its favor." (W.G.F.)

M1581 Jones, Marian Elder, " 'Me and My Book'," Georgia Review,
16:180-7, Spring, 1962.

[This is an account of a talk given by Margaret Mitchell at a
writers's club in Macon, Georgia, three weeks before Gone With
the Wind was published.] (G.C.)

M1582 Mathews, James W., "The Civil War of 1936: Gone With the Wind
and Absalom, Absalom!" Georgia Review, 21:462-9, Winter, 1967.

"Despite the conflicting judgment of Gone With the Wind and Absalom,
Absalom! by critics in 1936 and today, both have become classics,
the one the most successful historical romance ever written and the
other a masterpiece of psychological realism. Other than style, the
greatest difference between the two novels is interpretation of the
same events by Southerners." (D.P.)

M1583 Pusey, William Webb, III, "Gone With the Wind in Germany: Translation and Criticism (to 1940)," Kentucky Foreign Language Quarterly, 5:180-8, Fourth Quarter, 1955.

Compelling narrative technique, a sympathetic point of view toward
a lost cause, and the psychological study of a colorful heroine explain why Germans of the later 1930's shared the general enthusiasm
for the world's most popular novel. (W.G.F.)

M1584 Tucker, Scotti Mae, "An Argentine Gone With the Wind," Hispania,
50:69-73, March, 1967.

Although there are indications in Josefina Cruz's El viento sobre el
río that she knew Manuel Gálvez's Escenas de la guerra del Paraguay
--which treated the same historical period--the major influence on
her work was Margaret Mitchell's Gone With the Wind. The indebtedness "extends to setting, plot, characters and incidents." (D.P.)

M1585 Watkins, Floyd C., "Gone With the Wind As Vulgar Literature,"
Southern Literary Journal, 2:86-103, Spring, 1970.

Gone With the Wind is narrowly patriotic, prudish, melodramatic
and sentimental. (T.T.B.)

MITCHELL, SILAS WEIR

M1586 Hayne, Barrie, "S[ilas] Weir Mitchell (1892-1914)," American
Literary Realism, 2:149-55, 1969.

[This article outlines the history of the criticism of S. Weir Mitchell,
lists editions, reprints, and published manuscript material, notes
manuscript collections, recent critical articles, and areas needing
further attention.] (D.A.B.)

MITCHELL, WILLIAM ORMOND

M1587 Barclay, Patricia, "Regionalism and the Writer: A Talk with W. O.
Mitchell," Canadian Literature, No. 14, pp. 53-6, Autumn, 1962.

In spite of being labeled a regionalist, Mitchell maintains that "it is
the 'essentially human truth' that he wishes to reveal in his serious
work, whether his subject is a boy in search of the meaning of life,
or a man face to face with the fact of his own morality." (G.C.)

M1588 New, William H., "A Feeling of Completion: Aspects of W. O.
Mitchell," Canadian Literature, No. 17, pp. 22-33, Summer, 1963.

"In his two novels, The Kite and Who Has Seen the Wind, W. O.
Mitchell makes use of this transition [from childhood to maturity]
as a means to consider man's awareness of time and perception of
reality during his life's span on earth." (G.C.)

WHO HAS SEEN THE WIND

M1589 Tallman, Warren, "Wolf in the Snow, Part One: Four Windows on to Landscapes," Canadian Literature, No. 5, pp. 7-20, Summer, 1960.

The characters Philip Bentley in Ross's As For Me and My House, Brian O'Connal in Mitchell's Who Has Seen the Wind, David Canaan in Buckler's The Mountain and the Valley, Alan MacNeil in Mac-Lennon's Each Man's Son and Duddy Kravitz in Richler's The Apprenticeship of Duddy Kravitz share a profound sense of isolation which may be traced "to the ways in which each is alienated from the natural childhood country of ordinary family life." (D.P.)

MOBERG, VILHELM

M1590 Alexis, Gerhard T., "Vilhelm Moberg: You Can Go Home Again," Scandinavian Studies, 40:225-32, 1968.

". . . the motif of the childhood garden recurs insistently over the span of [Moberg's] writing career. I should like to inquire why and how well it is used in novels representing each of the past four decades." (D.A.B.)

THE EMIGRANTS--See
UTVANDRARNA

THE LAST LETTER HOME--See
UTVANDRARNA

UNTO A GOOD LAND--See
UTVANDRARNA

UTVANDRARNA

M1591 Alexis, Gerhard T., "Moberg's Immigrant Trilogy: A Dubious Conclusion," Scandinavian Studies, 38:20-5, 1966.

"I wish to focus on a specific and disburbing facet of the publication of The Last Letter Home. . . . This concluding work . . . was apparently not the translation of a single Swedish equivalent . . . but somehow of two Swedish novels. . . ." However, the American publishers cut these novels "by almost half, some sections were transposed, and others were summarized in other than the author's words. . . . The publishers distributed . . . in effect, a radical abridgement," without notifying the reader. (D.A.B.)

UTVANDRARNA   (cont'd)

M1592 Alexis, Gerhard T., "Sweden to Minnesota: Vilhelm Moberg's
Fictional Reconstruction," American Quarterly, 18:81-94,
Spring, 1966.

Moberg's trilogy dealing with the Swedish immigrant (The Emigrants,
1961; Unto a Good Land, 1954; The Last Letter Home, 1961), taken
as a whole, represents the major attempt in contemporary Scandina-
via to reconstruct in fictional terms the causes of the great nineteenth-
century exodus, the routes and methods of travel, and the outcome of
settlement." (W.G.F.)

M1593 Bouquet, Philippe, "L'Image de l'Amérique dans le cycle romanesque
Les Emigrants de Vilhelm Moberg," Études Germaniques, 24:452-63,
July-September, 1969.

Moberg's novel cycle is an excellent vehicle for displaying his "sense
of the dialectic of life, his sensibility to history, his art of nuance
and permits him to mix equally individual and collective destiny."
(J.R.R.)

M1594 Winther, Sophus Keith, "Moberg and a New Genre for the Emigrant
Novel," Scandinavian Studies, 34:170-82, August, 1962.

[This is a discussion of Moberg's novels: The Emigrants, Unto a
Good Land, and The Last Letter Home, translated by Gustaf
Lannestock.] (E.L.)

MOGIN, GEORGES--See
NORGE, GÉO

MOHRT, MICHEL

M1595 Sénart, Philippe, "Le Sudisme," La Table Ronde, No. 180, pp.
104-13, January, 1963.

Southernism, as represented in French literature by Mohrt and Yves
Berger, is not geographical, but moral and sentimental. It is not
merely a complaint about lost illusions, but in the work of Northern-
ers or Bretons like Mohrt a recourse against the severities of destiny. Mohrt has sympathy for oppressed minorities, difficult causes,
battles lost in advance. (T.T.B.)

MOLINA CAMPOS, ENRIQUE

M1596 Davison, Ned J., "Enrique Molina Campos: A Poet of the New
Spanish Generation," Bulletin of the Rocky Mountain Modern
Language Association, 22:22-8, March, 1968.

"Molina Campos is an accomplished poet who promises much. He
speaks in a voice wholly his own without falling into excessive
novelty; he carries with him the poetic tradition of his language; and
he bears the charge with maturity, deep sensitivity, and devotion to
his craft." (D.A.B.)

MOLL, ERNEST GEORGE

M1597 Gardiner, Thomas J., "The Poetry of E. G. Moll," Southerly,
25:173-81, No. 3, 1965.

The belief that this Australian poet "was essentially a regionalist
whose lyrical and narrative description of landscape and native"
defined his poetry is belied by an examination of some of his poems,
which reveal his impressive achievement as a lyricist. (D.A.B.)

MOMBERT, ALFRED

M1598 Haenicke, Diether, "Alfred Mombert: Beobachtungen zur Form
seiner Gedicht-Werke," German Quarterly, 40:41-57, January,
1967.

The characterization of Mombert as a "cosmic poet" is inaccurate;
his material is primarily chaos, which he strives to animate, to
form into a cosmos. Thus his insistence that no single lyric had
meaning except as a part of a total Gedicht-Werk. (R.H.L.)

M1599 Hermand, Jost, "Die Ur-Frühe: Zum Prozess des mythischen
'Bilderns' bei Mombert," Monatshefte, 53:105-14, March, 1961.

Before Mombert's lyrics proceed via expressionistic vacuity into a
conceptual disintegration, his symbolism harking back to the primeval
succeeds in reconciling the intellectual masculine element with the
terrestrial-feminine, the individual element with the collective unconscious. (R.H.L.)

MONDOR, HENRI

M1600 Groll, Henriette, "Henri Mondor," Cahiers des Saisons, No. 38, p. 319, Summer, 1964.

[These are souvenirs and a portrait of Mondor.] (T.T.B.)

MONROE, HARRIET

M1601 Lowe, Robert Liddell, "Edwin Arlington Robinson to Harriet Monroe: Some Unpublished Letters," Modern Philology, 60:31-40, August, 1962.

"Obviously, the editor and the poet were primarily at odds with one another on points of themes appropriate to the modern poet, and each was to remain stubbornly loyal to his principles." But each maintained respect for the other's integrity. (A.S.)

M1602 Zabel, Morton Dauwen, "H. M.: In Memory, 1860-1936," Poetry, 97:241-54, January, 1961.

Harriet Monroe's founding of Poetry magazine in 1912 was a coura- geous, forward-looking venture. Only a few people sensed that the new age of poetry was about to begin. Possessed of hard-headedness, enthusiasm and good judgment, in spite of some errors, she made a success of the magazine. She was an "explorer and adventurer to the last." (F.L.)

MONSARRAT, NICHOLAS

M1603 Jarrett, Thomas D., "The Talent of Nicholas Monsarrat," English Journal, 45:173-80, April, 1956.

Monsarrat "seems to depend too much on fine writing, contrivance, and superb reporting to sustain his novels, often at the expense of failing to present characters that are more than types. . . . he falls short when he must interrelate other people or probe deeply for the motives that lie beneath the actions of his characters." (K.M.W.)

MONTAGUE, CHARLES EDWARD

M1604 Irwin, W. R., "Experiment in Irony: Montague's A Hind Let Loose," Modern Fiction Studies, 3:141-6, Summer, 1957.

As an experiment in sustained irony, A Hind Let Loose is not bold enough. Montague adopts irony as a method and then deserts it, setting dulce and utile at odds, confounding his original purpose. (R.A.K.)

MONTALE, EUGENIO

M1605 Almansi, Guido, "Earth and Water in Montale's Poetry," Forum for Modern Language Studies, 2:377-85, October, 1966.

"Water, the sea, are for Montale, above all, symbols of death. . . . Life moves downhill towards this sea in a perennial descent, a painful wasting away towards aquatic annihilation, the suffered experience of a fall in which not only human beings, but vegetables, minerals, objects participate." (K.M.W.)

M1606 Cambon, Glauco, "Eugenio Montale: A Biographical Note," Quarterly Review of Literature, 11:304-6, 1962.

[This short biographical note includes an assessment of Montale's literary accomplishment.] (D.A.B.)

M1607 Cambon, Glauco, "Eugenio Montale's 'Motets': The Occasions of Epiphany," PMLA, 82:471-84, December, 1967.

"Through . . . inner experience, the persona has known heaven and hell and purgatory . . . now only the stoic acceptance of slowly dwindling life is left, with whatever minor consolations it may offer. . . . the poet's persona has grown from passionate youth to the sad wisdom of age, through the cycles of experienced time." (K.M.W.)

M1608 Cambon, Glauco, "Eugenio Montale's Poetry: A Meeting of Dante and Brueghel," Sewanee Review, 66:1-32, Winter, 1958.

"From a thorough reading, we may conclude, there emerges perhaps the best lyrical poet of the Italian twentieth century . . . one belonging to the great Western tradition which, with Proust, Joyce, Eliot and Faulkner, has explored the paradoxes of time, existence, finitude and memory, expressing outspokenly the impending disintegration of our civilization." (A.A.S.)

M1609 Caprioglio, Giuliana, "Intellectual and Sentimental Modes of Rapport with Reality in Montale's Ossi and Occasioni," Italian Quarterly, 49:51-66, 1969.

". . . it would appear that poetry and love pose themselves as the two poles between which the spectrum of possible rapports with reality vibrates; but while at the end of Ossi a voice of hope . . . raised itself . . . above the desert of . . . life . . . at the end of Occasioni . . . no voice of hope is raised, and to the cognitive desperation is added the sentimental desperation of the by now deluded hope of a salvation on the level of a human love." (D.A.B.)

M1610 Cluny, Claude Michel, "Les Poésies d'Eugenio Montale," La Nouvelle Revue Française, 15:503-9, March, 1967.

Far from the influence of Marinetti and Gabriele d'Annunzio, Montale discovers the setting which will be the frame of his work, in which the essential interrogation will be freed little by little from the contradictions of the being, as the style will break also, imperceptibly, with musical symbolism. (T.T.B.)

M1611 Gathercole, Patricia M., "Two Kindred Spirits: Eugenio Montale and T. S. Eliot," Italica, 3:170-9, September, 1955.

"Although critics have called attention to interesting parallels in the personalities and works of these eminent figures," the contrasts between them indicate rather than conscious imitation, "an affinity of mind." (D.P.)

M1612 Gerstenlauer, Wolfgang, "Italienische Lyrik der Moderne: Luce in Tenebra: Variationen eines Motivs in der Dichtung Eugenio Montales 'Für Giuseppe Bevilacqua'," Die Neueren Sprachen, 16:118-36, March, 1967.

Montale's evolution as an artist may be traced by studying his use of the contrast of light and darkness as a motif in a number of poems. (J.R.R.)

M1613 Hersey, Jane M., "Eugenio Montale: The Analysis of a Few Poems in the Tradition of The Waste Land," Bucknell Review, 5:29-40, No. 2, 1955.

Both poets "find the poetic object of their search in the symbol which jolts the consciousness into a momentary recreation of the past. Eliot took the path leading away from the waste land towards a religious reconciliation of time and eternity, while Montale seems to have struck a balance, however precarious, between 'Divine Indifference' and human memory." (K.M.W.)

M1614 Huffman, Claire L., "The Poetic Language of Eugenio Montale," Italian Quarterly, 47-48:105-28, 1969.

"The language of [Montale's] poetry is storicizzato . . . which means something quite different from being 'timely.' Only certain things can be said in verse . . . and this verse must have its own language. . . . The language of a poet is that which distinguishes him from other poets, and . . . from the newspaper reporter" and the conversationalist. (D.A.B.)

M1615 Livi, François, "Hommage à la poésie," La Table Ronde, No. 228, pp. 137-43, January, 1967.

Since 1925 Eugenio Montale has renounced the sentimentalism of twilights and idealized biographies of saints. His point of departure is more vast than that of Ungaretti. He is more like T. S. Eliot. Dino Campana, in life and work, resembles Gérard de Nerval. (T.T.B.)

M1616 Pipa, Arshi, "Memory and Fidelity in Montale," Italian Quarterly, 39-40:62-79, 1967.

"The present essay is an attempt to explore and map out the domain of memory in the work of Montale. . . . For this purpose I shall consider Montale's poetry in its distinct stages, beginning with Ossi di seppia, first . . . and second edition . . . through Le Occasioni . . . and Finisterre . . . to La bufera e altro . . . and Farfalla di Dinard. . . ." (D.A.B.)

M1617 Pipa, Arshi, "The Message of Montale," Italica, 39:239-55, December, 1962.

"Montale's poetry may be described as a masterful variation of a few themes, invariably concerned with ultimate problems: life, time, evil, freedom, love, and God. The answers proposed may not be entirely new; but they do have a highly personal and often an original accent." (K.M.W.)

M1618 Sampoli-Simonelli, Maria, "The Particular World of Eugenio
Montale: With Translations from Montale's Works by Mark Musa,"
Italian Quarterly, 3:42-55, 1959.

"To talk about Montale's poetics is above all to talk about his Ossi
di seppia (1925). His later collections of poems . . . do not modify
the position assumed and lived by Montale from his early poetic
experiences. . . ." (D.A.B.)

M1619 Singh, G., "Eugenio Montale," Italian Studies, 18:101-37, 1963.

Montale's "is the poetry of life-secrets guarded jealously, but not
too jealously to inspire a certain confidence between the poet and
his readers, and . . . in the poet himself. . . ." (G.C.)

M1620 Solmi, Sergio, "The Poetry of Montale," Quarterly Review of
Literature, 11:221-38, 1962.

"In the early work the situation was statically and naturalistically
universal: the creature confronted with the desolate machine of
cosmic necessity. In the late work the universalism is, so to speak,
particularized and historic: the poet tries to break through the lines
of an individual destiny and to make them tally, at least at some
point, with those of common human destiny." (D.A.B.)

LA BUFERA E ALTRO

M1621 Cambon, Glauco, "The Privacy of Language: A Note on Eugenio
Montale's 'Obscurity'," Modern Language Notes, 78:75-9,
January, 1963.

". . . close scrutiny will reveal that the good poems--and they are
a majority [in La Bufera e altro]--have a different kind of privacy.
They are . . . shrouded in modesty, and demand the highest tact
and the most loving insistence to yield their secret. There is
nothing opaque about genuine mystery." (K.M.W.)

ELEGIA DI PICO FARNESE

M1622 Rebay, Luciano, "I diàspori di Montale," Italica, 46:33-53,
Spring, 1969.

[This article, which is concerned with Montale's "Elegia di pico
Farnese," includes a correspondence between Montale and Roberto
Bazlen, who strongly admired and influenced the course of Italian
letters in the first half of the century.] (D.P.)

OCCASIONI

M1623 Pipa, Arshi, "Le Mythe d'un papillon: Montale et Anouilh, "
Revue de Littérature Comparée, 38:400-13, July-September, 1964.

Anouilh's Léocadia was written in 1938, and the last poems of
Montale's Occasioni were written in 1938-39. The inspiration for
"Elegia di pico Farnese," from Occasioni, bears a striking analogy
to Léocadia. "One is able to say without fear of error that the culmination of Léocadia very nearly approximates the shining aspiration
of Montale's poetry during a long period of gestation." (D.P.)

L'ORTO

M1624 Cambon, Glauco, "The Garden of Apocalyptic Memory, " Quarterly
Review of Literature, 11:288-94, 1962.

". . . 'L'Orto' holds a privileged position as a piece of spiritual
autobiography that concedes very little to the innocent reader in the
way of factual references, yet almost everything as far as internal
clues to the essential meaning go. . . . It is as if Dante's mystic
experience in Paradiso were being re-enacted here on earth, and
without the hope of final revelation, only the yearning for one."
(D.A.B.)

OSSI DI SEPPIA

M1625 McCormick, C. A., "Sound and Silence in Montale's Ossi di seppia, "
Modern Language Review, 62:633-41, October, 1967.

"With a poet like Montale, whose work is so curiously free from
'influences, ' we are bidden to enter into the poet's own world, to
try part against part and part against whole. Almost invariably the
most relevant comment on a Montale poem will come from another
Montale poem." (J.R.R.)

MONTEFORTE TOLEDO, MARIO

M1626 Lipp, Solomon, "Mario Monteforte Toledo: Contempory Guatemalan
Novelist, " Hispania, 44:420-7, September, 1961.

This is "an excellent example of the trajectory taken by the Latin
American novel": increasingly disciplined style, growing concern
for psychological themes, and continuing attempts to transcend
purely regional appeal. (C.O.)

MONTESQUIOU, ROBERT DE

M1627 Jullian, Philippe, "Le Péril mauve," Cahiers des Saisons, 41:57-63, Spring, 1965.

The theme of homosexuality and lesbianism so prevalent in contemporary literature stems largely from the works of Montesquiou, the inspiration of Proust. Although he was not a participant, slander has unjustly accused him of abjection and scandal. (T.T.B.)

M1628 LeSage, Laurent, "Proust's Professor of Beauty: Count Robert de Montesquiou," American Society of Legion of Honor Magazine, 27:65-76, Spring, 1958.

"Montesquiou was not only a model for Proust, but a real master, a 'professeur de beauté' as Proust had called him. But the pupil was a genius and soon surpassed the master, who was, after all, only an esthete. Montesquiou was left behind to ruminate the folly of putting more talent in his life than in his work." (K.M.W.)

MONTGOMERY, LUCY MAUDE

M1629 Miller, Muriel, "Who was Ephraim Weber?" Queen's Quarterly, 68:333-6, Summer, 1961.

Weber's recently published (1960) correspondence with L. M. Montgomery may bring him the "literary recognition denied him during his life." (G.B.M.)

MONTGOMERY, MARION

M1630 Colvert, James B., "An Interview with Marion Montgomery," Southern Review, 6:1041-53, October, 1970.

[This is a conversation with the author on a wide range of topics, including both his own works and those of other authors.] (K.M.W.)

MONTHERLANT, HENRY DE

M1631 Alheinc, Raoul, "Montherlant et le bovarysme," La Table Ronde, No. 103-4, pp. 208-15, July-August, 1956.

In Montherlant's work there are two themes which begin about 1927: the "crise du voyageur traque" and the "crise de l'homme de trente ans." The influence of Flaubert becomes more than intellectual;

he is a part of Montherlant's esthetic sensibility and animates his vision of life in work from Rose de Sable to Port-Royal. (C.D.S.)

M1632 Arthos, John, "The Montherlant Manner," French Review, 43:135-43, Special Issue No. 1, Winter, 1970.

Montherlant "wants above all else, in his plays as in his novels, in his epigrams, to impress us with the quality of his arrogance, and of his selfishness. . . . He does have a style, even a certain elegance. . . . We come to understand how much his licentiousness is complicated by his delight in wit and elegance, how much religion there is in his irreligion, and how much reticence in the ostentatious parade of the most personal matters." (D.P.)

M1633 Batchelor, J. W., "Religious Experiences in Henry de Montherlant's Dramatic Characters," Australian Journal of French Studies, 3:180-95, May-August, 1966.

". . . Montherlant is not an agnostic; he is an atheist. The problem posed, then, is to decide why and--perhaps more important--how such an atheist artist uses his vast intellectual awareness of religious problems and even theological doctrine itself to create characters and plays which are serious religious drama. . . ." (D.A.B.)

M1634 Becker, Lucille, "Pessimism and Nihilism in the Plays of Henry de Montherlant," Yale French Studies, No. 29, pp. 88-91, Spring-Summer, 1962.

"There is expressed throughout Montherlant's theatrical production a desire for death, providing that heaven be empty and death lead to nothingness. This desire is a natural outcome of the knowledge of the equivalence of all things, of the fact that virtue carries no more weight than vice." (D.P.)

M1635 Belli, Angela, "The Rugged Individualists of Henry de Montherlant," Modern Drama, 13:157-68, September, 1970.

"Montherlant's achievement is to awaken within us an awareness of what it means to be an aristocrat. He exhibits the extraordinary. And he reminds us that if there are no great heroes in our contemporary plays, it may well be because ordinary men perform no extraordinary deeds." (K.M.W.)

M1636 Blanc, André, "Montherlant est-il chrétien?" La Revue des Deux
Mondes, 140:190-201, March 15, 1968.

In his work Montherlant places himself in the line of esthetic paganism and rationalistic atheism, although attracted by certain forms
of religious life and certain Catholic attitudes which he admires.
Agnostic, rather than pure atheist as Sainte-Beuve, as the end of
life approaches he is ready to take the opposite odds of Pascal's bet.
(T.T.B.)

M1637 Blanchard, Jean-Marc, "Montherlant: La jeunesse, le désir, et la
mort," Romanic Review, 59:93-8, April, 1968.

In the writings of Montherlant "the young grow old, and death loses
its epic costume. That is the final glory of Montherlant." (D.P.)

M1638 Borel, Jacques, "La maconnerie collégiale de Montherlant,"
La Nouvelle Revue Française, No. 199, pp. 85-92, July, 1969.

Montherlant has a passion for adolescence. He returns in Les
Garçons to the universe of his first works, L'Exil, La Relève du
matin, etc. This school world has always been for him the elect,
the only breathable place. A real, vital woman does not appear in
any of his works. (T.T.B.)

M1639 Chiaromonte, Nicola, "Montherlant e il gusto del rigore,"
Il Mondo, 10:14, May 27, 1958.

Montherlant's ethical axiom, "to remain superior and thus in a
certain sense apart from himself, lucid at the cost of falling into the
delirium of solitary pride" also "dominates his theatre, inspires its
themes and makes of his heroes types of obsessives of severity, of
rigor." (V.R.)

M1640 Dopagne, Jacques, "Mors et fricum ou Montherlant et La Guerre
civile," La Nouvelle Revue Française, 13e anneé, No. 150, pp.
1080-5, June, 1965.

The singularity of Montherlant is the alternation of the writer who
is and who is not his characters, who, for more than forty years,
has been floundering around in a same and continual dilemma. It
is worse. It is not merely a question of alternation, but rather of
simultaneity. (T.T.B.)

M1641 Edney, David B., "L'Antithéâtre de Montherlant," La Revue des Deux Mondes, 142:331-7, February, 1970.

Montherlant's originality is to have expressed his nihilism under a form dazzling in appearance, uniting profound modern thought with a beautiful classic form. (T.T.B.)

M1642 Gobert, David L., "Identity in Diversity: Montherlant's Celles qu'on prend dans ses bras and La Ville dont le prince est un enfant," Symposium, 21:22-8, Spring, 1967.

"Celles qu'on prend dans ses bras and La Ville dont le prince est un enfant present a curious example of Montherlant's 'alternance' in intensity of movement, structure, character disposition, and resolution. Indeed, they represent alternative solutions to the same problem, and as such, appear as variations on a single theme." (K.M.W.)

M1643 Gobert, David L., "Structural Identity of La Reine morte and Le Maître de Santiago," French Review, 38:30-3, October, 1964.

With these plays "Montherlant has succeeded--more so than in other plays--in effecting a balance between the exigencies of two separate genres, the novel and the drama, the aesthetics of which, he has long contended, are not mutually exclusive." (R.B.W.)

M1644 Gouhier, Henri, "La religion dans le théâtre d'Henry de Montherlant," La Table Ronde, No. 212, pp. 5-11, September, 1965.

Montherlant envisions Christianity as a principle of surpassing the world as it is: a soul detached from the goods of this world and from itself; a liberation which rids the ego of passions and results in the annihilation of the ego itself. (T.T.B.)

M1645 Johnson, Robert B., "Definitions of Youth in the Theater of Montherlant," Modern Language Journal, 47:149-54, April, 1963.

". . . his young people--and his mature people, as well--seem to be static figures motionless within the dramatic framework. . . . at least where youth is concerned, [Montherlant writes] 'case history' plays, and case histories rarely offer satisfying conclusions. Static as his study of youth may be, it makes for good theater." (K.M.W.)

M1646 Kops, Henri, "Henry de Montherlant," Books Abroad, 31:229-32, Summer, 1957.

". . . Henry de Montherlant is peerless in the manner in which he possesses French [,] molding it to his every nuance of feeling and thought. . . ." "La Reine morte is a haunting romance of old Portugal spiced with his own brand of cynicism. . . ." Fils de personne is "an unrelenting modern drama of a father and son relationship. . . . in his last play, Port-Royal (1954), he makes the rebellion of the Sisters of that monastery a startlingly human and stirring historical event." (D.P.)

M1647 Montherlant, Henry de, "Carnets," La Nouvelle Revue Française, 3:1025-39, December, 1955.

[Excerpts from Montherlant's notebooks for 1931 reveal his thoughts on his work and on life and literature in general.] (M.M.)

M1648 Morreale, Gerald, " 'Alternance' and Montherlant's Aesthetics," French Review, 37:626-36, May, 1964.

". . . Montherlant possesses a comprehensive and complex aesthetic that enables him to move between two literary worlds: that of art for art's sake and that of so-called littérature engagée." (R.B.W.)

M1649 Norrish, P. J., "Montherlant as a moraliste," Australian Journal of French Studies, 1:307-24, September-December, 1964.

". . . the essential characteristic of Montherlant the moraliste. . . is his highly unusual moral viewpoint. This leads him to dwell mainly on the presence or absence in men, of certain qualities or capacities he believes to be pre-eminent. . . . he excels in making rich and provocative characters . . . of a single exalted morality." (D.P.)

M1650 Norrish, P. J., "Montherlant's Conception of the Tragic Hero," French Studies, 14:38-51, January, 1960.

Although Montherlant's heroes lack compassion and although their sufferings often seem more melodramatic than tragic, they celebrate some "much neglected virtue": integrity and "a sense of duty to one's principles" which is expressed in a pure and forceful language "which heightens their nobility." (R.A.B.)

M1651 Orcibal, Jean, "De Port-Royal au Cardinal d'Espagne," La Table Ronde, No. 148, pp. 26-32, April, 1960.

We should not be surprised to see the author of Maître de Santiago return to Castille for his Cardinal d'Espagne; he has demonstrated since Port-Royal a concern with themes common to those found in his picture of Paris of 1664 and that of Madrid of 1517. (D.P.)

M1652 Pivot, Bernard, "Montherlant," Réalités, No. 279, pp. 5-15, April, 1969.

For over thirty years, from Les Jeunes Filles to Les Garçons, Montherlant has been perfecting his craft as a novelist. Although an atheist, he is, paradoxically, a mystic; he is sensual, sensitive and cynical. (T.T.B.)

M1653 Price, Jonathan Reeve, "Montherlant: The Jansenist Libertine," Renascence, 19:208-16, Summer, 1967.

"Montherlant accepts the quicksilver of his soul, and he gives it free play. The Jansenist libertine, the soldier monk, the skeptic saint--these are the saints in Montherlant's pantheon. The human soul, in all its complexity, is the godhead. All that gives the self its freedom, its liberty to flow as it will, is morally good, for it leads to the one prerequisite, the unum necessarium, happiness." (D.P.)

M1654 Price, Jonathan Reeve, "Montherlant's Aesthetics," Modern Drama, 8:324-31, December, 1965.

Montherlant's "relation to his audience is a peculiar one, deriving from the concepts of renoncement, alternance, and the néant sublime. In fact, his plays seem to be designed to enable his spectators to experience many of the feelings he himself moves through." (K.M.W.)

M1655 Price, Jonathan Reeve, "Montherlant's Exemplar," Yale French Studies, No. 33, pp. 101-4, 1964.

"The image Montherlant has of Shakespeare is thus essentially the romantic one--that Shakespeare as an artist had the ability to enter into all beings equally, that he felt character was more important than mere action, that character consisted mainly in contradictory impulses. . . . But Montherlant has adapted the image so that Shakespeare will seem to be an example of his own conceptions as well." (K.M.W.)

M1656 Rey, John B., "The Search for the Absolute: The Plays of Henry de Montherlant," Modern Drama, 3:178-90, September, 1960.

"Montherlant is half-way right [in his plays] in shocking his audiences out of their complacency and apathy, in making them aware of spiritual values. But his audience is also half-way right in considering his heroes monsters." (C.K.L.)

M1657 Sola Balust, Luis, "Le Moment espagnol dans l'oeuvre de Montherlant," La Table Ronde, No. 148, pp. 34-40, April, 1960.

With Maître de Santiago and Port-Royal, Montherlant's Cardinal d'Espagne forms a grand Catholic trilogy; three different dramas, yet monothematic in its treatment of authentic Christianity, which is, however, seen more for psychological than for doctrinal aspects. (D.P.)

M1658 Turnell, Martin, "Adventurer Montherlant," Commonweal, 74:171-3, May 12, 1961.

"Montherlant is not merely an adventurer; he is a man of contradictions: Catholic and pagan; a soldier who detests modern warfare; a patriot who enjoys belaboring the fatherland; and--most important of all for an understanding of his work--a womaniser who at bottom hates women." His "most impressive achievement remains La Reine morte." (D.P.)

M1659 Vial, Fernand, "The 'Last' Plays of Henry de Montherlant," American Society of Legion of Honor Magazine, 32:31-47, No. 1, 1961.

[This is a discussion of Brocéliande, Don Juan, and Le Cardinal d'Espagne.] (D.A.B.)

LE CARDINAL D'ESPAGNE

M1660 Genevoix, Maurice, "Le Cardinal d'Espagne," La Table Ronde, No. 148, pp. 18-9, April, 1960.

"The strength of this proud, hard and nihilist play lies in its tender humanity, its love and its pity." (D.P.)

LE CARDINAL D'ESPAGNE (cont'd)

M1661 Gouhier, Henri, "Une Tragédie de l'homme caché," La Table Ronde, No. 148, pp. 20-5, April, 1960.

"Le Cardinal d'Espagne is, like Port-Royal, a work where the drama takes place in spirit and nearly without external episodes." (D.P.)

M1662 Massis, Henri, "Montherlant, homme de théâtre," La Table Ronde, No. 148, pp. 45-8, April, 1960.

"In Le Cardinal d'Espagne Montherlant has given us a language carrying truth and force, able to express the noblest thoughts and the most profound emotions. I know nothing, today, which equals it." (D.P.)

M1663 Montherlant, Henry de, "Notes sur Le Cardinal d'Espagne," La Table Ronde, No. 148, pp. 9-17, April, 1960.

[These notes are intended to clarify and to provide additional background on the characters and events in Le Cardinal d'Espagne.] (D.P.)

M1664 Peman, José Maria, "Une Tragédie des conflits," La Table Ronde, No. 148, pp. 41-4, April, 1960.

"In Le Cardinal d'Espagne Montherlant has not at all betrayed the Spanish spirit in writing a play which he himself considers as much psychological as historical. . . . To give full weight to the inner conflict Montherlant has . . . opposed Cardinal Cisneros to the queen." (D.P.)

M1665 Saint-Robert, Philippe de, "Une Tragedie de la grâce," La Table Ronde, No. 148, pp. 49-51, April, 1960.

"The miracle of Montherlant is the way in which he perpetually renews himself and always remains the same. Of the total oeuvre of Montherlant Le Cardinal d'Espagne is the most accomplished, the most perfect." (D.P.)

L'EXIL

M1666 Primeau, Marguerite-A., "L'Amour-passion dans L'Exil de Montherlant," French Review, 44:322-8, December, 1970.

In Montherlant's L'Exil "we are faced with two manifestations of the love passion: first, the stifling love of Geneviève for her son, and second, the hypertrophied friendship of Philippe for Sénac." In this work, as well as later, "Montherlant has arrayed himself with the young against their parents." (D.P.)

LE MAÎTRE DE SANTIAGO

M1667 Thiher, Allen, "Le Maître de Santiago and Tragic Affirmation," Romance Notes, 11:238-43, Winter, 1969.

Although its hero is a Christian mystic, this is the closest among Montherlant's plays to the spirit of classical Greek tragedy. (A.K.)

MALATESTA

M1668 Gerrard, Charlotte Frankel, "Montherlant's Malatesta: Pagan, Christian, or Nietzschean?" French Review, 41:831-8, April, 1968.

Malatesta "is a blasphemer who is innocently blind to the hatred and envy that surround him. Because of his repentance and love, he cannot be called an anti-Christ, but he must be considered a dubious Christian. He is much more pagan than Catholic in the appreciation he shows for literature, architecture, and the body. Original sin is a meaningless doctrine for this hero of varied passions and intense Nietzschean joy." (K.M.W.)

PORT-ROYAL

M1669 Blanc, André, "A Propos de Port-Royal," La Revue des Deux Mondes, No. 12, pp. 612-6, December, 1969.

Port-Royal is the most religious of Montherlant's plays. Paradoxically it best discloses the author's agnosticism. The Catholic religion for him is reduced to a language that he does not like, does not see, and understands only at the level of word and gesture. (T.T.B.)

PORT-ROYAL (cont'd)

M1670 Vial, Fernand, "Montherlant's Farewell to the Stage: Port Royal," American Society of Legion of Honor Magazine, 27:33-54, Spring, 1956.

"The essential merit of the play resides . . . in the boldness of its conception, the constantly sustained interest, the ingenuity in the combination of historical events and figures, and the extraordinary ability in transforming an abstruse point of theology, which holds no interest for a modern public, into a deeply human, stirring crisis. . . ." (K.M.W.)

M1671 Vial, Fernand, "Paris Letter," Renascence, 7:187-95, 1955.

[Among "some important events of a Catholic character" this "letter" mentions the Semaine des Intellectuals Catholiques which dealt with Mauriac's theme "What is man?" and the production of Montherlant's play Port-Royal.] (D.A.B.)

M1672 Weiss, Auréliu, "Montherlant et Port-Royal: Un Portrait de Soeur Angélique," Romance Notes, 10:1-6, Autumn, 1968.

The central conflict of the play, that between the church and the nuns of Port-Royal as dramatized through the characterization of Soeur Angélique, is really a broader expression of a demand for social and moral justice. (A.K.)

LA REINE MORTE

M1673 Johnson, Robert B., "The Ferrante Image in Montherlant's La Reine morte," French Review, 36:255-9, January, 1963.

La Reine morte is "a curiously ingenious drama of a single figure, Ferrante, surrounded by persons reflecting facets of his own personality; it may properly be termed a monologue play. The focus rarely slips from the central image, although it may fall temporarily upon other characters who always reflect the main image." (K.M.W.)

M1674 Montherlant, Henry de, "Souvenirs sur la création de La Reine morte," La Revue des Deux Mondes, pp. 481-5, October 15, 1966.

[These are Montherlant's recollections of critical, popular and official attitudes at the early performances of La Reine morte.] (D.P.)

LA REINE MORTE   (cont'd)

M1675 Weiss, Auréliu, "Montherlant et La Reine morte: Un Portrait d'Inès
de Castro," Revue des Langues Vivantes, 33:563-71, No. 6, 1967.

In creating Inès, Montherlant was deeply influenced by his Spanish
source, Velez de Guevara's play, which shows that Inès de Castro's
driving ambition was to continue reigning after death.   (D.-J.J.)

UN VOYAGEUR SOLITAIRE EST UN DIABLE

M1676 Saint-Robert, Philippe de, "Montherlant ou le voyage au bout du
jour," La Table Ronde, No. 169, pp. 16-20, February, 1962.

Montherlant claims that Un Voyageur solitaire est un diable, published more than thirty years after it was written, contains "the
things that today are dead in him and for him."   To the contrary,
this essay-diary-novel discloses a Montherlant quite like the one of
today.   (T.T.B.)

MONTIEL BALLESTEROS, ADOLFO

M1677 Garganigo, John F., "Gaucho Tierra y Don Segundo Sombra: dos
idealizaciones gauchescas," Revista Hispánica Moderna, 32:198-205,
July-October, 1966.

Gaucho Tierra by the Uruguayan Montiel Ballesteros takes up where
Don Segundo Sombra leaves off.   It directs our attention to the need
to live in contact with the earth, to a kind of self-definition for
Argentines and Uruguayans.   (C.O.)

MOOCK, ARMANDO

M1678 Ventura Agudiez, Juan, "Armando Moock y el sainete argentino,"
Duquesne Hispanic Review, 3:139-64, 1965.

The Chilean Moock finds the sainete or one-act play highly successful commercially.   But his original and more careful plays tend to
be overlooked.   (C.O.)

MOODY, WILLIAM VAUGHN

M1679 Brown, Maurice F., "Moody and Robinson," Colby Library Quarterly, Series 5, pp. 185-94, December, 1960.

"Neither Robinson nor Moody was essentially changed by the friendship, but early impulses in the personalities and poetry of the two men were certainly strengthened by their acquaintance. Robinson's example and dicta encouraged Moody to greater experiment with the immediate subject drawn from life and with simpler diction." (K.M.W.)

M1680 Cary, Richard, "Robinson on Moody," Colby Library Quarterly, Series 6, pp. 176-83, December, 1962.

"Robinson's response to Moody's first poetic play, The Masque of Judgment . . . [is contrasted against] the claim that Moody's success with this genre enticed Robinson into futile periods of experimentation and emulation." (K.M.W.)

M1681 Eckman, Frederick, "Moody's Ode: The Collapse of the Heroic," Texas Studies in English, 37:80-92, 1957.

Moody aimed "An Ode in Time of Hesitation" at "embodying a theme of idealistic patriotism in a vehicle of lofty language and heroic imagery." The poem has failed to appeal to later twentieth century audiences because of our time's distrust of the conventional hero-figure, the ceremonial public utterance, and the Shelleyan concept of the poet-lawmaker. (W.J.F.)

MOORE, BRIAN

M1682 Cronin, John, "Ulster's Alarming Novels," Eire: Ireland, 4:24-34, No. 4, 1969.

"Ulster, with its segregated schools, its residential ghettoes and its neanderthal politics produces novelists [like Michael McLaverty, Brian Moore, Forrest Reid or Maurice Leitch] who reflect its sectarian schizophrenia." (G.C.)

M1683 Foster, John W., "Crisis and Ritual in Brian Moore's Belfast Novels," Eire: Ireland, 3:66-74, Autumn, 1968.

"The dilemma faced by the heroes of Moore's novels, especially Devine in The Feast of Lupercal and Judith Hearne in The Lonely

MOORE, B.

Passion, is a primitive rather than twentieth-century dilemma.
It centers upon the characters's rejection by the community, partly
through their failure to weather successfully . . . the 'rites of
passage,' and partly through their transgression of deep-rooted
and unreasonable taboos associated with those rites." (K.M.W.)

M1684 Fulford, Robert, "Robert Fulford Interviews Brian Moore,"
Tamarack Review, No. 23, pp. 5-18, Spring, 1962.

[This interview explores Moore's novels, and elicits a range of
literary opinions from the author.] (D.P.)

M1685 Kattim, Naim, "Brian Moore," Canadian Literature, No. 18,
pp. 30-9, Autumn, 1963.

"The principal characters of Brian Moore are Irish, who come,
respectively, to Montreal, to New York, or to Belfast. In spite of
differing exterior circumstances his protagonists share a certain
vision of the world, attitudes towards events, men and the society
in which they live. It is this which gives the world of Moore its
unity and infuses his novels with a semblance of continuity in spite
of the peregrinations of his heroes." (D.P.)

M1686 Kersnowski, Frank L., "Exit the Anti-Hero," Critique: Studies in
Modern Fiction, 10:60-71, No. 3, 1968.

"Brian Moore's novels reveal an all too real conclusion for contemporary man: withdrawal from involvement in human pain and
pleasure. . . . when people find experience debunks expectation
. . . even the anti-hero is too optimistic, too idealistic a concept."
(K.M.W.)

M1687 Ludwig, Jack, "Brian Moore: Ireland's Loss, Canada's Novelist,"
Critique: Studies in Modern Fiction, 5:5-13, Spring-Summer, 1962.

"The world, Moore's third novel indicates, may be as well affirmed
by the failure as by the hero, by the fop as well as the king: the
insignificant man, like Bloom, can see the world significantly."
(K.M.W.)

M1688 Ludwig, Jack, "A Mirror of Moore," Canadian Literature, No. 7,
pp. 18-23, Winter, 1961.

Moore resembles Joyce in compassion (which he successfully combines with the ludicrous), although he lacks the latter's larger view

M1688   2776

of life. The Luck of Ginger Coffey succeeds for the first time in
presenting a convincing analysis of a principal character whose
personality completely permeates the style. (B.V.)

M1689 Sale, Richard B., "An Interview in London with Brian Moore,"
Studies in the Novel, 1:67-80, Spring, 1969.

[Moore discusses his writing in an interview.] (K.M.W.)

THE EMPEROR OF ICE-CREAM

M1690 Dahlie, Hallvard, "Brian Moore's Broader Vision: The Emperor of
Ice-Cream," Critique: Studies in Modern Fiction, 9:43-55,
No. 1, 1966.

Brian Moore, claimed only by Canada, was born in Ireland, lived
ten years in Canada and has resided in the United States since 1959.
The Emperor of Ice-Cream may "be regarded as the culmination of
Moore's concern with despair and failure, and it could mark the
beginning of a new trend in his fiction. [Includes a bibliography of
Moore's works and studies on that work.] (D.P.)

M1691 Hicks, Granville, "An Invitation to Live," Saturday Review,
48:97-8, September 18, 1965.

The Emperor of Ice-Cream "is almost certainly a more closely
autobiographical novel than anything [Brian Moore] has previously
written." In the book, "Moore has returned to Belfast and to his own
boyhood in that city. . . . He has waited twenty five years to tell this
story [of a young man's coming-of-age] and he has gained greatly in
perspective without losing a sense of immediacy." (D.P.)

MOORE, GEORGE

M1692 Acton, Harold, "George Moore and the Cunard Family," London
Magazine, 5:54-7, March, 1958.

The letters of Moore to Lady Cunard reflect the inspiration she was
for the writer. (D.B.D.)

M1693 Blissett, William F., "George Moore and Literary Wagnerism," Comparative Literature, 13:52-71, Winter, 1961.

Frequently alluding to Wagner, Moore attempts "to recapture for literature alone certain qualities of art realized for the first time by Wagner in terms of his composite art, specifically, he attempts to fuse dialogue, description, and narrative as Wagner had fused aria, recitative, and orchestra, in the interest of a unified effect." (R.J.G.)

M1694 Burkhart, Charles, "George Moore and Father and Son," Nineteenth-Century Fiction, 15:71-7, June, 1960.

Letters between George Moore and Edmund Gosse indicate that Moore stimulated Gosse into writing Father and Son, gave advice during its composition, but is not responsible, as is sometimes said, for its "subtleties and profundities." (F.C.T.)

M1695 Burkhart, Charles, "The Short Stories of George Moore," Studies in Short Fiction, 6:165-74, Winter, 1969.

Neglected since his death, Moore's short stories deserve critical attention. Moore preferred the ancient form of the tale to the modern single incident type. His unique theory of fiction explains this preference as well as the presence of elements of autobiography in every book. (B.K.N.)

M1696 Colum, Padraic, "Encounters with George Moore," Dublin Magazine, No. 2, pp. 49-55, March, 1962.

[Colum, as a young man, first met Moore at A. E.'s.] "George Moore represented the modern, the enfranchised." "This man, so expert in the use of language, so penetrating in his gaze into individuals, so much at home in the worlds of painting and music, was limited intellectually." Like other writers of his time, Moore had "a good conceit" of himself. (D.P.)

M1697 Garnett, David, "Some Writers I Have Known: Galsworthy, Forster, Moore, and Wells," Texas Quarterly, 4:190-202, Autumn, 1961.

Both Galsworthy and Forster appealed to the English intelligentsia for attacking "British complacency, smugness, conventionality, respectability, and love of money." George Moore was "a mysterious writer: a great goose and a great genius." H. G. Wells "saw quicker and farther than other men. He cared greatly for mankind. . . ." (D.P.)

M1698 Gerber, Helmut E., "Bibliography of George Moore," English Fiction in Transition, 1:32-5, Fall-Winter, 1957.

[This is an annotated bibliography of articles and news on George Moore published between 1950 and 1957.] (K.M.W.)

M1699 Gerber, Helmut E., "George Moore: An Annotated Bibliography of Writings About Him," English Fiction in Transition, 2:1-91, Summer-Fall, 1959.

[This is a two part annotated bibliography on George Moore of material published in books and periodicals, including signed reviews.] (K.M.W.)

M1700 Gerber, Helmut E., "George Moore: An Annotated Bibliography of Writings About Him: Supplement I," English Fiction in Transition, 3:34-46, No. 2, 1960.

[This is a supplement to the annotated bibliography by the same author which appeared in English Fiction in Transition, 2:1-91, No. 2, 1959.] (K.M.W.)

M1701 Gerber, Helmut E., "George Moore: An Annotated Bibliography of Writings About Him; Supplement II," English Fiction in Transition, 4:30-42, No. 2, 1961.

[This is the second supplement to the annotated bibliography by the same author which appeared in English Fiction in Transition, 2:1-91, No. 2, 1959.] (K.M.W.)

M1702 Gerber, Helmut E., "George Moore," English Literature in Transition, 11:50-4, No. 1, 1968.

[These are additions to the annotated bibliography of writings about George Moore which first appeared in English Fiction in Transition in 1959, with supplements and additions in subsequent numbers of ELT.] (D.P.)

M1703 Gerber, Helmut E., "George Moore," English Literature in Transition, 12:45-8, No. 1, 1969.

[These are additional items in ELT's annotated bibliography of writings about George Moore.] (D.P.)

MOORE, G.

M1704 Gerber, Helmut E., "George Moore: From Pure Poetry to Pure Criticism," Journal of Aesthetics and Art Criticism, 25:281-91, Spring, 1967.

". . . Moore did not simply parrot a handful of controversial French writers for the sole or main purpose of advertising himself. . . . he did not merely copy, unaltered, what he borrowed but used it in his own individual way in support of a consistently avowed artistic creed; and . . . the obvious, often provoking, surface statement . . . belie[s] the carefully made, real content." (K.M.W.)

M1705 Henn, T. R., "Moore and Yeats," Dublin Magazine, 4:63-77, No. 2, 1965.

[These are impressions of Moore, many of them Yeats's, from "The Sketch of a Great Man." "Shrewdness, wit, a genius that could never resist the twisting of the truth into an epigram: so Shaw, so Wilde." (G.C.)

M1706 Hough, Graham, "George Moore and the Novel," Review of English Literature, 1:35-44, January, 1960.

Moore's "characters are not coloured by any overwhelming emotional tincture of his own. This makes him very unlike most modern novelists; but it also means that he can see people simply as they are. . . . Objective, impersonal comprehension . . . becomes at its highest pitch a kind of charity. Moore the artist possessed this gift . . . [and] I believe that its presence in his works will be more perceived as the personal legend about him begins to fade." (D.A.B.)

M1707 Marcus, Phillip L., "George Moore's Dublin 'Epiphanies' and Joyce," James Joyce Quarterly, 5:157-61, Winter, 1968.

Joyce's one important predecessor in his treatment of Dublin in fiction was George Moore who in his Parnell and His Island and A Drama in Muslin unleashed "slashing indictments of virtually every aspect of Irish life." Although Moore's "epiphanies" cannot be claimed as sources for Joyce's early fiction "it is conceivable that Moore's work helped crystallize the elements of Joyce's personal vision by presenting a very similar vision in an organized pattern. . . ." (D.P.)

M1708 Noël, Jean, "George Moore et Mallarmé," Revue de Littérature Comparée, 32:363-76, July, 1958.

"It is now possible to say that Moore first met Mallarmé between the time the latter moved to Rue de Rome and February, 1876. The two continued to meet until 1897. Moore seems to have been receptive to and positively influenced by Mallarmé." (D.-J.J.)

M1709 Saul, George Brandon, "The Short Stories of George Moore," Poet Lore, 59:61-8, 1964.

George Moore wrote "a very few distinguished short stories, practically all gleanable from The Untilled Field." He often fails in his stories because he is "limited in sympathy and human perspective." (G.C.)

M1710 Schwab, A. T., "Irish Author and American Critic: George Moore and James Huneker," Nineteenth-Century Fiction, 8:256-71, March, 1954; 9:22-37, June, 1954.

[This is an exchange of letters between Moore and Huneker, who did more than any other to acquaint the American reading public with Moore's writings.] (D.P.)

M1711 Seinfelt, Fred, "Wagnerian Elements in the Writing of George Moore," Studies in the Humanities, 1:38-49, March, 1969.

Héloïse and Abélard, Ulick and Soracha, "Marban and Luachet," and "Liodin and Curithur" may "be related convincingly to some aspects of Tristan and Isolde. Also, in The Brook Kerith Moore was able to blend "the convoluted, musical sentences of Pater with the leitmotif technique of Wagner." (D.P.)

M1712 Stevenson, Lionel, "George Moore: Romantic, Naturalist, Aesthete," Études Anglaises, 21:362-6, October-December, 1968.

Students of English literature will refer to Jean C. Noël's George Moore: L'homme et l'oeuvre for "the record of the welter of competing themes and techniques in the eighties, the impact of dynamic French movements upon static English literary habits, and the elegantly frock-coated figure of George Moore at the very eye of the hurricane." (K.M.W.)

M1713 Stokes, Sewell, "A Conversation with George Moore," Listener, 63:222, 225, February 4, 1960.

[This is a recollection of an interview of Moore in 1929 during which Moore expressed his aversion to deposits dogs left on his doorstep, his detestation of Shaw's vulgarity, his great satisfaction with the later editions of his own books, and his continuing need to weed "daisies" from his texts.] (D.P.)

M1714 Weaver, Jack W., "An Exile Returned: Moore and Yeats in Ireland," Eire-Ireland, 3:40-7, Spring, 1968.

". . . his residence in Dublin was probably the most significant period of his creative existence. This was the period in which he helped to found the Irish Literary Theatre. This was the period in which he alternately quarreled and collaborated with Yeats. This was also the period that furnished materials for his masterpiece, Hail and Farewell." (K.M.W.)

M1715 Weaver, Jack Wayne, "Some Notes on George Moore and Professor Watson," English Literature in Transition, 6:147-50, No. 3, 1963.

Professor Sara Ruth Watson (ELT 6; No. 2, 1963) appears to be in error in identifying Dujardin as the source of Moore's knowledge of Palestrina (Edward Martyn is more likely), and in claiming that Moore lost interest in the Irish theatre after his collaboration with Yeats on Diarmuil and Grania. Actually, Moore and Yeats planned further collaborations. (D.P.)

THE BROOK KERITH

M1716 Brooks, Michael W., "George Moore, Schopenhauer, and the Origins of The Brook Kerith," English Literature in Transition, 12:21-31, No. 1, 1969.

"Few of Moore's readers were prepared to see him crown his kaleidoscopic career with a deeply felt statement of his private theology and, as a consequence, his achievement in The Brook Kerith has never been quite squarely faced." (K.M.W.)

CONFESSIONS OF A YOUNG MAN

M1717 Cassagnau, M., "Moore traducteur de lui-même," Revue de Littérature Comparée, 44:120-4, January-March, 1970.

CONFESSIONS OF A YOUNG MAN (cont'd)

Although George Moore co-translated his own Confessions of a Young Man into French, he allowed several errors to slip by. [Most of them are treated here.] (D.-J.J.)

M1718 Osborn, Neal J., "Optograms, George Moore, and Crane's 'Silver Pageant'," American Notes and Queries, 4:39-40, November, 1965.

The passages in George Moore's Confessions of a Young Man which describe optograms, or pictures imprinted on the retina of a creature immediately before death, appear to have influenced Stephen Crane's "Silver Pageant." (D.P.)

DIARMUIL AND GRANIA

M1719 Michie, Donald M., "A Man of Genius and a Man of Talent," Texas Studies in Literature and Language, 6:148-54, Summer, 1964.

Despite the constant quarrels between Yeats and George Moore when they collaborated in writing the play Diarmuil and Grania, the collaboration hastened Yeats's growth as a dramatist and indirectly influenced the rise of Synge as a dramatist. (W.G.F.)

A DRAMA IN MUSLIN

M1720 Chaikin, Milton, "Balzac, Zola, and George Moore's A Drama in Muslin," Revue de Littérature Comparée, 29:540-3, October-December, 1955.

Moore's third novel, A Drama in Muslin, "combines two themes, the first being foil to the second: the pettiness and sterility of Irish provincial society and the celebration of the natural desire of a maid for a mate. Moore got both [themes] from Balzac and Zola." (D.P.)

ESTHER WATERS

M1721 Bartlett, Lynn C., "Maggie: A New Source for Esther Waters," English Literature in Transition, 9:18-20, No. 1, 1966.

Maggie Younghusband "the purported author of an article entitled 'From the Maid's Point of View' which appeared in the August 1891 issue of The New Review" "may have contributed to the development of Esther Waters." (D.A.B.)

ESTHER WATERS (cont'd)

M1722 Jernigan, Jay, "The Forgotten Serial Version of George Moore's
Esther Waters," Nineteenth-Century Fiction, 23:99-103, June, 1968.

"Moore revised the serial portion . . . to develop his characterization of Esther as an unwed mother forced to choose between Fred,
an obviously good but dull man, and William, the seemingly penitent
but only quasi-respectable father of her child." Therefore, "a 'true
picture' of the development of Esther Waters as novel can exist only
with reference to this evolution of Esther Waters as character."
(D.A.B.)

M1723 Ohmann, Carol, "George Moore's Esther Waters," Nineteenth-
Century Fiction, 25:174-87, September, 1970.

"My purpose here is to look at Esther Waters (1894) bearing in mind
. . . the tension between Moore's adverse opinion of Zola's naturalism ('simple,' 'crude,' 'narrow') and his allegiance to certain of
Zola's prescriptions for fiction. Such a reading may . . . help to
order the relative strengths and weaknesses of the novel . . . [and]
suggest one or two reasons why Moore's work took the direction it
did after Esther Waters." (D.P.)

M1724 Sporn, Paul, "Esther Waters: The Sources of the Baby-Farm
Episode," English Literature in Transition, 11:39-42, No. 2, 1968.

". . . although Moore uses Waugh for the specifics of the baby-farm
episode, he continues to emulate Flaubert in his general . . . hostile
attitude toward the bourgeoisie. . . ." (K.M.W.)

EVELYN INNES

M1725 Watson, Sara Ruth, "George Moore and the Dolmetsches," English
Literature in Transition, 6:65-75, No. 2, 1963.

Arnold Dolmetsch's "concerts of old music suggested to . . . Moore
the character of Mr. Innes in . . . his only 'musical novel,' Evelyn
Innes (1898)." (G.C.)

HAIL AND FAREWELL

M1726 Cary, Meredith, "Yeats and Moore--An Autobiographical Conflict,"
Eire: Ireland, 4:94-109, Autumn, 1969.

HAIL AND FAREWELL (cont'd)

"Moore referred to <u>Hail and Farewell</u> as a novel and declared that, in order to achieve thematic unity, he had 'interpreted' the actions and personalities of the people whose names he used. Not surprisingly, however, Yeats failed to be comforted by, or even apparently to notice, that Moore had deliberately structured his characterization in such a way as to transform him into one of the 'types' of which literature is made." (D.A.B.)

M1727 Shumaker, Wayne, "The Autobiographer As Artist: George Moore's <u>Hail and Farewell</u>," <u>University of California English Studies</u>, 11:159-85, 1955.

An examination of Moore's artistry suggests "how much more than ordinarily is expected in autobiography can be accomplished by an author who is willing to expand on compositional technique the painstaking craftsmanship usually reserved for 'creative' art forms." (L.L.)

M1728 Setterquist, Jan, "Ibsen and Edward Martyn," <u>Edda</u>, 61:97-104, 1961.

"A rather malicious, yet magnificent full-length portrait of Martyn appears in George Moore's autobiography <u>Hail and Farewell</u>. Martyn had a "special interest in social and intellectual drama" and he, "Moore and Yeats were all united in a mutual effort of doing for Ireland what Ibsen had done for Norway." (G.C.)

A MERE ACCIDENT

M1729 Chaikin, Milton, "A French Source for George Moore's <u>A Mere Accident</u>," <u>Modern Language Notes</u>, 71:28-30, January, 1956.

Moore relied upon Zola's <u>La Faute de l'abbé Mouret</u> to a considerable degree. "The relationship between the two novels makes clear that, though he had abandoned the Zola purple passage and the 'scientific' trappings of naturalism, Moore did retain Zola's faith in the goodness of nature and the natural instinct. This faith is indeed the orientation of <u>A Mere Accident</u>. (K.M.W.)

MOORE, G.

A MODERN LOVER

M1730 Chaikin, Milton, "The Composition of George Moore's A Modern
Lover," Comparative Literature, 7:259-64, Summer, 1955.

A Modern Lover "does have historical importance, in the fact that
it introduced French methods of fiction to England: minute examination of detail, brilliant evocation of scene, contrived methods of
development, attention to pattern, consciousness of language, psychological realism, and exposure of the obscure corners of man's being."
(K.M.W.)

M1731 Niess, Robert J., "George Moore and Emile Zola Again,"
Symposium, 20:43-9, Spring, 1966.

The many similarities between the nude scenes in George Moore's
A Modern Lover and Emile Zola's L'Oeuvre strongly suggest direct
influence on L'Oeuvre, which was published later than A Modern
Lover. Zola's treatment of the scene demonstrates his superiority
as an artist. (D.P.)

A MUMMER'S WIFE

M1732 Chaikin, M., "George Moore's A Mummer's Wife and Zola,"
Revue de Littérature Comparée, 31:85-8, January-March, 1957.

"That George Moore's second novel, A Mummer's Wife (1885), is
an imitation of Zola is a commonplace. . . . Certain of the Zolaesque
features are readily identifiable . . . but the full extent of Moore's
dependence on Zola has not hitherto been revealed." (D.A.B.)

M1733 Heywood, C., "Flaubert, Miss Braddon, and George Moore,"
Comparative Literature, 12:151-8, Spring, 1960.

The novel which Kate Ede, George Moore's heroine in A Mummer's
Wife, occasionally reads "is clearly The Doctor's Wife (1864), a
novel by Miss Braddon which Moore read enthusiastically as a young
man. This novel . . . is almost certainly the earliest borrowing
from Flaubert in English literature, and is in addition a major source
of A Mummer's Wife." Miss Braddon had shown Moore how to domes-
ticate Flaubert "into the Victorian tradition of fiction." (D.P.)

A MUMMER'S WIFE   (cont'd)

M1734 Heywood, C., "D. H. Lawrence's The Lost Girl and its Antecedents
by George Moore and Arnold Bennett," English Studies, 47:131-4,
April, 1966.

". . . Lawrence's justifiable claim that his heroine was 'not morally
lost' gains point when his heroine is placed in her literary context
. . . [of] themes of English novelists who had in turn drawn substantially from Balzac, Flaubert and Zola. In this process, however, he
reserved a more searching criticism for the arguments in George
Moore's novel upon which he leaned more decisively" than Bennett's
novel. (D.P.)

A REMEMBRANCE

M1735 Bartlett, Lynn C., "George Moore's 'A Remembrance'," Notes
and Queries, 10:268-9, July, 1963.

George Moore's "A Remembrance," his tribute to his friend Mrs.
Bridger, was published first in 1891 in the August issue of The New
Review, not in 1906, as has been stated in Hone's The Life of George
Moore. (D.P.)

SISTER TERESA

M1736 Brown, Calvin S., "Balzac as a Source of George Moore's Sister
Teresa," Comparative Literature, 11:124-30, Spring, 1959.

In the cloister setting, choice of the main female character's name,
recognition of her from her musical performance, the dream of
breaking into a convent, and the appearance of the Carmelites in the
background, Moore's Sister Teresa shows influence, not of Balzac's
Honorine, but of his La Duchesse de Langcais. (F.C.T.)

STAGE MANAGEMENT IN THE IRISH NATIONAL THEATRE

M1737 Weaver, Jack Wayne, "'Stage Management in the Irish National
Theatre': An Unknown Article by George Moore?" English
Literature in Transition, 9:12-7, No. 1, 1966.

"Internal and external evidences" necessitate the assigning of "Stage
Management in the Irish National Theatre" to Moore. (G.C.)

THE SWEETNESS OF THE PAST

M1738 Cassagnau, M. G., "Moore s'inspire d'une poésie de Catulle Mendès," Revue de Littérature Comparée, 42:443-5, July-September, 1968.

"Moore's ['The Sweetness of the Past'] appears to have been strongly inspired by one of Mendès's short poems, ['Douceur du souvenir']. . . ." There is practically no doubt that Mendès's poem came before Moore's. (D.-J.J.)

THE UNTILLED FIELD

M1739 Cary, Meredith, "Saint Biddy M'Hale," Studies in Short Fiction, 6:649-52, Fall, 1969.

"At first glance . . . Biddy M'Hale may not seem to be an addition to a list of women through whom Irish writers have represented their native land. . . . However . . . when one analyzes Biddy's transformation from a canny neighborhood gossip into a 'local saint,' a symbolic function for the characterization emerges from the undeniable realism of the portrait." (D.A.B.)

M1740 Kennedy, Sister Eileen, S. C., "Moore's Untilled Field and Joyce's Dubliners," Eire-Ireland, 5:81-9, Autumn, 1970.

"External evidence proves that Joyce read Moore's book [The Untilled Field.] Internal evidence [in Joyce's Dubliners] indicates some similarity in themes and attitudes; the paralysis of so many of Ireland's inhabitants, the death-grip religion wielded, the quality of life in a country where frustration and repression were so common, the denial of beauty and of life-enhancing experience by a sacred puritanism, exile as the only hope for the individual--and over this, the concurrent attraction and repulsion for Ireland as each writer championed the priesthood of the artist. From Moore's uneven assortment . . . Joyce drew inspiration to shape a different, far greater book." (D.P.)

M1741 Kennedy, Sister Eileen, S. C., "The Source for Moore's Title, The Untilled Field," English Literature in Transition, 12:155, No. 3, 1969.

Although commentators have suggested that Moore drew his title from Turgenev's Virgin Soil or Psalm 65--"the untilled meadows overflow" --a more likely source is the seventh line of Shelley's sonnet "England in 1819," which was "another hymn against tyranny." (D.P.)

MOORE, MARIANNE

M1742 Borroff, Marie, "Dramatic Structure in the Poetry of Marianne
Moore," Literary Review, 2:112-23, Autumn, 1958.

The quotation of lines from Miss Moore's poems too briefly and out
of context do her injustice: evaluation must be based on synthesis
of the total structure rather than on the "felicitous statement" of
single lines. (E.T.)

M1743 Brumbaugh, Thomas B., "Concerning Marianne Moore's Museum,"
Twentieth Century Literature, 1:191-5, January, 1956.

Art works mentioned in Miss Moore's later poems serve a "slightly
more outgoing and didactic purpose than in the earlier poems."
(D.P.)

M1744 Brumbaugh, Thomas B., "In Pursuit of Miss Moore," Mississippi
Quarterly, 15:74-80, Spring, 1962.

[This is a small collection of letters from Marianne Moore to
Professor Brumbaugh, interspersed with a few very brief explanatory comments by the latter. The letters concern such things as
autographs, manuscripts, museum pieces, and attitudes toward
poets and poetry.] (J.L.A.)

M1745 Cecilia, Sister Mary, "The Poetry of Marianne Moore," Thought,
38:354-74, Autumn, 1963.

"The dominant themes that underlie the poetry of Marianne Moore
both support the integration of her affirmative subject matter and
demonstrate her positive philosophy of composition. Yet no single
theme is dominant, for each poem is thematically individualistic
in keeping with its poetic entity." (K.M.W.)

M1746 Engel, Bernard F., "A Democratic Vista of Religion," Georgia
Review, 20:84-9, Spring, 1966.

Marianne Moore, Wallace Stevens and William Carlos Williams
"have in common . . . not a set of doctrines but the insistence upon
the central importance of religious questions and the acceptance of
. . . inquiry into these questions as fundamental in the work of the
literary artist." (G.C.)

M1747 Engel, Bernard F., "Marianne Moore and 'Objectivism'," Papers of the Michigan Academy of Science, Arts and Letters, 48:657-64, 1963.

A central paradox in Marianne Moore's work is her commitment to ethical values and to the Objective emphasis on "the thing itself." As a result, she has developed as a poet of analogy, deeply concerned with the dichotomy of soul and body, spirit and matter. In her writing objects have more than phenomenological significance. (D.P.)

M1748 Fowlie, Wallace, "Jorge Guillén, Marianne Moore, T. S. Eliot: Some Recollections," Poetry, 90:103-9, May, 1957.

Jorge Guillén and Marianne Moore each had humility before their craft: Guillén concentrating on the essence and reality of poetry, Miss Moore concerned with the "immediate problems of the moment." Eliot had either " 'foresuffered all' in the life of our age or he had altered it irrevocably with his art." (D.P.)

M1749 Hall, Donald, "The Art of Poetry IV: Marianne Moore," Paris Review, No. 26, pp. 41-66, Summer-Fall, 1961.

[In this interview Miss Moore reminisces about the beginnings of her writing career at Bryn Mawr, her long life in Brooklyn, and her association with the Others group. She describes how a poem is formed for her, her editorship of the Dial, and her view that the poet and the scientist work analogously.] (D.P.)

M1750 Hartsock, Mildred E., "Marianne Moore: A 'Salvo of Barks'," Bucknell Review, 11:14-37, December, 1962.

Marianne Moore "has received almost every public honor that can be given a poet; yet the critical writing about her is a strange amalgam of patronizing praise and uneasy insistence upon her limitations." (K.M.W.)

M1751 Hayes, Ann L., "On Reading Marianne Moore," Carnegie Series in English, 11:1-19, 1970.

"Marianne Moore's poetry, her 'way of happening,' is one voice which has many tones, but two consistent qualities: concentration of interest which sometimes rises to intensity; and full honesty. The poet may beguile, delay, bewilder, enmesh us; she never deludes." (D.P.)

M1752 Jennings, Elizabeth, "Idea and Expression in Emily Dickinson, Marianne Moore and Ezra Pound," Stratford-upon-Avon Studies, 7:97-113, 1965.

"Emily Dickinson, Marianne Moore, Ezra Pound--these are three very different American poets. . . . Yet, when one examines them more closely, one realizes that what they share is a contemplative attitude towards men and affairs; they all look, appraise, annotate, and re-create." (D. P.)

M1753 Kennedy, X. J., "Marianne Moore," Minnesota Review, 2:369-76, Spring, 1962.

In Miss Moore's poetry "as much as possible is left unsaid . . . [and] the most bitterly opposing forces are held in truce." (G.C.)

M1754 Kenner, Hugh, "The Experience of the Eye: Marianne Moore's Tradition," Southern Review, 7:754-69, Autumn, 1965.

"Miss Moore's poems deal in many separate acts of attention: optical puns, seen by snapshot, in a poetic normally governed by the eye, sometimes by the ears and fingers, ultimately by the moral sense. It is the poetic of the solitary observer, for whose situation the usual meanings of a word like 'moral' have to be redefined." (J.M.D.)

M1755 Kenner, Hugh, "Meditation and Enactment," Poetry, 102:109-15, May, 1963.

Although "critical curiosity . . . has tended to leave Miss Moore's poems approvingly uninvestigated . . . she has accomplished things of general import to the maintenance of language that no one else has had the patience, the skill, the discipline, or the perfect unself-conscious conviction to adumbrate." (D.P.)

M1756 McCord, Howard, "Marianne Moore's Chinese Tadpoles," American Notes and Queries, 3:5-6, September, 1964.

Miss Moore first uses the image of the tadpole in her poem "The Labors of Hercules," apparently because "she wishes to draw an analogy between the head-heavy shape of a tadpole, and a musical note. . . ." In another use of the image in "Novices" "the context is one in which an image related to learning, language, writing and antiquity can be expected, and the Chinese tadpoles provide this." Miss Moore may have derived this image from Weiger's Chinese Characters, Peking, 1940. (D.P.)

M1757 Moore, Marianne, "Marianne Moore: A Self-Portrait," Esquire, 58:99, July, 1962.

[This is a brief outline of personality traits.] (K.M.W.)

M1758 Moore, Marianne, "Ten Answers: Letters from an October After-noon, Part II," Harper's Magazine, 229:91-8, November, 1964.

[Miss Moore answers ten questions for George Plimpton (Harper's, October, 1964) ranging from why she wears two watches to her keen interest in baseball.] (D.A.B.)

M1759 Olson, Elder, "The Poetry of Marianne Moore," Chicago Review, 11:100-4, Spring, 1957.

"Miss Moore is one of the very few major poets of our era who can reasonably be called classical." She treats "ordinary matters and normal mental conditions" in a "poetry of personal discussion. . . . She deals repeatedly with the hardest of all things to imagine: The fact perfectly known, or known, at any rate, far more perfectly than most of us know it." (M.J.B.)

M1760 Parkin, Rebecca Price, "Some Characteristics of Marianne Moore's Humor," College English, 27:403-8, February, 1966.

"With respect to humor, one can never relax in the conviction that one is in an Eden. In particular, the Eden of Miss Moore's humor is always tenanted by a teaching serpent." (K.M.W.)

M1761 Plimpton, George, "The World Series with Marianne Moore: Letter from an October Afternoon," Harper's Magazine, 229:50-8, October, 1964.

[This is an account of an October afternoon at the World Series with "that extraordinary poetess and her vision."] (D.A.B.)

M1762 Rees, Ralph, "The Armor of Marianne Moore," Bucknell Review, 7:27-40, May, 1957.

"Miss Moore's armor is anything that protects . . . contributes to individuality. . . . The armor which protects also shapes the per-sonality." To compose her armor, she uses compression, restraint, indirection. (M.H.)

M1763 Ruthven, Greystiel, "Charles Tomlinson--An Introduction,"
Gemini, 3:30-3, Spring, 1960.

Seeing Is Believing, the second book of poems by Tomlinson, a 33
year old Bristol University lecturer, shows the influence of America
and Marianne Moore. A visual poet using painters as his theme, his
lens is "designed in Britain, but ground in America." His efforts to
widen his "ethical implications" will fail unless he recognizes "the
human element." (K.M.)

M1764 Schulman, Grace, "Conversation with Marianne Moore,"
Quarterly Review of Literature, 16:154-71, Nos. 1-2, 1969.

[This is an edited transcript of a conversation with Miss Moore
about her methods of composition. The discussion took place on
April 30, 1967.] (D.P.)

M1765 Shankar, D. A., "The Poetry of Marianne Moore," Literary
Criterion, 5:141-7, Winter, 1962.

In Marianne Moore's poetry a "mastery of the conversational idiom
is . . . [her] finest achievement. . . . the speech-tone of her
poetry . . . needs to be emphasized." (G.C.)

M1766 Snodgrass, W. D., "Elegance in Marianne Moore," Western
Review, 19:57-64, Autumn, 1954.

English poetry depends upon some order of external elegance whereby sound, texture, rhythm, rhyme, word connotations, or imagery
may establish certain discreet (ironic) values. Much of Marianne
Moore's early poetry shows no such quality "because by a rhetorical
lack-of-surface-brilliance, she dulls her lines," although by juxtaposition of line to line or image to image she gains brilliant effects.
Something like elegance appears in the later poetry. This rise in
musicality is of a very personal sort, created by novel rhythms, by
extension of her normal uses of muted rhymes, and by intricate
internal rhyme and echo structures. (L.L.)

M1767 Stapleton, Laurence, "Marianne Moore and the Element of Prose,"
South Atlantic Quarterly, 57:366-74, Summer, 1958.

Largely concerned with her contemporaries, Marianne Moore's
prose is special: its strength derives from enlightened knowledge;
its weakness is in too few concessions to the reader. (W.B.B.)

M1768 Tomlinson, Charles, "Abundance, Not Too Much: The Poetry of Marianne Moore," Sewanee Review, 65:677-87, Autumn, 1957.

From her early poems through Like a Bulwark Miss Moore's "fundamental concerns do not change. Indeed, one might say that in the interaction of order and spontaneity Miss Moore had found the theme on which to variate all that follows and that the degree of her success has lain in the observance of the limits of her method." Also, "her characteristic achievements derive from an impersonality in the means of the poetry which, in fact, permits the fusion of both personal and impersonal in their most significant form." (D.P.)

M1769 Wasserstrom, William, "Marianne Moore, The Dial, and Kenneth Burke," Western Humanities Review, 17:249-62, Summer, 1963.

". . . if we would understand the reasons why The Dial . . . sought to establish Miss Moore's reputation and to publicize Burke's ideas, we must discover those points of conjunction which connect Miss Moore's unique career with Burke's extraordinary system." (M.G.)

M1770 Weatherhead, A. Kingsley, "Imagination and Fancy: Robert Lowell and Marianne Moore," Texas Studies in Literature and Language, 6:188-99, Summer, 1964.

"Just as Coleridge speaks of Milton and Cowley as possessing respectively 'highly imaginative' and 'very fanciful' minds, one may speak of Miss Moore as a poet of the fancy and Robert Lowell--the Lowell of Lord Weary's Castle--as one of the imagination." (W.G.F.)

M1771 Weatherhead, A. K., "Two Kinds of Vision in Marianne Moore," ELH, 31:482-96, 1964.

"When there are two views or attitudes present in a poem the cruder one is generally dismissed, usually implicitly, in favor of the accurate one; or the former is corrected by the latter. A study of the poet's use of the twofold approach [also] helps to reveal . . . the essential code . . . of the poet and her work: that truth and feeling must rest upon minutely perceived, finite detail." (D.A.B.)

APPARITION OF SPLENDOR

M1772 Parkin, Rebecca Price, "Certain Difficulties in Reading Marianne Moore: Exemplified in Her 'Apparition of Splendor'," PMLA, 81:167-72, June, 1966.

APPARITION OF SPLENDOR   (cont'd)

In "Apparition of Splendor" Miss Moore "makes it possible for the
reader in some measure to see and experience this reality [that
abnegation is assertion] as she herself has by juxtaposing such dis-
parates as a stylized rhinoceros, a moralized eighteenth century
fairy tale, and the metaphysical resemblances between a porcupine
and a Downeaster." (D.P.)

CRITICS AND CONNOISSEURS

M1773 Messing, Gordon M., "The Linguistic Analysis of Some Contemporary Non-formal Poetry," Language and Style, 2:323-9, 1969.

When Creeley's "I Know a Man" and Ginsberg's "A Supermarket in
California" are subjected to stylolinguistic and stylobehavioristic
analysis, Creeley's poem narrowly avoids banality, while Ginsberg's
poem, although often prosaic and undistinguished, comes to life
through literary parody. Marianne Moore's "Critics and Connoisseurs," has a much more complex appeal, is not amenable to linguistic analysis, and should be turned over "to the goddam literary
critics." (D.P.)

DREAM

M1774 Going, William T., "Marianne Moore's 'Dream': Academic By-
path to Xanadu," Papers on Language and Literature, 5:145-53,
Supplement, Summer, 1969.

Two major sources for "Dream" are Lionel Trilling's "A Valedic-
tory" (Encounter, March, 1965) and Jerome S. Shipman's "Herr
Bach at Northwestern" (Encounter, July, 1965). "Dream summarizes Shipman, refers to Trilling, and is "an ode to Bach and a
dream-nightmare in which the reader must mentally cope with timelessness. . . . " (W.E.K.)

THE FISH

M1775 Renick, Sue, "Moore's 'The Fish'," Explicator, 21: Item 7,
September, 1962.

The poem's unity comes "from a central consciousness that identifies itself with the movement of the sea." (B.K.)

THE ICOSASPHERE

M1776 Borroff, Marie, "Moore's 'The Icosasphere'," Explicator, 16: Item 21, January, 1958.

The various activities relate to social cooperation or disintegration. (B.K.)

IN DISTRUST OF MERITS

M1777 Fowler, Albert, "That I May Yet Recover," Fellowship, pp. 5-6, March, 1966.

What Marianne Moore said in "In Distrust of Merits," written during World War II, speaks with even greater intensity now as the United States is "fighting, fighting, fighting" in Viet Nam. Her plea is that "I/ may yet recover from the disease, My/ Self." (A.F.)

MATHEMATICS

M1778 Beloof, Robert, "Prosody and Tone: The 'Mathematics' of Marianne Moore," Kenyon Review, 20:116-23, Winter, 1958.

Generally, the poem's "lack of rhythmic pattern is the basis of its emotional texture." However, there is a "heightened," less mathematical, lyricism in the later poems. (K.W.)

THE MONKEYS

M1779 Miller, Lois, "I Went to the Animal Fair: An Analysis of Marianne Moore's 'The Monkeys'," English Journal, 52:66-7, January, 1963.

Moore's "The Monkeys" can be presented to older students to help them "gain and perhaps put into words some understanding of the artistry of the animal world." (K.M.W.)

TO A SNAIL

M1780 Warlow, Francis W., "Moore's 'To a Snail'," Explicator, 26: Item 51, February, 1968.

The poem "is a plastic demonstration of the idea 'style'; it is also a snail-style analogy recalling a seventeenth-century emblem poem." (D.P.)

TOM FOOL AT JAMAICA

M1781 Borroff, Marie, " 'Tom Fool at Jamaica' by Marianne Moore: Meaning and Structure," College English, 17:466-9, May, 1956.

The true subject of "Tom Fool" is the nature of the moral excellence which underlies superior action or performance. (D.B.D.)

MOORE, MERRILL

M1782 Basler, Roy P., "Proteus as Apollo: The Poetry of Merrill Moore," Literary Review, 1:233-47, Winter, 1957-8.

[This is a tribute to Merrill Moore as a person, a friend, and a doctor, with pertinent quotations from his poetry.] (E.T.)

M1783 Ciardi, John, "Merrill Moore: A Goodbye," Saturday Review, 40:27, October 12, 1957.

"Merrill Moore wasted more energy than most men have to live on, but what survives after the waste is still more than many more fashionable poets have accomplished. . . . Merrill Moore, at his best, has shown one of the ways in which poetry can shape itself, almost raw to immediate experience. He has kept alive the art of impromptu, and he has had the gift of energy. . . ." (D.P.)

M1784 Davidson, Donald, "The Thankless Muse and Her Fugitive Poets," Sewanee Review, 66:201-28, Spring, 1958.

". . . in general Moore's poems tended to be mere observation of the phenomenal aspects of life . . . they took the form of libertine sonnets, written in what seemed like marvelous improvisation. . . . Yet the practice of Tate and of other Fugitives except Moore [Ransom, Warren, Curry, Hirsch and Davidson], reveals them as struggling to unite the form of their poetry with the myth that ought to belong to it: or, to use the sublime term, the religious concepts and symbols that alone can validate the merely literary concepts and symbols and establish them as poetry in a realm impregnable to the attack of skeptical science." (D.P.)

MOORE, PAMELA

M1785 Hamblen, Abigail Ann, "Teen-Ager as Novelist: Pamela Moore," Midwest Quarterly, 7:355-65, July, 1966.

Pamela Moore's novels, Chocolates for Breakfast, The Horsey Set and Diana, are "violent, almost brutal, stories of sex and perversion and murder and defiance." However, the world of "reckless evil" Miss Moore describes should be ignored neither by "the student of American life nor the critic of popular fiction." (G.C.)

MOORE, THOMAS STURGE

M1786 Winters, Yvor, "The Poetry of T. Sturge Moore," Southern Review, 2:1-16, Winter, 1966.

Moore's "great achievements are Daimonassa, the first sonnet entitled 'Silence,' and 'From Titian'." Nevertheless, "there are many interesting works of less value; there are many beautiful passages; and there is the remarkable spectacle of his endeavor to understand the tradition into which he was born, and, at one and the same time, to save himself from it and to make something of it." (J.M.D.)

MORAES, DOM

M1787 Doherty, Francis, "Poetic Parable: A Note on the Poetry of Dom Moraes," Studies, 52:205-11, Summer, 1963.

Among the best verse of Moraes is "that which is presented as fable or dream, and a look at one of his poems ["One of Us"] yields something of interest both as a technical exercise and as a highlighting of a spiritual condition common enough in our civilization." (S.A.)

MORAES, VINICIUS DE

M1788 Lee, M. Owen, "Orpheus and Eurydice: Some Modern Versions," Classical Journal, 56:307-13, April, 1961.

No modern author has succeeded in retelling the classic myth of Orpheus and Eurydice as well as have Virgil, the poet of Sir Orfeo, or Politian, Monteverdi and Gluck. Cocteau's identification of himself with Orpheus is his most powerful symbol; Anouilh is limited by his pessimism; Tennessee Williams cannot bring the myth to life; and Moraes's version, as filmed by Marcel Camus, is too exotic. (D.P.)

MORALES, RAFAEL

M1789 Jiménez Martos, Luis, "Rafael Morales, entre los toros y la ciudad," La Estafeta Literaria, No. 397, pp. 8-9, June 1, 1968.

For twenty-five years poet of the bullfights and the city, specialist in the sonnet, Morales writes a vitalized and romantic poetry. He uses the adjective and the gerund freely, for molding and precision. His work shows the point of view that the human condition is the same; the only variable in man is his situation. (T.T.B.)

MORAND, PAUL

M1790 Jouhandeau, Marcel: "Paul Morand particulier et universel," NRF Bulletin, pp. 1-2, June, 1965.

Morand, recognized by Proust as his master, drew his tales in the same vein as Mérimée, Stendhal, Barbey and Villiers d l'Isle-Adam. His Bazar de la Charité recalls the Madame de of Louise de Vilmorin, just as Le Coucou et le roitelet seems to have the air of an anecdote of Chamfort. (T.T.B.)

M1791 Knowlton, Edgar C., Jr., "Chinese Elements in Paul Morand's 'Mr. U'," Chinese Culture, 5:34-51, March, 1964.

". . . Chinese influence, direct or indirect, on a twentieth-century European writer may result in an inspiring glimpse at Chinese civilization. . . . Morand's technique . . . not only makes effective use of an exotic theme, but handles the smallest details with craftsmanship." (K.M.W.)

M1792 Schneider, Marcel, "Situation de Morand," La Nouvelle Revue Française, 14e année, No. 158, pp. 291-8, February, 1966.

In 1944 Morand was regarded as the vestige of an abolished world. Today he has regained his supremacy. Maxims, portraits, characters, fables, tales, short stories are summed up by the notion of taste and are explained by love of ellipsis. (T.T.B.)

MORANTE, ELSA

M1793 McCormick, E. Allen, "Utopia and Point of View: Narrative Method in Morante's L'Isola di Arturo and Keyserling's Schwüle Tage," Symposium, 15:114-29, Summer, 1961.

"The problem . . . involves a particular kind of utopia, that of adolescence, seen from a particular point of view, that of the first person. The combination is . . . not a very common one, doubtless because the limited point of view inherent in first person narration is made doubly difficult by the fact of imperfect or immature vision." (K.M.W.)

MORAVIA, ALBERTO

M1794 Baldanza, Frank, "The Classicism of Alberto Moravia," Modern Fiction Studies, 3:309-20, Winter, 1957-58.

Moravia sees life about him with an agreeable moderation and an ancient simplicity, and he attempts to present it in a conclusive and profound form that will in itself reveal the hard concreteness of objective reality without losing any of the inner psychic coloring. (R.A.K.)

M1795 Baldanza, Frank, "Mature Moravia," Contemporary Literature, 9:507-21, No. 4, 1968.

"Moravia has staked out a clearly delimited province in contemporary Italian fiction. For those readers willing to grant him what Henry James would call his données, his recent work is consistently in the line of his major achievements, with a new access of contemplative wisdom." (D.A.B.)

M1796 Chiaromonte, Nicola, "Rome Letter: Moravia and the Theater," Partisan Review, 26:643-9, Fall, 1959.

"Moravia's work is an illuminating example of the relation between . . . the impulse to narrate and the impulse to dramatize. Very distant from drama because of its pervasive feeling of opacity of the world and the ambiguity of every human attitude, nevertheless his art also aspires to the nakedness of dramatic conflict as the solution of his most pressing torment, which is to rediscover necessity in a world in which everything seems to happen by chance or weakness or from a general lack of conviction." (D.P.)

M1797 De Dominicis, Anna Maria, and Ben Johnson, "The Art of Fiction--VI: Alberto Moravia," Paris Review, No. 6, pp. 17-37, Summer, 1954.

". . . whatever is autobiographical is so in only a very indirect manner, in a very general way. . . . I do not take, and have never taken, either action or characters directly from life. Events may suggest events to be used in a work later; similarly, persons may suggest future characters; but suggest is the word to remember."(K.M.W.)

M1798 Foster, Kenelm, "Alberto Moravia," Blackfriars, 43:221-30, 1962.

Moravia, who "seems . . . to be always haunted by the possibility of discovering some meaningful and satisfying relationship between the human soul and the reality which it comes from and confronts" is "now moving towards a 'mystical' view of reality." (G.C.)

M1799 Heiney, Donald, "Moravia's America," Western Humanities Review, 18:315-29, Autumn, 1964.

In Two Women and in many stories written after 1945, "American culture plays in important part. . . . America is maleness, farce, prepotenza, success. . . . Italian culture . . . represents the opposite: weakness, decadence, and failure." (G.C.)

M1800 Lancaster, Charles Maxwell, "Fantasy in Moravia's Social and Political Satire," Forum Italicum, 2:3-12, 1968.

"Moravia's appalling diagnostics of man's robot condition, though presented with all the graces of sophisticated art . . . must still be regarded as a distorted miniature and parody of the vast complex of total reality." (G.C.)

M1801 Mitchell, Bonner, "Moravia's Proletarian Roman Intellectuals," Modern Language Journal, 44:303-6, November, 1960.

Moravia's "La Romana and the two volumes of Racconti romani represent not just a new predilection in subject matter but also a rather daring narrative experiment . . . in the creation of a novel sort of fictitious narrator. . . . Moravia has chosen . . . to have his Roman works presented by characters belonging to the lower-class, unlettered milieux in which the action is set . . . not . . . for the sake of picturesqueness or of humorous effect but in search of a new mode of expression." (D.P.)

M1802 Moravia, Alberto, "About My Novels," Twentieth Century, 164:529-32, December, 1958.

"In my novels the problem of the relationship between man and reality is seen either in terms of the relationship between the intellectual and a social or emotional or economic situation, or in terms

of the relationship between such a situation and the intellectual.
. . . Naturally this explanation is partial and limited: it takes no
account of aesthetic and poetical values which . . . are the only ones
which really matter in a work of art." (D.A.B.)

M1803 Pacifici, Sergio J., "The Fiction of Alberto Moravia: Portrait of a
Wasteland," Modern Language Quarterly, 16:68-77, March, 1955.

A fresh view of Moravia's work reveals that although his vision is
limited his work has matured. The Italian middle class maintains
its indifference because love, integrity, and understanding do not
prevail. It remains to be seen whether Moravia will eventually
sympathize with his imaginative creatures and thus become a great
writer. (G.M.P.)

M1804 Ragusa, Olga, "Alberto Moravia: Voyeurism and Storytelling,"
Southern Review, 4:127-41, January, 1968.

In spite of great popularity and notoriety, "Moravia's case has not
yet been proved. . . . his work . . . is traditional in structure and
unimaginative in language. . . . his own dogmatic statements . . .
underline rather than mitigate its shortcomings. Moravia has by
and large been unable to renew himself." (D.P.)

M1805 Rimanelli, Giose, "Moravia and the Philosophy of Personal Existence,"
Italian Quarterly, 41:39-68, 1967.

"Moravia's work develops in three directions: the social, the Freudian and the existential." In Agostino (1945) and La disubbidienza
(1948), "the social aspect . . . remains in the background while the
psychological study, embroidered with the existential vision of the
world, becomes very detailed. . . ." (G.C.)

M1806 Rolo, Charles J., "Alberto Moravia," Atlantic Monthly, 195:69-74,
February, 1955.

Moravia vents his indignation against the bombastic and consolatory
cant that permeated Italian culture in the 1920's. With frankness and
unsensational spontaneity, but with classic simplicity, he documents
the truth of sex, and projects the "feel" of Italian life. He represents
sex as the connection between the cerebral modern and instinctual
nature. A pragmatic self-acceptance, Moravia believes, will enable
mankind to make the best of its purgatorial destiny. (C.P.)

AGOSTINO

M1807 Waldhorn, Hilda K., "Two Adolescents," Literature and Psychology, 12:43-51, Spring, 1962.

[Of Moravia's two adolescents Agostino is studied from both Freudian and Sullivanian points of view and Luca's development agrees completely with Anna Freud's description of the adolescent.] (D.P.)

L'AUTOMA

M1808 Pacifici, Sergio, "Alberto Moravia's L'Automa: A Study in Estrangement," Symposium, 18:357-64, Winter, 1964.

"L'Automa emerges as a study in estrangement, as a conscious effort to dramatize the kind of automatic life to which we have all, for mysterious reasons, fallen prey." (K.M.W.)

BEATRICE CENCI

M1809 Mastrangelo, Aïda, "Alberto Moravia as Dramatist," Quarterly Journal of Speech, 53:127-34, April, 1967.

"The exciting, brilliant, and violently clear surfaces of Beatrice Cenci are likely to obscure completely its real life and underlying form. . . . Beatrice's changing relation to Olimpio is only one strand, though an important one. In this structure Moravia rediscovers the tragic rhythm of the Greeks through his conception of modern realism." (D.P.)

IL DISPREZZO

M1810 Goldstone, Herbert, "The Ghost of Moravia," Sewanee Review, 63:665-71, 1955.

In A Ghost at Noon "Alberto Moravia tells about a confused but well-intentioned young writer's attempt to understand why his wife no longer loves him. . . . Unfortunately . . . we have more of a psychological who-done-it than a satisfying novel about lively, sharply drawn people." (D.P.)

A GHOST AT NOON--See
IL DISPREZZO

THE INDIFFERENT ONES--See
GLI INDIFFERENTI

GLI INDIFFERENTI

M1811 Pacifici, Sergio, "Alberto Moravia and The Age of Indifference,"
Symposium, 8:321-6, Winter, 1954.

Moravia's dominant themes are adolescence, lasciviousness, and
indifference. Gli Indifferenti (1929) dramatized a "moral condition"
of crisis; indifference represents "man's struggle to find himself in
a civilization without beliefs." Lack of a moral code explains the
"viciousness and futility" characterizing Moravia's fiction. Only
redefinition of our civilization's values can provide one. (J. L. B.)

M1812 Radcliff-Umstead, Douglas, "Moravia's Indifferent Puppets,"
Symposium, 24:44-54, Spring, 1970.

"Moravia's The Indifferent Ones is a novel of defeat. . . . Paralyzed
in the nonexistence of puppets, the Moravian characters attempt to
bring themselves to life. . . . What Moravia has created is a grotesque vision of characters unable to forge a meaningful existence."
(D. P.)

THE TIME OF INDIFFERENCE--See
GLI INDIFFERENTI

TWO ADOLESCENTS--See
AGOSTINO

MORE, PAUL ELMER

M1813 Duggan, Francis X., "Paul Elmer More and the New England
Tradition," American Literature, 34:542-61, January, 1963.

Although More doubted the importance of American literature, he
devoted a great deal of attention to New England writers because he
found that they reflected certain of his own religious and philosophical
positions. (W.G.F.)

M1814 Dunham, Barrows, "Paul Elmer More," Massachusetts Review,
7:157-64, Winter, 1966.

[These are reminiscences by an acquaintance of More's.] (K.M.W.)

M1815 Hanford, John Holly, "The Paul Elmer More Papers," Princeton
University Library Chronicle, 22:163-8, Summer, 1961.

[Announces the gift of More's papers to Princeton and explains the
new light they will throw on the development of Humanism in American
intellectual history.] (W.G.F.)

M1816 Lambert, Bryon C., "Paul Elmer More and the Redemption of
History," Modern Age, 13:277-88, Summer, 1969.

"More sought to establish those permanent principles upon which
literature and civilization could rest. As the years went by, More
found his platonism being transformed into Christian faith. . . ."
(D.A.B.)

M1817 Newell, Kenneth B., "Paul Elmer More on Byron," Keats-Shelley
Journal, 12:67-74, Winter, 1963.

Although More's essays on individual authors are . . . considered
either acceptable but unfruitful truisms or fruitful but unacceptable
moral judgments . . . [his] estimate of Byron in the Cambridge
Edition [of Byron's Complete Poetical Works] is . . . often read as
a contemporary authoritative, and even popular estimate." More
invested his critique of Byron with "ideas of 'classicism' and 'humanism' . . . as touchstones . . . and found Byron . . . sometimes
attaining and sometimes failing the requirements of great art."
(D.P.)

M1818 Tanner, Stephen L., "T. S. Eliot and Paul Elmer More on Tradition," English Language Notes, 8:211-5, December, 1970.

"Considering Eliot's familiarity with More's work, their common
interests, particularly with regard to religion, and the younger
man's admiration of the elder's wisdom, it seems certain that More
was a primary source for Eliot's ideas on tradition and the historical
sense in 'Tradition and the Individual Talent'." (D.P.)

M1819 Warren, Austin, "Paul Elmer More: A Critic in Search of Wisdom,"
Southern Review, 5:1091-111, Autumn, 1969.

Although More left no "impeccable and imperishable" book, he represented "the principles which are naturally so little insisted on by
men of specialized genius--that civilization is a corporative achievement . . . that society is held together by the presence in it of men
of general parts and powers, of intelligence and good will." (J.M.D.)

THE SHELBOURNE ESSAYS

M1820 Harding, Joan N., "An American Thinker," <u>Contemporary Review</u>, No. 1057, pp. 34-9, January, 1954.

"<u>The Shelbourne Essays</u> give expression to an eternal longing for a resting place for man's soul, and thereby lend to American criticism a fourth dimension, an infinite perspective, which lifts it above the merely social or ethical issues of the day into the purer, rarer atmosphere of true art." (D.P.)

MORENO, BALDOMERO FERNÁNDEZ--See FERNÁNDEZ MORENO, BALDOMERO

MORGAN, CHARLES

M1821 Duffin, Henry Charles, "Charles Morgan's Novels," <u>Contemporary Review</u>, No. 1107, pp. 123-8, March, 1958.

Morgan's novels, shamefully neglected, present a world good and beautiful, a world of intellectuals in which love and sex are important and humor not at all, where everything is significant and life has spiritual dimensions. In some of the novels the passion is sensual: in others, it is overlaid with poetry and philosophy. (F.L.)

M1822 Giffard, Hugh, "The Writer and the Naturalist," <u>Études Anglaises</u>, 23:3-5, January-March, 1970.

[These are reminiscences of Morgan by the lifelong friend whom Morgan called "my horticultural mentor."] (D.A.B.)

M1823 Harding, Joan, "Charles Morgan and the Metaphysic of Evil," <u>Contemporary Review</u>, No. 1138, pp. 638-42, November, 1960.

The earlier novels of Charles Morgan (before 1939) presented evil as negative, a failure of the creative imagination. The creative imagination Morgan defined as the "flash of communication between man and God." In <u>The River Line</u>, <u>The Judge's Story</u>, and <u>The Burning Glass</u>, however, evil has become a positive, militant force. (F.L.)

M1824 Harding, Joan N., "Three Plays by Charles Morgan," Contemporary Review, No. 1078, pp. 244-8, October, 1955.

In The Flashing Stream, The River Line, and The Burning Glass Mr.
Morgan treats three aspects of human responsibility in the atomic
and depersonalized age. His Platonic just man is one who has
achieved "singleness of mind." Such a character lacks dramatic
power because he is not subject to temptation. (F.L.)

M1825 Painting, David E., "Charles Morgan: A Revaluation," Anglo-
Welsh Review, 18:90-4, No. 42, 1970.

Morgan is "an accomplished artist" who deals "with sexual desire
in all its various forms, whether physical or spiritual; where the
longing of a man for perfect harmony with a woman and the eternal
truths of art, love and death are treated with a depth of feeling and
delicacy of language totally lacking in . . . so many nodern novelists. . . ." (D.A.B.)

SPARKENBROKE

M1826 Cazamian, Louis, "Sparkenbroke de Charles Morgan," Études
Anglaises, 19:164-7, 1966.

"Sparkenbroke is not a flawless novel; its very clear-sighted sense
of composition and equilibrium does not prevent some slow-moving
moments; its inspiration, at once sensual and delicate, is sometimes a bit dull; it is possible to detect a faintly morbid inclination
toward the indissoluble and paradoxical union of spirituality and
feverish ardor; but, we can hail in it a very rich thought, and the
full realization of a very beautiful talent." (D.-J.J.)

MORGENSTERN, CHRISTIAN

M1827 Hofacker, Erich, "Ruhe und Aufstieg im Werk Christian Morgensterns," Monatshefte, 52:49-61, February, 1960.

The repose following Morgenstern's early spiritual progression
consists of submergence in earthly beauty. Then, as spiritual and
physical are felt as one, his second period culminates in perception
of oneness between God and man. In his last years this synthesis
becomes a religious surrender, a happy readiness to be sacrificed.
(R.H.L.)

M1828 Stern, Guy, "A Case for Oral Literary History: Conversations with or about Morgenstern, Lehmann, Reinacher and Thomas Mann," German Quarterly, 37:487-97, November, 1964.

Literary facts established through oral history interviews with Christian Morgenstern, Wilhelm Lehmann, Eduard Reinacher, Thomas Mann and/or their associates demonstrate the great value of this new technique for literary historians. (D.P.)

GALGENLIEDER

M1829 Neumann, Friedrich, "Christian Morgensterns Galgenlieder: Spiel mit der Sprache," Wirkendes Wort, 14:332-50, October, 1964.

"As poet and artist Morgenstern turns his back to that which is earthly and observes it in hundreds of mirrors. Such reflected images distort a little but specifically thereby they also prevent false views which tempt one to confuse the appearance with the substance." (J.R.R.)

M1830 Roy, Albert, "Christian Morgenstern, Poet of the Galgenlieder," American-German Review, 27:4-7, February-March, 1961.

"Is this combination of artistic imagination and child-like love of life, of 'being earnest' and at the same time bubbling over with laughter, a disposition that may be called typically German, or is it merely typically Christian Morgenstern?" (J.R.R.)

GALLOWS SONGS--See
GALGENLIEDER

MORLEY, CHRISTOPHER

M1831 Bracker, Jon, "The Christopher Morley Collection at the University of Texas," Library Chronicle (University of Texas) 7:19-35, Summer, 1962.

[This is a description of the books and manuscripts from Morley's home and office, now in the University of Texas Humanities Research Center.] (W.G.F.)

M1832 Cousins, Norman, "The World of Christopher Morley, " <u>Saturday</u>
<u>Review</u>, 40:26, April 20, 1957.

Few contemporary essayists had a greater energy or inventiveness.
"Almost none knew better the beautiful distinction between humor and
wit. . . . He had a radar-like faculty for picking up the incongruous
and converting it on his scope into a readily identifiable form of
whimsy." (C.P.)

M1833 Lyle, Guy R., "Ethos of a Man of Letters, " <u>Emory University</u>
<u>Quarterly</u>, 19:137-43, Fall, 1963.

[This is a discusssion of Morley which stresses three ingredients of
his novels: wit, symbolism and fantasy, and "the expression of his
own engaging human qualities."] (G.C.)

M1834 Mandel, Siegfried, "Man with Gusto, " <u>Saturday Review</u>, 40:27,
April 20, 1957.

Morley's greatest popular success was his novel <u>Kitty Foyle</u>,
although <u>Thunder on the Left</u>, <u>Where the Blue Begins</u>, <u>The Haunted</u>
<u>Bookshop</u>, and <u>Parnassus on Wheels</u> are more typical fictions.
Actually, he was more at home with articles and essays, which
range "from literary dissections of Shakespeare to a description of
the pugilistic art of Dempsey. . . . Morley's writings reflect a
philosophic mind that was receptive to all experience." (D.P.)

M1835 Smith, Harrison, "Christopher Morley, " <u>Saturday Review</u>, 40:22,
April 13, 1957.

"Morley was a poet, novelist, essayist, critic of high rank. . . .
Although he was born in America he seemed to belong to London, to
Oxford, to the calmer tempo of British intellectual life. He was a
man in a hurry, a man who had too many talents, too much to say."
(D.P.)

M1836 White, William, "Morley on Whitman: Inédite, " <u>American Notes</u>
<u>and Queries</u>, 4:132-3, May, 1966.

A letter (printed here) from Morley to Horace Traubel reports that
Morley had first suggested the transfer of the authorized Whitman
edition from Kennerley to Doubleday, Page and Company. "Morley
was actively interested in Whitman: he mentions him in several
books, wrote at least eight essays on him, edited a selection from
<u>Leaves of Grass</u>, " as well as introductions to several collections
of Whitmaniana. (D.P.)

M1837 Williams, W. L. G., "Christopher Morley as I Remember Him,"
American Oxonian, 44:158-63, July, 1957.

As a young man, Morley said of himself: "I seem to be clever in a
superficial way, adaptable to my surroundings, and tho' not personally prepossessing yet not ill-mannered . . . and yet, curiously
enough, with plenty of self-depreciation, I think I have genuine
ability if I can find the appropriate channel for it." (K.M.W.)

MORRIS, MYRA

M1838 Macartney, Frederick T., "Myra Morris: A Memorial Note,"
Meanjin Quarterly, 26:457-8, 1967.

[This is a short memorial note to Myra Morris.] (K.M.W.)

MORRIS, WRIGHT

M1839 Bluefarb, Sam, "Point of View: An Interview with Wright Morris,
July, 1958," Accent, 19:34-46, Winter, 1959.

[This interview ranges from Wright Morris's beginnings as a writer,
through his assessment of the Midwest influence on his writing, to
some consideration of his work habits, the importance of nostalgia
in his writing, and comments on the future of the novel.] (D.P.)

M1840 Booth, Wayne C., "The Shaping of Prophecy: Craft and Idea in the
Novels of Wright Morris," American Scholar: 31:608-26,
Autumn, 1962.

"There is in [Wright Morris's] novels a constant, explicit dialectic
between two worlds--between what is really real and what, in our
ordinary experience, merely seems so. Almost obsessed, from the
beginning, with the poignance of a human life caught in a changing,
shifting world, he has in most of his novels gone back to the past,
caught the lives of his characters in flux, and tried to fix them by a
transforming vision of whatever is timeless. . . ." "What is important to us is that his great powers of observation are in the
service of an inventive gift that yields character after character,
placed and heightened in larger designs that are themselves a
delight." (D.P.)

M1841 Booth, Wayne C., "The Two Worlds in the Fiction of Wright Morris,"
Sewanee Review, 65:375-99, Summer, 1957.

In Morris's fiction, "the real world, gruesome as it is, is not as
real as it looks. To endure it . . . a man must . . . find a more
genuine reality" through heroism, imagination, and love: these take
him "Out of this World." (A.A.S.)

M1842 Carpenter, Frederic I., "Wright Morris and the Territory Ahead,"
College English, 21:147-56, December, 1959.

"His novels have all contributed to the traditional American myth
of new discovery and self-realization, although his criticism consciously asserts that this myth is deluded and dangerous." (M.J.O.)

M1843 Flanagan, John T., "The Fiction of Wright Morris," Studia
Germanica Gandensia, 3:209-31, 1961.

Morris is very much part of the American literary tradition. Of
all his works, "his Nebraska fiction seems the most impressive,
the most durable." (G.C.)

M1844 Guettinger, Roger J., "The Problem with Jigsaw Puzzles: Form
in the Fiction of Wright Morris," Texas Quarterly, 11:209-20,
Spring, 1968.

"Through form, Morris believes, fiction becomes fact." Characters
in Field and in Cause express Morris's own sentiments. In the type
of fiction Morris writes, he attempts to become one of the few who,
through mastery of the form of fiction, create and discover the
meanings veiled in the facts of man's experience." (W.G.F.)

M1845 Hunt, John W., Jr., "The Journey Back: The Early Novels of
Wright Morris," Critique: Studies in Modern Fiction, 5:41-60,
Spring-Summer, 1962.

Wright Morris's early books, which contain the seeds of his later
works, "are not mere apprentice pieces. . . . They are finished,
rewarding novels which justify in their own right the careful critical
attention his later books are beginning to receive." [Hunt discusses
My Uncle Dudley, The Man Who Was There, The Home Place, and
The World in the Attic.] (D.A.B.)

M1846 Linden, Stanton J. and David Madden, "A Wright Morris Bibliography,"
Critique: Studies in Modern Fiction, 4:77-90, No. 3, 1962.

"The following bibliography includes all of the published works of
Wright Morris known to the editors, as well as a generous, and
reasonably complete list of reviews, biographical information, and
general criticism. In the case of secondary materials, fullness
. . . has been emphasized. . . ." (D.P.)

M1847 Madden, David, "The Great Plains in the Novels of Wright Morris,"
Critique: Studies in Modern Fiction, 4:5-23, No. 3, 1962.

"The central recurring theme in Morris's novels, around which all
other themes and elements resolve and through which his vision is
focussed, is the effect of the hero upon his witnesses: the witnesses
become in some way transformed as a result of their relationship
with the hero, who seldom benefits himself." (D.A.B.)

M1848 Miller, James E., Jr., "The Nebraska Encounter: Willa Cather
and Wright Morris," Prairie Schooner, 41:165-7, Summer, 1967.

The vision and voices of Willa Cather and Wright Morris have been
shaped by their Nebraska experience. In these two writers is provided "an account of the twentieth-century experience [and] . . . a
foreshortened history of the American imagination." Morris's
world "is the Cather world inverted, made comfortable and prosperous, fatuous and tranquil, but filled with terrors that Ántonia
never imagined. . . ." (D.P.)

M1849 Morris, Wright, "Letter to a Young Critic," Massachusetts Review,
6:93-100, Winter, 1965.

[Wright Morris, in a letter to David Madden, comments on his
development as a writer, his creative process, and themes in his
work.] (G.A.S.)

M1850 Morris, Wright, "The Lunatic, the Lover, and the Poet," Kenyon
Review, 27:727-37, Autumn, 1965.

"As it did to Anderson, the word 'grotesque' is now clinging to me.
Nor am I alone." [Morris discusses European and American writers
who use the grotesque and he indicates its significance for "the
contemporary imagination."] (D.A.B.)

M1851 Morris, Wright, "National Book Award Address," Critique: Studies in Modern Fiction, 4:72-5, No. 3, 1962.

[This is the text of the address given by Wright Morris on the occasion of his receiving the National Book Award in 1967. Morris's text told of his feeling of self as the center of the universe, and the role of the writer in imposing order on the world around him by using "fragments of disorder."] (V.E.)

M1852 Morris, Wright, "The Origin of a Species, 1942-57," Massachusetts Review, 7:121-35, 1966.

[Morris discusses the origins and natures of his characters.] (K.M.W.)

M1853 Trachtenberg, Alan, "The Craft of Vision," Critique: Studies in Modern Fiction, 4:41-55, No. 3, 1962.

The "craft of vision" is the technique used by Wright Morris. A photographer, Morris incorporated photography into his writing, sometimes literally, sometimes as a literary device. Morris's use of photography and "photographic" narrative suggests a vision of Americans losing their illusions to focus on truth, to lose their "pastoral innocence" and gain "personal integrity." (V.E.)

M1854 Tucker, Martin, "The Landscape of Wright Morris," Lock Haven Review, No. 7, pp. 43-51, 1965.

An "example of the isolated American writer," Morris "owes a debt to Henry James, F. Scott Fitzgerald, Sherwood Anderson, D. H. Lawrence. . . . Frustration, yearning and unquenchable love are [perpetual] themes in Morris's literary and spiritual universe." (G.C.)

M1855 Waterman, Arthur E., "The Novels of Wright Morris: An Escape From Nostalgia," Critique: Studies in Modern Fiction, 4:24-40, No. 3, 1962.

The development of an escape from nostalgia is the theme which unifies and gives direction to the novels of Wright Morris. Morris's novels stress the lack of feeling which characterized the American experience in the past and define the necessity of discovering one's own nature in order to be fully alive. (V.E.)

MORRIS, W.

CEREMONY IN LONE TREE

M1856 Baumbach, Jonathan, "Wake Before Bomb: Ceremony in Lone Tree,"
Critique: Studies in Modern Fiction, 4:56-71, No. 3, 1962.

"The main preoccupations of Morris's novels: prohibitive isolation,
violence repressed and exploded, the castrating Female, the cas-
trated Male, the unlived life, the narcosis of nostalgia, the 'self-
unmade man,' the whimsical nature of the universe, are all assembled as if for the occasion in Ceremony in Lone Tree." (D.P.)

FIELD OF VISION

M1857 Leer, Norman, "Three American Novels and Contemporary Society:
A Search for Commitment," Wisconsin Studies in Contemporary
Literature, 3:67-86, Fall, 1962.

The "post-modern" novel (exemplified by Malamud's The Assistant,
Wright Morris's The Field of Vision, and Kerouac's The Dharma
Bums), starting in opposition to the fluid world of mass society,
records the search for relationship; implied is that the discovery of
individual identity is perhaps the beginning of a larger social commitment. (B.K.)

M1858 Madden, David, "The Hero and the Witness in Wright Morris's
Field of Vision," Prairie Schooner, 34:263-78, Fall, 1960.

"The central, recurring theme in Morris's works, around which all
other themes revolve and through which his vision is focused, is the
effect of the relationship between the hero and the witness. . . .
The effect, directly or indirectly, of the hero's unexpected, audacious gesture of heroism . . . provides a focus for all comments on,
and revelations in, the characters." (D.E.W.)

IN ORBIT

M1859 Garrett, George, "Morris the Magician: A Look at In Orbit,"
Hollins Critic, 4:1-12, 1967.

"In In Orbit . . . the relationships between events, people, and
things are as close and complex, as similar and different, as the
suggested quality inherent in all of Morris's work." In it, "the
design is crucially important and superbly achieved." (D.P.)

IN ORBIT (cont'd)

M1860 Madden, David, "Wright Morris's In Orbit: An Unbroken Series of Poetic Gestures," Critique: Studies in Modern Fiction, 10:102-19, No. 2, 1968.

"For every element in . . . In Orbit, some prototype exists in [Morris's] other books. . . . More poetically compressed, the major themes of his other novels are made new in this brief book. . . . Yet Morris never repeats himself, and the familiar never looked so new and strange as in this novel." (D.P.)

ONE DAY

M1861 Waterman, Arthur E., "Wright Morris's One Day: The Novel of Revelation," Furman Studies, 15:29-36, May, 1968.

"One Day . . . conveys the poverty of lives without love and renders the difficulty of a modern person finding his connection, his moment, his realization of how to live in a meaningful context." (G.C.)

MORSTIN, LUDWIK HIERONIM

M1862 Natanson, Wojciech, "Xanthippe's Champion," Polish Perspectives, pp. 69-72, May, 1963.

Author of about thirty plays, several novels and essays, Morstin is chiefly known outside of Poland for L'Epi de la Vierge, a novel concerning Copernicus, and Defense of Xanthippe. Far too little is known in the West about Polish theatre, but Morstin has been recognized in France, Germany and Switzerland. (T.T.B.)

MOTLEY, WILLARD

M1863 Weissgärber, Alfred, "Willard Motley and the Sociological Novel," Studi Americani, 7:299-309, 1961.

Motley's three novels, Knock on Any Door, Let No Man Write My Epitaph and We Fished All Night reveal that his "special aptitude is his clear perception of the weakness, faults, sins and crimes of Society." (G.C.)

MOURLET, MICHEL

M1864 Bancroft, David, "A Re-assessment of the Contemporary Film by
Two French Novelists," L'Esprit Créateur, 8:255-67, Winter, 1968.

Cayrol has become conscious of the supremacy of the filmed image
over the purely literary one, whereas Michel Mourlet maintains that
the novel and film are two fundamentally different forms of art that
can never be reconciled. (T.T.B.)

MPHAHLELE, EZEKIEL

M1865 Cartey, Wilfred, "The Realities of Four Negro Writers," Columbia
University Forum, 9:34-42, Summer, 1966.

"The absurdity of the question, whether the Negro writer shall write
as a Negro, is particularly patent here; for these are, in effect,
autobiographical novels. The writers have in common the accident
that each is dealing with the same theme--the debut of himself; and
he is a Negro. Whether in South Africa, Barbados, or Harlem, he
speaks from within the castle of his skin." (D.P.)

MROZEK, SLAWOMIR

M1866 Krynski, Magnus J., "Mrozek, Tango, and American Campus,"
Polish Review, 15:114-6, No. 2, 1970.

[This is a report of Slawomir Mrozek's visit to the Duke University
campus (Durham, N. C.) on May 6 and 7, 1970. Portions of an
interview with Mrozek, which appeared in the campus newspaper,
The Duke Chronicle, are reproduced.] (G.C.)

MUELAS, FEDERICO

M1867 Fernández-Braso, Miguel, "Federico de Cuenca," La Estafeta
Literaria, No. 413, p. 37, February 1, 1969.

Poet, extravagant literary orphan, Muelas is considered a conform-
ist because of the absence of rebellion and pain--an easy, superficial
judgment. He seeks to trample underfoot grief and confusion, avoid-
ing the cold, pompous and false by stressing love and mutual human
comprehension. (T.T.B.)

MUIR, EDWIN

M1868 Blackmur, R. P., "Edwin Muir: Between the Tiger's Paws,"
Kenyon Review, 21:419-36, Summer, 1959.

An "unprofessional poet," Muir wrote "runes" in which the Incarnation and Resurrection are dominant symbols of his traditional awareness of the past. (K.W.)

M1869 Bruce, George, "Edwin Muir . . . Poet," Saltire Review, 6:12-6,
Spring, 1959.

[This is an appreciation of the poet as a man, with brief biographical
notes, and an estimate of his work as a modern symbolist.] (E.T.)

M1870 Carruth, Hayden, "An Appreciation of Muir," Prairie Schooner,
32:148-53, Summer, 1958.

"This is not a review, but a tribute. . . . Muir is his own poet, he
needs no comparisons, and if his work does not quite attain the
superexcellence of Yeats, its qualities nevertheless are enough to
ensure its durability." (D.H.)

M1871 Carruth, Hayden, "To Fashion the Transitory," Poetry, 88:389-93,
September, 1956.

Muir's concern with time allies him with the metaphysical tradition
of modern poetry. Time takes on the "ancient aspect of the thief";
eternity is an extension of time or an existence in dream and memory
and in the later poems it is akin to conventional Christian belief.
(F.L.)

M1872 Eliot, T. S., O. M., "Edwin Muir: 1887-1959--An Appreciation,"
Listener, 71:872, May 28, 1964.

"I do not believe that technique was ever a primary concern with
Edwin. . . . under the pressure of emotional intensity, and possessed by his vision, he found almost unconsciously the right, the
inevitable way of saying what he wanted to say." He "will remain
among the poets who have added glory to the English language.
. . . There is the sensibility of the remote [Orcadian] islander
. . . who struggled to understand the modern world of the metrop-
olis in London, and finally the realities of Central Europe in Prague.
. . . And all of this experience is somehow concentrated into that
great, that terrifying poem of the atomic age--'The Horses'."
(D.P.)

M1873 Fowler, Helen, "To Be in Time: The Experience of Edwin Muir,"
Approach, No. 40, pp. 11-8, Summer, 1961.

Muir looked against the time scheme he shared with his literary
friends in order to become self-acquainted, to experience the several
layers in the inner-consciousness. He required of his imagination results, not solely for his art, but for reliving his life with meaning.
(A. F.)

M1874 Galler, David, "Edwin Muir," Poetry, 94:330-3, August, 1959.

Muir, caught between the deterministic God of his father and his own
questionings, was led from a Nietzschean "Indifference" and "Pity"
to existentialism. He embraces the Absurd; his realm is contradiction. He labors under a guilt from the "equivocal ignominy of non-
election" in the early poems. The guilt is never completely expiated.
(F. L.)

M1875 Garber, Frederick, "Edwin Muir's Heraldic Mode," Twentieth
Century Literature, 12:96-103, July, 1966.

"Heraldry, for Muir, is still another version of the language that
speaks, through dreams and archetypes, in the voice of the racial
unconscious. Until the publication of The Labyrinth in 1949, images
derived from armorial bearings bulk large in the totality of his
poems. Muir probably knew little about the complex traditions and
involuted nomenclature of this highly specialized art, but enough,
certainly, had attracted him, and so strongly, that we can rightfully
speak of his concern as an obsession." (D. P.)

M1876 Gill, Bernard, "Sunset Light: A Poet's Last Days," Western
Humanities Review, 14:283-8, Summer, 1960.

[This is a description by a neighbor of Muir in his last years.]
(M. H.)

M1877 Glicksberg, Charles I., "Edwin Muir: Zarathustra in Scotch Dress,"
Arizona Quarterly, 12:225-39, Autumn, 1956.

Muir's criticism is Nietzschean in character. Asserting that the
world is at bottom meaningless, Muir sees art as play, aspiring
towards "absolute meaninglessness." Yet, he says, reason gives
man "absolute empire over himself and the world." Such paradoxes
in his work are marks of his effort to affirm the wholeness of reality.
(A. A. S.)

M1878 Grice, Fred, "The Poetry of Edwin Muir," Essays in Criticism, 5:243-52, July, 1955.

Muir's first preoccupation is with Innocence, and his best poetry records the pilgrimage back to lost Innocence. His second theme, the conquest of Time, gives his poetry a depth and dignity unusual in modern verse. (D.B.D.)

M1879 Hamburger, Michael, "Edwin Muir," Encounter, 15:46-53, December, 1960.

To separate the "technique" of Muir's poetry from his vision would "offend against the integrity of his art." Beginning his poetic career when he was almost forty, Muir brought to his work a variety of experiences. In his poetry his experience of hardships overcome is as evident as is his philosophy. (V.E.)

M1880 Hassan, Ihab H., "Of Time and Emblematic Reconciliation: Notes on the Poetry of Edwin Muir," South Atlantic Quarterly, 58:427-39, Summer, 1959.

Written in distinctive though limited language, the allegorical and paradoxical poetry of Edwin Muir centers on the shapes and disguises of time: Muir grapples with the concept of recurrence in all his poems. The Christian character of his vision is seen in his latest poetry. (W.B.B.)

M1881 Hoffman, Daniel, "Edwin Muir: The Story and the Fable," Yale Review, 55:403-26, March, 1966.

The dreams and fancies serving Muir as fertile sources for his poetry are akin to the Jungian archetypes, inherent in the racial consciousness. His concept of reality was Platonic, his intellectual attitude that of late Romanticism. His "myth" ("fable") requires no Yeats-like revision of history; it is extracted from lived events, inner or outer. (F.L.)

M1882 Holloway, John, "The Poetry of Edwin Muir," Hudson Review, 13:550-67, Winter, 1960.

"The foundation of Muir's achievement as a poet is not a voguish manipulation of language, but the embodiment in verse of a deep and true apprehension of life"--an awareness that, though "the powers of evil were great, ultimately the powers of good and goodness were greater." (M.H.)

M1883 Hoy, Peter, "Edwin Muir Addenda: Checklist of Secondary Reference," Serif, 7:11-9, No. 1, 1970.

[This is a listing of 180 of "the more important chapters, essays, and reviews omitted from Elgin W. Mellown's 'A Checklist of Critical Writings about Edwin Muir'."]   (G.C.)

M1884 Jennings, Elizabeth, "The Living Dead--VII: Edwin Muir as Poet and Allegorist," London Magazine, 7:43-56, March, 1960.

"The most striking thing about the poetry of Edwin Muir is the slow sureness of its development. . . . Muir was a visionary poet whose poems were both the source and fulfillment of his vision; they did not crystallize a past experience but embodied it even while it was being experienced."   (M.H.M.)

M1885 Joselyn, Sister M., "Herbert and Muir: Pilgrims of Their Age," Renascence, 15:127-32, Spring, 1963.

"In a verse generally so impeccably one with its thought that it almost ceases to be art, Edwin Muir has well represented the modern man of religious sensibility, speaking in a new, existential voice which has also affinities with the great seventeenth-century metaphysicals" like Herbert.   (S.A.)

M1886 Marcel, Gabriel, "Edwin Muir," Études Anglaises, 13:10-25, January, 1960.

Muir's Autobiography confirms that his poetry is a function of "an effort to force his life to take shape" and that it is therefore essentially meditative.   (D.-J.J.)

M1887 Maxwell, J. C., "Edwin Muir's An Autobiography: An Error in Revision," Notes and Queries, 13:101, March, 1966.

The phrase "a fragment of that age swam up recently after being lost for more than sixty years" which appears in An Autobiography is identical to a sentence which appears in The Story and the Fable, substituting "sixty" for "forty." This "must have been the result of mere confusion."   (D.P.)

M1888 Mellown, Elgin W., "Autobiographical Themes in the Novels of Edwin Muir," Wisconsin Studies in Contemporary Literature, 6:228-42, Summer, 1965.

"Each novel centers upon one main character, a young man who in spite of apparent differences actually portrays the author. . . . The differences between these three fictional characters reflect the maturing of Muir's personality and the development of his understanding of himself." (W.G.F.)

M1889 Mellown, Elgin W., "The Development of a Criticism: Edwin Muir and Franz Kafka," Comparative Literature, 16:310-21, Fall, 1964.

"This essay is an examination of [Edwin Muir's]. . . criticism in order to show how its changes and developments afford insight into Kafka criticism in general." (C.E.N.

M1890 Merton, Thomas, "The True Legendary Sound: The Poetry and Criticism of Edwin Muir," Sewanee Review, 75:317-24, Spring, 1967.

"Muir's metaphysical insight into the numinous and sacred which does not underlie but actually is the ordinary reality of our world, was not an other-worldly mysticism." It is grounded in a deep and Human sympathy which seeks the "reconciliation of the inner and outer man." (D.M.M.)

M1891 Mills, Ralph J., Jr., "Eden's Gate: the Later Poetry of Edwin Muir," Personalist, 44:58-78, Winter, 1963.

Central to all of Muir's poetry and especially strong in his later work is his awareness of the essential duality of human existence: "the 'story'--the history of our daily lives and our personalities--and the 'fable'--the religious and mythological drama of man." (G.B.M.)

M1892 Mills, Ralph J., Jr., "Edwin Muir: A Speech from Darkness Grown," Accent, 19:50-70, Winter, 1959.

Muir's interest in the common estate of men leads to concentration on the deep well of childhood, "where memory, imagination, and the elements of the world mingle." He uses myth and image (e.g., mirror, mountain, light images) to probe "the meaning of time" and the hidden sides of life. (F.J.C.)

M1893 Morgan, Edwin, "Edwin Muir," Review, No. 5, pp. 3-10,
February, 1963.

"Muir was in search of a simplicity which the future was unlikely to
reveal except by a return to the past, and even the simplicity of the
past is more myth than reality." (W.G.F.)

M1894 Muir, Edwin, "Some Letters of Edwin Muir," Encounter, 26:3-10,
No. 1, 1966.

[After having reviewed a novel by Stephen Hudson, whose real name
was Sydney Schiff, Edwin Muir began a correspondence with Schiff
which went on for many years. Topics of the letters ranged from
literary discussions to personal gossip and began, in the 1930's,
to encompass the horrifying political changes which were taking
place in Europe at that time.] (V.E.)

M1895 Peschmann, Hermann, "Edwin Muir: A Return to Radical Innocence,"
English, 12:168-71, Summer, 1959.

Although Muir was aware of the social, political, and technical up-
heavals of his time, his poetry and prose show little trace. To him,
the "source and centre of mankind's dilemma lay elsewhere: in the
solving of those problems and the overcoming of those temptations
which militate against the self-integration of the individual soul."
(J.M.D.)

M1896 Porteous, Alexander, "The Status of Edwin Muir," Quadrant,
7:80-2, Winter, 1963.

"The stamp of one fine mind is strongly on all his poems, they
are informed by one individual voice, we are aware of . . . their
essential coherence, their largeness of reference, the worth and
power of their commentary on our lives." Muir is a major poet
of our time. (D.P.)

M1897 Raine, Kathleen, "Edwin Muir: An Appreciation," Texas Quarterly,
4:233-45, Autumn, 1961.

Edwin Muir's poems "seem to glow with some inner light. . . .
Time does not fade them, and it becomes clear that their excellence
owes nothing to the accidental circumstances of the moment at which
the poet wrote. . . . Edwin Muir, a poet who never followed fashion,
has in fact given more permanent expression to his world than other
poets who deliberately set out to be the mouthpieces of their generation." (D.P.)

M1898 Read, Herbert, "Edwin Muir," Encounter, 12:71-3, April, 1959.

[This is a brief memoir of Edwin Muir by Herbert Read, whose
career paralleled Muir's until the First World War. Muir never
lost his belief in immortality, having never undergone the disillusionment of the War, and found the perfect expression of his faith in the
Upanishads, the Hindu doctrine of the Self.] (V.E.)

M1899 Rosenthal, M. L., "Edwin Muir: 1887-1959," Nation, 188:392-3,
April 25, 1959.

"In Muir we have a great spokesman for the foiled humanistic ideal
of European man, and for the era in which that ideal began to lower
its flag in utter discouragement. The paltry lugubriosity of so much
contemporary British writing is transcended by the vastness of what
Muir implies--that once again the stars have 'thrown down their
spears' and 'watered heaven with their tears'." (D.P.)

M1900 Scholten, Martin, "The Humanism of Edwin Muir," College English,
21:322-6, March, 1960.

"It seems to me that what Muir is saying . . . is that the human
condition requires a realization of the qualities that made us human.
Again, however, one notes the imperative of . . . the enduring archetypal form and of the transient mortal expression. For Muir, human
existence has meaning only in relation to that which transcends it."
(M.J.O.)

M1901 Stanford, Derek, "Edwin Muir (1887-1959)," Contemporary Review,
No. 1119, pp. 145-7, March, 1959.

The search for a solution of or meaning to existence undertaken by
Edwin Muir derived from his unhappy youth. He saw his childhood
and youth as a myth and a dream, two terms which remained significant to him. In 1939 a realization of his Christianity resulted in
increased poetic production. (V.E.)

M1902 Summers, Joseph H., "Edwin Muir," Books Abroad, 34:123,
Spring, 1960.

"As a critic, Muir's tastes were wide. . . . From his early essays
on Joyce, Lawrence, and Eliot to the later ones on Shakespeare,
Kafka, Sterne, and Hölderlin, he showed his appreciation for almost
any writer who could achieve an individual vision. . . . As a poet,
also, Muir was chiefly concerned with inward vision rather than with

technical innovations." He was "a man who combined sensitivity and wit: who recognized and was moved by the condition of man . . . and who became a great writer partially because he was so sure that there are things more important than literature." (D.P.)

M1903 Summers, Joseph H., "The Achievement of Edwin Muir," Massachusetts Review, 2:240-60, Winter, 1961.

"Muir's achievement in poetry and prose is larger than the merely literary. . . . Implicit in all of his works is the recognition that there are things more important than literature: . . . those things in which the religious man recognizes the immediate work of God." (G.C.)

M1904 Watson, J. R., "Edwin Muir and the Problem of Evil," Critical Quarterly, 6:231-49, Autumn, 1964.

Scottish qualities are evident in the poetry of Edwin Muir, as is a "preoccupation with the fundamental questions of the human condition which extend the Scottish tradition and link it with the European." Due in part to a "search for completeness" Muir wrote in English and not in Scots. To Muir completeness meant an answer to the problem of evil and to basic questions on human conditions. (V.E.)

THE ANIMALS

M1905 Emig, Janet, "The Articulate Breath," English Journal, 52:540-1, 1963.

Muir's poem "The Animals" might serve effectively as a unit on language. Muir's deceptively simple poem on the importance of language as man's unique possession which sets him above other animals serves as a metaphor on its own theme. (V.E.)

THE JOURNEY BACK

M1906 Butter, Peter, "Edwin Muir: 'The Journey Back'," English (London), 16:218-22, Autumn, 1967.

"The Journey Back" is Edwin Muir's longest mature poem. Muir's difficult poetry reflects a long waking dream he experienced while being psychoanalysed. In "The Journey Back" the poet voyages backward in time, through images of Christianity to the collective unconscious, giving the reader a feeling of imprisonment in time. (V.E.)

THE TOY HORSE

M1907 Goodwin, K. L., "Muir's 'The Toy Horse'," Explicator, 23:
Item 6, September, 1964.

". . . the central image of the poem . . . should therefore probably
be interpreted . . . as a beast representing . . . the Jewish-Christian
religious tradition based on the Bible." (D.P.)

M1908 Scott-Craig, T. S. K., "Muir's 'Toy Horse'," Explicator, 24:
Item 62, March, 1966.

"The poem has a positive but not blatant Christian orientation."
(D.P.)

MUKHERJI, SHANKAR

M1909 Baumer, Rachel Van M., "Sankar: Twentieth-Century Kathak,"
Books Abroad, 43:487-98, Autumn, 1969.

The importance of medieval literary conventions in contemporary
Bengali literary composition can be seen by comparing the novels
of Sankar (Shankar Mukherji) to the techniques of the medieval kathak
or storyteller. (K.H.B.)

MUNCH-PETERSEN, GUSTAF

M1910 Mitchell, P. M., "The English Poetry of Gustaf Munch-Petersen,"
Orbis Litterarum, 22:352-62, 1967.

"Despite all semantic and syntactical difficulties" in Gustaf Munch-
Petersen's English poetry, "the ethical substance of the poetry--the
underlying and recurrent ideas--are identifiable and demonstrable."
(G.C.)

MUÑIZ, CARLOS

M1911 Cazorla, Hazel, "Simbolismo en el teatro de Carlos Muñiz,"
Hispania, 48:230-3, May, 1965.

Muñiz is more than a documentary realist, but he avoids the "dead
end" absurdism of Beckett and Ionesco. Rather, he continues the
esperpento or grotesque farce tradition of Valle-Inclán. (C.O.)

MUNK, KAJ

M1912 Madsen, Børge Gedsø, "Bjørnstjerne Bjørnson's Beyond Human Power and Kaj Munk's The Word," Modern Drama, 3:30-6, May, 1960.

Probably, Kaj Munk "felt Beyond Human Power as a challenge to his Christian faith, and this may have added impetus to his desire to write his own counterpart to it, the drama about the life-giving Word." (C.K.L.)

MUNRO, HECTOR HUGH

M1913 Bilton, Peter, "Salute to an N. C. O.," English Studies, 47:439-42, December, 1966.

Hector Munro (Saki) created characters who speak or act for him, showing their creator's underlying attitude. Literary history and academic criticism largely ignore Saki, despite his popularity. Saki showed life as a "source of constant surprise, shock--and interest." As he grew older his wit became more earnest and more bitter, and the end of his own life possessed a cruel irony that he might have written himself. (V.E.)

M1914 Drake, Robert, "Saki: Some Problems and a Bibliography," English Fiction in Transition, 5:6-26, No. 1, 1962.

Saki is a serious artist; his genius may not be a great one, but it burns with a "hard and gem-like flame." (W.D.)

M1915 Drake, Robert, "Saki's Ironic Stories," Texas Studies in Literature and Language, 5:374-88, Autumn, 1963.

"Saki's stories which are not humorous seem, if they have no other bond in common, to have a pervading irony. . . . This irony usually consists in the principal character's bringing about his own downfall by scorning as 'unreal' some aspect of total reality." (W.G.F.)

M1916 Gerber, H. E., and Philip Armato, "H. H. Munro ('Saki')," English Literature in Transition, 11:54-5, No. 1, 1968.

Abstracts in continuation of Robert Drake's "Saki: Some Problems and a Bibliography" (English Fiction in Transition, 5:1, 1962), include Peter Bilton's "Salute to an N. C. O." (English Studies, 46:439-42), Carl N. Jester's "The Foreign Correspondence (1902-

1903) of H. H. Munro" (Ph. D. Thesis at the University of Pennsylvania), and Bernard Peltzie's "Teaching Meaning Through Structure in the Short Story," (English Journal, 55:703-9, 719).   (V.E.)

M1917   Lambert, J. W., "Jungle Boy in the Drawing-Room," Listener, 55:211-2, February 9, 1956.

Although Munro wrote a history of Russia, two novels, several plays and many sketches, his reputation rests on his short stories.   "In them--in the best of them--prigs, snobs, bores, politicans, and other self-important comedians, spiteful old women, and silly, smug young ones are deliciously impaled."   (D.P.)

M1918   Overmyer, Janet, " 'Turn Down an Empty Glass'," Texas Quarterly, 7:171-5, Autumn, 1964.

Although Saki was never a best selling author he has caught the attention and respect of some major authors and critics, and his public "is faithful and growing."   His "stylistic blend of wit and cruelty" is especially brought to bear on those he regarded as fools. "His compassion and cruelty come into careful balance when he writes of children. . . . Interwoven with Saki's attitudes toward fools and children are four main themes . . .: supernatural beings and events, religion, hypocrisy, and death."   "Those characteristics of Saki's work that would seem to make it obsolete are mainly the surface ones of subject matter and style. . . . As a credo for modern man . . . the underlying philosophy . . . keep trying in the face of almost certain defeat . . . is not outworn."   (D.P.)

BEASTS AND SUPER-BEASTS

M1919   Stevick, Philip, "Saki's Beasts," English Literature in Transition, 9:33-7, No. 1, 1966.

Several stories from the collection of Beasts and Super-Beasts (1914) illustrate that "there is, behind the facile glass, an uncompromising honesty in much of Saki together with a remarkably prescient insight into the unconscious life of his characters."   (G.C.)

THE OPEN WINDOW

M1920   Peltzie, Bernard E., "Teaching Meaning Through Structure in the Short Story," English Journal, 55:703-9, 719, September, 1966.

THE OPEN WINDOW   (cont'd)

Mansfield's "The Fly" and Saki's "The Open Window" "demonstrate
how a formal characteristic, structure . . . may be used to open up
a story." (G.C.)

MUNTHE, AXEL

M1921 Tolstoi, Catherine, "Axel Munthe et le livre de San Michele, "
À la Page, No. 58, pp. 47-53, April, 1969.

Towards the end of his life and under the pressure of Henry James,
Munthe began to write, eventually being translated into twenty-five
languages. As a side-effect, his international success and the setting at Anacapri and the Bay of Naples brought about the foundation
of bird refuges at Capri and in Sweden. (T.T.B.)

MURDOCH, IRIS

M1922 Balakian, Nona, "The Flight from Innocence: England's Newest
Literary Generation, " Books Abroad, 33:260-70, Summer, 1959.

In England "there has emerged in the past five or six years a new
group of writers, all under forty, whose insight into the contemporary
scene is [easily] the most striking thing about their work. The most
interesting among them are the novelists: Kingsley Amis, John Wain,
Iris Murdoch, John Braine, and J. P. Donleavy--all writing in a
comic genre. . . . What they have in common . . . is an impious and
unromantic view in which anger figures as a detergent, clearing the
air for a new look at reality." (D.P.)

M1923 Baldanza, Frank, "Iris Murdoch and the Theory of Personality, "
Criticism, 7:176-89, Spring, 1965.

Iris Murdoch "maintains that the characteristic of the greatest
works of art is the assumption . . . that there are separate, autonomous, free persons . . . in the world. . . . it is the failure to
recognize the real, independent existence of other people that is
dangerous in [existentialism and solipsism] that dominate the modern
novel." (J.L.A.)

M1924 Baldanza, Frank, "The Murdoch Manuscripts at the University of Iowa: An Addendum," Modern Fiction Studies, 16:201-2, Summer, 1970.

[This is a discussion of "two misleading statements in William M. Murray's bibliographical description of the Murdoch manuscripts . . . in the special Modern Fiction Studies issue on that writer (15:445-448)."] (G.C.)

M1925 Berthoff, Warner, "Fortunes of the Novel: Muriel Spark and Iris Murdoch," Massachusetts Review, 9:301-32, Spring, 1967.

Muriel Spark and Iris Murdoch are two of the most productive and most admired writers of recent years. Not creators of master-pieces, these two writers are instead dedicated to the principle of a writer simply pursuing the business of writing, in order to survive psychically. Neither uses "expository and assertive prose" and both show "little prose imagination," but each possesses her own "voice as a writer." (V.E.)

M1926 Brierre, Anne, "Littérature anglo-irlandaise," La Revue des Deux Mondes, 140:84-91, January 1, 1968.

[These are critical analyses of the works of William Golding, Iris Murdoch and Elizabeth Bowen.] (T.T.B.)

M1927 Broich, Ulrich, "Tradition und Rebellion," Poetica, 1:214-29, April, 1967.

Recent novels by Wain, Amis and Murdoch all have a hero who seems a mixture of the mutually exclusive figures of the picaro and the pilgrim. The resulting character does not fit into traditional categories, for he is definitely a new creation of our own times. (J.R.R.)

M1928 Culley, Anne with John Feaster, "Criticism of Iris Murdoch: A Selected Checklist," Modern Fiction Studies, 15:449-57, Autumn, 1969.

[This checklist includes general studies, discussions of individual novels, and an index to the general studies and special studies not previously listed.] (G.C.)

M1929 Culley, Ann, "Theory and Practice: Characterization in the Novels
of Iris Murdoch," Modern Fiction Studies, 15:335-45, Autumn, 1969.

[This essay examines the close connection between Murdoch's moral
philosophy and her literary theory and shows how "her method of
characterization derives from her philosophical concept of personality."] (D.A.B.)

M1930 Demant, V. A., "El nuevo humanismo," Revista de Occidente,
No. 83, pp. 149-68, February, 1970.

Murdoch represents Christian humanistic conceptions in her recognition of the tragic, potential demonism in human power, technique
and sexual relations, which may take possession of the best human
beings. (T.T.B.)

M1931 Dick, Bernard F., "The Novels of Iris Murdoch: A Formula for
Enchantment," Bucknell Review, 14:66-81, May, 1966.

"Each of [Iris Murdoch's] novels is a variation on one theme:
theorizing, when wrenched from a concrete frame of reference, is
enchantment in the form of self-delusion. . . . [She] warns against
philosophical complacency or absolute norms as substitutes for contact with reality." (G.C.)

M1932 Emerson, Donald, "Violence and Survival in the Novels of Iris
Murdoch," Transactions of the Wisconsin Academy of Sciences,
Arts, and Letters, 57:21-8, 1969.

In Under the Net, The Bell, An Unofficial Rose, and The Time of
the Angels; Miss Murdoch presents a world "in which . . . violence
is a fact to which survival or destruction are alternatives." (G.C.)

M1933 Felheim, Marvin, "Symbolic Characterization in the Novels of Iris
Murdoch," Texas Studies in Literature and Language, 2:189-97,
Summer, 1960.

Miss Murdoch's characters are "a combination of strangeness and
reality. They are engaged in a series of actions which, though occasionally bizarre, are not altogether unrealistic." The characters
themselves are far more strange than the situations into which they
are plunged. (W.G.F.)

M1934 Fraser, G. S., "Iris Murdoch: The Solidity of the Normal,"
International Literary Annual, 2:37-54, 1959.

Iris Murdoch's Under the Net and Flight from the Enchanter are
"loosely episodic"; The Sandcastle and The Bell are "tightly plotted."
(G.C.)

M1935 German, Howard, "Allusions in the Early Novels of Iris Murdoch,"
Modern Fiction Studies, 15:361-77, Autumn, 1969.

". . . my purpose here is . . . to show the existence of some of the
allusive material in Miss Murdoch's first five novels and to suggest
the particular relevance of these details in each of the works."
(D.A.B.)

M1936 Gindin, James, "Images of Illusion in the Work of Iris Murdoch,"
Texas Studies in Literature and Language, 2:180-8, Summer, 1960.

Each of Miss Murdoch's novels "gives a symbolic identity to the
characters's desire to manufacture form and direction out of their
disparate experience." In each the attempt is unsuccessful; "the
general structure suggested by the title cannot meaningfully operate
in the fragmented, relative world." (W.G.F.)

M1937 Hall, James, "Blurring the Will: The Growth of Iris Murdoch,"
ELH, 32:256-73, June, 1965.

"In this injury-inflicting world, eros is over-matched against
aggressiveness. At some stage the individual naturally--not on existentialist principle--begins to think of regrouping, gathering his
scattered forces and centering on his best possibilities. The effort,
because it is a counter-attack, becomes a private attempt at rebirth,
vulnerable because unsupported in the confusing social fabric."
(G.A.S.)

M1938 Hall, William F., "Bruno's Dream: Technique and Meaning in the
Novels of Iris Murdoch," Modern Fiction Studies, 15:429-43,
Autumn, 1969.

In Iris Murdoch's novels, "it is possible to trace . . . two larger
patterns in terms of which [they] . . . may be grouped." "In the
first pattern . . . a character . . . moves . . . out of the world of
form, pattern and convention, into one of contingency." In the
second pattern, the direction is reversed. (G.C.)

M1939 Hall, William, " 'The Third Way': The Novels of Iris Murdoch, " Dalhousie Review, 46:306-18, Autumn, 1966.

Iris Murdoch's work may be examined in the light of what she has to say about philosophy. She offers the stance of "acceptance of the formless." This acceptance involves a "return to Kant's concept of the sublime." Miss Murdoch's vision is essentially a comic vision, and "though certain general preoccupations reign throughout . . . the separate novels display a remarkable variety of individual themes." (V.E.)

M1940 Heyd, Ruth, "An Interview with Iris Murdoch, " University of Windsor Review, 1:138-43, Spring, 1965.

[These are comments on the author's interview with Iris Murdoch during which Miss Murdoch discussed some of the basic problems in her novels.] (K.M.W.)

M1941 Hoffman, Frederick J., "Iris Murdoch: The Reality of Persons, " Critique: Studies in Modern Fiction, 7:48-57, Spring, 1964.

Miss Murdoch "is not an 'existential novelist, ' in the manner of Sartre, or even of Camus. But she is preoccupied with a set of human conditions that serve well to adorn a Sartrean text . . . . She is right to avoid both extremes of farce and tragedy." (W.G.F.)

M1942 Hoffman, Frederick J., "The Miracle of Contingency: The Novels of Iris Murdoch, " Shenandoah, 17:49-56, Autumn, 1965.

"I believe that in her novels she has struggled for a balance of symbol and 'intimate fact, ' and that she has reached a definition of human perfection in terms of 'love': that is, of a slow, often commonplace change in one person's view of another, which marks the 'heroism of quotidian'." "It is my contention that The Italian Girl is an exemplary work, illustrating beautifully Miss Murdoch's definition of 'love' and 'the idea of perfection.'. . ." (D.A.B.)

M1943 Hope, Francis, "The Novels of Iris Murdoch, " London Magazine, 1:84-7, August, 1961.

Readers "have been delighted by the grace of Miss Murdoch's writing, by its complexity and depth of imagination, by its extraordinary mixture of the real and the fantastic. . . ." Of her later work "The Sandcastle was often stiltedly written. . . . But The Bell . . . never falters for lack of a word or a phrase. Structurally, it is equally imposing. . . ." (D.P.)

M1944 Kauffmann, R. J., "The Progress of Iris Murdoch," Nation, 188:255-6, March 21, 1959.

Iris Murdoch is a "sophisticated philosopher" who tries to achieve through her novels a new vision of reality based on the uniqueness and significance of man. Through her "unsentimental concern for people" she has restored "high intelligence and virility to the English novel." In each novel she has shown a deepening and enrichment of her craft. (D.P.)

M1945 Kermode, Frank, "The House of Fiction: Interviews with Seven English Novelists," Partisan Review, 30:61-82, Spring, 1963.

[These interviews with Iris Murdoch, Graham Greene, Angus Wilson, Ivy Compton-Burnett, C. P. Snow, John Wain and Muriel Spark confirm that "the house of fiction has many windows. . . . designed as variations . . . within these limits [are] irreducibly complex personalities, a sadistic landscape, a gaunt country house full of secrets that cannot survive the preternatural explicitness of the inhabitants, a mountain of cheese."] (D.P.)

M1946 Kogan, Pauline, "Beyond Solipsism to Irrationalism: A Study of Iris Murdoch's Novels," Literature and Ideology, 2:47-69, 1969.

In her twelve novels written since 1954, Iris Murdoch "denies the possibility of knowledge about life, locates the sources of social evils in solipsism, and proposes an irrational theory of love . . . to release the decadent bourgeousie from this bondage of self-centredness." (G.C.)

M1947 Kuehl, Linda, "Iris Murdoch: The Novelist as Magician; The Magician as Artist," Modern Fiction Studies, 15:347-60, Autumn, 1969.

Iris Murdoch "appears to be irreconcilably divided between a contemporary proclivity towards novels of ideas and a nostalgic commitment to novels of character. . . . Her nostalgia for traditional but outmoded techniques makes her position obsolete." (G.C.)

M1948 Lodge, David, "Le Roman contemporain en Angleterre," La Table Ronde, No. 179, pp. 80-92, December, 1962.

Of the post-war writers, only Miss Murdoch has shown her lack of interest in social realism. She uses settings where she can depict individuals endowed with a fine sensitivity and make them move in

an intrigue as minutely regulated as a minuet. She is distinguished
from her contemporaries by the balanced construction, the finish
and the harmony of her novels. (T.T.B.)

M1949 McCabe, Bernard, "The Guises of Love," Commonweal, 83:270-3,
December 3, 1965.

Iris Murdoch has become fashionable as a novelist during the past
decade because her interests as a novelist have coincided with major
preoccupations of the reading public. For example, her protagonists,
who are alienated, are invariably in search of their own identities.
(D.P.)

M1950 Maes-Jelinek, Hena, "A House for Free Characters: The Novels
of Iris Murdoch," Revue des Langues Vivantes, 29:45-69, 1963.

". . . strongly indebted to existentialism," Iris Murdoch maintains
in her novels that "man exists . . . through action . . . and is responsible for his own life. The free act . . . proceeds directly from
instinctive life . . . [and] each man must find his own rules of conduct." (G.C.)

M1951 Martin, Graham, "Iris Murdoch and the Symbolist Novel," British
Journal of Aesthetics, 5:296-300, July, 1965.

"Iris Murdoch's most successful novels are . . . clearly within the
symbolist mode which she anathematizes in the Encounter article.
. . . But they . . . assert no symbolist autonomy from experience,
and as part of this the characters are made . . . resistant to the
schematic demands of the allegorical structure." (D.P.)

M1952 Meidner, Olga McDonald, "The Progress of Iris Murdoch,"
English Studies in Africa, 4:17-38, March, 1961.

The intellectual and the moralist threaten to oust the observer of
life at large and the stylist in Iris Murdoch's work. (R.K.)

M1953 Morrell, Roy, "Iris Murdoch: The Early Novels," Critical
Quarterly, 9:272-82, Autumn, 1967.

Whether Iris Murdoch has distorted human realities through the use
of extravagances of incident and symbol is "a vital question." In
The Sandcastle she shows a "drift into private worlds that hold no
future." In Under the Net she shows characters who "bump into each
other" as she had accused Sartre's characters of doing. In The Bell
she continues to write of "actions and their truthfulness." (V.E.)

M1954 Murdoch, Iris, "Against Dryness: A Polemical Sketch,"
Encounter, 16:16-20, January, 1961.

The chief feature of our present dilemma "is that we have been left
with far too shallow and flimsy an idea of human personality." However, "through literature we can re-discover a sense of the density
of our lives. Literature can arm us against consolation and fantasy
and can help us to recover from the ailments of Romanticism. . . .
But [to do this] . . . prose must recover its former glory, eloquence
and discourse must return." (D.P.)

M1955 Murdoch, Iris, "The Darkness of Practical Reason," Encounter,
27:46-50, July, 1966.

"Moral freedom . . . cannot, it seems to me, be defined without
reference to virtue. . . . To be free is . . . to exist sanely without
fear and to perceive what is real." In his Freedom of the Individual
"Hampshire sees the enemy of freedom in . . . the sinister influence
of will upon belief. . . . I would see the enemy of freedom as fantasy,
a bad use of imagination. . . ." (D.P.)

M1956 Murdoch, Iris, "A House of Theory," Partisan Review, 26:17-31,
Winter, 1959.

"The discrediting of theory [in England] has, then, taken place as a
result of a combination of different tendencies: Tory scepticism,
Benthamite scepticism, a Kantian protestant fear of 'superstitions,'
and more recently a dislike of Marxism, all apparently supported by
the anti-metaphysical destructive techniques of modern philosophy."
However, "all that the anti-metaphysical arguments make clear
. . . is that moral theorizing . . . is an activity whose purpose and
justification are moral." (D.P.)

M1957 Murdoch, Iris, "The Idea of Perfection," Yale Review, 53:342-80,
March, 1964.

The task of modern philosophers is "the provision of rich and fertile
conceptual schemes which help us to reflect upon and understand the
nature of moral progress and moral failure and the reasons for the
divergence of one moral temperament from another. And I would
wish to make my theory undercut its existential rivals by suggesting
that it is possible in terms of the former to explain why people are
obsessed with the latter, but not vice versa." (D.P.)

M1958 Murdoch, Iris, "The Sublime and the Beautiful Revisited," Yale
Review, 49:247-71, December, 1959.

". . . I think one may be enlightened by connecting the question: Is
the Liberal-democratic theory of personality an adequate one? with
the question: What is characteristic of the greatest literary works
of art?. . . . I shall be concerned here mainly with the novel, and I
approach the problem as a novelist concerned with the creation of
character." (D.P.)

M1959 Murdoch, Iris, "The Sublime and the Good," Chicago Review,
13:42-55, Autumn, 1959.

"Our direct apprehension of which works of art are good has just as
much authority, engages our moral and intellectual being just as
deeply, as our philosophical reflections upon art in general. . . .
Our aesthetic must stand to be judged by great works of art which
we know to be such independently. . . ." (D.P.)

M1960 Murray, William M., "A Note on the Iris Murdoch Manuscripts in
the University of Iowa Libraries," Modern Fiction Studies,
15:445-8, Autumn, 1969.

[This is a detailed description of the holograph manuscripts for
eight of Iris Murdoch's novels acquired by the University of Iowa
Library.] (G.C.)

M1961 O'Connor, William Van, "Iris Murdoch: The Formal and the Con-
tingent," Critique: Studies in Modern Fiction, 3:34-46, Winter-
Spring, 1960.

Iris Murdoch's four novels and her non-fiction reveal her indebtedness to Sartre, or "at least a view of the human situation very like
his." Further, Miss Murdoch feels that the recent emphasis on
formal control has limited the possibilities of the modern novel.
(G.O.)

M1962 Rose, W. K., "An Interview with Iris Murdoch," Shenandoah,
19:3-22, Winter, 1968.

[In this comprehensive interview Iris Murdoch presents her views
on life, art and philosophy.] (G.C.)

M1963 Souvage, Jacques, "The Novels of Iris Murdoch," Studia Germanica Gandensia, 4:225-52, 1962.

A conception of morality as " 'a technique for discovering more about what is real' . . . is central to all Iris Murdoch's work." (G.C.)

M1964 Weatherhead, A. K., "Backgrounds with Figures in Iris Murdoch," Texas Studies in Literature and Language, 10:635-48, Winter, 1969.

The paradigm of Murdoch's novels is that of a person entering and withdrawing from the orbit of an enchanter. Environment is broadly conceived, extending from a person's country to his body as the background of his mind. The drama of the novel is enacted not only between person and person but between person and environment. (M.R.)

M1965 Whiteside, George, "The Novels of Iris Murdoch," Critique: Studies in Modern Fiction, 7:27-47, Spring, 1964.

"Miss Murdoch is a realist and a realistic satirist. She looks at the world without romantic preconceptions, without bitterness or loathing. . . . Five of her seven novels are about main characters who develop romantic preconceptions, act on them, lose them, and thus are back where they started." (W.G.F.)

M1966 Widmann, R. L., "An Iris Murdoch Checklist," Critique: Studies in Modern Fiction, 10:17-29, No. 1, 1968.

[This checklist is arranged in four parts, covering all of Murdoch's work to date, plus reviews, general criticism and interviews. The four parts are: 1. novels and book length works arranged chronologically, followed by reviews both anonymous and alphabetically by author; 2. articles, alphabetically by title; 3. general criticism of Murdoch in books or parts of books; and 4. general criticism of Murdoch in articles and reviews.] (V.E.)

THE BELL

M1967 Gérard, Albert, "Iris Murdoch," Le Revue Nouvelle, 39:633-40, June 15, 1964.

The Bell is an ambitious work in which what might be called "schemes récurrents" are used to define at the same time both the conditions of a certain moral perfection and a hierarchy of modes of living. (W.G.F.)

THE BELL   (cont'd)

M1968 Jones, Dorothy, "Love and Morality in Iris Murdoch's The Bell, "
Meanjin Quarterly, 26:85-90, March, 1967.

Miss Murdoch has stated that " 'the essence of . . . [art and
morals] is love. . . . Love, and so art and morals, is the discovery
of reality.' This relationship between art, morality and love is the
central theme of . . . The Bell. " (G.C.)

M1969 Kaehele, Sharon, and Howard German, "The Discovery of Reality in
Iris Murdoch's The Bell, " PMLA, 82:554-63, December, 1967.

"In her novels Miss Murdoch tries to correct the current oversim-
plified concept of man by delineating with great persuasiveness both
the complexity and diversity of human beings and the complicated
relationship between the individual and society; in The Bell the ideas
which emerge from a very credible fictional world are concerned
with the inadequacy of absolute moral codes, the nature of love,
reality, the irrational, and freedom. " (D.A.B.)

M1970 McGinnis, Robert M., "Murdoch's The Bell, " Explicator, 28:
Item 1, September, 1969.

Both Murdoch's The Bell and Hauptmann's Die versunkene Glocke
"are about the interactions between a Christian community and its
pagan dissentients. " (D.P.)

M1971 Souvage, Jacques, "Symbol as Narrative Device: An Interpretation
of Iris Murdoch's The Bell, " English Studies, 43:81-96, April, 1962.

The Bell occupies a special position among Iris Murdoch's novels in
that it is steeped in morality. Its characters are seeking the Good
Life. The bell is the symbol of this moral life. Murdoch sees
maturity as "ability to live without illusion, " suggesting that illusion
is a "temptation to be resisted. " The symbol of the bell as the vision
that "the moral life is a search for objective reality" has been articulated into the plot by Murdoch.   (V.E.)

M1972 Wall, Stephen, "The Bell in The Bell, " Essays in Criticism,
13:265-73, July, 1963.

"The importance of the bell in this novel is that it assists in the
. . . unfolding [of the characters]. Its meaning is shifting, not
residual, and lies in its relation to the main characters in the story,
rather than in any property in itself. " (K.M.W.)

BRUNO'S DREAM

M1973 Ivasheva, V. V., "Ot Sartra k Platonu," Voprosy literatury, 13:134-55, November, 1969.

Although England didn't have its Heidegger, Jaspers, Sartre and Camus, some English writers, i.e., Iris Murdoch, approached existentialism. Her latest work, Bruno's Dream, is, however, Platonic in philosophy. In it she manifested a "victory of philosophic optimism over philosophic pessimism." (V.D.)

M1974 Thomson, P. W., "Iris Murdoch's Honest Puppetry--The Characters of Bruno's Dream," Critical Quarterly, 11:277-83, Autumn, 1969.

Even Iris Murdoch's admirers have been irritated by her "tendency towards extravaganza." The complaint that she over-agitates her "puppets" is heard, but it appears that this is essential to her writing. In Bruno's Dream the convention is not realistic, but ritualistic. Murdoch's characters must be distinguished by what they recognize rather than what they are. (V.E.)

THE FLIGHT FROM THE ENCHANTER

M1975 Meidner, Olga McDonald, "Reviewer's Bane: A Study of Iris Murdoch's The Flight From the Enchanter," Essays in Criticism, 11:435-47, October, 1961.

Iris Murdoch's The Flight From the Enchanter is "extremely interesting--a brilliant failure, highly original, superbly audacious, fatally over-ambitious." The "enchanter" of the title is complex, although seen as evil by others in the novel is really not as mysterious as he seems. The mixture of reality and symbolism is "confusing." (V.E.)

THE NICE AND THE GOOD

M1976 Baldanza, Frank, "The Nice and the Good," Modern Fiction Studies, 15:417-28, Autumn, 1969.

". . . 'the nice' and 'the good' of the title refers, respectively, to the kind of human love represented by the many pairings-off in the final chapters and to a selfless, transcendent spiritual love. A kind of selflessness, however, is common to the best of both loves. . . . Thus, the cause of the novel is toward the exorcism of the obsessive demons of selfish preoccupation. . . ." (D.A.B.)

THE RED AND THE GREEN

M1977 Kemp, Peter, "The Fight Against Fantasy: Iris Murdoch's The Red and the Green," Modern Fiction Studies, 15:403-15, Autumn, 1969.

The Red and the Green "is in the same tradition as the majority of Miss Murdoch's fictions, though noticeably less complex. . . ." (G.C.)

A SEVERED HEAD

M1978 Gregor, Ian, "Towards a Christian Literary Criticism," Month, 33:239-49, April, 1965.

"The two novels [Women in Love and A Severed Head] not only illuminate each other, but suggest something of the way in which the novel encapsulates the world where modern Christianity takes its shape and form." (D.A.B.)

M1979 Kenney, Alice P., "The Mythic History of A Severed Head," Modern Fiction Studies, 15:387-401, Autumn, 1969.

". . . A Severed Head demonstrates that the use of history is to illuminate the events of our own times, while the use of myth is to provide a framework for understanding the facts of our own experience." (G.C.)

UNDER THE NET

M1980 Bradbury, Malcolm, "Iris Murdoch's Under the Net," Critical Quarterly, 4:47-54, Spring, 1962.

Iris Murdoch's Under the Net was associated with the "angry" movement of the 1950's, but it is "dominated by an imagination of a strikingly different order from that of the other 'angries'." The hero, Jake, in many ways a typical hero of the fifties, is in the complex philosophical quandary of being torn between the aesthetic and the social. (V.E.)

M1981 Porter, Raymond J., "Leitmotiv in Iris Murdoch's Under the Net," Modern Fiction Studies, 15:379-85, Autumn, 1969.

". . . the initial attitude Jake [Donoghue] has toward life and the change he undergoes are not only dramatized through conversation

UNDER THE NET   (cont'd)

and action but also woven into the very texture of the novel through the author's use of diction, image and symbol." (G.C.)

M1982 Souvage, Jacques, "The Unresolved Tension: An Interpretation of Iris Murdoch's Under the Net," Revue des Langues Vivantes, 26:420-30, No. 6, 1960.

"The unresolved tension between theme and plot in Under the Net is . . . seen to be the outcome of the fact that this novel mirrors a divided idiosyncracy rather than a fully realized artistic consciousness." (D.P.)

M1983 Widmann, R. L., "Murdoch's Under the Net: Theory and Practice of Fiction," Critique: Studies in Modern Fiction, 10:5-16, No. 1, 1968.

"Miss Murdoch is not a great novelist . . . because she does not really create the free characters she finds essential in great art. She does follow some of her own theory, particularly in use of disciplined, aesthetic language and in presenting the accidental, unexpected, and fortuitous." (K.M.W.)

AN UNOFFICIAL ROSE

M1984 Pondrom, Cyrena Norman, "Iris Murdoch: An Existentialist?" Comparative Literature Studies, 5:403-19, December, 1968.

The themes of An Unofficial Rose indicate that Iris Murdoch shares many views with Jean-Paul Sartre, but also indicate her "dissociation from a simply existential position and show her to combine elements from both the existential and empirical traditions and from the metaphysical and social novel." (V.E.)

MURDOCH, WALTER

M1985 Craig, Clifford, "Memories of Walter Murdoch," Overland, 44:34-5, Autumn, 1970.

[These are memories of the small circle of intellectuals in Melbourne of which both Walter Murdoch and the author's father were members.] (K.M.W.)

M1986 Durack, Mary, "Walter Murdoch: The Man in the Mirror,"
Meanjin Quarterly, 28:217-20, June, 1969.

In Walter Murdoch's essays "realistic thinking, based on the study
of mankind, was always one of his strongest platforms, but nothing
ever led him to adopt a philosophy of despair." (G.C.)

M1987 Phillips, A. A., "Walter Murdoch: The Art of Good-Humoured
Devastation," Meanjin Quarterly, 28:221-3, June, 1969.

[This is a "good humoured" appreciation of Murdoch's accomplishment as an essayist.] (G.C.)

M1988 Triebel, Louis A., "Walter Murdoch: Australia's Premier Essayist,"
South Atlantic Quarterly, 49:556-67, Autumn, 1960.

Walter Murdoch's "essays are easy and conversational, whimsi-
cally humorous but wise, and often with a serious undertone. They
can well stand comparison with those of the masters of the genre."
(D.P.)

M1989 Triebel, Louis, "Walter Murdoch: Essayist," Meanjin Quarterly,
28:209-16, June, 1969.

Murdoch's essays reveal "literary quality," and economy of language. His "utterances" betray "neither weakness nor mawkish
statement." (G.C.)

MURRAY, GILBERT

M1990 Curgenven, Arthur. "Gilbert Murray: Some Memories,"
Meanjin Quarterly, 17:267-76, September, 1958.

"Gilbert Murray, as a public figure, won a twofold fame" as an
"eminent professor" and a "great humanist." "My subject here is
a third Gilbert Murray. During twenty years and more we were
near neighbours on Boar's Hill, near Oxford, and I saw a good deal
of him in his private life." (D.A.B.)

M1991 Panichas, George A., "A Tribute to Gilbert Murray," Classical
Journal, 53:62-6, October, 1957.

"It has been well said that Murray, through his outstanding translations of the great Greek dramas, 'brought Greek drama back to the
modern stage'." "To the modern war-torn world that has in one way

or another forgotten the significance of Hellenism . . . Murray
managed somehow to show the hollow meaning of material power.
He focused much needed attention on Hellenism. . . ." (D.P.)

M1992 Price, Lucien, "Gilbert Murray at Ninety," Atlantic Monthly,
197:76-9, January, 1956.

Both Shaw and Murray "are dramatists, but they are antithetical.
. . . Shaw's influence is wide; Murray's is deep, a force that works
in the cellarage among the massive arches of foundation thought.
Shaw, in spirit, is Hebraist; Murray is Hellenist." Yet, "the heart
of Murray's work is . . . in three of his finest books of scholarship
. . . [:] The Rise of the Greek Epic . . . Five Stages of Greek
Religion . . . [and] The Classical Tradition of Poetry. . . ."
(D.P.)

M1993 West, Paul, "Gilbert Murray: 'Civic Monk'," Dalhousie Review,
41:57-64, Spring, 1961.

"Murray emerges as one of the most active, most unshakable avators
of aristocratic humanism." "There is that quality of him: his sense
of belonging to a beleaguered generation, of witnessing an abysmal
militarism . . . his essentially civilized conscience. . . . It is a
wonder, then, that he showed so much balance, so little contumely."
(D.P.)

MURRAY, THOMAS C.

M1994 Conlin, Matthew T., O.F.M., "T. C. Murray: Ireland on the
Stage," Renascence, 13:125-31, Spring, 1961.

"Murray brought to the stage a realistic and fully sympathetic treatment of the religious spirit of the largest segment of Irish life, the
country." (R.K.)

M1995 Ó h-Aodha, Micheál, "T. C. Murray and Some Critics," Studies,
47:185-91, Summer, 1958.

"In at least six of his fifteen plays, Murray has given us not only
the most authentic expression of country ways but a profound criticism of life in rural Ireland. It is unlikely that he will ever be
surpassed in the distinctive genre of the peasant play." (D.A.B.)

MURRY, JOHN MIDDLETON

M1996 Beer, J. B., "John Middleton Murry," Critical Quarterly, 3:59-66, Spring, 1961.

Murry "lacked the positive assertions, the individual position which we look for in a great critic, but not the wise passiveness of a fine one." (J.N.P.)

M1997 Crépin, André, "John Middleton Murry et le sens állégorique de la vie," Études Anglaises, 14:321-30, October-December, 1961.

Murry saw his personal life as a symbolic parallel to and commentary on the state of society. (C.E.N.)

M1998 Fogle, Richard Harter, "Beauty and Truth: John Middleton Murry on Keats," D. H. Lawrence Review, 2:68-75, Spring, 1969.

"Like some other romantics, he knows and is obsessed with one great truth--Oneness--and without quite realizing it he is always striking inwards at it, though from many angles and directions. . . . Murry does not give the difficulties to be faced, the oppositions to be reconciled, enough provisional reality to convince us that he has really faced them, and has genuinely accomplished the romantic mission." (K.M.W.)

M1999 Girard, Denis, "John Middleton Murry, D. H. Lawrence et Albert Schweitzer," Études Anglaises, 12:212-21, July-September, 1959.

When they met in June 1913 it appeared to Murry and Lawrence that they had much in common. However, fundamental differences in their personalities and approaches to life manifested themselves. The break came in January 1926 (as confirmed in a previously unpublished Lawrence letter). In Son of Woman Murry explained Lawrence as a visionary and a philosopher; he was not "a great artist." In his last work Love, Freedom and Society, Murry acknowledged Lawrence's artistry, but, in his concentration on Lawrence's personality, compared him to Schweitzer. (D.P.)

M2000 Griffin, Ernest G., "The Circular and the Linear: The Middleton Murry--D. H. Lawrence Affair," D. H. Lawrence Review, 2:76-92, Spring, 1969.

". . . at a certain point for a short distance together, Murry and Lawrence met and felt that they had a common destiny; but Murry soon began a circuitous course separating at an ever greater distance from the tangential course of Lawrence." (D.P.)

M2001 Griffith, Philip M., "Middleton Murry on Swift: The Nec Plus Ultra of Objectivity?" D. H. Lawrence Review, 2:60-7, Spring, 1969.

"The two overriding and overlapping hypotheses that gave birth to his critical biography of Swift, highly personal and highly 'emotional' hypotheses [Swift's behavior to women and his scatology], make his view of Swift, at bottom, unsatisfactory and unreliable. Murry's book can scarcely live up to his aim at 'the nec plus ultra of objectivity'." (K.M.W.)

M2002 Heath, William W., "The Literary Criticism of John Middleton Murry," PMLA, 70:47-57, March, 1955.

Contemporary criticism neglects the valuable "system of literary evaluation" which preceded Murry's later romanticism. ". . . many of his apparently vague criteria and methods have concrete, but concealed, referents." Thus his present "banishment" is undeserved. (J.R.B.)

M2003 Kaufmann, R. J., "On Using an Obsessed Critic: John Middleton Murry," Graduate Student of English, 3:4-8, Winter, 1960.

There is great critical utility in Murry's "unprofessional" obsessions with life and morality. As an artist manqué, Murry read "to find out what he was thinking himself." Unlike the professional critics, too, Murry is not disturbed at his failure to unravel a mystery, to answer all questions. (E.L.)

M2004 Lea, F. A., "Murry and Marriage," D. H. Lawrence Review, 2:1-23, Spring, 1969.

Like Katherine Mansfield, Murry was a social déraciné, devoid, when they met, not merely of the ease of living which goes with a familiar society, but of all those accepted standards of good and bad, right and wrong, which most of us assimilate unconsciously and few of us ever question." [Includes a letter by Murry on marriage.] (D.P.)

M2005 Murry, Mary Middleton, "Katherine Mansfield and John Middleton Murry," London Magazine, 6:69-71, April, 1959.

[These are recollections of Katherine Mansfield and her second husband, John Middleton Murry.] (D.P.)

M2006 Seymour-Smith, Martin, "Zero and the Impossible," Encounter, 9:38-51, November, 1957.

Roy Campbell, Wyndham Lewis, Cary and Murry were alike in striving to create a poetic idiom, a language in which it is possible to communicate an apprehension of reality. Paradoxically, Campbell, the poet, was least successful, and Lewis came closest to success. (D.B.D.)

M2007 Stanford, Derek, "Middleton Murry as Literary Critic," Essays in Criticism, 8:60-7, January, 1958.

"Murry once distinguished between the 'scientists of art' . . . and the 'philosophic critic.'. . . The philosophic critic is concerned not with facts but with ranking intuitions in their right order. This was Murry's self-appointed labour; and though his writing is not closely systematic, there is an extraordinary consistency about it." (K.M. W.)

M2008 Stanford, Derek, "Middleton Murry as Literary Critic," South Atlantic Quarterly, 58:196-205, Spring, 1959.

A fine critic, John Middleton Murry stressed the importance of unity in great and small art. A romantic, he believed in "personal" contact between the critic and the work. Contentious, he was willing to defend his judgments. (W.B.B.)

M2009 Watson, J. H., "A Good Workman and His Friends: Recollections of John Middleton Murry," London Magazine, 26:51-5, May, 1959.

Murry was a hard worker, faithful friend, and provocative critic who preferred the company of workingmen to that of the literary coteries. (M.H.M.)

THE NECESSITY OF COMMUNISM

M2010 Rees, Richard, "Politics of a Mystic," D. H. Lawrence Review, 2:24-31, Spring, 1969.

Murry's The Necessity of Communism demonstrates "how much truth he was able to combine even in his worst writing with extravagant and intemperate fantasy. For the book does exhibit him almost at his worst. . . ." (D. P.)

THE PROBLEM OF STYLE

M2011 Bennett, James R., "The Problem of Style," D. H. Lawrence Review, 2:32-46, Spring, 1969.

"The most damaging defect [of Murry's The Problem of Style] is its omission of fundamental elements of imaginative literature. . . . Point of view . . . receives no mention. Although Murry recognizes the existence of the persona in literature, he focuses excessively upon the author. . . . Contemporary stylisticians will be offended especially by Murry's disregard of syntax. . . . But . . . a careful consideration of the whole of The Problem of Style will partly resolve these objections and allow it a continued place among valuable introductions to the critical reading of literature." (D. P.)

SHAKESPEARE

M2012 Thayer, C. G., "Murry's Shakespeare," D. H. Lawrence Review, 2:47-59, Spring, 1969.

"If some of Murry's personal qualities made it impossible for him to write a totally satisfying book on Shakespeare, they contributed to his writing an extraordinarily attractive one. . . . Murry was in effect an almost super-romantic critic who opened his consciousness to the enormous power of the Shakespearean influence. If he allowed himself to be ravished by Shakespeare, one can hardly accuse him of bad taste." (D. P.)

MUSIL, ROBERT

M2013 Baudry, Jean-Louis, "L'Intelligence en questions," Tel Quel, No. 13, pp. 64-6, Spring, 1963.

In Der Mann ohne Eigenschaften Musil started the conflict between action and contemplation, incarnated in the relations of man and woman. In <u>Drei Frauen</u> and to a lesser extent in <u>Vereinigungen</u> he continues his theme. (T.T.B.)

M2014 Berghahn, Wilfried, "Ärgernisse einer Musil-Deutung," <u>Neue Rundschau</u>, 74:284-96, No. 2, 1963.

Psychoanalytical analysis of an author, and interpretation of his works, are two different things. Kept separate, each can contribute profitably to the other. In <u>Robert Musil--Eine Einführung in das Werk</u>, Kaiser and Wilkins refuse to recognize limitations of method, and resort to flagrant misreadings to support preconceived conclusions. (R.H.L.)

M2015 Braun, W., "Musil's Siamese Twins," <u>Germanic Review</u>, 33:41-52, February, 1958.

By means of a highly experimental solution, Musil recreates that ancient state of <u>Gleichnis</u> and metaphor and the unity between reality and imagination which man has lost in modern times. His symbolic solution for the dilemma of our own generation makes his work one of the most daring and speculative novels of our time. (C.S.P.)

M2016 Brosthaus, Heribert, "Robert Musils 'Wahre Antithese'," <u>Wirkendes Wort</u>, 14:120-40, April, 1964.

Musil's mysticism is so illuminated by the clear powers of reason that "poetry embraces as a unity the polarity of the two realms [rationality and mysticism], which are divided from one another in time." (J.R.R.)

M2017 Henninger, Peter, "Le Dernier livre de Robert Musil," <u>Critique</u>, No. 221, pp. 841-52, October, 1965.

Throughout his career, Musil has not ceased laying claim to a part of his work, multiplying references to his previous works and recommencing repeatedly an historical account in which he tries to define the precise place and function of them. (T.T.B.)

M2018 Karthaus, Ulrich, "Musil-Forschung und Musil-Deutung: Ein Literaturbericht," <u>Deutsche Vierteljahrsschrift für Literaturwissenschaft und Geistesgeschichte</u>, 39:441-83, September, 1965.

[This is a critical survey of research concerning Musil, the texts of his works and their interpretation.] (J.R.R.)

M2019 Kermode, Frank, "Robert Musil," Kenyon Review, 28:224-30,
March, 1966.

Musil belongs "to the same class as Joyce and Mann." His novel,
The Man Without Qualities, "is a work of fantastic intelligence, of
pervasive eroticism, of completely original mysticism"; his stories
"suggest a map of reality with an orientation at first strange and unfamiliar." (G.S.)

M2020 Leppmann, Wolfgang, "Zum Goethebild bei Robert Musil, Hermann
Broch und Ernst Jünger," Monatshefte, 54:145-55, April-May, 1962.

Musil, Broch, and Jünger show in their concepts of Goethe a unanim-
ity which outweighs their disparity in biography, politics, and art.
The unifying characteristics they share with Goethe, despite their
modern familiarity with the abyss of despair, are: science, knowledge of man's mind in crisis, poetry as an autochtonous force.
(R.H.L.)

M2021 Müller, Gerd, "Mathematik und Transzendenz: Die Bedeutung
Novalis' für das Werk Robert Musils," Orbis Litterarum,
23:265-75, 1968.

Musil and Novalis are linked by a passion for exactness, thence for a
joining of the mathematical with the transcendental. They differ in
that Novalis is optimistic, Musil pessimistic. Analogy and continuity,
safe roads for Novalis, are for Musil no more than bridge piers,
leading over abysses from one unknown to another. (R.H.L.)

M2022 Pelz, Werner, "In Pursuit of Love," Listener, 17:778-9, May 3,
1962.

"What all Musil's writings have in common is this: like the Russian
novel . . . they are all attempts to explore a country without sign-
posts where everything has still to be established in the inner and
outer world of the characters." (K.M.W.)

M2023 Prawer, S. S., "Robert Musil and the 'Uncanny'," Oxford German
Studies, 3:163-82, 1968.

In his diary and letters "as in Der Mann ohne Eigenschaften, it is in
the sense of automatism, the sense of action without apparent meaning,
which is the chief factor" in Musil's attributions of the feelings of the
uncanny. Also, in Die Verwirrungen des Zöglings Törless "uncanny"
sensations "play a particularly important part." (D.P.)

M2024 Seidler, Ingo, "Das Nietzschebild Robert Musils," Deutsche Vierteljahrsschrift für Literaturwissenschaft und Geistesgeschichte, 39:329-49, September, 1965.

Nietzsche defined and delimited the problems which were poetically refashioned by Musil. (J.R.R.)

M2025 Silone, Ignazio, "Begegnung mit Musil," Forum, 12:82-5, February, 1965.

"Musil achieves original and enduring significance not as a philosopher, not as a scientist, not as the inventor of a new religion, but as an artist totally devoted to his work. The true incomparable strength and dignity of Der Mann ohne Eigenschaften is the author himself, who, struggling with his utopia, rests within this work like one buried alive." (J.R.R.)

M2026 Wilkins, Eithne, "The Musil Manuscripts and a Project for a Musil Society," Modern Language Review, 62:451-8, July, 1967.

[This is the history of the Musil manuscripts and of recent attempts to make them more available to interested persons.] (J.R.R.)

DIE AMSEL

M2027 Krotz, Frederick W., "Robert Musils Die Amsel, novellistische Gestaltung einer Psychose," Modern Austrian Literature, 3:7-38, Spring, 1970.

Musil has effected an identity between a schizophrenic paleosymbol and a novelistic symbol--the blackbird-nightingale-airplane. The novelistic symbol unites and expresses the various content levels of the narrative. (R.H.L.)

DREI FRAUEN

M2028 Boa, Elizabeth J., "Austrian Ironies in Musil's Drei Frauen," Modern Language Review, 63:119-31, January, 1968.

"How much Robert Musil belongs in, yet stands outside the Austrian literary tradition is nowhere more evident than in his trilogy of Novellen, Drei Frauen. . . . More than a restatement they represent, rather, a radical critique of these most Austrian preoccupations." (J.R.R.)

DREI FRAUEN (cont'd)

M2029 Kichberger, Lida, "Musil's Trilogy: An Approach to Drei Frauen, "
Monatshefte, 55:167-82, April-May, 1963.

"Grigia," "Tonka," and "Die Portugiesin, " the Drei Frauen,
reflect a timeless theme. They comprise an analogue of Freud's
analysis of the three choices in Merchant of Venice. While reflecting Musil's concern with Bachofen's principle of unlimited hetaerism,
they also demonstrate his superiority to timebound expressionism.
(R.H.L.)

M2030 McCormick, E. Allen, "Ambivalence in Musil's Drei Frauen: Notes
on Meaning and Method, " Monatshefte, 54:183-96, April-May, 1962.

These three stories well illustrate that the peculiar tone of Musil's
narratives depends on the paradoxical juxtaposition of clarity and
mystery--in Musil's words, Genauigkeit and Seele. Examples are:
the ambivalence of point of view, non-rational integration of language,
and resolution or insight through, but not necessarily in, tragedy.
(R.H.L.)

GRIGIA

M2031 Bedwell, Carol B., "Musil's 'Grigia': An Analysis of Cultural
Dissolution, " Seminar, 3:117-26, Fall, 1967.

". . . if the story . . . is regarded . . . from the point of view of
. . . sociology . . . Homo then becomes a collective hero whose
personal downfall is analogous to the decline of European culture in
the first two decades of the twentieth century. " (G.C.)

M2032 Hermand, Jost, "Musils 'Grigia', " Monatshefte, 54:171-82,
April-May, 1962.

The motifs are: the mine, interpretable as a tunnel into the subconscious; the gold, man's inchoate drives, also an epitome of
genuineness; the feminine, reproductive and destructive. The unifying basis is man's primeval and repressed religious-mythical
element. Not expressionistic and not a manifest, this story is essentially an analysis. (R.H.L.)

ISIS UND OSIRIS

M2033 Titche, Leon L., Jr., " 'Isis und Osiris': An Interpretation of
Robert Musil's Poem, " Kentucky Foreign Language Quarterly,
13:165-9, 1966.

"Robert Musil's poem 'Isis und Osiris' displays the hermaphroditic
theme within a solid mythological framework. " (G.C.)

THE MAN WITHOUT QUALITIES--See
DER MANN OHNE EIGENSCHAFTEN

DER MANN OHNE EIGENSCHAFTEN

M2034 Bauer, Gerhard, "Die 'Auflösung des anthropozentrischen Verhaltens'
im modernen Roman: Dargestellt an Musils Mann ohne Eigenschaften, "
Deutsche Vierteljahrsschrift für Literaturwissenschaft und Geistesgeschichte, 42:677-701, November, 1968.

Using Musil's Mann ohne Eigenschaften as an example, one may
assert that "in order to judge the modern novel justly, we must
balance the loss in understandability and formal completeness with
the gain in general problematics and the sharper awareness of form. "
(J.R.R.)

M2035 Braun, Wilhelm, "Moosbrugger Dances, " Germanic Review,
35:214-30, October, 1960.

In Der Mann ohne Eigenschaften Moosbrugger is the typical "unbe-
hauste Mensch" of our time. Despite his previous schizophrenic
alternation between unequivocal and metaphorical thinking, he enters
a new, mystic state when he dances in jail. Moosbrugger is a catalyst in the hero's striving for the original vital state of metaphor.
(R.H.L.)

M2036 Braun, Wilhelm, "Musil and the Pendulum of the Intellect, "
Monatshefte, 49:109-19, No. 3, 1957.

"If Musil wants primarily to reveal the intellectual crisis that was
reflected in the outbreak of the war, he clarifies specifically the
relationship on the one hand between various ideologies, and between
ideas and power on the other. " (J.R.R.)

DER MANN OHNE EIGENSCHAFTEN (cont'd)

M2037 Braun, Wilhelm, "Musil's 'Erdensekretariat der Genauigkeit und Seele,' a Clue to the Philosophy of the Hero of Der Mann ohne Eigenschaften," Monatshefte, 46:305-16, November, 1954.

"One alternative to grappling with the whole novel is to select one cardinal aspect of the book, in this case the philosophy of its main character, and try to analyze it in the hope that such a partial examination will illumine the work as a whole." (J.R.R.)

M2038 Braun, Wilhelm, "Musil's Musicians," Monatshefte, 52:9-17, January, 1960.

In Der Mann ohne Eigenschaften the hero's close friends, Walter and Clarisse, a married couple, are musicians. The ironical description of their playing helps Musil stress that it is emotional rather than physical union during which the borders between the ego and the world seem to vanish. (R.H.L.)

M2039 Braun, Wilhelm, "The Temptation of Ulrich: The Problem of True and False Unity in Musil's Der Mann ohne Eigenschaften," German Quarterly, 29:29-37, January, 1956.

". . . Ulrich's rejection of Arnheim and his fraud and his empire . . . contains the essence of the novel, the acceptance of true unity as the aim to be pursued." (J.R.R.)

M2040 Brosthaus, Heribert, "Zur Struktur und Entwicklung des 'anderen Zustands' in Robert Musils Der Mann ohne Eigenschaften," Deutsche Vierteljahrsschrift für Literaturwissenschaft und Geistesgeschichte, 39:388-440, September, 1965.

[The author gives a detailed analysis of what Musil might have meant by the "other state" in his unfinished novel Der Mann ohne Eigenschaften.] (J.R.R.)

M2041 David, Claude, "Form und Gehalt in Robert Musils Mann ohne Eigenschaften," Euphorion, 64:221-30, 1970.

Musil's novel "belongs in this series of novels--which today hardly exist anymore--which wanted to present a total picture of the times, a complete diagnosis of man, a total overview of one single gigantic work." (J.R.R.)

DER MANN OHNE EIGENSCHAFTEN (cont'd)

M2042 Heydebrand, Renate von, "Zum Thema Sprache und Mystik in Robert Musils Roman Der Mann ohne Eigenschaften," Zeitschrift für Deutsche Philologie, 82:249-71, 1963.

The theme of the disparity between language and mystical experience of the world is realized, with some variations, in Musil's novel, which embraces the spiritual movement of the decades around 1900 from a later, heightened viewpoint. (K.M.W.)

M2043 Holmes, F. A., "Some Comic Elements in Musil's Der Mann ohne Eigenschaften," German Life and Letters, 18:25-9, October, 1964.

Musil's novel "makes few concessions to the reader. . . . The reader is rarely allowed to feel, but he may laugh as well as think. Yet he laughs at rather than with. Underlying the comic is serious satire and reformatory zeal." (J.R.R.)

M2044 Holmes, F. A., "Two Studies in Musil's Der Mann ohne Eigenschaften," German Life and Letters, 15:202-9, April, 1962.

Musil risks the dangers of "too much reflection and abstraction in Der Mann ohne Eigenschaften" and "of the narrator playing too great a part and destroying the work by exerting a stranglehold on it. . . . the claustrophobic effect of the work is partly the result of the emphasis given to the narrator." (K.M.W.)

M2045 Rasch, Wolfdietrich, "Zur Entstehung von Robert Musils Roman Der Mann ohne Eigenschaften," Deutsche Vierteljahrsschrift für Literaturwissenschaft und Geistesgeschichte, 39:350-87, September, 1965.

Musil's many sketches for his unfinished novel may have literary merit and be of great interest, but we should not try to fit together the unused pieces. (J.R.R.)

M2046 Reichert, Herbert W., "Nietzschean Influence in Musil's Der Mann ohne Eigenschaften," German Quarterly, 39:12-28, January, 1966.

The various published and unpublished components of Musil's novel, from 1898 to 1942, reveal initially a pronounced influence of Nietzsche, exemplified in the hero Ulrich's espousal of Nietzschean relativism, then nihilism. Though later Ulrich pointedly rejects Nietzscheanism, subsequent fragments indicate that this rejection was not definitive. (R.H.L.)

DER MANN OHNE EIGENSCHAFTEN   (cont'd)

M2047 Roth, Marie-Louise, "1938: Eine Neuerscheinung im Bermann
Fischer Verlag: Der dritte Band des Mann ohne Eigenschaften,"
Euphorion, 61:196-205, August, 1967.

[Reproductions of the publisher's advanced announcements are included in this presentation of the factual basis for the many hypotheses concerning Musil's never completed novel.] (J.R.R.)

M2048 Seeger, Lothar Georg, "Ibsens Wildente und Musils 'Kakanien',"
German Quarterly, 43:47-54, January, 1970.

In a marginal note Musil compared his concept of the Habsburg
Austrian situation with the plight of Hjalmar Ekdal in The Wild Duck.
The land of unreality, "Kakanien' in Der Mann ohne Eigenschaften,
resembles the attic room in Ibsen's play. (R.H.L.)

M2049 Seeger, Lothar Georg, "Zur Funktion Ulrichs im Mann ohne
Eigenschaften: Musils 'Monsieur Le vivisecteur' in der Kakanischen
Experimentallandschaft," Colloquia Germanica, 2:299-321, No. 3,
1968.

"In the figure of Ulrich is realized the poetic vision of the new man
within that graspable by language. (J.R.R.)

M2050 Titche, Leon L., Jr., "The Concept of the Hermaphrodite: Agathe
and Ulrich in Musil's Novel Der Mann ohne Eigenschaften," German
Life and Letters, 23:160-8, January, 1970.

". . . indeed, any interpretation of [Musil's] novel must begin with
the [hermaphroditic] myth, in order to approach one level of understanding of Musil's characters and their own longings and attain-
ments." (J.R.R.)

M2051 Wilkins, Eithne, "Der Mann ohne Eigenschaften and Musil's
'Steinbaukastenzeit'," Oxford German Studies, 3:183-205, 1968.

"In part . . . the divergence between the plan and the execution [of
Der Mann ohne Eigenschaften] is accounted for by the author's
attitude toward time. . . . in at least two of the many references to
'Steinbaukasten' that he associates with 'unreal' time, the 'Steinbaukasten' is associated with fixed ideas. . . ." (D.P.)

DER MANN OHNE EIGENSCHAFTEN (cont'd)

M2052 Wilkins, Eithne, und Ernst Kaiser, "Monstrum in Animo:
Bemerkungen zu einem bisher im Original unveröffentlichten
Manuskript aus dem Nachlass Robert Musils," Deutsche
Vierteljahrsschrift für Literaturwissenschaft und Geistesgeschichte,
37:78-119, 1963.

"Musil's deeply rooted uncertainty concerning his material reveals
itself everywhere and the changes in concept resulting from this
demanded again and again the reshaping of the plot, not only as a
whole, but also in details." (J.R.R.)

M2053 Wilkins, Eithne, "Musil's 'Affair of the Major's Wife' with an
Unpublished Text," Modern Language Review, 63:74-93, January,
1968.

The 'Affair of the Major's Wife' in Robert Musil's novel, Der Mann
ohne Eigenschaften, is an example of what makes the work so fascinating and so difficult. Investigation of the 'affair' yields information about Musil's method of working and a clue as to why the novel
was unfinished at the author's death in 1942." (J.R.R.)

DIE SCHWÄRMER

M2054 Braun, Wilhelm, "An Approach to Musil's Die Schwärmer,"
Monatshefte, 54:156-70, April-May, 1962.

Through varying interaction between characters Musil seeks to prove
the autonomy of the emotions. The emotions continue to be operative,
with or without present cause. Intense emotion overrides distinctions
between imagination and reality. This makes possible the immediate
apprehension of truth through the emotions. (R.H.L.)

M2055 Braun, Wilhelm, "Musil's Anselm and 'The Motivated Life',"
Wisconsin Studies in Contemporary Literature, 8:517-27, Autumn,
1967.

"By expanding the scope of Anselm's character, by making evil the
necessary part of achievement, Musil underscores the universal
scope of his approach." (J.R.R.)

DIE SCHWÄRMER   (cont'd)

M2056 Braun, Wilhelm, "Musil's Die Schwärmer," PMLA, 80:292-8, June, 1965.

"We can look upon Musil's Die Schwärmer, his visionaries, as an experiment on the way to a new, balanced man." (J.R.R.)

M2057 Scharanz, Michael, "Robert Musils theatralische Sendung," Forum, 12:255-8, May, 1965.

Musil's Die Schwärmer [1911] "is determined not by what happens, but by what is thought. Therefore it is not interested in a result, in a solution in the sense of the traditional determined coming-to-an-end." A spiritual relationship to the theater of the absurd is perhaps suggested. (J.R.R.)

THE TEMPTATION OF QUIET VERONICA--See
DIE VERSUCHUNG DER VERONIKA

THREE WOMEN--See
DREI FRAUEN

TONKA

M2058 Braun, Wilhelm, "An Interpretation of Musil's Novelle Tonka," Monatshefte, 53:73-85, February, 1961.

The nameless hero symbolizes modern scientific man, and Tonka symbolizes naive femininity. Musil thus anticipates the theoretical divisive basis of Der Mann ohne Eigenschaften. In Tonka Musil makes the main point that objectivity cannot apply to human affairs, which are relatable only to the emotions of the present. (R.H.L.)

M2059 Sokel, Walter H., "Kleist's Marquise of O., Kierkegaard's Abraham, and Musil's Tonka: Three Stages of the Absurd as the Touchstone of Faith," Wisconsin Studies in Contemporary Literature, 8:505-16, Autumn, 1967.

"All three works deal with situations in which faith contradicting human reason and experience is the problem. . . . Yet the terms in which the problem is posed in each work and the solution given (or withheld) delineates a shift which makes comparison a means for gauging a profound and symptomatic change in the spiritual history of Western man." (J.R.R.)

UNIONS--See
VEREINIGUNGEN

VEREINIGUNGEN

M2060 Schröder, Jürgen, "Am Grenzwert der Sprache: Zu Robert Musils Vereinigungen," Euphorion, 60:311-34, 1966.

The language of Vereinigungen is a calculated language of equation and minimal transition, in which Musil puts the potentiality of language to the test with a relentlessness never after repeated. The line between the real and the possible, between Genauigkeit and Seele is reduced linguistically to such fineness that it is all but unnoticeable. (R.H.L.)

DIE VERSUCHUNG DER VERONIKA

M2061 Geulen, Hans, "Robert Musils Die Versuchung der Veronika," Wirkendes Wort, 15:173-87, June, 1965.

The unusual thing about Musil's novella is "that its author draws an 'individual' truth, a truth which we regard as possible, which we evaluate but which we are not in a position to accept in any point. Nevertheless, we have the impression that a view, an insight into a possible and splendidly thought-out existence was created by the imagination of the poet." (J.R.R.)

DIE VERWIRRUNGEN DES ZÖGLINGS TÖRLESS

M2062 Braun, Wilhelm, "The Confusions of Törless," Germanic Review, 40:116-31, March, 1965.

The confusions of the adolescent hero of Musil's first novel revolve about his inability to perceive that the aspects of onrushing emotional experience, conditioned by a childhood trauma, cannot be subsumed in the category of logic and reason. Finally he comes to assume the coexistence of both kinds of awareness. (R.H.L.)

M2063 García Ponce, Juan, "Musil and Joyce," James Joyce Quarterly, 5:75-85, Winter, 1968.

Musil's "Young Törless is partially a developmental novel with a structure similar to that of A Portrait of the Artist as a Young Man, but . . . within an essentially German narrative tradition. . . . the style anticipates the tense tautness of the action. . . . the dry direct language moves forward jerkily in brief and concise paragraphs. In immediate contrast stands the open and evocative style

DIE VERWIRRUNGEN DES ZÖGLINGS TÖRLESS (cont'd)

of A Portrait by Joyce, moving along in vast rhythmic waves. . . . In Young Törless what interests us is the nature of the experience, whereas in A Portrait of the Artist as a Young Man obviously what matters is the personal decision the protagonist reaches. . . . " (D.P.)

M2064 Golden, Harry, "The Square Root of Minus One: Freud and Robert Musil's Törless," Comparative Literature, 17:117-32, Spring, 1965.

Freud has been a particularly strong influence on the "adolescent novel" genre: Musil's Törless is the earliest adolescent novel, or novel of any sort, to show such influence. (C.E.N.)

M2065 Stopp, Elisabeth, "Musil's Törless: Content and Form," Modern Language Review, 63:94-118, January, 1968.

"Taken as a whole, the content and the form, the material and its structure, are related to one another in a wholly personal and distinctive way, resulting in a work which has the quality of life." (J.R.R.)

M2066 White, John J., "Mathematical Imagery in Musil's Young Törless and Zamyatin's We," Comparative Literature, 18:71-8, Winter, 1966.

"Zamyatin's We and Robert Musil's Young Törless belong to that small group of novels that have embodied abstract concepts symbolically into their subject matter." (J.R.R.)

VINZENZ UND DIE FREUNDIN BEDEUTENDER MÄNNER

M2067 Braun, Wilhelm, "Musil's Vinzenz und die Freundin bedeutender Männer," Germanic Review, 37:121-34, March, 1962.

The basic problem of this comedy foreshadows Der Mann ohne Eigenschaften. There are two basic attitudes toward the world, "one definite, sharp, logical, and tied to one's profession, the other hazy, imaginative, uncommitted." Musil would join the two in a new, metaphorical view of life. (R.H.L.)

YOUNG TÖRLESS--See
DIE VERWIRRUNGEN DES ZÖGLINGS TÖRLESS

MYERS, ELIZABETH

M2068 Braybrooke, Neville, "Elizabeth Myers, 1912-47: An Appreciation,"
Month, 22:165-71, 1959.

[This is a memorial to Elizabeth Myers.] (K.M.W.)

MYERS, LEOPOLD HAMILTON

M2069 Bottrall, Ronald, "L. H. Myers," Review of English Literature,
2:47-58, April, 1961.

Like Lawrence, Forster, and Virginia Woolf, Myers was concerned
with "the distinction between genuineness and fake or unhealthy attitudes: between first-hand experience and second hand experience."
(W.G.F.)

THE POOL OF VISHNU

M2070 Gupta, B. S., "An Obscure Allusion in L. H. Myers's The Pool of
Vishnu," Notes and Queries, 15:59-60, February, 1968.

The god Indra mentioned in Myers's book is a Buddhist rather than
a Hindu deity. (J.C.O.)

M2071 Sen Gupta, Bhim, "An Unknown Source of L. H. Myers's The Pool
of Vishnu," Revue des Langues Vivantes, 34:341-53, 1968.

The Pool of Vishnu derives its suggestive background from Paul
Brunton's The Quest of the Overself. (D.P.)

NABOKOV, VLADIMIR

N1   Appel, Alfred, Jr., "An Interview with Vladimir Nabokov,"
Wisconsin Studies in Contemporary Literature, 8:127-52,
Spring, 1967.

[This interview probes Nabokov's perceptions of affinities of
European and American writers with his writing, his assessment
of the value of criticism, his work habits, his views on Joyce,
most particularly of Ulysses, his experiences as a translator, and,
finally, offers insights into various scenes or characters in his
fiction.]   (D.P.)

N2   Berberova, Nina, "Nabokov in the Thirties," Tri-Quarterly,
17:220-33, Winter, 1970.

[This article recalls Nabokov in Paris in the thirties, when his
work first began to be published.] (A.S.W.)

N3   Bishop, Morris, "Nabokov at Cornell," Tri-Quarterly, 17:234-9,
Winter, 1970.

[The chairman of the committee which hired Nabokov at Cornell
reminisces about Nabokov's years teaching there.] (A.S.W.)

N4   Bitsilli, P. M., "The Revival of Allegory," Tri-Quarterly,
17:102-18, Winter, 1970.

A first reading of Sirin's [Nabokov's] works produces an impression
of an absence of rhythm, of artistic imperfection and lawlessness.
This "estrangement from life" is one of the prerequisites of an
allegorical art, as practiced by Gogol, Saltykov, and Sirin. (A.S.W.)

N5   Brenner, Conrad, "Nabokov: The Art of the Perverse, " New
      Republic, 138:18-21, June 23, 1958.

      "Vladimir Nabokov is an artist of the first rank, a writer in the
      great tradition. . . . Lolita is probably the best fiction to come out
      of this country . . . since Faulkner's burst in the thirties. He may
      be the most important writer now going in this country. He is
      already, God help him, a classic. He . . . now wields an English
      that a native young writer would kill for . . . [although] for the
      moment, he writes for the happy few. . . ." (D.P.)

N6   Bryer, Jackson R., and Thomas J. Bergin, Jr., "A Checklist of
      Nabokov Criticism in English, " Wisconsin Studies in Contemporary
      Literature, 8:316-64, Spring, 1967.

      [In this checklist a special effort has been made to include book
      reviews, and almost total coverage of articles and comment in
      books has been attempted.] (D.P.)

N7   Bryer, Jackson R., "Vladimir Nabokov's Critical Reputation in
      English: A Note and a Checklist, " Wisconsin Studies in Contem-
      porary Literature, 8:312-5, Spring, 1967.

      "But by far the single most notable--and deplorable--characteristic
      of Nabokov criticism is the disproportionate amount of attention
      devoted to Lolita and the resultant lack of serious comment on the
      other fiction, poetry, and translation. . . . it is striking what little
      critical ground has actually been covered by the literally hundreds
      of reviewers and scholars who have grappled with the intricacies of
      Nabokov's work." (D.P.)

N8   Dembo, L. S., "Vladimir Nabokov: An Introduction, " Wisconsin
      Studies in Contemporary Literature, 8:111-26, Spring, 1967.

      Although Nabokov's novels are not "themeless, they are, for the
      most part 'asocial.'. . . Characters like Humbert Humbert,Hermann
      and Kinbote are really more important for their artistic vitality than
      for the moral questions they raise, just as Luzhin's insanity is no
      comment on the rightness or wrongness of his life. . . . Invitation
      to a Beheading and Bend Sinister are not political disquisitions but
      vivid presentations of the hallucinative or introspective mind under
      certain political conditions." Nabokov "has created a magic-mirror
      that reflects a single image--that of the artist himself--no matter
      what is put in front of it." (D.P.)

N9   Elkin, Stanley, "Three Meetings," Tri-Quarterly, 17:261-5, Winter, 1970.

[This fictional description of two meetings parodies Nabokov's style.] (A.S.W.)

N10   Field, Andrew, "The Artist as Failure in Nabokov's Early Prose," Wisconsin Studies in Contemporary Literature, 8:165-73, Spring, 1967.

In his early works Nabokov occasionally confronts "the figure of the artist directly, and it is most curious that these direct statements concern artists who are failures either in their lives or their art." In Nabokov's case we may say that "when the artist is more important than his art . . . that is tantamount to saying that he is a false or failed artist." (D.P.)

N11   Gold, Herbert, "The Art of Fiction XL: Vladimir Nabokov: An Interview," Paris Review, No. 41, pp. 92-111, Summer-Fall, 1967.

[This interview elicits an apology for Nabokov's problems with English style; much information on writers who have not influenced Nabokov, and why they have not; explores a range of matters distasteful to Nabokov; and does not discuss the novel he is writing.] (D.P.)

N12   Grosshans, Henry, "The Great Vladimir," Research Studies (Washington State University), 35:264-8, 1967.

[This article reviews the recent gathering of criticism devoted to Nabokov--Wisconsin Studies in Contemporary Literature, 8:2, 1967 --and points out the weaknesses of a critical approach which relies overly on adulation and plot summary and which fails to utilize the perspective of Nabokov's time or his work as a whole.] (A.S.W.)

N13   Grosshans, Henry, " Vladimir Nabokov and the Dream of Old Russia," Texas Studies in Literature and Language, 7:401-9, Winter, 1966.

One of the elements of order in Nabokov's fiction "is the fine thread of golden memory of the Russia he left and to which he can never return. Much of his writing has been an attempt to breath life into a past that he has remembered and created. Through all his wanderings, he has carried his dream of old Russia with him as his dearest baggage, and in his works he has defended the cultural remnant that was cast away by the catastrophic events of this century." (D.P.)

N14   Hayman, John G., "After Lolita--A Conversation with Vladimir
Nabokov--with Digressions," Twentieth Century, 166:444-50,
December, 1959.

In Nabokov's case "the process of building a vocabulary was obviously a laborious one, but . . . one often feels that Nabokov is
actually building a language as he writes. . . . This verbal awareness and wit seems a full recompense for the loss . . . of his
untrammelled, rich, and infinitely docile Russian tongue. . . ."
"The instantaneous vision, the immediate which is also timeless--
this is what interests Nabokov and makes him contemptuous of the
social and didactic writer." (D.P.)

N15   Heidenry, John, "Vladimir in Dreamland," Commonweal,
90:231-4, May 9, 1969.

Vladimir Nabokov "may have countless passions . . . language above
all . . . in three tingling-entangling tongues: English for the long
stretch, French for the hard clichés of reality, and Russian for those
gem-bright intimacies and endearments that glow (but do not light the
way) along the misty, dream-specked time-space discontinuum of his
artifice. . . . All of Vladimir Nabokov's interests take place in the
inflowerite microworld of Dreamland: a world where . . . if you
passionately hope hard enough, whatever you want will happen."
(D.P.)

N16   Hicks, Granville, "A Man of Many Words," Saturday Review,
50:31-2, January 28, 1967.

"Nabokov's English vocabulary is not only remarkable for a writer
who was Russian born; it is phenomenal by any standards. . . .
Many of the difficult words . . . come from particular scientific
disciplines . . .; a few related to Lepidoptera . . . more from
physiology and medicine. . . . Many words seem to be made up
. . . from recognizable Latin roots. . . . He takes pleasure . . .
in using rare words and rare forms of words." ". . . as a stylist
Nabokov is [not] merely a gamester; on the contrary . . . he is
serious in intention and possessed of a marvelous command of the
resources of the English language." (D.P.)

N17   Ivask, George, "The World of Vladimir Nabokov," Russian Review,
20:134-42, April, 1961.

"Nabokov completely assimilates his impressions and transforms
what he sees into an entirely new vision of the world." (R.G.L.)

N18   Janeway, Elizabeth, "Nabokov the Magician," Atlantic Monthly, 220:66-71, July, 1967.

Nabokov's lifelong task has been a study in identity. His art is "an instrument of inquiry into reality, into the nature of the prison which holds us and of the creature which bruises its fists against those prison walls. His tricks are not an attempt to obscure reality, but to determine its nature by imitating it." (D.P.)

N19   Karlinsky, Simon, "Anya in Wonderland: Nabokov's Russified Lewis Carroll," Tri-Quarterly, 17:310-5, Winter, 1970.

Nabokov's translation of Alice . . . is one of the finest in any language because of his success with parodies and puns, and the beautifully caught and conveyed tone and diction of the original. (A.S.W.)

N20   Karlinsky, Simon, "Illusion, Reality, and Parody in Nabokov's Plays," Wisconsin Studies in Contemporary Literature, 8:268-79, Spring, 1967.

Nabokov's three verse plays Death, The Grandfather, and The [North] Pole are much indebted to Pushkin. The Event and The Waltz Invention both "benefit from Nabokov's literary mastery at its most original and inventive. Both plays are firmly connected with Nabokov's central preoccupation with creative imagination. . . . The Event can be described as a portrait of an artist as a coward, and The Waltz Invention as a portrait of an artist as a madman-politician." (D.P.)

N21   Lawrenson, Helen, "The Man Who Scandalized the World," Esquire, 54:70-4, August, 1961.

[This interview with Nabokov is followed by a discussion of his background and a brief history of Lolita.] (G.C.)

N22   Lee, L. L., "Duplexity in V. Nabokov's Short Stories," Studies in Short Fiction, 2:307-15, Summer, 1965.

"It is the concept of the double which is the Ariadne thread to lead us into and through the labyrinth of Vladimir's short stories. . . . his doubling is an artistic realization of the unity of opposites which is always in precarious balance over the abyss, a demonstration that the anomalous is a ready and perpetual threat." (D.P.)

N23   Lee, L. L., "Vladimir Nabokov's Great Spiral of Being, "
       Western Humanities Review, 18:225-37, Summer, 1964.

       Nabokov's statement that his life appears as a "colored spiral in a
       small ball of glass and that all things are essentially spiral in their
       relation to time" offers a key not only to his themes but to his
       methods: his images and characteristic devices such as mirror re-
       flections, spelling reversals, puns, sexual ambivalences, name
       echoes, etc.   (F.L.)

N24   Levin, Harry, "Literature and Exile, " Listener, 62:613-7, 1959.

       [This is a discussion of the exiles of Pasternak, Conrad, Nabokov,
       Dante, Heine, Mickewicz, Ovid, James, Joyce and Pound.] "The
       relation between the poet and the multitude, according to Vigny, is
       perpetual ostracism. . . . exile has often proved to be a vocation,
       reinforcing other gifts with courage and looking forward to a final
       triumph of independence over conformity. "]   (H.S.)

N25   Merivale, Patricia, "The Flaunting of Artifice in Vladimir Nabokov
       and Jorge Luis Borges, " Wisconsin Studies in Contemporary
       Literature, 8:294-309, Spring, 1967.

       "Both Borges and Nabokov could be called 'modern mannerists. '
       . . . Both Borges and Nabokov exploit, for their own thematic pur-
       poses, all the narrative tricks and devices of the Gothic fantasy
       writers of the last two centuries, and they blend mannerism and
       Gothicism together in their single most important parodic pattern,
       the metaphysical detective story. " (D.P.)

N26   Nabokov, Vladimir, " 'To Be Kind, to Be Proud, to Be Fearless'--
       Vladimir Nabokov in Conversation with James Mossman, " Listener,
       82:560-1, October 23, 1969.

       [This interview includes Nabokov's comments on some nineteenth
       century Russian novelists, his "pleasure and agony" in writing
       novels, his comments on Edmund Wilson and John Updike as critics
       of his writing, his appreciations of the Americans landing on the
       moon.] (D.P.)

N27   Pryce-Jones, Alan, "The Art of Nabokov, " Harper's Magazine,
       226:97-101, April, 1963.

       "For the art of Nabokov is less a novelist's art than a fabulist's.
       He does not see people as they are, but as they might have appeared

to the medieval constructor of a bestiary. His worlds are static. They may become tense with obsession, but they do not move or expand or break apart like the world of everyday reality." (D.P.)

N28 Purdy, Strother B., "Solux Rex: Nabokov and the Chess Novel," Modern Fiction Studies, 14:379-95, Winter, 1968-69.

"Of modern novelists, Vladimir Nabokov is probably the one who has made the most constant use of chess in his work, in ways at times obvious and at times obscure to his readers, and is one of the very few writers to compare the game to the artist's craft. . . . I offer the following notes on chess in several of his novels both to add to the critical appreciation of them and to consider what relevance chess can have to the business of the novel in general." (D.P.)

N29 Rovet, Jeanine, "Vladimir Nabokov: Le Démon de l'analogie," Les Temps Modernes, 21:2279-82, June, 1966.

Whether in Pale Fire, a satire of the American university, or Lolita, a satire of America, Nabokov's technique is that of a series of secret drawers, which lacks the final one. His world is that of the great Analogy, a rhythmic indifference of resemblances. (T.T.B.)

N30 [Sheehan, Donald], "Selected Bibliography of Nabokov's Work," Wisconsin Studies in Contemporary Literature, 8:310-1, Spring, 1967.

[This is a list of Nabokov's works in Russian and English, his translations of other writers, and translations into English of his Russian novels.] (D.P.)

N31 Smith, Peter Duval, "Vladimir Nabokov on His Life and Work," Listener, 68:856-8, November 22, 1962.

[Nabokov tells Peter Duval Smith of the influence of his Russian background on his work, his reason for writing, his methods, and the extent to which his personality is reflected by his characters.] (P.A.R.)

N32   Struve, Gleb, "Notes on Nabokov as a Russian Writer," Wisconsin
Studies in Contemporary Literature, 8:153-64, Spring, 1967.

"Nabokov's conception of literature as an artifice, his interest in,
and concern with, the problems of composition, of pattern, his out-
spoken contempt for any kind of 'message' in literature, be it social,
moral, or religious-philosophical, are all against the grain of the
Russian literary tradition. . . . What makes Nabokov even more
alien to the Russian literary tradition is his lack of sympathy with
. . . human beings as such." (D.P.)

N33   Vordtriede, Werner, "Die Masken des Vladimir Nabokov," Merkur,
20:138-51, February, 1966.

Nabokov is no Proust for the former is certain that that which has
disappeared can never return. "Thus arise his ironic dead ends,
his self-created worlds which have grown from hopelessness."
(J.R.R.)

N34   Williams, Carol T., "Nabokov's Dialectical Structure," Wisconsin
Studies in Contemporary Literature, 8:250-67, Spring, 1967.

"Thus, not only do the triadic movements of Nabokov's compositions
resemble Hegel's Dialectic, in which opposing processes in time or
the mind are interpreted as complements, but their conceptions of
art and life are also similar. Both emphasize the nobility of the
human striver as well as his destructiveness, and both reconcile the
mortal conflict in an aesthetic synthesis in which two opposing impulses are retained in stasis." (D.P.)

N35   Zimmer, Dieter E., "Der Erzähler Nabokov," Der Monat, No.
206, pp. 40-9, November, 1965.

Whenever we are about to pigeonhole Nabokov, we run into nothing
but paradoxes "which shows above all that something is wrong with
these categories--or that he is superior to them." (J.R.R.)

ADA OR ARDOR

N36   Alter, Robert, "Nabokov's Ardor," Commentary, 48:47-50,
August, 1969.

"Ada, which is surely one of the sunniest works of fiction written in
this century, sounds . . . like a dark drama of fatal, incestuous
passion." In it, "Nabokov's intricately wrought, elaborately figura-

ADA OR ARDOR   (cont'd)

tive style, with its painterly effects and its perspectivist mirror-games, transmutes objects of description, even the most pungently physical objects, into magical objets d'art." (D.P.)

N37   Appel, Alfred, Jr., "Ada Described," Tri-Quarterly, 17:160-86, Winter, 1970.

"Ada . . . is a love story, an erotic masterpiece, an Edenic fantasy, a philosophical investigation into the nature of time." It is "an act of accommodation that in the face of darkness asserts joy." (A.S.W.)

N38   Bok, Sissela, "Redemption Through Art in Nabokov's Ada," Critique: Studies in Modern Fiction, 12:110-20, No. 3, 1970.

"Ada can be read, therefore, as a confession . . . of a very unusual kind. . . . The confession is a quest for redemption which can only be partial; the transformation of the confession into a work of art produces but a melancholy and very local palliative. . . . It is a measure of Nabokov's achievement that he can approach such a task without falling into sentimentality or sententiousness." (D.P.)

N39   Johnson, Carol, "Nabokov's Ada: Word's End," Art International, 13:42-3, October, 1969.

"If anyone in our lamentable century is equipped to fulfill Flaubert's expressed wish of writing a novel 'about nothing,' surely it is Nabokov, who with Ada has succeeded in perpetrating a feat of style . . . to the virtual exclusion of substance, to the extent of 598 pages, in a language not his own." (D.P.)

N40   Kazin, Alfred, "In the Mind of Nabokov," Saturday Review, 52:27-9, 35, May 10, 1969.

Ada "simply has no counterpart just now for imaginative detail, for range of interest, for architectural form, for caprice and genius of language. It is prodigious." (D.P.)

BEND SINISTER

N41   Lee, L. L., "Bend Sinister: Nabokov's Political Dream," Wisconsin Studies in Contemporary Literature, 8:193-203, Spring, 1967.

BEND SINISTER (cont'd)

Bend Sinister is a vision "of madness, political and personal--a madness that is the dream which carried too far, begins to act in the world." The novel states "human values which must be upheld against those mad abstractions which . . . would destroy the mind and the body, treating man at best as only a machine." (D.P.)

DAR

N42   Malcolm, Donald, "A Retrospect," New Yorker, 40:198-205, April 25, 1964.

Nabokov's The Gift was written in the mid nineteen-thirties, and now translated and extensively revised. While "the ear repeatedly detects the accomplished, the assured, the very individual English voice of the contemporary Mr. Nabokov . . . one's literary sense is perpetually reminded that the substance of The Gift belongs to an earlier period in the author's career. . . . this subtle discrepancy between matter and tone produces an odd feeling of dislocation in time." (D.P.)

DESPAIR--See
OTCHAYANIE

EUGENE ONEGIN

N43   Brown, Clarence, "Nabokov's Pushkin and Nabokov's Nabokov," Wisconsin Studies in Contemporary Literature, 8:280-93, Spring, 1967.

After a sharp intake of breath, reviewers of Nabokov's translation of Pushkin's Eugene Onegin described it in varying degrees of passion as "preposterous, gauche beyond words, intentionally ugly, a travesty of a great work of art, sickeningly cute, incomprehensible." Actually, his translation "is the best that under the circumstances and under the sway of Nabokov's inexorable principles is possible." In this work "we become Nabokov reading Pushkin. It is literally a kind of aesthetic ecstasy. . . . To read Pushkin not with Nabokov but as Nabokov is an experience that leaves us pleased, instructed, and altered." (D.P.)

EUGENE ONEGIN   (cont'd)

N44   Gerschenkron, Alexander, "A Manufactured Moment?" <u>Modern
Philology</u>, 63:336-47, May, 1966.

Vladimir Nabokov's monumental edition of <u>Eugene Onegin</u> . . . has
everything: artistic intuition and dogmatic stubbornness; great ingenuity and amazing folly; acute observations and sterile pedantry;
unnecessary modesty and inexcusable arrogance. It is a labor of
love and a work of hate." "The work . . . is a monumental handi-
work . . . [which] contains real intuitions, numerous flashes of
brilliance, and a mass of solid learning. " It is "the fruit of enormous industry, skill and erudition. " (D.P.)

THE GIFT--See
DAR

INVITATION TO A BEHEADING--See
PRIGLASHENIE NA KAZN'

LOLITA

N45   Aldridge, A. Owen, "<u>Lolita</u> and <u>Les Liaisons dangereuses</u>,"
<u>Wisconsin Studies in Contemporary Literature</u>, 2:20-6, Fall, 1961.

The relationship between Valmont and Cécile in <u>Les Liaisons
dangereuses</u>, and its communication by innuendo and euphemism,
persiflage and humorous detachment, is the prototype of the relationship between Humbert and Lolita, and its communication. (B.K.)

N46   Appel, Alfred, Jr., "The Art of Nabokov's Artifice," <u>University
of Denver Quarterly</u>, 3:25-37, Summer, 1968.

Critics have not recognized Nabokov's unique contribution in creating the novel of parody, and thus, have underestimated his achievement. His <u>Lolita</u> "becomes a game-board on which, through parody,
he assaults the worst assumptions, pretensions, and intellectual
conventions of his readers. . . ." (D.P.)

N47   Appel, Alfred, Jr., "Backgrounds of <u>Lolita</u>," <u>Tri-Quarterly</u>,
17:17-40, Winter, 1970.

<u>Lolita</u> is a fiction concerning fiction, a story about the artist's
mastery of form, and "his triumph in art is but a heightened emblem of all of our own efforts to confront, order, and structure the

LOLITA (cont'd)

chaos of life, and to endure, if not master, the demons within and around us." (A.S.W.)

N48   Appel, Alfred, Jr., "Lolita: The Springboard of Parody," Wisconsin Studies in Contemporary Literature, 8:204-51, Spring, 1967.

". . . Lolita is not merely about sexual perversion but rather about love and the search for ineffable beauty, and as such . . . it is ultimately 'about' its own creation." The comic, the parodic nature of Lolita ultimately stems "from the depth of Vladimir Nabokov's profoundly humane comic vision; and the gusto of Humbert's narration, his punning language, his abundant delight in digressions, parodies, and games all attest to a comic vision that overrides the circumscribing sadness, absurdity, and terror of everyday life." (D.P.)

N49   Baker, George, "Lolita: Literature or Pornography?" Saturday Review, 40:18, June 22, 1957.

"Last December the French government, spurred on by the British government (which feared, logically enough, that copies of Lolita would find their way to England), invoked its obscenity laws against the novel. Then, to the surprise of almost everybody, the U.S. Customs Office pronounced the book unobjectionable. The paradoxical result: Lolita cannot be legally exported from France but after being smuggled out of France it can be legally imported into the U.S. . . . for the first time in history . . . 'France has shown herself to be more intolerant and more puritanical than an English-speaking country'." (D.P.)

N50   Balakian, Nona, "The Prophetic Vogue of the Anti-heroine," Southwest Review, 47:134-41, Spring, 1962.

In contrast with D. H. Lawrence's Lady Chatterly, modern writers show us the disparity between what is and what should be the relationship between men and women. Modern "anti-heroines" of Salinger, Capote, Tennessee Williams, Mailer, Mary McCarthy, Kerouac, and Nabokov exemplify the new realistic attitude. (D.P.)

LOLITA   (cont'd)

N51   Brick, Allan, "The Madman in His Cell: Joyce, Beckett, Nabokov,
and the Stereotypes," Massachusetts Review, 1:40-55, Fall, 1959.

Joyce's Ulysses, Beckett's novels from Murphy to Watt and Nabokov's
Lolita mount attacks against the stereotypes imposed on us by modern
mass culture. (D.P.)

N52   Butler, Diana, "Lolita Lepidoptera," New World Writing, No. 16,
pp. 58-84, 1960.

"In Lolita Nabokov has transformed his own passion for butterflies
into his hero's passion for nymphets. At least on one level, and as
a part of an elaborate literary game, little Dolores Haze is a butter-
fly." (D.P.)

N53   Campbell, Felicia Florine, "A Princedom by the Sea," Lock Haven
Review, 10:39-46, 1968.

". . . a prose parody of Poe's 'Annabel Lee' forms the motivation
for the hero's action and acts as a point of reference throughout the
novel." Humbert himself bears "a marked resemblance to a number
of Poe's heroes and . . . even . . . Poe himself. . . . [Also], a
comparison of Lolita and Ligeia . . . provides a number of amusing
contrasts. (G.C.)

N54   DuBois, Arthur E., "Poe and Lolita," CEA Critic, 26:1, 7,
March, 1964.

A number of "Poe 'recollections'" in his novel indicates that
"Nabokov has hidden in Lolita an essay on Poe." (G.C.)

N55   Dupee, F. W., "Lolita in America," Columbia University Forum,
2:35-9, Winter, 1959.

[This is an account of the long genesis, strange publication, and
surprising reception of Lolita.] (G.M.)

N56   Dupee, F. W., "Lolita in America," Encounter, 12:30-5,
February, 1959.

". . . Lolita probably sums up the process, compounded of fear and
fascination, disgust and laughter, by which [Nabokov] has become an
American writer." Inevitably, after a comedy of errors in censor-

LOLITA   (cont'd)

ship by the French government, after the U. S. Customs service declined to ban the book, and after these events were well publicized in the American press, the book became an immediate best seller with its publication by a reputable American firm. Oddly, the expected opposition in America has not developed. (D.P.)

N57   Dupee, F. W., "A Preface to Lolita," Anchor Review, No. 2, pp. 1-13, 1957.

"The book's general effect is profoundly mischievous like that of some diabolical distorting mirror in some particularly obscene amusement park. The images of life which Lolita gives back are ghastly but recognizable." (W.G.F.)

N58   Girodias, Maurice, "Lolita, Nabokov, and I," Evergreen Review, 9:44-7, 89-91, September, 1965.

[This is Girodias's account of his difficulties with Nabokov after Olympia Press published the first edition of Lolita.] (D.P.)

N59   Gold, Joseph, "The Morality of Lolita," British Association for American Studies Bulletin, n.s. No. 1, pp. 40-4, September, 1960.

Lolita is "as moral a novel as one could possibly hope for." Humbert learns that "love is a single and selfless dedication to an object for its own sake, and that existence is meaningless without such love." (G.C.)

N60   Green, Martin, "The Morality of Lolita," Kenyon Review, 28:352-77, June, 1966.

Nabokov represents a standard of art directly opposite Tolstoy's, "far out in the direction of freedom from all cultural-moral imperatives." But there is a "moral strategy" in Lolita: "a series of concessions, a self-criticism, a self-defense, and a moral theory of art." (G.S.)

N61   Harris, Harold J., "Lolita and the Sly Foreword," Mad River Review, 1:29-38, Spring-Summer, 1965.

Lolita fails as a great comic novel because it "is insufficiently comical. . . . just below its comic surface lurk essentially non-comic elements . . . traditionally found in the problematic,

LOLITA   (cont'd)

realistic novel--which is precisely what Dr. Ray's foreword asks
us to believe Lolita is not." (G.C.)

N62   Hiatt, L. R., "Nabokov's Lolita: A 'Freudian' Cryptic Crossword,"
American Imago, 24:360-70, Winter, 1967.

Although Nabokov denies the validity of Freudian readings of his
works, nevertheless "he knowingly but surreptitiously endows
Humbert with classical symptoms of the Oedipus complex." (J.M.D.)

N63   Hinchliffe, Arnold P., "Belinda in America," Studi Americani,
6:339-47, 1960.

Lolita "adds another chapter to the history of innocence and morality
which runs from . . . Hester Prynne to Temple Drake. . . .
'Humbert emerges . . . as a lone lost nineteenth century European
romantic in a crowded established twentieth century American
prison'." (G.C.)

N64   Hughes, D. J., "Character in Contemporary Fiction,"
Massachusetts Review, 3:788-95, Summer, 1962.

Generally, the contemporary novel falls short in characterization;
however recent works of Bellow and Nabokov, most particularly his
Lolita, "maintain the integrity and dignity of character" in modern
settings. (D.P.)

N65   Hughes, D. J., "Reality and the Hero: Lolita   and   Henderson
the Rain King ," Modern Fiction Studies, 6:345-64, Winter, 1960-61.

Nabokov's Lolita and Bellow's Henderson the Rain King are important novels--in theme, in structure, in their presentation of reality,
and in their demonstration of the novel in its present crisis. A
comparative analysis of their successes and failures illuminates
the problems of the contemporary novelist. (D.E.W.)

N66   Jones, David L., "Dolorès disparue," Symposium, 20:135-40,
Summer, 1966.

In Lolita "many of Nabokov's lyrical passages offer a light parody,
or at least a reminiscence, of the verbal ecstasies of Proust's
narrator. The strongest Proustian imprint, however, appears not
on Nabokov's style but on the narrative structure and content of

LOLITA   (cont'd)

Lolita." Finally, "the strength of each novel lies not in the consistency of the writer's tragic or comic control, but in the richness of the psychological world he creates." (D.P.)

N67   Josipovici, G. D., "Lolita: Parody and the Pursuit of Beauty," Critical Quarterly, 6:35-48, Spring, 1964.

"What gives Lolita a depth lacking in the earlier novels is that Humbert does in fact reach his goal. . . . By possessing Lolita, who was desirable precisely because she could not be possessed, Humbert seems to have destroyed everything in himself which had hitherto set him above the 'normal big males'." (D.P.)

N68   Malcolm, Donald, "Lo, the Poor Nymphet," New Yorker, 34:187-90, November 8, 1958.

It has been suggested that Nabokov wanted to write of romantic passion in the grand manner and could make such passion interesting to the contemporary reader only by disguising it as psychopathology; but "perhaps one might plausibly suggest that the artistic (as distinct from the clinical) interest of [Lolita] is all the justification its story requires." It is satire of a special kind in which vice or folly is regarded with "profound dismay and a measure of tragic sympathy." (W.G.F.)

N69   Mitchell, Charles, "Mythic Seriousness in Lolita," Texas Studies in Literature and Language, 5:329-43, Autumn, 1963.

"Lolita presents, in mythical form, first the problem and then the solution to the existential despair of its narrator, Humbert Humbert . . . . The mythic presentation and solution to this existential despair is that involving the Quest Hero searching for the realization of the spiritual image of self which transcends despair." (W.G.F.)

N70   Nabokov, Vladimir, "Lolita and Mr. Girodias," Evergreen Review, No. 45, pp. 37-41, February, 1967.

Mr. Girodias's recollection of the events leading to our "strained relations" subsequent to his publication of Lolita contains numerous factual errors and fails to indicate that our disagreements were entirely due to his repeated failures to render accounts and royalty payments according to the schedules he had contracted to meet. (D.P.)

LOLITA   (cont'd)

N71   Nabokov, Vladimir, "On a Book Entitled Lolita, "   Encounter,
12:73-6, April, 1959.

"The book developed slowly . . . [since] it had taken me some forty
years to invent Russia and Western Europe, and now I was faced
with the task of inventing America." Suggestions from American
publishers for revising the book were very amusing. "I am neither
a reader nor a writer of didactic fiction. . .: Lolita has no moral
in tow." "My private tragedy . . . is that I had to abandon . . . my
untrammelled, rich, and infinitely docile Russian tongue for a second-
rate brand of English. . . ." (D.P.)

N72   Nabokov, Vladimir, "On a Book Entitled Lolita, "   Anchor Review,
No. 2, pp. 105-12, 1957.

Lolita neither employs pornographic cliches, nor provides information about a country, a social class, or the author; it is not, as has
been charged, either allegorical or anti-American. American publishers's refusal to handle the book is based not on the treatment of
the theme, but on the theme itself, which is one of at least three that
they consider utterly taboo. (W.G.F.)

N73   Oliphant, Robert, "Public Voices and Wise Guys, "   Virginia
Quarterly Review, 37:522-37, Autumn, 1961.

In contemporary novels "one use of language . . . we might call the
'public voice, ' the . . . conventional voice of the author who attempts
to make a significant statement about experience. The other use of
language, that of Nabokov, might be called the voice of the 'wise guy, '
the voice which we cannot identify. . . ." "Perhaps the public voice
. . . is too pompous, too strident, too often wrong . . . The surface
statement of the wise guy, [such as Wright Morris, Mark Harris and
Nabokov], then, recognizes the conventions and limitations of language,
perspective, and reason. . . . it marks the first step toward phrasing questions in a world in which there are no easy answers." (D.P.)

N74   Phillips, Elizabeth, "The Hocus-Pocus of Lolita, "   Literature and
Psychology, 10:97-101, Autumn, 1960.

"Although an explanation of what the author calls the mechanism of
the novel risks spoiling a good joke, Vladimir Nabokov's Lolita is
a satire on an orthodox Freudian view of the life and writings of
Edgar Allan Poe." (J.M.D.)

LOLITA (cont'd)

N75   Rubin, Louis D., Jr., "The Self Recaptured," Kenyon Review, 25:393-415, Summer, 1963.

Wolfe's Look Homeward, Angel, Proust's Remembrance of Things Past, Hemingway's The Sun Also Rises are all autobiographical novels. "Autobiographical fiction . . . represents an attempt to triumph over time by converting that which happened in time . . . into an ordered and meaningful reality in language, complete and permanent in itself. The process is the form." In contrast, Nabokov's Lolita, although purportedly autobiographical, is not, "simply because no authorial personality is involved. . . ." (D.P.)

N76   Rubinstein, E., "Approaching Lolita," Minnesota Review, 6:361-7, Winter, 1966.

"At a time when pure artifice is held to be more personal than direct expression; when novelists . . . are exposing the incompatibility of narrative and personality; when the fine arts have rediscovered and exalted the unseemly everyday object--at such a time Lolita . . . assumes the authority of a document." (K.M.W.)

N77   Scott, W. J., "The Lolita Case," Landfall, 15:134-8, June, 1961.

The Indecent Publications Act, which at first seemed to have some value, has been shown to be restrictive to works of literary merit, as demonstrated in the Lolita case. (A.S.W.)

N78   Slonim, Marc, "Doctor Zhivago and Lolita," International Literary Annual, 2:213-25, 1959.

"Doctor Zhivago . . . is certainly one of the most important and representative novels of our century. . . . Lolita may not be a great book--but it certainly is a most curious and symptomatic phenomenon of the international (or cosmopolitan) spirit of Western Society." (G.C.)

N79   Strainchamps, Ethel, "Nabokov's Handling of English Syntax," American Speech, 36:234-5, October, 1961.

When Lolita appeared "most critics took occasion to praise the Russian-born author's command of the English language. . . . Actually, his English is so nearly first-rate and he uses it so inventively that the reader . . . prefers to overlook his small lapses.

LOLITA (cont'd)

. . . Most of Mr. Nabokov's difficulties are with English verbals
. . . unidiomatic ellipsis . . . clumsiness with articles . . . [and]
a few other doubtful constructions in Lolita that are fairly common
even in the writing of native speakers of English." (D.P.)

N80 Teirlinck, Herman, "Marginal Notes on Nabokov's Lolita," Literary
Review, 7:439-42, Spring, 1964.

In Lolita "Nabokov betrays his particularly perfidious and . . .
highly gifted ambiguity when he tries to cover up his autobiographical
traces. . . . And it is to the extent that his text may be regarded as
autobiographical that I feel justified in calling him pornographic."
(D.P.)

N81 Trilling, Lionel, "The Last Lover--Vladimir Nabokov's Lolita,"
Encounter, 11:9-19, October, 1958.

Although Lolita is not legally pornographic, it does certainly keep
erotic sensations before the reader. The book demolishes one of
the few taboos still able to shock: "the taboo about the sexual avail-
ability of very young girls." This device enables Nabokov to write
a modern novel set in the code of courtly love. Humbert is caught
in an unreasonable and illicit passion for a cruel mistress whom he
can never possess with any permanence. (D.P.)

N82 Trilling, Lionel, "The Last Lover: Vladimir Nabokov's Lolita,"
Griffin, 7:4-21, August, 1958.

Lolita is by intent a shocking novel about love and not about sex.
Nabokov meets the requirement of traditional illicitness in passion-
love in what must be the only terms now available to an author.
"The breaking of the taboo about the sexual unavailability of very
young girls has for us something of the force that a wife's infidelity
had for Shakespeare. H. H.'s relation with Lolita defies society as
scandalously as did Tristan's relation with Iseult. . . . It puts the
lovers, as lovers in literature must be put, beyond the pale of
society." (G.M.)

LOLITA   (cont'd)

N83   Uphaus, Robert W., "Nabokov's Künstlerroman: Portrait of the Artist as a Dying Man," Twentieth Century Literature, 13:104-10, July, 1967.

"Despite its melange of literary conventions, however, the novel [Lolita] is an overt parody of the Künstlerroman, presenting Humbert's fateful but comic commitment to an artistic ideal found to be wanting: it is the ideal of the soaring imagination disciplined by craft, but unencumbered by the commonplace. It is the ideal of the mind undisturbed by society; in short, it is a romantic ideal, an ideal purportedly above agony." (D.P.)

N84   Zall, Paul M., "Lolita and Gulliver," Satire Newsletter, 3:33-7, Fall, 1965.

"The external trappings of Lolita are patently reminiscent of Gulliver's Travels . . . [and] both Swift and Nabokov are concerned with mechanistic psychology, theories that dehumanize man down to mechanically operated parts--glands, repressions, projections, and so forth." (G.C.)

OTCHAYANIE

N85   Rosenfield, Claire, "Despair and the Lust for Immortality," Wisconsin Studies in Contemporary Literature, 8:174-92, Spring, 1967.

"Despair, which is Nabokov's revised translation of his Otchayanie, written thirty years before, is a novel about Doubles." In this novel, "paradoxically, the narrator's longing for a bodily double . . . is a modern perversion of the primitive's longing for immortality; it reveals the quality of his personal disintegration that he seeks his soul by destroying another's body." (D.P.)

PALE FIRE

N86   Berberova, Nina, "The Mechanics of Pale Fire," Tri-Quarterly, 17:147-59, Winter, 1970.

In Pale Fire, the structural surprise is that the symbolic level is the obvious, surface one, while the realistic level is only hinted at. Kinbote, the main character, is trying to restore his lost connection with reality, but he "has to be satisfied with some ad hoc knocked together passageways." (A.S.W.)

PALE FIRE   (cont'd)

N87   Field, Andrew, "Pale Fire: The Labyrinth of a Great Novel,"
Tri-Quarterly, 8:13-36, 1967.

". . . Pale Fire is a structure whose general plan and pattern are
so brilliant, so perfect, that the reader who follows after Nabokov
long enough can . . . continue on as a 'little Nabokov' without in any
way destroying or distorting the pattern . . . or even the 'universal
or ultimate truth' that seems to me to be present in this breathtak-
ingly simple and endlessly complex novel. . . . The primary pattern
--that is, the form as opposed to the theme--of Pale Fire is a complete and precise portrayal of the artist and his creation." It is "a
serious work of art and also one of the eight masterpieces of the
novel in this century. . . ." (D.P.)

N88   Handley, Jack, "To Die in English," Northwest Review, 6:23-40,
Spring, 1963.

In Pale Fire, even more than in Nabokov's earlier books, the reader
"may presume that the heart-stopping prose, the exploding congru-
encies, the magical elegancies and demonic intaglio are bait, re-
freshments for the weary traveler, signs of a distant world the
artificer has not completed yet, where death, heaven and hell exist
beyond the reach of metaphor--even beyond a resemblance to the
present simulacrum. . . . Pale Fire is the lattice of a future
crystal." (D.P.)

N89   Krueger, John R., "Nabokov's Zemblan: A Constructed Language of
Fiction," Linguistics, 31:44-9, 1967.

Nabokov's constructed language Zemblan appears in scattered words,
even several complete paragraphs, almost all with English glosses
in his novel Pale Fire. "On the basis of evident cognates and grammatical forms, Zemblan appears to be a West Germanic language
with overlays of Scandinavian (Swedish) and Slavic (Russian) borrowings, a few Romance words and a few words in which cognates are
not apparent. . . ." (D.P.)

N90   Levine, Jay Arnold, "The Design of A Tale of a Tub (with a
Digression on a Mad Modern Critic)," ELH, 33:198-227, 1966.

"Pale Fire is a new Dunciad with elements of A Tale of a Tub and
the Memoirs of Martinus Scriblerus." (D.P.)

PALE FIRE   (cont'd)

N91   Lyons, John O., "Pale Fire and the Fine Art of Annotation,"
Wisconsin Studies in Contemporary Literature, 8:242-9, Spring,
1967.

"Nabokov's Pale Fire is undoubtedly one of the wittiest . . . novels
since Joyce's Ulysses." The novel "has an impatience with cant and
injustice expressed in a full range of satirical rhetoric. . . . There
is [also] more than a little flippancy, innuendo, and playing of games
with words and events. . . ." It seems to inherit its "sly narrative
pose from Pope, Sterne, and Byron."   (D.P.)

N92   Riemer, Andrew, "Dim Glow, Faint Blaze--The 'Meaning' of Pale
Fire," Balcony, 6:41-8, 1967.

Pale Fire defies classification as a novel, and must be accorded a
new term, such as Northrop Frye's "Menippean Satire," as its
satire and parody are directed at the intellect and at the English
language itself.   (A.S.W.)

N93   Williams, Carol T., " 'Web of Sense': Pale Fire in the Nabokov
Canon," Critique: Studies in Modern Fiction, 6:29-45, Winter,
1963-64.

The separate parts of Pale Fire synthesize in a presentation of
Nabokov's views about life, art, and afterlife--that "the life that,
at its highest moments, is inhabited by the creative spirit and is a
work of art" is "the closest translation of timelessness possible in
the mortal condition."   (W.G.F.)

PNIN

N94   Mizener, Arthur, "The Seriousness of Vladimir Nabokov,"
Sewanee Review, 76:655-64, Autumn, 1968.

Chapter three of Pnin demonstrates that Nabokov's wit and ingenuity
have a serious purpose, for ". . . what is absurd is [Pnin's] ordi-
nariness . . . he is everyman; but the narrator's suggestions make
us see him as everyman in the fullest sense, as the glory, jest, and
riddle of the world."   (W.E.K.)

PRIGLASHENIE NA KAZN'

N95   Alter, Robert, "Invitation to a Beheading: Nabokov and the Art of Politics," Tri-Quarterly, 17:41-59, Winter, 1970.

"By emphasizing an elaborately self-conscious art both as its medium and its moral model, the novel affirms the thorough persistence of humanity in a world that is progressively more brutal and more subtle in its attempts to take us away from ourselves." (A.S.W.)

N96   Hughes, Robert P., "Notes on the Translation of Invitation to a Beheading," Tri-Quarterly, 17:284-92, Winter, 1970.

Invitation to a Beheading seems to have suffered less in the translation than many of Nabokov's other works, and the splendid verbal effects of the original are often captured. (A.S.W.)

N97   Moynihan, Julian, "A Russian Preface for Nabokov's Beheading," Novel, 1:12-8, Fall, 1967.

[This is an English translation of the preface to the Russian language edition of Invitation to a Beheading issued in Paris in 1966. This preface attempts to keep in mind both the member of Russian literary circles who is aware of literature abroad and the ordinary Soviet reader who does not know Nabokov's work, and also "to say something valid about Nabokov's importance for a reader of any nationality (or party) whatsoever."] (D.P.)

N98   Pifer, Ellen I., "Nabokov's Invitation to a Beheading: The Parody of a Tradition," Pacific Coast Philology, 5:46-53, 1970.

"In Invitation to a Beheading, literary artifice provides the reader with a radical insight into the problem of reality. Because men perceive differently, the only world they share is one of concrete particulars. . . . it is a dead world--a parody. Thus Nabokov's assessment of reality is as subversive to realism as his literary methods." (D.P.)

N99   Stuart, Dabney, "All the Mind's a Stage: A Reading of Invitation to a Beheading by Vladimir Nabokov," University of Windsor Review, 5:1-24, No. 2, 1969.

Nabokov labels Invitation to a Beheading accurately when he calls it "a violin in a void"; "and yet what the book suggests . . . is that the small transient strain of that violin is of more permanent value than the context in which it sounds. The possibility it poses is that our

PRIGLASHENIE NA KAZN' (cont'd)

predicaments--political, existential, or whatever--are basically
personal predicaments, the results of our habits of mind, our habits
of perception, our failure of imagination, and the way out of those
predicaments might be a new perspective, a reoriented way of
imagining ourselves." (D.P.)

THE REAL LIFE OF SEBASTIAN KNIGHT

N100   Fromberg, Susan, "The Unwritten Chapter in The Real Life of
Sebastian Knight," Modern Fiction Studies, 13:427-42, Winter,
1967-68.

"In The Real Life of Sebastian Knight, Nabokov expresses his belief
that artistic creation is a paradigm of the process which created the
'real' world; just as his characters are expressions and extensions of
his own soul, so he, and his characters, and everyone else may be
the expressions of the souls of the ultimate artificers of the natural
world." (D.P.)

N101   Johnson, W. R., "The Real Life of Sebastian Knight," Carleton
Miscellany, 4:111-4, Fall, 1963.

"Like Crusoe's memoir and Ossian's epics, [The Real Life of
Sebastian Knight] will be seen in the next century to have altered the
conventions of our writing and to have been a capsule of our tradition."
We must conclude "that Nabokov is one of those hoaxes that have to
be perpetrated at moments when the conventions of English writing
must suddenly expand and alter." (D.P.)

N102   Stegner, S. Page, "The Immortality of Art: Vladimir Nabokov's
The Real Life of Sebastian Knight," Southern Review, 2:286-96,
Spring, 1966.

"The Nabokovian gambits that one discovers in the better known
Lolita and Pale Fire--the parody of traditional forms and formulas,
the conjuror's allusions and illusions, the amused, sometimes
petulant, swipes at Freud and literary critics are all here in
Sebastian Knight." (J.M.D.)

THE REAL LIFE OF SEBASTIAN KNIGHT (cont'd)

N103   Stuart, Dabney, "The Real Life of Sebastian Knight: Angles of
Perception, " Modern Language Quarterly, 29:312-28, September,
1968.

This novel is "both a game of detection and a quest for self knowledge "; we are led toward "the identity . . . of a man who has died
of self-awareness" and has then "been reborn through the process of
observing himself reflected in a mirror." (G.S.)

NAIPAUL, VIDIADHAR SURAJPRASAD

N104   Derrick, A. C., "Naipaul's Technique as a Novelist, " Journal of
Commonwealth Literature, 7:32-44, July, 1969.

"As a satirist, Naipaul's most impressive achievements are The
Mystic Masseur and A House for Mr. Biswas. . . . At the same
time, however, these works clearly show his lack of compassion
and how completely destructive his mode of satire can be." (G.C.)

N105   Lee, R. H., "The Novels of V. S. Naipaul, " Theoria, 27:31-46,
1967.

"The main interest of the first novels lies . . . in the way in which
Naipaul defines his own attitude, and that of the society he portrays,
to . . . the change occurring in his own generation from a dominating respect for the past, to an acceptance of a new world, geograph-
ically and philosophically. . . . There is considerable pleasure to
be gained in . . . Naipaul's increasing ability to bring under control
the vivid life that surely and pervadingly fills the books, and gives
the work cohesion and unity." (D.P.)

N106   Maes-Jelinek, Hena, "V. S. Naipaul: A Commonwealth Writer?"
Revue des Langues Vivantes, 33:499-513, 1967.

". . . the strain experienced by Naipaul is peculiar to writers of the
Commonwealth. What is his dread of Trinidad, his repulsion for
India but the expression of his insecurity as a westernized, unattached
artist? . . . he should accept the reality of India and of Trinidad since
he is directly indebted to them for . . . [his] discover[y of] human
qualities which transcend race and nationality." (D.P.)

N107   Ormerod, David, "In a Derelict Land: The Novels of V. S. Naipaul," Contemporary Literature, 9:74-90, Winter, 1968.

Naipaul "sees the act of literary creation as being deeply involved with the desire to produce observations of a quasi-sociological nature." His analysis of West Indian society always springs from symbols of dereliction and fantasy. (A.S.W.)

A HOUSE FOR MR. BISWAS

N108   Krikler, Bernard, "V. S. Naipaul's A House for Mr. Biswas," Listener, 71:270-1, February 13, 1964.

"But for me, the great virtue of the book lies in its attachment to life . . . in its feeling for the tenacity of life." Naipaul's achievement rests with the delicacy and honesty with which he has rendered "the possibilities and limitations of . . . a single life, in a particular place. . . ." (D.P.)

N109   Ormerod, David, "Theme and Image in V. S. Naipaul's A House for Mr. Biswas," Texas Studies in Literature and Language, 8:589-602, Winter, 1967.

Although "at first sight, V. S. Naipaul's A House for Mr. Biswas . . . is a simple and direct novel . . . Naipaul's calculated simplicity should not obscure from us the fact that many of the novel's most telling effects are obtained by employing a consistent structure of imagery and near symbolism which . . . gives a consistency and immediacy to what would otherwise be a disorganized and rambling narrative." (D.P.)

NALÉ ROXLO, CONRADO

N110   Mazzara, Richard A., "Dramatic Variations on the Themes of El sombrero de tres picos: La zapatera prodigiosa and Una viuda difícil," Hispania, 41:186-9, May, 1958.

Nalé Roxlo's Una viuda difícil reveals influence of "not only the two versions of El sombrero de tres picos, but more particularly García Lorca's La zapatera prodigiosa." (A.C.H.)

N111 Tull, John F., Jr., "Influences and Attitudes in Nalé Roxlo's 'Mundo poético'," Hispania, 45:49-51, March, 1962.

Although Nalé Roxlo "has followed his own Muse from the very beginning . . . the profoundly modern character of his poetic attitudes and style" reveals a number of influences on his poetic output, stemming from other Hispanic poets of the generation of '27, from Heinrich Heine, and from Unamuno. He is "essentially a philosophical poet in . . . that the thoughts and imagery of his poetry may be understood to be articulations of his reflections on the meaning of life." (D.P.)

N112 Tull, John F., Jr., "La mujer en el teatro de Nalé Roxlo," Duquesne Hispanic Review, 3:133-7, 1964.

"In short, the truth is that the study of woman, whether as protagonist or as complement of man, turns out to be the key which opens the mytho-poetic world of the Argentine dramatist." (C.O.)

N113 Tull, John Frederick, Jr., "Nalé Roxlo's 'Chamico' Stories: A Dramatist's Apprenticeship," Hispania, 44:245-9, May, 1961.

A survey of Nalé Roxlo's humorous short stories reveals "his ability to reconstruct the complex patterns of association of his imagination in a vocabulary laden with metaphor and plays on words." (A.C.H.)

N114 Tull, John F., Jr., "Poesía y humorismo en la obra de Nalé Roxlo," Hispanófila, No. 14, pp. 41-4, 1962.

Poet by preference, humorist by necessity, Nalé approaches in the theater a synthesis of his two talents. (C.O.)

N115 Tull, John F., Jr., "Renunciation and Hope in Nalé Roxlo's Mature Poetry," Hispania, 46:533-5, September, 1963.

In his late poems Nalé "invokes . . . the virtues of renunciation, resignation, acceptance, and hope." However, "the mood of renunciation and hope in Nalé's mature poetry . . . is, in fact, the mask of an individual who has never found true internal peace." (D.P.)

N116 Tull, John F., Jr., " 'Simpatías' y 'diferencias' en los pastiches de Nalé Roxlo," Duquesne Hispanic Review, 1:1-6, No. 3, 1962.

The likes and dislikes of Nalé may be seen in his journalistic satires, later published in book form. (C.O.)

N117   Tull, J. F., Jr., "El teatro breve de Nalé Roxlo," Duquesne Hispanic Review, 6:37-40, No. 1, 1967.

As in his other works, Nalé flees from everyday reality and creates a fantasy of greater value. (C.O.)

N118   Tull, John F., Jr., "Unifying Characteristics in Nalé Roxlo's Theater," Hispania, 44:643-6, December, 1961.

"Nalé has shown in his four plays his ability to adapt his ideas about human experience and his imaginative view of human relationships to the dimensions, and limitations, of the theater. He has displayed . . . a command of language and form, and the unifying tendencies of a thoughtfully developed and consistent approach to life and to the theater. Finally . . . he has adequately demonstrated through his mastery of the techniques of the modern theater his accomplishments as the most original porteño dramatist since Sánchez. . . ." (D.P.)

JUDITH Y LAS ROSAS

N119   Tull, John F., Jr., "A Source of the Doubling of Characters in Judith y las rosas," Romance Notes, 2:21-2, Fall, 1960.

Nalé Roxlo may have borrowed the plot device of substituting characters from Giraudoux's Judith (1931). (G.B.M.)

NARAYAN, RASIPURAM KRISHNASWAMI

N120   Dale, James. "The Rootless Intellectual in the Novels of R. K. Narayan," University of Windsor Review, 1:128-37, Summer, 1965.

"The frustrated intellectual may be the cause of social upheaval and dislocation as in The Man-Eater of Malgudi, or the frustration experienced by the man with a western-style education may give rise to the inner tensions and conflicts which furnish the main themes of such novels as The English Teacher. . . ." (G.C.)

N121   Mehta, Ved, "The Train Had Just Arrived at Malgudi Station," New Yorker, 38:51-90, September 15, 1962.

"The dominant force" in Narayan's imaginary town of Malgudi "is ineluctable fate, playing one ironic trick after another on the simple inhabitants, who rise and fall a little blandly as fortune dictates." The difference between its inactivity and the activity of Faulkner's Yoknapatawpha County "may have something to do with the essences of America and India." (W.G.F.)

N121   2888

N122 Nazareth, Peter, "R. K. Narayan: Novelist," English Studies in Africa, 8:121-34, September, 1965.

" 'The naiveté of being human' is Narayan's theme. . . . He is at his best when dealing with . . . characters who are . . . 'ordinary.' . . . The darker conflicts of the human soul find no place in Narayan's work. . . ." (G.C.)

N123 Rao, V. Panduranga, "The Art of R. K. Narayan," Journal of Commonwealth Literature, 5:29-40, July, 1968.

Two cycles of spiritual experience can be traced in the total work of Narayan: in the first, "the introvert movement is centripetal," and in the second, "the extrovert movement is centrifugal." The cycle is completed from pure philosophy to pure mysticism or faith. (A.S.W.)

N124 Venkatachari, K., "R. K. Narayan's Novels: Acceptance of Life," Osmania Journal of English Studies, 7:51-65, No. 1, 1969.

"It is not 'resignation' that connotes passivity but 'acceptance' . . . of life, which is rooted in the Indian tradition, [that] imposes on . . . [Narayan's] novels a thematic pattern within which the lives of characters appear to be working themselves out. . . ." (G.C.)

N125 Walsh, William, "The Intricate Alliance: The Novels of R. K. Narayan," Review of English Literature, 2:91-9, October, 1961.

Narayan's work is "not in any limiting way regional. . . . The novels plot the rise of this intention [to attain 'a life freed from distracting illusions and hysterics'] into awareness, its recognition in a crisis of consciousness, and then its resolution." (R.J.G.)

N126 Walsh, William, "Sweet Mangoes and Malt Vinegar," Listener, 67:380-1, March 1, 1962.

Narayan's fiction, as yet little noticed critically, portrays middle class Indian life with a "subdued association of seriousness and comedy." (P.A.R.)

N127 Westbrook, Perry D., "The Short Stories of R. K. Narayan," Journal of Commonwealth Literature, 5:41-51, July, 1968.

Narayan's focus is on character and personality, and his viewpoint is gently ironic toward human failings. In his short stories, with their close observation of Indian life, he comes closest to his aim of providing pleasure and instruction to the masses through literature. (A.S.W.)

THE GUIDE

N128 Mukerji, Nirmal, "Some Aspects of the Technique of R. K. Narayan's The Guide," Western Humanities Review, 15:372-3, Autumn, 1961.

"The consistently braided time-scheme that the novelist employs in this book contributes towards a better and deeper understanding of the hero who is both a swindler and a holy man. . . . The novelist has [made] the photographic technique . . . applicable to the study of a fictional character." (G.C.)

N129 Narasimhaiah, C. D., "R. K. Narayan's The Guide," Literary Criterion, 4:63-92, Summer, 1961.

In Narayan's The Guide "characterization, setting, story, symbol, style . . . are functionally related to each other so as to create an artistic unity. . . . Narayan writes not merely with an intense social awareness of his own age but with the past of India in his bones. . . ." (D.P.)

NATHAN, GEORGE JEAN

N130 Angoff, Charles, "George Jean Nathan: A Candid Portrait," Atlantic Monthly, 210:45-8, December, 1962.

"The critical and psychological mystery about Nathan is a simple one: how did this fop, who knew nothing about slum life . . .come to be the champion of O'Neill and O'Casey, both of whom wrote so sincerely and so lovingly about the people of the slums? And how was it that [he] . . . saw through Noel Coward so readily--Noel Coward who wrote almost entirely about snobs and fops? . . . how was it that this same man . . . could see through the pretentiousness and hollowness and falseness of Clifford Odets?" (D.P.)

N131 Angoff, Charles, "George Jean Nathan: Superlative Dandy," New Republic, 150:17-20, January 4, 1964.

[This is Angoff's reconstruction of a conversation with Nathan shortly before his death. Topics covered include Mencken, Cornell University, O'Neill, beer, New York City, Scott Fitzgerald, Dreiser, Willa Cather, and Sean O'Casey.] (D.P.)

N132   Rudin, Seymour, "Playwright to Critic: Sean O'Casey's Letters to George Nathan," Massachusetts Review, 5:326-34, Winter, 1964.

[This article chronicles O'Casey's affection and friendship for Nathan, as expressed through his letters.] (A.S.W.)

NATHAN, ROBERT

N133   Roberts, Francis, "Robert Nathan: Master of Fantasy and Fable: An Interview," Prairie Schooner, 40:348-61, Winter, 1966.

[The interview covers Nathan's years at Harvard, his first novel Peter Kindred, his prose style modeled on Anatole France, his methods of writing, his use of "satiric fantasy," his emphasis on time in his novels, his eight years at Metro-Goldwyn-Mayer, and his views of the future of the novel.] (D.P.)

NAVEL, GEORGES

N134   Aubrey, Pierre, "Regards sur l'oeuvre de Georges Navel," PMLA, 78:417-21, September, 1963.

Under the peaceful surface of the work of Navel boils the violent passion of the ineradicable spirit of revolt. He did not think he could find his true place in a society with a revolutionary economy because he felt alienated from a society of workers. (W.G.F.)

NEIHARDT, JOHN G.

N135   Aly, Lucile F., "The Word-Sender: John G. Neihardt and His Audiences," Quarterly Journal of Speech, 43:151-4, April, 1957.

Neihardt's great success as a reader of his own poetry may be attributed, in part, to the moving power of the poetry itself. Additionally, he has natural advantages of "a striking appearance and a clear, resonant tenor voice." He trained himself to achieve "a flexible, resonant tone and a clear enunciation," and he pays great attention to the "techniques of phrasing, pause, and stress." (D.P.)

N136   Black, W. E., "Ethic and Metaphysic: A Study of John G. Neihardt," Western American Literature, 2:205-12, Fall, 1967.

"For Neihardt the search for the reality upon which he could predicate his life grew from a vision and an early study of Eastern philosophy." (W.G.F.)

N137 Flanagan, John T., "John G. Neihardt: Chronicler of the West," *Arizona Quarterly*, 21:7-20, Spring, 1965.

Neihardt "made a heroic effort to weld a classic form to native Western material. If his work is uneven and prolix, if probably his reach . . . exceeded his grasp, he deserves praise for his attempt." (G.C.)

N138 [Slote, Bernice D.], "Neihardt: Nebraska's Poet Laureate," *Prairie Schooner*, 41:178-81, Summer, 1967.

John G. Neihardt is a mystic and a realist, on a scale that "begins with the senses, goes to the understanding, and finally to the higher values. And there is another kind of sense--the awareness of other powers, other forces beyond understanding." (D.P.)

N139 Todd, Edgeley W., "The Frontier Epic: Frank Norris and John G. Neihardt," *Western Humanities Review*, 13:40-5, Winter, 1959.

Frank Norris expressed disappointment that no epic singer had sought to deal with the conquest of Western America. His views strikingly anticipated those of John G. Neihardt, who tried to fill the need in writing *A Cycle of the West*. (M.H.)

A CYCLE OF THE WEST

N140 Rothwell, Kenneth S., "In Search of a Western Epic: Neihardt, Sandburg, and Jaffe as Regionalists and 'Astoriadists'," *Kansas Quarterly*, 2:53-63, Spring, 1970.

John G.Neihardt in *A Cycle of the West*, Carl Sandburg in *The People, Yes*, and Dan Jaffe in *Dan Freeman* have produced the best examples of poems that might be called "Astoriads," accounts of the conquest of the American frontier that turn history into myth; as the frontier has faded, however, poets have turned from the outward settlement of the land to the inward settlement of the spirit. (W.G.F.)

NEILSON, JOHN SHAW

N141 Anderson, Hugh, "Green Singer," *Southerly*, 17:9-16, 1956.

Neilson "might be seen . . . as . . . a deliberate writer of deep sensibility who, in recording a simple yet vigorous sensuous life," rejected the sentimental and sought "an intellectual restraint in his lyricism." (G.C.)

N142   Anderson, Hugh, "A List of Uncollected Poems by Shaw Neilson,"
        Southerly, 17:37-8, 1958.

        [This is a list of uncollected poems from the Nhill Mail, the Bulletin
        (1905-1907), the Sydney Sun, the Bookfellow and the Clarion.]
        (G.C.)

N143   Chisholm, A. R., "The Celt in Shaw Neilson," Meanjin, 21:438-43,
        April, 1962.

        An examination of various possibilities for "Gaelic" influence on
        Neilson's work: language, themes, constructions, and mystical
        attitudes toward Nature. (R.L.G.)

N144   Chisholm, A. R., "Shaw Neilson's Metaphysic," Southerly,
        17:17-20, 1956.

        "Shaw Neilson's poetic nobility is instinctive . . . and as he turns to
        the sky (and the spring, and the simplicities of life and death) for his
        themes, he establishes with native ease a communion with the cosmos."
        (G.C.)

N145   Devaney, James, "John Shaw Neilson's Poems," Meanjin Quarterly,
        24:256-9, June, 1965.

        ". . . it remains a mystery how an unlettered man came to create
        the loveliest things with such consummate art." Shaw Neilson "did
        by instinct and his innate gift what scholar-poets try to do by close
        study of the subject and all the resources of the poet's workshop."
        (D.P.)

N146   Devaney, James, "Neilson's Manuscripts," Southerly, 17:34-6,
        1956.

        [These are examples of handwritten "doubtful words" in Neilson's
        manuscripts.] (G.C.)

N147   Howarth, L. I., "Neilsonian Gleanings," Southerly, 17:27-8, 1956.

        "The Unpublished Poems of Shaw Neilson, collected by . . . [James]
        Devaney, show the poet without the . . . touch [of A. G. Stephens]
        and give opportunity of studying his work as it first came from his
        hand." (G.C.)

N148   Howarth, R. G., "Shaw Neilson, 1872-1942," <u>Southerly</u>, 17:2-8, 1956.

Three poems are representative of "three different phases of . . . [Neilson's] mind." " 'Green Singer' represents him as the poet of spring, 'The Land Where I Was Born' as a lover of childhood and romance, 'The Orange Tree' as a mystic." (G.C.)

N149   McAuley, James, "Shaw Neilson's Poetry," <u>Australian Literary Studies</u>, 2:235-53, December, 1966.

Some inner strength, perhaps definable only as honesty and intuition, saved Shaw Neilson from the destroying excesses of Romantic and Symbolist poetry which, at the start of his career, strongly influenced him. Neilson's poetic diction became increasingly purified, and his sentiments came through finally with powerful sincerity. (S.T.)

N150   Oliver, H. J., "A More Versatile Neilson: The Manuscript Evidence," <u>Southerly</u>, 17:29-33, 1956.

Neilson's "<u>Notebooks</u> and the A. G. Stephens papers contain material that is indispensable if we are to be given an accurate assessment of Neilson as critic and expositor of his own work; as critic of the work of others; and as satirist and writer of humorous verse." (G.C.)

N151   Wright, Judith, "The Unshielded Eye: The Paradox of Shaw Neilson," <u>Quadrant</u>, pp. 61-75, Spring, 1959.

Shaw Neilson's "world is a world not of facts, but of meanings, in which the image is reality. Death is abroad in it, 'waiting with a watchful eye'; but love and spring and sunrise are the other persons in the parable that the world presents, and the lover and the poet are messengers of light as well as mourners of the passing." (D.P.)

NÉKRASOV, VIKTOR PLATONOVICH

N152   Nivat, Georges, "Victor Nékrasov," <u>La Table Ronde</u>, No. 185, pp. 51-60, June, 1963.

From <u>Les Tranchées de Stalingrad</u> (Prix Staline in 1947), which was almost an autobiographical account of the battle of Stalingrad, through <u>La Ville natale</u> in which it was a question of the non-combatants under the German occupation, and through <u>Kira</u>, concerning those deported to concentration camps, Nékrasov has employed the psychological monologue, borrowed doubtless from Hemingway. (T.T.B.)

NEMECEK, ZDENEK

N153   Nosco, Beatrice M., "Zdenek Nemecek (1894-1957), Poet of the Czech Emigrants," Slavic and East European Journal, 17:43-6, Spring, 1959.

Nemecek's work expresses the tragic view that "people are both innocently and intentionally wounded by blindness, by inability to learn the truth and thus they fight an unequal fight with an unknown force that for them only approaches the truth." (W.G.F.)

NEMEROV, HOWARD

N154   Harvey, Robert D., "A Prophet Armed: An Introduction to the Poetry of Howard Nemerov," Tri-Quarterly, 3:37-42, Fall, 1960.

Nemerov's novels and poems are characterized by wit and satire. His chief themes are childhood experiences, wartime violence, and nature. (E.T.)

N155   Nemerov, Howard, "Attentiveness and Obedience," London Magazine, 4:41-9, November, 1964.

Early on, like other neophyte poets of his generation, Nemerov pursued matters of style--irony, learning, ambiguity. Now simplicity and ease in the measure are primary in his set of values. (D.P.)

N156   Nemerov, Howard, "The Muse's Interest," Carleton Miscellany, 4:83-90, Spring, 1963.

Poetry's "opening of the ways is visible . . . wherever a poet illuminates human consciousness, or the consciousness of being human, which he does, perhaps, more by his way of speaking than by the morality or general truth of what it is he says." The power of poetry is "subversive, in that it is unpredictable and beyond control or purposive application to the immediate situation; without meaning to, perhaps without especially wanting to, poetry changes the mind of the world." (D.P.)

N157   Randall, Julia, "Genius of the Shore: The Poetry of Howard Nemerov,"
Hollins Critic, 6:1-12, June, 1969.

"Nemerov, then, does not seek to impose a vision upon the world so
much as to listen to what it says. He works in closer relationship
with literal meaning than is presently fashionable; consequently his
worst fault . . . is sententiousness, but his corresponding virtue is
a clarity whose object is not to diminish the mystery of the world but
to allow it to appear without the interposition of a peculiar individuality, or of fancy-work or arabesque. He is . . . a romantic poet;
he is a religious poet without religion; a prophet, especially in the
polemical and ironic mode, without portfolio." (D.P.)

NERUDA, PABLO

N158   Babilas, Wolfgang, "Die Oden Pablo Nerudas," Archiv für das
Studium der Neueren Sprachen und Literaturen, 204:161-79,
September, 1967.

Particularly in the late odes does Neruda's realism seek to show all
men the beauty and usefulness of elemental things. (J.R.R.)

N159   Belitt, Ben, "The Burning Sarcophagus: A Revaluation of Pablo
Neruda," Southern Review, 4:598-615, Summer, 1968.

"I shall assume . . . that the poetry of Pablo Neruda is part of
everything else I know and sense about work of genius everywhere
. . . that his work . . . resonates against literatures other than
his own . . . and that their resonance is the true measure of his
long traffic with the democracy of letters." (D.P.)

N160   Belitt, Ben, "The Mourning Neruda," Mundus Artium, 1:14-23,
Winter, 1967.

[This is an appreciative assessment of Neruda's The Stones of Chile,
Ceremonial Songs, and Full Powers, which includes considerable
quotation and paraphrase as well as some explication.] (J.M.D.)

N161   Bly, Robert, "The Surprise of Neruda," Sixties, No. 7, pp. 18-9,
Winter, 1964.

Neruda's poetry violates the rules of the "wise" critics. He combines surreal imagery with the "outer world," such things as the
United Fruit Company. He also proved that a politically committed
poet can be "wildly romantic and . . . sophisticated." (E.T.)

N162 Ellis, Keith, "Poema veinte: A Structural Approach," Romance Notes, 11:507-17, 1970.

Previous explicators have failed to take into account a key reference to "versos tristes." An exhaustive analysis reveals Neruda's debt to his predecessors as well as his similarities to his contemporaries. (C.O.)

N163 Gottlieb, Marlene, "La Guerra Civil española en la poesía de Pablo Neruda y César Vallejo," Cuadernos Americanos, 154:189-200, September-October, 1967.

The Spanish Civil War frees Neruda from his withdrawal and his spiritual isolation. But to Vallejo the war brings a personal awareness of his own human tragedy. Neruda opens to the world and finds joy and purpose in struggle. Vallejo withdraws into himself and finds strength in stoically bearing suffering. (C.O.)

N164 Gottlieb, Marlene, "Pablo Neruda, poeta del amor," Cuadernos Americanos, 149:211-21, November-December, 1966.

Contrary to popular belief, love continues to be an important theme in Neruda's poetry. Even his political works contain love poems. Love is still passion, but not despair as in his youth. His philosophy of hope has produced a love poetry of joy. (C.O.)

N165 Hamilton, Carlos D., "Itinerario de Pablo Neruda," Revista Hispánica Moderna, 22:286-97, July-October, 1956.

"From the Tercera Residencia, or rather from the poem 'Las furias y las penas,' the first after his conversion (to communism), there rises the present-day Neruda, prophetic and happy, embittered and erotic, involved and fiercely individualistic, coarse and poetic, with the greatest density of light in the midst of the complicated illogical imagery of his 'hermetic' poetry." (A.C.H.)

N166 Lozada, Alfredo, "Neruda y Schopenhauer," Revista Hispánica Moderna, 32:217-30, July-October, 1966.

Neruda may have read Schopenhauer. More probably, he read the works of Pío Baroja and Azorín, both strongly influenced by Schopenhauer during their early years. But Neruda's "Schopenhauerian" negativism is tied to a positive desire which goes beyond Schopenhauer's ethical solution. (C.O.)

N167   McGrath, Thomas, "The Poetry of Pablo Neruda," Mainstream,
        15:43-7, June, 1962.

        Neruda is a poet in whose work "one of the essentials of great poetry,
        continual surprise and revelation, in the language itself, is always
        present. The typical form which that revelation assumes in his work
        is that of the unexpected coupling of qualities. . . ." (R.L.G.)

N168   Navas-Ruiz, Ricardo, "Neruda y Guillén: un caso de relaciones
        literarias," Revista Iberoamericana, 31:251-62, July-December,
        1965.

        Pablo Neruda and Nicolás Guillén both evidence the influence of
        modern Brazil in their poetry. And both occasionally allow their
        art to suffer for the sake of ideology. (C.O.)

N169   Paseyro, Ricardo, "The Dead World of Pablo Neruda," Tri-Quarterly,
        15:203-27, Spring, 1969.

        As a poet Neruda "impoverishes the planet, heaping together an infor-
        mational and coarse slang; never does he make Being agree with lan-
        guage, he doesn't operate except on the most abject and inferior
        existence of things. Thus he betrays . . . all his rights and all his
        obligations; thus does he expatriate himself, forever, from poetry."
        (D.P.)

N170   Rojas, Manuel, "Apunte sobre el sentimiento de soledad en la
        poesía de Pablo Neruda," Cuadernos Americanos, 138:208-17,
        January-February, 1965.

        Solitude as a poetic theme is less important in Neruda since the
        Spanish Civil War. In this struggle, as well as in the teachings of
        his party, he finds peace and human company. (C.O.)

N171   Sánchez, Luis Alberto, "Pablo Neruda," Cuadernos Americanos,
        3:235-47, March-April, 1962.

        [This article traces the complicated poetic trajectory of Neruda,
        with pointed references to his biography.] (C.O.)

                RESIDENCE ON EARTH--See
                RESIDENCIA EN LA TIERRA

RESIDENCIA EN LA TIERRA

N172 Lozada, Alfredo, "Estilo y poesía de Pablo Neruda: Examen de la interpretación de Amado Alonso de Residencia en la tierra," PMLA, 79:648-63, December, 1964.

Alonso termed Neruda's language undisciplined, crude, incorrect, often seeming an awkward and incompetent translation. Lozada's detailed rebuttal discusses the intent and the impact of these numerous instances of "unfortunate" language and explicates the passages in question. (C.O.)

N173 Lozada, Alfredo, "Residencia en la tierra: Algunas correcciones," Revista Hispánica Moderna, 30:108-18, April, 1964.

Neruda's changes in later editions of certain poems shows the poet's concern for the creation as finished product. The changes evidence a tendency toward greater conciseness and a more fertile imagination. (C.O.)

N174 Simonis, Ferdinand, "Pablo Nerudas frühe Lyrik und die Residencias: Wege der Wandlung," Neophilologus, 51:15-31, January, 1967.

Neruda's Residencia en la tierra marked a major change in his work. (J.R.R.)

N175 Tolman, Jon M., "Death and Alien Environment in Pablo Neruda's Residencia en la tierra," Hispania, 51:79-85, March, 1968.

There is a thematic unity in Residencia which is more important than its apparently chaotic form or syntax. The theme of death is related to time, self-destruction, night and isolation. The correlative theme of solitude in an alien environment is related especially to distance, silence and falling. (C.O.)

LAS UVAS Y EL VIENTO

N176 Eshleman, Clayton, "Neruda: An Elemental Response," Tri-Quarterly, 15:228-37, Spring, 1969.

The Grapes and the Wind [Las uvas y el viento] is a bad book. . . . It is a 400 page travel journal versed as poetry. . . . it literally consists of memories, news topical to the Korean war and the division of Berlin, friends's deaths, potshots at non- and anti-Communist powers, instantly befriended martyrs, and it is ballasted by a promotion of Stalin . . . as world leader/savior." (D.P.)

NERVAT, MARIE

N177   Rat, Maurice, "Le Souvenir de Marie Nervat," <u>La Revue des Deux Mondes</u>, No. 7, pp. 19-24, July 1, 1969.

Like Marceline Desbordes-Valmore, Marie Nervat was an adept at pure, spontaneous, musing poetry. A feminine romantic similar to Gerard d'Houville, she described exotic landscapes, memories of her youth and her intimate sensations. (T.T.B.)

NERVO, AMADO

N178   Bratsas, Dorothy, "The Problem of Ideal Love in Nervo's Novels," <u>Romance Notes</u>, 9:244-8, 1968.

The material world, and especially sex, impede perfect love in this life. Carnal love is self-love. Utopia can come only after death. (C.O.)

N179   Holdsworth, Carole A., "Amado Nervo's 'Notas bibliográficas' in the <u>Revista Moderna</u>," <u>Romance Notes</u>, 10:300-3, 1969.

[This is a survey of Nervo's early journalistic criticism.] (C.O.)

N180   Leal, Luis, "La poesía de Amado Nervo: A cuarenta años de distancia," <u>Hispania</u>, 43:43-7, March, 1960.

The value of Nervo's poetry, in its transition from personal experience to philosophy, has diminished since his death. (A.C.H.)

NEVEUX, GEORGES

N181   Brée, Germaine, "Georges Neveux: A Theater of Adventure," <u>Yale French Studies</u>, No. 14, pp. 65-70, Winter, 1954-55.

Neveux's theatre, language, and themes are poetic. His principal idea is that "to live is to create, to <u>give</u> life not merely to receive it. Love is not an end in itself, but . . . the instrument of creation, initiator of all adventure, producer and reproducer of life." (L.L.)

N182   Pronko, Leonard C., "Georges Neveux: The Theatrical Voyage," <u>Drama Survey</u>, 3:244-52, Fall, 1963.

Georges Neveux is unknown in America although he is appealing, charming, amusing, poetic and theatrical, as may be confirmed by study of <u>Juliette ou la clé des songes</u>, <u>Le Voyage de Thésée</u>, <u>Plainte contre inconnu</u> and <u>Zamore</u>. (D.P.)

NEVEUX, POL

N183   Lebrau, Jean, "Le Souvenir de Pol Neveux," <u>La Revue des Deux Mondes</u>, 142:621-7, March, 1970.

Although best known for <u>Golo</u> and <u>La Douce Enfance</u>, Neveux's greatest work perhaps was <u>Richesses des bibliothéques provinciales</u>. (T.T.B.)

NEVILLE, EDGAR

N184   Wade, Gerald E., "Spain: Present-Day Theatre and Edgar Neville," <u>South Atlantic Bulletin</u>, 16:4-7, March, 1961.

Because it is impossible for Spanish playwrights to raise the large questions of social and political import that harrass the Spanish people, the most flourishing drama in an era of frivolous mediocrity is the <u>teatro evasionista</u>--as exemplified by Neville's smashing success <u>El baile</u>--"that uses fantasy in place of emotion and hence fails to arouse emotion in the spectators." (W.G.F.)

NEWBY, PERCY HOWARD

N185   Bufkin, E. C., "Quest in the Novels of P. H. Newby," <u>Critique: Studies in Modern Fiction</u>, 8:51-62, Fall, 1965.

Man's " 'timeless quest for wholeness and wisdom' . . . is indeed the principal matter of Newby's novels, shaping them both thematically and structurally. The hero-quester's search . . . deals with the spiritual, religious, moral, or psychological, and it centers on the individual, not society. . . ." Newby's "technique, looking forward while gazing backward, formulates the hero's problem, structures the complex design of narrative, and involves the reader himself as quester in an amazingly original manner." (D.P.)

N186   Dickerson, Lucia, "Portrait of the Artist as a Jung Man," <u>Kenyon Review</u>, 21:58-83, Winter, 1959.

The novels of P. H. Newby are elaborations of Jungian myths and archetypes and show an "ultimate concern . . . with that universal hero, man, his timeless quest for wholeness and wisdom, the One in the aspect of the Many." (K.W.)

N187   Mathews, F. X., "Newby on the Nile: The Comic Trilogy," Twentieth Century Literature, 14:3-16, April, 1968.

The trilogy of The Picnic at Sakkara, Revolution and Roses, and A Guest and His Going are seen as "satiric comedy concerned with the exposure of illusion, both individual and cultural." The satire particularly flourishes on the contradictions between the English and Egyptian character. (D.P.)

N188   Mathews, F. X., "Witness to Violence: The War Novels of P. H. Newby," Texas Studies in Literature and Language, 12:121-35, Spring, 1970.

"In his two-volume sequence, A Step to Silence (1952) and The Retreat (1953) . . . Newby poses most insistently the question of the responsibility of the private witness for a world of violence." His "approach to the war is perhaps best described . . . by the image of the witness. In an age of violence the witness is a mere spectator of, is blind to, reflects, or sees beyond irrational reality." (D.P.)

N189   Poss, Stanley, "Manners and Myths in the Novels of P. H. Newby," Critique: Studies in Modern Fiction, 12:5-19, No. 1, 1970.

Although Newby's body of work is large it reveals few signs of hasty or redundant work, "but rather an original and resourceful imagination pursuing its visions in deceptively traditional forms, chiefly that of the comedy of manners. The closely observed surfaces of these (usually) comic novels conceal a terrain that remains virtually unmapped by critics. . . ." However, his best books "form a volume of work which I am inclined to rank as one of the most substantial achievements in English fiction during the last two decades." (D.P.)

NEWLOVE, JOHN

N190   Ferns, John, "A Desolate Country: John Newlove's Black Night Window," Far Point, 2:68-75, 1969.

Black Night Window is more diffident and introspective than Newlove's previous work, and in the best poems "interior journeys are balanced by disinterested social awareness and genuine insights." (A.S.W.)

NEWMAN, FRANCES

N191   Drake, Robert Y., Jr., "Frances Newman: Fabulist of Decadence,"
Georgia Review, 14:389-98, Winter, 1960.

Miss Newman is "undeserving of such neglect as she has suffered at
the hands of serious readers since her death [1928]. Though her
production is slight [a few short stories and two novels] . . . her
fables abide as pertinent--and as sinister--as when they were
written." (R.J.G.)

N192   Symons, Julian, "About Frances Newman," London Magazine,
6:36-48, June, 1966.

Frances Newman should be noted in any history of the literature
between the wars. Her The Hard-Boiled Virgin and Dead Lovers
are Faithful Lovers, representative of the fresh American aestheticism of the 1920's, are true works of art. (D.P.)

NEXO, MARTIN ANDERSEN

N193   Koefoed, H. A., "Martin Andersen Nexo--Some Viewpoints,"
Scandinavica, 4:27-37, 1965.

". . . the 'universal value' . . . of Nexo's work has been firmly
established through its social-human rather than its social-political
aspects, whereas the 'actual value' of his revolutionary programme
. . . can be registered in Eastern Europe." (G.C.)

NICHOLSON, NORMAN

N194   Gardner, Philip, "The Provincial Poetry of Norman Nicholson,"
University of Toronto Quarterly, 36:274-94, April, 1967.

Among poets who treat regional and local themes Norman Nicholson
is the only true provincial poet. His work expresses an intimacy
derived from his membership in a Christian community; his poems
have facets of archetypal myth and universality. Central to his
ethos is the permanence of nature despite the impact of man. (D.P.)

N195   Morgan, K., "Some Christian Themes in the Poetry of Norman
Nicholson," Review of English Literature, 5:70-8, July, 1964.

". . . within a framework of generally orthodox Christian belief
[Norman Nicholson] stresses the need to respect the natural order;

to develop sensitivity to the 'voices' of the majestic and solitary heights; to accept as God's gifts the graces of the seasons. . .; to be willing to make a 'holy fool' of oneself as a way of truly inheriting the earth; to recognize the gospel of cooperative work as one solution to the problem of man's 'fallen' condition; to accept the potential meaning of the traditional symbols of the faith; to recognize the mysteries of the physical universe as analogies of some facets of metaphysical reality." (D.P.)

N196 Nicholson, Norman, "The Writer and His Background: The Second Chance," Listener, 70:343-4, September 5, 1963.

[These are Nicholson's recollections of his childhood and early youth in the town of Millom in the County of Cumberland, and how the town influenced Nicholson as a writer and as a man.] (D.P.)

NICOLSON, HAROLD

N197 Hudson, Derek, "Harold Nicolson," Quarterly Review, 305:163-71, 1967.

"As a writer [Harold Nicolson] has been gifted with a rare facility of expression. . . . But he has never descended to banality. And now that we can read his diary . . . we can recognize Harold Nicolson's mind as one of the most brilliant and stimulating of his time." (D.P.)

N198 Kronenberger, Louis, "Diary of a U-Man," Atlantic Monthly, 218:131-6, November, 1966.

"From its very beginnings. . . . [the life of Sir Harold Nicolson] has been multifaceted, polylingual, cosmopolitan, and at the same time monumentally English, ineradicably upper-class." In his Diaries and Letters "the self in Sir Harold speaks in many ways for many similar Englishmen. . . ." (D.P.)

NIEDECKER, LORINE

N199 Cox, Kenneth, "The Poems of Lorine Niedecker," Cambridge Quarterly, 4:169-75, No. 2, 1969.

"The poems hold attention by their quiet confidence. Their language is colloquial and elliptical to a degree that registers the feel of a place and the personality of a speaker before meaning. It is the speech of the American people, whittled clean." (K.M.W.)

NIMIER, ROGER

N200   Abirached, Robert, "Roger Nimier," La Nouvelle Revue Française,
No. 119, pp. 901-2, November, 1962.

"You will not live old. Otherwise you would make less enemies."
Nimier's work is studded with such premonitions and presages. He
was one of the authentic spokesmen of his generation and the principal inventor of modern romanticism. (T.T.B.)

N201   Spens, Willy de, "Roger Nimier," La Table Ronde, No. 178,
pp. 29-31, November, 1962.

Contrary to the critics, Nimier did not open "new perspectives."
Thanks to him, Montherlant, Drieu la Rochelle, Bernanos and
Giraudoux found a successor. From the sequels of naturalism,
immodest confessions and reporters's accounts disguised as fiction,
he turned away and restored the dignity of the novel as a work of
art. (T.T.B.)

NIMS, JOHN FREDERICK

N202   Shaw, Richard O., "Sanctity and the Poetry of John F. Nims,"
Renascence, 13:84-91, Winter, 1961.

Nims's poetry, though noted for its striking perceptual images, is
nearly always organized around a governing principle. (R.K.)

NIN, ANAÏS

N203   Lipton, Victor, "The Little Straw Basket," Prairie Schooner,
40:266-72, Fall, 1966.

Anaïs Nin's . . . diary of the years 1931-1934 . . . may well be one
of the last great diaries we will be privileged to see. . . . We have
in it an attempt to use the resources of unaided, pure artistic talent
that stands out in a world whose humans are cyborgian and whose art
is pop. . . . it appears to be a vindication of symbolism and surrealism . . . [which] does more than symbolism and surrealism ever
hoped to do: . . . it is, somehow magically, the symbolic and even
surreal concept made real and lived out." (D.P.)

N204 Nin, Anaïs, "Onze lettres à Anaïs Nin," Tel Quel, No. 20, pp. 3-11, Winter, 1965.

[These are eleven letters to the American novelist written between February and July 1933.] (T.T.B.)

N205 Zinnes, Harriet, "Anaïs Nin's Works Reissued," Books Abroad, 37:283-6, Summer, 1963.

Like D. H. Lawrence "Anaïs Nin is one of the few writers to understand modern woman's striving, her nervous relations with men floundering in a disintegrated society, men no longer sure of their position in that most primitive of relationships, that between man and woman." (C.E.N.)

SEDUCTION OF THE MINOTAUR

N206 McEvilly, Wayne, "Two Faces of Death in Anaïs Nin's Seduction of the Minotaur," New Mexico Quarterly, 38, No. 4 - 39, No. 1, pp. 179-92, Winter-Spring, 1969.

"Seduction of the Minotaur ought to be read . . . as music. Then we would understand readily enough the dynamic peace which pervades the glorious ending of the book, not a peace without strife . . . but a passionate serenity, a belief in the richness of life, a fullness, an illumination, a fire, gold." However, "at the very core [of the book] the novelist has let fall over the structure the shadow of death . . . a death of living . . . palpable, black, silent, ominous, sterile presence." (D.P.)

NIRALA--See
TRIPATHI, SURYA KANT

NKOSI, LEWIS

N207 Gérard, Albert, "Tragédies africaines," La Revue Nouvelle, 41:184-94, 1965.

Although the English-language theatre in Africa received no strong impetus until 1962, when a school of dramatic art was founded in Nigeria, it has already produced two powerful tragedies: The Rhythm of Violence by exiled South African Lewis Nkosi, which completely ignores African tradition, and Song of a Goat by Nigerian John Pepper Clark, which makes no allusion to modern Africa. (W.G.F.)

NOAILLES, ANNA DE

N208 La Rochefoucauld, Edmée de, "Anna de Noailles et le goût de l'éternel," La Revue de Paris, 63:90-102, January, 1956.

The theme of eternity appears in passages of the poet's work at various periods of her life. (M.M.)

NOËL, MARIE

N209 Crane, Christina, "Marie Noël's Achievements in Prose," Renascence, 9:132-9, Spring, 1957.

Marie Noël's prose writings are fresh and spontaneous, delineating a wide range of human emotions through her main themes of love, death and religion. (A.S.W.)

N210 Sutton, Howard, "Marie Noël: A Life in Song," American Society of Legion of Honor Magazine, 37:153-63, No. 3, 1966.

Marie Noël, "no less cogently than Mauriac and Bernanos . . . has sounded the abyss of metaphysical anguish and dramatically repre-sented the misery of man deprived of God. . . . [Her] depth and originality of concepts and the fitness of expression at times recall the Pensées of Pascal." (D.P.)

PETIT-JOUR

N210a Sutton, Howard, "Two Poets of Childhood: Marcel Proust and Marie Noël," Books Abroad, 41:261-6, Summer, 1967.

"Marie Noël's charming volume of childhood memories, Petit-jour, presents a number of analogies with parts of Marcel Proust's A la recherche du temps perdu, especially the Combray section . . . [al-though] there can be no question of a literary influence." (D.P.)

NOLAN, BRIAN--See
O'NOLAN, BRIAN

NORGE, GÉO

N211 Temmer, Mark, "The poetry of Géo Norge," Yale French Studies, No. 21, pp. 49-59, Spring-Summer, 1958.

"Norge's verse is in line with the traditional French ideal of formal elegance. It is poetry which, although anchored in the French past, leads to the present and future of men in general." (D.P.)

NORRIS, FRANK

N212   Coolidge, John S., "Lewis E. Gates: The Permutations of Romanticism in America," New England Quarterly, 30:23-38, March, 1957.

In his criticism of Frank Norris and elsewhere Gates's "anticipation--from impressionist premises--of [T. S.] Eliot's theory of tradition makes it . . . clear how essentially Romantic that theory is."(W.T.S.)

N213   Cooperman, Stanley, "Frank Norris and the Werewolf of Guilt," Modern Language Quarterly, 20:252-8, September, 1959.

"Frank Norris, as perhaps no other major figure among naturalist writers, combines . . . elements [of] . . . the duality between flesh and spirit, evil and purity. . . . especially in McTeague and Vandover and the Brute . . . these elements combine with a torturous sense of guilt and masochism. The result in both books is psychic disease and destructive ambivalence." (D.P.)

N214   Davison, Richard Allan, "Frank Norris's Thirteen Uncollected Newsletters," Notes and Queries, 11:71-3, February, 1964.

Frank Norris's thirteen Newsletters published in the Chicago American are important not only in delineating Norris's concept of naturalism; they also present his "views on contemporary authors and literary issues elucidating both his craft and his aesthetics." (D.P.)

N215   Davison, Richard Allan, "The Remaining Seven of Frank Norris's 'Weekly Letters'," American Literary Realism, 3:47-65, Summer, 1965.

[This is the first re-publication of seven "Weekly Letters" Frank Norris contributed to the Chicago American in 1901. The letters are important for their valuable commentary about publishing of the period, and for their statements of "Norris's critical views, personal and literary gossip."] (D.P.)

N216   Davison, Richard Allan, "An Unpublished Norris Discussion of Kipling," American Notes and Queries, 4:87, February, 1966.

[This reprints a "weekly letter" by Frank Norris in which he describes and analyzes Kipling's manner of composing verse rapidly and without correction.] (D.P.)

N217   Dillingham, William B., "Frank Norris and the Genteel Tradition,"
        Tennessee Studies in Literature, 5:15-24, 1960.

        Although "Norris's deviation from acceptable subject matter of fiction,
        his treatment of unpleasant details, and his Darwinism . . . com-
        pletely blinded his own generation and many critics afterwards to his
        kinship with the genteel tradition" his novels often "reveal him as
        strongly influenced by the same manners, morals, and restraints
        that molded the work of . . . writers of genteel literature." (D.P.)

N218   Filler, Louis, "Dreamers and the American Dream," Southwest
        Review, 40:359-63, Autumn, 1955.

        Dreiser, London, Norris were "not intellectual traitors who had gone
        over to the enemy of success," as K. Lynn suggests in The Dream of
        Success; "their value has lain . . . in what they unconsciously re-
        vealed about the people from whom they had sprung . . . having ex-
        perienced America . . . they have much to report. (F.F.E.)

N219   Francis, Herbert E., Jr., "A Reconsideration of Frank Norris,"
        Emory University Quarterly, 15:110-8, June, 1959.

        "If Norris's romantic nature often interfered in the clear execution
        of his themes, ironically much of his appeal is derived from that
        nature. . . ." Of his works, The Octopus and The Pit best reveal
        the "multiplicity of conflicting truths which so represent the conflict
        in the life of man." (G.C.)

N220   French, Warren, "Frank Norris (1870-1902)," American Literary
        Realism, 1:84-9, Fall, 1967.

        [This is a critical survey of the state of Norris scholarship, review-
        ing criticism, sources, and recent articles; locating manuscript
        collections, and indicating prime areas for further study.] (D.P.)

N221   Giles, James R., "Beneficial Atavism in Frank Norris and Jack
        London," Western American Literature, 4:15-27, Spring, 1969.

        Both Norris and London expressed their fear of the growth of the
        city through the concept of atavism. "Both writers made a distinc-
        tion between beneficial atavism and destructive atavism. . . . If
        the reversal occurs in the city, it is usually destructive; while a
        similar reversal on the high seas or on any 'frontier' is generally
        beneficial." (W.G.F.)

N222   Giles, James R., "Some Notes on the Red-Blooded Reading of Kipling by Jack London and Frank Norris," Jack London Newsletter, 3:56-62, 1970.

London and Norris both admired and were influenced by Kipling, whom they misinterpreted as glorifying brutality and racism. (A.S.W.)

N223   Goldsmith, Arnold L., "Charles and Frank Norris," Western American Literature, 2:30-49, Spring, 1967.

"Like Dreiser, Charles Norris was deeply concerned with literature of social reform. The same cannot be said of Frank, who, in his first five novels, really did not question such things as the structure of our capitalist economy . . . and the inequalities of American justice . . . but there seems to be no such pivotal point in the writing career of Charles." (K.M.W.)

N224   Hill, John S., "The Influence of Cesare Lombroso on Frank Norris's Early Fiction," American Literature, 42:89-91, March, 1970.

Norris's three stories "A Case for Lombroso," "A Reversion to Type" and "Son of a Sheik," demonstrate that he was influenced by Lombroso's theory "that physical characteristics reveal mental characteristics . . . [a] postulation . . . based on anthropological measurements. . . ." (D.P.)

N225   Hill, J. S., "Poe's 'Fall of the House of Usher' and Frank Norris's Early Short Stories," Huntington Library Quarterly, 26:111-2, November, 1962.

The direct influence of Poe's "Fall of the House of Usher" on Norris's "A Case for Lombroso" and "His Single Blessedness" includes "certain characteristics of hero and heroine--such as highly developed senses . . . [and] the mood of horror which Norris tries to create." (D.P.)

N226   Hill, John S., "The Writing and Publication of the Novels of Frank Norris," American Notes and Queries, 2:151-2, June, 1964.

[Listed here are the dates of the writing and publication of Norris's novels.] (D.P.)

N227 Hoffmann, Charles G., "Norris and the Responsibility of the Novelist,"
South Atlantic Quarterly, 54:508-15, October, 1955.

Norris's realistic, sincere, and purposeful novels insist upon his
belief that the novelist must mold public opinion. Although the novels
do not indicate Norris's steady development as an artist, they document his rejection of complete naturalism and his growing belief in
the regenerative power of love. (W.B.B.)

N228 Johnson, George W., "Frank Norris and Romance," American
Literature, 33:52-63, March, 1961.

"Although a pioneer in forming a viable tradition of American naturalism," the tension between the romantic and realistic approaches to
reality "contribute much to the vitality of his best work." (W.G.F.)

N229 Kwiat, Joseph J., "Frank Norris: The Novelist as Social Critic and
Literary Theorist," Arizona Quarterly, 18:319-28, Winter, 1962.

Norris "considered the novel as a social instrument and the novelist
as a person with social responsibilities in performing his literary
duties." (G.C.)

N230 Kwiat, Joseph J., "Frank Norris: The Novelist as Social Critic and
Literary Theorist," Die Neueren Sprachen, 9:385-92, 1954.

Frank Norris "was too frequently downright naive and uncertain in
his knowledge of his own position. His discussion . . . of what he
considered to be the major aesthetic issues (for example: life vs.
literature; realism vs. romance; accuracy vs. truth; constructing
vs. exploring) is by and large over-simplified, vacillating and contradictory. But once the theoretical limitations of his mind are understood . . . Norris manages to give . . . a sense of the intellectual struggle through which one novelist expressed some of the
leading ideas and attitudes of an important stream of writers . . .
within the American environment." (D.P.)

N231 Labrie, Rodrigue E., "The Howells-Norris Relationship and the
Growth of Naturalism," Discourse, 11:363-71, Summer, 1969.

Frank Norris was "the most Zolaesque of the American naturalists
in his selection of large themes, the sensational and often sordid
treatment of contemporary affairs and the belief in the necessity of
the novel being used . . . to expose evil, and ultimately to improve
the lot of mankind." Although he viewed Howells's genteel realism
with impatience, the younger writer did respect Howells's craftsmanship and was grateful for his influential support of his own career.(D.P.)

N232   Millgate, Michael, "The Novelist and the Businessman: Henry
        James, Edith Wharton, Frank Norris," Studi Americani, 5:161-89,
        1959.

        "It is perhaps a fundamental weakness in James, not simply that he
        failed to deal with business and businessmen . . . but that the social
        and human area in which he worked . . . became progressively
        narrower. . . . The great interest of Edith Wharton's work, on the
        other hand, is that, unrestricted by the Jamesian inhibitions, she is
        able to bring to bear the Jamesian techniques upon important socio-
        economic questions that James himself regards . . . from a great
        distance. At the same time she does not have the devouring energy
        which Norris displays in The Octopus and . . . sections of The Pit.
        . . ." (D.P.)

N233   Piper, Henry Dan, "Frank Norris and Scott Fitzgerald,"
        Huntington Library Quarterly, 19:393-400, August, 1956.

        Fitzgerald's indebtedness to Frank Norris "was limited for the most
        part to the younger writer's early formative years--for Fitzgerald
        in his later and greatest work is, after all, not really a naturalist or
        even a realist." However, the influence of Vandover and the Brute
        on The Beautiful and Damned and "May Day" is clear, explicit and
        direct. (D.P.)

N234   Pizer, Donald, "Evolutionary Ethical Dualism in Frank Norris's
        Vandover and the Brute and McTeague," PMLA, 76:552-60,
        December, 1961.

        A close examination of Vandover and the Brute and McTeague
        demonstrates "that though Norris was attracted by Zola and by con-
        temporary science, he was by no means a materialistic determinist.
        He was instead what can be called an evolutionary dualist, and much
        of his fiction draws upon the possibilities of conflict, of symbolism,
        and of sensationalism within this system for its power and for its
        inner coherence." (D.P.)

N235   Pizer, Donald, "Frank Norris's Definition of Naturalism,"
        Modern Fiction Studies, 8:408-10, Winter, 1962-63.

        An examination of Norris's "A Plea for Romantic Fiction," his
        "Zola as a Romantic Writer," and his unknown "Weekly Letter" in
        the Chicago American of August 3, 1901 makes it clear that he "con-
        ceived of naturalism as a fictional mode which illustrated some fun-
        damental truth of life within a detailed presentation of the sensational
        and low." (D.P.)

N236   Pizer, Donald, "The Masculine-Feminine Ethic in Frank Norris's
        Popular Novels," Texas Studies in Literature and Language,
        6:84-91, Spring, 1964.

        Moran of the Lady Letty, Blix and A Man's Woman constitute a kind
        of trilogy which develops clearly and forcefully the theme of the
        correct relationship of man and woman, which is closely related to
        Norris's beliefs about man's ethical nature. (W.G.F.)

N237   Pizer, Donald, "Romantic Individualism in Garland, Norris and
        Crane," American Quarterly, 10:463-75, Winter, 1958.

        "Garland, Norris and Crane all exhibit qualities of romantic individ-
        ualism [as] . . . an integral part of their intellectual make-up. In
        Garland and Crane it is manifested by a belief in the validity . . . of
        the individual artist's perception of life. . . . In Norris it is imag-
        inatively embodied in an acceptance of intuitively derived Truth."
        (D.P.)

N238   Schneider, Robert W., "Frank Norris: The Naturalist as Victorian,"
        Midcontinent American Studies Journal, 3:13-27, Spring, 1962.

        In Norris's fiction traditional moral and ethical assumptions, center-
        ing on the Victorian sexual code, war with progressive determinism,
        and it is this combination "that brings philosophical confusion to his
        novels." (R.B.W.)

N239   Todd, Edgeley W., "The Frontier Epic: Frank Norris and John G.
        Neihardt," Western Humanities Review, 13:40-5, Winter, 1959.

        Frank Norris expressed disappointment that no epic singer had
        sought to deal with the conquest of Western America. His views strik-
        ingly anticipated those of John G. Neihardt, who tried to fill the need
        in writing A Cycle of the West. [Part 1 of "The Frontier and Amer-
        ican Literature: A Symposium."] (M.H.)

N240   Walker, Don D., "The Western Naturalism of Frank Norris,"
        Western American Literature, 2:14-29, Spring, 1967.

        In the wilderness, Norris saw the primeval world, which encouraged
        in man a reversion to a brutish past. (A.S.W.)

BLIX

N241 Stronk, James B., "John Kendrick Bangs Criticizes Norris's
Borrowings in Blix," American Literature, 42:380-6, November,
1970.

John Kendrick Bangs's essay "The Compleat Novelist," which appeared in Literature (New York, November 17, 1899), although
"ostensibly a bantering review of [Norris's] light novel Blix . . . is
in fact a satirical article . . . intended to discredit Norris for
unoriginality. . . ." The essay "was probably the first adverse
criticism of Norris's method as a novelist. . . ." (D.P.)

McTEAGUE

N242 Childs, James, "The First Draft of McTeague: 1893," American
Notes and Queries, 3:37-8, November, 1964.

Internal evidence suggests that McTeague was begun as early as
February, 1893; it is unlikely that composition began before that
date. (D.P.)

N243 Dillingham, William B., "The Old Folks of McTeague," Nineteenth-
Century Fiction, 16:169-73, September, 1961.

"Rather than a 'romantic flaw,' the sub-plot [of McTeague] intensi-
fies and broadens Norris's theme and is an integral part of the
novel's structure. . . . Every important step in the progress of the
old pair's romance marks a stage in the deterioration of McTeague
and Trina. . . . The destinies, the 'very souls' of all the characters
. . . are the 'sport of chance'." (J.D.S.)

N244 Hill, John S., "Trina Sieppe: First Lady of American Literary
Naturalism," University of Kansas City Review, 29:77-80,
October, 1962.

". . . Trina Sieppe, McTeague's wife, is a true counterpart to her
husband in that she is the first well-created female character to be
used to depict naturalism in American fiction." (G.C.)

McTEAGUE (cont'd)

N245   Johnson, George W., "The Frontier Behind Frank Norris's
McTeague," Huntington Library Quarterly, 26:91-104, November,
1962.

"As a crucial and representative national experience, the loss of
the frontier was of the greatest imaginative import" to Frank Norris.
This fact is reflected in McTeague and also in Norris's collected
critical essays, Responsibilities of the Novelist. (S.A.)

N246   Kaplan, Charles, "Fact into Fiction in McTeague," Harvard
Library Bulletin, 8:381-5, Autumn, 1954.

The dental lore in McTeague seems to have been drawn from Norris's
reading of Thomas Fillebrown's A Textbook of Operative Dentistry
which Norris had borrowed from the Harvard College Library in
1894. (D.P.)

N247   Pizer, Donald, "Nineteenth-Century American Naturalism: An
Essay in Definition," Bucknell Review, 13:1-18, December, 1965.

The American naturalistic novel "asserts the value of all life by
endowing the lowest character with emotion and defeat and with
moral ambiguity. . . . Thus, the melodramatic sensationalism and
moral 'confusion' . . . should really be incorporated into a normative definition of the mode and be recognized as its essential constituents." Norris's McTeague, Dreiser's Sister Carrie and Crane's
The Red Badge of Courage illustrate this definition and the range of
variation within it. (D.P.)

A MAN'S WOMAN

N248   Sherwood, John C., "Norris and the Jeannette," Philological
Quarterly, 37:245-52, April, 1958.

The early chapters of Norris's A Man's Woman, which describe the
arctic adventures of Ward Bennett, appear to be drawn primarily
from the published accounts of the Jeannette disaster. For his novel
Norris borrowed not only general outlines, but small details, striking
incidents, and many other episodes, all of which make Norris's novel
more vivid and memorable through "the accumulation of a wealth of
exact and convincing detail." (D.P.)

THE OCTOPUS

M249 Brunvand, Jan Harold, "Type 1365A in <u>The Octopus</u>," <u>Western</u>
<u>Folklore</u>, 22:192-3, July, 1963.

"There is an apparent allusion to Tale Type 1365A <u>The Obstinate</u>
<u>Wife Falls into a Stream</u>" in chapter one of Book II of Frank Norris's
<u>The Octopus</u>, a variety of the story which "has not been reported in
the United States." (D.P.)

N250 Davison, Richard Allan, "An Undiscovered Early Review of Norris's
<u>Octopus</u>," <u>Western American Literature</u>, 3:147-51, Summer, 1968.

The Chicago <u>American</u> published on April 6, 1901 a review, by
Wallace Rice, of <u>The Octopus</u>, which may be the earliest review and
also one of "the most extensive early critical treatments of . . .
Norris's greatest novel." [The review is reprinted here in its
entirety.] (D.P.)

N251 Folsom, James K., "Social Darwinism or Social Protest? The
'Philosophy' of <u>The Octopus</u>," <u>Modern Fiction Studies</u>, 8:393-400,
Winter, 1962-63.

Although most critics have been disturbed by the apparently illogical
ending of <u>The Octopus</u>, the more credible assumption is that the
ending "might be highly ironic, that Presley might just possibly not
have the slightest idea of what he is talking about." (D.P.)

N252 Pizer, Donald, "Another Look at <u>The Octopus</u>," <u>Nineteenth-Century</u>
<u>Fiction</u>, 10:217-24, December, 1955.

The criticism that Norris fails to distinguish the moral and amoral
worlds, and free will and determinism, stems from "a lack of understanding of Presley's role as a developing character" and from the
"assumption that Presley's thoughts represent Norris himself."
Personal freedom and cosmic determinism are not incompatible in
Norris's mind. (G.M.P.)

N253 Pizer, Donald, "The Concept of Nature in Frank Norris's <u>The</u>
<u>Octopus</u>," <u>American Quarterly</u>, 14:73-80, Spring, 1962.

". . . the guiding system of ideas in the novel is an evolutionary
theism which attributes to nature the powers and qualities usually
assigned to a personal, supernatural diety." Its flaws are, therefore, "not those of the relationship of parts to the whole," but those

THE OCTOPUS   (cont'd)

arising from translating supernatural literally into natural and from "the traditional paradoxes of religious faith." (W.G.F.)

N254   Pizer, Donald, "Synthetic Criticism and Frank Norris: Or, Mr. Marx, Mr. Taylor, and The Octopus," American Literature, 34:532-41, January, 1963.

Norris's basic attitude in The Octopus corresponds less to "the polarity between the kingdom of love and the kingdom of power," which Leo Marx finds probably "the dominant theme in American literature" than to "the capacity of the popular mind to maintain without a sense of contradiction the opposing ideals of cultural primitivism and industrial progress." (W.G.F.)

N255   Vance, William L., "Romance in The Octopus," Génre, 3:111-36, 1970.

"The Octopus is not the romantic epic Presley hoped to write. . . . It is a book about a man who wished to write such a work, but could not. Nor could Norris." "The failure of The Octopus as an artistic creation . . . [is] rooted in the excessively literary character of the book, the last thing Norris could have wished." (D.P.)

N256   Walker, Philip, "The Octopus and Zola: A New Look," Symposium, 21:155-65, Summer, 1967.

". . . the crucial differences between . . . The Octopus and [Zola's] novels that it most closely resembles--Germinal, La Terre, and La Bête humaine--may be found in the different kinds and amounts of realism, romanticism, and symbolism that they contain and the different ways these elements are combined." ". . . while in Zola metaphor tends to serve primarily as a means for effecting the flight of the poet from the springboard of factual observation and documentary realism to the greater truth of symbol and revelation, Norris's imagery, lacking any strongly cohesive poetic or metaphysical vision to express, tends to be more purely rhetorical, more subordinate to his frankly romanticizing fancy. . . ." (D.P.)

VANDOVER AND THE BRUTE

N257   Astro, Richard, "Vandover and the Brute and The Beautiful and
        Damned: A Search for Thematic and Stylistic Reinterpretations,"
        Modern Fiction Studies, 14:397-413, Winter, 1968-69.

        Fitzgerald's "The Beautiful and Damned, while embodying many of
        the typically refreshing stylistic qualities found in all of Fitzgerald's
        works, is patterned largely after Frank Norris's second novel,
        Vandover and the Brute." (D.P.)

N258   Pizer, Donald, "The Problem of Philosophy in the Novel,"
        Bucknell Review, 18:53-62, Spring, 1970.

        Fictional practice often varies from philosophical statements made
        by novelists. Norris in Vandover and the Brute employs a Darwin-
        ian passage as a metaphor of fear in a novel which insists that artists
        are the victims of their own demonic natures. In one passage in
        Sister Carrie Dreiser condemns Carrie for establishing an immoral
        relationship with Drouet although the general thrust of the novel is
        to approve this and subsequent alliances as the method which allows
        her spiritual development. (D.P.)

NORTON, CHARLES ELIOT

N259   Marsden, Malcolm M., "Discriminating Sympathy: Charles Eliot
        Norton's Unique Gift," New England Quarterly, 31:463-83,
        December, 1958.

        Norton's "gift" is best seen in his effect on the literary careers of
        Lowell, Ruskin, James, Edith Wharton, and others." (W.T.S.)

NOSSACK, HANS ERICH

N260   Plard, Henri, "La Jeune Fille et la mort: Das kennt man, de Hans
        Erich Nossack," Études Germaniques, 23:12-36, January-March,
        1968.

        Nossack's prose style helps convey the author's message of how the
        individual must preserve his private rights in a civilization of col-
        lective, organized and taxed pleasures. (J.R.R.)

N261   Prochnik, Peter, "Controlling Thoughts in the Work of Hans Erich Nossack," German Life and Letters, 19:68-74, October, 1965.

"The world Nossack portrays in his books is a fusion of ours and the rarefied atmosphere of das Jenseits where there is not always an identifiable, welcome refuge." (J.R.R.)

N262   Prochnik, Peter, "First Words: The Poetry of Hans Erich Nossack," Modern Language Review, 64:100-10, January, 1969.

"That the public should be discouraged by Nossack's work is understandable, but that they should be discouraged from reading it, is an alarming testimony to man's inability to confront himself." (J.R.R.)

NOURISSIER, FRANÇOIS

N263   Abirached, Robert, "Vivre en Suisse?" La Nouvelle Revue Française, No. 135, pp. 509-13, March, 1964.

One wonders why a novelist stops writing novels at 30 and turns to autobiographical, personal works, even though such may be the logical sequence of Bleu comme la nuit. Apparently he is only beginning to settle the account of his adolescence. (T.T.B.)

N264   Messadié, Gérald, "Un Caméléon nommé François Nourissier," Cahiers des Saisons, No. 38, pp. 373-6, Summer, 1964.

Nourissier was a veritable Jekyll and Hyde in several domains: love, religion, family, politics, friendships. As Hegel would say, Nourissier is an "unhappy conscience." (T.T.B.)

NOVAK, SLOBODAN

N265   Kodić, Ante, "Slobodan Novak," Books Abroad, 38:367-70, Autumn, 1964.

Novak (b. 1924) is the leading writer of short stories in Yugoslavia's postwar generation. His "writing is calm, measured, filled with constant lyrical undertones." (C.E.N.)

NOVÁS CALVO, LINO

N266   Souza, Raymond D., "Two 'Lost' Stories of Lino Novás Calvo,"
Romance Notes, 9:49-52, 1967.

Two forgotten stories from the 30's show Novás's early concern for
personal disorientation and innovative technique. (C.O.)

NOWLAN, ALDEN

N267   Fraser, Keath, "Notes on Alden Nowlan," Canadian Literature,
No. 45, pp. 41-51, Summer, 1970.

"Dedicated honestly and humbly to his art, equally at home in more
than one genre, Alden Nowlan furnishes an unhip, thoroughly non-
academic world with splashes of exquisite insight. . . . his work
reveals relentless growth, while his regional qualities continue to
endure." (D.P.)

NOYES, ALFRED

N268   Sencourt, Robert, "Alfred Noyes," Contemporary Review,
No. 1113, pp. 118-20, September, 1958.

Alfred Noyes, victim of the change in taste from the Victorian
toward the modern, wrote much vigorous work of which the world
is generally unaware. At heart he remained a Victorian, regarding
with "amused scorn" the changes in the poetic method that came to
England from America witn Ezra Pound. (F.L.)

N269   Stanford, Derek, "Alfred Noyes: 1880-1958," Catholic World,
188:297-301, January, 1959.

The best work of Noyes belonged to an "earlier body of more popular
poetry. . . . Rhythm was always his forte, and by its employment
he was able to express what would otherwise have appeared tritely
sentimental. . . . The world to which his rhythms belong is that of
the music-hall with its songs, the drawing-room with its middle-
class ballads." (D.P.)

N270   Stanford, Derek, "The Poetic Achievement of Alfred Noyes,"
English, 12:86-8, Autumn, 1958.

"In Alfred Noyes . . . there existed two strains of mind seldom
discoverable together. The first was a vein of popular imagination

[The Barrel-Organ, A Highwayman, Dick Turpin's Ride, A Song of Sherwood, Drake, Tales of the Mermaid Tavern] . . . . The second strain was one of scientific curiosity [The Torchbearers, The Unknown God, Voltaire] . " (J.M.D.)

OATES, JOYCE CAROL

O 1   Kuehl, Linda, "An Interview with Joyce Carol Oates," Commonweal, 91:307-10, December 5, 1969.

[This interview concentrates on Miss Oates's novels, with comments on influences on her work, and her assessment of the comparative rewards of writing fiction and writing poetry.] (D.P.)

O'BRIEN, EDNA

O 2   McMahon, Sean, "A Sex by Themselves: An Interim Report on the Novels of Edna O'Brien," Eire-Ireland, 2:79-87, Spring, 1967.

". . . Miss O'Brien's literary reputation was established by The Country Girls--her first and best book--and later affirmed by the second, The Lonely Girl. These novels told of the adolescence and early womanhood of two young girls from Co. Clare. Their story is continued in Girls in Their Married Bliss but the book was so . . . angry, and to many readers so sordid, that there was considerable disappointment when it appeared. Yet when the three novels are read together and in sequence the girls are seen to contain the seeds of their own fate." "If we regard the [later] sequence of novels as a kind of Pilgrim's Progress, then Miss Pilgrim is finding it difficult to climb out of the slough of despond." (D.P.)

O 3   Sheehy, Michael, "Irish Literary Censorship," Nation, 208:833-6, June 30, 1969.

Miss O'Brien's marked preoccupation with sex, particularly the experimental type, has caused five of her six books to be banned, and her most recent one is not yet out of danger. The Irish censorship board is conditioned mainly by the Irish Catholic Church, whose Irish Index reads like a guide to modern literature. (T.T.B.)

THE COUNTRY GIRLS

O 4   Senn, Fritz, "Reverberations," <u>James Joyce Quarterly</u>, 3:222, Spring, 1966.

Mrs. Edna O'Brien seems to make effective use of one of the most memorable passages from Joyce's "The Dead" in her description of snow falling in Ireland on page 99 in her novel <u>The Country Girls</u>. (D.P.)

A PAGAN PLACE

O 5   O'Brien, Edna, "Edna O'Brien Talks to David Heycock about Her New Novel, <u>A Pagan Place</u>," <u>Listener</u>, 83:616-7, May 7, 1970.

"I wanted this time, in <u>A Pagan Place</u>, to get into the kingdom of childhood. I wanted to get the minute-to-minute essence of what it is when you're very young, when you're both meticulously aware of everything that's going on around you and totally uncritical. . . . And of course the only place I could set it is in Ireland where all my association, all my dreams and all my experience is. . . . I was brought up very much on mythology and folk-tales, and on verse, and I wanted, as I always do, to write an extremely non-literary book." (D.P.)

O'BRIEN, FLANN--See
O'NOLAN, BRIAN

O'BYRNE, DERMOT

O 6   Saul, George Brandon, "Of Tales Half-Forgotten," <u>Arizona Quarterly</u>, 18:151-4, Summer, 1962.

O'Byrne's tales have not achieved wide distribution. And this is especially "a shame in the light of their fusion of imagination, suggested racial recall, and verisimilitude." (R.G.L.)

O'CASEY, SEAN

O 7   Ayling, Ronald, "The Autobiographies of Sean O'Casey," <u>Research Studies</u> (Washington State University), 37:122-9, June, 1969.

The autobiographical works of Sean O'Casey have been both praised and condemned by critics. Though some have stated that O'Casey's reputation may ultimately rest more on the autobiographical works than on the plays, others have condemned them, but rarely on literary grounds. A detailed and exhaustive study is needed which will provide a comprehensive evaluation. (V.E.)

O 8   Ayling, Ronald, "Sean O'Casey and His Critics," New Theatre Magazine, 8:5-19, No. 1, 1968.

"Reviewing O'Casey criticism to the present, one is immediately struck by the irrelevance of much of it and by the number of false or misleading approaches to be encountered. At the same time, many important aspects of his writings remain unexplored . . . notably, practical consideration of stagecraft in his drama and objective literary evaluation of the autobiographies." (D.P.)

O 9   Baggett, Patricia, "Sean O'Casey's Development of a Basic Theme," Dublin Magazine, 31:25-34, October-December, 1956.

In most of his plays O'Casey attempts to discover "the meaning of the struggle for existence. . . ." The answer is seen in his heroes's actions: one struggles to eat, to lead the people, and to establish a utopian kingdom. But O'Casey ultimately becomes a "destructive critic" who has lost his creativity. (J.L.B.)

O 10   Benstock, Bernard, "A Covey of Clerics in Joyce and O'Casey," James Joyce Quarterly, 2:18-32, Fall, 1964.

"It becomes apparent that the writer emerging from Catholic Ireland, regardless of his faith or disbelief, carried with him a preoccupation with his nation's religion and the representatives of the Church. For O'Casey the problem synthesized itself into a dominant struggle seen primarily along a political scale, with the clergy . . . either supporting the prevailing deathhold of reactionary ideals masked as religion, or in rebellion against them. . . . Joyce's characters, clergymen as well as laymen, were personifications of his own . . . subjective responses to life in Ireland. The effect of the cleric to Joyce is essentially pernicious . . . while for O'Casey the effect varies with the perspective of the particular clergyman. . . ." (D.P.)

O 11   Benstock, Bernard, "Kelly, Burke and Shea," James Joyce Quarterly, 8:124-6, Fall, 1970.

"On occasion in his autobiographies O'Casey isolated a trio of . . . 'Micks' for special attention, and although they function differently at each instance, the same names are applied to them: Kelly, Burke

and Shea. They take on a life of their own. . . . What they represent
. . . are those faceless and soulless who are outside the pale, the
deformers of life both for themselves and for anyone over whom they
can exert their influence." (D.P.)

O 12   Benstock, Bernard, "The Mother-Madonna-Matriarch in Sean
O'Casey," Southern Review, 6:603-23, Summer, 1970.

". . . not all of . . . [O'Casey's] older women are gentle creatures
nor are all his mothers active and positive. Countering the quartet
of venerated women [Juno Boyle, Susan Casside, Mrs. Breydon,
Bessie Burgess] is a galaxy of lesser lights, women torn between
holding on to the best that is in life and a destructive pettiness and
self-interest that is their spiritual death." (G.C.)

O 13   Carens, James F., "Four Letters: Sean O'Casey to Oliver St. John
Gogarty," James Joyce Quarterly, 8:111-8, Fall, 1970.

Both Gogarty and O'Casey "waged a lifelong laughing-war on the
smug-minded. . . . These four letters . . . suggest that by the end
of the 'twenties the two men knew well how much they had in common."
(D.P.)

O 14   Carpenter, Charles A., "Sean O'Casey Studies Through 1964,"
Modern Drama, 10:17-23, May, 1967.

[This checklist attempts reasonable comprehensiveness for biographical, critical, and other scholarly studies of O'Casey.] (D.P.)

O 15   Coston, Herbert Hull, "Sean O'Casey: Prelude to Playwrighting,"
Tulane Drama Review, 5:102-12, September, 1960.

"During his years in Ireland Sean O'Casey's development progressed
by a series of rejections." However, "in the early 1920's he eagerly
assumed the artist's role, for it meant to him not simply an opportunity for personal expression and recognition, but a way to bring
order out of chaos, to reduce to essence the many experiences and
questions that sprawled in his mind, and to assert the social truths
that he knew. The themes of his drama lay already in his mind;
his characters lived all around him; he needed only to be made aware
of the dramatic possibilities of the material that he had at hand."
(D.P.)

O 15   2926

O 16   Cowasjee, Saros, "The Juxtaposition of Tragedy and Comedy in the
        Plays of Sean O'Casey," Wascana Review, 2:75-89, No. 1, 1967.

        "Broadly speaking, illusion and reality are translated into terms of
        comedy and tragedy in O'Casey's plays: the frequency of the clashes
        between the former determining the rapidity of alternation of comedy
        and tragedy." O'Casey "mixes the moods because he himself feels
        the pathetic irony of the life he is depicting." (D.A.B.)

O 17   Cowasjee, Saros, "O'Casey Seen Through Holloway's Diary,"
        Review of English Literature, 6:58-69, July, 1965.

        Holloway "has left behind many anecdotes narrated to him by the
        dramatist, which add to our knowledge of the man and his plays.
        . . . Holloway [also] throws more light on the realistic basis and
        origin of O'Casey's characters than any other source." (G.C.)

O 18   De Baun, Vincent C., "Sean O'Casey and the Road to Expressionism,"
        Modern Drama, 4:254-9, December, 1961.

        ". . . Sean O'Casey's application of expressionistic techniques
        actually began not with The Silver Tassie (1928), but with The
        Plough and the Stars (1926)." (C.K.L.)

O 19   Edwards, A. C., ed., "The Lady Gregory Letters to Sean O'Casey,"
        Modern Drama, 8:95-111, May, 1965.

        [These are the letters the editor has been able to find written by
        Lady Gregory to Sean O'Casey.] (G.A.S.)

O 20   Esslinger, Pat M., "The Irish Alienation of O'Casey," Eire-
        Ireland, 1:18-25, Spring, 1966.

        Before his exile O'Casey was alienated "from things Irish" as a
        result of his recognition of the chasm between the Anglo-Irish and
        the native Irish; the poverty of the native Irish; and the indifference
        of the church to the needs of the slum dwellers. His communist
        affiliation in 1913 completed his alienation from Ireland. The aliena-
        tion brought a decline in dramatic power, but, in providing the
        distance to see objectively, allowed him to "create his finest tragedy."
        (D.P.)

O 21   Esslinger, Pat M., "Sean O'Casey and the Lockout of 1913: Materia
        Poetica of the Two Red Plays," Modern Drama, 6:53-63,
        May, 1963.

        The Great Lockout of 1913 "was not only responsible for two of . . .
        [O'Casey's] most expressionistic dramas, The Star Turns Red and
        Red Roses for Me, but is also the origin of . . . [his] Communistic
        views. . . ." (G.C.)

O 22   Fitzgerald, John J., "Sean O'Casey's Dramatic Slums," Descant,
        10:26-34, Fall, 1965.

        "O'Casey had been born and brought up in the Dublin slums . . . he
        writes . . . from resentful experience. The world of the slums is
        the world of O'Casey's plays, but since he is an artist, O'Casey is
        able to transmute the raw facts of tenement life into a dramatic
        vision. He takes this sociological phenomenon of the perpetual
        wrangling which characterizes the life of the poor and makes it serve
        contrapuntally to the main music of his dramatic action." (D.P.)

O 23   Freedman, Morris, "The Modern Tragicomedy of Wilde and O'Casey,"
        College English, 25:518-27, April, 1964.

        "The tragicomedy in Wilde comes from his acceptance of his world
        as a man, an acceptance violated by his rejection of it as an artist.
        . . . The tragicomedy in O'Casey . . . comes not from despair,
        conscious or unconscious, but from a full sense of the immense, the
        truly absurd, spread of man's possibility. In their quite different
        ways, Wilde and O'Casey set the tragicomic tone for the later drama
        of Beckett and Ionesco. . . ." (D.P.)

O 24   Hogan, Robert, "The Experiments of Sean O'Casey," Dublin
        Magazine, 33:4-12, January, 1958.

        "What critics call O'Casey's formlessness is not the aimless sprawl-
        ing of a talented amateur, but experiments with form and, in the last
        plays, experiments in synthesis, in the juxtaposition of techniques
        from different genres. O'Casey's later plays have . . . the tremen-
        dous formal complexity of one of the few still growing and experimen-
        tal talents of the modern theatre." (D.A.B.)

O 25   Hogan, Robert, "The Haunted Inkbottle: A Preliminary Study of Rhetorical Devices in the Late Plays of Sean O'Casey," James Joyce Quarterly, 8:76-95, Fall, 1970.

"Certain characteristics of [O'Casey's] middle style--particularly its highly colored and romantic diction--recur as elements in the style of the late plays. These late plays . . . are versions of pastoral; and their style is a complex mixture of most of the elements of O'Casey's early style, plus the addition of a few new devices. . . . the late plays . . . differ radically in tone, and so the overall style has in different plays different emphases." (D.P.)

O 26   Hogan, Robert, "O'Casey's Dramatic Apprenticeship," Modern Drama, 4:243-53, December, 1961.

Sean O'Casey's early unpublished plays are brilliant forecasts of the later plays that established his international reputation as a major dramatist. (C.K.L.)

O 27   Krause, David, "O'Casey and Yeats and the Druid," Modern Drama, 11:252-62, December, 1968.

[These are biographical reflections prompted by publication of a collection of O'Casey's prose.] (R.C.B.)

O 28   Krause, David, "The Playwright's Not For Burning," Virginia Quarterly Review, 34:60-76, Winter, 1958.

". . . since the opposing theories of drama which . . . [Yeats and O'Casey] defended represent a conflict that has often confronted the dramatist, it is significant to examine the background out of which the conflict developed, the main arguments on both sides, and . . . those aspects of . . . [The Silver Tassie] which provoked the conflict." (G.C.)

O 29   Krause, David, "The Principle of Comic Disintegration," James Joyce Quarterly, 8:3-12, Fall, 1970.

"Joyce, O'Casey and Beckett . . . were comic myth-makers of their own liberation. They survived because they were cunning enough to construct their own mythology of self-exile. . . ." O'Casey "will always remain 'a master of the knockabout in . . . that he discerns the principle of disintegration in even the most complacent solidities, and activates it to their explosion'." (D.P.)

O 30 Krause, David, " 'The Rageous Ossean': Patron-Hero of Synge and O'Casey, " Modern Drama, 4:268-91, December, 1961.

The hero of Celtic myth, the warrior-bard Oisin (Joyce's Ossean), "just as Cuchulain was Yeats's patron-hero . . . indirectly served in a similar role for Synge and O'Casey." (C.K.L.)

O 31 Krause, David, "Sean O'Casey: 1880-1964, " Massachusetts Review, 6:233-51, Winter-Spring, 1965.

[This is a recounting of the author's last visit with O'Casey and some observations on his life and work.] (G.A.S.)

O 32 Larson, Gerard A., "An Interview with Mrs. Sean O'Casey, " Educational Theatre Journal, 17:234-9, October, 1965.

[Mrs. O'Casey reminisces about her husband.] (G.C.)

O 33 Lewis, Allan, "Sean O'Casey's World, " Nation, 181:555-6, December 24, 1955.

O'Casey is "a dialectical materialist with a dash of Shelley." In him is "a bit of Yeats and a great deal of Gorky." The world of his dramas is the working man's kitchen, not the middle-class living room or the aristocratic drawing room. In Red Roses for Me, he presents the conflict between Sheila (selfishness and social irres- ponsibility) and Ayamonn (fellowship and trade-union humanitarian- ism). (T.C.L.)

O 34 McHugh, Roger, "The Legacy of Sean O'Casey, " Texas Quarterly, 8:123-37, Spring, 1965.

"O'Casey's world was a world 'in chassis' because he saw its in- humanity, the isolation of individuals, the apprehension of doom, the repeated pattern by which 'the texture of life is forever tusked by the forces of darkness'," yet "in O'Casey, as in Swift and Langland, a positive set of values guided the brain that directed the scalpel." (W.G.F.)

O 35 McHugh, Roger, "Sean O'Casey and Lady Gregory, " James Joyce Quarterly, 8:119-23, Fall, 1970.

Although normally Lady Gregory and Sean O'Casey "would have been separated by barriers of class, of belief, (or disbelief) and by loca- tion" they were drawn together by common interests in the arts. (D.P.)

O 36   Mercier, Vivian, "The Riddle of Sean O'Casey," Commonweal, 64:366-8, July 13, 1956.

The question often asked is what caused the deterioration of O'Casey after the great trio of The Shadow of a Gunman, Juno and the Paycock, and The Plough and the Stars? The question might better be asked: "In view of all the formless, tasteless, wordy and sentimental rubbish that he has written before and since, how did he ever produce those three works of authentic genius? . . . It is clear that events in the national life and in O'Casey's private life . . . conspired to sharpen that view of his fellow men--one part compassion and two parts satire--which stamps its hallmark on the three great early plays." Also, the triumvirate of W. B. Yeats, Lady Gregory, and Lennox Robinson gave O'Casey excellent advice in shaping his plays, advice which was not available to him when he moved to England.   (D.P.)

O 37   O'Casey, Sean, "The Bald Primaqueera," Atlantic Monthly, 216:69-74, September, 1965.

We must reject the theatre of decay and despair, the theatre of Artaud, Ionesco, Pinter, and the many films of mystery and horror of Alfred Hitchcock. These are the visions of the Primaqueera, the savage who looks "through a lens which reflects back into the mind of the onlooker." "The world has many sour noises; the body is an open target. . . . It is full of disappointments, and too many of us have to suffer . . . a world that aches bitterly till our time here ends. Yet, even so, each of us, one time or another, can ride a white horse, can have rings on our fingers and bells on our toes, and if we keep our senses open . . . we shall have music wherever we go." (D.P.)

O 38   O'Casey, Sean, "Sean O'Casey Concerning James Joyce," Massachusetts Review, 5:335-6, Winter, 1964.

[These are three letters to Professor Joseph Prescott, Wayne State University, about O'Casey's admiration for Joyce.] (G.A.S.)

O 39   Parker, R. B., "Bernard Shaw and Sean O'Casey," Queen's Quarterly, 73:13-34, Spring, 1966.

". . . G. B. S. ran unbroken, like a golden thread . . . through the tattered weave of the younger man's career. Affection and admiration for Shaw were obviously dominating passions in O'Casey's life. . . ." He "was O'Casey's hero and dramatic model right from the start. . . ." (D.P.)

O 40   Rees, Leslie, "Remembrance of Things Past: On Meeting Sean
O'Casey," Meanjin Quarterly, 23:414-20, December, 1964.

[This is a description of a dinner and conversation with Sean O'Casey
and his wife.] (A.S.W.)

O 41   Ritchie, Harry M., "The Influence of Melodrama on the Early Plays
of Sean O'Casey," Modern Drama, 5:164-73, September, 1962.

"O'Casey states that he learned plot, music and tableau from melodrama. . . . O'Casey used the melodramatic techniques . . . to
lull the Abbey audience into a false sense of security, a mood essential for his ultimately satiric purpose." (G.C.)

O 42   Rogoff, Gordon, "Sean O'Casey's Legacy," Commonweal, 81:128-9,
October 23, 1964.

O'Casey was often the center of a storm, but "when the dust of
battle settled, a responsive, gentle, lyric artist was revealed. . . ."
When O'Casey exiled himself from Ireland "the theatre without the
playwright lost more than the playwright without the theatre." (D.P.)

O 43   Rollins, Ronald G., "Form and Content in Sean O'Casey's Dublin
Trilogy," Modern Drama, 8:419-25, February, 1966.

"O'Casey's Dublin tragi-comedies stand . . . as organically fused
dramas designed to examine scrupulously the paradoxical Irish
menaced by extended disorder." They are examples of "hybrid
drama of sardonic comedy and ironic tragedy." (G.C.)

O 44   Rollins, Ronald G., "Sean O'Casey's Mental Pilgrimage,"
Arizona Quarterly, 17:293-302, Winter, 1961.

O'Casey's "entire, restless life . . . has been a quest for certain
ideal human types, and for religious, economic, and political
systems that will accelerate, not retard, man's material and spiritual growth." (R.G.L.)

O 45   Rudin, Seymour, "Playwright to Critic: Sean O'Casey's Letters to
George Jean Nathan," Massachusetts Review, 5:326-34, Winter,
1965.

[The author gives details from the letters but does not reprint them.
They reveal lively, honest attitudes toward the theater by the critic
and the playwright.] (G.A.S.)

O 46   Smith, B. L., "O'Casey's Satiric Vision," <u>James Joyce Quarterly</u>, 8:13-28, Fall, 1970.

". . . O'Casey's satiric vision gives both continuity and unity to the kaleidoscopic variety of his work. . . ." His "satire is developmental and does not emerge as fully mature until near the end of the transitional period. . . . Like satirists before him, O'Casey . . . earned himself the enmity of the establishment. . . . But . . . O'Casey's satiric vision includes ample room for joy and laughter, for having a good time and loving life in the process." (D.P.)

O 47   Snoddy, Oliver, "Sean O'Casey as Troublemaker," <u>Eire-Ireland</u>, 1:23-38, Winter, 1967.

Sean O'Casey was "one of the main agents of the acrimony evinced by the Irish Citizen Army against the Irish volunteers. His republicanism was broadly published, and received much heated criticism in response. He resigned from the Citizen Army in 1914 after his attempt to oust the Countess Markievicz failed. ". . . the pouting resignation of O'Casey, the emigration . . . of Larkin, the accession of Connolly to command and the outbreak of the World War I, all hastened a reappraisal and . . . change in Labor's attitude towards the Irish Volunteers." (D.P.)

O 48   Worth, Katharine J., "O'Casey's Dramatic Symbolism," <u>Modern Drama</u>, 4:260-7, December, 1961.

Symbolism is "an intrinsic part of the dramatic process in O'Casey's plays, whether it functions in a fantastic or realistic context." (C.K.L.)

      THE BALD PRIMAQUEERA

O 49   Murphy, Robert P., "Sean O'Casey and 'The Bald Primaqueera'," <u>James Joyce Quarterly</u>, 8:96-110, Fall, 1970.

"The heart of the article ['The Bald Primaqueera'] is an attack on Antonin Artaud's theater of cruelty." However, "it is clear from the many parallels in structure, use of language, and dramaturgical techniques that O'Casey, despite his protestations to the contrary, is firmly in the tradition of Artaud's theater of cruelty as translated into practicable drama by Ionesco." (D.P.)

BEDTIME STORY

O 50 Smith, Bobby L., "The Hat, the Whore, and the Hypocrite in
O'Casey's Bedtime Story," Serif, 4:3-5, June, 1967.

"O'Casey draws freely from the farce, melodrama, and situation-
comedy traditions for this episodic expose of the 'decline and fall
into the drab and malicious menace of puritanism.' Angela
Nightingale is the only vital person on stage as she lives her song of
life; she combines vitality, paganism, and sense of humor in her
lucrative professions of con-artist and whore." (K.M.W.)

COCK-A-DOODLE DANDY

O 51 Daniel, Walter C., "The False Paradise Pattern in Sean O'Casey's
Cock-a-Doodle Dandy," CLA Journal, 13:137-43, 1969.

". . . when the play is read as a loose reversal of the paradox of
the Fortunate Fall, it not only becomes particularly meaningful as
important dramatic literature, but Michael Marthraun becomes an
ingenious character creation in his ironic contrast to Archangel
Michael in Paradise Lost." (G.C.)

O 52 Rollins, Ronald, "Clerical Blackness in the Green Garden: Heroine
as Scapegoat in Cock-a-Doodle Dandy," James Joyce Quarterly,
8:64-72, Fall, 1970.

"Cock-a-Doodle Dandy, satiric extravaganza, duplicates virtually
all the main aspects of scapegoat ceremonies. . . ." The play
"synthesizes ancient ceremonial formulas to censure severe, in-
flexible custodians of conduct who are too quick to punish free spirits."
(D.P.)

O 53 Rollins, Ronald G., "O'Casey's 'Cock-a-Doodle Dandy," Explicator,
23: Item 8, September, 1964.

"The deliberate arrangement of stage properties in Scene I . . . is
designed to expose Ireland as a bleak, backward, and superstitious
island largely devoid of beauty and joy and acutely afraid of innovation and change." (D.P.)

COCK-A-DOODLE DANDY   (cont'd)

O 54   Smith, Bobby L., "Satire in O'Casey's Cock-a-Doodle Dandy,"
Renascence, 19:64-73, Winter, 1967.

"Cock-a-Doodle Dandy, like virtually all of O'Casey's later plays,
is a morality play. . . . The drama . . . is a religious experience.
Its satire is a weapon directed against the knavish hypocrisy and the
malignant sickness that lie at the heart of his modern society."
(G.C.)

THE DRUMS OF FATHER NED

O 55   Marcus, Phillip L., "Addendum on Joyce and O'Casey," James
Joyce Quarterly, 3:62-3, Fall, 1965.

Mr. Benstock in his "A Covey of Clerics in Joyce and O'Casey,"
(James Joyce Quarterly, Vol. 2, No. 1) omits mention of an allusion
to Ulysses in O'Casey's The Drums of Father Ned "that provides the
clinching evidence that Father Ned . . . is meant to be a portrait of
the Deity Himself."   (D.P.)

FEATHERS FROM THE GREEN CROW

O 56   Ayling, Ronald, "Feathers Finely Aflutter," Modern Drama,
7:135-47, September, 1964.

The collection of Feathers from the Green Crow reveal O'Casey
evolving from nationalist to socialist. His strong opinion always
involved him in controversies with his best friends who did not
understand him.   (G.A.S.)

HALL OF HEALING

O 57   Kosok, Heinz, "Sean O'Caseys Hall of Healing," Die Neueren
Sprachen, 19:168-79, April, 1970.

For the uniformly grey world of naturalistic drama, O'Casey substitutes, in Hall of Healing, a many-shaded picture in which dark
tones predominate but do not overrule. It is precisely because he
has not been limited by the established forms and precepts of
naturalism that O'Casey has been capable of such a singular accomplishment. (G.C.)

JUNO AND THE PAYCOCK

O 58   Coakley, James and Marvin Felheim, "Thalia in Dublin: Some
Suggestions about the Relationships between O'Casey and Classical
Comedy," Comparative Drama, 4:265-71, Winter, 1970.

"O'Casey's persistent use of Roman equivalents, then, is one basis
of the play [Juno and the Paycock]. Just as the characters reflect
their sources, so, too, the play may be described as Roman in
shape. The plot is complicated by trickery . . . and by turns of
fortune. . . . Moreover, the vigorous dialogue reminds one . . .
of the colloquial speech so notable in Plautus. At once farcical and
sad, compassionate and severe, the mixture of genres with classical
sources works in Juno to fine effect." (D.P.)

O 59   Greany, Helen T., "Some Interesting Parallels: Pope and the
Paycock," Notes and Queries, 5:252-3, June, 1958.

The Paycock "affirm[s] the . . . sentiment" of Pope's famous
encomium   'An honest Man's the noblest work of God' . . . to Joxer
in the final act of O'Casey's play." (G.C.)

KATHLEEN LISTENS IN

O 60   Hethmon, Robert, "Great Hatred, Little Room," Tulane Drama
Review, 5:51-5, June, 1961.

The Abbey Theatre produced O'Casey's Kathleen Listens In, "a no-
holds-barred, deadly accurate satire of warring contemporary
Ireland," only a few months after the great success of The Shadow
of a Gunman. The play closed within a week and was never revived.
At the first performance "the laughter was all on the stage, the
despair and sense of total catastrophe altogether in the audience.
Out of the savagery of Ireland's civil war came the savage mockery
of Kathleen Listens In." (D.P.)

NANNIE'S NIGHT OUT

O 61   Ayling, Ronald, "Nannie's Night Out," Modern Drama, 5:154-63,
May, 1962.

In Nannie's Night Out there are "flashes of drama which anticipate
themes and incidents in O'Casey's later plays. But they are only
touches in the play. . . . The rest of the play is mediocre."
(G.C.)

THE PLOUGH AND THE STARS

O 62   Armstrong, W. A., "The Sources and Themes of The Plough and the
Stars," Modern Drama, 4:234-42, December, 1961.

Sean O'Casey's Drums Under the Windows (1945) and The Story of
the Irish Citizen Army (1919) "reveal some of the sources of his
tragedy The Plough and the Stars and elucidate some of its main
themes." (C.K.L.)

O 63   Ayling, Ronald, "Character Control and 'Alienation' in The Plough
and the Stars," James Joyce Quarterly, 8:29-47, Fall, 1970.

"In this essay we have examined alienation effects in The Plough
with reference only to characterisation. . . . The skilful structural
patterning . . . reinforces the play's theme and helps realise . . .
the author's social attitude. . . . O'Casey's wish to communicate
the universal significance of poverty and of modern warfare . . .
led to his . . . creative experiments" which were similar to Brecht's
Verfremdungseffekt. (D.P.)

O 64   Kaufman, Michael W., "The Position of The Plough and the Stars
in O'Casey's Dublin Trilogy," James Joyce Quarterly, 8:48-63,
Fall, 1970.

"The Plough which concludes the trilogy [The Shadow of a Gunman,
Juno and the Paycock, and The Plough and the Stars] dramatically,
but begins it chronologically, focuses in the clearest way the simultaneity of beginning and end, and in its position suggests that this
cycle of death and destruction will repeat itself endlessly unless man
can exercise his rational sanity and exhibit humane sympathy to
break the chain of delusion and suffering." (D.P.)

O 65   Saurel, Renée, "Un Dramaturge inconfortable," Les Temps
Modernes, 17e année, No. 193, pp. 1938-44, June, 1962.

The Plough and the Stars is to O'Casey's work what Baal and In the
Jungle of Cities is to that of Brecht. Less rigorous than Brecht,
O'Casey will deliver himself in his last works to the same denuncia-
tions of puritanism, clericalism, militarism and capitalism, without
ever elaborating clearly a doctrine. (T.T.B.)

THE PLOUGH AND THE STARS   (cont'd)

O 66   Smith, Bobby L., "Satire in The Plough and the Stars: A Tragedy
        in Four Acts," Ball State University Forum, 10:3-11, Summer,
        1969.

        "In The Plough and the Stars a bitter artist portrays the wide
        variance between the pomp, parade, and splendor that men take war
        to be and the deprivation, gore and death that war is." (G.C.)

        PURPLE DUST

O 67   McLaughlin, John J., "Political Allegory in O'Casey's Purple Dust,"
        Modern Drama, 13:47-53, May, 1970.

        ". . . beneath the ripples of surface laughter [in Purple Dust] runs
        a powerful current of revolutionary prophecy: a political allegory
        of the destruction of capitalism and the victory of militant socialism."
        (G.C.)

O 68   Rollins, Ronald G., "O'Casey's Purple Dust," Explicator,
        26: Item 19, October, 1967.

        "O'Casey resorts to mythic patterns to impart provocative dimensions
        to his satiric drama." (D.P.)

O 69   Rollins, Ronald G., "Shaw and O'Casey: John Bull and His Other
        Island," Shaw Review, 10:60-9, May, 1967.

        Both Shaw's John Bull's Other Island and O'Casey's Purple Dust
        "study English expeditions to Ireland. . . . the exposure of the
        mental and spiritual torpidity and economic stagnation that invari-
        ably follow when people develop a paralyzing preoccupation with the
        remote and the illusory . . . emerges as the major objective of both
        works." (G.C.)

        RED ROSES FOR ME

O 70   Malone, Maureen, "Red Roses for Me: Fact and Symbol,"
        Modern Drama, 9:147-52, September, 1966.

        Red Roses for Me "is bound more closely than any other [O'Casey
        play] to memories of his early life in Ireland and to the history tak-
        ing shape there in 1913; yet . . . it is here more than anywhere else
        in his work that we are conscious of the artist raising . . . facts to
        a poetic level beyond the reach of mere journalism." (G.C.)

THE SHADOW OF A GUNMAN

O 71 Armstrong, William A., "History, Autobiography, and The Shadow of a Gunman," Modern Drama, 2:417-24, February, 1960.

O'Casey, in The Shadow of a Gunman, "does provide a realistic cross-section of life in a Dublin slum in 1920" but "a comparison between the play and certain parts of his autobiography, Inishfallen, Fare Thee Well (1949) reveals that the personal element in the play is more important than the historical one. . . ." (C.K.L.)

O 72 Dunkel, Wilbur Dwight, "Theology in the Theater," Theology Today, 16:65-73, April, 1959.

". . . while one praises J. B. as an artistic masterpiece, even in its denial of the Christian faith, the Christian must regret that the early premises of this work of art were not fulfilled." James Forsyth's "Heloise deals with the theology of Abelard . . . rather than the letters of this articulate pair of lovers." The dramatization of Greene's The Power and the Glory by Dennis Cannan and Pierre Bost "develops forceful theological concepts." Compassion is "the pervasive quality of O'Neill's latest play, A Touch of the Poet." Budd Schulberg and Harvey Breit's The Disenchanted "poses the theological question . . .: 'What has happened to me?' " "In The Shadow of a Gunman Sean O'Casey . . . still tilts his lance at the Roman Catholic Church and its ritual. . . ." These recent productions pay great attention to theological principles. (D.P.)

O 73 Rollins, Ronald G., "O'Casey and Synge: The Irish Hero as Playboy and Gunman," Arizona Quarterly, 22:217-22, Autumn, 1966.

The heroes of O'Casey's The Shadow of a Gunman and Synge's The Playboy of the Western World both illuminate a common theme: the Irishman's obsession with the heroic personality and his easy deception by the false and flamboyant. Synge's protagonist grows to be the hero people thought him to be, while O'Casey's protagonist accepts his inability to be the character he has pretended to be. (D.P.)

THE SILVER TASSIE

O 74   Rollins, Ronald G., "O'Casey's The Silver Tassie," Explicator, 20: Item 62, April, 1962.

Act I, "commingling some of the symbols and traditional procedures of the Christian religion with some of the ritualism peculiar to the Dionysiac festival of ancient Greece, is erected around a sacrificial motif." (B.K.)

O 75   Rollins, Ronald G., "O'Casey, O'Neill and Expressionism in The Silver Tassie," Bucknell Review, 10:346-9, May, 1962.

"O'Casey's chance acquaintance with Eugene O'Neill's The Hairy Ape . . . strongly impelled the Irish dramatist to discard his previous dramatic manner. . . . The Silver Tassie, adapting the imaginative and flexible dramatic technique of O'Neill and other expressionists, integrates symbolism and realism into a unique and penetrating critique of the holocaust of war." (D.A.B.)

THE STAR TURNS RED

O 76   Rollins, Ronald G., "O'Casey's The Star Turns Red: A Political Philosophy," Mississippi Quarterly, 16:67-75, 1963.

"The Star Turns Red is clearly a labored, declamatory drama of ideas which, while exploiting political antagonism, outlines the formula which revolutionists should follow in order to succeed." (G.C.)

WITHIN THE GATES

O 77   Ayling, Ronald, "The Poetic Drama of T. S. Eliot," English Studies in Africa, 2:247-50, Summer, 1959.

[In a letter to Ayling, Eliot indicates that O'Casey's Within the Gates may have subconsciously influenced the composition of The Family Reunion.] (D.P.)

O 78   Goldstone, Herbert, "The Unevenness of O'Casey: A Study of Within the Gates," Forum (Houston), 4:37-42, Winter-Spring, 1965.

Often in Within the Gates the dull drab lives that O'Casey portrays are one-sided and uninteresting, yet the play "redeems itself by

WITHIN THE GATES   (cont'd)

sensuous richness, the striking power and variety of its images of
contrast, and the ecstatic, explosive force of Jannice's character."
(A.S.W.)

O 79   Rollins, Ronald G., "O'Casey's Within the Gates," Explicator,
29: Item 8, September, 1970.

In Within the Gates O'Casey uses "the timeless patterns of Christian
and pagan myths to illuminate personality and to throw into high and
sharp relief both the paralysis and potential of another wasteland."
(G.C.)

O 80   Todd, R. Mary, "The Two Published Versions of Sean O'Casey's
Within the Gates," Modern Drama, 10:346-55, February, 1968.

The first version, published before the play was produced, was
much changed and strengthened in plot, character, and statement
of theme for the second version, shaped in the laboratory of the
living stage.   (R.C.B.)

O'CONNOR, EDWIN

O 81   Dooley, Roger B., "The Womanless World of Edwin O'Connor,"
Saturday Review, 47:34-6, March 21, 1964.

In I Was Dancing "the lengths to which Mr. O'Connor will go to
avoid dealing with women characters (a tendency already apparent
in the other novels) here reaches a ludicrous extreme." A careful
excursion through all the O'Connor novels brings up the question:
"How can any novelistic world be called definitive, complete, or
even wholly real which is so hemmed in by the . . . taboos of Irish
Puritanism that not only sex or love but marriage itself is viewed,
if at all, suspiciously, from afar, and the only felt emotional relationships are between grotesque old men and their middle-aged sons?"
(D.P.)

O 82   Jones, Howard Mumford, "Politics, Mr. O'Connor and the Family
Novel," Atlantic Monthly, 218:117-20, October, 1966.

"Beginning with The Last Hurrah, O'Connor started a series of
experiments in narrative by indirection. . . . In The Edge of
Sadness O'Connor shifted to first-person narrative, making Father
Hugh the chronicler of his own dishonor and his own recovery. . . .

The indirect method is pushed to its limits in <u>All in the Family</u>"
in which "politics is the occasion, not the theme, of the story."
(D.P.)

O 83   Kelleher, John V., "Edwin O'Connor and the Irish-American
Process," <u>Atlantic Monthly</u>, 222:48-52, July, 1968.

Edwin O'Connor "was very Irish. . . . he had the Irish capacity for
being instantaneously right on any topic that interested him, and he
would thereupon argue his position with a fluent precision that filled
me with envy." "Most of his humor is backward-looking . . .
[although] in most ways Ed O'Connor was a present-minded man.
He was urbane, well informed, concerned with politics as a citizen,
full of the sense of how much needs desperately to be done here and
now, and always very interested in the young. He was impatient
with sentimental, unhistorical praise of the good old days." (D.P.)

THE EDGE OF SADNESS

O 84   Rank, Hugh, "O'Connor's Image of the Priest," <u>New England
Quarterly</u>, 41:3-29, March, 1968.

". . . the book is Father Hugh Kennedy's story, whether he, as
narrator denies it or not. It is the story of the regeneration of a
priest, a story of sanctity in the modern world, of a man coming
to terms with himself, and with God." "The expression of faith, in
a faithless age, is a difficult task because too many Pollyannas have
debased the meaning of hope. ". . . O'Connor joins J. F. Powers
as a leader in breaking away from a priestly stereotype which had
dominated [American literature] for nearly a century." (D.A.B.)

O 85   Sandra, Sister Mary, S.S.A., "The Priest-Hero in Modern
Fiction," <u>Personalist</u>, 46:527-42, October, 1965.

In Edwin O'Connor's <u>The Edge of Sadness</u>, J. F. Powers's <u>Morte
D'Urban</u>, Bernanos's <u>The Diary of a Country Priest</u>, and Graham
Greene's <u>The Power and the Glory</u> "the common conflict existing
between the priest-hero and his culture is, in reality, a complex of
conflicts resulting from the interdependence of a man and his culture.
. . . For the priest-hero in these novels, coming to terms with his
culture is an essential part of coming to terms with himself."
(D.P.)

THE LAST HURRAH

O 86   Boulger, James D., "Puritan Allegory in Four Modern Novels,"
Thought, 44:413-32, Autumn, 1969.

"The use of Puritan allegory . . . lifts The Last Hurrah, By Love
Possessed, Invisible Man, and Herzog to the level of serious and
lasting importance." (D.P.)

O 87   Goodwin, George, Jr., "The Last Hurrahs: George Apley and Frank
Skeffington," Massachusetts Review, 1:461-71, May, 1960.

"Much of what is unique in Massachusetts politics stems from the
fact that the state received an overwhelming proportion of Irish
immigrants. . . ." Both George Apley (The Late George Apley)
and Frank Skeffington (The Last Hurrah) "help to explain much"
of this uniqueness. (G.C.)

O'CONNOR, FLANNERY

O 88   Abbot, Louise Hardeman, "Remembering Flannery O'Connor,"
Southern Literary Journal, 2:3-25, Spring, 1970.

[These are remembrances of Flannery O'Connor.] (T.T.B.)

O 89   Alice, Sister Rose, S. S. J., "Flannery O'Connor: Poet to the
Outcast," Renascence, 16:126-32, Spring, 1964.

"Miss O'Connor peoples her stories not with burnt-out intellectuals
but with feverish quasi-primates in whom religion becomes allied
with sheer animal cunning." And yet her works are "highly moral
and constructed within the Christian frame of reference," although
it takes a certain skill to see "beyond the sensational to the spiritual."
(S.A.)

O 90   Bassan, Maurice, "Flannery O'Connor's Way: Shock, with Moral
Intent," Renascence, 15:195-9, 211, Summer, 1963.

Within the "narrow range of theme and subject-matter she has allowed
herself to explore," Flannery O'Connor writes with an "exquisite
sense of perfection"; "setting aside the question of whether one need
embrace her values," she is "one of the best writers of fiction we
have." (S.A.)

O 91   Baumbach, Jonathan, "The Acid of God's Grace: The Fiction of
        Flannery O'Connor," Georgia Review, 17:334-45, Fall, 1963.

        O'Connor's novels demonstrate a theological pattern in the explora-
        tion of a world of evil and decay. As in Wise Blood, the rite de
        passage is reversed: central characters have fallen and only after
        moving through evil do they discover God; and through extreme
        penance they achieve redemption. (W.A.F.)

O 92   Bertrande, Sister, "Four Stories of Flannery O'Connor," Thought,
        37:410-26, Autumn, 1962.

        "The Partridge Festival," "The Comforts of Home," "The Enduring
        Chill," and "A View of the Woods" demonstrate that "the action of
        redemptive grace upon the lowly, the ignorant, the deprived, and a
        sensitive use of scriptural parallels constitute her purpose, plan and
        pattern." (G.C.)

O 93   Brittain, Joan, "The Fictional Family of Flannery O'Connor,"
        Renascence, 19:48-52, Fall, 1966.

        "In order of the most frequently occurring types of characters,"
        O'Connor's fictional family "includes adolescents, young single
        males, widows, widowers, bachelors, old maids, whole families,
        and finally, children." The characters, "once developed, rarely
        change from one story to another." (S.A.)

O 94   Brittain, Joan T. and Leon V. Driskell, "O'Connor and the Eternal
        Crossroads," Renascence, 22:49-55, Autumn, 1969.

        "O'Connor's characters, Georgians nearly all of them, embody her
        search for a location at which the exigencies of time and place will
        have relevance to the larger scope of eternity." (S.A.)

O 95   Burns, Stuart L., "Flannery O'Connor's Literary Apprenticeship,"
        Renascence, 22:3-16, Autumn, 1969.

        After looking closely at the early stories we know they "are not
        masterpieces. They are valuable not because they reveal a finished
        portrait but rather because they provide a sense of the preliminary
        sketches which preceded it." (S.A.)

O 96   Burns, Stuart L., " 'Torn by the Lord's Eye': Flannery O'Connor's
        Use of Sun Imagery," Twentieth Century Literature, 13:154-66,
        October, 1967.

        "This study of sun imagery in Flannery O'Connor's fiction is by no
        means comprehensive. . . . But it is possible to state with some
        confidence that its main function is to define man's attitude toward
        God and, conversely, God's toward man. It gives us a sense of
        man's relation to the natural world he inhabits as well as his rela-
        tion to the spiritual world with which he is so often in conflict.
        Through extended use, Miss O'Connor has established a brilliant
        and comprehensive symbol that is psychologically, biologically and
        theologically appropriate." (D.P.)

O 97   Carlson, Thomas M., "Flannery O'Connor: The Manichaean
        Dilemma," Sewanee Review, 77:254-76, Spring, 1969.

        "The Manichaean dilemma appears in every story. Often it repre-
        sents the ultimate flaw in the perception of the protagonist."
        (W.E.K.)

O 98   Cheney, Brainard, "Flannery O'Connor's Campaign for Her
        Country," Sewanee Review, 72:555-8, Autumn, 1964.

        "It occurs to me here that she accomplished what she set out to do
        to an astonishing degree. She got attention. She got reaction. And
        I believe that she got across her Christian vision to a significant
        public." (G.C.)

O 99   Cheney, Brainard, "Miss O'Connor Creates Unusual Humor Out of
        Ordinary Sin," Sewanee Review, 71:644-52, Autumn, 1963.

        "It has remained to Flannery O'Connor . . . to create a brand of
        humor based on the religious point of view. . . . The genius of
        Miss O'Connor's humor is that she nowhere appears the partisan of
        human fallibility. This is the initial requirement of the orthodox
        outlook. . . . That sense of conscience, that nakedness before God,
        is the source of religious realism and the premise for Miss O'Connor's
        humor." (D.P.)

O 100   Coffey, Warren, "Flannery O'Connor," Commentary, 40:93-9,
        November, 1965.

        [This retrospective view of Flannery O'Connor emphasizes her
        Catholic Jansenistic background which made her short stories sharp
        investigations of the pain and the torture of sex.] (G.A.S.)

O 101   Coleman, Richard, "Flannery O'Connor: A Scrutiny of Two Forms
of Her Many-Leveled Art," Phoenix, No. 1, pp. 30-66, 1966.

O'Connor's writing may be approached through a self-portrait. Both
forms of her art are "symbolic, metaphoric, ironic, satiric, comic,
tragic, and mysterious." Both betray a "gift for seeing" and "the
strength of faith." (G.C.)

O 102   Detweiler, Robert, "The Curse of Christ in Flannery O'Connor's
Fiction," Comparative Literature Studies, 3:235-45, No. 2, 1966.

". . . four of the main constituents of fiction as they are employed
by Miss O'Connor are informed and determined by corresponding
religious elements, and . . . she, simultaneously, converts those
elements into the structure and content of good literary art."
(G.C.)

O 103   Dowell, Bob, "The Moment of Grace in the Fiction of Flannery
O'Connor," College English, 27:235-9, December, 1965.

". . . Miss O'Connor's fiction is primarily concerned with man's
life-and-death spiritual struggle. The protagonist, rebelling against
belief, forces a crisis that reveals to him his haughty and willful
misconception of reality, at which time he experiences . . . his
'moment of grace'." (G.C.)

O 104   Drake, Robert, " 'The Bleeding Stinking Mad Shadow of Jesus' in
the Fiction of Flannery O'Connor," Comparative Literature Studies,
3:183-96, No. 2, 1966.

O'Connor's major theme "is that the Christian religion is a very
shocking, indeed a scandalous business . . . and that its Savior is
an offense and a stumbling block, even a 'bleeding stinking mad'
grotesque to many. . . . He terrifies before He can bless." (G.C.)

O 105   Drake, Robert, "The Paradigm of Flannery O'Connor's True
Country," Studies in Short Fiction, 6:433-42, Summer, 1969.

O'Connor's absolute devotion to writing about the time and place of
which she had "fundamental heart and head knowledge," and thus
revealing the essential human condition through the particular,
makes her an outstanding example for any fiction writer. (B.K.N.)

O 106   Driskell, Leon, " 'Parker's Back' vs. 'The Partridge Festival':
Flannery O'Connor's Critical Choice," Georgia Review, 21:476-90,
Winter, 1967.

"To have included 'The Partridge Festival' with its bleak doctrinal
insistence upon carnality and its concomitant burdens in Everything
That Rises Must Converge would have totally broken Miss O'Connor's
thematic pattern for the book. Her inclusion of 'Parker's Back'
raised no such problems." (G.C.)

O 107   Eggenschwiler, David, "Flannery O'Connor's True and False
Prophets," Renascence, 21:151-61, Spring, 1969.

Most critics agree about what Miss O'Connor has rejected, but not
about what she affirms. In hope of clearing this up, it is worthwhile
"to analyze conflicting forms of religious values in Miss O'Connor's
works." (S.A.)

O108   Feeley, Sister M. Kathleen, S.S.N.D., "Thematic Imagery in the
Fiction of Flannery O'Connor," Southern Humanities Review,
3:14-32, Winter, 1968.

Flannery O'Connor makes excellent use of poetic imagery in her
writings. Her own phrase "reasonable use of the unreasonable" is
the key to some of her images. Her primary theme--"the reaction
of man to the fact of Redemption"--does not detract from the "artistic
excellence" of her work. Imagery is briefer but no less powerful in
the short stories than in the novels. (V.E.)

O 109   Friedman, Melvin J., "Flannery O'Connor: Another Legend in
Southern Fiction," English Journal, 51:233-43, April, 1962.

[The essay attempts to define "what is unique in Flannery O'Connor's
talent."] (D.A.B.)

O 110   Hart, Jane, "Strange Earth, the Stories of Flannery O'Connor,"
Georgia Review, 12:215-22, Summer, 1958.

Flannery O'Connor's works have the grotesque stamp of the Southern
Gothic school, yet there is "a strong sense of rich red-clay reality
underlying and reinforcing all her work." (W.G.F.)

O 111   Hawkes, John, "Flannery O'Connor's Devil," <u>Sewanee Review</u>, 70:395-407, Summer, 1962.

Miss O'Connor's fiction is comic, but it is also serious; and it acquires tension and force from the two major components of her imagination--the apocalyptic and the demonic. It is the demonic which "speaks with a new and essential shrewdness about what Nathanael West called 'the truly monstrous'." (A.S.)

O 112   Hendin, Josephine Gattuso, "In Search of Flannery O'Connor," <u>Columbia Forum</u>, 13:38-41, Spring, 1970.

"O'Connor wrote about what she knew best: what it means to be a living contradiction. . . . [She] became more and more the pure poet of the Misfit, the oppressed, the psychic cripple, the freak--of all of those who are martyred by silent fury and redeemed through violence." (D.A.B.)

O 113   Hicks, Granville, "A Writer at Home with Her Heritage," <u>Saturday Review</u>, 45:22-3, May 12, 1962.

[These are views of Flannery O'Connor at her home in Milledgeville.] (G.C.)

O 114   Jacobsen, Josephine, "A Catholic Quartet," <u>Christian Scholar</u>, 47:139-54, Summer, 1964.

"Each of these [Catholic] writers comes to the living material from a totally diverse angle; each has a characteristic or dominant approach. At the risk of oversimplification, it is possible to say that Muriel Spark's implementation is that of style, Greene's that of paradox, Mr. Powers's that of discipline and Miss O'Connor's that of mystery." (D.P.)

O 115   Kann, Jean Marie, O. S. F., "Everything That Rises Must Converge," <u>Catholic World</u>, 204:154-9, December, 1966.

[These are personal reminiscences of Flannery O'Connor and a discussion of her interest in the work of Teilhard de Chardin.] (D.A.B.)

O 116   Kirkland, William M., "Flannery O'Connor: The Person and the Writer," East-West Review, 3:159-63, Summer, 1967.

"I had never heard of Flannery O'Connor in 1954, when I came to Milledgeville . . . to become rector of the little Episcopal church there." ". . . I find it next to impossible to separate the Flannery O'Connor I knew from the legend of the writer. . . . She was such a strange mixture--gothic, apocalyptic, and modern. Through her characters, she dared to poke fun at scientific man's grandiose achievements. . . . Yet, she was quick to remind critics that there was more than one kind of humanism; hers was the pre-reformation, Thomas More, kind. Yet, while she could seem cold and aloof . . . no one . . . could doubt her compassion and her liking for people. Certainly no one ever questioned her genuineness." (D.P.)

O 117   Le Clézio, J. M. G., "L'Univers de Flannery O'Connor," La Nouvelle Revue Française, 13e année, No. 153, pp. 488-93, September, 1965.

O'Connor depicts man as a prisoner in a cursed universe. Consequently he can only be a fanatic. His ideas have more importance than his daily acts because they motivate them. Reality no longer has such importance. Interior motivation is what counts. (T.T.B.)

O 118   Lensing, George, "De Chardin's Ideas in Flannery O'Connor," Renascence, 18:171-5, Summer, 1966.

"The danger inherent in reading Flannery O'Connor . . . is to call her a disciple of the grotesque, a victim of violent and morbid preoccupation. She is ultimately more than an heir of the Gothic tradition, and it is her sense of the comic which adds another dimension, frequently overlooked, to her fiction." (S.A.)

O 119   Lorch, Thomas M., "Flannery O'Connor: Christian Allegorist," Critique: Studies in Modern Fiction, 10:69-80, No. 2, 1968.

"Miss O'Connor repeatedly insisted that her religious beliefs in no way restricted her freedom as a writer. . . . But what one sees and 'what is' differ from observer to observer, and as the allegories in her works reveal, Flannery O'Connor underestimated the extent to which what was real for her was determined by her religious faith." (D.A.B.)

O 120   McCarthy, John F., "Human Intelligence versus Divine Truth:
         The Intellectual in Flannery O'Connor's Works," English Journal,
         55:1143-8, December, 1966.

         "If there must be a conflict between human intelligence and divine
         truth (and if man is human and God is divine there must always be
         such a conflict), there is no question as to the side on which Flannery
         O'Connor's sympathies lay." Her position has been stated in Antigone:
         " 'There is no happiness where there is no wisdom; No wisdom but in
         submission to the gods. . .'." (D.A.B.)

O 121   McCown, Robert, S. J., "Flannery O'Connor and the Reality of
         Sin," Catholic World, 188:285-91, January, 1959.

         "Flannery O'Connor's phenomenal power of giving life to her charac-
         ters is due to a complex mastery of her art which renders with rapid
         precision their psychological makeup. What Mr. Esty [Commonweal,
         (March 7, 1958)] mistakes for the gratuitous grotesque is, much of
         the time, none other than this realism in picturing living, breathing,
         sweating humanity." (D.A.B.)

O 122   Maloof, Saul, "On Flannery O'Connor," Commonweal, 90:490-1,
         August 8, 1969.

         "The range of Flannery O'Connor's occasional prose . . . is neces-
         sarily limited, and many of her readers will take exception . . . to
         this or that formulation--on the South, on 'pornography' and 'obscen-
         ity,' on some marginal matters; but . . . what is important is the
         luminosity and intensity of her best pages on the nature of fiction--
         the suppleness and radiance of her intelligence and the acerbity of
         her wit; and . . . the body of work that underlies and amplifies
         them." (D.P.)

O 123   Mary-Alice, Sister, O.P., "My Mentor, Flannery O'Connor,"
         Saturday Review, 48:24-5, May 29, 1965.

         Soon after Sister Mary-Alice met Flannery O'Connor in 1960 Miss
         O'Connor agreed to " 'take on criticizing your work . . . if you'll
         take on praying for mine.'. . . From her first letter to her last
         she was outspoken in her constructive criticism." She "was the
         humblest person I have ever met." (D.P.)

O 124 May, John R., S. J., "The Pruning Word: Flannery O'Connor's Judgment of Intellectuals," Southern Humanities Review, 4:325-38, Fall, 1970.

O'Connor offers us a complete and consistent revelation of the futility of an intellectual life-style. "In fact, there is no intellectual anywhere in her fiction who escapes the judgment of her vision." (A.S.W.)

O 125 Meaders, Margaret Inman, "Flannery O'Connor: 'Literary Witch'," Colorado Quarterly, 10:377-86, Spring, 1962.

[These are reminiscences and biographical data about Flannery O'Connor by a fellow Georgian.] (G.C.)

O 126 Montgomery, Marion, "Flannery O'Connor's Territorial Center," Critique: Studies in Modern Fiction, 11:5-10, No. 3, 1969.

"O'Connor's fiction has a territorial center to its spiritual geography in the regions of the Inferno, rather than in the Purgatorio or Paradiso." She often makes her actions horrifying to produce a more drastic effect. (B.K.N.)

O 127 Montgomery, Marion, "Miss O'Connor and the Christ-Haunted," Southern Review, 4:665-72, Summer, 1968.

O'Connor "was in a position to see the surface of lives, of which we make a great deal of sentimental nonsense, in relation to a more profound view of life. In the disparity between the two views, the larger (hers) including the lesser, lies in a comedy in Dante's sense of the term." (G.C.)

O 128 Montgomery, Marion, "A Note on Flannery O'Connor's Terrible and Violent Prophecy of Mercy," Forum (Houston), 7:4-7, Summer, 1969.

Denial "involves one's looking at the immediate world without penetrating it. Such refusal inevitably makes that world a mirror. But when one comes to the point of recognizing his own 'grinning' reflection in the immediate world . . . he may at last begin to see into the world." (K.M.W.)

O 129   Montgomery, Marion, "O'Connor and Teilhard de Chardin: The
Problem of Evil," Renascence, 22:34-42, Autumn, 1969.

Although both O'Connor and Teilhard believe in the "sacred worth of
created nature," O'Connor obviously "agrees with Claude
Tresmontant's doctrinal position which he expresses in rejecting
Teilhard's vision, particularly attacking Teilhard's concept of
original sin." (S.A.)

O 130   Nance, William L., "Flannery O'Connor: The Trouble with Being a
Prophet," University Review, 36:101-8, December, 1969.

". . . there is no need to search Miss O'Connor's lectures and
essays to determine her role as critic and truth-revealer, for she
has made that attitude one of the central dramatic concerns of her
fiction." (D.A.B.)

O 131   Quinn, Sister M. Bernetta, O. S. F., "View From a Rock: The
Fiction of Flannery O'Connor and J. F. Powers," Critique: Studies
in Modern Fiction, 2:19-27, Fall, 1958.

Writing from the Catholic point of view provides Flannery O'Connor
and J. F. Powers with "a vantage point in the universe." Yet for
both these artists, "the exercise of their craft is a literary, not a
therapeutic, matter. Without trying to remedy it . . . they record
what they see, though there is a difference, in Miss O'Connor's
favor, in the depths to which they see." (G.O.)

O 132   Rubin, Louis D., Jr., "Flannery O'Connor: A Note on Literary
Fashions," Critique: Studies in Modern Fiction, 2:11-8, Fall, 1968.

Miss O'Connor's success is not dependent upon her treatment of
fashionable subjects--Roman Catholics and Southern rural characters.
"These are images, conventions; it is the universal insight embodied
in them and given form by them that gives [her stories] impact."
(G.O.)

O 133   Rupp, Richard H., "Flannery O'Connor," Commonweal, 79:304-7,
December 6, 1961.

In Flannery O'Connor's stories "only the materially and spiritually
destitute (the freaks and the ignorant, the crazed and the innocent)
shall see God. . . . They are modern instances of the Christian
paradox, the Sermon on the Mount." (M.G.)

O 134   Shear, Walter, "Flannery O'Connor: Character and Characterization," Renascence, 20:140-6, Spring, 1968.

"The detached recording of the personality only faintly veils the
ferocity underneath the rather casual but persistent notation of
speech, illogic, and contradiction and almost totally disguises
her peculiar sympathy for her characters, a sympathy which
seems connected with rather settled conclusions about human limitations." (S.A.)

O 135   Shinn, Thelma J., "Flannery O'Connor and the Violence of Grace,"
Contemporary Literature, 9:58-73, Winter, 1968.

Flannery O'Connor completed her mission--"to wake the sleeping
children of God"--before her death. She believed that modern man
must be "struck" by God's mercy or grace with a violence equal to
that of contemporary life. (P.J.R.)

O 136   Smith, J. Oates, "Ritual and Violence in Flannery O'Connor,"
Thought, 41:545-60, Winter, 1966.

"The violent and ritualistic world of Flannery O'Connor's fiction is
neither realistic nor naturalistic but surrealistic, a series of
parables that are harshly and defiantly spiritual." (G.C.)

O 137   Snow, Ollye Tine, "The Functional Gothic of Flannery O'Connor,"
Southwest Review, 50:286-99, Summer, 1965.

The novels and short stories of Flannery O'Connor, especially the
two short stories "Everything That Rises Must Converge" and "A
Good Man is Hard to Find," reflect the theme of the "grotesqueries
of man's defiant, sometimes stupid disobedience of God." Reflected
also is O'Connor's debt to eighteenth century Gothic devices, which
"function organically and artistically in her writing." (V.E.)

O 138   Spivey, Ted R., "Flannery O'Connor's View of God and Man,"
Studies in Short Fiction, 1:200-6, Spring, 1964.

O'Connor demonstrates that to know the truth is not enough. Only
"the leap of faith . . . can bring back the love which will banish
destructiveness." She ends with the paradoxical hope and prophecy
that "through the motiveless criminal shall come a new man free of
the Devil." (P.J.R.)

O 139 Stelzmann, Rainulf, "Shock and Orthodoxy: An Interpretation of
Flannery O'Connor's Novels and Short Stories," Xavier University
Studies, 2:4-21, March, 1963.

In O'Connor's works, "God is very much alive as the creator of the
world and the Lord who does not leave man alone. In fact, He sometimes overpowers man and seems to rescue him by force from his
self-dug pitfalls." (G.C.)

O 140 Stephens, Martha, "Flannery O'Connor and the Sanctified-Sinner
Tradition," Arizona Quarterly, 24:223-39, Autumn, 1968.

Miss O'Connor's works have been "crudely misread" by critics
viewing her as a characteristically Southern writer. She belongs
more properly with Eliot, Mauriac, Greene, Bernanos--writers
concerned with "the high capability of the desperately-driven sinner
for true belief and holiness." (S.T.C.)

O 141 Stern, Richard, "Flannery O'Connor: A Remembrance and Some
Letters," Shenandoah, 16:5-10, Winter, 1965.

[These are several letters from Flannery O'Connor to Richard Stern
and some reminiscences of her visit to the University of Chicago in
1959.] (G.C.)

O 142 Sullivan, Walter, "The Achievement of Flannery O'Connor,"
Southern Humanities Review, 2:303-9, Summer, 1968.

"In her amalgamation of the two traditions--the Christian and the
agrarian--she developed the only truly original voice among her
Southern contemporaries." Ultimately, however, "the level of her
accomplishment must be established principally by fifteen stories.
. . ." (G.C.)

O 143 Taylor, Henry, "The Halt Shall be Gathered Together: Physical
Deformity in the Fiction of Flannery O'Connor," Western Humanities Review, 22:325-38, Autumn, 1968.

Physically deformed persons are led to think about themselves more
deeply than physically intact people so that they are peculiarly well-
equipped to come to grips with the spiritual problems which are so
important in Miss O'Connor's fiction. (B.D.G.)

O 144   Thorp, Willard, "Suggs and Sut in Modern Dress: The Latest
Chapter in Southern Humor," Mississippi Quarterly, 13:169-75,
Fall, 1960.

Although the influence of the tradition of early Southern humor on
contemporary Southern fiction is difficult to document, much recent
Southern writing is humorous. The fantastic, sometimes horrifying,
humor of Faulkner, Capote, O'Connor, and McCullers parallels
similar fantasies in George Washington Harris and Henry Junius
Nott, although much of that tradition of Southern humor was extremely
realistic. (D.P.)

O 145   True, Michael D., "Flannery O'Connor: Backwoods Prophet in the
Secular City," Papers on Language and Literature, 5:209-23,
Spring, 1969.

O'Connor's heroes are "backwoods prophets in the secular city,
who carry some overt manifestation of God's 'grace' to the modern
world." (W.E.K.)

O 146   Vandekieft, Ruth M., "Judgment in the Fiction of Flannery O'Connor,"
Sewanee Review, 76:337-56, Spring, 1968.

O'Connor's hero is "the essence of the existential man, and his life
is all encounter." Only the major question matters; all else is given
over to the devil. Against the "deep" but ill-educated hero is ranged
the educated skeptic or the soft-hearted humanitarian. (D.M.M.)

O 147   Walsh, Thomas F., "The Devils of Hawthorne and Flannery
O'Connor," Xavier University Studies, 5:117-22, June, 1966.

"In their fiction Hawthorne and O'Connor use the devil to prove to
man that he is still the old Adam. . . . However, Hawthorne's
vision is more tragic than satiric. O'Connor's vision is more comic,
and her characters are more susceptible to God's saving grace."
(D.P.)

O 148   Wedge, George F., "Two Bibliographies: Flannery O'Connor,
J. F. Powers," Critique: Studies in Modern Fiction, 2:59-70,
Fall, 1958.

"Both bibliographies follow the same plan: they list (1) books, (2)
fiction in magazines, (3) articles and reviews by Flannery O'Connor
or J. F. Powers, (4) bibliographical material and (5) articles or
parts of books about Miss O'Connor or Mr. Powers." (D.A.B.)

O 149   Wylder, Jean, "Flannery O'Connor: A Reminiscence and Some
Letters," North American Review, 255:58-65, Spring, 1970.

At the Writer's Workshop at the University of Iowa in 1947-1948
Flannery O'Connor was reluctant to discuss the work of other
students; she contributed little in class about herself. Her correspondence reveals a particular fondness for peacocks and other exotic
birds. Many of her short stories were originally conceived as chapters for Wise Blood before it was published. (D.P.)

THE ARTIFICIAL NIGGER

O 150   Byrd, Turner F., "Ironic Dimension in Flannery O'Connor's 'The
Artificial Nigger'," Mississippi Quarterly, 21:243-51, Fall, 1968.

Flannery O'Connor's "'The Artificial Nigger' . . . reflects . . .
the consummate artistry with which she blends classic literary
allegory and theology; yet this story is misread at its most crucial
point. . . . The failure to detect the ironic mode (with particular
concern for her point of view) as the basis of Miss O'Connor's technique, has led many to accept Mr. Head's judgment of his condition
in the denouement as a true moment of grace, rather than as an
extension of his stubborn, misguided, self-proclaimed omniscience."
(D.P.)

O 151   Hays, Peter L., "Dante, Tobit, and 'The Artificial Nigger',"
Studies in Short Fiction, 5:263-8, Spring, 1968.

"Mr. Head, in this amazingly complex short story, is compared to
and contrasted with Vergil--who is guide and spiritual tutor to Dante,
but learns nothing on the trip himself--and with the angel Raphael
('God heals')--who is also a geographical guide, moral preceptor,
and not, unlike Vergil with Dante, the cause of healing the blindness
of the elder Tobias (or Tobit)." (D.A.B.)

THE CRUCIFIED NIGGER

O 152   Muller, Gilbert H., "The City of Woe: Flannery O'Connor's Dantean
Vision," Georgia Review, 23:206-13, Fall, 1969.

There are many affinities between "The Crucified Nigger," and
Dante's passage through the inferno. Through her use of this particular allegorical construction, based as it is on The Divine Comedy,
Miss O'Connor renews traditional themes and presents a Hell within
the modern city. (B.D.G.)

THE DISPLACED PERSON

O 153   Fitzgerald, Robert, "The Countryside and the True Country,"
Sewanee Review, 70:380-94, Summer, 1962.

Contrary to the opinion of a Time reviewer, Flannery O'Connor's
"The Displaced Person" develops its theme lucidly, and the theme
is that "estrangement from Christian plenitude is estrangement
from the true country of man." And the main character is "the
worthy protagonist of a tragic action." (A.S.)

O 154   Joselyn, Sister M., O.S.B., "Thematic Centers in 'The Displaced
Person'," Studies in Short Fiction, 1:85-92, Winter, 1964.

"The fullest exploitation of the two thematic centers, the peacock
and the Displaced Person, and their analogue, Christ, is reached
in this final revelation that the displacer is the displaced. The
denouement in the story's 'overthought' coincides exactly with the
maximum revelation of the 'underthought'." (P.J.R.)

O 155   Male, Roy R., "The Two Versions of 'The Displaced Person',"
Studies in Short Fiction, 7:450-7, Summer, 1970.

Major differences have been overlooked between the first appearance
of O'Connor's "The Displaced Person" in Sewanee Review, Autumn,
1954 and its appearance in A Good Man Is Hard to Find in 1955. The
earlier version ends with the death of Mrs. Shortley; it is part one
of the revised story. The revised version has also been altered to
prepare for the shift of point of view to Mrs. McIntyre and to develop
the foreshadowing of the final catastrophe in the expanded tale. (D.P.)

EVERYTHING THAT RISES MUST CONVERGE

O 156   Burke, John J., Jr., S.J., "Convergence of Flannery O'Connor and
Chardin," Renascence, 19:41-7, 52, Fall, 1966.

The title of O'Connor's posthumous short stories, Everything That
Rises Must Converge, is derived from the writings of Teilhard de
Chardin, and both the title story and the whole volume should be
viewed in relationship to those writings. (S.A.)

O 157   Esch, Robert M., "O'Connor's 'Everything That Rises Must
Converge'," Explicator, 27: Item 58, April, 1969.

"At the end . . . the eyes of Julian's mother symbolize the ultimate
rejection of Julian." (D.P.)

EVERYTHING THAT RISES MUST CONVERGE   (cont'd)

O 158   Kane, Patricia, "Flannery O'Connor's Everything That Rises Must Converge," Critique: Studies in Modern Fiction, 8:85-91, Fall, 1965.

"The Lame Shall Enter First," "A View of the Woods," and "Everything That Rises Must Converge," all from Miss O'Connor's last collection, Everything That Rises Must Converge, "will bear comparison with the high standard set in Miss O'Connor's earlier work. . . . these stories, like the earlier ones, show Miss O'Connor to be the Catholic and Southern writer that she called herself." However, "the stories can and should be seen in the particular. . . ." (D.P.)

O 159   Maida, Patricia Dinneen, " 'Convergence' in Flannery O'Connor's 'Everything that Rises Must Converge'," Studies in Short Fiction, 7:549-55, Fall, 1970.

The title for this story was derived from Teilhard de Chardin's The Phenomenon of Man, and the allusion to Chardin's theory of "convergence" enriches the story, which ends in a convergence of opposing forces. O'Connor is less optimistic than Chardin. However, Julian does achieve a revelation that may redeem him in the sense of making him the man he could become. (D.P.)

O 160   Sullivan, Walter, "Flannery O'Connor, Sin, and Grace: Everything That Rises Must Converge," Hollins Critic, 2:1-8, 10, September, 1965.

"It was Flannery O'Connor's contention that the strange characters who populate her world are essentially no different from you and me. That they are drawn more extravagantly, she would admit, but she claimed that this was necessary because of our depravity: for the morally blind, the message of redemption must be writ large." (K.M.W.)

GOOD COUNTRY PEOPLE

O 161   Jones, Bartlett C., "Depth Psychology and Literary Study," Midcontinent American Studies Journal, 5:50-6, Fall, 1964.

The Flannery O'Connor story, "Good Country People," demonstrates a "better methodology" of psychological criticism. (R.B.W.)

A GOOD MAN IS HARD TO FIND

O 162 Brittain, Joan Tucker, "O'Connor's A Good Man Is Hard to Find,"
Explicator, 26: Item 1, September, 1967.

"Structurally, Miss O'Connor emphasizes through her many stories
of violence the need for man's 'conversion' from isolation from God
to acceptance." (D.P.)

O 163 Hamblen, Abigail Ann, "Flannery O'Connor's Study of Innocence and
Evil," University Review, 34:295-7, June, 1968.

"Foolish Innocence and senseless Evil . . . are doomed to wander
the earth, suffering, and inflicting pain and, paradoxically, they are
linked by a single set of values." (D.A.B.)

O 164 Marks, W. S., III, "Advertisements for Grace: Flannery O'Connor's
'A Good Man Is Hard to Find'," Studies in Short Fiction, 4:19-27,
Fall, 1966.

"In 'A Good Man Is Hard to Find' . . . the action of the story expands parabolically into a narrative of modern man's general sin-
sickness. . . . the plot concerns the tragi-comic destruction of
some Florida-bound Georgians, chiefly through the senile offices of
a grandmother who craftily, if unintentionally, detours her son and
his family into the hands of a homicidal mania called the Misfit."
In the final analysis, "it is not brilliance of invention one misses in
'A Good Man Is Hard to Find,' but something of real human dignity
and 'the mere sensuous sympathy of dust for dust'." (D.P.)

O 165 Martin, Sister M., O.P., "O'Connor's 'A Good Man Is Hard to
Find'," Explicator, 24: Item 19, October, 1965.

"Only when faced with death does the grandmother admit her responsibility to more than social standards. . . ." (D.P.)

O 166 Montgomery, Marion, "Miss O'Connor's 'Good Man'," University
of Denver Quarterly, 3:1-19, Autumn, 1968.

In spite of her Christian view of life O'Connor anchors her fiction
"in the literal world." She begins with the negative aspects of life,
deleting "all modern justifications of evil as an accident of existence."
However, she demonstrates at the climax the "terror of mercy,"
thus bringing "good out of evil, through her creations." For example,
the grandmother in the climax of "A Good Man Is Hard to Find" identifies the Misfit, who is a Satan figure, as one of her children. (D.P.)

A GOOD MAN IS HARD TO FIND   (cont'd)

O 167   Rubin, Louis D., Jr., "Two Ladies of the South," Diliman Review,
3:334-47, October, 1955.

"Where Miss Welty's fiction hovers [in The Bride of the Innisfallen],
where her style is veiled, shimmering, elusive, Miss O'Connor's
approach [in A Good Man Is Hard to Find] is direct, precise,
bounded." (W.G.F.)

O 168   Rubin, Louis D., Jr., "Two Ladies of the South," Sewanee Review,
63:671-81, Autumn, 1955.

"For each of the tales in The Bride of the Innisfallen, the plot is the
character's discovery of himself, and events all occur for that final
purpose. The progress of Miss Welty's art is in . . . the match-
lessly revealed moment of knowledge and feeling in a perfect inutility
of place. . . . Where Miss Welty's fiction hovers, where her style
is veiled, shimmering, elusive, Miss O'Connor's approach is direct,
precise, bounded." "There is a great deal of compassion in her
work, but it is always compassion for characters because they are
human beings with human limitations. . . . The moral consciousness
that runs throughout . . . A Good Man Is Hard to Find can accept
evil, but not try to find excuses for it." (D.P.)

GREENLEAF

O 169   Asals, Frederick, "The Mythic Dimensions of Flannery O'Connor's
'Greenleaf'," Studies in Short Fiction, 5:317-30, Summer, 1968.

"What Miss O'Connor presents in 'Greenleaf' is a kind of smaller
modern version of Euripides's Bacchae with Mrs. May as the
Pentheus figure whose refusal to acknowledge the essential physical
and spiritual terms of life calls down upon her the fittingly ironic
punishment of the gods." "In all its complex artistry, 'Greenleaf'
is a central expression of Flannery O'Connor's vision, one of the
most pregnant renderings of her conception of the divine harmony
that embraces nature, man, and God." (D.P.)

THE LAME SHALL ENTER FIRST

O 170   Asals, Frederick, "Flannery O'Connor's 'The Lame Shall Enter
First'," Mississippi Quarterly, 23:103-20, 1970.

THE LAME SHALL ENTER FIRST   (cont'd)

A "reading" of the story which concentrates on the "richness and coherence of language and imagery in that work not only . . . demonstrate[s] the fineness and complexity of her art but . . . suggest[s] that without some such close attention to the density of texture, we are likely to misapprehend the larger meanings of her 'poetically' conceived fiction." (G.C.)

THE LIFE YOU SAVE MAY BE YOUR OWN

O 171   Griffith, Albert J., "Flannery O'Connor's Salvation Road," Studies in Short Fiction, 3:329-33, Spring, 1966.

In "The Life You Save May Be Your Own," Miss O'Connor shows that Mr. Shiftlet leads a meaningful spiritual life "only insofar as his life corresponds with the pattern set by Christ," and only thus can he save others and himself. (P.J.R.)

PARKER'S BACK

O 172   Browning, Preston, Jr., " 'Parker's Back': Flannery O'Connor's Iconography of Salvation by Profanity," Studies in Short Fiction, 6:525-35, Fall, 1969.

O'Connor maintains the integrity of both the natural and metaphysical by refraining from writing an uplifting parable about the fall and redemption of a sinner, by maintaining the comic tone, and by guarding the story's naturalistic surface from being undermined by propagandistic motives. (B.K.N.)

O 173   Fahey, William A., "Flannery O'Connor's 'Parker's Back'," Renascence, 20:162-6, Spring, 1968.

This important story reveals O'Connor's talent for "marvelously accurate dialogue" and shows again that she makes scenes "with the deft touch of a master." (S.A.)

O 174   Gordon, Caroline, "Heresy in Dixie," Sewanee Review, 76:263-97, Spring, 1968.

"Parker's Back," Flannery O'Connor's last story, is illuminated by a comparison with Flaubert's The Temptation of St. Anthony. Both works involve the denial of hypostatic union. O'Connor often investigates heresy in her fiction. (D.M.M.)

A STROKE OF GOOD FORTUNE

O 175   Montgomery, Marion, "Flannery O'Connor's 'Leaden Tract Against Complacency and Contraception'," Arizona Quarterly, 24:133-46, Summer, 1968.

Stanley Edgar Hyman formulated this harsh criticism of "A Stroke of Good Fortune" because he read it as a trivial exercise in naturalism rather than a significant, technically superb, and humorous analogue to the Annunciation. (S.T.C.)

THE VIOLENT BEAR IT AWAY

O 176   Bowen, Robert O., "Hope vs. Despair in the New Gothic Novel," Renascence, 13:147-52, Spring, 1961.

". . . if we weigh The Violent Bear It Away seriously, we are forced to conclude that its truth is that there is no hope in this world or the next. . . . O'Connor in this novel is an enemy of literature and life, for the book is a pointless bit of comic book sentimentality." (G.C.)

O 177   Burns, Stuart L., "Flannery O'Connor's The Violent Bear It Away: Apotheosis in Failure," Sewanee Review, 76:319-36, Spring, 1968.

"A close examination of the text reveals that the novel makes a single, penetrating, and devastatingly ironic comment on the state of religion in modern society." The Tarwaters, "grotesques," have a truer vision of reality in their apparent insanity than does normal man. The city is asleep as Tarwater goes to seek it, and he, like his great-uncle, will be unable to awaken it. (D.M.M.)

O 178   Davis, Jack and June Davis, "Tarwater and Jonah: Two Reluctant Prophets," Xavier University Studies, 9:19-27, Spring, 1970.

". . . O'Connor drew directly upon the myth of Jonah to establish the pattern for her protagonist's experience in The Violent Bear It Away. This analogy not only draws the novella into the context of Christian mythology, it also explains the function of violence in the work." (G.C.)

O 179   Duhamel, P. Albert, "Flannery O'Connor's Violent View of Reality," Catholic World, 190:280-5, February, 1960.

"Many aspects of [O'Connor's] writing which have puzzled critics-- her directness of phrasing, her reduction of character and setting to

THE VIOLENT BEAR IT AWAY   (cont'd)

essentials, her avoidance of any hint of sentimentalizing--can now be understood [in The Violent Bear It Away] as the direct consequence of the application to art of what might be called a 'violent' [or prophetic] view of reality."   (D.A.B.)

O 180   Fahey, William A., "Out of the Eater: Flannery O'Connor's Appetite for Truth," Renascence, 20:22-9, Autumn, 1967.

In The Violent Bear It Away the episode in which Tarwater leaves his Uncle Rayber's house at night to visit a revivalist chapel is only "a single element in the narrative of the pursuit" but has ramifications that spread throughout the book.   (S.A.)

O 181   Ferris, Sumner J., "The Outside and the Inside: Flannery O'Connor's The Violent Bear It Away," Critique: Studies in Modern Fiction, 3:11-9, Winter-Spring, 1960.

"The Violent Bear It Away is not only a subtle and profound and disturbing study of spiritual states but a great religious novel. Miss O'Connor has shown that a Christian tragedy can be written; for in her novel fate and doom do not conspire against man." Her theology is Catholic, although none of her characters in the novel are. (G.O.)

O 182   Jeremy, Sister, C.S.J., "The Violent Bear It Away: A Linguistic Education," Renascence, 17:11-6, Fall, 1964.

"Miss O'Connor's skill as an artist lies in her ability to endow each of Tarwater's teachers with an individual voice which, while personal and idiosyncratic, yet expresses the attitude of a class in the dialect appropriate to that class."   (S.A.)

O 183   McCown, Robert M., S.J., "The Education of a Prophet: A Study of Flannery O'Connor's The Violent Bear It Away," Kansas Magazine, pp. 73-8, 1962.

"There are two basic abstractions underlying the actions and characters of this work . . . faith in the supernatural and--in dramatic opposition--unbelief." The former is "represented by the spirit of prophecy," the latter by "the spirit of rationalism or naturalism." (G.C.)

THE VIOLENT BEAR IT AWAY   (cont'd)

O 184   Muller, Gilbert H., "The Violent Bear It Away: Moral and Dramatic Sense," Renascence, 22:17-25, Autumn, 1969.

"All of O'Connor's fiction is permeated with the moral sense, and to make it a viable property she relies heavily on . . . the dramatic sense." In The Violent Bear It Away one can see a "perfect coincidence" of these senses.   (S.A.)

O 185   Nolde, Sister M. Simon, O.S.B., "The Violent Bear It Away: A Study in Imagery," Xavier University Studies, 1:180-94, Spring, 1962.

"Three strands of imagery underline the novel's development. Eucharistic imagery, including images of bread, fish and hunger, and images of silence are introduced in part one. . . . images describing the prophetic vocation are introduced in part two. . . ." (G.C.)

O 186   Smith, Francis J., S.J., "O'Connor's Religious Viewpoint in The Violent Bear It Away," Renascence, 22:108-12, Winter, 1970.

"As a Christian and a Catholic, like Flannery O'Connor, one can sympathize and cheer for anyone, any backwoods idiot, who is in pursuit of his own salvation and that of others, but as a reader of The Violent Bear It Away one fails to be amused or interested in antic religiosity." (D.A.B.)

O 187   Trowbridge, Clinton W., "The Symbolic Vision of Flannery O'Connor: Patterns of Imagery in The Violent Bear It Away," Sewanee Review, 76:298-318, Spring, 1968.

O'Connor's images and metaphors are often meant to be taken literally. In The Violent Bear It Away, the image of fish, of bread, of the fire and water which produce them, and of the road which leads young Tarwater to the words of prophetic command provide a key to the novel. (D.M.M.)

WISE BLOOD

O188   Asals, Frederick, "The Road to Wise Blood,"   Renascence, 21:181-94, Summer, 1969.

A close analysis of O'Connor's early stories shows "those first gropings toward a subject and technique which were to fuse so successfully in Wise Blood."   (S.A.)

O 189   Burns, Stuart L., "The Evolution of Wise Blood,"   Modern Fiction Studies, 16:147-62, Summer, 1970.

Flannery O'Connor's Wise Blood requires not only attention to the novel, but close examination of the five short stories published independently between 1948 and 1952, four of which were eventually incorporated in the novel. It is clear that Miss O'Connor "began Wise Blood with a story, or perhaps with a character, but not with a theme. During the evolution of the novel all three elements were considerably altered."   (D.P.)

O 190   Burns, Stuart L., "Structural Patterns in Wise Blood,"   Xavier University Studies, 8:32-43, Summer, 1969.

In Wise Blood, O'Connor uses "water, sex, and coffin symbolism . . . [to] help illuminate the theme. . . . These patterns provide insight into Hazel [sic] Motes's motivation in his lifelong struggle to cope with the question of Christ."   (G.C.)

O 191   Gordon, Caroline, "Flannery O'Connor's Wise Blood,"   Critique: Studies in Modern Fiction, 2:3-10, Fall, 1958.

What sets Miss O'Connor's work apart from that of her contemporaries and makes her one of the most original of modern writers is the theological frame-work implicit in her fiction. All her characters, like Haze Motes of Wise Blood, are displaced persons, "victims of a rejection of the Scheme of Redemption." (G.O.)

O 192   Lawson, Lewis A., "Flannery O'Connor and the Grotesque: Wise Blood,"   Renascence, 17:137-47, 156, Spring, 1965.

Wise Blood is the most grotesque work in Southern fiction and demonstrates that there is no place in O'Connor's world "for any norms; from her vantage point the entire world did not look grotesque, since her audience did not recognize the normative value of faith." (S.A.)

WISE BLOOD   (cont'd)

O 193   Littlefield, Daniel F., Jr., "Flannery O'Connor's Wise Blood: 'Unparalleled Prosperity' and Spiritual Chaos," Mississippi Quarterly, 23:121-33, 1970.

". . . an analysis of Miss O'Connor's use of the motif of material prosperity in Wise Blood show[s] the relationship that prosperity has to the distortion of spiritual purpose." (G.C.)

O 194   Rechnitz, Robert M., "Passionate Pilgrim: Flannery O'Connor's Wise Blood," Georgia Review, 19:310-6, Fall, 1965.

Haze Motes's self-mutilation is paradoxical; total commitment to his atheism becomes his highest affirmation of God's existence, and in the final pages of the novel he is possessed by this god. (A.S.W.)

O'CONNOR, FRANK

O 195   Brenner, Gerry, "Frank O'Connor, 1903-1966: A Bibliography," West Coast Review, 2:55-64, Fall, 1967.

[This bibliography is designed to indicate the range of O'Connor's achievement as a "man of letters."] ". . . the thematic unity and development of ideas . . . make the entirety of his work greater than the sum of its parts and . . . give him literary merit worthy of study. . . ." (D.A.B.)

O 196   Brenner, Gerry, "Frank O'Connor's Imprudent Hero," Texas Studies in Literature and Language, 10:457-69, Fall, 1968.

". . . the clash between judiciousness and the correlatives of imprudence, impulsiveness, irrationality, and immorality marks out the central line of his short fiction. What starts in his stories as simply a celebration of individuality . . . later flowers into more serious ways of expressing individuality." (G.C.)

O 197   Flanagan, Thomas, "Frank O'Connor, 1903-1966," Kenyon Review, 28:439-55, September, 1966.

O'Connor was a fiery, brilliant, magnificent man, deeply involved with the Ireland that he loved and attacked. Of his hundred stories, at least twenty are "as fine as any in our literature"; the stories in Guests of the Nation and Crab Apple Jelly are especially noteworthy. (G.S.)

O 198   Fowler, Albert, "Challenge to Mood in Frank O'Connor," Approach, No. 23, pp. 24-7, Spring, 1957.

"His zest for life in all its contradictory variety keeps him from playing the prophet of doom, and The Holy Door, longer than most of his tales, affords him more scope to develop a conviction that man can overcome the adverse and the perverse, given time to engage them." (A.F.)

O 199   McHugh, Roger, "Frank O'Connor and the Irish Theatre," Eire-Ireland, 4:52-63, Summer, 1969.

[This discussion of O'Connor's relationship with the Abbey Theatre includes analyses and discussion of The Invincibles, Moses's Rock, and The Statue's Daughter.] (D.A.B.)

O 200   Saul, George Brandon, "A Consideration of Frank O'Connor's Short Stories," Colby Library Quarterly, Series 6, No. 8, pp. 329-42, December, 1963.

[The essay provides an overview of O'Connor's achievement as a short story writer. A bibliography is included.] (D.A.B.)

O 201   Weiss, Daniel, "Freudian Criticism: Frank O'Connor as Paradigm," Northwest Review, 2:5-14, Spring, 1959.

The short story "Judas" is about an Oedipal situation, yet the author was unaware of this at the time of writing; "My Oedipus Complex," on a similar Freudian situation, was written with iconoclastic deliberation. (R.K.)

O 202   Whittier, Anthony, "The Art of Fiction XIX: Frank O'Connor," Paris Review, No. 17, pp. 43-64, Autumn-Winter, 1957.

[In this interview Frank O'Connor discusses his work, his experiences, and his opinions about modern literature.] (D.A.B.)

JUDAS

O 203   Kramer, C. R., "Experimentation in Technique: Frank O'Connor's 'Judas'," Dublin Magazine, 8:31-8, Nos. 1-2, 1969.

That O'Connor "was continually . . . trying to provide the correct amount of detail in order for his reader to understand the development of the story is illustrated by a study of 'Judas' . . . [of which] there are five different published versions. . . . Each version shows that O'Connor thought that the exposition in the preceding version had been excessive, the final version being stripped of almost every detail not immediately relevant to the experience being narrated." (K.M.W.)

A SET OF VARIATIONS

O 204   O'Connell, Shaun, "A Net of Revelations," Massachusetts Review, 10:610-3, Summer, 1969.

"O'Connor's range might not be vast, but his eyes are clear, his ear is sharp, his heart is big and his craft is sufficient to his needs. The stories in A Set of Variations might be short and narrow, but they are more than small favors. . . ." (D.P.)

UPROOTED

O 205   Gerber, Helmut E., "O'Connor's 'Uprooted'," Explicator, 14: Item 7, October, 1955.

The two brothers journey from disillusionment to a brief encounter with innocence. (B.K.)

O'CONNOR, WILLIAM VAN

O 206   O'Connor, William Van, "The Writer and the University," Texas Quarterly, 3:51-63, Summer, 1960.

"The university, in a more complicated way than ever before, has involved itself with the living arts--music, painting, literature. . . . the university is now one of the creators of culture as well as the custodian of it. This is why so many writers now live on a campus rather than on the Left Bank or in Greenwich Village." (D.P.)

O 207   Weber, Brom, "A Tribute to William Van O'Connor," Modern Fiction Studies, 15:463-6, Winter, 1969.

"A practical critic rather than a formulator of new theories, O'Connor wrote pioneering studies of Wallace Stevens, William Faulkner, Ezra Pound, and other contemporaries. . . . he generally upheld the tenets of New Criticism. . . . Nevertheless . . . he was perceptively generous to critics whose values and methods he found questionable." (D.P.)

O 207

ODETS, CLIFFORD

O 208   Hughes, Catharine, "Odets: The Price of Success," Commonweal, 78:558-60, September 20, 1963.

"There is something more than usually ironic in the fact that Odets, starting out as the 'symbol' of revolt in American theater should ultimately have come to the point where . . . he was singled out as the symbol of its opposite." His "sentiment--and his career--were almost an American prototype: the early overwhelming success and acclaim; the attempts to repeat it; the still-young relegation to the land of Whatever-Became-of." Although Odets was not a great writer his talent was "destroyed by the easy fanfare, the quick buck of Hollywood." (D.P.)

O 209   Mendelsohn, Michael J., "Clifford Odets and the American Family," Drama Survey, 3:238-43, Fall, 1963.

"But it is the family as a social organism . . . that most often occupies Odets's attention. . . . the playwright's feelings have undergone a change from rebellion (Awake and Sing!) through search (Night Music) to cohesiveness (The Flowering Peach). . . ." (D.P.)

O 210   Mendelsohn, Michael J., "Odets: The Artist in Wonderland," Drama Critique, 9:31-4, Winter, 1966.

Odets's motion picture career can be roughly divided into three periods: 1936-38, 1943-47, and 1955-61. His name . . . appeared on only seven produced films," although he probably contributed to twenty scripts or more. Odets found various rationalizations for his continued presence in Hollywood, and hoped frequently to return to playwrighting, but "was never destined to write as his own man again." (D.P.)

O 211   Odets, Clifford, "How a Playwright Triumphs," Harper's Magazine, 233:64-70, 73-4, September, 1966.

[This monologue--which centers on Odets's early career from Awake and Sing! through his Hollywood days and his success with Golden Boy--also comments on the pressures to tailor plays to ideological concepts, and the way he developed his ideas for his plays.] (D.P.)

O 212 Shuman, R. Baird, "Thematic Consistency in Odets's Early Plays," Revue des Langues Vivantes, 35:415-20, 1969.

"The themes of non-fulfillment, personal isolation, and loneliness are the most prominent and consistent themes in the four earliest plays, and Odets developed them in one way or another throughout the remainder of his career." (A.S.W.)

O 213 Usigli, Rodolfo, "Mis encuentros con Clifford Odets," Hispania, 46:689-92, December, 1963.

Mexico's foremost playwright recalls a stormy scene with Odets in 1939, and uses the occasion to comment on the fate of Odets's work in Mexico and the debilitating effects on an artist's work of the "consuming monsters" of Broadway and Hollywood. (C.O.)

O 214 Willett, Ralph, "Clifford Odets and Popular Culture," South Atlantic Quarterly, 69:68-78, Winter, 1970.

Clifford Odets, the playwright, torn between the ideology of Broadway drama and the popular and financial appeal of Hollywood, tried to represent lower middle class idealism but eventually "succumbed to total despair . . ." as he saw his art deteriorate. (P.M.C.)

AWAKE AND SING!

O 215 Burt, David J., "Odets's Awake and Sing!" Explicator, 27: Item 29, December, 1968.

"Ralph's final words . . . actually contribute structural unity to the play . . . ." (D.P.)

O 216 Haslam, Gerald W., "Odets's Use of Yiddish-English in Awake and Sing!" Research Studies (Washington State University), 34:161-4, September, 1966.

"Odets utilized four major types of lexical or grammatical aberrations in constructing a believable stage Yiddish-English: (1) prepositional differences; (2) sentence order; (3) verb variations; (4) Yiddish loans." (G.C.)

AWAKE AND SING!   (cont'd)

O 217   Kaplan, Charles, "Two Depression Plays and Broadway's Popular
Idealism," American Quarterly, 15:579-85, Winter, 1963.

"There is no evidence that Kaufman and Hart deliberately conceived
of You Can't Take It With You as a reply" to Clifford Odets's Awake
and Sing! but the former play turns the situation of the latter upside
down and "taken together they offer a revealing glimpse into the ways
of the theatre in the Depression era." (W.G.F.)

WAITING FOR LEFTY

O 218   Shuman, R. Baird, "Waiting for Lefty: A Problem in Structure,"
Revue des Langues Vivantes, 28:521-6, November-December, 1962.

Waiting for Lefty might distort "conventional structure development,
but it is developed quite in accordance with the basic elements of
dramatic structure when it is viewed episode by episode." (G.C.)

O'DONOVAN, MICHAEL--See
O'CONNOR, FRANK

O'DOWD, BERNARD PATRICK

O 219   Todd, F. M., "The Poetry of Bernard O'Dowd," Meanjin Quarterly,
pp. 91-7, March, 1955.

O'Dowd's "preconceptions about poetry were wrong and, while he
had the poet's imagination, he lacked above all the poet's sense of
reality. For real things he substituted political abstractions, ab-
stracted emotions, generalisations which his imagination never
made concrete. Yet for all his . . . limitations, O'Dowd's poetry
was part of a self-conscious effort to create an Australian poetic
culture." (D.P.)

O'FAOLÁIN, SEÁN

O 220   Braybrooke, Neville, "Seán O'Faoláin: A Study," Dublin Magazine,
31:22-7, April-June, 1955.

O'Faoláin's dilemma: how to write freely in Ireland when "Catholicism and nationalism are at loggerheads." His solutions: write of
a "demi-paradisal state" before St. Patrick's time when this conflict did not exist, or, defy the religious, for "One cannot attempt a
sinless literature of sinful man." (J.L.B.)

O 221   Braybrooke, Neville, "Seán O'Faoláin: Conjurer of Eden,"
        Renascence, 8:59-63, Winter, 1955.

        Seán O'Faoláin's novels deal with the Irish struggle for national,
        spiritual, and sexual emancipation. In novels such as A Nest of
        Simple Folk, A Purse of Coppers, Teresa and Other Stories, and
        Come Back to Erin, O'Faoláin's simple characters look to an Eden-
        like Ireland of the past, using the symbolism of the garden and often
        finding themselves in Gethsemane instead of Eden. (V.E.)

O 222   Doyle, Paul A., "Chekhov in Erin: Seán O'Faoláin's Career as Short
        Story Writer," Four Quarters, 17:16-21, January, 1968.

        "Like Chekhov, O'Faoláin is a realist who can blend truth with mood
        and poetry so that his portrayal of existence is enhanced by nuances
        and subtleties. . . . Overall, O'Faoláin is more poetic and more
        contemplative than Chekhov but less ironic and a bit less detached.
        Like Chekhov, O'Faoláin is basically an optimist." (D.P.)

O 223   Doyle, P. A., "Seán O'Faoláin and The Bell," Eire-Ireland,
        1:58-62, Fall, 1966.

        "The Bell, perhaps the most literally significant publication printed
        in Ireland since AE's Irish Statesman, first appeared in October,
        1940 under the editorship of Seán O'Faoláin. . . . The Bell regarded
        itself as an arbiter of taste for modern Ireland." "In addition to
        deploring censorship, Gaelicism, and willingness to compromise
        with authoritarianism and mediocrity, O'Faoláin attempted to shake
        Ireland out of its insular viewpoints." All in all, "for his work in
        encouraging and advancing Ireland's literary, social, and political
        accomplishments and awareness," O'Faoláin justly deserves to be
        known as the "first Irish man of letters." (D.P.)

O 224   Doyle, P. A., "Seán O'Faoláin as a Novelist," South Atlantic
        Quarterly, 66:566-73, Autumn, 1967.

        Although each of O'Faoláin's three novels has certain shortcomings
        as an extended fictional narrative, they all include memorable epi-
        sodes and characters and portray with much truth and accuracy
        Ireland's rebellions and struggles for independence. (J.L.A.)

O 225 Kelleher, John V., "Seán O'Faoláin," Atlantic Monthly, 199:67-9, May, 1957.

As the leading Irish writer of today, he has translated his romanticism into "a patriotism, a concern for tradition and the urge to express the unexpressed potentialities" of contemporary Irish life. He moves with sureness because he has worked out and defined the understanding of Ireland to which romanticism first impelled him." (C.P.)

O 226 O'Faoláin, Seán, "Seán O'Faoláin's Dublin," Critic, 24:14-25, April-May, 1966.

[This is a pictorial tour of Dublin on the fiftieth anniversary of the Easter rising, with text by O'Faoláin and photographs by Bard Failte Eireann.] (D.P.)

O 227 Saul, George Brandon, "The Brief Fiction of Seán O'Faoláin," Colby Library Quarterly, Series 7, pp. 69-74, June, 1965.

Seán O'Faoláin is "a gifted writer with moments of moving lyric power, whatever his limitations of theme and attitude." His short stories "seem at best, in their strained effort to project livid character out of the complex of religion, politics and sex O'Faoláin habitually exploits, no better than second-rate." (D.P.)

O 228 Tenenbaum, Louis, "Two Views of the Modern Italian: D. H. Lawrence and Seán O'Faoláin," Italica, 37:118-25, June, 1960.

". . . Lawrence found the sensual emphasis in Italian life exaggerated. His moralistic strain . . . acted as a modifying influence on his paganism, and made him a sometimes affectionate, sometimes irritable critic. In O'Faoláin, admiration for the Italians is so warm that it overwhelms the criticism he occasionally makes, and leads him to a supreme tribute. . . ." (D.P.)

COME BACK TO ERIN

O 229 Doyle, P. A., "Whitman and Seán O'Faoláin," Walt Whitman Review, 16:117-9, December, 1970.

In Come Back to Erin Seán O'Faoláin "has made one of the most appropriate and meaningful uses of Whitman material in twentieth-century fiction." His "use of Whitman's poetry in the novel is extremely effective in conveying and emphasizing scene, atmosphere,

COME BACK TO ERIN   (cont'd)

and historical time, and in developing convincing and appropriate characterization." (D.P.)

THE SILENCE OF THE VALLEY

O 230   Hopkins, Robert H., "The Pastoral Mode of Seán O'Faoláin's 'The Silence of the Valley'," Studies in Short Fiction, 1:93-8, Winter, 1964.

"When read in this pastoral context of tensions between primitivism and progress, love and power, nature and civilization, Seán O'-Faoláin's 'The Silence of the Valley' becomes a truly great example of twentieth-century short fiction." (P.J.R.)

O'FLAHERTY, LIAM

O 231   Doyle, P. A., ed., "A Liam O'Flaherty Checklist," Twentieth Century Literature, 13:49-51, April, 1967.

[Books, booklets, essays, poems, short stories in periodicals by O'Flaherty are listed as well as criticisms of O'Flaherty.] (D.P.)

O 232   Mercier, Vivian, "Man Against Nature: The Novels of Liam O'-Flaherty," Wascana Review, 1:37-46, No. 2, 1966.

O'Flaherty's "most ambitious and greatest novel, Famine, offers the same basic confrontation, man versus nature, as his second novel, The Black Soul, or many of the stories and sketches in Spring Sowing. Yet the thirteen years that lie between the two latter books and Famine were largely devoted to other themes . . . by no means so well suited to O'Flaherty's novelistic gifts." (D.A.B.)

O 233   Murray, Michael H., "Liam O'Flaherty and the Speaking Voice," Studies in Short Fiction, 5:154-62, Winter, 1968.

At his best O'Flaherty is "one of the finest craftsmen of the short narrative." However, "whenever he rejects the straight narrative . . . for the short story of philosophical statement, artless grace gives way to inappropriate imagery, careless structure, and tedious repetition." (D.P.)

O 234 Saul, George Brandon, "A Wild Sowing: The Short Stories of Liam O'Flaherty," Review of English Literature, 4:108-13, July, 1963.

Although the quality of Liam O'Flaherty's short stories is uneven, the best are of "striking quality." ". . . the O'Flaherty who counts is both gripping and panoramic. . . . On the other hand . . . his apparent lyricism is sometimes suggestive of the bogus . . .; and his minute descriptions and psychological meanderings can become very tedious. . . ." (D.P.)

   THE INFORMER

O 235 Doyle, Paul A., "O'Flaherty's Real View of The Informer," Dublin Magazine, 8:67-70, No. 3, 1970.

". . . in the light of his [O'Flaherty's] correspondence with Edward Garnett [his editor] . . . The Informer must be reevaluated and considered not as a potboiler but as an artistic study in characterization, an analysis of evil confronting and conquering a physically gigantic but mentally confused protagonist." (G.C.)

O'GORMAN, NED

O 236 Kelly, Richard, "In Praise of Beauty: Ned O'Gorman," Renascence, 17:171-9, Summer, 1965.

Ned O'Gorman "offers both vigor and a deep sense of mystery to an age of poetry that at one extreme defies the rational and well-wrought poem and at the other the Emotional Self that clinically unfolds itself in metaphoric prose." (S.A.)

O'GRADY, ROHAN

O 237 Troost, Betty Todd, "O'Grady's Classic: O'Houlihan's Jest," Critique: Studies in Modern Fiction, 10:78-84, No. 1, 1967.

Rohan O'Grady's "major themes are the nature of heroes, the loss of innocence, the tension between the dream and the reality, the instinctive attraction of mystery versus reason, O'Houlihan's Jest is a parable of all these. . . ." (D.P.)

O'HARA, FRANK

O 238 Berkson, Bill, "Frank O'Hara and His Poems," Art and Literature, 12:53-63, Spring, 1967.

Frank O'Hara's poems "grew out of a process of natural selection. . . . It is a poetry of nouns and pronouns. . . ." His poetic voice "abounds with personality . . . [but] it does not seem affected or eccentric. . . ." "Breadth, endurance and a vision of oneself alive with living things are the master qualities of his longer poems." (D.P.)

O'HARA, JOHN

O 239 Podhoretz, Norman, "Gibbsville and New Leeds: The America of John O'Hara and Mary McCarthy," Commentary, 21:269-73, March, 1956.

"Sharing O'Hara's angle of vision, one begins to believe that to learn where a man was born, educated and buys his clothes is to know virtually all there is to know about him." McCarthy's A Charmed Life "is a satiric portrait of a community of intellectuals" in which every man's "movement of his spirit is taken account of and used in evidence against him." (D.P.)

O 240 Portz, John, "John O'Hara Up to Now," College English, 16:493-9, 516, May, 1955.

Appointment in Samarra remains O'Hara's finest piece; in the rest of his work O'Hara avoids the serious artist's responsibility to interpret what he sees and reports. (R.W.S.)

O 241 Schanche, Don A., "John O'Hara is Alive and Well in the First Half of the Twentieth Century," Esquire, 72:84-6, 142-9, August, 1969.

For more than thirty years John O'Hara has been painting "his unique portrait of America in the first half of the twentieth century . . . in sparing, brilliantly organized paragraphs all mentally constructed, reconstructed and revised again before they ever touch paper. . . . In most of his stories and books, flawless dialogue marches page after page, carrying with it scene, action, characterization and the agonies or joys of his fictional people. He is never arcane, never prolix. . . ." (D.P.)

O 242 Waterman, Rollene, "Appt. with O'Hara," Saturday Review, 41:15, November 29, 1958.

Since shortly after his father died, when he worked on the local paper in Pottsville, Pennsylvania, John O'Hara wanted to be a writer. After the success of Appointment in Samarra he went to Hollywood as a scriptwriter. "'My writing took an upward turn after A Rage to Live in 1948. . . . I don't rewrite and I don't outline. Newspaper work taught me to get it right the first time'." (D.P.)

O 243 Weaver, Robert, "Twilight Area of Fiction: The Novels of John O'Hara," Queen's Quarterly, 66:320-5, Summer, 1959.

"In his four Pennsylvania novels John O'Hara has written much of the social history of a small corner of America. . . . There is much to be said for novelists who are willing to try to capture the texture of a place and a time, and the novel properly deals with that mundane world that wears away at us day by day." (D.A.B.)

APPOINTMENT IN SAMARRA

O 244 Bier, Jesse, "O'Hara's Appointment in Samarra: His First and Only Real Novel," College English, 25:135-41, November, 1963.

"In his first and only important work O'Hara seemed bent on examining that collaboration between predetermining forces and a virtual principle of weak American character which conspired against adulthood." (R.J.G.)

O 245 Donaldson, Scott, "Appointment with the Dentist: O'Hara's 'Naturalistic Novel'," Modern Fiction Studies, 14:435-42, Winter, 1968-69.

Although critics have been puzzled by Julian English's suicide in O'Hara's Appointment in Samarra, his death "is made inevitable by the kind of world he lives in and its psychological effect upon him." "Julian's tragedy is that he accepts society's judgment as both inevitable and final . . . rejected by others, he rejects his own existence rather than take the slide down the status ladder." (D.P.)

O 246 Hierth, Harrison E., "The Class Novel," CEA Critic, 27:1, 3-4, December, 1964.

Edith Wharton in her The House of Mirth and John O'Hara in his Appointment in Samarra are both "very obviously class conscious. . . . both look at class distinction with a perceptive eye. . . . Both recognize the effects of social stratification on the individual. Both are extremely sensitive to and skillful in delineating the subtler gradations of social status. Each is cognizant of the dangers inherent in violating social convention. In the work of each there is a strong element of determinism." (D.P.)

O'KELLY, SEUMAS

O 247   Saul, George Brandon, "The Verse, Novels and Drama of Seumas
O'Kelly," Eire-Ireland, 2:48-57, Spring, 1967.

Although O'Kelly has been overshadowed by Yeats, Stephens, and
Joyce, his work is worthy of attention. His undistinguished collection
of verse, Rauns and Ballads is notable for its interest in people.
The Lady of Deerpark is the best of his two novels; his two tragedies,
The Shuiler's Child and The Bride demonstrate his significance as a
dramatist. He is "the equal of any English writing dramatist of the
contemporary theater." (D.P.)

THE WEAVER'S GRAVE

O 248   Rose, Marilyn Gaddis, "An Irish Widow of Ephesus: Seumas O'Kelly's
The Weaver's Grave," Eire-Ireland, 2:58-62, Spring, 1967.

The Weaver's Grave is an Irish version of the "consolable widow plot"
which involves a dutiful fourth wife, three old cronies of her dead husband, and two young gravediggers. The novella contrasts the old
men's scornful view of the world with the young men's praise. The
widow rejects the scornful view and accepts life and its optimism from
the young gravedigger who leaps over the open grave to kiss her. (D.P.)

OKIGBO, CHRISTOPHER

O 249   Dathorne, O. R., "African Literature IV: Ritual and Ceremony in
Okigbo's Poetry," Journal of Commonwealth Literature, 5:79-91,1968.

"Okigbo . . . transmutes all experience into ceremony." "All types
of influences can be found in Okigbo's verse" but he is not "a derivative poet, or at best a welder of two traditions of versifying. . . .
part of his success derives from his distinctive, private voice. . . .
His poetry is full of allusions to a private mythological world. . . ."
His "verse shows man in the process of striving towards a god." (D.P.)

O 250   Whitelaw, Marjory, "Interview with Christopher Okigbo, 1965,"
Journal of Commonwealth Literature, 9:28-37, 1970.

[This interview was recorded in Ibadan, two years before Okigbo's
death in the Nigerian civil war. Okigbo regards himself as a poet
rather than as an African poet. Négritude is a special kind of platform poetry; there is no kind of agreement in Nigeria, either French
or English, on writing poetry. Although I am a Christian, I do not

feel uprooted from my own village gods. "I believe that writing poetry is a necessary part of my being alive, which is why I've written nothing else."] (D.P.)

OKUDZHAVA, BULAT

O 251   Krasuxin, Genadij G., "To grusten on, to vesel on. . . ,"
Voprosy literatury, 12:40-55, September, 1968.

Okudzhava is a real poet; people love to hear him, for his poetry is emotional, live, and effective. An emotional poet has a right to use poetic license and to move away occasionally from traditional syntax and grammar. (V.D.)

O 252   Kunjaev, Stanislav, Jr., "Inercija akkompanementa," Voprosy literatury, 12:30-9, September, 1968.

Okudzhava's poetry is "empty"--it lacks ideas. Therefore the poet uses artificial devices to reinforce his heroes. He also sings his own poetry to the accompaniment of a guitar. (V.D.)

OLDENBOURG, ZOË

O 253   Hoffmann, Leon-François, "Notes on Zoë Oldenbourg's Destiny of Fire," Yale French Studies, No. 27, pp. 127-30, Spring-Summer, 1961.

Destiny of Fire is an artistic success because it harmonizes "historical reality" and "human truth." "The Albigensians's destiny was fire precisely because their lives were played out in the Languedoc of the twelfth and thirteenth centuries. But their response to the challenge they faced is as old as man's fate; it will not disappear until Man or the Gods put an end to human existence." (D.P.)

OLESHA, IURIĬ KARLOVICH

O 254   Čudakova, Marietta O., "Poètika Jurija Oleši," Voprosy literatury, 12:120-35, April, 1968.

Olesa's prose, in essence, does not have dialogue. Between a reader and the world in which Oleša's characters function exists a third world--that of appearance [Schein]. The key to Oleša's prose is "zreliscnost." (V.D.)

O 255   Harkins, William E., "The Philosophical Stories of Jurij Oleša,"
<u>Orbis Scriptus</u>, 92:349-54, 1966.

The early stories of Jurij Oleša are concerned with antitheses such
as idealism vs. materialism and vitalism vs. mechanism. Often
the opposition is young vs. old. Oleša's light irony and spontaneity
make him unique among philosophical fiction writers. (V.E.)

O 256   Nilsson, Nils Åke, "Through the Wrong End of Binoculars: An
Introduction to Jurij Oleša," <u>Scando-Slavica</u>, 11:40-68, 1965.

"In his view on art and life Oleša is . . . connected with some well-
known Russian masters of 'fantastic photography' but he also stands
out as an interesting representative for a general trend in Western
literature." (A.S.W.)

O 257   Pertsov, V. O., "K sozidatelyam novogo mira," <u>Voprosy literatury</u>,
13:75-89, November, 1969.

Olesha's literary characters served as a vehicle for his own
<u>Weltanschauung</u>. Despite a sharp conflict in the "new world,"
Olesha's heroes talk and do not act. (V.D.)

O 258   Pertsov, Victor, "Selected Work of Yuri Olesha," <u>Soviet Literature</u>,
November, 1956.

Author of a novel, <u>Envy</u>, a book for children, <u>Three Fat Men</u>, and a
series of short stories, Yuri Olesha "seeks to reveal and affirm the
material nature of the world, to convey in tangible form the primary
nature of being in relation to the mind." (B.B.)

THE CONSPIRACY OF FEELINGS--See
ZAGOVOR CHUVSTV

ENVY--See
ZAVIST'

ZAGOVOR CHUVSTV

O 259   Dukore, Bernard F., and Daniel C. Gerould, "Socialist Salami and
Soviet Avant-Garde: Olyesha's <u>The Conspiracy of Feelings</u>,"
<u>Drama and Theatre</u>, 7:17-9, 1968.

"In the plays by Teller and Brecht, there is hope and longing for the
revolutionary world still to be born. In Olyesha's play . . . there

ZAGOVOR CHUVSTV (cont'd)

is a futile yearning for the old bourgeois world and an absurd dream
of re-establishing the heroic emotions and gestures of the past."
(G.C.)

ZAVIST'

O 260 Harkins, William E., "The Theme of Sterility in Olesha's Envy,"
Slavic Review, 25:443-57, September, 1966.

"Envy is dominated by the theme of castration and sterility, a sterility extending to all areas of life, including those of career and creativity." (D.P.)

O 261 Piper, D. G. B., "Yuriy Olesha's Zavist': An Interpretation,"
Slavonic and East European Review, 48:27-43, January, 1970.

Olesha's Zavist' "is a personal testament, whose theme . . . is
essentially the clash between the artist and society." (D.P.)

OLMO, LAURO

O 262 Rodriguez Puértolas, J., "Tres aspectos de una misma realidad en
el teatro español contemporáneo: Buero, Sastre, Olmo,"
Hispanófila, 31:43-58, September, 1967.

The theater of these writers represents three serious approaches to
the concrete reality of today's Spain. Each tries to outline a contemporary problem and to oblige the audience to become involved. Each
shows, consciously, Brecht's concern for truth, and each rejects a
non-involved or "artistic" theater. (C.O.)

OLSEN, TILLIE

O 263 O'Connor, William Van, "The Short Stories of Tillie Olsen,"
Studies in Short Fiction, 1:21-5, Fall, 1963.

"When Miss Olsen is at her best, as in 'Tell Me a Riddle,' she is a
writer of tremendous skill and power. Her productivity has been
small, but she would not have to write a great deal more than she
has to earn a place among the eminent writers of short stories."
[The article also includes brief discussions of "Hey, Sailor, What
Ship," "O Yes," and "I Stand Here Ironing."] (D.A.B.)

OLSON, CHARLES

O 264   Butterick, George, "A Charles Olson Checklist," West Coast Review, 2:25-31, Spring, 1967.

[This list attempts "not only to catalogue critical reaction of all kinds to Olson, but also to reveal his relation to his contemporaries, some biographical information, his successes as a Melville scholar, and finally, at least some indication of recognition abroad."] (D.P.)

O 265   Malanga, Gerard, "The Art of Poetry: XII," Paris Review, No. 49, pp. 177-204, Summer, 1970.

[In this interview Olson answers--and doesn't answer--questions about why he chose to be a poet, the influence of Ezra Pound on his writing, which poets he (Olson) influenced, how he writes his poems, his views of schools of poetry and his impressions of the United States.] (D.P.)

THE KINGFISHERS

O 266   Combs, Maxine, "Charles Olson's 'The Kingfishers': A Considera- tion of Meaning and Method," Far Point, 4:66-76, 1970.

Unlike Eliot, Olson maintains that "Christianity is inadequate to cope with a changing world . . . and he places the responsibility for the situation on the refusal of the West to find . . . a course of action which genuinely deals with the actualities as they exist." (G.C.)

OLSON, ELDER

O 267   Gray, J. M., "Aristotle's Poetics and Elder Olson," Comparative Literature, 15:164-75, Spring, 1963.

When Olson fails as a critic his failure can be "attributed to his mis- understanding of Aristotle's significance as a philosopher and partic- ularly as an aesthetician." (C.E.N.)

OLSSON, HAGAR

O 268   Stormbom, N.-B., "Inward Journey: The Works of Hagar Olsson," American-Scandinavian Review, 52:261-6, 1964.

"Hagar Olsson has always sought the strong and secret currents in the depths of the human soul. . . . Man is exhorted never to stop, but always seek and be on the way. The direction is inward, and through inner self to the universal." (K.M.W.)

O'NEILL, EUGENE

O 269 Alexander, Doris M., "Eugene O'Neill and Light on the Path," Modern Drama, 3:260-7, December, 1960.

The catalyst that set off O'Neill's alignment with the mystics and individualists was a book by Terry Carlin entitled Light on the Path. (C.K.L.)

O 270 Alexander, Doris M., "Eugene O'Neill as Social Critic," American Quarterly, 6:349-63, Winter, 1954.

"The main trend in O'Neill's social criticism is negative. He condemns the capitalist state, but sees no hope for man in any other kind of state. Whatever hope he sees for man lies in individuals who may have the courage to possess their own souls." (H.S.)

O 271 Alexander, Doris M., "Eugene O'Neill, 'The Hound of Heaven,' and the 'Hell Hole'," Modern Language Quarterly, 20:307-14, December, 1959.

Servitude, Welded and Days Without End all "dramatize the 'Hound of Heaven' theme: that is, flight from love and acceptance with an ultimate surrender into love and faith"; this parallelism shows that Days Without End is non-Catholic and directly in O'Neill's line of development. (G.S.)

O 272 Andreach, Robert J., "O'Neill's Use of Dante in The Fountain and The Hairy Ape," Modern Drama, 10:48-56, May, 1967.

The influence of the Commedia on The Fountain is explicit; parallels with The Hairy Ape are present although more obscurely. (D.P.)

O 273 Björk, Lennart A., "The Swedish Critical Reception of O'Neill's Posthumous Plays," Scandinavian Studies, 38:231-50, August, 1966.

Repeatedly, "the Swedish critics expressed their admiration for the deepened knowledge of human character which O'Neill evidenced in these late plays; they were impressed by his insight into and compassion for, human weaknesses; his hope for, and assertion of, human endurance." (G.C.)

O 274   Bowling, Charis Crosse, "The Touch of Poetry: A Study of the Role
of Poetry in Three O'Neill Plays," CLA Journal, 12:43-55,
September, 1968.

"When O'Neill wishes to be poetic, he becomes so through the use of
the situations, the prose dialogue. . . . And when O'Neill does use
the actual words or verse of other writers, he does so because the
verse is a natural and necessary part of the scene . . . and, more
important, because his characters feel that they need the words of
someone else to help them in the particular situation in which they
find themselves." (K.M.W.)

O 275   Brashear, William R., "O'Neill and Shaw: The Play as Will and
Idea," Criticism, 8:155-69, Spring, 1969.

"O'Neill's was essentially the voice of the 'will' . . .; Shaw's was
the voice of the intellect." Although both read Schopenhauer and
Nietzsche, "ironically what Shaw . . . did not grasp was the 'vital'
principle itself," thus remaining superficial, intellectual, and
comic. O'Neill, portraying wills in conflict with this world force,
achieved tragic profundity. (J.L.A.)

O 276   Bryer, Jackson R., "Forty Years of O'Neill Criticism: A Selected
Bibliography," Modern Drama, 4:196-216, September, 1961.

[This is "a selected compilation which seeks to present the most
significant articles, books, and book sections written about O'Neill
between 1920 and 1960. . . . Foreign language criticism has not
been included. . . . In addition, most reviews of O'Neill plays have
not been included."] (D.P.)

O 277   Busch, C. Trent and Orton A. Jones, "Immortality Enough: The
Influence of Strindberg on the Expressionism of Eugene O'Neill,"
Southern Speech Journal, 33:129-39, Winter, 1967.

The influence of Strindberg on O'Neill is confirmed not only through
O'Neill's tributes to the older playwright, but also from his use of
expressionistic devices and similarities in style. The influence is
most apparent in The Emperor Jones, The Hairy Ape and The Great
God Brown. (D.P.)

O 278   Chaitin, Norman C., "O'Neill: The Power of Daring," Modern Drama, 3:231-41, December, 1960.

"O'Neill's trajectory presents the only accomplished life of any playwright in our country. The most American of our playwrights, and the most universal . . . his [personal] drama had a beginning, a middle and an end." He did not sell the American dream for nothing; he made it pay.   (C.K.L.)

O 279   Chen, David Y., "Two Chinese Adaptations of Eugene O'Neill's The Emperor Jones," Modern Drama, 9:431-9, February, 1967.

O'Neill was principally responsible for bringing expressionism to modern Chinese drama. His direct influence may be seen in Hung Shen's The Yama Chao, which is essentially a Chinese recension of The Emperor Jones. Also, Ts'ao Yü's The Wild owes many expressionistic devices to The Emperor Jones.   (D.P.)

O 280   Chiaromonte, Nicola, "Eugene O'Neill (1958)," Sewanee Review, 68:494-501, Summer, 1960.

"O'Neill . . . bears the brunt of the whole of reality, without understanding it." But "it is the moralist . . . in him which refuses to turn to the intellect"; hence his plays "reach in the end the essential effect of drama: they lead us to reflect on the reason for the action." (A.A.S.)

O 281   Churchill, Allen, "Portrait of a Nobel Prize Winner as a Bum," Esquire, 47:98-101, June, 1957.

Eugene O'Neill lived as a bum on the Buenos Aires waterfront, an experience from which came the "first inspiration for his plays and much of the dark brooding comprehension of human nature that made all his plays great." From the men and women he met during these days came his understanding of human character and how little of himself a man shows to the world.   (V.E.)

O 282   Cole, Lester, and John Howard Lawson, "Two Views on O'Neill," Masses and Mainstream, 7:56-63, June, 1954.

[This is comment by Lester Cole on the article "The Tragedy of Eugene O'Neill" by John Howard Lawson. Taking exception to Lawson's statements that O'Neill was incorruptible, Cole asserts that because O'Neill's work did not reflect "current bourgeois fashions" it declined in popularity in the 1930's. Lawson refutes these claims and states that O'Neill's complex class struggle must be considered by Marxist criticism to place him "correctly in relation to the history of his time."] (V.E.)

O 283 Dahl, Lisa, "The Attributive Sentence Structure in the Stream-of-Consciousness-Technique, with Special Reference to the Interior Monologue Used by Virginia Woolf, James Joyce and Eugene O'Neill," Neuphilologische Mitteilungen, 68:440-54, 1967.

The attributive sentence structure, which uses loose modifiers, is a definite syntactical device to demonstrate the process of thought. Woolf, Joyce, even O'Neill in Strange Interlude employ the device, although each uses it differently. (D.P.)

O 284 Dahlström, Carl E. W. L., "Dynamo and Lazarus Laughed: Some Limitations," Modern Drama, 3:224-30, December, 1960.

". . . while our greatest American dramatist was successful in exploiting some matters of psychological import, he was unable to give artistic treatment to the ferment in religion, science, and existence. Lazarus Laughed and Dynamo are both witnesses to endeavors that failed." (C.K.L.)

O 285 Daiches, David, "Mourning Becomes O'Neill," Encounter, 16:74-8, June, 1961.

[This is a discussion of the personal experiences which influenced O'Neill's art.] (H.S.)

O 286 Davenport, William H., "The Published and Unpublished Poems of Eugene O'Neill," Claremont Quarterly, 11:11-20, 37-44, No. 1, 1963.

". . . in these poems . . . there appear to be keys to a more complex personality than even the popular notion affords--of a man . . . who could like a Titan one moment battle with the gods and in the next grovel and grope perplexedly in the darkness, striving for personal identity and universal meaning." (G.C.)

O 287 Doyle, Rev. Louis F., S. J., "The Myth of Eugene O'Neill," Renascence, 17:59-62, 81, Winter, 1964.

O'Neill's achievement is vastly overrated. It is "very difficult to escape the conclusion that greatness was thrust on the man by those who had a vested interest in the commercial possibilities of the son of Monte Cristo: the producers, including the Theatre Guild, the publishers, Hollywood, and other such entrepreneurs." (S.A.)

O 288 Driver, Tom F., "On the Late Plays of Eugene O'Neill," Tulane Drama Review, 3:8-20, December, 1958.

The continued dominance of O'Neill over the serious American theatre derives from his relevance to "vibrant concerns of the [American] audience," through his preoccupation with death in his late plays. (D.P.)

O 289 Engel, Edwin A., "Ideas in the Plays of Eugene O'Neill," Selected Papers from the English Institute, 22:101-24, 1964.

"Throughout most of his career O'Neill . . . preferred to treat ideas that are universal and abstract: Man, Life, Death, Love, Hate. The relation between man and man did not interest him at all. . . ." (D.P.)

O 290 Engel, Edwin A., "O'Neill, 1960," Modern Drama, 3:219-23, December, 1960.

O'Neill's last plays, "composed around 1940, have crowned the distinguished earlier career, not only culminating but surpassing (in depth, power, truth) the pieces which earned him his original reputation." (C.K.L.)

O 291 Fagin, N. Bryllion, "Eugene O'Neill," Antioch Review, 14:14-26, March, 1954.

"In the thirty-odd plays . . . [O'Neill] has left us, mere sobriety at times substitutes for tragic eloquence. Yet the high seriousness with which he approached his themes, his characters, and the art of playwriting has been of incalculable benefit to the American drama." (H.S.)

O 292 Falb, Lewis W., "The Critical Reception of Eugene O'Neill on the French Stage," Educational Theatre Journal, 22:397-405, December, 1970.

O'Neill "was instantly recognized [in France] as a dramatist of talent and importance, but he never achieved popular success." French re- viewers most welcomed his qualities of "originality, strength, and vigour, occasionally even [his] social and philosophical interests. . . ." He has been most condemned for his naturalism, his primi- tivism, and for being melodramatic. (D.P.)

O 293   Falk, Doris V., "That Paradox, O'Neill," Modern Drama,
        6:221-38, December, 1963.

        O'Neill's "best plays are those in which the vision is single and the
        action is unified. The comedy in the play . . . is clearly and hon-
        estly there--not just grinning behind the mask of tragedy--and there
        is no mechanical division between the two. They are inextricably
        combined to provide a real paradox, not merely a contradiction and
        canceling out." (D.P.)

O 294   Falk, Signi, "Dialogue in the Plays of Eugene O'Neill," Modern
        Drama, 3:314-25, December, 1960.

        "It is obvious that when O'Neill worked from experience and observa-
        tion, when he let the characters speak for themselves, and out of
        themselves, he wrote some of his best dialogue. When he worked on
        a grander scale, his handling of the spoken word was pretentious and
        overdone." (D.A.B.)

O 295   Fitzgerald, John J., "The Bitter Harvest of O'Neill's Projected
        Cycle," New England Quarterly, 40:364-74, September, 1967.

        "The truncated and dismembered corpus of his projected nine-play
        cycle on the material of aggrandizement of a nineteenth-century
        American family [A Tale of Possessors Self-Dispossessed] is a
        melancholy testimonial both to the inevitable mathematics of
        mortality and to the perfectionist tendency of O'Neill. . . ." (H.S.)

O 296   Fleisher, Frederic, "Eugene O'Neill and 1912," Moderna Språk,
        53:232-40, No. 3, 1959.

        During his stay at a sanatorium in 1912 O'Neill first began to find
        himself as a playwright. A Moon for the Misbegotten, The Iceman
        Cometh, and Long Day's Journey Into Night--all staged in this year
        --share autobiographical elements and the theme of the necessity to
        withdraw from reality. (D.P.)

O 297   Fleisher, Frederic, "Strindberg and O'Neill," Symposium,
        10:84-94, Spring, 1956.

        Strindberg's influence on O'Neill, overemphasized in O'Neill's
        Nobel Prize acceptance speech in 1936, was strongest during 1918-
        1923. It is seen in cyclical structure (The Road to Damascus and
        The Emperor Jones) and in the destruction of a man by a "super-
        woman" (Married and Beyond the Horizon). (J.L.B.)

O 298   Freedman, Morris, "O'Neill and Contemporary American Drama," College English, 23:570-4, April, 1962.

"Much of American drama lies in his shadow, but we pretend he is not there. . . . The failure of modern American drama may be found in its uncomfortable relation to [the intensely serious] O'Neill." (R.J.G.)

O 299   Frenz, Horst and Frederic Fleisher, "Eugene O'Neill and the Royal Dramatic Theater of Stockholm: The Later Phase," Modern Drama, 10:300-11, December, 1967.

Since 1923 O'Neill has had an unusual prominence in Swedish theater, a prominence that contributed to his being awarded the Nobel prize. (D.P.)

O 300   Frenz, Horst, "Notes on Eugene O'Neill in Japan," Modern Drama, 3:306-13, December, 1960.

". . . the Japanese critics were greatly interested in Eugene O'Neill not merely as a dramatist but also as a man. . . . In O'Neill the critics discovered a man consciously articulating his views of life and death, a man of mystic quality whose preoccupation was with the nature of 'behind life.' They favored such plays as The Hairy Ape and The Iceman Cometh, for they saw in them the expression of the playwright's disillusionment with modern civilization and his opposition to America and western materialism." (D.P.)

O 301   Gelb, Arthur and Barbara Gelb, "The Catholicism of Eugene O'Neill," Critic, 23:18-23, April-May, 1965.

Eugene O'Neill formally renounced his faith as a youth after a rigid Catholic upbringing, and never returned to the church. Although, "on his deathbed . . . [he] had resigned himself to damnation, he left a body of work illuminated, ironically, by the religion he had renounced." (D.P.)

O 302   Gelb, Arthur and Barbara Gelb, "Start of a Long Day's Journey: The New London Youth of Eugene O'Neill," Horizon, 2:25-40, March, 1960.

The summers spent in New London made an "indelible impression" on O'Neill and gave him settings for at least three plays and parts of more. (J.P.H.)

O 303   Goldman, Arnold, "The Vanity of Personality: The Development of Eugene O'Neill," Stratford-upon-Avon Studies, 10:29-51, 1967.

"The underlying movement of an O'Neill drama . . . is a fluctuation and oscillation, a flow and ebb forever turning back upon itself." "O'Neill came to found the very being of his people on ambivalences and polarities. . . . [he] appears not to have needed to work with heroes, or characters who would win through to . . . audience shared satisfaction." (D.P.)

O 304   Granger, Bruce Ingham, "Illusion and Reality in Eugene O'Neill," Modern Language Notes, 73:179-86, March, 1958.

"Here then, O'Neill would have us believe, is the dilemma confronting modern man: illusion brings order out of the chaos of the present but incapacitates him for meaningful action, and yet without illusion life is intolerable for all but the sturdy few like Lavinia Mannon and Larry Slade." (M.J.O.)

O 305   Griffin, Ernest G., "Pity, Alienation and Reconciliation in Eugene O'Neill," Mosaic, 2:66-76, Fall, 1968.

O'Neill was uncertain about the meaning of pity: "Was it an essential motivating force in human community . . . or did it alienate man from his true being, reducing him from hero to victim?" (G.C.)

O 306   Groff, Edward, "Point of View in Modern Drama," Modern Drama, 2:268-82, December, 1959.

The dramatic techniques or methods of such modern dramatists as Pirandello, O'Neill, Arthur Miller, Strindberg, Brecht, and Wilder "have a common aim: to make the playform more subjective by associating the dramatic events with the consciousness of individual characters who may participate in the action or merely narrate the story presented on the stage." (D.P.)

O 307   Halfmann, Ulrich, "Ironie und Symbolik in den Dramentiteln O'Neills," Die Neueren Sprachen, 18:322-35, July, 1969.

The titles of O'Neill's plays are very consciously and densely structured abbreviations of their contents. (J.R.R.)

O 308 Hamilton, Gladys, "Untold Tales of Eugene O'Neill," Theatre Arts, 40:31-2, 88, August, 1956.

[These are the recollections of Mrs. Clayton Hamilton of the long association between the Hamiltons and O'Neill, beginning in 1914. Mr. Hamilton was instrumental in persuading the elder O'Neill to pay the tuition for Eugene to study playwriting with George Baker at Harvard, and was helpful and supportive to Eugene O'Neill through-out his career. Excerpts from several letters from O'Neill to the Hamiltons are printed here.] (D.P.)

O 309 Hanzeli, Victor E., "The Progeny of Atreus," Modern Drama, 3:75-81, May, 1960.

The notion that one finds no possible remedy to fate in the actions of free men has been dramatically demonstrated by Eugene O'Neill and Jean-Paul Sartre. (C.K.L.)

O 310 Hartman, Murray, "Strindberg and O'Neill," Educational Theatre Journal, 18:216-23, October, 1966.

From his recognition of Strindberg in 1913, "O'Neill consciously adapted Strindberg's form and subject matter to native materials." Both authors shared "intellectual backgrounds, which included the pessimist Schopenhauer; Nietzsche, the alienated pagan 'superman'; Ibsen, the social realist; and Maeterlinck, the mystic poet." But Strindberg's influence can be also credited to O'Neill's recognition of him as a kindred spirit. Both authors explored "new techniques for presenting their insights into psychological and emotional states. . . . both authors ran the gamut of [expressionistic], romantic, naturalistic, and historical plays. . . . Their legacy may be the basic endowment of modern drama." (D.P.)

O 311 Hastings, Warren H., and Richard F. Weeks, "Episodes of Eugene O'Neill's Undergraduate Days at Princeton," Princeton University Library Chronicle, 29:208-15, Winter, 1968.

[These are reminiscences of O'Neill by two classmates and friends during their Freshman year, O'Neill's single year as a Princeton undergraduate.] (K.M.W.)

O 312   Herbert, Edward T., "Eugene O'Neill: An Evaluation by Fellow
        Playwrights," Modern Drama, 6:239-40, December, 1963.

        [These are brief evaluative comments on O'Neill by Paul Green,
        Thornton Wilder, Sean O'Casey, Arthur Miller, and Clifford Odets.]
        (D.P.)

O 313   Highsmith, James M., "O'Neill's Idea of Theater," South Atlantic
        Bulletin, 33:18-21, November, 1968.

        Eugene O'Neill never formulated theories of drama verbally because
        of his constantly changing and developing ideas. Nevertheless his
        basic idea of drama can be discerned from letters, articles, and
        interviews and can be seen to be that "drama is to approximate life,"
        but also "to transform life into art" through the medium of the
        theater and that the "presentation itself is to acquire ritualistic
        value." (V.E.)

O 314   Hoffmann, Gerhard, "Lachen und Weinen als Gestaltungsmittel der
        dramatischen Grenzsituation: Zum Verhältnis von direkten und
        indirekten Ausdrucksformen im Drama O'Neills," Jahrbuch für
        Amerikastudien, 15:101-22, 1970.

        Laughter and weeping carry a structural function in O'Neill's plays.
        As leitmotifs and symbols they support the pace of the plays and
        enhance emotional crises. They may also elucidate subconscious
        feelings and motives of characters in the plays. (D.P.)

O 315   Hofmannsthal, Hugo von, "Eugene O'Neill," Tulane Drama Review,
        5:169-73, September, 1960.

        Eugene O'Neill is "the foremost living American playwright. . . .
        his work is throughout essentially of the theatre. Each play is clear-
        cut and sharp in outline, solidly constructed from beginning to end.
        . . . The essential dramatic plot . . . is invariably linked to and
        revealed by that visual element which the . . . modern theatre de-
        mands. The dialogue is powerful, often direct, and frequently
        endowed with a brutal though picturesque lyricism." (D.P.)

O 316   Holtan, Orley I., "Eugene O'Neill and the Death of the 'Covenant',"
        Quarterly Journal of Speech, 56:256-63, October, 1970.

        In A Touch of the Poet and More Stately Mansions, the two remain-
        ing plays of the proposed eleven play cycle, A Tale of Possessors
        Self-Dispossessed, O'Neill discusses "the contradictions of American

experience . . . equality, and simplicity as opposed to the reality of
urban corruption, greed and complexity. . . ." (H.S.)

O 317   Keane, Christopher, "Blake and O'Neill: A Prophecy," <u>Blake</u>
<u>Studies</u>, 2:23-34, Spring, 1970.

Blake's <u>Tyger</u>, prophesied what O'Neill's <u>Hairy Ape</u> confirms--the
destruction of man's creativity and inspiration by the industrial
society. (D.P.)

O 318   Klavsons, Janis, "O'Neill's Dreamer: Success and Failure,"
<u>Modern Drama</u>, 3:268-72, December, 1960.

"Hurt by the practical failure of the optimistic philosophers, hurt by
increasing American materialism, O'Neill withdrew the dreamer
from the preacher's post and turned him into a pathetic and frequently
timid character." (C.K.L.)

O 319   Krutch, Joseph Wood, "O'Neill the Inevitable," <u>Theatre Arts</u>,
38:66-9, February, 1954.

"It was O'Neill who wrote and who successfully demanded recognition
for the American playwright's declaration of independence and charter
of liberty." (H.S.)

O 320   Langford, Richard E., "Eugene O'Neill: The Mask of Illusion,"
<u>Stetson Studies in the Humanities</u>, No. 1, pp. 65-75, 1963.

O'Neill's major "plays are not the morose, pessimistic view of life
that both his admirers and detractors say they are: they are "positive, noble expressions of one man's understanding of the human
dilemma." (G.O.)

O 321   Lee, Robert C., "Eugene O'Neill's Approach to Play Writing,"
<u>Drama Critique</u>, 11:2-8, Winter, 1968.

O'Neill wrote plays to escape his inner conflicts, structuring a
world where his emotional needs could dominate. He revised little
until the failure of <u>Dynamo</u>, which was caused by his ordeal of
divorce. He preferred to let his emotions take charge, limiting
planning to the writing of scenarios. (D.P.)

O 322   Lee, Robert C., "Eugene O'Neill's Remembrance: The Past Is the Present," Arizona Quarterly, 23:293-305, Winter, 1967.

O'Neill's last plays--The Iceman Cometh, Long Day's Journey Into Night, and A Moon for the Misbegotten--are among his greatest dramatic achievements, but they are also "psychoneurotic explosions that he trapped himself into reliving endlessly." (J.C.)

O 323   Lee, Robert C., "The Lonely Dream," Modern Drama, 9:127-35, September, 1966.

"Alienation sums up the O'Neill artist. Like O'Neill himself, the artist character pines for a plateau of peace. He wants to belong to life in some tangible, permanent way. Since he does not find this unattainable security, he flails away in all directions. His ultimate dream . . . is of death itself." (D.P.)

O 324   Leech, Clifford, "Eugene O'Neill and His Plays," Critical Quarterly, 3:242-56; 339-53, Autumn, Winter, 1961.

[Part I is a brief discussion of O'Neill's life and an examination of his early drama. Part II identifies The Iceman Cometh and Long Day's Journey Into Night as "concerned with what Aristotle called 'anagnorisis' or 'discovery,' with the idea of a Second Coming, and with . . . despair, the impulse to suicide."] (H.S.)

O 325   LoCicero, Vincent, "Schnitzler, O'Neill, and Reality," Journal of the International Arthur Schnitzler Research Association, 4:4-26, No. 3, 1965.

The veils and masks which preoccupy both O'Neill and Schnitzler involve failure to recognize or accept what another person really is, preference for the persona-mask rather than the real person, and the delusion that all aspects of reality or of a person can be intellectually grasped and possessed. (A.S.W.)

O 326   McCarthy, Mary, "Americans, Realists, Playwrights," Encounter, 17:24-31, July, 1961.

The realists of the American theater are Arthur Miller, Tennessee Williams, William Inge, Paddy Chayevsky, the Elmer Rice of Street Scene and Eugene O'Neill. "Unlike the other playwrights, who make a journalistic claim to neutral recording, Arthur Miller admittedly has a message." (G.C.)

O 327 McDonnell, Thomas P., "O'Neill's Drama of the Psyche,"
Catholic World, 197:120-5, May, 1963.

"The key to the secret of O'Neill's power lies in the fact that his
work was autobiographical. In the dissolution of values all around
us, he dramatized the plight of the spiritually dispossessed, an
autobiographical and intensely agonizing search for a self he could
not find." (R. J. G.)

O 328 Machts, Walter, "Das Menschenbild in den Dramen Tennessee
Williams," Die Neueren Sprachen, 10:445-55, October, 1961.

Williams's characters turn away from God and find their salvation
in unconscious, vitalist forces, which can satisfy their individual
needs. This picture is more hopeful than that offered by O'Neill,
who, like Williams, can only accept the realm of the worldly.
(U. C. K.)

O 329 Miller, Jordan Y., "The Georgia Plays of Eugene O'Neill,"
Georgia Review, 12:278-90, Fall, 1958.

The religious conventionality of Days Without End and the domestic
sentimentality of Ah, Wilderness!, the plays written during O'Neill's
four years in Georgia, and even his isolated home at Sea Island were
all part of the author's retreat from reality and surrender to the
"romantic" element in his nature. (W. G. F.)

O 330 Nethercot, Arthur H., "The Psychoanalyzing of Eugene O'Neill,"
Modern Drama, 3:242-56, December, 1960.

"To what extent was Eugene O'Neill to be regarded as a student and
practitioner of the 'new psychology,' as it was denominated?" is
a complex problem of O'Neill criticism. (C. K. L.)

O 331 Nethercot, Arthur H., "The Psychoanalyzing of Eugene O'Neill,"
Modern Drama, 3:357-72, February, 1961.

"It is very unlikely that this evolution in O'Neill's plays [from an
active outer world to an inner world where nothing is important]
can be attributed alone to the increasingly psychoanalytic approach
in them. But no matter what people thought of the influence of
psychoanalysis on O'Neill as a playwright, most of them would have
agreed that . . . he would have made an excellent psychoanalyst
himself." (D. P.)

O 332   Nethercot, Arthur H., "The Psychoanalyzing of Eugene O'Neill: Postscript," Modern Drama, 8:150-5, September, 1965.

[This is a postscript to Nethercot's article "The Psychoanalyzing of Eugene O'Neill," Modern Drama (December 1960 and February 1961).] "This then, is a Pyrrhonic postscript designed to prove out of O'Neill's own mouth that his knowledge of [psychoanalysis] was both earlier in its beginnings and more pervasive in its effects than he wanted the world to believe." (D.A.B.)

O 333   O'Neill, Eugene and Oliver M. Sayler, "The Artist of the Theater: A Colloquy," Theatre Arts, 41:23-4, 86, June, 1957.

[This is the reconstruction of a colloquy which took place between the critic Oliver M. Sayler and Eugene O'Neill at the Peaked Hill Bar in Provincetown, Massachusetts in Midsummer, 1921. The colloquy ranges over the philosophic base of drama, demands of the new theatre, and forecasts the theatre of the future.] (D.P.)

O 334   O'Neill, Joseph P., S. J., "The Tragic Theory of Eugene O'Neill," Texas Studies in Literature and Language, 4:481-98, Winter, 1963.

". . . in re-creating the Greek concept of fate in terms of modern psychology, O'Neill is not presenting a drama of pure determinism. His insight into human nature, dim though it be, is sufficient to indicate that regardless of how influential the forces of the universe are, they are not coercive; that man is ultimately responsible for his own destiny." (W.G.F.)

O 335   Pallette, Drew B., "O'Neill and the Comic Spirit," Modern Drama, 3:273-9, December, 1960.

O'Neill's last plays, produced since the Second World War, have shown "a good deal of rowdy comedy, involving tricks, invective, and a militantly disrespectful mocking of the pretentious." In these plays, "the comic and the humorous play an organic part." (C.K.L.)

O 336   Pallette, Drew B., "O'Neill's A Touch of the Poet, and His Other Last Plays," Arizona Quarterly, 13:308-19, Winter, 1957.

". . . in order to appreciate A Touch of the Poet one must see it in the context of the rest of O'Neill's later produced work. In these terms it unexpectedly expands the ideas that tie these plays together, and gives new complexity to the picture they provide of the dramatist's final views." (A.A.S.)

O 337 Parks, Edd Winfield, "Eugene O'Neill's Quest," <u>Tulane Drama</u> <u>Review</u>, 4:99-107, Spring, 1960.

". . . O'Neill's quest for a valid faith has shifted from the philosophical to the personal. . . . As his faith in the abstract idea or
the philosophic or theological doctrine waned, he substituted for it
the warmth of human love [which] . . . gives a mellow underlying
richness to the otherwise dark autobiographical plays." (D.P.)

O 338 Pettegrove, James P., "Eugene O'Neill as Thinker," <u>Maske und</u> <u>Kothurn</u>, 10:617-24, 1964.

"O'Neill teaches the unity of body and soul, the identity and divinity
of Eros and Agape. . . . A religion combining the mysteries of life
and love with rites designed to free the spirit from its burden of
guilt and fear is either asserted or clearly implied in eight or more
of O'Neill's plays." (G.C.)

O 339 Pommer, Henry F., "The Mysticism of Eugene O'Neill," <u>Modern</u> <u>Drama</u>, 9:26-39, May, 1966.

"O'Neill's type of mysticism was suprarational rather than irrational.
Never anti-intellectual, its role was not to contradict or ignore empirical evidence, but to supplement what man had learned through
other forms of knowing." "The intellectual core of O'Neill's mysti-
cism--the interrelatedness of all processes and the inevitability of
all events--was consistent with and probably reinforced by the determinism he frequently expressed." (D.P.)

O 340 Quinn, Arthur H., "A Letter from Eugene O'Neill," <u>Arizona</u> <u>Quarterly</u>, 13:293-4, Winter, 1957.

[In this letter O'Neill is perplexed by critics who call him a "sordid
realist," a "grim pessimistic naturalist," and a "lying Moral
Romanticist." "I'm always acutely conscious of the Force behind
. . . and of the eternal tragedy of Man . . . to make the Force
express him. . . . And my profound conviction is that this is the
only subject worth writing about. . . ."] (D.P.)

O 341 Raleigh, John Henry, "Eugene O'Neill," <u>English Journal</u>,
56:367-77, 475, March, 1967.

Eugene O'Neill "is <u>the</u> major American playwright, not only intrinsi-
cally, that is, because <u>The Iceman Cometh</u> and <u>Long Day's Journey</u>
<u>Into Night</u> are the most powerful plays written on this continent, but

also extrinsically, because he is the major historical force in the development of serious American drama." (D.P.)

O 342 Raleigh, John Henry, "Eugene O'Neill," Ramparts, 2:72-87, Spring, 1964.

"The most potent writer of the American twentieth century as well as its most fascinating literary personality and imagination, he belongs in the dark tradition of Poe and Melville, but has an affinity to modern American novelists and a lasting place in world literature." O'Neill's suffering emphasizes that "literary genius is precisely this capacity for remaining in a perpetual maelstrom of powerful and con- flicting emotions." (E.F.S.)

O 343 Reardon, William R., "O'Neill Since World War II: Critical Reception in New York," Modern Drama, 10:289-99, December, 1967.

". . . the reputation of O'Neill was solidified in the period since World War II. A dozen of his major dramas have been presented, including those of his mature period as well as outstanding efforts from the 1920's." (D.P.)

O 344 Riegel, Kurt, "Zum Thoreau-Echo im Spätwerk O'Neills," Germanisch-Romanische Monatsschrift, 18:191-9, April, 1968.

"Investigation shows that O'Neill to a certain extent depersonalizes and objectifies material borrowed from Thoreau when adapting it into the complex of A Touch of the Poet and More Stately Mansions. (J.R.R.)

O 345 Roy, Emil, "The Archetypal Unity of Eugene O'Neill's Drama," Comparative Drama, 3:263-74, Winter, 1969-70.

"Although many of [O'Neill's] plays are based directly or obliquely on classical or Biblical myth, he is at his most effective, it seems, when he creates or parallels not myth but an individual fantasy expressing a symbolic action, equivalent and related to the myth's expression of a public rite." (D.P.)

O 346 Roy, Emil, "Eugene O'Neill's The Emperor Jones and The Hairy Ape as Mirror Plays," Comparative Drama, 2:21-31, Spring, 1968.

"The Emperor Jones (1920) and The Hairy Ape (1921-22), are Eugene O'Neill's most successful experiments in expressionism.

Considering the similarities in their cyclic structures, mock-
heroic protagonists and archetypal symbolism, they are mirror
plays whose aspects parallel or complement one another's correspondences." (D.P.)

O 347 Rubinstein, Annette, "The Dark Journey of Eugene O'Neill,"
Mainstream, 10:29-33, April, 1957.

Eugene O'Neill's "dark journey" through life is exemplified by his
autobiographical play Long Day's Journey Into Night. "Who is the
villain, who the victim?" Central to the play is the tragic, powerful figure of the father, who demonstrates that essential causes are
undecipherable and that character as well as fortune depends on the
"inscrutable decrees of a malicious fate." (V.E.)

O 348 Salem, James M., "Eugene O'Neill and the Sacrament of Marriage,"
Serif, 3:23-35, June, 1966.

"In Welded [O'Neill] showed that adultery was never acceptable; in
Desire Under the Elms, Mourning Becomes Electra, and Strange
Interlude, that adultery was a step toward complete decay and destruction; and in Days Without End, that only through the power of
the cross could an adulterer atone for his sin." (G.C.)

O 349 Schuh, Oscar Fritz, "Eugene O'Neill und seine Dramen,"
Universitas, 17:235-44, March, 1962.

O'Neill's recognition that things go on in man's unconscious and subconscious which only rarely penetrate the conscious is of paramount
importance to an understanding of his work. (M.G.)

O 350 Stamm, Rudolph, "'Faithful Realism': Eugene O'Neill and the
Problem of Style," English Studies, 40:242-50, August, 1959.

In his last plays (The Iceman Cometh, Long Day's Journey into
Night, A Moon for the Misbegotten, and A Touch of the Poet),
"the dramatist perfected a style that can properly be called his own,
and he found a valid solution of his language problem. (C.K.L.)

O 351 Stroupe, John H., "Eugene O'Neill and the Creative Process,"
English Record, 21:69-76, October, 1970.

". . . Eugene O'Neill was an obsessive craftsman. . . . his plays
are a consistent chronological record of a mind in torment. . . .
But what is less obvious . . . is how O'Neill's artistry emerges

through his particular habit of work. My purpose is to detail O'Neill's physical method of composition and to include in this analysis several excerpts from correspondence between O'Neill and Saxe Cummins (O'Neill's literary editor . . .) which have never been published." (D.P.)

O 352 Thurman, William R., "Journey Into Night: Elements of Tragedy in Eugene O'Neill," Quarterly Journal of Speech, 52:139-45, April, 1966.

". . . there should be in [tragic drama] a quality of affirmation in even the darkest representations of human experience. . . . The victory of the spirit may not appear, but it must be at least a credible possibility. . . ." O'Neill fails "to relate the realities and contingencies of experience to any satisfying and positive exposition of the human condition bereft of faith." (D.A.B.)

O 353 Törnqvist, Egil, "Ibsen and O'Neill: A Study in Influence," Scandinavian Studies, 37:211-35, August, 1965.

Eugene O'Neill publically acknowledged his literary debt to Nietzsche and Strindberg. The influence of Ibsen he noted early in his career, but in later years he grew more skeptical and negative. In his early play Recklessness, for example, the influence of A Doll's House can be clearly seen. In fact, though O'Neill denied any debt to Ibsen, the influence of the Norwegian playwright may be traced in many of O'Neill's works. (V.E.)

O 354 Törnqvist, Egil, "Nietzsche and O'Neill: A Study in Affinity," Orbis Litterarum, 23:97-126, 1968.

". . . whether the resemblances should be attributed to a conscious or unconscious identification on O'Neill's part or to a basic spiritual affinity between the two men leading to similar manifestations [is not clear]. . . . the evidence suggests a mingling of all three aspects. But . . . only a basic spiritual affinity can explain the scope and depth of Nietzsche's impact on O'Neill's writings." (K.M.W.)

O 355 Törnqvist, Egil, "Personal Addresses in the Plays of O'Neill," Quarterly Journal of Speech, 55:126-30, April, 1969.

". . . this brief survey may suffice to indicate O'Neill's interest in personal addresses as an element of characterization. Always indicative of the mental relations between the characters, the designations they give each other are often revealing also in other aspects:

when ambiguous, they frequently relate to the 'pipe dream' theme so central for O'Neill; when typifying, they suggest the universal implications that can nearly always be felt in his work." (D.A.B.)

O 356 Törnqvist, Egil, "Personal Nomenclature in the Plays of O'Neill," Modern Drama, 8:362-73, February, 1966.

". . . throughout his work [O'Neill] has indeed taken pains to call his characters by their 'right' names, that is, names which add to our understanding of them and, indirectly, of the world in which they draw their breath and have their being." (D.A.B.)

O 357 Valgemae, Mardi, "O'Neill and German Expressionism," Modern Drama, 10:111-23, September, 1967.

Because of disclaimers by O'Neill, the influence on him of the avant-garde German expressionist dramatists, particularly Georg Kaiser, has not been noted. Yet his techniques have more in common with the Germans than with Strindberg. (D.P.)

O 358 Vena, Gary A., "The Role of the Prostitute in the Plays of Eugene O'Neill," Drama Critique, 10:129-37, Fall, 1967.

The prostitute plays many roles in O'Neill's plays. Two types predominate: the ordinary lady of the night who sells her favors for money, and the "spiritually virginal . . . ubiquitous and eternal" woman. (D.P.)

O 359 Vena, Gary A., "The Role of the Prostitute in the Plays of Eugene O'Neill," Drama Critique, 11:9-14, Winter, 1968.

In O'Neill's later plays the prostitute abrogates the romantic ideal and she is the eternal woman. She is the answer to "man's longing for both sexual and spiritual fulfillment." (D.P.)

O 360 Vena, Gary A., "The Role of the Prostitute in the Plays of Eugene O'Neill," Drama Critique, 11:82-8, Spring, 1968.

In his autobiographical plays Long Day's Journey into Night and A Moon for the Misbegotten "O'Neill's spiritual quest is scarred with unfulfillment. His preoccupation with the opposed images of mother and whore is a manifestation of a perversity which was both subtly and intermittently apparent in his playwrighting. He gradually elevated the prostitute's role . . . finally merging the two antithetical and conflicting types--the mother and the whore--in such a way as to suggest that they join hands in a shameful conspiracy to destroy the soul with love." (D.P.)

O 361 Waith, Eugene M., "Eugene O'Neill: An Exercise in Unmasking," Educational Theatre Journal, 13:182-91, October, 1961.

"The characteristic structure of an O'Neill play . . . is determined by a movement toward unmasking, which is often also a movement of the principal characters toward discovery of the stance they must take toward the fundamental problems of existence." (D.A.B.)

O 362 Walton, Ivan H., "Eugene O'Neill and the Folklore and Folkways of the Sea," Western Folklore, 14:153-69, July, 1955.

O'Neill made extensive use of sailor folklore "to develop atmosphere and general verisimilitude, to present characters and foreshadow action, and in at least three plays to supply the central motif." (A.S.W.)

O 363 Whitman, Robert F., "O'Neill's Search for a 'Language of the Theatre'," Quarterly Journal of Speech, 46:153-70, April, 1960.

In his search for a dramatic medium to explore the human soul, O'Neill tried methods as radical as any attempted in the American theatre. All called "attention to themselves rather than to what they were intended to reveal." He did not return to his "natural language" of realism until he had found with it, and the help of whiskey, he could say the same thing better. (W.G.F.)

O 364 Winther, Sophus K., "Eugene O'Neill: The Dreamer Confronts His Dream," Arizona Quarterly, 21:221-33, Autumn, 1965.

"O'Neill recognized the fearful pressure of outward circumstances on man's life and destiny, and he uses these outward forces to dramatize the genuine tragedy of human life . . . the impossibility of harmonizing [man's] dream of . . . perfection with the actuality of his life and world." (G.C.)

O 365 Winther, S. K., "Strindberg and O'Neill: A Study of Influence," Scandinavian Studies, 31:103-20, August, 1959.

"In [Strindberg] O'Neill not only saw revealed a vision of the tragic failure of life, he also saw the dramatic technique by which the inner conflicts that torture man were exposed so that all might see." (G.C.)

O 366 Wolfson, Lester M., "Inge, O'Neill, and the Human Condition,"
Southern Speech Journal, 22:221-32, Summer, 1957.

O'Neill's Long Day's Journey Into Night "is one of the great dramas
of the recent theatre, showing with love and truth the condition of
modern man in search of himself." Journey, as well as The Iceman
Cometh, A Moon for the Misbegotten, and Inge's Come Back, Little
Sheba, Picnic, and Bus Stop share "a desperate aloneness, a radical
feeling of alienation . . . in part a consequence of blurred notions of
good and evil, of innocence and responsibility. . . ." However, Inge
has received an "over-zealous critical acclaim. . . ." (D.P.)

O 367 Wylie, Max, "Aspects of E. G. O.," Carrell, 2:1-12, June, 1961.

Some of the basic resemblances between O'Neill and Jonathan Swift
"as intellectual odd-balls and social anomalies, are astonishing."
Principal among them are their attitudes toward women, children,
and doctors; their severe anxiety, suspiciousness, stinginess,
marked bi-sexuality, and general hypochondriasis. (W.G.F.)

O 368 Young, Stark, "Eugene O'Neill: Notes from a Critic's Diary,"
Harper's Magazine, 214:66-71, 74, June, 1957.

O'Neill's story sometimes "limps," the style is often flat, the
thought sometimes sophomoric, but he touches greatness because
of his deep compassion. His intention and "the dark center of it"
enable him to "break your heart" in spite of his limitations. (F.L.)

AH, WILDERNESS!

O 369 Adler, Jacob H., "The Worth of Ah, Wilderness!" Modern Drama,
3:280-8, December, 1960.

". . . Ah, Wilderness! is a distinguished play." It deals with the
ever-recurrent problems of loneliness, misunderstanding, vice,
self-indulgence, tyranny, prejudice, and hints of violence and
revenge. (C.K.L.)

O 370 Going, William T., "O'Neill's Ah, Wilderness!" Explicator,
29: Item 28, November, 1970.

The inexact quotation from the Rubáiyát for the title of the play
seems to represent O'Neill's commentary on the "Wilderness of
maturing youth." (D.P.)

AH, WILDERNESS!   (cont'd)

O 371   Herron, Ima Honaker, "O'Neill's Comedy of Recollection: A
Nostalgic Dramatization of 'The Real America'," CEA Critic,
30:16-8, January, 1968.

"... youthful experiences in several rural and small-town commu-
nities" "not only account for O'Neill's deep personal affection for
Ah, Wilderness! but help explain why, in a nostalgic mood, he once
thought of the American small town, as it existed at the turn of the
century, as 'the real America'." (D.P.)

O 372   Shawcross, John T., "The Road to Ruin: The Beginning of O'Neill's
Long Day's Journey," Modern Drama, 3:289-96, December, 1960.

Ah, Wilderness! is a play of "biographical import depicting that
time of adolescent innocence which all men pass through just before
they are rudely made aware that life can be a bitter experience ...
and that a long journey down a road to ruin awaits some before tears
and blood exculpate their dead." (C.K.L.)

ANNA CHRISTIE

O 373   Frazer, Winifred L., "Christ and Poseidon: Man versus God in
Anna Christie," Modern Drama, 12:279-85, December, 1970.

"Perhaps, looked at in the light of Greek myth, [Anna Christie]
has a unity which it seems to lack if viewed merely as a naturalistic
American drama." (D.A.B.)

O 374   McAleer, John J., "Christ Symbolism in Anna Christie," Modern
Drama, 4:389-96, February, 1962.

"... the present writer wishes merely to distinguish O'Neill's
debt to Sherwood Anderson for the concept of Christ symbolism and
to the Anima Christi for providing a device on which to structure
Christ symbolism in this particular drama...." Unfortunately,
"O'Neill, in attempting to use a medieval prayer as an agent synthesizing the Christ of the Passion and Anna Christie as a single
character representing mankind, undertook to do more than he
could reasonably manage." (D.P.)

BEYOND THE HORIZON

O 375 Dave, R. A., "Have We Lost the Tragic Sense? Eugene O'Neill's
Beyond the Horizon: A Study," Literary Criterion, 6:26-35, No. 4,
1965.

"If the idea of the Immanent Will overshadows Hardy's tragic view,
the psychological preoccupations blur Eugene O'Neill's vision of
tragedy. More often than not he fails to measure up to a tragic
stature, he becomes only pathetic. He none the less lays bare the
unfathomable depths of human life and shows the beauty of human
soul in the midst of disaster and death." (K.M.W.)

O 376 Roy, Emil, "Tragic Tension in Beyond the Horizon," Ball State
University Forum, 8:74-9, Winter, 1967.

Beyond the Horizon fully develops for the first time motifs--"girl
pursues reluctant boy" and the quest for rebirth--which would preoccupy O'Neill for the rest of his career. (A.S.W.)

DAYS WITHOUT END

O 377 Chiaromonte, Nicola, "O'Neill cattolico," Il Mondo, 11:14,
February 10, 1959.

In Days Without End, O'Neill wanted to go to the roots of the problem
of God and of Evil in the modern world. He did not succeed since
"on the one hand the problem was equivocal, and on the other, though
O'Neill was a confused writer, he was incapable of lying or of betraying his own suffering, which was real." (V.R.)

DESIRE UNDER THE ELMS

O 378 Conklin, Matthew T., "The Tragic Effect in Autumn Fire and
Desire Under the Elms," Modern Drama, 1:228-35, February,
1959.

"Although each author treated the same themes and used a similar
set of characters in a rural setting, the tragic effects of the two
plays are so vastly dissimilar as to warrant a comparative study."
(C.K.L.)

DESIRE UNDER THE ELMS (cont'd)

O 379 Frenz, Horst, "Eugene O'Neill's Desire Under the Elms and Henrik Ibsen's Rosmersholm," Jahrbuch für Amerikastudien, 9:160-5, 1964.

The influence of Strindberg on O'Neill has obscured Ibsen's role in the development of the American playwright. Both Rosmersholm and Desire Under the Elms share place as "a significant agent recognized as exerting a compelling power in the lives of those who are close to it. . . . People in both houses have second sight. . . . Both plays depict a period of transition. . . . Both in O'Neill and in Ibsen the admission of love is followed by disillusion and then by the true fulfillment of this love. . . . In both plays the heroine herself sets in motion the machinery that brings about her destruction." Both plays "are distinguished by the special place they occupy in the total work of the author . . . [and] in each the central theme is identical, that of a struggle to escape a burden of guilt and to achieve an inner integrity." (D.P.)

O 380 Hartman, Murray, "Desire Under the Elms in the Light of Strindberg's Influence," American Literature, 33:360-9, November, 1961.

Hardly a plot element in the play cannot be traced to Strindberg. "The basic situation, where the young man has seen his beloved mother worked to death by a hard father and then has had to bear the usurpation of her position by an aggressive stepmother, has its origin in The Son of a Servant." (W.G.F.)

O 381 Hays, Peter L., "Biblical Perversions in Desire Under the Elms," Modern Drama, 11:423-8, February, 1969.

Desire Under the Elms "is, if not controlled, then at least shaped by an intellectual idea and a message: that the harsh, loveless and covetous Puritanical religion practiced by Ephraim Cabot is a perversion of religion that cripples love and destroys men." (D.P.)

O 382 Lau, Joseph S. M., "Two Emancipated Phaedras: Chou Fan-yi and Abbie Putnam as Social Rebels," Journal of Asian Studies, 25:699-711, August, 1966.

Chou Fan-yi, in Ts'ao Yü's Thunderstorm "has perhaps the closest resemblance to the traditional tragic hero, for, like Abbie Putnam in O'Neill's Desire Under the Elms, she is essentially a woman of passion, though its nature and the manner they react to it are characteristically different." (H.S.)

DESIRE UNDER THE ELMS (cont'd)

O 383   Macgowan, Kenneth, "O'Neill and a Mature Hollywood Outlook,"
Theatre Arts, 42:79-81, April, 1958.

[This is a discussion of the film Desire Under the Elms as produced
in 1958 by Don Hartman.] (H.S.)

O 384   Meyers, Jay R., "O'Neill's Use of the Phèdre Legend in Desire
Under the Elms," Revue de Littérature Comparée, 41:120-5,
January-March, 1967.

"A strong case can be made for identifying the Phèdre legend as the
direct source of the play. O'Neill's variant of the story treated
dramatically by Euripides and Racine provides us with the clearest
explanation of his purposes." (H.S.)

O 385   Papajewski, Helmut, "Realismus und Verfremdung in der Symbolik
von O'Neills Desire Under the Elms," Germanisch-Romanische
Monatsschrift, 16:410-25, October, 1966.

"Thus we see that in the motif complexes in which the tragic problem
in Desire Under the Elms is essentially expressed, O'Neill is striving simultaneously for a realistic functional context and for an adequate expression of the magical." (J.R.R.)

O 386   Racey, Edgar F., Jr., "Myth as Tragic Structure in Desire Under
the Elms," Modern Drama, 5:42-6, May, 1962.

Desire Under the Elms relies for its mythic or classical source "on
the Hippolytus of Euripides (and perhaps, on Racine's treatment of
the theme). . . ." The play "combines a traditional tragic theme
(the Oedipus legend) with a dramatic reconciliation in the interests
of a higher virtue (Justice)." (D.P.)

O 387   Reardon, William R., "The Path of a Classic: Desire Under the
Elms," Southern Speech Journal, 31:295-301, Summer, 1966.

Desire Under the Elms was originally misjudged, but mature criticism helped it achieve its present position in spite of being absent
from the stage for almost thirty years. (D.P.)

DESIRE UNDER THE ELMS   (cont'd)

O 388   Roy, Emil, "O'Neill's Desire Under the Elms and Shakespeare's King Lear," Die Neueren Sprachen, 15:1-6, January, 1966.

Desire Under the Elms owes theme, imagery, and moral character to King Lear. However, Shakespeare's play relies on a universally accepted belief, while O'Neill's play appears mad, unable to make contact.   (D. P.)

O 389   Winther, Sophus Keith, "Desire Under the Elms: A Modern Tragedy," Modern Drama, 3:326-32, December, 1960.

"In this play, for the first time, O'Neill begins to see the problem of tragedy in modern drama as opposed to the classical and traditional interpretations." Here, in Desire Under the Elms, he departs from the Aristotelian interpretation.   (C. K. L.)

THE GREAT GOD BROWN

O 390   Berkelman, Robert, "O'Neill's Everyman," South Atlantic Quarterly, 58:609-16, Autumn, 1959.

The Great God Brown can be read as a play tracing the journey of a twentieth-century Everyman: Dion Anthony is the artist in everyone; William Brown is everyone's practical side. But O'Neill's wish to disclose the truth about modern man was distorted by his desire to attack worldly success.   (W. B. B.)

O 391   Metzger, Deena P., "Variations on a Theme: A Study of Exiles by James Joyce and The Great God Brown by Eugene O'Neill," Modern Drama, 8:174-84, September, 1965.

The Great God Brown and Exiles "are variations on a single theme despite their variant philosophic base and technique. They both investigate the difference between conventional and original thought, between habit and commitment. They both investigate the pain which occurs to people separated by two worlds and the duplicity of those who try to manipulate this separation to their advantage. . . . Basically, O'Neill saw human experience as personal, transient, and subjective. . . . In every way, Joyce's approach differed from O'Neill's. . . . Instead of ecstasy, he presents epiphany; instead of catharsis, he evokes stasis. Joyce's drama is more intellectual than O'Neill's, and his conclusions are not personal."   (D. P.)

THE GREAT GOD BROWN (cont'd)

O 392 Sogliuzzo, A. Richard, "The Uses of the Mask in The Great God Brown and Six Characters in Search of an Author, " Educational Theatre Journal, 18:224-9, October, 1966.

"An analysis of the technique of the masks employed in The Great God Brown and Six Characters . . . reveals that O'Neill and Pirandello used the mask to express different themes, and neither was primarily concerned with the mask as a means to express the psychological conflict of the many masks of human personality. " (D.A.B.)

O 393 Valgemae, Mardi, "Albee's Great God Alice, " Modern Drama, 10:267-73, December, 1967.

"The parallels between Tiny Alice and The Great God Brown suggest that in breaking away from the realistic mode, Albee has been influenced . . . by Eugene O'Neill. " (D.P.)

O 394 Valgemae, Mardi, "Eugene O'Neill's Preface to The Great God Brown, " Yale University Library Gazette, 43:24-9, July, 1968.

[Printed here is the autograph draft of the foreward to The Great God Brown, with a typed transcript and extensive commentary.] (D.P.)

THE HAIRY APE

O 395 Clark, Marden J., "Tragic Effect in The Hairy Ape, " Modern Drama, 10:372-82, February, 1968.

Yank's progress is from an unthinking, prideful brute to a man tormented by unanswerable questions. Even from a hero at the lowest level of humanity can come an affirmation of human dignity. (R.C.B.)

O 396 Das, P. N., "The Alienated Ape, " Literary Half-Yearly, 11:53-69, No. 1, 1970.

"This play [is] . . . in the centre of O'Neill's concern which . . . is . . . the relation . . . between man and God and this deep concern with problems of belonging and alienation places O'Neill among the avant-garde artists of our time. " (G.C.)

THE HAIRY APE   (cont'd)

O 397   Gump, Margaret, "From Ape to Man and from Man to Ape,"
Kentucky Foreign Language Quarterly, 4:177-85, Fourth Quarter,
1957.

In Hauff's "Der Affe als Mensch," "an ape is permitted to ape
civilized man and to deceive the citizens of a small town . . .; in
Kafka's . . . 'Ein Bericht für eine Akademie,' the ape actually
becomes a man, at least superficially; in O'Neill's play _The Hairy
Ape_, the hero is seen by others as an ape and comes to consider
himself as such; and in Huxley's novel, _Ape and Essence_, human
society is run by apes before its final ruin." Over the years the
satires on this theme have become increasingly bitter, increasingly
pessimistic as to the future.   (D. P.)

O 398   Rollins, Ronald G., "O'Casey, O'Neill and Expressionism in _The
Silver Tassie_," Bucknell Review, 10:346-9, May, 1962.

"O'Casey's chance acquaintance with Eugene O'Neill's _The Hairy
Ape_ . . . strongly impelled the Irish dramatist to discard his previous dramatic manner. . . . _The Silver Tassie_, adapting the
imaginative and flexible dramatic technique of O'Neill and other
expressionists, integrates symbolism and realism into a unique and
penetrating critique of the holocaust of war." (D. A. B.)

HUGHIE

O 399   Alexander, Doris, "The Missing Half of _Hughie_," Tulane Drama
Review, 11:125-6, Summer, 1967.

Problems in _Hughie_ are the result of its first being produced posthumously, without O'Neill to oversee the staging, and from the fact
that in it O'Neill attempted, with limited success, to combine elements of the talking film and live dramatic performance.   (D.P.)

O 400   Cohn, Ruby, "Absurdity in English: Joyce and O'Neill,"
Comparative Drama, 3:156-61, Fall, 1969.

Anglo-American playwrights rarely incorporate "a sense of metaphysical anguish at the absurdity of the human condition," which
Esslin views as the theme of Absurd theatre. Such anguish is contained in Joyce's _Exiles_ and the Nightown chapter of _Ulysses_, as
well as in O'Neill's _Hughie_.   (D.P.)

THE ICEMAN COMETH

O 401 Andreach, Robert J., "O'Neill's Women in The Iceman Cometh, " Renascence, 18:89-98, Winter, 1966.

An examination of the theological implications of The Iceman Cometh explains "why O'Neill's males have ambivalent feelings toward Mary and all females who are figures of Mary." (S.A.)

O 402 Brashear, William R., "The Wisdom of Silenus in O'Neill's Iceman, " American Literature, 36:180-8, May, 1964.

"The concentration on biographical detail in current criticism has, perhaps, obscured the more fundamental characteristic of [O'Neill's] genius--his tragic vision." This element is best explored by concentrating on The Iceman Cometh, which is distinguished from a purely naturalistic work like The Lower Depths by the "solidly founded 'urge toward life' and the profound ennoblement of 'hopeless hopes'." (W.G.F.)

O 403 Chabrowe, Leonard, "Dionysus in The Iceman Cometh, " Modern Drama, 4:377-88, February, 1962.

"O'Neill thus seems to have derived The Iceman Cometh from Lazarus Laughed in almost every aspect of its action and characters. . . . Once again this was a celebration of life by means of its embodiment in ritual forms, which is to say by means of singing and dancing about it. The underlying aesthetic idea was that only through ritual could the audience be made to experience a Dionysian communion with life itself." (D.P.)

O 404 Day, Cyrus, "The Iceman and the Bridegroom: Some Observations on the Death of O'Neill's Salesman, " Modern Drama, 1:3-9, May, 1958.

"The Iceman Cometh is a play about the death of a salesman; its central theme is the relationship between men's illusions and their will to live. . . . [Unlike] Arthur Miller's Willie Loman . . . [who] is adrift in contemporary American society, Hickey is adrift in the universe. . . . By an extraordinary reconciliation of opposites [O'Neill] equates the drunken Hickey with the secular savior Freud and the Christian savior Christ, and at the same time rejects the gospels preached by both." (D.A.B.)

THE ICEMAN COMETH   (cont'd)

O 405   Lee, Robert C., "Evangelism and Anarchy in The Iceman Cometh,"
Modern Drama, 12:173-86, September, 1969.

The Iceman is O'Neill's culmination and his demise and is a denial
of any other experience of faith in his plays. Long Day's Journey
sums up O'Neill's life, while Iceman sums up all life.   (T.T.B.)

O 406   LoCicero, Donald, "Arthur Schnitzler and Eugene O'Neill: Masks,
Pipe-Dreams, and Reality," Journal of the International Arthur
Schnitzler Association, 4:27-42, No. 3, 1965.

"The object of this study will be to point out the similarities of
Der grüne Kakadu and The Iceman Cometh in their involvement with
the problem of reality."   (D.P.)

O 407   Presley, Delma Eugene, "O'Neill's Iceman: Another Meaning,"
American Literature, 42:387-8, November, 1970.

O'Neill may have been acquainted with the underworld meaning of
"ice-man," "one who makes ostentatious gifts of worthless or
trivial things."   (W.G.F.)

O 408   Roy, Emil, "The Iceman Cometh as Myth and Realism," Journal of
Popular Culture, 2:299-313, Fall, 1968.

"The irresolvable paradox which finally suspends Slade between equal
but opposite versions of nullity interworks endlessly with Iceman's
other major elements: the play's revelations of hate motivating love
entangle not only Hickey but Slade and Parritt; the play's parodies of
Christian ritual, social reform and family unity tie in with the prevailing sense of suppressed crimes and words; its constant conflicts
of questionings and withholdings result from a conspiracy of false
brotherhood created by arrested hostility."   (D.P.)

O 409   Wright, Robert C., "O'Neill's Universalizing Technique in The
Iceman Cometh," Modern Drama, 8:1-11, May, 1965.

The critics charge that the play is a nihilistic, overdrawn picture of
futility; however, "the deliberate building of density, then, along
with the encouragement of audience identification with the spirit of
man and the use of the universal language of ritual, myth, and
symbol, are the universalizing techniques O'Neill uses in The Iceman
Cometh." The repetition and length are necessary to achieve the
vision. (G.A.S.)

IN THE ZONE

O 410 Goldhurst, William, "A Literary Source for O'Neill's In the Zone, " American Literature, 35:530-4, January, 1963.

"Certain elements in the play bear a striking resemblance to an almost forgotten short story by Arthur Conan Doyle entitled 'That Little Square Box'." (W.G.F.)

LAZARUS LAUGHED

O 411 Alexander, Doris M., "Lazarus Laughed and Buddha, " Modern Language Quarterly, 17:357-65, December, 1956.

"Intrinsic to the character of O'Neill's redeemer in Lazarus Laughed are many of the characteristics of Gautama the Buddha, for Lazarus is a composite of saviours." "If one adds to the Christ, the Dionysus the Zarathustra, in Lazarus, the image of Gautama the Buddha, the character of O'Neill's Lazarus becomes fairly understandable. " (D.A.B.)

O 412 Day, Cyrus, "Amor Fati: O'Neill's Lazarus as Superman and Savior, " Modern Drama, 3:297-305, December, 1960.

[This essay considers "some of the ways in which Nietzsche's philosophy is revealed in Lazarus Laughed." It also touches briefly on "O'Neill's failure . . . to transmute Nietzsche's ideas into effective drama."] (C.K.L.)

O 413 Törnqvist, Egil, "O'Neill's Lazarus: Dionysus and Christ, " American Literature, 41:543-54, January, 1970.

In Lazarus Laughed, O'Neill may have made the central figure resemble Dionysus, Jupiter, and Christ in order "to demonstrate the highly ironical fact that the Dionysiac savior is received or understood no better than the Christian one." The syncretism of the play is an accurate description of the religious spirit of the Graeco-Roman world. (W.G.F.)

LONG DAY'S JOURNEY INTO NIGHT

O 414   Cerf, Walter, "Psychoanalysis and the Realistic Drama," Journal of Aesthetics and Art Criticism, 16:328-36, March, 1958.

Eugene O'Neill's Long Day's Journey into Night and Arthur Laurents's A Clearing in the Woods show that psychological realism and artistic realism are mutually incompatible and that psychologically retrospective plays, despite intellectual interest, are essentially without emotional impact. (M.J.O.)

O 415   Downer, Alan S., "Tragedy and 'The Pursuit of Happiness': Long Day's Journey Into Night," Jahrbuch für Amerikastudien, 6:115-21, 1961.

"Long Day's Journey Into Night demonstrates convincingly the possibilities for the equivalent of tragic experience in the drama of the living room . . . the room which limits and defines the action, and the living which is the action. For nobody dies. This is the tragedy of survival," of failure in the modern pursuit of happiness. (R.J.G.)

O 416   Finkelstein, Sidney, "O'Neill's Long Day's Journey," Mainstream, 16:47-51, June, 1963.

[This is a general discussion of O'Neill's play prompted by the appearance of the motion picture version of Long Day's Journey Into Night directed by Sidney Lumet.] (G.C.)

O 417   Krutch, Joseph Wood, "O'Neill's Last Play--Domestic Drama with Some Difference," Theatre Arts, 40:25, 89-91, April, 1956.

"Long Day's Journey Into Night is intensely personal and directly autobiographical. . . . The play is a determined attempt to face those external circumstances which made him the desperate man (and perhaps helped make him the arresting playwright) he was." (D.P.)

O 418   Lawrence, Kenneth, "Dionysus and O'Neill," University Review, 33:67-70, October, 1966.

[This is a comparison of O'Neill's Long Day's Journey Into Night to "the rite of Dionysus." (H.S.)

LONG DAY'S JOURNEY INTO NIGHT   (cont'd)

O 419   Raleigh, John Henry, "O'Neill's Long Day's Journey into Night and
New England Irish-Catholicism," Partisan Review, 26:573-92,
Fall, 1959.

The culture of New England Irish-Catholicism "provides the folkways
and mores, the character types, the interrelationships between
characters, and the whole attitude toward life that informs Long
Day's Journey and gives it its meaning." (R.K.)

O 420   Redford, Grant H., "Dramatic Art vs. Autobiography: A Look at
Long Day's Journey Into Night," College English, 25:527-35,
April, 1964.

"It is as poetry, as dramatic art, and not as autobiography that
Long Day's Journey Into Night should be judged." (D.A.B.)

O 421   Rothenberg, Albert, "Autobiographical Drama: Strindberg and
O'Neill," Literature and Psychology, 17:95-114, Nos. 2-3, 1967.

Although Strindberg wrote many autobiographical plays, The Father
typifies some differences between his and O'Neill's approach.
"Strindberg wrote manifestly autobiographical plays throughout his
life. . . . in contrast, O'Neill's Long Day's Journey Into Night was
one of his last plays [and O'Neill suppressed it]." (J.M.D.)

O 422   Winther, Sophus Keith, "O'Neill's Tragic Themes: Long Day's
Journey into Night," Arizona Quarterly, 13:295-307, Winter, 1957.

"Long Day's Journey into Night combines in one action the great
themes O'Neill developed in all his tragedies. . . . He has revealed
the father, the home, and the sources of his philosophy in one
dramatic action which embraces the meaning of all his plays and
unites us to him in the universal tragedy of man." (A.A.S.)

MARCO MILLIONS

O 423   Stroupe, John H., "O'Neill's Marco Millions: A Road to Xanadu,"
Modern Drama, 12:377-82, February, 1970.

"O'Neill's preliminary notes for Marco Millions indicate that as he
approached a writing of the play, he sought information from Marco
Polo's own travels and from Yule's introductory materials. . . .
His intent was satirical, his focus economic. In forming Marco, he

MARCO MILLIONS   (cont'd)

sought only the information which allowed him . . . to satirize the American businessman and to show the tragedy inherent in American culture." (D.A.B.)

A MOON FOR THE MISBEGOTTEN

O 424   Fitzgerald, John J., "Guilt and Redemption in O'Neill's Last Play: A Study of A Moon for the Misbegotten," Texas Quarterly, 9:146-58, Spring, 1966.

"In Aristotelian terms, O'Neill seems to be trying to effect a triple purgation. . . . the act of writing the play was a form of self-therapy for his own feelings of familial guilt; the whole action revolves around the purgation of James Tyrone; and although O'Neill did not call his drama a tragedy . . . [it] does subserve the tragic end of purging the audience of pity and fear." (W.G.F.)

O 425   Krutch, Joseph Wood, "Genius Is Better Than Talent," Theatre Arts, 38:22-3, October, 1954.

"The two paradoxes of Eugene O'Neill are the almost unbelievable difference in quality between individual plays, and a certain technical clumsiness in even the best of them. . . . He had . . . a measure of real genius, but he was curiously devoid of talent. . . . Both of these paradoxes are glaringly illustrated in A Moon for the Misbegotten, which . . . has a few powerful scenes and a few flashes of memorable dialogue. But it is certainly not one of his best plays, and the over-all execution is cruder than in some quite early works. . . ." (D.P.)

O 426   Welch, Mary, "Softer Tunes for Mr. O'Neill's Portrait: Police Close O'Neill Play," Theatre Arts, 41:67-8, 82-3, May, 1957.

"Having had direct, personal contact with [O'Neill], I would like to add some warmer, softer tones to what I feel is an overly stark and limited portrait of O'Neill [as an isolated "lonely, passionate, tormented genius"]. [The author appeared in the first production of A Moon for the Misbegotten.] (D.A.B.)

MORE STATELY MANSIONS

O 427 Hartman, Murray, "The Skeletons in O'Neill's Mansions," Drama Survey, 5:276-9, Winter, 1966-67.

"More Stately Mansions is in its totality a drama manqué. There is too much exposition and unmotivated conflict before the play begins to cohere. . . . it is nostalgic to hear these last echoes of one of the representative voices of the century, fulminating to the end against the dehumanization of man. . . ." (D.P.)

O 428 Real, Jere, "The Brothel in O'Neill's Mansions," Modern Drama, 12:383-9, February, 1970.

"In spite of the embryonic nature of this work and the derivative nature of its style and technique from earlier O'Neill plays, More Stately Mansions was given a highly unified thematic form by its author. The recurring references in both dialogue and in the development of the characters's actions all support the premise that man prostitutes himself for material gain, even to the point of treating human relationships as property to be possessed." (D.P.)

MOURNING BECOMES ELECTRA

O 429 Alexander, Doris M., "Captain Brant and Captain Brassbound: The Origin of an O'Neill Character," Modern Language Notes, 74:306-10, April, 1959.

"No one can blame O'Neill for this extraordinarily complete literary theft, for he was probably totally unaware of it, and his stolen Shaw character fits beautifully into Mourning Becomes Electra, a play overwhelmingly original in philosophy and psychology. . . ." (M.J.O.)

O 430 Asselineau, Roger, "Mourning Becomes Electra as a Tragedy," Modern Drama, 1:143-50, December, 1958.

Mourning Becomes Electra is a modern realization of Aristotelian tragedy, flawed by its lack of a "distinctive style." (D.P.)

O 431 Dickinson, Hugh, "Eugene O'Neill: Anatomy of a Trilogy," Drama Critique, 10:44-56, Winter, 1967.

O'Neill found it necessary to find a retributive force as a substitute for the supernatural in order "to give a sense of ineluctable fate" to

MOURNING BECOMES ELECTRA (cont'd)

his audience which did not believe in gods or supernatural retribution.
In Mourning Becomes Electra he achieved by this means a drama of
"mythic grandeur." (D.P.)

O 432 Dickinson, Hugh, "Eugene O'Neill: Fate as Form," Drama
Critique, 10:78-85, Spring, 1967.

Mourning Becomes Electra is not deterministic, although characters
act and their acts have consequences. In the play O'Neill reshapes
the classical myth, denies fate and develops this paradox: "the
subconscious becomes the mother of demons, the dead become the
pursuing furies, and man goes inward to a hell of his own choosing."
(D.P.)

O 433 Frenz, Horst and Martin Mueller, "More Shakespeare and Less
Aeschylus in Eugene O'Neill's Mourning Becomes Electra,"
American Literature, 38:85-100, March, 1966.

"The comparison of Hamlet and Mourning Becomes Electra will not
only prove that these two plays show similarities in plot wherever
there are plot differences between Hamlet and the Oresteia but also
to help define the fundamentally different concept of action that
separates O'Neill's trilogy from the Oresteia." (W.G.F.)

O 434 Hill, Philip G., "Dramatic Irony in Mourning Becomes Electra,"
Southern Speech Journal, 31:42-55, Fall, 1966.

". . . the pervading irony of the entire trilogy is . . . the family
curse that operates as 'Fate' to drag each member of the Mannon
family back to face the sins of his ancestors. . . . Furthermore . . .
O'Neill has made use of one central irony for each of the three plays
in" Mourning Becomes Electra. (D.P.)

O 435 Lecky, Eleazer, "Ghosts and Mourning Becomes Electra: Two
Versions of Fate," Arizona Quarterly, 13:320-38, Winter, 1957.

Though Ibsen's play and O'Neill's have been compared with their
Greek counterparts, "the analogies between the two modern plays
are equally significant, for they help reveal the structure and meaning of each of these modern versions of fate." (A.A.S.)

MOURNING BECOMES ELECTRA   (cont'd)

O 436   Pratt, Norman T., Jr., "Aeschylus and O'Neill: Two Worlds,"
Classical Journal, 51:163-7, January, 1956.

"The whole significance of the trilogy (Mourning Becomes Electra)
rests upon psychotic and neurotic impulses" ending in annihilation
which unhappily "exemplifies the ideas which dominate current
literature and thought." In contrast, we have seen briefly in the
Oresteia (Aeschylus) a view comprehending the entire human scene
which restores tranquility and order. (M.J.O.)

O 437   Ramsey, Warren, "The Oresteia since Hofmannsthal: Images and
Emphases," Revue de Littérature Comparée, 38:359-75, July-
September, 1964.

Hofmannsthal's Elektra "is interesting in its own right, for reasons
of style, texture and construction. It further provides a series of
familiar plot-positions against which versions of the Oresteia as
various as those of Jeffers (The Tower Beyond Tragedy), O'Neill
(Mourning Becomes Electra), Giraudoux (Électre), Sartre (Les
Mouches) and Eliot (Family Reunion) may be viewed." (D.P.)

O 438   Stafford, John, "Mourning Becomes America," Texas Studies in
Literature and Language, 3:549-56, Winter, 1962.

"In Mourning Becomes Electra American history is seen to have
been plagued by an Evil Fate, a Force created by the Puritan denial
of Love and Beauty," which "corrupts the lives of the powerful ruling families in the rising American industrial society especially."
(W.G.F.)

O 439   Weissman, Philip, M. D., "Mourning Becomes Electra and The
Prodigal: Electra and Orestes," Modern Drama, 3:257-9,
December, 1960.

"The Prodigal is as reflective of today's generation as O'Neill's
[Mourning Becomes Electra] mirrored the mood of the preceding
generation. For both O'Neill and [Jack] Richardson are clairvoyant
spokesmen of their respective eras." (C.K.L.)

S. S. GLENCAIRN

O 440 Rust, R. Dilworth, "The Unity of O'Neill's S. S. Glencairn,"
American Literature, 37:280-90, November, 1965.

"Although the plots of the four episodes are somewhat different in
nature and although the episodes had been, and still could be, acted
as one-act plays, the coherence of the combined plots into a single
plot line justifies their being bound together into one cycle play."
(W.G.F.)

STRANGE INTERLUDE

O 441 Brashear, William R., "O'Neill's Schopenhauer Interlude,"
Criticism, 6:256-65, Summer, 1964.

An important "aspect of Schopenhauer's philosophy . . . not touched
by" Doris Alexander's "Strange Interlude and Schopenhauer"
(American Literature, 25:213-28) is "the theory of time and . . .
the present . . . in The World as Will and Idea." This "provides
the intellectual framework" of the play.   (J.L.A.)

TOMORROW

O 442 Brashear, William R., "'To-morrow' and 'Tomorrow': Conrad
and O'Neill," Renascence, 20:18-21, 55, Autumn, 1967.

By comparing O'Neill's only short story, "Tomorrow," and Conrad's
earlier work of the same title, we can begin to answer the previously
unanswered question, to what extent did Conrad influence O'Neill?
(S.A.)

A TOUCH OF THE POET

O 443 Alexander, Doris, "Eugene O'Neill and Charles Lever," Modern
Drama, 5:415-20, February, 1963.

"Eugene O'Neill turned to the novels of Charles Lever for the
historical background he needed" for A Touch of the Poet. "He
took from Lever only facts. Nothing in Lever influenced O'Neill's
plan for [his 'cycle of nine plays'], a grand study of fatal patterns
recurring in generation after generation of Americans, the plan of
his Tale of Possessers Self-Dispossessed." (D.A.B.)

A TOUCH OF THE POET   (cont'd)

O 444   Dunkel, Wilbur Dwight, "Theology in the Theater," Theology Today, 16:65-73, April, 1959.

". . . while one praises J. B. as an artistic masterpiece, even in its denial of the Christian faith, the Christian must regret that the early premises of this work of art were not fulfilled." James Forsyth's "Heloise deals with the theology of Abelard . . . rather than the letters of this articulate pair of lovers." The dramatization of Greene's The Power and the Glory by Dennis Cannan and Pierre Bost "develops forceful theological concepts." Compassion is "the pervasive quality of O'Neill's latest play, A Touch of the Poet." Budd Schulberg and Harvey Breit's The Disenchanted "poses the theological question . . . : 'What has happened to me?' " "In The Shadow of a Gunman Sean O'Casey . . . still tilts his lance at the Roman Catholic Church and its ritual. . . ." These recent productions share great attention to theological principles.   (D. P.)

O 445   Krutch, Joseph Wood, "In an Earlier Era: The O'Neills on Stage Once More," Theatre Arts, 42:16-7, 71, October, 1958.

"Any hitherto unknown play by O'Neill would be of interest. There are many reasons why A Touch of the Poet is especially interesting, and one of them pertains to what the play enables us to guess concerning the intention of the whole cycle."   (H. S.)

O 446   Marcus, Mordecai, "Eugene O'Neill's Debt to Thoreau in A Touch of the Poet," Journal of English and Germanic Philology, 62:270-9, April, 1963.

"Eugene O'Neill's late play A Touch of the Poet is heavily indebted to the life and writings of Henry David Thoreau for the conceptions of three characters and for much thematic material."   (H. S.)

THE WEB

O 447   Fish, Charles, "Beginnings: O'Neill's The Web," Princeton University Library Chronicle, 27:3-20, Autumn, 1965.

"The Web is not an isolated effort, but one which connects significantly with later work in respect to stagecraft, theme, character, and experimentation with language."   (G. C.)

O'NOLAN, BRIAN

O 448   Benstock, Bernard, "The Three Faces of Brian Nolan," <u>Eire-Ireland</u>, 3:51-65, Autumn, 1968.

"In most ways O'Nolan was his own man, or more precisely three men divided against themselves. A hard drinker and Dublin pub wit, he was consubstantially closer to his journalistic self, the Myles na Gopaleen of the <u>Irish Times</u>, than he was to his artistic self, the Flann O'Brien who produced his literary masterpiece <u>At Swim-Two-Birds</u> in 1939, the year Joyce published <u>Finnegans Wake</u>." (D.A.B.)

O 449   Wain, John, "'To Write for My Own Race': The Fiction of Flann O'Brien," <u>Encounter</u>, 29:71-2, 74-85, July, 1967.

O'Brien's <u>At Swim-Two-Birds</u> is "just about the only real masterpiece in English that is far too little read and discussed. . . ." In an individual way it is related to the work of Eliot, Pound and Joyce. O'Brien's <u>The Hard Life</u> and <u>The Dalkey Archive</u> also are worthy of attention. (D.A.B.)

AT SWIM-TWO-BIRDS

O 450   Janik, Del Ivan, "Flann O'Brien: The Novelist as Critic," <u>Eire-Ireland</u>, 4:64-72, Winter, 1969.

Flann O'Brien's <u>At Swim-Two-Birds</u> is strongly influenced by Joyce in matters of style and content, and, indeed, provides an ironic commentary on <u>A Portrait of the Artist as a Young Man</u>. In the novel, Stephen's aloofness, his problems with religious and other authority, and his aesthetic theory provide the basis for extended parody. (D.P.)

O 451   Lee, L. L., "The Dublin Cowboys of Flann O'Brien," <u>Western American Literature</u>, 4:219-25, Fall, 1969.

Although it is hard to imagine cowboys in Dublin, in <u>At Swim-Two-Birds</u> Flann O'Brien (a pseudonym) uses "that archetypal American figure" to give most clearly one of his major meanings: "Adam has been thrown out of the Garden." (W.G.F.)

THE THIRD POLICEMAN

O 452   Benstock, Bernard, "Flann O'Brien in Hell: The Third Policeman,"
Bucknell Review, 17:67-78, May, 1969.

O'Brien's The Third Policeman, which was first published in 1967,
actually was written in 1940, immediately after At Swim-Two-Birds.
Although O'Brien described it as an endless journey through hell,
the protagonist's experiences vary from terrifying to delightful. The
book is a comic novel. (D.P.)

OPPEN, GEORGE

O 453   Dembo, L. S., "The 'Objectivist' Poet: Four Interviews,"
Contemporary Literature, 10:155-219, Spring, 1969.

[These are interviews with four "Objectivist" poets, George Oppen,
Carl Rakosi, Charles Reznikoff, and Louis Zukovsky. The concept
of "Objectivism" was formulated by Zukovsky in 1931, and "Oppen,
Reznikoff, and Rakosi, though denying the existence of a unifying
ideology, all had personal interpretations of 'objectivism' that gave
shape to their poetry." (D.P.)

OPPENHEIM, E. PHILLIPS

O 454   Stokes, Sewell, "Mr. Oppenheim of Monte Carlo," Listener,
60:344-5, September 4, 1958.

[These are reminiscences of the author who "had taken the lid off
Monte Carlo for thousands, millions, of readers the world over."]
(D.A.B.)

ORLOVITZ, GIL

O 455   Chatfield, Hale, "Literary Exile in Residence," Kenyon Review,
31:545-53, No. 4, 1969.

"What Orlovitz's poetry is mainly 'about' . . . is the mind that has
written it and the mind that can read it. Orlovitz's approach to
poetry will . . . be compared by some to Jackson Pollock's approach
to painting. . . . The poem is the world's words and Orlovitz's mind;
the painting is the world's pigments and Pollock's hands." (H.S.)

O 456   Orlovitz, Gil, "Some Autobiographical Words," Literary Review,
         2:197-9, Winter, 1958-59.

         [Orlovitz speaks about his life to date and about the "four major
         projects in poetry and one in fiction [which] presently engage . . .
         [his] work."] (H.S.)

ORLOVSKY, PETER

O 457   Glaser, Alice, "Back on the Open Road for Boys," Esquire,
         60:48-9, 115, July, 1963.

         [This interview with Ginsberg and his fellow beat poet Peter Orlovsky
         took place in Benares, India. Ginsberg and Orlovsky are "probably
         the only two Beats still on the open road."] (D.P.)

ORTEGA Y GASSET, JOSÉ

O 458   Anido-Meulener, Gastón, "La polémica Unamuno-Ortega y Gasset,"
         Duquesne Hispanic Review, 4:91-9, 1965.

         "The forty year debate between Unamuno and Ortega developed from
         preoccupations which aspired to a revision of the Spanish spirit; the
         resolution of the question was instrumental in deciding fundamental
         matters of Spanish style." (D.P.)

O 459   Aponte, Barbara B., "A Dialogue between Alfonso Reyes and José
         Ortega y Gasset," Hispania, 49:36-43, March, 1966.

         Correspondence reveals a coldness in Ortega's attitude toward
         Reyes after 1947, though no reason is apparent. Reyes never
         faltered in his respect for the master. (C.O.)

O 460   Baker, Clifford H., "The Role of Ideas in Ortega's Ontology,"
         Romance Notes, 3:21-4, Spring, 1962.

         Ortega is concerned with the relationship between ideas and human
         life, which is the basic reality. Ideas have reality only in reference
         to particular circumstances, so there can be no such thing as
         abstract or eternal ideas. (T.T.B.)

O 461   Campbell, Brenton, "Free Will and Determinism in the Theory of Tragedy: Pérez de Ayala and Ortega y Gasset," Hispanic Review, 37:375-82, July, 1969.

Two apparently contrary views of tragedy are really conciliable. Ayala associates tragedy with necessity, Ortega with freedom; but Ayala focuses on the spectator, Ortega on the tragic hero. (C.O.)

O 462   Caponigri, A. Robert, "Contemporary Spanish Philosophy," Modern Age, 13:169-76, Spring, 1969.

[This is a survey of Spanish philosophy from its nineteenth century antecedents to its present-day followers of Ortega.] (C.O.)

O 463   Corrigan, Robert, "José Ortega y Gasset: Master Teacher," Kentucky Foreign Language Quarterly, 10:129-32, 1963.

"Ortega has been called the political educator of his generation. . . . Indeed, [he] . . . was first and above all else a teacher--one whose powerful influence in the classroom, through his work as a writer, publisher, lecturer, and inspirer of youth has earned for him the right to be considered the systematic educator of his beloved Spain." (D.P.)

O 464   Giménez Caballero, Ernesto, "Las generaciones españolas," La Estafeta Literaria. No. 391, p. 8, March 9, 1968.

As founder and guiding light of La Gaceta Literaria, Ortega introduced surrealism into Spain, launched the lyrical vanguard, revealed functional architecture, at the same time presenting expositions of Spanish, European and American books and offering extraordinary monographs by Góngora and Unamuno. (T.T.B.)

O 465   Johannet, René, "Ortega y Gasset," La Revue des Deux Mondes, pp. 321-5, November 15, 1955.

The part of Ortega y Gasset's work which will remain is perhaps a "collection of his thoughts, if one decides to isolate them, gather them. He has the gift of sonorous, laconic and striking phrases." (M.M.)

O 466   Maldonaldo-Denis, Manuel, "Ortega y Gasset and the Theory of the
Masses," Western Political Quarterly, 14:676-90, September, 1961.

Ortega's mass man is usually a psychological type, not a member of
a sociological class. But even in The Revolt of the Masses his use
of the term has at least four connotations. (C.O.)

O 467   Morón Arroyo, Ciriaco, "Álgebra y logaritmo: Dos metáforas de
Ortega y Gasset," Hispania, 49:232-7, May, 1966.

From 1904 to 1914 Ortega went through a rationalist phase. After-
wards he moved closer to the "supra-rationalism" which was the
hallmark of Unamuno. (C.O.)

O 468   Orringer, Nelson R., "Ortega y Gasset's Sportive Theories of
Communication," Modern Language Notes, 85:207-34, March, 1970.

The idea of "sport" informs Ortega's views on words and gestures
from the 1920's on and is not limited to his vitalist-oriented phase
(1920-27). Further, his sportive notion must be evaluated in the
context of his ethics, epistemology, and esthetics. (C.O.)

O 469   Raley, Harold G., "Ortega y el problema de la verdad," Revista de
Estudios Hispánicos, 2:81-90, 1968.

In Ortega "philosophy deals as much with life as with logic; as much
with seriousness as with gaiety; as much with desperation as with
sport. The same truth may be discovered in these differing human
manifestations as in the dichotomy between the risible and the tragic.
(D.P.)

O 470   Read, Herbert, "High Noon and Darkest Night: Some Observations
on Ortega y Gasset's Philosophy of Art," Journal of Aesthetics and
Art Criticism, 23:43-50, Fall, 1964.

Ortega's "dehumanized" art was a kind of extremism, thus anti-
popular and unsatisfactory. The concept reveals Ortega as the
intellectual failing to understand that art which corresponds to the
"dark night of the soul." (C.O.)

O 471   Rexach, Rosario, "España en Unamuno y Ortega," Revista
Hispánica Moderna, 33:262-79, 1967.

"Unamuno and Ortega, respectively, brought passion and reason to
bear on Spain. And nobly contested each other in this study." (D.P.)

O 472 Rodríguez-Alcalá, Hugo, "José Ortega y Gasset and Jean-Paul Sartre on Existence and Human Destiny," <u>Research Studies</u> (State College of Washington), 24:193-211, September, 1956.

Basically Ortega and Sartre agreed on problems of existence and destiny. Indeed, Ortega made these ideas "familiar to Spanish-speaking readers long before Sartre ever dealt with them." (D.P.)

O 473 Rodríguez-Luis, Julio, "La discusión sobre la novela entre Ortega y Baroja," <u>La Torre</u>, 10:85-125, April-June, 1962.

[This summary of the well known polemic between Ortega y Gasset and Baroja, beginning in the twenties, laments the absence of a "happy medium" between the intense psychological probing and the academic discipline demanded by Ortega, and the apparently formless, wandering, fast-paced works of Baroja.] (C.O.)

O 474 Schwartz, Egon, "Ortega y Gasset and German Culture," <u>Monatshefte</u>, 49:87-91, February, 1957.

Ortega admired Germany while seeing the dangers and corruption of the Empire. Ultimately his position is symbolized by his attitude towards Goethe, whose spirit was grand enough to mirror an epoch. (C.O.)

O 475 Schwartz, Kessel, "Ortega y Gasset and Goethe," <u>Hispania</u>, 43:320-7, September, 1960.

Ortega's "interest in Goethe's attitude towards life, then, reflects his own eternal search and can be broken down into various headings such as the meaning of existence, the necessity for action, and the attempt to find one's essence." (A.C.H.)

O 476 Sebastian, Elmer G., "José Ortega y Gasset: World Crises and the Unification of Europe," <u>Hispania</u>, 46:490-5, September, 1963.

The crisis of our modern age is due in part to the outmoded nation-state. Thus every step toward a unified Europe, as called for by Ortega, is necessary in the scheme of "historical reason." (C.O.)

O 477 Weber, Frances, "An Approach to Ortega's Idea of Culture: The Concept of Literary Genre," <u>Hispanic Review</u>, 32:142-56, April, 1964.

Ortega's ambiguous understanding of culture leads to two discrepant notions of the novel genre. They derive from his division of reality into material substance on the one hand and interpretation and idea on the other. (C.O.)

O 478   Werrie, Paul, "Grâces et disgrâces du roman espagnol," La Table Ronde, Nos. 248-9, pp. 110-33, September-October, 1968.

[This is an analysis of the tendencies of Ortega y Gasset, Baroja, Cela, Aldecoa, Espina and Tomás Salvador.] (T.T.B.)

O 479   Winecoff, Janet, "The Spanish Novel from Ortega to Castellet: Dehumanization of the Artist," Hispania, 50:35-43, March, 1967.

The novelists of the Ortega-oriented Generation of '25 and those of the contemporary nouveau roman in Spain constitute a highly un-Spanish phenomenon. In both cases they manifest the ascendancy of theoretical considerations among practitioners of the novel genre. (C.O.)

THE DEHUMANIZATION OF ART--See
LA DESHUMANIZACIÓN DEL ARTE

LA DESHUMANIZACIÓN DEL ARTE

O 480   Frank, Joseph, "The Dehumanization of Art," New Republic, 140:16-8, June 1, 1959.

"Ortega's essay on The Dehumanization of Art [written in 1925] is still among the best efforts to define and interpret the radical break in continuity between modern art and the whole Renaissance tradition of representation. . . ." However, "nothing dates Ortega's essay more than . . . his view of modern art as its own self-negation. . . . From our vantage point, it is clear that modern culture did not take the road that Ortega predicted . . . he did not forsee how deep and radical that crisis [in modern culture] was--nor how profoundly it was reflected in the dehumanization of art." (D.P.)

O 481   Newberry, Wilma, "Aesthetic Distance in García Lorca's El público: Pirandello and Ortega," Hispanic Review, 37:276-96, April, 1969.

El público "is an extremely important document because it shows García Lorca's very special reaction to Pirandello. . . . Lorca, realizing that his type of lyrical theater could not exist unless a certain aesthetic distance were maintained, wrote El público to il-

LA DESHUMANIZACIÓN DEL ARTE   (cont'd)

lustrate the damage caused by extreme forms of Pirandellism, to
criticize these forms, and then to manifest his rejection of them.
. . . García Lorca may have been inspired by Ortega y Gasset['s
La Deshumanización del arte.]"   (D.P.)

O 482   Shaw, D. L., "A Reply to Deshumanización: Baroja on the Art of
the Novel," Hispanic Review, 25:105-11, April, 1957.

An overview of this lengthy polemic shows apparent agreement on
two points: the intranscendence and the pervasive irony of modern
art. But ultimately, for Ortega art is escape from, while for
Baroja it is an exploration of human reality.   (C.O.)

     GOETHE FROM WITHIN--See
     PIDIENDO UN GOETHE DESDE DENTRO

     IDEAS SOBRE LA NOVELA

O 483   McDonald, E. Cordel, "The Modern Novel as Viewed by Ortega,"
Hispania, 42:475-81, December, 1959.

Ortega's Ideas sobre la novela considers the crisis of the novel and
these norms: "the psychological foundations on which the novelist
rests his novelistic structure; the peculiarly unique novelistic
cosmos which he creates; the method and techniques by which he
best achieves these ends."   (A.C.H.)

     NOTES ON THE NOVEL--See
     IDEAS SOBRE LA NOVELA

     PIDIENDO UN GOETHE DESDE DENTRO

O 484   Lawson, Richard H., "Ortega's Goethe from Within," Research
Studies (State College of Washington), 24:212-24, September, 1956.

Basic to Ortega's proposal in his "Goethe desde dentro" "for a new
sort of biography of Goethe . . . [which] will depart from the evident
contradiction between the Naturfrömmigkeit which inspires Goethe's
relationships with the universe, and the constant preoccupation with
his own life . . . is Ortega's notion that Goethe was not true to his
destiny, that he was unauthentic." In his desire to be original
Ortega has succumbed to the temptation to produce a subtle paradox
in his analysis.   (D.P.)

LA REBELIÓN DE LAS MASAS

O 485   Weiss, Robert O., "The Levelling Process as a Function of the
Masses in the View of Kierkegaard and Ortega y Gasset," Kentucky
Foreign Language Quarterly, 7:27-36, 1960.

Søren Kierkegaard in his The Present Age and Ortega y Gasset in
his The Revolt of the Masses "demonstrate most clearly the malignant dynamics of the masses, and as the active principle therein, a
function which they called 'levelling'." (D.P.)

THE REVOLT OF THE MASSES--See
LA REBELIÓN DE LAS MASAS

ORTON, JOE

O 486   Lahr, John, "Artist of the Outrageous," Evergreen Review,
14:30-4, 83-4, February, 1970.

"Joe Orton was the comedian of the dark side of the contemporary
soul; the vituperative anti-Christ isolated by his anarchist rage and
cynical in his desolation." His farces "make an audience confront
the schizophrenic patterns of their lives, rather than evade them.
By making a carnival of man's stupidity and superstition, by exposing the condition of social insanity, his plays hold out to an audience
the possibility of humility and care." (D.P.)

ORWELL, GEORGE

O 487   Barr, Donald, "The Answer to George Orwell," Saturday Review,
40:21, 30-2, March 30, 1957.

Critics to the contrary, "Orwell's work was not essentially topical,
as we can see if we compare his first novel, Burmese Days, published in 1934, with his last, 1984, published fifteen years later.
In that interval, a hellish revolution in politics took place, and the
possibilities of total despotism were demonstrated, yet the two
books are startlingly similar." "In his literary life he passed
through five moods . . . coming . . . in succession . . . to dominate his brain": revulsion, atonement, the rediscovery of England,
tension, and "an unforgiving realization of the inadequacy of man."
(D.P.)

O 488   Beadle, Gordon, "George Orwell and Charles Dickens: Moral
         Critics of Society," Journal of Historical Studies, 2:245-55, 1969-70.

         "The similarity between Orwell and Dickens can be traced to the
         acceptance of a common moral and intellectual tradition, while the
         period in which they lived partially accounts for the difference.
         Orwell's work reflects the despair and justifiable fears of the first
         half of the twentieth century, just as Dickens reflects the naive faith
         in man and progress that so characterized mid-Victorian England."
         (D.A.B.)

O 489   Beadon, Roger, "With Orwell in Burma," Listener, 81:755,
         May 29, 1969.

         [These are recollections of Orwell, whom Beadon knew as Eric A.
         Blair in Burma from 1922 to 1927.]   (D.P.)

O 490   Brander, Laurence, "George Orwell: Politics and Good Prose,"
         London Magazine, 1:64-71, April, 1954.

         "Prose for Orwell was a weapon in political warfare. It was the
         instrument by which he retained and expressed his individuality and
         he cared for it exceedingly." Orwell " 'is unique in being immensely
         serious [about the dangers to liberty of officialese], and in connecting
         good prose with liberty.'. . . His method is to expose the forces
         against clear writing and thinking. . . . His life was dedicated to the
         defence of liberty and this he felt was the whole duty of a writer in a
         political age." (D.P.)

O 491   Burns, Wayne, "George Orwell: Our 'Responsible' Quixote,"
         West Coast Review, 2:13-21, Spring, 1967.

         Before World War II Orwell established himself as champion of the
         values of the common, decent man, largely for his defense of tradi-
         tional Western ideals and for his battles with the intellectual left.
         He became skeptical of his earlier values after World War II, but
         1984, ironically, has been widely read as an anti-communist tract.
         (D.P.)

O 492   Colquitt, Betsy Feagan, "Orwell: Traditionalist in Wonderland,"
         Discourse, 8:370-83, Autumn, 1965.

         "The body of Orwell's writings affirms that his general intellectual
         position was always traditional; his early works show commitment
         to such beliefs with the tenacity and aplomb of Carroll's heroine if

not with her optimism." But the last novels suggest the plight of a tragic, modern Alice "whose wonderland is an anti-utopia." (W.G.F.)

O 493 Cook, Richard, "Rudyard Kipling and George Orwell," Modern Fiction Studies, 7:125-35, Summer, 1961.

". . . despite the immense variance in their political outlooks [Kipling and Orwell] shared a number of fundamental attitudes" of "respect for the individual, a sense of responsibility, and, above all, a code of personal decency and honor. . . . For all its smugness, insularity, and hypocrisy, Kipling's world, in Orwell's eyes, seemed preferable to the world that had succeeded it." (D.P.)

O 494 Cosman, Max, "George Orwell and the Autonomous Individual," Pacific Spectator, 9:74-84, Winter, 1955.

Orwell's basic questions relate to the individual and society. His protagonists are dogged by failure in art, religion, and politics. His final message: "the individual . . . cannot stand up to society; his doom is destruction." Sympathetic and humane, Orwell gave "the novel of ideas an airing" and increased its audience. (J.L.B.)

O 495 Cosman, Max, "Orwell's Terrain," Personalist, 35:41-9, Winter, 1954.

"His [Orwell's] virtues . . . are positive. Whether in commentary, in fiction, or in treatise, he has that sagacity and courage, that mother-wit and grip on fundamentals which we sum up in the term 'common sense'." (H.S.)

O 496 Dooley, D. J., "The Limitations of George Orwell," University of Toronto Quarterly, 28:291-300, April, 1959.

"His books are interesting, not as warnings of a prophet who realized the truth before anyone else, but as portraits of the mind of a man who . . . imprisoned himself inside the game [of revolutionary politics] he played." (F.J.P.)

O 497 Dunn, Avril, "My Brother, George Orwell," Twentieth Century, 169:255-61, March, 1961.

[These are reminiscences.] (R.K.)

O 498   Edrich, Emanuel, "George Orwell and the Satire in Horror,"
         Texas Studies in Literature and Language, 4:96-108, Spring, 1962.

         "The most striking conclusion" to come from George Orwell's
         analysis of power "forms the foundation for the extreme horror that
         permeates" 1984. The conclusion is that "power can fully realize
         itself only when it is inflicting pain and thereby assuring itself that
         its subjects are obedient not because they want to be but because
         they are forced to be." (W.G.F.)

O 499   Fen, Elisaveta, "George Orwell's First Wife," Twentieth Century,
         168:115-26, August, 1960.

         Eileen O'Shaughnessy was "sophisticated, fastidious, highly intelli-
         gent and intellectual. . . . [She] was perhaps no less gifted, though
         in different ways, than the man she married." (H.S.)

O 500   Fiderer, Gerald, "Masochism as Literary Strategy: Orwell's
         Psychological Novels," Literature and Psychology, 20:3-21, No. 1,
         1970.

         Orwell's schoolboy experiences may account for the ambivalent sado-
         masochism that manifests itself in his works through frequent refer-
         ences to rods, punishments, and whippings. (J.M.D.)

O 501   Fitzgerald, John J., "George Orwell's Social Compassion,"
         Discourse, 9:219-26, Spring, 1966.

         "To most well read Americans [Orwell] is merely a safe anti-
         Communist. His two best known works, Animal Farm and 1984,
         clearly establish him as a secure anti-totalitarian. But Orwell was
         not just a negative thinker who was simply against something. A
         rare harmony resounds in both his life and works, for a deep social
         compassion not only animates his books but also motivated his
         mature life." (D.A.B.)

O 502   Fixler, Michael, "George Orwell and the Instrument of Language,"
         Iowa English Yearbook, No. 9, pp. 46-54, Fall, 1964.

         Orwell's "whole moral attitude toward linguistic usage is based on
         the assumption that the evolution of language was related to ideo-
         logical evolution (language and thought were for him directly and
         invariably involved each with the other), and that both were influ-
         enced, or capable of being influenced, by consciously deliberate
         literary and linguistic actions." (W.G.F.)

O 503 Fyvel, T. R., "A Case for George Orwell?" <u>Twentieth Century</u>, 160:254-9, December, 1956.

The canonization of George Orwell by the political Right is due to his early writings such as <u>The Road to Wigan Pier</u> in which he scathed Left Wing intellectuals. In reality Orwell was an active Socialist all of his life though he avoided extremism and the narrow view. His complex personality must be studied fully in order to be understood. (V. E.)

O 504 Fyvel, T. R., "George Orwell and Eric Blair: Glimpses of a Dual Life," <u>Encounter</u>, 13:60-5, August, 1959.

"Biographical literary criticism is dangerous even where we know a great deal about the subject. It is doubly so in Orwell's case because he was so secretive over the stages by which he changed himself from Eric Blair (his real name) into the personality of George Orwell. . . ." (H.S.)

O 505 Glicksberg, Charles I., "The Literary Contribution of George Orwell," <u>Arizona Quarterly</u>, 10:234-45, Autumn, 1954.

The key to George Orwell's character is in <u>Down and Out in Paris and London</u> which demonstrates his belief that there is no real gulf between rich and poor. Practically all of Orwell's novels deal with the corruption of society and the evil influence of wealth and power. (V. E.)

O 506 Green, Martin, "British Decency," <u>Kenyon Review</u>, 21:505-32, Autumn, 1959.

"The new type I should call the decent man--as opposed to the gentle-man--or the Anglo-Saxon moralist, or the Anglo-Saxon rebel. In this century all the most central and vital examples have been essen-tially rebellious. . . . What is always essential is its puritanism. . . a concern with right and wrong so keen as to set the tone of the whole personality, an eagerness to draw sharp, exclusive lines . . . a distrust of all connoisseurship in experience, all aestheticism. . . . the four men who embody most vitally this idea of England and Englishness, are D. H. Lawrence, F. R. Leavis, George Orwell, and Kingsley Amis." (D.P.)

O 507 Griffin, C. W., "Orwell and the English Language," Audience, 7:63-76, Winter, 1960.

"As Orwell reminds us, we are not powerless, even as individuals, in the fight against slovenly language. The Existentialists, sociologists, bureaucrats, and mind-molders get away with their verbal crimes only because their readers are passive." (D.P.)

O 508 Hollis, Christopher, "George Orwell and His Schooldays," Listener, 51:382-3, March 4, 1954.

[These are recollections of a classmate of Orwell at Eaton.] "I would not say that he was a typical old Etonian, but then it is . . . peculiarly easy for an old Etonian not to be a typical old Etonian. His private school may . . . have played its part in driving him to spiritual loneliness, and this loneliness certainly was sharpened and embittered by a life in Burma . . . but I think that Eton had a good deal to do with the unique courage with which he gave expression to that spiritual loneliness." (D.P.)

O 509 King, Carlyle, "The Politics of George Orwell," University of Toronto Quarterly, 26:79-91, October, 1956.

To Orwell, "the prime political facts, then, are money and the class distinctions which are the by-products of more or less money; the main political objectives must consequently be an equitable distribution of income and destruction of the stone walls of class. . . . That is why Orwell became a socialist, remained one to the end of his life and devoted all his literary powers to persuading his fellows to line up on the side of justice and decency." (D.P.)

O 510 Lutman, Stephen, "Orwell's Patriotism," Journal of Contemporary History, 2:149-58, April, 1967.

"Patriotism as a theme connects up with many of the other dominant themes in Orwell's work; it acted for Orwell as 'the bridge between the future and the past' and its unconscious persistence through time and change comes up briefly in 1984 in the proles. Patriotism was part of the defence against totalitarianism as Orwell saw it during the war, and a hope for the future." (D.P.)

O 511 Mander, John, "George Orwell's Politics: I," <u>Contemporary Review</u>, 197:32-6, January, 1960.

Orwell's novels are didactic monologues, since the author is so much involved. He is paradoxical in his presentation of the working class, at the same time stating a theory of progress and supporting class loyalty--each person staying in his own class. He has basically conservative ideas. He is against change, but even here he is paradoxical. (F.L.)

O 512 Mander, John, "George Orwell's Politics: II," <u>Contemporary Review</u>, 197:113-9, February, 1960.

Orwell represents a fundamental paradox: he is both revolutionary and conservative. His theory of history is the "devil's parody" of the Historical Dialectic: "There must always be revolutions" is the first premise; "all revolutions are entirely useless" is the second. "Trotskyism" covers the basic principle of his socialism: his faith in the working class. (F.L.)

O 513 Mellichamp, Leslie, "George Orwell and the Ethics of Revolutionary Politics," <u>Modern Age</u>, 9:272-8, Summer, 1965.

"Orwell was not unaware of important implications of the Terror-- its foreshadowing of modern totalitarian methods, for instance--but he displays no consciousness of the ethical quicksand that follows a subjection of means to ends, especially when this is coupled with an attack on absolutes. . . . what Dickens knew intuitively, Koestler apparently had to learn inductively . . . Orwell . . . may have never learned." (D.P.)

O 514 O'Flinn, J. P., "Orwell on Literature and Society," <u>College English</u>, 31:603-12, March, 1970.

". . . in the body of his essays and reviews he [Orwell] emerges as one of the first English writers to indicate that literature does not spring up in an economic and political void but is an integral part of the society that produces it." (H.S.)

O 515 Orwell, George, "Some Letters of George Orwell," <u>Encounter</u>, 18:55-65, January, 1962.

[This is a selection of twenty-one letters, February 2, 1936-July 28, 1949, "to Cyril Connolly, Richard Rees, Stephen Spender, T. R. Fyvel and others."] (H.S.)

O 516   Potts, Paul, "Quixote on a Bicycle: In Memoriam George Orwell,
         1903-1950," London Magazine, 4:39-47, March, 1957.

         A journalist only as Swift and Hazlitt were journalists, Orwell was
         better than anything he wrote. Independent, generous, honest, brave,
         "his life was a duel fought against lies; the weapon he chose, the
         English language." (D.B.D.)

O 517   Powell, Anthony, "George Orwell: A Memoir," Atlantic Monthly,
         220:62-8, October, 1967.

         "I want to put on record not so much . . . his courage . . . but
         what I remember of him as a friend . . . with whom, in spite of
         differing opinions on almost every subject, I seem so often to have
         had such oddly enjoyable times." (D.P.)

O 518   Quintana, Ricardo, "George Orwell: The Satiric Resolution,"
         Wisconsin Studies in Contemporary Literature, 2:31-8, Winter, 1961.

         Satire offered Orwell in Animal Farm and in 1984 a style, a way to
         keep in balance his belief in life and his equal belief in absolute evil.
         (B.K.)

O 519   Rieff, Philip, "George Orwell and the Post-Liberal Imagination,"
         Kenyon Review, 16:49-70, Winter, 1954.

         "What drives the Liberal imagination beyond itself is precisely the
         ascendancy of imagination, no longer confident in its liberal-
         Christian forms. Orwell was the perfect liberal, neither passive
         nor unimaginative. Yet at the same time there was in Orwell a
         residual ambiguity typical of the finest liberalism." (H.S.)

O 520   Rovere, Richard H., "George Orwell," New Republic, 135:11-5,
         September 10, 1956.

         Orwell's writing avoided the unique or eccentric in human behavior,
         but shunned conformity and mediocrity as well. Orwell is notably a
         social prophet, a critic of fanaticism, a man of firm principle.
         (G.K.)

O 521   Shannon, Jean, "George Orwell: The Writer and His Political
         Commitments," Unisa English Studies, 4:21-33, November, 1969.

         ". . . I wish to examine briefly certain of Orwell's ideas with regard
         to power, freedom of the Press, nationalism and Socialism . . . in

order to try to show that he is a didactic writer, and that his 'thought' or 'message' is vital to his writing." (D.P.)

O 522   Smith, W. D., "George Orwell," Contemporary Review, No. 1085, pp. 283-6, May, 1956.

"To call . . . George Orwell an optimist is missing the head of the nail by a mile. He is the incurable pessimist. . . . Part of this pessimism . . . is due to the fact that Orwell has little or no belief in the goodness of human nature. He hates human beings, and above all he hates himself. Through all his writings there is this sadistic streak. . . ." (H.S.)

O 523   Spence, J., "George Orwell," Theoria, 13:15-26, 1959.

"George Orwell . . . speaks to us with an intensely personal voice, revealing a man vitally committed to the political and social issues of his day. . . . Orwell's approach to political and social problems was based on a profound respect for the individual. . . . And this may explain why at times he turned to the novel as a medium for expressing his concern at the fate of the underprivileged both in England and abroad." (D.P.)

O 524   Strachey, John, "The Strangled Cry," Encounter, 15:3-18, November; 23-37, December, 1960.

Koestler's Darkness at Noon "was the first book to begin to reveal the far-reaching consequences upon the mind and spirit of the West of the rejection of Communism." The theme "of the falsification of the past," which, "together with physical torture, was to make Orwell hag-ridden for the rest of his life," first appeared in Animal Farm, his masterpiece. In 1984 "Orwell lent his powerful, detailed, concrete imagination to the task of describing a nightmare, in order, if possible . . . to avert it." Whittaker Chambers "is a writer possessing major powers, but also capable of dreadful failures. . . ." Pasternak's Zhivago "completes, and at the same time transcends, the reaction against mechanical or 'mechanistic' materialism." Thus, "against the awful sterility of this new dogma [of Communist rationalism] the strangled cry of the writers of the literature of reaction has been raised." (D.P.)

O 525   Symons, Julian, "Orwell: A Reminiscence," <u>London Magazine</u>,
        3:35-49, September, 1963.

        Orwell "remained a libertarian Socialist until he died, and those who
        read into the bitterness of <u>1984</u> a change in his essential beliefs are
        mistaken. He would have been horrified by the way in which his
        name and his work have given comfort to the Right. . . . Finally,
        his unique merit rested in the fact that . . . he always welcomed and
        even invited the assaults of life." (D.P.)

O 526   Thompson, Frank H., Jr., "Orwell's Image of the Man of Good
        Will," <u>College English</u>, 22:235-40, January, 1961.

        "Surrounded by Orwell's clear look at what is and firmly embedded in
        his old-fashioned truthfulness, the images lead to a double view of
        the man of good will: what he means as a representative modern
        man and how uncomfortably close he is to us." (M.J.O.)

O 527   Trocchi, Alexander, "A Note on George Orwell," <u>Evergreen Review</u>,
        2:150-5, No. 6, 1958.

        "In his concern for the day to day movement of sociological currents,
        he [Orwell] never seriously concerned himself with the fact that . . .
        everything is filtered through the prism of self, that it is not enough
        to control what is acting upon one from without, and that is precisely
        when men in their organisational zeal forget this that freedom dies."
        (H.S.)

O 528   Voorhees, Richard J., "George Orwell as Critic," <u>Prairie Schooner</u>,
        28:105-12, Summer, 1954.

        "The interest in the ordinary man which characterizes the fiction and
        political essays of George Orwell also characterizes his literary
        criticism. Because of this interest Orwell was led to a diligent ex-
        amination of popular novels . . . and . . . certain pulp magazines."
        Through such a study "Orwell gets an insight into the readers's minds."
        (H.S.)

O 529   Voorhees, Richard J., "George Orwell: Rebellion and Responsibility,"
        <u>South Atlantic Quarterly</u>, 53:556-65, October, 1954.

        "Undoubtedly, Orwell felt a nostalgia for much in the nineteenth
        century and a hatred for much in the twentieth, but he did not imagine
        that . . . any period in the past was a golden age. And, although
        earnestly devoted to Socialism, he did not naively suppose that it

would change the essential nature of human life . . . in which there was much more to be suffered than enjoyed. Human life, however, was a good thing, and the suffering was to be accepted. . . . George Orwell was a combination of toughness and of sensibility that never tended to neurosis." (D.P.)

O 530 Voorhees, Richard J., "Orwell's Secular Crusade," Commonweal, 61:448-51, January 28, 1955.

Central to an understanding of Orwell are his views "of nationalism, power, responsibility, poverty, and religion." His definition of nationalism is extremely broad; most nationalists share a desire for power. He regards intellectuals as largely irresponsible. "The point he wishes to make about poverty is not that it is melodramatic or sinister, but that it is dull." He was persistently and unrelentingly hostile to religion. Perhaps "more important than the lack of imagination which kept the quality of poetry almost entirely out of Orwell's books was the lack of imagination which often kept the quality of mercy out . . . he . . . found it difficult to be charitable." (D.P.)

O 531 Wadsworth, Frank W., "Orwell as a Novelist: The Early Work," University of Kansas City Review, 22:93-9, Winter, 1955.

"Revealing the social/political purpose which will govern subsequent novels, Burmese Days shows as well the technical unevenness typical of Orwell's work in this genre. The novel is remarkable for the amount of intrusive comment on the part of the author." "However, the novel's weaknesses are to a great extent balanced by Orwell's power of observation and resultant ability to create vivid, realistic settings for his narrative." "All in all, A Clergyman's Daughter (1935) is his poorest novel. It suffers more than the rest from Orwell's inability to keep himself out of his story, revealing . . . a frequently intrusive personal antagonism. . . . The novel's most serious weakness is structural, however." (D.P.)

O 532 Wadsworth, Frank W., "Orwell as a Novelist: Orwell's Later Work," University of Kansas City Review, 22:285-90, June, 1956.

"If Coming Up for Air represents Orwell's first awareness, organized but incomplete, of the 'after-war,' and 1984 the full length dramatization of what this 'after-war' will be like, Animal Farm represents his vision of how such a state will come about. Its allegorical methods and its surface faithfulness to Russian history do not limit its significance." (L.L.)

O 533 Wagner, Geoffrey, "The Novel of Empire," Essays in Criticism, 20:229-42, April, 1970.

The English novel of empire, as written by Conrad, Kipling, Forster, Orwell and others, is not only concerned with "the creation of character through colonial hardships," but, very often "the regeneration of those 'back home'." (D.P.)

O 534 Wain, John and George Woodcock, "On George Orwell," Commentary, 47:28-30, June, 1969.

It is a question whether or not Orwell "found his natural place once again in the sectarian Left." (E.S.F.)

O 535 Wain, John, "Orwell and the Intelligentsia," Encounter, 31:72-80, June, 1968.

[This essay (written after the publication of The Collected Essays, Journalism and Letters of George Orwell, 1961) finds "it necessary to withdraw the caveat that Orwell is unfair to the intelligentsia."] (H.S.)

O 536 Warncke, Wayne, "George Orwell's Critical Approach to Literature," Southern Humanities Review, 2·484-98, Fall, 1968.

Orwell's "involvement in the struggle for human freedom and decency is unquestionable; and it is the most important single factor influencing his essays on literature from the briefest reviews to the more extended and better known studies...." (D.A.B.)

O 537 Warncke, Wayne, "George Orwell's Dickens," South Atlantic Quarterly, 69:373-81, Summer, 1970.

"Liking a writer is not the same thing as being like him, even though Orwell found many of his own sentiments reflected in Dickens's work." (H.S.)

O 538 Warncke, Wayne, "The Permanence of Orwell," University Review, 33:189-96, March, 1967.

"... Orwell came to recognize the essential crisis of his time ... [as] a crisis of the human individual who held within his own hands the fate of the liberal Western culture. Orwell's legacy to future generations is the emphatic living of that recognition." (D.P.)

O 539 Way, Brian, "George Orwell--The Political Thinker We Might Have
Had," Gemini, 3:8-18, Spring, 1960.

Orwell's political development was tragic. Nineteen Eighty-Four is
not a culmination, but a decline into despair which smothers all
"positive impulses" and has "enfeebled" the Labour movement.
Instead of giving Britain a Socialist thought "rooted in the decency of
British radicalism and the Protestant democratic tradition," he
"degenerated into pessimistic conservatism." (K.M.)

O 540 Woodcock, George, " 'I Wasn't Born for an Age Like This': Was
Smith? Was Jones? Were You?" Esquire, 66:142-5, 207-11,
September, 1966.

"Orwell was too solitary to be a symbol and too angry to be a saint.
But he succeeded in becoming a writer who set down, in the purest
English of his time, the thoughts and fantasies of an individual mind
playing over the common problems of our age. What made him
exceptional . . . was the fact that he also tried to work out his
theories in action and then to give his actions shape in literature."
(D.P.)

O 541 Yorks, Samuel A., "George Orwell: Seer over His Shoulder,"
Bucknell Review, 9:32-45, March, 1960.

Although obviously and avowedly committed to didacticism, Orwell's
art derives its real power from its emotive qualities, its ability to
create a real feeling of grime, squalor, and discomfort. (M.H.M.)

ANIMAL FARM

O 542 Davis, Robert Murray, "Politics in the Pig-pen," Journal of
Popular Culture, 2:314-20, Fall, 1968.

Orwell's Animal Farm "represents a major shift in his fictional
method from reportage to fable. . . . it seems plausible . . . that
the form and many of the details of Animal Farm were influenced by
an American children's book, Wiggins for President." (D.P.)

O 543 Gulbin, Suzanne, "Parallels and Contrasts in Lord of the Flies and
Animal Farm," English Journal, 55:86-90, 92, January, 1966.

Orwell's Animal Farm and Golding's Lord of the Flies share striking
similarities in theme, setting, motivation; they share significant incidents of bloodshed which motivate breakdown of established order;

ANIMAL FARM   (cont'd)

they share conflict for leadership, key henchmen to enforce compli-
ance, one character with mystic insight into situations, comparable
symbols, and parallel use of irony. However, whether Golding was
directly influenced by Orwell is still conjectural. (D.P.)

O 544   Lee, Robert A., "The Uses of Form: A Reading of Animal Farm,"
Studies in Short Fiction, 6:557-73, Fall, 1969.

Orwell's choice of the beast fable precluded his former role as
polemicist. His need to attack social evils could be subsumed into
an artistic mode which by its very nature provided irony and contrast,
and, hence, criticism. (B.K.N.)

BURMESE DAYS

O 545   Lee, Robert A., "Symbol and Structure in Burmese Days: A Revaluation," Texas Studies in Literature and Language, 11:819-35,
1969.

"Both Orwell's character and his political acumen are worthy of the
highest praise, but it is time to appreciate his imaginative creations
for the same qualities we look for in any other artist." (H.S.)

O 546   Meyers, Jeffrey, "The Ethics of Responsibility: Orwell's Burmese
Days," University Review, 35:83-7, December, 1968.

Orwell is "responsible, active, rejecting the horrors of the modern
world and committing himself to change them." He has a "close
kinship--in his intense feeling of guilt . . . and commitment--to the
French novelists, particularly Malraux and Sartre, who began to
write during the interwar years, the 'age of guilt'." (H.S.)

DOWN AND OUT IN PARIS AND LONDON

O 547   Kubal, David L., "Down and Out in Paris and London: The Conflict
of Art and Politics," Midwest Quarterly, 12:199-209, 1970.

Orwell's "powers of observation and use of detail . . . make Down
and Out more than simply a tract. Throughout the book there is an
underlying moral horror, the presence of a highly sensitive conscience reacting to a diseased society." (H.S.)

DOWN AND OUT IN PARIS AND LONDON   (cont'd)

O 548   Smyer, Richard I., "Loss of Innocence in George Orwell's Down and Out in Paris and London," South Dakota Review, 8:75-83, Winter, 1970.

"To appreciate fully the significance of this early work . . . we must realize that in addition to being a more or less chronologically arranged record of personal experiences with the external, social world, Down and Out is a guilt-burdened expression of lost sexual innocence, a symbolic statement of the narrator's anxiety regarding sensual experience." (D.P.)

ENGLAND, YOUR ENGLAND

O 549   Rogers, Daniel, " 'Look Back in Anger'--to George Orwell," Notes and Queries, 9:310-1, August, 1962.

Jimmy Porter's attacks upon his brother-in-law echo George Orwell's essay "England, Your England." (W.G.F.)

HOMAGE TO CATALONIA

O 550   Edrich, Emanuel, "Naïveté and Simplicity in Orwell's Writing: Homage to Catalonia," University of Kansas City Review, 27:289-97, Summer, 1961.

"To bring his audience to an acceptance of his point of view" [In Homage to Catalonia] Orwell uses to advantage "the exploitation of naïveté." He establishes himself . . . as the innocent but sincere figure . . . victimized by the forces of ruthlessness and chicanery." (R.G.L.)

KEEP THE ASPIDISTRA FLYING

O 551   Kubal, David L., "George Orwell and the Aspidistra," University Review, 37:61-7, October, 1970.

"Keep the Aspidistra Flying . . . very clearly marks George Orwell's transition from protest to commitment." (H.S.)

KEEP THE ASPIDISTRA FLYING   (cont'd)

O 552 Wadsworth, Frank W., "Orwell as Novelist: The Middle Period,"
University of Kansas City Review, 22:189-94, March, 1956.

George Orwell's Keep the Aspidistra Flying is typical in its tale of
a middle class man's struggle to defy the middle class code in order
to find meaning in existence. The novel is also typical in its weaknesses and strengths such as strong attention to detail and sympathy
for those caught in the horrors of middle and lower class existence.
(V.E.)

NINETEEN EIGHTY-FOUR

O 553 Barr, Alan, "The Paradise Behind 1984," English Miscellany,
19:197-203, 1968.

"Central to Christianity is the notion that our earthly lives primarily
anticipate and determine our hereafters. Corollary to this is the
effort to build a heaven on earth. This latter is the hope that Orwell
ironically parades and mercilessly shatters in . . . Nineteen Eighty-
Four." (G.C.)

O 554 Browning, Gordon, "Toward a Set of Standards for Everlasting Anti-
Utopian Fiction," Cithara, 10:18-32, December, 1970.

Examples of the anti-Utopian genre typically include some form of
salutary warning, remote or exotic settings, a considerable degree
of scientific or rational backgrounding, and card-board characters
with ideational or moralistic functions, attempting to become credible
as human beings. Of the genre Zamiatin's We is the most intense,
Huxley's Brave New World the most readable and clever, and Orwell's
1984 the most successful in generating a sense of urgency and terror.
(D.P.)

O 555 Deutscher, Isaac, "1984: Le Mysticisme de la cruauté," Les
Temps Modernes, 114-115:2205-18, June-July, 1955.

1984 lacks originality because Orwell borrowed the idea, intrigue,
characters, symbols, and atmosphere from the Russian writer
Eugenii Zamyatin's novel We. Orwell added the element of sado-
masochism, however, which became the novel's dominant leitmotif.
(L.L.)

3045   O 555

NINETEEN EIGHTY-FOUR   (cont'd)

O 556   Elsbree, Langdon, "The Structured Nightmare of 1984," Twentieth Century Literature, 5:135-41, October, 1959.

"1984 is, then, a shocking and powerful novel which derives much of its forcefulness from its structure as a nightmare in which there is no escape from the grotesque series of images and events. These images and events, each representing a commentary upon the possible fate of humans in an overcentralized economy, increasingly point to the individual's loss of self-identity." (D.P.)

O 557   Geering, R. G., "Darkness at Noon and Nineteen Eighty-Four: A Comparative Study," Australian Quarterly, 30:90-6, September, 1958.

The works of Koestler and Orwell, "which [are] most characteristically exemplified in Darkness at Noon and Nineteen Eighty-Four, [are] primarily analyses of the achievement, the exercise, and the effects of power." However, in Nineteen Eighty-Four, Orwell carries "the analysis of totalitarianism a stage further" than does Koestler in Darkness at Noon. (G.C.)

O 558   Gerber, Richard, "The English Island Myth: Remarks on the Englishness of Utopian Fiction," Critical Quarterly, 1:36-43, Spring, 1959.

"All three great English island fictions [Utopia, Gulliver's Travels, and Robinson Crusoe] are . . . thin: strangely focussing mirrors of abstraction. . . ." Later, "the thin myth of English utopian fiction . . . appears in certain of Wells's works, in Brave New World and in 1984." (D.P.)

O 559   Gleckner, Robert F., "1984 or 1948?" College English, 18:95-9, November, 1956.

Orwell's novel should not be read as a frightening prophecy or simply as an attack on the Soviet system. Its terrors are applicable to our own lives, and it condemns the elimination of "objective truth" in all countries. (E.L.)

NINETEEN EIGHTY-FOUR   (cont'd)

O 560   Harris, Harold J., "Orwell's Essays and 1984," Twentieth Century Literature, 4:154-61, January, 1959.

"Most of the themes and many of the characters in the novel represent a further development of themes dealt with and characters glimpsed in the essays, but the one overwhelming theme in 1984-- the terrible inadequacy of the individual--belongs to that work alone and inheres in its every part." (D.P.)

O 561   Howe, Irving, "The Fiction of Anti-Utopia," New Republic, 146:13-6, April 23, 1962.

"Eugene Zamiatin (We) is a dissident from Communism; George Orwell (1984) is a heterodox socialist; Aldous Huxley (Brave New World) a scion of liberalism. . . . The work of these authors is a systematic release of trauma, a painful turning upon their own presuppositions. It is a fiction of urgent yet reluctant testimony, forced by profoundly serious men from their own resistance to fears they cannot evade." (D.P.)

O 562   Howe, Irving, "Orwell: History as Nightmare," American Scholar, 25:193-207, Spring, 1956.

"How remarkable a book 1984 really is can be discovered only after a second reading. It offers true testimony, it speaks for our time. And because it derives from a perception of how our time may end, it trembles with an eschatological fury that is certain to create among its readers . . . the most powerful kinds of resistance." (H.S.)

O 563   Kegel, Charles H., "Nineteen Eighty-Four: A Century of Ingsoc," Notes and Queries, 10:151-2, April, 1963.

Orwell may have picked the date for the action of his novel because it would mark the centenary of the founding of three major English socialistic organizations. (W.G.F.)

O 564   Kessler, Martin, "Power and the Perfect State: A Study in Disillusionment as Reflected in Orwell's Nineteen Eighty-Four and Huxley's Brave New World," Political Science Quarterly, 72:565-77, December, 1957.

NINETEEN EIGHTY-FOUR   (cont'd)

In Brave New World and Nineteen Eighty-Four "the system works
splendidly . . . precisely because . . . maintenance of the status
quo has become the supreme goal to which all other non-operational
values, such as truth, happiness, freedom, must be and are subordinated. . . . It is against this sort of operational determinism
that Huxley and Orwell rebel." (D.P.)

O 565   Knox, George, "The Divine Comedy in 1984," Western Humanities
Review, 9:371-2, Autumn, 1955.

Many "startling structural and thematic parallels" exist between the
Divine Comedy and Orwell's 1984. (D.P.)

O 566   Lyons, John O., "George Orwell's Opaque Glass in 1984,"
Wisconsin Studies in Contemporary Literature, 2:39-46, Fall, 1961.

Glass, in a reversal of its usual function, is a chief symbol to communicate the limited vision of the conditioned in 1984. Orwell fails
to communicate how the conditioners arrive at their vision. (B.K.)

O 567   Maddison, Michael, "1984: A Burnhamite Fantasy?" Political
Quarterly, 32:71-9, January-March, 1961.

The two main sources for 1984 are Zamyatin's We and James
Burnham's The Managerial Revolution, which furnishes the model
for the twenty-odd pages in the middle of 1984 of The Theory and
Practice of Oligarchical Collectivism by the legendary Emmanuel
Goldstein. (D.P.)

O 568   Malkin, Lawrence, "Halfway to 1984," Horizon, 12:33-9, Spring,
1970.

Orwell's "critics find him gloomy because he returned to classical
stoicism and abandoned progress. But without the relativism of
ideology to organize human affairs, only the stark absolutes of
human character remain. What Orwell is saying is that, now or in
1984, they are the things that really matter." (D.P.)

O 569   Miller, Cecil, "Orwell and Literature," American Scholar, 26:128,
Winter, 1956-57.

"It becomes clear finally that what we are witnessing in [Irving
Howe's] 'Orwell: History as Nightmare,' [AS, Spring, 1956] is not

NINETEEN EIGHTY-FOUR   (cont'd)

an assessment of Orwell's book but a transvaluation of values. . . .
In this process, 1984 is not the subject but a touchstone." (D.P.)

O 570   New, Melvyn, "Ad Nauseam: A Satiric Device in Huxley, Orwell,
and Waugh," Satire Newsletter, 8:24-8, Fall, 1970.

". . . by associating moral corruption with regurgitation, the
satirist makes his moral point dramatically and emphatically. Of
particular interest is the occurrence of this device in . . . Aldous
Huxley's Brave New World, George Orwell's 1984, and Evelyn
Waugh's Vile Bodies. Moreover, in all three works the nausea
occurs in juxtaposition with a clear statement of the author's normative values, in each case expressed by an allusion to Shakespeare.
And finally, in each instance, the nausea seems to be in response to
another character's enthusiastic endorsement of a 'brave new world'."
(D.P.)

O 571   Nott, Kathleen, "Orwell's Nineteen Eighty-Four," Listener,
70:687-8, October 31, 1963.

Orwell's Nineteen Eighty-Four . . . is a work of imagination. Its
political judgments, if any, are expressed symbolically: they are
not realistic analysis or factual description. . . . Nevertheless . . .
his book is to be taken as realistic, a warning, even a prophecy.
Nineteen Eighty-Four was a black Utopia, a threatening fantasy of
the future." (D.P.)

O 572   Ranald, Ralph A., "George Orwell and the Mad World: The Anti-
Universe of 1984," South Atlantic Quarterly, 66:544-53, Autumn,
1967.

1984 depicts a world in which all values are reversed or turned upside down. In this world the only means of communication is through
inflicting or suffering pain. The desired norm suggested by this
satirical anti-world is one in which communication could be through
rational discourse. (J.L.A.)

O 573   Richards, D., "Four Utopias," Slavonic and East European Review,
40:220-8, 1962.

"The purpose of this study is to discuss the ideological connection
between Dostoyevsky's 'Legend of the Grand Inquisitor,' Zamyatin's
My (We), Huxley's Brave New World and Orwell's 1984, examining

NINETEEN EIGHTY-FOUR   (cont'd)

first the two Russian works and then their English successors."
"With the threat of global annihilation in the air Orwell's description
of world war now seems underwritten and the nightmare of Dostoyevsky
and Zamyatin, the rational Utopia--even Huxley's scientific Utopia--
seem not merely unhorrific, but almost attractive."   (D.P.)

O 574   Schmerl, Rudolf B., "Fantasy as Technique," Virginia Quarterly
Review, 43:644-56, Autumn, 1967.

Forster's essay on fantasy "which does not quite define fantasy,
illuminates almost all its relevant elements." Modern political
fantasies--such as Huxley's Brave New World and Orwell's 1984--
"are satiric projections of sociological perspectives, not literary
creations. . . . To suspend disbelief when reading a fantasy may
mean to fail to understand it." (D.P.)

O 575   Smith, Marcus, "The Wall of Blackness: A Psychological Approach
to 1984," Modern Fiction Studies, 14:423-33, Winter, 1968-69.

Orwell's "protagonist" in 1984, Winston Smith, "is clearly and carefully developed along familiar Oedipal lines and an accurate understanding of 1984 must take this into account and consider why he be-
haves the way he does and how this affects the total meaning of
Orwell's novel." (H.S.)

O 576   Thale, Jerome, "Orwell's Modest Proposal," Critical Quarterly,
4:365, 367-8, Winter, 1962.

"The large and immediately applicable political ideas in 1984 . . .
have more often than not been a distraction from the real character
of the novel. . . . What is wrong with the world of 1984, however,
is not so much its political structure as the intolerable quality of its
life; 'it struck him that the truly characteristic thing about modern
life was not its cruelty and insecurity, but simply its bareness, its
dinginess, its listlessness'." (H.S.)

O 577   Voorhees, Richard J., "Nineteen Eighty-Four: No Failure of Nerve,"
College English, 18:101-2, November, 1956.

Orwell, a brave man, and suspicious of political prediction, "did
not turn coward and prophet of doom" in writing 1984. (E.L.)

NINETEEN EIGHTY-FOUR (cont'd)

O 578   Warncke, Wayne, "A Note on 1984," Hartwick Review, 3:60-1,
Fall, 1967.

1984 is a warning against the trend of liberal societies to over
organize life, which denies possibilities of self-fulfillment. Unlike
other anti-utopian novels, 1984 is not ironic. It is, instead, a
demonstration of what could happen; the satire focuses in on man's
vulnerability to tyranny. (D.P.)

O 579   Willison, Ian, "Orwell's Bad Good Books," Twentieth Century,
157:354-66, April, 1955.

Nineteen Eighty-Four depicts the "superiority of the public world
. . . and the utter dereliction of the private consciousness." There
is no "dramatic tension" between the individual and the public world
because the "hero" must capitulate to the "controlled insanity" of
the public point of view. (J.R.B.)

O 580   Woodcock, George, "Utopias in Negative," Sewanee Review,
64:81-97, Winter, 1956.

Zamiatin's We clearly influenced Huxley's Brave New World and
Orwell's 1984 in details and in structure. "Already, in banning . . .
We a generation ago, the Communists showed their realization that
the development of the anti-Utopian novel must end in a direct attack
on their own methods and aims. In 1984 . . . what in Zamiatin was
remote satire on the Communists has now become direct. But . . .
Orwell [also] indicates a general tendency towards the Utopian form
of society. . . . the two aspects--the satirical and prophetic--are
complementary. . . . what gives 1984 its peculiar force is the way
in which it accepts Zamiatin's hints of the continuity between the
present and the possible Utopian future, and shows that these may
be . . . actual parts of a new social structure even now forming
around us." (D.P.)

THE ROAD TO WIGAN PIER

O 581   Hoggart, Richard, "George Orwell and The Road to Wigan Pier,"
Critical Quarterly, 7:72-85, Spring, 1965.

"Wigan Pier, more than any other book of Orwell's, shows a host of
contradictions in his thinking--between an absolutist and a tolerantly
gentle man; between a resilient man . . . and a dark despairer . . .

THE ROAD TO WIGAN PIER   (cont'd)

between a pessimist and an optimist who believed in the eventual triumph of ordinary good sense." (H.S.)

O 582   Wolheim, Richard, "Orwell Reconsidered," Partisan Review, 27:82-97, Winter, 1960.

"What makes The Road to Wigan Pier a piece of journalism isn't its content, nor the urgency with which it is written, nor exactly its style. It is, rather, the particular attitude that the author adopts toward his subject matter." (H.S.)

SHOOTING AN ELEPHANT

O 583   Keskinen, Kenneth, "'Shooting an Elephant': An Essay to Teach," English Journal, 55:669-75, September, 1966.

"Shooting an Elephant," better than 1984 or Animal Farm, reveals Orwell's style and talent as a writer. (H.S.)

WHY I WRITE

O 584   Foley, Joseph, and James Ayer, "Orwell in English and Newspeak: A Computer Translation," College Composition and Communication, 17:15-8, February, 1966.

[Using an IBM computer, the text of George Orwell's essay "Why I Write" was translated into his invented language "Newspeak." Comparative texts are included in this article to show how the uncaring computer can be programmed to corrupt the text, thus illustrating Orwell's point in 1984 about the destruction of language.] (V.E.)

ORY, CARLOS EDMUNDO DE

O 585   Hernández, Antonio, "Carlos Edmundo de Ory," La Estafeta Literaria, No. 433, pp. 13-4, December 1, 1969.

Denounced as the lyrical son of patafísica francesa, Ory is the founder of postismo, together with Eduard Chicharro and Silvano Sernesi. In his poetry all that is finished, concluded and immobile does not exist. (T.T.B.)

OSBORNE, JOHN

O 586 Amette, Jacques-Pierre, "Osborne, Pinter, Saunders & Cie,"
La Nouvelle Revue Française, No. 205, pp. 95-9, January, 1970.

Pinter's theater resembles an aquarium. His ambiguity, double-
meanings and incongruity in a theater of silence resemble a cruel
Chekhov with touches of Freud, whereas Osborne merely borrows
the forms of conventional theater to demolish it with its own
instruments. (T.T.B.)

O 587 Bailey, Shirley Jean, "John Osborne: A Bibliography," Twentieth
Century Literature, 7:118-20, October, 1961.

[The major writings of Osborne are listed--plays, and essays--as
well as an extensive reporting of critical and biographical writings
about Mr. Osborne.] (D.P.)

O 588 Bonnerot, Louis, "John Osborne," Études Anglaises, 10:378-91,
October-December, 1957.

"John Osborne comes from the same spiritual family as J. J.
Rousseau and D. H. Lawrence. With him as with them, it is feeling,
blood, and heart which rules the whole being. . . . The word human
gives us the vibration of all of Osborne's work and is sufficient to
tell him apart from his more intellectual acolytes who are on the
same crusade." (D.-J.J.)

O 589 Brustein, Robert, "The Backward Birds," New Republic, 149:28-31,
October 19, 1963.

"Crude, unsophisticated, unskeptical, the new English dramatists
[Osborne and Wesker] demonstrate that politics and art can no more
be synthesized than doctrine and truth; what their ideology gives
them in vitality, it takes away in complication." (W.F.)

O 590 Deming, Barbara, "John Osborne's War Against the Philistines,"
Hudson Review, 11:411-9, Autumn, 1958.

Osborne frequently substitutes anger and assertion for understanding
and perception. (M.H.)

O 591   Gersh, Gabriel, "The Theater of John Osborne," <u>Modern Drama</u>, 10:137-43, September, 1967.

Osborne has contributed more than anyone else to the last decade of British drama. He has been an author "continuously in search of a style . . . the only convention he has made his own is the tirade." (D. P.)

O 592   Hollis, Christopher, "Keeping Up with the Rices," <u>Spectator</u>, No. 6747, pp. 504-5, October 18, 1957.

"Angry young men" like the playwright Osborne constitute a "revolt of those who have come, as it were, within sight of a literary and cultured life, but who have found themselves barred out from a proper share in that life. It is the revolt of the envious. . . ." (M. H.)

O 593   Hunter, G. K., "The World of John Osborne," <u>Critical Quarterly</u>, 3:76-81, Spring, 1961.

John Osborne has now produced a fair body of work for the interested reader; although each play is different from its predecessors the same themes, notably "the opposition between self-expression and restraint" turn up again and again. Osborne's widely praised " 'truth to life' . . . is obtained only by starting at a point remote from ordinary experi- ence." Finally, "if one is going to be as angry as Mr. Osborne, one must find a target large enough to sustain it. The 'world' of Paul Slickey is too small, too parochial, too monomaniac to convey the important things that Osborne has to say." (D. P.)

O 594   Karrfalt, David H., "The Social Theme in Osborne's Plays," <u>Modern Drama</u>, 13:78-82, May, 1970.

"The great barrier that Osborne believes must be broken down, both in the world of his plays and in the actual world in which those plays are read and are seen performed, is the barrier between those who respond to feeling and those who do not." (H.S.)

O 595   Kennedy, Andrew K., "Old and New in London Now," <u>Modern Drama</u>, 11:437-46, February, 1969.

[This essay discusses and compares the works of Stoppard (<u>The Real Inspector Hound</u> and <u>Rosencrantz and Guildenstern are Dead</u>), Osborne (<u>Time Present</u> and <u>The Hotel in Amsterdam</u>), and Pinter (<u>Landscape</u> and <u>The Homecoming</u>).] (H.S.)

O 595   3054

O 596   Lahr, John, "Poor Johnny One Note," Evergreen Review, 12:61-3, 93-5, December, 1968.

"At thirty-eight, twelve years after his initial success, Osborne's latest plays, Time Present and The Hotel in Amsterdam, show his literary muscle turning to flab, his ruthless self-examination going to sleep amidst his now lavish surroundings." Osborne "is not a master of ambiguity, but of statement; he does not know the articulateness of silence but the bravura of theatrical speech. His texts are loose, strangely undisciplined; he mismanages language instead of infusing it with greater clarity." (D.P.)

O 597   Nicoll, Allardyce, "Somewhat in a New Dimension," Contemporary Theatre, 20:77-95, 1963.

Although Osborne's Look Back in Anger is generally viewed as "a turning point in the history of the modern British theatre," actually the dramatic themes advanced by Osborne, Wesker, Pinter and others bear important and fundamental similarities to those of the playwrights of the Edwardian and early Georgian periods. (D.P.)

O 598   Scott-Kilvert, Ian, "The Hero in Search of a Dramatist: The Plays of John Osborne," Encounter, 9:26-30, December, 1957.

Although he has effectively voiced the new standards of the post-war British young people, Mr. Osborne's growth will be limited unless he begins to take as his subjects, heroes from a "wider range of human action and interests." (D.B.D.)

O 599   Sigal, Clancy, "Looking Back Without Anger," Commonweal, 92:186-8, May 8, 1970.

In the late '50's "angry" included "almost every writer in Britain under 40. . . ." Later, under the pressure of events "the 'angry' artists began to disperse--but not to disappear." Among those still active are John Osborne, Kenneth Tynan, Kingsley Amis, Lindsay Anderson, John Braine, Shelagh Delaney, Bernard Kops, Doris Lessing, Christophe Logue, Joan Littlewood, Karel Reisz, Tony Richardson, Alan Sillitoe, John Wain, and Arnold Wesker. (D.P.)

O 600   Worth, Katherine J., "Shaw and John Osborne," Shavian, 2:29-35, No. 10, 1964.

Although "the Socialist element in Osborne's drama is at first sight the single feature of his work most strikingly reminiscent of Shaw," the two playwrights also share affinities in rhetorical power, capacity for detachment, interest in the sexually bizarre and unorthodox, habits of distributing dramatic sympathy, and in the way they "create opportunities for their actors to . . . do turns, improvise, dress up, strike attitudes and play the fool." Indeed, more than any other recent playwright, Osborne shares with Shaw his "special blend of serious social purpose and exuberant theatrical display." (D.P.)

LOOK BACK IN ANGER

O 601   Barker, Clive, "Look Back in Anger--The Turning Point: An Assessment of the Importance of John Osborne's First Play in the Development of British Theatre," Zeitschrift für Anglistik und Amerikanistik, 14:367-71, 1966.

Look Back in Anger bridged the gap between the old school, a theatre based on emotional rather than social relationships of characters, and the new school, in which the social situation of the characters is accurately observed and recorded. (A.S.W.)

O 602   Dyson, A. E., "Look Back in Anger," Critical Quarterly, 1:318-26, Winter, 1959.

"Look Back in Anger is a play which increases understanding both of the tormented and their torments," reminding "us what our rebel moralists are apt to be like, and of the strange mingling of sensitivity and cruelty, insight and wilfulness, idealism and cynicism in their make-up that can make life terrible for those who know them, and yet offer rewards as well." (J.N.P.)

O 603   Faber, M. D., "The Character of Jimmy Porter: An Approach to Look Back in Anger," Modern Drama, 13:67-77, May, 1970.

"What Look Back in Anger actually presents us with is an orally fixated neurotic who projects his own psychological shortcomings onto the external environment." The story "vividly demonstrates the impossibility of detaching Jimmy's . . . social and political attitudes from the requirements of the unconscious mind." (H.S.)

O 604   Graef, Hilda, "Why All This Anger?" Catholic World, 188:122-8, November, 1958.

[This is an essay, dealing with the concept of "anger" in John Osborne's Look Back in Anger. The play "may well be considered the essence of all that our 'angry young men' stand for--or against."] (H.S.)

LOOK BACK IN ANGER   (cont'd)

O 605   Graham, John, "A Tale of a Stifling Dog," Tamarack Review, 7:53-67, Spring, 1958.

The Australian Ray Lawler's play The Summer of the Seventeenth Doll, is more successful than Osborne's Look Back in Anger because Lawler concentrates more on characterization based on a well-formulated concept of the nature of life. John Osborne fails because he does not, like Lawler, portray characters who are caught in the "old net of passion, fear, pride, and delusion" that has always been the subject matter for great drama.   (D.E.W.)

O 606   Huss, Roy, "John Osborne's Backward Half-Way Look," Modern Drama, 6:20-5, May, 1963.

"No matter how influential Osborne's role has been in staking out a path of social protests for other dramatists and novelists to follow, in . . . Look Back in Anger . . . he fails to give a dramatic context to such themes."   (H.S.)

O 607   Rogers, Daniel, "'Look Back in Anger'--to George Orwell," Notes and Queries, 9:310-1, August, 1962.

Jimmy Porter's attacks upon his brother-in-law echo George Orwell's essay "England, Your England." (W.G.F.)

O 608   Rollins, Ronald G., "Carroll and Osborne: Alice and Alison in Wild Wonderlands," Forum (Houston), 7:16-20, Summer, 1969.

Osborne uses Lewis Carroll's Alice's Adventures in Wonderland "as an archaic prototype, as an analogy which frequently duplicates and illuminates the action as recorded in Look Back in Anger." (G.C.)

O 609   Spacks, Patricia Meyer, "Confrontation and Escape in Two Social Dramas," Modern Drama, 11:61-72, May, 1968.

A comparison of A Doll's House and Look Back in Anger shows Osborne less successful than Ibsen in clearly portraying his characters and their meanings. (R.C.B.)

LOOK BACK IN ANGER   (cont'd)

O 610   Weiss, Samuel A., "Osborne's Angry Young Play," Educational
Theatre Journal, 12:285-8, December, 1960.

"On first view, Look Back in Anger suffers from the apparent chaos
of its hero's emotional distemper. But on close analysis the play
takes on a coherence and shape that reveals a tight core of related
thinking and feeling." (H.S.)

LUTHER

O 611   Dennis, Nigel, "Out of the Box," Encounter, 17:51-3, August, 1961.

"Mr. John Osborne's Luther is not a pioneer work; it is an act of
consolidation. . . . It is the form of the biography, the epic, and
many novels; it is 'chapters' strung together with selected 'intervals'
for whisky and the powder-room; it is also a free verse, with the
poet looking only to himself for his disciplines and bound by nothing
. . . but historical respect." (H.S.)

O 612   Denty, Vera D., "The Psychology of Martin Luther," Catholic
World, 194:99-105, November, 1961.

"Although based on considerable research, Luther is neither a
historical, religious nor polemic play; rather it is a character study
strongly influenced by twentieth-century psychological concepts and
Brechtian theater technique. Each scene reveals Luther's character
development, which is primarily that of a rebel and almost accidentally that of a social revolutionary." (H.S.)

O 613   Marowitz, Charles, "The Ascension of John Osborne," Tulane
Drama Review, 7:175-9, Winter, 1962.

Luther, while marred by structural and intellectual shortcomings,
proves that Osborne has "the ability to grasp dramatic ideas and the
language to convey them on a hard, bright poetic level." (W.A.F.)

O 614   O'Brien, Charles H., "Osborne's Luther and the Humanistic
Tradition," Renascence, 21:59-63, Winter, 1969.

Osborne's play "restates traditional humanistic views of the Reformation with a peculiarly modern stress on the unconscious forces in
Luther's psyche and on the Reformation's failure in dealing with
social protest." (S.A.)

LUTHER   (cont'd)

O 615   Rosselli, John, "At Home with Lucifer," Reporter, 25:50-3,
October 12, 1961.

"Luther shows that Osborne has extended his grasp and come nearer
than before to writing a play that is a whole satisfying shape rather
than a string of effective scenes, but his fingers can still slip."
(R.J.G.)

O 616   Rupp, Gordon, "Luther and Mr. Osborne," Cambridge Quarterly,
1:28-42, Winter, 1965-66.

"There are in this play . . . fine insights, great obtuseness." "As
we listen to this highly complicated psychological interpretation read
into or out of chancy little bits of historical evidence which have haphazardly survived, we wonder whether it wouldn't be simpler in the
end to think that perhaps Christian theology has some meaning: that
the language of the Church might after all have the more important
clues." (D.A.B.)

TOM JONES

O 617   Battestin, Martin C., "Osborne's Tom Jones: Adapting a Classic,"
Virginia Quarterly Review, 42:378-93, Summer, 1966.

"It is pleasant to think of this film, a comic masterpiece of our new
Age of Satire, standing in the same relation to Fielding's classic,
as, say, Pope's free imitations of Horace stand in relation to their
original. In an impressive variety of ways, both technical and
thematic, Osborne and Fielding's Tom Jones is a triumph in the
creative adaptation of a novel to the very different medium of the
cinema." (H.S.)

THE WORLD OF PAUL SLICKEY

O 618   Findlater, Richard, "The Case of P. Slickey," Twentieth Century,
167:29-38, January, 1960.

In The World of Paul Slickey "Osborne deserves the highest praise
for setting out to stretch the musical to such limits, for his boldness
in challenging the preconceived ideas of London audiences, for his
enterprise in attempting so much so soon. Yet . . . the writing is
too often slack, stale, and forcible-feeble work. . . ." Also, the
author "is apparently unable to write singable and scannable lyrics"
and the score is disastrous. (D.P.)

OSORIO, MIGUEL ÁNGEL

O 619　Echeverri Mejía, Oscar, "Porfirio Barba Jacob, caballero de la angustia," La Estafeta Literaria, No. 364, pp.8-9, February, 1967.

Barba Jacob, among present-century Colombian poets, is one of the greatest importance. His life is depicted in his style and technique, particularly his childhood, voyages and many changes of name. (T.T.B.)

OSTENSO, MARTHA

O 620　Mullins, S. G., "Some Remarks on Theme in Martha Ostenso's Wild Geese," Culture, 23:359-62, 1962.

The "influence" and "literary significance" of this novel "rest on its exceptionally well-developed theme and on the successful integration of this theme . . . [that] materialism cannot supply nor . . . substitute for happiness . . . by means of symbol and exemplification, in the structure of the novel." (G.C.)

OSTER, PIERRE

O 621　Chessex, Jacques, "La Grande Année ou quelques remarques sur Pierre Oster," La Nouvelle Revue Française, 12e année No. 144, pp. 1068-72, December, 1964.

Oster is a poet whose voice has the power to impose his universe instantaneously, a universe of which he is the sole and irreplaceable witness. He shares this privilege with the greatest, with poets as different as Claudel, Éluard or Char. (T.T.B.)

OWEN, WALTER

O 622　Tinker, Edward Larocque, "Walter Owen: Interpreter of Spanish Epic Poetry," Books Abroad, 29:289-93, Summer, 1955.

In his translations of Martín Fierro, Owen achieved his aim of presenting "Spanish epics that read like original English poems," with the diction and idiom of the time. (F.F.E.)

OWEN, WILFRED

O 623   Cohen, Joseph, "Critic's Key: Poem or Personality: An Aubade,"
English Literature in Transition, 12:96-7, No. 2, 1969.

Rather than discussing matters of fact or interpretation, or differing
critical approaches or conclusions, Gertrude White ("Critic's Key:
Poem or Personality?" ELT, 11:174-9, No. 3, 1968) has chosen to
launch an "uncalled-for acrimonious personal attack" on me for
reasons which remain incomprehensible. There is "plenty of room
for new work on Owen" and her new insights (if any) would be welcome. (D.P.)

O 624   Cohen, Joseph, "In Memory of W. B. Yeats--and Wilfred Owen,"
Journal of English and Germanic Philology, 58:637-49, October, 1959.

Yeats's exclusion of Wilfred Owen's poetry from his Oxford Book of
Modern Verse was not so much on the basis of personal animosity,
but in support of a poetic principle no longer popular. Yeats objected
to Owen's "excessively Romantic diction," and to his successful
contention through his poetry of grounds other than "the joy of battle"
as themes for war poetry. (D.P.)

O 625   Cohen, Joseph, "Owen Agonistes," English Literature in Transition, 8:253-68, No. 5, 1965.

"Any final assessment of Owen's achievement must now take into
account the strong evidence that he was 'an idealistic homosexual
with a religious background.' His homosexual proclivities play a
major role in the expression of anger and pity and their presence
cannot be denied." (D.P.)

O 626   Cohen, Joseph, "Wilfred Owen: Fresher Fields than Flanders,"
English Literature in Transition, 7:1-7, No. 1, 1964.

Wilfred Owen's first rank among the minor English poets is now
assured, and the body of his poetry, except for some juvenilia, is
now in print. Unfortunately, the early editions of his poetry were
corrupted through editorial inadequacies. Even the Day-Lewis
edition, claimed as authoritative, relied heavily on Blunden's substitutions and conflations. (D.P.)

O 627 Cohen, Joseph, "Wilfred Owen in America," Prairie Schooner, 31:339-45, Winter, 1957.

Wilfred Owen's reputation with American poets and critics rests on their "realization that his verses captured and expressed the essence of twentieth century war, i. e., its totality, with more clarity, forcefulness, compassion and accomplishment than did the verse of his contemporaries." Unfortunately, this appreciation has yet to be shared by the American public. (D.P.)

O 628 Cohen, Joseph, "Wilfred Owen's Greater Love," Tulane Studies in English, 6:105-17, 1956.

". . . Owen was above all a spiritual poet. . . . The distinguishing spiritual element in his poetry is a thoroughly developed religious concept which he called the greater love. Its source . . . is to be found in the impact on his thinking made by the life of Jesus." "It is my belief that Owen's ultimate status . . . must rest primarily on his orthodox evocation of the greater love." (D.P.)

O 629 Fletcher, John, "Wilfred Owen Re-edited," Études Anglaises, 17:171-8, April-June, 1964.

Recent studies and editions make study of Owen's work easy and fruitful. He is a master of irony, image and symbol and the best poet to come out of WWI. (C.E.N.)

O 630 Fowler, Albert, "The Pity is the Music: Benjamin Britten's War Requiem," Approach, No. 50, pp. 40-4, Winter, 1964.

Benjamin Britten's use of Owen's poetry in the War Requiem joins him with Owen's statement: My Subject is War, and the Pity of War." Where Owen said, "The poetry is the pity," Britten says, "The music is the pity." (A.F.)

O 631 Freeman, Rosemary, "Parody as a Literary Form: George Herbert and Wilfred Owen," Essays in Criticism, 13:307-22, October, 1963.

"By both George Herbert and Wilfred Owen certain styles of poetry were successfully directed into a new framework with the preservation of the evocative qualities of the form to which they had first belonged. Both adopt the formulae of love poetry but direct them to other occasions. The principle is a principle of parody. . . . The impression is not ironic, only suggestive of a more profound meaning." (D.P.)

O 632   Hazo, Samuel J., "The Passion of Wilfred Owen," <u>Renascence</u>, 11:201-8, Summer, 1959.

Owen is more than a "war poet" because "in his best poems, which are his testament, he has transfigured rather than narrowed this experience." (K. L.)

O 633   Masson, David I., "Wilfred Owen's Free Phonetic Patterns: Their Style and Function," <u>Journal of Aesthetics and Art Criticism</u>, 13:360-9, March, 1955.

In Owen's poetry, the "internal alliterative/assonant patterns with their kinesthetic and musical shapefulness, function (like the verbal mythopoeia) as a counter-affirmation. They compensate for Owen's discordant half-rhymes . . . support the heroic affirmations in his poetry . . . form a litany or charm against 'panic and emptiness'." (L. L.)

O 634   Spear, Hilda, "Wilfred Owen and Poetic Truth," <u>University of Kansas City Review</u>, 25:110-6, Winter, 1958.

Owen's poetry reflects his spiritual development. His early work was modelled upon that of the Romantics, but the war caused him "to interpret things afresh." He rejected conventional ideas of heroism, maintaining that true heroes were those who laid down their lives without hate. (G. K.)

O 635   Stallworthy, Jon, "W. B. Yeats and Wilfred Owen," <u>Critical Quarterly</u>, 11:199-214, Autumn, 1969.

"Undistracted by compassion, unmoved by the prospect of suffering, [Yeats] . . . sees, and accepts, the rise and fall of civilizations, the loosing of 'the blood dimmed tide,' with less emotion than the young Wilfred Owen. . . . So Yeats, the poet of distance, past and future, failed to recognize the poet of the foreground, the here and now; Owen. . . ." (K. M. W.)

O 636   White, Gertrude M., "Critic's Key: Poem or Personality?" <u>English Literature in Transition</u>, 11:174-9, No. 3, 1968.

The question of whether the details of Wilfred Owen's life furnish evidence of latent homosexuality supplies no key to Owen's poetry, and leaves untouched the reality, the impact, and the integrity of his poems. (A. S. W.)

O 637 White, William, "Wilfred Owen (1893-1918): A Bibliography,"
Serif, 2:5-16, December, 1965.

[Previously uncollected articles, reviews, etc. of Wilfred Owen are
compiled for the first time, along with an up-date of the bibliographical material found in Welland's 1963 study of the poet.] (V.E.)

O 638 White, William, "Wilfred Owen: Bibliographical Notes and Addenda,"
Serif, 7:25-7, March, 1970.

[This is an updating of "the Wilfred Owen bibliography, published in
book form in The Serif Series: Bibliographies and Checklists (Kent,
Ohio: Kent State University Press, 1967), including a number of
items which were not in the original _Serif_ list. . . ."] (D.A.B.)

ALL SOUNDS HAVE BEEN AS MUSIC

O 639 Bentley, Christopher, "Wilfred Owen and Gustave Flaubert,"
Notes and Queries, 17:456-7, December, 1970.

Critics have suggested the influence of Jules Romaine and Laurent
Tailhade on the writings of Wilfred Owen. Two apparent reminiscences from _Madame Bovary_ in Owen's fragment "All Sounds Have
Been As Music" suggest the need to identify further French influences on the poetry of Owen. (D.P.)

GREATER LOVE

O 640 Freeman, Rosemary, "Wilfred Owen's 'Greater Love'," _Essays in
Criticism_, 16:132-3, January, 1966.

James J. Hill's "suggestion that the biblical allusion at the end of
'Greater Love' (_Essays in Criticism_ 15:476-7) is better identified
with Christ's rebuke to the woman of Jerusalem in St. Luke 23:28-9"
is too literal. The last line is deliberately ambiguous to allow Owen
to reinforce "the contrast between the sacrifice of death in the soldiers and the 'beauty and purity of life.'. . ." (D.P.)

O 641 Hill, James J., Jr., "Wilfred Owen's 'Greater Love'," _Essays in
Criticism_, 15:476-7, October, 1965.

". . . the poem's final line implicitly reinforces the tragic irony
that death has more real value than life by ironically devaluating
the natural consequence of a woman's love, i.e. giving birth to
new life." (K.M.W.)

PURPLE

O 642 Hill, James J., Jr., "The Text of Wilfred Owen's 'Purple'," <u>Notes and Queries</u>, 10:464, December, 1963.

"C. Day Lewis's gloss . . . on the word <u>King</u> in line 10 of Wilfred Owen's poem 'Purple' is unnecessary because of the existence of the poet's own manuscript authority for the word. On an early draft of the poem the word <u>King</u> is clearly legible. . . ." (K.M.W.)

THE SHOW

O 643 Cohen, Joseph, "Owen's 'The Show'," <u>Explicator</u>, 16: Item 8, November, 1957.

The poem combines images from <u>The Dynasts</u> and from Yeats's poem, "The Shadowy Waters." (B.K.)

STRANGE MEETING

O 644 Gose, Elliott B., Jr., "Digging In: An Interpretation of Wilfred Owen's 'Strange Meeting'," <u>College English</u>, 22:417-9, March, 1961.

In "Strange Meeting" "Owen achieves 'aesthetic distance' and 'universality' by means of descent into the unconscious where a strange meeting of external and internal man takes place." (M.J.O.)

OWENS, WILLIAM A.

O 645 Owens, William A., "Writing a Novel: Problem and Solution," <u>Southwest Review</u>, 40:254-61, Summer, 1955.

Owens's novel <u>Walking on Borrowed Land</u> grew out of his southern childhood. The unusual case of a white man writing a novel about negroes reflected Owens's desire as a novelist to make others see and know and understand a way of life. The novel's success is due to his ability to submerge himself into his characters and their way of life. (V.E.)

PAGNOL, MARCEL

P1   Achard, Marcel, "Marcel Pagnol mon ami," À La Page, No. 26, pp. 1142-60, August, 1966.

Although Topaze is a marvelous dramatic feat, it is inferior to Marius, Fanny and César. As film producer and author, Pagnol has given an authentic masterpiece in La Femme du boulanger. Some critics believe he has found his forte in the novel; however, this is a debatable question. (T.T.B.)

P2   Koëlla, Charles E., "The Teachers's Gallery of Marcel Pagnol," Modern Language Journal, 40:405-8, November, 1956.

No one in French literature has given us such an animated gallery of pedagogues, from the teacher at a children's school (Topaze) to the University professor (Jazz), as has Marcel Pagnol in his plays and film scripts. (W.G.F.)

P3   Pagnol, Marcel, "Comment est né 'Monsieur' Topaze," À La Page, No. 8, pp. 246-76, February, 1965.

[These are souvenirs of Jacques Théry, André Malraux, André Antoine, Vincent Scotto, etc. during the 1920's. The origin of the character Topaze was inspired by Pagnol's father with additions drawn from the conversation of his father with friends.] (T.T.B.)

P4   Pagnol, Marcel, "Mes débuts d'auteur dramatique," À La Page, No. 2, pp. 20-7, August, 1964.

[These are souvenirs of Pagnol, from professor to playwright, tracing the influence of Paul Nivorix, J.-P. Liausu and Robert de Thiac on his early plays.] (T.T.B.)

P 5   Pagnol, Marcel, "Mes débuts au cinéma," <u>À La Page</u>, No. 31, pp. 79-106, January, 1967.

[These are memoirs of Pagnol concerning his beginnings as a movie writer and his experiences with Raimu, Alex Korda, Robert T. Kane, etc.] (T.T.B.)

P 6   Vial, Fernand, "Provence and Provençals in the Works of Marcel Pagnol," <u>American Society of Legion of Honor Magazine</u>, 35:29-47, No. 1, 1964.

Provence "has furnished [modern] French literature with a striking array of singular types." Among these authors Pagnol's treatment of Provence is notable for the truthfulness of his portraits. His characters in his plays <u>Marius</u>, <u>Fanny</u> and <u>César</u>, his autobiographical <u>Souvenirs d'enfance</u>, and his novel <u>L'Eau des collines</u>, are "lively, good fellows at heart, prompt to anger and equally prompt to forgiveness. There is, of course, a caricatural element in Pagnol's picture and many burlesque scenes, but they are only exaggerations of authentic aspects. . . ." (D.P.)

SOUVENIRS D'ENFANCE

P 7   Caldecott, C. E. J., " 'Cigale ou fourmi'? Pagnol as an Auto-biographer," <u>Modern Languages</u>, 50:152-60, December, 1969.

Marcel Pagnol's <u>Souvenirs d'enfance</u>, although autobiography, surprises with "lyrical self-expression" as he recounts experiences of his youth which were eventually incorporated into his novels. The work is "a clear, consistent portrait of the writer in his youth." (P.M.C.)

PALACIO VALDÉS, ARMANDO

P 8   Childers, J. Wesley, "Sources of Palacio Valdés's 'Las burbujas'," <u>Hispania</u>, 41:181-5, May, 1958.

The principal sources of Palacio Valdés's short story, "Las burbujas," "are found in variants of the ancient Grecian legend about the cranes of Ibycus, which reappear in Arabic, general European, and Spanish folklore. (A.C.H.)

PALMA, RICARDO

P9   Monguió, Luis, "Sobre un milagro en Meléndez, Palma y Barrios,"
      Revista Hispánica Moderna, 22:1-11, January, 1956.

      Of a miracle attributed to Friar Martín de Porres, Meléndez gives
      an impression of truth and devotion in Tesoros verdaderos de las
      Indias; Palma's technique of the Tradiciones peruanas communicates
      his skepticism in Los ratones de Fray Martín; Barrios's psycho-
      logical curiosity focused on miraculous phenomena helps to reveal
      the characters of El hermano asno. (A.C.H.)

P10   Reedy, Daniel R., "Las 'Tradiciones en salsa verde' de Ricardo
      Palma," Revista Iberoamericana, 32:69-77, 1966.

      These unpublished short pieces are structurally similar to Palma's
      other "tradiciones." However, their outstanding characteristic is
      their piquant, even scabrous, humor. (C.O.)

P11   Rubman, Lewis H., "Ricardo Palma y el problema de la poesía
      romántica," Revista Iberoamericana, 32:113-21, 1966.

      For Palma, poetry is a romantic extravagance at once appealing and
      unworthy of trust. He never resolves, as does Heine, the two oppos-
      ing tendencies within his work. (C.O.)

P12   Schraibman, Joseph, "An Unpublished Letter from Galdós to Ricardo
      Palma," Hispanic Review, 32:65-8, January, 1964.

      [The letter published here "is Galdós's first published letter to a
      Latin-American writer. . . . The letter is by far Galdós's longest
      . . . and offers a most interesting testimony . . . of his literary
      modus operandi and of certain traits of personal psychology."]
      (D.P.)

      PALMER, EDWARD VANCE--See
      PALMER, VANCE

      PALMER, HERBERT

P13   Stanford, Derek, "Herbert Palmer: 'Twentieth-Century Isaiah',"
      Poetry Review, 49:224-7, 1958.

      Herbert Palmer's poetry exhibits a wide range of expression. His
      verse collection The Old Knight presents indignation, grief, humor

and melancholy. The Ride From Hell, which is his "most closely unified volume," consists of twelve pieces, a prologue and epilogue, a page of epigraphs, and notes. It is a "colloquy of the spirit with God and of man's heart and mind with his own sense of evil." The Ride From Hell is a book with vitality, clarity, and power. (V.E.)

PALMER, JANET GERTRUDE--See
PALMER, NETTIE

PALMER, NETTIE

P14   Hope, A. D., et al, "The Prose of Nettie Palmer," Meanjin Quarterly, 18:225-38, July, 1959.

"It has been Nettie Palmer's greatest strength as a writer and as a person that she has always taken her status as a complete human being for granted; and so she has been able to capture the best out of each environment in which she has found herself. . . ." (G.C.)

P15   Hotimsky, C. M., and Walter Stone, "A Bibliographical Checklist," Meanjin Quarterly, 18:264-9, July, 1959.

[This is a bibliography of works and articles on the Palmers, including a selected checklist of their contributions to the Sydney Bulletin, 1916-1937 and Meanjin, 1941-1959.] (G.C.)

PALMER, VANCE

P16   Barnes, John, "The Man of Letters," Meanjin Quarterly, 18:193-205, July, 1959.

Palmer's fiction is "an important contribution to Australian literature in three respects: it is based on a mature feeling of nationality; it is distinguished by a sure sense of form and artistry; and it explores the inner realities of ordinary life in a way unattempted by any other Australian novelist." (G.C.)

P17   Fitzpatrick, Brian, "The Palmer Pre-eminence," Meanjin Quarterly, 18:211-7, July, 1959.

Vance and Nettie Palmer "pervade the Australian climate of opinion and taste. . . ." Vance Palmer has an "ability to be always contemporary and interested." He and his wife have been responsible for historical work on Australian situations and personages. Nettie has also written literary biography and memoirs. The Palmers are in

the "select small company of estimable twentieth century biographers
and historians who have animated the 'great empty spaces' of the
Australian past." (V.E.)

P18   Hotimsky, C. M., and Walter Stone, "A Bibliographical Checklist,"
Meanjin Quarterly, 18:264-9, July, 1959.

[This is a bibliography of works by and articles on the Palmers,
including a selected checklist of their contributions to the Sydney
Bulletin, 1916-1937 and Meanjin, 1941-1959.] (G.C.)

P19   Lindsay, Jack, "The Novels," Meanjin Quarterly, 18:146-72,
July, 1959.

"In this essay I hope to examine the novels [of Vance Palmer] and
assess how deep the artistic truth, how fully the works accord with
the rhythms and patterns of national development." (G.C.)

P20   Macartney, Keith, "The Plays," Meanjin Quarterly, 18:182-92,
July, 1959.

Vance Palmer's plays are "perhaps more significant for . . .
potentialities than for . . . actual achievement." Palmer's best
known plays are found in an anthology called The Black Horse. The
title play is perhaps the "most successful of all Palmer's dramas."
The Prisoner, Travellers, and Telling Mrs. Baker are less successful. Hail Tomorrow is a four act play concerning the Queensland
shearer's strike of the 90's. As a social document the play is important, and the characters are natural, but the play is not too successful as drama. The "parts are better than the whole." (V.E.)

P21   Moore, T. Inglis, "Vance Palmer's Aid to Writers," Meanjin
Quarterly, 18:206-10, July, 1959.

Palmer gave "inspiration to writers by standing foursquare for the
highest literary values, by giving writers personal help and guidance,
and by working unremittingly to advance our literary development."
(G.C.)

P22   Palmer, Nettie, "Remembrance of Things Past," Meanjin Quarterly,
20:297-301, September, 1961.

[These are recollections of Nettie Palmer concerning her marriage
to Vance Palmer in England shortly before the first World War, of
their two visits to France, and of their return to England as mobiliza-

tion for the war began, and of Vance and Nettie's writings at the time.] (D.P.)

P23   Phillips, A., "The Short Stories[of Vance Palmer]," Meanjin Quarterly, 18:173-81, July, 1959.

Vance Palmer's earliest short stories are characterized by purity of line, undecorated; they are strongly Australian in tone. Later, he moved from "an anecdotal to a psychological or symbolic emphasis," still drawing his "nourishment from the roots of the Australian imagination." (D.P.)

P24   Ward, Russel, et al, "Vance Palmer: Homo Australiensis," Meanjin Quarterly, 18:239-63, July, 1959.

Vance Palmer may be remembered as a writer who "did more than any other man to explore and illuminate the nature of this 'elusive quality residing in Australians'." Palmer takes his nationality for granted and his work is a "truer and more profound reflection of contemporary Australian life" because of this fact. Palmer's characters are farmers, fishermen, school teachers and workingmen, and in them resides the "elusive quality" which contains the "essence of Australianism." [Eleven Australian writers here give opinions of Palmer.] (V.E.)

GOLCONDA

P25   Hope, A. D., "Vance Palmer Reconsidered," Southerly, 16:203-9, 1955.

In his unfavorable review of Vance Palmer's Golconda, McKellar missed the point of the novel. Though Palmer's characters are unreal, they are not unrealistic. They lack life, but not liveliness. By comparing Golconda with the complementary The Passage the point of Palmer's novels can be seen. Palmer stresses the dominance of "place and scene in Australian life." As a novelist he rejects intimacy and dramatic intensity for his poet's vision. (V.E.)

PANNWITZ, RUDOLF

P26   Weltmann, Lutz, "Eminent European: An Approach to the Work of Rudolf Pannwitz," German Life and Letters, 9:306-12, July, 1956.

"The way in which Dante had absorbed the oriental elements of European culture in his Commedia was an example to Pannwitz.

Goethe's religion of 'Gottes ist der Orient, Gottes is der Okzident'
--is an integral part of Pannwitz's Weltanschauung. His writings
. . . aim at the rejuvenation of our civilization." (L. L.)

PANOVA, VERA

P27   Lampert, Katherine, "A Propos of Vera Panova," Gemini, pp. 38-9,
January, 1960.

The novels of Vera Panova may be surveyed on the premise that "The
Soviet writer is a human being before he is Soviet, and he writes out
of his own temperament; but he writes inside the Soviet milieu: it is
a part of him and he is a part of it." Contradictory critical estimate
of Panova is evidence of the complexity and stimulation in the current
Soviet Literary scene. (K. M.)

PAPINI, GIOVANNI

P28   Golino, Carlo L., "Giovanni Papini and American Pragmatism,"
Italica, 32:38-48, March, 1955.

". . . the particular overtone of the necessity of action which is
fundamental in Pragmatism did have definite repercussions on the
Italian scene through the personalities of Papini and the other members of Leonardo, and this gave a powerful jolt to . . . the somnolent
provincialism which had affected a great part of Italian cultural life
to that time." (G. C.)

P29   Livi, François, "Les Bonnes Adresses du passé," La Table Ronde,
No. 231, pp. 129-32, April, 1967.

For fifty years Papini played a major role in Italian intellectual life.
In turn philosopher, poet, essayist, acrid and unjust critic, polemicist, he incorporated the worries and gropings of a whole generation.
Like Curzio Malaparte, he was a man at grips with the contradictions
of life. (T. T. B.)

P30   Maranzana, Mother Clelia, "Papini: Warrior at Rest," Catholic
World, 186:45-9, October, 1957.

[This is an admiring discussion of Papini's life, work and religious
conviction.] (G. C.)

P31   Montagna, Gianni, "Papini: L'Homme, son oeuvre, son évolution spirituelle," Les Lettres Romanes, 12:19-34, February, 1958.

[This is a review of Papini's life and conversion to Catholicism, together with a short discussion of his major books.] (K. L.)

LE BUFFONATE

P32   Wilson, Lawrence A., "The Possible Original of Papini's Dottor Alberto Rego," Italica, 38:296-301, December, 1961.

Dottor Alberto Rego of La Gatta pensante, the twelfth of "twenty amusing pieces" published in 1914 "under the descriptive title Le Buffonate," is modeled after Enrico Ferri, "one of the most influential Italian positivists and originator of criminal sociology." (G. C.)

THE DEVIL--See
IL DIAVOLO

IL DIAVOLO

P33   Gullace, Giovanni, "Giovanni Papini and the Redemption of the Devil," Personalist, 43:233-52, April, 1962.

". . . the author undertakes the hard task of convincing us that Satan should be treated with Christian charity, and, when his arguments are logically unconvincing, he resorts to lyric tension." (G. C.)

P34   Gullace, Giovanni, "Giovanni Papini e il Diavolo," Italica, 33:193-204, September, 1956.

Conversion to Catholicism changed Papini's purely literary interest in the Devil to Christian compassion and love. His novel, The Devil, attempts to "present the pure truth concerning the rebel angel . . . to explain the need for the Devil in this world, to emphasize the injustice of our hate towards him . . . to conclude that the Devil merits salvation and we who are good Christians should strive for his redemption." (V. R.)

PARDO BAZÁN, EMILIA

P35 Brent, Albert, "The Novels of Elena Quiroga," Hispania, 42:210-3, May, 1959.

The novels of Elena Quiroga reveal influences of Pardo Bazán and the existentialists. "Her novels possess that power of sustained attraction, which Ortega y Gasset calls 'imperviousness'." (A.C.H.)

P36 Davis, Gifford, "Pardo Bazán, Juan Valera, and Literary Fashion," Romance Notes, 11:315-21, 1969.

[This is a résumé of an 1897 newspaper polemic about Naturalism.] (C.O.)

P37 Dendle, Brian J., "The Racial Theories of Emilia Pardo Bazán," Hispanic Review, 38:17-31, January, 1970.

In common with many nineteenth-century scientists, "race plays an important role in Pardo Bazán's literary and social theories, she accepts doctrines of racial temperament, racial superiority and antagonism, and even, at times, racial purity and racial atavism. Her racial theories are above all apparent in the novels Una cristiana and La prueba. . . . Her concept of racial heredity reveals a greater degree of determinism and pessimism than do the naturalistic theories of Zola and Blasco Ibáñez." (D.P.)

P38 Giles, Mary E., "Color Adjectives in Pardo Bazán's Novels," Romance Notes, 10:54-8, 1968.

The novels of Emilia Pardo Bazán differ in theme, technique, and style between her early Naturalist works and her later Modernist style. She used standard adjectives in her early novels in their literal sense; more abstract meanings were applied in later works. Pardo Bazán selected color adjectives in accordance with the theme and technique of each novel, to the extent of enhancing the adjectives with neologisms, Gallicisms, and other foreign words in her later work. (V.E.)

P39 Giles, Mary E., "Impressionist Techniques in Descriptions by Emilia Pardo Bazán," Hispanic Review, 30:304-16, October, 1962.

Her early novels show the influence of Zola's espousal of Impressionistic techniques, especially in the treatment of sunlight and haze. Her three last novels show a rediscovery of Impressionism under the impact of literary Modernism. (C.O.)

P40   Giles, Mary E., "Pardo Bazán's Two Styles," Hispania, 48:456-62,
       September, 1965.

       Earlier estimates of Pardo Bazán which emphasize her affinities to
       the French naturalistic novel have "resulted in an unfortunate neglect
       of her as a stylist and a descriptive artist." Her "acknowledged
       masterpieces, Los pazos de Ulloa and La madre naturaleza, high-
       light her early period of writing, when she was strongly influenced
       . . . by French Naturalism. . . . In those novels between 1890 and
       1905 . . . [she] ceased, in general, to follow the Naturalistic vogue.
       . . . Pardo Bazán had come to grips with her penchant to keep pace
       with literary currents and had settled for an independent position."
       Her "last three novels indicate a tendency to discard complex
       structure and long sentences and to cultivate her período breve . . .
       which characterizes much Modernist writing." (D. P.)

P41   Hilton, Ronald, "Doña Emilia Pardo Bazán: Neo-Catholicism and
       Christian Socialism," Americas, 11:5-18, 1954.

       Doña Emilia Pardo Bazán "was one of Spain's most enlightened
       representatives of Neo-Catholicism and Christian Socialism"
       although towards the end of her career "she became more and more
       an exponent of direct action, without religious theorizing." (D. P.)

P42   Kronik, John W., "Emilia Pardo Bazán and the Phenomenon of
       French Decadentism," PMLA, 81:418-27, October, 1966.

       "With her comments on French decadentism Pardo Bazán . . . laid
       before her educated countrymen the traits and precepts of the
       decadent mode and told them what she thought of it. Decadentism
       never did gain an avid following in Spain . . . but the inroads that
       the worthiest elements of the esthetic of decadence were to make
       into Spanish literature, poetry in particular, did so with forceful
       assistance from Pardo Bazán." (D. P.)

P43   Sánchez, Porfirio, "How and Why Emilia Pardo Bazán Went from
       the Novel to the Short Story," Romance Notes, 11:309-14, 1969.

       "In her final period, Pardo Bazán will be concerned with only one
       firmly outlined cause . . . going along with the current literary
       movements of that time, with novelists who concentrated on the
       psychology of their characters rather than on external action."
       (C. O.)

LA CUESTIÓN PALPITANTE

P44   Davis, Gifford, "The 'coletilla' to Pardo Bazán's La cuestión palpitante," Hispanic Review, 24:50-63, January, 1956.

An analysis of the polemic on naturalism reveals the extent of Pardo Bazán's acceptance of Zola's doctrines. She does not reverse "her previous judgments, but under the influence of criticism . . . and in the exchange of debate, her wording and spirit moved at least fractionally toward greater theoretical acceptance of naturalism, and thus more accurately portrayed her practice." (A.C.H.)

LA MADRE NATURALEZA

P45   Kirby, Harry L., Jr., "Pardo Bazán, Darwinism, and La madre naturaleza," Hispania, 47:733-7, December, 1964.

Pardo Bazán's uncollected Darwin study, "Reflexiones científicas contra el darwinismo," published in 1877, is chiefly important in revealing her "belief in the relative importance of heredity and environment and it clearly depicts her desperate attempt to assert her religious beliefs while bringing them into harmony with Darwinism. . . . This same attitude is expressed fictionally in La madre naturaleza, published . . . ten years after the Darwin study." Although "the overall tone created in the novel is one of pessimism and doubt," at the end of the novel "Pardo Bazán is attempting to assert her religious beliefs and bring them into artful harmony with her scientific beliefs as she had done ten years earlier in her study on Darwinism." (D.P.)

P46   Knox, Robert B., "Artistry and Balance in La madre naturaleza," Hispania, 41:64-70, March, 1958.

Pardo Bazán's La madre naturaleza "consists of a well-balanced blend of varied elements and. . . naturalism, though an important ingredient, is hardly a dominant one." (A.C.H.)

LOS PAZOS DE ULLOA

P47   Lott, Robert E., "Observations on the Narrative Method, the Psychology, and the Style of Los pazos de Ulloa," Hispania, 52:3-12, March, 1969.

"In Los pazos de Ulloa there is every indication of a thoroughly realistic narrative method and style. But, because of religious and

LOS PAZOS DE ULLOA   (cont'd)

philosophical beliefs, because of the euphemistic treatment of potentially crude or shocking details and situations, and because of restraint in the use of style features and images, Pardo Bazán falls short of full-fledged naturalism. Yet . . . the theme, settings, and characterizations are believably and incisively presented and the varying stylistic and imagistic nuances correspond perfectly to the shifts in mood, tone, and point of view." (D.P.)

LA SIRENA NEGRA

P48   Giles, Mary E., "Symbolic Imagery in La sirena negra," Papers on Language and Literature, 4:182-91, Spring, 1968.

"Pardo Bazán's symbolist handling of imagery in La sirena negra is consistent with her general tendency to draw inspiration for theme, technique, and style from various literary quarters. Her essential literary eclecticism . . . caused her to expand the vision of reality inherited from the realistic Spanish novel of the nineteenth century, and the symbolism of imagery in La sirena negra is one means by which she sought to probe the nature of reality in a unique, inventive way and to go beyond the confines of the peninsular literary conventions." (D.P.)

P49   Sánchez, Porfirio, "La dualidad mística en La sirena negra de Pardo Bazán," Hispania, 53:189-97, May, 1970.

"In conclusion, we have attempted to explain some ideas about the dual mysticism of Emilia Pardo Bazán in La sirena negra. We hope to have shown that the mysticism in this work, as in all its predecessors, is the expression of an anguished and tortured soul which wins through darkness and pessimism to obtain the repose of clear emotions." (D.P.)

PAREJA Y DIEZ CANSECO, ALFREDO

P50   Schwartz, Kessel, "Alfredo Pareja y Diez Canseco, Social Novelist," Hispania, 42:220-8, May, 1959.

The works of the Ecuadorian novelist demonstrate that "Pareja expressed his horror at the cruelty of man towards man, but he also affirmed the power of love as a redeeming force. . . . He has used in his writing all the twentieth-century techniques: the flashback, the stream-of-consciousness, the dialogue carrying action forward, and the interior monologue." (A.C.H.)

PARKER, DOROTHY

P51   Brown, John Mason, "High Spirits in the Twenties," Horizon,
       4:33-41, July, 1962.

       When Robert Sherwood, "fresh from battle in his Canadian uniform,"
       joined the staff of Vanity Fair he found himself "amid an array of
       talents as original as his own." Robert Benchley "was a wit who had
       no malice in him. . . ." Dorothy Parker's "smile was radiator
       warm; her manners perfect. . . . To those she did not like or who
       bored her, she was a stiletto made of sugar." In the early twenties
       the trio, now separated from Vanity Fair, formed a luncheon group
       at the Algonquin, which included Franklin Pierce Adams, Woollcott,
       Heywood Broun, Marc Connelly, George S. Kaufman, Frank Sullivan,
       Deems Taylor, Harold Ross, Laurence Stallings and others, a group
       famous for wisecracks, puns and frivolity. "Among these Round
       Tablers, Sherwood stood out like a grandfather's clock." (D.P.)

P52   Captron, Marion, "The Art of Fiction XIII: Dorothy Parker,"
       Paris Review, No, 13, pp. 72-87, Summer, 1956.

       [This interview with Dorothy Parker concerns her work.] (G.C.)

P53   Cooper, Wyatt, "Whatever You Think Dorothy Parker Was Like,
       She Wasn't," Esquire, 70:57, 61, 110-4, July, 1968.

       "Biographies will be written about her . . . but . . . they won't get
       anywhere near the truth of her. How can they? The truth of her
       was that complex, and complex truths resist examination." (G.C.)

P54   Winn, Janet, "Capote, Mailer and Miss Parker," New Republic,
       140:27-8, February 9, 1959.

       The recent Truman Capote, Norman Mailer and Dorothy Parker
       television program moderated by David Susskind turned into a debate
       between Capote and Mailer on virtually every topic discussed. Miss
       Parker contributed little to the occasion beyond her presence.
       Capote made excellent sense, demolishing Mailer's remarks at every
       point, albeit politely. (D.P.)

PARRA, NICANOR

P55   Williams, Miller, "A Talk with Nicanor Parra, " Arizona Quarterly,
       23:144-51, Summer, 1967.

       [This is an interview with one of Chile's best-known poets.]   (J.C.)

P56   Williams, Miller, "A Talk With Nicanor Parra, " Shenandoah,
       18:71-8, Autumn, 1966.

       [This interview took place in Santiago de Chile.]   (C.O.)

PARRA, TERESA DE LA

P57   Schade, George D., "Las memorias de Mamá Blanca: A Literary
       Tour de Force, " Hispania, 39:157-60, May, 1956.

       "Not only do Teresa de la Parra's exquisite phrasing and graceful
       mastery of style set her several notches above most of her contem-
       poraries in Spanish American literature; her delicate sense of humor
       --witty, urbane, tempered in its irony, gentle in its mockery, never
       biting or vicious--adds greatly to the fine quality of her work. "
       (A.C.H.)

PASCOLI, GIOVANNI

P58   Ukas, Michael, "Nature in the Poetry of Giovanni Pascoli, "
       Kentucky Foreign Language Quarterly, 13:51-9, 1966.

       Giovanni Pascoli, in his treatise "Il Fanciullino, " indicates a
       "vital connection" between poetry and the various creatures, phenom-
       ena, and objects of nature. He equates poetry with everything that is
       pure and beautiful; it can arise "only out of unblemished innocence. "
       To compose a poem one must be young at heart. It follows that
       poetry itself renders a "moral and social service to mankind. " To
       all that is chaotic and discordant Pascoli applies the term impoetico.
       Pascoli links all nature and each thing becomes a conscious being in
       its own right. "Only understanding of the world and all its creatures
       can lead to the poetical harmony . . . so dear to Pascoli's heart. "
       (V.E.)

PASINETTI, PIER-MARIA

P59   Houston, M. T. and S. N. Rosenberg, "The Onomastics of
Pasinetti," Italian Quarterly, 10:33-44, 1966.

For his novel Rosso Veneziano Pasinetti has named his characters
with special care. The surnames Partibon and Fassoli are characteristically Venetian. The Partibons have simple Italian names,
while the Fassola names suggest the "neo-Roman bombast of the
Fascists." Also, names have been chosen with similar care for
Pasinetti's La Confusione. The onomastic richness of both novels
is an "indisputable and striking element of Pasinetti's fictional art."
(V.E.)

LA CONFUSIONE

P60   Della Terza, Dante, "Contemporary Italian Novelists: Language and
Style in P. M. Pasinetti's La Confusione," Italian Quarterly,
7:64-76, 1964.

Pasinetti's La Confusione aims at "the metaphorical dissimulation
and transposition of places, circumstances and events." Three
examples of Pasinetti's "anti-romantic, anti-naturalistic narrative
technique" are the sculptor Clement Blumenfeld, the woman
Genziana Horst, and Bernardo Partibon, whose presence in the novel
is the "most singular discordant presence." These characters represent to Pasinetti "all those in that world which is his who fight
hypocrisy with love." (V.E.)

PASO, ALFONSO

P61   Dowling, John C., "The Theater of Alfonso Paso," Modern Language
Journal, 45:195-9, May, 1961.

[This is an introductory survey of the works of this prolific dramatist,
followed by a list of his plays.] (C.O.)

PASOLINI, PIER PAOLO

P62   Carella, Ada, "Un Apôtre incroyant: Pier Paolo Pasolini,"
La Table Ronde, No. 203, pp. 72-9, December, 1964.

Patronized and encouraged by Moravia, Pasolini has not been influenced by him. His best known novels (Ragazzi di vita and Una Vita
violenta) show his Marxist tendencies, but a collection of poems,

Le Ceneri de Gramsci, does not hesitate to attack the party. His
literary work concentrates on the society which has appeared since
1946 on the fringes of large cities, living by expedients, theft and
poverty. (T.T.B.)

P63   Della Terza, Dante, "Il realismo mimetico di P. P. Pasolini, "
        Italica, 38:306-13, December, 1966.

        "Pasolini is a unique example of a writer-critic who divides the act
        of artistic creation into two distinct periods. There is, beside the
        narrative invention, a concern with style, and it is interesting to
        note that Pasolini formulates his narrative requirements, vitalizing
        and expanding his own linguistic choices, at the time the Italian
        writer is attempting to resolve the crisis of neo-realism in a
        completely nominal sense. " (D.P.)

P64   O'Neill, T., "Il filologo come politico: Linguistic Theory and Its
        Sources in Pier Paolo Pasolini, " Italian Studies, 25:63-78, 1970.

        Pasolini's novels "will undoubtedly be of prime interest to the
        historical philologist as documentary evidence of a renewed interest
        in the linguistic problem which characterized the 'fifties in Italy. "
        In his poetry, "dialect has a . . . function . . . of a private, un-
        changing language through which is expressed the private, unchanging
        world of the poet . . . but also that of a reaction against Fascist
        culture and conformity. . . . dialect in the 'Roman' novels . . . is
        used to provide . . . an alternative to a language in crisis, a basis
        on which can be constructed a new language commensurate with a
        new social reality. " (D.P.)

P65   O'Neill, Thomas, "A Problem of Character Development in
        Pasolini's Trilogy, " Forum for Modern Language Studies, 5:80-4,
        January, 1969.

        Recognition of socio-ideological elements as contributory factors in
        the spiritual development of Pasolini merely indicates its complexity
        and confirms that the problem of character development is not purely
        an aesthetic one. (J.R.R.)

BICICLETTONE

P66   O'Neill, Thomas, "Pier Paolo Pasolini: Biciclettone," Modern
Languages, 50:11-3, March, 1969.

Biciclettone is "an excellent introduction to the more complex novels
of Pasolini, for . . . we have in nuce all the thematic and stylistic
material" later developed. The theme is sympathy for "those who
live on the margin of society." The style is Neorealism, "short
sentences . . . light brush strokes" and predominant dialogue.
(J.L.A.)

PASTERNAK, BORIS LEONIDOVICH

P67   Annenkov, G., "Pasternak and the Martyrology of Soviet Writers,"
Texas Quarterly, 3:189-92, Autumn, 1960.

[This is a memoir.] (M.H.)

P68   Aucouturier, Michel, "The Legend of the Poet and the Image of the
Actor in the Short Stories of Pasternak," Studies in Short Fiction,
3:225-35, Winter, 1966.

In Pasternak the actor's role demands a complete giving of himself,
an acceptance of unlimited risk. The poet, similarly, "is not the
author of his legend, but . . . the slave of a higher and more significant work than his own person." (P.J.R.)

P69   Aucouturier, Michel, "The Metonymous Hero or the Beginnings of
Pasternak the Novelist," Books Abroad, 44:222-7, Spring, 1970.

[This is a discussion of Pasternak's use of metonymy in his
Spektorski and Tale.] (G.C.)

P70   Erlich, Victor, "The Concept of the Poet in Pasternak," Slavonic
Review, 37:325-35, 1959.

Pasternak's "work does not so much project a coherent and dramatically effective image of the poet as dramatize . . . the power which
brings the poem into being. Is not that joy of heightened perception,
of passionate seeing, which provides the emotional leitmotiv of
Pasternak's poetry, the essential quality and the unique prerogative
of creative imagination?" (D.P.)

P71   Ford, R. A. D., "The Poetry of Boris Pasternak," Queen's
Quarterly, 67:673-7, 1960.

Russian lyric poetry is "the greatest submerged literary treasure of
the twentieth century," largely due to the difficulty of translating
Russian poetry into English. This treasure was relatively unknown
in the West before the granting of the Nobel Prize to Boris Pasternak,
partly through politics. George Reavey's The Poetry of Boris
Pasternak is not altogether successful in its attempt to retain the
command of form and music of the words in the Russian original.
Reavey's book does provide facts of Pasternak's life, recollections,
a bibliography and a brief critical commentary on ninety two poems.
(V. E.)

P72   Frank, Victor S., "A Matter of Conscience: Boris Pasternak and
the Russian Tradition," Dublin Review, 234:222-6, 1960.

All major Russian writers from Pushkin to Pasternak have been in
conflict with the authorities, since Russian writers have been required to become the "vehicle of the nation's conscience." The
Literary Foundation, originally formed to organize a society to
protect the professional and personal interests of its members, has
become a channel for awards to writers who have pleased the society.
Against this background Boris Pasternak's Dr. Zhivago sounds "once
again the voice of Russia's conscience." (V. E.)

P73   Frank, Victor S., "The Meddlesome Poet: Boris Pasternak's Rise
to Greatness," Dublin Review, 232:49-58, Spring, 1958.

The artistic integrity revealed in Pasternak's life and poetry speaks
well for the quality of his only full-length novel, Dr. Zhivago, soon
to be translated into English. (W.T.S.)

P74   Gifford, Henry, "Pasternak and the 'Realism' of Blok," Oxford
Slavonic Papers, 13:96-106, 1967.

"Pasternak can be seen as the true successor to Blok in Russian
poetry. . . . These poets have in common an idea of the artist's
responsibility, and of his character. . . . Pasternak follows a
poetic system unlike that of Blok; he belongs to another generation;
his training and many of his interests were different. But there is
an essential bond between them nowhere . . . so manifest as in
Pasternak's comments on realism." (D. P.)

P75 Gijsen, Marnix, "A Note on Pasternak," Books Abroad, 35:132-3, Spring, 1961.

[This is Pasternak's correspondence with a Belgian (1958-60).] (C.E.N.)

P76 Grigorieff, Dmitry Felix, "Pasternak and Dostoevskij," Slavic and East European Journal, 17:335-42, Winter, 1959.

Dostoevsky and Pasternak share similar metaphysical ideas, significant for a complete appreciation of their art, about an eschatological upheaval in the coming of Christ, life as the Highest Essence sustaining the created world, and the ethically spiritless and esthetically trivial approach to life of modern humanistic civilization. (W.G.F.)

P77 Gupta, Nolini Kanta, "Boris Pasternak, An Indian Viewpoint," Russian Review, 19:248-53, July, 1960.

"Pasternak's poetry is characterized by this tragic sensitivity, a nostalgia woven into the fabric of utterance, its rhythm and imagery, its thought and phrasing." (R.G.L.)

P78 Harari, Manya, "Pasternak," Twentieth Century, 164:524-8, December, 1958.

After having refused the Nobel Prize under pressure, being expelled from the Writer's Union, and attacked in the Soviet press as well as at a meeting attended by Khrushchev, Pasternak sent a letter to Khrushchev and one to Pravda in which he declared "that he wishes it to be known that he loves Russia and has never wished her any harm and that he does not accept the interpretation placed upon his views by Suskov and Novy Mir." (D.P.)

P79 Harvie, J. A., "The Poems of Boris Pasternak," Meanjin Quarterly, 25:326-31, September, 1966.

"While there is much that is portentously trivial in his work, the best of Pasternak is superb. He is superb when he abandons his complicated verbal acrobatics to speak with the directness of Lermontov or Pushkin, and when metaphor and direct vision fuse in the incandescence of pure poetry." (D.P.)

P80   Hughes, Olga Raevsky, "Pasternak and Cvetaeva: History of a
        Friendship," Books Abroad, 44:218-21, Spring, 1970.

        ". . . the published works provide sufficient material for establish-
        ing a general outline and for determining the prevailing tone of the
        friendship between the two poets, for reflections of their friendship
        can be found not only in the letters and autobiographies, but in their
        poetry as well." (G.C.)

P81   Ivask, Ivar, "Introduction: The Poplar is King," Books Abroad,
        44:195-200, Spring, 1970.

        [Printed here are four letters from Pasternak to Ivask, thanking him
        for his poems and gifts of books, and commenting on literary matters.]
        (D.P.)

P82   "Judgment on Pasternak," Survey, No. 60, pp. 134-63, July, 1966.

        [This is an account of a meeting of Moscow writers held in 1958.
        Pasternak's work is called "redolent of pure and unadulterated pre-
        revolutionary decadence." Pasternak is condemned also for selling
        his novel abroad and a resolution is passed against him.] (V.E.)

P83   Levin, Elena, "Nine Letters of Boris Pasternak," Harvard Library
        Bulletin, 15:317-30, October, 1967.

        "These nine letters from Boris Pasternak to George Reavey . . .
        cover the years between 1931 and 1960. . . . Their documentary
        importance lies in the fact that they are addressed to a prospective
        translator . . . and that in them Pasternak wants to put across . . .
        the nature of his literary aims and the external limitations under
        which he must labor." (D.P.)

P84   Levin, Harry, "Literature and Exile," Listener, 62:613-7,
        October 15, 1959.

        [This is a discussion of the exiles of Pasternak, Conrad, Nabokov,
        Dante, Heine, Mickiewicz, Ovid, James, Joyce and Pound.] "The
        relation between the poet and the multitude, according to Vigny, is
        perpetual ostracism. . . . exile has often proved to be a vocation,
        reinforcing other gifts with courage and looking forward to a final
        triumph of independence over conformity." (H.S.)

P85   Livingstone, Angela, "Pasternak's Early Prose," <u>AUMLA</u>, No. 22, pp. 249-67, November, 1964.

Boris Pasternak simplified his style after about 1932. His youthful style is "mannered, dense with accumulations of imagery, often obscure. . . ." Simplicity and naturalness were always his expressed ideal, however. Six stories written between 1915 and 1931, "The Stroke of Appeles," "Letters from Tula," "The Childhood of Luvers," "Aerial Ways," "The Tale," and "Safe Conduct," may be linked to Pasternak's ideas of simplicity and creativity. (V.E.)

P86   Livingstone, Angela, "Pasternak's Last Poetry," <u>Meanjin Quarterly</u>, 22:388-96, December, 1963.

The poems of personal confession and descriptions of natural or urban scenes composed during and after the writing of <u>Dr. Zhivago</u> are among the last poems that Boris Pasternak wrote. They share feelings of "the positive expectation of the future, the last look at the world he has loved, the attitude of willingness, readiness to be close to it, and the personal impotence." (D.P.)

P87   Magidoff, Robert, "The Life, Times and Art of Boris Pasternak," <u>Thought</u>, 42:327-57, Autumn, 1967.

Pasternak was generally recognized, with Esenin and Mayakovsky, as one of the three leading Russian poets in the early 1920's; he was most influential on many Soviet poets, although he remained independent of all poetic movements except the Acmeists, the Futurists, and the Imagists. His roots lay within the traditions of Russian literature of all periods. The great purge "seems to have resulted in the emergence of Christianity as a major theme in Pasternak's prose and poetry. . . . Pasternak's conception of Christ . . . is reflected in <u>Doctor Zhivago</u>--in the novel itself and in Zhivago's poems." (D.P.)

P88   Markov, Vladimir, "An Unnoticed Aspect of Pasternak's Translations," <u>Slavic Review</u>, 20:503-8, October, 1961.

In a strong tradition of Russian translation, Pasternak's work is unusual for the great freedom he allows himself, which results in a highly idiomatic and vital Russian, while preserving the intentions of the original. However, in certain passages in <u>Hamlet</u> and <u>Faust</u>, as well as other works, he used translation as a pretext "to do what he could not do in his original poems: tell the truth about his own life, discuss problems of his generation, engage in polemics with authorities." (D.P.)

P89   Matlaw, Ralph E., "A Visit with Pasternak," Nation, 189:134-5,
       September 12, 1959.

       Pasternak asserted that in Dr. Zhivago the totality of the work is
       important, not the details, yet he displayed an interest in symbolism
       which indicated that symbolic details meant more to him than he was
       consciously aware of. His choice of poems, he also maintained, was
       controlled by the demands of the whole novel. (G.K.)

P90   Merton, Thomas, "The Pasternak Affair in Perspective," Thought,
       34:485-517, Winter, 1959-1960.

       The award of the 1958 Nobel Prize for Literature to Pasternak was
       a literary rather than a political event, and "the essentially spiritual
       character of the Pasternak affair . . . is precisely its greatest
       importance. . . . Those who have been struck by the religious
       content of his work have been responding . . . not so much to a
       formal Christian witness as to a deep and uncompromising spiritu-
       ality." (D.P.)

P91   Milosz, Czeslaw, "On Pasternak Soberly," Books Abroad, 44:200-9,
       Spring, 1970.

       "Pasternak was a man spellbound by reality, which was for him
       miraculous. He accepted suffering because the very essence of life
       is suffering, death, and rebirth. And he treated art as a gift of the
       Holy Spirit. We would not know, however, of his hidden faith with-
       out Doctor Zhivago. His poetry . . . was too fragile an instrument
       to express, after all, ideas." In his novel "he created a new myth
       of the writer, and we may conjecture that it will endure in Russian
       literature. . . ." (D.P.)

P92   Mottley, Robert C., Jr., "Boris Pasternak: The Late Phase,"
       Shenandoah, 13:42-7, Autumn, 1961.

       "Most of Pasternak's work is characterized by an urge for freshness
       of air, body, and soul. His art was a cry of joy at the wonder of
       life, a deep conviction of man's resurrection, a perpetual pursuit of
       a Holy Grail from many Damascuses towards many Romes." (D.P.)

P93   Muchnic, Helen, "Toward an Analysis of Boris Pasternak," Slavic
       and East European Journal, 15:101-5, 1957.

       "Feeling for Pasternak is the theme of art, not its method, and his
       world is not the stuff of dreams but a world of cognitions and per-

ceptions. In the last analysis, reality is unknowable; it is emotionally apprehended and deflected by emotions. But art approaches a knowledge of it. . . . Pasternak's own work can be explained as the allegorical speech of direct feeling, a language composed of the interchangeable images of a transposed reality, through which power alone is expressed." (D.P.)

P94   Pasternak, Boris, "Three Letters," <u>Encounter</u>, 15:3-6, August, 1960.

[These are the texts of three recent letters to Stephen Spender.] (M.H.M.)

P95   Paul, Sherman, "An Art of Life: Pasternak's Autobiographies," <u>Salmagundi</u>, 14:17-33, 1970.

"Pasternak's autobiographies are those of a poet. That is their distinction. They are almost wholly concerned with the poet's self, with its nature, gift, or genius, with its nurture and development, and with its persistence, at whatever cost, in continuing to be itself. . . . We learn little or nothing from Pasternak about family, love affairs, marriages, divorce, children, recognition honors, social world and political life." (K.M.W.)

P96   Payne, Robert, "Boris Pasternak," <u>Literary Review</u>, 2:315-33, Spring, 1959.

Pasternak's novels, letters, essays, and poems show him as a perfectionist involved with the conflicting problems of responsibility, freedom, and individuality. [Included is a selection of Pasternak's poems translated by George Reavey.] (E.T.)

P97   Poggioli, Renato, "Boris Pasternak," <u>Partisan Review</u>, 25:541-54, Fall, 1958.

Pasternak, as is revealed by a survey of his life work, deserves to be "honored as poet as well as novelist." (R.K.)

P98   Reznikoff, Daniel, "Notes sur Pasternak," <u>Cahiers des Saisons</u>, 47:216-8, Autumn, 1966.

Metaphors and images are Pasternak's preferred means of expression. In its ensemble his work is an autobiography poetically expressed, telling us of himself, what he has seen, felt, thought and liked on earth. (T.T.B.)

P99   Ruge, Gerd, "Conversations in Moscow," <u>Encounter</u>, 11:29-31,
        October, 1958.

        [Interviews were arranged with Vladimir Dudentsev, Ilya Ehrenburg,
        and Alexei Surkov. Thus an opportunity existed for talking with a
        popular but officially attacked novelist, with a famous older writer
        who imagines himself above the bickerings of policy, and the power-
        ful secretary of the Writers's Union. The three give a varied picture
        of literary life in Russia. Of interest are their attitudes toward
        Pasternak.] (D. B. D.)

P100   Šilbajoris, Rimvydas, "The Conception of Life in the Art of
        Pasternak," <u>Books Abroad</u>, 44:209-14, Spring, 1970.

        "To Pasternak, life is not a statistical concept, a sum total of
        individual existences, absolute and hermetical, like grains of sand,
        but rather, like the sea, it is a single dynamic entity, on the surface
        of which you and I are its configurations." (D. P.)

P101   Šilbajoris, Rimvydas, "Pasternak and Tolstoj: Some Comparisons,"
        <u>Slavic and East European Journal</u>, 11:23-34, Spring, 1967.

        Pasternak and Tolstoj treat similarly such topics as death, life, and
        truth. Both authors "were Christian humanists in the best tradition
        of Russian literature." (V. D.)

P102   Sinyavsky, Andrei, "On Boris Pasternak," <u>Encounter</u>, 26:45-50,
        April, 1966.

        "In half a century of Pasternak's writing . . . he remained faithful
        until the end . . . to a series of ideas, principles, and partialities.
        One of Pasternak's deep convictions was that true art is always
        greater than itself, for it testifies to the significance of being, the
        greatness of life, the immeasurable value of human existence. . . .
        the presence of greatness shows in the unaffected liveliness of what
        is being told, in the heightened awareness and poetic inspiration of
        the artist . . . although the subject may be only the snow falling or
        the forest stirring." (D. P.)

P103   Stepun, Fedor, "Boris Leonidowitsch Pasternak: Der 'Fall'
        Pasternak," <u>Die Neue Rundshau</u>, 70:145-61, No. 1, 1959.

        <u>Doctor Zhivago</u> represents the artistic and spiritual culmination of a
        non-political poet, whose roots are to be found between, rather than
        in, the pre-revolutionary groups centering about Gorki on the socio-

logical side and Mayakovski on the expressionistic side. Pasternak prefers metonymy to metaphor, Verinnerlichung to objectivity. (R.H.L.)

P104   Struve, Gleb, "Boris Pasternak about Himself and His Readers," Slavic Review, 23:125-8, March, 1964.

[This article comments on a short essay by Pasternak on Rilke, and the relationship between a writer and his reader. The piece has never before appeared in translation and is generally unknown to Russian readers.] (D.P.)

P105   Terras, Victor, "Boris Pasternak and Romantic Aesthetics," Papers on Language and Literature, 3:42-56, Winter, 1967.

"But clearly Pasternak's joyful vision of life and nature, full of childlike wonder, is in its ethos and in its pathos quite different from Blok's. Pasternak's conception of the symbolic nature of poetry is the corollary of a monistic world view. . . . Pasternak's imagery and phraseology are concrete and vigorous, original and future-directed. . . . Pasternak's aesthetic is certainly closer to romantic than to Kantian aesthetics." (D.P.)

P106   Terras, Victor, "Boris Pasternak and Time," Canadian Slavic Studies, 2:264-70, Summer, 1968.

Unlike Maiakovskii or Mandel'shtam, Pasternak "has no argument with time. His time experience is ahistorical and panchronistic. He is a man fascinated by the powerful and steady flow of time, and overwhelmed by the joyous feeling of being a part of it." (D.P.)

P107   Tomiinson, Charles, "Poetry and Silence," Poetry, 96:108-11, May, 1960.

Pasternak's poetry places great moral strength in the words "silence" and "stillness," as is done much later in Dr. Zhivago. The words "restore the measure of what is essentially human." Pasternak's schooling as a Symbolist probably motivated this emphasis. Tsvetayeva wrote in 1922: "His speech (in conversation) is like the interruption of primordial muteness." (F.L.)

P108   Turkevich, Ludmilla B., "Boris Leonidovich Pasternak," Books
        Abroad, 33:26-8, Winter, 1959.

        "Nature, Love, and Revolution are Pasternak's principal themes.
        Nature . . . is an inspiration, a symbol, a means of communication,
        and it is, above all, man's link to immortality. . . . For Pasternak
        Love is sometimes strange, incomprehensible, and wilful, and it is
        always elemental. The third theme is the Revolution which was once
        portrayed as a liberating and ennobling force promising a new life.
        . . . Now its visage is ugly, dripping with blood." (D.P.)

P109   Weidlé, Wladimir, "A Contemporary's Judgment," Books Abroad,
        44:215-7, Spring, 1970.

        Pasternak "was always a poet, whether writing verse or prose.
        This I did not deny in my 1928 article in spite of its title. He has
        consistently grown in stature since then, has of his own free will
        repudiated all that impeded his growth, and has become a giant
        among the pygmies of Soviet literature. . . ." (D.P.)

                THE ADOLESCENCE OF ZHANYA LUVERS--See
                DETSTVO LYUVERS

                THE CHILDHOOD OF LUVERS--See
                DETSTVO LYUVERS

                DETSTVO LYUVERS

P110   Livingstone, A., "The Childhood of Luvers: An Early Story of
        Pasternak's," Southern Review, 1:74-84, 1963.

        Written in 1917, the story "shows no sign of the political and social
        upheavals of that year in Russia." It could be called "a Christian
        story"; at least "it seems to prove that Christianity is natural."
        Additionally, The Childhood of Luvers "in a number of respects"
        looks forward to Doctor Zhivago. (S.T.)

                DOKTOR ZHIVAGO

P111   Angeloff, Alexander, "Water Imagery in the Novel Doctor Zhivago,"
        Russian Language Journal, No. 81/82, pp. 6-13, February-March,
        1968.

        Pasternak's literary force is "not so much the state of mind he seeks
        to express as the language in which he expresses it." In Dr. Zhivago

DOKTOR ZHIVAGO (cont'd)

the "essence of death and the relationship between life and death"
are portrayed by water imagery, specifically in "the vitality of man's
relationship to man and to nature itself." "Water imagery is a device
to stop time and the stream of life so as to unite the communication of
language and the meaning of existence." (V.E.)

P112 Arndt, Walter, "Dr. Zhivago--Freedom and Unconcern," South
Atlantic Bulletin, 25:1-6, May, 1959.

The novel is composed of "three interbraided strands," an external
plot and accounts of two affairs: the first that between the intellectual
and artist, Zhivago, and socialism; the other between Zhivago and
Lara. This is a personal affair which becomes a refuge as the first
affair turns into a nightmare. (W.G.F.)

P113 Avegno, Hamilton P., "Some Notes on Pasternak's Doctor Zhivago
and Bernanos's Joy," Xavier University Studies, 1:26-33, April,
1961.

Boris Pasternak's Dr. Zhivago and George Bernanos's Joy may be
compared by asking these questions: is the novel informed, are
elements of character, tone, incident, style, etc. compatible, does
the novel achieve organic form, and does the novel have a symbolic
level of meaning? Pasternak's theme is easier to dramatize and
manipulate. Joy answers the second question better than Zhivago,
as it does the third. Joy is obviously a symbolic novel; Zhivago is
more tragic and epic than it is symbolic. Though both works are
quite different there are "tenuous rays of attraction and revulsion
issuing from each in the direction of the other." (V.E.)

P114 Baird, Sister Mary Julian, R. S. M., "Pasternak's Vision of the
Fair Rowan Tree," Catholic World, 189:427-31, September, 1959.

"In one of the key chapters [of Doctor Zhivago], Zhivago . . .
describes . . . a vision of the one woman, Mary, the Mother of
God." (G.C.)

P115 Baird, Sister M. Julian, R. S. M., "Pasternak's Zhivago--Hamlet
--Christ," Renascence, 14:179-84, Summer, 1962.

In the so-called supplement-in-verse to Doctor Zhivago "the deepest,
truest, most telling Pasternak is to be found. . . . And if it is safe to
say that Pasternak is Zhivago, it is equally true that from the poems

DOKTOR ZHIVAGO (cont'd)

arise two further identifications: Zhivago is Hamlet, and, climactically, Zhivago is Christ." (S.A.)

P116   Bayley, John, and Donald Davie, "Argument: I. Doctor Zhivago's Poems," Essays in Criticism, 16:212-9, April, 1966.

Bayley: "Professor Davie might be said to translate most feelingly and most ingeniously the weakest, the least emancipated of the poems." Davie: It is the task of the translator "to make as good an English poem as possible," even if his original is "a less than good poem." (G.C.)

P117   Bowman, Herbert E., "Doctor Zhivago," Northwest Review, 2:59-67, Spring, 1959.

The atmosphere of the novel is the atmosphere of poetry. Pasternak approaches his story poetically, not fictionally. The method is lyrical and objective; the images and metaphor are those of poetry. (E.T.)

P118   Bowman, Herbert E., "Postscript on Pasternak," Survey, No. 36, pp. 106-10, 1961.

"What is especially disappointing in so much that has been written is that the major meaning of the book . . . has inspired so little genuine excitement. It is as if Pasternak had presented us with . . . a great simple gift and we spent all of our time fussing with the wrappings. . . . For the greatness of Dr. Zhivago lies primarily in the revelation that . . . 'life is a glory.' It is this great open secret . . . that Pasternak has enshrined in his novel." (D.P.)

P119   Chiaromonte, Nicola, "Pasternak's Message," Partisan Review, 25:127-34, Winter, 1958.

". . . in the over-all equilibrium of the work, it is certainly the Tolstoyan inspiration that predominates, particularly in the expression of the religious emotion of the individual's dependence on the life of the cosmos and the noble pride that comes from this dependence." (G.C.)

DOKTOR ZHIVAGO (cont'd)

P120 Chiaromonte, Nicola, "Il valore del Dottor Zivago, " Il Mondo, 10:11-2, December, 1958.

"The modern novel by its very nature attempts to set itself up against official history and against that which individuals live day by day without understanding its meaning, the true history of men." This is what Boris Pasternak wanted to do in Doctor Zhivago whose "importance as a work of art lies in the fact that its author has given us for the first time a human image, humanly suffered and judged, of our inhuman times." (V.R.)

P121 Christesen, Nina, "Notes on Three Soviet Novels, " Meanjin Quarterly, 17:87-91, 1958.

In the last few years several novels have appeared in Soviet Russia which give emphasis to the humanist tradition: Dudintsev's Not by Bread Alone, Pasternak's Dr. Zhivago, and Leonov's The Russian Forest. (A.S.W.)

P122 Christesen, Nina, and Vance Palmer, " "Pasternak's Doctor Zhivago: A Discussion, " Meanjin Quarterly, 17:356, 448-60, 1959.

[This is a transcript of a discussion which followed the awarding of the Nobel Prize for Literature to Boris Pasternak. The novel, though containing political overtones, is primarily a work of art. The discussion covers Pasternak's personality, the novel Dr. Zhivago, and the Nobel Prize in general.] (V.E.)

P123 Clough, Wilson O., "Dr. Zhivago's Hamlet, " Western Humanities Review, 13:425-8, Autumn, 1959.

"Taken within the context of the novel, then, Dr. Zhivago has indeed left behind him one poem of personal communication. Like an uncertain Hamlet, he views the drama unfolding before him after the revolutionary 'overture' of 1917, which had aroused his initial enthusiasm. . . . Yet he accepts the inevitable end and his own destiny. Perhaps he is even a kind of Hamlet to his Mother Russia. . . ." (D.P.)

DOKTOR ZHIVAGO   (cont'd)

P124   Daniel, John, "A Note on Doctor Zhivago," Anglo-Welsh Review, 9:39-42, 1959.

Pasternak's political views "are a curious mixture of the unexpected and the almost obvious." Pasternak's view of Zhivago is that the simple existence of such a man is hope for the future. Zhivago's attitude towards the revolution is based on his concern for the human personality, founded on his faith in Christ's Incarnation. This respect for personality causes Pasternak to reject attempts to re-shape life. The novel is an appealing "poet's novel," although it has defects. (V.E.)

P125   Deutsch, Babette, " 'Talent for Life' in a New Russian Novel," Harper's Magazine, 217:71-6, September, 1958.

"At one point the doctor remarks that talent 'in the highest and broadest sense means talent for life.' The novel is a study of the degree to which diverse individuals possess that talent, and what it means in terms of twentieth-century history." (G.C.)

P126   Deutscher, Isaac, "Pasternak and the Calendar of the Revolution," Partisan Review, 26:248-65, Spring, 1959.

"The most striking characteristic of Boris Pasternak's Doctor Zhivago is its archaism. . . . The book . . . is utterly unrelated to the Russia of the 1950's. . . . It is a parable about a vanished generation." "Doctor Zhivago is a political novel par excellence. . . ." Its "chief character . . . and . . . the other figures . . . dwell on the revolution's failure, on its inability to solve any prob-lems, on the violence it has done to the human personality. . . . Christianity remains the hope and refuge. . . . It is from this quasi-fatalistic Christianity that finally springs Pasternak's ethereal note of reconciliation. . . ." (D.P.)

P127   Dyck, J. W., "Doktor Živago: A Quest for Self-Realization," Slavic and East European Journal, 6:117-24, No. 2, 1962.

"Živago's entire life is a chain of experiences which have gradually shaped, molded, and destroyed him. The following will, therefore be . . . some thoughts on the conception of Živago's self-realization and how this self-realization progresses step by step through his experience of freedom, his views on culture, and his understanding of history. . . . in Dr. Živago these three are closely interwoven." (D.P.)

DOKTOR ZHIVAGO (cont'd)

P128   Frank, Victor S., "A Russian Hamlet: Boris Pasternak's Novel,"
        Dublin Review, 232:212-24, Autumn, 1958.

        Doctor Zhivago reveals Pasternak as a man "passionately aware of
        the primacy of spirit over matter" and one to whom "human history
        does not make sense outside of Christ." (W.T.S.)

P129   Gayn, Mark, "A Party at the Kremlin: Soviet Literary Rebels,"
        Queen's Quarterly, 65:549-67, Winter, 1959.

        Because Pasternak is not a muckraker (as are Dudintsev and other
        literary rebels of the period 1952-7), the appearance of Doctor
        Zhivago, coming just when the Party thought it had brought the
        rebelling writers under control, revealed the seriousness of internal
        social problems and the extent of the widespread intellectual unrest.
        (G.M.)

P130   Gerschenkron, Alexander, "Notes on Dr. Zhivago," Modern
        Philology, 58:194-200, February, 1961.

        ". . . what is so anti-Soviet about the novel is its being so clearly
        pre-Soviet. Its language, its central figure, and its main theme all
        belong to the main stream of Russian literature of the nineteenth
        century." It reaffirms the ideals of an intelligentsia which the
        Soviets have labored to exterminate. (A.S.)

P131   Gifford, Henry, "Dr. Zhivago: The Last Russian Classic," Essays
        in Criticism, 9:159-70, April, 1959.

        "Doctor Zhivago is the last Russian Classic. . . . It presages a
        renewal of the tradition. When Russian literature begins again it
        will surely stem from Doctor Zhivago." (D.P.)

P132   Hampshire, Stuart, "Doctor Zhivago: As From a Lost Culture,"
        Encounter, 11:3-5, November, 1958.

        "The difficulty that this novel presents . . . is the difficulty that
        any carefully composed and long meditated work of part presents.
        It is naïve art, in Schiller's special sense of the word, but far from
        naïve . . . in its composition. . . . The English translation . . .
        allows one to guess that the vocabulary of the original is rich and
        elaborate, particularly in descriptions of nature and in dialogues of
        the poor. . . . The whole book is informed by an intense feeling for

DOKTOR ZHIVAGO (cont'd)

everything that is distinctively Russian by a characteristic kind of
mystical patriotism. . . ." (D.P.)

P133 Harari, Manya, "On Translating Zhivago," Encounter, 12:51-3,
May, 1959.

". . . the problem is whether to transliterate into . . . good English
. . . or to try, at the same time, to keep the tone of the original.
In our translation we were influenced by Pasternak's insistence . . .
on the need to keep the tone and to write 'in a natural and lively way'."
(G.C.)

P134 Harari, Manya, "Red for Beauty: Some Problems of Translating
from the Russian," Twentieth Century, 165:223-34, March, 1959.

As a result of the immensely different structure of Russian and
English and "the lack of a common background between the Russian
and the English reader . . . the English version of Zhivago loses
much of the richness of the original." Pasternak's "language is
never mannered or vulgar, yet in it thieves can curse, witches cast
their spells and intellectuals discuss abstractions. It can be earthy,
violent, and it can rise from one moment to the next to the height of
lyricism." (D.P.)

P135 Hayward, Max, "Doctor Zhivago and the Soviet Intelligentsia,"
Soviet Survey, No. 24, pp. 65-9, April-June, 1958.

Dr. Zhivago becomes a social outcast not for political reasons, but
because of his rejection of Bolshevik assumptions about man, life,
and history. The revolution was doomed, as Pasternak saw it,
because it was "trying to revert to a conception of man which had
been made obsolete by the advent of Christianity." The funeral of
Zhivago symbolizes the death of Soviet intelligentsia. The book ends
on a note of optimism, though, as Zhivago's friends look over his
poems, which they feel represent the freedom of the spirit of the
Soviet people. (V.E.)

P136 Hayward, Max, "Pasternak's Dr. Zhivago," Encounter, 10:38-48,
May, 1958.

Dr. Zhivago presents a contrast between the typical Russian obyvatel
(the person who is indifferent to politics but whose submission is yet
resilient and whose passivity preserves integrity of judgment) and the
fanatic. (D.B.D.)

DOKTOR ZHIVAGO   (cont'd)

P137   Howe, Irving, "Freedom and the Ashcan of History," Partisan Review, 26:268-75, Spring, 1959.

"Mr. Deutscher writes as a theorist who believes that the irrevocable progress of History is floating the Communist state. His assault upon Pasternak derives from a fundamental identification . . . with that progress." Actually, "through his doomed yet exemplary struggle to maintain the life of contemplation . . . Zhivago comes to represent . . . all that which in human life must remain impervious to the manipulation of the party-state and its ideology." (D.P.)

P138   Ignatieff, Leonid, "A Philosopher Who Lived His Philosophy: Yuri Zhivago," Queen's Quarterly, 75:703-17, Winter, 1968.

In Dr. Zhivago "the dominant theme of the whole work was life, life lived in spite of the gravest conditions, difficulties and dangers." (S.T.C.)

P139   Iswolsky, Helene, "The Voice of Boris Pasternak," Commonweal, 69:168-70, November 14, 1958.

[This is a biographical-critical approach to Pasternak's novel.] "In order to understand the many complexities of Doctor Zhivago, we should go back to . . . an earlier period, when Pasternak's own poetic genius was shaped." (J.M.D.)

P140   Ivask, George, "A Note on the Real Zhivagos," Russian Review, 25:405-8, October, 1966.

"I do not believe that one can find among the real Zhivagos some hints and allusions to this family, whose wealth and importance is rather exaggerated. . . ." (G.C.)

P141   Jackson, Robert L., "Doktor Živago and the Living Tradition," Slavic and East European Journal, 18:103-18, Summer, 1960.

Doctor Zhivago is closely related to War and Peace. Both depict "the individual as essentially powerless in the great tidal movements of history. But in War and Peace this powerlessness of the individual is tragic only when it is unrecognized or denied by the individual: in Doctor Zhivago it is unconditionally tragic." (W.G.F.)

DOKTOR ZHIVAGO (cont'd)

P142 Jackson, Robert L., "The Symbol of the Wild Duck in Dr. Zhivago,"
Comparative Literature, 15:39-45, Winter, 1963.

The wild duck episode is "apocalyptic in meaning"; it "presages the
tragedy of Zhivago and his world." (C.E.N.)

P143 Lamont, Rosette C., " 'As a Gift . . .': Zhivago, the Poet,"
PMLA, 75:621-33, December, 1960.

The poems of the Appendix disclose "the significant and indestructible
part of the life of the hero, which preserves in art his evanescent
moments of happiness and despair." (B.K.)

P144 Lehrman, Edgar H., "A Minority Opinion on Doctor Zhivago,"
Emory University Quarterly, 16:77-84, Summer, 1960.

Doctor Zhivago lacks the artistic unity of a great novel; further, its
hero does not sufficiently inspire our passionate involvement with
his fate. (R.K.)

P145 Livingstone, Angela, "Allegory and Christianity in Doctor Zhivago,"
Melbourne Slavonic Studies, 1:24-33, 1967.

In Doctor Zhivago Pasternak "has written with his metaphysics carefully before him and he has worked at details always with the overall
picture in mind [which] . . . has dictated the whole structure of
events and experiences in the novel. . . ." (D.P.)

P146 Lohenbill, F., "Doctor Zhivago and the Russian Revolution,"
Contemporary Issues, 11:1-10, May-June, 1961.

Pasternak's ideas about the Russian revolution are mirrored in
Doctor Zhivago's change from enthusiastic idealism to disillusion
and revulsion at violence and programmatic "reshaping life."
Pasternak's treatment of the revolution, distorted by feelings, is
not historically objective. Stalin's "planned barbarism" is not dis-
criminated from the earlier revolution. (K.M.)

P147 Loose, Gerhard, "Pasternak's Dr. Zhivago," Colorado Quarterly,
7:259-70, Winter, 1959.

[The now well-known story of the "publication, recognition and
denunciation" of Dr. Zhivago is retold followed by comments on

DOKTOR ZHIVAGO (cont'd)

the life of Pasternak and the concern of his novel, a work of "striking epic quality."] (D.H.)

P148　MacBride, Winifred, "Dr. Zhivago: Novel into Film," Journal of
Russian Studies, 18:20-5, No. 1, 1969.

Although many omissions of material from the novel for the film
can be justified on the basis of achieving reasonable length and
clarity, a number of omissions seriously distort Pasternak's intentions. Again, the overemphasis on the love story of Lara and Yurij
in the film, as well as the introduction of sentimental details, serves
to cheapen and simplify the message of the novel. (D.P.)

P149　MacIntyre, Alasdair, "Dr. Marx and Dr. Zhivago," Listener,
61:61-2, January 8, 1959.

The limitations of Russian critics of Doctor Zhivago have prevented
them from seeing "that the Marxist insights which they value so
highly are central to Pasternak's novel." Although Zhivago is the
protagonist, "the Revolution is a presence before which all the
characters tend to insignificance. . . ." Thus, "the diagnosis of
Dr. Zhivago's predicament has to be made in terms of the young
Dr. Marx's concept of human nature and its alienation." (D.P.)

P150　Mallac, Guy de, "Zhivago versus Prometheus," Books Abroad,
44:227-31, Spring, 1970.

"I would like to discuss here Pasternak's philosophy of natural
authenticity, as propounded in . . . Doctor Zhivago, and to show
how this desire for fulfillment through natural values clashes with
the Promethean dream of the Soviet era--since this conflict can be
seen as a basic tension in Pasternak's book." (D.P.)

P151　Markov, Vladimir, "Notes on Pasternak's Doctor Zhivago,"
Russian Review, 18:14-28, January, 1959.

"Besides being a work of art, Dr. Zhivago is clearly an ideological
novel. The themes of Christianity, death, freedom, truth, revolution, 'shared happiness,' history in general, nature and art in their
relation to the individual human being can be clearly seen." (R.G.L.)

DOKTOR ZHIVAGO (cont'd)

P152 Matlaw, Ralph E., "Mechanical Structure and Inner Form: A Note on War and Peace and Dr. Zhivago," Symposium, 16:288-95, Winter, 1962.

Structural parallels exist between the two novels. However, comparison is misleading because "the fundamental assumptions about history and about the form of the novel are completely different." (M.G.)

P153 Moreau, Jean-Luc, "The Passion According to Zhivago," Books Abroad, 44:237-43, Spring, 1970.

"Not only did Pasternak belong to the generation that reaped the heritage of Blok's; Christ, come late into his work as into that of his predecessor, completes in the poems of Doctor Zhivago the cycle of his Passion begun in 'The Twelve'." (D.P.)

P154 Obolensky, Dimitri, "The Poems of Doctor Zhivago," Slavic and East European Review, 40:123-35, 1962.

". . . the three basic themes . . . nature, love, and the author's views on the meaning and purpose of life--occupy an equally central position in the book as a whole; . . . the themes of nature and of human love . . . [have] always been typical of Pasternak's work; and . . . [his] reflections on the fundamental problems of human existence . . . are clarified and completed in this cycle of twenty-five poems." (D.P.)

P155 Oldham, Janet, "Dr. Zhivago and Babbitt," English Journal, 48:242-6, May, 1959.

In 1930 Sinclair Lewis was awarded the Nobel Prize primarily on the basis of Babbitt; in 1958 Boris Pasternak was similarly honored for Doctor Zhivago. "In each of the books the chief protagonist is not a person but a society: middle-class urban America in Babbitt, Mother Russia in Doctor Zhivago. . . . Both authors denounce conformity as the curse of their societies." "Nature is insignificant to Babbitt. . . . In Doctor Zhivago nature is an integral part of the story." "In each novel plot is subservient to the promulgation of ideas." (D.P.)

DOKTOR ZHIVAGO (cont'd)

P156   Page, Alex, "Doctor Zhivago in the Classroom," CEA Critic,
21:1, 10-1, March, 1959.

Doctor Zhivago "is a highly ambitious, complex, 'big' novel. . . .
Its subject is the fate of people and, equally important, the fate of
a man caught in chaos--his tiny part in championing that chaos and
his determination to preserve a vestige of life despite it." (D.P.)

P157   Powers, Richard Howard, "Ideology and Doctor Zhivago," Antioch
Review, 19:224-36, Summer, 1959.

Many American critics have overrated Doctor Zhivago. It is, in
fact, political, irreligious, and inartistic in its pleading for special
privilege and in certain failures of sympathy. Politics (and poor
artistry) may be defined as supporting or creating "sanctions for a
particular apportionment of rights and privileges." (F.C.T.)

P158   Prausnitz, Walther G., "Doctor Zhivago," Discourse, 2:171-88,
July, 1959.

"Pasternak's novel is one of the rare, great, permanent testaments
of art, and . . . the novel will live because of this and not because it
was written by a Russian during a time when Western man was
anxiously looking for an easing of political tension." (W.G.F.)

P159   Reeve, F. D., "Doctor Zhivago: From Prose to Verse," Kenyon
Review, 22:123-36, Winter, 1960.

"The most unusual aspect of Pasternak's Doctor Zhivago is the group
of poems which constitutes the seventeenth section of the novel."
These poems "are formal, tight, organized, immediately different
from the structure of the other sixteen sections. Their function is
. . . dependent on their formal excellence: they continue and comment on the rest of the novel just because of their artistic self-
sufficiency." (D.P.)

P160   Rowland, Mary and Paul Rowland, "Doctor Zhivago: A Russian
Apocalypse," Religion in Life, 30:118-30, Winter, 1960-61.

Doctor Zhivago was intended to "'resemble and continue the Revelation of St. John.'. . . The resemblances between the two works . . .
are many, striking, and unmistakable. . . . The chief purpose of
both revelations--St. John's and Pasternak's--is to give courage to

DOKTOR ZHIVAGO (cont'd)

persecuted, confused, despairing people by reminding them that
their struggle is part of . . . the continuing warfare between the
forces of God and Satan, of Good and Evil, of Life and Death."
(D.P.)

P161   Rowland, Mary and Paul Rowland, "Larisa Feodorovna: From
Another World," Kenyon Review, 22:493-501, Summer, 1960.

"In the person of beautiful, vital, erring Larisa Feodorovna,
Pasternak has created an eidolon of Russia--mother, nurse,
teacher of life, beloved land--whose figure is an integral part of
the rich nature imagery, of the love, defeat, and final triumph
woven into the tapestry of Doctor Zhivago." (D.P.)

P162   Rowland, Mary and Paul Rowland, "Pasternak's Use of Folklore,
Myth, and Epic Song in Doctor Zhivago," Southern Folklore
Quarterly, 25:207-22, December, 1961.

"From the wealth of material in the novel we have selected a few
examples--well known in Russia but little known here--which will
illustrate Pasternak's method and at the same time shed maximum
light on his philosophic message." (R.J.G.)

P163   Rowland, Paul and Mary Rowland, "The Mission of Yury and Evgraf
Zhivago," Texas Studies in Literature and Language, 5:199-218,
Summer, 1963.

"Our thesis, then, is that Doctor Zhivago . . . was a resolute
physician who deliberately remained with his stricken patient, Russia,
and sacrificed himself in an effort to save her. Together with his
brother Evgraf . . . Yury Andreyevich, metaphorically speaking,
descended into hell to set his countrymen free . . . [by loosing] their
spiritual fetters." (D.P.)

P164   Ruge, Gerd, "A Visit to Pasternak," Encounter, 10:23-4,
March, 1958.

[In this interview concerning Dr. Zhivago, Pasternak insists that
he had "the sense of obligation to bear witness, to provide a document
of the age" and to do it "by prose, by something that might well cost
more labour, more effort, more time, and whatever else."] (D.P.)

DOKTOR ZHIVAGO (cont'd)

P165   Šajković, Miriam Taylor, "Notes on Boris Pasternak's Doktor
Živago," Slavic and East European Journal, 4:319-30, Winter, 1960.

Doctor Zhivago concerns a change in ideas about both the individual
and society. The concept of the individual moves from "the idealistic position of immortality as memory" to "a clear belief in the
Christian sense of eternal life." The concept of society moves from
an idealistic enthusiasm for the socialist revolution in Russia to the
"higher realism" of sobornost--"the abiding felt communion" of man
with nature and man. (W.G.F.)

P166   Šilbajoris, Rimvydas, "The Poetic Texture of Doktor Živago,"
Slavic and East European Journal, 9:19-28, No. 1, 1965.

The narration is "so intense and true to the sources of life that it
communicates on the same level as poetry does, and this is what
constitutes the poetic texture of Doktor Živago. The book may be
read both as a novel and as a poem, because in it Pasternak succeeded
in speaking the language, not of poetry or prose in particular, but that
of art itself, as he understood it." (D.P.)

P167   Slonim, Marc, "Doctor Zhivago and Lolita," International Literary
Annual, 2:213-25, 1959.

"Doctor Zhivago . . . is certainly one of the most important and
representative novels of our century. . . . Lolita may not be a great
book--but it certainly is a most curious and symptomatic phenomenon
of the international (or cosmopolitan) spirit of Western Society."
(G.C.)

P168   Steussy, R. E., "The Myth Behind Dr. Zhivago," Russian Review,
18:184-98, July, 1959.

"It is my thesis that Dr. Zhivago is first and foremost a work constructed around . . . the myth of the inevitability of the Revolution
[of] . . . October 1917. . . ." (D.P.)

P169   Strachey, John, "The Strangled Cry," Encounter, 15:3-18,
November; 23-37, December, 1960.

Koestler's Darkness at Noon "was the first book to begin to reveal
the far-reaching consequences upon the mind and spirit of the West
of the rejection of Communism." The theme "of the falsification of

DOKTOR ZHIVAGO (cont'd)

the past, " which, "together with physical torture, was to make Orwell hag-ridden for the rest of his life, " first appeared in Animal Farm, his masterpiece. In 1984 "Orwell lent his powerful, detailed, concrete imagination to the task of describing a nightmare, in order, if possible . . . to avert it. " Whittaker Chambers "is a writer possessing major powers, but also capable of dreadful failures. . . ." Pasternak's Zhivago "completes, and at the same time transcends, the reaction against mechanical or 'mechanistic' materialism. " Thus, "against the awful sterility of this new dogma [of Communist rationalism] the strangled cry of the writers of the literature of reaction has been raised. " (D.P.)

P170   Struve, Gleb, "The Hippodrome of Life: The Problem of Coincidences in Doctor Zhivago, " Books Abroad, 44:231-6, Spring, 1970.

Many commentators have regarded the numerous coincidences in Doctor Zhivago as a weakness in composition. However, "not only are those coincidences part of a deliberature structural pattern, but they also have a deeper meaning and are expressive of the main thematic design of the novel. " (D.P.)

P171   Tiernan, Katherine, "Pasternak's 'Hamlet' (from Doctor Zhivago), " Explicator, 24: Item 45, January, 1966.

In his poem "Hamlet" in Doctor Zhivago "Pasternak has chosen to align the role of Hamlet with that of Christ in terms of his own conception of the pre-ordained self-sacrifice of the artist in society. " (D.P.)

P172   Urbanski, Edmund S., "Revolutionary Novels of Gironella and Pasternak, " Hispania, 43:191-7, May, 1960.

Gironella's Los cipreses creen en Dios and Pasternak's Doctor Zhivago espouse a belief in God and justice. "Both Gironella and Pasternak condemn the revolutionary chaos and civil war as well as the threats and inquisitorial terror of police states. " (A.C.H.)

P173   Vickery, Walter, "Symbolism Aside, Doktor Živago, " Slavic and East European Journal, 17:343-8, Winter, 1959.

The principal impact of Doctor Zhivago, and its claim to greatness derive not from its more abstruse and esoteric aspects, but from the doings, personalities, lives, and fates of the main characters. " (W.G.F.)

DOKTOR ZHIVAGO (cont'd)

P174   Wain, John, "The Meaning of Dr. Zhivago," Critical Quarterly,
10:113-37, Spring-Summer, 1968.

"Zhivago, like Christ, has triumphed by submitting. . . . He builds
his whole life on a deep act of choice, choosing his death and choosing his resurrection." (D.P.)

P175   Wall, Bernard, "A Great New Russian Novel," Listener, 60:387-8,
September 11, 1958.

Boris Pasternak's Dr. Zhivago "is plainly one of the great books of
our time and the only masterpiece we have had from Russia since
the Revolution. . . . deeply rooted in the Russian tradition . . . it
uses symbolism that has grown as unfamiliar to us as the . . . icons
of Kiev. . . . The style . . . is charged with a kind of restrained
classical poetry. . . ." (D.P.)

P176   Wilson, Edmund, "Legend and Symbol in Doctor Zhivago,"
Encounter, 12:5-16, June, 1959.

". . . the whole book is an enormous metaphor for the author's
vision of life. The personalities of Yury and Larisa stream back
into wider reaches, a realm in which their contours and features are
lost, in which they become indefinables, unclassifiable poetic elements that can only be conveyed by imagery; and it is not only the
imagery of these metaphors but their rhythms of recurrence, their
alienations, their confluences and interfusions that express the real
sense of Zhivago." (D.P.)

P177   Wilson, Edmund, "Legend and Symbol in Doctor Zhivago," Nation,
188:363-73, April 25, 1959.

"The more one studies Doctor Zhivago the more one comes to realize
that it is studded with symbols and significant puns, that there is
something in it of Finnegans Wake and something of the cabalistic
Zohar, which discovers a whole system of hidden meanings in the
text of the Hebrew Bible. . . . poetic symbolism . . . has been
plotted and planned by the author" to achieve "another dimension."
(D.P.)

DOKTOR ZHIVAGO (cont'd)

P178   Zaslove, Jerald, "Dr. Zhivago and the Obliterated Man: The Novel and Literary Criticism," Journal of Aesthetics and Art Criticism, 26:65-80, Fall, 1967.

"In this paper I wish to establish a context beginning with Tolstoy's sense of reality, that shows the novel is a failure and that the exact nature of Pasternak's response to life and art is a consequent comment on the state of criticism and aesthetics in our time." (D.P.)

PATCHEN, KENNETH

P179   See, Carolyn, "The Jazz Musician as Patchen's Hero," Arizona Quarterly, 17:136-46, Summer, 1961.

"Becaust Patchen is experimenting cautiously, and has taken over the parts of the jazz form that were essential to his ultimate success . . . there is a good chance that Patchen will be able to effect the merger of poetry and jazz." (R.G.L.)

PATEL, RAVJI

P180   Joshi, Suresh, "Life Against Death: The Poetry of Ravji Patel," Books Abroad, 43:499-503, Autumn, 1969.

Beneath the "simplicity of his poetic texture," Patel reveals a "complex artistic sensibility." He transformed Gujarati poetry into a "living art" by "sighing rapturously about his own death." (K.H.B.)

PATERSON, ANDREW BARTON

P181   Heseltine, H. P., " 'Banjo' Paterson: A Poet Nearly Anonymous," Meanjin Quarterly, 23:386-402, 1964.

Paterson's is "a special kind of minor poetry--an Arcadian poetry. It removes its material and attitudes to the realm of myth, and in so doing makes them permanently available to later readers." (A.S.W.)

P182   Long, Gavin, "Young Paterson and Young Lawson," Meanjin Quarterly, 23:403-13, December, 1964.

[This is a survey of verse contributed to The Bulletin in the late 1880's and early 1890's by Lawson and Paterson which includes a brief comparison of their works.] (G.C.)

P183 Semmler, Clement, "Kipling and A. B. Paterson: Men of Empire and Action," Australian Quarterly, 39:71-8, June, 1967.

A. B. Paterson "applied a romantic imagination to the Australian outback in precisely the same way as Kipling did to the empire at large. And just as Paterson has left in his writing an idealized vision of the bush and its courageous, philosophical and independent people . . . so too Kipling left for succeeding generations a vision of Empire that is . . . a saga in intrepidity and men pushing onwards into an unknown. . . ." (D.P.)

PATON, ALAN

P184 Callan, Edward, "The Art of Nadine Gordimer and Alan Paton: Introductory Remarks," English Studies in Africa, 13:291-2, March, 1970.

Nadine Gordimer and Alan Paton, who share a South African heritage, "differ in their insights into the significance of this heritage and also in their manner of expressing those insights." In Miss Gordimer's writing "one is likely to recoil with a sense of shock at the sight of one's own haggard face staring back from the mirror of her art. . . . Alan Paton's two great novels, Cry, the Beloved Country and Too Late the Phalarope . . . reach beyond realism, and even beyond tragedy to the mythological or spiritual worlds of resurrection and restoration." (D.P.)

P185 Paton, Alan, "Beware of Melancholy," Christianity and Crisis, 25:233-4, November 1, 1965.

[This short essay expresses Paton's view of the stance which persons who assume an active role in South African politics must take and makes clear his personal acquaintance with the problems of the South African people that ultimately gives authenticity to his fictional characters.] (E.F.S.)

P186 Rooney, F. Charles, "The Message of Alan Paton," Catholic World, 194:92-8, November, 1961.

Paton's technique is weakened by a tendency to "profess his heart" in passages which "do not have conviction or a natural flavor; they are superfluous, extrinsic." (R.L.G.)

CRY, THE BELOVED COUNTRY

P187   Baker, Sheridan, "Paton's Beloved Country and the Morality of Geography," College English, 19:56-61, November, 1957.

[This is a discussion of the Christian symbolism in Cry, the Beloved Country, with special reference to the hill and valley as heaven and earth.] (K. L.)

P188   Bruell, Edwin, "Keen Scalpel on Racial Ills," English Journal, 53:658-61, December, 1964.

Alan Paton's Cry, the Beloved Country and Harper Lee's To Kill a Mockingbird, both novels which deal with racial themes, are linked by "the twin powers of compassion and understanding." "In both novels the initial truth . . . is manifest--that the motives of children are basically kind and decent until the grown-ups get to them." (D. P.)

P189   Gailey, Harry A., "Sheridan Baker's 'Paton's Beloved Country'," College English, 20:143-4, December, 1958.

"Seldom . . . have I read a short article (CE, Nov. 1957) with so much promise that was compounded of so much unproven speculation." (M. J. O.)

P190   Marcus, Fred H., "Cry the Beloved Country, Strange Fruit: Exploring Man's Inhumanity to Man," English Journal, 51:609-16, December, 1962.

"Strange Fruit contrasts sharply with Cry, the Beloved Country. While both novels deal with Negro-white relationships under strained conditions, their emphasis and tonal qualities differ. Paton combines his sociological sophistication with simple lyric expression. Lillian Smith, however, has created a novel of explosive force with endless levels of psychological complexity." (D. P.)

TOO LATE THE PHALAROPE

P191   Baker, Sheridan, "Paton's Late Phalarope," English Studies in Africa, 3:152-9, September, 1960.

Too Late the Phalarope suffers from imported "literary" features; compassion turns sentimental. (R. K.)

PAULHAN, JEAN

P192   Abirached, Robert, "La Précaution inutile," <u>La Nouvelle Revue</u>
<u>Française</u>, No. 197, pp. 774-8, May, 1969.

"For Paulhan the short story is the privileged place where the writer
is able to exhibit the varieties of language with its good and bad will,
its semblance of artifice and its artless mechanics." (D.P.)

P193   Amer, Henry, "Jean Paulhan: Un Guide modeste," <u>La Nouvelle</u>
<u>Revue Française</u>, No. 197, pp. 922-6, May, 1969.

[This article discusses Paulhan's personal and intellectual traits.]
(D.P.)

P194   Belavel, Yvon, "Pas Facile à lire," <u>La Nouvelle Revue Française</u>,
No. 197, pp. 790-9, May, 1969.

Jean Paulhan wished to reinvent rhetoric. He failed to liberate
certain laws of expression, although he believed himself to be influential in dissipating "the illusion of great words." Perhaps Paulhan
is the Leibnitz of criticism of the future. (D.P.)

P195   Blanchot, Maurice, "La Facilité de mourir," <u>La Nouvelle Revue</u>
<u>Française</u>, No. 197, pp. 743-64, May, 1969.

Rapport with death plays an unrecognized role in the stories of
Paulhan. (D.P.)

P196   Boissonnas, Édith, "Les Mots," <u>La Nouvelle Revue Française</u>,
No. 197, pp. 702-3, May, 1969.

In his work Paulhan had the ability to simplify for others. This
seems strange, for his writings bear witness to a tendency to develop
nuances, to meander. (D.P.)

P197   Borel, Jacques, "Les Clés de Jean Paulhan," <u>La Nouvelle Revue</u>
<u>Française</u>, No. 197, pp. 927-30, May, 1969.

[These are keys to Paulhan's work as poet, as critic of literature
and art.] (D.P.)

P198   Bosquet, Alain, "Sur quelques phrases de Jean Paulhan, "
        La Nouvelle Revue Française, No. 197, pp. 814-8, May, 1969.

        [Explained here are some statements in letters of Paulhan which
        were written between 1950 and 1967.] (D.P.)

P199   Boulanger, Daniel, "Croquis, " La Nouvelle Revue Française,
        No. 197, pp. 674-6, May, 1969.

        [These are affectionate memoirs.] (D.P.)

P200   Bourgeade, Pierre, "Jean Paulhan et les philosophes, " La Nouvelle
        Revue Française, No. 163, pp. 170-3, July, 1966.

        Contrary to the philosophers for whom prose alone is pure, either
        as the selected instrument of reason or the necessary instrument of
        action, Paulhan does not make these distinctions. He seizes the
        language and returns it to us, in its fundamental ambiguity. (T.T.B.)

P201   Caillois, Roger, "Touches pour un portrait sincère, " La Nouvelle
        Revue Française, No. 197, pp. 734-40, May, 1969.

        [These are notes on the work and life of Jean Paulhan.] (D.P.)

P202   Chessex, Jacques, "Singulier plaideur, " La Nouvelle Revue
        Française, No. 197, pp. 782-6, May, 1969.

        Jean Paulhan isn't in a hurry; he does not promise miracles; he does
        not force. However, when one has accompanied him in his digres-
        sions, followed his oblique steps, when one has made Paulhan's
        doubts his, seen his reasons and his astonishments, admitted his
        objections and his examples, the truth of his enterprise seems
        natural and clear. (D.P.)

P203   Clerval, Alain, "Un Démocrate, Jean Paulhan, " La Nouvelle
        Revue Française, No. 197, pp. 931-7, May, 1969.

        Paulhan supported democratic ideals throughout his long life, al-
        though he was criticized for not being a member of the partisans in
        the Second World War. (D.P.)

P204   Dhôtel, André, "Jean Paulhan et le mystère," La Nouvelle Revue
Française, No. 197, pp. 829-35, May, 1969.

Paulhan is not a simple grammarian who has no other role than to
study the minor details of language and rhetoric. His research is a
critical research. (D.P.)

P205   Elsen, Claude, "Jean Paulhan et le Zen," La Nouvelle Revue
Française, No. 197, pp. 857-63, May, 1969.

The confluence of Buddhism, Taoism and Zen was most influential
on Paulhan's work. Personal letters of Jean Paulhan support this
thesis. (D.P.)

P206   Esteban, Claude, "Paulhan, peinture, perception," La Nouvelle
Revue Française, No. 197, pp. 888-96, May, 1969.

Paulhan is a patient and perceptive critic of painting. (D.P.)

P207   Etiemble, René, "Jean Paulhan ou le langagier contre le linguistique,"
La Nouvelle Revue Française, Nos. 186-7, pp. 969-85, June-July,
1968.

Whereas Valéry does not know what he is talking about when he tries
to explain how he composes a poem, and Benda accuses Bergson of
faults which are implicit in his own work, and Alain's experiments
on etymology are no better than those of Claudel, Paulhan's study of
language helps to deliver us from the tyranny of linguistics and thus
to prepare us for the coming Renaissance. (T.T.B.)

P208   Etiemble, [René], "Paulhan, épistolier," La Nouvelle Revue
Française, No. 197, pp. 897-902, May, 1969.

Paulhan's correspondence would destroy his standing as an angel
with some; it would exorcise his reputation as a devil for many; it
would reduce him to being a brother of mankind. (D.P.)

P209   Ferenczi, Thomas, "Jean Paulhan et la linguistique moderne,"
La Nouvelle Revue Française, No. 197, pp. 800-13, May, 1969.

Paulhan introduced to linguistics the study of the phrase and in so
doing modified the traditional opposition of language to the word.
(D.P.)

P210   Follain, Jean, "Paulhan l'attentif," <u>La Nouvelle Revue Française</u>, No. 197, pp. 713-4, May, 1969.

Paulhan was curious, attentive. This characteristic dominated his life, enriched his thought. (D.P.)

P211   Furnal, Roland, "Prose en l'honneur de Jean Paulhan," <u>La Nouvelle Revue Française</u>, No. 197, pp. 677-82, May, 1969.

Paulhan was a grammarian, a poet, a philosopher, a letter writer, a polemist, a Chinese scholar, a creator of splendors. (D.P.)

P212   Gracq, Julien, "Entre l'écriture et la lecture," <u>La Nouvelle Revue Française</u>, No. 197, pp. 741-2, May, 1969.

Paulhan wrote with great courage, he wrote with a singular originality which contributed to an uneasiness between writer and reader. (D.P.)

P213   Grenier, Jean, "L'Émerveillement," <u>La Nouvelle Revue Française</u>, No. 197, pp. 836-40, May, 1969.

[These are reflections on the thought and character of Paulhan.] (D.P.)

P214   Gyergyaï, Albert, "Souvenirs sur Jean Paulhan," <u>La Nouvelle Revue Française</u>, No. 197, pp. 663-9, May, 1969.

[These are recollections of a friendship and correspondence which began shortly after the first World War and ended with Paulhan's death in 1968.] (D.P.)

P215   Harvitt, Hélène, "An Appraisal of Jean Paulhan," <u>French Review</u>, 31:432-6, April, 1958.

[This is a consideration of articles on Paulhan which were published in <u>Cahier des Saisons</u> in April-May, 1957.] (F.M.L.)

P216   Hellens, Franz, "Adieu à Jean Paulhan," <u>La Nouvelle Revue Française</u>, No. 197, pp. 731-3, May, 1969.

[This is a fond, sentimental farewell.] (D.P.)

P217   Jouhandeau, Marcel, "Hommage à Jean Paulhan," La Nouvelle
Revue Française, No. 197, pp. 654-5, May, 1969.

The subtlety and precision of his language gave Paulhan a magic
power. (D.P.)

P218   Judrin, Roger, "Feuilles mortes," La Nouvelle Revue Française,
No. 197, pp. 659-62, May, 1969.

Paulhan is religious by Protestant standards. He searches for
enlightenment in the country of the Aztecs. He admires the mystic
philosophers. He does not yet believe; he is prepared to believe.
(D.P.)

P219   Lefebve, Maurice-Jean, "Cet homme de confiance," La Nouvelle
Revue Française, No. 197, pp. 687-90, May, 1969.

The qualities which this reliable man passes on to posterity are
preciosity, subtlety, scrupulousness, a certain astuteness, and a
return to simplicity, naturalness, spontaneity and innocence. (D.P.)

P220   Liger, Christian, "Vers une ethique," La Nouvelle Revue Française,
No. 197, pp. 841-56, May, 1969.

With logical precision, Paulhan developed a number of intellectual
rapports with first causes and the ends toward which his spirit drew
him. One may see the effects in his books; most significantly in
Une Main sous les Pierres. (D.P.)

P221   Mallet, Robert, "Jean Paulhan ou la leçon d'insolite," La Nouvelle
Revue Française, No. 197, pp. 691-5, May, 1969.

The ease with which Paulhan practiced the unwonted must be admired.
Ostensibly this characteristic could be taken for an affectation, a
premeditated attempt to astonish, to provoke, to stun. However,
this was his true nature. (D.P.)

P222   Martine, Claude, "Un Ferme soutien," La Nouvelle Revue Française,
No. 197, pp. 683-6, May, 1969.

[This is a memoir of Paulhan as editor of the Nouvelle Revue
Française.] (D.P.)

P223   Masson, André, "Jean Paulhan devant la peinture," La Nouvelle Revue Française, No. 197, pp. 877-80, May, 1969.

Paulhan preferred Georges Braque to other painters. The subjects chosen by Braque sometimes seemed to be rejoinders to topics of Paulhan. (D.P.)

P224   Mauriac, Claude, "Président de la république des lettres," À la Page, No. 64, pp. 52-3, October, 1969.

Paulhan dedicated his work to specifying the connection between meaning and words, having less at heart, however, the purification of literature than that of writers. (T.T.B.)

P225   Michaux, Henri, "En songeant à l'avenir," La Nouvelle Revue Française, No. 197, pp. 656-8, May, 1969.

Jean Paulhan should be rediscovered in the future. Clever with thoughts, he knew how to engage in free logic, practicing all manipulations, all tactics. (D.P.)

P226   Morand, Paul, "Le Voyage en Suisse," La Nouvelle Revue Française, No. 197, pp. 787-9, May, 1969.

Paulhan's visit to Switzerland in 1945 not only resulted in his Voyage en Suisse; it served to define to him with precision the duality of his nature: moral elegance, inflexible pride, physical beauty as against sincerity, honesty, and kindness. (D.P.)

P227   Noulet, É., "Rhétorique profonde," La Nouvelle Revue Française, No. 197, pp. 765-70, May, 1969.

The perfect critic and the perfect explorer, Paulhan always held at the center of his meanderings a profound rhetoric. (D.P.)

P228   Oster, Pierre, " 'Ici commence mon désespoir d'écrivain'," La Nouvelle Revue Française, No. 197, pp. 870-6, May, 1969.

Paulhan threw himself into a prolonged examination of the ambiguities peculiar to language. (D.P.)

P229   Parain, Brice, "Une Vie pleine," La Nouvelle Revue Française,
       No. 197, pp. 825-8, May, 1969.

       Paulhan was a disciple of Descarts, while at the same time being
       influenced by Zen Buddhism. This seems strange, since he was
       attuned to his times. In his first stories he demonstrated a bond
       with surrealism; he has been allied with Paul Éluard; he had also
       affinities with rationalists such as Léautaud. He is, finally, a
       classicist. (D.P.)

P230   Paulhan, Jean, "Correspondance," La Nouvelle Revue Française,
       No. 197, pp. 988-1041, May, 1969.

       [These letters, written by Paulhan from 1908 to 1968, were to
       Jouhandeau, Artaud, Gide, Étiemble, Édith Thomas, Suarès,
       Braque, and many others.] (D.P.)

P231   Peignot, Jérôme, "Paulhan la belette et le 'petit Robert',"
       La Nouvelle Revue Française, No. 197, pp. 819-24, May, 1969.

       The first principle upon which the work of Paulhan is constructed
       denies not only to words but also to language the ability to arrive at
       a definition of language. (D.P.)

P232   Perros, Georges, "Le métier d'être ou les instants bien employés,"
       Critique, No. 235, pp. 979-89, December, 1966.

       It is with words, with language that Paulhan is so amusing. In his
       careful impatience, he deducts in advance, pockets, notes, waits.
       There is no length in his work, yet it is not concise. It is, instead,
       economy, propriety, generous elimination. (T.T.B.)

P233   Picon, Gaëtan, "D'une double enterprise," La Nouvelle Revue
       Française, No. 197, pp. 903-8, May, 1969.

       [This article describes Paulhan's double role as the editor of
       La Nouvelle Revue Française and as a prolific and important author.]
       (D.P.)

P234   Pieyre de Mandiargues, André, "J. P.," La Nouvelle Revue
       Française, Nos. 186-7, pp. 986-96, June-July, 1968.

       With Paulhan it is never a question of a beautiful novel or admirable
       poem. Most often it is the rarity, the natural, the clarity, insolence
       or humor which are praised, and always the figure of the author and

the virtues of vocabulary and expression which form less a critical
opinion than a portrait. (T.T.B.)

P235   Pieyre de Mandiargues, André, "Partie gagnée," La Nouvelle
Revue Française, No. 197, pp. 649-53, May, 1969.

Paulhan insisted on the equality and identity of contraries: (good
and bad, high and low, hot and cold, light and dark). He had a
spiritual discipline, a unique intellectual honesty. (D.P.)

P236   Porquerol, Élisabeth, "Le Nîmois ou l'attraction de l'ennemi,"
La Nouvelle Revue Française, No. 197, pp. 709-12, May, 1969.

Paulhan was a native of Nîmes, where language is often used to
describe the opposite of feeling and thought. Irony, humor predominate. Metaphor, symbol are constant aspects of this language.
(D.P.)

P237   Régnier, Yves, "Les Yeux de Jean," La Nouvelle Revue Française,
No. 197, pp. 696-701, May, 1969.

[These last letters and reflections of Jean Paulhan and Yves Régnier
are much concerned with cats.] (D.P.)

P238   Sébastien, Robert, "Avec Jean Paulhan," La Nouvelle Revue
Française, No. 197, pp. 704-8, May, 1969.

[These are fond memories of Jean Paulhan.] (D.P.)

P239   Segonds, Jean-Philippe, "Jean Paulhan-Valery Larbaud:
Entrentiens familiers," La Nouvelle Revue Française, No. 197,
pp. 715-30, May, 1969.

[This is an exchange of letters between Paulhan and Larbaud from
1923 to 1935, the years of their greatest friendship. A brief introduction by Segonds is included.] (D.P.)

P240   Spens, Willy de, "Un Guerrier exemplaire," La Nouvelle Revue
Française, No. 197, pp. 779-81, May, 1969.

Paulhan volunteered for a regiment of Zouaves in the first World
War; however, he believed in peace, in humanity, in sanity. (D.P.)

P241   Thévenin, Paule, "Le Bouquet de violettes de Jean Paulhan, "
La Nouvelle Revue Française, No. 197, pp. 909-21, May, 1969.

Artaud's long friendship with Paulhan began in 1923 when Paulhan,
then secretary to Jacques Rivière, editor of La Nouvelle Revue
Française, wrote to Artaud to refuse the publication of his poems in
the NRF. (D.P.)

P242   Wogensky, Robert, "Celui qui aimait les peintres, " La Nouvelle
Revue Française, No. 197, pp. 881-7, May, 1969.

He was one of those very rare men who were not blinded by intelligence and culture. He mistrusted peremptory affirmations, knowing that infallible reasons are never secure, that the lines are never
right, and that thinkers, sages, or artists cannot, finally, resolve
questions. (D.P.)

P243   Zylberstein, Jean-Claude, "Bibliographie, " La Nouvelle Revue
Française, No. 197, pp. 1042-55, May, 1969.

[This is a descriptive list of articles, reviews, exhibition catalogues,
and books authored by Paulhan, arranged chronologically.] (D.P.)

LE CLAIR ET L'OSCUR

P244   Jaccottet, Philippe, "En Relisant Le Clair et l'obscur, " La Nouvelle
Revue Française, No. 197, pp. 864-9, May, 1969.

The most serious misunderstanding of Paulhan now is the general
lack of comprehension of the authority of his language among the
phrase-makers; his sense of justice is rejected among the fanatics;
his subtle balance in our firmament is not appreciated. (D.P.)

LES FLEURS DE TARBES

P245   Minon, Jean-Michel, "Actualité des Fleurs de Tarbes, " Revue des
Langues Vivantes, 25:188-91, No. 3, 1959.

Paulhan's efforts to rehabilitate literary criticism by establishing a
new rhetoric have gone virtually unnoticed. Yet the Terreur he
denounced has but augmented since the publication of his Fleurs de
Tarbes. "Only through a universal study of the modes of expression
can we put an end to the insufficiencies of criticism. " (R.C.F.)

PROGRÈS EN AMOUR ASSEZ LENTS

P246   Dalmas, André, "Le Spectateur," La Nouvelle Revue Française, No. 197, pp. 771-3, May, 1969.

Progrès en amour assez lents, a brief story still little known fifty years after it appeared, seems mysterious, suspenseful, devoted to love. (D.P.)

PAUSEWANG, GUDRUN

P247   Glenn, John, "Gudrun Pausewang and Der Weg nach Tongay: A New Voice in German Literature," Studies in Short Fiction, 7:556-63, 1970.

Fräulein Pausewang, although a very talented writer, has "not been widely acclaimed by either the academic community or the reading public" since "her works contain neither the profanity and eroticism often found in best-sellers, nor the stream-of-consciousness philosophizing of many literary novels. The style is simple, almost austere, the model of clarity." The "definite modern element in Fräulein Pausewang's novels . . . most readily demonstrable in Der Weg nach Tongay is the bold conception of man's relation to God." (D.P.)

PAUSTOVSKII, KONSTANTIN

P248   Urman, Dorothy Fuldheim, "Konstantin Paustovskii, Marcel Proust and the Golden Rose of Memory," Canadian Slavic Studies, 2:311-26, Fall, 1968.

"For Proust art was a subjective intellectual exercise in analyzing a man's soul. Paustovskii displays a gentle, compassionate heart as he lays bare before us the life of his moment in the Space-Time continuum. . . . In neither Proust nor Paustovskii is there grandeur. Proust was too cultivated, Paustovskii too gentle. . . . Proust chronicled the world he knew. . . . Paustovskii shows the collapse of that world. . . ." (D.P.)

PAVESE, CESARE

P249   Biasin, Gian-Paolo, "The Smile of the Gods," <u>Italian Quarterly</u>, 10:3-32, 1966.

". . . in the Mediterranean mythology Pavese seems to have found himself and the world, without tensions. By going to the origins of mystery, 'which, being irrational, brings us to the universal,' Pavese has found the fraternal bond between himself and others, without, however, overcoming his solipsism. . . ." (D.P.)

P250   Biasin, Gian-Paolo, "Lo straniero sulle Colline: Cesare Pavese," <u>Modern Language Notes</u>, 81:1-21, January, 1966.

"In <u>Dialoghi con Leucò</u> Pavese turned to the classics to discover universal truth; in <u>La luna e i falò</u> he returned to his hills to rediscover universal truth: in the first book he achieved a clear metaphysics, in the second a profound subjectivity." (D.P.)

P251   Chase, Richard H., "Cesare Pavese and the American Novel," <u>Studi Americani</u>, No. 3, pp. 347-69, 1957.

Cesare Pavese "illustrates the stylistic and ideological effects of [the Italian] contact with the American corpus of literature; to which he went for its 'regionalism' and . . . 'rinnovamento linguistico nella prosa italiana.'. . ." He "without question found some liberation for his intuition in his contact with American novelists and poets; and although . . . this 'borrowing' was a complex one . . . it certainly shaped the general form, structure and dialogue of his stories. . . ." (D.P.)

P252   Deguy, Michel, "Pavese poète," <u>La Nouvelle Revue Française</u>, No. 202, pp. 598-608, October, 1969.

The <u>Dialogues with Leuco</u> are a key for the reading of all Pavese's poems, in which the men are essentially mortals speaking to divinities or mythological sirens and trying to rationalize death and nothingness. (T.T.B.)

P253   Fales, Angela Bianchini, "Cesare Pavese e le sue opere posthume," <u>Italica</u>, 31:160-9, September, 1954.

"Pavese, shy and pensive writer, lived his difficult and lonely years locked in the world of his poetry and his interior life. He has left behind [in his posthumous works] the means to trace his love affair with death." (D.P.)

P254   Fernandez, Dominique, "Cesare Pavese, poète," La Nouvelle
        Revue Française, No. 126, pp. 1076-81, June, 1963.

        Known as essayist and novelist, Pavese was first of all a poet.
        Desirous of opposing to D'Annunzianism and its sequels a simple,
        spoken poetry without embellishment or declamation, he wanted "to
        make each poem a récit," which resulted in a sort of anti-poetry
        purged of every musical sortilege, reduced to a look cast honestly
        on the world. (T.T.B.)

P255   Fiedler, Leslie A., "Introducing Cesare Pavese," Kenyon Review,
        16:536-53, 1954.

        "The real unity which is discoverable in Pavese's work under its
        superficial shifts from realism to regionalism, from the political
        to the archetypal, is his preoccupation with the meanings of America;
        as essayist, poet, novelist, translator and critic, his chief effort
        was directed toward defining, discovering an America for his coun-
        try and his time." (G.C.)

P256   Flint, R. W., "Translating Cesare Pavese," Delos, 1:152-64, 1968.

        "A major literary figure by Italian standards . . . Cesare Pavese
        had the kind of essentially lyric and confessional genius that seems
        to spill over almost automatically into legend and scandal; he was,
        in a word, naïve. . . . My purpose here is to . . . rescue him from
        the suspicion of having become popular for the wrong reasons and to
        justify the very high estimation in which he is held by a few intelligent
        and experienced people." (D.P.)

P257   Ginzburg, Natalia, "Portrait of a Friend," London Magazine,
        8:21-7, May, 1968.

        ". . . it remained for him to conquer mundane reality: but this was
        forbidden and impregnable to him, who had both thirst and disgust
        for it; and thus he was only able to gaze at it as from distant spaces."
        (K.M.W.)

P258   Heiney, Donald, "Pavese: The Geography of the Moon," Contempo-
        rary Literature, 9:522-37, 1968.

        Pavese "belongs with Stendhal and Rimbaud," all those who believe
        that " 'the final-and primary--reason for making a story is the
        impulse to bring into form the irrational and indistinct that lurks at
        the bottom of our experience'." (G.C.)

P259   Hood, Stuart, "A Protesant Without God: On Cesare Pavese,"
       Encounter, 26:41-8, No. 5, 1966.

       "What gives Pavese's writing its laconic power is his own detach-
       ment, his refusal to make moral or political judgments. . . .
       Politically, Pavese was too honest to believe that good and evil lie
       wholly on one side or the other." (D.P.)

P260   Leiner, Wolfgang, "L'uomo solo. Das Problem der Einsamkeit bei
       Pavese," Die Neueren Sprachen, 15:122-8, March, 1966.

       "[Pavese's] suicide was the final impressive confirmation of the life
       experiences of many of his narrative figures, of Pavese's own life
       experiences: the acknowledgment of the impossibility of freeing
       oneself from the shaft of loneliness." (J.R.R.)

P261   Marshall, Robert G., "Additional Items on Pavese's American
       Criticism," Italica, 9:268-72, December, 1962.

       [Listed here with commentary are four book reviews by Pavese and
       the preface to his translation into Italian of Christopher Morley's
       The Trojan Horse. These items, not included in Pavese's collection
       of critical articles on American literature, Letteratura americana e
       altri saggi (Turin 1952), "may help . . . to throw additional light on
       the understanding of the subject."] (D.P.)

P262   Rimanelli, Giose, "The Conception of Time and Language in the
       Poetry of Cesare Pavese," Italian Quarterly, 8:14-34, 1964.

       Pavese's poems "are suffused with an ineffable feeling that transcends
       reason." Also, they "are primarily a series of landscapes at once
       governed and united by a primordial rhythmic background which cre-
       ates and recreates the myth of existence." (D.P.)

P263   Rimanelli, Giose, "Myth and De-Mythification of Pavese's Art,"
       Italian Quarterly, 49:3-39, 1969.

       "The difference between Pavese and his contemporaries is that the
       latter used the mythic past . . . as a simile in that, for them, to
       believe in history transformed into legend would have been equivalent
       to a rejection of their poetics. Instead Pavese, with the help of myth,
       dramatizes the experiences of his contemporaries, and encompasses
       them within himself." (K.M.W.)

P264   Tenenbaum, Louis, "Character Treatment in Pavese's Fiction,"
        Symposium, 15:131-8, Summer, 1961.

        In his fiction Pavese adopted "a fragmentary, episodic method of
        character presentation which generally resulted in violence to the
        chronological and the sequential. The focus of unity, the transcen-
        dental relationship existent between the personages and the physical
        and spiritual environment is lucidly delineated, but this process . . .
        requires that no one character monopolize either the author's or the
        reader's attention to the point that he destroys the harmony and pro-
        portion of the narrative form." (D.P.)

             LAVORARE STANCA

P265   Foster, David William, "The Poetic Vision of Le colline: An
        Introduction to Pavese's Lavorare stanca," Italica, 42:380-90,
        No. 4, 1965.

        ". . . Pavese turns a coldly critical eye upon his material, ruthlessly
        scrutinizing it and unmercifully portraying the bitterest of realities."
        His "particular anguish is that of the poet who is both a part of and
        external to his poetic world." (G.C.)

             LA LUNA E I FALÒ

P266   Freccero, John, "Mythos and Logos: The Moon and the Bonfires,"
        Italian Quarterly, 4:3-16, 1961.

        In Pavese's The Moon and the Bonfires "Nuto saw the death of Santu
        and could never again contemplate an act of violence. Cinto saw the
        burning of his home and put down his knife forever. It remains for
        these two to teach the lesson of brotherly love to the rest of mankind.
        The two bonfires have served to awaken them into a new life and have
        therefore done some good in spite of the violence." (D.P.)

P267   Norton, Peter M., "Cesare Pavese and the American Nightmare,"
        Modern Language Notes, 77:24-36, 1962.

        ". . . The Moon and the Bonfires may . . . be read as a kind of
        doom-haunted parable of our times. The book's dualistic structure
        . . . is typical of our deranged culture in which black and white,
        hep and square, fascist and communist attack each other across a
        no-man's-land of imagined stability." (G.C.)

THE MOON AND THE BONFIRES--See
LA LUNA E I FALÒ

PAZ, OCTAVIO

P268   Bosquet, Alain, "Octavio Paz, ou le séisme pensif," La Nouvelle
Revue Française, 14:1071-5, December, 1966.

The words of Paz over the last fifteen years serve to qualify him as
one of the rare poets seized viscerally by paroxysm and wisdom. At
each page his contradictory outbursts clash, multiply, form a strange,
a balanced yet unbalanced aberration. (T.T.B.)

P269   Durán, Manuel, "Libertad y erotismo en la poesía de Octavio Paz,"
Sur, No. 276, pp. 72-7, May-June, 1962.

The poetry of Octavio Paz, Mexico's leading contemporary poet, is
dominated by several central themes or concerns: solitude, communion, liberty and eroticism. (D.P.)

P270   Durán, Manuel, "Liberty and Eroticism in the Poetry of Octavio
Paz," Books Abroad, 37:373-7, Autumn, 1963.

Paz is the most important contemporary Mexican poet. His poetry
is "dominated by two or three central and organizing experiences,
points of departure and points of arrival: solitude, communion,
liberty, eroticism." (C.E.N.)

P271   Durand, José, "Octavio Paz: A Mexican Poet-Diplomat," Américas,
15:30-3, July, 1963.

The writings of Octavio Paz, poet and diplomat, show his strong
attachment and passion for Mexico, although he has lived, traveled
and studied in many parts of the world and has opened himself to
many influences. He is "a passionate and contradictory soul, with
lucid intelligence and sensibility, and an adventurous imagination
that . . . will confess to horror, repugnance, or tenderness. And
also, irremediably, beauty." (D.P.)

P272   Duvignaud, Jean, "Le Poète et l'amibe," La Nouvelle Revue
Française, No. 133, pp. 118-24, January, 1964.

In El laberinto de la soledad, Paz has seized and understood the living woof and thread of his own culture, as few poets have. The
European seeks in death something the world has not given him.

There is a mysticism of love and a love of mysticism. In his
Homenaje y profanaciones, Paz contrasted the eroticism of Eastern
practices, the rigorous obsession of the flesh transformed by volup-
tuousness or the exaltation of desire. (T.T.B.)

P273   Fein, John M., "The Mirror as Image and Theme in the Poetry of
        Octavio Paz," Symposium, 10:251-70, Fall, 1956.

The mirror image is an "obsession or at least a fixation of Paz."
It is an object that "suggests absence of limits, an object which by
definition is not subject to the usual laws of spacial measurement."
His search for meaning in the mirror is ultimately a negative one
and is, in many ways representative of twentieth century man.
(B.B.)

P274   King, Lloyd, "Surrealism and the Sacred in the Aesthetic Credo of
        Octavio Paz," Hispanic Review, 37:383-93, July, 1969.

"Paz has argued that the sacred is above all made manifest through
poetic consciousness issuing in the poem. Poetic experience fulfills
the demiurgic function of imagination and puts man in touch with his
original religious perceptions long clouded by institutional Religion."
(C.O.)

P275   Souza, Raymond D., "The World, Symbol and Synthesis in Octavio
        Paz," Hispania, 47:60-5, March, 1964.

"Paz is an ambitious poet who has dealt with many of the numerous
individual and social problems that exist in the world today. At a
time in which the distinguishing attitude has been one of negation,
Paz has chosen to raise an affirmative voice characterized by an
almost mystical optimism." (C.O.)

EL LABERINTO DE LA SOLEDAD

P276   Sirgado, Isabel M. Cid de, "En torno a El laberinto de la soledad
        de Octavio Paz," Hispanófila, 37:59-64, September, 1969.

"Aspects of Octavio Paz's Laberinto reveal general characteristics
of the author's thought. Religion, poetry and love are three essential
elements in his work; each may be analyzed sui-generis. In Paz
conscience is a substitute for God; God, in Laberinto is lord of
nothing. Poetry is a means to create a revolution for oneself, and
love [in Laberinto] opposes its social identification with marriage."
(D.P.)

LIBERTAD BAJO PALABRA

P277 Rambo, Anne Marie Remley, "The Presence of Woman in the Poetry of Octavio Paz," Hispania, 51:259-64, May, 1968.

In Paz's major collection, Libertad bajo palabra, woman appears in three forms: (1) universal image, (2) the beloved, (3) transformed and fused with nature. Love of woman is the key to the search for a metaphysical union which is the central theme of Paz's philosophy. (C.O.)

PIEDRA DE SOL

P278 Bernard, Judith, "Myth and Structure in Octavio Paz's Piedra de sol," Symposium, 21:5-13, Spring, 1967.

"Patterned on a primitive cosmological view but utilizing the most sophisticated references and techniques, this work represents the primeval cyclical state in which opposites were united in a pure existence outside of limitations of space and time." (C.O.)

P279 Meloche, Verna M., "El ciclo de Paz: Ideas sobre Piedra de sol de Octavio Paz," Hispanófila, No. 13, pp. 45-51, September, 1961.

The "sun stone" of the title refers to a primitive clock. Here it is the 584 day clock of Venus--love--the only reality for man. (C.O.)

P280 Nelken, Zoila E., "Los avatares del tiempo en Piedra de sol de Octavio Paz," Hispania, 51:92-4, March, 1968.

The Aztec Calendar is transformed into a poem as unique as its source. The poem presents Paz's four cardinal aspects of Time: (1) Time immemorial, the beginning of beginnings; (2) historical time, the succession of events; (3) psychological time, emotion before history and life; (4) religious time, the "privileged instant" of mystic union with Being. (C.O.)

P281 Nugent, Robert, "Structure and Meaning in Octavio Paz's Piedra de sol," Kentucky Foreign Language Quarterly, 13:138-46, 1966.

"Existence is, for Paz, the individual being as he reaches out . . . with another body, other men, all nature. . . . Paz attempts to reconcile his solitude with utterance." (C.O.)

PUERTA CONDENADA

P282   Segall, Brenda, "Symbolism in Octavio Paz's 'Puerta condenada'," Hispania, 53:212-9, May, 1970.

The boarded-up door of the title is typical of the symbols Paz uses to reflect the desolation and confusion within himself as well as in the world. The system of symbols expresses an unrelieved despair. (C.O.)

LA RAMA

P283   Leal, Luis, "Una poesía de Octavio Paz," Hispania, 48:841-2, December, 1965.

"In 'La rama' Paz has given us his concept of reality. Reality, according to Paz, is capable of transformation; thus . . . the young pine with its growing shoots, may be transformed by the magic of poetry into the symbol of poetry; the bow and the arrow." (D.P.)

SUN STONE--See
PIEDRA DE SOL

PEAKE, MERVYN

P284   Morgan, Edwin, "The Walls of Gormenghast: Introduction to the Novels of Mervyn Peake," Chicago Review, 14:74-81, Autumn-Winter, 1960.

Peake's novels give an impression of relevance to life that is all the more extraordinary because it might seem incompatible with the undoubtedly "Gothic material . . . which Peake doesn't hesitate to incorporate." (W.G.F.)

PÉGUY, CHARLES

P285   Béguin, Albert, "Péguy and the Communion of Saints," Cross Currents, 7:193-200, Summer, 1957.

"There is hardly an important page of his work or an aspect of his belief that ought not to be linked up with that happiness which he felt in meditating on the communion of saints." For Péguy, this communion was symbolized by "a chain of unbreakably linked fingers" encompassing past, present and future and leading to a victory over time. (W.J.L.)

P286   Borgal, Clément, "Charles Péguy et Alain-Fournier," La Table Ronde, No. 202, pp. 68-78, November, 1964.

Péguy and Fournier had a number of points in common other than their friendship. Both were of peasant origin and had a love of the countryside. Both were faithful to their childhood teachings and had an obsession with purity to the highest degree. (T.T.B.)

P287   Braun, Sidney D., "An Unpublished Letter from J. Schlumberger to André Suarès," French Review, 39:533-5, February, 1966.

[This letter comments on Suarès's book Péguy, published in 1915, and corroborates Suarès's portrait of Péguy.] (D.P.)

P288   Chauchard, Paul, "Deux fils de l'espérance," La Table Ronde, No. 207, pp. 79-84, November, 1964.

In spite of evident differences, there are many analogies in the works of Péguy and Teilhard de Chardin. The same modern world is the object of meditations on war. The same love of nature and of human works animates their works, as well as the same disappointment before their ambiguity, the same obsession with salvation. (T.T.B.)

P289   Delaporte, Jean, "L'Expérience spirituelle de Péguy," La Table Ronde, No. 202, pp. 39-59, November, 1964.

From 1897 to 1907, Péguy forged his own objective method of knowledge and applied it to a concrete analysis of the times as well as to the outline of a philosophy of history. In 1910 his socialistic Jeanne d'Arc became Christian and Péguy experienced a refound faith, rediscovery of the catechism and acceptance of the Church. This is fidelity of grace. His last period, 1912-1914, is characterized by fidelity of action. (T.T.B.)

P290   Delaporte, Jean, "Péguy et le catholicisme française au début du siècle," La Table Ronde, No. 299, pp. 43-59, February, 1967.

It took thirty years and two wars for Péguy's work to be studied in depth. One has finally discovered that, behind the national poet and moralizing writer to which he had been reduced, there is a philosopher Péguy, a theologian Péguy, and even a prophet Péguy. (T.T.B.)

P291   Fowlie, Wallace, "Péguy as Poet," <u>Commonweal</u>, 66:594-5, September, 1957.

After reviewing contemporary work on Péguy, it is clear that "only the mere beginnings of Péguy's justification as a poet have been written." (W.J.L.)

P292   Fraisse, Simone, "Péguy et la Sorbonne," <u>Revue d'Histoire Littéraire de la France</u>, 70:416-34, May-June, 1970.

Péguy attacked the Sorbonne on several occasions because it never gave him the recognition he craved. (D.-J.J.)

P293   Fumet, Stanislas, "Péguy 'd'un seul tenant'," <u>La Table Ronde</u>, No. 202, pp. 18-38, November, 1964.

Péguy, in the <u>Mystères</u> of Jeanne d'Arc, depicted her as his image, the portrait of his soul and its transfiguration. She is a socialistic Jeanne, just as Péguy was at 23 or 24. The other influence on the work of Péguy is found in the Dreyfus Affair, which he treated as a Christian mysticism and frequently confused with Jeanne d'Arc. (T.T.B.)

P294   Gilmary, Elizabeth, "Péguy's Madonna," <u>Renascence</u>, 6:112-6, Spring, 1954.

"Briefly, the whole life of Péguy was akin to a pilgrimage. From his peasant childhood through his youth of unbelief, he sought the eternal shrine of the Virgin. His heart was always going home to her." (W.J.L.)

P295   Guillemin, Henri, "Péguy et Jaurès," <u>Les Temps Modernes</u>, 18ᵉ année, No. 194, pp. 78-108, July, 1962.

One finds curious discrepancies in Péguy's writing. In 1899 he sided with Juarès in favor of Waldeck-Rousseau. In 1910 he declared Juarès a part of "our national shame." Yet in 1901 he reproached Juarès for too much idealism and generosity. The more one attempts to find valid ethical or ideological reasons for Péguy's combat with Juarès, the less apparent they become. (T.T.B.)

P296   Guy, Basil, "Notes on Péguy the Socialist," <u>French Studies</u>, 15:12-29, January, 1961.

"Such as they are, these notes deal first with biographical data regarding Péguy's political activity until approximately 1905, and then attempt to evaluate its importance for his later works and our interpretation of them." (W.J.L.)

P297   Guyon, Bernard, "Fidélités ou reniements," <u>La Table Ronde</u>, No. 202, pp. 61-7, November, 1964.

Péguy accords a primordial importance to the virtue of fidelity but the curve of his life and his successive stands on various questions often make him appear as an infidel and renegade. (T.T.B.)

P298   Hardré, Jacques, "Charles Péguy et Albert Camus: Esquisse d'un parallèle," <u>French Review</u>, 40:471-84, February, 1967.

Parallel situations in the life and works of Péguy and Camus reveal some striking resemblances. Sharing similar formation and tastes, they share also the same love of humanity, the same respect for justice and the same devotion to truth. Both seek happiness--Camus, in vain by revolt against the absurd; Péguy, in belief in God. (S.M.K.)

P299   Hardré, Jacques, "Péguy et les classiques," <u>South Atlantic Bulletin</u>, 34:12-5, November, 1969.

Péguy's preferences were the Greek authors which determined not only his attitude towards classical and modern French authors but the choice of characters in his own works. (T.T.B.)

P300   Henry, Sister Mary, C.S.J., "Péguy's Debt to Pascal," <u>L'Esprit Créateur</u>, 2:55-65, Summer, 1962.

". . . the imprint of both the personality and the work of Pascal was a decisive factor in [Péguy's] intellectual and spiritual formation and in his orientation toward a deep comprehension of man and of Christianity. . . . Pascal brings to Péguy a personal doctrine and helps him to be more truly himself. . . . to a certain degree it is thanks to Pascal that the work of Péguy reaches metaphysical, psychological and spiritual depth. . . . essentially Pascalian themes are re-presented by Péguy with renewed freshness and pertinency." (D.P.)

P301   Jones, Grahame C., "Graham Greene and the Legend of Péguy,"
Comparative Literature, 21:139-45, Spring, 1969.

Péguy's personality rather than his writings has marked the works
of Graham Greene, although fundamental differences exist between
their attitudes. "Greene sees the world in the unrelieved colors of
evil and corruption; whereas Péguy with his simple peasant attachment to the earth, glorifies the world as God's own creation redeemed by Christ." (D.P.)

P302   Jussem-Wilson, Nelly, "Péguy et ses premiers commentateurs
d'outre-Manche," Revue de Littérature Comparée, 36:121-30,
January-March, 1962.

Today the Anglo-Saxon public has all but forgotten Péguy. Immediately preceeding and following the war of 1914, however, Péguy was
one of the most discussed and appreciated French authors. [This is
a chronicle of that enthusiastic reception.] (D.-J.J.)

P303   Kelly, Mother M. Louis, "Charles Péguy: Rassembleur des siècles
de l'humanisme chretien," Romance Notes, 2:16-20, Fall, 1960.

Péguy's special gift as a religious writer is his ability to make us
touch objects and see reality. (G.B.M.)

P304   Nugent, Robert, "Péguy and Charity," Renascence, 9:32-5, 1956.

[This article concerns Péguy's attempt to create ". . . a new ethic
of action for France, one which he exemplified in his death on the
Marne." There are frequent references to his Holy Innocents and
Corneille's Polyeucte.] (W.J.L.)

P305   Queffélec, Henri, "Racine, Péguy et le silence," La Table Ronde,
No. 168, pp. 44-53, January, 1962.

Péguy's energetic repulsion towards Racine amounted almost to an
allergy, but one which implied resemblances of composition. Both
had the same taste for mysticism and the same respect for literature
and for a public. (T.T.B.)

P306   Schmitt, Hans A., "Charles Péguy: Autobiographer," Renascence,
9:68-76, Winter, 1956.

"His prose, especially, is rich in autobiographical detail. His discourse, no matter what the subject, is constantly interrupted by

intensely personal asides which give the reader a striking two-dimensional view. Péguy simultaneously presents to his public the idea and its source and environment." (W.J.L.)

P307 Schmitt, Hans, "Charles Péguy: The Man and the Legend, 1873-1953," Chicago Review, 7:24-37, Winter, 1953.

[This article traces Péguy's relations with socialism and the Church. It concludes with a summary of critical and popular reaction to his work.] (W.J.L.)

P308 Schmitt, Hans A., "Charles Péguy's Rise to Fame," Renascence, 10:129-36, 1958.

Peguy's "rise to fame was rapid. Rewards of a substantial nature came to him as early as 1909. . . . In part, at least, this was due to his ability to inspire undying loyalty in some and unqualified distaste in others." He was "a self-made man. Neither influence nor protection of any substantial sort smoothed his path to fame." (D.P.)

P309 Sussex, R. T., "Charles Péguy," Meanjin Quarterly, 19:184-92, June, 1960.

[This is a general consideration of Péguy's life and thought with occasional references to his style.] (W.J.L.)

P310 Turnell, Martin, "A Hero of Our Time--Péguy," Commonweal, 85:251-4, December 2, 1966.

"Péguy cannot be judged in purely literary terms. He is not for me what is ordinarily understood by a great writer, but I have no doubt that he was a great man. He was a powerful personality. He had grasped certain 'basic verities' and was determined to put them across to the public. He succeeded in spite of the faultiness of his instrument because of the man he was." (D.-J.J.)

P311 Weber, Eugen, "A Persistent Prophet--Péguy," French Review, 27:337-45, April, 1954.

From April 1913 on, "Péguy's work, in print or in talk, would be to prepare France for the war which he considered as inevitable as the dawn, and in many ways as hopeful. And his campaigns in this role were carried on, quite inevitably, on two fronts. For Péguy was a prophet and, as such, a moralist." (D.P.)

P312   Wilson, Nelly, "A Contribution to the Study of Péguy's Anti-Intellectualism: Early Revolt against the Spirit of the Sorbonne," *Symposium*, 20:63-78, Spring, 1966.

Although Péguy's war against "l'esprit de la Sorbonne" is generally regarded to have begun as an aftermath to the Dreyfus Affair, "we hope to show that Péguy reacted against the spirit of the Sorbonne [which was] . . . inseparably linked in his mind with the spirit of modern times, long before his denunciation of 'la trahison des clercs.' The latter was a resumption of hostilities . . . into which the Dreyfus Affair . . . had introduced an uneasy truce." (D.P.)

P313   Wilson, N., "Ernst Stadler and Charles Péguy: Notes on the Fiction and Facts of a Relationship," *Modern Language Review*, 57:551-5, October, 1962.

"The evidence available at present would suggest that the exchange of ideas" between Péguy and Stadler during World War I "across trenches is fiction, but that a pre-war exchange of ideas between the two poets may well be fact." (S.T.B.)

JEANNE D'ARC

P314   Onimus, Jean, "Les Sources de la Jeanne d'Arc de Péguy," *Revue d'Histoire Littéraire de la France*, 62:381-99, July-September, 1962.

A study of his sources shows how Péguy altered his models to create his own Jeanne d'Arc. (D.-J.J.)

NOTRE JEUNESSE

P315   Jussem-Wilson, Nelly, "L'Affaire Jeanne d'Arc et l'Affaire Dreyfus: Péguy et Notre Jeunesse," *Revue d'Histoire Littéraire de la France*, 62:400-15, July-September, 1962.

"Notre Jeunesse is the work of a man who felt out of place in his century: he is a Christian who wants to remain a humanist and who finds himself at odds with those who fight religion under the humanist flag, and with those who seek in Christianity the weapons to eliminate the old French tradition of humanism." (D.-J.J.)

TEMPORAL AND ETERNAL--See
NOTRE JEUNESSE

PENZOLDT, ERNST

P316   Gump, Margaret, "Ernst Penzoldt: Ein Humanist unserer Zeit, "
German Quarterly, 39:42-54, January, 1966.

Eleven years after his death Penzoldt is still little known in America.
His works were described by Thomas Mann as "contributions to
humanity." In these works Penzoldt is revealed as a non-militant
pacifist, as a humanist who saw no conflict between being both a
German and a citizen of the world. (R.H.L.)

PERCY, WALKER

P317   Blouin, Michael T., "The Novels of Walker Percy: An Attempt at
Synthesis, " Xavier University Studies, 6:29-42, February, 1967.

"Dichotomization and syncretism are the cultural diseases from
which Percy's heroes suffer," but for redemption, Percy returns
in both of his novels to "the family in its archetypal, evolutionary,
and religious dimensions." (A.S.W.)

P318   Bradbury, John M., "Absurd Insurrection: The Barth-Percy Affair,"
South Atlantic Quarterly, 68:319-29, Summer, 1969.

John Barth and Walker Percy, similar Southern existential novelists,
treat absurdist protagonists similarly, although they are qualitatively
discrete in style and background. Both men lead their characters
through miasmas of rejection, alienation, and despair. "The new
Southern world is a tragi-comic absurdity. . . . It produces existential despair . . . cosmopsis, suicide." (P.M.C.)

P319   Brown, Ashley, "An Interview with Walker Percy, " Shenandoah,
18:3-10, Spring, 1967.

[Percy discusses his early years, his background in psychiatry,
his use of the existential mode, and his two novels The Last Gentleman and The Moviegoer.] (K.M.W.)

P320   Cheney, Brainerd, "Secular Society as Deadly Farce, " Sewanee
Review, 75:345-50, Spring, 1967.

"Mr. Percy's satiric illumination of Orgasm Only worship, that has
had so pervasive a literary vogue in this country, is done in large
perspective and fully." Despite the verbal nihilism of his characters,
Percy implants in them a hope which is not dead. (D.M.M.)

P321   Cremeens, Carlton, "Walker Percy, The Man and the Novelist: An Interview," Southern Review, 4:271-90, April, 1968.

[This interview elicits Percy's views of the modern South, the state of Southern fiction, influences on his work--primarily Russian and French novelists--and his writing procedures.] (D.P.)

P322   Lawson, Lewis A., "Walker Percy's Indirect Communications," Texas Studies in Language and Literature, 11:867-900, Spring, 1969.

". . . the influence of Kierkegaard on Dr. Percy's thought can hardly be overemphasized. Allusions and references to the Danish writer abound in his nonfiction articles, and both The Moviegoer and The Last Gentleman begin with mottoes from the same source." (H.S.)

P323   Lawson, Lewis A., "Walker Percy's Southern Stoic," Southern Literary Journal, 3:5-31, Fall, 1970.

". . . admiration of the Stoic attitude as it was embodied in William Alexander Percy and his class, but rejection of the attitude as being irrelevant to the present generation, has remained with Walker Percy. Such a dialectic provides the essence of the relationship between the protagonist and the representative of the past, the father figure, in both of his novels" The Moviegoer and The Last Gentleman. (K.M.W.)

P324   Lehan, Richard, "The Way Back: Redemption in the Novels of Walker Percy," Southern Review, 4:306-19, April, 1968.

"While there are many differences between the novels of Faulkner and Walker Percy, both these Southern writers share the same point of view, although Percy's characters are less concerned with the reasons for the moral and physical collapse of their world and more concerned with how to come to terms with everyday problems." (J.M.D.)

P325   Maxwell, Robert, "Walker Percy's Fancy," Minnesota Review, 7:231-7, 1967.

Walker Percy's The Moviegoer and The Last Gentleman "are two magnificent novels. . . ." He "is as gifted a narrator as we are likely to find today. . . . He is outfitted with flawless pitch, an absolute ear necessary to the detailing of how our moment-to-moment concourse becomes small treason. . . . Especially, here is one of the really pure contemporary prose styles; fluid, idiomatic, many-leveled, always personal; an intensity built out of the comedian's throwaway gifts. The man writes beautifully. . . ." (D.P.)

THE MOVIEGOER

P326   Atkins, Anselm, "Walker Percy and Post-Christian Search," Centennial Review, 12:73-95, Winter, 1970.

[This is an "attempt to clear up the muddle (caused by various critical interpretations of the character John "Binx" Bolling in Percy's The Moviegoer) by indicating the philosophical and theological framework within which Binx's search is conceived, and by showing how his search . . . explains his actions and attitudes."] (H.S.)

P327   Henisey, Sarah L., "Intersubjectivity in Symbolization," Renascence, 20:208-14, Summer, 1968.

By the end of The Moviegoer the main characters are beginning to be "integrated with the world. They have discovered how much they are alike through communication, through a symbolization which achieves intersubjectivity." (S.A.)

P328   Hoggard, James, "Death of the Vicarious," Southwest Review, 49:366-74, Autumn, 1964.

Percy's The Moviegoer "does not seem remarkable or glorious--its tone is too nonchalant for that; but on reflection one realizes that a man, under his own stamina, has come to grips with responsibility; and perhaps one is surprised that there is nothing terrifying in it." (S.A.)

P329   Thale, Jerome, "Alienation on the American Plan," Forum (Houston), 6:36-40, Summer, 1968.

Percy's novel about alienation is successful because of his "happy facility for inventing or revivifying metaphors for familiar concerns --moviegoing, exile, the horizontal and vertical searches." (A.S.W.)

P330   Thale, Mary, "The Moviegoer of the 1950's," Twentieth Century Literature, 14:84-9, July, 1968.

The Moviegoer may be placed against Miss Lonelyhearts, for a better examination of Percy's character Binx Bolling. "While

THE MOVIEGOER (cont'd)

Shrike, though magnificent, is limited in his interests and in his expression, Binx has a broader insight into other people and a greater variety of voices. This range of his knowledge and expression is integral to The Moviegoer. Only a man who has passed beyond a phase of being 'sensitive and articulate' can see the people around him as 'dead,' can feel the anguish for a world that might be, a rage-turned-to-irony for the world that is." (D.P.)

P331   Van Cleave, Jim, "Versions of Percy," Southern Review, 6:990-1010, October, 1970.

"I want to look first at [William Alexander Percy's] Lanterns on the Levee as it relates to Walker Percy's characterization of and attitude toward Aunt Emily in The Moviegoer; then to examine in detail Binx Bolling's response to the idealistic form of unauthenticity and his eventual, if not necessarily permanent, shared consciousness with his cousin Kate Cutrer." (D.P.)

PERCY, WILLIAM ALEXANDER

P332   Spalding, Phinizy, "A Stoic Trend in William Alexander Percy's Thought," Georgia Review, 12:241-51, Fall, 1958.

Percy's work has been misrepresented as without contemporary application because his noteworthy poems are set in the past and written in traditional forms; but his approach to the problem of change and reform, based on the Classical Stoical philosophy, has universal significance. (W.G.F.)

LANTERNS ON THE LEVEE

P333   Van Cleave, Jim, "Versions of Percy," Southern Review, 6:990-1010, October, 1970.

"I want to look first at [William Alexander Percy's] Lanterns on the Levee as it relates to Walker Percy's characterization of and attitude toward Aunt Emily in The Moviegoer; then to examine in detail Binx Bolling's response to the idealistic form of unauthenticity and his eventual, if not necessarily permanent, shared consciousness with his cousin Kate Cutrer." (D.P.)

PÉRET, BENJAMIN

P334   Caws, Mary Ann, "Péret and the Surrealistic World," <u>Romance</u>
        <u>Notes</u>, 11:233-7, Winter, 1969.

        "The most direct of all the surrealist poets, and perhaps the only
        one to write consistently automatic poems, he casually displays the
        effortless perfect language of abundance and explosion that was
        demanded also of the Dada poet. In view of this, it is particularly
        interesting to examine, if briefly, his own attitude toward the
        language of surrealism, which he meant to be the chief instrument
        of man's liberation." (D.-J.J.)

P335   Caws, Mary Ann, "Péret: Plausible Surrealist," <u>Yale French</u>
        <u>Studies</u>, No. 31, pp. 105-11, May, 1964.

        "Péret is the most faithful poet of Surrealism because he is never
        untrue to its theory; he is the only one constantly at ease in auto-
        matic writing. . . . In his spontaneous writing, image follows image
        with no apparent effort on the part of the poet. The reader is con-
        scious . . . of a flow of images all consistent with a world in which
        the poet is at home. . . . Péret's poems . . . do have a structure,
        sometimes exterior, sometimes interior." (D.P.)

P336   Caws, Mary Ann, "Péret's <u>Amour sublime</u>--just another <u>Amour</u>
        <u>fou</u>?" <u>French Review</u>, 40:204-12, November, 1966.

        Péret is a surrealist poet, faithful to the principles of the movement.
        A re-examination of the poet's works presently out of print may prove
        him to be an equal to André Breton. The love theme in Péret clearly
        establishes his link with the surrealist movement. (S.M.K.)

P337   Caws, Mary Ann, "Péret and the Surrealist Word," <u>Romance Notes</u>,
        11:233-7, Winter, 1969.

        Péret's extremely spontaneous poems contain an expression of poetic
        theory of language that goes beyond self-consciousness. (A.K.)

P338   Matthews, J. H., "Mechanics of the Marvelous: The Short Stories
        of Benjamin Péret," <u>L'Esprit Créateur</u>, 6:23-30, Spring, 1966.

        Péret places his stories in a universe released from the restrictions
        of our own. He borrows from the real to elaborate the surreal.
        "The manner in which he undertakes to dispose of the disparity which
        exists in the world we call normal between the familiar and unthought-
        of is a distinctive feature of his narrative method." (T.T.B.)

P339   Prigioni, Pierre, "Benjamin Péret: Das Gewissen seiner Zeit,"
        Germanisch-Romanische Monatsschrift, 14:188-97, April, 1964.

        Present revival of surrealistic art brings renewed interest in this
        little known French poet who felt poetry should give a complete pic-
        ture of life and that the poet should fight for new human rights,
        should accuse society of its crimes. [This brief survey closes with
        a bibliography of the late poet's published works.] (J.R.R.)

PÉREZ DE AYALA, RAMÓN

P340   Beck, Mary Ann, "La realidad artística en las tragedias grotescas
        de Ramón Pérez de Ayala," Hispania, 46:480-9, September, 1963.

        Ayala's sardonic view of life stems from experiences of childhood
        and youth, and is best exemplified in a novel such as Belarmino y
        Apolonio, rather than in Tigre Juan and its sequel. (C.O.)

P341   Campbell, Brenton, "The Esthetic Theories of Ramón Pérez de
        Ayala," Hispania, 50:447-53, September, 1967.

        [This is a synthesis of Ayala's ideas as scattered through some
        sixty years of literary journalism. General areas treated are
        esthetic perception, the nature of art, esthetic creation, and the
        function of art.] (C.O.)

P342   Campbell, Brenton, "Free Will and Determinism in the Theory of
        Tragedy: Pérez de Ayala and Ortega y Gasset," Hispanic Review,
        37:375-82, July, 1969.

        Two apparently contrary views of tragedy are really conciliable.
        Ayala associates tragedy with necessity, Ortega with freedom; but
        Ayala focusses on the spectator, Ortega on the tragic hero. (C.O.)

P343   Chapman, Arnold, "Waldo Frank in the Hispanic World: The First
        Phase," Hispania, 44:626-34, December, 1961.

        Shortly before Waldo Frank visited Madrid in 1924 and at the begin-
        ning of his crusade to unite the Americas with cultural bonds, Pérez
        de Ayala began a series of articles condemnatory of the United States,
        the articles supposedly in review of H. G. Wells's The Future of
        America. Waldo Frank responded in print, pointing out many of the
        fallacies Pérez de Ayala had taken from Wells. (D.P.)

P344 Fabian, Donald L., "Bases de la novelística de Ramón Pérez de Ayala," Hispania, 46:57-60, March, 1963.

The task of the critic, for Ayala, is to elucidate and justify the intent and achievement of the artist. The novelist must give first importance to his characters, to his moral foundations, and to the classic principles of beauty and restraint. Technique as such is secondary, a professional attribute. (C.O.)

P345 Fabian, Donald L., "Pérez de Ayala and the Generation of 1898," Hispania, 41:154-9, May, 1958.

Pérez de Ayala's early novels exhibit the generational preoccupation with Spain's decadence in politics, religion and literature. (A.C.H.)

P346 Fabian, Donald L., "The Progress of the Artist: A Major Theme in the Early Novels of Pérez de Ayala," Hispanic Review, 26:108-16, April, 1958.

Ayala's Tinieblas en las cumbres, A. M. D. G., La pata de la raposa, and Troteras y danzaderas present the development of the artist in three phases from egotism ("forms") through aridity ("clouds") to maturity ("norms"). (A.C.H.)

P347 Hartsook, John H., "Literary Tradition as Form in Pérez de Ayala," Romance Notes, 6:21-5, 1964.

[Pérez de Ayala allays reader anxiety and achieves unified form by ironic allusion to epic and Cervantine tradition.] (C.O.)

P348 Livingstone, Leon, "The Theme of the Paradoxe sur le comédien in the Novels of Pérez de Ayala," Hispanic Review, 23:208-23, July, 1954.

"Throughout the novels of Ramón Pérez de Ayala runs a predominant theme . . . indispensable to the understanding of this writer. This motif is a variation on Diderot's thesis, expounded in the Paradoxe sur le comédien, that the great actor . . . is successful in the portrayal of emotions precisely to the degree that he does not feel them." (D.P.)

P349   Rand, Marguerite C., "Pérez de Ayala: Poet, Novelist, and Essay-
       ist," Hispania, 45:662-9, December, 1962.

       [This is a summary of his career on the occasion of his death with
       special emphasis on his poetry, his essays, and his interest in the
       United States.] (C.O.)

P350   Schraibman, José, "Cartas inéditas de Pérez de Ayala a Galdós,"
       Hispanófila, No. 17, pp. 83-103, 1963.

       [These are letters written from 1905 to 1917.] (C.O.)

P351   Shaw, D. L., "On the Ideology of Pérez de Ayala," Modern
       Language Quarterly, 22:158-66, 1961.

       Pérez de Ayala "occupies an important position in the ideological
       pattern which underlies the literature of the Generation of 1898.
       . . . Ayala's change to his later [serene] outlook . . . localiz[es]
       the decline of authentic '98 sensibility as a creative force in modern
       Spanish literature." (D.P.)

            BELARMINO Y APOLONIO

P352   Leighton, Charles A., "La parodia en Belarmino y Apolonio,"
       Hispanófila, No. 6, pp. 53-5, 1959.

       Although both elements and objects of the parody seem obvious,
       there is room for doubt. In any case, it is important to recognize
       that these characters have lived beyond the limited time of their
       topical reference. (C.O.)

P353   Weber, Frances, "Relativity and the Novel: Pérez de Ayala's
       Belarmino y Apolonio," Philological Quarterly, 43·253-71, April,
       1964.

       ". . . the relativity of reality, its fragmentation into many different
       points of view . . . [is] the underlying theme of [Pérez de Ayala's]
       best novel, Belarmino y Apolonio." ". . . the novel is a carefully
       wrought image of the relativity of truth. Yet at the center of this
       ingenious contrivance is an absurd story about two crazy shoe-
       makers. . . ." "By making the crazy shoemaker the spokesman
       for his own beliefs, Pérez de Ayala fuses comedy and a doctrine of
       love [into] . . . the often paired gestures of affirmation [which]
       bring together the infinite fragments of reality." (D.P.)

LA CAÍDA DE LOS LIMONES

P354   Noble, Beth, "The Descriptive Genius of Pérez de Ayala in La caída
de los limones," Hispania, 40:171-5, May, 1957.

"La caída de los limones, generally considered a good exposé of the
cacique system but inferior to the other two novelas poemáticas
(Prometeo, Luz de domingo), is . . . an excellent psychological
novel and a little masterpiece of descriptive style with striking
plasticity of language and subtle juxtaposition of visual, symbolic,
and abstract reality." (A.C.H.)

PROMETEO

P355   Fabian, Donald L., "Action and Idea in Amor y pedagogía and
Prometeo," Hispania, 41:30-4, March, 1958.

Pérez de Ayala's Prometeo shares with Unamuno's Amor y pedagogía
"an obvious similarity in certain incidents of the plots." But Ayala's
novelette is a thesis novel. "Unamuno's novel . . . rises to a climax
whose effect is essentially emotional." (A.C.H.)

P356   Johnson, Ernest A., "The Humanities and the Prometeo of Ramón
Pérez de Ayala," Hispania, 38:276-81, September, 1955.

Ayala's ironic rendering of the Odyssey suggests that humanity is
best characterized, not by the exceptional man, the "leavening,"
but by the broad masses which serve as footing for the rest. (C.O.)

PROMETHEUS--See
PROMETEO

LA REVOLUCIÓN SENTIMENTAL

P357   Soldevila-Durante, Ignacio, "Ramón Pérez de Ayala: De 'Sentimental
Club' a 'La revolución sentimental'," Cuadernos Hispanoamericanos
No. 181, pp. 5-19, January, 1965.

"Sentimental Club," a forgotten early story of Pérez de Ayala, links
him with the London literary scene of that time (1909), as well as
with the ideas of Shaw, J. Huxley, and H. G. Wells. A revised version of the story (1959) reveals quite a different man. (C.O.)

SENTIMENTAL CLUB--See
LA REVOLUCIÓN SENTIMENTAL

PÉREZ GALDÓS, BENITO

P358   Alfaro, María, "Tres heroínas nefastas de la literatura española,"
Cuadernos Americanos, 140:246-54, May-July, 1965.

Doña Perfecta of Galdós, La Tía Tula of Unamuno, and Bernarda
Alba of Lorca could only have existed in Spain. Incarnating a
blindly conceived sense of virtue, they each bring about ruin and
destruction. They lack human kindness; they are slaves to their
obsessions. (C.O.)

P359   Alfieri, J. J., "The Double Image of Avarice in Galdós's Novels,"
Hispania, 46:722-9, December, 1963.

Paired characters, frequent in Galdós, are particularly negative
when motivated by greed. Symbolically the "avarice pairs" recall
the traditional mortal sin as well as suggesting the modern capitalist;
technically they are a part of Galdós's pervasive gemelismo. (C.O.)

P360   Alfieri, J. J., "Galdós Revaluated," Books Abroad, 42:225-6,
Spring, 1968.

"The recent trend in Galdósian studies shows a reaction against the
critics who have overstated the novelist's accomplishments. The
need to re-examine Galdós, to accept him on his own terms and
within the framework of his own epoch has been apparent for some
time and is now being met by competent scholarship." (D.P.)

P361   Andrade Alfieri, Graciela, and J. J. Alfieri, "El lenguaje familiar
de Pérez Galdós," Hispanófila, No. 22, pp. 27-73, 1964.

Considered radical in his day, Galdós used the language of the
streets in his novels without fear of critic or Academy. [A 35-page
lexicon of idiomatic expressions in Fortunata y Jacinta is included.]
(C.O.)

P362   Andrade Alfieri, Graciela and J. J. Alfieri, "El lenguaje familiar
de Galdós y de sus contemporáneos," Hispanófila, 28:17-25, 1966.

"Our intention in this article is to compare the colloquial language
of Galdós with that of other novelists of his time, and to especially
consider selected novels of Alarcón, Clarín, Pardo Bazán, Valera

which vary from Galdós's practice." Galdós made much more frequent use of colloquialisms "in communicating reality and humanity in his descriptions." (D.P.)

P363   Ángeles, José, "Baroja y Galdós: Un ensayo de diferenciación," Revista de Literatura, 33:49-64, January-June, 1963.

In spite of the commonplace that Galdós is a precursor and model for Baroja and his generation, the differences are enormous. The great objectivity of Galdós is quite incompatible with the subjectivity of Baroja. (C.O.)

P364   Ángeles, José, "Galdós en perspectiva," Revista de Estudios Hispánicos, 3:105-16, 1969.

The tendency to link Galdós to the following "Generation of '98" is mistaken. For reasons of style and philosophy, differences are more noteworthy than similarities. (C.O.)

P365   Ángeles, José, "¿Galdós precursor del noventa y ocho?" Hispania, 46:265-73, May, 1963.

In spite of the commonplace of literary history, the differences between Galdós and the Generation of '98 are fundamental and widespread. They may be discussed under as many as ten headings. (C.O.)

P366   Bacarisse, S., "The Realism of Galdós: Some Reflections on Language and the Perception of Reality," Bulletin of Hispanic Studies, 42:239-50, 1965.

If language is material reality, not a means of presenting it, then "writing is realistic to the extent that the conceptual and logical properties of language are neutralized giving the illusion of perceptual acquaintance with content." (C.O.)

P367   Blanquat, Josette, "Galdós et la France en 1901," Revue de Littérature Comparée, 42:321-45, July-September, 1968.

"Galdós is at the head of the anti-clerical campaign in Spain. . . . We have tried to clarify the anti-clericalism of Galdós, the reasons which motivated him through the course of his life, and the nuances which distinguished [his anti-clericalism] from French anti-clericalism." (D.P.)

P368   Bonet, Laureano, "Clarín ante la crisis de 1898," Revista de Occidente, 25:100-19, April, 1969.

The novelist Galdós, most representative of the Restoration, presents an ideological trajectory similar to that of Clarín: juvenile and optimistic defender of middle-class values. Clarín's republican pragmatism and cultural hispanicism is more clearly evident. (T.T.B.)

P369   Casalduero, Joaquín, "Conjunción y divergencia de vida y arte en Galdós," Hispania, 53:828-35, December, 1970.

Although it is traditional to seek biographical sources for fictional events and characters, numerous examples from the life and works of Galdós underline the importance of studying also the divergencies. (C.O.)

P370   Casalduero, Joaquín, "Galdós: De Morton a Almudena," Modern Language Notes, 79:181-7, March, 1964.

Unfortunately we lack a comprehensive study of Galdós by theme. "In our time a work of art forms part of an epoch; it conforms to a system of references in which new life or new aspects may often be seen, because it has acquired a series of resonances and complementary values which did not exist when the work was created." (D.P.)

P371   Chamberlin, Vernon A., "Galdós and Galdósistas in the United States: On the Fiftieth Anniversary of the Author's Death," Hispania, 53:819-27, December, 1970.

[This is an overview of Galdós scholarship in the United States since 1920.] (C.O.)

P372   Chamberlin, Vernon A., "A Galdósian Statement in 1899 Concerning Dramatic Theory," Symposium, 24:101-10, Summer, 1970.

The united contribution of Pérez Galdós on page 638 of volume one of the Revista Nueva is "a frank and intimate revelation" which "indicates that at that date Galdós had, at least temporarily, abandoned his Messianic vision of the theater in favor of a theory of drama that was essentially novelistic." (D.P.)

P373   Chamberlin, Vernon A., "Galdós's Sephardic Types," <u>Symposium</u>, 17:85-100, Summer, 1963.

"In conclusion, then, an examination of the Sephardic characters [in <u>Aita Tettauen</u> and <u>Carlos VI, en la rápita</u>] reveals that even when Galdós worked from reference sources instead of living models, realism of speech and personal names were an important part of his creativity. . . . many of his characters . . . appear more convincingly realistic than those of eye-witness Alarcón who actually lived for a time in a Sephardic home. . . . Finally . . . he reveals a sense of fairness toward all groups, shows compassionate understanding for the plight of the <u>Sephardim</u>, and is, as always, an advocate of religious toleration." (D.P.)

P374   Chamberlin, Vernon A., "Galdós's Use of Yellow in Character Delineation," <u>PMLA</u>, 79:158-63, March, 1964.

". . . Galdós used yellow as a conscious, effective facet of his characterization technique throughout the major part of his long literary career [to] . . . reflect . . . the common Occidental notion of yellow as a symbol of opprobrium." For Galdós <u>personajes</u> afflicted by the sins of "fanatical religious intransigence . . . and lust for wealth . . . needed to be stigmatized clearly with the opprobrious color of illness, the social outcast, and the devil." (D.P.)

P375   Chamberlin, Vernon A., "The <u>Muletilla</u>: An Important Facet of Galdós's Characterization," <u>Hispanic Review</u>, 29:296-309, October, 1961.

As in his English predecessor Dickens, Galdós makes extensive use of the "speech tag" to individualize his characters and set them in the reader's mind. (C.O.)

P376   Correa, Gustavo, "Tradicion mística y cervantismo en las novelas de Galdós, 1890-97," <u>Hispania</u>, 53:842-51, December, 1970.

Although the influences of Tolstoy and of the New Testament are clear in Galdós's later works, he himself reminds us of the indigenous idealism and mysticism typified by Santa Teresa and Don Quixote. (C.O.)

P377   Curland, David J., "Galdós and the Advanced Class in High School,"
        Hispania, 52:873-6, December, 1969.

        Doña Perfecta and Gloria can profitably be assigned for reading and
        discussion in the advanced high school class. (C.O.)

P378   Davison, Ned J., "Galdós's Conception of Beauty, Truth and Reality
        in Art," Hispania, 38:52-4, March, 1955.

        Fragmentary remarks in speeches and journalism reveal that Galdós
        holds a largely coherent view of literary art. To him nothing is
        more beautiful than reality, which consists of "pure emanations of
        truth." (C.O.)

P379   Eoff, Sherman, "Galdós y los impedimentos del realismo,"
        Hispanófila, No. 24, pp. 25-34, 1965.

        In his realism Galdós is typically plebian and uncommitted emotion-
        ally. Thus he is less highly regarded than contemporaries such as
        Dostoyevsky or Zola. (C.O.)

P380   Fedorchek, Robert M., "The Ideal of Christian Poverty in Galdós's
        Novels," Romance Notes, 11:76-81, 1969.

        A voluntary commitment to live in poverty brings suffering and hard-
        ship. But unlike charity or fraternity, it is of clearly divine inspira-
        tion, "an efficacious means of serving God." (C.O.)

P381   Gillespie, Gerald, "Galdós and the Unlocking of the Psyche,"
        Hispania, 53:852-6, December, 1970.

        "The arbitrariness of an existence dictated by unconscious, irrational
        forces flowing out of the psyche did not mean a reductio ad absurdum.
        The unconscious mind was still anchored in the bedrock of natural
        law." (C.O.)

P382   Hafter, Monroe Z., "Ironic Reprise in Galdós's Novels," PMLA,
        76:233-9, June, 1961.

        "The present essay focuses on Galdós's developing skill with internal
        repetitions from La fontana de oro . . . through the rich complex-
        ities of the novels written between 1886-89 to their almost stylized
        simplicity in El abuelo (1897). . . . the variety of verbal echoes,
        the mirroring of one character in another, the unconscious illumina-
        tion each may offer the other, underscore the increasingly intimate

wedding of form and matter with which Galdós came to unfold his narratives." (D.P.)

P383   Heck, Francis S., "Dos mujeres sin alma: La Pharisienne y Doña Perfecta," Duquesne Hispanic Review, 4:79-89, 1965.

No definite answer may be given to the question whether Galdós's Doña Perfecta influenced Mauriac's La Pharisienne, or indeed whether Mauriac knew the work of Galdós. (D.P.)

P384   Paolini, Gilberto, "The Benefactor in the Novels of Galdós," Revista de Estudios Hispánicos, 2:241-9, 1968.

True charity, for Galdós, is a unifying force which knows no limits of person or class. It is "a levelling force with a sanctifying resultant." (C.O.)

P385   Pattison, Walter T., "How Well Did Galdós Know English?" Symposium, 24:148-57, Summer, 1970.

In spite of claims by Galdós and others "our conclusions . . . must be that Galdós did not learn English as a child. Later on, when Dickens became his admired master, he made an effort to familiarize himself with the language, but his progress was minimal . . . . After several trips to England he still did not speak the language fluently. . . ." (D.P.)

P386   Penuel, Arnold M., "The Ambiguity of Orozco's Virtue in Galdós's La incógnita and Realidad," Hispania, 53:411-8, September, 1970.

The complex nature of reality is reflected in the character Orozco, whose nearly obsessive generosity is tinged with guilt, egotism, pride, and puritanical deprivation. (C.O.)

P387   Rogers, Douglass, "The Descriptive Simile in Galdós and Blasco Ibáñez: A Study in Contrasts," Hispania, 53:864-9, December, 1970.

In general, Ibáñez favors a poetic or descriptive simile, Galdós a humorous one. Thus Ibáñez is usually pictorial while Galdós may be conceptual. (C.O.)

P388   Schraibman, Joseph, "Cartas inéditas de Galdós," Symposium,
        16:115-21, Summer, 1962.

        [These are eight previously unpublished letters of Galdós.]   (R.J.G.)

P389   Schraibman, José, "Cartas inéditas de Pérez de Ayala a Galdós,"
        Hispanófila, No. 17, pp. 88-103, 1963.

        [These are letters written from 1905 to 1917.]   (C.O.)

P390   Schraibman, Joseph, "Dreams in the Novels of Pérez Galdós,"
        Literature and Psychology, 10:91-6, Autumn, 1960.

        "The present study is the result of an examination of the one hundred
        and seventy dreams which appeared in the thirty-one social novels
        [of Galdós] written between 1870 and 1915, a period which encom-
        passes Galdós's entire literary career. The word dream is used
        here in its broadest sense. . . ." Galdós should be included "in a
        prominent place among those creative writers who in their intuitive
        understanding of human nature anticipated the later findings of an
        experimental science." (D.P.)

P391   Schraibman, José, "El ecumenismo de Galdós," Hispania,
        53:881-6, December, 1970.

        "Galdós was most critical of the hypocrisy of the church in Doña
        Perfecta. In later works he appeared to question the nature of true
        religion, while his vision of the church as an institution also gained
        in complexity. In Ángel Guerra the church as an institution is un-
        able to respond to the question of how man achieves a total integra-
        tion and perfection, which is a dichotomy between "biology" and
        "mysticism" never resolved at the end of the work. Torquemada y
        San Pedro concludes with the Torquemada salvation equally uncertain.
        . . .   Seen from this perspective Misericordia is a contrapuntal
        symphony on the theme of charity.   In this work, Galdós has chosen,
        through the character of Benina, to create a symbol of . . . the ever-
        present Spanish problem [of charity and the religious conscience.]"
        (D.P.)

P392   Schraibman, Joseph, "An Unpublished Letter from Galdós to Ricardo
        Palma," Hispanic Review, 32:65-8, January, 1964.

        [The letter published here "is Galdós's first published letter to a
        Latin-American writer. . . . The letter is by far Galdós's longest
        . . . and offers a most interesting testimony . . . of his literary
        modus operandi and of certain traits of personal psychology."] (D.P.)

P392   3150

P393   Shoemaker, William H., "Galdós y La Nación," Hispanófila,
       No. 25, pp. 21-50, 1965.

       [This is a survey of the contributions of Galdós to the Madrid news-
       paper, La Nación from 1865 to 1868, followed by an annotated catalog
       of 131 articles.] (C.O.)

P394   Steele, Charles W., "The Krausist Educator as Depicted by Galdós,"
       Kentucky Foreign Language Quarterly, 5:136-42, Third Quarter,
       1958.

       Through the characters of León Roch and Máximo Manso, Galdós,
       although sympathetic to the Krausist educational program for Spain,
       emphasizes the unreality of the program for the country because of
       the gap between these progressive educators and the average Span-
       iard. (W.G.F.)

P395   Woodbridge, Hensley C., "Benito Pérez Galdós: A Selected
       Annotated Bibliography," Hispania, 53:899-971, December, 1970.

       "This bibliography is intended for graduate students in the field and
       for the non-Galdósian Spanish teacher who may . . . want . . . to
       know what has been published on a given subject or work by Galdós.
       The Galdós expert will necessarily find the comprehensive bibli-
       ography by Suárez of greater use to him than this selective bibli-
       ography of approximately 400 items." (D.P.)

P396   Zviguilsky, A., "Tourguéniev et Galdós," Revue de Littérature
       Comparée, 41:117-20, January-March, 1967.

       Although we have searched vainly for the two letters Tourgeniev
       sent to Galdós at the end of his life, the letters do exist, as is con-
       firmed by a conversation Yakovlev had with Galdós, a year after
       Tourgeniev's death, and other contemporary accounts. At the start
       of his career Galdós saw himself as a disciple of Tourgeniev. The
       two authors share continuing concern with truth and justice, and are
       notable for the clarity and precision of their style. However, Galdós
       seems to have been more influenced by Tolstoy than by Tourgeniev.
       (D.P.)

AITA TETTAUEN

P397   Colin, Vera, "Tolstoy and Galdós's Santiuste: Their Ideology on War and Their Spiritual Conversation," Hispania, 53:836-41, December, 1970.

Galdós had copies of Tolstoy's Ma Religion and Souvenirs de Sébastopol and thus knew of Tolstoy's religious conversion. A similar case, though telescoped, is seen in Galdós's Santiuste in Aita Tettauen. (C.O.)

EL AMIGO MANSO

P398   Davies, G. A., "Galdós's El amigo Manso: An Experiment in Didactic Method," Bulletin of Hispanic Studies, 39:16-30, 1962.

Galdós leaves the ideological stereotypes and the schematic fictitious setting to create a novel didactic by indirection and allusion. He also gives a more satisfactory analysis of psychology and of real society. (C.O.)

P399   Hafter, Monroe Z., "Le crime de Sylvestre Bonnard: A Possible Source for El amigo Manso," Symposium, 17:123-9, Summer, 1963.

Anatole France's Le crime de Sylvestre Bonnard apparently influenced the composition of Pérez Galdós's El amigo Manso, the basic likeness focusing "on the title heroes who are both respected scholars. . . ." (D.P.)

P400   Price, R. M., "The Five Padrotes in Pérez Galdós's El amigo Manso," Philological Quarterly, 48:234-46, April, 1969.

The four padrotes noted in Manso's study by Doña Javiera in chapter three of El amigo Manso are "a device which illuminates the character of Manso and the complex texture of the whole novel. With regard to Manso, they are an ironic detail. . . . The padrotes also throw light on the variety of devices and interests in the novel as a whole. . . ." (D.P.)

P401   Russell, Robert H., "El amigo Manso: Galdós with a Mirror," Modern Language Notes, 78:161-8, March, 1963.

In El amigo Manso "Galdós is taking a stand against the uselessness of purely theoretical knowledge. But the person who receives the most upsetting and transforming education is Manso the teacher,

EL AMIGO MANSO (cont'd)

Manso the novelist. Manso's growing consciousness of the reality
around him and of the ways of dealing with it, is remarkably similar
to Galdós's own artistic development. . . . El amigo Manso is as
much concerned with literature as it is with education. " (D.P.)

AQUÉL

P402 Chamberlin, Vernon A., "The Riddle in Galdós's 'Lost' Sketch
Aquél, " Symposium, 15:62-6, Spring, 1961.

Galdós's Aquél is the only one of the eighty-six sketches contained
in Los españoles de ogaño presented in the form of a riddle. "In
all probability, Galdós, a life-long Madrilenean vago and realistic
author par excellence, chose to create Aquél as he himself had experienced the role--with the vago as the center of conjecture. "
(D.P.)

CÁDIZ

P403 Brown, Donald F., "More Light on the Mother of Galdós, "
Hispania, 39:403-7, December, 1956.

The character of Doña María in the early historical novel, Cádiz,
closely resembles Galdós's mother. It is clear that the liberal
deals most harshly with the reactionary woman here, as he had in
similar novelistic situations before. (C.O.)

LA CORTE DE CARLOS IV

P404 Rogers, Paul Patrick, "Galdós and Tamayo's Letter-Substitution
Device, " Romanic Review, 45:115-20, April, 1954.

"With . . . boldness, almost arrogance [Galdós] appropriated
Tamayo's [letter-substitution] stratagem for the culminating point
of the action in one of his most entertaining episodios, La corte de
Carlos IV (1873). . . . The case under consideration is an excellent
example of the way in which he made appropriated material his own."
(D.P.)

LA DE BRINGAS

P405   Shoemaker, William H., "Galdós's Classical Scene in La de Bringas," Hispanic Review, 27:423-34, October, 1959.

The Rosalía-Refugio mistress-turned-servant scene "was a lineal descendant of Plautus's Asinaria, through either the Aquilana (of Torres Naharro) or some other hereditary line, Spanish or foreign." (A.C.H.)

LA DE LOS TRISTES DESTINOS

P406   Shoemaker, William H., "Galdós's La de los tristes destinos and its Shakespearean Connections," Modern Language Notes, 71:114-9, February, 1956.

In spite of Galdós's well known admiration for Shakespeare, the title of his La de los tristes destinos, one of his Episodios nacionales, was drawn directly or indirectly from a speech in the Cortes on July 4, 1865 by the statesman Antonio Aparisi y Guijarro. (D.P.)

LA DESHEREDADA

P407   Hafter, Monroe Z., "Galdós's Presentation of Isidora in La desheredada," Modern Philology, 60:22-30, August, 1962.

In La desheredada "one chapter may give way to the next with no apparent transition, but the continuing commentary on Isidora connects one to another. It is in this way that Galdós gives to a wide social spectrum his coherent artistic expression of a woman's folly and tragedy. With a daring which far exceeded that of the contemporary Spanish works of realism or naturalism, he . . . forg[ed] a characterization of uncommon dimension." (D.P.)

P408   Petit, Marie-Claire, "La desheredada, ou le procès du rêve," Romance Notes, 9:235-43, 19681

"It is not by chance that La desheredada begins in an asylum where an inmate attacks her contemporaries so convincingly that their derangement appears greater than her own. The confusion is necessary: she shows the interpenetration of two worlds that the walls cannot separate." (D.P.)

LA DESHEREDADA   (cont'd)

P409   Rodgers, Eamonn, "Galdós's La desheredada and Naturalism, "
Bulletin of Hispanic Studies, 45:285-98, 1968.

Galdós's novel is typical of Naturalism, Spanish style: critical of
Romantic idealism, often didactic, but not subscribing to the doctrine
of determinism.   (C.O.)

THE DISINHERITED LADY--See
LA DESHEREDADA

DOÑA PERFECTA

P410   Brown, Donald F., "An Argentine Doña Perfecta: Galdós and
Manuel Gálvez, " Hispania, 47:282-7, May, 1964.

Manuel Gálvez, like Pérez Galdós in his Doña Perfecta, has used
the idea of a domineering matriarch as a central protagonist in his
Perdido en su noche.   For Galdós, Doña Perfecta employs her
mojigatería as a means "to the end of dominating, getting her way,
and destroying her opponents.   She appears good, but is not."
Gálvez's Graciana, on the other hand, is misguidedly religious:
"She is more human and convincing, less the all-black villain type
found in Galdós."   (D.P.)

P411   Jones, C. A., "Galdós's Second Thoughts on Doña Perfecta,"
Modern Language Review, 54:570-3, October, 1959.

Two editions of Galdós's Doña Perfecta were published in 1876, both
editions being identified as the first.   Variants between these two
versions "are to be found chiefly in the letters appended to the novel
and purporting to have been written by Doña Perfecta's brother-in-
law, Don Cayetano Polentinos, to a friend in Madrid." ". . . the
later version gives evidence of a very much better taste, and of a
greater artistic sense."   (D.P.)

P412   Mazzara, Richard A., "Some Fresh Perspectivas on Galdós's
Doña Perfecta, " Hispania, 40:49-56, March, 1957.

Though clearly a novel of thesis, Doña Perfecta yields also to a
study of creative technique.   It has not only ideas and arguments but
a "feeling for life" as well.   (C.O.)

DOÑA PERFECTA   (cont'd)

P413   Sánchez, Roberto G., "Doña Perfecta and the Histrionic Projection
of Character," Revista de Estudios Hispánicos, 3:175-90, 1969.

The dramatic force of this novel resides primarily in the title
character, that of Doña Perfecta; the novel does not manage to avoid
melodrama but rather glories in it. (C.O.)

P414   Sisto, David T., "Doña Perfecta and Doña Bárbara," Hispania,
37:167-70, May, 1954.

The protagonists in Pérez Galdós's Doña Perfecta and Gallegos's
Doña Bárbara share important psychological identities. One may
wonder whether "Perfecta in her intolerance, religious bigotry, and
self-satisfaction of moral code, or Bárbara in her uncontrolled
barbarism, sadistic passion, and rampant nihilism" is more dangerous. (D.P.)

P415   Sisto, David T., "Pérez Galdós's Doña Perfecta and Louis
Bromfield's The Good Woman," Symposium, 11:273-80, Fall, 1957.

Although there are dangers of exaggerating in drawing such similarities and there is no implication of direct influence, "the basic
similarities between the two women and between other personages
of the two stories . . . are nevertheless of interest to observers of
creative perception and the literary process." (B.B.)

P416   Weber, Robert J., "Galdós and Orbajosa," Hispanic Review,
31:348-9, October, 1963.

[A letter Galdós published in Apuntes on April 5, 1896 states his
pessimism about the limited effect the character Orbajosa in Doña
Perfecta had had in demonstrating the merits of liberalism to Spain.
The letter probably refers to the dramatic version of the novel, first
staged in 1896.] (D.P.)

EPISODIOS NACIONALES

P417   Antón, Angel, "Galdós, historiador y novelista," Die Neueren
Sprachen, 10:455-61, October, 1962.

Hans Hinterhäuser's Die "Episodios nacionales" von Benito Pérez
Galdós is an important contribution to Galdós scholarship, although
it contains several factual errors. Hinterhäuser also overestimates

EPISODIOS NACIONALES   (cont'd)

the historical accuracy of Unamuno and underestimates that of
Galdós; likewise, contrary to what Hinterhäuser claims, Baroja is
an admirer rather than a denigrator of Galdós.   (U.C.K.)

P418   Obaid, Antonio H., "Galdós y Cervantes," Hispania, 41:269-73,
September, 1958.

[A study of the Episodios nacionales reveals Galdós's admiration for
Cervantes's Don Quixote.] (A.C.H.)

P419   Obaid, Antonio H., "La Mancha en los Episodios nacionales de
Galdós," Hispania, 41:42-7, March, 1958.

The association of La Mancha with Don Quixote is seen in the quixotic
characters of Galdós. "The preoccupation in landscape and its effects on conduct, which so greatly interested the writers of the
Generation of '98 already appears some years before in Galdós's
Episodios." (A.C.H.)

P420   Obaid, Antonio H., "Sancho Panza en los Episodios nacionales de
Galdós," Hispania, 42:199-204, May, 1959.

Cervantes's influence on Galdós is seen in a half dozen characters
of Sancho Panza type in the first three series of the Episodios
nacionales. (A.C.H.)

P421   Pattison, Walter T., "The Prehistory of the Episodios nacionales,"
Hispania, 53:857-63, December, 1970.

A careful check of notebooks, correspondence, and newspaper
articles shows that Galdós had a detailed plan for his series of historical novels, and that his interest pre-dates publication of the
first novel by five years. (C.O.)

LA FAMILIA DE LEÓN ROCH

P422   López-Morillas, Juan, "Galdós y el krausismo: La familia de León
Roch," Revista de Occidente, 20:331-57, March, 1968.

Influenced by Azcárate, Galdós in his work and some characters
espouses the puritanical precept of Christian rationalism, joining
the pedagogical ideas of Kraus, Rousseau, Pestalozzi and Froebel.
(T.T.B.)

LA FAMILIA DE LEÓN ROCH (cont'd)

P423   Rodríguez, Alfred, "Algunos aspectos de la elaboración literaria de La familia de León Roch," PMLA, 82:121-7, March, 1967.

The source for Galdós's La familia de León Roch could well have been Jules Michelet's Le Prêtre, la famille et la femme. Many parallels and affinities, particularly in anti-religious theme, exist between Galdós's novel and Michelet's work, which thirty years earlier had created a religious controversy in France. (D.P.)

LA FONTANA DE ORO

P424   Hafter, Monroe Z., "The Hero in Galdós's La fontana de oro," Modern Philology, 57:37-43, August, 1959.

"Lázaro, the hero of La fontana de oro, is a frequently inept young man, a pawn in others's schemes, and . . . nearly the cause of a disaster to his own party. What is problematic about him is in part his unheroic character and in part his failure to stand out with vividness or interest. . . . This discussion . . . has two purposes: to show textually how Galdós presents Lázaro and to explain his vision of the hero through an examination of the novelist's earlier and contemporary writings." (D.P.)

P425   Johnson, Carroll B., "The Café in Galdós's La fontana de oro," Bulletin of Hispanic Studies, 42:112-7, 1965.

"Far from being a mere touch of local colour . . . the café in this novel . . . is a vital, functioning part of an integrated artistic unit, La fontana de oro." (C.O.)

P426   Smieja, Florian, "An Alternative Ending of La fontana de oro," Modern Language Review, 61:426-33, July, 1966.

Galdós introduced in the second edition (1871) of La fontana de oro an alternative ending (published here) which he dropped in succeeding editions. "By returning to his original ending . . . Galdós the artist proved that in his constant search for the fitting solution he was capable of substituting an inferior one, but that he also had the good sense, and the courage, to restore his first idea." (D.P.)

FORTUNATA Y JACINTO

P427   Armistead, S. G., "The Canarian Background of Pérez Galdós's
        echar los tiempos," Romance Philology, 7:190-2, February, 1954.

        Pérez Galdós's expression, echar los tiempos, "is, then, an es-
        sentially Canarian idiom, a recollection of the author's youth, which
        he has adapted and interpolated into the speech of his Madrilenian
        characters in Fortunata y Jacinto." (D.P.)

P428   Braun, Lucille V., "Galdós's Re-Creation of Ernestina Manuel de
        Villena as Guillermina Pacheco," Hispanic Review, 38:32-55,
        January, 1970.

        [This is a study of characterization and other fictional techniques as
        Galdós transforms a historical personage into a key novelistic charac-
        ter in Fortunata y Jacinto.] (C.O.)

P429   Brooks, J. L., "The Character of Doña Guillermina Pacheco in
        Galdós's Novel Fortunata y Jacinto," Bulletin of Hispanic Studies,
        38:86-94, 1961.

        The rich angel of charity, while apparently saintly as well, is tightly
        bound to class interest and to oversimplified religious dogma. Her
        charitable impulses are wrongly motivated and often ineffective.
        (C.O.)

P430   Calley, Louise Nelson, "Galdós's Concept of Primitivism: A
        Romantic View of the Character of Fortunata," Hispania, 44:663-5,
        December, 1961.

        Fortunata, representing an idealized folk, is best understood in
        terms of an eighteenth century primitivism related to Rousseau's
        noble savage. (C.O.)

P431   Engler, Kay, "Notes on the Narrative Structure of Fortunata y
        Jacinto," Symposium, 24:111-27, Summer, 1970.

        "Fortunata y Jacinto . . . represents a synthesis of the techniques
        of Galdós's narrative art at the heighth of his creative genius. . . .
        It is a monumental work. . . . Its structure is highly complex, and
        it offers a wealth of narrative techniques, some of great originality
        for the period when they were introduced." (D.P.)

FORTUNATA Y JACINTO (cont'd)

P432   Randolph, E. Dale A., "A Source for Maxi Rubín in Fortunata y
Jacinto," Hispania, 51:49-56, March, 1968.

Galdós's novelistic clinical case may owe its detail to a widely
known psychological treatise of the day, Henry Maudsley's The
Pathology of Mind (1879). (C.O.)

P433   Smith, Paul C., "Cervantes and Galdós: The Duques and Ido del
Sagrario," Romance Notes, 8:47-50, 1967.

Two selected passages reveal similar attitudes of condemnation for
parasitic types of the leisure classes. They suggest that Galdós
was thinking of the Cervantes passage when he composed his own.
(C.O.)

P434   Zahareas, Anthony, "The Tragic Sense in Fortunata y Jacinto,"
Symposium, 19:38-49, Spring, 1965.

"What is remarkable about the novel is the artistry with which Galdós
has woven various distinct tragedies--psychological, moral, social--
into one. He effectively dramatizes the clash of human values which,
inevitably, destroys man, creates misery, and wastes excellence.
Paradoxically, the novel is complex despite the simple plot. . . ."
In Fortunata y Jacinto "Galdós captures the tragic implications of
humanity . . . through man's everyday psychological performance."
(D.P.)

GLORIA

P435   Zamora, Charles A., "Tiempo cíclico: Estructura temporal en
Gloria de Galdós," Hispania, 46:465-70, September, 1963.

"In this analysis we hope to reveal, for the first time, how Galdós
employed cyclic time. In the whole of his work, no more definite
and specific fact is ever mentioned among the prototypical and
universal values which Galdós aspired to give to his creations."
(D.P.)

JUAN MARTÍN EL EMPECINADO

P436 Lovett, Gabriel H., "Some Observations on Galdós's Juan Martín el Empecinado," Modern Language Notes, 84:196-207, March, 1969.

Juan Martín el Empecinado "is in some ways one of the most important books of Galdós dealing with the War of Independence. Its importance . . . is due to Galdós's felicitous rendering in fictionalized form of what was easily the most essential historical aspect of the war against Napoleon and to his ability to give epic grandeur to this aspect through a truly heroic figure." (D.P.)

LEON ROCH--See
LA FAMILIA DE LEÓN ROCH

LA LOCA DE LA CASA

P437 Carney, Hal, "The Two Versions of Galdós's La loca de la casa," Hispania, 44:438-40, September, 1961.

Galdós's play, contrary to uncritical opinion, is not derived from a dialogued novel of the same name. Both versions are the same stage play--before and after cuts. Neither resembles his true dialogued novels. (C.O.)

MARIANELA

P438 Blanco, Louise S., "Origin and History of the Plot of Marianela," Hispania, 48:463-7, September, 1965.

The story "Les Aveugles de Chamouny" by Charles Nodier, the Wilkie Collins novel, Poor Miss Finch, and popular interest in the operation for cataracts, all combine to provide plot material and topicality for Marianela. (C.O.)

P439 Jones, C. A., "Galdós's Marianela and the Approach to Reality," Modern Language Review, 56:515-9, October, 1961.

In Marianela "Galdós is suggesting that if opposing reality or trying to reconcile it with one's ideals leads to disaster . . . the success which accompanies the heedless acceptance of reality is a relative and superficial success which takes no account of the deeper needs and qualities of humanity. . . . Marianela emerges as an experiment . . . in the search for an answer to the problem of how a man can come to terms with reality." (D.P.)

MARIANELA   (cont'd)

P440   Ruiz, Mario E., "El idealismo platónico en Marienala de Galdós,"
Hispania, 53:870-80, December, 1970.

A study of metaphor and structure leads to the Platonic nature of the
novel. Galdós seeks the ideal absolute, but through the changeable
data of the senses. (C.O.)

P441   Wellington, Marie A., "Marianela: Nuevas dimensiones,"
Hispania, 51:38-48, March, 1968.

"Marianela is an important work because it represents the concili-
ation of the ideas of Comte with those of Galdós and because it prefigures the evolution of thought in the novels to succeed it." (D.P.)

MI CALLE

P442   Hoar, Leo J., Jr., " 'Mi calle': Another 'Lost' Article by Galdós,
and a Further Note on His Indebtedness to Mesonero Romanos,"
Symposium, 24:128-47, Summer, 1970.

"Mi calle," purportedly the study of a street in Madrid, is important since "it reveals new or hitherto unknown biographical data about
one of Galdós's early residences in Madrid. It is also an explicit
example of how Galdós was directly influenced by specific works of
Mesonero Romanos. Most important, it "demonstrates that Galdós
actually novelizes within the frame of what at first glance appears to
be a cuadro de costumbres, a genre notably undistinguished for much
more than pleasant scenes and anecdotal treatment of tipos and local
color." [The article is reproduced here.]   (D.P.)

MISERICORDIA

P443   Allen, Rupert C., "Pobreza y neurosis en Misericordia, de Pérez
Galdós," Hispanófila, 3:35-47, 1968.

Galdós's theme is not simply urban poverty, but the effects of such
poverty on its victims. Thus Benina, hardly a saint, ends overcome
by the same pathological neurosis as the characters around her.
(C.O.)

MISERICORDIA (cont'd)

P444 Chamberlin, Vernon A., "The Significance of the Name Almudena in Galdós's Misericordia," Hispania, 47:491-6, September, 1964.

The supposedly Arabic name of Galdós's blind beggar is actually a reference to a well known eleventh century church, still prominent in Madrid and central to both Church and State traditions. (C.O.)

LOS PEPES

P445 Shoemaker, William H., "Los Pepes of Galdós in 1868 and 1887: Two Stages of His Style," Hispania, 53:887-98, December, 1970.

". . . when Galdós resurrected his 1868 artículo de costumbres from the Madrid daily newspaper La Nación in order to send it nineteen years later to the Buenos Aires daily La Prensa, he felt obliged to make a serious and thorough adaptation. . . .the number, the pervasive extent and the kinds of alterations give ample evidence of a considered word-by-word rewriting. . . . chiefly, his own criteria for the subject had undergone a change. . . . The resulting essay, a critical, weighty, and more informative essay, thus came to be significantly different from the sketch of tipos from which it had started." [The two versions are published here in parallel columns.] (D.P.)

LO PROHIBIDO

P446 Chamberlin, Vernon A., "Galdós's Chromatic Symbolism Key in Lo prohibido," Hispanic Review, 32:109-17, April, 1964.

Galdós consistently used a color symbolism as a device of characterization. He outlines his chromatic "moral map" in Lo prohibido (1885). (C.O.)

TORMENTO

P447 Durand, Frank, "Two Problems in Galdós's Tormento," Modern Language Notes, 79:513-25, December, 1964.

Although the function of Ido del Sagrario's novel in Galdós's Tormento is problematic, and the interjection of Galdós social criticism appears to be superfluous, actually, "the development of Ido's novel within Tormento and the interaction of the two works absolve Galdós of any charge of gratuity. . . . Similarly, Galdós's social commen-

TORMENTO (cont'd)

tary complements the character analyses so as to deepen and enrich the reader's understanding of the action." (D.P.)

P448　Rodgers, Eamonn, "The Appearance-Reality Contrast in Galdós's Tormento," Forum for Modern Language Studies, 6:382-98, October, 1970.

"What makes Tormento a masterpiece is the lucidity of its insight into the moral quality of everyday life. . . . If by the end of the novel we feel no inclination to laugh at Ido, it is because we know that nearly all the other characters, and by extension, the whole of humanity, are engaged in a more insidious and harmful type of falsificación than this poor starving hack-writer. . . . The working out . . . of the appearance-reality contrast (the terms of which come to stand respectively for 'life as people apprehend it' and 'life as it really is') is fundamental to Galdós's method." (D.P.)

P449　Rodríguez, Alfred, "Sobre el contenido y el uso líricos en Tormento," Romance Notes, 8:204-6, 1967.

In spite of the much touted prosaic nature of his works, Galdós is able to make effective use of themes and even images from the most "lyrical" of his contemporaries. (C.O.)

TORQUEMADA EN EL PURGATORIO

P450　Bosch, Rafael, "La influencia de Echegaray sobre Torquemada en el Purgatorio, de Galdós," Revista de Estudios Hispánicos, 1:243-53, 1967.

Although Galdós's novel clearly echoes Echegaray's play, there are essential differences. Galdós pushes no thesis and presents no idealized characters. In character, incident, and language he strives for verisimilitude. (C.O.)

TORQUEMADA EN LA HOGUERA

P451　Baüml, B. J. Zeidner, "The Mundane Demon: The Bourgeois Grotesque in Galdós's Torquemada en la hoguera," Symposium, 24:158-65, Summer, 1970.

"Pérez Galdós's Torquemada en la hoguera exemplifies [the] trans-mutation of the pre-realistic to a thoroughly realistic bourgeois

TORQUEMADA EN LA HOGUERA   (cont'd)

grotesque. . . . Galdós's technique of stylistic and structural integration of this essentially pre- and anti-realistic phenomenon into his
novelistic realism [may be] posited [by the concept] that the grotesque
is capable of existing only in the immediate juxtaposition of fear-
generating evil and the ludicrous in a given situation or individual.
. . ."   (D.P.)

P452   Ullmann, Pierre L., "The Exordium of Torquemada en la hoguera,"
Modern Language Notes, 80:258-60, March, 1965.

In Torquemada en la hoguera Galdós has given us an introduction
"closely akin to the proem of a romance de ciego. "Through this
device the author warns "the sophisticated reader against mature
involvement in the work" and projects "the sublimation of malice
essential to a convincing mélange of buskins and socks. . . ."
(D.P.)

TORQUEMADA Y SAN PEDRO

P453   Weber, Robert J., "Galdós's Preliminary Sketches for Torquemada
y San Pedro," Bulletin of Hispanic Studies, 44:16-27, 1967.

Three preliminary character sketches for his 1895 novel show that
Galdós did careful ground work for his novels. They are also
examples of his views on the close relations of literature and
medicine. (C.O.)

ZARAGOZA

P454   Rodríguez, Alfred, "Galdós's Use of the Classics in Zaragoza,"
Modern Language Notes, 79:211-3, March, 1964.

"Zaragoza (1874) is one of the first of Galdós's works in which
classical elements appear extensively, and it is not altogether surprising to find both a touch of genius in their use and a dash of
pedantic immaturity in their repetition." (D.P.)

PÉROL, JEAN

P455   Amette, Jacques-Pierre, "Jean Pérol," La Nouvelle Revue
Française, No. 194, pp. 276-9, February, 1969.

At times approaching uncertain wavering and tiresome impressionism,

Pérol's poetry is saved by a fluid style and the introduction of fantasy into his realism. (T.T.B.)

PERROS, GEORGES

P456 Liger, Christian, "Georges Perros ou la marche à pied," La Nouvelle Revue Française, No. 184, pp. 701-9, April, 1968.

Perros has sensed the terrible power of language; words are the look of the Medusa, which petrify life. What matters beautiful form if the world, the thought and the rest must die? His form is the octosyllabic verse, in which he recounts a life, childhood, youth, theater, encounters, literature, women, the woman and children. (T.T.B.)

PERRY, GEORGE SESSIONS

P457 Brown, John Mason, "King-Sized Texan: George Sessions Perry," Saturday Review, 42:14-5, 40, August 15, 1959.

[This is biographical information about Perry with a discussion of his "beautiful folk novels . . . Walls Rise Up (1939), and Hold Autumn in Your Hand (1941)."] (H.S.)

PERSE, SAINT-JOHN

P458 Ahston, Dore, "St.-John Perse's Guadeloupe," Kenyon Review, 23:520-6, Summer, 1961.

[Many influences, allusions and resonances of St.-John Perse's poetry with Guadeloupe, where he spent his first eleven years, are commented on as a result of Dore Ashton's visit to the Island.] (D.P.)

P459 Baldner, R. W., "St.-John Perse as Poet-Prophet," Proceedings of the Pacific Northwest Conference on Foreign Languages, 17:123-8, 1966.

"The role of seer and prophet appeared late in Perse's poetic career. Although Anabase, a vision apparently inspired by the great migrations of the yellow horde, is more historical in its implications than prophetic of man's destiny, it does contain the germ of the prophetic role in certain passages spoken by the Prince. This almost-epic poem of startling color and movement also channeled the poet's style into strophic verse form so admirably suited to the nature of his message and which he would henceforth use exclusively." (D.-J.J.)

P460   Carmody, Francis J., "Saint-John Perse and Several Oriental
        Sources," Comparative Literature Studies, 2:125-51, No. 2, 1965.

        Perse's synopsis to Anabase may be made "more precise by com-
        parisons with other of Perse's narratives and . . . his poetics [may
        be examined] in the light of the influence on Anabase, Exil, and Vents
        of Herodotus, Ammianus Marcellinus and the Book of Job. It is only
        of secondary interest that the action of Anabase occurs for the most
        part in Asia Minor and Persia; more important is the poet's reason
        for using this particular narrative." (D.P.)

P461   Chapin, Katherine Garrison, "Saint-John Perse: Some Notes on a
        French Poet and an Epic Poem," Sewanee Review, 66:33-43,
        Winter, 1958.

        Perse's poems are "histories of the soul"--"the work of a writer
        who stands at a crossroads, a Janus figure who faces both east and
        west, looking backward and forward." Perse's imagery is exact
        and purposeful, his scope vast, his meaning multi-layered. (A.A.S.)

P462   Colt, Byron, "St.-John Perse," Accent, 20:158-69, Summer, 1960.

        "Perse is one of the few men undertaking 'reactionary' works in our
        time who has been able successfully to make a certain spiritual
        reversion." "In Perse . . . the love of the god for men resembles
        invective, and we find in the predestined violence of natural things
        the same tragic, exultant view which is characteristic of Nietzsche."
        (D.P.)

P463   Colt, Byron, "St.-John Perse," Modern Language Quarterly,
        21:235-8, September, 1960.

        Following a route different from that of other symbolists, Perse
        "found his way around the Christian religion to the spiritual home-
        land which Nietzsche reached in his maturity." (G.S.)

P464   Connell, Allison B., "Saint-John Perse and Valery Larbaud,"
        French Review, 41:11-22, October, 1967.

        The prose of Valery Larbaud was profoundly influenced by the early
        poetry of Saint-John Perse, and Perse was a great admirer of
        Larbaud. "The most important quality shared by Perse and Larbaud
        is a perpetual renewal of the intellectual conquest." (D.P.)

P465   Cranston, Mechthild, " 'L'Activité du Songe' in the Poetry of
        Saint-John Perse," Forum for Modern Language Studies,
        2:356-67, October, 1966.

        "Like every true poet, Saint-John Perse is forever singing but one
        song. For the Guadeloupean poet, this song is the song of the sea.
        The oneness of Perse's poetry lies in the double nature of that sea:
        sea of childhood, innocence and peace, but also of temptation and
        war. Two main principles can be derived from this ambiguity:
        that of violence, which rules in the world of action, and that of
        acquiescence, governing the sphere of dreams. These mutually
        oppose each other and are, by turns, opposed by death and, pos-
        sibly, ennui." (D.-J.J.)

P466   Fowlie, Wallace, "Poems that Sing of Man," Saturday Review,
        43:22-3, November 19, 1960.

        "If only one word were allowed for describing the subject matter of
        this poet, we would have to say it is history. His is a work relating
        the secular and the spiritual efforts of man to see himself as a part
        of the natural world, to tame the hostile powers of the world, to
        worship the endlessly renewed beauty of the world, to conjugate his
        ambitions and dreams with the changes and the modifications of
        time." (D.-J.J.)

P467   Gaster, Beryl, "Saint-John Perse," Contemporary Review,
        199:129-31, March, 1961.

        "To the uninitiated the actual bulk of Saint-John Perse's writings
        seems astonishingly small. . . . Yet the verse form is always
        perfect, every line is polished and each word-picture and individual
        word underlying the philosophy so chosen that it defies quotation.
        . . . the imagery is outstanding . . . its wonder lies in the way it
        transmutes the very stuff of Pliny and Linnaeus and Darwin into
        poetry." (D.P.)

P468   Guerre, Pierre, "In the High House of the Sea: Meetings with
        Saint-John Perse," Yale Review, 50:308-17, December, 1960.

        [These are impressions of visits with Saint-John Perse in his "high
        house by the sea" on the Southern coast of France.] (D.P.)

P469   Guillou, Jean, "Karukéra, île natale de St.-John Perse?" French
        Review, 39:281-7, November, 1965.

        Throughout St.-John Perse's works appear glimpses of his native
        Guadeloupe, colored by his childish and adolescent years, beautiful,
        vegetal and exotic but conforming only to the viewpoint of the white
        settler. (T.T.B.)

P470   Hartley, Anthony, "Saint-John Perse," Encounter, 16:41-4,
        February, 1961.

        Perse's poetry is memorable for its celebration of the objects of
        reality and for the calm assurance with which it accepts the tragic
        dilemma of mankind. (M.H.M.)

P471   Knodel, Arthur J., "The Unheard Melody of Saint-John Perse,"
        Romanic Review, 50:195-206, October, 1959.

        In Perse's "anti-sonic" theory "only the inner ear can hear as a
        single chord the complex harmonic structure of . . . poems; and
        then all the more will it be true that the succession of chords can
        be fused into a melody only by that same inner ear." (R.G.L.)

P472   Little, Roger, "The Image of the Threshold in the Poetry of
        Saint-John Perse," Modern Language Review, 64:777-92,
        October, 1969.

        "The virtue, then, of the threshold, beach, dawn, and noon is a
        precariousness which heightens awareness." (J.R.R.)

P473   Little, Roger, "Language and Imagery in Saint-John Perse,"
        Forum for Modern Language Studies, 6:127-39, April, 1970.

        "There are two obvious ways in which Perse reveals his attachment
        to language. The first shows in his technical mastery and his sen-
        sitivity to philology, the second in his extensive use of language
        itself as an image. Not only is language likened to things; things
        are likened to language. The various manifestations of language
        become images in their own right, so creating the curious situation
        in which the tool becomes an integral part of the end product."
        (D.-J.J.)

P474   Little, Roger, "T. S. Eliot and Saint-John Perse," Arlington
        Quarterly, 2:5-17, Autumn, 1969.

        Certain verbal echoes of Perse linked with particular rhythms,
        imagery and preoccupation, may be found in Eliot's more serious
        poems from Ash Wednesday onwards.   (T.T.B.)

P475   McCormick, James, "Just an Impression," Kenyon Review,
        23:336, Spring, 1961.

        [This is a brief report of Perse's acceptance of the Nobel Prize for
        Literature in Stockholm.] (D.P.)

P476   McMahon, Joseph H., "A Question of Man," Commonweal,
        73:407-9, January 13, 1961.

        "What is excellence? It is, Léger seems to say, the movement
        through which man defines himself by giving values to his civiliza-
        tion. But the definition is not easily made, because it depends on
        the willingness to accept pain, to elect the unpleasant but productive
        choice rather than the pleasant and destructive one." (D.-J.J.)

P477   Martin du Gard, Maurice, "Les Mémorables: Dejeuner au quai:
        Alexis Léger, Laval et Mandel," La Revue des Deux Mondes,
        140:188-90, January 15, 1968.

        [This is a brief souvenir.] (D.P.)

P478   Muner, Mario, "Saint-John Perse, Char, and 'La Poésie
        irresponsable'," AUMLA, No. 19, pp. 5-20, May, 1963.

        Both Saint-John Perse and René Char, representatives of the
        'poetic current,' descend from a line beginning with Rimbaud:
        "poetry that cannot be conceived unless the poet attains a sort of
        voyance and almost of irresponsibility." Lack of true stylistic form,
        however, makes their work barren. (S.T.)

P479   Nelson, C. E., "Saint-John Perse: A Way to Begin," Books
        Abroad, 36:275-9, Autumn, 1962.

        Structure and point of view are the major problems for the reader
        of Perse. (C.E.N.)

P480   Nelson, C. E., "Saint-John Perse and T. S. Eliot," Western Humanities Review, 17:163-71, Spring, 1963.

"This essay . . . is an attempt to turn to critical advantage the co-incidental conjunction of two major poets who to a large extent treated the same subject but as agents of different intellectual and artistic temperaments." (R. J. G.)

P481   Paz, Octavio, "St.-John Perse: Poet as Historian," Nation, 192:522-4, June 17, 1961.

In Perse's poetry "a single verbal stream flows, uninterruptedly from Eloges to Chronique. Perse's language swallows up events, transmutes them and then . . . redeems them. Everything that has taken place in the last fifty years . . . is fitted into the work. . . . Histories of our age, they are at the same time the account of an exile that has no end. . . . The planet itself is a migrant body." (D. P.)

P482   Paulhan, Jean, "Énigmes de Perse," La Nouvelle Revue Française, No. 119, pp. 773-89, November, 1962; No. 121, pp. 74-83, January, 1963.

Perse breaks with modern poetry and reunites all that is separated. He presents an epic without a hero. The whole earth passes in review in his work; however, the hero may very well be Perse himself at various stages of his career. In each line of his work, one finds a figure of speech. Far from being distributed at random, these follow a rigorous order. Although Perse has indicated a disgust and horror for rhetoric, never was there a language more rhetorical. (T. T. B.)

P483   Paulhan, Jean, "Énigmes de Perse, III," La Nouvelle Revue Française, No. 133, pp. 6-17, January, 1964.

Perse is assailed by ambiguities. He takes the part of the West against Asia, Asia against the West. He supports the dreamer against the man of action, then the man of action against the dreamer. He draws near and then moves away from the world of things. (T. T. B.)

P484   Pieyre de Mandiargues, André, "À l'honneur de la chair," La
Nouvelle Revue Française, No. 113, pp. 872-5, May 1, 1962.

With more force than the Latin poets, Jean Second, Donne or even
Baudelaire, Saint-John Perse has celebrated the love of the flesh.
At times his crudity and brutality recall Martial but the loftiness
and quality of accent are the gifts of the modern poet. "He has no
other purpose than to elevate man by making him aware and proud
of his virility." (T.T.B.)

P485   Raine, Kathleen, "St.-John Perse: Poet of the Marvelous,"
Encounter, 29:51-61, October, 1967.

". . . Like the symbolists, St.-John Perse not only assumes but
affirms and uses as the instrument of his art the law of harmony
which subsists in and unifies the cosmos; his universe is neither
arbitrary nor indeterminate; and is governed by that symmetry,
unity and accord in which Plotinus discovers the essence of 'the
beautiful'." (D.-J.J.)

P486   Roditi, Eduoard, "Commerce with Saint-John Perse," Adam
International Review, 30:186-91, 1963-5.

"Today, I can look back on thirty-five years of the strangest nodding
acquaintances with Saint-John Perse. . . . When I was sixteen, I
would have mentioned Perse . . . in the same breath as Nerval,
Baudelaire, Rimbaud, Lautréamont . . .; today I look upon him as
. . . a poet of the same intentional quality as José-Marie de Hérédia
or Valéry." (D.P.)

P487   Roudiez, Leon S., "The Epochal Poetry of Saint-John Perse,"
Columbia University Forum, 4:27-31, Fall, 1961.

"It is simply a matter for regret, considering the world-wide appeal
of a writer like Camus, that similar themes and symbols (strangers,
exile, kingdoms, deserts, the sea) have not drawn more readers to
the discovery of Perse." (W.F.)

P488   Senghor, Léopold-Sédar, "Saint-John Perse ou poésie du royaume
d'enfance," La Table Ronde, No. 172, pp. 16-36, May, 1962.

"The originality of Saint-John Perse does not reside in the figures
that he employs, but in the fashion which he uses them, in the
mastery of his language. . . . What makes the genius of Saint-John
Perse is that, although a creole, rooted in the Antilles, in his pro-

fession of diplomacy and his omnivorous curiosity, he goes beyond all these elements and expresses the civilization of the universal." (T.T.B.)

P489   Strauss, Walter A., "Saint-John Perse: Poet of Celebration," Emory University Quarterly, 14:100-11, June, 1958.

Saint-John Perse "perceives the cumulative pattern of cosmic restlessness not merely in terms of elemental forces of nature that unleash elemental energies in man; these forces also liberate man's ability to praise--to sing rhapsodies--and to lament--to sing threnodies; and so Perse correlates man's deeds and man's song in one and the same breath of dithyrambic intoxication. The celebration moves in the direction of the epic as well as the lyric." His "lines are lofty, detached from specific orientations in time and space, and appear to be . . . the collective product of the human race rather than the work of one man." (D.P.)

P490   Vidan, Ivo, "Saint-John Perse's Visit to Conrad: A Letter by Alexis Saint-Leger Leger to G. Jean-Aubry," Conradiana, 2:17-22, Spring, 1969-70.

[A letter from Saint-John Perse to Jean-Aubry contains vividly remembered details of a visit to Conrad's home in 1912. The text of the letter is given in French and in English translation with extended comments.] (D.P.)

   AMERS

P491   Guicharnaud, Jacques, "Vowels of the Sea: Amers by Saint-John Perse," Yale French Studies, No. 21, pp. 72-82, Spring-Summer, 1958.

"Amers, a vast epic and lyric metaphor, is based on twofold relationships: the Poet and those for whom he speaks; the Poet and his subject; his "heroes" and the Sea; his "heroes" and men in general; the Sea and the acts of Man, etc." (D.P.)

   ANABASE

P492   Knodel, Arthur J., "Towards an Understanding of Anabase," PMLA, 79:329-43, June, 1964.

Saint-John Perse's Anabase "is admittedly difficult and highly condensed. . . . The strangeness of the poem's idiom, however, is

ANABASE (cont'd)

greatly diminished when one is familiar with the rest of Saint-John
Perse's works, especially the earlier poems and the vast later
poem, Vents. But . . . the extraordinary tone of Anabase helps
the sensitive reader to surmount the sometimes bafflingly cursive
shorthand of the poem." It is "a haunting poem that is perhaps
unique in French literature. . . ." (D.P.)

P493   Turnell, Martin, "The Epic of St.-John Perse," Commonweal,
70:376-8, July 17, 1959.

"I have suggested that Anabase is still Perse's most impressive
work. And that is true. A great deal of his poetry is written like
Claudel's in what the French call the verset, which corresponds to
'verse of the Bible.' This form gives his poetry its freedom, richness and sweep. At the same time its very freedom is a temptation
from which he does not altogether escape in his later works. He
does not manage to avoid repetition or the creation of images for
the sheer pleasure of creating them, whether they are necessary to
the design of the poem or not." (D.-J.J.)

P494   Weinberg, Bernard, "Saint-John Perse's Anabase," Chicago
Review, 15:75-124, Winter-Spring, 1962.

In Anabase "a prosodic lyricism--the constant use of the song form
--is added to the fundamental lyricism of the organizing conception."
(K.L.)

BIRDS--See
OISEAUX

CHRONIQUE

P495   Benamou, Michel, "Chronique de Saint-John Perse," French
Review, 34:480-2, April, 1961.

"Far from being . . . a period at the end of the work of Saint-John
Perse, Chronique stands out in the world created by the poet through
his concept of reality. The space-time structure, the counterpoint
of his pastoral and sea images, the movement of his style, all support the central thrust of his poetry: to give to man a domain where
he can feel most noble and most free." (D.P.)

CHRONIQUE (cont'd)

P496 Fowler, Helen, "This Great Age according to Saint-John Perse,"
Approach, No. 39, pp. 41-2, Summer, 1961.

Chronique is "about as uneven as a masterly poem can be." The
poet heightens the intensity of his images by gnomic sayings which
often sound profound but are actually meaningless. (A.F.)

EXIL

P497 Little, J. Roger, "Elements of the Jason-Medea Myth in Exil by
Saint-John Perse," Modern Language Review, 61:422-5, July, 1966.

"Other stories of exile and deprivation are certainly present [in
Perse's Exil], but the Jason-Medea theme persists, and provides an
argument for taking the four poems as a single unit rather than as
separate works." (J.R.R.)

NEIGES

P498 Knodel, Arthur J., "The Imagery of Saint-John Perse's Neiges,"
PMLA, 70:5-18, March, 1955.

Neiges has been neglected in studies of Perse. Analysis of its
imagery reveals a "highly personal idiom," use of nature imagery,
and the "centripetal" organization of images (convergence of images
around a central metaphor) frequent in his later work. (J.R.B.)

P499 Koerber, Cécile, "Saint-John Perse: Neiges," French Review,
37:22-30, October, 1963.

"The spiritual evolution which constitutes the thread of Neiges is
not an abstract concept expressed by the aid of images. Rather, the
images evolve by themselves, intersect, multiply, leading thus to
the development of the idea. The vocabulary is so diverse: fine,
effervescent, ships, depots, sky and water, song, festivals and
palm groves offer a multitude of terms in which the abstract and
the concrete join with the journalistic and the exotic, the spiritual
and the material to suggest a cosmic dimension." (D.P.)

OISEAUX

P500   Raine, Kathleen, "St.-John Perse's Birds," Southern Review,
        3:255-61, January, 1967.

        Oiseaux is the result of "the collaboration of two masters each long
        established in his art, who have indeed converged from opposite
        poles, Braque through cubism and the avant-garde, St.-John Perse
        by way of Rimbaud and Claudel." "Of all the poems of St.-John
        Perse Oiseaux is, in image and vocabulary, the most austere. . . .
        with a few master strokes the mature poet knows perfectly how to
        achieve those highly characteristic and perfectly wrought poetic
        figurations." (D.P.)

PESSOA, FERNANDO

P501   Biderman, Sol, "Mount Abiegnos and the Masks: Occult Imagery in
        Yeats and Pessoa," Luso-Brazilian Review, 5:59-74, June, 1968.

        "Owing to their common interests [in the occult] Yeats and Pessoa
        employed common hermetic images in their art: Mount Abiegnos,
        the Rose and the Cross, the Initiation, the illusory nature of death,
        and the Mask." "Both Yeats and Pessoa, like the French Surrealists,
        attempt to establish magic knowledge as the corollary of poetry.
        Dissatisfied with existing religions, both sought mystic ascension
        through art." (D.P.)

P502   Hamburger, Michael, "Fernando Pessoa," Agenda, 6:104-12,
        Nos. 3-4, 1968.

        "The most extreme case of multiple personality and self-division in
        modern poetry is that of the Portuguese poet Fernando Pessoa
        (1885-1935)." Dividing himself into four authors of different names,
        he explores reality and establishes the full identity of his multiple
        selves. (C.O.)

P503   Lind, Georg R. and Ulrich Suerbaum, 'Dichter in fremden Sprachen:
        zu bisher unveröffentlichten englischen Gedichten Fernando Pessoas,"
        Poetica, 2:237-71, April, 1968.

        [This discussion of literary works composed in languages other than
        the poet's native one centers on some previously unpublished works
        in English written by the Portuguese poet Fernando Pessoa.]
        (J.R.R.)

P504   Roberts, William H., "The Figure of King Sebastian in Fernando Pessoa," Hispanic Review, 34:307-16, October, 1966.

Pessoa's elegy to President Sidonio Paes is unique in its extensive use of the Sebastian theme. He envisioned Sebastian as metaphysical, beyond the reach of reason--akin to the ideal, then, and to madness. (C.O.)

P505   Roditi, Edouard, "Fernando Pessoa, Outstanding among English Poets," Literary Review, 6:372-85, Spring, 1963.

Fernando Pessoa wrote in Portuguese and English with equal ease. He also wrote under six pen names, each representing a specific idiom. Thus he has probably the most split personality of any modern writer. He was a "simulator, mythomaniac, and inventor of hoaxes designed primarily to fool himself." (E.T.)

PETERKIN, JULIA

P506   Durham, Frank, "Mencken as Midwife," Menckiana, No. 32, pp. 2-6, Winter, 1969.

Although DuBose Heyward, John Bennett, and Hervey Allen formed the Poetry Society of South Carolina in part, at least, because of "their outrage at the apparently anti-Southern disquisitions of Henry Louis Mencken," he was really, in his Machiavellian way, attempting to encourage the formation of a Southern literature. He was also responsible for the first appearances in print of Julia Peterkin. (D.P.)

PEYREFITTE, ROGER

P507   Hyams, Edward, "Peyrefitte," Kenyon Review, 24:484-500, Summer, 1962.

Peyrefitte is "a satirist without being a reformer"; his books are half fiction and half autobiography or "documentary satire," with insufficient integration of the two elements so far. (G.S.)

P508   Thiébaut, Marcel, "Roger Peyrefitte," La Revue de Paris, pp. 150-1, August, 1956.

Peyrefitte has written four good books: Les Amities particulières, Mort d'une mère, Du Vesuve à l'Etna, and Jeunes proies. He utilizes public curiosity or malignity too ingeniously in all four. (L.L.)

L'EXIL DE CAPRI

P509   Fitzgibbon, Constantine, "The Exile of Capri by Roger Peyrefitte,"
        Encounter, 17:81-2, November, 1961.

        Peyrefitte's The Exile of Capri "is a slightly fictionalized biography
        . . . constructed about the life of a rich, French, homosexual poet-
        aster by the name of Fersen who was born in 1880 and died of dope
        in 1923." In the book "Peyrefitte has kept his eye firmly on one
        theme throughout. The result is a work of pseudo-history . . . a
        chronique scandaleuse, of international, high society perversion.
        . . . Every scandal of the sort is brought out for an airing from
        Verlaine, through Wilde, Krupp, Moltke, Douglas, to even more
        recent scandals." On balance, "The Exile of Capri is a very silly
        book indeed." (D.P.)

        THE EXILE OF CAPRI--See
        L'EXIL DE CAPRI

PHILIPPE, CHARLES-LOUIS

P510   Barberet, Gene J., "Charles-Louis Philippe Fifty Years After,"
        Books Abroad, 34:13-6, Winter, 1960.

        Critics generally ignore the author of Bubu of Montparnasse because
        "his well meaning concern with humanitarian ideas led to an exag-
        gerated partisanship of the poor at the expense of a sense of artistic
        proportion." (W.G.F.)

P511   Demorest, J.-J., "Le Primitivisme de Charles-Louis Philippe,"
        French Review, 29:306-13, February, 1956.

        Primitivism so dominates Philippe's work--"I don't think a writer
        need have any culture . . . only a taste for the savage"--that not
        even Gide could overcome the public's indifference toward Philippe.
        "There are those who demand of a writer that he be human. Emi-
        nently more informed than Philippe, the lettered world would not
        pardon his naivety." (R.C.F.)

PHILLIPS, DAVID GRAHAM

P512   McGovern, James R., "David Graham Phillips and the Virility
Impulse of the Progressives," New England Quarterly, 39:334-55,
September, 1966.

"The foregoing discussion of the personality of Phillips from the
standpoint of his behavior and writing . . . reveals his high readiness of response to Progressivism. The wealthy class, in general,
was unacceptable to Phillips because it projected his fears of indo-
lence and passivity. The reformer was acceptable because . . . he
hoped that vigorous reform would eradicate those signs of effeminacy
in American life which disturbed him. His feminist sympathies represented a deep, unconscious association . . . which demonstrated
his desire to receive aggression from women. In all this, Phillips
transferred his highly personal feelings to politics and society,
rationalizing them into a Progressive ideology which facilitated real
socio-economic problems." (D.P.)

P513   Ravitz, Abe C., "David Graham Phillips (1867-1911)," American
Literary Realism, 3:24-9, Summer, 1968.

[This is a survey of Phillips criticism and bibliography, and suggestions for studies and editions currently needed.] (A.S.W.)

P514   Spangler, George M., "The Confession Form: An Approach to the
Tycoon," Midcontinent American Studies Journal, 10:5-18, Fall,
1969.

"In the four years from 1902 to 1905 Henry K. Webster, David
Graham Phillips and Robert Herrick all used the confession form
to present their portraits of the tycoon," probably because "the
form freed them of the obligation to create the illusion of a complete
naturalistic account." (W.G.F.)

P515   Stallings, Frank L., Jr., "David Graham Phillips (1867-1911): A
Critical Bibliography of Secondary Comment," American Literary
Realism, 3:1-35, Winter, 1970.

[This is an annotated bibliography of books and articles about
Phillips.] (D.P.)

PICHAMURTHI, N.

P516   Kanakasabapathy, C., "A New Voice in Tamil Poetry," Books
Abroad, 43:526-9, Autumn, 1969.

N. Pichamurthi, essentially an imagist, is the "new voice" in Tamil
poetry. He is concerned with the breakdown of Indian traditions and
of reality itself. He advocates classicism in art and his view of
nature is similar to Whitman's. (K.H.B.)

PICHETTE, HENRI

P517   Shattuck, Roger, "A Poet's Progress: Henri Pichette," French
Review, 32:111-9, December, 1958.

Since Les Epiphanies--"the most promising poetic event of the post
war decade"--Pichette has "trundled himself through a complex
evolution which seems to leave him facing in several directions at
once. . . . The circumstances of his career seem to reveal a division in his attitude toward his art--an uncertainty whether poetry is
life unto itself or a moyen de parvenir." (R.C.F.)

PICÓN-SALAS, MARIANO

P518   Loveluck, John, "Picón-Salas," Revista Iberoamericana, 31:263-76,
1965.

[This is a survey of the life and work of this Venezuelan essayist
(1901-1965) on the occasion of his death.] (C.O.)

PIERCE, OVID WILLIAMS

P519   Betts, Doris, "The House by the River: Ovid Williams Pierce,"
South Atlantic Quarterly, 64:283-95, Summer, 1965.

In three novels, one yet unpublished, Pierce has employed and
transcended regional elements to depict " 'life in its fundamental
terms'," In each, the theme of "the effect on man of time" is
conveyed through the image of a house, man's "piece of permanence," beside a river, "the flow of Time." (J.L.A.)

PIEYRE DE MANDIARGUES, ANDRÉ

P520 Abirached, Robert, "D'Un merveilleux moderne," La Nouvelle Revue Française, No. 126, pp. 1070-5, June, 1963.

Baroque by sensuality, lover of strangeness and disturber of habits, Pieyre de Mandiargues is saturated with animism and fetichism. Yet in his eroticism enters no libertinism or wantonness, in the conventional sense, because love in his eyes does not consist of a society game. (T.T.B.)

P521 Bosquet, Alain, "La Poésie d'André Pieyre de Mandiargues," La Nouvelle Revue Française, No. 146, pp. 298-304, February, 1965.

To separate the novelist from the essayist and the latter from the poet is useless in the case of Pieyre de Mandiargues. In all the genres he is engaged in a labyrinth of images. His four volumes of collected verse develop through the baroque and modern Gongorism to the point where his poetry is purified of verbal adornments to permit the perception of the heart and spirit of the author. (T.T.B.)

P522 Haig, Stirling, "André Pieyre de Mandiargues and Les pierreuses," French Review, 39:275-80, November, 1965.

Throughout Pieyre de Mandiargues's works, whether short stories, récits, poetry or essays, the one unifying element is the fantastic or the panic, in the etymological sense. Although a late surrealist, he mingles with such characteristics the romanticism of a Hugo, the gratuitousness of a Kafka, and the metamorphosis and metaphysics of physical reality. (T.T.B.)

P523 Les Six, "Les Prix littéraires," La Revue des Deux Mondes, 6:474-5, December 1, 1967.

Pieyre de Mandiargues might be placed in the line of a Villiers de l'Isle-Adam, who was acquainted with surrealism, as well as with Sade. He has the tincture of the affected, the unusual and the fantastic, implacably bent towards shattering love by eroticism and obsessed by death. (T.T.B.)

PIL'NYAK, BORIS

P524   Bristol, Evelyn, "Boris Pil'nyak," <u>Slavic and East European</u>
<u>Review</u>, 41:494-512, 1963.

Boris Pil'nyak's "fundamentally romantic orientation enabled him
initially to welcome the revolution. . . . During the later 1920's
and 1930's . . . his manner of writing did develop in the direction
of realism, omitting much that had been ornamental . . . [although]
his attempt to adjust to Soviet circumstances was unsuccessful.
. . ." "Pil'nyak's poignancy and rhetoric . . . add to the interest
of his work. . . ." (D.P.)

P525   Hayward, Max, "Pilnyak and Zamyatin," <u>Survey</u>, No. 36,
pp. 85-91, 1961.

"It was in 1929 that one distinctive Soviet device, the campaign of
vilification against certain chosen scapegoats with the object of ter-
rorising a particular group into submission, was first applied to
intellectuals. The campaign against Boris Pilnyak and Evgeni
Zamyatin [who occupied strategic positions in the Soviet literary
worlds] was a rehearsal for the sort of campaign which was to become commonplace later. . . . the victimization of the two writers
[as in later cases] was the signal for a sharp change in literary
policy and a general purge. The alleged offenses of the writers
were of relatively little importance . . . compared with the terroris-
tic effects for which they offered a suitable pretext." (D.P.)

P526   Wilson, Peter, "Boris Pilnyak," <u>Survey</u>, No. 46, pp. 134-42, 1963.

Boris Pilnyak was regarded as "one of the most promising Soviet
writers by Trotsky and other, less exalted, critics." (G.C.)

PINCHERLE, ALBERTO--See
MORAVIA, ALBERTO

PIÑERA, VIRGILIO

P527   Aragones, Juan Emilio, "Virgilio Piñera, autor cubano,"
<u>La Estafeta Literaria</u>, No. 436, p. 34, January 15, 1970.

The Cuban dramatist, Piñera, has multiple resonances: Ionesco,
Beckett, Pinter and Albee, as is particularly evident in <u>Dos viejos</u>
<u>pánicos</u>. (T.T.B.)

PINERO, ARTHUR WING

P528   Davies, Cecil W., "Pinero: The Drama of Reputation," English, 14:13-7, Spring, 1962.

Sir Arthur Wing Pinero's greatness and neglect stem from the same cause; his concentration on reputation in his comedies and tragedies. Reputation no longer is of vital concern to us; thus Pinero does not seem relevant. Moreover, he lacked the literary qualities of Ibsen. Nevertheless, he was an important influence on his young contemporaries, and his "great grim dramas" should be revived, since they depict the nobility of his time and provide magnificent vehicles for women. (D.P.)

P529   Pearson, Hesketh, "Pinero and Barrie: A Backstage View," Theatre Arts, 42:56-9, July, 1958.

[These are personal recollections of Arthur Pinero who "from the production of The Second Mrs. Tanqueray in 1893 until the outbreak of World War II . . . was the playwright-autocrat of the British theatre" and his "only competitor as a successful dramatist James Barrie . . . [who] though he scored more popular successes as a playwright . . . never received as much deference. . . ."] (D.P.)

THE SECOND MRS. TANQUERAY

P530   Nethercot, Arthur H., "Mrs. Warren's Profession and The Second Mrs. Tanqueray," Shaw Review, 13:26-8, 1970.

". . . there is evidence inadvertently produced . . . that Pinero's play [The Second Mrs. Tanqueray] was at least a crystalizing factor in Shaw's mind when he decided to write his own version of the character and actions of the Woman with a Past (Mrs. Warren's Profession). . . ." (H.S.)

PINGET, ROBERT

P531   Bann, Stephen, "Robert Pinget," London Magazine, 4:22-35, October, 1964.

The influence of Beckett and Robbe-Grillet on Pinget has been exaggerated, while his distinctive style has been overlooked. Pinget's development has been an "attempt to fashion a new realism--a new technique . . . which does not falsify experience. . . . Pinget's writing . . . demonstrates . . . forcibly how the exploration of new forms can lead to new possibilities of sympathy." (D.P.)

P532   Cismaru, Alfred, "Robert Pinget: An Introduction," American
        Benedictine Review, 19:203-10, June, 1968.

        ". . . although the disciple [Beckett] has eclipsed the master, he
        [Pinget] deserves to be considered independently, for he occupies an
        increasingly important place in contemporary letters." (R.C.F.)

P533   Knapp, Bettina L., "Une Interview avec Robert Pinget," French
        Review, 42:548-54, March, 1969.

        In the same intimate spirit that characterizes his novels, Pinget
        discusses the meaning and the developmental technique used in all
        his works--"The only thing which interests me is to capture a tone"
        --especially in light of such influences as Beckett, the Nouveau
        Roman, and the Theater of the Absurd. (R.C.F.)

P534   Magny, Olivier de, "Voici dix romanciers . . . Robert Pinget,"
        Esprit, 7-8:47-9, July-August, 1958.

        With incomparable verve, Robert Pinget has locked himself into a
        dangerous position. The heroes of Pinget carry themselves as
        identity cards, scrupulously completed with a name which does not
        exist. (D.P.)

P535   Micha, René, "Une Forme ouverte du langage," Les Temps
        Modernes, No. 201, pp. 1484-90, February, 1963.

        With few exceptions Pinget has had recourse to a unilateral dialogue.
        Since the je is inconceivable without the tu and the je-tu relationship
        is defined by reversibility, discourse is meaningless unless it re-
        ceives a reply. In Pinget, the je addresses the tu in vain. In
        L'Inquisitoire the dialogue appears more clearly as the confession
        of the moi alone. This "inquisitory interrogation" does not discover
        truth. It is truth itself. (T.T.B.)

P536   Perros, Georges, "Pinget ou le matériau," Critique, No. 225,
        pp. 150-4, February, 1966.

        Pinget does not play with words but he makes them play together.
        At times they are difficult to grasp, but they astonish and present
        a comprehensible description. In his play with present and past
        times, the time which does not pass is more important than that
        which does. (T.T.B.)

P537   Rose, Marilyn Gaddis, "Robert Pinget's Agapa Land," Forum
       (Houston), 8:68-70, No. 1, 1970.

       "Within the fluid meridional boundaries of Robert Pinget's fictional
       French province, natives never seem to live in its historic seat
       Agapa. . . . But they can live nearby on the road to it, and they can
       all visit it from time to time. . . . Pinget's province [is] itself a
       verbal game--sometimes eluding us like a summer mirage but
       steadily growing in density and traditions. Pinget's world, like
       Balzac's or Faulkner's, is consistent, self-contained, easily recog-
       nizable." (D.P.)

              L'INQUISITOIRE

P538   Steisel, Marie-Georgette, "Pinget's Method in L'Inquisitoire,"
       Books Abroad, 40:267-71, Summer, 1966.

       The "immense bite of life" Pinget promises in L'Inquisitoire "is
       only accessible to the reader once [he] . . . has become sensitive
       to the Pinget method. . . . Pinget's aim is not to tell a story. . . .
       To succeed in giving to the reader a tangible sensation, tactile so
       to speak, of the reality of another being [Pinget himself], is precisely
       what Pinget is seeking." (R.C.F.)

                  THE INQUISITORY--See
                  L'INQUISITOIRE

              QUELQU'UN

P539   Kuhn, Reinhard, "Robert Pinget: Quelqu'un," Novel, 1:93-5,
       Fall, 1967.

       Quelqu'un "is not a novel of 'being' but of 'becoming.' The quest is
       constantly broken off, only to be resumed again for no apparent pur-
       pose, and around the intermittent search for the piece of paper there
       accumulates a body of tentative assumptions, made up of an amalgam
       of realistic observations and enumerations, of daydreams and remem-
       brances of the past, of the snapshots in a family album and a tele-
       vision series. . . . Out of this ambiguous matter in constant flux
       there gradually emerges not a story, but a world, the run-down
       world of the shabby boarding house." (D.P.)

PINTER, HAROLD

P540   Amend, Victor E., "Harold Pinter: Some Credits and Debits,"
Modern Drama, 10:165-74, September, 1967.

Pinter "lacks that quality of greatness we so ardently desire in great
plays that move us . . . [although he] is the most accomplished
dramatist writing in English for the Theater of the Absurd." (D.P.)

P541   Amette, Jacques-Pierre, "Osborne Pinter, Saunders & Cie,"
La Nouvelle Revue Française, No. 205, pp. 95-9, January, 1970.

Pinter's theater resembles an aquarium. His ambiguity, double-
meanings and incongruity in a theater of silence resemble a cruel
Chekhov with touches of Freud, whereas Osborne merely borrows
the forms of conventional theater to demolish it with its own instruments. (T.T.B.)

P542   Aragones, Juan Emilio, "Dos herméticas piezas breves de H.
Pinter," La Estafeta Literaria, No. 363, p. 31, February, 1967.

In The Lover Pinter presents an unconventional farce which can
easily be overdone with disastrous effects. The Collection is more
hermetic, being rooted in an aprioristic confusion, typical of the
author's technique, which admits no clear distinction between the
true and the false. (T.T.B.)

P543   Ashworth, Arthur, "New Theatre: Ionesco, Beckett, Pinter,"
Southerly, 22:145-54, No. 3, 1962.

In plot, character and dialogue, the "Drama of the Absurd," is "a
complete rejection of realism." Sources for this drama are to be
found in Chekhov, Strindberg, Claudel and Jarry. Ionesco is both
the center of the movement and its best dramatist. (S.T.)

P544   Bensky, Lawrence M., "The Art of the Theatre III: Harold Pinter:
An Interview," Paris Review, No. 39, pp. 13-37, Fall, 1966.

[This interview ranges from the beginning of Pinter's writing career,
to how his background in acting influenced his playwrighting; notes
that Beckett and Kafka--not Ionesco--have been influences, comments
on several of his plays, indicates that one should not pay attention to
critics, and contends that he--Pinter--is "a very traditional playwright."] (D.P.)

P545   Bernhard, F. J., "Beyond Realism: The Plays of Harold Pinter,"
        Modern Drama, 8:185-91, September, 1965.

        "Despite their patina of realism, Pinter's plays [The Caretaker,
        The Birthday Party, The Room, A Slight Ache, and Night School]
        are clearly something other than the faithful imitations of life so
        characteristic of many of his contemporaries. Especially in his
        use of language, Pinter demonstrates his essentially suprarealistic
        quality. . . . the words have a consistent rhythmic construction and
        a symbolic change that lift them beyond conventional realism."
        (H.S.)

P546   Boulton, James T., "Harold Pinter: The Caretaker and Other Plays,"
        Modern Drama, 6:131-40, September, 1963.

        In his plays, notably The Birthday Party and The Caretaker, Pinter
        "is concerned with 'subtle experiences' but he sets out to evoke
        rather than exhaustively to depict or narrate them; by suggestion,
        hints, variations in intensity of mood . . . he involves the audience
        in an imaginative comprehension of the dramatic situation. . . ."
        (H.S.)

P547   Brown, John Russell, "Dialogue in Pinter and Others," Critical
        Quarterly, 7:225-43, Autumn, 1965.

        "On first hearing, as an impatient acquaintance, Pinter's plays, like
        his dialogue, can seem banal; their size, colour, delicacy and weight
        depend on the actor's ability to transmit under the text the deep and
        necessarily consistent truth of behavior they discovered in long re-
        hearsal." (H.S.)

P548   Brown, John Russell, "Mr. Pinter's Shakespeare," Critical
        Quarterly, 5:251-65, Autumn, 1963.

        The new dramatists, most particularly Pinter, Beckett and Ionesco,
        have had to create a new audience able to appreciate "a more inward,
        a deeper, a wider or a more precarious reality than can easily be
        viewed in life or in the exhibition of some clear narrative upon the
        stage," and in so doing they have created an audience better able to
        respond to "Shakespeare's presentation of human nature, his intuitive
        skill in using the stage as a means of viewing deeply and widely."
        (D.P.)

P549   Callen, A., "Comedy and Passion in the Plays of Harold Pinter," _Forum for Modern Language Studies_, 4:299-305, July, 1968.

"Intent on penetrating the inner chambers of the modern mind, Pinter has . . . forsaken traditional use of plot, consequential speech forms and logical action. But he has evolved a highly stylised theatrical language, blended delicately with naturalistic techniques, which, when successful, results in a vivid evocation of familiar problems that progresses excitingly from comedy to tragedy." (D.P.)

P550   Cohn, Ruby, "Latter Day Pinter," _Drama Survey_, 3:367-77, Winter, 1964.

Pinter's most obsessive theme is "the ambiguous relationship between appearance and reality." (D.P.)

P551   Cohn, Ruby, "The World of Harold Pinter," _Tulane Drama Review_, 6:55-68, Spring, 1962.

"Pinter's drama savagely indicts a System which sports maudlin physical comforts, vulgar brand names, and vicious vestiges of a religious tradition. Pinter's villains descend from motorized vans to close in on their victims in stuffy, shabby rooms. The System they represent is as stuffy and shabby. . . . The essence of the Pinter victim is his final sputtering helplessness." (K.M.W.)

P552   Dias, Earl J., "The Enigmatic World of Harold Pinter," _Drama Critique_, 11:119-24, Fall, 1968.

In spite of his assertions, Pinter is a serious artist with a great deal to say. His _The Birthday Party_, _The Caretaker_, and _The Homecoming_ condemn the false values of contemporary society; they consider the struggle for domination and the urge to violence. Among his dramatic devices are the pause, the speech of recall, curtain scenes, ambiguity, and common speech. (D.P.)

P553   Dick, Kay, "Mr. Pinter and the Fearful Matter," _Texas Quarterly_, 4:257-65, Autumn, 1961.

"Creating tension is part of this dramatist's pattern, a suspense which superficially verges on the farcical but simultaneously hints at grim revelation." Also, "Pinter's characters are able to concentrate on their strangely limited topics of dialogue no matter how these may be at variance with what is being said by other characters at that particular moment. Pinter is well aware how devastating every word is in this business of communication. . . . Pinter's 'fearful communication' becomes clearer with each new play." (D.P.)

P554   Dukore, Bernard, "The Theatre of Harold Pinter," Tulane Drama Review, 6:43-54, Spring, 1962.

The theatre of Harold Pinter "is a picture of contemporary man beaten down by the social forces around him. It is a picture of man without identity and without individuality, of man crushed into a rigid social mold. . . . It is a picture of the powerlessness of modern man, and the plays are frightening. It is a picture of the absurdity of the human condition . . . and the plays are comic. But . . . overpowering the laughter, there is a cry of despair from a well of human hopelessness." (D.P.)

P555   Esslin, Martin, "Pinter and the Absurd," Twentieth Century, 169:176-85, February, 1961.

Harold Pinter is closely linked with "The Theatre of the Absurd." (R.K.)

P556   Esslin, Martin, "Pinter Translated," Encounter, 30:45-7, March, 1968.

"Neither the social comedy of language in Pinter nor Pinter's poetic use of cadence and pause appears in the German version of the plays. What remains is something of the plot, something of the characters as revealed by their actions rather than their words. And that is precious little." (K.M.W.)

P557   Gillen, Francis, " '. . . Apart from the Known and the Unknown': The Unreconciled Worlds of Harold Pinter's Characters," Arizona Quarterly, 26:17-24, Spring, 1970.

Tea Party and The Homecoming dramatize "the division between a world which the major character knows because he can touch it and a world whose reality he occasionally glimpses but cannot prove by any of his instinctual criteria for reality. . . ." (S.T.C.)

P558   Hinchliffe, Arnold P., "Mr. Pinter's Belinda," Modern Drama, 11:173-9, September, 1968.

Pinter's plays from The Caretaker to The Homecoming have been involved with sex, and particularly with the role of woman with her possible ambiguities of wife, mother, and whore. (R.C.B.)

P559   Hughes, Catharine, "Pinter Is as Pinter Does," Catholic World, 210:124-6, December, 1969.

"But the dedicated symbol hunters . . . are missing the point: Pinter is as Pinter does. The importance of his work is what takes place on the stage." In his recent Silence and Landscape, "in the moments from the past that help to ward off the present . . . it is not so much that past that is important as its effect on the present." In these plays the "refusal to make contact has been carried to its farthest extreme thus far. The contrapuntal monologues in both plays are heavily interspersed with troubled silences. . . ." Pinter's "world remains the world of words, and of silences that sometimes speak louder than words." (D.P.)

P560   Kennedy, Andrew K., "Old and New in London Now," Modern Drama, 11:437-46, February, 1969.

[This essay discusses and compares the works of Stoppard (The Real Inspector Hound and Rosencrantz and Guildenstern are Dead), Osborne (Time Present and The Hotel in Amsterdam), and Pinter (Landscape and The Homecoming).] (H.S.)

P561   Kunkel, Francis L., "The Dystopia of Harold Pinter," Renascence, 21:17-20, Autumn, 1968.

"The Birthday Party is fully as obscure as The Homecoming, and a bit more mysterious, if less absurd. . . . These two dramas . . . combine to form a portrait of modern society as degenerate." (D.P.)

P562   Lahr, John, "Pinter and Chekhov: The Bond of Naturalism," Drama Review, 13:137-45, Winter, 1968.

Pinter has Chekhov's passion for the objective but the world he must portray lacks the pastoral background found in Chekhov. It is a world of terror and dehumanization. (J.C.O.)

P563   Lahr, John, "Pinter the Spaceman," <u>Evergreen Review</u>, 12:49-52, 87-90, June, 1968.

"While the new novel has set out to paint the surfaces of the objective world . . . the drama of Harold Pinter has come closest to capturing that relationship between Man and Nature as the basis of the artistic revolt in the other arts. Pinter is a storyteller, not a scientist; but his images of the world chronicle the wrench which has been thrown into the Newtonian machine." (D.P.)

P564   Lübbren, Rainer, "Robbe-Grillet, Pinter, und <u>Die blaue Villa in Hongkong</u>," <u>Die Neue Rundschau</u>, 78:119-26, No. 1, 1961.

Robbe-Grillet's earlier works, as well as Harold Pinter's full-length plays, provide, in accordance with Robbe-Grillet's critical theory, a non-metaphoric reality on which the reader can test his own relationship with the world. Robbe-Grillet's latest novel is dominated by the whim of its author, and founders on incomprehensibility. (R.H.L.)

P565   Morrison, Kristin, "Pinter and the New Irony," <u>Quarterly Journal of Speech</u>, 55:388-93, December, 1969.

"What Pinter seems to be doing, among other things, is contributing to the formation of a new kind of irony, a reversal in audience-expectation, a surprisingly consequent contrast between what the audience knows and what the characters know. In his plays of menace this kind of dramatic irony shifts the fear of being an object of hate from the stage into the audience. . . ." (D.P.)

P566   Nelson, Gerald, "Harold Pinter Goes to the Movies," <u>Chicago Review</u>, 19:33-43, No. 1, 1966.

"Quite simply, then, Pinter is making movies because they move--fast or slow, from here to there depending on exactly which effect he wants to achieve. He is making movies because on the screen he can determine the focus, direct attention, regulate rhythm, juxtapose events, and yet still feel that the audience is being drawn along. He is making movies because here seems to be . . . freedom for the artist to control and perfect movement which, for Pinter's purposes, is reason enough." (D.P.)

P567   Orley, Ray, "Pinter and Menace," Drama Critique, 11:125-48,
       Fall, 1968.

       Pinter's plays are concerned with menace and terror. In his plays
       a character undermines other characters and often is undermined
       himself. The greatest terror is that of a universe which cannot be
       understood. In his early plays Pinter explores the forces that press
       upon man from without; the later plays concentrate on internal psycho-
       logical stress. (D.P.)

P568   Palmer, David S., "A Harold Pinter Checklist," Twentieth Century
       Literature, 16:287-96, October, 1970.

       [This checklist reports printings of Pinter's works and unpublished
       writings, as well as biography, studies, reviews and discography of
       his plays, gathered internationally.] (D.P.)

P569   Pesta, John, "Pinter's Usurpers," Drama Survey, 6:54-65, Spring-
       Summer, 1967.

       Pinter insists "on the precariousness of man's existential security.
       . . . [His] device for expressing this theme has been the 'Usurper,'
       a menacing figure who . . . undermines the security of other charac-
       ters. . . . Pinter's handling of the theme of usurpation is still evolv-
       ing." (D.P.)

P570   Pinter, Harold, "Writing for Myself," Twentieth Century, 169:172-5,
       February, 1961.

       [These are recollections of his first experiences as a playwright.]
       (R.K.)

P571   Schechner, Richard, "Puzzling Pinter," Tulane Drama Review,
       11:176-84, No. 2, 1966.

       "Thus I believe the essential characteristic of Pinter's work is its
       conceptual incompleteness. Structurally each play . . . begins,
       develops, ends, and each part is organically joined to the others.
       But . . . the 'conceptual world' out of which the plays emerge, is
       sparse, fragmented. The outside world is frequently hardly alluded
       to. Past experience is brought into focus only with great difficulty.
       . . . The plays--as aesthetic entities--are completed, but the
       conceptual matrices out of which the action arises are left gaping."
       (D.P.)

P572 Storch, R. F., "Harold Pinter's Happy Families," Massachusetts Review, 8:703-12, Autumn, 1967.

"Pinter's plays are largely about the running away from certain family situations. . . . By dislocating our attention from the common sense view of things he makes us alive to primitive fears, destroys the rational façade of the adult mind, and lays bare regressive fantasies." (D.P.)

P573 Thornton, Peter C., "Blindness and the Confrontation with Death: Three Plays by Harold Pinter," Die Neueren Sprachen, 17:213-23, May, 1968.

"In Pinter's work, even his earliest, every action, every word, and indeed every silence, counts: apparently casual hints accumulate significance as the image of which they form a part grows more complex." (J.R.R.)

P574 Walker, Augusta, "Messages from Pinter," Modern Drama, 10:1-10, May, 1967.

Pinter has "two types of subject matter: one, the little allegory about life, death, and cosmic concepts, the other, the undercurrents and drives in human relationships." [Discussed are The Dumbwaiter, The Room, The Collection, A Slight Ache and The Caretaker.] (D.P.)

BIRTHDAY PARTY

P575 Hoefer, Jacqueline, "Pinter and Whiting: Two Attitudes Towards the Alienated Artist," Modern Drama, 4:402-8, February, 1962.

"For all its loose construction and awkward expression, Whiting's Saint's Day has the urgency of an alarm. More lyric than dramatic, never sentimental, it moves by the authenticity of its portrayal of the artists who betray society. Tense and highly charged in contrast, Pinter's Birthday Party nevertheless has the finality of a post mortem. . . . the brilliant sharp lines and scenes serve to strip [the artist] of all identity." (D.P.)

THE CARETAKER

P576   Cook, David and Harold F. Brooks, "A Room with Three Views: Harold Pinter's The Caretaker," Komos, 1:62-9, 1967.

"In a minor tour-de-force, by means of a myth which has a dynamic, progressive action, Pinter presents his picture of a condition, which is static. In The Caretaker the immediate events, and also the underlying question for the audience, have dramatic shape, and move forward from situation through development to catastrophe, which is then felt to have been inevitable. The progress attempted has been abortive: there is the tragic waste. . . . But the people in their attempt . . . win tragic sympathy. There is farce, but it is tragic farce." (D.P.)

P577   Gallagher, Kent G., "Harold Pinter's Dramaturgy," Quarterly Journal of Speech, 52:242-8, October, 1966.

"The Caretaker presents Pinter's amoral world. Society, individuality, samaritanism, technology, even the standard techniques of playwriting are all questioned through dramaturgical distortions that force heightened attention to extra-dramatic issues as well as to the action of the play. Hyper-reality added to realism creates an absurd microcosmos in which unexpected distortion becomes acceptable, and comedy bears a burden of savagery." (K.M.W.)

P578   Goodman, Florence Jeanne, "Pinter's The Caretaker: The Lower Depths Descended," Midwest Quarterly, 5:117-26, Winter, 1964.

Pinter, unlike the majority of the writers in the theatre of the absurd, uses language in a rather traditional way to communicate ideas. He may believe that the characters cannot communicate with each other, but he is aware that the artist can communicate with his audience. (A.S.W.)

P579   Minogue, Valerie, "Taking Care of the Caretaker," Twentieth Century, 168:243-8, September, 1960.

Most critics of The Caretaker "have seen it as a sort of socialized sociological document. Few have explored the content and ideas of the play. . . ." Pinter's use of lower-class speech, "despite its apparent air of banality, and its inconsequences . . . [produces] effects [which] are fresh and revealing. . . . In The Caretaker, discomforts, evasions, and pretensions flash like headlights on a dark road. . . . The illusions are less expertly integrated, the

THE CARETAKER (cont'd)

supposed realities less solidly entrenched, the fears, confusions, and delusions of grandeur nearer the surface than they are in most of us." (D.P.)

THE COLLECTION

P580   Mayersberg, Paul, "Harold Pinter's The Collection," Listener, 68:26, July 5, 1962.

"The only thing Pinter has in common with Ionesco is a contemporary theatrical idiom: an emphasis on the inadequacy of language to cope with the human predicament." He "is not a dramatist of the Absurd. . . . For Pinter reality is a social reality; and The Collection has a logic, a social and psychological logic, that is in opposition to the theatre of the Absurd." (D.P.)

THE DUMB WAITER

P581   Cohn, Ruby, "The Absurdly Absurd: Avatars of Godot," Comparative Literature Studies, 2:233-40, No. 3, 1965.

Beckett's En Attendant Godot, Pinter's The Dumb Waiter, and Bromberg's Defense of Taipei (unpublished) all "reflect Absurdity in absurdity. More explicitly than most Absurdist plays, they deal with the transcendental. . . . For all the differences in plot, the pattern is strikingly similar; for all the differences in language, all the plays probe more deeply than the surface level of their words." (D.P.)

THE DWARFS

P582   Sykes, Arlene, "Harold Pinter's Dwarfs," Komos, 1:70-5, 1967.

Pinter's radio play The Dwarfs should "be enjoyed for its own sake; it is also an example of the way Pinter seems to respond, quickly and sensitively, to a new dramatic medium. . . . The Dwarfs . . . has far more vivid descriptive writing than any of the stage plays. . . . The weight of evocative description, the flexibility, and sense of intimacy, make The Dwarfs a radio play to its very bones." (D.P.)

THE HOMECOMING

P583   Dukore, Bernard F., "A Woman's Place," <u>Quarterly Journal of</u>
<u>Speech</u>, 52:237-41, October, 1966.

In <u>The Homecoming</u> "Pinter presents a cluster of interwoven images:
battles for power among human animals, mating rites, and a dominant
wife-mother in a den of sexually maladjusted males. The various
repetition and patterns . . . convey a vividly theatrical image of lust
and power, and of lust used for power." (D.P.)

P584   Franzblau, Abraham N., "A Psychiatrist Looks at <u>The Homecoming</u>,"
<u>Saturday Review</u>, 50:56, April 8, 1967.

"Pinter has fashioned a <u>menage-à-cinq</u> out of four ill-assorted
characters and Ruth. However, her open door will afford them as
much heterosexual gratification as they can take, while, from the
excitement of the others, each will gain his secret homosexual
pleasure. . . . through . . . Ruth . . . the opening disequilibrium
is . . . stabilized, misery and discontent are banished, hopeful
excitement prevails, and the dramatic conflict is perfectly resolved."
(D.P.)

P585   Free, William J., "Treatment of Character in Harold Pinter's <u>The</u>
<u>Homecoming</u>," <u>South Atlantic Bulletin</u>, 34:1-5, November, 1969.

"Pinter's plays communicate the impression of absurdity not by
presenting us that idea through conventional dramatic technique
. . . but by making absurdity the essence of dramatic technique
itself. That is why his plays are so disturbing and controversial
and why . . . we must learn to take a fresh look at Pinter characters." (K.M.W.)

P586   Ganz, Arthur, "A Clue to the Pinter Puzzle: The Triple Self in
<u>The Homecoming</u>," <u>Educational Theatre Journal</u>, 21:180-7, May,
1969.

Although "<u>The Homecoming</u> . . . [is] bizarre and mysterious on the
surface, it has a tightly controlled sequence of significant actions
and, most notably, a rich pattern of symbolic relationships among
the characters which, more than any other factor, makes the play
not an exercise in obscurity but an extraordinarily illuminating experience." (D.P.)

THE HOMECOMING   (cont'd)

P587   Hewes, Henry, "Probing Pinter's Play," Saturday Review,
50:56-8, 96, April 8, 1967.

[These are answers of Pinter and actors in The Homecoming to
questions about the play.]   (D.P.)

P588   Mast, Gerald, "Pinter's Homecoming," Drama Survey, 6:266-77,
Spring, 1968.

In The Homecoming, as in his other plays, Pinter begins with the
familiar and transforms it into something bizarrely unfamiliar,
working on the premise that life is not as "logical," as clearly
patterned, as we would like to believe.   (A.S.W.)

P589   Morris, Kelly, "The Homecoming," Tulane Drama Review,
11:185-91, No. 2, 1966.

The "root concern for 'simple action' with 'simple effect' locates
Pinter in a special type of modern comedy of manners. No ideas
but in acts: wisdom lies in the discovery of immediate theatrical
means." (G.C.)

P590   States, Bert O., "Pinter's Homecoming: The Shock of Nonrecog-
nition," Hudson Review, 21:474-86, Autumn, 1968.

The arresting quality of Pinter's play is in part achieved by its
characters's possessing an ironic vision of action which is not
shared by the audience. Such irony is a defense against any single
failure of moral sense and the "exhaustion of a set of inherited
images." (D.M.M.)

P591   Warner, John M., "The Epistemological Quest in Pinter's The
Homecoming," Contemporary Literature, 11:340-53, Summer,
1970.

". . . Pinter must resort to metaphors replete with violent inver-
sions of conventional morality to make his audience see the decadence
of its whole materialistic, rationalistic culture; for The Homecoming
is a drama which describes man's plight in the godless world of
science and reason." (D.P.)

A SLIGHT ACHE

P592 Burkman, Katherine H., "Pinter's A Slight Ache as Ritual,"
Modern Drama, 11:326-35, December, 1968.

The replacement of the dying god by a new god as the mate of the
fertility goddess provides the structure for Pinter's play. (R.C.B.)

TEA PARTY

P593 Canaday, Nicholas, Jr., "Harold Pinter's Tea Party: Seeing and
Not-Seeing," Studies in Short Fiction, 6:580-5, Fall, 1969.

"Tea Party is a virtuoso treatment of the metaphor of sight. . . .
The obscurity and distortion that characterize the structural development of the story are relevant to the central metaphor of sight: what
is first blurred becomes disconcerting double vision by the end."
(H.S.)

PINTOR, GIAIME

P594 Heiney, Donald, " 'Americana' by Giaime Pintor," Western
Humanities Review, 17:203-12, Summer, 1963.

[This essay by Giaime Pintor, Italian anti-fascist, is a review of
Vittorini's Americana, an anthology of American literature, which
was later published in emasculated form, by action of the fascist
censors. In the review, published posthumously, Pintor attacked
Soldati's America Primo Amore and Cecchi's America Amara, both
official Italian experts on America, notable for their "wooden cultural
conservatism."] (D.P.)

PIOVENE, GUIDO

P595 Forti, Edgard, "L'Oeuvre de Guido Piovene," Critique, No. 203,
pp. 314-29, April, 1964.

From Lettere di una novizia (1941), through Gazetta nera (1943),
Pietà contro pietà (1946), I falsi redentori (1949) and Le Furie
(1963), Piovene deals with the question of the lie, the equivocal and
conjugal hatred. The inspiration of Gazetta nera is related to that
of Jouhandeau, whereas Pietà contro pietà contains the equivalent
of certain themes of the early works of Camus. (T.T.B.)

PIRANDELLO, LUIGI

P596   Bander, Robert G., "Pulcinella, Pirandello and Other Influences on De Filippo's Dramaturgy," Italian Quarterly, 46:39-72, 1968.

Pirandello "cannot be said to have been a major influence on De Filippo." "The tradition of Pulcinella, the Italian playwrights he has learned from, the dialect theatre of Naples, and the life of the city itself--all these forces have been influential in forming De Filippo's art." (D.P.)

P597   Bartocci, G., "Pirandello as Novelist," AULLA Proceedings, 9:71-4, 1965.

Pirandello's novels "lack unity and continuity [and do] . . . not follow the schemata of the traditional novel." Pirandello frees himself from the fetters of Naturalism and Verism; his character "is not the product of heredity, environment or a political regime. . . . his sufferings derive . . . from the grief of being alive, from the afflictions of conscious life." With Il fu Mattia Pascal Pirandello "introduces the real 'pirandellian' hero. . . . The dissolution of the personality . . . will reach its extreme consequences in Uno, nessuno e centomila." (D.P.)

P598   Baumann, Bedrich, "George H. Mead and Luigi Pirandello: Some Parallels between the Theoretical and Artistic Presentation of the Social Role Concept," Social Research, 34:563-607, September, 1968.

These conclusions may be drawn from the shared bodies of ideas of Mead and Pirandello: 1) The "sociological implications" of Mead's work explain "various cultural phenomena and relevant artistic creations." 2) "Eminent artists . . . articulate . . . relevant social problems. . . ." 3) ". . . the sociology of literature" makes "the real significance of literature and drama" more evident. (G.C.)

P599   Bergin, Thomas G., "Luigi Pirandello: "Pathfinder--and More," Books Abroad, 41:413-4, Autumn, 1967.

"The greatness of Pirandello demands our attention, compels our study, and justifies our right to analyze and distinguish. . . . as a creator, innovator, and theorist it would be hard to find his equal in his generation." (D.P.)

P600   Cecchetti, Giovanni, "Beneath Pirandello's Naked Masks,"
        Forum Italicum, 1:244-58, December, 1967.

        ". . . Pirandello called his collected plays Maschere nude (Naked
        Masks). . . . by 1935 they had grown into thirty one volumes. . . .
        He devoted his energies to the theater rather late, and saw it simply
        as a means of setting forth his personal view of life in a different
        way." ". . . for Pirandello social pressures . . . determine not
        only man's behavior, but man's actual identity. The individual may
        believe in existing per se, independently of what others may think,
        but it is nothing but an illusion. We are only the masks that society
        has imposed upon us, and can be nothing else." (D.P.)

P601   Chiaromonte, Nicola, "Libertà di Pirandello," Il Mondo, 12:14,
        November 1, 1960.

        To Pirandello is due "the rediscovery of the original nature of the
        theatre, of its first raison d'être, which is the link between the Ego
        and the others." "The culminating moment of this discovery" and
        of the freedom implicit in it "is the Six Characters." (V.R.)

P602   Chiaromonte, Nicola, "Pirandello and the Contemporary Theatre,"
        World Theatre, 16:224-37, 1967.

        "For the main characteristic of Pirandello's plays, namely, the
        presence of the intellect as the prime mover of the dramatic action,
        is to be found at the basis of every important development in the
        contemporary theatre. . . ." (D.P.)

P603   Costa, Orazio, "Six Characters, Right You Are . . . and Henry IV,"
        World Theatre, 16:248-55, 1967.

        Six Characters in Search of an Author, Right You Are--If You Think
        You Are, and Henry IV demonstrate "that Pirandello had taken the
        European theatre to the end of its bourgeois cycle by renovating it
        totally: plot, characters, settings. Pirandello, fully aware of the
        futility of the plot, reduced the argument to an interchangeable
        canvas; he rediscovered, in the characters's sufferings, the only
        dignity worthy of containing and expressing life; he stripped the stage
        of its decorative tinsel and restored it to the nudity of its primary
        function, that of a machine." (D.P.)

P604   Della Fazia, Alba, "Pirandello and His French Echo Anouilh," Modern Drama, 6:346-67, February, 1964.

"Jean Anouilh's work reveals Pirandellian influences to a greater extent than that of any other modern French dramatist." (D.P.)

P605   Della Fazia, Alba, "Pirandello's Mirror Theatre," Renascence, 15:37-40, Fall, 1962.

In Pirandello's Ciascuno a suo modo and Trovarsi "the antagonism between the reflection and the mirror, or between a perverted, criminal society and the purity of the individual ends, then, either in actual death or in the symbolic death of an objective reality." (D.P.)

P606   Fabbri, Diego, "A Rip in a Paper Sky," World Theatre, 16:218-23, 1967.

Pirandello's "whole production is a puppet show: puppets who, more or less, are aware of the 'rip in the paper sky'--and to this unexpected hole which deeply disturbs his characters, Pirandello himself always applies his searching look, unsuccessfully attempting to see what lies on the other side." (D.P.)

P607   Freedman, Morris, "Moral Perspective in Pirandello," Modern Drama, 6:368-77, February, 1964.

Pirandello's "unrelenting insistence on the art-reality opposition is subordinate to moral matters and has final meaning in the context of highly particularized human situations." (D.P.)

P608   Groff, Edward, "Point of View in Modern Drama," Modern Drama, 2:268-82, December, 1959.

The dramatic techniques or methods of such modern dramatists as Pirandello, O'Neill, Arthur Miller, Strindberg, Brecht, and Wilder "have a common aim: to make the playform more subjective by associating the dramatic events with the consciousness of individual characters who may participate in the action or merely narrate the story presented on the stage." (D.P.)

P609   Gullace, Giovanni, "Pirandello e l'esistenzialismo," Forum
Italicum, 1:267-78, December, 1967.

"Pirandello has been considered to be one of the direct precursors
of existential literature, having anticipated the significance of
motives of being. I need to say "anticipated" because Pirandello
remained misunderstood and incomprehensible for many long years:
only after the first World War was his work viewed affirmatively,
when the process of breaking down traditional values had reached
its tragic epilogue." (D.P.)

P610   Hainaux, René, "Pirandello," World Theatre, 16:216-7, 1967.

"The anguished questions [Pirandello] fired at the public of the 20's
and the 30's are precisely those which are troubling the present-
day audience. Pirandello undoubtedly continues to disconcert most
spectators and . . . most theatre people; his undelimitable characters and unravellings that unravel nothing still disquiet us. But
today, Pirandello comes not as a shock that jars but as one which
moves and affects us." (D.P.)

P611   Hatzantonis, Emmanuel, "Luigi Pirandello, Kostas Uranis, e la
Grecia," Forum Italicum, 1:336-44, December, 1967.

"Kostas Uranis met Pirandello in Lisbon in Autumn, 1931 at the
Fifth International Congress of Critics, which was concerned with
the influence of the revolutionary era created by the Sicilian playwright." Through Uranis, Pirandello was to have a major influence
on the development of modern Greek drama and cinema. (D.P.)

P612   Heffner, Hubert C., "Pirandello and the Nature of Man," Tulane
Drama Review, 1:23-40, June, 1957.

Pirandello did not create tragic or comic figures because the condition of life, he felt, was a mixture of the two. Pirandello confused
art and nature when he confused personality and character; therefore,
he wrote about the common man more as an animal mechanism than
as a human being. (F.J.H.)

P613   Herman, William, "Pirandello and Possibility," Tulane Drama
Review, 10:91-111, Spring, 1966.

"The plays of Pirandello are dense with word, argument, thesis,
aesthetic declaration and outright lecture. . .: the loquaciousness
we find in his dialogue is certainly related to the fertility of his

imagination. . . . In the case of Pirandello, the mind that was disposed to make theatre found a perfect solution: the great hue and cry raised by passion wherever it goes. The tumultuous histrionics suited the nature of his overproduction admirably." (D.P.)

P614   Illiano, Antonio, "Pirandello e i primi critici," Forum Italicum, 1:289-301, December, 1967.

"The Italian critics and public of the first twenty years of this century can only be accused of hostility and insensibility when confronted with the genius of Pirandello; his recognition in his own country was determined, in the last analysis, by the clamorous foreign successes which appeared after the first stagings of Sei personnagi and Enrico IV. . . . However, Pirandello's success beyond the Alps was due in no small part to the triumphant reception given to Sei personnagi by Manzoni in Milan on September 27, 1921." (D.P.)

P615   James, Norman, "The Fusion of Pirandello and Brecht in Marat/ Sade and The Plebeians Rehearse the Uprising," Educational Theatre Journal, 21:426-38, No. 4, 1970.

The most noticeable influences on Peter Weiss's Marat/Sade and Günter Grass's The Plebeians Rehearse the Uprising are Brecht and Pirandello, Brecht for his alienation effect, and Pirandello for his ability to "convey a world in which there are no fixed points in space and time, but in which various points in space and time illuminate each other. . . ." (D.P.)

P616   Lawrence, Kenneth, "Luigi Pirandello: Holding Nature up to the Mirror," Italica, 47:61-77, Spring, 1970.

Pirandello's theme of Art versus Life "is the cornerstone idea supporting the great trilogy. . .: Sei personnagi in cerca d'autore (1921), Ciascuno a suo modo (1924), and Questa sera si recita a soggetto (1930). . . . The principal thesis informing the trilogy is the incommensurability involved in the transference of Life to Art, or more specifically, to the theater. Pirandello shows us the agonizing difficulty attendant upon the carrying of life to the stage." (D.P.)

P617   Leighton, Charles H., "Alejandro Casona's 'Pirandellism',"
        Symposium, 17:202-14, Fall, 1963.

        Pirandello's influence here is minimal. Casona rejects Pirandello's
        psychological solutions, assumes a single unified truth, though with
        several perspectives, and contents himself with artistic exploitation
        of Pirandello's solipsism. (C.O.)

P618   Lueders, Perry H., "Pirandello: Reality, Illusion and the Void,"
        Xavier University Studies, 1:158-61, No. 4, 1962.

        In Pirandello's "country drama" Liola, pessimism and pain remain
        softened because of the comparative simplicity of the characters,
        but in the "city dramas," It's So and Henry IV, the illusion is
        constant and the pain more severe. (A.S.W.)

P619   Matthei, Renate, "Die Provokation der Maske," Merkur, 21:547-56,
        June, 1967.

        "It seems to me that Pirandello is today again much closer to us
        [than is absurd theater]. Where awareness of catastrophe recedes,
        then pressure must be increased and neurosis shown as that which
        it is: not the consequence of a metaphysical misfortune, but the
        result of a social or political condition whose mechanism forces the
        individual into a wrong adaptation." (J.R.R.)

P620   Maurino, Ferdinando D., "Pirandello: The Plausible Absurd,"
        Forum Italicum, 1:259-66, December, 1967.

        In Pirandello's plays "we do not encounter a sustained pathos, as
        we do in the greater plays of Shakespeare. . . . Yet the Pirandello
        who made possible the Theatre of the Absurd . . . remains its
        prototype and master." "His world is a gigantic galaxy in the
        stratosphere soaring ever higher in search of relief for man's
        isolation, for his mental and spiritual tumult. . . . In such a state
        Pirandello's characters can exist, and their grotesque behavior
        becomes then a plausible absurd." (D.P.)

P621   May, Frederick, "A Neglected Article by Luigi Pirandello,"
        Italian Quarterly, 6:30-45, 1962.

        The "condemned and rapid survey of the (then) contemporary Italian
        novel" which Pirandello contributed to the April, 1934 issue of
        Fortnightly Review, may not be "a great addition to the opera of
        Luigi Pirandello, but it is not one we can afford to neglect" since

Pirandello "was not only haunted by <u>his own</u> characters; he was possessed by those evolved by other writers." (D.P.)

P622   May, Frederick, "Polyaretus: Some Notes on Ulysses in the Dramatic Works of Luigi Pirandello," <u>Komos</u>, 1:105-14, 1967.

"Ulysses is one of Pirandello's most fruitful classical sources. . . . He is a tension of loss and gain, of gangster and aristocrat of the mind. Often he provides Pirandello with that range of man comprehended in the satyr . . . so prompting an exploration of all that is Panic in the Sicilian writer's work. Above all, he is a delicate measure of the protean, and, as such, the movement within so much of Pirandello's poetry. . . . It is this quality which raises him from symbol or extensive metaphor to paradigm of entelechy." (D.P.)

P623   May, Frederick, "Three Major Symbols in Four Plays by Pirandello," <u>Modern Drama</u>, 6:378-96, February, 1964.

Three favorite symbols of Pirandello--the mirror, water and greenness--appear prominently in <u>Six Characters in Search of an Author</u>, <u>Henry IV</u>, <u>A Dream (But Perhaps It Isn't)</u> and <u>Man, Beast and Virtue</u>. (G.C.)

P624   Newberry, Wilma, "Aesthetic Distance in García Lorca's <u>El público</u>: Pirandello and Ortega," <u>Hispanic Review</u>, 37:276-96, April, 1969.

<u>El público</u> "is an extremely important document because it shows García Lorca's very special reaction to Pirandello. . . . Lorca, realizing that his type of lyrical theater could not exist unless a certain aesthetic distance were maintained, wrote <u>El público</u> to illustrate the damage caused by extreme forms of Pirandellism, to criticize these forms, and then to manifest his rejection of them. . . . García Lorca may have been inspired by Ortega y Gasset['s <u>Deshumanización del arte</u>.]" (D.P.)

P625   Newberry, Wilma, "Cubism and Pre-Pirandellianism in Gómez de la Serna," <u>Comparative Literature</u>, 21:47-62, Winter, 1969.

In the works of Gómez de la Serna and Pirandello "cubist" techniques are applied in drama. Stage conventions are exposed and talked about, traditional illusionism is shattered, and the audience is made conscious of the medium itself. (J.C.O.)

P626   Newberry, Wilma, "Echegaray and Pirandello," PMLA, 81:123-9,
March, 1966.

Echegaray is a playwright "who shows kinship not only with his
literary ancestors, but one who is also a link from the past to the
twentieth century, so ably represented by Luigi Pirandello." (D.P.)

P627   Newberry, Wilma, "The Influence of Pirandello in Two Plays of
Manuel and Antonio Machado," Hispania, 48:255-60, May, 1965.

In Las adelfas the Machados give their version of the theme of the
many-sided nature of truth, but without carrying Pirandello's ideas
to the extreme. In El hombre que murió en la guerra they pose the
problem of personality, translating it to the Spain of the Generation
of '98. (C.O.)

P628   Newberry, Wilma, "Luca de Tena, Pirandello, and the Spanish
Tradition," Hispania, 50:253-61, May, 1967.

"Luca de Tena's plays, then, show the direct influence of Pirandello,
amply supported by Spanish theatrical tradition, and modified by his
approach as a popular entertaining playwright. Perhaps the fact
illustrated so clearly in Luca de Tena's plays that Pirandellism is
based securely on Spanish tradition accounts for the strong influence
of Pirandello in the theater of the members of the generation of '98
and beyond to the present time." (C.O.)

P629   Newberry, Wilma, "Pirandello and Azorín," Italica, 44:41-60,
March, 1967.

"In summary, 'Pirandellism' is an essential component of the work
of this important member of the Generation of '98, and Azorín's
admiration of and affinity for Pirandello are undeniable." Azorín
"consistently uses methods associated with Pirandello, such as the
gamut of the theater-within-the theater techniques . . . and
Pirandello's personality themes. . . . In his experimental plays
Azorín artistically combines "Pirandellism plus Golden Age Spanish
techniques and ideas, plus [his] own original art . . . to conform to
the needs of his generation. . . ." (D.P.)

P630   Newberry, Wilma, "A Pirandellian Trilogy by Jacinto Grau,"
        Forum Italicum, 1:309-24, December, 1967.

        In Tabarín, Las gafas de don Telesforo o un loco de buen capricho,
        and Bibí Carabé Jacinto Grau "becomes a full-fledged member of
        the group of playwrights inspired by Pirandello and Pirandellism."
        Indeed, Grau has written "one of the most important examples of
        Pirandello's great impact beyond the borders of Italy." (D.P.)

P631   Norwood, W. D., Jr., "Zen Themes in Pirandello," Forum
        Italicum, 1:349-56, December, 1967.

        "Certain of the major themes of . . . Luigi Pirandello . . . form a
        pattern of ideas that are essentially Eastern and specifically Zen."
        (D.P.)

P632   Petrorska-Giudici, Marija, "Pirandello a Praga," Forum Italicum,
        1:345-8, December, 1967.

        [This is a survey of the performances and influence of Pirandello in
        Czechoslovakia, from his first mention in an article in 1903 to the
        present day.] (D.P.)

P633   "Pirandello in the World," World Theatre, 16:355-66, 1967.

        [These are comments by Shunjiro Aoe, playwright; Orestes Caviglia,
        actor and director; Boro Draskovic, director; Kamal Eid, director;
        Nabil El-Alfy, director; Vaclav Hudecek, director; Jean Mercure,
        actor and director; Rogerio Paulo, actor and director; Ursula
        Pueschel and Helfried Schoebel, directors: and Takashi Sugawara,
        director, on their indebtedness to Pirandello, his influence on their
        colleagues, and the relevance of his plays to "fundamental problems
        of our day."] (D.P.)

P634   Pirandello, Luigi, "The Art of Humour," Massachusetts Review,
        6:515-20, 1965.

        [This is a translation by John Patrick Pattinson of "a section from
        Chapter V and most of Chapter VI of Part Two" of Pirandello's long
        essay "L'Umorismo," based on the revised and augmented version
        first published in 1920.] (D.P.)

P635   Pirandello, Luigi, "An Autobiographical Sketch, " Forum Italicum,
        1:241-2, December, 1967.

        [This is "the English translation of the autobiographical sketch which
        Pirandello wrote in German and sent to E. Gagliardi, a Swiss
        journalist and critic. Gagliardi inserted it in his profile . . . 'Luigi
        Pirandello: Ein italienischer Erzähler, ' Nation (Berlin), No. 37
        (1905). This is one of the first articles on Pirandello ever to appear
        outside Italy." The original German of Pirandello is also printed
        here.] (D.P.)

P636   Pirandello, Luigi, "On Humor, " Tulane Drama Review, 10:46-59,
        Spring, 1966.

        "Let's conclude: humor is the feeling of polarity aroused by that
        special activity of reflection which doesn't hide itself, which doesn't
        become . . . a form of feeling, but its contrary, following the feel-
        ings step by step, however, as the shadow follows the body." (D.P.)

P637   Poggioli, Renato, "Pirandello in Retrospect, " Italian Quarterly,
        No. 4, pp. 19-47, Winter, 1958.

        Pirandello's plays are not mere vehicles for ideas, but have at their
        center a humanity and a constant search for characters who are real
        people, not only reflections of people. (A.S.W.)

P638   Radcliff-Umstead, Douglas, "Pirandello and the Puppet World, "
        Italica, 44:13-27, March, 1967.

        "It is to the theatre of Luigi Pirandello that one must turn to find
        characters who, although they appear to be made of wood, are really
        contrasted in a desperate tension. Afraid of their emotions and
        crushed by overwhelming circumstances, Pirandellian characters
        protect themselves by functioning like puppets." In essence, "the
        puppet theme in Pirandello's work has portrayed modern man in his
        desperate attempt to impart meaning to life." (D.P.)

P639   Radice, Raul, "Ups and Downs of Pirandello's Theatre in Italy, "
        World Theatre, 16:238-47, 1967.

        ". . . the reasons for the silence that encompassed [Pirandello's]
        work once he was dead and which led to his virtual banishment from
        the Italian stage just as his plays were meeting with even greater
        success at world level are still difficult to understand . . . [although]
        Pirandello was never completely banished from the Italian stage.

. . . For the centenary of his birth, Pirandello reigns on all the major Italian stages . . . because the centenary coincides with a moment when his art is deeply and widely appreciated." (D.P.)

P640   Rizzo, Gino, "Directing Pirandello Today," <u>Tulane Drama Review</u>, 10:76-85, Spring, 1966.

". . . Pirandello integrates his <u>ars poetica</u> into his own art and anticipates the treatment of reality on fragmented levels which is the mark of this century's great art. He approaches reality on the basis of its many probable levels. . . . I still think the way to do Pirandello is to present him as one of the first European writers to contribute to the fragmentation of traditional structures." (D.P.)

P641   Rizzo, Gino, "Luigi Pirandello in Search of a Total Theatre," <u>Italian Quarterly</u>, 45:3-26, 1968.

"The progressively more open form witnessed by the plays of the 'trilogy' [<u>Six Characters in Search Of An Author</u>, <u>Each In His Own Way</u>, <u>Tonight We Improvise</u>], puts Pirandello at the head not only of the avant-garde movements of his time, but also of the most recent experimentations and innovations undertaken by the neo avant-garde of the Sixties." (G.C.)

P642   Romeo, Luigi, "Pirandello linguista," <u>Forum Italicum</u>, 1:302-8, December, 1967.

"We should not be surprised that Pirandello made his entrance into the academic world with a study of the dialect of Girgenti, since we must recall that all great Italian writers since Dante have always had a foot in the linguistic-philological field. . . . Pirandello . . . follows this tradition, with the difference that he was the first contemporary man of letters to write a doctoral dissertation [his <u>Laute und Lautenwicklung der Mundart von Girgenti</u>] on a linguistic subject." (D.P.)

P643   Rosenberg, Marvin, "Pirandello's Mirror," <u>Modern Drama</u>, 6:331-45, February, 1964.

"In all but the self-questioning plays, Pirandello's characters find that the firm selves they believe they own are in fact made up of evanescent hopes, impulses, wishes, fears, social pressures, the instincts of the animal inheritance. . . . Hence his characters usually wander as in a hall of mirrors, thinking they look for reality, while, in fact, they desperately try to find safe illusions--'ideals'-- to live by." (D.P.)

P644 Scherer, Jacques, "Marivaux and Pirandello," Modern Drama, 1:10-4, May, 1958.

"The article aims at . . . showing how the new ideas on the theatre that have been made familiar by the work of Pirandello can rightly clarify, in a retrospective way, certain aspects of the comedies of Marivaux." (D.P.)

P645 Sedwick, Frank, "Unamuno and Pirandello Revisited," Italica, 33:40-51, March, 1956.

"It must be concluded that these likenesses are only similar reactions by two men of nearly identical aesthetic principles who wrote in like intellectual climates." (C.O.)

P646 Sinicropi, Giovanni, "Arte e vita nelle opere di Luigi Pirandello," Italica, 38:265-95, December, 1961.

"The problem of the rapport of Art and Life in the work of Pirandello must then be analyzed in the light of the need to explain, to justify, to find the primary rationale in the life of an artist and of his thought. To Pirandello the spiritual is more important than the authentic because it signifies a rapport of spirit and fact, of being and creating, which is never static in his spiritual and artistic world, but proceeds with the same logic which governs his will to find a true and certain passage towards the essence of Being." (D.P.)

P647 "Some Selected Works on Pirandello," World Theatre, 16:270, 1967.

[Listed here are book length studies of Pirandello in Italian, French, English, and German.] (D.P.)

P648 Squarzina, Luigi, "Each in His Own Way and We Know Not How," World Theatre, 16:256-62, 1967.

["The following are some of the notes drafted by Luigi Squarzina" while working on "his historic productions of Each in His Own Way and We Know Not How."] (D.P.)

P649 Starkie, Walter, "Luigi Pirandello: 1867-1967," Theater Annual, 23:1-8, 1967.

"Pirandello's theatre makes a wide appeal to the thoughtful theatre public of today because its essence is the marrow of contemporary ideas, of modern anxieties and pessimism." Although dramatists in many countries admired him it was France "which adopted him as its own." No one "since Ibsen has given Europe so totally renewed a conception of the theatre, a more violently original artistry together with so personal a technique." (D.P.)

P650   Tillona, Zina, "La morte nelle novelle di Pirandello," Forum Italicum, 1:279-88, December, 1967.

The characters in Novelle per un anno live, suffer and make others suffer, searching in vain for love, struggling helplessly with life. . . . Death, the one irrevocable and inexorable reality in a life given to illusion and delusion, becomes the driving agent of many stories [of Pirandello.]" (D.P.)

P651   Vicari, Antonio, "I miti di Luigi Pirandello," Italica, 44:28-40, March, 1967.

For Pirandello "myth, then, must be directed towards the accession of the ideal state. . . . In the drama of the Pirandellian world myth represents the final phase [of his art]: the catharsis." (D.P.)

P652   Vittorini, Domenico, "Luigi Pirandello as I saw Him," Symposium, 8:113-23, Summer, 1954.

[These are recollections of a series of conversations between Pirandello and the author. Pirandello speaks of the influences which shaped his work, of his themes, religion, politics, the art of his contemporaries, and literary criticism.] (J.R.B.)

P653   Weiss, Auréliu, " 'The Remorseless Rush of Time'," Tulane Drama Review, 10:30-45, Spring, 1966.

Pirandello "was convinced that any communication between men is based on misunderstanding" and "felt compelled to proclaim his doubts to an audience which he pictured in his works as . . . incapable of understanding themselves and even less the desires and personalities of others." (G.C.)

P654   Whitfield, J. H., "Pirandello and T. S. Eliot: An Essay in Counterpoint," English Miscellany, 9:329-57, 1958.

". . . at the root, the purposes of Eliot and Pirandello are contrary. For the latter, all order is illusory, and we have to lift the lid . . . to find the inconsistencies lurking underneath. But for the former, the order in reality is a derivative and an earnest of the order outside the world in which we live." Finally, "in the last resort it is Pirandello who offers hope in life, and Eliot who counsels us in despair." (D.P.)

CIASCUNO A SUO MODO

P655   Dukore, Bernard F., and Daniel C. Gerould, "Explosions and Implosions: Avant-Garde Drama Between World Wars," Educational Theatre Journal, 21:1-16, March, 1969.

Witkiewicz's surrealist play The Water Hen, Ernest Toller's expressionist drama Man and the Masses, Brecht's epic play Saint Joan of the Stockyards, and Pirandello's example of theatricalism Each In His Own Way "dramatize different versions of revolution, social and artistic. . . . Witkiewicz, Toller, Brecht, and Pirandello are innovators . . . : revolutionaries demanding fundamental changes in society, in the mind, and in the theatre." (D.P.)

P656   Squarzina, Luigi, "Notes for Each in His Own Way," Tulane Drama Review, 10:87-90, Spring, 1966.

[These are director's interpretive notes and comments.] (G.C.)

COSÌ È (SE VI PARE)

P657   Sticca, Sandro, "The Drama of Being and Seeming in Schnitzler's Anatol and Pirandello's Così è (se vi pare)," Journal of the Arthur Schnitzler Research Association, 5:4-28, Summer, 1966.

"In the shattering search to distinguish between reality and illusion . . . Schnitzler's and Pirandello's Weltanschauung reveals a profound relativism which in both dramas seeks primarily to point out the unavailability of objective truth in the intelligible world and the consequent effort of the individual to see that world as an expression of his personality. . . ." (G.C.)

DIANA AND TUDA--See
DIANA E LA TUDA

DIANA E LA TUDA

P658   Feng, Carole B., "Reconciliation of Movement and Form in <u>Diana</u> <u>and Tuda</u>," <u>Modern Drama</u>, 10:410-5, February, 1968.

Pirandello contrasts, by means of two sculptors, the antithetical views that only life matters and that only art matters. But he then fuses the two ideas in terms of a work of art as a living moment preserved through form. (R.C.B.)

EACH IN HIS OWN WAY--See
CIASCUNO A SUO MODO

ENRICO IV

P659   Bentley, Eric, "Il Tragico Imperatore," <u>Tulane Drama Review</u>, 10:60-75, Spring, 1966.

In <u>Henry IV</u>, Pirandello gives us "the <u>experience</u> of a man with Pirandellian <u>opinions</u>, a man who has applied himself to the Pirandellian task of 'constructing himself.'. . . The point is that 'Henry' <u>always failed</u>." (G.C.)

P660   Savage, Edward B., "Masks and Mummeries in <u>Enrico IV</u> and <u>Caligula</u>," <u>Modern Drama</u>, 6:397-401, February, 1964.

". . . Pirandello and Camus in these two plays, <u>Henry IV</u> and <u>Caligula</u> demonstrate the continuing high significance of the actor and of the play as a form [by their use of] <u>artificial</u> or <u>unrealistic</u> elements. . . ." (D.P.)

IL FU MATTIA PASCAL

P661   Leal, Luis, "La función de los personajes españoles en <u>Il fu Mattia</u> <u>Pascal</u>," <u>Forum Italicum</u>, 1:325-35, December, 1967.

<u>Il fu Mattia Pascal</u> is the first work in which Pirandello abandons naturalism for psychological realism. In the novel the Spanish characters "serve three functions: to create cosmopolitan atmosphere, to add a note of humor and to unite the world of Mattia Pascal to that of Adriano Meis." (D.P.)

LA GIARA

P662   Blanquat, Josette, "D'Une jarre à un moulin à vent," Revue de
Littérature Comparée, 40:294-302, April-June, 1966.

The image of the jar in La Giara is charged with meaning and comes
to suggest, along with the action of the piece, the movement of a
silent meditation on man, his character, his imprisoned state, his
aspiration towards liberty and the affirmation of that liberty in
humor. (F.M.L.)

THE GIANTS OF THE MOUNTAIN--See
I GIGANTI DELLA MONTAGNA

I GIGANTI DELLA MONTAGNA

P663   Strehler, Giorgio, "The Giants of the Mountain," World Theatre,
16:263-9, 1967.

[These are director's notes on Pirandello's The Giants of the
Mountain by "one of the greatest contemporary directors."] (D.P.)

HENRY IV--See
ENRICO IV

THE JAR--See
LA GIARA

THE LATE MATTIA PASCAL--See
IL FU MATTIA PASCAL

THE MAN WITH THE FLOWER IN HIS MOUTH--See
L'UOMO DAL FIORE IN BOCCA

THE MOUNTAIN GIANTS--See
I GIGANTI DELLA MONTAGNA

RIGHT YOU ARE! (IF YOU THINK SO)--See
COSÌ È (SE VI PARE)

SEI PERSONAGGI IN CERCA D'AUTORE

P664 Bentley, Eric, "Father's Day: In Search of Six Characters in Search of an Author," Drama Review, 13:57-72, Fall, 1968.

"To me the deepest . . . interpretation of the search for an author would stress neither God nor literary authorship but fatherhood, and I like to think I derive this choice . . . from the text." Six Characters "is a supreme achievement that says something profound about the theatre and about life seen as theatre and seen by means of theatre." (D.P.)

P665 Clark, Hoover W., "Existentialism and Pirandello's Sei Personaggi," Italica, 43:276-84, September, 1966.

"The peculiar situation presented as subject matter in Sei Personaggi, in which characters of the theater are contrasted with people in real life . . . gives rise to many themes which occur also in the literary works of modern existentialists, e. g.: denunciation of a world which does not appear to be as it should be, scorn for those who are content with the world as it is, general attitude of pessimism, choice of the absurd against the very absurdity of existence, frenzy to negate and destroy. . . ." (D.P.)

P666 Hewes, Henry, "Two Masterpieces in Search of an Audience," Saturday Review, 38:25, December 31, 1955.

[This is a consideration of Six Characters in Search of an Author and Finnegans Wake.] (D.P.)

P667 Illiano, Antonio, "Pirandello's Six Characters in Search of an Author: A Comedy in the Making," Italica, 44:1-12, March, 1967.

Pirandello's Six Characters in Search of an Author "has several meanings, several layers of reality adding up to an unconcluded and unconcluding plurality. In spite of a seemingly philosophical surface, it does not try to preach any moral or philosophy, not excluding skepticism. A definition of Six Characters . . . must take into account the fact that the play is, first and foremost, a highly sophisticated and artistic re-enactment of relativism-in-the-making." (D.P.)

SEI PERSONAGGI IN CERCA D'AUTORE   (cont'd)

P668   Kennedy, Andrew K., "Six Characters: Pirandello's Last Tape,"
Modern Drama, 12:1-9, May, 1969.

Pirandello's handling of the tension between full, rhetorical speed
and minimal speed points toward a dialogue of fragments and cries.
(R.C.B.)

P669   Kernan, Alvin B., "Truth and Dramatic Mode in the Modern Theater:
Chekhov, Pirandello, and Williams," Modern Drama, 1:101-14,
September, 1958.

"Despite very real differences in technique and tone in these three
plays [Chekhov's The Sea Gull, Pirandello's Six Characters in
Search of an Author, and Williams's Streetcar Named Desire], they
all turn on the fundamental and often noted similarity between life
and the stage, of the problem of the individual in 'constructing' a life
and the author in constructing a play. And their plays are perfect
images for our time, for they reveal our characteristic relativism,
concern for epistemology, pragmatism, and unwilling acquiescence
in naturalism." (D.P.)

P670   Kligerman, Charles, M. D., "A Psychoanalytic Study of
Pirandello's Six Characters in Search of an Author," Journal of
the American Psychoanalytic Association, 10:731-44, October, 1962.

In Six Characters in Search of an Author "Pirandello seems to have
crystallized the main psychic conflicts of his life, beginning in
childhood and elaborated in mature years. Seldom has a man described so vividly the confrontation with his own unconscious and
subsequent rejection of it. . . . By the use of his inventive genius
he was able to project the pathological material artistically, create
a magnificent achievement, and thus preserve his own integration."
(D.P.)

P671   Nolan, David, "Theory in Action: Pirandello's Sei Personaggi,"
Forum for Modern Language Studies, 4:269-76, July, 1968.

"The dramatic action of Sei personaggi in cerca d'autore is based on
the dialectic of the creative process, as understood by Pirandello."
(J.R.R.)

SEI PERSONAGGI IN CERCA D'AUTORE   (cont'd)

P672   Sogliuzzo, A. Richard, "The Uses of the Mask in The Great God
       Brown and Six Characters in Search of an Author," Educational
       Theatre Journal, 18:224-9, October, 1966.

       "An analysis of the technique of the masks employed in The Great
       God Brown and Six Characters . . . reveals that O'Neill and
       Pirandello used the mask to express different themes, and neither
       was primarily concerned with the mask as a means to express the
       psychological conflict of the many masks of human personality."
       (D.A.B.)

           SIX CHARACTERS IN SEARCH OF AN AUTHOR--See
           SEI PERSONAGGI IN CERCA D'AUTORE

           L'UOMO DAL FIORE IN BOCCA

P673   Loriggio, Franco, "Life and Death: Pirandello's Man With a Flower
       in His Mouth," Italian Quarterly, 47-48:151-60, 1969.

       ". . . constantly overcoming the fear of death to live: this very
       basic therapy allows the man to talk, to laugh, to avoid committing
       any desperate act. Towards a similar goal . . . strive most of
       Pirandello's characters and ultimately his plays: plenitude, the
       union of opposites, or paradox conquered. . . . Man With a Flower
       in His Mouth affirms, it celebrates." (K.M.W.)

       PLATH, SYLVIA

P674   Alvarez, A., "Sylvia Plath," Tri-Quarterly, No. 7, pp. 65-74,
       Fall, 1966.

       "The achievement of [Sylvia Plath's] final style is to make poetry
       and death inseparable. The one could not exist without the other.
       . . . In a curious way the poems read as though they were written
       posthumously. It needed not only great intelligence and insight to
       handle the material of them, it also took a kind of bravery. Poetry
       of this order is a murderous art." (D.P.)

P675   Ames, Lois, "Notes Toward a Biography," Tri-Quarterly, No. 7,
       pp. 95-107, Fall, 1966.

       "Sylvia Plath's life has already taken on the quality of a legend . . .
       [which] has made any reconstruction of her life, not to mention

critical estimation of work, additionally difficult. What follows is an account of her which, however skeletal, is at least fairly accurate." (D.P.)

P676　Bagg, Robert, "The Rise of Lady Lazarus," Mosaic, 2:9-36, No. 4, 1969.

"In the case of Sylvia's three predecessors [Yeats, Eliot, and Robert Lowell], their varying solutions had this in common: they acknowledged . . . that their conception of the self . . . always incurred a diminution, a partial defeat for the self fighting to preserve its autonomous happiness. Sylvia, however, who finds the world more insidious and intolerable than any of the others, is not bound by any metaphysical belief in the self's limitations." (K.M.W.)

P677　Boyers, Robert, "Sylvia Plath: The Trepanned Veteran," Centennial Review, 13:138-53, Spring, 1969.

"Time and again in . . . [her] poems, Plath becomes the thing or person imagined and described, so that cumulatively the poems evolve an image not of a single human victim, but of a monstrous, abstract victim whose condition is general and unavoidable." (G.C.)

P678　Claire, William F., "That Rare, Random Descent: The Poetry and Pathos of Sylvia Plath," Antioch Review, 26:552-60, Winter, 1966-67.

"Grief, a crazy, jig-saw humor, and destructive undertones comprise the basis of the poetry. . . . Her insistent desire was to have the reader hear, feel, and experience her own ordeal." (J.L.A.)

P679　Cox, C. B. and A. R. Jones, "After the Tranquillized Fifties: Notes on Sylvia Plath and James Baldwin," Critical Quarterly, 6:107-22, Summer, 1964.

"The last poems of Sylvia Plath draw their compulsive intensity not so much from their element of naked confession but from this assumption that in a deranged world a deranged response is the only possible reaction of the sensitive mind. . . . This 'intense breakthrough into very serious, very personal emotional experience' is also powerfully demonstrated in prose by James Baldwin's novel, Another Country. . . ." (D.P.)

P680 Davison, Peter, "Inhabited by a Cry: The Last Poetry of Sylvia Plath," Atlantic Monthly, 218:76-7, August, 1966.

"Sylvia Plath was a greatly but unevenly gifted woman who took the trouble, and had the intellectual resources, to train herself for a decade as a poet. . . . her early work, written in her twenties . . . showed an unusual sense of rhythm, a vocabulary that had a long, accurate reach, and a protean talent kept under severe control. . . . Sylvia Plath's talent . . . did not bloom into genius until the last months of her life when . . . she stood at the abyss of existence and looked steadily, courageously, with holy curiosity, to the very bottom. . . . the resultant poetry has a bone-chilling authority that could not have been achieved except by steady staring." (D.P.)

P681 Dyson, A. E., "Sylvia Plath," Tri-Quarterly, No. 7, pp. 75-80, Fall, 1966.

"It was only in the last two years of her life that . . . the dark undercurrent of her experience became a new and fierce possession, and a terrible beauty was born. Between The Colossus and the very late poems, there was a period when her earlier work took on a new, almost ethereal quality . . . where a longing for death more explicit than anything expressed earlier is transmuted. . . . And then . . . having mastered form, she transcended it, and the central drama of her troubled consciousness was wholly released." (D.P.)

P682 Hoyle, James F., "Sylvia Plath: A Poetry of Suicidal Mania," Literature and Psychology, 18:187-203, 1968.

An examination of the subject matter and techniques employed in Plath's poetry reveals that "the coherence of her work is that of an excited artistic working at both the production of lyric poems and the death of herself." (J.M.D.)

P683 Hughes, Ted, "Notes on the Chronological Order of Sylvia Plath's Poems," Tri-Quarterly, No. 7, pp. 81-8, Fall, 1966.

[This chronology of Miss Plath's poems also mentions circumstances, sources, or inspirations in their composition.] "Surveyed . . . with attention to the order of composition, I think the unity of her opus is clear. Once the unity shows itself, the logic and inevitability of the language . . . becomes more obviously what it is--direct, and even plain, speech." (D.P.)

P684   Jones, A. R., "Necessity and Freedom: The Poetry of Robert
        Lowell, Sylvia Plath and Anne Sexton," Critical Quarterly,
        7:11-30, Spring, 1965.

        "Robert Lowell, Sylvia Plath and Anne Sexton are all extremely
        traditional poets . . . in the sense that they see the tradition of
        poetry as a living and growing force, which must be constantly
        extended in order to be kept vitally alive. All three poets are self-
        conscious and accomplished craftsmen, who delight in the poet's
        traditional role of maker; and all three are incidentally concerned
        in trying to define a specifically contemporary sensibility. . . . But,
        above all, these poets are willing to experiment, to take chances and
        to run risks." (D.P.)

P685   Newman, Charles, "Candor Is the Only Wile: The Art of Sylvia
        Plath," Tri-Quarterly, No. 7, pp. 39-69, Fall, 1966.

        "At its height, her poetry expresses that 'extensive feeling' which
        Freud claims we lose as the cost of enduring and is regained only
        in pathological guises. . . . in the final poems there is no boundary
        between life and death, mind and artifact. The ultimate persona is
        that of transcendence. . . . Sylvia Plath evolved in poetic voice
        from the precocious girl, to the disturbed modern woman, to the
        vengeful magician, to--Ariel--God's Lioness." (D.P.)

P686   Oberg, Arthur K., "Sylvia Plath and the New Decadence,"
        Chicago Review, 20:66-73, No. 1, 1968.

        ". . . it is in bringing whatever tendencies were either implicit or
        explicit in modern art to a deadly perfection that she evidences the
        confusion of life and art which we associate with decadence." (G.C.)

P687   Ostriker, Alicia, " 'Fact' as Style: The Americanization of Sylvia,"
        Language and Style, 1:201-12, Summer, 1968.

        Reading Sylvia Plath's The Colossus and Ariel, then, on the
        assumption . . . that the poetry has nothing to do with the suicide
        . . . there remains the startling phenomenon of a poet finding her
        own voice . . . through an almost complete reversal of stylistic
        direction. . . . the poetic strength of Ariel lies in its fusion of
        personal voice with national voice in an Americanization which takes
        the form of strict--or strident--insistence on immediate factual
        reality; and second, that this strength, mostly missing in The
        Colossus, is achieved in Ariel by means of a poetic technique, again
        essentially American, which consists in taking poetic risks." (D.P.)

P688   Perloff, Marjorie, "Angst and Animism in the Poetry of Sylvia Plath,"
        Journal of Modern Literature, 1:57-74, No. 1, 1970.

        Sylvia Plath's is an "oracular poetry." Her vision of reality sees
        human beings as "dead, inanimate, frozen, unreal, while everything
        that is non-human is intensely alive, vital, potent." (D.P.)

P689   Plath, Sylvia, "The Writer and His Background: Ocean 1212-W,"
        Listener, 70:312-3, August 29, 1963.

        "My childhood landscape was not land but the end of the land--the
        cold, salt, running hills of the Atlantic. I sometimes think my
        vision of the sea is the clearest thing I own. I pick it up, exile that
        I am . . . and in one wash of memory the colours deepen and gleam,
        the early world draws breath." When "my father died, we moved
        inland. Whereon those nine first years of my life sealed themselves
        off like a ship in a bottle--beautiful, inaccessible, obsolete, a fine,
        white flying myth." (D.P.)

P690   Sexton, Anne, "The Barfly Ought to Sing," Tri-Quarterly, No. 7,
        pp. 89-94, Fall, 1966.

        [This is a sketch of Sylvia Plath and two poems written to com-
        memorate her death.]   (D.P.)

P691   Sumner, Nan McCowan, "Sylvia Plath," Research Studies,
        (Washington State University), 38:112-21, June, 1970.

        ". . . the depth of Plath's dissatisfaction with her life or of the
        profounder disillusionment with our society . . . underlies all . . .
        she published--a disillusionment which cannot be revealed except
        by recognizing and comprehending her specific psychological
        disturbances." In her work, "using age-old metaphors to express
        the ages-older human desire to start afresh, to cleanse by destroy-
        ing all, to experience pain and fear in preference to growing numb
        and satiated, Plath combines the mythological with the most recent
        psychological insights to create a rich and terrible portrait of life
        in contemporary society." (D.P.)

P692   Taylor, Eleanor Ross, "Sylvia Plath's Last Poems," Poetry,
        109:260-2, January, 1967.

        The last poems, impatient and urgent, are concerned with (1) the
        special experience that is woman's, including an "underlying
        rejection" of being a woman, and (2) death, with attendant "suffer-

ing, wounds, and ignominy." The poems are sometimes hasty, prosy, and few have light touches. (F.L.)

PLIVIER, THEODOR

P693   Wilde, Harry, "Vom Proletarier zum Bürger: Theodor Plivier," Politische Studien, 18:45-55, January-February, 1967.

[Plivier's biographer here summarizes the author's development from "proletarian" to "bourgeois" writer.] (J.R.R.)

PLOMER, WILLIAM

P694   Doyle, John Robert, Jr., "The Poetry of William Plomer," Sewanee Review, 75:634-61, Autumn, 1967.

William Plomer's poetry uses elements of his own experience, sometimes comic, to present a quiet affirmation of man in the face of disaster. (D.M.M.)

MUSEUM PIECES

P695   Mudrick, Marvin, "Humanity Is the Principle: Museum Pieces," Hudson Review, 7:615-7, Winter, 1955.

In Museum Pieces "Mr. Plomer's mosaic of acute anecdotes and observations is the history of . . . not quite stubborn enough anachronisms. Toby, who never learns to do the little things well, overcomes his futile versatility and charm to run through career after career, as painter, playwright, novelist, milliner, his life a series of abandoned experiments,' until . . . he has nothing trivial left except . . . suicide." (D.P.)

PLUNKETT, JAMES

P696   MacIntyre, Thomas, "Some Notes on the Stories of James Plunkett," Studies, 47:323-7, Autumn, 1958.

". . . the stories contained in The Trusting and the Maimed reveal . . . Plunkett in four major roles: (i) social critic; (ii) student of child psychology and behaviour; (iii) sympathetic observer of the inimitable Dublin scene; (iv) the artist sensitively touching on the futilities of existence." ". . . the pallid characterization, awkward symbolism and featureless prose of Plunkett show that he has . . . derived little from Joyce. . . ." However, "his quick-stabbing realism is his own particular vein. . . . he is original and sincere, and his work has that vital feeling that certain things do matter." (D.P.)

PLUNKETT, JOSEPH

P697   Dillon, Geraldine, "Joseph Plunkett," Dublin Magazine, 5:63-5,
        No. 1, 1966.

        [These are recollections by Geraldine Dillon of her brother Joseph
        Plunkett, Irish poet, editor of The Irish Review, and active in Irish
        politics.] (D.P.)

P698   Kennelly, Brendan, "The Poetry of Joseph Plunkett," Dublin
        Magazine, 5:56-62, No. 1, 1966.

        Although "Joseph Plunkett is probably the least known of the Rising
        poets . . . we should remember that he had a unique visionary
        intensity; that some of his best poetry is born out of deep inner
        conflict; that he was concerned with the problems of good and evil
        in a way that Pearse and MacDonagh were not; and that occasionally,
        despite all his uncertainties, he speaks with a mystical certainty,
        insight and authority." (D.P.)

PLUTZIK, HYAM

P699   Kaehele, Sharon and Howard German, "In Pursuit of a Precious
        Ghost: Hyam Plutzik's Horatio," Laurel Review, 8:53-64, No. 1,
        1968.

        Although Hyam Plutzik's Horatio "is an original work of great merit,"
        it has received little attention from critics. "Plutzik uses the
        characters and events of Hamlet as the donnee for a long poem in
        which Horatio describes his efforts to protect Hamlet's reputation
        during the fifty years after Hamlet's death. . . . Embodied in the
        episodes and made immediate and concrete by the texture of the
        poetry are Plutzik's ideas about the self, truth, and time; his ideas
        form a kind of modern Aristotelianism. . . ." (D.P.)

PODHORETZ, NORMAN

P700   Goldberg, S. L., "The Education of Norman Podhoretz: Or, I Was a
        Teen-Age Intellectual," Critical Review, 12:83-106, 1969.

        ". . . all literature can do about [the mess society's in] . . . is, at
        its best, explore and clarify it, or, at its worst, merely reflect it;
        while all literary criticism can do . . . is to distinguish, as finely
        as possible, how far works of literature are doing one or the other."
        (K.M.W.)

P701   Podhoretz, Norman, "Making It: The Brutal Bargain," Harper's Magazine, 235:59-67, December, 1967.

["This is an account of a young Brooklyn Jew's first confrontation with the abrasive issue of class."] (D.P.)

MAKING IT

P702   Garrett, George P., "My Silk Purse and Yours: Making It, Starring Norman Podhoretz," Hollins Critic, 5:1-13, February, 1968.

"Basically a classic example of the bildungsroman of the nineteenth century, [Making It] includes such diverse contemporary types as the Jewish novel, the College novel, the Army novel, the American-in-Europe novel, with lesser elements from the novel of espionage, the roman a clef, the works of Horatio Alger. . . . It is . . . extremely literary. . . . there is clever use of the conventions of the Pornographic novel. . . ." This book "is poetic, a statement of the eternal paradox of man's goals in the only world he knows for sure. . . ." (D.P.)

POLGAR, ALFRED

P703   Pollak, Felix, "Alfred Polgar: An Introduction," Tri-Quarterly, No. 2, pp. 35-9, Fall, 1959.

The work of Alfred Polgar (1875-1955) has not been adequately translated and is little known in this country. (E.T.)

POLLOCK, CHANNING

P704   Turner, Darwin T., "Jazz-Vaudeville Drama in the Twenties," Educational Theatre Journal, 11:110-6, May, 1959.

Among American Jazz-Vaudeville plays written in the decade of experimentation between 1920 to 1930, John Howard Lawson's Processional, John Dos Passos's The Garbage Man, J. P. McEvoy's God Loves Us, and Channing Pollock's Mr. Moneypenny are out-standing, although none were completely successful. Probably "the major reason for the death of Jazz-Vaudeville social criticism in drama was the inability of the playwrights to enrich their dramas with thought and significance which would transcend the superficial appeal of the novelty of the technique." (D.P.)

POMBO, RAFAEL

P705   Orjuela, Héctor A., "Rafael Pombo y la poesía antiyanqui de
Hispanoamérica," Hispania, 45:27-31, March, 1962.

Pombo (1833-1912) heads a list of Romantic and post-Romantic poets
who make a major theme of an anti-Yankee protest. The resolution
of the Cuban problem and the nature of America's struggle against
Communist infiltration will determine if such a list continues to
grow. (C.O.)

PONCELA, ENRIQUE JARDIEL--See
JARDIEL PONCELA, ENRIQUE

PONCELA, SERRANO

P706   Mainer, José-Carlos, "La primera persona narrativa en Francisco
Ayala y Serrano Poncela," Insula, No. 242, pp. 3-4, January, 1967.

Several modes of first person narration and their precedents may be
differentiated in Spain. Ayala and Serrano clearly continue the
picaresque and costumbrista traditions of a morally based criticism
of society in crisis. (C.O.)

PONGE, FRANCIS

P707   Bosquet, Alain, "Rêverie sur le premier Ponge," La Nouvelle
Revue Française, 14e année, No. 163, pp. 98-106, July, 1966.

Although defining incessantly an essence, Ponge is an artist in prose
rather than a philosopher. His person is less dear than his word.
He confronts and contemplates the thing, which he isolates until unity
becomes the symbol of the species and a perfect world, a cosmogeny,
is made. (T.T.B.)

P708   Chappuis, Pierre, "L'Ivresse lucide de Ponge," La Nouvelle Revue
Française, No. 178, pp. 667-71, October, 1967.

Pretension and modesty, clarity and confusion, creative impulse
checked by critical reflection, the distance from the word to the
thing or idea, from the matter to the mind, verbal play on words
and gibberish--all these are hallmarks of Ponge's work. (T.T.B.)

P709   Douthat, Blossom Margaret, "Le Parti pris des choses?"
        French Studies, 13:39-51, January, 1959.

        Ponge is the "existential poet par excellence. His concept of the
        world, his esthetic, his morality likens him to Sartre--a great deal
        more than Sartre thinks. For, in spite of the differences that
        separate them--differences for that matter reducible in large part
        to the nature of each's artistic vocation--the fundamental choice
        found in each work is the same: a prejudice perpetually renewed in
        man's favor." (D.-J.J.)

P710   Greene, Robert W., "Francis Ponge, Metapoet," Modern Language
        Notes, 85:572-92, May, 1970.

        Ponge "celebrates the explosive rise of differentiation and definition,
        the birth of consciousness. And since consciousness and formulation
        are the same for Ponge, his poetry is of necessity metapoetic, turned
        in on itself, watching itself and guiding itself as it comes into being."
        (F.M.L.)

P711   Hahn, Otto, "Les Ambiguïtés de Ponge," Les Temps Modernes,
        17e année, No. 190, pp. 1362-6, March, 1962.

        The thirty-four pages of My Creative Method contain many contra-
        dictions concerning Ponge's ideas about the quality of the object,
        the object itself and the idea of the object. They also furnish an
        explanation: "Ponge has a disgust for ideas, for systems." (T.T.B.)

P712   Lawall, Sarah N., "Ponge and the Poetry of Self-Knowledge,"
        Contemporary Literature, 11:192-216, Spring, 1970.

        Ponge's ideal of a "coldly calculated expression that analyzes its
        own perceptions," his mode of verbal experimentation, and his
        appreciation of contemporary artists are all echoed in the sixties
        in works by Bonnefoy, Dupin, and Du Bouchet. (K.H.B.)

P713   Ponge, Francis, "My Creative Method," Quarterly Review of
        Literature, 15:146-64, Nos. 1-2, 1967.

        [This is a series of letters from Francis Ponge, written between
        December 1947 and April 1948, in which he describes and explains
        his creative method.] (D.P.)

P714   Richard, Jean-Pierre, "Les Partis pris de Ponge," La Nouvelle
        Revue Française, 12e année, No. 136, pp. 629-55, April, 1964.

        Mustism, insensitivity, debility and infirmity are the great themes
        of Ponge's works. By giving speech to things he finds new phenomena
        of words and speech, but, at the end of the poem, the object returns
        to silence, just as in Mallarmé. (T.T.B.)

P715   Sartre, Jean-Paul, "Der Mensch und die Dinge: Über den Dichter
        Francis Ponge," Die Neue Rundschau, 73:229-67, Nos. 2-3, 1962.

        Ponge seems at first to be obsessed with things and any and all
        words to describe these things. But, in fact, exact nomenclature is
        his purpose. He regards his tissue of words as having a perceptible
        existence. His art, however, actually exceeds the scope of his
        materialism. (R.H.L.)

P716   Temmer, Mark J., "Francis Ponge: A Dissenting View of His
        Poetry," Modern Language Quarterly, 29:207-21, June, 1968.

        The high praise heaped on Ponge by Sartre and others is undeserved,
        since Ponge is a derivative and flawed artist; he seems likely to
        "remain a literary oddity." (G.S.)

P717   Thibaudeau, Jean, "Les 'Poésies' de Ponge," Critique, 21:753-62,
        August-September, 1965.

        Ponge's work has always aroused violent reactions because avoiding
        as much as possible the misunderstandings by which a writer can
        render literature tolerable is the very principle of his progression.
        (T.T.B.)

P718   Willard, N. M., "A Poetry of Things: Williams, Rilke, Ponge,"
        Comparative Literature, 17:311-24, Fall, 1965.

        ". . . several poets writing in the wake of imagism and symbolism
        . . . are united by a desire to create a poetry based on the careful
        examination of concrete things as the way to attain poetic truth.
        (F.M.L.)

LA CHÈVRE

P719   Douthat, Blossom, Margaret, "Francis Ponge's Untenable Goat,"
        Yale French Studies, No. 21, pp. 172-81, Spring-Summer, 1958.

        [This is an extended explication of the prose-poem "The Goat"
        which appears in translation in the same issue of Yale French
        Studies.]   (D.P.)

        LE GRAND RECUEIL

P720   Jaccottet, Philippe, "Notes quant au Grand recueil," La Nouvelle
        Revue Française, No. 112, pp. 689-94, April 1, 1962.

        Ramuz, Claudel and Ponge are alike in their passion for matter and
        a certain horror of the mind and ideas, but Ponge is superior in his
        bold imagery. His boldness is accompanied by a complexity which
        is decisive and justified. It is surprising but condensed and spar-
        kling and not blind like that of the surrealists. (T.T.B.)

P721   Plank, David G., "Le Grand recueil: Francis Ponge's Optimistic
        Materialism," Modern Language Quarterly, 26:302-17, June, 1965.

        Ponge tried to convey in complex verse the truth "of a new man, the
        man of the future with all the power of his mind, heretofore enchained,
        now freed from the impediments of communication." (G.S.)

            THE GOAT--See
            LA CHÈVRE

        PONTEN, JOSEF

P722   Dyck, J. Wilhelm, "Josef Ponten's Visit to America," American-
        German Review, 24:23-5, February-March, 1958.

        Josef Ponten's chief task, as he saw it, was "to focus the attention
        of the world on the wandering German." Unfortunately, the author's
        death in 1941 "prevented him from writing the cycles which were to
        present the problems of the German immigrants in North and South
        America. . . . many of the impressions gleaned from his travels
        . . . remain in the form of letters and notes. . . . I have received
        . . . a copy of the letters Ponten wrote to his friend and critic
        Friedrich Riessner, while he was travelling 15,000 miles through
        the United States." (D.P.)

P723   Dyck, J. W., "Thomas Mann and Josef Ponten," German Quarterly, 35:24-33, January, 1962.

"This article attempts to point to this gap of literary criticism [i.e., the failure to examine Mann's strong attraction to Ponten] and to expound the Mann-Ponten relationship in the light of sources other than the well-known Rundschau letter." (J.R.R.)

P724   Tennyson, Georg, "An Unknown Essay by Josef Ponten on the Design of Volk auf dem Wege," Monatshefte, 52:71-8, February, 1960.

In a previously almost unknown essay (1938), published now for a wider audience, Ponten successfully justifies the structure of his series of novels on Auslandsdeutschtum. Critics have carped at this structure, although they were ignorant of Ponten's real plan. (R.H.L.)

PONTOPPIDAN, HENRIK

P725   Jones, W. Glyn, "Henrik Pontoppidan (1857-1943)," Modern Language Review, 52:376-83, July, 1957.

"Without him it is unlikely that the realist novels of the twentieth century . . . would ever have existed in their present form." (W.T.S.)

POIRIER, LOUIS--See
GRACG, JULIEN

POOLE, ERNEST

P726   Hart, John E., "Heroism Through Social Awareness: Ernest Poole's The Harbor," Critique: Studies in Modern Fiction, 9:84-94, No. 3, 1966-67.

"The Harbor is more than a novel of strikes or of social protest; it is the story of humanity in search of its destiny. . . . [Poole's] flair for idealism, his concern for the rights of people, his questioning spirit of revolt link him to the tradition of Jefferson and Emerson, of Zola and Whitman and Shaw." (D.P.)

POPOVIC, ALEKSANDAR

P727   Czerwinski, E. J., "Aleksandar Popovic and Pop-Theater: Beyond
the Absurd," Comparative Drama, 3:168-75, Fall, 1969.

Popovic, Yugoslavian playwright, "has finally found a style that has
only one thing in common with Absurdist or Metaphoristic drama,
and that is freedom of expression." He has a social conscience, he
writes to entertain, his themes are universal, and his plays contain
political satire. (D.P.)

P728   Czerwinski, E. J., "Aleksandar Popovic: Belgrade's Poet of the
Streets," Books Abroad, 43:347-53, Summer, 1969.

Popovic is a "dramatist who has isolated and arrested . . . within
an artistic framework . . . the spontaneous flow of thought, molded
by folk-poetic expressions, from a people's tongue." His "gift is
writing superb dialogue supported often by a mere wisp of a plot."
(W.W.)

PORTER, BERNARD H.

P729   Blake, Harriet S., "The Leaves Fall in the Bay Area: Regarding
Bern Porter and Four Little Magazines," Colby Library Quarterly,
Series 9, pp. 85-104, June, 1970.

In the 1940's and '50's much of Bern Porter's time "was spent in
California, where he contributed considerable material to little
magazines and was particularly active in the formation and publication of "The Leaves Fall, Circle, Berkeley, and Broadside. An
exhaustive examination of Porter's writing, photography, and art
work in these little magazines confirms that his "major contribution
is in the field of non-commercial publication." (D.P.)

P730   Cary, Richard, "Bern Porter Chronology," Colby Library
Quarterly, Series 9, pp. 65-7, June, 1970.

[This is a detailed chronology of Bern Porter, from his birth in 1911
through 1969.] (D.P.)

P731   Cary, Richard, "Bern Porter's Friends in Books," Colby Library
Quarterly, Series 9, pp. 114-29, June, 1970.

"The quantity and quality of Porter's association in the precincts of
sci-art are demonstrably impressive. It is, however, the impact,

the interpenetration and effect of these associations that irresistibly elevates the stature of Bern Porter as champion of the fledgling, the unheralded and the disfavored." (D.P.)

P732   Higgins, Dick, "Thinking about Bern Porter," <u>Colby Library Quarterly</u>, Series 9, pp. 82-4, June, 1970.

"The Porter generation was never torn between the conflicts of identity, of being sometimes a composer and sometimes a philosopher, sometimes a designer and sometimes an essayist. The common denominator was always this business of noticing things . . . and Bern Porter is a very great noticer of things. It must always be Springtime in him . . . that he can maintain the innocence of his eye and not stereotype himself." (D.P.)

P733   Schevill, James, "Bern Porter: Further Notes on <u>The Roaring Market and the Silent Tomb</u>," <u>Colby Library Quarterly</u>, Series 9, pp. 68-81, June, 1970.

"The developments of the 1950s and 1960s have vindicated the practicality of many of Porter's ideas. The attempt in these years to abolish the divisions between painting, sculpture, and the performing arts, to bring all of the media together, became the dominant trend. . . . In the end . . . the current generation of artists and scientists . . . are shaped by an age of satire and black humour, while Porter belongs more to the idealistic, transcendental tradition that still believes in the rational benefits to be gained from the liberation of the American imagination." (D.P.)

P734   Simon, Renée B., "Bern Porter: A Bibliographical Sampling," <u>Colby Library Quarterly</u>, Series 9, pp. 105-13, June, 1970.

"Bernard Porter is a man of vast creative talents. In this brief sampling of his imprints [from 1944 to 1965] . . . the entries . . . represent the kind of creative endeavors he felt it important to encourage and reflect, to that extent, the man." (D.P.)

PORTER, ELEANOR

P735   Allentuck, Marcia E., "Old Books: <u>Pollyana</u> by Eleanor H. Porter," <u>Georgia Review</u>, 14:447-9, 1960.

Although Eleanor H. Porter's <u>Pollyanna</u> is "almost embarrassingly encumbered by the trappings of indiscriminate gladness and the Panglossian denial of the cogency of the daemonic, its burden of the

redeeming power of love and human participation places it in the
tradition of those works which find man's adjustment and growth
more arresting than his disenchantment and fall." (D.P.)

PORTER, HAL

P736   Burns, Robert, "A Sort of Triumph over Time: Hal Porter's Prose
        Narratives," Meanjin Quarterly, 28:19-28, Autumn, 1969.

        Porter's two styles, one of a highly structured prose (used in the
        novels and most of the short stories), and that of a loose "matter-
        packed prose," are expressive of his contrasting attitudes towards
        time: the first suggests that men are the subjects of time; the second
        that men can defeat time. (S.T.)

P737   Lord, Mary, "A Contribution to the Bibliography of Hal Porter,"
        Australian Literary Studies, 4:405-9, 1970.

        [This is a supplement to the Libraries Board of South Australia's
        Bibliography of Hal Porter (1966), including relevant items to the
        end of 1968.] (K.M.W.)

P738   Lord, Mary, "Hal Porter's Comic Mode," Australian Literary
        Studies, 4:371-82, 1970.

        "The early attempts to control and direct response are transformed
        into an attitude, a satiric stance, from which the material is
        interpreted at least as much as it is described. . . . Porter's
        satire is a method of indirection in which meaning emerges by
        inference out of the way the material is presented, and comment is
        implicit in the style and in a balance of opposing viewpoints."
        (K.M.W.)

P739   Ward, Peter, "The Craft of Hal Porter," Australian Literature,
        5:19-25, December, 1963.

        "Australian literature has not yet greatly benefited from Hal
        Porter's talents, but it is possible to predict that it will. Whether
        this will be through the novel or the short story, or through the
        theatre, is naturally anyone's guess. The Tower is undoubtedly his
        most finely controlled and fully realized work . . . but it lacks the
        sense of involvement with and commitment to larger issues that was
        so humanly satisfying in A Handful of Pennies. I am tempted to call
        him a Literary Dandy." (D.P.)

THE WATCHER ON THE CAST-IRON BALCONY

P740   Geering, R. G., "Hal Porter, the Watcher," Southerly, 24:92-103,
No. 2, 1964.

"The strongly personal subject matter of much of Porter's work and
his highly individual rendering of such material (the artist and the
portrait) are fascinatingly revealed in The Watcher on the Cast-Iron
Balcony," one of the very best of all Australian autobiographies.
(S.T.)

PORTER, KATHERINE ANNE

P741   Allen, Charles A., "Katherine Anne Porter: Psychology as Art,"
Southwest Review, 41:223-30, Summer, 1956.

"Her theme is the betrayal of life through the hostility that develops
if physical and social needs are repeatedly and consistently frustrated."
An analysis of leading stories shows how she employs imagery, tone,
and language to present this theme. (F.F.E.)

P742   Allen, Charles A., "The Nouvelles of Katherine Anne Porter,"
University of Kansas City Review, 29:87-93, December, 1962.

Katherine Anne Porter's four short novels share a focus on the
individual "as the victim of a hostile society." Noon Wine reveals
the hostile motivation of an ostensibly moral character; Old Mortality
probes the psychology of a Southern belle; Pale Horse, Pale Rider is
concerned with the contraries of illness and health, individuality and
conformity and life and death, while The Leaning Tower explores the
German national character. (D.P.)

P743   Baker, Howard, "The Upward Path: Notes on the Work of Katherine
Anne Porter," Southern Review, 4:1-19, January, 1968.

One may take issue with the critics who would call Katherine Anne
Porter's point of view "negative" and "skeptical." Her "peculiar
wisdom" is "archaic," her modernism is informed by a classic
view of life and a sense of the primitive civilizations of man.
(J.M.D.)

P744   Cruttwell, Patrick, "Swift, Miss Porter, and the 'Dialect of the
        Tribe'," Shenandoah, 17:27-38, Summer, 1966.

        ". . . many writers have felt more than interest [in the English
        language]," they have also felt "a degree of responsibility for the
        language and of concern about the way it seems to be going." Two
        such writers were Jonathan Swift and Katherine Anne Porter.   (H.S.)

P745   Curley, Daniel, "Katherine Anne Porter: The Larger Plan,"
        Kenyon Review, 25:671-95, Autumn, 1963.

        Miss Porter succeeds in her "Miranda" stories, when she treats "a
        human being simply as a human being"; she fails when she enlarges
        her context, as in Ship of Fools. (G.S.)

P746   Greene, George, "Brimstone and Roses: Notes on Katherine Anne
        Porter," Thought, 36:421-40, Autumn, 1961.

        Porter cannot be easily classed with the other American novelists of
        her period. Her "private note" stems partly from formal considera-
        tions, such as resistance to "experimental tricks," and partly from
        an avoidance of "social thesis" fiction and from a compulsion to
        "explore the scope and sanctions of human love." (R.L.G.)

P747   Hagopian, John V., "Katherine Anne Porter: Feeling, Form, and
        Truth," Four Quarters, 12:1-10, November, 1962.

        Miss Porter's writing is most notable for its "emotional charge, the
        intensity of feeling . . . manifested in language." She is preoccupied
        with feeling and form. Her characters are complex; she has a
        mastery of symbolism, often hidden. Her narrative method is
        characterized by indirect dialogue or monologue; her basic concern
        is with self-discovery. (D.P.)

P748   Johnson, James William, "Another Look at Katherine Anne Porter,"
        Virginia Quarterly Review, 36:598-613, Autumn, 1960.

        "A few basic themes, an adroit use of symbols, a limpid prose
        style--these combine in Miss Porter's stories to the propagation
        of a fictional point of view which is amazingly consistent and
        complete." (J.P.H.)

P749 Keily, Robert, "The Craft of Despondency: The Traditional
Novelists," Daedalus, 92:220-37, Spring, 1963.

". . . there is a sizeable group of mid-century writers who have
taken the novel pretty much as they found it after the First World
War and set about sustaining and embellishing it rather than introducing revolutionary innovations in form and function." Most notable
among these "for sheer mastery of language, eccentricity of characterization, precision, and popularity" are Evelyn Waugh and Graham
Greene in England and Katherine Anne Porter in America. (D.P.)

P750 Lopez, Hank and Katherine Anne Porter, "A Country and Some
People I Love," Harper's Magazine, 231:58-68, September, 1965.

[This interview with Miss Porter centers on her concern with Mexico,
its politics, history and culture.] (G.C.)

P751 Marsden, Malcolm H., "Love as Threat in Katherine Anne Porter's
Fiction," Twentieth Century Literature, 13:29-38, April, 1967.

Miss Porter portrays the relationship between love and hostility in
three ways: 1) Since a sincere lover is over-demanding rather than
indifferent, he tends to arouse resentment in his lover. A quarrel
is the means to purge this hostility and reaffirm the love; 2) in
another type of story, the existence of certain factors may make it
impossible for the beloved to rid himself of hostile feelings towards
the person who threatens his identity; 3) in another kind of story, a
character's fear of extinction has become so exaggerated that he has
withdrawn from and rejects a vital human relationship. These three
ways, already defined in Miss Porter's stories, are present in Ship
of Fools. (D.P.)

P752 Nance, William L., "Katherine Anne Porter and Mexico," Southwest
Review, 55:143-53, Spring, 1970.

"The fondness for Mexico . . . [expressed] in Miss Porter's essays
and interviews of the past few years is the reflection of a bond
between deeply kindred spirits. Perhaps it is also a nostalgia for
the time and place where the best of possible dreams first came to
fruition, and the impossible dream seemed closest to coming true."
(K.M.W.)

P753   Nance, William L., "Variations on a Dream: Katherine Anne
       Porter and Truman Capote," Southern Humanities Review,
       3:338-45, Fall, 1969.

       "The career of Truman Capote has been as marked by deliberate
       change as Katherine Anne Porter's has been by a sort of deliberate
       fixity. While her dramatization of the paradisal vision seems only
       to confirm a feeling of captivity, Capote's use of a similar kind of
       dream seems to have been for him a means of liberation." (K.M.W.)

P754   Partridge, Colin, " 'My Familiar Country': An Image of Mexico in
       the Work of Katherine Anne Porter," Studies in Short Fiction,
       7:597-614, Fall, 1970.

       Miss Porter's Mexican sojourn in the 1920's was a formative
       influence on her life and writing. During this period she developed
       from journalist to short story writer, through the replacement of
       adventure by experience. The dramatization of a "moment of
       experience" became a basic structural element in her early fiction.
       (D.P.)

P755   Porter, Katherine Anne, "From the Notebooks of Katherine Anne
       Porter: Yeats, Joyce, Eliot, Pound," Southern Review, 1:570-3,
       Summer, 1965.

       [These are reminiscences of Yeats, Eliot, Pound, and chiefly,
       Joyce.] (J.M.D.)

P756   Porter, Katherine Anne, "On First Meeting T. S. Eliot,"
       Shenandoah, 12:25-6, Spring, 1961.

       [These are Miss Porter's recollections of Eliot at a party after the
       New York opening of The Cocktail Party.] (D.P.)

P757   Poss, S. H., "Variations on a Theme in Four Stories of Katherine
       Anne Porter," Twentieth Century Literature, 4:21-9, April-July,
       1958.

       "The Circus," "Old Mortality," "Pale Horse, Pale Rider," and
       "The Grave" form a quasi-bildungsroman pattern, since they
       "manifest that typical structure of the genre which may be described
       as a secular version of the medieval notion of life as a pilgrimage."
       (D.P.)

P758   Ruoff, James, "Katherine Anne Porter Comes to Kansas," <u>Midwest</u> <u>Quarterly</u>, 4:305-14, February, 1963.

[During a visit to the University of Wichita in 1961, Porter discusses the sources of her material, her use of symbolism in "The Grave," her literary contemporaries, and some background to the collection <u>Flowering Judas</u> and the novel <u>Ship of Fools</u>.] (K.M.W.

P759   Ryan, Marjorie, "<u>Dubliners</u> and the Stories of Katherine Anne Porter," <u>American Literature</u>, 31:464-73, January, 1960.

The theme of <u>Dubliners</u>, "the hopelessness and futility of many lives," is the dominant theme in Miss Porter's work, but she has a more comprehensive view than Joyce and goes beyond him in "dramatizing her belief that trying to repress all irrational impulses actually means releasing and justifying the most destructive." (W.G.F.)

P760   Ryan, Marjorie, "Katherine Anne Porter: <u>Ship of Fools</u> and the Short Stories," <u>Bucknell Review</u>, 12:51-63, March, 1964.

"The satiric, ironical undertones of the stories have become the dominant tones of the novel; the dominant lyrical, poetic tones of the stories have become the undertones of the novel. This different blend gives us a different and more complex treatment of characters and experiences familiar to us from the stories." (K.M.W.)

P761   Schwartz, Edward Greenfield, "The Fictions of Memory," <u>Southwest Review</u>, 45:204-15, Summer, 1960.

Miss Porter's "art is an art of remembering, its subject the artist's personal recollections. Miss Porter looks within, regards with steady eye the one reliable reality--the writer's self." (J.P.H.)

P762   Schwartz, Edward, "The Way of Dissent: Katherine Anne Porter's Critical Position," <u>Western Humanities Review</u>, 8:119-30, Spring, 1954.

". . . Miss Porter's critical position may sometimes seem ambiguous, at times even contradictory. Her preference for the conscious artist . . . may seem to contradict her advocacy of an organic theory apparently akin to that of Whitman. . . . And her concept of the poet as 'seer' . . . may not be entirely compatible with her notion of the poet as being like other men. . . . But the most striking paradox in Miss Porter's position emerges [in] . . . her negation of the orthodoxy of her Catholic family, of her denial of social and political authoritarianism. . . . For Miss Porter--ironically, in view of her skepticism--declares her faith in the continuity of human life through art." (D.P.)

P763   Sullivan, Walter, "Katherine Anne Porter: The Glories and Errors of Her Ways," Southern Literary Journal, 3:111-21, No. 1, 1970.

"She has followed her heart as far as it would take her, and in one sense, it was while she was trying to follow it even further that it played her false. . . . But it gave us 'Noon Wine' and 'Pale Horse, Pale Rider' and several other small masterpieces. It is because these are so very fine that we dare complain that she did not give us more." (K.M.W.)

P764   Sutherland, Donald, "Ole Woman River: A Correspondence with Katherine Anne Porter," Sewanee Review, 74:754-67, Summer, 1966.

[This correspondence was exchanged between Katherine Anne Porter and Donald Sutherland, as well as between Gertrude Stein and Donald Sutherland. These letters reveal biographical information about Miss Porter as a person and as a writer.] (H.S.)

P765   Thompson, Barbara, "The Art of Fiction XXIX: Katherine Anne Porter: An Interview," Paris Review, No. 29, pp. 87-114, Winter-Spring, 1963.

[This interview probes influences on Miss Porter's writing--Shakespeare, Dante, Montaigne, Voltaire, the eighteenth century novelists--her Southern background, her restless spirit, her philosophy of life and writing, her patterns of work and her writing techniques, and special problems in writing Ship of Fools.] (D.P.)

P766   Van Zyl, John, "Surface Elegance, Grotesque Content: A Note on the Short Stories of Katherine Anne Porter," English Studies in Africa, 9:168-75, September, 1966.

Opposing the idea "that the novelist wants us to take the world of the novel for the real world, [Miss Porter] rather provides points of reference between the world of the imagination and the world of reality, and her characters achieve some sort of self-knowledge when the two worlds meet. Untidy, grotesque reality meets the organized, elegant experience" of art. (K.M.W.)

P767   Warren, Robert Penn, "Uncorrupted Consciousness: The Stories of Katherine Anne Porter," Yale Review, 55:280-90, December, 1965.

Paradoxically, Miss Porter's stories are at once "fixed" against shifting fashions, and are profoundly modern. She confronts and explores inner tensions, convinced that "truth" is found in the process of living, not in stasis. Her analyses of motives are not clinical reportage; she believes in Evil as a reality. (F.L.)

P768   Welty, Eudora, "The Eye of the Story," Yale Review, 55:265-74, December, 1965.

Katherine Anne Porter writes of the interiors of life and uses a minimum of sensory imagery. Her stories are moral ones about love, hate and death. Rejection, desertion, betrayal (things done to human love) are common points of encounter. Outrage is her most often expressed emotion; time one of the main factors in her work, the "eye" of her stories. She writes of the spirit, and time for the spirit is eternity. (F.L.)

THE CRACKED LOOKING-GLASS

P769   Wiesenfarth, Brother Joseph, F.S.C., "Illusion and Allusion: Reflections in 'The Cracked Looking Glass'," Four Quarters, 12:30-7, November, 1962.

"The Cracked Looking-Glass has resonances with Henry James's "The Beast in the Jungle" and "In the Cage." It is concerned with "the accommodation of a woman's illusion to reality." The mirror symbol has special complexities in function and meaning, changing meanings and having, at times, several meanings simultaneously. (D.P.)

THE DOWNWARD PATH TO WISDOM

P770   Hartley, Lodwick, "Stephen's Lost World: The Background of Katherine Anne Porter's 'The Downward Path to Wisdom'," Studies in Short Fiction, 6:574-9, Fall, 1969.

Several complex and esoteric glosses have been suggested for Katherine Anne Porter's "The Downward Path to Wisdom." However, "the best possible approach to the story . . . is in Philip Horton's . . . biography of Hart Crane . . . particularly the first chapter. . . ." (D.P.)

FLOWERING JUDAS

P771   Bluefarb, Sam, "Loss of Innocence in 'Flowering Judas',"
        CLA Journal, 7:256-62, March, 1964.

        "In . . . 'Flowering Judas,' there is a . . . loss of innocence through
        an initiation. But the shock, and the paralysis that follows, do not
        necessarily lead to an 'equal but opposite' reaction. . . . What is
        produced in Laura . . . is a change in tempo of her work in the
        Mexican revolutionary movement. . . ." Her loss of innocence "does
        not bring that work to a stop; it merely brakes it to a slower pace."
        (H.S.)

P772   Bride, Sister Mary, O.P., "Laura and the Unlit Lamp," Studies in
        Short Fiction, 1:61-3, Fall, 1963.

        " 'Flowering Judas,' then . . . is a condemnation not of chastity but
        of that peculiar spiritual deadness so much feared and decried in
        medieval spiritual treatises under the title of 'accedia.' It is a
        paralysis of the will, induced through a refusal on the part of the
        soul to make a resolute choice between good and evil." (D.P.)

P773   Flood, Ethelbert, O.F.M., "Christian Language in Modern
        Literature," Culture, 12:28-42, March, 1961.

        [This is a comparison of "Christian" elements in Porter's "Flower-
        ing Judas," Greene's The End of the Affair, and Mann's Joseph and
        his Brothers.] "A writer, attempting to elicit response from his
        readership, can fashion a desired reaction by playing on the impres-
        ions the Christian tradition has made on the common mind." (H.S.)

P774   Gottfried, Leon, "Death's Other Kingdom: Dantesque and Theological
        Symbolism in 'Flowering Judas'," PMLA, 84:112-24, January, 1969.

        "Because of the absence of any viable faith in 'Flowering Judas,' it
        is a portrayal of a hell without a heaven." Through its "complex,
        parodic symbolism of life and death, salvation and damnation, good
        and evil," the story's "rich symbiosis of religious and political
        imagery offers a profound and moving experience of the failure of
        two of the great faiths of our epoch." (D.P.)

FLOWERING JUDAS (cont'd)

P775   Gross, Beverly, "The Poetic Narrative: A Reading of 'Flowering
        Judas'," Style, 2:129-39, Spring, 1968.

        ". . . 'Flowering Judas' is a story and not a poem. The final point
        about its poetic language and form is that they are there to support
        the telling of a story. . . . And the story's moral and dramatic con-
        sequence comes precisely from the subordination of its narrative
        energy in favor of this poetic evocation of a state of mind." (H.S.)

P776   Madden, David' "The Charged Image in Katherine Anne Porter's
        'Flowering Judas'," Studies in Short Fiction, 7:277-89, Spring,
        1970.

        The real-life image on which Miss Porter based the scene of Laura
        and Braggioni in Laura's room was itself charged with feeling and
        meaning. Elements of Laura's worlds, exterior and interior, join
        in a pattern of images drawn from this charged image. Each aspect
        of Laura's psychological and physical quandary is implicit in images
        that recur and cluster. The contrast in "Flowering Judas" between
        the stasis of its images and the immediacy of the present tense
        creates a tension that increases the effect of the "basic image
        technique." (D.P.)

P777   Redden, Dorothy S., " 'Flowering Judas': Two Voices: Studies in
        Short Fiction, 6:194-204, Winter, 1969.

        Accepting the hypothesis that Porter's outlook is essentially and
        irrevocably dual rather than unitary explains much about this cryptic
        story, particularly the basic role of tension. (B.K.N.)

            THE GRAVE

P778   Bell, Vereen M., " 'The Grave' Revisited," Studies in Short
        Fiction, 3:39-45, Fall, 1965.

        Professor Curley ("Treasure in 'The Grave'," Modern Fiction
        Studies, Winter, 1963-64) "makes certain interpretive judgments
        . . . [which] I cannot help regarding as gratuitous, if not wrong-
        headed. . . ." "The Grave" "is a story about emotions and intuitions
        that are vague and formless. . . ." It is an example of the modern
        short story which "has abandoned the old preoccupation with formal
        plot and has concentrated more upon the lyric expression and
        evocation of moods, feelings, intuition. . . ." (D.P.)

THE GRAVE   (cont'd)

P779   Brooks, Cleanth, "On 'The Grave'," Yale Review, 55:275-9,
December, 1965.

"The Grave" is a splendid example of Miss Porter's almost unbelieve-
able economy and her seeming simplicity, which in fact, is full of
subtleties and "sensitive insights." So personal for Miranda is the
story and yet so enlarged by its special context that it states a social
and philosophical content as well as a ritualistic one of growing up.
(F.L.)

P780   Curley, Daniel, "Treasure in 'The Grave'," Modern Fiction
Studies, 9:377-84, Winter, 1963-64.

In "The Grave" the "Christian fable appears in its entirely with the
final phase of redemption cleverly disguised in the really obvious
treasure in the grave." The story stands as a metaphor for much
of the rest of Katherine Anne Porter's work. (D.P.)

P781   Joselyn, Sister M., O.S.B., " 'The Grave' as Lyrical Short Story,"
Studies in Short Fiction, 1:216-21, Spring, 1964.

" 'The Grave' . . . may be taken as representative of a class of
short stories which retain the essentials of narrative yet incorporate
elements generally associated with poetry to reflect and enrich
consciousness." (H.S.)

P782   Kramer, Dale, "Notes on Lyricism and Symbols in 'The Grave',"
Studies in Short Fiction, 2:331-6, Summer, 1965.

". . . a work of art cannot be limited to a simple meaning, or even
to a single profound meaning." In " 'The Grave' symbols . . .
challenge sympathies as well as the intellect, stimulating the reader
into a greater, if subliminal and unrecognized, acceptance of the
artist's effort to seize significance from flowing and vanishing
senses." (H.S.)

P783   Prater, William, " 'The Grave': Form and Symbol," Studies in
Short Fiction, 6:336-8, Spring, 1969.

The "relationship [between the] aspect of human behavior [and] the
careful construction [of 'The Grave'] becomes evident at the end of
the story, at which point the reader is able to see how the form of
the story has led up to the revelation of the most significant meaning
of the symbolic 'grave' of the title." (H.S.)

HACIENDA

P784   Hendrick, George, "Katherine Anne Porter's 'Hacienda',"
        Four Quarters, 12:24-9, November, 1962.

        "Hacienda" is much more than an ironic comedy of manners. It is
        a brilliant narrative of disengagement, of isolation; it is "a short
        novel of the lost generation." (D.P.)

P785   Perry, Robert L., "Porter's 'Hacienda' and the Theme of Change,"
        Midwest Quarterly, 6:403-15, July, 1965.

        Change also "applies to individuals, and here also the possibility for
        change is illusory. . . . people are what they are and cannot become
        something different, at least not overnight. Man is enslaved by his
        own nature, which is, in turn, the inevitable product of his heritage,
        and although he may try, he cannot escape its influence." (K.M.W.)

        THE JILTING OF GRANNY WEATHERALL

P786   Barnes, Daniel R., and Madeline T. Barnes, "The Secret Sin of
        Granny Weatherall," Renascence, 21:162-5, Spring, 1969.

        There is considerable indication that Granny's jilting "was attended
        by one further complication--pregnancy--and that Granny's sense of
        guilt for her pre-marital transgression has continued to plague her
        all those years." (S.A.)

P787   Becker, Laurence A., " 'The Jilting of Granny Weatherall': The
        Discovery of Pattern," English Journal, 55:1164-9, December,
        1966.

        The story of "The Jilting of Granny Weatherall" is "the total design
        which the reader discovers as the various threads of obscure
        information are . . . seen to adhere, to support, and to give
        substance to the whole." (D.P.)

P788   Cowser, Robert G., "Porter's 'The Jilting of Granny Weatherall',"
        Explicator, 21: Item 34, December, 1962.

        Granny Weatherall's betrayal by death, "the second jilting," is more
        important to the theme of the story than the first jilting by George.
        (B.K.)

THE JILTING OF GRANNY WEATHERALL   (cont'd)

P789   Wiesenfarth, Joseph, "Internal Opposition in Porter's 'Granny
       Weatherall'," Critique: Studies in Modern Fiction, 11:47-55, No. 2,
       1969.

       In "The Jilting of Granny Weatherall," "we are asked to see that
       the problem of existence has been vexing and difficult for Granny
       and that she has not satisfactorily solved it."   (G.C.)

P790   Wolfe, Peter, "The Problems of Granny Weatherall," CLA Journal,
       11:142-8, December, 1967.

       " 'The Jilting of Granny Weatherall' commands our serious interest
       because of its technical artistry and its generous, humane under-
       standing of man's eternal efforts to discover for himself a free,
       purposeful existence, i.e., to formulate a transcendent concept of
       life within which he can live with spiritual and moral dignity."
       (K.M.W.)

       MARÍA CONCEPCIÓN

P791   Hafley, James, " 'María Concepción': Life among the Ruins,"
       Four Quarters, 12:11-7, November, 1962.

       "María Concepción "demonstrates how meaning in fiction is often a
       function of verbal form. The story is, essentially, words in pattern:
       the story achieves its meaning through the words--and the order of
       the words is the story.   (D.P.)

       NOON WINE

P792   Pierce, Marvin, "Point of View: Katherine Anne Porter's Noon
       Wine," Ohio University Review, 3:95-113, 1961.

       "The present essay seeks to follow the pattern of the point of view,
       to see how and why it works as it does, in the belief that such an
       inquiry will help the reader to discover the essence of the story.
       (J.M.D.)

P793   Porter, Katherine Anne, "Noon Wine: The Sources," Yale Review,
       46:22-39, September, 1956.

       Characters, scene, and plot of Noon Wine come from flashes of
       childhood memory, given form partly through sensitivity to social

NOON WINE (cont'd)

and moral patterns understood long after the experiences, but
sensed even at the time. All elements in the story are composites;
why the author recalls certain incidents she does not know. (F.L.)

P794 Smith, J. Oates, "Porter's Noon Wine: A Stifled Tragedy,"
Renascence, 17:157-62, Spring, 1965.

Although Noon Wine has received little critical attention, "it is one
of Porter's finest works of art. . . ." It has the "material for
tragedy," but Porter, "as if all tragedy were predicated upon
romanticism, refuses to exploit it or to transform it into existential
comedy as Faulkner, Beckett and Conrad often do." (S.A.)

P795 Walsh, Thomas F., "The Noon Wine Devils," Georgia Review,
22:90-6, Spring, 1968.

Benét, in "The Devil and Daniel Webster," is "interested in the
bare mechanics of the Faust myth as a way of humorously developing his folk material in a tribute to the stirring oratory of Daniel
Webster. [Miss Porter's] Noon Wine, on the other hand, is concerned with justice and related problems which have ever fascinated
mankind. . . ." (D.P.)

THE OLD ORDER

P796 Kaplan, Charles, "True Witness: Katherine Anne Porter,"
Colorado Quarterly, 7:319-27, Winter, 1959.

In the recent paperback compilation of Miss Porter's short stories,
under the title of The Old Order, the author and her central character investigate the relationship of the past to the present in a search
for personal truth. (D.H.)

P797 Pinkerton, Jan, "Katherine Anne Porter's Portrayal of Black
Resentment," University Review, 36:315-7, June, 1970.

In these stories "in which her main theme is a wish to understand
her own past . . . [Katherine Anne Porter] shows . . . an understanding of the bitterness behind seemingly 'harmonious' black-white
relationships." (G.C.)

PALE HORSE, PALE RIDER

P798   Yannella, Philip R., "The Problems of Dislocation in 'Pale Horse,
Pale Rider'," Studies in Short Fiction, 6:637-42, Fall, 1969.

In " 'Pale Horse, Pale Rider' . . . one clearly sees the problems of
the spatially dislocated individual, the problem of the self vis-á-vis
twentieth-century strategies of containment, and the burden of moral
improvisation thrust upon the modern sensibility." (H.S.)

P799   Youngblood, Sarah, "Structure and Imagery in Katherine Anne
Porter's 'Pale Horse, Pale Rider'," Modern Fiction Studies,
5:344-52, Winter, 1959-60.

"A consideration of structure and imagery in [Pale Horse, Pale
Rider] . . . illuminates the dimensions of both . . . [Porter's]
work and her reputation." (G.C.)

SHIP OF FOOLS

P800   Alexander, Jean, "Katherine Anne Porter's Ship in the Jungle,"
Twentieth Century Literature, 11:179-88, January, 1966.

Although Ship of Fools may seem cold and cynical, it was really
prepared for long ago in Miss Porter's early stories. "Ship of
Fools, brilliantly questioning the motions of personality and society
gives us no promise, but only the mind's pleasure in seeing the
worst." (D.P.)

P801   Connolly, Francis X., "Lettre de New York," La Table Ronde,
No. 176, pp. 88-92, September, 1962.

Mrs. Porter is difficult to classify in terms of literary conventions.
Her novel , Ship of Fools, depends on the quickness of the reader to
discern her intentions and method. She considers it a foregone
conclusion that her readers do not expect continuity or a story with
a plot or even a dominant point of view. Her method is the intellectually refined use of the myth. (T.T.B.)

P802   Finkelstein, Sidney, "Ship of Fools," Mainstream, 15:42-8,
September, 1962.

"Porter's Ship of Fools is not the great and profound novel that
current criticism has made it out to be. . . ." (H.S.)

SHIP OF FOOLS   (cont'd)

P803   Hartley, Lodwick, "Dark Voyagers: A Study of Katherine Anne
       Porter's Ship of Fools," University Review, 30:83-94, December,
       1963.

       Ship of Fools does not reflect "the possibility of a universal order
       above the chaos of life, but rather the dark chaos of life itself."
       (R.G.L.)

P804   Heilman, Robert B., "Ship of Fools: Notes on Style," Four
       Quarters, 12:46-55, November, 1962.

       In Ship of Fools style is "a window of things and people, not a
       symbolic aggression of ego upon them." Miss Porter's style fuses
       other styles; it is without mannerisms.   (D.P.)

P805   Hendrick, George, "Hart Crane Aboard the Ship of Fools: Some
       Speculations," Twentieth Century Literature, 9:3-9, April, 1963.

       Events between Hart Crane and Katherine Anne Porter in his year
       in Mexico shortly before his tragic death have been incorporated
       fictionally in Miss Porter's Ship of Fools. Some of Crane's
       characteristics seem to have been apportioned among Denny,
       Echegaray, and Baumgartner."   (D.P.)

P806   Hertz, Robert Neil, "Sebastian Brant and Porter's Ship of Fools,"
       Midwest Quarterly, 6:389-401, July, 1965.

       "Ship of Fools is plainly not a conventional fictional narrative, and
       it does not lend itself unprotestingly to familiar critical descriptions
       and proscriptions." "Having taken for her own use the well known
       'image' of man's mortal voyage, Miss Porter is saying, in effect,
       that her novel is a kind of acquatic Pilgrim's Progress."   (H.S.)

P807   Joselyn, Sister M., "On the Making of Ship of Fools," South
       Dakota Review, 1:46-52, May, 1964.

       "A comparison of the eleven previously published chapters with
       Ship of Fools reveals in general that the author eliminated almost
       nothing from the episodes, although she re-arranged them, that she
       re-wrote the sections meticulously . . . that she composed approx-
       imately twenty-eight 'bridges' . . . . These alterations had
       important thematic effects: new stress upon the allegorical sig-
       nificance of the journey . . . firmer chronology, the creation of

SHIP OF FOOLS (cont'd)

several climactic points in the action . . . and new emphasis upon some of the characters and their stories. . . ." (K.M.W.)

P808   Liberman, M. M., "The Responsibility of the Novelist: The Critical Reception of Ship of Fools," Criticism, 8:377-88, Fall, 1966.

Ship of Fools which has received a mixed critical reception, "argues that romantic literary conventions do not work in the modern world, and images are then even more remote from the idea of a novel than a study of its formal properties alone would suggest." (G.C.)

P809   Liberman, M. M., "The Short Story as Chapter in Ship of Fools," Criticism, 10:65-71, Winter, 1968.

Why condemn Ship of Fools as a bad novel? It is "more properly read, not as a novel by any useful formal or historical definition, but as a kind of modern apologue." (S.A.)

P810   Liberman, M. M., "Some Observations on the Genesis of Ship of Fools: A Letter from Katherine Anne Porter," PMLA, 84:136-7, January, 1969.

". . . a letter from Miss Porter to Malcolm Cowley in 1931 . . . tends to . . . support a reading of Ship of Fools as an apologue by felicitous predisposition, rather than as a novel by misguided intention." (G.C.)

P811   McIntyre, J. P., "Ship of Fools and Its Publicity," Thought, 38:211-20, Summer, 1963.

Ship of Fools is a rationalistic novel; it lacks imagination and is reminiscent in some ways of Hawthorne and of Melville's Confidence Man. It is American in theme, British in structure. It questions whether justice can exist without love, and whether faith in human affairs can be achieved without love. It is replete with a sophisticated irony. (D.P.)

P812   Miller, Paul W., "Katherine Anne Porter's Ship of Fools: A Masterpiece Manqué," University Review, 32:151-7, Winter, 1965.

The weak construction of the novel results from the "failure on the part of a great short story writer to adapt her materials perfectly to the very different requirements of the novel." (W.G.F.)

SHIP OF FOOLS (cont'd)

P813   Plante, Patricia R., "Katherine Anne Porter: Misanthrope
        Acquitted," Xavier University Studies, 2:87-91, December, 1963.

        "The Ship of the world may presently be filled with Fools who have
        lost their compass and who spend their voyage practicing inhumani-
        ties upon each other. . . . With the anguish of one who truly cares,
        [Porter] is now asking for a re-beginning." (K.M.W.)

P814   Ruoff, James and Del Smith, "Katherine Anne Porter on Ship of
        Fools," College English, 24:396-7, February, 1963.

        [Here Porter discusses "the origins of the novel, the difficulty she
        experienced as a short story writer working in a new form, and the
        paradoxical relationship of the ideas in the novel to her actual
        experiences and moral values."] (G.C.)

P815   Solotaroff, Theodore, "Ship of Fools and the Critics," Commentary,
        34:277-86, October, 1962.

        "Far from being a profound account of the 'ship of this world on its
        voyage to eternity,' Ship of Fools is . . . an account of a tedious
        voyage to Europe . . . that has been labored over for twenty years
        by a writer who, late in life, is venturing, hence revealing, little
        more than misanthropy and clever technique." (P.A.R.)

P816   Walton, Gerald, "Katherine Anne Porter's Use of Quakerism in
        Ship of Fools," University of Mississippi Studies in English,
        7:15-23, 1966.

        Walton has not attempted to establish David Scott as a Quaker, but
        "points to the characters as being people who outwardly struggle
        with some burdensome inner will; and . . . the view that Katherine
        Anne Porter consciously selected Quakerism, the religion of David
        Scott's early youth, to be the cause of David's struggle of wills."
        (K.M.W.)

P817   Wescott, Glenway, "Katherine Anne Porter: The Making of a Novel,"
        Atlantic Monthly, 209:43-9, April, 1962.

        [This is an appreciation of Katherine Anne Porter, by a personal
        friend, and a consideration of all that went into the composition of
        Ship of Fools from its inception in 1931.] (D.P.)

THEFT

P818   Givner, Joan, "A Re-Reading of Katherine Anne Porter's 'Theft',"
        Studies in Short Fiction, 6:463-5, Summer, 1969.

        The theme of Katherine Anne Porter's "Theft" "is self-delusion in
        the face of evil. . . ." (D.P.)

P819   Prager, Leonard, "Getting and Spending: Porter's 'Theft',"
        Perspective, 11:230-4, Winter, 1960.

        "The protagonist is a woman and the purse which she has lost can
        readily be seen as sexual symbol; her problem of self-identity is
        concretely presented as the woman who is starving emotionally in
        the Wasteland of urban anonymity and alienation. But on another
        level, and this the most far-fetching, purse means value, the lost
        purse uncertainty of values, the stolen purse betrayal of self."
        (J.W.W.)

P820   Stein, William Bysshe, " 'Theft': Porter's Politics of Modern Love,"
        Perspective, 11:223-8, Winter, 1960.

        " 'Theft' evokes the pathos of the loss of self-identity in the modern
        world" through the disintegration of traditional religious authority.
        The protagonist's infatuation with sexual passion is reduced to a
        "Theft" of selfhood, the inevitable consequences of the betrayal of
        the holistic ideal of Christian love. (J.W.W.)

PORTER, WILLIAM SIDNEY

P821   Barban, A. M., "The Discovery of an O. Henry Rolling Stone,"
        American Literature, 31:340-1, November, 1959.

        The Rolling Stone, published by O. Henry in Austin, Texas from 1894
        to 1895, has been uniformly believed to have begun with Volume I,
        No. 3, since earlier issues could not be found. The discovery of a
        copy of Volume I, No. 2 now makes it probable that the humorous
        newspaper began, as others do, with Volume I, No. 1. (D.P.)

P822 Current-Garcia, Eugene, "O. Henry's Southern Heritage,"
Studies in Short Fiction, 2:1-12, Fall, 1964.

The most prominent qualities of O. Henry's fiction, "his playfulness
and fondness for the exotic, the exaggerated, and the picturesque;
his awareness of the distinctive differences between Northern and
Southern aims; and especially his sympathetic feeling for changing
Southern attitudes--are all products of a Southern literary heritage."
(P.J.R.)

P823 Gallegly, J. S., "Backgrounds and Patterns of O. Henry's Texas
Badman Stories," Rice Institute Pamphlet, 62:1-32, October, 1955.

"Young Willie Porter came to LaSalle County [Texas] in 1882. He
could not have picked a more favorable time--or a better place--to
gain acquaintance with material for his desperado stories." (H.S.)

P824 Long, E. Hudson, "O. Henry (William Sidney Porter) (1862-1910),"
American Literary Realism, 1:93-9, Fall, 1967.

[This is a bibliography of first editions, collections, letters, bibliographies, biographies, materials concerning his trial, and supplementary articles and essays. Primary materials are listed in
chronological order; supplementary titles alphabetically by author.]
(K.M.W.)

P825 Saroyan, William, "O What a Man Was O. Henry," Kenyon Review,
29:671-5, 1967.

"One story after another of O. Henry's that I read as a kid made me
feel not only that each was a living thing that was my own, but that
the whole unimportant human race was a living thing that was my
own." (G.C.)

CABBAGES AND KINGS

P826 McLean, Malcolm D., "O. Henry in Honduras," American Literary
Realism, 3:39-46, 1968.

Cabbages and Kings appears to be "the most exaggerated, overdrawn,
ludicrous picture of life in Latin America that has ever strained the
fantasy of modern man, but" a close look at "Honduras, the diminu-
tive real-life republic which provided the inspiration for those stories"
proves it to be a "very realistic, true-to-life presentation of manners
and customs which O. Henry had recorded with photographic accuracy."
(K.M.W.)

POULET, GEORGES

P827   Miller, J. Hillis, "Geneva or Paris? The Recent Work of Georges
        Poulet," University of Toronto Quarterly, 39:212-28, April, 1970.

        "This essay is an attempt to assess the significance of the many
        books and essays Poulet has published since 1963. I shall also set
        Poulet's criticism against the challenging new developments in
        literary criticism appearing now in Paris under the impact of
        structuralism and current reinterpretations of Nietzsche, Marx,
        and Freud." (F.M.L.)

P828   Miller, J. Hillis, "The Literary Criticism of Georges Poulet,"
        Modern Language Notes, 78:471-88, December, 1963.

        [This is a discussion of Poulet's critical techniques and methodology.]
        "Poulet's criticism remains faithful to its exclusive commitment to
        human consciousness, and . . . follows the mind of mankind as it
        uncovers the limitless riches of interior space." (F.M.L.)

POUND, EZRA

P829   Agresti, Olivia Rossetti, "In Commemoration: The Ambassador,"
        Pound Newsletter, No. 8, pp. 19-20, October, 1955.

        "It is not in a lunatic asylum, but as an 'ambassador at large' that
        Ezra Pound is needed if America is to play wisely and well the part
        of world leadership that fate has forced on her. And nowhere would
        this 'Ambassador' be more welcome than in Italy." (D.P.)

P830   Alvarez, A., "Ezra Pound: The Qualities and Limitations of
        Translation-Poetry," Essays in Criticism, 6:171-89, April, 1956.

        Pound is at his best when he gets on the inside of a foreign work and,
        not translating it, recreates it outwards, writing Latin verse, for
        instance, in English, putting the strengths of other languages into
        English verse. (D.B.D.)

P831   Baldner, Ralph W., "Ezra Pound: Image of Theophile Gautier,"
        Arizona Quarterly, 14:246-56, Autumn, 1958.

        Pound's revolt against the Georgians was analogous to Gautier's
        revolt against Romanticism. Pound's imagistic principles closely
        resemble the poetic standards Gautier advocated. Further, Pound's
        masculine, energetic temperament, his Bohemianism, his vigorous

assistance to younger writers, his passion for Chinese culture--all were characteristic of Gautier also. (A.S.)

P832   Bergman, Herbert, "Ezra Pound and Walt Whitman," American Literature, 27:56-61, March, 1955.

Pound's attitude toward Whitman was mixed but in a previously unpublished essay (1909) Pound says, "His (Whitman's) message is my message." (R.W.S.)

P833   Berryman, John, "A Tribute," Agenda, 4:27-8, October-November, 1965.

"He [Pound] seems to have proposed to himself, very early on, two things: to become a great poet, and to alter the formal direction of literature in English. . . . He has accomplished both." (H.S.)

P834   Bornstein, George J. and Hugh H. Witemeyer, "From 'Villain' to 'Visionary': Pound and Yeats on Villon," Comparative Literature, 19:308-20, Fall, 1967.

Pound saw Villon as a "naive" poet without self-consciousness or dramatization. Yeats's early conception of Villon agrees with Pound's, but after 1919 he spoke of Villon as self-dramatizing and concerned with a good-evil antagonism. (J.C.O.)

P835   Boselli, Mario, "Alcune osservazioni sui saggi critici di Ezra Pound," Nuova Corrente, 5-6:70-9, January-June, 1956.

Pound's preoccupation with "charged language" was influenced by both the pragmatic and Bergsonian atmosphere he matured in, with the relationships of word-object, literature-history, etc., synthesizing the classico-romantic nature of his criticism . . . and poetry. (V.R.)

P836   Bowers, Frederick, "Arthur Hugh Clough: The Modern Mind," Studies in English Literature, 6:709-16, Autumn, 1967.

"Both Pound and Clough feel superior to their age--one as a youth 'born to inglorious days,' the other as a cultural . . . exile, punished for 'non-esteem of self-styled "his betters" '--and to the 'accelerated grimaces' and 'gewgaws' which formed the standards of their times's taste. Clough's 'Anglo-savage' is Pound's 'half-savage'." (H.S.)

P837   Bradbury, Malcolm, "A Visit to Ezra Pound," Twentieth Century,
        159:604-6, June, 1956.

        Is Pound insane or a traitor? If insane, he should be treated as
        insane; if a traitor, he should be imprisoned or pardoned. There
        seems little evidence of insanity; his treachery must consist in
        his act of broadcasting from wartime Italy rather than in his
        materials. (R.A.K.)

P838   Brooke-Rose, Christine, "Ezra Pound: Piers Plowman in the
        Modern Waste Land," Review of English Literature, 2:74-88,
        April, 1961.

        "Both Pound and Langland are fundamentally moralists, both
        intransigent and idealistic, each hammering at what he believes to
        be the root of human evil." (W.G.F.)

P839   Bryer, Jackson R., "Pound to Joyce on Ulysses: A Correction,"
        American Notes & Queries, 4:115-6, April, 1966.

        D. D. Paige, on pp. 150-1 of his 1950 edition of The Letters of
        Ezra Pound, has erroneously dated a letter from Pound to Joyce in
        1919. Actually, from external evidence the letter must have been
        written in late October or early November of 1920. (D.P.)

P840   Bynner, Witter, "From Mexico," Pound Newsletter, No. 10,
        pp. 15-6, April, 1956.

        "But after all I enjoy the vehemence--when I can decipher it. Or
        his vehemence against my preferring Laotzu to Confucius for final
        import. And I enjoy Pound's poetry--when I can decipher it. . . .
        In the ponderings of the Cantos I grant that for me there is too much
        ponderous ore; but I maintain that in Pound's poetry when the veins
        are pure they are as pure as any." (D.P.)

P841   Cambon, Glauco, "La poesia di Pound come esperienza spaziale, "
        Nuova Corrente, 5-6:81-91, January-June, 1956.

        "The poet's consciousness constitutes the meeting-place of all time
        and all space, the ideal place in which history annuls its chronology
        and manifests itself as a series of eternal archetypes." (V.R.)

P842 Cann, Louise Gebhard, "With the Pounds in Paris, A Memoir,"
Pound Newsletter, No. 8, pp. 24-7, October, 1955.

[These are recollections of Mrs. Cann, who with her husband, took
over Ezra Pound's studio in Paris in 1923 on the eve of his departure
for Rapallo.] (D.P.)

P843 Carne-Ross, D. S., "New Metres for Old: A Note on Pound's
Metric," Arion, 6:216-32, Summer, 1967.

Pound has brought to poetry in English "some of the formal resources
of Greek poetry," most specifically, a recurring or constant metrical phrase. His Sapphic hendesyllabic line is most notable for its
stress and quantity. His two major innovations are falling rhythms
and trisyllabic feet. (D.P.)

P844 Carruth, Hayden, "Ezra Pound and the Great Style," Saturday
Review, 49:21-2, 56, April 9, 1966.

Pound is unique in having created the magnificent style--"the huge,
concrete, multiform artifice that transmits to us the impersonal
light beyond art, and from the artist himself drops away." His best
poetry "attracts every literate sensibility without reference to
temperament or sympathy; it transcends taste." (W.K.)

P845 Carruth, Hayden, "On a Picture of Ezra Pound," Poetry,
110:103-5, May, 1967.

"It is an ordinary half-tone reproduction. . . . [which shows] . . .
the flashing white hair and beard, the dark, deep, almost blind-
looking eyes, the attitude of stubborn concern. . . ." It is possible
"that Pound himself re-invented the poetic line as the unit of poetry,
variable and end stopped . . . that Pound was as closely associated
with Eliot as with Williams throughout their lives, that . . . he
damned London as heartily as he did Concord, and that his immense
influence has descended equally . . . through the entire conspectus
of Anglo-American writing." Finally, that "Pound had the first and
clearest view of the inter-objective relationship between poetry and
nature. . . ." (D.P.)

P846 Chace, William M., "Ezra Pound and the Marxist Temptation,"
American Quarterly, 22:714-25, Fall, 1970.

"Ezra Pound's politics . . . are a dramatically exaggerated instance
of the artist caught between the aesthetic standards and the political

exigencies of his time. . . . Perhaps it is this kind of understanding of his situation, an understanding rooted in Marx, which can save Pound from being preserved forever in literary histories as a mysterious, and most regrettable, aberration." (H.S.)

P847   Chute, Desmond, "In Commemoration: Poet's Paradise, A Memoir," Pound Newsletter, No. 8, pp. 12-4, October, 1955.

[These are recollections of "over twenty years, in close touch with the work--poetic, musical and humanitarian--of Ezra Pound."] (D.P.)

P848   Connolly, Cyril, "The Break-Through in Modern Verse," London Magazine, N.S. 1:27-40, June, 1961.

Modern poetry in England began early in the century with the poetic revolution wrought by Pound and Eliot, and the mature Yeats who had learned from Pound. By the first World War "the Pound-Eliot streams have become a river. . . ." (D.P.)

P849   Corrigan, Matthew, "The Poet's Intuition of Prose Fiction: Pound and Eliot on the Novel," University of Windsor Review, 2:33-51, Fall, 1966.

["Much consideration (though different) on each of . . . [Pound's and Eliot's] parts has gone into prose-fiction. The purpose of this paper is to examine their ideas on this issue and to see how these evolved through their critical analyses of certain trends in fiction and of specific novelists themselves."] (H.S.)

P850   Corrigan, Robert A., "Ezra Pound and the Bollingen Prize Controversy," Midcontinent American Studies Journal, 8:43-57, Fall, 1967.

The controversy over the award of the Bollingen Prize to Ezra Pound in 1949 by the Library of Congress may mark a high point in the dominance of formalistic criticism in American letters and "may also reflect the degree to which the reaction against the new orthodoxy had already set in." [This is accompanied by an extensive bibliography]. (W.G.F.)

P851 Cory, Daniel, "Ezra Pound: A Memoir," Encounter, 30:30-9, No. 5, 1968.

[This is an account of meetings and associations with Pound in America and Italy during the period 1932-1962.] (H.S.)

P852 Creeley, Robert, "A Note Followed by a Selection of Letters from Ezra Pound," Agenda, 4:11-21, October-November, 1965.

[These are recollections of Pound's influence on writers "coming of age" in the 1940's, followed by "selections from Pound's letters to Robert Creeley March 1950 to October 1951."] (H.S.)

P853 Cummings, E. E., "Letters of E. E. Cummings to Ezra Pound," Paris Review, No. 39, pp. 55-87, Fall, 1966.

[This "representative selection from the letters of E. E. Cummings to Ezra Pound . . . appear here just as Cummings wrote them, with his often eccentric punctuation and his verbal byplay intact." The correspondence published here begins in 1930 and ends in January, 1955.] (D.P.)

P854 Davenport, Guy, "The Perpendicular Honeycomb: Pound, de Gourmont and Frobenius," Meanjin Quarterly, 14:492-501, December, 1955.

"To go to Pound's sources is to confirm the accuracy of perception with which he brought across a value--intact--or caught a nuance; it is not a matter of seeing behind the scenes, of prying. . . . To respond . . . to the analytical de Gourmont and . . . to the historian Frobenius is . . . to project into . . . complex epic forms of knowledge created or gathered by those who know." (H.S.)

P855 Davie, Donald, "Second Thoughts: III, F. R. Leavis's 'How to Teach Reading'," Essays in Criticism, 7:231-41, July, 1957.

Leavis's reply to Pound is in error when he argues that technique is non-transferable, and it begs the question of the use of translations that Pound squarely faced. The over-all effect of Leavis's essay was to prolong confusion about the relationship between English literature and, especially, the literatures of Europe. (D.B.D.)

P856   Davie, Donald, "Yeats and Pound," Dublin Magazine, 30:17-21,
October-December, 1955.

"Is he [Pound], like Yeats . . . calling up his own opposite, the
phase antithetical to his own? Or is he, unlike Yeats but like Synge,
seeking in the various idioms of these various personae a dialect in
which he can express himself 'objectively'?" (H.S.)

P857   Demetz, Peter, "Ezra Pound's German Studies," Germanic Review,
31:279-92, December, 1956.

Despite his inability to master the German language, Pound always
believed in and put into intellectual action Goethe's idea of Welt-
literatur. (E.L.)

P858   Diggins, John P., "The American Writer, Fascism, and the
Liberation of Italy," American Quarterly, 18:599-614, Winter, 1966.

The contrast in anti-Fascist novelist John Horne Burns's The Gallery
"between a meretricious America and an Arcadian Italy" recalls pro-
Fascist Ezra Pound's "contrast between a defiled America . . . and
a Medieval Italy where "Beauty alone" prevails. Whatever their
ideological differences, both the Fascist poet and the liberal novelist
were measuring the seamy vices of the new world against the supposedly noble virtues of the old." (W.G.F.)

P859   Dos Passos, John, et al, "Aftermath: The Question of Ezra Pound,"
Esquire, 48:12-20, December, 1957.

[This is a "reprint" of some of the "pertinent excerpts" of letters
Esquire received regarding Richard H. Rovere's article discussing
Pound's stay in St. Elisabeth's hospital in Washington, D. C.]
(H.S.)

P860   Duncan, Robert, "The Lasting Contribution of Ezra Pound,"
Agenda, 4:23-6, October-November, 1965.

". . . from 1950 on a new poetry began to appear deriving its music
from the ground Ezra Pound had given us in his theory and practice
forty years earlier, from the composition by phrase which Pound
had advanced to the high art of The Pisan Cantos (1949). . . ."
(H.S.)

P861   Duncan, Ronald, "Religion," Agenda, 4:56, October-November, 1965.

"Pound has an integrated sensibility. The range of his interests is not a diffusion, or a kind of dilettantism as has been suggested, but it is the result of a vitality which perceives a connection in all things." (H.S.)

P862   Elliott, George P., "On Pound--Poet of Many Voices," Carleton Miscellany, 2:79-103, Summer, 1961.

"The magnitude of what Pound set himself, first as a poet, then as a citizen of the world, would have appalled anyone more sure of himself than Pound was. . . . The size of the task, and rage at his inadequacy, broke him." His "chief scapegoats were America, the bankers and the Jews. . . . Fascism was not immoderate enough for him. . .: he adopted nazi anti-semitism." One marvels "that a man with qualities and gifts of so noble a kind could choose a course of political action so vile, that one man could in some measure deserve comparison to both Yeats and Eichmann." (D.P.)

P863   Ellmann, Richard, "Ez and Old Billyum," Kenyon Review, 28:470-95, September, 1966.

Pound and Yeats had a close relationship that began in 1908 and went through various stages: Yeats as old master; Pound as humble adviser and not-so-humble critic; both as mutual advisers and aesthetic antagonists; finally both as "uncles." Often in sharp disagreement about poetic theory and practice, they still "face each other in unending debate." (G.S.)

P864   Emery, Clark M., "Pound as Mauberley," History of Ideas News Letter, 4:6-8, January, 1958.

Spector is wrong in indicating that Pound is disinterested in society (HINL, 3:2-5); he has devoted his life to an attempt to fight the causes of war. Pound is known for his personal generosity and his intellectual involvement in the amelioration of social evils. (K.L.)

P865   Faas, Egbert, "Formen der Bewusstseinsdarstellung in der dramatischen Lyrik Pounds und Eliots," Germanisch-Romanische Monatsschrift, 18:172-91, April, 1968.

Pound rarely achieved the all-embracing presentation of the human psyche that Eliot had already captured in Prufrock. (J.R.R.)

P866   Fang, Achilles, "Fenollosa and Pound," Harvard Journal of Asian Studies, 20:213-38, June, 1957.

[This is a discussion of "the three books [Ernest Francisco] Fenollosa and Pound jointly produced ['Noh' on Accomplishment, A Study of the Classical Stage of Japan; The Chinese Written Character as a Medium for Poetry; and Cathay], without any judgment of their importance in the Anglo-American literary world."] (H.S.)

P867   Farmer, David, "An Unpublished Letter by Ezra Pound," Texas Quarterly, 10:95-104, Winter, 1967.

[This is a reproduction of a letter from Pound, dated February 3, 1927, explaining his influence on the Chicago Renaissance.] (W.G.F.)

P868   Faulkner, Peter, "Yeats, Ireland and Ezra Pound," Threshold, No. 18, pp. 58-68, 1963.

"Pound was undoubtedly a dynamic missionary for 'modernism,' but in Yeats's case he had the undeniable advantage of preaching to one who was already converted. . . . Yeats's strong national feeling [and the influence of Synge] led him" to a more vigorous and catholic critical theory including a preference for simple and direct poetry. (R.J.G.)

P869   Ferkiss, Victor C., "Ezra Pound and American Fascism," Journal of Politics, 17:173-97, May, 1955.

[This essay concerns itself with Pound's views as an "American Fascist." Items discussed include: "Pound's Basic Philosophy: Its Relationship to His Poetry and Economics," "Pound's Interpretation of History," "Pound's Political Philosophy," and "Pound's Anti-Semitism."] (H.S.)

P870   Finkelstein, Sidney, "Ezra Pound's Apologists," Mainstream, 14:19-34, January, 1961.

[This essay is "not . . . written to intimate in any way that those who spoke up for Pound should have remained silent, or called for him to be shot. It is only to state that poets, writers and publicists of any kind, should specially be principled people and try to find a morally principled position."] (H.S.)

P871   Fitzgerald, Robert, "Gloom and Gold in Ezra Pound, " Encounter,
        7:16-22, July, 1957.

        In his Chinese Classic Anthology and in many of his Cantos, "at the
        other end of historical time and terrestrial space [Pound] lives, in
        princely imagination, through texts with which he can be at ease
        perhaps because they are untouched by the tragic conviction and
        faith of the West." But in Pound's radio harangues from Rome "he
        who had praised the sane construction, the clear moving line, the
        fine thing held in the mind, had ended in ramshackle and noisome
        fantasy, in a clogged and static obsession--no fine thing held in his
        mind but the most vulgar and violent of contemporary passions."
        (D.P.)

P872   Fitzgerald, Robert, "A Note on Ezra Pound, 1928-56, " Kenyon
        Review, 18:505-18, Autumn, 1956.

        It is ironic that Pound's "self-centered human pride" is an offense
        against "his own standards . . . himself," and the realm of
        "princely imagination" of his earlier years. Nevertheless his "place
        in . . . poetry is not in question and with every year it becomes
        better discriminated and understood." (G.M.P.)

P873   Fitzgerald, Robert, "Notes on Ezra Pound, 1928-1956, " Nouva
        Corrente, 5-6:35-48, January-June, 1956.

        An examination of the contrast between Pound's earlier and later
        works not only indicates his literary development, but also indicates
        the critical impressions of a younger poet. (V.R.)

P874   Friedrick, Otto, "Ezra Pound: The Guide to Kulchur, " New World
        Writing, 17:161-202, 1960.

        "Pound actually lacked most of the qualities that are normally
        considered essential to producing good criticism. He absolutely
        could not write two sentences of good English prose. . . . His
        critical method was often limited to quoting long passages of poetry
        he admired, with a few epigrams separating the extracts." (H.S.)

P875   Gallup, Donald, " 'Boobliography' and Ezra Pound, " Texas
        Quarterly, 10:80-92, Winter, 1967.

        The bibliographer of contemporary literature has the opportunity of
        producing a useful work unencumbered with trivialities. Particular
        problems in collecting Pound's works for description were encoun-

tered in his ephemera, in later editions, in his periodical appearances, in his editorial appearances, although by and large Pound's
own correspondence and other records have survived. (D.P.)

P876   Gallup, Donald, "T. S. Eliot and Ezra Pound: Collaborators in
        Letters," Atlantic Monthly, 225:48-62, January, 1970.

        Pound, according to Eliot, was much concerned with helping to
        improve the writing of talented writers, to formulate the literary
        tenets best suited to the twentieth century, and to support little
        magazines. He helped Eliot and other writers of talent to modernize
        their writing and find publishers. (W.E.K.)

P877   Gershman, Herbert S., "Ezra Pound to Littérature," Modern
        Language Notes, 74:608-9, November, 1959.

        A letter from Pound, printed in Littérature No. 16 (1920), p. 48,
        summarily and humorously lists worthy contemporary English
        authors. (M.J.O.)

P878   Goacher, Denis, "Pictures of Ezra Pound," Nimbus, 3:24-32,
        No. 4, 1956.

        [This is a visit with Pound during his confinement to St. Elizabeth's
        federal hospital for the insane in Washington, D.C.] (H.S.)

P879   Goodwin, K. L., "Ezra Pound's Influence on Literary Criticism,"
        Modern Language Quarterly, 29:423-38, December, 1968.

        "Pound's direct influence on the content and techniques of criticism
        in the present century has been neither extensive nor significant"
        but his "gestures and slogans" helped to introduce new and forgotten
        writers. (G.S.)

P880   Graves, Robert, "These Be Thy Gods, O Israel," New Republic,
        134:16-9, 17-8, February 27, March 5, 1956.

        Yeats, Pound, Eliot, Auden and Dylan Thomas have been set up as
        living idols. However, Yeats had "wit, industry, a flexible mind,
        a good ear . . . but nothing to say. . . ." "Pound's sprawling,
        ignorant, indecent, unmelodious, seldom metrical Cantos . . . are
        now compulsory reading in many ancient centers of learning."
        "Eliot pasted fragments of the Elizabethan ornate against skillfully
        chosen examples of the modern nasty . . .; and in his notes asked
        the reader to find . . . a connecting thread of sense." Auden "is

as synthetic as Milton . . . his real talent is for light verse."
Dylan Thomas "was drunk with melody, and what the words were
he cared not." (D.P.)

P881   Guiliani, Alfredo, "Le ragiono metriche di Ezra Pound (Il problema
della cetra)," Nuova Corrente, 5-6:105-10, January-June, 1956.

"Pound's metric exercises, inspired by a fresh perception of the
musical quality of the quantitative measure and by the intention to
restore to modern poetry the old measure in new terms, achieve
their goal in the verses of the Cantos." (V.R.)

P882   Hall, Donald, "The Art of Poetry V: Ezra Pound: An Interview,"
Paris Review, No. 28, pp. 22-51, Summer-Fall, 1962.

[This interview covers various aspects of the Cantos, free verse,
the impact of the modern world on poetry, Pound's opinions of
contemporary poets, his relations with Yeats, Ford, Eliot and
visual artists, his early life in America and England, his interest
in monetary reform, his radio broadcasts from Italy in the Second
World War, his plans for completing and revising the Cantos, and
his sense of isolation as an American in Italy.] (D.P.)

P883   Hayman, David, "Pound at the Wake or the Uses of a Contemporary,"
James Joyce Quarterly, 2:204-16, Spring, 1965.

"Whatever his contribution to the character of Shaun and HCE and
whatever his role as friend or enemy of Joyce, Pound was more than
a subject in the Wake. Joyce exploited him as he did other contemporaries as an historical landmark. . . . Pound's language, in his
letters . . . demonstrated to what extent words could be distorted
and emotionally loaded without a loss of meaning. . . . His distortions are certainly not the only source of Joyce's night-language
in the Wake. . . . However . . . Joyce's use of them . . . points
towards influence. . . . In one way or another Pound's eccentricities,
his foibles and follies, his passions, wit and rage have all been
woven into Joyce's night-weave. . . ." (D.P.)

P884   Hesse, Eva, "Von der Nationalität des Dichters," Akzente,
15:354-82, August, 1968.

"Pound's connection to the country of his birth . . . adheres rather
to a kind of spirit which is rooted deep in the past and which even if
it may be lost for his lifetime, is capable of regeneration in the
future." (J.R.R.)

P885   Holder, Alan, "The Lesson of the Master: Ezra Pound and Henry James," American Literature, 35:71-9, March, 1963.

From the beginning of his career "Ezra Pound has displayed a continual awareness of Henry James and his works," producing in 1918 a long essay on the older writer. Through the years the artist James "has continually served Pound as a great exemplar of literary dedication and achievement." (D.P.)

P886   Honig, Edwin, "That Mutation of Pound's," Kenyon Review, 17:349-56, Summer, 1955.

Pound's " 'abrupt mutation of poetic form and idiom' " is less a "revolution in poetic idiom" and more a "style" and thus the man. The merits of Pound and Eliot are not denied, but the poetry of their contemporaries who write without personal idiom "deserves equal if not more attention." (G.M.P.)

P887   Hubbell, Lindley Williams, "Yeats, Pound and Nō Drama," East-West Review, 1:70-8, 1964.

Through Pound's contact with Yeats and because of Pound's translations of Ernest Fenollosa's manuscripts, the influence of Nō on Yeats was "overwhelming." (H.S.)

P888   Hummel, John, "The Provençal Translations," Texas Quarterly, 10:47-51, Winter, 1967.

Pound was concerned with the quantitative determinate in Provençal poetry, as a poetic devise, which derives from the fact that troubadour poetry was written to be sung. His early interest in Provençal poetry was technical, but that interest was sustained by his realization that "they also reflected positional possibilities that were of tremendous concern to him." (D.P.)

P889   Hurwitz, Harold M., "Ezra Pound and Rabindranath Tagore," American Literature, 36:53-63, March, 1964.

Pound's attitude changed greatly after Tagore's success. While the Indian poet was unknown, Pound vigorously championed him; but "when the English public accepted the Indian and used Pound's own words to praise him, Pound, apparently shocked to find himself part of the herd, quickly denounced him." (W.G.F.)

P890   Hutchins, Patricia, "Ezra Pound and Thomas Hardy," Southern
        Review, 4:90-104, January, 1968.

        [This is a general survey of the relationship between Pound and
        Hardy, including letters written by Pound in the years between 1920-
        1925.] (J.M.D.)

P891   Hutchins, Patricia, "Ezra Pound as Journalist," Twentieth Century,
        167:39-48, January, 1960.

        Pound not only did sterling duty as music critic, but provided an
        "excellent analysis of the tendencies and ideas running through the
        various popular magazines" of the day (i.e. The Hibbert Journal,
        Blackwoods and the Quarterly Review.) (H.S.)

P892   Hutchins, Patricia, "Ezra Pound in Kensington," New World
        Writing, 11:203-13, 1957.

        [This is information about Pound and the people he met during his
        stay in the London suburb of Kensington, 1908-1920.] (H.S.)

P893   Hutchins, Patricia, "Ezra Pound's 'Approach to Paris'," Southern
        Review, 6:340-55, April, 1970.

        Evidence from a number of sources (including several letters pub-
        lished here for the first time) indicates that Pound's interest in
        French poetry began much earlier than is generally recognized.
        (J.M.D.)

P894   Hutchins, Patricia, "Letters from Ezra Pound," Twentieth
        Century, 164:355-63, October, 1958.

        "When the Letters of Ezra Pound appeared in 1950, unfortunately no
        reproductions were included to suggest his highly original methods
        of communication. It would then have been seen that as regards
        style, he is above all concerned with sound, with a tone of voice,
        accent, intonation, the speed of words in relation to meaning."
        (H.S.)

P895   Hutchins, Patricia, "Yeats and Pound in England," Texas
        Quarterly, 4:203-16, Autumn, 1961.

        [This is an account of the Yeats/Pound relationship from Pound's
        arrival in London in 1908 until his marriage in 1914.] (D.P.)

P896   Hynes, Sam, "The Case of Ezra Pound," Commonweal,
        63:251-4, December 9, 1955.

        Even while confined in St. Elizabeth's Hospital Pound "will go on
        blasting usury and preaching Social Credit, praising Mussolini and
        damning Roosevelt. . . . And however wrong-minded we may think
        all this is in a citizen of a democracy, we must, I think, admire it,
        however grudgingly, in the uncompromising poet." (H.S.)

P897   Hynes, Samuel, "Whitman, Pound and the Prose Tradition,"
        Selected Papers from the English Institute, pp. 110-36, 1961.

        ". . . Whitman's principal influence on later American poets (and
        specifically . . . on the work of Ezra Pound) has been through his
        role of 'poet of things'." ". . . Pound's briefest lyrics and his vast
        epic have a common root in the theories of the prose tradition--
        they all belong to . . . the poetry of things." Clearly, Whitman and
        Pound also share "the common concern with America's future, the
        hieratic conception of the poet, the notion that 'the topmost proof of
        a race is its own born poetry,' the inclination toward science and
        away from organized religion, the preoccupation with the modern,
        the sense of the need for new methods in new circumstances. In
        technique there are the catalogues, the foreign languages, the wide-
        ranging vocabularies, the freed meter, and a common hostility
        toward ornament." (D.P.)

P898   Jennings, Elizabeth, "Idea and Expression in Emily Dickinson,
        Marianne Moore and Ezra Pound," Stratford-upon-Avon Studies,
        7:97-113, 1965.

        "Emily Dickinson, Marianne Moore, Ezra Pound--these are three
        very different American poets. . . . Yet, when one examines them
        more closely, one realizes that what they share is a contemplative
        attitude towards men and affairs; they all look, appraise, annotate,
        and re-create." (D.P.)

P899   Jones, A. R., "Notes Toward a History of Imagism: An Examina-
        tion of Literary Sources," South Atlantic Quarterly, 60:262-85,
        Summer, 1961.

        The history of Imagism "has been misinterpreted by interested
        parties," chief among whom were Ezra Pound and Ford Madox
        Ford. By 1907 T. E. Hulme had conceived the essential features
        of Imagism. Pound disseminated Hulme's ideas and made them
        his own. (W.B.B.)

P900   Kenner, Hugh, "Art in a Closed Field," Virginia Quarterly Review,
        38:597-613, Autumn, 1962.

"I am going to argue (1) that the recent history of imaginative
literature . . . is closely parallel to the history of mathematics
during the same period; (2) that a number of poets and novelists in
the last century [for example, Flaubert, Joyce, Beckett and Pound]
stumbled upon special applications of what I shall call by mathematical analogy, the closed field; (3) that this principle has since been
repeatedly extended, to produce wholly new kinds of literary works;
and (4) that it is worth knowing about . . . because it helps you . . .
to think more coherently and usefully about the literature of both our
own time and times past." (D.P.)

P901   Kenner, Hugh, "Blood for the Ghosts," Texas Quarterly, 10:67-79,
        Winter, 1967.

Through his whole poetic career, Pound has been preoccupied with
absorbing, modifying and regenerating the cadences and rhythms of
poets of many languages and periods, informing these with his own
enormous, vital craft and producing a poetic sensitively alive to
impressions from troubadour's song to Whitman. (D.P.)

P902   Kenner, Hugh, "Ezra Pound and Chinese," Agenda, 4:38-41,
        October-November, 1965.

"Intermittently, over a span of fifty years, Pound has drafted verse
or prose with a Chinese text open beside him, but the exact process,
and hence the exact relationship between Chinese and English, has
varied continually." (H.S.)

P903   Kenner, Hugh, "Ezra Pound und das Geld," Neue Deutsche Hefte,
        4:22-40, No. 2, 1967.

"One can easily say that he should not have tried to understand the
world at all or definitely not to order it or give advice to the orderers;
he should have remained with his books, in the interior of his poem;
his life would have been calmer but his poem unimaginably different."
(J.R.R.)

P904   Kenner, Hugh, "Ezra Pound and Money," Agenda, 4:50-5, October-
        November, 1965.

"With the appearance of Impact, tightly and intelligently edited by
Noel Stock, we are at last in a position to grasp the extra-literary

preoccupations about which Pound was making such a fuss in the 1930's and 1940's, to the great distress of disciples whose curiosity stopped with the technique of verse." (H.S.)

P905   Kenner, Hugh, "MAO[4] or Presumption," Shenandoah, 21:84-93, Spring, 1970.

In 1915 Pound "had the impertinence to publish Cathay, in 1916 Certain Noble Plays of Japan, and in 1917 Noh, or Accomplishment," to the distress of Amy Lowell, since "the Orient was Amy's by right of Lowellship." Amy was concerned to "knock a hole in Ezra Pound's translations . . . clearly, his weak flank was Fenollosa. . . ." In partnership with Florence Wheeler Ayscough, who had been born in Shanghai, Miss Lowell began doing "translations" of her own, with the intention of proving that Pound's translations were incorrect. Unfortunately, Fir Flower Tablets are unreadable today through Amy Lowell's "impregnable vulgarity." Meanwhile, after many delays, Pound's refinement of Fenollosa's "The Chinese Written Character as a Medium for Poetry" began appearing in the Little Review. (D.P.)

P906   Kermode, Frank, "The New Apocalyptists," Partisan Review, 33:339-61, Summer, 1966.

The sense of crisis is one way to give order and design to the past, present, and future. Each era has its own crisis or apocalypse. A sense of ending can come at any time. "In general we seem to combine a sense of decadence in society . . . with a technological utopianism." Pound seems to be "an instance of a poet's failure to see that a poetic regression toward paradigms of justice," unlike a political regression, need not involve "immeasureable horror" or "loss of reality." (V.E.)

P907   La Zebnik, Jack, "The Case of Ezra Pound," New Republic, 176:17-20, April 1, 1957.

[This discussion of Pound considers the actions which led to his confinement in St. Elizabeth's, and whether his imprisonment was "cruel and unusual punishment."] (H.S.)

P908   Lemaire, Marcel, "Some Recent American Novels and Essays," Revue de Langues Vivante, 28:70-8, 1962.

[This essay appraises several books which consider "the controversial figure of the American poet Ezra Pound."] Also, John Steinbeck, in The Winter of Our Discontent, although "concerned with the ambiguous problem of good and evil . . . is not very successful in bringing home to the reader some of his inner certitudes." Finally, William Styron's Set this House on Fire "misses its point, firstly because the two heroes raise the question 'whether (they) could possibly have a soul worth saving' and secondly because the author has failed to select . . . [those] facts, scenes, people, notations and feelings . . . that might objectify his point of view. . . ." (H.S.)

P909   Levi, Peter, "Pound and the Classics," Agenda, 4:42-5, October-November, 1965.

". . . in Pound's poetry the tap-root of the Renaissance is not really a matter of information, gods, the classics; it is his own poetic bone and ability. This of course is why we can feel the sap in his words so strongly." (H.S.)

P910   Levin, Harry, "Literature and Exile," Listener, 62:613-7, October 15, 1959.

[This is a discussion of the exiles of Pasternak, Conrad, Nabokov, Dante, Heine, Mickewicz, Ovid, James, Joyce and Pound.] "The relation between the poet and the multitude, according to Vigny, is perpetual ostracism. . . . exile has often proved to be a vocation, reinforcing other gifts with courage and looking forward to a final triumph of independence over conformity." (H.S.)

P911   Lipke, William C., and Bernard W. Rozran, "Ezra Pound and Vorticism: A Polite Blast," Wisconsin Studies in Contemporary Literature, 7:201-10, Summer, 1966.

William Wees, in "Ezra Pound as a Vorticist" (WSCL, 6:56-72), describes Pound's career as a vorticist, but vorticism needs to be more clearly understood. "Pound's own vorticism is as elusive to define as Rilke's 'impressionism'." (P.J.R.)

P912   Loftus, Beverly J. G., "Ezra Pound and the Bollingen Prize: The Controversy in Periodicals," Journalism Quarterly, 39:347-54, Summer, 1962.

An analysis of "over fifty articles and editorials appearing . . . between 1949 and 1951 in twenty magazines" help to determine positions "for" and "against" Pound, his award of the "Bollingen Prize," and "the federal government's sponsorship of an award in the arts. . . ." (H.S.)

P913   Lottmann, Herbert R., "The Silences of Ezra Pound," Texas Quarterly, 10:105-28, Winter, 1967.

At eighty-two years of age Pound frequently lapsed into long silences, became very shy with new acquaintances. [Described is a dinner with Pound and nine or ten others in Paris, on the occasion of the publication in French of ABC of Reading.]   (D.P.)

P914   Lowell, Robert, "A Tribute," Agenda, 4:22, October-November, 1965.

"Ezra Pound's writings belong to the moment of experimental explosion--Stravinsky, Schoenberg, Picasso, Rilke, Joyce, Eliot, Proust. His work, like theirs, is alive with a radiant daring we now seem to have lost."   (D.P.)

P915   Lucas, John, "Our Foreign Agents: Rock Drill Dinner-Date," Carleton Miscellany, 1:91-4, Summer, 1960.

[This is a reconstruction of a dinner with Pound in Rapallo in March, 1959. Pound "said that anger is good, that patience is necessary, that optimism is paramount, that substance is all. Of his life here: 'I got out of Paris in 1924 because things were more interesting here.' Of his recent ordeal: 'I last heard from [Sister] Bernetta [Quinn] when they sprung me from the bughouse.' Of his work in progress: 'How many is it up to now?' And of certain old foes: I say with Violet [Hunt] there are two kinds of people I dislike on sight, the crocodile type and the foetus face, which looks as though it had never been properly born'."]   (D.P.)

P916   McNaughton, William, "Ezra Pound's Meters and Rhythms," PMLA, 78:136-46, March, 1963.

Three statements by Pound indicate the development of his versification through forty years: "To break the pentameter, that was the first heaven"; "Poetry atrophies when it gets too far from music"; "Metre is the articulation of the total sound of a poem."   (B.K.)

P917   McNaughton, William, "Pound's Translations and Chinese Melopoeia," Texas Quarterly, 10:52-6, Winter, 1967.

"Pound, in one way or another, has accounted for every effect in the Chinese original. . . . Pound's willingness thus to depart slightly from the original in order more accurately to produce these effects is one of the major reasons for the immense superiority of Pound's translations to others's translations."   (D.P.)

P918   McShane, Frank, et al, "Letters: The Case for Pound," London
        Magazine, 3:68-74, July, 1963.

        [Letters from Frank McShane, G. S. Fraser, William Cookson,
        Michael Alexander, and Ronald Duncan are printed here in rebuttal
        of Robert Conquest's article on Pound in the April, 1963 issue of
        London Magazine.] (D.P.)

P919   McShane, Frank, " 'To Establish the Facts': A Communication on
        Mr. A. R. Jones and Ford Madox Ford," South Atlantic Quarterly,
        61:260-5, Spring, 1961.

        A. R. Jones, in his article on Imagism has discounted the importance
        of Ford as a luminary in London literary circles, and as an influential
        figure, as against Hulme, Pound and others, in the "prewar poetic
        movements that culminated in Imagism," although Ford was directly
        and indirectly influential on the formation of Imagism as a literary
        movement dedicated to "precise observation and rendering of images."
        (D.P.)

P920   Martin, W., "Freud and Imagism," Notes and Queries, 8:470-1,
        474, December, 1961.

        "Although the first of Freud's books to be translated into English
        did not appear until . . . after the publication of the Imagist
        Manifesto, it seems that Pound was unwittingly indebted to Freud."
        "In describing the effect of the Image upon a reader Pound . . . may
        have been indebted to T. E. Hulme's exposition of Bergson's theory
        of Intensive Manifolds. . . . The aesthetic theory of Imagism can
        thus be seen largely as a product of its time." (D.P.)

P921   Merchant, W. Moelwyn, "Ezra Pound," Critical Quarterly,
        1:277-87, Winter, 1959.

        ". . . Pound's work has the fullest integrity: wholeness, unity; it
        proceeds from passionate conviction. . . . His failures of obscurity,
        or of blurring violence in public statement, are to be related to his
        work as a whole. . . ." (J.N.P.)

P922   Miner, Paul, "Pound, Haiku, and the Image," Hudson Review,
        9:570-84, Winter, 1956-57.

        Pound's "interest in haiku [and] . . . his Japanese studies . . . show
        that they are not the poor cousins among his literary relations, but
        rather enjoy a prominent place alongside Latin and Provençal poetry."
        (H.S.)

P923   Montgomery, Marion, "Ezra Pound's Angry Love Affair with America," Journal of Popular Culture, 2:361-9, Winter, 1968.

Ezra Pound was, "young and old, a revolutionary activist, bent on confronting the establishment with force. . . . The war he waged, focusing his attack upon the political and academic segments, was one engaging mind against mindlessness, in the interest of a significant order out of chaos. . . . He did not, nor could he, approve anarchy. . . . The very cause of his [almost singlehanded] engagement . . . was a conviction that the political and academic establishment itself presented the appearance of orderliness while actually being aspects of a general chaos . . . leading inevitably to a destruction of America, the country he so passionately loved, the most conspicuous aspect of that decay being the dissolution of its language." (D.P.)

P924   Montgomery, Marion, "Ezra Pound's Problems with Penelope," Southern Humanities Review, 3:114-23, Spring, 1969.

Pound's sense of "responsibility to poetry on society's behalf" approaches religious fanaticism. His poetic practice best represents his theory, through demonstrating "innovation from within strict form"; in his poetry image is not ornament but "the word beyond formulated language." His obscurity derived from his abandoning discursive language; his fascination with Mussolini grew out of his image of the poet as dictator. (D.P.)

P925   Montgomery, Marion, "Ezra Pound's Search for Family," Georgia Review, 22:429-36, Winter, 1968.

"Having set aside that larger family Eliot chose, whose mystical relation of father to children Dante pictures . . . Pound also put too much aside the natural family, electing to put his expectations in that larger family of man we call the state. But the natural family . . . provides an order and safeguards against chaos. . . . As Pound's heirs in art, we are much enriched by his eighty-year struggle on our behalf. But his struggle is finally more limited than is necessary to our survival as whole beings, members one of another." (D.P.)

P926   Montgomery, Marion, "Homage to Ezra Pound," Denver Quarterly, 3:1-17, Winter, 1969.

Pound's Cantos lacks unity; they are an "intricate web anchored in dark, uncertain regions of art and history." The Pisan Cantos are

Pound at his best, human as never before. Pound is both an Oedipus and a Don Quixote. (D.P.)

P927 Moore, Marianne, "A Note," _Agenda_, 4:22, October-November, 1965.

"Pound is the most contagious teacher I have known--deadly in earnest, at the same time, indigenously piquant." (H.S.)

P928 Nänny, Max, "Ezra Pound's Visual Poetry and the Method of Science," _English Studies_, 43:426-30, October, 1962.

". . . this basically nominalistic axiom of Pound's epistemology is one of the main foundations of the pronounced visual quality of his poetry. For in order to render the particularized facts of reality most adequately in his poetry Pound must have recourse to the most particularizing of all perceptions: to visual perception." (K.M.W.)

P929 Nist, John, "Ezra Pound: Young Poets, Beware!" _Approach_, No. 38, pp. 5-9, Winter, 1961.

Fascination with Pound as poet and critic is dangerous for emulators. His erudition reinforces his predilection for images, fear of emotional slither, lack of narrative thrust, preference for texture at the expense of structure. (A.F.)

P930 Olmstead, Edwin G., "Usher Burdick and Ezra Pound," _North Dakota Quarterly_, 28:66-8, Summer, 1960.

Pound was released from St. Elizabeth's Hospital because of House Resolution 403, introduced into Congress by Usher L. Burdick, Representative from the State of North Dakota. This Resolution stated "that the committee on the Judiciary . . . is authorized and directed to conduct a full and complete investigation and study of the sanity of Ezra Pound. . . . to determine whether there is justification for his continued incarceration. . . ." (H.S.)

P931 Olson, Paul A., "The Bollingen Controversy Ten Years After: Criticism and Content," _Prairie Schooner_, 33:225-9, Fall, 1959.

[Olson takes in turn "Sentimentality," "Fascist Belief," and "Incoherence" as manifested in the _Cantos_ to focus on the argument "that poets the likes of Pound demand critics" with certain of the characteristics of Dr. Johnson.] (J.N.P.)

P932   Orsini, G. N. G., "Pound and Italian Literature," <u>Sewanee Review</u>,
        68:465-72, Summer, 1960.

        Pound's scholarship is naive and ill-informed. His edition of
        Cavalcanti is based on an unreliable text, and the edition has been
        called "monstrous" by competent judges. "In almost twenty years
        he never succeeded in decently learning our [the Italian] language."
        (A.A.S.)

P933   Pack, Robert, "The Georgians, Imagism, and Ezra Pound: A Study
        in Revolution," <u>Arizona Quarterly</u>, 12:250-65, Autumn, 1956.

        Pound's Imagism was intended to destroy and replace the stale
        poetry of the Georgians. Yet if Georgian verse was chiefly bad
        rhetoric, Imagism, too, failed seriously, for its perceptions lacked
        meaning. "In order to deal with ideas, poetry must be metaphorical
        not imagistic. . . ." Nevertheless, Pound gave poetry new stylistic
        sharpness and freshness. (A.A.S.)

P934   Palandri, Angela Jung, "Ezra Pound Revisited," <u>West Coast
        Review</u>, 2:5-8, Winter, 1968.

        [This is an account of a visit to Pound at his home in Rapallo, Italy,
        fifteen years after a first visit. Pound's home is described; he is
        not sure he will complete the <u>Cantos</u>.] (D.P.)

P935   Palandri, Angela Jung, " 'The Stone Is Alive in My Hand'--Ezra
        Pound's Chinese Translations," <u>Literature East and West</u>,
        10:278-91, September, 1966.

        Admitting Pound's inaccuracies of translation, "which warrant the
        righteous indignation of the formidable scholars and sinologists . . .
        his strongest defense is perhaps that of Mencius (372-289 B.C.), who
        warned millennia ago against over-literal as well as over-fanciful
        interpretations of the Odes. . . . Whatever his inaccuracies in
        translation, Pound's attempt is to comprehend the poems."
        (K.M.W.)

P936   Paolucci, Anne, "Ezra Pound and D. G. Rossetti as Translators of
        Guido Cavalcanti," <u>Romanic Review</u>, 51:256-67, December, 1960.

        ". . . the struggle of the conscious artist for mastery of expression,
        the loving care with which every word is examined and weighed, the
        laboring . . . for adequate representation make Pound's transla-
        tions infinitely more interesting than those of Rossetti." (R.G.L.)

P937   Parkinson, Thomas, "Yeats and Pound: The Illusion of Influence,"
Comparative Literature, 6:256-64, Summer, 1954.

"Both poets from 1908 to 1917 were starting from Yeats's early
poetry, but they moved from this starting point to ends that were in
fact mutually incompatible. They met, profited, grew apart
aesthetically, but remained tenuously joined by personal affection.
. . . But Yeats--not Pound--made Yeats a major poet." (K.M.W.)

P938   Patmore, Brigit, "Ezra Pound in England," Texas Quarterly,
7:68-81, Autumn, 1964.

[These are reminiscences of Pound's experiences among the British
literati before World War I.] (K.M.W.)

P939   Permoli, Piergiovanni, "Appunti sull imagismo in America e in
Russia," Nuova Corrente, 5-6:155-64, January-June, 1956.

In Esenin and the Russian futurists, Pound's "imagism" found a
favorable environment. Though developing in a different cultural
atmosphere and taking inspiration from a different poetic experience,
it acquired its own distinct characteristics. (V.R.)

P940   Porter, Katherine Anne, "From the Notebooks of Katherine Anne
Porter--Yeats, Joyce, Eliot, Pound," Southern Review, 1:570-3,
Summer, 1965.

[These are reminiscences of Yeats, Eliot, Pound, and chiefly,
Joyce.] (J.M.D.)

P941   Pound, Ezra, "An Autobiographical Outline," Paris Review,
No. 28, pp. 18-21, Summer-Fall, 1962.

[This is an autobiographical outline, written for Louis Untermeyer
in Rapallo in 1932.] (D.P.)

P942   Racey, Edgar F., Jr., "Pound and Williams: The Poet as Renewer,"
Bucknell Review, 11:21-30, March, 1963.

"According to Williams [The Pound Newsletter, VIII (October 1955),
2-7], Pound's role may be finally conceived, not in terms of his
erudition . . . but rather in terms of his influence on the metric of
American poetry, and, by extraction, on the structure of that poetry."
"Culture . . . is incorporated in the personality of the poet (who
assimilates the river, the town, the male and female, and history).

Williams, then, is the ultimate sanction, as perceiver, for the myriad subject matter which is Paterson; history is insignificant because it is part of his experience." (H.S.)

P943   Rachewiltz, Mary de, "Ezra Pound at Eighty," Esquire, 65:114-6, 178-80, April, 1966.

[Pound's daughter speaks of "the after-image (elliptical), activities (volcanic), and interests (intense) of the poet in his time of energetic tranquillity."] (H.S.)

P944   Rachewiltz, Mary de, "Tempus Loquendi," Texas Quarterly, 10:36-9, Winter, 1967.

[These are introductory comments by Ezra Pound's daughter on the occasion of "Make it New: Articles delivered at a Symposium on Translation and Metrical Innovation: Aspects of Ezra Pound's Work." Her plea: "It is urgent for America to recognize the propaedeutic, cleansing and antiseptic value of Pound's work and the integrity behind the man."] (D.P.)

P945   Rattray, David, "A Weekend with Ezra Pound," Nation, 185:343-9, November 16, 1957.

[This is an account of a weekend spent with Jean Marie Châtel, Miss Martinelli, Mrs. Pound and Pound during his confinement to St. Elizabeth's Hospital in Washington, D. C.] (H.S.)

P946   Reche, Denis, "Pour Ezra Pound," Tel Quel, No. 11, pp. 17-24, Fall, 1962.

Adopting Cummings's axiom that a poem is what cannot be translated, Pound, with Hilda Doolittle, launched a revolution, using the poem as the opportunity for a constant renewal of poetic vision. Now that American imagism has, however, come full circle to its point of departure, Pound is thinking of future quests. (T.T.B.)

P947   Reck, Michael, "A Conversation between Ezra Pound and Allen Ginsberg," Evergreen Review, 19:27-9, 84, June, 1968.

[This conversation took place in Venice, in October, 1967, shortly before Pound turned eighty two. Pound was in one of his silences, appeared morose and depressed about his poetry: "Any good I've done has been spoiled by bad intentions--the preoccupation with ir-relevant and stupid things." Ginsberg assures Pound of the continu-ing relevance and importance of his poetry.] (D.P.)

P948   Ringer, Gordon, "Notes on the Present State of Pound Studies, "
Shenandoah, 6:64-6, Summer, 1955.

"It is ironic that after fifty years of making it new, Pound has been
seized upon by academic conspiracy against the academy, fragmented
and institutionalized into a 'safe' classic. It is tragic that the editors
of the Analyst and [Pound] Newsletter haven't told their graduate
students that their work is supposed to make sense. And it is
monstrous that the Newsletter, which owes so much to Pound, is
betraying the cause of understanding it professes to serve." (D.P.)

P949   Rizzardi, Alfredo, "Saeva Indignatio di Ezra Pound, " Nuova
Corrente, 5-6: 1-8, January-June, 1956.

Pound's poetry being an "uninterrupted . . . juxtaposition of human
reality and economic and moral irreality" in which we live the poet
thus spoke out against the economic oppression of usury from a
fascist pulpit, though in his "naive anti-semitism" he could not know
nor imagine the excesses of the Nazis. (V.R.)

P950   Rorem, Ned, "Ezra Pound as a Musician, " London Magazine,
7:10, 27-41, January, 1968.

Pound's one act opera Le Testament, his Antheil and the Treatise of
Harmony with Supplementary Notes by Ezra Pound, and his comments
on new music in New Age from 1917 to 1920, where he wrote under
the name William Atheling and his Varia, which appeared in New
Masses and New Criterion, confirm his wish to revolutionize the
music, as well as the poetry, of his day. (D.P.)

P951   Rose, W. K., "Ezra Pound and Wyndham Lewis: The Crucial
Years, " Southern Review, 4:72-89, January, 1968.

[This is a reconstruction of the relationship between Lewis and
Pound during the decade of 1910-1920.] (J.M.D.)

P952   Rosenthal, M. L., "Ezra Pound: The Poet as a Hero, " Forum
(Houston), 3:29-32, Fall-Winter, 1960.

Pound's prose and poetry are characterized by the "authority of the
self-appointed leader." The "authority of his tone and style" is
enhanced by his experiments with translation, attempts to capture
the essence of other poets in the language and rhythms of present day
English. (J.P.H.)

P953   Rovere, Richard, "The Question of Ezra Pound," Esquire, 48:66-80, September, 1957.

[This is a summary, mainly biographical, of Pound's life: the experiences which influenced his work, his "broadcasts" from fascist Italy, and his confinement in St. Elizabeth's Hospital in Washington, D. C.] (H.S.)

P954   Ruthven, K. K., "Ezra Pound, Alice Kenny and the Triad," Landfall, 23:73-84, 1969.

[Printed here is the controversy between Ezra Pound, and Frank Morton, one of the editors of the New Zealand periodical Triad, with some comments on Miss Alice A. Kenny, who regularly contributed verse and short stories to Triad, and had received some faint approval from Pound. Morton was strongly opposed to Vorticism and other manifestations of modernism.] (D.P.)

P955   Salomon, Louis B., "The Pound-Ruskin Axis," College English, 16:270-6, February, 1955.

A comparison of the social and political thinking of Ezra Pound and John Ruskin (and the similarities are many) "enable[s] us to see Pound in somewhat clearer perspective than was possible in the more heated atmosphere of a few years ago." (R.S.)

P956   Schneidau, Herbert N., "Pound and Yeats: The Question of Symbolism," ELH, 32:220-37, June, 1965.

Actually Yeats's occultism influenced the young Pound rather than Pound's influencing Yeats toward symbolism. (G.A.S.)

P957   Schneidau, Herbert N., "Vorticism and the Career of Ezra Pound," Modern Philology, 65:214-27, February, 1968.

"Vorticism was an alliance of artists, launched in 1914 to promote the work of Wyndham Lewis, Henri Gaudier-Brzeska, Edward Wadsworth and others; but it was led, in part, by Ezra Pound. . . ." (H.S.)

P958   Schutz, Alexander H., "Pound as Provençalist," Romance Notes, 3:58-63, Spring, 1962.

Pound, although not a dilettante, made errors in his translations of Provençal and was evidently not aware of some of the scholarly material available. (S.T.B.)

P959   Sechi, Giovanni, "Decadenza e Avanguardia in Ezra Pound,"
        Nuova Corrente, 5-6:184-95, January-June, 1956.

        Pound retained the "irrepressible vitality" of his American predeces-
        sors and mastered some of the expressive techniques of the Europe-
        ans: "verbal activism . . . the rational line . . . rejection of
        formalism . . . universality of metaphoric expression . . . simul-
        taneity of perception, etc." (V.R.)

P960   Smith, Richard Eugene, "Ezra Pound and the Haiku," College
        English, 26:522-7, April, 1965.

        "Pound may appear to have written a Haiku in the English language.
        . . . Such is not the case, however. Although Pound seems to have
        grasped the external method of expression employed by Haiku poets,
        he does not seem to have understood their conception of the intrinsic
        nature of the 'true' Haiku." (K.M.W.)

P961   Spector, Robert Donald, "Eliot, Pound, and the Decline of the
        Conservative Tradition," History of Ideas News Letter, 3:2-5,
        April, 1957.

        While Eliot and Pound are related to Matthew Arnold in their
        conservatism; they differ from him in their complete rejection of
        the modern world and their hopeless attitude about an improvememt
        of society. This is demonstrated in their poetry which is so obscure
        it can be appreciated only by a coterie and which thus shows a
        contempt of their audience. (K.L.)

P962   Spector, Robert Donald, "Pound as Pound," History of Ideas News
        Letter, 4:9-10, January, 1958.

        [Spector replies to Emery (see pp. 6-8) by stating that he does not
        answer his basic argument; that Pound's poetry is "deliberately
        idiosyncratic to the point of obscurity," and shows contempt of his
        audience.] (K.L.)

P963   Spencer, Benjamin T., "Pound: The American Strain," PMLA,
        81:457-66, December, 1966.

        "From Pound's temperament and behavior and from his explicit
        statements about America and her literature one can undoubtedly
        derive a complex of interrelated traits and attitudes suggesting an
        'ineradicable Americanism'; to reach a similar conclusion through
        a scrutiny of his belletristic modes is more difficult. . . ."
        (W.G.F.)

P964   Stock, Noel, "Ezra Pound and an American Tradition," Agenda,
       3:4-10, June, 1961.

       "Pound blames the literati for allowing monetary knowledge to
       become separated from general literary culture." (W.G.F.)

P965   Stock, Noel, "Ezra Pound and the Sense of Responsibility," Modern
       Age, 5:173-8, Spring, 1961.

       Pound's sense of responsibility is reflected in "his efforts to keep
       clear the channels of communication; to get answers from people in
       a position to know and to communicate these answers to literary
       colleagues, senators--to anyone, in fact, who might be likely to
       pass such information around or act on it." (K.M.W.)

P966   Stock, Noel, "Ezra Pound's Central Judgments on Contemporary
       Literature," Quadrant, 6:5-17, Winter, 1962.

       Pound's critical theories led him to reject most of the "accepted
       literature of the age" (especially between 1913 and 1922). His own
       choices--Frost, Joyce, Lawrence, Eliot--were not otherwise
       praised. Yet Pound's judgments "forced the literary world to take
       notice of unwanted work of the highest importance." (S.T.)

P967   Stock, Noel, "Innovation through Translation," Texas Quarterly,
       10:40-6, Winter, 1967.

       Imagination, innovation, enthusiasm, enjoyment, the feeling for
       language, are the characteristics Pound brings to his work as a
       translator. It was he who reintroduced us to "the point of being
       able to consider poems in foreign languages as poems and works of
       art rather than as simply fodder for editors and translators." (D.P.)

P968   Stock, Noel, "Modern Poetry and the Norm of Language," Texas
       Quarterly, 4:134-44, Winter, 1961.

       Pound and Eliot returned English verse to the norm of the language
       by incorporating "certain elements of the spoken language into the
       texture of verse which is contrived and 'artificial' and not at all
       simple" and by delivering "poetry from reliance upon explanatory
       passages linking together and commenting on the nuggets of
       intensity." (W.G.F.)

P969   Stock, Noel, "Verse Is a Sword: Unpublished Letters of Ezra Pound," X, A Quarterly Review, 1:258-65, 1960.

[These letters of Pound, written between 1935 to 1940, to Gladys Bing, Sir Ernest Benn, William Carlos Williams, E. E. Cummings, G. K. Chesterton, John Masefield, Dorothy L. Sayers, Herbert Read, C. H. Douglas, Archibald MacLeish, and James Laughlin range from monetary reform, literary matters, and the need for fellowships for creative writing to stipulations on the printing of Cantos 52/7.] (D.P.)

P970   Strickland, G. R., "Flaubert, Ezra Pound, and T. S. Eliot," Cambridge Quarterly, 2:242-63, Summer, 1967.

The influence of Flaubert on Pound and Eliot "is very far-reaching indeed and can be seen in their meditations as poets and critics on matters apparently far removed from any with which Flaubert was concerned himself. . . . Eliot and Pound derived from Flaubert certain habits of thought which can be seen in a sophisticated quasi-omniscience." (D.P.)

P971   Sullivan, J. P., "Ezra Pound's Classical Translations," Texas Quarterly, 10:57-60, Winter, 1967.

Classical critics and scholars have found themselves puzzled and horrified by the revolutionary nature of Pound's dealings with the classics, particularly as he abandoned the literal, abandoned the familiar Victorian verse and replaced it with a poetic language which juxtaposed the ancient with the modern and employed imagistic association. (D.P.)

P972   Tanselle, Thomas, "Ezra Pound and a Story of Floyd Dell's," Notes and Queries, 8:350-2, September, 1961.

Dell used Pound as a model for the central character in "Jessica Screams," a story of "the conflict between a person of artistic temperament and the middle-class philistinism of a small town." (W.G.F.)

P973   Tanselle, G. Thomas, "Two Early Letters of Ezra Pound," American Literature, 34:114-9, March, 1962.

Two letters (Philadelphia, 1911 and Paris, 1911) from Pound to Floyd Dell "are important because in them Pound discusses his ideas about poetry, his opinion of contemporary literary criticism, and influences on his own work." (H.S.)

P974   Teele, Roy E., "A Balance Sheet on Pound's Translation of Noh
        Plays," Books Abroad, 39:168-70, Spring, 1965.

        "The historical and literary value of Pound's translation remains,
        but for a sound and wide knowledge of Noh plays, readers should
        now turn elsewhere." (C.E.N.)

P975   Teele, Roy E., "The Japanese Translations," Texas Quarterly,
        10:61-6, Winter, 1967.

        Unlike most of his other translations, Pound's Japanese translations
        were done with only a secondhand knowledge of the language. In
        terms of "achieving in the new language something of the effect of
        the original," it is very difficult to fault his haiku and noh play
        renditions, but rhymically and metrically Pound typically is at
        variance with the originals. (D.P.)

P976   Thirwall, John C., "The Quality of Mercy Was Not Strained: A
        Footnote Followed by a Letter," Pound Newsletter, No. 8, pp. 22-3,
        October, 1955.

        [This is a brief description of the relationship between Ezra Pound
        and William Carlos Williams, followed by a letter from Williams to
        Babette Deutsch about Pound, written in 1943.] (D.P.)

P977   Tucker, William P., "Ezra Pound, Fascism, and Populism,"
        Journal of Politics, 18:105-7, February, 1956.

        "Despite the cogency of Professor Ferkiss's study of 'Ezra Pound
        and American Fascism' " in the May 1955 issue of Journal of Politics,
        "his analogies between American fascism and assumed characteris-
        tics of American populism are overdrawn." (D.P.)

P978   Wain, John, "The Prophet Ezra v. 'The Egotistical Sublime',"
        Encounter, 33:63-70, August, 1969.

        [These are reflections on Pound, Eliot, and Joyce.] (D.P.)

P979   Wain, John, "The Reputation of Ezra Pound," London Magazine,
        2:55-64, October, 1955.

        By his work and advice to Yeats and Eliot, "Pound did more to
        establish the characteristic English poetry of the twentieth century
        than anyone else." An "expert verbal mechanic" whose Cantos are
        "a collection of magnificent fragments," he has "inhabited a cleaner,
        simpler and saner world than anything that actually exists. . . ."(J. L. B.)

P980   Wang, John C., "Ezra Pound as a Translator of Classical Chinese
        Poetry," Sewanee Review, 73:345-57, Summer, 1965.

        "Compared with other translators of . . . classical odes, Mr. Pound
        may again suffer from the accusation of being a free translator. But
        credit must go to him that he is the one who really recreates the
        original spirit of the odes." (H.S.)

P981   Wees, William C., "England's Avant-Garde: The Futurist-Vorticist
        Phase," Western Humanities Review, 21:117-28, Spring, 1967.

        "Futurism was an important part--but only part--of the shaping
        forces that brought about Blast and Vorticism. . . . The Vorticists
        were inclined to convert images of life into mechanical, geometrical,
        and even monumental forms. . . . Here Worringer and Hulme meet
        on a common ground with Ezra Pound, who carried to Vorticism the
        Imagists's liking for the sharply defined line, the sculptured and
        clean-cut image, and with Wyndham Lewis . . . whose . . . prose
        [w]as machine-like, 'static,' and monumental. . . ." While
        Vorticism lasted it "gave England and avant-garde movement that
        for a brief period rivaled anything the Continent produced. . . ."
        (D.P.)

P982   Wees, William C., "Ezra Pound as a Vorticist," Wisconsin Studies
        in Contemporary Literature, 6:56-72, Winter-Spring, 1965.

        "Vorticism came at the crucial point in Pound's development as a
        poet. . . . In the Vorticists's art he found not only a new way of
        seeing things, but, as the Cantos have proved, a new way of saying
        things, as well." (W.G.F.)

P983   Wees, William C., "Pound's Vorticism: Some New Evidence and
        Further Comments," Wisconsin Studies in Contemporary Literature,
        7:211-6, Summer, 1966.

        Pound's letters support the view that for him Vorticism became "an
        aesthetic not limited to art, an artistic frame of reference on which
        to build the economics, politics and general view of 'kulcher' we
        find in the later essays and cantos." (P.J.R.)

P984   Wieners, John, "Ezra Pound at the Spoleto Festival, 1965,"
        Agenda, 4:68-9, October-November, 1965.

        [This is an account of Pound's visit to the Spoleto Festival, with
        mention of his readings, i.e., "translations from the Chinese and

Provençal . . . [followed by his reading of] Robert Lowell's translation of the XVth Canto from Dante's Inferno."]   (H.S.)

P985   Wigginton, Waller B., ed., "A Homer Pound Letter," Rendezvous, No. 4, pp. 27-9, No. 2, 1969.

[This letter was written in 1925 by Homer Pound, Ezra's father, to Mrs. Susie Boice Trego, editor of the Idaho Republican. The letter demonstrates "Homer Pound's close relationship to his son and reports his continuing in Idaho. . . ."]   (H.S.)

P986   Wigginton, Waller, "The Pounds at Hailey," Rendezvous, No. 4, pp. 31-68, No. 2, 1969.

"This account . . . is offered as a small contribution towards a definitive biography of Ezra Pound, which, of course, has yet to be written, Ezra, despite his epitaph, still being alive."   (H.S.)

P987   Willard, Charles B., "Ezra Pound and the Whitman 'Message'," Revue de Littérature Comparée, 31:94-8, January, 1957.

"Whitman often said that his poems had only begun his theme.   Ezra Pound, in the early years of his career, believed that he was destined to complete this theme and to promulgate the Whitman message. . . . The message he felt he shared with Whitman had to do with the future of America."   (H.S.)

P988   Willard, Charles B., "Ezra Pound's Appraisal of Walt Whitman," Modern Language Notes, 72:19-26, January, 1957.

"For a few years after 1909 Pound was much concerned with Whitman. . . . After this early critical wrestling, Pound referred to Whitman less often; but when he did, it was either to point out that Whitman is after all one of the American 'greats' or to wonder how so weak an artist could have succeeded so well."   (H.S.)

P989   Willard, Charles B., "Ezra Pound's Debt to Walt Whitman," Studies in Philology, 54:573-81, October, 1957.

"Pound's literary life and work in the first few years of his career show the influence of a rather thorough knowledge of Whitman." Not only did Pound and Whitman share certain poetic themes and practices, but both were poseurs, centers of coteries, and were harried by censors.   (C.K.L.)

P990 Yoshikawa, Kōjirō, "An Interview with Ezra Pound," East-West Review, 1:212-7, 1964.

[This is a meeting with Pound at St. Elizabeth's Hospital, Washington, D. C. Pound briefly explains the differences between eastern and western "nature."] (H.S.)

CANTOS

P991 Alexander, Michael, "On Rereading the Cantos," Agenda, 4:4-10, October-November, 1965.

"To sum up on the Cantos so far, one can safely say that in technical accomplishment and variety of invention they rank with the best long poems in the language." (H.S.)

P992 Baumann, Walter, "Pound and Layamon's Brut," Journal of English and Germanic Philology, 68:265-76, April, 1969.

The source of "a block of text near the middle of Canto 91 "is Layamon's Brut. An analysis of his reliance on the Brut sheds light on Pound the historiographer as much as on Pound the seeker of the immortal design." (G.C.)

P993 Cambon, Glauco, "William Carlos Williams and Ezra Pound: Two Examples of Open Poetry," College English, 22:387-9, March, 1961.

"Even a local sampling from the two impressive bodies of unconventional verse [Pound's Thrones and Williams's Paterson Book V] will serve to throw some light on their vital affinity." (M.J.O.)

P994 Campbell, K. T. S., "The Purification of Poetry--A Note on the Poetics of Ezra Pound's Cantos," British Journal of Aesthetics, 8:124-37, 1968.

In The Cantos "the inward intuition of Light and the outward programme of political and financial action form nuclei for groups of images whose polarity corresponds to a division of mood and tonality fundamental to the entire poem." (H.S.)

CANTOS (cont'd)

P995   Carruth, Hayden, "The Poetry of Ezra Pound," <u>Perspectives USA</u>, 16:129-59, Summer, 1956.

Premier American expatriate, Imagist, Vorticist, impressario, introducer and helper of the great, Pound has created his monument in his complex <u>Cantos</u>, which treat the "truth of history," and in his superb translations from many languages. The <u>Cantos</u> fail as a poem but only as other unrealizable masterpieces do. Pound "restored integrity to the language." He should be freed. (J.L.B.)

P996   Clark, Thomas, "The Formal Structure of Pound's <u>Cantos</u>," <u>East-West Review</u>, 1:97-144, 1964.

"The work of the poet, then, is to transmit 'forms': ethical, aesthetic, emotional, universal. 'The mind making forms can verbally transmit them when the mental voltage is high enough.' This is the root of Pound's method of organizing the <u>Cantos</u>. . . ." (H.S.)

P997   Cookson, William, "Some Notes on <u>Rock-Drill</u> and <u>Thrones</u>," <u>Agenda</u>, 4:30-7, October-November, 1965.

"It [<u>Rock-Drill</u>] can be divided into two parts: 85-89 are historical, didactic; 90-95 is an immense lyric . . . showing a kind of beauty that has not been present in English since medieval times. . . . <u>Thrones</u> is one of the most solid historical achievements of the <u>Cantos</u>. While illuminating the earlier parts of the poem it is a coherent structure in itself resting upon . . . monuments to justice and good government." (H.S.)

P998   Cowan, James C., "The Classical Figure as Archetype in Pound's <u>Cantos</u>, I-XXX," <u>Twentieth Century Literature</u>, 6:25-32, April, 1960.

"Ezra Pound's <u>Cantos</u> . . . gain structural unity through the three basic thematic motifs of descent into Hades, metamorphosis, and archetype-variant patterns which Pound sees as inherent in his subject matter of mythic, literary, and historical fragments. . . . The three basic thematic motifs are fused in a single theme: the degeneration throughout history of the ethical values represented in what Pound calls 'the factive personality' and the possible regeneration of these values through revitalization of fragments from the usable past." (D.P.)

CANTOS (cont'd)

P999   D'Agostino, Nemi, "Sulle origini dei Cantos," Nuova Corrente,
        5-6:92-102, January-June, 1956.

        The basis of the Cantos is formed on the extended use of ellipses
        as in Browning's Sordello, Pound's love of the fertile past as
        opposed to the arid present, and what Croce calls the highly
        "intuitive poetic intuition" of Pound. (V.R.)

P1000   Davenport, Guy, "A Collation of Two Texts of the Cantos," Pound
        Newsletter, No. 6, pp. 5-13, April, 1955.

        [This is a collation of the differences in 278 lines between the first
        and second printings of the Cantos by New Directions, 1948, and
        the Faber and Faber edition published last year.] (D.P.)

P1001   Davenport, Guy, "Ezra Pound's Radiant Gists: A Reading of
        Cantos II and IV," Wisconsin Studies in Contemporary Literature,
        3:50-64, Spring-Summer, 1962.

        Cantos II and IV dramatize transformation or metamorphosis.
        (B.K.)

P1002   Davenport, Guy, "Persephone's Ezra," Arion, 7:165-99, Summer,
        1968.

        "The early interpreters of The Cantos tended to see the poem as a
        study of the man of willed and directed action, personae of Odysseus.
        It is now clear that the poem rests in a deeper, stiller sense of
        humanity, the city and its continuity, symbolized by the goddess of
        field and citadel wearing the sanctuary of her people as a crown."
        (H.S.)

P1003   Davie, Donald, "Adrian Stokes and Pound's Cantos," Twentieth
        Century, 160:419-36, November, 1956.

        To suggest the relationship between Pound's Cantos and the writings
        of Adrian Stokes directs attention upon Mr. Stokes as an original
        thinker and shows how criticism of Pound can avoid the pitfalls of
        would be conclusive judgments and mere source hunting. (R.A.K.)

CANTOS   (cont'd)

P1004 Davie, Donald, " 'Forma' and 'Concept' in Ezra Pound's Cantos,"
Irish Writing, 36:160-73, Late Autumn, 1956.

Yvor Winters's statement that Pound's Cantos leave one now knowing
"whether we have any ideas or not" is accurate, but is not derogatory
criticism: the state of "not knowing" is exactly what Pound strives
to create in readers's minds. Full knowledge will come only when
the Cantos are finished. (R.A.B.)

P1005 De Bedts, Ruth, "The Ideogrammatic Method in the Cantos of Ezra
Pound," Florida Review, No. 2, pp. 30-9, Spring, 1958.

The true significance of the ideograms comprising the Cantos lies
in their relationship to one another. "The great difficulty in reading
the Cantos lies in discovering these relationships." (W.G.F.)

P1006 Evans, David W., "Ezra Pound as Prison Poet," University of
Kansas City Review, 23:215-20, March, 1957.

Pound's poetry has often been found "chaotic." The Pisan Cantos
(composed during his war imprisonment) marks an advance over
his earlier work in use of description and detail; it also displays
greater unity and economy of expression. Pound's rigid adherence
to time sequence and use of contrast particularly contribute to these
effects. (G.K.)

P1007 Fang, Achilles, "Aspects of the Cantos: V: Notes on China and the
Cantos," Pound Newsletter, No. 9, pp. 3-5, January, 1956.

"I submit that the Cantos, at least the most important parts, are
variations on themes of Confucian and pseudo-Confucian writers,
among which latter I would include John Adams, Thomas Jefferson,
Martin Van Buren, J. Q. Adams, and even Homer. . . ." (D.P.)

P1008 Foster, John L., "Pound's Revision of Cantos I-III," Modern
Philology, 63:236-45, February, 1966.

"Though it is impossible to say just what caused Pound to revise the
beginning of his poem so drastically, a comparison of the first and
present versions of Cantos I-III go far toward providing an answer.
Some of the most basic elements of the Cantos . . . are missing
from Pound's conception of it in 1917." (H.S.)

CANTOS (cont'd)

P1009 Frohock, W. M., "The Revolt of Ezra Pound," Southwest Review, 44:190-9, Summer, 1959.

The principal subject of Cantos is the rejection of life as it is now lived. The structure is a kind of intential incoherence, comparable to Celine's Journey to the End of the Night. Cantos ultimately belongs to the category of poetry of revolté. (J.P.H.)

P1010 Fussell, Edwin, "Dante and Pound's Cantos," Journal of Modern Literature, 1:75-87, No. 1, 1970.

The Cantos may be described as "simultaneously a secularized and a re-paganized version of the Commedia." Pound transmutes Dante's values and fuses the Commedia with Greek epics. Brief allusions to Dante's writing are scattered through the Cantos. (D.P.)

P1011 Goacher, Denis, "Ezra Pound's Cantos," Listener, 68:357-8, September 6, 1962.

". . . many intelligent people complain of the technical difficulties and 'obscurities' of The Cantos when in fact they are really refusing to consider the ideas and perceptions Pound displays, alike in his poetry and his prose work." (H.S.)

P1012 Grigsby, Gordon K., "Newspeak in Pound's Cantos," South Atlantic Quarterly, 62:51-6, Winter, 1963.

Pound's ideogrammic method, which purports to present particulars and sensory experience directly, without any distortion by subjective selection or organization, raises the question how the Cantos can express any "sustained coherent" ideology. They can't. "What we get from the anti-thought of the Cantos is poor thought." (J.L.A.)

P1013 Gross, Harvey, "Pound's Cantos and the Idea of History," Bucknell Review, 9:14-31, March, 1960.

Pound's concept of history as "myth" existing in the present only and of "usury" as the master key to history make the Cantos, ultimately, a failure both as history and as poem because they deny the ordering function of the mind. (M.H.M.)

CANTOS (cont'd)

P1014 Halperen, Max, "Old Men and New Tools: The Chinese Cantos of Pound," Trace, No. 52, pp. 1-8, Spring, 1964.

Each of the Chinese Cantos of Pound's long poem (Numbers 522-61) has "an emphasis different from that of its neighbors." In the group the reader is brought full circle from Canto 52, "where religion in the West was seen as divorced from economic attitudes" to Cantos 60 and 61 in which East and West are at last opposed and the Chinese reject Christianity as "immoral." (W.G.F.)

P1015 Highet, Gilbert, "Beer-bottle on the Pediment," Horizon, 3:116-8, January, 1961.

Pound's Cantos are a "dump containing some beautiful fragments of antique and Oriental sculpture (often disfigured by careless handling), some outrageous fakes, loads of personal trivia, some bits of filth, many promising but embryonic artistic sketches, and a huge scree of pure rubbish." (J.P.H.)

P1016 Hlawatsch, Wolfhard, "Ezra Pounds Weg zum Licht: Eine Interpretation von Canto XV," Die Neueren Sprachen, 18:551-7, 1969.

Modern man has lost the knowlege of his intellectual and spiritual depravity. Pound's desire is again to restore this knowledge. He wants to lead modern man out of the thicket of ignorance, through the purgatory of mistakes and to the light of perception. (H.S.)

P1017 Hutchins, Patricia, "Ezra Pound's Pisa," Southern Review, 2:77-93, Winter, 1966.

Since "the Cantos as a whole require a pre-knowledge of situation before they become luminous", a visit to the scene of Pound's confinement along with certain biographical details elucidates the Pisan Cantos. (J.M.D.)

P1018 Hynes, Samuel, "Pound and the Prose Tradition," Yale Review, 51:532-46, Summer, 1962.

Ezra Pound, true to his adherence to the "prose tradition" in poetry (emphasis upon plain speech, presentation of facts, distrust of rhetoric, personality and didacticism), created in the Cantos a poem which is historically and critically important, but lacking in significant action, authority, and order. (F.L.)

CANTOS (cont'd)

P1019 Jackson, Thomas H., "The Adventures of Messire Wrong-Head," ELH, 32:238-55, June, 1965.

Malatesta in the Cantos "has much in common with the particular Odysseus of Homer and with Pound's own Odysseus--a conqueror, something of a free-booter, a highwayman, perhaps, a destroyer of cities." (G.A.S.)

P1020 Kenner, Hugh, "'Rock Drill': A Review of Cantos 88-89," Pound Newsletter, No. 8, pp. 15-7, October, 1955.

"The function of these cantos is to specify the complaint against nation-wide usury in terms of a particular case from American history . . . and to make use of Benton's admirably lucid and civilized statements of the case to indict the unreality of the currency circulating in a nation which has relinquished its control over monetary issue." (D.P.)

P1021 Kenny, H. A., "Pound's Cantos: The Failure of an Epic," Critic, 19:9-10, 72, June-July, 1961.

The Cantos fails as an epic because Pound is its hero, although he brought a sense of history, a gift of languages and an ear "for the magnificent English line" to his epic. His lack of integrating philosophy and the absence of originality are flaws, but the failure of the Cantos derives from his inability to achieve "the Augustinian greatness that could at once give us himself, true and entire, and in all humility, and yet be hero, human and divine." (D.P.)

P1022 Landini, Richard G., "Confucianism and the Cantos of Ezra Pound," Topic: A Journal of the Liberal Arts, 6:30-42, Fall, 1966.

The Confucian ethic elucidates Pound's criticism of twentieth century Western civilization. It not only provides the basis of Pound's examination of the shortcomings of that civilization but also provides the correctives for the errors in the politico-economic and ethical character of the age. (J.M.D.)

P1023 Landini, Richard G., "Vorticism and the Cantos of Ezra Pound," Western Humanities Review, 14:173-81, Spring, 1960.

Vorticism, which, "unlike Imagism, places emphasis upon energy, upon the subjective source of the image rather than the image itself,"

CANTOS (cont'd)

is particularly important to contemporary poetry because Pound's Cantos, "one of the most controversial and most rewarding" of twentieth-century poems was written under the Vorticist discipline. (W.G.F.)

P1024 Neame, Alan, "The Pisan Cantos VI: Speech and Penalty," European, 10:351-63, February, 1958.

[This is a protest against Pound's imprisonment, together with an annotated reprint of Cantos LXXIV, lines 43-77.] (E.L.)

P1025 Oakes, Loisann, "An Explication of Canto LXXV by Ezra Pound," Wisconsin Studies in Contemporary Literature, 5:105-9, Summer, 1964.

" '--not of one bird but of many' refers to Gerhart Münch's transcription of Clement Janequin's four voice chanson, Reveilles-vous" (1539). "The ideogram is the music itself, an example of recreation." (W.G.F.)

P1026 Olson, Paul A., "Pound and the Poetry of Perception," Thought, 35:331-48, September, 1960.

"The poetry of perception, Pound's kind of verse, deals with the seen world, the act of perception, the finer sensations. The poetry of vision, Eliot's kind . . . is interested in the seen thing . . . only as it intimates some meaning beyond itself." The Cantos include "heightened perceptions, the record of what has been or might be imagined by various historical personages. Or they are part of the satiric machinery of the poem. . . ." "In all sections what counts is the orderliness, the justice, the visual accuracy of the language, not its typological richness or mystical insight. What counts is the closeness to nature, scientifically observed . . . which then must form the basis of intelligent political action." (D.P.)

P1027 Øverland, Orm, "Ezra Pound and Wilfred Scawen Blunt: A Footnote to Canto 81," Notes and Queries, 14:250-2, July, 1967.

In Blunt's "With Esther" "Pound recognized two important themes of his own Cantos: the durability of what has true life and value as opposed to the transience of the dross of vanity. . . . The vanity he is able to denounce in the midst of his trials is the same 'poor stuff' Blunt had learned to see through." (K.M.W.)

CANTOS (cont'd)

P1028 Owen, Earl Ben, "Social Credit and the Cantos," Pound Newsletter, No. 2, pp. 6-10, April, 1954.

[This is a glossary of terms in the economic theories of Clifford Hugh Douglas, followed by a bibliography of his major works. His theories "recur in many contexts throughout the Cantos. A minimum of these theories, especially as they relate to money, banking, and 'high finance,' is necessary if we are to understand what Pound is talking about."] (D.P.)

P1029 Paige, D. D., "Aspects of the Cantos: III: Three New Cantos," Pound Newsletter, No. 6, pp. 2-4, April, 1955.

"These notes are intended to serve as a gnomon and not as an explication de texte" of Cantos 85, 86, and 87. (D.P.)

P1030 Peachy, Frederic, "Aspects of the Cantos: IV: The Greek Element in the Cantos," Pound Newsletter, No. 8, pp. 8-10, October, 1955.

"These notes are not the place to catalogue exhaustively Pound's knowledge and use of Greek. That knowledge is extensive, and his use of it eclectic. . . . But . . . the employment of Greek in the Cantos is sensitive, purposeful and precise." (D.P.)

P1031 Pearce, Roy Harvey, "Ezra Pound's Appraisal of Walt Whitman: An Addendum," Modern Language Notes, 74:23-8, January, 1959.

". . . in the Pisan Cantos Pound sets out at once to establish and interpret his relationship to Whitman--and does so in a way to signify that he has come to define his own career and the burden of his poetry as being, in some basic aspects, quite Whitmanian." (M.J.O.)

P1032 Pearce, R. H., "Toward an American Epic," Hudson Review, 12:362-77, Autumn, 1959.

"I mean to . . . offer what amounts to a theory of the American epic and a summation of the sort of poetics it has striven so hard, so desperately, to put into action. I shall take as my exemplars three poems--[Barlow's] The Columbiad, [Whitman's] Song of Myself, and the Cantos. These are heroic poems, but of a curious sort. For, instead of celebrating, affirming, and memorializing a hero . . . the poet of the American epic . . . tried and continues to try to

CANTOS (cont'd)

create a hero. And his means to that creation was, and remains,
the very act of the poem itself. " (D.P.)

P1033   Peterson, Leland D., "Ezra Pound: The Use and Abuse of History,"
American Quarterly, 17:33-47, Spring, 1965.

" I myself find the first forty-one cantos the most satisfying and
those following much less so, mainly because I seldom find myself
arguing with the poet's treatment of history in the earlier cantos,
but from canto XLII . . . I find my aesthetic responses inhibited by
. . . a frequently arbitrary and completely irresponsible treatment
of history." (W.G.F.)

P1034   Pound, Ezra, "Ezra Pound: A Prison Letter," Paris Review,
No. 28, p. 17, Summer-Fall, 1962.

[This is "an explanatory note to the censor at the Pisa Detention
Camp where Pound was held after the war. That officer, in censor-
ing Pound's correspondence (which included the MSS of verse on its
way to Pound's publishers) apparently suspected the Pisan Cantos
were in fact coded messages. Pound is writing to explain this is
not the case."] (D.P.)

P1035   Rachewiltz, Mary de, "Traduzione Integrale," Arion, 6:208-15,
Summer, 1967.

Three aspects of Pound's Cantos are: "(1) the Cantos considered
as translation; (2) the problems of retranslating certain passages
of the Cantos into their original language; and (3) the mark which
coaching me in the translation of the Cantos into Italian has left upon
the poet's later work, and the humanizing effect of Mediterranean
humanitas." (H.S.)

P1036   Read, Forrest, "The Pattern of the Pisan Cantos," Sewanee
Review, 65:400-19, Summer, 1957.

The "same Inferno-Purgatorio-Paradiso patterns--experience
subjected to time, experience which is symbolic of timelessness,
and experience in timelessness itself; and the process by which the
sensibility moves from reception through creation to articulation--
animate the Commedia and the Pisan Cantos." (A.A.S.)

CANTOS (cont'd)

P1037 Reck, Michael, "Reading the Cantos: Pound's Fugal Music,"
Commonweal, 83:93-5, October 22, 1965.

Although difficult the Cantos is an "extraordinarily beautiful and
rewarding poem. . . . What gives difficulty is the range of reference." "The Cantos bring all history before us, live and of this
moment--one of their brilliant achievements. . . . Seemingly
disparate objects are described seriatim . . . perceived together,
they express a sentiment, a mood, or an atmosphere. . . . In
addition to the fact that every line of the Cantos is interesting for
its rhythm and verbal melody, the whole structure has a musicality.
As in music, themes appear and are repeated . . . as a horn may
suddenly resound amid the strings in an orchestra." (D.P.)

P1038 Rosen, Aaron, "The Enormous Dream--Its Rhetoric: A Review,"
Pound Newsletter, No. 10, pp. 6-9, April, 1956.

"Pound . . . has constructed his Cantos almost entirely with his
literal ear, and this is both marginal and central in a peculiar way."
"What we have, however, with the Pisan Cantos and more especially
with Rock-Drill, is a greater freedom and rapidity of reference
while maintaining the same order of meaning: a structure open to
the significance of putting one's 'quidities' through as many contexts
as possible to the sheer exhaltation of mobility." (D.P.)

P1039 Russell, Francis, "The Cantos of Ezra Pound," Contemporary
Issues, 10:117-42, May-June, 1960.

Although Pound has "an extraordinary gift for words" and the Cantos
express an occasional charm, Pound's work is an enigmatic melange
lacking structural integrity because it is based on accidents of
Pound's life. Pound lacks a sense of history, shows "a deteriorating
reasoning power, misunderstands and misapplies the ideogram,
elevates the preoccupation of the moment to a dogma," and demonstrates a "gross lack of judgment." (K.M.)

P1040 Slatin, Myles, "A History of Pound's Cantos I-XVI, 1915-1925,"
American Literature, 35:183-95, May, 1963.

"The Cantos is an 'action' poem, free to move improvisationally
and accidentally in any direction as the process of composition
clarifies what is implicit in its material, and in directions which
could not possibly have been foreseen at the beginning." (K.M.W.)

CANTOS (cont'd)

P1041 Vasse, William, "Aspects of the Cantos: II: American History and the Cantos," Pound Newsletter, No. 5, pp. 13-9, January, 1955.

"Pound has constructed his scale of measurement in these cantos fact by fact, each fact from a document of American history. If some of the facts seem obscure, they are, nevertheless . . . facts that Pound thinks his readers ought to be acquainted with and which he uses, both to create an image of balanced action and to contribute to that larger picture of ideas moving into right action that is the Cantos." [Included is an appendix which corrects names and dates in the Cantos which differ from the Works of John Adams, the major source for the poem.] (D.P.)

P1042 V[asse], W[illiam], "A Note on the Text of the Chinese Cantos," Pound Newsletter, No. 6, pp. 15-6, April, 1955.

[This is a listing of typographical errors in Chinese names of the China Cantos "discovered by comparing these Cantos with their source: Histoire générale de la Chine (Paris, 1777).] (D.P.)

CATHAY

P1043 Benton, Richard P., "A Gloss on Pound's 'Four Poems of Departure'," Literature East and West, 10:292-301, September, 1966.

"Pound tells us that the poems in Cathay ['Separation on the River Kiang,' 'Taking Leave of a Friend,' 'Leave-taking near Shoku,' and 'The City of Choam'] were done for the most part from the Chinese of Rihaku, from the notes of the late Ernest Fenollosa, and the decipherings of Professors Mori and Ariga. Thus Pound's Japanese aids account for his Japanese substitutions of Chinese names in the poems." (H.S.)

P1044 Lee, Pen-Ti, and Donald Murray, "The Quality of Cathay: Ezra Pound's Early Translations of Chinese Poems," Literature East and West, 10:264-77, September, 1966.

". . . when Pound began his career as a translator of Chinese [Cathay] he was a brilliant improvisor in an unfamiliar field, an improvisor who concealed a great deal of ignorance with an almost equal amount of bluff. The ignorance and perhaps the bluff as well did injury to the poetry." (H.S.)

P1044   3296

HOMAGE TO SEXTUS PROPERTIUS

P1045 Drew-Bear, Thomas, "Ezra Pound's Homage to Sextus Propertius," American Literature, 37:204-10, May, 1965.

"This essay is an attempt to reconstruct Pound's trains of thought as he wrote these twelve poems, following some of the . . . at least half-conscious associations . . . by which Pound recreated the poetry of Propertius, not in a stilted translation but as living English poetry. . . ." (W.G.F.)

P1046 Ruthven, K. K., "Propertius, Wordsworth, Yeats, Pound, and Hale," Notes and Queries, 15:47-8, February, 1968.

W. G. Hale took Pound's Homage to Sextus Propertius for a poor translation rather than an "imitation" in the neo-classical sense because the allusion to Wordsworth and the parody of Yeats which help to identify the work as an imitation are obscure and easily misinterpreted. (J.C.O.)

P1047 Sullivan, J. P., "The Poet as Translator: Ezra Pound and Sextus Propertius," Kenyon Review, 23:462-81, Summer, 1961.

Homage to Sextus Propertius is a creative adaptation of Propertius in contemporary terms; it involves an implied criticism of the Roman poet, a Poundian defense of the poet's freedom, and an interesting application of modern poetic techniques to the problem of translation. (G.S.)

P1048 Sullivan, J. P., "Pound's Homage to Sextus Propertius," Agenda, 4:57-61, October-November, 1965.

"Pound's Homage to Sextus Propertius was in many ways ahead of its time and its revolutionary character undoubtedly led to the gross misunderstanding and critical dispraise it received." (H.S.)

P1049 Sullivan, J. P., "Pound's Homage to Propertius: The Structure of a Mask," Essays in Criticism, 10:239-50, July, 1960.

Homage to Propertius examined in relationship to Mauberley shows that "it was the Roman poet who first became the mask through which Pound registered his protest at the monstrous state of society and culture in which he found himself living." (G.O.)

HUGH SELWYN MAUBERLEY

P1050 Bueltmann, Faith, "Mauberley's 'Medallion'," Notes and Queries, 205:149, April, 1960.

A possible source for the first line of "Medallion" is George Meredith's descriptions of Clara Middleton in The Egoist. (W.G.F.)

P1051 Donoghue, Denis, "James's The Awkward Age and Pound's Mauberley," Notes and Queries, 17:49-50, February, 1970.

Pound's long essay on James in two 1918 issues of the Little Review suggest that his own Hugh Selwyn Mauberley was influenced by the satiric chapters of The Awkward Age. (K.H.B.)

P1052 Emslie, Macdonald, "Pound's Hugh Selwyn Mauberley, I, iii, 13-16," Explicator, 14: Item 26, January, 1956.

Tokalon, the trade name of inexpensive cosmetics, conveys modern commercialism of classical and Christian values. (B.K.)

P1053 French, A. L., "Mauberley: A Rejoinder," Essays in Criticism, 16:356-9, July, 1966.

"Pound's allusions [in Mauberley] are . . . a sort of cultural short-hand, based upon an unacceptably naive apprehension of the values involved." (H.S.)

P1054 French, A. L., "'Olympian Apathein': Pound's Hugh Selwyn Mauberley and Modern Poetry," Essays in Criticism, 15:428-45, October, 1965.

"The achievement of Mauberley (and also of The Waste Land) is supposed to be that they capture the mood of a whole society and civilization: the poet's response to his age is universalised and becomes profoundly representative. . . . Eliot and Pound . . . had made a modern poetry possible, [and] had shown young poets ways . . . to come to grips with modern life. . . ." (H.S.)

P1055 Giovannini, G., "Pound's 'Hugh Selwyn Mauberley, I, iii, 22'," Explicator, 16: Item 35, March, 1958.

Though not tyrannical, our government is incapable of supporting culture, Pound asserts. (B.K.)

HUGH SELWYN MAUBERLEY (cont'd)

P1056 Knox, George, "Glaucus in Hugh Selwyn Mauberley," English Studies, 45:236-7, June, 1964.

Allusions to Odysseus in Pound's Hugh Selwyn Mauberley are clear but "aspects of Glaucus legendry may also be detected." Pound's fascination with the word "glauque" and with eye-water imagery has been pointed out. Hugh Selwyn Mauberley "dramatizes the end of one stage in the pilgrimage and the start of another, a parable-quest of the alienated artist in the first two decades of the twentieth century." The deepest levels of the poem have not yet been read. (V.E.)

P1057 Malkoff, Karl, "Allusion as Irony: Pound's Use of Dante in Hugh Selwyn Mauberley," Minnesota Review, 7:81-8, No. 1-2, 1967.

". . . there is one set of allusions in particular which . . . provides a consistent ironic framework for the poem. . . . These allusions make it possible to read Hugh Selwyn Mauberley as a parody of Dante's Commedia." (D.P.)

P1058 Reiss, Christopher, "In Defense of Mauberley," Essays in Criticism, 16:351-5, July, 1966.

"A. L. French's attack on Hugh Selwyn Mauberley (Essays in Criticism, October, 1965) is more a symptom of a change in critical fashion than anything else." French's criticisms of Pound (his "obscurity," "aloofness" and "futility") are nothing more than "misconceptions." (H.S.)

P1059 Sanavio, Piero, "Hugh Selwyn Mauberley," Nuova Corrente, 5-6: 165-83, January-June, 1956.

The technical devices of Mauberley, synthesized from the Epitaphe of Corbiere, L'Ode pour l'election de son sepulchre of Ronsard and Propertius, via Laforgue, indicate the importance of the poem as the first positive step towards the structure of the Cantos, and as an influence on W. C. Williams, T. S. Eliot, E. Sitwell, and W. H. Auden. (V.R.)

HUGH SELWYN MAUBERLEY (cont'd)

P1060 Spanos, William V., "The Modulating Voice of Hugh Selwyn Mauberley," Wisconsin Studies in Contemporary Literature, 6:73-96, Winter-Spring, 1965.

"Once it is acknowledged that the modulating voice of the epitaph is Mauberley's, we are in a position to discover the tight dramatic logic that it gives to the entire sequence." The poem is neither personal confession nor parody, but "catharsis, or, more precisely, . . . exorcism by externalization." (W.G.F.)

P1061 Sutton, Walter, "Mauberley, The Waste Land, and the Problem of Unified Form," Contemporary Literature, 9:15-35, Winter, 1968.

Pound's Hugh Selwyn Mauberley, rather than the Cantos, is most appropriately compared with Eliot's The Waste Land. Eliot's work has greater formal unity, but Pound's in general outlook is "more in keeping with the intellectual temper of the twentieth century." (P.J.R.)

IN A STATION OF THE METRO

P1062 Iwamoto, Yoshiyuki, "Pound's 'In a Station of the Metro'," Explicator, 19: Item 30, February, 1961.

"The precarious position of the petals to the bough symbolizes the predicament in which man finds himself . . . lonely, isolated from others, and yet living with them." (B.K.)

P1063 Lasser, Michael L., "Pound's 'In a Station of the Metro'," Explicator, 19: Item 30, February, 1961.

"The diverse petals, multiform and various, and the almost onomatopoetically characterized bough are infinitely more real, more individualized and personalized, than the blank faces. . . . Pound reveals nothing of didactic or aesthetic grandeur here, but he does accomplish a quick, pleasing . . . flirtation with poetry." (D.P.)

NEAR PERIGORD

P1064 Connolly, Thomas E., "Ezra Pound's 'Near Perigord': The Background of a Poem," Comparative Literature, 8:110-21, Spring, 1956.

" 'Near Perigord' . . . is an attempt by Pound to plumb the hidden depths of the boisterous, twelfth-century, fighting baron poet," Bertran de Born, by examining one of Bertran's own poems from three points of view: first historically, then imaginatively, and finally dramatically. (G.M.P.)

P1065 Schmidt, Gerd, "Ezra Pound: 'Near Perigord'," Die Neueren Sprachen, 18:502-12, October, 1969.

"We want to attempt to redraw the twisted lines of the poem in order to arrive in this manner at a better understanding of its complex structure." (J.R.R.)

A PACT

P1066 D'Avanzo, Mario L., "Pound's 'A Pact'," Explicator, 24: Item 51, February, 1966.

"The poem is actually a very carefully organized expression of the organic relationship Pound's poetry has with Whitman's." (D.P.)

PAPYRUS

P1067 Collinge, N. E., "Gongyla and Mr. Pound," Notes and Queries, 5:265-6, June, 1958.

In "Papyrus" Pound "is guilty, under the heading of academic faults, only of a conscious exploitation of an accidentally marred original poem--and perhaps of confusing parchment with papyrus." (H.S.)

P1068 Kenner, Hugh, "The Muse in Tatters," Agenda, 6:43-61, No. 2, 1968.

"The Sapphic fragment concerning Gongyla, which in 1916 yielded Pound his 'Papyrus' is actually parchment, one of three such parchment scraps, torn by good fortune from a book destroyed centuries ago. . . . They were salvaged from among masses of illegible papyrus scraps that came to Berlin from Egypt in 1896." (H.S.)

PAPYRUS (cont'd)

P1069 Kenner, Hugh, "The Muse in Tatters," Arion, 7:212-33, No. 1-2, 1968.

[This is a consideration of the Sapphic fragments which provided Pound his materials for "Papyrus."] (D.P.)

PORTRAIT D'UNE FEMME

P1070 Giannone, Richard J., "Eliot's 'Portrait of a Lady' and Pound's 'Portrait D'Une Femme'," Twentieth Century Literature, 5:131-4, October, 1959.

"Pound struggles vigorously for intensity by paring away the excesses and trimmings, what he understands to be undramatic, and treats only the special, vital, dramatic moment. Eliot's poem shows a striving for tightly packed poetry but embodies matters associated with the central situation--soft ironies, motives, responses and his mingling of a very subtle observation with the unexpected backhanded cliché." (D.P.)

THE RETURN

P1071 Israel, Calvin, "Imitation and Meaning in Ezra Pound's 'The Return'," Lock Haven Review, No. 8, pp. 31-6, 1966.

"Since Pound's poem is in one movement of free verse, with no concession to [Henri de] Régnier's frequent rhymes, and in short-ness and exactness corresponds to the theories of the Imagists, it is difficult to deny the similar rhythms, line cuts, manner of repetition, corresponding expressions, and other echoes. The stylistic similarities [between Regnier's work and Pound's 'The Return'] are apparent. . . ." (H.S.)

THE SEAFARER

P1072 Bessinger, J. B., "The Oral Text of Ezra Pound's 'The Seafarer'," Quarterly Journal of Speech, 47:173-7, April, 1961.

Pound's ". . . reading of 'The Seafarer' has the added value . . . of throwing a little light on the author's attitude to the poem considered purely as a translation." The recordings preserve with evident fidel-ity the poet's reading style, the measured, moderate tempo of which adapts easily to sardonic or elegiac, energetic or muted variations in tone." (H.S.)

SEPARATION ON THE RIVER KIANG

P1073 Graham, D. B., "From Chinese to English: Ezra Pound's 'Separation on the River Kiang'," Literature East and West, 13:182-95, 1969.

Pound's "Separation on the River Kiang" is a translation which "preserves whatever factual content of the Chinese original is poetically useful and discards those details that are not." (H.S.)

THE WOMEN OF TRACHIS

P1074 Dick, Bernard F., "Sophocles Com-Pounded," Classical World, 54:236-7, 1961.

Pound's Women of Trachis, a "version" of Sophocles's Trachiniae, "is not tragedy at all, but, despite the author's pretensions of cosmic symbolism, emerges as a burlesque of Greek tragic poetry--caustic, pedestrian, and often in dubious taste." (H.S.)

P1075 Earp, Frank Russell, "The Women of Trachis: A Symposium," Pound Newsletter, No. 5, p. 4, January, 1955.

"It is a good and vigorous translation and probably would go well on the stage. But the language of the dialogues hardly suggests Sophocles, whose language is as near perfect as human language can be, given the conventions of Athenian tragedy." (D.P.)

P1076 Lattimore, Richard, "The Women of Trachis: A Symposium," Pound Newsletter, No. 5, pp. 4-5, January, 1955.

"The values of the original are consistently sacrificed to those of the translator. . . . Sophocles does not come through at all. The effect is that of a kind of serious burlesque . . . an adroit, stimulating and consistent adaptation." (D.P.)

P1077 Mason, H. H., "Creative Translation: Ezra Pound's Women of Trachis," Cambridge Quarterly, 4:244-72, No. 3, 1970.

"The compliment that Pound deserves is to have his version properly edited with a detailed running commentary. For . . . the surprising merits of Women of Trachis will come out best when the Greek text is printed opposite Pound's and the felicities of his translation are brought out locally, almost in every word. For then I think it will appear how much creative thinking has gone into Women of Trachis." (D.P.)

THE WOMEN OF TRACHIS (cont'd)

P1078 Peachy, Frederic, "The Women of Trachis: A Symposium,"
Pound Newsletter, No. 5, pp. 6-8, January, 1955.

Pound "seems incapable of entering, as Sophocles could, into the
lives and thoughts and feelings of diverse characters: for they must
all conform to Pound's way. . . . Though the version is marred by
the slovenliness of the Cantos, it can never be that bad. For the
ever young and vigorous apprentice is working this time from a
model . . . pretty near perfection. . . . Pound, in teaching us how
to read . . . has also taught us how to read Pound." (D.P.)

P1079 Sutherland, Donald, "Ezra Pound or Sophocles," Colorado Quarterly,
8:182-91, Autumn, 1959.

Ezra Pound, an "amateur of genius," has given us a version of
Women of Trachis ("This particular classic can fairly enough be said
to be negligible or Pound's use of it vicious, and the Culture to which
it contributes neither ours nor living,") which "will not really dull
the contemporaneity of Sophocles, try as it does." (J.N.P.)

POURRAT, HENRI

P1080 Temmer, Mark J., "Henri Pourrat's Trésor des contes," French
Review, 38:42-51, October, 1964.

Pourrat failed to reproduce the vital quality of the folktale "because
his conception of the Volkseele and the pastoral ideal were too
rudimentary and the embroidered mantle of folklore too thin to hide
his intellectual and artistic shortcomings." (R.B.W.)

POWELL, ANTHONY

P1081 Brooke, Jocelyn, "From Wauchop to Widmerpool," London Magazine,
7:60-4, September, 1960.

The characteristic of Powell's fiction that makes him so widely
respected is his deliberate rejection of all the time-honored tricks
of the novelist. (M.H.M.)

P1082 Herring, H. D., "Anthony Powell: A Reaction against Determinism,"
Ball State University Forum, 9:17-21, Winter, 1968.

In A Question of Upbringing, A Buyer's Market, The Acceptance
World and other works, Powell "embodies a fuller understanding of
the true limitations of human beings in relation to their opportunities
for choice and action than many . . . writers who have reacted against
the idea of man as wholly controlled by pre-established conditions."
(H.S.)

P1083 Hynes, Sam, "Novelist of Society," Commonweal, 70:396-7,
July 31, 1959.

"Powell's preoccupation with time, and the way in which he moves
backward and forward over social causes and effects, gives his
novels a Proustian form. . . . Like Proust (and like James) Powell
organizes his meditations around social occasions, each occasion
stimulating recollections and speculations about the characters
involved, and their relations to each other." (H.S.)

P1084 Powell, Anthony, "Anthony Powell: Some Questions Answered,"
Anglo-Welsh Review, 14:77-9, 1964.

[In a letter to Roland Mathias, Powell discusses his family genealogy
and his "associations with Wales and the Welsh March."] (H.S.)

P1085 Radner, Sanford, "Powell's Early Novels: A Study in Point of View,"
Renascence, 16:194-200, Summer, 1964.

Increased recognition came with Anthony Powell's series called A
Dance to the Music of Time, but the author has been writing novels
since the early 30's. These novels are virtually unknown in America.
Of his first three novels, Afternoon Men, Venusburg, and From a
View to a Death, the latter "may very well be the best of early
Powell." Powell's last prewar novel, What's Become of Waring,
shows a definite advance in technique. His early novels clearly
indicate how the author "struggled with the problem of point of view"
before finding the solution he used in later works. (V.E.)

P1086 Russell, John, "Quintet from the '30s: Anthony Powell," Kenyon
Review, 27:698-726, Autumn, 1965.

The first novels that Powell published in the 30s are differentiated
from the later series by "highly finished short scenes and scrolls of
dialogue." The wide array of characters is unified by a quest for
power. (G.S.)

P1087 Voorhees, Richard J., "Anthony Powell: The First Phase,"
Prairie Schooner, 28:337-44, Winter, 1954.

The characters in Afternoon Men (1931), Venusberg (1932), and
From a View to a Death (1933), suggest characters from the early
Aldous Huxley, without possessing, however, their wit and learning.
Agents and Patients (1936) mixes comedy with neurosis and stupidity.
Two novels published in the Fifties "are almost pedantically elaborate
investigations of the past." The early novels display tragedy and
comedy growing out of the same materials, showing that "if human
beings are preposterous they are also pathetic, that if their lives are
farcical they are also deadly serious." (J.L.B.)

THE MUSIC OF TIME

P1088 Bergonzi, Bernard, "Anthony Powell: 9/12," Critical Quarterly,
11:76-86, Spring, 1969.

"The ultimate question is, how far can The Music of Time continue
as the great comic work that it has, so far, essentially been? And,
then, how can it end?" Powell's "sceptical, empirical, untheoretical
vision does not seem capable of a final, large-scale resolution. With
this conviction, one regards the whole work at the three-quarter
point with . . . a certain muted disquiet about its future." (H.S.)

P1089 Davis, Douglas M., "An Interview with Anthony Powell, Frome,
England, June 1962," College English, 24:533-6, April, 1963.

The Music of Time will occupy twelve volumes. After The Kindly
Ones, which brings the series to the outbreak of World War II,
"there will be three novels on the war and three after. What I hope
to do . . . is show the changes in English society . . . from 1914 to
the present, but that is only secondary to the investigation of human
character. As for Widmerpool, I don't think I ever planned to have
him take 'charge' the way he has. But I don't mind, really." (D.P.)

P1090 Hall, James, "The Uses of Polite Surprise: Anthony Powell,"
Essays in Criticism, 12:167-83, April, 1962.

It is essential to "look at the where of its [The Music of Time]
comedy--specifically, at the dramatic conflicts and the underlying
sense of character and society." (H.S.)

THE MUSIC OF TIME   (cont'd)

P1091   McCall, Raymond G., "Anthony Powell's Gallery," <u>College English</u>, 27:227-32, December, 1965.

In <u>A Dance to the Music of Time</u> Anthony Powell "dramatizes changes in the manners of English middle and upper classes effected by two world wars. . . ." The character Jenkins, who appears throughout the series is endowed with a "strong sense of pictorial composition and the ability to 'frame' episodes." Art and painter images are always associated with Jenkins. Characters are often described as resembling subjects of paintings. The allusions to art in the novels "attest to the human desire to discover order in the welter of experience." (V.E.)

P1092   Mizener, Arthur, "A Dance to the Music of Time: The Novels of Anthony Powell," <u>Kenyon Review</u>, 22:79-92, Winter, 1960.

In his <u>The Music of Time</u> Powell shows the ludicrousness and underlying sadness of people in a decaying twentieth century, making his point not through dogma or abstraction but through "beautifully realized" human characters, rich images, and a meaningfully loose design. (G.S.)

P1093   Quesenbery, W. D., Jr., "Anthony Powell: The Anatomy of Decay," <u>Critique: Studies in Modern Fiction</u>, 7:5-26, Spring, 1964.

"Casual and episodic as <u>The Music of Time</u> appears to be, it is in fact a disciplined and complexly organized work." Through the "brief lives" of his characters, "Powell explores the two major movements of the age: the decline of British power and prestige and changes in the social structure of English life." (W.G.F.)

P1094   Radner, Sanford, "The World of Anthony Powell," <u>Claremont Quarterly</u>, 10:41-7, No. 2, 1963.

"Powell . . . has created a rich and variegated world, even though he apparently concerns himself with only a narrow segment of English upper class society. . . . Powell's is the most comprehensive world created by a twentieth century novelist writing in English. The evidence for this theory is Powell's series of novels, <u>Dance to the Music of Time</u>." (H.S.)

THE MUSIC OF TIME   (cont'd)

P1095   Ruoff, Gene W., "Social Mobility and the Artist in Manhattan Transfer and The Music of Time," Wisconsin Studies in Contemporary Literature, 5:64-76, Winter-Spring, 1964.

Dos Passos's and Powell's seemingly disparate novels are basically alike in using society in flux as their subject matter and "particularly in their presentation of the artist's reaction to a social order that is constantly breaking apart and realigning." (W.G.F.)

P1096   Vinson, James, "Anthony Powell's Music of Time," Perspective, 10:146-52, Summer-Autumn, 1958.

"In examining The Music of Time, comparison is instructive with that twentieth century classic of social decay, Proust's Remembrance of Things Past. Both are told from a first-person point of view, both create a richly diverse upper-middle and upper class society; both are concerned with the decay of that society and the workings of time towards that decay; both deal with pattern and shifting relationships in that society." (H.S.)

P1097   Voorhees, Richard J., "The Music of Time: Themes and Variations," Dalhousie Review, 42:313-21, Autumn, 1962.

Powell's fiction falls into two periods, the division occurring with his non-fictional study of John Aubrey. (R.K.)

P1098   Woodward, A. G., "The Novels of Anthony Powell," English Studies in Africa, 10:117-28, September, 1967.

". . . the whole tendency of . . . [Powell's] later and major work, the sequence of novels entitled The Music of Time, shows a resolute avoidance of any slanted, pre-determined scheme into which people and events are to be fitted." (H.S.)

P1099   Zigerell, James J., "Anthony Powell's Music of Time: Chronicle of a Declining Establishment," Twentieth Century Literature, 12:138-46, October, 1966.

A series flawed by a general slackness in design, Powell's Music of Time is insufficiently assertive. The main character, Nicholas Jenkins "does not stand as a character whose changes of outlook and fortune and whose growth in maturity fully engage a reader's sympathetic attention." (D.P.)

POWERS, JAMES FARL

P1100 Hagopian, John V., "The Fathers of J. F. Powers," <u>Studies in Short Fiction</u>, 5:139-53, Winter, 1968.

Although one of J. F. Powers's characters states that all problems are at bottom theological, the author "does not as a rule deal directly with theological problems." Powers's first clerical story, "Lions, Harts, Leaping Does," considered by many to be Powers's greatest, is the most "tenderly elegaic" of his stories. In "Prince of Darkness" the tone is more "viciously satiric." While the first story portrays a "lean and saintly cloistered friar, whose only desire is to be worthy of God's approval," the second story is of a "fat, boorish, incompetent curate . . . whose fervent desire is to find a secure niche. . . ." (V.E.)

P1101 Hertzel, Leo J., "Brother Juniper, Father Urban and the Unworldly Tradition," <u>Renascence</u>, 17:207-10, 215, Summer, 1965.

"Much of the fiction of J. F. Powers may be viewed as an exploration of the prudence of religious practice in our time over against the extravagant, perhaps extreme, Christian tradition of the past." (S.A.)

P1102 Jacobsen, Josephine, "A Catholic Quartet," <u>Christian Scholar</u>, 47:139-54, Summer, 1964.

"Each of these [Catholic] writers comes to the living material from a totally diverse angle; each has a characteristic or dominant approach. At the risk of oversimplification, it is possible to say that Muriel Spark's implementation is that of style, Greene's that of paradox, Mr. Powers's that of discipline and Miss O'Connor's that of mystery." (D.P.)

P1103 Malloy, Sister M. Kristin, O. S. B., "The Catholic and Creativity: J. F. Powers," <u>American Benedictine Review</u>, 15:63-80, March, 1964.

[In this interview, which concentrates on the philosophy and the authorship of J. F. Powers, he states that he has avoided "the usual kind of thing, <u>Elmer Gantry</u>, <u>Going My Way</u>, or <u>The Cardinal</u>, as the case may be. I might avail myself in a general way of the feelings readers have about such clerical characters, but I would never go at it like that. . . ."] (D.P.)

P1104 Phelps, Donald, "Reasonable, Holy and Living," Minnesota Review, 9:57-62, No. 1, 1969.

J. F. Powers "is the only American Catholic author . . . who has mastered comedy of manners within a specifically Catholic terrain. . . . We must not mistake the smallness of Powers's focus, which is the smallness . . . of stringent compression. . . . The cardinal grace involved here is Powers's submission of his art, of his intelligence, to the imminence of his faith." (D.P.)

P1105 Poss, Stanley, J. F. Powers: The Gin of Irony," Twentieth Century Literature, 14:65-74, July, 1968.

The chief theme in J. F. Powers's short stories and novels takes the form of a dialogue between a Secular Wise Man and a Fool of God; in Morte D'Urban, Father Urban is both. "In short Powers's works reveal a fortunate though somewhat paradoxical blend of serious, perhaps monumental themes and a dry de-romanticized, ironic treatment." (D.P.)

P1106 Quinn, Sister M. Bernetta, D. S. F., "View From a Rock: The Fiction of Flannery O'Connor and J. F. Powers," Critique: Studies in Modern Fiction, 2:19-27, Fall, 1958.

Writing from the Catholic point of view provides Flannery O'Connor and J. F. Powers with "a vantage point in the universe." Yet for both these artists, "the exercise of their craft is a literary, not a therapeutic, matter. Without trying to remedy it . . . they record what they see, though there is a difference, in Miss O'Connor's favor, in the depths to which they see." (G.O.)

P1107 Scouflas, George, "J. F. Powers: On the Vitality of Disorder," Critique: Studies in Modern Fiction, 2:41-58, Fall, 1958.

The countering motifs of order and disorder are of primary significance in nearly all of Powers's stories. The Church represents an established pattern of order; opposed to it is the disorder of the "world." (G.O.)

P1108 Sisk, John P., "The Complex Moral Vision of J. F. Powers," Critique: Studies in Modern Fiction, 2:28-40, Fall, 1958.

J. F. Powers has the rare gift in a modern writer--"the ability to imagine virtue--but he also has the ability to portray virtue in its complex relations with evil . . . [and] the ability to confront ambivalence." (G.O.)

P1109 Steichen, Donna M., "J. F. Powers and the Noonday Devil,"
American Benedictine Review, 20:528-51, 1969.

"Powers's acedy has been a misfortune for the literary world not
because of its effect on his viewpoint . . . but because it seems to
have destroyed the impetus that kept him at work, and has threatened
to silence his remarkable talent. It is not only his characters whom
he has come to see as doomed to failure; he has made it clear that he
regards it as a central truth about life." (D.P.)

P1110 Wedge, George F., "Two Bibliographies: Flannery O'Connor, J. F.
Powers," Critique: Studies in Modern Fiction, 2:59-70, Fall, 1958.

"Both bibliographies follow the same plan: they list (1) books, (2)
fiction in magazines, (3) articles and reviews by Flannery O'Connor
or J. F. Powers, (4) bibliographical material and (5) articles or
parts of books about Miss O'Connor or Mr. Powers." (D.A.B.)

THE FORKS

P1111 Kelly, Richard, "Father Eudix, the Judge and the Judged: An
Analysis of J. F. Powers's 'The Forks'," University Review,
35:316-8, June, 1969.

In "The Forks" "Powers has placed in a rectory an old worldly
traditionalist and a young, idealistic radical--and the drama that
unfolds from their interaction is what the story is about. On the
surface, Powers seems to be satirizing the worldly Monsignor and
lauding the saintly curate, but . . . Father Eudix, like his biblical
counterpart who foolishly buried his one talent, is found wanting in
his stewardship." (D.P.)

KEYSTONE

P1112 Kirvan, John J., C. S. P., "Ostergothenburg Revisited," Catholic
World, 198:308-13, February, 1964.

"A proper understanding of the more important incidents [in the short
story 'Keystone'] would seem to be the most direct route to the meaning of the story. One especially, the building of a new cathedral,
would seem to illuminate not only this story but the entire body of
Powers's work." (H.S.)

MORTE D'URBAN

P1113 Bates, Barclay W., "Flares of Special Grace: The Orthodoxy of
J. F. Powers," Midwest Quarterly, 11:91-106, Autumn, 1969.

". . . the burden of this paper will be that Morte D'Urban does indeed
answer questions--and answers them according to orthodox Catholic
belief, which many readers find incomprehensible." (S.T.C.)

P1114 Collignon, Joseph P., "Powers's Morte D'Urban: A Layman's
Indictment," Renascence, 16:20-1, 51-2, Fall, 1963.

In Morte D'Urban, a major American novel, "there is no suggestion,"
as there are in Powers's earlier short stories, "that Father Urban's
life may have been of value in spite of setbacks, no hint that the Church
will march triumphant. . . ." This novel lacks "the quality of hope."
(S.A.)

P1115 Dolan, Paul J., "God's Crooked Lines: Powers's Morte D'Urban,"
Renascence, 21:95-102, Winter, 1969.

By the end we "have seen all we need to understand the man and his
complex relations with his world and himself. As superior he is as
remote and mysterious and alien as the Latin with which he is
invested. He has learned, and so have we, something about being a
winner. (S.A.)

P1116 Hagopian, John V., "Irony and Involution in J. F. Powers's Morte
D'Urban," Contemporary Literature, 9:151-71, Spring, 1968.

"Drained of the distorting perspective of Father Urban's hilarious
wit and the rich evocative details, the plot [of Morte D'Urban] can
be seen as the experience of a man who uses the priesthood as an
instrument for worldly success until a traumatic event shocks him
into awareness that compromise with the mammon of iniquity is
morally and spiritually degrading. Then, as his mortal self declines,
he gradually sets his own soul in order, without false piety and even
without conscious deliberation." (D.P.)

P1117 Hynes, Joseph, "Father Urban's Renewal: J. F. Powers's Difficult
Precision," Modern Language Quarterly, 29:450-66, December,
1968.

"Morte D'Urban is a series of trials manifesting and justifying title
and epilogue"; the middle chapters of the novel are unified, cumulative,
tragicomic, leading logically to the "morte." (G.S.)

MORTE D'URBAN (cont'd)

P1118 O'Brien, Charles F., "Morte D'Urban and the Catholic Church in America," Discourse, 12:324-8, Summer, 1969.

In Morte D'Urban "Powers uses the Arthurian motif to render the historical and cultural themes. Much of Father Urban's 'quest,' in terms of the Arthurian motif, involves the search for acceptance. Many of his 'trials' likewise reflect the course of traditional Catholicism in adjusting to American society. Father Urban is, like Arthur, a mythic hero and Morte D'Urban is a mythic history of the Catholic Church in America." (D.P.)

P1119 Sandra, Sister Mary, S. S. A., "The Priest-Hero in Modern Fiction," Personalist, 46:527-42, Autumn, 1965.

In Edwin O'Connor's The Edge of Sadness, J. F. Powers's Morte D'Urban, Bernanos's The Diary of a Country Priest, and Graham Greene's The Power and the Glory "the common conflict between the priest-hero and his culture is, in reality, a complex of conflicts resulting from the interdependence of a man and his culture. . . . For the priest-hero in these novels, coming to terms with his culture is an essential part of coming to terms with himself." (D.P.)

P1120 Stewart, D. H., "J. F. Powers's Morte D'Urban as Western," Western American Literature, 5:31-44, Spring, 1970.

"The difficulty of Morte D'Urban lies in its complexity. . . . We must begin with the proposition that Powers has attempted to weave two very different life-styles simultaneously into his narrative: the WASPish 'American way of life' and ecclesiastical Catholicism." (H.S.)

THE VALIANT WOMAN

P1121 Barnet, Sylvan, "Powers's 'The Valiant Woman'," Explicator, 20: Item 56, March, 1962.

The title is a quotation from the Douay version of Proverbs XXXI, a picture of the ideal Hebrew wife: Mrs. Stoner is obviously and ironically a "valiant woman." (B.K.)

POWYS, JOHN COWPER

P1122 Adkinson, R. V., "A Short Guide to Powysland," Revue de Langues Vivantes, 32:78-81, 1966.

Of the "three great narratives" of John Cowper Powys, "Wolf Solent is packed with dense, suggestive imagery. . . ." In A Glastonbury Romance "romance and nature are made 'to blend into a more general and unmediated occultism.' In Jobber Skald the conflict of mind and nature does not seem so fierce. . . ." Additionally, "during the nineteen-thirties Powys published his autobiography and several philosophical works . . . [and] his fiction at this time, too, has a denser metaphysical content." (D.P.)

P1123 André, Robert, "La Sensibilité de John Cowper Powys," La Nouvelle Revue Française, No. 152, pp. 299-304, August, 1965.

Obsessed by sadistic impulses, Powys developed a sensitivity which surpassed that of Proust, refusing to dissect the various reasons for the actions of his characters but recording faithfully the impressions and the nuances. (T.T.B.)

P1124 Aury, Dominique, "John Cowper Powys," La Nouvelle Revue Française, No. 129, pp. 495-501, September, 1963.

Finally released from his sadistic obsessions of rapes, tortures and massacres, Powys retained that ferocious and prodigious joy manifest through all his work. Poet, philosopher or novelist, he is the prophet of a single idea: that one can be happy. (T.T.B.)

P1125 Aury, Dominique, "Reading Powys," Review of English Literature, 4:33-7, January, 1963.

J. C. Powys's novel Jobber Skald tells a "confused story . . . impossible to summarize clearly from memory alone." What remains after reading Powys is "illumination," the "light of another kind of life." In Powys there is "something mad which breaks through the fixed forms of reality to reveal the burning heart." His work "quivers . . . with this universal raging love for all beings and created things." His work changes and in some way liberates the reader and "one is held captive for ever." (V.E.)

P1126 Churchill, R. C., "Not Least Llewelyn," <u>Review of English</u>
<u>Literature</u>, 4:68-75, January, 1963.

"John's personal influence upon Llewelyn was profound, and they
were both . . . very subjective writers. But if we follow their work
in chronological order, from their one effort in collaboration,
<u>Confessions of Two Brothers</u> (1916) onwards, it is not long before
we find their paths diverging, if not in all matters, yet in some of
the most important. . . ." (H.S.)

P1127 De Wet, Oloff, "Visit to John Cowper Powys," <u>Texas Quarterly</u>,
11:91-116, Autumn, 1968.

[This is an account of a meeting and conversation with Powys and
with Phyllis Playter at Powys's home; followed by a description of
the completion of a sculpture (death mask) upon Powys's death.]
(H.S.)

P1128 Gregory, Alyse, "A Famous Family," <u>London Magazine</u>, 5:44-53,
March, 1958.

[This is biographical information about members of the Powys
family, especially about the female members, i. e., Gertrude,
Philippa, Lucy and Marian. "Legends about the male members of
the family have sprouted and burgeoned . . . but no one, as far as I
have been able to determine, has written of the girls."] (H.S.)

P1129 Gresset, Michel, "John Cowper Powys," <u>La Nouvelle Revue</u>
<u>Française</u>, No. 182, pp. 290-305, February, 1968.

Powys in 1929 was reputed a belated beginner of 57 years of age,
with the publication of <u>Wolf Solent</u>, the first of his great novels.
However, with <u>Wood and Stone</u> (1915), <u>Rodmoor</u> (1916) we have
already the psychological molds into which he pours his own subjective material, a romantic and even philosophical projection of
the tension inherent to the personality of the author. (T.T.B.)

P1130 Hansbury, Michael, "John Cowper Powys and Some Catholic
Contacts," <u>Month</u>, 30:299-303, November, 1963.

"By choosing Polytheism [Powys] evaded having to reconcile an
Almighty, All-holy Ruler of the world with the existence of the evil
that so distressed him." (R.J.G.)

P1131   Miller, Henry, "The Immortal Bard," Review of English Literature, 4:21-4, January, 1963.

"The secret of his joyous wisdom may be found in his little books which deal with life and art, with everyday philosophy and the cultivation of the sensual nature." Wolf Solent, the Autobiography and A Glastonbury Romance are such works. (H.S.)

P1132   Peate, Iorwerth C., "John Cowper Powys: Letter Writer," Review of English Literature, 4:38-40, January, 1963.

[This is correspondence between I. C. Peate and Powys 1944-1947. Letters from Powys include mention of Albert Schweitzer, religion, God, Christian names, writing, and speaking.] (H.S.)

P1133   Priestley, J. B., "The Happy Introvert," Review of English Literature, 4:25-32, January, 1963.

"The unhappy introvert in modern literature . . . is to be expected. What is unexpected and so really surprising is a writer of power . . . who seems as happy as the rest seem unhappy. John Cowper Powys is an original, perhaps in this sense a unique figure in modern writing, because he can be fairly described as a happy introvert." A Philosophy of Solitude, In Spite of and his Autobiography are "happy" works. (H.S.)

P1134   Robillard, Douglas, "Landscape with Figures: The Early Fiction of John Cowper Powys," Studies in the Literary Imagination, 1:51-8, October, 1968.

"One of Powys's excellences as a writer is his ability to describe large, impressive, panoramic scenes, full of people, movement, contrast, and color. . . . Powys uses such scenes [in Woodland Stone, Rodmoor, Ducdame, Wolf Solent and A Glastonbury Romance] as focal points for the meeting of opposing forces and ideas, for the confrontation of friends and enemies, and for the dramatic exposition of theme." (H.S.)

P1135   Tolchard, Clifford, "Letters from John Cowper Powys," Meanjin Quarterly, 23:89-92, March, 1964.

[These are four letters September 10, 1942, February 1, 1943, March 2, 1943 and January 21, 1957 from Powys to Clifford Tolchard. ". . .John Cowper is the letter writer par excellence."] (H.S.)

P1136 Wilson, Angus, "'Mythology' in John Cowper Powys's Novels," Review of English Literature, 4:9-20, January, 1963.

". . . both Porius [Porius] and Wolf [Wolf Solent] seem to participate very deeply in John Cowper Powys's own thoughts, feelings and imaginations, so that the reader is inevitably drawn to conclude that the highly subjective metaphysical views of these two heroes . . . must reflect the inner life of the author." (H.S.)

A GLASTONBURY ROMANCE

P1137 Brooke, Jocelyn, "On Re-reading A Glastonbury Romance," London Magazine, 3:44-51, April, 1956.

Long-winded, wasteful of his dramatic effects, and heavily indebted to numerous writers, John Cowper Powys nevertheless achieved in A Glastonbury Romance the full flowering of his genius for inspired nonsense, imaginative intensity, and skillful caricature. The novel may be fairly described as a masterpiece, "the great English epic of sensuality and cerebral perversion." (D.B.D.)

P1138 Knight, G. Wilson, "Lawrence, Joyce, and Powys," Essays in Criticism, 11:403-17, October, 1961.

"With Powys's 'massed weight,' 'world' and 'release' we may compare Joyce's word-play on terrestrial and feminine 'hemispheres' to define Bloom's ultimate solution . . .; Mellors's praise of a 'bottom as could hold the world up' in Lady Chatterley's Lover. . . . Powys's prose unfurls with an unhurried and unperturbed ease that goes far to witness its authority; and on the strength of his revelatory passages the tormenting obsessions of Swift, the tragic lives of Byron and Wilde, the sex-agonies of Lawrence and obscenities of Joyce, may all receive, in retrospect, a new sympathy and justification." (D.P.)

LUCIFER

P1139 Anderson, John Redwood, "John Cowper Powys's Lucifer: An Appreciation," Dublin Magazine, 32:37-43, July, 1957.

". . . in this conjunction of Chance, ultimate Annihilation, and the Will, Lucifer, like all its predecessors, save alone the Divine Comedy, and Faust, has fallen into the pit that lies in wait for all those who attempt this greatest kind of poetry--the philosophical kind: the pit of self-contradiction." (H.S.)

OWEN GLENDOWER

P1140 Brebner, John A., "Owen Glendower: The Pursuit of the Fourth Dimension," Anglo-Welsh Review, 18:207-16, February, 1970.

"Although subtitled 'An Historical Novel,' Owen Glendower cannot be defined easily by the neat little definitions of most literary criticism. The magnitude of its scope, the complexity of its vision, and the ingenuity of its technique defy facile categorization." (H.S.)

P1141 Knight, G. Wilson, "Owen Glendower," Review of English Literature, 4:41-52, January, 1963.

J. C. Powys's Owen Glendower shows "amazing artistry"; it is a work in which historical exactitude is accompanied by a profound metaphysic. "People in Owen Glendower are characterized by their eyes." The female characters are "not outstandingly drawn," but the male characters are "varied and rich." Many of the main characters appear in bisexual terms. Natural descriptions are "exactly integrated into the story," as where Harlech is described as blending sun and sea, which can be compared to the story's blending of "upstanding action and elemental endurance." (V.E.)

POWYS, LLEWELYN

P1142 Churchill, R. C., "Not Least Llewelyn," Review of English Literature, 4:68-75, January, 1963.

"John's personal influence upon Llewelyn was profound, and they were both . . . very subjective writers. But if we follow their work in chronological order, from their one effort in collaboration, Confessions of Two Brothers (1916) onwards, it is not long before we find their paths diverging, if not in all matters, yet in some of the most important. . . ." (H.S.)

P1143 Gregory, Alyse, "A Famous Family," London Magazine, 5:44-53, March, 1958.

[This is biographical information about members of the Powys family, especially about the female members, i. e., Gertrude, Philippa, Lucy and Marian. "Legends about the male members of the family have sprouted and burgeoned . . . but no one, as far as I have been able to determine, has written of the girls."] (H.S.)

POWYS, THEODORE FRANCIS

P1144 Buning, M., "Folly Down Revisited: Some New Light on T. F. Powys," English Studies, 50:588-97, December, 1969.

"As in William Faulkner, the strange people and situations of . . . [Powys's] novels assume symbolic qualities, and upon re-reading a mythopoeic pattern unfolds itself, held together by a distinctive poetic style and a vision of life at once profound and disturbing." (H.S.)

P1145 Carr, W. I., "T. F. Powys: A Comment," English, 15:8-12, Spring, 1964.

Some of the reasons for critical neglect of T. F. Powys may be ascribed to the "kind and degree of his originality." His work is isolated from everything except his own "Dorset experience." One must admit a similarity in Powys's villains in such novels as Mr. Weston's Good Wine and Innocent Birds. "At the centre of Powys's art there is the profoundest respect for human beings and the life they are given." Powys's individuality shows in the form and themes of his work. (V.E.)

P1146 Gregory, Alyse, "A Famous Family," London Magazine, 5:44-53, March, 1958.

[This is biographical information about members of the Powys family, especially about the female members, i. e., Gertrude, Philippa, Lucy and Marian. "Legends about the male members of the family have sprouted and burgeoned . . . but no one, as far as I have been able to determine, has written of the girls."] (H.S.)

P1147 Hopkins, Kenneth, "The Second Brother: A Note on T. F. Powys," Review of English Literature, 4:59-67, January, 1963.

"A reader of T. F. Powys must inevitably pause after a time to consider what manner of man this was, for writings so singular and strange must call up an interest in their creator. . . . his life affords scant material for biography . . . [but] his early essay Soliloquies of a Hermit . . . is a key to his character." (K.M.W.)

P1148 Pouillard, M., "T. F. Powys conférencier à Eastbourne 1902-03,"
Études Anglaises, 22:346-50, October-December, 1969.

"Theodore Francis Powys, unlike his brothers John and Llewelyn,
detested public speaking, even among close friends. . . . [His] life
[was] essentially secret and uneventful." It is thus interesting that
he taught history and literature most successfully at a school for
young girls in Eastbourne for two years. His experience was important in contributing to his views on pedagogy. Characteristically,
"when given a task T. F. Powys applied himself seriously." (D.P.)

P1149 Steinmann, Martin, Jr., "The Symbolism of T. F. Powys,"
Critique: Studies in Modern Fiction, 1:49-63, Summer, 1957.

"Of the Georgians, T. F. Powys is surely the furthest removed
from realism and naturalism and the farthest gone in symbolism"--
a symbolism "in a different tradition from that of the other
Georgians." (W.T.S.)

P1150 Steinmann, Martin, Jr., "Water and Animal Symbolism in T. F.
Powys," English Studies, 41:359-65, December, 1960.

"Powys's characters and his settings constitute an allegorical world
in which the interactions of symbolic characters in symbolic settings
figure a meaning: theme, rather than scientific law, is its master."
While water figures as a symbol of death, animals have a more
complex role: "they function figuratively . . . as well as literally
and, hence, symbolically." (K.M.W.)

MR. WESTON'S GOOD WINE

P1151 Riley, A. P., "The Original Ending of Mr. Weston's Good Wine,"
Review of English Literature, 8:49-55, April, 1967.

The revised conclusion in Powys's novel is far superior to the
original because "the allegory is effectively and coherently concluded
instead of being dropped short of completion." (S.T.C.)

PRADA, MANUEL GONZÁLEZ--See
GONZÁLEZ PRADA, MANUEL

PRADO NOGUEIRA, JOSÉ LUIS

P1152   Hernández, Antonio, "José Luis Prado Nogueira," La Estafeta
Literaria, No. 422, pp. 11-2, June 15, 1969.

Prado Nogueira's poetry is that of actuality. It is confessional and
dry, describing his customary world with equal despair and attention,
giving testimony of his time and his own situation in it. (T.T.B.)

P1153   López Anglada, Luis, et al, "Premios 'Estafeta Literaria' 1969,"
La Estafeta Literaria, No. 430, pp. 116-20, October 15, 1969.

[These are judgments and bibliography of the poet Prado Nogueira,
who was awarded the poetry prize for Despedida provisional.]
(T.T.B.)

PRAED, ROSA CAMPBELL

P1154   Bielenstein, Gabrielle Maupin, "Affinities for Henry James?"
Meanjin Quarterly, 16:196-9, June, 1957.

Henry James's The Portrait of a Lady and Rosa Praed's Affinities
"exhibit a conspicuous identity of plot and character." (D.P.)

PRATOLINI, VASCO

P1155   Rosengarten, Frank, "A Crucial Decade in the Career of Vasco
Pratolini (1932-1942)," Modern Language Notes, 79:28-46,
January, 1964.

Pratolini's writings on literary, political, and social topics in Il
Bargello (1932-1937), in Campo di Marte (1938-1939), and in such
magazines as Incontro and La Ruota (1940-1942) reveal the development of those "human and literary values that were to inspire his
creative work in the postwar years." (K.M.W.)

METELLO

P1156   Piroue, Georges, "Metello de Vasco Pratolini," Monde Nouveau
Paru, No. 102, pp. 103-6, July, 1956.

This novel attempts a certain definition of history; history not made
on the battlefields or in ceremonies, history not solely the province
of kings or heads of state. Pratolini, however, has not only de-
dramatized history, but literature as well. (E.L.)

UNA STORIA ITALIANA

P1157 Rosengarten, Frank, "Vasco Pratolini's Una storia italiana and the Question of Literary Realism," Italica, 40:62-72, March, 1963.

Vasco Pratolini's trilogy Una storia italiana (Metello, Lo scialo, and I fidanzati del mugnone) describes aspects of Italian life from 1875 to 1945. In his article "Questioni sul realismo" Pratolini defines the "method and purpose of realism" as being able to "uncover and reveal historical truth" and to "express this truth through characters." In Una storia italiana Pratolini sought to "move from intimate memories to chronicle to history" and to "discover through the character . . . the most profound secret, perhaps the essential truth," of Italy's national history. (V.E.)

PRATT, EDWIN JOHN

P1158 Cogswell, Fred, "E. J. Pratt's Literary Reputation," Canadian Literature, No. 19, pp. 6-12, Winter, 1964.

Speculation arises as to whether "Pratt's conjectured final position in the world of letters will ultimately be radically different" from Bliss Carman's. Both poets created a large amount of work of a "high degree of technical competence" upon a limited range of themes. Pratt "combines sophisticated . . . poetic technique . . . erudition and . . . timeliness in choice of themes" with an obsessive poetic vision that is almost incredibly primitive. (V.E.)

P1159 Daniells, Roy, "Ned Pratt: The Special Quality," Canadian Literature, No. 21, pp. 10-2, Summer, 1964.

Pratt's "special and unique quality" was "largeness of mind." Responsive to people, he "relived the old virtues of the Canadian literary tradition." He was unique for his "massive simplicity of purpose" and "enforced immediacy of . . . daily response to life." (V.E.)

P1160 Davey, Frank, "E. J. Pratt: Apostle of Corporate Man," Canadian Literature, No. 43, pp. 54-66, Winter, 1970.

"In E. J. Pratt we quite plainly have a committed and somewhat uncritical spokesman for the values of industrial man." He continually presents "both the machinery of technology and the machinery of social organization as man's best way to salvation." (G.C.)

P1161 Dudek, Louis, "Poet of the Machine Age," <u>Tamarack Review</u>,
No. 6, pp. 77-80, Winter, 1958.

"The characteristic quality of Pratt's poetry . . . is derived from
his primary vision of life: it is a language of mechanism, of fact,
of naked energy. . . . Pratt, more than any other modern poet one
can think of, has written the poetry of science and the machine age."
(D.P.)

P1162 Frye, Northrop, "Ned Pratt: The Personal Legend," <u>Canadian
Literature</u>, No. 21, pp. 6-9, Winter, 1964.

Pratt is "the only figure in Canadian literature . . . great enough to
establish a personal legend." As editor of <u>Canadian Poetry Magazine</u>
he took poetry "too seriously." Never anti-intellectual, he "stuck to
the essentials of university work" without compromising his poetry.
(V.E.)

P1163 Horwood, Harold, "E. J. Pratt and William Blake: An Analysis,"
<u>Dalhousie Review</u>, 39:197-207, Summer, 1959.

William Blake's influence on E. J. Pratt is clear. Their styles have
much in common, though Blake's is difficult and Pratt's easy. Both
poets "see things readily in cosmic proportions." In <u>The Great Feud</u>
Pratt manages to give cosmic proportions to biology. Like Blake,
Pratt holds pacifist views as seen in his poems <u>They Are Returning</u>
and <u>Dunkirk</u>. "Perhaps the essence of Pratt's greatness lies . . .
in his attainment of a coherent mythology." Pratt is the first
Canadian poet of "real consequence." (V.E.)

P1164 Livesay, Dorothy, "The Polished Lens: Poetic Techniques of Pratt
and Klein," <u>Canadian Literature</u>, No. 25, pp. 33-42, Summer, 1965.

"For me, Pratt is a self-made poet; Klein a natural one, possessing
a Blakeian simplicity. Pratt remained a story-teller to the end . . .
collecting artefacts and arranging them cunningly, without committing
his deeper self. . . . Klein . . . probed inwards to the human soul,
revealing its possibilities for creative joy as well as its predilections
for darkness, madness." (D.P.)

P1165 Sharman, Vincent, "Illusion and an Atonement: E. J. Pratt and
Christianity," <u>Canadian Literature</u>, No. 19, pp. 21-32, Winter, 1964.

A Christian interpretation of the poetry of E. J. Pratt would be
erroneous and "limiting to the intent of his poetry." Of Pratt's

Collected Poems only ten can be construed as being Christian. Pratt views Christ "not as divine, but as the 'perfection of natural evolution in man'." The Iron Door is "Pratt's earliest, most complete, expression of a sense of the illusion of belief in Christian afterlife." In his great epic Brebeuf and His Brethren and in his poem Titanic the poet expresses the theme of religious illusion once more. (V.E.)

P1166   Smith, A. J. M., "The Poet," Tamarack Review, No. 6, pp. 66-71, Winter, 1958.

E. J. Pratt's principle theme is "man's Promethean struggle with the blind forces of nature." His writing is notable for its irony leavened with compassion, its humor, and his wit, which is often resonant with the metaphysical conceit. His poetry has shown a continuous development. (D.P.)

P1167   West, Paul, "E. J. Pratt's Four-Ton Gulliver," Canadian Literature, No. 19, pp. 13-20, Winter, 1964.

Edwin John Pratt is considered by Newfoundlanders to be "the best of their several hundred outstanding poets." He epitomizes the "earthiness and vitality for which Newfoundlanders are known and, in some cases, loved." Pratt's poetry in general has "the same childlike quality, the same obsession with force, grandeur and immensity as boys's adventure stories." He has an "underlying view of an impersonal universe surviving through a prearranged calculation of favourable chances." Pratt is still profoundly influenced by the sea. (V.E.)

THE CACHALOT

P1168   Gibbs, Robert J., "The Living Contour: The Whale Symbol in Melville and Pratt," Canadian Literature, No. 40, pp. 17-25, Spring, 1969.

Where does the significance of the whale as a symbol begin and end in Melville's Moby Dick and E. J. Pratt's The Cachalot? Or is there any significance? Both works feature a great whale, "a clash of titanic forces" and a mutually destructive conclusion. Like Melville, Pratt uses the rhythm of words to create the rhythm of whale and ocean, but Pratt also makes use of the rhythm of the poem itself. "Symbolic meaning is inherent in the artistic process itself . . . individual interpretation may enrich the book for us, but what counts is the architecture of the book itself." (V.E.)

PRÉVERT, JACQUES

P1169 Bouthoul, Gaston, "Jacques Prévert et un siècle de poésie martiale,"
Les Lettres nouvelles, 56:91-101, January, 1958.

The first World War, with its systematic destruction, ended the
poetic tradition celebrating individual heroes of battle. Prévert is
the most representative of the new poet who rejects completely the
martial virtues. Prévert believes that war causes the social
hierarchy that supports oppression: that it is promulgated by fathers
who wish to destroy their sons: and in consequence he denounces
"les maîtres" in every sphere. (K.L.)

P1170 Greet, Anne Hyde, "Negation and Affirmation in Jacques Prévert's
Word Games," Wisconsin Studies in Contemporary Literature,
7:131-41, Summer, 1966.

Prévert satirizes bourgeois institutions and language ("clichés,
euphemisms, and other misleading or meaningless phrases") through
word-games "based upon a literal approach towards figurative expressions." These verbal paradoxes help create a world of logical fantasy
giving insights into human nature and showing the defeat of language as
used by rationalists. (P.J.R.)

P1171 Hammond, Robert, "Humorous Word-Play in the Poetry of Jacques
Prévert," Pacific Coast Philology, 1:59-65, April, 1966.

"Two principal varieties may be discerned in Prévert's humor. One
is the word-play of innocent merriment, the child-like émerveillement
devant le verbe. The other is a more sophisticated set of games,
which presupposes external referents and by so doing adds satire and
social criticism to the verbal sport." (D.-J.J.)

P1172 Poujol, Jacques, "Jacques Prévert ou le langage en procès,"
French Review, 31:387-95, April, 1958.

Prévert's poetry is essentially verbal. Language is not merely the
means of expression but constitutes the very subject of his poems.
He endeavors to rediscover the true meaning of words. (F.M.L.)

PRÉVOST, JEAN

P1173 Bertrand, Marc, "Jean Prévost disciple d'Alain," <u>Modern Language Notes</u>, 80:618-22, December, 1965.

Although Jean Prévost was a disciple of Alain, his works display originality and independence of mind. (F.M.L.)

PRICE, REYNOLDS

P1174 Barnes, Daniel R., "The Names and Faces of Reynolds Price," <u>Kentucky Review</u>, 2:76-91, No. 2, 1968.

By the manner and mode in which Price employs proper names in his fiction, he has succeeded in mastering the genres of both the pastoral novel and the comic romance. (A.S.W.)

P1175 Eichelberger, Clayton L., "Reynolds Price: 'A Banner in Defeat'," <u>Journal of Popular Culture</u>, 1:410-7, Spring, 1968.

Reynolds Price's <u>A Long and Happy Life</u>, <u>A Generous Man</u>, and <u>The Names and Faces of Heroes</u> have all received mixed reviews. Price is "concerned with love between ordinary people." The "ordinary" young people of Price's novels are extraordinary enough to rise beyond the mundane, but fail to do so. The "banner of defeat" flies over them. Each person has the chance to live up to his or her potential but, by giving way to conformity at the crucial moment, misses the chance. "Buried beneath the mound of conformity lies sacrificed individuality." (V.E.)

P1176 Kaufman, Wallace, "A Conversation with Reynolds Price," <u>Shenandoah</u>, 17:3-25, Summer, 1966.

[In a recorded conversation held at his North Carolina home, Reynolds Price talks about his life and writing. Initially a poet, Price turned to novels because he "knew the poems weren't any good." Faulkner has not been an influence on his work, "technical or otherwise." Eudora Welty has been a strong influence, not on technique but on his life, by first showing him that serious writing could be done about his Southern background and life. Symbolism is of little consequence in his work: "more nonsense . . . is talked about symbols now than about any other single aspect of fiction."] (V.E.)

P1177 Price, Reynolds, "A Long and Happy Life: Fragments of Ground-work," <u>Virginia Quarterly Review</u>, 41:236-47, Spring, 1965.

[These are excerpts from his notebooks which he offers "as a fragmentary demonstration of the ways in which one writer attempted to comprehend--and prepared to transmit--one story, one knot of people who arrived, unsummoned but welcome, in his mind, his life."] (S.A.)

P1178 Stevenson, John W., "The Faces of Reynolds Price's Short Fiction," <u>Studies in Short Fiction</u>, 3:300-6, Spring, 1966.

"The controlling theme of Reynolds Price's fiction is the revelation that comes through the quest for self-knowledge, not in any intellectual sense but in the discovery that meaning and identity are found in giving, and in giving is learned the fulfillment of love." (P.J.R.)

A GENEROUS MAN

P1179 Price, Reynolds, "New for the Mineshaft," <u>Virginia Quarterly Review</u>, 44:641-58, Autumn, 1968.

"<u>A Generous Man</u>, however imperfect . . . whatever its place in the Sweepstakes-in-the-sky, discovered holes in a number of its readers--in their appreciative agility . . .; in their senses of humor; their control of panic at the sight of the body engaged in its own delight and continuance; in short, in their lives. . . . The meaning of <u>A Generous Man</u> is itself, its physical shape which is both the product of its meaning and the container, limiter, protector. . . . Anyone who has chosen to read it at all can discover its full content in how-it-looks--not in what it says. . . ." (D.P.)

PRICHARD, KATHARINE SUSANNAH

P1180 Hewett, Dorothy, "Excess of Love: The Irreconcilable in Katharine Susannah Prichard," <u>Overland</u>, 43:27-31, Summer, 1969-70.

"In the clash between the artist's pagan and poetic sensibility . . . and the moralising Marxist religieuse, it is the latter who finally wins the battle. Yet given the climate of critical thought, the narrowness of provincial horizons, and her own limitations, the outcome was perhaps inevitable." (K.M.W.)

P1181   Lindsay, Jack, "The Novels of Katharine Susannah Prichard,"
Meanjin Quarterly, 20:366-87, December, 1961.

The particular quality of her work reveals a conflict "between a
preoccupation with the insistent and immediate demands of life and
a need to struggle for the fullest artistic concentration and precision."
Resisting any tincture of superficial aestheticism, she presents a
"realistic representation of the world of work." (R.L.G.)

P1182   Malos, Ellen, "Some Major Themes in the Novels of Katharine
Susannah Prichard," Australian Literary Studies, 1:32-41, June,
1963.

Prichard's "main fault as a writer is really that the particular
quality of her love of the soil and of those who live in a close relationship with it . . . the source of her best writing, has also prevented
her from interpreting the lives of her people as deeply and fully as a
truly great writer is able to do." Black Opal, Working Bullocks and
Coonardoo are representative works. (H.S.)

P1183   Prichard, Katharine Susannah, "Some Perceptions and Aspirations,"
Southerly, 28:235-44, No. 4, 1968.

[Prichard discusses the aims of her work, and the experience on
which she drew for her writing.] (A.S.W.)

P1184   Roland, Betty, "Requiem for K. S. P." Overland, 44:29-31,
Winter, 1970.

[These are personal reminiscences of the author's acquaintance with
Katharine Prichard at home in Australia and in Moscow.] (K.M.W.)

PRIESTLEY, JOHN BOYNTON

P1185   Braine, John, "Lunch with J. B. Priestley," Encounter, 10:8-14,
June, 1958.

One of the most undervalued of living English writers, Priestly has
lost critical esteem because of the quantity and unevenness of his
work. His very best, however, is better than the works of more
fashionable writers. (D.B.D.)

P1186   Fuchs, Konrad, "J. B. Priestley," <u>Die Neueren Sprachen</u>, 15:221-6, May, 1966.

In Priestley's novels the times influence man and determine his fate without being able to change his innate character. (J.R.R.)

P1187   Nigot, Georges, "Les Ouvrages récents de J. B. Priestley," <u>Études Anglaises</u>, 10:231-4, July-September, 1957.

As author of novels, short stories, plays and essays, Priestley continues to be an "extraordinarily able" and energetic writer of "invincible readability." (J.H.A.)

P1188   Nigot, Georges, "Le Théâtre de J. B. Priestley," <u>Études Anglaises</u>, 10:322-34, October-December, 1957.

Already established as novelist and essayist, in 1932 Priestley turned to the theatre "to prove he was capable of thinking and creating as a dramatist and not necessarily as a novelist." The extreme diversity of the thirty plays to follow affirms that "Priestley's theatre is a fine example of professional integrity and artistic skill, of methodic lucidity and intelligent goodness." (R.C.F.)

P1189   Rogers, Ivor A., "The Time Plays of J. B. Priestley," <u>Extrapolation</u>, 10:9-16, December, 1968.

Priestley is one of the few nineteenth or twentieth century playwrights to explore fully in his plays a scientific concept--that of the dimensions, implications, and relativity of time. (A.S.W.)

P1190   Skloot, Robert, "The Time Plays of J. B. Priestley," <u>Quarterly Journal of Speech</u>, 56:426-31, December, 1970.

"The time plays of J. B. Priestley usually reach a point of diminishing returns somewhere in the second act. . . . Priestley's craftsmanship is usually excellent, but his ideas are insubstantial when his own or unconvincing when borrowed from others. . . . Yet Priestley's plays . . . despite their numerous failings . . . are truly unique and significant for their attempt in the theatre to expand human consciousness in its time perception." (D.P.)

P1191 Smith, Grover, "Time Alive: J.W. Dunne and J. B. Priestley,"
South Atlantic Quarterly, 56:224-33, April, 1957.

The time-writings of Priestley are the best imaginative treatment
of Dunne's philosophy of serial time. Priestley's time-plays reveal
characters awaking to eternal reality and recognizing the significance
of a meaningful existence. A philosophy like Dunne's may sustain a
literary work, but usually it only multiplies the eccentricities of
literature. (W.B.B.)

LITERATURE AND WESTERN MAN

P1192 Mercier, Vivian, "Priestley on Literature," Commonweal,
73:40-5, October 7, 1960.

In Literature and Western Man "Priestley has written . . . less a
literary history than a lengthy essay, in which Western literature
is treated as a symptom and at the same time a potential cure for
the disease of Western Man." (H.S.)

PRINCE, FRANK TEMPLETON

P1193 Inglis, Fred, "F. T. Prince and the Prospects for Poetry,"
Denver Quarterly, 1:23-44, Autumn, 1966.

Prince's poetry, with its rich and varied language and subtle rhythms,
is poetry within a major tradition; it affirms life and is sufficiently
courageous and intelligent to look beyond life. (A.S.W.)

PRISCO, MICHELE

P1194 Ricciardelli, Michael, "Prisco and the Modern Predicament,"
Books Abroad, 41:47-8, Winter, 1967.

Prisco's Una spirale di nebbia "transcends characters and episodes,
time and space, to show the crisis of modern man, 'tremendously
alone,' living in a society of prejudices, hypocrisies, doubts, and
uncertainties." (A.S.W.)

PRITCHETT, VICTOR SAWDON

P1195 Scott-Jones, R. A., "The Five Mr. Pritchetts," New Republic, 135:17-8, August 20, 1956.

"Mr. V. S. Pritchett has a big reputation, but it ought to be five times as great. . . . There is the . . . Pritchett who has written so many interesting essays about books. . . the writer of travel books. . . the short story writer. . . the novelist (of satire and grave student of the human heart). . . . in all these fields he excels and can be favorably compared with the best writers of our time. . . ." (L. L.)

PROKOSCH, FREDERIC

P1196 Carpenter, Richard C., "The Novels of Frederic Prokosch," College English, 18:261-7, February, 1957.

The forceful and vivid writing of Prokosch deserves wide notice. He illuminates the essential nature of man's place in the world by the surrealistic device of the waking dream, in which "all is strange yet impregnated with significance." Reality is thrown out of focus so that we may see the "real" reality behind it. (E. L.)

P1197 Cluny, Claude Michel, "Frederic Prokosch," La Nouvelle Revue Française, No. 155, pp. 886-93, November, 1965.

The Asiatics (1935) prefigures all subsequent work of Prokosch down to and including The Sisters (1962), the ensemble of which characterizes him as part of the uprooted writers that each American generation has known since Melville. His novels are attempts at the exploration of the self through space and time. (T. T. B.)

P1198 Lefebve, Maurice-Jean, "Frederic Prokosch et la deception essentielle," Monde Nouveau, No. 104, pp. 86-92, October, 1956.

Prokosch's insistence on the fantastic is a method for uncovering reality. In his Storm and Echo, "myth becomes indiscernable from reality." (E. L.)

PROUST, MARCEL

P1199 Alderman, Sidney S., "Young Proust's Search for Lost Time,"
<u>South Atlantic Quarterly</u>, 57:39-54, Winter, 1958.

The titles of Proust's main work have been painfully mistranslated.
In the recently discovered <u>Jean Santeuil</u> and <u>Contre Sainte-Beuve</u>
the young Proust was already perfecting his style, already searching
for lost time, already preparing <u>À la recherche du temps perdu</u>.
(W.B.B.)

P1200 Alley, John N., "Proust and Art: The Anglo-American Critical
View," <u>Revue de Littérature Comparée</u>, 37:410-30, July-September,
1963.

[This article presents, with abundant quotations, the opinions of a
wide variety of Anglo-American critics over a period of several
decades. The comments center on Proust's concern for the arts,
especially literature, music and painting.] (W.J.L.)

P1201 Almansi, Guido, "The 'Italian Proust'," <u>Adam International Review</u>,
31:115-8, Nos. 310-11-12, 1966.

Early critics of Italo Svevo linked him with Proust, even suggested
that Proust had directly influenced <u>La coscienza di Zeno</u>. However,
Svevo only read Proust late in life; Proustian traces in his work are
more apparent than real. "He is the naive historian who studies the
past in order to understand the present, not the romantic who attempts to recreate it." (D.P.)

P1202 Bailey, Ninette, "Les Modalités du temps et la notion de l'acte
libre: un aspect négligé de la pensée proustienne," <u>French Studies</u>,
11:28-37, January, 1957.

Proust's philosophical speculations are weakened because he refuses
to face the reality of human freedom, even though his own psychology
should have led him to affirm it. Yet Proustian determinism, which
results in individual passivity, allows the artist to treat effectively
all the forces to which man has been submitted. (R.A.B.)

P1203 Bailey, Ninette, "La Rôle des couleurs dans la genèse de l'univers
proustien," <u>Modern Language Review</u>, 50:188-96, April, 1965.

Proust's use of colors is no mere imitation of the Impressionists;
in remaking the world from materials of his own choosing, he

realized "a transformation of all that is real by having it pass
through the magic prism of colors." (J.R.R.)

P1204 Bersani, Jacques, "Proust exposé," <u>Critique</u>, Nos. 219-20,
pp. 781-5, August-September, 1965.

Proust is the most pathetic of all writers. He lacks the romantic
exaltation of a Balzac, or Hugo, even that of a Musset. He placed
all his talent in the living setting of his works. (T.T.B.)

P1205 Bersani, Jacques, "Proust et Dada: Deux lettres inédites de
Marcel Proust à Philippe Soupault et à André Breton," <u>Revue
d'Histoire Littéraire de la France</u>, 65:260-8, April-June, 1965.

"Doesn't the brief exchange of letters in 1920 prove that beyond
apparent differences there existed a deep similarity between Proust
and Breton, and that both sacrificed to the . . . ambition . . . to
transform the world and enable man to find not only time but the
nature he had lost?" (D.-J.J.)

P1206 Bibesco, Princesse, "Les Courants de l'inspiration anglaise,"
<u>Adam International Review</u>, 25:62-4, No. 260, 1957.

[These are Princesse Bibesco's souvenirs of Proust.] (D.-J.J.)

P1207 Brée, Germaine, "The Enchanted World of Marcel Proust,"
<u>American Society of Legion of Honor Magazine</u>, 33:9-27, No. 1,
1962; 35:151-69, No. 3, 1964.

"All Proust's world derived its beauty in part from the recreation
of a time that has gone by. . . ." "Proust . . . 'saved' his
frivolous, nonchalant epoch, saved it for us, with its inimitable
troupe of characters." (F.M.L.)

P1208 Brée, Germaine, "From <u>Jean Santeuil</u> to <u>Time Regained</u>,"
<u>Bucknell Review</u>, 6:16-21, No. 3, 1956.

<u>Jean Santeuil</u> and <u>Contre Sainte-Beuve</u> reveal that the creative
process which culminated in À la recherche du temps perdu was
arduous and that the idea for the overall structure of that novel
"came slowly." (F.M.L.)

P1209   Brée, Germaine, "Les Manuscrits de Marcel Proust," French Review, 37:182-7, December, 1963.

[This article considers the impact of the release to the public of a large number of the novelist's manuscripts. The problems involving the genesis and development of Proust's works are, if anything, more complex than they had seemed.] (W.J.L.)

P1210   Brée, Germaine, "Marcel Proust: Changing Perspective," Australian Journal of French Studies, 1:104-13, January-April, 1964.

The plethora of emerging works by Proust points out the need for creating firm textual foundations and basing future research and re-evaluations on the newly accumulated data. (F.M.L.)

P1211   Brée, Germaine, "Marcel Proust: Manuscripts Lost and Found," AULLA Proceedings, 2:7, 1964.

Since the 1952 publication of Jean Santeuil, much new material by Proust has emerged. Accurate texts now need to be established-- a difficult but essential task. (F.M.L.)

P1212   Brée, Germaine, "Le 'Moi oeuvrant' de Proust," Modern Language Review, 61:610-8, October, 1966.

"In that which concerns his own work, Proust is a clairvoyant artist. The doctrinal exposé, the melange of theory and conviction, of rhetoric and images and even the failure of his demonstration create a complete and revealing ensemble." (J.R.R.)

P1213   Briand, Charles, "Proust--homme d'affaires," Adam International Review, 31:123-6, Nos. 310-11-12, 1966.

By his own admission, Proust considered himself to be a good accountant, and records show that he also had extensive business holdings. (D.-J.J.)

P1214   Brooke, Jocelyn, "Proust and Joyce: The Case for the Prosecution," Adam International Review, No. 297-8, pp. 5-66, 1961.

Various "disciples, apologists and exegetists" of Proust and Joyce "have inflated the reputations of two important and highly gifted writers . . .: Joyce scholars . . . by condoning or explaining away Joyce's failures and defects . . . [and] Proustians . . . [not so much by trying] to justify Proust's lapses as [by] simply fail[ing] to mention them." (D.P.)

P1215 Cattaui, Georges, "Proust et les lettres anglo-américaines," La Table Ronde, No. 192, pp. 36-47, January, 1964.

German, Italian, and often French literature left Proust indifferent, but he confessed that his development had been tremendously influenced by English and American writers, especially George Eliot, Hardy, Stevenson, and Emerson, but also Shakespeare, Ruskin, Browning, Meredith, Thackeray, Carlyle, and William Morris. (T.T.B.)

P1216 Champigny, Robert, "Temps et reconnaissance chez Proust et quelques philosophes," PMLA, 73:129-35, March, 1958.

Proust is essentially anti-Bergsonian and, although he shares some similarities with Schopenhauer and Spinoza, it is Kierkegaard with whom the novelist has the greatest affinity. (W.J.L.)

P1217 Channon, Henry, "How I Met Proust," Adam International Review, 25:68-70, No. 260, 1957.

[These are recollections of a series of meetings with Proust in 1918 in wartime Paris. ". . . I remember Proust's gentleness, his sensitiveness that was almost an illness, his hot hands and sad, wonderful eyes, his rather tawdry elegance and the determined parting of his incredibly black hair."] (D.P.)

P1218 Church, Margaret, "Kafka and Proust: A Contrast in Time," Bucknell Review, 7:107-12, December, 1957.

Proust is a durational writer, attaching "importance directly to the inner continuous atmosphere of the mind"; Kafka, however, is a Platonic thinker concerned with man in general rather than the individual man, with the myth or parable rather than the painstaking analysis of a Leopold Bloom. (J.R.R.)

P1219 Cocking, J. M., "Marcel Proust: The Novelist of Memory," Listener, 54:660, 663, October 20, 1955.

"Proust had the sensibility of a poet, the critical, though perhaps not the creative, intelligence of a philosopher, and a scientist's interest in minute observation. He also had . . . an ordinary memory which was outstandingly retentive and capacious; a memory for facts, ideas, scraps of gossip, tricks of speech and behaviour. He also had insight into the tricks and subterfuges of his own mind in its attempt to come to terms with life. . . ." (D.P.)

P1220 Cocking, J. M., "Proust and Music," Essays in French Literature, No. 4, pp. 13-29, November, 1967.

". . . Proust's thinking on and around his reactions to music may have helped him to know himself and to write his book. Music was, for him, first a kind of mnemonic . . . bound up with his own particular experiences. Then it was a way of enriching those experiences. Then it became a way of abstracting emotional patterns from a number of experiences. Finally it became a structure, a way of dominating and patterning those emotions." (D.P.)

P1221 Cocking, John, "Some English Influences on Proust," Adam International Review, 25:92-9, No. 260, 1957.

". . . the English influences [on Proust] were important. If the tendency to poeticise the real without transforming it seems to me eminently French, I think that Proust learned his impressionistic precision from Ruskin. George Eliot helped him to the notion of an imaginative capital laid up in childhood, providing in later life diminishing means which only memory could subsidize; while from Ruskin's thought and Ruskin's prose Proust forged an instrument whereby he could re-inject imagination into a dreary world." (D.P.)

P1222 Cocteau, Jean, "Marcel's Nautilus," Adam International Review, 25:56-7, No. 260, 1957.

[This is a recounting of evenings in Marcel Proust's home in the Boulevard Haussmann, where the author read sections of Du côté de chez Swann to his guests.] (D.P.)

P1223 Cohn, Robert G., "Proust and Mallarmé," French Studies, 24:262-75, July, 1970.

". . . what makes Proust closer to Mallarmé than almost any other writer . . . is the combination of stubborn ambition projected through an iron will, brilliant intellect, fused with deep sensuality into the mid-product of imagination, controlled or articulated by exquisite French taste." (F.M.L.)

P1224 Cook, Gladys E., "Marcel Proust: From Analysis to Creation," <u>Bucknell Review</u>, 8:17-37, November, 1958.

Proust's literary technique improved considerably from <u>Jean Santeuil</u> to <u>À la recherche du temps perdu</u>. He discovered the benefits of first-person narration; learned the art of composition, how to pre-pare emotional responses, how to build up suspense, how to skill-fully depict character via dialogue and how to use "metaphor and suggestion instead of flat statement or obvious comparison. . . ." (F.M.L.)

P1225 Cruickshank, John, "The Shifting World of Proust," <u>Critical Quarterly</u>, 8:220-8, Autumn, 1966.

"Through the revelation of involuntary memory and its application to literature he brought the shifting realities of the self and the external world into a relationship in which . . . life is conveyed with an immediacy that renews our sense of its complexity, its transience and its beauty." (W.J.L.)

P1226 Deakin, William, "D. H. Lawrence's Attacks on Proust and Joyce," <u>Essays in Criticism</u>, 7:383-403, October, 1957.

Lawrence's criticism, in his "Surgery for the Novel," that Proust's and Joyce's methods permitted their inclusion of large amounts of trivia in their work has a certain justification. Lawrence missed, however, the "enlargement of moral understanding" which both writers achieved as a result of their techniques. (D.B.D.)

P1227 Duc de Gramont, "Proust as I Knew Him," <u>London Magazine</u>, 2:21-30, November, 1955.

[These are recollections of Proust and the milieu in which he and the writer moved from their meeting in 1901 until Proust's death.] (J.L.B.)

P1228 Fauconnier, R., "Proust en exil," <u>Symposium</u>, 8:134-7, Summer, 1954.

Much time and effort has been expended on Proust's allusions to Bergson and to Freud. Yet the novelist's "exile" in his small room in Paris, because of his asthma, has been substantially ignored despite the many valuable insights it provides into the nature of the Proustian universe. (W.J.L.)

P1229 Ferré, André, "Si Marcel Proust etait encore parmi nous,"
Adam International Review, 25:104-6, No. 260, 1957.

"If he were with us now, we would still be assimilating his message
and not already profiting from his lesson, as we are today."
(D.-J.J.)

P1230 Fould, Elisabeth, "Marcel in My Youth," Adam International
Review, 31:51-61, Nos. 310-11-12, 1966.

[These are recollections of Marcel Proust, whom Elisabeth Fould
(Vicomtesse de Nantois) met in 1891, when Proust was twenty years
of age. Proust already exhibited minute powers of observation, was
always impeccably dressed.] (D.P.)

P1231 Fowlie, Wallace, "Proust and the French Novel," Sewanee Review,
71:569-84, Autumn, 1963.

Proust is the only novelist since 1850 whose work, in structure and
intensity, is comparable with Balzac's. And "Balzac and Proust
helped to make the novel into much more than a story. It communicates a vision and a wisdom." It is "a spiritual exercise." (A.S.)

P1232 Friedman, Melvin J., "The Novels of Samuel Beckett: An Amalgam
of Joyce and Proust," Comparative Literature, 12:47-58, Winter,
1960.

Beckett's novels have developed in directions implied in his essay
on Joyce and his monograph on Proust. His point-of-view characters
have the sense of time and the impulse for self-identification of
Proust's. From Joyce, Beckett drew the concentration of his
characters upon "things" and their habit of cataloging them.
(F.C.T.)

P1233 Gautier-Vignal, Louis, "The Proust I Knew: An Infernal Circle,"
Adam International Review, 31:62-72, Nos. 310-11-12, 1966.

[This is a recollection of a first meeting with Proust in his flat in
June, 1914. Gautier-Vignal had already read Du côté de chez Swann
several times, having been given a copy of the work by the Lucien
Daudets. Daudet had reviewed the book in Le Figaro as a great
literary event.] (D.P.)

P1234 Gerhardi, William, "Resurrection and Proust," Adam International Review, 25:70-1, No. 260, 1957.

"Where Proust is at his purest is in his involuntary resuscitations of a moment lifted clean out of Time. It is in my identification of an authentic experience of my own out of the body with that sudden breath of unalloyed reality of which Proust speaks . . . which can be traced through my autobiographical novel, Resurrection." (D.P.)

P1235 Girard, Marcel, "Proust et Zola," Adam International Review, 25:111-2, No. 260, 1957.

"Under [Proust and Zola's] different colors, it is possible to grasp the similarity of their great design: the transmutation of the chaotic and unstable world into a recreated and rethought universe, according to the injunctions of art, against Time." (D.-J.J.)

P1236 Girard, René, "De l'experience romanesque au mythe oedipiem," Critique, No. 222, pp. 899-924, November, 1965.

In À la recherche, Proust attempts to penetrate the world of the favored Others, whereas in Jean Santeuil the protagonist possesses all that is lacking to the narrator of À la recherche. He exercises over the Others an irresistible charm and is a projection of the desire revealed in the latter novel. (T.T.B.)

P1237 Glikin, Gloria, "The 'I' and the 'She'," Adam International Review, 31:41-4, Nos. 310-11-12, 1966.

In the 1920's Dorothy Richardson "had not only been enraptured by Proust. . . . She had also seen . . . the relationship of her own fiction to his, and perceived as well the nature of the fundamental difference between them. Instead of writing 'through consciousness, she observed, Proust was writing 'about consciousness,' a vastly different thing. . . . Behind their separate choices, however, lay a common ground of motive and purpose. . . . Both had double aims as writers: art and self-portrayal; and . . . in finding the method of fiction suited to their autobiographical intentions, Dorothy Richardson and Proust appear to have also learned that the very process of discovery was the theme of their art." (D.P.)

P1238 Greshoff, C. J., "Proust as Symbolist Novelist," Standpunte, 81:5-15, 1969.

"Proust, by relating through analogy and metaphor a great number of disparate experiences and objects, establishes in the Baudelairian sense 'correspondances' which, multiplied ad infinitum, should eventually arrive at One." (F.M.L.)

P1239 [Grinlea, Miron], "In Search of Our Proust," Adam International Review, 25:6-53, No. 260, 1957.

[This is an account of the tribulations and rewards in gathering Proustiana for this special issue on Marcel Proust, with extended comment by and about Violet and Sydney Schiff, Marie Nordlinger-Riefstahl, Laure Hayman, the Prince and Princesse Bibesco, a visit to Illiers, and comments on celebrated scholars of Proust.] (D.P.)

P1240 Harper, Ralph, "Remembering Eternity: St. Augustine and Proust," Thought, 34:569-606, Winter, 1959-60.

"For Proust the Way is art, the marshalling of the debris of nostalgia. For Augustine the Way is humility, the learning of the incarnation. Both Augustine and Proust knew the joy of remembering what we have never really known; this is the formula of their common humanity." (D.P.)

P1241 Hodson, W. L., "Proust's Methods of Character Presentation in Les Plaisirs et les jours and Jean Santeuil," Modern Language Review, 57:41-6, January, 1962.

Proust uses three methods--the "simple," the "multilateral," and the "hidden observer"--"to show his characters evolving in Time or to give the reader some insight into their natures by revealing unsuspected features." (G.B.M.)

P1242 Hornsby, Jessie L., "Le 'Nouveau roman' de Proust," L'Esprit Créateur, 7:67-80, Summer, 1967.

Proust, as predecessor of the new novel, attempted to depict a mental architecture of time. The most important characters are in perpetual change. The dematerialization of the characters and the dissipation of the character of the hero is particularly pertinent to the new novel. (T.T.B.)

P1243 Houston, John Porter, "Literature and Psychology: The Case of Proust," L'Esprit Créateur, 5:3-13, Spring, 1965.

In his creation of characters Proust liberated the narrow, somewhat mechanical concepts of personality in which Flaubert and Zola were confined. His innovations in the portrayal of characters did not transform the novel, for he has had few distinguished imitators-- the most striking one being Lawrence Durrell, whose Justine owes much to Proust. (T.T.B.)

P1244 Hübner, Wolfgang, "Antike Unterweltmythen bei Marcel Proust," Arcadia, 3:181-94, No. 2, 1968.

"All mythological similes open up the perspective onto a complex world which contains both the true and the untrue at the same time. They correspond to Marcel's fairy tale manner of experimenting as well as to Proust's manner of thinking." (J.R.R.)

P1245 Hudson, Stephen, "Marcel Proust," Cornhill, No. 1045, pp. 57-61, Autumn, 1965.

Proust's "uniqueness consisted less, I think, in his obvious posses- sion to an outstanding degree of gifts and charms than in his use of them. . . . no one I have ever known combined in his own person so many attractive qualities and could bring them into play so spontane- ously. Yet . . . there was an impalpable objectivity about him, an aloofness felt rather than observed . . . while the dominant con- sciousness lay behind them. . . . It was, I believe, in the depth and capacity of this ultimate consciousness that his uniqueness lay, as it is there that the source of his creative power and sensibility is to be found." (D.P.)

P1246 Inoué, Kynichiro, "Les Aubépines, fleurs proustiennes," Adam International Review, 25:129-31, No. 260, 1957.

"The sentiments that these flowers stirred in little Marcel would later be the feelings of art and love which he would decipher and recreate in his work." (D.-J.J.)

P1247 Jackson, Elizabeth R., "The Genesis of the Involuntary Memory in Proust's Early Works," PMLA, 76:586-94, December, 1961.

The emergence of the three separate forms of involuntary memory-- dream sentiment, and aesthetic memory--along with other basic features of Proust's affective memory may be traced through its

involuntary character, its structural function, and its intricate
mechanism in the early works of Proust. (B.K.)

P1248 Jefferson, Louise M., "Proust and Racine," <u>Yale French Studies</u>,
No. 34, pp. 99-105, June, 1965.

"Racine was . . . such an artistic fixture in Proust's literary
vocabulary that he became a standard reference in Proust's writing."
Racine, "as Proust's most revered literary idol, provided him with
an example of true artistic finesse on the common ground of violent
human emotions. Racine's theatre . . . was an ever-present
reference and inspiration as Proust expertly and creatively found
his way through the labyrinth of experiences and ideas amassed
throughout his own lifetime, and recorded them for posterity."
(D.P.)

P1249 Johnson, Pamela Hansford, "Six Proustian Reconstructions,"
<u>Adam International Review</u>, 25:71-4, No. 260, 1957.

[This is an analysis and discussion of the six Proustian reconstructions done by Pamela Johnson at the suggestion of Rayner Heppenstall
for broadcast by the B. B. C. Included is an extract from "Madame
de Charlus," the third reconstruction.] (D.P.)

P1250 Jones, David L., "Proust and Doderer: Themes and Techniques,"
<u>Books Abroad</u>, 37:12-5, Winter, 1963.

"Many Proustian approaches unavoidably strike the reader of the
two major novels of Heimito von Doderer, certainly one of the most
exciting and accomplished of contemporary [Austrian] writers."
(C.E.N.)

P1251 Laporte, Roger, "Naissance de la littérature," <u>La Nouvelle Revue
Française</u>, No. 175, pp. 81-91, July, 1967.

Proust, after Balzac and Stendhal, has carried the classic psychological novel to a level never before reached. A serious study of
jealousy, perception, habit and, of course, memory cannot do
without Proust. He is the founder of the concept, so important to
modern literature, which has for its object language itself. (T.T.B.)

P1252 Lauris, Georges de, "L'Ami qu'il pouvait être," <u>Adam International</u> <u>Review</u>, 25:59-61, No. 260, 1957.

"Marcel lived with a constant and sometimes sad intensity. He was open to all resonances. A word of Mme. de Chevigne or of Mme. Straus joined a phrase of Maeterlinck, a thought of Joubert or of Bergson. Proust amused himself sometimes, he was even subject to foolish laughters. His conversation was brilliant but, as I recollect, his thought contained an underlying mysteriousness." (D.P.)

P1253 LeSage, Laurent, "Proust's Professor of Beauty: Count Robert de Montesquiou," <u>American Society of Legion of Honor Magazine</u>, 27:65-76, 1958.

"Montesquiou was not only a model for Proust, but a real master, a 'professeur de beauté' as Proust had called him. But the pupil was a genius and soon surpassed the master, who was, after all, only an esthete. Montesquiou was left behind to ruminate the folly of putting more talent in his life than in his work." (K.M.W.)

P1254 Louria, Yvette, "Recent Studies of Proust's Stylistic and Narrative Techniques," <u>Romanic Review</u>, 58:120-6, April, 1967.

Three recent critical works on Proust place emphasis on the development of new techniques by the author and an examination of his method of adapting these to the telling of a story. (S.M.K.)

P1255 Lowery, Bruce, "Proust et James," <u>Cahiers des Saisons</u>, No. 38, pp. 377-84, Summer, 1964.

The characters of Proust and James dream of life before living it, dream of individuals before knowing them well. They thus become victims of a sort of inevitable self betrayal. Even confronted with reality they can not always adapt themselves to it. Instead of accepting people just as they are, they prefer their illusions. (T.T.B.)

P1256 Lynes, Carlos, Jr., "Marcel Proust: His Vision and His Symbols," <u>Sewanee Review</u>, 63:500-9, Summer, 1955.

"A number of recent critics . . . have already made it clear to us that the keys to unlock the portals of the Proustian edifice are to be found, not in Saint-Simon or Balzac, but in Nerval, Baudelaire, and even Mallarmé." (D.-J.J.)

P1257 Macksey, Richard A., "Marcel Proust and the 'Chant d'un Rossignol': An Unpublished Letter," Modern Language Notes, 77:463-9, December, 1962.

[This letter to Mrs. John Work Garrett herein reproduced in its entirety "sheds some light on the novelist's metamorphic method and raises once again the pernicious question of the models. . . . [It] reflects the impending crisis of Proust's forced removal from the Boulevard Haussmann . . . and rehearses several of the favorite themes of the professional invalid. . . ."] (R.C.F.)

P1258 McMahon, Joseph H., "From Things to Themes," Yale French Studies, No. 34, pp. 5-17, June, 1965.

"If Jean Santeuil is the history of a young man's escape from the various threats imposed by the things, À la recherche is the history of a mature man's escape from social habits and conventions whose tyranny would eventually be worse than that of the things. . . ." "A Proustian theme . . . [as presented in À la recherche] is a literary rendering of the forces of life which lie behind every anecdote, every isolated event . . . which for Proust, locates and contains reality." (D.P.)

P1259 Maurois, André, "Marcel Proust," À la Page, No. 22, pp. 575-88, April, 1966.

Proust renewed the art of the novel and brought to the world of art the ideas of the philosophers and the vocabulary of the scholars of the turn of the century. He gave the true impression of time and revived the past through the evocation of involuntary memory, produced by the coincidence between a present sensation and a recollection. (T.T.B.)

P1260 Maurois, André, "Situation de Marcel Proust," Adam International Review, 25:54-5, No. 260, 1957.

"What we admire in him now is . . . the natural tone, the verity of the conversations, the scientific rigor of the vocabulary and the familiar poetry. The moral truths which he has put forth remain true because they are immutable, as much so as human nature. As for esthetic principles, this great artist remains the modern who has written with the greatest accuracy about the creative process. Proust's place in literature has never been surer than in 1955." (D.-J.J.)

P1261 Mauzi, Robert, "Les Complexes et les signes: Diversité et convergence de la critique proustienne," Critique, No. 225, pp. 155-71, February, 1966.

There is diversity and convergence in Proustian criticism. Some critics stress the structures of a conscience and the birth of an esthetic, beginning with Jean Santeuil and developing into a mystic-esthetic revelation, at the end of Le Temps retrouvé. Others do not stress memory and time but the sign and truth, in which the notions of the Recherche are the sign, the meaning and the presence. (T.T.B.)

P1262 May, Gita, "Chardin vu par Diderot et par Proust," PMLA, 72:403-18, June, 1957.

Diderot and Proust were both literary artists who appreciated the still lifes, dead animals, and portraits of Chardin, Diderot mainly by esthetic analysis and Proust by study of psychological effects. They carried into their fiction Chardin's principle of expressing "l'universal . . . en se confinant au particulier, au concret et au quotidien." (F.C.T.)

P1263 Mein, Margaret, "Flaubert, a Precursor of Proust," French Studies, 17:218-37, July, 1963.

"Both writers have in common this effort to reincarnate the soul of memory in the portion of the past to which it belongs. By his own exploration in depth, Flaubert has prepared the way for Proust, and both stand indomitable in their search to renew time. . . ." (P.F.L.)

P1264 Moloney, Michael F., "The Enigma of Time: Proust, Virginia Woolf, and Faulkner," Thought, 32:69-85, Spring, 1957.

"Whereas Bergson the philosopher was concerned primarily with psychological time, Proust the artist could not nor did he attempt to escape the operation of chronological time. . . . Mrs. Woolf sought through the creative activity of the intellect not only to stay the moment but to expand it into an eternity. . . ." Faulkner "cannot envision the possibility of man's mastery of time because the past being the only time which he accepts there is no room for indetermination." (D.P.)

P1265 Monge, Jacques, "Un Précurseur de Proust: Fromentin et la mémoire affective," Revue d'Histoire Littéraire de la France, 61:564-88, October-December, 1961.

Fromentin is a true precursor of Proust in his use of memory. Unfortunately this debt has gone unnoticed. (D.-J.J.)

P1266 Morris, C. B., "Pedro Salinas and Marcel Proust," Revue de Littérature Comparée, 44:195-214, April-June, 1970.

Salinas translated Proust and was receptive to his works, especially Du côté de chez Swann and À l'ombre des jeunes filles en fleurs. Among important parallels of word and theme are those dealing with women and the artist's need to superimpose his own personality. (C.O.)

P1267 Mortimer, Raymond, "Autant ou mieux qu'hier," Adam International Review, 25:78-9, No. 260, 1957.

The work of Proust, although uneven, stands the test of time and rereading. (D.-J.J.)

P1268 Murray, Jack, "The Esthetic Dilemma in Marcel Proust," French Review, 36:125-32, December, 1962.

To contemplate beauty one must "have recourse to a device that is a poor second to a timeless vision of the beautiful. . . . Memory confers a mixed blessing, however, by engendering a basic dissatisfaction. It hints at a greater beauty to which no human experience can possibly attain." (R.B.W.)

P1269 Murray, Jack, "Mind and Reality in Robbe-Grillet and Proust," Wisconsin Studies in Contemporary Literature, 8:407-20, Summer, 1967.

The literary raison d'être of Proust and Robbe-Grillet seems to be based on the subjectivity-objectivity, art versus science, or mind versus reality antithesis. (P.J.R.)

P1270 Naughton, Helen Thomas, "A Contemporary Views Proust," L'Esprit Créateur, 5:48-55, Spring, 1965.

Prior to Proust, novelists limited themselves to the search for motives of action. Absurdity had been stressed by Dada and the Surrealists. Proust fixed with his gaze the subconscious which had flowed unchecked. He refused to accept the notion of human absurdity, of the unfathomability of the human soul. (T.T.B.)

P1271 Naumann, Manfred, "Studie über Proust," Weimarer Beiträge, 13:916-49, No. 6, 1967.

Socialist criticism should not praise Proust for fighting battles long since won nor should it reject him in toto as a bourgeois, since he was capable of fashioning a valid work of art. (J.R.R.)

P1272 O'Brien, Justin, "Proust Confirmed by Neurosurgery," PMLA, 85:295-7, March, 1970.

Proust's theory of involuntary memory has been confirmed by neurosurgeons who, electrically stimulating parts of the cerebral cortex, activate strips of time long forgotten. This demonstrates the existence of a permanent record of the stream of consciousness in the brain. (F.M.L.)

P1273 Ortega y Gasset, José, "Time, Distance, and Form in Proust," Hudson Review, 11:504-13, Winter, 1958-59.

In Proust, "memory . . . becomes itself the very thing described." Thus, Proust's situations are static and dynamic, and, because he rejects external frameworks, and defines "by reference to . . . inner form," his observations are minute: "He is the inventor of a new distance between us and things." (M.H.)

P1274 Painter, George D., "How Proust Met Miss Barney," Adam International Review, 29:28-30, No. 294, 1962.

After a year of correspondence the meeting of Proust and Miss Natalie Clifford Barney towards November, 1921 was not a success. The visit was late at night, Proust spoke of "nothing but persons in high society." He was dressed in a black tail-suit and "looked like a corpse laid out in a coffin." (D.P.)

P1275 Pardee, W. Hearne, "The Images of Vision," Yale French Studies, No. 34, pp. 19-23, June, 1965.

Proust's "abstract visual imagery . . . dramatize[s] his philosophy in concrete terms, in his attempt to distill a superessential light from the visual world. The senses are by nature only passive. . . . But Proust's inner sense is active and creative, attuned to the light of poetry; it deals in the harmonies of near-transparent colors . . . although light here is still made visible only by its corruption." (D.P.)

P1276   Pasquali, Costanza, "Una lettera di Proust," Studia Neophilologica, 32:117-22, No. 1, 1960.

[This is a facsimile and typescript of the French text of an unpublished letter to Giuseppe-Napoleone Primoli, with notes and commentary in Italian.] (F.J.P.)

P1277   Piñera, Humberto, "Tempo de Proust en el tiempo de Machado," La Torre, 13:137-54, January-April, 1965.

The ideas of Bergson and Heidegger are clearly reflected in the ideas of Antonio Machado. But as a poet, Machado is closer to Proust. He feels time in the same way. He makes similar extensive use of memory and dream, and creates a similar mood of tedio or tempo lento. (C.O.)

P1278   Porel, Jacques, "Reminiscences of Proust," American Scholar, 27:331-42, Summer, 1958.

[This is an English translation of a section from Porel's Fils de Réjane, recounting his acquaintance with Proust.] (F.J.P.)

P1279   Poulet, Georges, "L'Espace proustien," La Nouvelle Revue Française, No. 121, pp. 32-56, January, 1963; No. 122, pp. 243-64, February, 1963.

The phenomenon of Proustian remembrance not only causes the mind to waver between two distinct epochs but to choose between mutually incompatible places. Consequently, his work is not only a search for lost time, but for lost space. Thanks to memory, time is not lost, and, if it is not lost, neither is space. Alongside of time recaptured is recaptured space, or, more precisely, space finally captured. (T.T.B.)

P1280   Poulet, Georges, "L'Espace proustien (III)," La Nouvelle Revue Française, No. 123, pp. 442-68, March, 1963.

Places which exist only independently of each other are connected by Proust via travel, superposition and juxtaposition. Proustian time is spatialized time, time juxtaposed. It could not be otherwise from the moment Proust conceived temporal reality under the form of a series of tableaux successively presented, which appear at the end, simultaneously, outside of time but not outside of space. (T.T.B.)

P1281 Proust, Marcel, "Marcel Proust: Quatre lettres à son frère Robert," La Nouvelle Revue Française, No. 209, pp. 744-50, May, 1970.

[These are personal letters, containing literary criticism, written from 1914 to 1920 to his brother.] (T.T.B.)

P1282 Pugh, Anthony R., "A Forgotten Article by Proust: 'Un Dimanche au conservatoire'," Modern Language Review, 53:87-91, January, 1958.

Proust's little-known article is here reprinted as an early example (1895) of his ability to express one sensation in terms of another and his "method of linking together different themes and ideas." (W.T.S.)

P1283 Pugh, Anthony R., "A Proust Bibliography," Adam International Review, 25:121-6, No. 260, 1957.

[This bibliography, although not exhaustive, is an attempt to pull together chronologically Proust's books and articles published from 1888 to 1922. Reprints of articles are included; À la recherche and its published extracts, with one exception, are not. Letters are not listed.] (D.P.)

P1284 Riefstahl-Nordlinger, Marie, "Memories of Marcel Proust," Listener, 63:749-51, April 28, 1960.

"As his books reached me, I found and I still discover, between the lines, messages intended for me alone and which none other can decipher. And this friendship, these memories of my youth, maintain and strengthen my devotion to France." (P.F.L.)

P1285 Riva, Raymond T., "Death and Immortality in the Works of Marcel Proust," French Review, 35:463-71, April, 1962.

"Physical death is certainly of little importance to Proust, the important life being less physical than psychic, within the minds of men." Here one may attain an immortality through memory or, more importantly, by artistic creation. (R.B.W.)

P1286 Rogers, Brian G., "The Role of Journalism in the Development of
Proust's Narrative Techniques," French Studies, 18:136-44,
April, 1964.

". . . Proust's occasional contributions to the Figaro and other
journals . . . [show] him taking a stand on questions concerned with
the art of fiction itself, criticizing the works of others in an attempt
to clarify his own position. Second, we can see him instinctively
adopting a new standpoint from which he can develop fictional techniques [for] . . . continuous narrative. Third, we can trace the
influence upon Proust's developing style and technique of the newly
acquired freedom which he found in the discursive essay and, finally,
conclude that the reappearance of this freedom within a fictional plan
provided him . . . with the formula he needed to express himself
most fully." (D.P.)

P1287 Ryan, James, "Descriptions of Music by Proust and Gustavo Adolfo
Bécquer," Hispania, 46:274-8, May, 1963.

"Proust and Bécquer can evoke [sounds], each in his way, better
than most writers." (C.O.)

P1288 Salvan, Albert J., "Recent Posthumous Proust Publications,"
American Society of Legion of Honor Magazine, 27:313-29, 1958.

The discovery of two unpublished works, Jean Santeuil and Contre
Sainte-Beuve "have cleared the baffling mystery of Proust's
apparent lack of creativity between 1896 and 1910." Both works
display an intellectual maturity and a dynamic poetic creativity.
(P.F.L.)

P1289 Saussine, Renée, "Si l'ardeur qui dure devient lumière," Adam
International Review, 25:99-101, No. 260, 1957.

In a July 1893 article on Henri de Saussine's Le Nez de Cléopâtre,
Proust's first themes are already evident. (D.-J.J.)

P1290 Savage, Catherine H., "Nostalgia in Alain-Fournier and Proust,"
French Review, 38:167-72, December, 1964.

"One can surmise, then, that Proust's nostalgia was more
individually centered than that of Alain-Fournier, who frequently
revealed a longing for a God-centered belief . . . [and was] tempted
by the idea of the Christian Paradise." (D.P.)

P1291 Schiff, Violet, "A Letter from Marcel Proust written at Cabourg in 1912 to a Young Man of 18, and Now Published for the First Time," London Magazine, 3:26-6, June, 1956.

[Deceived in friendship by an eighteen year old, Proust's disappointment and sensitivity are evident in a letter written to this vain and inconsiderate young man.] (P.F.L.)

P1292 Schiff, Violet, "A Night with Proust," London Magazine, 3:20-2, September, 1956.

"I believe Marcel Proust to have been one of the most angelic human beings that ever lived." "He was completely disinterested, unself-protective, fantastically generous, loving and lovable." (P.F.L.)

P1293 Schiff, Violet, "Proust Meets Joyce," Adam International Review, 25:64-5, No. 260, 1957.

[This is an account of probably the only meeting between Marcel Proust and James Joyce, which took place in Paris.] (D.P.)

P1294 Shattuck, Roger, "Making Time: A Study of Stravinsky, Proust, and Sartre," Kenyon Review, 25:248-63, Spring, 1963.

Proust and Sartre "share the sense of music being another time, a newly created order of things"; Stravinsky also controls time and "shapes an art that reaches a universal order of communion." (G.S.)

P1295 Smithner, Eric, "Les Poupées intérieures de Marcel Proust," French Review, 32:520-6, May, 1959.

In Proust's world, the men fabricate ideal women and fall in love with them. The dichotomy between the object of the fantasy and the fantasy itself causes these men a great deal of sorrow; however, it also leads to self-knowledge. (D.-J.J.)

P1296 Sonnenfeld, Albert, "Tristan for Pianoforte: Thomas Mann and Marcel Proust," Southern Review, 5:1004-18, Autumn, 1969.

"In the works of Thomas Mann and Marcel Proust, the Wagnerite of the piano bench is an important ironic representation of the authors's own youthful fervor as acolytes at the pagan altars of Bayreuth. And if in later years they were to mock the excessively pious faithful, they never forswore the faith." (J.M.D.)

P1297 Soucy, Robert, "Proust's Aesthetic of Reading," <u>French Review</u>, 41:48-59, October, 1967.

". . . Proust suggests that good reading rather than being an escape from reality is a means of experiencing it more fully, a means of sharpening one's intellectual and emotional awareness of life. In this, the act of reading is not unlike the act of creating." (W.J.L.)

P1298 Stockwell, H. C. R., "Proust and Reality," <u>Adam International Review</u>, 25:106-10, No. 260, 1957.

"Proust hated to forget anything, whether the shape of a hat or a line of Racine. He had to get his facts straight . . . mainly because he thought of himself as a man dealing with facts from which he hoped to deduce rigorous laws. . . . On the other hand Proust could not tolerate reality; it hurt him. . . . he used ordinary reality as a means to the ideal. . . ." (D.P.)

P1299 Tadié, Jean-Yves, "Proust et le 'nouvel écrivain'," <u>Revue d'Histoire Littéraire de la France</u>, 67:79-81, January-March, 1967.

"What Proust liked in Giraudoux and Morand was the reflection of his own vision, his own lesson in the mirror of their images." (D.-J.J.)

P1300 Todd, Robert E., "Proust and Redemption in <u>Waiting for Godot</u>," <u>Modern Drama</u>, 10:175-81, September, 1967.

"Thus the question as to whether or not Godot is God is resolved finally in . . . the less arbitrary conclusion that Godot is the redeemer, or metaphysical entity in whom modern man no longer really believes, yet whose existence, paradoxically enough, remains modern man's most ardent desire or hypothetical imperative." (D.P.)

P1301 Torre Campoy, Manuel de la, "El carácter de Marcel Proust," <u>La Estafeta Literaria</u>, No. 385, p. 25, December 16, 1967.

The marvel of his work is explained by the immensity of Proust's suffering, by the true martyrdom of his real life. To illness, homosexuality and the capacity to feel definite affections is joined in heart-rending fashion in Proust an absolute inertia before life. (T.T.B.)

P1302 Tougas, Gérard, "Marcel Proust devant la critique anglo-saxonne: Quelques aspects," Revue de Littérature Comparée, 30:102-6, January-March, 1956.

". . . for the French critic, the man and the product of his thought, the work, are two; for the Anglo-saxon critic, they constitute a totality." Thus, "despite the unprecedented amount of English criticism provoked by Proust, the condemnation of the man has been unjustly extended to his work." (R.C.F.)

P1303 Tukey, Ann, "Notes on Involuntary Memory in Proust," French Review, 42:395-402, February, 1969.

". . . involuntary memory, like mystic experience, is noetic (in a certain way), transient, passive, and appears to follow, psychologically, the stages of mystic trance." Nevertheless, "the term 'mystic' and mystic experience as used by James do not definitively summarize the intellectual nature and aesthetic value of involuntary memory in Proust." (W.J.L.)

P1304 Urman, Dorothy Fuldheim, "Konstantin Paustovskii, Marcel Proust and the Golden Rose of Memory," Canadian Slavic Studies, 2:311-26, Fall, 1968.

"For Proust art was a subjective intellectual exercise in analyzing a man's soul. Paustovskii displays a gentle, compassionate heart as he lays bare before us the life of his moment in the Space-Time continuum. . . . In neither Proust nor Paustovskii is there grandeur. Proust was too cultivated, Paustovskii too gentle. . . . Proust chronicled the world he knew. . . . Paustovskii shows the collapse of that world. . . ." (D.P.)

P1305 Vigneron, Robert, "Marcel Proust: Creative Agony," Chicago Review, 12:33-51, Spring, 1958.

[An English version of articles in French in Modern Philology, November, 1941, pp. 159-95, and March, 1945, pp. 212-30, this extended essay charts the moral condition of Proust during the fifteen years before the "illumination" which led to À la recherche du temps perdu.] (B.M.S.)

P1306 Vigneron, Robert, "A propos d'une prétendue lettre de Proust à Vallette," Modern Philology, 52:131-3, November, 1954.

Contrary to the information in the catalogue Autographes et documents historiques by Théodore Tausky (Summer, 1952-53, pp. 50-51, No. 21137), which indicates that a letter by Proust was sent to Vallette, the letter was actually written to Auguste Marguillier, editor for the Gazette des Beaux Arts and its supplement, Chronique des Arts et de la Curiosité; the chief business of the letter was to communicate Proust's offer to collaborate with M. Marguillier on the newspapers which he edited. Parts of the letter illustrate Proust's interest in certain English engravings and his ingeniously politic methods of protecting himself from unexpected incursions on his private life. (A.A.S.)

P1307 Watson, D. R., "Sixteen Letters of Marcel Proust to Joseph Reinach," Modern Language Review, 63:587-99, July, 1968.

[These letters are preceded by a short commentary which discusses Proust's interest in the Dreyfus Affair, his concern with the anti-clerical campaign of the Combes cabinet, and especially the nature of his relationship with Reinach and the reasons behind its termination.] (W.J.L.)

À LA RECHERCHE DU TEMPS PERDU

P1308 Alden, Douglas W., "Proustian Configuration in Jean-Christophe," French Review, 41:262-71, November, 1967.

". . . the numerous similarities between Jean-Christophe and À la recherche du temps perdu . . . although they do not prove an influence, lead to the conclusion that these two authors had far more in common than either would recognize." (W.J.L.)

P1309 André, Robert, "Walter Pater et Marcel Proust," La Nouvelle Revue Française, No. 126, pp. 1082-9, June, 1963.

The reading of Pater, as well as of Ruskin, helped Proust to conceive with more clarity the sense of À la recherche du temps perdu. Both, in the domain of art, drew the same conclusions, namely, that the faculty of discovering the real resides in the power to distinguish and fix fugitive and delicate details. (T.T.B.)

À LA RECHERCHE DU TEMPS PERDU (cont'd)

P1310 Auchincloss, Louis, "Proust's Picture of Society," Partisan Review, 27:690-701, Fall, 1960.

Never "in fiction or outside of it, has there been so brilliant or so comprehensive a study of the social world. In fact, it stands so above its nearest competitors as to seem in retrospect almost the only picture of society in all literature." (W.J.L.)

P1311 Bailey, Ninette, "Symbolisme et composition dans l'oeuvre de Proust: Essai de lecture colorée de la recherche du temps perdu," French Studies, 20:253-66, July, 1966.

[This is a study of the symbolic use of colors in Proust's À la recherche du temps perdu.] (D.P.)

P1312 Baker, Joseph E., "Ivory Tower as Laboratory: Pater and Proust," Accent, 19:204-16, Autumn, 1959.

"Not only does Proust set forth the same esthetic theory as Pater, and develop it; he has in À la recherche du temps perdu produced the greatest masterpiece in conformity with that theory since Pater wrote 'style'." (W.J.L.)

P1313 Barnes, Annie, "Le Jardin de Marcel Proust: Pour le cinquantenaire des 'Jeunes filles en fleurs'," Modern Language Review, 64:546-54, July, 1969.

Proust tells us that "Even without being a creative artist every human being has an interior garden . . . [where] not only all art is true, but also all life is spiritual--the true life." (J.R.R.)

P1314 Barnes, Annie, "Le Retour des thèmes dans la recherche du temps perdu et l'art de Proust," Australian Journal of French Studies, 6:26-54, January-April, 1969.

Although Proust sought to incarnate his theories rather than to expound them overtly, illness and finally death, prevented him from completing this task. Examination of corrected proofs and manuscripts show how Proust, through the recurrence of themes tried to achieve this goal of literary incarnation. (F.M.L.)

À LA RECHERCHE DU TEMPS PERDU   (cont'd)

P1315 Bell, William S., "Proust's Un Amour de Swann: A Voyage to
Cytherea," L'Esprit Créateur, 5:26-37, Spring, 1965.

Like Baudelaire's voyager, Proust, the narrator, sets out on a
quest for the country of love and finds it sterile. In both cases,
love is an actively destructive force. At the end of the voyage,
Baudelaire's adventurer, like Swann, finds there only his own
image. (T.T.B.)

P1316 Beznos, Maurice J., "Aspects of Time According to the Theories
of Relativity in Marcel Proust's À la recherche du temps perdu: A
Study of the Similitudes in Conceptual Limits," Ohio University
Review, 10:74-102, 1968.

A comparative analysis of Proust's work and Einstein's theories
yields the conclusion: "Proust and Einstein seem to have employed
in their works . . . certain comparable functional components to
yield comparable descriptions of Time and the universe." (J.M.D.)

P1317 Birn, Randi Marie, "Love and Communication: An Interpretation of
Proust's Albertine," French Review, 40:221-8, November, 1966.

The closer one is attached to a person, the more difficult it is to
grasp his character since it is not separated from his own. A study
of Albertine demonstrates that love is not a means of communication
and does not put an end to isolation. (S.M.K.)

P1318 Birn, Randi Marie, "The Windows of Imagination in À la recherche
du temps perdu," Pacific Coast Philology, 5:5-11, 1970.

"In À la recherche du temps perdu window imagery serves as a
gauge of a character's emotional receptiveness." It also "documents
one aspect of the laborious process which guides Marcel towards his
vocation." (F.M.L.)

P1319 Black, Carl John, Jr., "Albertine as an Allegorical Figure of Time,"
Romanic Review, 54:171-86, October, 1963.

". . . in her very amorphousness and ambiguity, Albertine assumes
the form of time as conceived in the novel . . . a sort of great and
complex image through which Proust expresses the mysteries of
human time. . . . Albertine conveys more completely than any other
character the fundamental meaning of À la recherche du temps perdu
and thus becomes the central figure of Marcel's narration."(R.C.F.)

À LA RECHERCHE DU TEMPS PERDU   (cont'd)

P1320   Bondanella, Peter E. and J. E. Rivers, "Sacripant and Sacripante: A Note on Proust and Ariosto," Romance Notes, 11:4-7, Autumn, 1969.

Elstir's painting of Odette as "Miss Sacripant" invites a comparison of Swann's love to that of Sacripante and Angelica in Orlando Furioso. (A.K.)

P1321   Brée, Germaine, "Proust's Combray Church: Illiers or Vermeer?" Proceedings of the American Philosophical Society, 112:5-7, February, 1968.

"To conclude, Proust . . . consistently compares works of art to optical devices that help us to rescue from oblivion the vague, undeveloped impressions lost to us in our conscious life. Vermeer's View of Delft seems to have served as just such an optical device for Proust, one of several. There is a kind of kinship between Illiers and Vermeer's Delft. . . . The View of Delft, perhaps because it has a spatial analogy with the Illiers of Proust's childish perceptions, may have . . . activat[ed] the vague impressions stored in his mind . . . as a patterned and ordered whole, with strong aesthetic potentialities, creating a vivid long-term impression." (D.P.)

P1322   Brée, Germaine, "Proust's Dormant Gods," Yale French Studies, No. 38, pp. 183-94, May, 1967.

"Through the figures of legend and mythology, Proust reaches out toward a vision of reality, diversified and yet consistently illustrative of a unique theme. The Greeks offered him their myths from which he drew, in order to give substance to his own myth on art. . . . It is to the Orphic mysteries rather than to the Greek tragics that Proust's vision is keyed . . . Proust's ambition was to awaken and free the dormant god in his reader, to urge him to . . . become a creator." (D.P.)

P1323   Cattaui, Georges, "Albertine retrouvée: Alfred Agostinelli a-t-il inspiré La Prisonniére?" Adam International Review, 25:80-4, No. 260, 1957.

Alfred Agostinelli was, from time to time, Proust's chauffeur and secretary from 1907 to 1914, before he was killed in an airplane crash. "Although it would be an exaggeration to say that Agostinelli is Albertine, undoubtedly he contributed several traits of character." (D.P.)

À LA RECHERCHE DU TEMPS PERDU (cont'd)

P1324 Cattaui, Georges, "Le Cinquantenaire de Swann et la critique proustienne," Critique, No. 198, pp. 958-69, November, 1963.

After a half century Du côté de chez Swann has lost nothing of its youth. The "lost time" in question was a "lost paradise" and the "search" was a "quest for the Holy Grail." Like his master Baudelaire, Proust wanted to realize "scientifically the absolute by making it the object of knowing." (T.T.B.)

P1325 Chua, C. L., "Proust's Un Amour de Swann," Explicator, 26: Item 69, May, 1968.

". . . what the Sonata tells Swann, and what Un Amour de Swann tells us, is that if we are able to transfigure a ridiculous love affair or an insane existence into a work of art, then we will have achieved something of permanence." (D.P.)

P1326 Clarac, Pierre, "À la recherche du temps perdu: Histoire d'une vocation (Documents inédits)," Adam International Review, 25:88-92, No. 260, 1957.

Swann and Guermantes are hardly more than the history of the deceptions by which a young man approaches the calling of novelist; however, one must search in his guises, and not in his spirit, for the secret of his beauty. . . . This theme of deception . . . appears and reappears on all the pages of Guermantes." (D.P.)

P1327 Cocking, J. M., "Proust and Combray," London Magazine, 1:59-73, December, 1954.

In À la recherche du temps perdu "the most self-contained, the brightest, the sun from which all other worlds borrowed some degree of reflected light was Combray. Whenever Marcel looks for the origin of those values, attitudes and expectations which set the course of his life, and determine the measure of his happiness, it is to Combray that he must return; and when he comes to present his past in the radiance of the involuntary memory, it is around Combray that the halo shines most convincingly." (D.P.)

À LA RECHERCHE DU TEMPS PERDU   (cont'd)

P1328   Cook, Albert, "Proust: The Invisible Stilts of Time," <u>Modern</u>
<u>Fiction Studies</u>, 4:118-26, Summer, 1958.

"The time which is the very essence of the novel, manipulated by
Stern and others, is rendered by Proust in the very actuality of its
process, is rendered as intimating, in all aesthetic surface and
spiritual depth, the conquest of natural time by the represented
quality of time."   (R.A.K.)

P1329   Cunningham, William, "Giorgione Transfigured--A Note on Proust's
Method," <u>Romance Notes</u>, 9:12-5, Autumn, 1967.

". . . Proust . . . does not hesitate to rearrange the facts concerning
even major paintings in order to create something which has a logic
and an aesthetic value only when seen in the context of his own purpose." (F.M.L.)

P1330   Curtis, Jean-Louis, "Time after Death," <u>Adam International</u>
<u>Review</u>, 31:73-114, Nos. 310-11-12, 1966.

"The narrator in <u>À la recherche du temps perdu</u> attends a reception
given by the daughter of Robert de Saint-Loup and Gilberte Swann in
contemporary Paris. This provides the text for this brief Proustian
evocation. . . . Included at this reception [are] . . . M. Mauriac,
M. Malraux, M. Paulhan. . . . the text in the last chapter [is]
attributed to M. André Breton. . . ." (D.P.)

P1331   Daniel, Vera J., "Proustian Time," <u>Contemporary Review</u>,
No. 1095, pp. 185-6, March, 1957.

Germaine Brée's recent study presents the structure of <u>Remembrance</u>
<u>of Things Past</u> as culminating in the transition element borne on
time's stream.   The subjective experience related demands the first
person point of view. (F.L.)

P1332   Dobbs, Annie-Claude, "Rousseau et Proust: 'Ouvertures' des
<u>Confessions</u> et d'<u>À la recherche du temps perdu</u>," <u>L'Esprit</u>
<u>Créateur</u>, 9:165-74, Fall, 1969.

The commentary of both authors invites one to consider as distinct
and inseparable from the rest of the work the first six books of the
<u>Confessions</u>, and <u>Combray</u> of the other author. The construction of
both is unequivocal. The last lines of the Sixth Book and of <u>Combray</u>

À LA RECHERCHE DU TEMPS PERDU   (cont'd)

are both the closing and the beginning. In spite of their independency both are organically indissociable from the ensemble.   (T.T.B.)

P1333   Duncan, J. Ann, "Imaginary Artists in À la recherche du temps perdu," Modern Language Review, 64:555-64, July, 1969.

"The orchestration of the four versions of the theme of artistic discovery, presented dramatically and successively in the first movement of the novel, relegated to an underlying motif in the second, reappears in contrapuntal form in the third before achieving its final synthesis." (J.R.R.)

P1334   Friedman, Gabrielle, "La Symbole de la sculpture mortuaire chez Proust," French Review, 30:5-12, October, 1956.

"The symbolism of the sculpture is restricted to two themes . . . the petrification of the Proustian person at the moment of death" and the moment when the narrator is struck by the resemblance between the gothic statues and the people of Combray." (D.H.)

P1335   Garrett, Helen T., "Marcel Proust's Vision of the French Social Hierarchy," Modern Language Forum, 40:95-103, December, 1955.

In À la recherche du temps perdu, the France depicted by Proust is an essentially democratic country "in which social hierarchy is nothing but an illusion, where it is perfectly possible to rise from one class into another and to be accepted by the reigning aristocracy." (F.M.L.)

P1336   Genette, Gérard, "Proust palimpseste," Tel Quel, No. 12, pp. 60-72, Winter, 1963.

Proust's work is a palimpsest in which are entangled and confused several figures and meanings, all present at the same time and capable of being deciphered only in their inextricable totality. (T.T.B.)

P1337   Gerstel, Eva Maria, "Proust's Conception of Nature," Rice University Studies, 11:23-32, Summer, 1965.

"Since Proust does not believe in a discontinuity between life in the outside world and that in the mental world, he is able to integrate nature into his being so as to make it a part of his 'moi-successifs' and to portray spiritual realities." (F.M.L.)

À LA RECHERCHE DU TEMPS PERDU   (cont'd)

P1338   Graham, Victor E., "Proust's Alchemy," Modern Language Review, 60:197-206, April, 1965.

The author offers a comparison which can be evoked to emphasize the sequential nature of À la recherche du temps perdu as it builds up to the stunning climax of Le Temps retrouvé: "From one important point of view, [the novel] is simply the story of how Proust came to write his novel, and in his long search for a raison d'être, the author might be said to be a sort of alchemist pursuing the quest for the philosopher's stone." (J.R.R.)

P1339   Graham, Victor E., "Water Imagery and Symbolism in Proust," Romanic Review, 50:118-28, April, 1959.

"Proust is undeniably lucid in his expression, but his work also provides examples of provocative private symbols which, once we are aware of them, increase immeasurably our appreciation of the novel À la recherche du temps perdu and its unity." (R.G.L.)

P1340   Gray, Stanley E., "Phenomenology, Structuralism and Marcel Proust," L'Esprit Créateur, 8:58-74, Spring, 1968.

"Proust's novel presents us with dualistic problems which the author has not entirely solved himself but which . . . suggest avenues to solution. Structuralist approaches can contribute much, but the only kind of analysis offering solutions appropriate to the problems seems to be a phenomenological one because only phenomenology resolves the subject-object duality in the particular ways suggested by Proust himself, ways that lead to unification." (D.P.)

P1341   Grubbs, Henry A., "Sartre's Recapturing of Lost Time," Modern Language Notes, 73:515-22, November, 1958.

"May I suggest that Sartre was taking a wry pleasure in making La Nausée an ironic counterpart of À la recherche du temps perdu; a reduced model, ironic, modern, realistic, a little sordid--in a word, a poor man's Proust." (M.J.O.)

P1342   Grubbs, Henry, "Two Treatments of a Subject: Proust's La Regarder dormir and Valéry's La Dormeuse," PMLA, 71:900-9, December, 1956.

To compare Valéry's sonnet with Proust's fragment from La

À LA RECHERCHE DU TEMPS PERDU   (cont'd)

Prisonnière--two fine treatments of the same subject, a man watching the beloved asleep--is to demonstrate a "profound difference between the intent and the method of prose fiction and . . . 'pure' poetry." (B.K.)

P1343   Gülich, Elisabeth, "Die Metaphorik der Erinnerung in Prousts À la recherche du temps perdu," Zeitschrift für Französische Sprache und Literatur, 75:51-74, April, 1965.

This study of Proust's metaphorical presentation of memories concludes that "the fabric of memories corresponds not only to Proust's theory of memory but also to his technique of presentation; through the tying of the threads of memory there emerges a pattern of high artistic quality which makes clear at the same time the strictly thought out and ingeniously executed composition of the work of art." (J.R.R.)

P1344   Gutwirth, Marcel, "Swann and the Duchess," French Review, 38:143-51, December, 1964.

"When Swann said he was dying, the Duchess would not have her evening marred by sorrow. She could not reach out to him, her friend, from amidst her whirl of temporalities. . . . To make the Duchess and the aesthete meet at last in the eternity of art, to bring Swann's way in touch with Le côté de Guermantes, this is one achievement of Marcel's victorious quest." (W.J.L.)

P1345   Heiney, Donald, "Illiers and Combray: A Study in Literary Geography," Twentieth Century Literature, 1:17-26, April, 1955.

Many parallels may be drawn between Illiers, where Proust spent his boyhood vacations, and Combray, the fictional town in À la recherche du temps perdu, and a number of dissimilarities also exist. The creative, imaginative sources of Proust's novel are drawn out of his experiences, refined, modified, embellished. (D.P.)

P1346   Heppenstall, Rayner, "Morel," Twentieth Century, 165:482-92, May, 1959.

At the core of Proust's literary portrait of Morel, there seems to lie some "phantom resentment at whose precise nature we can only guess." (F.M.L.)

À LA RECHERCHE DU TEMPS PERDU   (cont'd)

P1347   Hicks, Eric C., "Swann's Dream and the World of Sleep," Yale French Studies, No. 34, pp. 106-16, June, 1965.

". . . the poetry of dreams, as indeed all poetry in Remembrance of Things Past, must be in some way related to realities which lie beyond the realm of immediate perception." Thus, "the dream recounted in the closing pages of Swann in Love is a poetic presentation culled from the hidden reality of the dreamer's former selves." (D.P.)

P1348   Hoog, Armand, "Time, Fate and Photography in the World of Marcel Proust," American Society of Legion of Honor Magazine, 32:49-60, No. 1, 1961.

"The symbolic importance of the acquisition of photographs or of their ritualistic use is one of the keys to Proust." Time for him is "a strange gallery of fascinating, disseminated photographs." (F.M.L.)

P1349   Houston, John Porter, "The Grandparents of Proust's Narrator: A Conflation," Philological Quarterly, 42:134-7, January, 1963.

"The two families depicted in Du côté de chez Swann are a conflation of the fourfold grandparental families of reality. The grandmother represents the maternal grandparents, the grandfather, the parental ones. . . . He abandons biological fact in describing the narrator's grandparents in order to create an artistic pattern better structured and more incisive than a real situation." (R.C.F.)

P1350   Houston, J. P., "Temporal Patterns in À la recherche du temps perdu," French Studies, 16:33-44, January, 1962.

Proust's temporal patterns are based on "natural temporal units: the day, the season, the year; but he presents them subjectively, as they are distorted by memory. . . ." He abandoned "the realist-naturalist technique which is based on chapter forms rather than temporal patterns." (F.M.L.)

P1351   Houston, John Porter, "Thought, Style, and Shape in Proust's Novel," Southern Review, 5:987-1003, Autumn, 1969.

"Proust's novel is an example--rare in modern literature--of the transmutation of complex metaphysical ideas into the concreteness

3363   P1351

À LA RECHERCHE DU TEMPS PERDU   (cont'd)

of art." Although Kant has served as Proust's original inspiration, Proust's thought is tempered by the pessimism of Schopenhauer. (J.M.D.)

P1352   Howard, R. G., "The Construction of an Episode in À la recherche du temps perdu," Australian Journal of French Studies, 4:74-85, January-April, 1967.

"The episode of Jupien's encounter with the Baron de Charlus in the courtyard of the Hôtel de Guermantes" was built up by Proust "from a number of primitive ideas in Contre Sainte-Beuve" and even earlier, and demonstrates that for Proust "considerations of plausibility counted heavily . . . in constructing his plots." (F.M.L.)

P1353   Hulin, J. P., "Joseph Milsand, maître à penser de Marcel Proust," Revue de Littérature Comparée, 30:419-24, July-September, 1956.

"Indirectly, the study of Milsand's influence tends to prove that, with Proust, reflection on esthetics preceded novelistic creation: an order which the final layout of the novel did not suggest." (D.-J.J.)

P1354   Hyde, John K., "Proust, His Jews and His Jewishness," French Review, 39:837-48, May, 1966.

". . . [Proust's] Jews are not endowed with a particular ethnic identity. Proust has seen them chiefly as components of the society he depicts. . . . In sum, the richness which they afford the novel can be ascribed chiefly to their role as agents against whose presence worldly success and human foible are exploited and developed." (R.C.F.)

P1355   Jackson, Elizabeth R., "The Crystallization of À la recherche du temps perdu 1908-1909," French Review, 38:157-66, December, 1964.

[With Proust's personal notebook as source, the problems of dating the novel's birth, the relationship of the novel to the study on Saint-Beuve, and whether Proust experienced "a 'revelation' . . . whereby all doubts concerning the nature of artistic creation and the nature of his book were resolved simultaneously" are examined.] (R.C.F.)

À LA RECHERCHE DU TEMPS PERDU   (cont'd)

P1356 Johnson, J. Theodore, Jr., "From Artistic Celibacy to Artistic
Contemplation," Yale French Studies, No. 34, pp. 81-9, June, 1965.

In À la recherche du temps perdu "the virtues of erudition, memory
and sensitivity lead Swann neither to the core of art nor to a pro-
founder understanding of himself and of others, but rather to a world
peripheral to art and reality, an esthetic limbo where virtues are
tainted by the vice of idolatry." (D.P.)

P1357 Johnson, Pamela Hansford, F. R. S. L., "Marcel Proust: Illusion
and Reality," Essays by Divers Hands, 32:58-71, 1963.

"Proust is so complex a writer that we are over-tempted to find short-
hand contractions for what we read into him. We catch the illusion, and
the reality escapes us: we debate the reality, and we lose the illusion.
...He is...far nearer to Balzac than has been realized...." (D.P.)

P1358 Johnson, Pamela Hansford, "Proust 1900," Encounter, 14:21-8,
February, 1960.

"In every serious novel there is a climacteric year . . . in which
the characters come to their full ripeness . . .: it is . . . the
moment before the decline into dust of mildness. . . . In À la
recherche du temps perdu it is . . .1900." (R.C.F.)

P1359 Johnson, Pamela Hansford, "A Single Saint-Loup," London
Magazine, 2:54-63, July, 1955.

Saint-Loup, "Proust's one serious attempt at the study of sexual
ambivalence," was probably not originally conceived as a homosexual. But Proust brilliantly develops this characterization from
ambiguities intuitively introduced at the beginning, although "his final
degradation seems to me wholly arbitrary and absurd." (J.L.B.)

P1359a Jones, David L., "Dolorès disparue," Symposium, 20:135-40,
Summer, 1966.

In Lolita "many of Nabokov's lyrical passages offer a light parody, or
at least a reminiscence, of the verbal ecstasies of Proust's narrator.
The strongest Proustian imprint, however, appears not on Nabokov's
style but on the narrative structure and content of Lolita." Finally,
"the strength of each novel lies not in the consistency of the writer's
tragic or comic control, but in the richness of the psychological
world he creates." (D.P.)

À LA RECHERCHE DU TEMPS PERDU (cont'd)

P1360 Jones, Peter, "Knowledge and Illusion in À la recherche du temps perdu," Forum for Modern Language Studies, 5:303-22, October, 1969.

Proust's narrator "tries to fuse his epistemological views largely founded on idealism, with the realism . . . essential to his role as narrator." He discovers that "knowledge is possible, even if it is, in a sense, always knowledge of the past; but its presentation is as difficult as its attainment." (R.O.R.)

P1361 King, Clifford, "The Laughter of Marcel Proust," Adam International Review, 25:126-9, No. 260, 1957.

"Proust is in all senses a serious writer, but he is also a very funny one." In À la recherche "the quality and quantity of his comedy rang[es] from faint irony to passages that recall Dickens" although he "has very little . . . of Dickens's concern for his characters." (D.P.)

P1362 Kolb, Philip, "An Enigmatic Proustian Metaphor," Romanic Review, 54:187-97, October, 1963.

The ambiguity of the metaphor which associates Aunt Léonie's forehead with the unfortunate word "vertèbres"--which led to the novel's rejection and to Proust's being ill-judged by readers--is attributable to a typographical error, subsequently overlooked due to Proust's "cavalier manner of correcting proof." (R.C.F.)

P1363 Kolb, Philip, "Proust's Protagonist as a'Beacon'," L'Esprit Créateur, 5:38-47, Spring, 1965.

The real protagonist of Proust's novel is not Time, as has been suggested, but the Narrator. Strictly speaking, Time is just a major theme, closely interwoven with that of Memory. (T.T.B.)

P1364 Kostis, Nicholas, "Albertine: Characterization through Image and Symbol," PMLA, 84:125-35, January, 1969.

"As seen through these images [flower, sea, bird] she [Albertine] is characterized by constant change on both the physical and psychological levels. . . . The imagery concerning Albertine, therefore, offers a clear demonstration of the Proustian conception of the human condition, and takes its place within the framework of the entire novel." (R.C.F.)

À LA RECHERCHE DU TEMPS PERDU (cont'd)

P1365 Languth, William, "The World and Life of the Dream," Yale French
Studies, No. 34, pp. 117-8, 120-30, June, 1965.

"Book and dream here begin in quiet association, imperceptibly
gathering from the first tiny increments the relationship which they
are to intermingle and confer on one another through the length of
their necessary work toward release. Boundless but circumscribed,
empty though pregnant, sleep is the key through which Proust can
approach dream and death and oblivion beyond, in which all things
are fused, all longings are no more. Sleep precedes dream, but
sleep and death are one. Death leads to oblivion, and so the oblivion
of sleep is one with death and dream. These are the sturdy nothings
of which structure is built." (D.P.)

P1366 Larcher, P. L., "Le Secret de Combray," Adam International
Review, 25:74-7, No. 260, 1957.

"Combray is in effect the symbol of the world which each of us is
able to recreate, to surround oneself in; it is the result of one's
personal experience, assimilated and integrated in one's character
and enhanced in value by the harmonies of one's inner life. It is
that which one discovers in Illiers after having penetrated the work
of Proust. . . ." (D.P.)

P1367 La Rochefoucauld, Edmée de, "La Maison de Tante Léonie,"
Adam International Review, 25:61-2, No. 260, 1957.

[This is a description of the house of Elisabeth Amiot, the model
for Tante Léonie.] (D.-J.J.)

P1368 LeSage, Laurent, "A Day in Proust's Combray," American Society
of Legion of Honor Magazine, 31:85-94, No. 2, 1960.

[This is a visit to Illiers, the Combray of Du côté de chez Swann.]
(F.M.L.)

P1369 Lettelier, Piere, "Avec Swann sur un Escalier (Extrait dún ouvrage
à paraitre prochainement)," Die Neueren Sprachen, 15:499-506,
November, 1966.

[This is a discussion of the symbolism contained in Proust's
detailed description of l'Escalier des Geants.] (J.R.R.)

À LA RECHERCHE DU TEMPS PERDU   (cont'd)

P1370   Lewis, Philip E., "Idealism and Reality," Yale French Studies,
No. 34, pp. 24-8, June, 1965.

In À la recherche du temps perdu "the narrator's experience of
eternity involves . . . the displacement of fictitious, one-dimensional,
Newtonian time by a full, comprehensive, integrating Time, whose
causal progression . . . precludes futile concerns for the future.
. . . In this temporal framework, Proustian reality thus represents
a strain of idealism, since only the mind can effect the transcendance
of time. But more importantly, as it is experienced, this reality is
simultaneously . . . a universe derived from external phenomena
and validated by internal relationships subconsciously established in
Time." (D.P.)

P1371   Linn, John Gaywood, "Notes on Proust's Manipulation of Chronology,"
Romanic Review, 52:210-25, October, 1961.

"Certain of Proust's allusions to plays, or to theatrical events such
as the Paris performances of the Russian Ballet, serve to establish
the effect of the passage of time and the chronology of particular
events in À la recherche du temps perdu." (R.G.L.)

P1372   Linn, John Greenwood, "Proust's Theatre Metaphors," Romanic
Review, 49:179-90, October, 1958.

"Throughout the whole of the vast work," (À la recherche du temps
perdu), "Proust has included more than twenty . . . metaphors, of
varied lengths, drawing on theatre, drama, and stage. . . . These
theatrical metaphors provide a useful perspective on Proust's grand
plan." (R.G.L.)

P1373   Lockspeiser, Edward, "Gabriel Fauré and Marcel Proust, "
Listener, 65:985, June 1, 1961.

"The long personal and musical relationship between Proust and
Fauré . . . has a direct bearing on À la recherche du temps perdu,
Proust's profound inquiry into the workings of the unconscious mind
brought to the surface by the myriad associations of music. Proust
believed that only music could illuminate this hinterland of the
conscious mind. In a sense, À la recherche du temps perdu is itself
a musical work, employing musical devices of construction, notably
in the constantly changing significance throughout the twelve volumes
of the 'petite phrase' and the Vinteuil sonata, the device of the

À LA RECHERCHE DU TEMPS PERDU (cont'd)

Wagnerian Leitmotiv. . . . we can be sure that among the works of
Fauré . . . one or another helped to create the visions of the 'little
phrase'." (D.P.)

P1374 Luchting, Wolfgang A., "Hiroshima, mon amour, Time, and
Proust," Journal of Aesthetics and Art Criticism, 21:299-313,
Spring, 1963.

Both artists utilize flashbacks "interwoven with the narration . . .
to annul the normal time perspective" but to different ends.
"Resnais does not wish the past to reside in the present, he pushes
it back into its own realm. Proust celebrates the past, searches it,
makes it into the present, and lives in it." (R.C.F.)

P1375 March, Harold, "The Imprisoned," Yale French Studies, No. 34,
pp. 43-54, June, 1965.

In À la recherche du temps perdu "the prisoner theme, although just
as important as that of homosexuality, is less conspicuous. For one
thing, the term la prisonnière, in the feminine, applies explicitly to
Albertine. . . . For another, the imprisonment is always a metaphor,
and a hackneyed one at that. . . ." (D.P.)

P1376 Marks, Jonathan E., "The Verdurins and Their Cult," Yale French
Studies, No. 34, pp. 73-80, June, 1965.

"Since Proust was a potent satirist, it is no surprise that in
Remembrance of Things Past the snobs receive a torrid, masterful
roasting at the hands of their former dévoté. He depicts them
mercilessly . . . in the narrator and his family, in Legrandin, in
the Verdurins, in the company of Mme. de Saint-Euverte, in the
Princesse des Laumes, in the Guermantes. . . . A glimpse at the
'cult of the Verdurins' gives us some idea of what Proust saw in
le beau monde. . . . We see its attempts to maintain an eternal
rigidity, its estrangement from the world of human action and
advancement, its inability to recognize that it possesses the very
faults it most despises." (D.P.)

P1377 Moss, Howard, "The Two Ways," Sewanee Review, 70:451-63,
Summer, 1962.

For Proust, memory, "embalmer of original enchantments . . .
is the only human faculty that can outwit the advance of chronological

À LA RECHERCHE DU TEMPS PERDU (cont'd)

time. Art, the embalmer of memory, is the only human vocation in which the time regained by memory can be permanently fixed." These are "the saving graces" of Remembrance of Things Past. (A.S.)

P1378   Murray, Jack, "Dinners at Rivebelle: A Study in Proust's Search for the 'Moi Profond'," Modern Language Quarterly, 24:267-73, September, 1963.

The treatment of time in one section of À l'ombre des jeunes filles en fleurs reveals how Proust "released memory . . . from its restricted role as a subsidiary instrument of unification and placed it in the far more important position it deserved as that wealth within us which orients us to ourselves as souls living in time. . . ." (G.S.)

P1379   Murray, Jack, "The Mystery of Others," Yale French Studies, No. 34, pp. 65-72, June, 1965.

In À la recherche du temps perdu "otherness does emerge as a theme for all those who read the novel today . . . because the novels and works of literary criticism coming after Proust have made present-day readers sharply aware of the theme. For Proust, however . . . otherness was a constant and unnamed barrier between himself and the people around him. . . ." "The principal value of Proust's treatment of the theme of otherness is that, by having had almost to invent it, he was able to make it a natural and even harmonious creation of his own being." (D.P.)

P1380   Murray, Jack, "Proust's Beloved Enemy," Yale French Studies, No. 32, pp. 112-7, October, 1964.

In À la recherche du temps perdu "Proust wished to show us that he had survived the tremendous snares which Paris had set before him at every stage of his existence and had left an eternal monument to himself. . . . Seen in this way, Paris was the scene of a titanic struggle for Proust. But it was a struggle in which Proust was not only victorious but also infinitely enhanced by the impressive stature of his beloved enemy." (D.P.)

À LA RECHERCHE DU TEMPS PERDU (cont'd)

P1381 Murray, Jack, "Proust's Robert de Saint-Loup and the Diagnostic Eye," Texas Studies in Literature and Language, 6:68-75, Spring, 1964.

"As Saint-Loup's case comes to show, Proust had an ultimately pathological concept of the human personality and, while the diagnostic approach could suggest various interpretations of a person's behavior, the result of overapplying such a technique is a sense of ambiguity." (W.G.F.)

P1382 Murray, Jack, "Proust's Views on Perception as a Metaphoric Framework," French Review, 42:380-94, February, 1969.

"Proust's recurrent insistence on the shortcomings or peculiarities of the human sensory apparatus is a source of bizarre perspective, supplying new and unexpected dimensions in the descriptions of various human experiences." (F.M.L.)

P1383 Nitzberg, Howard, "À la recherche du temps perdu: Mirror-Image as a Level of Extratemporal Existence," French Review, 34:440-4, April, 1961.

In Proust's mirror images the agent of the reflection recognizes "a strong sentiment of existence in reverse, when he himself becomes the very reflection of his image, extratemporal." (R.B.W.)

P1384 Nolting-Hauff, Ilse, "Prousts À la recherche du temps perdu und die Tradition des Prosagedichts," Poetica, 1:67-84, January, 1967.

"Proust's Recherche thus does not simply stand generally in the tradition of pre-Romanticism and Romanticism; in it are also re-united several different branches of tradition emerging from pre-Romanticism." (J.R.R.)

P1385 O'Brien, Justin, "An Aspect of Proust's Baron de Charlus," Romanic Review, 55:38-41, February, 1964.

Charlus, who in the Faubourg St.-Germain was "the arbiter of elegance" has the "quirk of scatological references in angry state-ments." These references usually occur when "he is castigating someone else for a lack of taste. . . ." (F.M.L.)

À LA RECHERCHE DU TEMPS PERDU   (cont'd)

P1386   O'Brien, Justin, "Fall and Redemption in Proust," <u>Modern</u>
<u>Language Notes</u>, 79:281-3, May, 1964.

As in religious art of the Middle Ages and Renaissance, Proust has
subtly reminded us, at the moment of his hero's Redemption, of his
initial Fall from grace, which necessitated that Redemption. It is
possible that Proust invoked the painting of the Madonna by Mantegna,
consciously or unconsciously, in his parallel of two capital moments
in <u>Le Temps retrouvé</u>.   (T.T.B.)

P1387   O'Brien, Justin, "Proust and 'le joli langage'," <u>PMLA</u>, 80:259-65,
June, 1965.

". . . by creating characters who speak 'le joli langage,' other
characters who comment on and condemn it, and still others who
use it while simultaneously criticizing others for doing so, Proust
viewed himself as it were from the outside and transcended in his
work his own personal addiction to that peculiar style." (F.M.L.)

P1388   O'Brien, Justin, "Proust's Use of Syllepsis," <u>PMLA</u>, 69:741-52,
September, 1954.

Syllepsis, "a shortened, tightened form of antithesis" was used by
Proust as an ironic device and as "a telescoped metaphor. . . ."
Syllepses are found "throughout the sixteen volumes of <u>À la recherche</u>
<u>du temps perdu</u> at the rate of once every sixty pages." (F.M.L.)

P1389   Painter, George D., "How Charlus Met Morel," <u>Adam International</u>
<u>Review</u>, 25:84-7, No. 260, 1957.

"Léon Delafosse was a thin, vain, ambitious, blond young man, with
icy blue eyes and diaphanously pale, supernaturally beautiful features.
. . . The young pianist was clearly an important original of . . .
Morel. But the model for the suffering and moral ruin brought upon
Charlus by Morel came from Baron Doazan and his Polish violinist,
not from the relationship between Montesquiou and Delafosse."
(D.P.)

P1390   Pasco, Allan H., "Albertine's Equivocal Eyes," <u>Australian Journal</u>
<u>of French Studies</u>, 5:257-62, September-December, 1968.

". . . Proust purposefully altered Albertine's eye colour in order
to provide imagerial support for the changes taking place in Marcel

À LA RECHERCHE DU TEMPS PERDU   (cont'd)

as well as in Albertine." Proust "seemed to have wanted her to
exemplify the reality of all people who constantly change and who
are forever unknowable." (F.M.L.)

P1391   Philip, Michel, "The Hidden Onlooker," Yale French Studies,
No. 34, pp. 37-42, June, 1965.

The act of seeing "is especially characteristic of a certain number
of passages in À la recherche du temps perdu; these passages are
all the more remarkable because in each one the Narrator partici-
pates in an eminently revealing event. The passages . . . are: the
erotic scene between Mlle Vinteuil and her friend at Montjouvain,
the initial meeting between Jupien and Charlus in the courtyard of
the Guermantes's mansion, and the flagellation of Charlus in a house
of assignations." (D.P.)

P1392   Pugh, Anthony, "A Note on the Text of Swann," Adam International
Review, 25:101-4, No. 260, 1957.

"One of the most fascinating problems confronting the Proust scholar
is the growth of the novel, from the straightforward structure of 1912
to the rambling mosaic of 1922," particularly since "careful scrutiny
of the manuscripts and proofs of the post-war volumes show that on
practically every page Proust, improving his novel in one direction,
created havoc in another." (D.P.)

P1393   Reddick, Ryan, "Proust: The 'La Berma' Passages in Proust's
À la recherche du temps perdu," French Review, 42:683-92,
April, 1969.

"The passages in which la Berma appears represent in little a
development in the narrator's thinking about the imagination which
is analogous to his 'education' in the novel as a whole." (F.M.L.)

P1394   Riva, Raymond T., "Marcel Proust: An Immodest Proposal,"
Criticism, 10:217-24, Summer, 1968.

À la recherche du temps perdu is "far more internal and interiorized
than most of us have thought or been willing to accept. Therefore
we must investigate far more thoroughly Proust's concepts of love
and sexuality, so as to discover what we have been almost ignoring
for many years." (S.A.)

À LA RECHERCHE DU TEMPS PERDU   (cont'd)

P1395   Riva, Raymond T., "A Probable Model for Proust's Elstir,"
Modern Language Notes, 78:307-13, May, 1969.

". . . Proust, in creating Elstir, chose a model who closely
reflected in his graphic art Proust's own vision in his literary art.
And the burden of evidence shows this initial model to be the
American, Thomas Alexander Harrison." (F.M.L.)

P1396   Roditi, Édouard, "Proust Recaptured," Kenyon Review, 30:23-39,
No. 1, 1968.

"Only in French literature can we find as complete a record [as
in À la recherche] of the evolution of a metropolitan society which
still has a broader significance than the world described by most
other great novelists." (D.-J.J.)

P1397   Rogers, Brian, "Narrative Tones and Perspectives in Proust's
Novel," Modern Language Review, 50:207-11, April, 1965.

"Proust's conception of reality and of the past finds, in the double
perspective of the 'two' narrators of À la recherche, a method of
translating a whole attitude to life, underlining his own assertion
that À la recherche is 'not a matter of technique, but of vision'."
(J.R.R.)

P1398   Rose, Marilyn Gaddis, "If Proust Had Been British,"
D. H. Lawrence Review, 1:63-71, Spring, 1968.

If we juxtapose the characters of Swann in Love with personalities of
London intellectual and social life of the early twentieth century we
could see a British Remembrance of Things Past. "During these
years, Russell and Whitehead finished Principia Mathematica,
Phillip Morrell became a parliamentary spokesman, his wife had a
legendary salon, Edith Sitwell was gestating Façade (1923),
Lawrence wrote several of his major works, and Beatrice Elvery
made a home for Gordon Campbell." (D.P.)

P1399   Rowland, Michael, "Contre Sainte-Beuve and Character Presentation
in À la recherche du temps perdu," Romance Notes, 8:183-7,
Spring, 1967.

Proust's presentation of Dr. Cottard in À la recherche du temps
perdu is a dramatization of what he considered the inherent weakness

À LA RECHERCHE DU TEMPS PERDU   (cont'd)

of Sainte-Beauve's method of literary criticism; i.e. the failure "to give due attention to the disparity between the two completely different entities found within the same creative person: the self which is seen by society and the self which produces works of art." (F.M.L.)

P1400   Rubin, Louis D., Jr., "The Self Recaptured," Kenyon Review, 25:393-415, Summer, 1963.

". . . when we say that a novel . . . is 'autobiographical,' we are not talking about biographical details; we are talking about a temporal relationship which is built into the way the novel is told and is part of the formal experience of it. A necessary part of the meaning of such a novel is the shaping and ordering of the past through memory," as may be seen in Proust's Remembrance of Things Past and Wolfe's Look Homeward, Angel.   (F.M.L.)

P1401   Queneau, Raymond, "The Unfinished Symphony," Adam International Review, 25:65-6, No. 260, 1957.

". . . Proust is, with Joyce, one of the first to have constructed a novel." Not only is there a large-scale plan for À la recherche, "the inner individual sections are themselves scrupulously planned. . . . [although] most of this delicate internal balance was destroyed when Proust tripled his text by his endless modifications and additions."   (D.P.)

P1402   Samuel, Maurice, "The Concealments of Marcel: Proust's Jewishness," Commentary, 29:8-22, January, 1960.

The linked themes of Jewishness and homosexuality are deliberately concealed, throughout Remembrance of Things Past, by the complex subterfuge of the confusion of identity of "Proust" and "Marcel." (M.H.M.)

P1403   Sarlet, Claudette, "La Sonate de Vinteuil et le thème du temps chez Marcel Proust," Revue de Langues Vivantes, 24:443-57, No. 6, 1958.

In the passages in À la recherche relative to Vinteuil's sonata, Proust seems to have been most sensitive to the flow of time. He reconstitutes the temporality of the musical work by the use of numerous verbs and adjectives without actually creating images or metaphors. (F.M.L.)

À LA RECHERCHE DU TEMPS PERDU (cont'd)

P1404 Savage, Catherine, "Death in À la recherche du temps perdu," Forum (Houston), 4:7-11, Spring-Summer, 1963.

Proust's treatment of death is a key to understanding his entire literary vision. ". . . one may say that death plays multiple roles in À la recherche du temps perdu and that the author approaches it from several angles, seeking to consider every possible sense it has for man and probing into its meaning. . . ." (F.M.L.)

P1405 Seiden, Melvin, "Proust's Marcel and Saint-Loup: Inversion Reconsidered," Contemporary Literature, 10:220-40, Spring, 1969.

"This much, though, is clear: Saint-Loup as invert has less emotional coherence than he had had so long as we, in our innocence, took him to be what he seemed to be in the passion and virility of his stormy affair with Rachel. . . . If Marcel's heterosexuality is a lie, then Saint-Loup is the sacrifice Marcel offers to the truth." (D.P.)

P1406 Shattuck, Roger, "Proust's Stilts," Yale French Studies, No. 34, pp. 91-8, June, 1965.

In the final two paragraphs of Montaigne's last essay and in the closing paragraphs of Proust's À la recherche both authors introduce the metaphor of stilts. ". . . the stilts metaphor in these two works has a related, not an identical meaning. It lays off the distance between Montaigne's resolutely down-to-earth attitude and the elevated stance from which Proust could at last see life whole and worth living. And those same objects stand for both authors's refusal of the sublime." (D.P.)

P1407 Sheridan Smith, A. M., "Madeleine and the Proust," London Magazine, 7:66-74, April, 1967.

[Printed here in translation is the report of the reader Jacques Madeleine for the publisher Eugène Fasquelle, to whom Proust had submitted the manuscript of the first two volumes of À la recherche in 1912.] (D.P.)

P1408 Simons, Madeleine A., "Les Regards dans À la recherche du temps perdu," French Review, 41:489-504, February, 1968.

Through analysis and interpretation of exterior signs such as speech and physical traits, Marcel Proust gave his characters changing

À LA RECHERCHE DU TEMPS PERDU   (cont'd)

images and revealed the complexity and contradictions of their
inmost being. (S.L.K.)

P1409 Slater, Maya, "Some Recurrent Comparisons in À la recherche du
temps perdu," Modern Language Review, 62:629-32, October, 1967.

Three recurrent comparisons in À la recherche du temps perdu are:
the music of Bach with the human voice; M. de Vaugoubert with
tennis; the young actress at Balbec with the atmosphere of exclusive-
ness. (F.M.L.)

P1410 Spalding, P. A., "Why I Wrote the Index," Adam International
Review, 25:120-1, No. 260, 1957.

The intention of the Index to Remembrance of Things Past is to
locate and identify characters (350) and subjects in the 4277 pages
of Scott Moncrieff's translation of Proust's novel. (D.P.)

P1411 Steen, James T., "Values and Difficulties in the Art of Marcel
Proust," Carnegie Series in English, No. 5, pp. 67-81, 1959.

Proust stands "as something of a contradiction in the twentieth
century--an individual of genius, great accomplishment, and great
cultivation, a great nonspecialist, representing in the art of fiction
the culmination and end of a cultural age, just as those parts of his
novel which deal with social manners and mores represent the
culmination and the end of the old European society. This is what
makes his book so huge and singular a reading experience and one
that is so inaccessible to so many moderns. . . . Terms such as
Realism, Romanticism, Naturalism, Symbolism, and the like, fall
away before the immensity of what he has done. . . ." (D.P.)

P1412 Sticca, Sandro, "Anticipation as a Literary Technique in Proust's
À la recherche du temps perdu," Symposium, 20:254-62, Fall,
1966.

Proust used anticipation as a manifest and conscious artistic device
in the revelation of events and character. It was an important
technique toward the realization of the novel. (C.O.)

À LA RECHERCHE DU TEMPS PERDU   (cont'd)

P1413   Sullivan, Dennis G., "On Vision in Proust: The Icon and the
Voyeur," Modern Language Notes, 84:646-61, May, 1969.

Objects in Proust's work "will appear through a number of metaphorical modalities that share the implication of figure and ground
"such as bas-relief, profile, portrait or silhouette." Such images
are called icons. On the other hand: "Whenever we come upon that
Proustian being who is wrong, who, unlike the narrator, apprehends
a reality independent of the necessity of his death, and whenever this
being sees, he shall see as the voyeur." (W.J.L.)

P1414   Sutton, Howard, "Two Poets of Childhood: Marcel Proust and Marie
Noël," Books Abroad, 41:261-6, Summer, 1967.

"Marie Noël's charming volume of childhood memories, Petit-jour,
presents a number of analogies with parts of Marcel Proust's À la
recherche du temps perdu, especially the Combray section . . .
[although] there can be no question of a literary influence." (D.P.)

P1415   Taylor, Rosalie, "The Adult World and Childhood in Combray,"
French Studies, 22:26-36, January, 1968.

The protagonist finally comes to terms with the world by exchanging
erroneous childhood daydreams for faith in idealism and art and by
grafting this faith onto his adult intellect. This is implicit in
Combray and made clear in Le Temps retrouvé. (T.T.B.)

P1416   Thibaudeau, Barbara, "Condemned to Lie," Yale French Studies,
No. 34, pp. 55-63, June, 1965.

"The theme of falsehood occupies a very large place in À la recherche
du temps perdu. . . . This theme is used in the general examination
of the human personality and in the definition of individual characters;
it serves as the basis or genesis for revelations about the complex
and frequently deceptive nature of the human character, of social and
personal relationships, of reality itself; and it often provides the
occasion for a certain, somewhat ironic, humor. Lying is presented
as one of the most universal manifestations of the human character.
. . . This essay will be chiefly concerned with its presentation in
relation to Marcel in his double role as principal actor in the drama
and narrator of the material which constitutes the novel." (D.P.)

À LA RECHERCHE DU TEMPS PERDU   (cont'd)

P1417   Tolmachev, M. V., "Impressionist-Classicist Tensions," Yale
French Studies, No. 34, pp. 29-35, June, 1965.

"What is of interest to us in Proust? Of course not his symbolism,
painted in the colors of Bergsonian philosophy, nor the harmful sides
of his psychologism, nor his idealistic conception of art in general.
The aspects of Proust's work that remain significant are the ones in
which he adheres to the traditions of realistic French literature.
Nor is it possible to omit Proust's achievements in the investigation
of the dialectic of the human soul. . . . The key to . . . the
significance of À la recherche lies in distinguishing between the past
which is decadent and historically transient, and the part which
belongs to the history of the progressive development of French
literature." (D.P.)

P1418   Van Ghent, Dorothy, "The Pattern in the Carpet: Some Recent
Analyses of Fiction," Yale Review, 46:435-42, March, 1957.

Dr. Milton Miller's new study of Proust contributes to understanding
of Remembrance, in spite of certain "psychological crossword
puzzles," understandable only by psychiatrists. It shows that
Proust worked with "screen memories" and symbols growing out
of buried memories, all of which he manipulated in multiple forms
and reappearances. (F.L.)

P1419   Vance, Vera Lindholm, "Proust's Guermantes as Birds," French
Review, 35:3-10, October, 1961.

An examination of Proust's bird imagery provides a corrective to
overemphasis on the inanimate floral and water imagery. In
particular, Proust characterizes the Guermantes with bird imagery
"that mediates between the less than human and the celestial."
(R.B.W.)

P1420   Vinson, James, "Anthony Powell's Music of Time," Perspective,
10:146-52, 1958.

"In examining The Music of Time, comparison is instructive with
that twentieth-century classic of social decay, Proust's Remembrance
of Things Past. Both are told from a first-person point of view, both
create a richly diverse upper-middle and upper class society; both
are concerned with the decay of that society and the workings of time
towards that decay; both deal with pattern and shifting relationships in
that society." (H.S.)

À LA RECHERCHE DU TEMPS PERDU (cont'd)

P1421 Virtanen, Reino, "Proust's Metaphors from the Natural and the Exact Sciences," PMLA, 69:1038-59, December, 1954.

Proust made skillful use of scientific metaphor (drawn from biology, chemistry, physics, mathematics, astronomy, etc.) to illuminate the psychological and social phenomena presented in À la recherche du temps perdu. (J.R.B.)

P1422 Waters, Harold A., "The Narrator, Not Marcel," French Review, 33:389-92, February, 1960.

". . . it would seem that Proust did not wish his hero to be called Marcel. Furthermore, the custom may be harmful to the best-intentioned and most sensitive critics in a way Proust hoped would not occur: he wanted his hero to remain distinct from himself. . . ." It would be better were critics to use terms such as protagonist or narrator. (W.J.L.)

À L'OMBRE DES JEUNE FILLES EN FLEURS--See
À LA RECHERCHE DU TEMPS PERDU

ALBERTINE DISPARUE--See
À LA RECHERCHE DU TEMPS PERDU

BY WAY OF SAINTE-BEUVE--See
CONTRE SAINTE-BEUVE

THE CAPTIVE--See
À LA RECHERCHE DU TEMPS PERDU

CITIES OF THE PLAIN--See
À LA RECHERCHE DU TEMPS PERDU

CONTRE SAINTE-BEUVE

P1423 Brée, Germaine, "Le 'Moi oeuvrant' de Proust," Modern Language Review, 61:610-8, October, 1966.

"The critical principles which take shape in these texts [Contre Sainte-Beuve] are those which govern the development of his [Proust's] own work." (D.-J.J.)

CONTRE SAINTE-BEUVE (cont'd)

P1424 Switzer, Richard, "The Madeleine and the Biscotte," French Review, 30:303-8, February, 1957.

"Proust's . . . essay Contre Sainte-Beuve contains in its preface a toast and tea ritual which is surprising for its basic identity with the Petite Madeleine episode, and at the same time for its radical differences in matter of detail. . . . A comparison of the two affords some fascinating insights into the genesis and development of some of Proust's ideas." (W.J.L.)

P1425 Trilling, Lionel, "Proust as Critic and the Critic as Novelist," Griffin, 7:4-13, July, 1958.

In Contre Sainte-Beuve, "Proust's insistence that we cannot assume that the poet-person is identical with the man-person constitutes the only theoretical ground of his case against Sainte-Beuve." This essay is "not only an extensive and cogent polemic against Sainte-Beuve but also what amounts to a sketch for Remembrance of Things Past." (G.M.)

LE CÔTÉ DE GUERMANTES--See
À LA RECHERCHE DU TEMPS PERDU

LA FUGITIVE--See
À LA RECHERCHE DU TEMPS PERDU

THE GUERMANTES WAY--See
À LA RECHERCHE DU TEMPS PERDU

JEAN SANTEUIL

P1426 Alden, D. W., "Jean Santeuil," Saturday Review, 39:14-5, February 18, 1956.

"Imperfect though this early novel may be, we will discover in it not a rudimentary Proust but one who is already capable of accomplishing a great work. In spite of occasional triteness . . . he is the master of his metaphors and is fully capable of rendering in words the beauty of an object. That is to say he is already one of the greatest poets in French prose. Simultaneously, he is one of the great novelists. . . . Furthermore he is a profound thinker. . . ." (D.P.)

JEAN SANTEUIL   (cont'd)

P1427 Barzun, Jacques, "Proust's Way," Griffin, 5:4-13, April, 1956.

Jean Santeuil, "the diary of a sensualist who reflects," is fiction
without story or plot. Balzac and Stendhal 'haunt' Proust: . . .
Balzac already has Proust's theme of the invasion of the old
aristocracy . . . by the top layer of the bourgeoisie": Stendhal's
"Life of Henry Brulard now reads like a telegraphic version of
Proust. . . ." (G.M.)

P1428 Bell, William Stewart, "The Prototype for Proust's Jean Santeuil,"
Modern Language Notes, 73:46-50, January, 1958.

"It was doubtless because of this parallelism [of artistic force
destroyed by life in higher society] between the case of the Chanoine
[Jean-Baptiste de Santeuil], as glimpsed in the letters of La Bruyére
and as represented in Saint-Simon, that Proust chose to call his hero
Jean Santeuil." (M.J.O.)

P1429 Brée, Germaine, "Jean Santeuil: An Appraisal," L'Esprit Créateur,
5:14-25, Spring, 1965.

In sharp contrast to Pleasures and Days, Proust's Jean Santeuil is
an ambitious and intricate novel abounding in skillfully narrated
passages ranging from the delicate to the quasi-Balzacian. Nevertheless, Proust did not succeed in creating an integrated fictional
world. (T.T.B.)

P1430 Hopkins, Gerard, "A Note on Jean Santeuil," Adam International
Review, 25:110-1, No. 260, 1957.

Three sections of Jean Santeuil--"La mer à la montagne," "Begmeil
en Hollande," and "Impressions retrouvées" "deal with a form of
experience [customarily known as 'affective memory'] which is
central to all Proust's work. . . ." (D.P.)

P1431 Kolb, Philip, "In Time the Seed Will Grow: The Genesis of Jean
Santeuil," Adam International Review, 25:112-9, No. 260, 1957.

The scarcity of paper in the rustic village Beg-Meil in Brittany,
where Proust and his friend Reynaldo Hahn spent September to
October 1895 of an extended vacation provides confirming evidence
that the first eight chapters of Jean Santeuil were composed at Beg-
Meil. Proust was to continue with the novel for the next four years,

JEAN SANTEUIL (cont'd)

finally abandoning it late in 1899 after it had grown to an unpublishable length. (D.P.)

P1432 Kolb, Philip, "Proust's Portrait of Juarès in Jean Santeuil," French Studies, 15:338-49, October, 1961.

The model for Couzon in Jean Santeuil must be Jean Juarès, who was first elected to the legislature as a Republican when only twenty-six. He had joined the Socialist Party after the miners's strike at Carmaux, and was re-elected on that ticket in 1893. (D.P.)

P1433 O'Brien, Justin, "The Wisdom of the Young Proust," Romanic Review, 45:121-34, April, 1954.

"Still in his twenties . . . Proust already possessed a gift for generalization and frequently mastered a lapidary form of expression." In Jean Santeuil "it is possible to find no fewer than 112 reflections and maxims. . . ." (F.M.L.)

P1434 Slater, Maya, "L'Inconnu: A Fragment of Jean Santeuil," Modern Language Review, 65:778-84, October, 1970.

The L'Inconnu episode in the collection Textes retrouvés edited by Kolb and Larkin, contains "the germs of many situations that will recur later in Proust." (F.M.L.)

P1435 Stern, Richard G., "Proust and Joyce Underway: Jean Santeuil and Stephen Hero," Kenyon Review, 18:486-96, Summer, 1956.

Critics have tended to undervalue the worth of Proust's Jean Santeuil and the remarkably similar early work of Joyce, Stephen Hero. "Stephen Hero is the work of a brilliant stylist, analyst and wit who had such other literary gifts as a sense of pace, a feeling for proportion . . . who was astonishingly perceptive, knowledgeable . . . and emotionally original." Jean Santeuil projects "less sense of continuity than in Stephen Hero, and yet . . . it is dominated by Jean's discovery that position, love, society, power, knowledge, pain, and grief are meaningful only in the creative memory which is art." (D.P.)

JEAN SANTEUIL   (cont'd)

P1436 Turnell, Martin, "Proust's Early Novel," <u>Commonweal</u>,
63:333-5, December, 1955.

Proust's <u>Jean Santeuil</u> is not so much a sketch for the later
<u>Remembrance of Things Past</u> as his first attempt to write a major
novel. It was discarded as a failure, though it possesses much
freshness and directness. In contrast to his later novel, it contains
little rancor toward the nobility, less sexual abnormality, and no
use of the great themes of "time lost" and "time regained."
(T.C.L.)

PORTRAITS DE PEINTRES

P1437 Johnson, J. Theodore, Jr., "Proust's Early <u>Portraits de peintres</u>,"
<u>Comparative Literature Studies</u>, 4:397-408, No. 4, 1967.

"Proust's fragile <u>Portraits de peintres</u> contains the seeds of a
number of essential elements of the later novel. . . . they constitute
one of the extremely rare examples of the collaboration of both
writer and musician [Reynaldo Hahn] in the transposition into their
own respective arts of the art of the painter."   (R.C.F.)

LA PRISONNIÈRE--See
À LA RECHERCHE DU TEMPS PERDU

REMEMBRANCE OF THINGS PAST--See
À LA RECHERCHE DU TEMPS PERDU

SODOME ET GOMORRHE--See
À LA RECHERCHE DU TEMPS PERDU

THE SWEET CHEAT GONE--See
À LA RECHERCHE DU TEMPS PERDU

LE TEMPS RETROUVÉ--See
À LA RECHERCHE DU TEMPS PERDU

TIME REGAINED--See
À LA RECHERCHE DU TEMPS PERDU

WITHIN A BUDDING GROVE--See
À LA RECHERCHE DU TEMPS PERDU

PSICHARI, ERNEST

P1438 Moylan, Paul A., "Ernest Psichari's Mystical Heroism, "
Renascence, 21:103-9, Winter, 1969.

"The intellectual crisis . . . in France at the beginning of the
twentieth century generated in many of her writers a feeling of
restlessness. . . . Ernest Psichari (1883-1914) stands out among
these neo-romantic idealists by dint of his mystic identification of
his own highly personal struggle with his country's need for
deliverance from . . . a delusive pacifism." (D.P.)

PURDY, ALFRED WELLINGTON

P1439 Bowering, George, "Purdy: Man and Poet, " Canadian Literature,
No. 43, pp. 24-35, Winter, 1970.

[This is a biographical essay discussing Purdy's life and works.]
(A.S.W.)

P1440 Stevens, Peter, "In the Raw: The Poetry of A. W. Purdy, "
Canadian Literature, No. 28, pp. 22-30, Spring, 1966.

In Purdy's best poetry he "has won his way to a medium which will
include both realism and romanticism . . . illustrating his personal
concerns and his individuality." (A.S.W.)

PURDY, JAMES

P1441 Baldanza, Frank, "Playing House for Keeps with James Purdy, "
Contemporary Literature, 11:488-510, Autumn, 1970.

In Purdy's works are both tortured love relationships and ersatz
parental-familial relationships, illustrating the assumption that
American society is afflicted, through material affluence, with a pernicious form of anaesthesia that separates it from reality. (A.S.W.)

P1442 French, Warren, "The Quaking World of James Purdy, " Stetson
Studies in the Humanities, No. 1, pp. 112-22, 1963.

Purdy has moved from giving concrete form to the nightmare of
modern life in "63: Dream Palace" through a surrealistic satire
of our loveless world in Malcolm to the Portrayal in The Nephew
of the faint hope of a dream that cannot stop our world from quaking,
but "might prevent its shattering by giving people the vision to move
with it." (W.G.F.)

P1443 French, Warren G., "The Quaking World of James Purdy," Scope,
       1:45-7, Spring, 1961.

       Purdy is especially concerned with "the individual's attempt to
       establish communication with others in a hostile, hysterical world,
       a quaking world that seems about to fragment under the intolerable
       pressures of suspicion and selfishness into a million jagged, mean-
       ingless pieces." (W.G.F.)

P1444 Herr, Paul, "The Small, Sad World of James Purdy," Chicago
       Review, 14:19-25, Autumn-Winter, 1960.

       "Purdy, by rigidly excluding all love from his world (or satirizing
       it or making it grotesque), seems to be saying that this is precisely
       what is lacking in America today." (W.G.F.)

P1445 McNamara, Eugene, "The Post-Modern American Novel," Queen's
       Quarterly, 69:265-75, Summer, 1962.

       The novels of Gaddis, Griffin, Purdy, and Styron are all technically
       innovative and are all involved with the themes of isolated love in our
       modern world and the search for a father. (A.S.W.)

P1446 Maloff, Saul, "James Purdy's Fictions: The Quality of Despair,"
       Critique: Studies in Modern Fiction, 6:106-12, Spring, 1963.

       "The 'loss of identity'--that fashionable contemporary deprivation--
       is nowhere made more actual than in Purdy's work: it is paramountly
       his subject, without chic and without cheating; the 'condition' we all
       talk about is the substance of his art, and he has discovered for it
       marvelously right metaphors and symbols." (W.G.F.)

P1447 Pomeranz, Regina, "The Hell of Not Loving: Purdy's Modern
       Tragedy," Renascence, 16:149-53, Spring, 1964.

       "James Purdy writes of the unspoken, sub-surface level which is
       man's existence in the contemporary world" and in his two novels
       and his short stories "sees loss of self and loss of human love and
       identity as man's greatest tragedy." (S.A.)

P1448 Schott, Webster, "James Purdy: American Dreams," Nation,
       198:300-2, March 23, 1964.

       "James Purdy has a vision of our society dead and decaying, and he
       lives and writes in sorrow over the corpse." As he wrote in a recent

letter, "All my work is a criticism of the United States, implicit not explicit." (W.F.)

P1449 Skerrett, Joseph Taylor, Jr., "James Purdy and the Works: Love and Tragedy in Five Novels," Twentieth Century Literature, 15:25-33, April, 1969.

Purdy's view of life is a tragic one. "The only kind of love man is capable of offering is a 'ravening' love. . . . The tragic action of each novel is played out against a background of more than vaguely symbolic chaos in the natural order and/or disruption of the social order." (D.P.)

CABOT WRIGHT BEGINS

P1450 Boyers, Robert, "Attitudes toward Sex in American 'High Culture'," Annals of the American Academy of Political and Social Sciences, No. 376, pp. 36-52, March, 1968.

"Probably the most talented, serious, and proclaimed champion of apocalyptic sexuality in this country is Norman Mailer, whose . . . An American Dream is a pop-art caricature of . . . banal and ludicrous" ideas, although "his imagination is teeming with invention and his metaphors have the reach of genius." Jeremy Larner's Drive devotes considerable attention "to the possibilities of apocalyptic orgasm." Ken Kesey's One Flew over the Cuckoo's Nest is "an indictment of modern society, and . . . an exploration into the . . . subtly repressive mechanisms we . . . build into the fabric of our daily lives. Kesey's solution . . . is . . . the releasing of . . . the twin resources of laughter and uninhibited sexuality. . . ." Barth's The End of the Road treats "sex as a means of relief from painful reality, though not as a means of transforming that reality. . . ." James Purdy's Cabot Wright Begins "is a novel about a rapist, and incidentally about everything in the modern world. . . ." Philip Roth's "Whacking Off" "recounts an adolescence and a young adulthood tainted by the spectral presence of masturbation and the fear of exposure." In our most gifted writers "human sexuality cannot be considered apart from other essential elements of the human personality. Where . . . sexual encounter has been reduced to the grinding of organs, at least we have been made aware of our impoverishment as men." (D.P.)

CABOT WRIGHT BEGINS (cont'd)

P1451 Ryan, Marjorie, "Four Contemporary Satires and the Problem of
Norms," Satire Newsletter, 6:40-6, Spring, 1969.

Norms of modern satire, as represented by Heller's Catch-22,
Purdy's Cabot Wright Begins, Barth's The Floating Opera, and
Berger's Reinhart in Love differ distinctively from the traditions
of earlier satire. These norms are of feeling rather than intellect
the individual rather than society; norms expressed in these fictions
are radical, subjective. These works cannot be read by the same
standards of satires of the past. (D.P.)

DADDY WOLF

P1452 Burris, Shirley W., "The Emergency in Purdy's 'Daddy Wolf',"
Renascence, 20:94-8, Winter, 1968.

"James Purdy's comic monologue 'Daddy Wolf' in Children Is All is
somewhat less comic if the reader sees it as a comment on man's
spiritual and sexual aridity and his dependence on mechanical
contrivances as a substitute for God." (S.A.)

P1453 Grinnell, James W., "Who's Afraid of 'Daddy Wolf'?" Journal of
Popular Culture, 3:750-2, Spring, 1970.

Purdy's enigmatic story, "Daddy Wolf" belongs to the category of
his fiction "which in a tragicomic way portrays the squalor of poor
Southern whites living in northern urban slums. . . ." The repeated
references to the breakfast cereal Cream of Wheat appear to be
based on an "advertising campaign of the early 1950's that used Al
Capp's dauntless comic strip hero, Li'l Abner, as a salesman. . . .'
Purdy has his beleaguered 'hero' . . . an All-American boy who
believes in the dream of success--eat and love Cream of Wheat."
(D.P.)

MALCOLM

P1454 Daiches, David, "A Preface to James Purdy's Malcolm," Antioch
Review, 22:122-30, Spring, 1962.

"At first one is tempted to call Malcolm a symbolic fantasy, but
. . . the more we read the book the more we come to realize that
the characters and events are not symbolic of something or of some
things; they are themselves, and their haunting comic mystery
derives from their being so very much themselves." (W.G.F.)

MALCOLM (cont'd)

P1455 French, Warren, with Marc Rosenberg, "The Beast That Devours Its Young," CCC: The Journal of the Conference on College Composition and Communication, 13:4-8, May, 1962.

Both The Catcher in the Rye and Purdy's Malcolm "depict youth caught up, and ultimately destroyed" by a "phony" world. "Young people will always feel closer to Holden than to Malcolm," but Malcolm is "a stronger condemnation of a society which, like some carnivorous beast, devours its young." (W.G.F.)

P1456 Krummel, Regina Pomeranz, "Two Quests in Two Societies," English Record, 17:28-32, April, 1967.

Dostoevsky's Crime and Punishment and Purdy's Malcolm offer versions of the search for a father. Both protagonists share meaningless lives because they lack a connection between themselves and their structured society. Raskolnikov's father refuses to aid the beaten horse; Malcolm's father leaves him waiting at the hotel. Raskolnikov finds a father through Sonia's love; Malcolm is betrayed to satisfy his women's vanity. (D.P.)

P1457 Lorch, Thomas M., "Purdy's Malcolm: A Unique Vision of Radical Emptiness," Wisconsin Studies in Contemporary Literature, 6:204-13, Summer, 1965.

"Purdy's first novel exhibits artistry of the highest order: he establishes control over a variety of juxtaposed styles and a bizarre spectrum of characters and incidents; his precise, economical, yet stylized language and action achieve a hard gem-like clarity; and his comic perspective never falters." (W.G.F.)

P1458 Schwarzschild, Bettina, "The Forsaken: An Interpretive Essay on James Purdy's Malcolm," Texas Quarterly, 10:170-7, Spring, 1967.

Purdy's Malcolm is fourteen, "the age when in a primitive culture he would have undergone puberty rites" as a tribally controlled initiation into manhood. He is abandoned, however, by his father, so that he develops "not towards life and self-realization . . . but under the misguidance of Mephistopheles towards destruction and death." (W.G.F.)

THE NEPHEW

P1459 Schwarzschild, Bettina, "Aunt Alma: James Purdy's The Nephew," University of Windsor Review, 3:80-7, Fall, 1967.

"In The Nephew, James Purdy unfolds the story of Alma Mason, the Puritan spinster, who through the death of the nephew she loved [and did not know] emerged from the cursed darkness into the blessed light." (A.S.W.)

PUTRAMENT, JERZY

P1460 Neveux, Jean B., "Un Demi-siècle d'historie et d'histories en Pologne," La Table Ronde, No. 202, pp. 106-11, November, 1964.

Relying on modern history for inspiration in his novels, Putrament mingles the virtues and the vices of the novelist and journalist. His masterpieces are two novelettes, Swieta kulo (The Sacred Ball) and Poczatek eposu (Beginning of an Era), 1944. His tales of Poland in the form of ethical and political chronicles appeared in Kronika Obyczajów, 1959. These themes are renewed in 1963 with Arka Noego (Noah's Ark) and Pasierbowie (The Unloved). (T.T.B.)

PYNCHON, THOMAS

P1461 McNamara, Eugene, "The Absurd Style in Contemporary American Literature," Humanities Association Bulletin, 19:44-9, No. 1, 1968.

Perhaps the absurd style, as exemplified in the novels of Thomas Pynchon and Heller's Catch-22, has reached the limit beyond which it becomes a parody of itself. (A.S.W.)

P1462 Sklar, Robert, "The New Novel, U. S. A.: Thomas Pynchon," Nation, 205:277-80, September, 1967.

Pynchon is the only major writer of fiction in America for those under thirty. V. reaches beyond the genre of black humor, and The Crying of Lot 49 helps us understand V. Pynchon is concerned with fact, science and technology, dualities and the entrance of another world into this one. He well exemplifies the "greater philosophical and metaphysical sophistication" that Borges indicates may be a major characteristic of fiction of the future. (D.P.)

P1463 Wasson, Richard, "Notes on a New Sensibility," Partisan Review, 36:460-77, No. 3, 1969.

Thomas Pynchon creates "an ironic juxtaposition of fools and foolish theories" in rejecting both "the notion that myth can be used to order the chaos of history" and "the modernist consensus over the nature of myth and metaphor." He attempts to achieve a literature able "to cope spontaneously with experience." (D.P.)

P1464 Young, James D., "The Enigma Variations of Thomas Pynchon," Critique: Studies in Modern Fiction, 10:69-77, April, 1968.

In Pynchon's fiction "the significance of human experience, freed from the usual categories of abstraction, is defined partly by speculation and partly by experience that one feels should be significant." (A.S.W.)

V.

P1465 Hall, James, "The New Pleasures of the Imagination," Virginia Quarterly Review, 46:596-612, Autumn, 1970.

Pynchon's V., like other modern fantasy novels, interlaces "social comedy with fantasy, live hopes with ideal ones," and suggests, but does not specify, a possibility of being. (A.S.W.)

P1466 Hausdorff, Don, "Thomas Pynchon's Multiple Absurdities," Wisconsin Studies in Contemporary Literature, 7:258-69, Autumn, 1966.

"Perhaps the underlying weakness [of V.] rests not with the ambitious size and sweep of the novel or its mass of details but with its attempt to integrate antithetical points of view. The numerous parallels with the temper and technique of Henry Adams, coupled with the Absurd affirmation that Pynchon strives for, hint at unresolved ambiguities in his outlook. Adams . . . retained an important measure of consistency in his design; Pynchon never quite achieves this. . . . Nevertheless . . . Pynchon is an unusual talent and V. a remarkable book." (D.P.)

P1467 Koch, Stephen, "Imagination in the Abstract," Antioch Review, 24:253-63, Summer, 1963.

Both Susan Sontag in The Benefactor and Thomas Pynchon in V. criticize "the modern tendency to allow the imagination to enthrall rather than to enlarge human capabilities." (D.P.)

V. (cont'd)

P1468 Larner, Jeremy, "The New Schlemihl," Partisan Review, 30:273-6, Summer, 1963.

Pynchon's V. "loses the fight against mechanical domination and becomes only one more symptom of the disease it portrays." (D.P.)